THE
CAMBRIDGE
ECONOMIC HISTORY

GENERAL EDITORS: M. M. POSTAN, Professor Emeritus of Economic History in the University of Cambridge; D. C. COLEMAN, Professor of Economic History in the University of Cambridge; and PETER MATHIAS, Chichele Professor of Economic History in the University of Oxford

VOLUME VII, PART 1

THE
CAMBRIDGE
ECONOMIC HISTORY
OF EUROPE

VOLUME VII

THE INDUSTRIAL ECONOMIES: CAPITAL, LABOUR, AND ENTERPRISE

PART I
BRITAIN, FRANCE, GERMANY, AND SCANDINAVIA

EDITED BY

PETER MATHIAS

Chichele Professor of Economic History in the University of Oxford, and Fellow of All Souls College

AND

M. M. POSTAN

Professor Emeritus of Economic History in the University of Cambridge, and Fellow of Peterhouse

CAMBRIDGE UNIVERSITY PRESS

CAMBRIDGE

LONDON · NEW YORK · MELBOURNE

1978

Published by the Syndics of the Cambridge University Press
The Pitt Building, Trumpington Street, Cambridge CB2 1RP
Bentley House, 200 Euston Road, London NW1 2DB
32 East 57th Street, New York, NY 10022, USA
295 Beaconsfield Parade, Middle Park, Melbourne 3206, Australia

First published 1978

Printed in Great Britain at the
University Press, Cambridge

Library of Congress Cataloguing in Publication Data (Revised)
Main entry under title:
The Cambridge economic history of Europe from the decline of
the Roman empire.
Includes bibliographies and indexes.
Vol. 2 planned by Sir John Clapham and Eileen Power,
edited by M. Postan and E. E. Rich.
CONTENTS: v. 1. The agrarian life of the middle ages.
v. 2. Trade and industry in the middle ages.
v. 3. Economic organization and policies in the middle ages.
1. Europe – Economic conditions. 2. Europe – History.
I. Clapham, Sir John Harold, 1873–1946, ed.
II. Power, Eileen Edna, 1889–1940, joint ed.
HC 240.C3   330.9′4   41–3509

ISBN 0 521 21590 0   part 1
ISBN 0 521 21591 9   part 2
ISBN 0 521 21124 7   the set of two parts

CONTENTS

CHAPTER I

Introduction: The Inputs for Growth   1

By ROBERT M. SOLOW, Professor of Economics, Massachusetts Institute of Technology, and
PETER TEMIN, Professor of Economics, Massachusetts Institute of Technology

BRITAIN

CHAPTER II

Capital Formation in Great Britain

By C. H. FEINSTEIN, Lecturer in Economics and Politics, and Fellow of Clare College, Cambridge

CHAPTER III

Labour in Great Britain

By SIDNEY POLLARD, Professor of Economic History, University of Sheffield

CHAPTER IV

Industrial Entrepreneurship and Management in Great Britain

By PETER L. PAYNE, Professor of Economic History,
University of Aberdeen

FRANCE

CHAPTER V

Capital Investment and Economic Growth in France, 1820–1930

By MAURICE LÉVY-LEBOYER, Professor of Economic History,
University of Paris (Nanterre)

CHAPTER VI

Labour in the French Economy since the Revolution

By YVES LEQUIN, Lecturer in Contemporary History,
University of Lyon

CHAPTER VII

Entrepreneurship and Management in France in the Nineteenth Century

By CLAUDE FOHLEN, Professor of History,
University of Paris (Sorbonne)

GERMANY

CHAPTER VIII

Capital Formation in Germany in the Nineteenth Century

By R. H. TILLY, Professor of Economic and Social History,
University of Münster

CHAPTER IX

Labour in German Industrialization

By J. J. LEE, Professor of Modern History, University College, Cork

CHAPTER X

Entepreneurs and Managers in German Industrialization

By JÜRGEN KOCKA, Professor of History,
University of Bielefeld

SCANDINAVIA

CHAPTER XI

Labour and Capital in the Scandinavian Countries in the Nineteenth and Twentieth Centuries

By K.-G. HILDEBRAND, Professor of Economic History,
Uppsala University

NOTES

BIBLIOGRAPHIES

TABLES

BRITAIN

FRANCE

GERMANY

SCANDINAVIA

ILLUSTRATIONS

PREFACE

The editors must begin their preface to this volume with apologies for its belated appearance. Such apologies have unfortunately become a customary feature of editorial prefaces to most volumes in this series, but this volume has suffered from delays greater than usual, which demands an apology correspondingly humbler and fuller. The tragic death of one of the editors, David Joslin, in October 1970 was a bitter blow for the volume, as for economic history more widely. This volume has also been afflicted by all the penalties of collective authorship, and above all by the failure of some contributors to deliver their chapters in time, and of others to deliver them at all. For this the editors and their plans are partly to blame. In planning the three concluding volumes of the series – the sixth, the seventh and the eighth – the editors have tried to depart from the assortment of themes in standard treatises of economic history. As these volumes are intended to cover the history of industrialized countries during and after their industrialization, the editors thought it appropriate to relate their contents to the theoretical and historical problems of industrialization and economic growth. So instead of following the established conventions and dividing the field into sections devoted respectively to agriculture, industry, commerce and economic policy, the editors have tried to redefine the themes assigned to contributors with due regard for the problems of economic development. They devoted the first of the three volumes, the sixth in the series, to the external factors, the 'parameters' of the economic process – geographical expansion, demographic change, technical progress – and have planned the present volume, the second of the group, to focus on the economic process in the narrower sense of the term, and in doing so to deal separately with the main factors of production – labour, capital, and entrepreneurship. Needless to say, the commissioning of separate histories of individual factors of production country by country, and still more their writing, was bound to raise innumerable difficulties. It is not for nothing that the classical or 'neoclassical' notion of 'production function' with its implied distinctions between individual factors of production has recently come under fire from many economists. Their theoretical argument is that in their operation the so-called 'factors' combine so indissolubly that all attempts to treat them as separate entities must distort the view of the economic process. The distortions would be even more obvious and deterrent to historians concerned with actual occurrences than to economists operating with idealized models.

All these difficulties, both theoretical and practical, were foreseen in planning the volumes. The editors did not – indeed dare not – take sides in the debate for and against neo-classical economics and its pet concept of 'production function'. Their decision to group the chapters round the individual 'factors' did not signify their acceptance of the 'production function' as the true mirror of life. They have adopted it as a purely heuristic convenience: a set of hooks on which to hang historical facts and interpretations in the best, i.e. the most relevant, order. Yet even so, questions of definition and relevance were bound to be raised, and the editors were not surprised that their brief should have necessitated protracted discussions with the authors and repeated revisions of their drafts, all resulting in prolonged delays. The difficulty of conforming to the editors' brief may have been to some extent responsible for the failure of at least one of the authors to deliver his contribution. After repeated postponements over a period of at least four years, the economic historian who had undertaken the chapter on labour in the United States decided to withdraw altogether. The withdrawal came too late to make it possible to commission the chapter from anyone else, and has forced the editors to go to print with this gap in the volume.

Equally troublesome has been the difficulty of confining individual chapters to the themes allotted to them. The editors had anticipated and allowed for a great deal of overlapping between individual chapters. The overlaps have in fact turned out to be not so wide as to obscure the main outlines of the volume; overlaps there nevertheless are, and they perhaps deserve special apology in this preface. In at least one chapter, the Scandinavian, the author has, with the editors' encouragement, dispensed with the demarcations. For reasons of space, the Scandinavian countries could not be allotted a number of words necessary to accommodate separate chapters on individual factors of production. The editors accordingly entrusted the chapter to one author with the request to deal in a more integrated way with developments in the whole of Scandinavia.

The editorial plan of the volume also accounts for what may seem to be gaps and inconsistencies of both chronology and geography in individual chapters. The chronological inconsistency is perhaps more apparent than real. The commencing and terminal dates of the stories differ widely from chapter to chapter. Whereas in some of the chapters, especially those dealing with the United Kingdom, the starting dates go back to the eighteenth century, in some other chapters, e.g. those concerned with Scandinavia and Japan, the account is mainly confined to the second half of the nineteenth century. This, however, is as it should be. Readers need not be reminded that in economic history calendar dates are not as true an indication of historical time as they would be in

narratives of political history. Economic phenomena and processes occurring in different places at different dates can be sufficiently alike and
closely enough related to be treated as essentially contemporaneous,
even though their contemporaneity is not chronological. However,
'philosophical contemporaneity' cannot be invoked to justify all the
inconsistencies of chronological limits. In some cases uniformity in the
commencing and concluding dates could not be enforced without doing
violence to the actual timing of economic development in different
countries. In some other cases the authors were for justifiable reasons
unable to accommodate their chapters to the dates proposed by the
editors. For example, the chapter on capital formation in the United
Kingdom does not go beyond the mid nineteenth century, as Dr
Feinstein felt that he had said what he wanted to say about the period
after 1860 in another place; while in Professor Kahan's chapter the
availability and coherence of the data, as well as the distribution of
emphasis in past historical discussion, impelled the author to concentrate his story of capital formation in Russia upon the period 1890–1913.

The geographical inconsistencies can nearly all be put down to
practical exigencies. In the strict sense of the series title – the Economic
History of Europe – the volumes should have been confined to
Europe, and should have included all the European countries without
exception. The editors have, however, been compelled to overstep the
geographical limits in some respects and to draw back from them in
others. As the main preoccupations of the series are economic and
historical, the editors have chosen to interpret the adjective 'European'
in the sense of 'modern' or 'developed' and accordingly to include the
United States and Japan. On the other hand they have not been able to
include into the volume such individual European countries as Holland
and Belgium, Italy, Spain and Portugal, Austria, and Switzerland.
Some of the reasons for the exclusion were accidental – mainly the
editors' inability to find economists capable or willing to deal with
these countries' development historically, or historians prepared to
rewrite their histories in a manner appropriate to this volume. The
editors were also restricted by lack of elbow room. The space that could
have been allotted to some of the smaller countries individually would
have been too exiguous to enable the authors to deal with their topics in
the manner of the other chapters, or to tempt them to do so. However,
the editors hope that the conception of the volume as a whole may make
the omission of these countries less damaging than it might have been
in a volume differently composed. As its main preoccupation is with
the problems thrown up in the process of industrialization, it is fortunate that most of these problems were shared by several countries and
are as a rule discussed in the different local contexts in some chapter or

another. This, however, is small consolation to historians to whom local contexts are the very essence of the problem. The gaps are, in other words, real, and all that can be hoped for is that they would be filled should a second edition of this volume be called for.

M. M. P.
P. M.

October 1977

CHAPTER I

Introduction: The Inputs for Growth

I

The purpose of this volume is to advance our understanding of industrial development by describing the progress of what economists call the 'factors of production', i.e. the inputs out of which food, clothing, and shelter are made. It is by no means clear, however, that the increase in our ability to produce food, clothing, and shelter that we call 'the industrial revolution' was a direct result of an increase in the factors of production. In fact, the relation between the traditional factors of production – land, labour, and capital – and the ability of an economy to produce is far more complex than the use of the words 'inputs' and 'outputs' might suggest. We therefore introduce the discussion of the factors of production by an attempt to set forward the relations between these factors and industrial development that is the subject of this book.

It is a great abstraction to talk of the economy as a whole and of only a few factors of production. The uses of such an abstraction are obvious: it enables us to make generalizations, to compare countries with each other, and to direct our research into areas of potential usefulness. But there are also limitations to this usefulness, limitations that are directly related to the ability of this abstraction to tell us something interesting about a complex world. The relationship between the factors of production and the process of industrialization to be described shortly holds good only under a variety of restrictive assumptions. If one agrees that these assumptions are roughly true, then the relation and the resultant discussion will appear useful. But if these assumptions appear less appropriate than some others, the limitations of this relation may be more apparent than its uses. We cannot here enter into the technical discussion of alternative assumptions; instead we simply assert that they are a useful and informative set.[1]

We need, first of all, some index to tell us when an industrial revolution takes place, how fast it is progressing, and how far it goes. Some index of human welfare might seem appropriate to indicate the existence and extent of such a revolution, but an index of welfare is too broad for our present purposes. There are many things that affect the happiness of people, and the state of the economy is only one of them. People who have eaten to satiety are not always happier than those who eat more lightly. We are all familiar with discontent in wealthy societies and with unhappiness coming from non-economic causes. There are even those who say that the overall psychological state of mankind is not susceptible of alteration by economic means. Each man, this theory says, will worry according to his nature. If he is poor, he may worry about his poverty. But if he is rich, he will find something else to worry about.

It is not necessary to hold to this extreme theory to see that a measure of welfare is too broad for our present concerns. It is enough to realize that we do not have the means to disprove such a theory to know that the link between the industrial revolution and welfare is quite tenuous. For example, historians have been debating for many years whether workers were better off in the early years of the industrial revolution than they had been previously.[2]

Another possible measure is an index of structural change. The terms 'industrial revolution' and 'industrialization' are often used interchangeably, and the place of industry in the economy would tell us something about the process to which these terms refer. It is a valid measure, however, only if there is some fixed relation between the industrial revolution and the place of industry in the economy, i.e. if there is a pattern which every country must follow to achieve its revolution. The diversity of historical experience has disabused us of this simple notion, and while industry plays a more important role in societies that have had an industrial revolution than in societies that have not, the extent of this role is determined by many as yet unknown factors, and the difference between economies that have and have not industrialized today lies more in the differences in efficiency between various sectors in the different economies than in the relative sizes of these sectors.[3] Just as a measure of welfare is too broad for our purposes, a measure of structural shifts within the economy is too narrow.

Since we have found one bowl of porridge to be too hot and one too cold, it is obvious that the third will be just right. Looking into one well-stirred bowl, we find the following: 'The characteristic which distinguishes the modern period in world history from all past periods is the fact of economic growth.'[4] Economic growth, or the ability of the economy to produce ever more goods and services of value to its members, is a more restricted measure than changes in welfare, because it looks only at the goods and services produced by the economy. We presume that, all other things being equal, an increase in these goods and services would increase welfare, but we do not know that other things remained the same when economic production was increased. On the other hand, economic growth is a broader measure than structural change, for an economy can grow in many ways and with many different types of structural change. It is the results of structural change that concern us, and we use them as our index of industrialization.[5]

Many people have seen the progress of industrial development in the expansion of the railways, the growth of coal production, and other such activities. We have to decide if our measure of production is to be the simple sum of these activities. The problem is that some of the coal production of the nineteenth century was used to fuel railways. If we count both activities separately, therefore, we are counting some of the coal production twice: once when the coal was mined and again when it was used to power locomotives. We have phrased this problem in specific terms, but a similar problem arises whenever the output of one industry is the input of another.

It is obviously preferable not to count the same activity twice. To avoid doing so, we do not count the total production of the economy in constructing our measure of economic growth; we count only the production of those goods destined directly for use by consumers. We call these goods 'final goods' to distinguish them from the 'intermediate goods' that are inputs to further production.

The distinction between intermediate and final goods is easier to make in theory than in practice. We cannot discover the disposition of everything produced by the economy, and we must make rules that allow us to deal with groups of commodities and services. The most widely used rule is that goods and services bought by consumers are final goods, while those bought by business firms are intermediate goods.

This rule, like any general rule, has implications that must be recognized. For instance, it costs more to live in the city than in the country. Food must be brought to the city; people must travel to work; living space is more expensive. If people like to live in cities and would choose to live there even if there were no economic incentives for them to do so, then these extra expenses are part of consumption, i.e. final goods. On the other hand, if people do not like to live in cities and live there only because they need to be near places of employment, then these extra expenses are a cost to them of working in the cities. They are then part of the cost of production of goods made in the cities, and they should be classified as intermediate goods and not included in our measure of economic growth. We have no way of discovering the preferences of all urban dwellers; our rule assumes that they work in the city in order to live there, as opposed to living in the city in order to work there.

Consider another example. Flour that is used to make bread in a bakery is clearly an intermediate product. Is flour that is purchased by a housewife to make bread at home the same? We conventionally consider housewives as consumers, and this flour therefore is considered a final good. As with the costs of urban living, we assume implicitly that housewives bake bread at home because they enjoy doing so and not because this is a necessary part of maintaining a family. This assumption is appropriate to industrialized twentieth-century societies where housewives have the option of buying bread; it is less relevant for pre-industrial societies. It has the added implication that as activities get taken out of the home and incorporated into businesses that sell their services, our measure of economic growth increases even though the volume of goods produced may not have changed.[6]

Finally, let us take a somewhat esoteric problem. How should we treat the consumption of slaves? From the point of view of the slave-owner, slaves were part of his capital, and their consumption was the cost of maintaining this capital. Clearly, the consumption of slaves was an intermediate good to the slave owner, similar in all respects to fuel for locomotives. To the slave, on the other hand, his consumption represented a final product of the economy, and he would have thought that it should be counted as such. In addition to deciding how to treat goods and services bought by consumers, consequently, we have to decide who are the consumers. A slaveowner in the American South before the Civil War may well have had a different index of economic growth than we – believing that all men are equal and to be counted as consumers – would construct today.

This rule tells us how to construct our measure, but it does so in a method that is not suitable for all uses. The coal mines, to return to our original example, sell most of their products to other firms, and their output does not appear directly in this measure of total output. If we wish to integrate our measure with studies of coal production we need to construct our measure in a way that allows us to make the transition from industry to nation.

A railway buys the coal that it uses. If we attribute to the railway the total value of its product used by consumers we are counting the value of the coal in this product, even though it was not produced by the railway. To avoid this, we talk of something called 'value added', which is the value of an industry's products less the value of the intermediate goods purchased by that industry, i.e. the value of the industry's services over and above the cost of the materials it purchased. Since we derive the value added by subtracting all the intermediate products from each industry's total, we can add the value added in different industries to get our total measure. We get the same total as before because the value of the bread purchased in a store equals the value added by the farmer, the baker, the wholesaler, and the retailer. And we can see the amount added to our total by each industry, whether or not it produces goods for final consumption.

This method also gives us a way to connect our total with the factors of production. If we subtract the intermediate goods purchased from the firm's receipts, we are left with the firm's value added. This equals the firm's payments for inputs other than intermediate goods, i.e. for labour, for capital (including profit and depreciation), and for raw materials not produced by other firms. A firm's value added, in other words, equals the sum of its payments to the factors of production. And our measure of an economy's output can be seen as either the sum of the final goods produced, the sum of the value added in different industries, or the sum of the payments to the factors of production. This measure, of course, is called national product or national income by economists. (These terms have slightly different meanings but can be used as synonyms here.) We measure economic growth by changes in national income, and these changes are equivalent to changes in the payments to the factors of production.

II

We said earlier that the relation between the national product and the factors of production used to produce it was complex. And so it is. For while payments to the factors of production have to rise with the national product, the quantities of these factors used may not rise in exact proportion to the rise in output. And the national product itself might rise because of a rise in the value of the commodities and services being produced, and not because of an increase in the quantity produced. If we wish to talk of the volume of production and its relation to the quantities of factors used, we must first find a way to transform the sum of values that we have called national product into a measure that is independent of price, i.e. into 'real' national product.

Were there only one unalterable commodity, and consequently only one price, the problem would be trivial: dividing the value of production at different times by the price at that time would give a measure of the quantity produced. Similarly, if all prices changed together, one price would be as good as another to use for deflation, and the problem would be solved. But when there are many goods, and when prices do not move together, it is necessary to choose what price or combination of prices to use for deflation. The measure of the goods and services produced – i.e. of real national product – that will emerge will depend on the choice made; obviously, there is no unique measure of real national product.

The problem may be restated as follows: when prices and quantities do not move together, it is necessary to choose a scheme whereby the changes in the various quantities are weighted to produce an average change. Various weighting schemes have been named after nineteenth-century investigators. A Paasche index is one that uses prices of the current year as weights; a Laspeyres index is one that uses prices of the initial year of the series as weights. In other words, a Paasche index uses the weights of the observer looking backward; a Laspeyres index uses the weights of a man at the start of the historical period being considered looking forward. (These gentlemen actually computed price indexes, but the problems are the same. Reading this discussion with 'price' substituted for 'quantity' and vice versa will show the problems as they encountered them.) As each observer uses the prices of his period as weights, each observer will give heavier weight to those industries with the higher relative price, i.e. the higher price relative to the prices of other industries. If there is a systematic relationship between the movements of relative prices and the growth of industries, there will be a consistent difference between the two measures.

Some writers have seen the industrial revolution as a result of spontaneous innovations. According to this view, the pattern of demand stayed relatively stable. Innovations in some industries lowered the price of their products, and people consumed more of them. (Expansions took place primarily by shifts of supply curves and movements along demand curves.) There was thus a negative correlation between price and quantity changes; those industries whose relative prices fell the most were also the industries whose output rose the most. An observer looking forward into the future would have seen rapid expansion in the industries he associated with relatively high prices; an observer looking back would see relatively slow expansion in the industries he associated with relatively high prices. The Laspeyres index would show a higher rate of growth than the Paasche index.

Is this a realistic – albeit simplified – view of industrialization? The reader is referred to the essays in the preceding volume of this *History* for informed opinion (particularly the chapter by David S. Landes). Tests of this proposition by the use of index numbers have shown that the discrepancy anticipated from this theory can be found in indexes of machinery output, but that it may not be present in indexes of consumer-goods industries.[7] We may hypothesize that in the production of capital goods, shifts of supply curves were more important in the expansion of production than shifts of demand curves, while shifts of both types of curves were equally important in the expansion of consumer-goods production. But this is not the place to analyse the industrial revolution; we want only to point out the possibility of systematic differences between index numbers.

The important question now arises of whether the story of the growth of real economic output can be translated into a story about the growth of the conventional productive inputs. Do the historically observed increments in the supply of labour, capital goods, and land (or natural resources) 'explain' economic growth? The very notion of an industrial revolution suggests not; historians would presumably be surprised to discover that all that happened in the second half of the eighteenth century was that the supplies of labour, capital, and natural resources began to grow more rapidly than they had done before. But even if there is more to the story than that, it is still a matter of some interest and importance to discover what part of the growth of output can be explained by the growth of inputs, and what part remains to be explained in other ways.

We must first state what we mean by 'explain'. It is not a matter of 'ultimate' explanation, of asking whether land is the mother of output and labour the father, or vice versa. If we were to say that a factor explains output if it is indispensable to the process of production, then to all intents and purposes we could explain output thrice over. Our notion of explanation is incremental. We want to account for changes in output by changes in the various inputs, to the extent that we can. 'Account for' is perhaps more descriptive than 'explain'. We wish to account for changes in output by changes in input much as one would account for changes in the area of a rectangle by the historical changes in the lengths of its sides. The differences are, first, that we have no prior definitional relation between output and inputs as we have between the area of a rectangle and the lengths of its sides; and, second, that we do not even know that changes in output can be accounted for completely by changes in inputs, and indeed we suspect the reverse.

In order to perform this accounting, we need to know something about the historical time-paths of what economists call the 'marginal products' of the factors of production. We need answers – approximate answers – to questions like this: In such and such a year, if employment had been higher (or lower) by 1,000 average workers and everything else had been the same, how much higher (or lower) would output have been? It is plain that such questions can have only rough answers, if they have answers at all. How are 'average workers' defined? Are we to imagine them appearing or disappearing in London, in Bristol, or all over the country in proportion to the existing supply of labour? Is everything else to be unchanged – even the stock of houses, which after all are capital goods? We will recur to some of the difficulties of principle and practice later; but some such estimates have to be produced if any analytical connection is to be made between the growth of inputs and the growth of output.

If the marginal product of a factor is known or knowable, then knowing it is almost equivalent to knowing a slightly more convenient quantity, the 'elasticity of output with respect to a particular factor of production', a kind of proportional marginal product. It answers in principle the question: In such and such a year, if employment had been higher (or lower) by 1 per cent and everything else had been the same, what percentage increase (or decrease) in output would have been registered? These elasticities are natural concepts in the kind of accounting that we are trying to do. To be precise, over some interval of time, the appropriate measure of the contribution of a particular input to the average annual rate of growth of output is given by the product of the average annual rate of growth of the input and the elasticity of output with respect to that input.[8] To ask whether the growth of productive inputs 'explains' the growth of output is simply to ask whether the sum of such products is equal to the rate of growth of output itself. Following Domar, we call the excess of the rate of growth of output over the sum of these products – if it exists – the 'residual'.[9]

It is significant that the residual does exist and is sometimes of substantial size; and the significance is more than merely descriptive. We mentioned earlier that the national product is so defined as to be equal to the national income (apart from minor discrepancies arising primarily from the tax and subsidy operations of government). All that the economy produces in any year is necessarily recorded as the income of one of the factors of production, as wages, rent, interest, or profits – although it is not always clear which, as in the case of the family-owned and family-operated business. Now consider the rates of return for the various factors of production: the annual wage per man, the annual rent per acre of land, the annual rate of profit on capital. If there were no residual, any increase in the rate of return to one or more factors of production could come about only at the expense of a fall in the rate of return to one or more of the remaining factors of production. The wage cannot rise unless the rate of profit, say, falls.

In other words, if in fact the growth of output were fully accounted for by the growth of inputs, then history could not record simultaneous increases in the real wage rate of a given grade of labour and in the rate of profit, nor even an increase in one while the other remained constant. The importance of the residual is that it provides the output, so to speak, out of which can come all-round increases in the rewards to factors of production.

There are exceptions to this rule, the most important of which derives from increasing returns to scale. If an economy automatically grows more efficient as it grows in absolute size, so that for instance a 10 per cent increase in all the factors of production generates a larger percentage increase in total output, then the increment over and above

10 per cent is available to support an increase in all rates of return to factors of production. The status of increasing returns to scale in contemporary industrial economies is still an unsettled question; but we would hazard the guess that in the large modern economies increasing returns to scale is probably considerably less important than the residual as a source of increased output. For the time and circumstances of the industrial revolution, however, there seems to be no basis for such a presumption, and the importance of economies of scale is an open question for research.

It is worth emphasizing, in this context, that 'internal' economies of scale, such as would be connected with an increase in the size of the individual factory, are only part of the problem. 'External' economies, i.e. reductions in cost connected with the finer specialization made possible by an increase in the size of the economy as a whole, may be at least as important, especially at early stages of industrialization. The part of economic growth that can be attributed to increasing returns to scale is assimilated, after a fashion, to a story about the growth of conventional inputs.

III

It is time we commented on the practical difficulty of carrying out this sort of analysis. We have mentioned that two kinds of numbers are required to make the connection between the growth of output and the growth of inputs. They are estimates of the rates of growth of real output and of the supplies of the various factors of production, and estimates of the elasticity of output with respect to each of the factors of production.[10]

We have already discussed some of the problems encountered in measuring the growth of real output. The problems of measuring the growth of inputs are similar but not identical. We now turn to a consideration of their unique characteristics.

It is easy to provide definitions of the three traditional factors of production – land, labour, and capital – but hard to translate these definitions into workable rules for use. There are many factors of production, and this triad represents only a particular way of separating these myriad factors into distinct groups for analysis. The first problem is how to determine where any particular factor belongs.

'Land' consists of the sum of all natural resources possessed by an economy, i.e. those earning assets not created by man. 'Labour' includes that part of the population able and willing to contribute to economic production. And 'capital' is the sum of earning assets created

by man; it is often called 'reproducible capital' to distinguish it from
land ('nonreproducible capital').

Business units of the economy employ the services of these three
factors to produce goods and services. The definitions have been given
in terms of the stock of the three factors, i.e. the amount of the factors
available to the economy, but the entire stock of land, labour, and
capital is not used to produce goods and services in any one year; the
services of these factors are used instead. In addition to defining the
stock of these factors, therefore, we must provide a means for evaluating
the input of each factor to production.

We begin our discussion with labour. Labour differs from the other
two traditional factors of production in at least one important way.
People can improve their level of well-being by working to increase
their income – i.e. their ability to purchase goods and services produced
by others – but they can also increase their well-being by abstaining
from work. The alternative to using land or capital is to let them stand
idle, which does not increase anyone's happiness. But the alternative to
working is leisure, which provides pleasure directly to the workers involved.[11]

The market for labour, therefore, is unlike the market for other
factors of production. Competing against the various 'productive' uses
of labour is the additional demand for time for leisure. In general, when
the price of a commodity rises, it becomes profitable for firms to substitute the production of the now higher-priced commodity for other
production (or at least it never becomes profitable to switch the other
way). When the price of labour rises, this effect is present: workers are
inclined to substitute labour for leisure, as they can buy more of the
goods they desire for a given quantity of work. However, there is also
another influence at work. A higher wage means that a man doing the
same amount of work as before has a higher income than before. He
may want to spend this income on goods he can buy, but he may also
wish to consume all or part of it in increased leisure. A rise in wages
therefore may actually decrease the amount of labour supplied, if what
we may call the 'income effect' increasing the desire for leisure offsets
the 'substitution effect' by which labour is made more attractive. In
this case, we talk of a 'backward-bending' supply curve of labour, because the quantity of labour supplied falls as the price rises. A backward-
bending supply curve can be an obstacle to industrialization, for increases in the productivity of workers can be offset by declines in the
amount of labour supplied. This is an obstacle that cannot be present
with either of the other factors; it is a historical question whether it was
present for labour.

The historical question is compounded because the distinction between work and leisure is itself comparatively modern. Religious ritual appears as a leisure-time activity in modern life, but it was far more serious in pre-modern society. It is doubtful whether men who believed in the active intervention of supernatural beings in human affairs viewed religious observances as recreation. Similarly, the domestic worker producing cloth or other articles would have been hard pressed to say when the 'productive' activity stopped and the duties of being a housewife or the recreation of sitting and talking began. The process of fixing a work week is distinct from the process of varying it – they may involve entirely different forces and have quite dissimilar effects on production.

Let us start our discussion of how to measure the services of labour by considering the services of a single worker, or alternatively a set of identical workers.

The simplest index of labour services is the size of the labour force. This index is often the only one permitted by the data. In fact, the labour force itself often is not observed but instead derived from demographic data by assuming stable participation rates, either for the population as a whole or for groups within the population. As the limitations of the data will remain severe, this measure will continue to be used. But let us ask, as we did with the measure of the national product, what is being measured.

To count the number of people who can work is to measure the potential labour input rather than the actual input: no account is taken of unemployment. It is virtually impossible to find reliable data on unemployment before the twentieth century, and no correction for unemployment is possible. Consequently, the measure of potential input that we use does not quite match a measure of actual output. (On the other hand, if output is estimated by using data on capacity, as is common in industry studies, the two measures do match.)

Similarly, no account is taken of the different amounts that people work when they do work. This implicitly assumes that the output to be associated with a man's labour is independent of how long he works: a man working an eight-hour day is assumed to produce as much as one working a ten- or twelve-hour day. The question about the backward-bending supply curve raised above disappears; we do not care how much a person works, because he always produces the same amount. In addition, the history of the nineteenth century becomes very hard to understand. Starting early in the century, workers demanded shorter working hours. They were adamantly and consistently opposed by their employers (excepting a few aberrant industrialists like Robert Owen). If the employers stood to lose nothing by reducing the hours of work, why did they object? It seems unlikely that their fear of the workers' vices was strong enough to explain their actions.

There are several factors that could cause output to remain the same when the length of the working day changes. If people work harder when they work shorter hours, if they damage fewer machines and make fewer mistakes when they are working less and are less tired, if their morale improves when their hours fall, their productivity in any given time may rise. The hypothesis that the intensity of work rises when the duration of work falls poses a problem like the problem of the backward-bending supply curve. In that case, there were two offsetting influences affecting the amount of labour offered at a given wage rate. There is no theoretical way to tell which was stronger at any moment of time; it is an empirical question. Similarly, the extent to which the increased intensity of work offsets a reduction in its duration is an empirical question. And, as often happens, several answers have been proposed (all by investigators studying the twentieth century).

No investigator thinks that the change in intensity is exactly the same as the change in duration for all conditions. On the other hand, they seem to agree that there is a maximum output attainable from any individual and that this maximum is obtained well before complete physical exhaustion sets in. Lloyd G. Reynolds asserted that the maximum output came when a person was working between forty and fifty hours a week. Edward F. Denison, in his study of economic growth in the United States, said that a person produced his maximum output when he worked about forty-nine hours a week (the normal working week in 1929). In his later, more comprehensive study, Denison assumed that the point of maximum output was reached for non-farm workers when they were working ten hours a week more than they worked in 1960, or about fifty-four and fifty-nine hours a week for the United States and northwest Europe respectively. (Denison assumed that the output per man-year of agricultural workers was independent of the hours worked, i.e. that the offset was exact and complete throughout the reported range.) Finally, P. J. Verdoorn asserted that an individual produced the most when he worked sixty hours a week.[12]

Even though these findings vary in detail, there is general agreement that a man working more than sixty hours a week is producing less than a man working fewer hours. It is probable that the ability to sustain long hours has increased over time as nutrition and factory experience have grown, making this conclusion valid for the nineteenth century as well. These findings imply, therefore, that a ten-hour day probably was not the most efficient use of labour in the nineteenth century, and that longer working days definitely resulted in smaller total output than the same workers would have produced had they worked shorter hours.

Should we believe this inference, or should we re-examine our method of dealing with changes in hours today? The essays in this volume may suggest some answers.

We have switched easily from talking about the intensity of effort to talking of hours per week, but there are many ways of reducing the hours that people work. Hours per day, days per week, and weeks per year are all subject to change. Does it make any difference which way the change is made? The preceding discussion assumed that all changes took place within the unit of a week, but longer weekends and vacations may also increase the efficiency of workers while on the job. We know even less about the effects of vacations than we do about the effects of variations in the length of the work week; historical judgements may help us out.

For example, it has been estimated that there were 111 feast days a year under the *ancien régime*.[13] Workers in eighteenth-century France consequently worked, on average, a five-day week (assuming that whatever they did on feast days was not work). This may have represented fewer hours of work than the more usual nineteenth-century six-day week, or it may simply have represented a different allocation of hours within a week. In any case, did it affect the productivity of labour?

The discussion so far has treated the problem of a homogeneous labour supply, whether composed of a solitary worker or of many identical labourers. Let us now consider the problem of diverse workers. The labour force will no longer be an adequate index of labour services, because it does not show changes in the quality of labour. There are many ways in which workers differ from one another; we must ask if these differences are likely to change the rate of growth of the labour force and, if so, how we can adjust our data.

First, workers differ in intelligence. In the absence of any evidence or reason to the contrary, we may assume that the distribution of intelligence among people remains constant over time. When the size of the labour force increases, the quantity of intelligent – and of less intelligent – people rises in exact proportion to the labour force. Similarly, although intelligent people can be expected to earn more than less intelligent ones, the distribution of salaries based on intelligence alone may be expected to remain constant, and the changes of any one wage can be used as an index of the movements of all wages. Therefore, we do not have to take explicit account of differences in intelligence among workers.

Second, workers differ in the skills they possess. (We distinguish here between skills learned on the job and those that are the results of formal education.) If these skills were purely the product of experience, if everyone acquired them as he aged, and if the age composition of the work force remained constant, then job skills could be treated in exactly the same way as intelligence. There would always be a pool of job skills, and this pool would increase with the size of the labour force: no specific account would need to be taken of it. Although everyone does not acquire skills at the same rate, we could assume that aptitudes are constant and ignore these differences as we have ignored differences in intelligence. If the age structure changes, a simple correction could be made.

But the relationship between skill and experience cannot be treated so simply. As jobs changed, the importance of experience changed. As traditional apprenticeship programmes were abandoned, the communication of skills was altered. As education became more widespread, the aptitude for on-the-job instruction undoubtedly rose. As workers became more used to factory discipline, their willingness to learn probably also increased. And as workers became more adapted to urban life, their ability to focus on their jobs probably rose too. An adjustment should be made in the measure of labour input to account for these changes. The method could follow that for education – to be described shortly – but the size is not clear. Empirical work must precede an explicit measure.

Third, workers differ in their educational backgrounds. The main problem with education can be seen by making a few extreme assumptions. Let us assume first that people learn nothing of economic value in school that they would not have learned in any case. The economic function of school then would be to sort out the intelligent people – those who finish school – from less intelligent people – those who do not finish – even though the intelligent people would have been as productive as they actually were even if they had not attended school. We would observe that the people with the most schooling earned the highest salaries, but we would not want to increase our estimates of labour input when the level of education rose as a result; the distribution of salaries in this case would be the distribution caused by differences in intelligence, which we have seen remains constant over time. (It may still be rational to have schools even if they teach nothing of economic value. Their sorting function may be worth their cost, and people may enjoy school as they enjoy leisure.)

Now let us assume the reverse, namely that there are no differences in native intelligence and that differences among workers are produced purely by education. Then any salary differentials would relate not to the constant distribution of intelligence but to the fruits of schooling. As the educational level of the population increased, we would want to show the quality of labour services being used increasing with it. Or, to use current terminology, we would want to show an increase in 'human capital' along with the increase in the labour force. (The valuation of this capital would pose the same problems as the valuation of any kind of capital – to be discussed shortly – although it is normally included with labour in discussions of production.)

It is fair to assume that one man earns twice as much as another because he produces twice as much (subject to qualifications to be mentioned in connection with labour mobility). It follows that the high wages of a university-educated worker reflect his high productivity, which comes in turn (by our assumption) from his education. We can construct an index of labour services, therefore, in the same way that we constructed an index of real national product. We find the wages of workers with different educational levels in some base period, and we use these wages as weights to combine the numbers of workers with these educational levels at each point in time. We will not have valued the stock of 'human capital', but we will have an index of the extent to which it augments the services of uneducated labour. It will be recalled that we constructed this index under the assumption that there are no differences in native intelligence – only differences in education.

Clearly, neither this assumption nor the alternative extreme assumption that education teaches nothing is valid. The true condition lies somewhere in between, wage differentials reflecting differences in both education and intelligence. The question then is how much of the differences to ascribe to education – a question to which no satisfactory answer has been given. Denison assumed that three-fifths of the wage differentials were due to education, measuring differentials from the wage of a worker who left school at the age of fourteen. In other words, Denison assumed that the salary differentials that would have been observed had all workers been exactly as intelligent as actual workers with eight years of schooling would have been three-fifths as large as the actual differentials.[14] There is no good way to test this assumption, because we have no way to separate the results of education from intelligence: our tests for intelligence are being revealed increasingly as tests of education. It is not clear how much historical work can contribute to the resolution of this dilemma.

However, unless we use an *ad hoc* assumption like Denison's, we cannot show educational investment as an element in the increase in national product. For if we do not use such an assumption, we have no way of separating the return to education from the fruits of native intelligence.[15] Either we must omit this important input from our discussion or else enter it according to a conventional method whose value has yet to be tested.

The preceding discussion has treated differences among workers, but there can also be changes in the character of the labour force coming from changes in the nature of the labour market. For example, there are many barriers to labour mobility. A worker may have to travel to find the best job, and he may be unwilling or unable to do so. He may refuse to leave a traditional occupation for one he is more suited for. He may not be able to enter into the social class that is needed to fill a job he could otherwise ably perform. As a result, the labour force may not be used to its fullest capacity. If the relationship between the actual productivity of the labour force and its perfect-market potential remained constant, we would not have to worry about it; like differences in intelligence, it would remain internal to the analysis. On the other hand, if the geographical and occupation mobility of labour increased – as it did during the industrial revolution – then there would be an increase in labour services in addition to the growth in the size of the labour force.

In general, we do not have to take account of the characteristics of the labour force that stay constant over time. We are interested in measuring changes in the services of labour supplied, and if all components of a disparate aggregate move together, we can use any one component as an index of change. On the other hand, if different components are changing at different rates, then we are faced with an index-number problem exactly analogous to the problem we faced in measuring the national product. Of course we have to determine the nature and identify the causes of the differences between workers before we can tell which is which. We have to decide in each case if an attribute is inborn and immutable – and will therefore vary with the size of the labour force as a whole – or is the result of changing circumstance – and will change at a rate all its own.

IV

These problems, however, pale to insignificance compared to the complexity of valuing the services of capital and land. We have a naive measure of labour services in the labour force. There are many difficulties with this naive index, and we try to improve upon it; but it represents a fairly advanced starting point. We do not have this advantage when we discuss reproducible and non-reproducible capital, and we must start from scratch.

We must first distinguish the two kinds of capital from intermediate goods. We stated above that goods and services bought by business firms were intermediate goods. We now amend that definition to say that of the goods and services purchased by business firms, those that are used up within one year are intermediate goods. Goods or services that last longer than a year we will classify as capital, including them with 'capital' or with land depending on whether or not they are reproducible. Coal bought by a railway is an intermediate product, but rails are capital because they last more than a year.

The distinction is important. We measure the national product on a yearly basis, and we want to have a measure that treats all years symmetrically. A railway typically uses most of the coal it buys within a year, and it is left at the start of the next year in the same position that it was in originally. On the other hand, a railroad that buys rails in one year has them on hand in the next. It is better off at the start of the second year than at the start of the first, and if we classified rails as an intermediate good we would observe an unexplained increase in the production of railroad services. To avoid this, we classify the rails as capital, and only their depreciation, i.e. the amount by which they are used up, is subtracted from output to get value added. The undepreciated portion of the rails is carried over from one year to the next as capital, and the excess of the production of capital over its depreciation is defined as investment and is added to consumption to give national income or product.[16]

This discussion points to two ways of formulating a measure of the reproducible capital stock. We could add together all the undepreciated capital existing in the economy at any one time; or we could add together the investments from past years, discounting them to allow for the intervening depreciation. The two measures are conceptually the same; the problem – as always – is that prices change. The cost of building a brick factory in 1840 differs sharply from the cost of reproducing that same building today and also from the cost of a modern pre-stressed concrete building that could serve the same purpose. At which price should we value the factory?

This question is of great theoretical importance, for the very nature of capital is at stake. In choosing a price by which to value the factory built in 1840, we are selecting its contemporary equivalent. This might be a modern reproduction of the 1840 factory, duplicating in every detail the nineteenth-century construction, or it might be a modern concrete and glass factory with the same floor space. In the one case, it is the physical characteristics that define the unit of capital; in the other, the economic.

The theoretical importance of this question, however, is matched by the difficulty of applying it in historical studies. We have enough data for recent years to make a choice between alternative concepts of capital, but we do not have enough data for the eighteenth and nineteenth centuries to use price indexes based on either of the choices just outlined. Let us therefore examine the assumptions implicit in the measures that can be used.

The worst – but not unusual – situation is where there is no separate price index for capital at all. Investment is then deflated by a wholesale price index to get a value for real capital formation. Without a standardized commodity, no price index is possible, and most wholesale price indexes concentrate on uniform commodities such as agricultural products and cloth. They do not generally include the prices of many capital goods, and we will not go too far wrong in this discussion if we make the slightly inaccurate assumption that wholesale price indexes measure the prices of consumption goods.

Deflating investment by the price of consumption goods denies that there is any separate commodity called 'capital'. Investment is then the act of putting aside consumption goods for future years, of accumulating inventories of consumption goods as opposed to consuming them. This can be seen by the following argument. Prices at any one time measure the relative costs of producing different commodities. If a country chooses to invest one pound or one franc less this year than last, it can thereby produce one pound's or one franc's worth of extra consumption goods. By extension, if a country chooses to invest nothing at all, it could then produce more consumption goods equal in value to the investment forgone.[17] Investment therefore represents consumption forgone, and we can measure it by the amount of consumption forgone, i.e. by valuing it as we value the past production of consumption goods.

A slightly better situation exists when we have a price index specially constructed to value investment which measures the prices of inputs to capital formation: wood, bricks, iron (steel for the late nineteenth century), and the labour used to combine these elements into capital. This situation is better because it opens another alternative to us, but this new price index has many of the characteristics of the old. It too denies the existence of capital goods, valuing the investment of the past by the resources used as opposed to the capital produced. It is as if the economy used its resources to accumulate inventories of intermediate goods, raw materials, and labour, whose work could be measured by the value of these items at a later date.

We initiated this discussion of capital by differentiating capital from intermediate goods. Capital, we said, consisted of inventories – goods produced in one year but not used till a later year. To value the capital stock we need to know what kind of goods comprise these inventories, and the choice of price indexes is the same as the choice of assumptions on this very question. Using a wholesale price index assumes that the inventories are composed of consumer goods (or their equivalent);

using the prices of inputs, that they are composed of these inputs. In either case, investment is simply the accumulation of inventories. There is no form of production recognized as capital goods and valued separately from other goods.

This is a theory of investment popular among Austrian economists at the end of the nineteenth century, and it is more appropriate to agricultural than to industrial societies. Wine and trees improve with age, and an economy can productively use its resources by holding inventories of these commodities. Generalizing from these and similar examples, the Austrians concluded that postponing consumption was in itself productive. Capital formation became inventory accumulation, and capital became the ability to wait.

No one denies that the ability to postpone is an important aspect of capital, but few people today would agree that this ability is the only aspect of capital worth considering. It is not enough just to accumulate inventories; it matters what goods you inventory. And we do not just store consumer goods or inputs to production. We construct special goods to store, goods distinguished by their usefulness in production over time. We call these goods 'capital goods', and it would be nice to value our inventory of these goods in a way that takes account of our changing ability to produce them. The construction of a price index suitable for this use poses many problems, but the nature of the available data limits the relevance of these problems to the topics dealt with in this volume, and we shall not consider them here.[18]

Instead we turn to a qualitative distinction that can be made between different kinds of capital formation. As the size of the labour force – measured by one of the methods already discussed – changes, the size of the capital stock must change in order to keep constant the ratio of capital to labour. Capital formation that accompanies a rise in the labour force and serves only to maintain the existing capital–labour ratio is called 'capital-widening'. On the other hand, capital formation that increases the ratio of capital to labour is called 'capital-deepening'. Capital-deepening can take place whether or not the labour force is increasing, and capital-widening and -deepening can take place simultaneously.

We have suggested that a rise in the national product is a hallmark of industrial development. It is reasonable to go further and to say that a rise in the national product per capita should be the appropriate measure. This measure has the disadvantage of ignoring any increases in the population caused by industrial development, but it has the advantage of focusing attention on the increase in a typical individual's ability to consume.[19] And if it is used, the distinction between capital-widening and capital-deepening is very important. In an economy with a growing labour force, some investment is required simply to maintain the existing output per capita – by maintaining the existing capital per worker – and investment to increase the output per capita must be in addition to this capital-widening. A given amount of investment, therefore, will cause a smaller increase in the national income per head in a country with a rapidly growing population than in one with a less rapidly growing or stable population. Even if we cannot discover the exact rate at which the capital stock grew, therefore, it is often illuminating to know how capital formation was divided between capital-widening and capital-deepening.

We turn our attention now to the remaining factor of production: land, by which we mean raw materials or 'non-reproducible capital'. Countries differ in their endowments of natural resources, and it is appropriate to take account of this fact in the explanation of economic production. But the problems of measurement encountered in the discussion of labour and capital are as nothing when compared with the difficulty of measuring raw materials. As with capital, there is no naive measure of land similar to the labour force for labour. But unlike capital, natural resources were not produced and are not reproducible, and there is consequently no easy way to value them or the cost of their production.

The problem is further complicated by the capricious nature of technology. The value of the minette ores of Lorraine was vastly increased by the discovery of the Thomas process for using ores containing phosphorus in the Bessemer converter. The value of palm oil and related products was raised by their substitution for tallow and other animal products in the manufacture of soap. Similarly, deposits of oil, aluminium, uranium, etc. were valueless before technology advanced to the point where they could be used in the production of goods or services.

And as if these problems were not enough, there is also the problem of discovery. The New World was composed of many riches, but what was its value to the Old before it had been discovered? The United States paid $15,000,000 for the Louisiana Purchase; it is hard to know what deflator would translate that price into the present value of the American Great Plains. The lands surrounding the Persian Gulf gave no evidence for many years of the liquid wealth lying beneath them; for all we know, the land we stand on may have similar undiscovered treasures beneath it.

It is interesting and useful to chronicle the discovery and exploitation of these resources, but we would like to know the total amount of natural resources available to each country to unify our discussion of land with that of the other inputs. For the reasons just listed, however, we can only find a measure of tl e resources in use at any given time – the value of those not in use or not even yet discovered being impossible to know. Half a loaf is better than none, and we turn to a measure of this type.

The crudest measure – but by the same token the easiest to use – is the area of a country, or alternatively its population density. This measure assumes that resources are spread evenly over the earth and is consequently of little help except in extreme cases, such as a comparison of nineteenth-century Australia with twentieth-century India. The quantity of one particular resource, like arable land or coal, is an alternative measure, but it is too restrictive a measure for use in any but specific, narrowly defined inquiries. And if we say that the sum of several different resources should be used, we are faced with the index-number problem deriving from the different valuation of different resources over time.

Some function of exports can also be used as an index of resource endowments.[20] Countries tend to export the products whose production depends on the utilization of resources they possess in relative abundance, and the ratio of exports to the national product gives an index of the resource endowment. The measure, however, is seriously flawed. The United States is obviously well endowed with natural resources, yet its exports are much smaller in relation to its national product than the exports of many less well-endowed but smaller countries. British foreign trade was large in the nineteenth century as a result of Britain's free-trade policy. And all exports fell in the 1930s, even though the world was not deprived of its natural resources by the depression in world trade. The size of a country, the nature of its mercantile policies and the state of international affairs – as well as natural-resource endowments – affect the volume of a country's exports. Nevertheless, a better index of resource endowments is hard to find.

V

Suppose that, somehow, estimates are constructed of the rates of growth of real output and of the employment of the main factors of production. Without those estimates there is no possibility of even posing the quantitative question about the extent to which the growth of inputs accounts for the growth of output. Even with them, the calculation of an answer requires another ingredient, the marginal products or output-elasticities of each of the inputs, or at least their average values during the period of time in question.[21] These elasticities have a status quite different from that of the rates of growth. They are not at all directly observable quantities but must be inferred.

There are essentially only two ways in which this can be done. One is by direct statistical inference from observations on output and input quantities, as one might estimate a demand curve from observations on price, quantity, and related variables. There are many advantages to this approach, but it has the substantial handicap of requiring a large number of observations over a fairly wide range of independent variation in input quantities. No such statistical record is likely to be available for periods more than a century in the past; indeed, even with contemporary data it is not easy to fulfil the requirement for independent variation in input quantities. Perhaps the most that can be expected of historical data on input and output quantities is that they serve as a check on conclusions derived by indirect methods.

The indirect approach to the estimation of marginal products and output–input elasticities rests on the proposition from economic theory that, under competitive market conditions, the return to a unit of each factor of production (measured in units of output) will approximate its marginal product. This is equivalent to saying that the fractional share of the return to a factor of production in the distribution of the output it has helped to produce will be an estimate of the elasticity of output with respect to that factor.

The great advantage of this approach, of course, is that it requires only data on factor returns – wage rates, rents, profits – or the proportional distribution of the product of the economy or industry among the various inputs. This sort of information may be available even in the absence of usable data on the quantities of inputs and outputs. The disadvantage of the indirect approach is that its validity depends on strong assumptions: that the markets for land, labour, and capital are approximately competitive, and that they are approximately in equilibrium (i.e. that factor returns do not differ from marginal products as a signal that the organization of production is in the process of adapting to change). These assumptions are not easy to swallow in ordinary times; they may be misleading in times of extraordinarily rapid and thoroughgoing change. If that is so, the data themselves may provide a warning by moving sharply or systematically. Suitably checked, this is probably the only way that the accounting exercise can be done, if it can be done at all.

Even if it can be done and if part of the growth of output can be imputed to the growth of inputs and the remainder segregated as a residual, the result can have only the rough validity of a parable or abstract model, a relation among statistical aggregates. When one says that over two decades the increase in labour input accounted for a specified part of the growth of output, one is saying that if employment had grown a bit more slowly than in fact it did, output would have grown a bit more slowly than in fact it did, and one is saying by how much. Now 'labour' and 'output' (and 'capital' and 'land') are particular statistical constructs. At the level of detail there are many ways, perhaps infinitely many ways, in which a small difference in the rate of growth of the aggregate 'labour input' might have occurred: the geographical balance, the industrial composition, the occupational structure might each or all have been different. Corresponding to each of those ways, the fine detail of output might have responded in alternative ways. And while some statistical 'stock of capital' remains constant, particular capital goods are ageing and are being replaced by new varieties. Only under the most special circumstances will there exist any exact relation among the aggregates so that one could say: Had the rate of growth of one input been greater or less by so much, the other inputs growing as they did, the rate of growth of output would have been so much higher or lower.

Nevertheless, one has the notion that there are times when the residual contribution to the growth of output is very large, and times when it is relatively small. It is probably possible, with available data and more or less aggregative methods, to distinguish one set of circumstances from the other.

Suppose, then, that one is able to estimate the rate of growth of output over some interval, and the contribution of each broad input to that rate of growth (i.e. the product of the rate of growth of the input and the estimated elasticity of output with respect to the input). Suppose the sum of the calculated contributions falls short of the rate of growth of output and leaves a residual.[22] If Nature abhors a vacuum, accountants abhor discrepancies. Can we say anything about the sources of the residual, even if we cannot account for it in quantitative terms?

Some of the things that can be said have already been mentioned, but it is well to gather them together here. Generally speaking, the residual is made up of two kinds of items. The first we can call measurement errors, though that name is misleading. The errors in question are not merely statistical (there will be plenty of those, but they might be expected to be unbiased) but rather systematic conceptual errors that tend to underestimate the rate of growth of inputs. The second sort of component that goes to make up the residual consists of genuine increases in productivity, and these can happen in any of several ways.

Among the measurement errors – or 'specification errors', as an econometrician would call them – the most important has already figured in our discussion. Over historical time, the supplies of the factors of production change both in quantity and in quality. Labour becomes better educated, healthier, more skilled, more or less adapted to industrial work. Capital goods become more or less durable, more accurate, more efficient; and eventually they are utterly transformed. In principle, one should count each grade of worker, each physically different piece of equipment, as a separate factor of production. In practice one often lumps them together as labour and capital.

The effect of lumping these disparate inputs together into a few large aggregates – even if one distinguishes between educated and uneducated labour – is to disregard much if not all of the increase in the quality of the inputs. The growth of the inputs used in production is consequently underestimated; and the proportion of output that cannot be explained by the growth of these inputs is overestimated. The size of this overestimate in contemporary data is a matter of some dispute.[23]

It should be remarked that inadequate allowance for improved quality of output may cause the rate of growth of output to be underestimated also. Correcting this bias has the reverse effect of adding to the unexplained residual. On the other hand, in economies at that stage of development in which self-sufficiency and local barter are giving way to the market, the coverage of statistical series is likely to widen, and the rate of growth of output to be overestimated. This sort of error verges on the merely statistical and suggests that even statistical errors may impart a bias to measured rates of growth for intervals of time long enough to make a difference.

Even after the best possible adjustment is made for quality changes in inputs and output, a positive residual is likely to remain as a reflection of a genuine increase in the productivity of the economic system. It is this increase in productivity that is available for all-round increases in the rewards to factors of production of constant quality. (Some part of the apparent increase in wage rates, however, is a result of the rise in the average quality of labour input; it is not part of a general rise in wages, as would be apparent if each grade of labour were accounted as a separate factor of production.) This true increase in productivity can be sub-classified according to its source. The three main sources are increasing returns to scale, improved efficiency in the allocation of resources, and technological progress, but it is exceedingly difficult to get any idea of their relative importance.

We have already mentioned the possible importance of economies of large-scale production as a source of economic growth. The economist distinguishes between internal economies that have to do with the scale of the individual producing unit and external economies that have to do with the possibility of extended specialization of function as the whole economy grows in scale. The exploitation of economies of scale is often, perhaps usually, accompanied by changes in the technique of production. In principle, increasing returns to scale should be distinguishable from genuine technological progress, because the changes in technique that merely accompany changes in scale should be reversible. Let an economy experience prolonged contraction and, in the absence of technological progress, techniques should revert to what they were before. But in fact, of course, one does not observe prolonged decay of whole economies (though studies of individual industries might throw light on this question). Increase in scale and increase in technical knowledge occur together, so that even sophisticated statistical analysis will have a hard time separating the effects of one from the effects of the other.

A second source of higher productivity is the achievement of a more efficient allocation of existing resources among industries and localities. In most industrial economies, even those that have been industrialized for a long time, there appear to be industries and occupations where the marginal products (and the earnings) of labour and other factors of production are lower than elsewhere. These are usually contracting industries (agriculture, especially small-scale agriculture, is of course the main example), but they are not contracting fast enough to keep the returns to factors from falling below those available elsewhere in the economy. In these circumstances, any transfer of resources from low-productivity employment to high-productivity employment has the effect of increasing real output as measured, with no corresponding increase in the total of inputs. Gains of this kind may be most available at times of rapid industrialization, or whenever the composition and location of economic activity are changing substantially. The immobility that holds resources in low-productivity employment need not be exclusively a matter of habit or non-pecuniary advantage or lack of information. It may be, for instance, that the pace of movement of labour from agriculture to industry is limited by the rate of capital investment in industry (and in housing). In this case, there is a sense in which the whole increment of output accompanying the shift of resources might be attributed to the capital input. But, equally, there is a point in distinguishing this kind of gain output from the kind that occurs when additional capital investment increases the productivity of other resources already engaged in industry.

Potential gains from the improved allocation of resources can be realized in other ways: from the elimination of monopolistic restriction of output, for example, or from the end of discriminatory practices in the employment of women, Negroes, or others. These are likely to be smaller, if only because their incidence affects a small fraction of the labour force.

The last major component of the residual growth of output is, of course, technological progress itself. One rather expects this to be a big component most of the time and especially at the times that tend to be labelled as First, Second, or Third Industrial Revolutions. For this reason, much attention has been lavished on the pure theory of technological change. No way has been found, however, to measure directly the contribution of technological progress to the growth of output. Studies of patent statistics and the like have been inconclusive.[24] The usual routine, in the absence of anything better, is to treat technological progress as the ultimate residual. One identifies as many of the components of economic growth as one can, and what is left provides at least an upper limit to the contribution of technological change.

This is particularly unsatisfying to the historian, who is aware of technological change primarily as a concrete phenomenon taking place in particular industries in particular localities. It is clear that neither extreme will do. The aggregative method, apart from its excessive indirectness, has the defect of concentrating all the errors of measurement of all the other factors into economic growth in the residual one, technological change. The wholly microeconomic approach has the defect that while a particular invention can be described with accuracy, its implications for economic growth are to be found not only in the industry in which the invention occurs but diffused through the whole economy. The contrast between the two ways of describing and analysing technological change suggests an experiment. The method of isolating the contribution of inputs to the growth of output, leaving a residual component of productivity increase, can be applied to the outputs and inputs of a single industry as well as to a whole economy. It would be interesting to conduct such an analysis for an industry and to compare the results with the economic historian's record of actual concrete changes in technology, in the same industry. One would hope for some correspondence.

If the object is to account for the growth of output, it is clearly the application of an invention in production rather than the invention itself that counts. To the extent that a particular innovation requires, for its application, labour with special skills or major investment in capital equipment of a novel kind, these requirements may govern the pace at which the innovation is introduced into production. This is another example of interaction among sources of economic growth that is much harder to handle in practice than in theory. Should the addition of this novel kind of capital be recorded as a rise in the input of capital or in the residual?

Since the statistics of inputs and outputs can reveal the consequences of technological changes only as they are applied, no distinction appears between the application of newly created knowledge and the diffusion or imitation of technical knowledge already in existence for some time. The distinction is an important one, but it has to be made extra-statistically. The point of the preceding paragraph is that the story of diffusion of new technology may be in many cases part of the story about inputs.

In any case, the relation between inputs and outputs that we have been discussing is a relatively mechanical one. It has to do with the evolution of productivity, and in that formal sense it explains the increase of output that we call economic growth. There are other, at least equally important, things to be said, but this method cannot say them. It can say that the growth of employment accounts for so much growth of output, and so much more when the improved quality of labour is given appropriate weight. It cannot say why the supply of labour did not increase faster or slower, or why it was not more or less mobile from place to place, from country to city, from farm to factory. Nor does it cast any light on the reverse influence: the extent to which, for instance, the evolution of the labour force was a response to the rise in wages, or a matter of demography, or something more complicated.

Analogously, it is important to know how much of the growth of output is attributable to capital investment. But it is at least as interesting to ask how that investment was motivated and financed. Was the willingness to invest primarily a reaction to the emergence of profit opportunities in industry? Or was it motivated otherwise? Or was the supply of saving the main limitation on the achieved growth of capital? In any case, a question arises about the sources of saving, whether the appearance of wholly new ones or the expansion of the old.

It seems, then, that economic development can be viewed in terms of the evolution of the main inputs, but it is a partial view, with something left out at either end. At one end, when the contributions of the broad factors of production to the growth of output have been evaluated, there will be something left over. This residual, or a substantial part of it, may be identifiable with technological progress. The difficult job remains of coordinating that indirect measure with a more circumstantial account of the course of invention and innovation.

At the other end, the evolution of inputs itself needs to be explained, with neither quantity nor quality slighted. The explanation will no doubt run in part in economic terms, as a response to changes in prices and incomes, output and its distribution. This reflex is what makes the economy an interrelated system. There will also be part of the explanation that runs in terms of attitudes and beliefs, chance and force. This is what keeps the economy from being an isolated system.

CHAPTER II

Capital Formation in Great Britain[1]

I. *Justification*

> Conjecture: an opinion formed on slight or defective
> evidence or none.

The above definition conveys very well the true character of many of the results which emerge from the exercise which follows: the estimation of capital accumulation over the period 1760–1860. As will soon be abundantly clear, the sources at present available for this period do not provide the evidence which would enable one to construct even moderately respectable estimates for certain key sectors – notably manufacturing – and hence for the whole economy. At crucial points we are able to proceed only by reliance on conjecture and speculation. The results are accordingly of limited pretension and humble status; the most that can be claimed for them is that they may indicate the broad orders of magnitude of the extent of the capital expenditures in each decade on both fixed assets and inventories, at home and abroad, and of the corresponding growth of the stock of capital; the approximate distribution, by sector, of domestic fixed capital; and the broad pattern and rate of change of capital over the hundred-year period in relation to the growth of population and of the national economy.

What justification is there for attempting at this stage to construct new estimates for the economy as a whole, when so much still remains to be done on the individual sectors which can alone provide a proper foundation for aggregate estimates? Partly the answer is to be found in the great historical importance of this period of early industrialization in Britain, the uncertainty surrounding the existing estimates, and the desirability of bringing together the estimates for individual sectors which have resulted from investigations undertaken since the last synthesis was prepared. Partly – and perhaps paradoxically – the justification for a new estimate lies in the view that a more ambitious and more systematic estimate has something special to contribute. By seeking to make continuous and comprehensive estimates at constant prices for both capital formation and the capital stock, we obviously create additional difficulties and impose greater burdens on an already weak foundation; but to offset this there is the benefit we derive from the framework of an interlocking system. For example, evidence about the capital stock can be used to make or corroborate estimates for the capital flows, and the need both to reconcile the various components of the system and to consider continuous series provides controls and checks not otherwise accessible.

A further justification, and one which is explained more fully below, is that despite all their limitations these series enable us to construct a new basis for the post-1860 estimates of the capital stock which is substantially more reliable than anything hitherto available.

This chapter is thus primarily devoted to an attempt to establish some rough orders of magnitude for capital formation in each decade from 1760 to 1860 and for the capital stock at four dates, 1760, 1800, 1830, and 1860 – the former measured at both current and constant prices, the latter at constant prices. It is a measure of the difficulties facing quantitative research in this area that despite much enterprising work in recent years a comprehensive set of estimates of this nature is still not available.

The existing estimates are reviewed in section II, and this is followed in section III by brief notes on the conceptual basis of the present estimates and on the procedure used to correct for changing prices. The discussion of the methods adopted to obtain the present estimates of reproducible domestic fixed capital (capital formation and capital stock) occupies section IV, and section V is devoted to the remaining components: circulating capital, farm crops and livestock, overseas assets, and land. The overall results are then compared with the existing estimates in section VI. Finally, in section VII we explore briefly some implications of our main findings and of their relationship to the growth of population and real income.

We shall thus be exclusively concerned with the extent and pattern of capital formation as viewed from the side of investment in real assets;[2] no attempt is made to consider the other side of this process, the flow of savings to finance the construction or acquisition of the capital goods.[3]

II. *The Existing Estimates*

CAPITAL FORMATION[4]

Until quite recently, empirical evidence about levels or rates of capital formation during and immediately after the industrial revolution was almost totally lacking. For the economy as a whole, writers either made no attempt at quantitative assessment, or else relied on *a priori* judgements, as in the much-debated propositions of Rostow and W. Arthur Lewis, regarding the proportion of national income devoted to capital accumulation. For individual sectors a few separate indicators could be assembled; and this approach was most fully exploited by Gayer,

Rostow, and Schwartz, using series in various physical units for brick production, fir timber imports, ships built, and railway mileage opened, together with some related financial series such as new home and foreign issues and the amounts authorized in parliamentary bills for canals and turnpikes.[5]

The first real advance on this front was made in the early 1960s by Phyllis Deane.[6] While still not seeking to provide comprehensive measurements for all sectors at a uniform date, she reviewed the existing evidence – including the work of writers and statisticians of the eighteenth and nineteenth centuries – and offered new estimates for capital expenditure on selected items at various dates. These included enclosures, house-building, roads, docks, shipping, cotton textiles, and iron. This covered a sufficiently large part of the aggregate for Miss Deane to feel justified in drawing a number of tentative conclusions, among which were estimates of the rate of capital formation, i.e. of net capital formation including inventories and foreign investment, expressed as a percentage of net national income. We can summarize these as follows:

Starting from a long-term average of not more than 3 per cent in the seventeenth and early eighteenth centuries,[7] the rate of capital formation began to rise in the middle decades of the eighteenth century; by the end of the century it had reached a 'sustained average of more than 5%' and 'may have somewhat exceeded 6% – most of the shift being attributable to the last quarter';[8] both capital and income rose after the end of the French wars, but at roughly the same pace until the beginning of the railway era in the 1830s; from there on the ratio of capital formation to income again began to increase, moving upwards to about 10 per cent by the later 1850s.[9]

The next major contribution was made by Sidney Pollard in a paper presented in 1965.[10] Here, for the first time, an attempt was made to construct estimates – described with due caution as 'possible orders of magnitude' – which aimed at complete coverage of all capital expenditure in Great Britain at four specified dates. These estimates are summarized in Table 1, together with an estimate of the gross national income and of the corresponding rate of gross capital formation.

Though Pollard had estimated the ratio of gross capital formation to gross national income and Miss Deane had worked with the net rate, he concluded that his results showed that the earlier estimates had seriously understated the proportion of income allocated to investment. This seems plausible: in particular, it is likely that the attempt to extrapolate from partial evidence to a national total without making separate estimates for the missing items could lead to an underestimate, especially for investment in industry and trade. However, as Pollard would readily

Table 1. *Gross Capital Formation, Great Britain, 1770–1835:*
Possible Order of Magnitude suggested by Pollard (£m)

	c. 1770	c. 1790–3	c. 1815	c. 1830–5
1. Gross domestic fixed capital formation	7·2	13·3	21·9	31·0
2. Stockbuilding	1·5	2·0	2·5	2·5
3. Foreign investment and bullion	0·7	0·7	0·7	6·5
Total	9·4	16·0	25·1	40·0
4. Gross national income	140	175	310	360
5. Total as % of 4	6½	9	8	11

SOURCE. Pollard, 'Growth and Distribution of Capital', I, p. 362.

acknowledge, his own estimates were very uncertain, and the issue cannot be settled without further evidence.

Since our main concern in this section is with gross domestic fixed capital formation (line 1 of Table 1), we may look more closely at the components of Pollard's estimates for this item. These are set out in Table 2. Subsequent work on the period covered by Table 2 has been

Table 2. *Gross Domestic Fixed Capital Formation, Great Britain,*
1770–1835: Possible Order of Magnitude suggested by Pollard (£m)

	c. 1770	c. 1790–3	c. 1815	c. 1830–5
1. Agriculture	2·7	3·6	5·3	4·6
2. Transport (incl. ships)	1·3	2·4	3·9	6·7
3. Building	2·3	5·1	8·5	11·5
4. Manufacture, trade, etc.	0·9	2·2	4·2	8·2
Total	7·2	13·3	21·9	31·0
5. Total as % of gross national income	5	7½	7	8½

SOURCE. As for Table 1.

devoted to some of the much-needed investigation in detail of capital formation in particular sectors, including inland transport, agriculture, and textiles; we may defer further reference to these studies until we come (below) to our attempt to make new estimates.

From 1830 onwards, however, we now have a further pioneering study by Miss Deane giving annual estimates of gross domestic fixed capital formation in the United Kingdom at both current and 1900 prices.[11] We may compare the opening years of this new series with Pollard's estimates for Great Britain (i.e. excluding Ireland) for the early 1830s (Table 3).

It is disconcerting to find that Miss Deane's new estimate is only half as large as Pollard's old one. In making the comparison we must allow for the possibility of differences in the scope of the individual sectors, but both estimates relate to substantially the same concept of capital formation. It is unhappily clear from Table 3 that the two leading

Table 3. *Gross Domestic Fixed Capital Formation, 1830–5: Comparison of Estimates by Deane and Pollard (£m p.a.)*

	Deane (UK)	Pollard (GB)
1. Transport		
Water (incl. ships)	2·2	2·5
Road[a]	2·0	2·2
Rail	0·6	2·0
Total (transport)	4·8	6·7
2. Residential building	6·0	10·0
3. Agriculture[b]	—	4·6
4. Industry, trade, etc.	2·9	8·2
5. Public buildings, etc.	2·0	1·5
Total	15·7	31·0

[a] Pollard omits expenditure on horses and carriages.
[b] Deane omits expenditure on land-clearing, drainage, etc.

SOURCES. Deane, 'New Estimates', 111; Pollard, 'Growth and Distribution of Capital', I, p. 362.

authorities are in serious disagreement over the level of gross domestic fixed capital expenditure in the early 1830s, and until this can be resolved similar doubt must attach to their respective estimates for earlier and later years. Equally, comment on, and analysis of, the course and consequences of capital formation must prove unrewarding as long as discrepancies of this magnitude exist.

The differences are largest in agriculture and in industry, trade, etc. In the case of the former, Miss Deane specifically omitted expenditure on land-clearing and drainage and appears also to have omitted farm buildings other than dwellings,[12] whereas Pollard made generous allowance for these assets. For industry, trade, etc. both estimates are exceptionally vulnerable and lack any real foundation. It is in this context that Crouzet has criticized Pollard: 'even a cursory glance at his sectoral estimates seems to reveal some bias towards selecting the highest figures wherever an alternative is available, and pushing upwards many estimates'.[13] Against this we might note that my comparison of Miss Deane's estimates with those which I prepared for the period from 1856 to 1914 led me to conclude that her capital-formation series for the second half of the nineteenth century was in general substantially too low from 1870 onwards, and that the shortfall applied particularly to her allowance for investment in industry, trade, etc.[14]

CAPITAL STOCK

When we turn to the pre-1860 estimates of the stock of fixed capital there is much less to report: quantitative research has not been appreciably advanced since 1889, when Sir Robert Giffen published his study *The Growth of Capital*.[15] In this the first of his own estimates relates to 1863 (though described as 1865), but Giffen also included an historical retrospect, calling attention to estimates of capital and national wealth put forward by earlier writers at various dates from 1679 to 1833. The most important of these contemporary estimates are summarized in Table 4, together with Giffen's own calculation for 1863.

Table 4. *Contemporary Estimates of the National Wealth, 1688–1863 ($£m$)*

Date	Author	Area	Reproducible capital[a]	Land	Furniture, 'plate', specie, etc.	Total
1688	King–Davenant	England	112	180	28	320
1800	Beeke	GB	665	825	250	1,740
1812	Colquhoun	GB	837	1,079	211	2,127
1832	de Pebrer[b]	GB	1,112	1,438	293	2,843
1863	Giffen	UK	3,749	1,864	500	6,113

[a] Including buildings and equipment, inventories, farm capital, and overseas assets.
[b] Obtained by adding one-third to Colquhoun's estimates; thus, not an independent assessment.

SOURCE. Giffen, *The Growth of Capital* (1889), 43 and 72–108.

These estimates have been frequently discussed and used, most recently by Deane and Cole and by Pollard,[16] but no new estimates of the stock of capital have appeared, apart from the series published in 1972,[17] which begins only in 1855 (considered below, p. 78). Although all the contemporary estimates have something of value to tell us, they are gravely deficient as a basis for long-run measurements of the capital stock designed for use in analysing the contribution of capital to the growth of the national income. Quite apart from the uncertainty of the data underlying the estimates, there are four critical comments which must be made.

First, all are wholly or largely derived by capitalizing estimates of income (profits and rents), and the conceptual basis of a capital series derived in this way is quite different from that underlying the conventional (perpetual inventory) national accounting estimates of capital. The essence of the conventional method is an objective cumulation of *actual past capital outlays*, revalued at the replacement cost of a given year.[18] By contrast, the essence of the 'Giffen method' is a subjective valuation of *expected future incomes*,[19] and the result will be strongly influenced by the profitability of the given year and by the view taken with regard to future prospects. There is, moreover, an inherent ambiguity in this method, and it is not clear to what extent the procedure allows for the depreciation of the capital assets.[20] Second, the overall capital–output ratios which can be calculated from such estimates simply reflect the capitalization rates (number of years' purchase) applied by Giffen and his predecessors in making the original estimates for each of the components of the capital stock, and thus provide no additional information.

The third point is that, for various reasons, the weakest item in the total is the estimate for capital in industry and trade. In the earlier estimates – for example, those of Beeke and Colquhoun – the main problem is simply the lack of data on trading profits; in later estimates, including Giffen's, the problem is to know what proportion of the profit of unincorporated enterprises represents a return on capital as opposed to the reward for the labour services of the owners. Giffen, following a suggestion by R. Dudley Baxter, capitalized one-fifth of the profits of 'trades and professions', but there is very little warrant for this.[21] Given the interest and importance of this sector, this weakness is particularly unfortunate. Finally, the method does not enable us to distinguish between fixed capital and inventories or – in the earlier estimates, including Giffen's for 1863 – between domestic and overseas assets.

For the capital stock, as for the capital-formation series, our review of the current situation thus points to the urgent need for further research. For the former, we have no modern investigation, and the contemporary estimates are of limited value. For the latter, we find some notable advances in recent years, but the position is still very unsatisfactory. We have Pollard's four benchmark estimates for the period before 1830 (Tables 1 and 2), but these suggest an appreciably higher rate of investment than that given by Phyllis Deane (Table 3). From 1830 onwards we have Miss Deane's annual series, but it is only half of the level of Pollard's at its starting point and is also well below my estimates for the latter part of the century.

III. *Concepts and Prices*

We begin the presentation of our new estimates with a brief discussion of the relevant concepts, and we then describe the indices which we use to correct for changes in price.

CONCEPTS AND DEFINITIONS

When dealing with reproducible fixed assets we shall be concerned with two basic series. The annual flow of *investment*, I_t, represents capital expenditure on domestic reproducible fixed assets (gross domestic fixed capital formation) and covers both new investment and replacement. It is measured either in current prices, i.e. the prices prevailing in the year in which the expenditure was incurred, or at constant prices, i.e. with all expenditure revalued at the prices of a given year. The corresponding stock estimate is G_t, the end-year gross stock of reproducible fixed assets. For this the actual outlays on the acquisition or construction of all reproducible fixed assets are revalued at the prices of a given year, and all assets remain in the stock at this valuation, regardless of their age or condition, until they are retired (scrapped or sold).

When both the flow, I_t, and the stock, G_t, are valued in the prices of the same year, i.e. at constant prices, they may be related by inclusion of a third series, R_t, the flow of assets *retired* at the end of their working lives as determined by depreciation and obsolescence. For this purpose the assets retired (scrapped or sold) would be taken at their original cost, revalued at the prices of the given year. We thus have the basic identity:

$$G_n = \sum_{t=0}^{n} (I_t - R_t)$$

and if we assume that all assets are automatically retired at the end of their working life of L years,[22] we have:

$$G_n = \sum_{t=0}^{n} (I_t - I_{t-L}) = \sum_{t=n-L}^{n} (I_t)$$

To measure the gross stock at any date, we thus need to estimate the flow of investment expenditure for L years preceding that date for each type of asset included in the stock – i.e. for as many years back as are required to cover the working life of each type of asset. Once we know the stock at any one date we can also cumulate by means of the basic relationship:

$$G_n = G_{n-1} + I_n - R_n$$

It would be possible to extend this set of *gross* estimates by a corresponding set of *net* flows and stocks in which provision would be made for depreciation of the fixed assets, but it did not seem desirable to add a further and even more arbitrary set of estimates at this stage.

For further discussion of the conceptual basis of the estimates the reader is referred to official studies such as *Sources and Methods*,[23] in which the current estimates for the United Kingdom are discussed, and to *National Income, Expenditure and Output*[24] for notes on the broadly comparable estimates for the years 1856–1948, preceding the official estimates. Within the very severe constraints imposed by the extent and quality of the data available, we have attempted to make the present estimates consistent in concept and definition with those for later years.

Two aspects warrant special mention. Firstly, the correction for movements in price. Reference has been made, in the above discussion of the basic concepts, to the need for evaluation of the capital outlays at the prices of a given year. Prices may change because the cost of construction of an asset of given type and quality changes owing to movements in the price of the inputs or in the productivity of the capital-goods sector; or they may change because the quality of the asset has changed as a result of technical progress embodied in new vintages of the asset. In general the price data we have can measure only the first of these causes of change, and even that with only minimal accuracy. We therefore implicitly treat any improvement in the efficiency and productivity of an asset, in excess of the corresponding increase in its cost of construction, as an increase in its quality; we do not treat it as a fall in the price – and thus a rise in the quantity – of a unit of capital of given quality. This procedure is imposed on us by the data but fortunately is also justifiable on theoretical grounds.[25] It has important implications for the measurement of the contribution of capital to the growth of output: the increase in efficiency of the capital goods is reflected as a rise in the measure of output per unit of capital, not in the measure of the capital stock.

Secondly, our measure of gross capital formation is a fairly narrow one, and as far as possible we exclude expenditure on maintenance and repairs. We shall, however, have to reckon with the fact that in some sectors it is extremely difficult to distinguish between outlays which represent new capital formation (i.e. those which will yield benefits in future accounting periods) and outlays which represent maintenance (i.e. those which do not add to the original life of the asset or improve the service which it yields), and this necessarily imparts a further element of approximation to our estimates.[26] This applies particularly in sectors such as agriculture, roads, and canals, where we rely in part on accounting records which made no distinction between new work and repairs. However, we have preferred to make a rough separation rather than accepting a very gross estimate including repairs. We do so partly because the very gross concept is less relevant and interesting for most purposes, and partly because its use would destroy comparability with estimates for other sectors and with estimates of total capital formation in later periods.

ADJUSTMENT FOR CHANGING PRICES

For some analytical purposes we require series for capital outlays at current prices; for other purposes, series at constant prices are needed. This case for two series is reinforced by the practical consideration that in some sectors of the economy the best starting point is an estimate in current prices, while in others we can make most progress by working first in the prices of a given year.

These arguments for constructing two sets of estimates have immediately to be weighed against the formidable problems created by the lack of suitable data on price changes. It is not only that we are rarely able to find actual price quotations for capital goods, but also that for much of the period we have great difficulty in getting even the data on movements in the costs of labour and materials used by the capital-goods industries, which in later periods provide a broadly acceptable substitute for asset prices.[27] Nevertheless the variations in prices within the period we cover are so great, especially during and immediately after the Napoleonic Wars, that it seems essential to make some correction; however uncertain the extent, we can at least be confident of the direction. It also seems preferable to use the most relevant of the specific price and wage series available, rather than relying on the much broader existing wholesale price indices, all of which are dominated by the movements in the prices of agricultural products.

We have accordingly compiled three main indices, each combining series for labour[28] and materials[29] used in the production of capital goods:[30]

(i) For houses and other buildings, an unweighted average of building wages and of the price of materials. The materials index is itself an unweighted average of the prices of imported fir timber and of bricks from 1760 to 1820 and of timber, bricks, and iron from 1810 to 1860, with the two indices spliced at 1810–20.

(ii) For agricultural works and buildings, a weighted average of agricultural wages (weight 4), timber (1), and bricks (1).

(iii) For plant and machinery, an index of engineering wages (weight 2) combined with indices for iron (1), and timber (1) for 1780–1820 and with iron only (weight 2) for 1810–60.

The three indices are set out in Table 5 as decade averages with 1851–60 = 100. It will be seen that they measure only the changes in the prices of some of the main inputs, and no allowance is made for changes in productivity in the building and engineering industries, even as measures of the cost of labour and materials, the series are thus very

Table 5. *Price Indices, 1760–1860 (average 1851–60 = 100)*

	(1) Houses and other buildings	(2) Agricultural works and buildings	(3) Plant and machinery	(4) General index of wholesale prices
1761–70	53	55	—	88
1771–80	56	56	—	95
1781–90	59	58	81	102
1791–1800	76	80	109	121
1801–10	121	126	150	152
1811–20	130	129	138	154
1821–30	114	98	117	109
1831–40	106	98	111	104
1841–50	100	97	102	93
1851–60	100	100	100	100

SOURCES

(1)–(3) See text, pp. 37–8 and notes 28–30.

(4) Based on the following indices of domestic and imported commodity prices – mainly wholesale prices and import unit values – spliced at the overlapping decades: for 1761–70 to 1791–1800, average of Schumpeter–Gilboy indices for consumer goods and producer goods; for 1791–1800 to 1841–50, Gayer–Rostow–Schwartz index for domestic and imported commodities; and for 1841–50 to 1851–60, Rousseaux's overall index. For all three indices see B. R. Mitchell, *Abstract of British Historical Statistics* (1962), 468–73.

imperfect. To the extent that productivity change in the construction of machinery is neglected, the index will overstate the rise in prices over the century; as a result the level of capital expenditure at current prices will be understated in years before 1851–60. Note, however, that the estimates at constant prices and the capital stock are not affected since the price index is not used in making these estimates (see below, p. 56).

The index for buildings rises by roughly 150 per cent between 1761–70 and 1811–20 and then drops by almost 25 per cent by the 1840s. In the first phase, building wages double while the index of materials rises threefold; in the second, wages show a slight setback in the 1820s and 1830s and then a small increase, and material prices fall sharply in each of these decades. The index for agricultural buildings and works follows broadly the same course but declines more sharply in the 1820s, when there is a swift fall in agricultural wages. The 'plant and machinery' index shows a steep fall between the peak of 1801–10 and the end of the period, essentially because of the greater influence of the large reduction in prices of iron and timber.

In the last column of Table 5 a general index of wholesale commodity prices is shown, both for comparison with the indices for capital goods and because it will be needed in section V. In addition to these major indices we also make use of special indices for individual sectors; these are described separately in section IV below.

IV. *Sources and Methods of Estimation*

We are now ready to embark on the main task – the estimation of gross domestic fixed capital formation and of the gross stock of domestic reproducible fixed assets. For the former we give estimates for each decade from 1761–70 to 1851–60, at constant prices of 1851–60 in Table 6 and at current prices in Table 7. For the stock we give estimates in Table 8 at 1851–60 prices, at four dates – 1760, 1800, 1830, and 1860 – reference in each case being to the end of the year. Of these, the 1860 estimates have been the main focus of our attention, and the earlier estimates are progressively more conjectural; despite this, they are given in order to provide some perspective in which to view the growth of the capital stock. All the estimates relate to Great Britain only.[31]

The detailed estimates are based on a classification which is in part by sector of activity and in part by type of asset, and we have thirteen separate estimates which are grouped in the tables on a sectoral classification under four headings: Residential and Social, Agriculture, Industry and Commerce, and Transport. The estimation procedures are described below in the same sequence in which the series are set out in Tables 6, 7, and 8. The description is designed to provide sufficient information about the major sources and methods and to permit future writers to make appropriate criticisms and revisions, but no attempt is made to specify every detail or to justify all the procedures and assumptions employed.

The logical order, if we could always follow the procedure suggested by the second equation on p. 35 above, would be to begin with the flow series for gross domestic fixed capital formation, and to derive from these the estimates for the gross stock of fixed assets. In practice, however, the limitations of the available data are such that in a number of sectors, including most of those which are of greatest importance for the estimates, we are compelled to reverse the procedure: we begin with an estimate of the stock of capital, obtained by some means other than accumulation of capital formation (e.g. from some count of the

Table 6. *Gross Domestic Fixed Capital Formation, Great Britain, 1761–1860, at Constant Prices* (£m p.a., decade averages, at 1851–60 prices)

	1761-70	1771-80	1781-90	1791-1800	1801-10	1811-20	1821-30	1831-40	1841-50	1851-60
Residential and Social										
1. Dwellings	1·49	1·38	2·17	3·35	4·58	5·82	8·91	10·28	7·60	10·25
2. Public buildings and works	0·15	0·14	0·22	0·33	0·46	0·58	1·07	1·54	1·52	2·05
Agriculture										
3. Farm buildings, improvements, and equipment	2·18	2·62	3·31	4·26	4·06	4·45	4·08	4·71	6·16	6·90
Industry and commerce										
4. Industrial and commercial buildings	0·97	0·73	2·13	2·20	3·04	4·16	6·81	8·52	8·15	10·99
5. Industrial machinery and equipment	0·27	0·11	1·10	0·88	0·84	1·28	2·65	3·51	4·18	5·65
6. Mining and quarrying	0·08	0·04	0·08	0·16	0·12	0·25	0·28	0·63	0·88	1·71
7. Gas and water	—	—	—	—	—	0·19	0·23	0·45	1·05	2·32
Total (industry and commerce)	1·32	0·88	3·31	3·24	4·00	5·88	9·97	13·11	14·26	20·67
Transport										
8. Railways	—	—	—	—	—	0·10	0·10	3·67	14·11	8·78
9. Roads and bridges	0·53	0·52	0·53	0·49	0·47	0·78	1·15	1·19	1·02	1·01
10. Carriages and coaches	0·20	0·20	0·30	0·40	0·50	0·60	0·80	1·00	1·30	1·70
11. Canals and waterways	0·22	0·50	0·25	1·04	0·70	0·57	0·52	0·47	0·19	0·17
12. Docks and harbours	0·02	0·04	0·05	0·07	0·68	0·42	0·30	0·45	0·85	1·46
13. Ships	0·53	0·77	0·98	1·13	1·12	1·31	1·39	2·17	2·42	5·00
Total (transport)	1·50	2·03	2·11	3·13	3·47	3·78	4·26	8·95	19·89	18·12
Total	6·64	7·05	11·12	14·31	16·57	20·51	28·29	38·59	49·43	57·99

Table 7. *Gross Domestic Fixed Capital Formation, Great Britain, 1761–1860, at Current Prices (£m p.a., decade averages)*

	1761–70	1771–80	1781–90	1791–1800	1801–10	1811–20	1821–30	1831–40	1841–50	1851–60
Residential and social										
1. Dwellings	0·79	0·77	1·28	2·55	5·54	7·57	10·16	10·90	7·60	10·25
2. Public building and works	0·08	0·08	0·13	0·25	0·55	0·76	1·22	1·64	1·52	2·05
Agriculture										
3. Farm buildings, improvements and equipment	1·20	1·47	1·92	3·41	5·12	5·74	4·00	4·62	5·98	6·90
Industry and commerce										
4. Industrial and commercial buildings	0·51	0·41	1·26	1·67	3·68	5·41	7·76	9·03	8·15	10·99
5. Industrial machinery and equipment	0·22	0·09	0·89	0·96	1·26	1·77	3·10	3·90	4·26	5·65
6. Mining and quarrying	0·04	0·02	0·05	0·12	0·15	0·32	0·32	0·67	0·88	1·71
7. Gas and water	—	—	—	—	—	0·27	0·32	0·52	1·01	2·32
Total (industry and commerce)	0·77	0·52	2·20	2·75	5·09	7·77	11·50	14·12	14·30	20·67
Transport										
8. Railways	—	—	—	—	—	0·10	0·10	3·85	15·25	8·78
9. Roads and bridges	0·33	0·33	0·39	0·49	0·63	1·03	1·19	1·15	0·99	1·01
10. Carriages and coaches	0·10	0·10	0·18	0·30	0·60	0·78	0·92	1·05	1·30	1·70
11. Canals and waterways	0·13	0·29	0·16	0·74	0·71	0·54	0·55	0·48	0·19	0·17
12. Docks and harbours	0·01	0·02	0·03	0·05	0·62	0·44	0·30	0·43	0·83	1·46
13. Ships	0·27	0·41	0·51	0·87	1·52	1·81	1·39	2·24	2·51	5·00
Total (transport)	0·84	1·15	1·27	2·45	4·08	4·70	4·45	9·20	21·07	18·12
Total	3·68	3·99	6·80	11·41	20·38	26·54	31·33	40·48	50·47	57·99

Table 8. *Gross Stock of Domestic Reproducible Fixed Capital, Great Britain, 1760–1860 (£m at 1851–60 replacement cost)*

	1760	1800	1830	1860
Residential and social				
1. Dwellings	191	248	390	599
2. Public works and buildings	19	25	37	80
Agriculture				
3. Farm buildings, improvements, and				
equipment	210	270	340	430
Industry and commerce				
4. Industrial and commercial buildings	25	75	204	460
5. Industrial machinery and equipment	9	26	61	160
6. Mining and quarrying	2	4	8	35
7. Gas and water	—	—	4	42
Total (industry and commerce)	36	105	277	697
Transport				
8. Railways	—	—	2	268
9. Roads and bridges	15	28	47	66
10. Carriages and coaches	2	5	9	23
11. Canals and waterways	8	23	35	37
12. Docks and harbours	1	3	15	42
13. Ships	12	22	31	68
Total (transport)	38	81	139	504
Total[a]	490	730	1,180	2,310

[a] Rounded to nearest £10m.

stock of assets), and then derive the corresponding capital flow from this. Accordingly, we begin with the stock estimates in some cases, with the flow in others.

I. RESIDENTIAL DWELLINGS

This item covers all dwellings: houses, farmhouses, lodging-houses, and the dwellings component of residential shops and pubs.[32] The number of inhabited houses in England and Wales at the end of each decade from 1800 onwards is given in the decennial Reports on the Census of Population.[33] We have extrapolated this series back to 1761 by reference to the movement of population[34] and on the assumption that the number of persons per dwelling increased slightly during the population upsurge of the late eighteenth century, rising from 5·5 in 1761 to the census-based figure of 5·8 in 1801.[35] In considering the evidence on this point it is necessary to distinguish between persons per home and persons per family, a distinction not always made, or easy to make, in contemporary enumerations. The assumption that the mean *houseful* size rose over the period – though with little change in mean *household* size – is based primarily on the conclusions drawn by Richard Wall after a systematic survey of all the available material.[36]

For Scotland the Census figures are not usable before 1881 because of confusion in the treatment of the many tenements containing two or more separate dwellings, and a rough estimate was made by assuming that the number of persons per dwelling changed in the same way as in England and Wales between 1761 and 1881. Combining these two series gives the number of dwellings in Great Britain at the end of each decade from 1760 to 1860. For our four benchmark years the figures (in millions) are 1·45, 1·87, 2·93, and 4·35.

The increase in the number of houses between each decennial figure represents effectively the number of new houses built in each decade less the number demolished. Lacking any direct information on demolition, we have attempted to construct a series which seems plausible in relation to (a) the size and age composition of the stock of houses at the beginning of each period, which broadly governs the number of houses likely to be ready for demolition; (b) the number of new houses built during each decade, which might broadly determine the rate at which demolition was undertaken; and (c) an assumed average life of just over 100 years. These assumptions lead to a very approximate series for houses demolished, taken as 40 per cent of the inter-censal increase for the decades 1761–70 to 1841–50, 35 per cent for 1851–60 to 1861–70, and 30 per cent for the remaining decades down to 1901–10.[37]

If dwellings were always built, on average, to a uniform standard of size and quality, we could treat these estimates of the decennial building and of the stock of dwellings as being measured in comparable units, which we could then proceed to value. In fact, of course, this is not the case, and we must first make some correction for the overall effect on dwellings of the extension of building regulations, the general rise in the standard of living, improvements in the standards of public health and sanitation affecting housing, and changes in the type of materials used. We have very little direct evidence on the effect of these factors, but have assumed that there was on average no appreciable change until 1810, and that thereafter housing standards began to rise – at first rather slowly, at an assumed annual rate of 0·1 per cent from 1811 to 1820 and 0·2 per cent from 1821 to 1840; and then a little more rapidly, by 0·5 per cent, from 1841 to 1860, as the building improvement laws began to take effect in a succession of major urban areas, and living standards began to rise, not for all but certainly for many groups within the population. These assumptions would mean, for example, that the average new house built in 1860 would be roughly 15 per cent bigger and better than the corresponding dwelling of 1810 or earlier.[38]

Our estimates of the dwellings built in each decade and of the stock of dwellings at the four benchmark dates can then be adjusted to comparable units of 1851–60 standard. For the stock, the standardized figures (in millions) become 1·28, 1·65, 2·60, and 4·00.

At this stage we attempted a partial check on our estimates of the number of (standardized) houses built in each decade by relating them to the widely used series for the output of bricks from 1791 to 1849.[39] It appeared from this that the present estimates understated the level of house-building in 1791–1800 and 1821–30 and overstated it in the two intervening decades. Close correspondence with the brick series is, of course, not to be expected: a changing proportion of houses was made with stone and timber, and bricks were used in fluctuating and unknown quantities for other purposes including canals, farm buildings, mills, factories, and warehouses; also, no allowance is made for changes in stocks of bricks. However, the discrepancy seemed too large to be

Table 9. *Relationship of House-Building to Brick Output, 1791–1850*

	Output of bricks (millions)	House-building (standardized houses, thousands)	Implied bricks per house
1791–1800	6,410	223	28,700
1801–10	8,250	305	27,100
1811–20	8,630	388	22,200
1821–30	12,310	594	20,700
1831–40	13,370	685	19,500
1841–50	10,560	507	20,800

SOURCE. See text.

explained by these factors, and a rough adjustment was made to the initial estimates, adding some 30,000 houses to the previous estimate for the number built in 1791–1800, subtracting 20,000 in 1801–10 and 30,000 in 1811–20, and adding 20,000 in 1821–30. These adjustments thus cancel out and so involve no change in the initial estimates of the total number of dwellings in 1830 and subsequent years or in those for 1790 and earlier. They represent adjustments of moderate proportions (the largest is 17 per cent in 1791–1800, the smallest 3 per cent in 1821–30) in the estimates of houses built, but of very small proportion (2 per cent or less) in the estimates of the total stock of dwellings in 1800, 1810, and 1820, from which the series for the numbers built was derived by difference, and can thus readily be accepted as plausible.

After these adjustments the relationship to the brick series is as shown in Table 9. The sharp drop in the implied figure for bricks per house between 1801–10 and 1811–20 suggests that the estimate of the number of houses built may be too low in the first decades (or too high in the last four – but these are likely to be more reliable), though this may be partly accounted for by the canal boom.

Finally, we can value the estimates at the average price per dwelling for houses built in 1851–60. We take this average price as £150 – this represents the cost of a house built at 1851–60 prices to 1851–60 standards, and is assumed to include an allowance for the costs of street improvements provided by builders and estate developers.[40]

There is no direct procedure by which we can obtain the required estimate of the average cost of dwellings. One very indirect method is to extrapolate back to 1851–60 the average cost per dwelling derived primarily from the 1907 Census of Production, the first comprehensive return of the value of work on new houses in Great Britain. This yields an 1851–60 average price of about £125, but both the base figure and the extrapolation over more than half a century are rather uncertain.[41]

A second possibility is to break the problem down by dealing separately with each of the main categories of dwelling. This is the method underlying the estimate actually adopted, and it leads to a figure which may at first glance appear rather high but is in fact quite reasonable when the upper end of the tremendous range in the standard

Table 10. *Average Cost of Houses in 1860 (at 1851–60 prices) based on Classification by Annual Value*

Annual value £		Number (thousands)	Per cent of total	Possible estimate of cost (1851–60 prices) £
Under 5		2,070	47·6	30
5	10	1,115	25·6	70
10	15	520	12·0	120
15	20	280	6·4	180
20 and under	30	135	3·1	300
30	50	120	2·8	500
50	100	73	1·7	1,000
Over 100		37	0·8	5,000
Total		4,350	100·0	Weighted average £138

SOURCE. See text.

of houses built is fully taken into account. Fortunately, we have fairly reliable sources on which to base a detailed classification by annual value of the total stock of inhabited houses in Great Britain in 1860,[42] and with this as the framework it turns out that plausible estimates of the cost at 1851–60 prices for each of eight categories of house are consistent with a weighted overall average of about £150. Almost half the 1860 stock of houses are taken at an estimated cost at 1851–60 prices (but actual standards) of only £30;[43] and a further quarter are taken at £70.[44] The cost rises through £120 to £180 for the next two categories, covering the better class of urban houses and rural cottages built in moderate numbers in the first half of the nineteenth century; and then through £300 and £500 to £1,000 for the smaller number of really substantial town and country houses built for the most prosperous of the commercial and professional classes.[45] Finally, for the top (and open-ended) group of some 37,000 of the grandest town and country residences we take a rather arbitrary but not, I think, excessive figure of £5,000.[46]

The result of a classification on this basis is set out in Table 10. The estimates adopted thus lead to a weighted average of £138 for the cost at 1851–60 prices of the total stock of houses in Great Britain in 1860. However, since we have previously attempted to allow for the improvement in the size and quality of houses built after 1810 by reducing all estimates of houses built to comparable units at 1851–60 standards, we must now make a corresponding upwards adjustment to the estimated cost; this gives us a figure of £150 for the cost at 1851–60 prices of houses of 1851–60 standard.[47] The same figure can be applied to the standardized estimates of houses built in each decade or to those in the stock at the earlier benchmark dates, if we assume that there were no significant changes in the relative composition of the houses built.

A third source of information, which became available only after the preliminary draft of this chapter had been completed, is the extensive collection of data assembled by C. W. Chalklin in his important study of the building process in a representative group of seven provincial towns in the period 1740–1820. Chalklin states his conclusions with respect to the average cost of *new* dwellings in the early nineteenth century as follows:

My own evidence, concerning provincial urban figures alone, cannot of course be used to estimate a national average, but I believe that such an average may have been at least as high as £150. Although the smallest new tenements in provincial towns cost only about £60–£80 after 1800, and country cottages as little as £40–£60, the *average* would have been pushed up strongly by the (relatively few) houses in the £500–£1,500 price range, which included some farmhouses as well as town houses and of course, the dwellings of intermediate value.[48]

Some allowance should be made for the difference in dates, but this may be taken as broadly confirming the present estimate.

We thus take the standardized figures for new building in each decade and for the stock of dwellings at the four dates at an average value of £150 per dwelling, and this gives the series for capital formation at 1851–60 prices in Table 6 and for the stock of dwellings in Table 8. To obtain capital formation at current prices for Table 7, the series at 1851–60 prices was multiplied by the price index for buildings in the first column of Table 5.

2. PUBLIC BUILDINGS AND WORKS

This series is intended to cover all public buildings including town halls, schools,[49] hospitals, museums, workhouses, prisons, and churches, and also sewers and sewage disposal works. On the basis of two contemporary estimates we can put the value of the civilian public buildings and works in 1800 at roughly £25 million at 1851–60 prices.[50] This represents 10 per cent of our estimate of the value of the stock of dwellings at that date.

Given this, we have assumed that the value of the gross stock of public buildings in 1760 was also 10 per cent of the value of dwellings, and further, that capital formation in each decade from 1761–70 to 1811–20 was 10 per cent of the corresponding expenditure (at constant and current prices respectively) on dwellings. We have then assumed an increase in the ratio to 12 per cent in 1821–30, 15 per cent in 1831–40, and 20 per cent in 1841–60. This increase is designed in the first place to capture the substantial expenditure in these decades on state and civic buildings, including Buckingham Palace, the Houses of Parliament, the British Museum, the National Gallery, and the Public Record Office, all financed by the Treasury, as well as the Royal Exchange and the Coal Exchange in London, St George's Hall in Liverpool and the Town Hall in Birmingham, the Ashmolean and Fitzwilliam Museums, Lincoln's Inn, and the National Gallery of Scotland, and numerous other exchanges, markets, town halls, and other monuments to the growing size and prosperity of urban Britain.[51] Secondly, the rise in the series is intended to cover the gradual expansion of capital outlays by the emerging local government institutions in the fields of public health and sanitation.[52]

To complete the estimates of the value of the gross stock of these assets, it was further assumed that they had an average life of 100 years; the stock in 1830 was taken as equal to 40 per cent of the stock in 1760 plus the cumulated expenditure at 1851–60 prices from 1761 to 1830, and the stock in 1860 as equal to the cumulative total of capital expenditure over the preceding century.

3. AGRICULTURE

This important component of domestic capital accumulation covers all capital outlays by both landowners and tenants on farm buildings (other than dwelling-houses); on enclosures, reclamation, drainage, and other improvements to the land; on farm roads (especially in association with enclosures); and on carts, equipment, and machinery. It does not cover livestock or horses, which are dealt with in section V below.

We begin the estimates for this sector with a series for capital formation at current prices derived by estimating the average gross rent in each decade and expressing the capital expenditure by both landowners and tenant farmers as a proportion of that gross rent. This procedure is adopted as a way of obtaining an indication of the likely order of magnitude: we can estimate the total rent for land in Great Britain, and we have evidence from some estates of the proportion of rent devoted to improvements. It is not assumed that the level of capital expenditure is directly determined by the level of rent received. The series for the gross rent of land in Britain is reasonably well founded. From 1842 onwards we know the gross rent of land (including tithes) assessed for Schedule A of the Income Tax, and we also have the earlier Schedule A assessment for 1806, 1808, 1810, and 1814.[53] For 1800 we have Beeke's carefully considered estimate,[54] and we have taken the gross rent in 1760 as £20 million.[55] We then interpolated between these benchmarks to complete the estimates for 1760–1842, using the series on farm rents compiled by Thompson and by Norton, Trist, and Gilbert.[56] The resulting series is shown in the first column of Table 11.

The proportion of gross rent to be regarded as being expended on capital outlays is a much more difficult and uncertain item to estimate. Holderness has recently discussed the problems of estimating capital formation in agriculture and has provided some valuable leads,[57] but his own work is still in progress, and we must await its completion to obtain adequate estimates for this sector. To make the present very provisional estimates we have taken capital expenditure on new works and improvements by landlord and tenant as amounting to 6 per cent of the gross rental in the 1760s, and then rising steadily to a peak during the great upsurge in enclosures and improvement which occurred from about 1795 to 1815 under the influence of rapidly increasing demand and the greatly inflated levels to which prices of agricultural products soared during the Napoleonic Wars. The decade averages adopted (second column of Table 11) partly conceal this peak but nevertheless show investment at current prices increasing threefold from £1·9 million per annum in the 1780s to £5·7 million per annum in 1811–20. The ratio is lowered during the years of post-war depression and then moved upward again to cover the substantial outlays on drainage in the Fens and the heavy clay lands under the stimulus of technical advances and parliamentary loans, and the more general investment in farm buildings and covered yards, in iron implements and steam machinery, which (together with improved techniques and use of fertilizers) helped to make these mid-century decades the 'golden age' of British farming. The resulting estimates show investment increasing by some 70 per cent between the 1820s and the 1850s.

Table 11. *Fixed Capital Formation in Agriculture: Farm Buildings, Improvements, and Equipment, Great Britain, 1761–1860*

	(1) Gross rent (excluding farmhouses) (£m p.a.)	(2) Capital expenditure as % of gross rent	(3) Capital expenditure at current prices (£m p.a.)	(4) Price index (1851–60 = 100)	(5) Capital expenditure at 1851–60 prices (£m p.a.)
1761–70	20	6	1·20	55	2·18
1771–80	21	7	1·47	56	2·62
1781–90	24	8	1·92	58	3·31
1791–1800	31	11	3·41	80	4·26
1801–10	32	16	5·12	126	4·06
1811–20	41	14	5·74	129	4·45
1821–30	40	10	4·00	98	4·08
1831–40	42	11	4·62	98	4·71
1841–50	46	13	5·98	97	6·16
1851–60	46	15	6·90	100	6·90

SOURCES. (1) and (2) see text. (3) = (1) × (2). (4) = col. 2 of Table 5. (5) = (3)/(4).

The full details of the estimation and the resulting series for capital expenditure at current and 1851–60 prices are set out in Table 11. The assets are assumed to have an average life of 100 years,[58] and the series at constant prices in column 5 is then cumulated over the century from 1761 to give the 1860 value of the stock of fixed capital in agriculture, some £430 million. Before proceeding further this result may be compared with two alternative estimates to provide a check on both the 1860 stock and the underlying estimates of capital expenditure. The first check is made by deducting £30 million from the total for 1860 to cover the implements, carts, etc. provided by the tenants,[59] and dividing the estimated value of the landlords' capital by the total area of agricultural land in Great Britain (crops and grass), taken as about thirty-one million acres. This gives a capital value per acre of some £13. To evaluate this result we can compare it with the estimate by R. J. Thompson (for England and Wales) that the capital outlay incurred by landowners for drainage and fencing, farm roads, and buildings averaged

£12 per acre.[60] This figure must however be adjusted in two respects. Firstly, it includes the cost of the farmhouse and farm cottages which should be excluded for the present purpose since they are covered in our estimates of dwellings: this would reduce Thompson's figure by £4 or £5 per acre. Secondly, his estimate explicitly excludes any initial outlay on felling, clearing and grubbing or marling, and allowance for this and similar costs would roughly offset the deduction for houses.[61] We are thus left with an estimate of about £12 per acre, suggesting that our estimate may be marginally on the high side.

The second and more uncertain alternative valuation is obtained by dividing the rent of land into that part which in Ricardo's terms represents the payment for 'the original and indestructible powers of the soil' and that part which is 'paid for the use of the capital which had been employed in ameliorating the quality of the land and in erecting such buildings as were necessary to secure and preserve the produce',[62] and capitalizing the latter. Various authors have estimated the proportion of the rental which might be regarded as the interest on the buildings and improvements, and the best-supported of these fall in a range from 25 to 50 per cent.[63] If we take 40 per cent and apply this to the £48 million for the rent of land as assessed for Schedule A in 1860 (after deducting £2 million for farm-houses), we have a figure of some £19 million, and if this is capitalized at twenty years' purchase[64] we obtain a capital value of £380 million to which (say) £30 million should be added for implements etc. provided by the tenants. The resulting total of £410 million could easily be varied either way – for example, by taking a lower proportion of the rent than 40 per cent, or by taking slightly more than twenty years' purchase as the multiplier – but it broadly confirms the order of magnitude of the present estimates of capital formation and capital stock.[65]

To complete the capital stock series we first require an estimate for 1760. The farm land in Britain at that date might be valued at some £500 million at current prices,[66] but the greater part of that would be pure rent, since by that date only limited improvements had as yet been undertaken.[67] If we take the proportion represented by buildings and improvements at a rather arbitrary 25 per cent,[68] this puts their value at £125 million, and deflation by the price index for agriculture assets raises this to £210 million for the value of the stock in 1760 at the prices of 1851–60. We further assume that 70 per cent of these assets survived to 1800 and 40 per cent to 1830,[69] and the value of the stock at these dates is then obtained from the sum of these survivals from 1760 plus the cumulated fixed capital expenditure from 1761 to the respective dates.

4. INDUSTRIAL AND COMMERCIAL BUILDING

We turn next to the industrial and commercial sector, for which there are four separate series, covering in aggregate all buildings and equipment in manufacturing, building, distribution, catering, mining, quarrying, and gas and water supply.

For these buildings the only reliable evidence available for any date in the nineteenth century is the assessment, for tax purposes, of the gross annual value (equivalent to gross rental) of trade premises. We therefore begin with the gross annual value in 1860 and from this is derived the estimated gross stock. This in turn provides a basis for the estimates of capital formation. It might be desirable to separate industrial from commercial buildings, but since there is no reliable statistical basis for the division, and since the distinction was in practice somewhat blurred, particularly for the eighteenth and early nineteenth centuries, we have not attempted to do so.

The statistics of trade premises exempt from Inhabited House Duty were not published until 1874–5. For years from 1842–3 these buildings were assessed (on the same basis) for Schedule A of the Income Tax, but the amount of the assessment was not distinguished in the published statistics from those for dwellings and other buildings. The derivation of the implicit gross annual value of trade premises in 1860 is explained in the Appendix, and is estimated at £25·5 million. This covers lock-up shops, the trade component of residential shops, hotels, pubs, stores and warehouses, offices, factories, and other trade premises.

In order to convert this annual value into estimates of the 1860 gross stock at prices of 1851–60, we assume that the ratio of the gross stock to the annual value is the same for these buildings as for dwellings.[70] The annual value of dwellings in 1860 is taken as £33 million (see below, p. 96), and the value of the 1860 gross stock at 1851–60 prices as estimated above was £600 million, giving a multiplier of 18.[71] Applying this to the annual value yields an estimate of some £460 million for the 1860 gross stock of industrial and commercial buildings.

To complete the estimates, we then divide the stock into two parts,[72] each assumed to have been accumulated over a period of 80 years. One part covers the factory buildings, warehouses, and offices, and it is assumed that capital expenditure on these buildings was proportional to the increase in industrial production.[73] This component thus rises rapidly in the last four decades (from £1·4 million per annum in 1811–20 to £6·5 million in 1851–60), reflecting both the increase in mills and factories required for the swift expansion of manufacturing output, and also the development of commercial architecture to provide the great cities with the massive bank and insurance premises, commercial chambers, and warehouses which were becoming common in the early Victorian period.[74] The second part of the stock covers the small but numerous residential and lock-up shops and the public houses and coffee houses, and for these it is assumed that capital formation moved in proportion to construction of dwellings.[75] This component thus starts at a higher level but rises much more sedately after 1820.

The sum of these two components is the series at 1851–60 prices in Table 6, and the standard index of building prices (Table 5) was applied to this to give the alternative series at current prices. Finally, the gross stock in 1760 at 1851–60 prices was assumed to be £25 million, with 60 per cent of this surviving to 1800 and 15 per cent to 1830,[76] and the gross stock in 1800 and 1830 could then be estimated as the sum of the surviving pre-1760 stock plus the cumulated expenditure to the respective dates.[77]

5. MACHINERY, EQUIPMENT, ETC. IN MANUFACTURING AND BUILDING

This series represents one of the most important and interesting aspects of capital formation in the early stages of industrialization, but it is the one for which we have probably the least information. It should cover all the new machinery and plant which symbolizes the industrial revolution: Cartwright's looms and Watt's steam engines, Cort's iron-works and Wedgwood's potteries, the machine tools of Maudslay and Nasmyth, the new iron machinery introduced in breweries and paper-mills, flour-mills, and chemical works. It should also include all the many survivals of older hand-working equipment, together with the tools, implements, utensils, and other minor items which are individually small but collectively important. Unfortunately, the textile industry is the only one for which we have some basis for direct estimates, and even here it is only for the cotton trade that moderately reliable information is available. We begin with estimates of the stock of machinery, etc. in textiles and move from this to cover the rest of manufacturing and building. We then derive from this the series for capital formation.

A widely used method of estimating the cost of fixed capital in the spinning sector of the cotton industry was to express the total cost (i.e. mill, power, preparatory machinery, and spindles) in terms of the price per spindle. Similarly the capital expenditure on the weaving sheds could be expressed in terms of the cost per loom. We have attempted to apply this method both to cotton and to the other branches of the textile industry. In each branch we take the numbers of spindles and looms in Great Britain in 1861, as shown by the Factory Inspectors' *Returns*, and value these at a figure intended to represent the replacement cost (at 1851–60 prices) of the mills and machinery. To this we add an estimate for hosiery and lace manufacture, and for printing, bleaching, and dyeing works. The detailed figures and sources are set out in Table 12, and it will be evident that for sectors other than cotton the estimates are very approximate indeed.

Table 12. *Fixed Capital in the Textile Industry of Great Britain, 1860*

	(1)	(2)	(3)	(4)
		Power	1851–60 replacement	Total
	Spindles	looms	cost per unit	value
	(thousands)		£ s. d.	(£m)
Cotton				
spinning	30,267		1 4 0	36·3
weaving		398	24 0 0	9·6
Woollen and worsted				
spinning	3,447		2 10 0	8·6
weaving		65	70 0 0	4·5
Silk				
spinning	1,337		1 4 0	1·6
weaving		11	40 0 0	0·4
Flax, etc.				
spinning	656		4 0 0	2·6
weaving		10	42 0 0	0·4
Lace and hosiery				4·0
Finishing trades (cotton)				14·0
				82·0

SOURCES

(1) and (2) 1861 *Returns*, PP 1862, LV.

(3) *Cotton*. A steady 24s. per spindle for the all-in cost of a *new* mill is quoted by a succession of writers, including Ashton in 1841, Baines in 1857, the Factory Inspectors in 1871, and Ellison in 1886: for all these see M. Blaug, 'The Productivity of Capital in the Lancashire Cotton Industry during the Nineteenth Century', *Economic History Review*, 2nd ser., XIII (1961), 372–4. (The only exception discovered was J. Platt, the textile machinery manufacturer, who gave a figure of 18s. in 1866: 'On Machinery for the Preparing and Spinning of Cotton', *Proceedings of the Institute of Mechanical Engineers*, 1866, 240. This was possibly a time when prices were still depressed by the 'famine'.) For weaving, the same sources – Baines, the Factory Inspectors, and Ellison, again quoted by Blaug – are agreed on the figure of £24 per loom as the comprehensive cost of new weaving sheds.

Woollen and Worsted. I have not come across any direct statements regarding the capital cost per spindle required for spinning wool. A figure of about £3 15s. 0d. per spindle in 1824 can be derived from the records of the Trowbridge firm of J. and T. Clark reproduced in R. P. Beckinsale, *The Trowbridge Woollen Industry* (1951), 113, 122, 130, 137, 180, and 191, but this is probably too high as a capital cost for spinning only since the firm had invested considerable sums in equipment for the finishing work on cloth produced by independent weavers. A more appropriate estimate is perhaps the £2 6s. od. per spindle indicated by the 1837 data for Black Dyke worsted mills given in E. M. Sigsworth, *Black Dyke Mills* (1958), 171–3 and 207–8. A capital cost about double that for spinning cotton is plausible, given the additional preparation which equipment and machinery required for wool (carding, combing, etc.), and is supported by the Returns of Horsepower, which show 18·4 h.p. per thousand spindles in woollen and worsted factories compared with 9·6 per thousand spindles in cotton. For weaving there is again a lack of information; as yet I have discovered only two estimates. The first is Heaton's statement (made without giving a specific source) that in the 1830s 'a power loom shed could be built and equipped with 50 looms for about £5000', i.e. about £100 per loom. See H. Heaton, 'Financing the Industrial Revolution' (1937), reprinted in Crouzet (ed.), *Capital Formation*, 86. The second is in the evidence given by Sir Jacob Behrens to the Royal Commission on the Depression in Trade and Industry in 1886, where it is stated that the total cost (including land) of a complete mill with all equipment for 500 broad and 500 narrow looms would be about £70,000 (PP 1886, xxi, *Minutes of Evidence*, Q. 6716). The same figure of £70 per loom has been adopted for the 1850s, and it is assumed to include equipment for dyeing and finishing, hence its high level relative to the capital costs for weaving in the other textile trades.

Silk. There is again very little information, and the estimates are based largely on the evidence of one of the leading manufacturers, Joseph Grout, given in 1831 to the Select Committee on the Silk Trade, PP 1831–2, xix, *Minutes of Evidence*, Q. 10, 295–303. His figure for looms is £34 10s. od. ('exclusive of the steam engines') and this has been raised to £40 to cover the engines. The cost of his mills (excluding the looms but including land) works out at about £1 8s. od. per spindle and it was assumed that for the 1850s the cost was the same as for cotton-spinning.

Flax, Jute, and Hemp. For spinning the figure used was given by T. Greenwood, 'On Machinery Employed in the Preparation and Spinning of Flax', *Proceedings of the Institute of Mechanical Engineers*, 1865, 123. For weaving the estimate was given by W. Charley, *Flax and its Products in Ireland* (1862), 92.

Lace and Hosiery. The cost of fixed capital is based largely on W. Felkin, *A History of the Machine-Wrought Hosiery and Lace Manufactures* (1867), 396–7 and 449, and the estimates for 1831 and 1886 quoted in Blaug, 'Productivity of Capital', 371–4.

Finishing trades. Taken as 30 per cent of the fixed capital in cotton-spinning and weaving, based on *ibid.*, 372–4.

The resulting estimate of the total gross stock of reproducible fixed assets in the textile industry, at 1851–60 prices, thus comes out at £82 million. The share of machinery in this (including engines and accessories) would be about 65 per cent, or £53 million.[78] This covers only the mechanized factories, and we must make a small addition for the equipment of hand workers, who still survived in 1861 in some sectors, notably woollen spinning and weaving.[79] The difference of some 450,000 between the 1861 Census of Population count of the occupied population in textile production and the 1861 Factory Inspectors' Returns of numbers employed in textile factories provides one clue to the extent of hand working in Great Britain at that date.[80] An allowance of £10 per head for equipment, etc. for this group would add £4·5 million, bringing the total for the textile industries to about £58 million.

We next use this result as a starting point for a highly conjectural extension to cover the remaining manufacturing industries. The only statistics which cover the whole of the manufacturing sector in 1860 are those for the occupied population given in the Census of Population, and we take this as our 'control', multiplying the number of workers by estimates of capital per head to obtain the total stock. According to the 1861 census there were some 3·6 million workers in manufacturing; these can be divided into five main groups, as shown in the first column of Table 13. For the factory sector of textiles, the estimate of £53

Table 13. *Stock of Machinery and Equipment in Manufacturing,*
Great Britain, 1860

	(1) Occupied population (thousands)	(2) Machinery per worker £	(3) Stock at 1851–60 replacement cost (£m)	
Textiles				
Factory	730	73	53	
Hand	450	10	5	
Total (textiles)			—	58
Metal-making, engineering, and shipbuilding	650	75	49	
Clothing	1,030	5	5	
Other manufacturing[a]	730	60	44	
Total (non-textile)			—	98
Total	3,590	43		156

[a] Includes food and drink, chemicals, wood and furniture, paper and printing, pottery, glass, and furs and leather.

SOURCES
(1) Booth, 'Occupations of the People of the United Kingdom', 415–19; see also note 80 below.
(2) See text.
(3) Textiles: see text; others: col. (1) × col. (2).

million obtained above yields a figure of some £73 for the replacement cost (at 1851–60 prices) of machinery and equipment per factory worker, and we allowed £10 per head for the hand workers. With these as guidelines we assume that for the metal-making, shipbuilding, and engineering industries the machinery per worker would average roughly the same as in the textile factories, say £75 per worker; for the substantial numbers engaged in making clothing (tailors, dressmakers, boot- and shoemakers, etc.) we take £5 per head; and for the remaining industries we assume an average of £60, about 20 per cent below the textile factories.[81] It would obviously be desirable to check the order of magnitude for as many as possible of the individual industries other than textiles and clothing, but it has not been possible to do this for the present chapter. It should be stressed, however, that the two estimates given for the metal and engineering industries and for the residual group are intended as averages – it is not suggested that they are appropriate for each industry within the two groups. In the former category, for example, the capital-intensive metal-making sector has to be set against the large number of workers employed in small and imperfectly mechanized workshops in the mechanical engineering trades: Clapham[82] discusses a return of the numbers employed in industry at the census of 1851 showing that of 677 English and Welsh engine and machine-makers who made returns, 447 employed one to nine men and a further 90 employed ten to nineteen; only 34 employed 100 or more.

Applying the above estimates to the numbers occupied gives an estimate of £98 million for industries other than textiles, and of £156 million for manufacturing as a whole. Some small allowance should also be made for equipment used in building and contracting, in which some 630,000 were occupied in 1861, and we add £4 million for this sector (roughly £6 per head), bringing our estimate of the total gross stock in manufacturing and building to £160 million.

To estimate the gross stock at earlier dates we assume that it grew proportionately with the index of industrial production;[83] this assumption of a constant capital–output ratio is clearly unsatisfactory, but there does not at present appear to be a better method of estimation. This gives estimates, at 1851–60 prices, of £9 million in 1760, £26 million in 1800, and £61 million in 1830.[84] We may compare the figure for 1800 with Sir Frederick Eden's estimate in 1803 that the sum invested in 'steam engines and other expensive machinery' was not less than £40 million.[85] Adjustment for the fall in prices to 1851–60 would lower this to perhaps £30 million, which is broadly consistent with the present estimate.

The estimates of capital formation at 1851–60 prices are obtained by assuming a life of forty years for these assets: that is, the stocks at each benchmark date are assumed to have been accumulated over the preceding period of forty years, the expenditure being allocated by decade *pro rata* to the increase in industrial production.[86] The price index in column 3 of Table 5 was then used to convert to current prices.

6. MINING AND QUARRYING

For this sector we again begin with an estimate of the stock of capital in 1860. The estimate covers all fixed assets and all forms of mining and quarrying, though it is based largely on data for coal-mining.

In the early years of the present century it was frequently suggested that the capital cost in coal-mining was 10s. per ton. This was, for example, the figure used by Flux in the Final Report on the 1907 Census of Production (p. 35); and it was defended as a reliable estimate before the Sankey and Samuel Commissions of 1919 and 1925. The origins, basis, and accuracy of the estimate were discussed and clarified in evidence to these Commissions by Lord Stamp and others,[87] and it appears from this that the estimate was originally put forward as an average for the 1890s and that it relates to the replacement cost of the fixed assets (shafts, equipment, etc.) in coal mines. The major component of the capital expenditure in mining is the labour cost, and as miners' wages in the 1850s were between 20 and 30 per cent below the level of the 1890s,[88] a significantly lower cost per ton would be appropriate for the replacement cost of the end-1860 stock at 1851–60 prices. It is also necessary to make allowance for the fact that shafts sunk before 1860 would not have been as deep as those of the later period. We therefore take a figure of 7s. per ton as the cost appropriate for 1860 at 1851–60 prices. To get a corresponding figure for the earlier benchmark dates we reduce this to 6s. for 1830 and to 5s. for 1760 and 1800 to allow for the shallower pits of the earliest collieries.[89]

These estimates are then applied to the series for the tonnage of coal produced in Britain[90] to obtain the gross stock of capital in coal-mining at 1851–60 prices at the four dates. For the 1860 output of £80 million tons this gives a value of £28 million, and an addition for iron ore, copper, and other mines and for quarries raises this to some £35 million.[91] A proportionate adjustment was made to the estimates for the three earlier dates.

Estimates of capital formation at 1851–60 prices were then obtained by assuming that these estimated stocks of capital were accumulated over a life of some forty years and that expenditure per decade was proportional to the increase in coal output. The standard index of building prices was then used to convert this series to current prices.

7. GAS AND WATER

We here rely on unpublished estimates of capital formation at current and 1900 prices kindly made available by B. R. Mitchell. For the gas industry he compiled estimates of cumulative capital cost for a sample of undertakings, and he expressed these in terms of the cost per head of the population in the area covered by the undertaking. Census of Population data were then used to expand this to cover all areas with a supply of gas. This was done for each census year from 1821, and the increment in the series over the decade was taken as the capital expenditure at current prices.

For water supply Mitchell drew on parliamentary papers and company reports to make similar estimates of accumulated capital expenditure at decade intervals from 1811 onwards for a sample of areas, and again he used population statistics to extend this to cover the total supply. As with gas the increase over the decade was taken as the capital expenditure at current prices.

These series at current prices are combined in Table 7 (with an addition for gas of £1 million for the decade 1811–20). Mitchell's corresponding series at 1900 prices were converted to 1851–60 prices to obtain the estimates for Table 6, and these were in turn cumulated over the period from 1811 to obtain the capital stock estimates for 1830 and 1860 for Table 8. The 1860 stock of £42 million (at 1851–60 prices) is evenly divided between gas supply and water supply.

8. RAILWAYS

We now move on to six separate estimates of capital formation in transport, beginning with the railways.

Estimates of capital expenditure on the permanent way and works and on railway rolling stock have been made by B. R. Mitchell from 1831 and by A. G. Kenwood from 1825.[92] Mitchell's estimate is consistently somewhat higher, particularly from 1845 onwards.[93] It includes estimated expenditure on renewals but excludes repairs, purchases of land, and transfer payments such as interest, subscriptions to other companies, and purchases of existing lines. We have adopted this series for the present estimates. It is limited to expenditure on the railways and does not include ancillary assets such as canals, docks, or hotels, which we cover elsewhere. The estimates are derived from the accounts of the railway companies and are subject to certain reservations regarding the accounting practices adopted in allocating expenditure to capital or revenue account; however, they are certainly among the most reliable of the series included in the present estimates.

Mitchell's estimates at current prices are shown in Table 7 (with a notional addition for 1811–30); his series at constant (1869) prices, obtained by constructing special price indices for work on the permanent way and for rolling stock,[94] has been adjusted to constant prices of 1851–60 to get the series in Table 6. This series was in turn cumulated over the period from 1811 to get the capital stock estimates in 1830 and 1860 for Table 8.

9. ROADS AND BRIDGES

In the case of roads we have to deal with an asset to which the application of the conceptual approach outlined above (p. 35) is particularly difficult. A basic assumption underlying that approach is that we are dealing with assets which are newly created by specific capital outlays on construction or purchase, maintained by expenditure on repairs during a finite lifetime, and then discarded at the end of that life as a result of depreciation and obsolescence.[95] Road-building does not normally conform to this pattern. We do occasionally have the creation of a new road in the period we are considering, but more commonly we have work undertaken on roads originally constructed centuries before – in some cases going back to the Roman era – and this work simultaneously involves elements of improvement and of repair. A further and equally fundamental difficulty is that the accounts kept by the authorities responsible for this expenditure typically distinguish only the type of outlay (e.g. labour, materials, etc.) but not the nature of the work, so that it is generally impossible to separate new work from repairs on the basis of the recorded information. One solution would be to abandon the distinction and include all repairs in the estimates of gross investment. However, for the reasons given above (p. 37) this was considered unsatisfactory, and we have preferred to take a proportion of the total expenditure as representing new work and major improvements, even though the choice of the proportion would necessarily have to be fairly arbitrary.

We begin with estimates of capital formation based largely on work by J. E. Ginarlis. In an unpublished dissertation Ginarlis has estimated what he terms 'quasi-net' expenditure on roads.[96] This covers new work and improvements, all expenditure on repairs and maintenance, and parliamentary and legal fees, but it excludes transfer payments such as purchase of land, compensation, and interest. His estimates cover the expenditure on the turnpikes, bridges, and parish roads and also the small amount of direct government expenditure on roads and bridges.

For the turnpikes Ginarlis computed estimates of quasi-net expenditure for 1822–56 from data compiled from parliamentary returns.[97] He extrapolated this series back to 1750 by an elaborate and careful procedure which involved a classification of all turnpikes according to their date of origin, mileage, and level of expenditure in the 1820s, as well as the use of a small sample of account books of turnpike trusts for the pre-1820 period. Each trust was allocated a pattern of expenditure over the period from 1750 (or from its origin, if formed after that date) to 1820 on the basis of the growth of expenditure shown by a sample trust of corresponding length and level of expenditure in the 1820s.[98] This series was extended to the end of the 1850s from the *Abstract of Turnpike Trust Expenditure* available for this period in Parliamentary Papers.[99] It was generally recognized that the activities of the turnpike trusts brought about a considerable improvement in the quality of Britain's roads,[100] so that it is appropriate that we should take a substantial proportion of Ginarlis's quasi-net expenditure to represent new works and improvements, and we have taken 60 per cent of his series as the measure of capital formation as we have defined it.[101]

The second component of the estimates covers the 96,000 miles of parish roads. For these Ginarlis based his estimates on returns to parliament for 1812–14, 1827, 1837–9, 1841, and 1847,[102] interpolated and extrapolated to cover the period 1750–1850 by means of data derived from a sample of parish surveyors' account books.[103] The sample is very small (1 per cent or less of expenditure in 1813) and the reliability of the series accordingly rather poor. The series again covers both maintenance and improvements, and the former would account for a much larger share of expenditure than was the case with the turnpikes. However, there is evidence of some improvement in the standard of parish roads over the period,[104] and we have taken a very arbitrary 20 per cent of Ginarlis's series to represent capital formation. From 1851 the series can be extrapolated to 1860 on the basis of the *Abstracts of Highway Expenditure*.[105]

Finally, Ginarlis has constructed a series for capital expenditure by bridge trusts and companies,[106] and we add this to the adjusted estimates for turnpikes and parish roads to obtain the series for capital formation at current prices in Table 7 above. It does not cover capital expenditure on road-making associated with the work of either the enclosure commissioners in rural areas or the improvement commissioners and private builders in urban areas; an implicit allowance for the former is included in the previous estimates for farm buildings and improvements, and for the latter in the series for residential building.

To convert the series to 1851–60 prices for Table 6 a special index was used, combining an index for labourers' earnings represented by the series for agricultural wages (weight 2);[107] and an index for the price of materials, represented by the series given by Ginarlis for the cost of gravel (weight 1).[108]

The value of the stock of roads and bridges in 1860 (at 1851–60 prices) was then taken as the accumulated total of capital expenditure over the eighty years from 1781, giving an estimate of £66 million. To obtain the stock at the earlier dates we first need some estimate of the stock in 1760, and we take this at a very uncertain £15 million,[109] of which one-half is assumed to survive to 1800 and one-eighth to 1830. The stock at these two dates is then obtained from the accumulated capital expenditure from 1761 to the respective dates, added to the surviving value of the pre-1760 roads.

As a first step towards an evaluation of these results we may note that the turnpikes account for £44 million of the estimated £66 million for the value of the stock of roads in 1860 at 1851–60 prices, and that there were approximately 27,000 miles of turnpike roads in Great Britain at that date.[110] The implied cost of construction is thus some £1,630 per mile. This is broadly corroborated by other evidence on construction costs. Sir James McAdam informed a Select Committee in 1836 that the cost of a gravel road four inches thick constructed on the principles he and his father followed would be £1,760 per mile.[111] Another source quotes figures of 1s. 2d. to 1s. 6d. per square yard for the cost of macadam roads in Scotland in the 1860s, and 1s. 6d. per square yard for macadam roads six inches thick in Birmingham in the early 1850s; assuming an average width of twelve yards, this works out at a cost per mile of roughly £1,200 to £1,600.[112]

A similar calculation for the estimate of £22 million for the value in 1860 of the 115,000 miles[113] of parish roads and highways yields a construction cost of £190 per mile, and if we assume an average width for these roads of about six yards[114] this is roughly 4d. per square yard. This may be compared with a cost of 1d. to 2d. per yard, varying with the quality of stone to be broken, quoted by McAdam for lifting a rough road and rendering it 'smooth and solid', and a cost of 3d. per yard for lifting, etc. plus 4d. per yard for three inches of extra stone, which he quoted as his price in a letter to the trustees of a turnpike road.[115] The present estimate thus appears to be of roughly the right order of magnitude; without an appropriately weighted average compiled from much more detailed information on both the mileage and the construction costs of each of a range of different categories of road, we cannot make a more precise check.

10. CARRIAGES AND COACHES

This estimate is intended to cover all carriages and coaches used for passenger transport, whether privately owned or hired, and some part of the vehicles used for goods transport.[116] The horses are included with livestock in section V.

We begin with the series for the stock of capital, obtained from estimates of the number of vehicles at each of the four benchmark dates and of their average (1851–60) price. For the numbers we rely largely on official statistics: various categories of carriage and coach were subject to taxation or licensing from the mid eighteenth century onwards, and though the coverage of the duties and licences varied over time and the underlying statistics were not published before 1810, we have fairly comprehensive information for 1810–28 and for 1854–69, so that we have a moderately secure basis for the main estimates.[117] The average prices at which these are valued are rather more approximate; but fortunately we have sufficient information to deal separately with six categories of vehicle, and we are thus less liable to be substantially in error than if we attempted a single average for all sizes and types.[118] For 1860 this yields an estimate for the gross stock of some £23 million, covering over 280,000 carriages, coaches, and omnibuses.

The estimates of capital expenditure at 1851–60 prices were derived from the stock estimates on the assumption that the average life of the vehicles was around fifteen years. For 1810–24 we can check this with the aid of statistics derived from a tax levied for a few years on carriages and carts made for sale.[119] We have no suitable means of adjusting this for price changes, and as a very rough approximation the standard index of building prices (Table 5) was used to convert the estimates to current prices.

11. CANALS AND WATERWAYS

Canals present similar problems to those encountered in the estimates for roads, and we attempt to deal with them in a similar fashion. We begin with the estimate for capital formation at current prices, built up from three components.

The first covers all work on *new* construction of canals and inland waterways and is derived from estimates of the mileage opened in each decade and of the average cost per mile of new work. For the former we use the series compiled by Ginarlis for the mileage of canals, and of rivers on which expenditure had been incurred to improve navigation.[120] It rises from 990 miles in 1760 to 1,750 in 1780, 2,690 in 1800, 3,190 in 1820, and 3,470 in 1840. For the average construction cost per mile we have relied on the figure for twenty-five canals assembled by Hadfield[121] together with information in Ginarlis.[122]

The second component is designed to cover the expenditure on improvements of existing canals and is confined to the period 1760–1840. For this we have taken Ginarlis's estimates of quasi-net expenditure (defined as for roads),[123] deducted the above estimate of new work, and then assumed that 20 per cent of the balance (representing approximately the expenditure on repairs and improvements) could be taken as an estimate of the outlays on improvements.

To convert the combined series for these first two components from current to 1851–60 prices we used a special index combining building wages (weight 2) and brick prices (weight 1). The aggregate value of the expenditure on new work and improvements over the century to 1860 comes to some £34 million at 1851–60 prices,[124] and we take this as the value of the stock (before adding in the third component) in 1860. The new work alone accounts for some £27 million, equivalent to a construction cost (at 1851-60 prices) of roughly £7,700 per mile, and we applied this to the mileage in 1760 to obtain the corresponding value of the canals at that date. The value in 1800 and 1830 was then obtained by assuming that the opening stock depreciated steadily at a rate of 10 per cent per decade (i.e. over a life of 100 years) and adding on the accumulated capital outlays from 1761 to the respective dates.

The third components covers the barges, pumping engines, hoists, and other ancillary equipment. G. B. Poole reckoned the value of these assets at £3 million in 1850.[125] We have assumed that the value at other dates was proportional to the mileage opened, and capital formation at 1851–60 prices was obtained by spreading the stock at the end of each decade over the two preceding decades – this represents an assumed life of 20 years for these assets. The standard index of machinery prices was used to convert this series to current prices. The stock and flow estimates for these items were then added to the corresponding estimates for the first two components to obtain the series shown in Tables 6 to 8.

12. DOCKS AND HARBOURS

For investment outlays on docks and harbours at current prices we have relied on information assembled by D. Swann for the period 1761–1830,[126] and on unpublished estimates by Mitchell covering the period from 1756 to 1914. These were based on a number of sources, including the accounts of dock companies and port authorities and a valuable parliamentary return of government expenditure.[127] This series was deflated by the index used above for canals to get the estimates at 1851–60 prices. We have taken the capital stock in 1760 at a notional £1 million and cumulated subsequent capital formation to get the value of the stock at the later dates.

13. SHIPS

The last item to be considered is shipping,[128] under which heading we cover all merchant vessels (whether cargo, passenger or fishing, coastal, or ocean-going) but not naval vessels. The series for gross capital formation at prices of 1851–60 is derived by valuing the tonnage built at an appropriate cost per ton. For the former, the main component is the tonnage built and first registered in Britain, statistics for which are available from 1787 onwards, with steamers distinguished from sailing ships after 1814.[129] For 1760–86 we have no record of annual shipbuilding, but the register of total tonnage belonging to Britain was compiled from 1788 onwards, and the tonnage built from 1760 to 1786 was estimated by assuming that the ships on the register in 1788 had been constructed or purchased over the previous twenty-five years, with an upward trend in the series.[130]

Craig has rightly insisted on the need to supplement the shipbuilding in British yards by allowing for the tonnage bought by British owners from outside the United Kingdom, particularly from the colonies in British North America[131] and also – after the repeal of the Navigation Laws in 1849 – from the United States. For 1821–60 a series is available in the parliamentary papers showing the tonnage of colonial-built vessels registered each year at each of the ports of the United Kingdom, but it is impossible to reconcile these figures with other returns, compiled by the same department, showing the total tonnage of colonial-built vessels registered at each port at the end of 1831, 1841, and 1846.[132] It seems that the annual series seriously understate the extent to which British shipowners were acquiring ships from the colonies, and we have constructed alternative estimates by spreading the total tonnage registered at the above dates over the preceding twenty years in proportion to the total tonnage built and registered in the colonies.[133] For years after 1846 there does not appear to be any published return of the tonnage of colonial-built vessels on the register at any one date, and we have assumed that the proportion of colonial-built vessels bought by British owners was about the same in 1847–60 (which includes the boom years of the mid-fifties) as in 1841–6. This gives a series for the colonial tonnage bought by British owners, rising from 100,000 tons in the 1820s to 400,000 tons in the 1840s and 500,000 tons (some 30 per cent of the tonnage of sailing ships built in British yards) in the 1850s.[134]

For the final component – the ships bought from the United States and other foreign countries after 1849 – we have taken the annual returns of foreign-built tonnage registered in Great Britain, available for 1850 to 1860.[135]

We thus have four categories of tonnage and require four estimates of the average value at prices of 1851–60. The first and most important is the estimate for home-built sailing vessels, for which we take £15 per registered ton to cover the replacement cost (at 1851–60 prices) of the hulls and of the masts, yards, and other fittings required to make the vessel 'ready for sea'. There is no lack of individual examples of shipbuilding costs, and once again the uncertainty arises in trying to strike an appropriate average within a wide range. For example, Hutchins quotes figures for British shipbuilding costs in 1860 varying from £16 16s. to £21 per ton for fourteen-year first-grade wooden ships, coppered and fitted with double outfits, down to £10 for low-grade eight-year vessels.[136] From all the evidence available an average of £15 seems about right for the whole range of sailing vessels and boats constructed in Britain.[137]

For the British-built steamers we take the 1851–60 price per gross ton of £25 10s.[138] given by Maywald, and raise this by 55 per cent to a price per net registered ton of £40.[139] The tonnage built in the Colonies was significantly cheaper than the British – that was its attraction for British owners and speculators – and prices were quoted varying from £10 to as little as £3 10s. per ton. The American ships purchased in the 1850s were generally of better quality and would have cost around £10 to £15 per ton. We have taken overall averages of £7 for colonial tonnage and £10 for United States tonnage.[140] The four components were valued and aggregated to give the estimates for capital formation at 1851–60 prices in Table 6.

The estimates of capital formation at current prices were then obtained by means of a price index combining engineering wages and timber prices[141] with equal weights. This gives an implicit price per ton for the sailing ships of around £8 in the period 1760–90, rising to £20 in 1801–20 and dropping back to about £15 from 1821 onwards. This is broadly consistent with the information available for these periods.[142]

The estimates of the value of the gross stock of merchant ships at replacement costs of 1851–60 were arrived at by valuing the tonnage on the register in England, Wales, and Scotland at the four benchmark dates. For 1860 we use the estimates of colonial and foreign tonnage described above (p. 65) to allocate the tonnage of sailing vessels on the register between British-, colonial-, and foreign-built, and value each of these, and the steamers, at the average 1851–60 prices given above. Similarly, for 1830 we distinguish colonial from British sailing vessels. For 1760 the total tonnage was estimated by extrapolating backwards from the start of the register in 1788, using a series for the tonnage of English-owned shipping given by R. Davis.[143]

V. *Circulating Capital, Overseas Assets, and Land*

Our aim in this section is to provide some rough orders of magnitude for three further categories of tangible wealth and, where appropriate, of their associated flows.

The first category is circulating capital in the form of stocks (inventories) and work in progress in industry, trade, and agriculture. This covers (1) non-farm stock-in-trade, i.e. stocks of home-produced and imported raw materials, semi-manufactured products, work in progress, and finished goods held by manufacturers and traders; and (2) farm crops (harvested and standing) and livestock, including horses whether used on farms or elsewhere in the economy. This circulating capital, together with the fixed capital already covered in section IV, constitutes the major part of domestic reproducible wealth.[144] We also estimate the changes in the circulating capital to derive series for stock-building – the value, at either current or constant (1851–60) prices, of the physical increase in stocks and work in progress – and these are added to the corresponding series for gross domestic fixed capital formation to obtain total capital formation.

The second category is the accumulated holding of overseas assets by British residents, net of assets in Britain owned by non-residents. This category differs from those previously estimated in that it covers both physical and financial assets. The assets and liabilities are valued on acquisition at their original cost, and the cumulative estimates require an adjustment to express this in terms of replacement at 1851–60 prices, but no adjustment is made for subsequent appreciation or depreciation of the assets.[145] Together with these assets we cover the holdings of gold and silver coin and bullion.[146] The change in the holdings of overseas assets and of gold and silver represents net investment abroad, and series for this – again valued at either current or 1851–60 prices – are added to the corresponding series for domestic capital formation to obtain estimates of total investment by Great Britain.

The final category of wealth to be covered is land, in which we include the unimproved value of farm land, the land underlying dwellings and other buildings and structures, and the value of standing timber. This is by far the most important component of non-reproducible tangible domestic wealth, and it is included because of its value and interest and for comparison with the estimates of reproducible domestic wealth and overseas assets.[147]

The estimates for all four categories are, at best, reasonable approximations, but they should serve to supplement the series in Tables 6–8 for reproducible fixed capital and to permit a broad assessment of the changing structure and rates of growth of the national wealth and investment of Great Britain in the century from 1760 to 1860.

I. NON-FARM STOCK-IN-TRADE

If we have hitherto laboured to make bricks without straw we have now to work without benefit of either straw or clay. Isolated series of stocks held are available for a few commodities,[148] but these provide no possible basis for an overall estimate; and no direct count of aggregate non-farm inventories was attempted prior to the post-war Censuses of Production (1948) and Distribution (1950).

The nearest approach to an overall total for the nineteenth century is an estimate which can be derived from the statistics of Fire Insurance Duty. In 1864, shortly before the duty was finally abolished, a reduced rate was charged on insurance of 'any Goods, Wares or Merchandise being Stock in Trade, or of any Machinery, Fixtures, Implements or Utensils used for the purpose of any Manufacture or Trade'.[149] From the return of the duty collected in 1863-4 at the reduced and higher rates it can be calculated that the value of the insured stock-in-trade, machinery, etc. was 33 per cent of the total value of property insured; applying this to the property insured in Great Britain in 1860 gives a figure of some £330 million.[150] If we then deduct from this our estimate of the value of industrial machinery and equipment in 1860 (Table 8), we are left with £170 million for the stock-in-trade.

This may safely be taken as the lower limit for the value of stock-in-trade, since even though the estimate for machinery, etc. may be somewhat too low (cf. p. 78 below), it is certain that not all stock-in-trade and machinery was insured and that the property which was covered was not always insured at its full value.[151] However, we are told that 'the destructible stock of producers and traders' was the 'most completely insured' of all forms of property,[152] and given the extent to which the practice of fire insurance had developed by 1860 it would seem likely that the full value of non-farm stock-in-trade in 1860 would be somewhere in the range of £200-250 million.

The only other estimate we have found is that made by Sir Frederick Eden, Chairman of the Globe Insurance Company, for c. 1800. This was derived as follows:[153]

British manufactures for home consumption	£76,000,000
for exportation	40,000,000
Foreign merchandise in Great Britain	40,000,000
	156,000,000

Of which total amount it is supposed that one-fourth is insurable or £39,000,000.

For a distant star to guide us between these two points we look to the twentieth century, and we find that the book value of non-farm stock-in-trade and work in progress in the inter-war years amounted to some 20 per cent of total final expenditure (i.e. GDP plus imports) at current prices, and that in the post-war period the ratio for 1948-58 was around

30 per cent and dropped by the late 1960s to 25 per cent.[154] We might expect there to be a downward trend in the ratio of stocks to turnover during the nineteenth century, and particularly after 1830, as improvements in transport and communication reduced the relative size of the stocks it was necessary to hold at each stage of the process of production and distribution,[155] though this might possibly be offset to some extent by an increase in the variety of goods offered.

Table 14. *Non-Farm Stock-in-Trade, 1760–1860*

	1760	1800	1830	1860
1. Final expenditure (£m)	120	294	392	858
2. Stocks as % of 1	30	30	30	25
3. Stocks at current prices (£m)	36	88	118	215
4. Price index (1851–60 = 100)	90	128	106	103
5. Stocks at 1851–60 prices (£m)	40	69	111	209

In the light of the foregoing discussion, we derive estimates of the value of non-farm stock-in-trade at current prices at the four benchmark dates by assuming that they amounted to 30 per cent of total final expenditure in 1760, 1800, and 1830, and 25 per cent in 1860.[156] A general index of wholesale prices was then used to value the resulting estimates at prices of 1851–60.[157] The successive stages are set out for the selected years in Table 14. The estimates of non-farm stock-in-trade at 1851–60 prices in line 5 are carried to Table 15, rounded to the

Table 15. *Stock of Circulating Capital, Overseas Assets, Coin and Bullion, and Land, Great Britain, 1760–1860ᵃ (£m at 1861–60 prices)*

	1760	1800	1830	1860
Circulating capital				
Non-farm stock-in-trade	40	70	110	210
Farm crops, livestock, and horses	140	190	220	240
Total	180	260	330	450
Overseas assets				
Accumulated net holdings of overseas assets	—20	10	90	360
Gold and silver coin and bullion	20	30	60	100
Total	0	40	150	460
Land				
Farm land (including woodlands)	900	940	990	1,000
Other	60	100	190	420
Total	960	1,040	1,180	1,420

ᵃ All values rounded to the nearest £10m.

SOURCE. See text, section V.

nearest £10 million as a reminder of their very approximate character.

From line 5 we can also estimate the value of stock-building at constant prices: the annual rate averages less than £1 million for 1760 to 1800, then rises to £1·4 million from 1800 to 1830 and to over £3 million over the last three decades to 1860. For the series shown in

Table 16. *Stockbuilding and Net Investment Abroad,*[a] *1761–1860*
(*£m p.a., decade averages, at current and constant prices*)

	Value of physical increase in stock and work in progress		Net investment abroad[b]	
	at current prices	at 1851–60 prices	at current prices	at 1851–60 prices
1761–70	1·0	1·0	0·5	0·5
1771–80	2·0	2·0	0·5	1·0
1781–90	2·0	2·0	1·5	1·5
1791–1800	3·5	3·0	1·5	1·5
1801–10	1·5	1·0	−3·0	−2·0
1811–20	3·0	2·0	7·5	5·0
1821–30	4·5	4·0	8·5	7·5
1831–40	3·5	3·5	4·5	4·5
1841–50	4·5	5·0	6·5	6·5
1851–60	3·5	3·5	20·0	20·0

[a] Rounded to nearest £0·5m.
[b] Including net changes in gold and silver coin and bullion.
SOURCE. See text, section V.

Table 16 we extend these results (by the same procedure as was used above) in order to obtain estimates of stockbuilding in each decade; the resulting series is then revalued at current prices.[158]

2. FARM CROPS, LIVESTOCK, AND HORSES

A continuous series of official agricultural statistics is not available for Great Britain until 1867, but fortunately the importance of farming attracted several careful investigators, and their studies, together with estimates of farm output and capital compiled after 1867, provide a reasonable starting point for the present estimates.[159] Even so, however, the final results necessarily involve a fair measure of conjecture and approximation, particularly with regard to the relationship of the feed crops to the valuation of the livestock.

Our initial objective is to estimate the value, at 1851–60 prices at the four selected dates, of (a) stocks of harvested and standing crops, (b) livestock, and (c) horses. The total of these items covers the major part of tenants' or occupiers' capital, but we exclude the machinery, equipment, etc. – which has already been covered in the comprehensive estimate for fixed capital in agriculture (see p. 48 above) – and include non-farm horses.

For the farm crops we begin with estimates of production or of crop acreage and yields at each of the four benchmark dates for wheat, barley, oats, and rye.[160] The estimated production of each crop was valued at the average *Gazette* prices of 1851–60.[161] The resulting series was then raised by 60 per cent to cover peas, beans, potatoes, turnips and other fodder crops, flax, and hops.[162] Finally, it was assumed, following Boreham,[163] that stocks of harvested and standing crops represented 85 per cent of crop production.[164]

For livestock we have made estimates of the numbers in Great Britain at the four selected dates,[165] and valued these on a basis intended to correspond roughly to store prices of 1851–60. These were taken to be: for all cows, heifers, and other cattle, an average of £9 10s.; for sheep and lambs, an average of £1 15s.; and for pigs, £2.[166] The resulting values were then raised by 2 per cent to cover asses, goats, and poultry; and, finally, the estimates for 1760, 1800, and 1830 were reduced by 20, 10, and 5 per cent respectively as a very rough allowance for the improvement in the weight and quality of the livestock over the period.[167] The estimates of farm and non-farm horses at the four dates were valued at an average (1851–60) price of £20.[168] The result of these estimates is:

	1760	1800	1830	1860
Harvested and standing crops	£56m	£69m	£83m	£89m
Livestock	66m	89m	99m	109m
Farmhorses	16m	27m	28m	25m
Other horses	4m	11m	14m	17m
Total	£142m	196m	224m	240m

These totals are rounded to the nearest £10 million and carried to Table 15.

As a rough test of the reliability of the above estimates, we may note that if they are expressed in terms of the capital per acre (taking the total area of cultivated land in Great Britain at a steady 30 million acres up to 1860) and adjusted to current prices by means of an index of wholesale prices for agricultural products,[169] we get the following:

	1760	1800	1830	1860
Farmers' capital, £ per acre	3·5	10·6	8·0	8·4

These figures seem reasonable when compared with previous estimates of tenants' capital for corresponding dates, including £4 per acre given by Arthur Young for England and Wales for 1770, £10 per acre suggested by Stevenson for 1800, £6 to £7 per acre suggested by Mc-Culloch for 1837 and 1846, £9 10s. per acre obtained by adjusting Boreham's estimate for 1867–73 for the United Kingdom to 1860 prices, and £8 per acre obtained by adjusting Turnbull's result for 1874 for the United Kingdom to 1860 prices.[170]

Finally, we can derive estimates of the contribution of farm crops and livestock to stock-building at 1851–60 prices by taking the change in the series shown above. Expressed as a rate per annum we have an average of £1·4 million for 1760–1800, £0·9 million for 1800–30, and £0·5 million for 1830–60. For the purposes of Table 16 we interpolate very roughly between the benchmark estimates to obtain the average for each decade. The series is then adjusted by the general index of wholesale prices[171] to get estimates at current prices.

3. NET HOLDINGS OF OVERSEAS ASSETS

From 1815 onwards we have Imlah's carefully constructed series for the net export of capital, obtained by estimating the annual balance on current account and deducting the estimated net imports of gold and silver bullion and specie.[172] To obtain estimates of the accumulated net holdings of overseas assets in terms of 1851–60 purchasing power, we accept Imlah's starting point of a net credit of £10 million at the end of 1815, and cumulate on this the net credit in each quinquennium, deflated by the general index of wholesale prices.[173] This gives the required values for 1830 and 1860.

For 1760 we have detailed estimates from both British and Dutch sources, indicating that total Dutch investment in Britain at that date was between £25 million and £30 million, and allowance for other foreign holdings would raise this to some £30–5 million.[174] The extent of British investment abroad to be set against that is unknown, but we may say £10–15 million and put the net *debit* in 1851–60 prices at £20 million. For 1800 we take foreign holdings in Britain as reduced to some £25–30 million,[175] and raise British investments abroad to some £35–45 million, making a net credit of some £10 million.[176] These results are shown for the four benchmark dates in Table 15.

For Table 16 we need estimates of the flow of capital abroad in each decade at current and 1851–60 prices. From 1815 to 1860 we have Imlah's estimates for the former and the deflated series for the latter. For 1760 to 1815 we interpolate between the estimates of the accumulated net credit abroad, assuming a broadly steady increase in British holdings of foreign assets and adjusting foreign investment in Britain in the light of the available information.[177]

4. GOLD AND SILVER COIN AND BULLION

One part of the net imports of gold and silver would be used for the manufacture of plate, jewellery, etc., and this does not affect the present estimates.[178] The remainder would be added to Britain's monetary holdings of coin and bullion, and since these represent a potential claim on foreigners they can be regarded as equivalent to overseas assets, with changes in the amount of monetary gold and silver treated as part of net investment abroad.[179]

Various estimates are available regarding the gold and silver coin in circulation in Britain in the nineteenth century,[180] and in the light of these we take the coin in circulation at the four selected dates, together with the bullion held by the Bank of England,[181] as:

	1760	1800	1830	1860
Bullion and specie	£20m	£30m	£60m	£100m

The same values are entered in Table 15, since the price of gold was broadly the same in 1851–60 as at the selected dates.

The annual net increase in the monetary holdings of gold and silver is thus some £0·25 million between 1760 and 1800, £1 million from 1800 to 1830, and £1·3 million from 1830 to 1860. These estimates form the basis for the series incorporated in Table 16 with interpolation in the light of the sources quoted above.[182]

5. FARM LAND (INCLUDING WOODS AND PLANTATIONS)

To form a rough estimate of the unimproved value of farm land we take estimates of the gross rent (including tithes) of farm lands and buildings at the four selected dates, and capitalize these at twenty-five years' purchase for 1760, twenty-eight years for 1800 and 1830, and thirty for 1860.[183] We then deduct from this the estimated value of farm buildings, drainage, and other improvements.[184] The resulting value of unimproved farm land at current prices is:

	1760	1800	1830	1860
Farm land	£380m	£630m	£820m	£1,020m

This is assumed to include the capital value of woods and plantations.[185] To obtain the series at constant prices, we could deflate by an index of land prices, but no suitable index is available.[186] Instead, we have adjusted the value of unimproved farm land in 1860 to 1851–60 prices, giving £1,000 million, and assume that the value would be the same for the earlier years at constant prices except to the extent that new land was brought into cultivation by enclosure of waste, heath, and moor, the drainage of marsh and fen, etc. The precise extent of this addition to the area of agricultural land is not known but seems likely to have been about three million acres, increasing the acreage by about 5 per cent between 1760 and 1800, by a further 5 per cent to 1830, and by about 1 per cent to around thirty-one million acres in 1860.[187] The estimates obtained on this basis are shown in Table 15.[188]

6. OTHER LAND

The value of urban land rent in England and Wales has been estimated by Singer at £14 million in 1861.[189] This represents 26 per cent of the gross rental (as assessed for Schedule A) of houses and other non-farm buildings. If we take the same proportion of (a) the gross rent for houses, etc. in Scotland, and (b) the gross income of railways, mines, and other property not covered by Schedule A, this would raise the total urban rent to some £21 million,[190] and if this is capitalized at twenty years' purchase it gives a capital value of some £420 million,[191] of which the land underlying dwellings and that underlying industrial and commercial buildings account for some £160 million and £150 million respectively, and the land for the railways for some £70 million.[192]

The estimates of the value of land at 1851–60 prices at the three earlier dates were obtained by assuming that the ratio of land to buildings and works was the same as in 1860 for each of the four items (dwellings; industrial and commercial buildings; railways; mines, canals, and gasworks). The resulting series is shown in line 6 of Table 15.

VI. *Comparison with Other Estimates*

The estimates for the component series in sections IV and V have already been compared, wherever possible, with estimates made by others or with estimates which we could derive by alternative procedures, and the following comments are confined to comparisons covering total fixed capital formation and the total stock of capital.

FIXED CAPITAL FORMATION

For total gross domestic fixed capital formation we can make the first comparison with the 'orders of magnitude' suggested by Pollard, to which we referred in section I. The comparison is not exact, because of the different dates to which the estimates relate; but with this reservation, we see from Table 17 that the new estimates lie very far below Pollard's for *c.* 1770 and well above his for *c.* 1815. Fixed capital formation thus increases over the period at a rate more than double that previously suggested. For the final date, *c.* 1830–5, the two estimates agree quite well.

Table 17. *Gross Fixed Capital Formation, Great Britain, c. 1770–1835: Comparison with Pollard's Estimates (£m p.a. at current prices)*

	c. 1770	*c.* 1790–3	*c.* 1815	*c.* 1830–5
1. Pollard	7·2	13·3	21·9	31·0
2. Feinstein: Present estimates	4·0	11·4	26·5	28·2
3. 1 minus 2	3·2	1·9	−4·6	2·8
4. 3 as % of 2	80	17	−17	10

SOURCE

Line 1: Pollard, 'Growth and Distribution of Capital', 362.

Line 2: See Table 7 above. The estimate taken for comparison for *c.* 1770 is the average for the decade 1771–80; for *c.* 1790–3, the average for 1791–1800; and for *c.* 1815, the average for 1811–20. For 1830–5, the present estimates for each item for 1831–40 were allocated between the two quinquennia in the proportions indicated by the annual estimates made for that decade by Deane, 'New Estimates'. (Miss Deane has very kindly made available the separate estimates underlying her published totals.)

Examination of the components (see Tables 2 and 7) shows even greater discrepancies. For *c.* 1770, all the present estimates are lower than Pollard's except for transport, and the absolute difference is greatest in agriculture and buildings (dwellings and public buildings). For *c.* 1790–3 the estimate for buildings is responsible for almost all of the difference in the two totals, and the other sectors agree moderately well. At the next date, *c.* 1815, there is again one sector which accounts for the greater part of the difference between the two estimates, but on this occasion it is manufacturing and trade. If the expansion over the period 1770–1815 is measured by expressing the level of gross domestic fixed capital formation at current prices *c.* 1815 as a ratio to the level *c.* 1770, we have the following contrast:

	Pollard	Present estimate
Agriculture	2·0	3·9
Transport	3·0	4·0
Building	3·7	9·8
Manufacturing, trade, etc.	4·7	14·9
Total	3·0	6·7

The discrepancies in the movement over this period are thus smallest for transport and largest for manufacturing, trade, etc.; and the overall impression given by the new estimates is thus substantially different.

For 1830–5 we can extend the comparison with Pollard to cover also the first years of Miss Deane's series. Their two estimates have already been compared with each other (see Table 3 and pp. 31–2 above) and found to show completely different orders of magnitude for fixed capital formation in Britain on the eve of the railway era. Table 18 now

Table 18. *Fixed Capital Formation, 1830–5: Comparison with Estimates by Pollard and Deane (£m p.a. at current prices)*

	(1)	(2)	(3)
			Feinstein:
	Pollard	Deane	present
	(GB)	(UK)	estimate (GB)
1. Dwellings	10·0	6·0	8·7
2. Public building and works, etc.	1·5	2·0[a]	1·5
3. Agriculture	4·6	—[b]	3·4
4. Industry and commerce	8·2	2·9	9·5
5. Transport	6·7	4·8	5·1
Total	31·0	15·7	28·2

[a] Includes expenditure on new works and buildings by navy, army, and ordnance departments, and on naval vessels (Deane, 'New Estimates', 111). These items are not treated as capital expenditure in the present estimates: see Feinstein, *National Income*, 192.

[b] Farm implements and machinery are included by Deane in the estimates for industry and commerce; farm buildings and works are omitted altogether (*op. cit.*, 111).

SOURCES

(1) Pollard, 'Growth and Distribution of Capital', 362.

(2) Deane, 'New Estimates', 104, and unpublished information kindly provided for the individual sectors.

(3) See Table 7 above, and the note to Table 17.

indicates that the new estimate is only £3 million (10 per cent) *below* Pollard's, with compensating differences of £1 to £1·5 million on all the main items, whereas it is over £12 million (44 per cent) *above* Deane's estimate. There is a broad measure of agreement on public buildings and works and transport (lines 2 and 5), but the present estimate is substantially higher than Deane's for dwellings, and there is a second major discrepancy in the key sector of industry and commerce, where the present estimate of £9·5 million is over three times the £3 million suggested by Deane. The third significant difference, in agriculture, is not a question of estimation, since Deane explicitly omitted the expenditures on farm buildings, land-clearing, drainage, and other improvements.

The same three sectors – industry and commerce, agriculture, and (to a lesser extent) dwellings – account for most of the differences which we find if we continue the comparison with Deane's estimates down to 1860. This is done in Table 19. The discrepancy is broadly steady in

Table 19. *Fixed Capital Formation, 1831–60: Comparison with Deane's Estimates* (£m p.a., decade averages, at current prices)

	1831–40	1841–50	1851–60
1. Deane (UK)	22·9	34·5	39·7
2. Feinstein: present estimate (GB)	40·5	50·5	58·0
3. 2 minus 1	17·6	16·0	18·3
4. 3 as % of 2	43	32	32

SOURCES

Line 1: Deane, 'New Estimates', 104.
Line 2: See Table 7 above.

absolute terms and so drops a little in size relative to the present estimates, but it is still extremely high (32 per cent) in the 1850s. A more detailed comparison of the components is made in Table 20 for the 1850s, and the picture this reveals is fully representative of the two earlier decades. Miss Deane would presumably not wish to defend the

Table 20. *Fixed Capital Formation, 1851–60, by Sector: Comparison with Deane's Estimates* (£m p.a., decade average, at current prices)

	(1) Deane (UK)	(2) Feinstein: present estimate (GB)
1. Dwellings	7·4	10·3
2. Other public buildings and works	4·9[a]	2·0
3. Agriculture	—[b]	6·9
4. Industry and commerce	9·0	20·7
5. Transport	18·4	18·1
Total	39·7	58·0

[a] See note *a* to Table 18.
[b] See note *b* to Table 18.

SOURCES

(1) Deane, 'New Estimates', 104, and unpublished information kindly provided for the individual sectors.
(2) Table 7 above.

omission of farm buildings and works, so that the main disagreement over estimation is concentrated on the level of capital expenditure in the industrial and commercial sector: £9 million per annum in Deane against £21 million according to the new estimate. Despite all the uncertainty regarding the estimates obtained for this sector, it is hard to believe that they overstate the true level so seriously that they should be reduced by more than half – particularly for the period 1831–60, for which they have a reasonably secure foundation in the assessments for Schedule A and the Inhabited House Duty. Since this sector is of such importance, not only for the estimates but also for our understanding of economic developments in this period, one obvious conclusion to be drawn from the analysis of Tables 18, 19, and 20 is that this is the area in which future research on capital formation should be concentrated.

The final comparison which can be made with a comprehensive estimate of gross fixed capital formation arises at the point where the present estimates overlap those which I have previously published for the years from 1856 onwards. This is given in Table 21 and can be done

Table 21. *Fixed Capital Formation 1856–60, by Type of Asset: Comparison with Previous Estimates, by Sector: (£m p.a. at current prices)*

	(1) Feinstein: previous estimates (UK)	(2) Feinstein: present estimates (GB)
1. Dwellings	6	9·5
2. Non-residential buildings and works		
a. Farm	—	7·0
b. Railways, docks, and harbours	8	8
c. Others	7	18·5
3. Plant and machinery	10	7
4. Ships	5	5
5. Vehicles	1	3
Total	37	58

SOURCES

(1) Feinstein, *National Income*, Table 39, p. T85, and supporting worksheets.
(2) Table 7 above, average for 1851–60, spread between the two halves of the decade (see the note to Table 17), and roughly allocated by type of asset.

only by type of asset, not by sector. The present estimates are higher by some £21 million (36 per cent), and of this over £8 million is accounted for by the farm buildings and works and the carriages and coaches which were omitted from the previous estimates (reflecting, to a large extent, their origin in the rather different economic circumstances of 1907);[193] while a further £11 million appears in the other buildings and works (line 2c of Table 21), mainly relating to the industrial and commercial buildings. This again calls for further investigation of this sector, but on the evidence now available I would consider the present estimate appreciably more reliable than the earlier extrapolation from the 1907 benchmark.[194] A further difference, in the opposite direction, occurs in the estimates for plant and machinery (line 3), and though it is smaller than that for the buildings it is not negligible. In this case I find it more difficult to take a view on the relative merits of the two estimates derived by totally independent and different procedures. However, taking the estimates as a whole, it seems clear that the previous estimate of £37 million per annum for the late 1850s was too low, and I would feel reasonably confident that the true value lies within a margin of error of ±15 per cent of the present estimates.

CAPITAL STOCK

For the estimates of the gross stock of fixed capital the only alternative estimates we have for comparison with the present results are the series which I published in 1972, starting in 1855 and classified by type of asset. Table 22 reveals the enormous discrepancy between these two attempts to value the stock of fixed assets: the previous estimate of £3,380 million is 46 per cent higher than the present figure of £2,310 million. The difference in prices underlying the two estimates (1860 replacement cost for the former, and the average of 1851–60 for the latter) is negligible,[195] but some allowance should be made for the exclusion of Ireland from the present estimates, and this might raise them by some 5 per cent.[196] This would still leave a great gulf of over £900 million.

The disagreement is at its worst in the estimate for plant, ships, and vehicles, and within this it arises primarily in the value of industrial plant and equipment. It is smallest for non-residential buildings and works, but within this aggregate the amount allowed in the present estimate for industrial and commercial buildings (£460 million) is substantially less than the amount of around £800 million implicit in the earlier work. This is partially offset by the larger value which the present estimates assign to farm buildings and works. Finally, there is a serious difference over the estimates for dwellings.

This is not the place for a full investigation of these discrepancies, but it seems desirable to make a brief comment. The earlier estimates were obtained by taking the end-1920 figures at 1930 replacement cost from the study of capital formation in the inter-war period,[197] making a small addition for Southern Ireland so as to cover the whole of the British Isles, adjusting from 1930 to 1900 prices, and then extrapolating backwards by means of a reversal of the perpetual inventory formula.[198] Finally a further price adjustment was made to convert from 1900 to current prices, so as to obtain, for example, the estimate for 1860 at 1860 replacement cost used in the comparison in Table 22.[199] It was always

Table 22. *Gross Capital Stock in 1860: Comparison with Previous Estimate (£m at replacement cost)*

	(1) Feinstein: present estimates (GB at 1851–60 replacement cost)	(2) Feinstein: previous estimate (UK at 1860 replacement cost)
1. Dwellings	600	850
2. Other buildings and works	1,370	1,630
3. Plant, ships, and vehicles	340	900
4. Total	2,310	3,380

SOURCES

(1) Table 8 above, with an approximate allocation of certain items by type of asset.
(2) Feinstein, *National Income*, Table 46, p. T103.

recognized that this indirect route was likely to lead to very unreliable results,[200] but obviously the full extent of the probable error was not correctly anticipated. The crucial question for the present is whether the new estimates can be regarded as likely to be more nearly correct and, if not, where the true estimate will fall between £2,400 million and £3,400 million. As a first step towards an answer, we may note that errors of overstatement could enter the results published in 1972 if:

(a) the initial benchmark obtained for the inter-war years was too high: in this connection, it is a critical consequence of the method that what may be a fairly minor error relative to the level of the stock in 1920 or later will be carried backwards as an unchanging absolute amount (at constant prices) and could then be a very large error relative to the level of the stock in 1860;[201]

(b) the estimates of gross fixed capital formation deducted from the end-1920 stock were too low; or

(c) the estimates of capital scrapped or sold, which are added to the 1920 stock as it is extrapolated back to earlier years, were too high.

A preliminary reconsideration of the 1972 estimates suggests that there are compensating errors in all three categories. In particular, it seems likely that the inter-war benchmark for commercial buildings was seriously overstated and that the estimates for dwellings and for industrial buildings and works (including mining) were also too high,[202] and that the estimates of capital expenditure, especially on non-residential building, were too low.[203] As a partial offset, the allowance for machinery and equipment scrapped was too high,[204] and the earlier estimates made too little allowance for the scrapping of farm assets during the late-nineteenth-century depression in the arable farming areas.[205]

It seems likely that correction for these factors would eliminate most of the differences shown in Table 22; but it is also, of course, possible that the present estimates are too low for some sectors, and this seems most likely to be the case for industrial machinery and equipment. As a very tentative conclusion at this stage, we might say that we expect the true value of the 1860 stock of fixed capital assets in Great Britain to lie between £2,200 million and £2,800 million, but a firm judgement will require a good deal of further research.

To round off this discussion of our methods and results we can compare the present estimate of national wealth in 1860 with Giffen's estimate, adjusted so as to be broadly comparable in coverage.[206] However, as we have already noted,[207] the two estimates differ conceptually, and close agreement is not to be expected. A valuation by Giffen's method should be lower than the present estimate to the extent that it allows for depreciation of fixed assets; it might be higher or lower to the extent that capitalization of future prospects diverges from the accumulation of actual past outlays.

As the comparison in Table 23 shows, the present total is only £120 million, or 3 per cent below the adjusted Giffen estimate. If the estimate for lands is excluded on the grounds that the source and the method used for the present estimate of the total are essentially the same as for Giffen's,[208] the discrepancy is still only 3 per cent though the sign changes, i.e. the present estimate is then marginally higher. This outcome is, however, the reflection of some compensating differences. The present estimate is one-third higher for houses and other buildings, and the difference would be substantial even if farmhouses were added to Giffen's estimate. It is also higher for mines, gas and water supply, canals, etc., where there is some reason to think that Giffen capitalized at too low a rate.[209] Our estimates are substantially lower than Giffen's for farmers' capital, on which Giffen had been the subject of criticism by contemporaries,[210] and for the domestic and foreign capital, fixed and circulating, of industry and trade, etc., where Giffen's method is particularly uncertain,[211] but where the present estimates are also highly conjectural.

The comparison in Table 23 is also of interest in bringing out the very heterogeneous character of some of the items covered by a single figure in Giffen's estimate, and in emphasizing the potentially misleading nature of some of his titles, e.g. 'lands' or 'houses'.

Table 23. *National Capital, Great Britain, 1860: Comparison with Giffen's Estimate (£m)*

	(1) Feinstein: present estimate	(2) Giffen (adjusted)	(3) (2)—(1)
1. Lands			
a. Farm land (unimproved)	1,000		
b. Buildings and improvements	400		
	—— 1,400	1,610	210
2. Houses, etc.			
a. Dwellings	600		
b. Industrial and commercial buildings	460		
c. Land	310		
	—— 1,370	890	—480
3. Farmers' capital			
a. Farm crops, livestock, horses	240		
b. Implements, tools, etc.	30		
	—— 270	490	220
4. Businesses, etc.			
a. Industrial machinery and equipment	160		
b. Non-farm stock-in-trade	210		
c. Ships, carriages, coaches	90		
d. Overseas assets	360		
	—— 820	1,010	190
5. Railways			
a. Buildings, rolling stock, track, etc.	270		
b. Land	70		
	—— 340	350	10
6. Mines, etc.			
a. Mines, gasworks, water supply, canals, etc.	110		
b. Land	40		
	—— 150	110	—40
7. Government and local property			
a. Roads and bridges	70		
b. Docks and harbours	40		
c. Public works and buildings	80		
	—— 190	200	10
	4,540	4,660	120

SOURCES

(1) See Tables 8 and 15 above. The value of gold and silver coin and bullion has been omitted since this item is not covered by Giffen; the estimates for non-farm land have been allocated to their respective buildings and structures in lines 2c, 5b, and 6b; and £30m for farmers' implements, etc. has been transferred from 1b to 3b.

(2) Giffen's published estimate for 1865 was £6,114m ('On Recent Accumulations of Capital in the United Kingdom', *J. R. Stat. Soc.*, XLI (1878), 11; also *Growth of Capital*, 43). This has been adjusted (*a*) to exclude his estimate of £500m for movable

property not yielding income: (*b*) to exclude army and navy property, taken at a very round £100m; (*c*) to exclude some £35m for Ireland from the remaining items on the basis of the proportions shown by Giffen for 1885 (*Growth of Capital*, 163–5); and (*d*) to change the underlying income estimates to correspond more closely with an estimate of the capital stock in 1860 by moving from the income of 1864–5 used by Giffen to the income of, e.g. 1860–1 for assessments on a current-year basis, or of 1862–3 where the average of the three preceding years was assessed for tax. The assessments used were those given by Giffen, 'Recent Accumulations', 29–30. This reduces the total by a further £510m.

VII.   *Capital Accumulation and Economic Growth*

In this final section we step back to look at the broad outlines of the results we have obtained and to make a preliminary analysis of some of their main implications for an understanding of the process of economic growth of the British economy from the pre-industrial condition of 1760 through the industrial revolution and the transformation of agriculture and transport to the industrialized and urbanized society of 1860.

As will be painfully clear to anyone who has studied the preceding pages, there have been very few items for which precise, objective, and comprehensive data could be found: we have hardly any records of actual capital expenditure or statistics of the number of assets of a particular type constructed or in place. In almost every case we have had to rely on fragmentary evidence held together by a multitude of more or less arbitrary assumptions. In the main, however, these have been specific and self-contained assumptions concerning, for example, the rate of improvement in the standard of dwellings, the proportion of farm rents represented by capital expenditure, the level of capital per head in textiles relative to other manufacturing industries, the average cost of sailing ships, the yield per acre of farm crops, and so on. With a few exceptions, we have not assumed a particular relationship between the level or growth of capital and the level or growth of population or of real national product.[212] Thus it is legitimate and may also be interesting to explore the consequences of all the assumptions and conjectures which have been made, and to see what they imply at an aggregate level about the growth and structure of the capital stock[213] and capital formation, and their relationship to population and real GNP. In what follows we shall make a preliminary attempt to do this; we shall not explicitly qualify every comment ('If the estimates are approximately correct . . .'), but the very large margins of error must, of course, be kept in mind throughout.

CAPITAL, POPULATION, AND OUTPUT

In Table 24 we look first at the levels and rates of growth of three of the main aggregates for the stock of capital: fixed capital, fixed and circulating (domestic reproducible) capital, and total capital or national wealth, including land and overseas assets. The first two measures of capital show broadly the same result: over the century to 1860, they rise to over four times their initial level, at an average annual rate of

Table 24. *Levels and Rates of Growth of the Stock of Capital, Great Britain, 1760–1860*

	(1) Fixed capital	(2) Domestic reproducible capital	(3) National wealth
A. End-year levels (£m at 1851–60 prices)			
1760	490	670	1,630
1800	730	990	2,070
1830	1,180	1,510	2,840
1860	2,310	2,760	4,640
B. Growth rates (% p.a.)			
1761–1800	1·0	1·0	0·6
1801–30	1·6	1·4	1·0
1831–60	2·3	2·0	1·6
1761–1860	1·6	1·4	1·0

SOURCES

(1) Table 8 above.
(2) = (1) plus total circulating capital (Table 15).
(3) = (2) plus land and overseas assets (Table 15).

growth of about $1\frac{1}{2}$ per cent per annum (compound); the rate of expansion is marginally greater for fixed capital than for domestic reproducible capital. The inclusion of land in the third series – total national wealth – slows down the rate of growth of this measure to about 1 per cent per annum. We defer further consideration of the differences between the three measures of capital to a later stage, where we examine the changes in the composition of the stock of capital (p. 87 below); for the moment, we confine our attention to the domestic reproducible capital.

The main series for reproducible capital, population, and real output[214] are set out in Table 25. The levels of the three primary series and their corresponding ratios – capital per head of the population, output per head of the population, and capital per unit of output – are shown

Table 25. *Levels and Rates of Growth of Capital, Population,*
and Output, Great Britain, 1760–1860

	(1)	(2)	(3)	(4)	(5)	(6)
	Domestic repro-ducible capital (£m at 1851–60 prices)	Popula-tion (millions)	Real output (GDP) (£m at 1851–60 prices)	Capital per head	Output per head	Capital/output ratio
				(£ at 1851–60 prices)		
A. End-year levels						
1760	670	7·87	90	85	11	7·4
1800	990	10·76	140	92	13	7·1
1830	1,510	16·34	310	92	19	4·9
1860	2,760	23·13	650	120	28	4·3
B. Growth rates (% p.a.)						
1761–1800	1·0	0·8	1·1	0·2	0·3	−0·1
1801–30	1·4	1·4	2·7	—	1·3	−1·2
1831–60	2·0	1·2	2·5	0·9	1·3	−0·4
1761–1860	1·4	1·1	2·0	0·3	0·9	−0·6

SOURCES

(1) Total fixed capital (Table 8 above) plus circulating capital (Table 15).
(2) Deane and Cole, *British Economic Growth*, 6, and Mitchell, *Abstract*, 6–7 (includ-ing allowance for the armed forces and merchant service in 1801 and 1831).
(3) GNP at factor cost in 1860 from Deane, 'New Estimates', 104, adjusted to exclude Ireland on the basis of Deane and Cole, *op. cit.*, 335, and converted to 1851–60 prices; extrapolated to 1830 on the basis of Deane, 'New Estimates', 98, to 1800 on the basis of Deane and Cole, *op. cit.*, 282, and to 1760 using the Deane and Cole indices but with 1800 weights, *op. cit.*, 78–9. This final link (1760–1800) is particularly uncertain. To obtain GDP at 1851–60 factor cost, this series was then adjusted to exclude net property income from abroad: Imlah, *Economic Elements in the Pax Britannica* (1958), 70–2.
(4) = (1)/(2). 　　　　　　　(5) = (3)/(2). 　　　　　　　(6) = (1)/(3).

in the upper part of the table for the benchmark dates, and the rates of growth are given in the lower part.

While reproducible capital increased fourfold over the century at a rate of about $1\frac{1}{2}$ per cent per annum, population expanded threefold at a rate of about 1 per cent per annum, and so capital per head shows a modest increase. As shown in column 4 of Table 25 it rises (at 1851–60 prices) from £85 in 1760 to £120 in 1860. Real output outpaces both capital and population over the century, increasing more than sevenfold at a rate of some 2 per cent per annum. There is thus a persistent down-ward trend in the capital–output ratio at a rate of about 0·5 per cent per annum.

The same relationship can be expressed in a slightly different way by noting that a rise in capital per head of population, at a rate of less than 0·5 per cent per annum, was accompanied by – and in some degree associated with – a rise in output per head of population, at about 1 per cent per annum. The degree of association and the nature of the causal relationships between the growth of output and the growth of capital must be left as subjects for further investigation.[215]

If we now look more closely at the pattern of growth *within* the century, we see that the estimates in Table 25 show a steady increase in the rate of growth of reproducible capital, from about 1 per cent per annum in the first of the three sub-periods distinguished in the table (1761–1800) to about $1\frac{1}{2}$ per cent per annum in the second (1801–30) and 2 per cent in the third (1831–60). In the first two periods population more or less keeps pace with capital, so that almost all of the increase in capital per head observed previously in fact occurs in the final three decades, when it rises from £92 to £120 (at constant prices), at a rate of about 1 per cent per annum.

Output rises at about the same rate as capital from 1760 to 1800, but thereafter it goes ahead much more rapidly, particularly in the three decades 1801–30 before the coming of the railways, and the capital–output ratio falls from about 7 in 1800 to just over 4 in 1860.[216]

CAPITAL, LABOUR, OUTPUT, AND PRODUCTIVITY

Up to this point we have considered the relationship of capital to output and population. However, in the context of an analysis of the growth of productivity, to which we now turn, the relevant variable is not population but labour. From 1800 onwards we have a very approximate estimate of the labour force (total occupied population), derived from the Census of Population, and this shows an increase from 4·8 million in 1801 to 7·2 million in 1831 and 10·8 million in 1861.[217] The corresponding participation rates are: 44, 44, and 47 per cent[218] – i.e. the rate of growth of the labour force was the same as that of the total population from 1800 to 1830 (1·4 per cent per annum) and only marginally faster from 1830 to 1860 (1·4 as against 1·2 per cent per annum). If we assume in the light of this that there was also no significant change in the overall participation rate in the period from 1760 to 1800, we can extend the labour series back to 1760. We can then make a very broad analysis of the productivity of both labour and capital.[219] We take as the most appropriate measure of capital the domestic reproducible assets. The corresponding measure of real output is again the gross domestic product. The relevant series are set out in Table 26, together with estimates of the combined input of labour and capital and of the 'residual' or output per unit of total inputs.[220]

Table 26. *Inputs, Output, and Total Factor Productivity, Great Britain, 1760–1860*

	(1) Output	(2)	(3) Inputs	(4)	(5)	(6) Productivity	(7)
	GDP at constant factor cost	Labour	Domestic reproducible capital	Total inputs	Output per worker	Output per unit of capital	Output per unit of total inputs
A. End-year levels (index: base = 100)							
1760	14	32	24	28	44	58	50
1800	21	44	36	40	48	58	52
1830	48	67	55	61	72	87	79
1860	100	100	100	100	100	100	100
B. Growth rates (% p.a.)							
1761–1800	1·0	0·8	1·0	0·9	0·2	—	0·3
1801–60	2·6	1·4	1·7	1·5	1·2	0·9	1·0
1801–30	2·8	1·4	1·4	1·4	1·4	1·4	1·4
1831–60	2·5	1·4	2·0	1·7	1·1	0·5	0·8
1761–1860	2·0	1·1	1·4	1·3	0·8	0·5	0·7

SOURCES

(1) See column (3) of Table 25 above.
(2) See text, p. 85.
(3) Total fixed capital (Table 8) plus circulating capital and land (Table 15), all at 1851–60 prices.
(4) Cols. (2) and (3) combined with equal weights on basis of roughly equal distribution of factor incomes between labour and property (profits plus rent, adjusted to exclude the estimated pure rent of land) in 1860: see Feinstein, *National Income*, Table 18, p. T44.

(5) = (1)/(2).
(6) = (1)/(3).
(7) = (1)/(4).

Our major findings with respect to the growth of output, capital, an labour inputs and productivity between 1760 and 1860 may be summarized as follows:[221]

(i) Real output (GDP) increased at a rate of about 1 per cent per annum from 1760 to 1800 and then accelerated to about $2\frac{1}{2}$ per cent from 1800 to 1860.

(ii) The labour force increased at just under 1 per cent per annum from 1760 to 1800 and at just under $1\frac{1}{2}$ per cent from 1800 to 1860.

(iii) The growth rate of the domestic reproducible capital stock increased steadily, rising from 1 per cent per annum in 1760–1800 to $1\frac{1}{2}$ per cent per annum in 1800–30, and to 2 per cent per annum in 1830–60.

(iv) The rate of increase of the combined inputs was thus about 1 per cent per annum from 1760 to 1800 and $1\frac{1}{2}$ per cent from 1800 to 1860.

(v) Capital and labour grew at about the same rate from 1760 through to 1830, so that there was effectively no change in the capital-labour ratio in these seven decades. In the last three decades the ratio did rise, as capital per worker increased at a rate of about $\frac{1}{2}$ per cent per annum.

(vi) In the first four decades output and inputs grew at about the same rate, so that there was effectively no improvement in the productivity of labour, or of labour and capital combined. From 1800 to 1860, however, we find that output per worker and per unit of capital increased at about 1 per cent per annum, and the 'residual' or total factor productivity also increased at 1 per cent. The rate of growth of total productivity is greater from 1800 to 1830 than from 1830 to 1860 because of the slower growth of capital in the first of these sub-periods.

(vii) With minor exceptions the main break in trend rates of growth, as indicated by the above summary, occurs around the end of the eighteenth century, with outputs, inputs, and productivity all growing appreciably more rapidly from 1800 to 1860 than from 1760 to 1800.

CHANGES IN THE STRUCTURE OF NATIONAL WEALTH

A detailed picture of the changes in the structure of national wealth is set out in Table 27, in order to provide more information about the forces underlying the trends in total capital input described in the preceding pages. The percentage composition of total national wealth is shown by type of asset in the upper part of the table and by economic sector in the middle part, and the lower part gives the percentage composition of domestic reproducible capital by sector and type of asset.

The major feature of the first part of the table is the decline in the

Table 27. *Composition of National Wealth, 1760–1860, by Type of Asset and by Sector (per cent)*

	1760	1800	1830	1860
A. National wealth by type of asset				
1. Fixed assets	30	35	42	50
2. Circulating capital	11	13	11	9
3. Domestic reproducible capital	41	48	53	59
4. Land	59	50	42	31
5. Total domestic capital	100	98	95	90
6. Overseas assets[a]	—	2	5	10
National wealth	100	100	100	100
B. National wealth by sector				
1. Residential and social	16	16	19	18
2. Agriculture	77	68	55	36
3. Industry and commerce	5	10	16	23
4. Transport	2	4	5	13
5. Overseas assets[a]	—	2	5	10
National wealth	100	100	100	100
C. Domestic reproducible capital by sector and type of asset				
1. Residential and social	31	28	28	24
2. Agriculture: fixed	31	27	22	16
3. Agriculture: circulating	21	19	15	9
4. Industry and commerce: fixed	5	11	18	25
5. Industry and commerce: circulating	6	7	7	8
6. Transport	6	8	9	18
Total	100	100	100	100

[a] Including gold and silver.

SOURCE. Estimates at 1851–60 prices in Tables 8 and 15 above. Components may not add to totals because of rounding.

relative importance of land and of circulating capital. The given, non-reproducible component of national wealth increased at a rate of less than $\frac{1}{2}$ per cent per annum over the whole century, and its share in the national wealth (which was growing at about 1 per cent per annum) thus fell from about 60 per cent in 1760 to 30 per cent in 1860. In assessing this trend, it must be remembered that the very large increase in the price of farm land relative to other prices (see note 188), and the increase in urban site values, have the effect of giving land a much larger weight relative to other assets, at the given base-period prices (1851–60), than it would have if land and other assets were valued at current prices in each period. Circulating capital in agriculture, industry, and trade also grew quite slowly (the rate was just under 1 per cent per annum), and there was a consequent fall in its share of national wealth, from a peak of 13 per cent in 1800 to 9 per cent in 1860. The categories which rise in importance are fixed capital and overseas assets. The former's share of the national wealth rises strongly from 30 per cent to 50 per cent; the latter's share rises from nothing to 10 per cent. The changing ratio of fixed to circulating capital which emerges from this process is thus quite striking: from 3:1 in 1760 to 5:1 a hundred years later.

The outstanding feature of the classification by sector in the middle part of Table 27 is the diminution of the share of national wealth in the agricultural sector. At the beginning of the century under review, agriculture accounted for 77 per cent of the total; by the end its share had plummeted to 36 per cent – that is, its relative importance had been halved. This huge change in the significance of the capital in agriculture reflects principally the fall in the relative importance of land already noted; fixed and circulating capital in agriculture held its share of the total steady at about 22 per cent until 1830 and then dropped to 14 per cent. The proportion of the national wealth in the form of housing and public buildings was broadly unchanged throughout the century, and it was the three remaining sectors which came to occupy a more prominent position in the nation's wealth. Between 1800 and 1860, the transformation of the economy is reflected in the rise in the share of industry and commerce from 10 per cent to 23 per cent, of transport from 4 per cent to 13 per cent, and of overseas assets from 2 per cent to 10 per cent.

The last part of Table 27, in which land and overseas assets are excluded, is in some ways the most interesting. It again shows a marked fall in the importance of capital in agriculture, with a decline from over half the total in 1760 to one-quarter in 1860. Both fixed and circulating capital in agriculture experience this continuous downward trend in their relative importance, the former from 31 per cent of domestic reproducible capital in 1760 to 16 per cent in 1860, and the latter from 21 per cent to 9 per cent. The share of residential and social capital also falls, though less dramatically, from 31 per cent to 24 per cent. By contrast, industrial and commercial capital rises very steeply, from 11 per cent of the total in 1760 to 18 per cent in 1800 and 33 per cent in 1860. A notable feature of this increase is that it is almost entirely due to the expansion of the stock of fixed assets; these assets increase at a rate of some 3 per cent per annum and consequently enhance their position from a lowly 5 per cent in 1760 to a dominant 25 per cent in 1860, by when they are larger than any other category shown in Table 27. A further consequence of these trends is the sharp rise in the ratio of fixed to circulating capital within the industrial and commercial sector. In 1760 the value of fixed capital was marginally less than the value of inventories; by 1800 it was considerably higher, and the ratio of fixed to circulating capital was 1·5:1; by 1830 the ratio was 2·5:1, and by 1860 it had climbed to 3·3:1. Finally, we may note that fixed capital in transport also shows a substantial increase, mainly after 1830, when the construction of the railways lifted the share of this sector from 9 per cent to 18 per cent.

THE INVESTMENT RATIO

One of the major issues which has been discussed with regard to capital formation is the investment (or savings) ratio, the proportion of national income devoted to investment. To see the implications of the present estimates for the hypothesis that an increase in the ratio is an essential feature of the industrialization process,[222] we turn to Table 28. All three of the investment series set out there show broadly the same picture. Gross domestic fixed capital formation (line 5) rises from about 7 per cent of GDP[223] in the 1760s and 1770s to a peak of 11 per cent in the period of rapid industrial advance from 1791 to 1800, then drops back a fraction during the war years, and thereafter remains remarkably steady at a rate of 10 or 11 per cent of income all the way down to 1851–60. The picture shown by the other two ratios is essentially the same. Total investment (line 7) rises from 8 per cent of national income in 1761–70 to 14 per cent in 1791–1800, falls quite sharply during the wartime decade 1801–10, bounces back to 13 per cent in the following decade, and then remains obstinately at about that level for the remainder of the period.[224]

There are two major conclusions to be drawn from the present estimates:

(i) Contrary to the view tentatively advanced by Deane and Cole and now widely (and sometimes dogmatically) accepted,[225] the investment ratio did rise during the eighteenth century, and by quite a substantial margin: on the evidence of line 7 of Table 28, it rose from 8 per cent in the 1760s (and presumably somewhat less than this earlier in the century) to 14 per cent in the 1790s.

(ii) After the recovery from the wartime dip in the ratio at the beginning of the nineteenth century, there was no further increase; and – again contrary to the view generally held – the investment ratio was not significantly lifted by the railway-construction booms of the 1840s

Table 28. Investment and Domestic Product, 1760–1860

	1761–70	1771–80	1781–90	1791–1800	1801–10	1811–20	1821–30	1831–40	1841–50	1851–60
1. Gross domestic fixed capital formation[a] (£m p.a.)	6·5	7·0	11·0	14·5	16·5	20·5	28·5	38·5	49·5	58·0
2. Total domestic investment[a] (£m p.a.)	7·5	9·0	13·0	17·5	17·5	22·5	32·5	42·0	54·5	61·5
3. Total investment[a] (£m p.a.)	8·0	10·0	14·5	19·0	15·5	27·5	40·0	46·5	61·0	81·5
4. GDP[b] (£m p.a.)	95	100	110	135	160	200	275	365	450	595
5. 1 as % of 4	7	7	10	11	10	10	10	11	11	10
6. 2 as % of 4	8	9	12	13	11	11	12	12	12	10
7. 3 as % of 4	8	10	13	14	10	14	14	13	14	14

[a] (1)–(3): decade averages at 1851–60 prices, rounded to nearest £0·5m.
[b] (4): decade averages at 1851–60 prices, rounded to nearest £5m.

SOURCES

(1) Table 6 above.
(2) = (1) plus stockbuilding, second column of Table 16.
(3) = (2) plus overseas investment, last column of Table 16.
(4) Real GDP at factor cost at 1851–60 prices using the sources listed in the notes to column 3 of Table 25, but taking annual averages per decade. For 1831–60, annual estimates are available as the basis for this; for 1801–30, the figures at decade intervals have been averaged (e.g. 1801–10 equals half of 1801 and 1811); and for 1761–1800, the decennial averages have been adjusted so that, for example, 1761–70 equals four-tenths of 1755–64 plus six-tenths of 1765–74. The level of the series is very uncertain throughout. See also note 223 above.

and 1850s. Investment, of course, was rising through the first half of the nineteenth century, but so too was income, and the level of investment relative to income did not change appreciably.

If these findings are confirmed by further studies of the trends of capital accumulation and GDP, they will have some significance for the analysis of such issues as the role of capital in the process of industrialization and the effects of early industrialization on the material standard of living of the working classes.

CHANGES IN THE STRUCTURE OF INVESTMENT

Two aspects of the changing structure of investment are set out in Table 29. The upper part shows, firstly, the investment in additions to stocks as a percentage of fixed capital formation and, secondly, the net investment abroad as a percentage of total domestic investment. Within the main productive sectors, i.e. industry, commerce, and agriculture (line 1a), the additions to stocks average almost 40 per cent of the fixed capital accumulation in the period 1761–1800, and this drops to an average of about 20 per cent in the first six decades of the nineteenth century. There is thus a marked decline in the relative importance of investment in stocks and work in progress. If the stockbuilding is expressed as a percentage of total domestic fixed capital formation (line 1b), the ratio declines from an average of about 20 per cent in 1761–1800 to just under half this level (9 per cent) in 1801–60. Line 2 shows net investment abroad steady at about one-tenth of domestic investment in the last four decades of the eighteenth century, and negative during the capital inflow of 1801–10; it then rises to over one-fifth in the two decades 1811–30, falls back sharply to eighteenth-century proportions in the next two decades, and finally climbs to record levels to equal one-third of the domestic investment in 1851–60.

The lower part of Table 29 indicates the very considerable changes which occurred in the composition of domestic fixed capital formation during this century of industrialization and modern economic growth. The outstanding – but not unexpected – features are:

(i) There is an uninterrupted fall in the share of investment in farm buildings and improvements, from 35 per cent at the beginning of the period (1761–80) to 12 per cent at the end.

(ii) The share of fixed investment absorbed by the industrial and commercial sector rises from under 20 per cent in the first two decades to an average of about 26 per cent in the period 1781–1820 and to over 33 per cent in the period 1821–60. Within this sector the share of buildings changes relatively little after 1780, and the upward trend in the total for the sector is essentially due to the increased investment in

Table 29. *The Structure of Investment, 1761–1850 (per cent)*

	1761–70	1771–80	1781–90	1791–1800	1801–10	1811–20	1821–30	1831–40	1841–50	1851–60
1. Stockbuilding as % of fixed capital formation										
a. Industry, commerce, and agriculture	29	57	30	40	12	19	30	19	24	13
b. Total economy	15	28	18	21	6	10	14	9	10	6
2. Net investment abroad as % of total domestic investment	7	11	11	9	–11	22	23	11	12	33
3. Structure of domestic fixed capital formation by sector and type of asset[a]										
a. Residential and social	25	22	21	26	30	31	35	30	18	21
b. Agriculture	33	37	30	30	25	22	16	13	13	12
c. Industry and commerce										
Buildings	15	10	19	15	18	20	24	22	16	19
Machinery	4	2	10	6	5	6	9	9	9	10
Mining, gas, and water	1	—	1	1	1	2	2	3	4	7
Total (industry and commerce)	20	12	30	23	24	29	35	34	29	36
d. Transport										
Railways	—	—	—	—	—	—	—	9	28	15
Ships	8	11	9	8	7	6	5	6	7	9
Other	14	18	10	14	14	12	10	8	5	7
Total (transport)	22	29	19	22	21	18	15	23	40	31
e. Total	100	100	100	100	100	100	100	100	100	100

[a] Components may not add to totals because of rounding.

SOURCES. All the underlying estimates are decade averages at 1851–60 prices.

Part 1a: Table 16, second column as % of Table 6, lines 3–7.   Part 1b: Table 16, second column, as % of Table 6, lines 1–13.
Part 2: Table 16, last column as % of Table 6 (total) plus Table 16, second column.   Part 3: Table 6.

machinery and equipment in manufacturing, mining, and the utilities. These assets – the capital goods that (together with the railways) most directly embody the technological changes which give this period its great historical significance – increase their share from 5 per cent or less in the mid eighteenth century to 17 per cent a century later.

(iii) The first canal boom makes its presence evident in the 1770s, but in general the share of fixed capital devoted to transport is steady at about one-fifth of the total until the end of the 1830s, when it leaps to double that proportion under the impact of the great railway boom of the 1840s. In that decade the railways alone account for some 28 per cent of domestic fixed capital formation; but this was not sustained, and the proportion dropped sharply to 15 per cent in the 1850s. Investment in ships is broadly stable at around 8 per cent of the total for most of the period; while investment in the other assets (roads, carriages, canals, and docks) is steady – and substantial – at around 14 per cent of the total for the first five decades (1761–1810) but in the next five decades shows a marked decline, to end at about 6 per cent in the period 1841–60.

(iv) Three phases are apparent in the capital expenditure on dwellings and public buildings and works (line 3a of Table 29). From 1761 to 1800 they account for about 23 per cent of the total; their share then rises sharply to about 32 per cent in the next four decades (1801–40) and finally falls back to about 20 per cent in the last two decades, to make way for the huge programme of railway construction.

APPENDIX

Number and Gross Annual Value of Buildings in 1860

The major sources of statistical information about buildings in the nineteenth century are the decennial Census of Population enumerations of inhabited and uninhabited houses from 1801; the assessments, for Schedule A of the Income Tax, of the gross annual value of all buildings (except farm buildings and farmhouses occupied by tenant farmers, which were assessed with land) from 1842–3; and the assessments, for Inhabited House Duty, of the number and gross annual value (equivalent to gross rental) of buildings charged with duty from 1851–2, supplemented from 1874–5 with corresponding details for buildings exempt from duty. By using all three of these sources we can compile an estimate of the number and annual value of buildings in Britain in 1860.

The number of inhabited houses at the end of each decade was given in the Census of Population *Reports* for England and Wales.[226] The census definition of houses covered private dwellings, farmhouses, residential shops, hotels, clubs, public houses, hospitals, and schools, as well as warehouses, offices, etc. when inhabited by resident caretakers. Blocks of flats and blocks of shops with residences above were each reckoned as one house.[227] The census gives only an aggregate figure for the stock of buildings (until 1911), and in order to get a more detailed picture we must turn to the Inhabited House Duty statistics. The duty was levied from 1796 to 1834 and was reintroduced in 1852–3, but it is only from 1874–5 that full statistics are given for the build- ings exempt from duty (i.e. those with a gross annual value of less than £20, and those not used as dwellings) as well as for those charged. Thus 1880 is the earliest year for which we can make a full comparison of the census and Inhabited House Duty enumerations; it is instructive to do this even though it lies outside our period. The number of inhabited houses in Great Britain at the census of 1881 was 5,570,000. In 1880–1, the number of dwelling-houses, residential shops, hotels, pubs, etc. and farmhouses assessed for duty was 5,413,000, to which we must add some 300,000 farmhouses with an annual value of less than £20 which were not covered by the assessment[228] – i.e., a total of 5,713,000. This is some 143,000 (2½ per cent) in excess of the census figure, and we thus have a broad confirmation of the census total and a reasonable indication of its coverage.[229]

We cannot make a similar comparison for 1860, but we can use the House Duty and other statistics[230] to make a broad classification of the estimated total of 4,350,000 inhabited houses, derived from the 1861 census for England and Wales plus an estimate for Scotland; this classification is shown in Table 30.

Table 30. *Number of Houses in Britain in 1860 (thousands)*

	Annual value less than £20	Annual value £20 or more	Total
Dwelling-houses	3,365	345	3,710
Farmhouses	300	20	320
Residential shops	135	135	270
Hotels, pubs, etc.	—[a]	50	50
Total	3,800	500	4,350

[a] Included with dwelling-houses.

We now turn from the number of houses to their annual value as assessed for Income Tax and Inhabited House Duty, and with the aid of one key assumption (see Table 31, note *a*) we obtain the classification shown in Table 31.

Combining the census data with the results of Table 31 we thus have the following picture for all inhabited houses in 1860:

	Number	Annual value	Average value
Private houses (incl. farmhouses)	4,030,000	£30·6m	£7·6
Residential shops, hotels, pubs, etc.	320,000	10·4m	32·5
	4,350,000	£41·0m	£9·4

Table 31. *Gross Annual Value of Buildings in Great Britain in 1860* (£m)

	Annual value less than £20	Annual value £20 or more	Total
Dwelling-houses	12·1[a]	16·5[b]	28·6
Residential shops, hotels, pubs, etc.	2·0[b]	8·4[b]	10·4
Farmhouses	1·2[c]	0·8[b]	2·0
Hospitals, etc.	—	—	0·4[d]
Trade premises	—	—	17·5[e]
Total			58·9[f]

[a] The annual value of these premises is assumed to be 85 per cent of the value of dwelling-houses of £20 or more, based on the ratio in reassessment years from 1874–5 onwards when both categories are given. The residential shops, etc. are estimated to account for £2·0m of this, calculated as 135,000 at an average value of £15 (cf. Stamp, *British Incomes and Property*, 118).
[b] Houses, etc. charged with House Duty as given in the Inland Revenue *Reports*.
[c] 300,000 farmhouses (see p. 95 above) assumed to have an average annual value of £4 per annum.
[d] Estimated on basis of assessments from 1874–5 onwards.
[e] Obtained as a residual; covers lock-up shops, factories, warehouses, etc.
[f] The total gross annual value of all houses, etc. assessed to Schedule A in 1860–1 (adjusted for understatement by interpolation between the reassessment years 1857–8 and 1861–2 – see Stamp, *op. cit.*, 31–6 and 50), plus the estimated value of farmhouses assessed to Schedule A as lands.

SOURCE. *Reports of H.M. Commissioners of Inland Revenue.*

The important conclusion to be drawn from this is the disproportionate weight in terms of annual value – and thus of cost of construction – of the relatively small number of residential shops, hotels, etc. Since we must include all the 320,000 shops, hotels, etc. in our total in order to make up the *number* of inhabited houses as shown by the census, we divide the residential shops, etc. into a 'dwelling' component, assumed to have the same average value as the private houses, and a 'shop' component, accounting for the remainder. We thus have a final figure of 4,350,000 private houses at an aggregate annual value in 1860 of £33·0 million (£28·6 million for the dwelling-houses, £2·0 million for the farmhouses, and £2·4 million for the 'dwellings' component of the residential shops, etc.). For the industrial and commercial buildings we have a corresponding annual value of £25·5 million, made up of £8·0 million for the 'shop' component of the residential shops, etc. and £17·5 million for the trade premises, covering lock-up shops, factories, warehouses, etc.

These two estimates together cover the main categories of building. Among those not covered are (a) hospitals, museums, churches, prisons, and other public buildings; (b) farm buildings; (c) buildings associated with mines or with gas and water supply; and (d) buildings on railway premises. These are included in the estimates in lines 2, 3, 6, 7, and 8 of Tables 6–8 respectively.

CHAPTER III

Labour in Great Britain[1]

I. *The Industrial Revolution: Economic Models of the Labour Market*

In Britain, the hundred years or so between *c.* 1750 and *c.* 1850 saw the competition of what is conventionally called the industrial revolution, and with it the corresponding transformation of the labour force from its traditional structure into a modern industrial working class. These changes constituted a stage in an irreversible social evolution, the creation of modern industrial capitalism. The new character given to society included the emergence of new classes and of new relationships between classes.

The period as a whole has a certain unity and is marked off without much difficulty as the transitional link between relatively more stable economic relations that preceded it and a re-stabilized, but different, framework that followed. Economic theorists who lived through it, beginning with the 'classics' of Political Economy, as well as more recent writers on economic development, have been inclined to treat it as a particular and indeed unique phase with certain laws and characteristics of its own. As far as the market for labour in this period is concerned, there has been a remarkable and indeed striking unanimity among them and among all observers. The general axiom is that in this period as a whole the market operated against labour, and that wages tended therefore to be at or near subsistence levels.

The mercantilist writers of the seventeenth and eighteenth centuries had looked upon labour as merely a factor of production, which, in a competitive world in which most industry was highly labour-intensive, should be obtained at the lowest possible cost. By and large, they were not concerned with labour as being made up of consumers whose satisfaction was the end of the productive process.[2] With the rise of individualist political economy, however, the latent clash between these two conceptions emerged into the open. Their humanism obliged economic writers to agree that high or rising wages were desirable and were a sign of economic success.[3] At the same time, their concern for the progress of society as a whole, seen implicitly or explicitly from the point of view of the capitalist–entrepreneur or, as in the case of Malthus, from that of the landowner, often led them to emphasize the benefits of low wage rates. This ambiguity was clearly reflected in the uncertainty about the specific issue of whether high or low real wages were more likely to induce labour to work hard – an objective considered desirable by all. Some, from Defoe and Mandeville to William Temple and Arthur Young, plumped for low wage rates; others, among them Sir James Steuart, Malachy Postlethwayt, James Anderson, and Adam Smith, tended to prefer the incentive of high wages for most workers and were mindful of the internal market created thereby: 'Men are forced to labour now', commented Steuart, 'because they are slaves to their own wants . . . Wants promote industry, industry gives food, food increases numbers.'[4] Malthus, unable to decide between the two, opted for a 'moderate scarcity' of labour, with wages neither too high nor too low, to make 'the lower classes of people do more work, and become more careful and industrious'.[5] With Adam Smith and Malthus, however, we enter a new phase of economic thought, for now that the political economists were satisfied with the political basis of the social framework and its class relations, they turned from a consideration of what ought to be to a description of what was.

Adam Smith found it natural – as did all others who lived through the industrial revolution – to begin by assuming that wages were normally at subsistence level. They could not fall below it, as by definition the race of labourers would not then survive. But, writing before the consequences of massive industrialization and urbanization became visible, Smith was optimistic enough to believe that a sustained increase in capital, as long as it was increasing ahead of the supply of labour, could keep wages well above the survival minimum for long periods, though ultimately the supply of population would catch up and bring wages down again. Some of his successors were even less hopeful for labour.

Malthus's pessimism derived from his naive theory of population, although it might also be argued – bearing in mind the occasion of the writing of the first version of his essay – that he began with the conviction that the majority must always remain poor and picked on the existing population theories of Wallace, Townsend, and others as his means of proving it. Be that as it may, the outcome was that while for Adam Smith increasing population was a sign of progress, for Malthus it was a guarantee of stagnation.[6] The Malthusian theory was welcomed by those who wanted to reform the Poor Law drastically against the interests of labour: ratepayers eager to cut poor rates, and employers eager for a pool of willing labour.[7] Only thus can we explain why it was that the Malthusian analysis enjoyed the greatest vogue in the period 1815–34, when it was most demonstrably untrue, since British agriculture, far from being unable to supply the necessary food, was expanding fast[8] and was in a crisis of overproduction for the majority of those years. Malthus was in fundamental disagreement with the majority of his profession over such issues as the Corn Laws and the law of the market, yet even they all accepted at least a part of his unrealistic population theory.

John Barton, another contemporary, held a rise in wages to be self-defeating, since it would reduce profits and thereby reduce the funds out of which future wages could be paid. He also believed that wages were paid out of circulating capital only, and that the increasing proportion of fixed capital in the total was bound to reduce the demand for labour and depress the wage level on a long-term view. Barton, indeed, saw the mechanism of industrialization as one in which it was the fall in the value of money which raised prices faster than wages, thus permitting profits to rise and offering greater employment while real wages were held down. These higher profits in manufacturing would draw capital – including some of the wages found – away from the land into industry, so that the agricultural employer would get higher profits, but the workers would get no higher wages while the prices of things bought by him would increase. It would take many years before higher profits would attract capital back to the land, just as it would take many years (up to twenty-one in the case of skilled workmen) before any Malthusian effects could be felt in the labour market. This analysis recalls the more recent theory of E. J. Hamilton, though the latter saw the fall in the incidence of rents and other fixed payments, rather than wages, as the source of the boon to profits.[9]

Ricardo came to accept much of Barton's analysis in a later edition of his *Principles*, but his own pessimism had a slightly different basis. Diminishing returns on land would, in the long run, raise the share of rent and diminish the share of wages and profits combined. Since wages could not fall below subsistence, it was profit rates which would bear the reduction, cutting accumulation and thereby the demand for labour while the labour supply increased. In some respects, Ricardo's was a doctrine of capital shortage: at any given level of technology, there were never enough savings to match up with all the potential labourers, and in consequence, unemployment and disguised unemployment kept labour's bargaining position weak. Thus wages would be firmly held down.[10]

'Subsistence' was, of course, an elastic term for the Ricardians, even for the more rigid of them like J. R. McCulloch. They would admit that if wages rose or fell for any temporary cause, the new level might fairly quickly come to be accepted as 'normal' or 'necessary'; thus, McCulloch, comparing the agricultural wages in some Southern counties with those of Yorkshire and the Northeast which were nearly twice as high, concluded that 'this comparative lowness of their wage is at once a consequence and a cause of the depressed condition of the peasantry in the counties referred to'.[11] With this somewhat question-begging proviso, the Ricardians as a whole assumed subsistence wages in their reasoning – though it has been doubted if Ricardo himself held to it consistently.[12]

The 'colonizers' differed from the other writers on economic matters in having to defend certain specific measures, from which they promised themselves greater prosperity for labour. But they, too, had been reared on Ricardian soil and assumed labour to be depressed in the Britain of their day. Wilmot-Horton, arguing for his programme of 'Systematic Emigration', based himself on the observation that the supply of labour exceeded the demand for it.[13] Wakefield (and Torrens) assumed that there was a glut both of labour and of capital in the mother country, which could be remedied by combining them with land overseas. Wakefield anticipated Marx in other respects also, predicting the decline of the lower middle classes into the ranks of the proletariat, and a revolt of the latter; but, unlike Marx, he hoped to avert such an outcome, in a country 'in which the subject order, composing the bulk of the people, are in a state of gloomy discontent arising out of excessive numbers', by opening up the colonies.[14]

Perhaps the most pessimistic view of wages in that stage of development was that expressed by Marx. According to him, not only would wages not rise: their tendency was to be depressed even further. The main economic mechanism for depressing them was the 'industrial reserve army', the numerous workers who would inevitably be rendered unemployed, part-employed, or casually employed by the progress of capitalism, and who could always be used to turn the terms of collective bargaining in the employer's favour. Marx had no difficulty in showing that such an 'army' existed as an important element in the British industrial revolution, both as a factor undermining the bargaining position of labour in general, and as an explanation of certain features of the phenomenon of the trade cycle in particular: 'Taking them as a whole, the general movements of wages are exclusively regulated by the expansion and contraction of the industrial reserve army . . . corresponding to the periodical changes of the industrial cycle.'[15]

That there was a general labour surplus, over and above the special problems of declining skills and declining industries, was a commonplace among working men in the 1830s and 1840s and among keen observers like Mayhew.[16] It was one of the main drives behind the repeated land schemes mooted by Owenists, by Poor Law reformers and by the Chartists. In O'Connor's words:

The first use the land would be to them was to ease the labour market of its surplus; the second was to create a certainty of work for the people; and the third was to create a natural rate of wages in the artificial market; for so long as there was a surplus to fall back on, or a workhouse from which to procure labour, so long would work be uncertain and wages low.[17]

In the long term, the industrial reserve army was seen by Marx as a product of the irreversible, and accelerating, change in the structure of capital itself. According to this reasoning, technical progress and competition ensure that there is ever more and more constant capital, which does not create employment, and an ever smaller share (though perhaps absolutely a rising quantity) of variable capital, which does. The reserve army will thus become larger and depress wages: not primarily, as Barton and Ricardo thought, because there would be too little capital, but because there would be too much.[18] Marx's analysis did, however, probe much deeper, and he observed more acutely than his contemporaries did. Among the ideas introduced by him into the mainstream of economic debate was his recognition that the trade cycle was an integral part of development, and that the level of wages depended not only on impersonal economic forces but also on deliberate action by employers as a class. There was here a struggle for power which had political, social, legal, and other aspects, and there were countervailing forces, so that 'the laws regulating wages are very complicated, sometimes one predominates and sometimes another, according to circumstances, [and] therefore they are in no sense iron but on the contrary very elastic'.[19]

In the second half of the nineteenth century, interest in the wage level during the Industrial Revolution lapsed somewhat. Economic writers were more concerned with the rise in real wages in their own time than with their alleged stagnation before. Marshall, though holding to a marginalist explanation of the wage level for his own time, agreed that in previous eras wages had depended on a socially acceptable subsistence minimum, plus a percentage for skill, and that the population mechanism helped to keep it there. But generally, theories which abstracted from social or political factors or which assumed that workers all make individual contracts [20] when the fact that they do not is one of the most decisive influences on the wage level – could have little relevance for explaining the early stages of industrialization.

Recent preoccupation with economic development has again focused attention on the position of labour in the British industrial revolution. The most significant new model is that of W. Arthur Lewis, according to which industrialization with 'unlimited supplies of labour' [21] may be viewed as taking place in two sectors – an 'agricultural' traditional sector characterized by endemic disguised unemployment, in which labour is therefore paid at subsistence level; and an 'industrial' sector able to draw labour from the former, in any quantities desired, by paying wages only slightly higher than those in the 'agricultural sector', without forcing up wages against itself to inhibit its own expansion. C. P. Kindleberger[22] believes that this dual economy operated in Britain in the first half of the nineteenth century (but not after 1850, when the agricultural labour supply is said to have become exhausted, and real wages therefore began to rise in both sectors), and there is much good evidence both for disguised unemployment on the land at that time and for a widening productivity differential between agriculture and industry.[23] Habakkuk's analysis also rests on an abundance of labour, i.e. labour that was both low in cost and elastic in supply, but it is not always clear whether he speaks of labour as abundant in any absolute sense or only in relation to the USA. Significantly, he exempts from this tendency not only the decades after 1850 but also most of the eighteenth century, which therefore also became, according to him, a period of comfortable wage rises.[24] The mechanism suggested by E. L. Jones was slightly different again: here agricultural change was driving farms in less favourably placed areas out of production, by virtue of raising productivity in more favoured areas. This agricultural population thus displaced had to turn to industry for survival in the early stages of industrialization. The motive force was therefore a push rather than a pull.[25]

Compared with classical and particularly neo-classical theory, the views of these present-day development economists and historians have the great merit of recognizing that labour was not perfectly mobile and that non-economic factors played a part in the friction. Indeed, in terms of current economic theory, the idea of 'abundant' labour, noted by every historical observer, makes no sense unless, indeed, the equilibrium wage level lay below a true absolute survival minimum:[26] at the actual wage level, labour supply should be neither abundant nor short, but just meeting demand.

There is thus an impressive degree of agreement among observers of the British industrial revolution that it was characterized by low wages and abundant labour, and that the cheap and elastic labour supply itself played an instrumental part in the progress of industrialization. 'The whole Industrial Revolution of the last 200 years', Hicks stated in an oft-quoted aside, 'has been nothing else but a vast secular boom, largely induced by the unparalleled rise in population.'[27] The earlier belief in poverty as the sole stimulus to work may no longer have been universal, and the lure of consumption goods was increasingly stressed; but virtually every model contains both the need to keep down wage rates in order to leave high profits for further investment, and the problem created by the consequent low level of demand on the part of the mass of the population.

This unanimity about the historical facts is all the more remarkable in view of the enormous variety of the models used to explain them. The impression of labour abundance must have been powerful indeed to unite observers as diverse as those quoted here. Similarly, although every economist saw a different mechanism by which labour was supplied to the employments needing it, they all had at least this much in common: that each was envisaged as a simple one-way movement, from country to town, from agriculture to industry, from domestic employment to factory.[28]

Both these groups of assumptions are open to challenge in view of the evidence now available about the labour market during the industrial revolution. Both contain a large element of truth: the bargaining position of labour was generally poor, and net movement of labour was in one direction rather than another. But the models available are too simple to do full justice to the complex and often contradictory movements by which the demand and supply for labour were adjusted to each other in the century *c.* 1750–1850. The deviations from the general trend were as important and as significant as the conformity, and to these deviations we must now turn.

A MULTIPLICITY OF LABOUR MARKETS

It is well known that there was nothing like a single national labour market at the beginning of the period, nor was such a market operating very smoothly even at the end, though its creation is one of the chief features of the hundred years of change.[29] Even the most general and common wages – those of agricultural and general labourers – were widely different as between regions, and they moved in different ways. In the course of the eighteenth century, Northern wages overtook those of the rural South and West, and in the first half of the nineteenth the gap was widened further still, appearing to make the labour market less rather than more perfect: if agricultural wages in 1770, according to Arthur Young, were 10 per cent higher in the North than in the South, by 1850 the difference had risen to 37 per cent.[30] In Scotland in the 1790s, the ratios between the highest and lowest rates were as high as three to one.[31] There were equally striking differences within the regions, not only between town and country but also between one town and another very similar one. It is important to note that these were not temporary differences, about to be ironed out by the forces of the market; on the contrary, as contemporaries were well aware, these were often self-reinforcing distinctions, in which cultural heritage, social expectations, and even physical stamina might play as large a part as economic opportunity. It has been argued very persuasively that it was the lower efficiency of the poorly paid labourer which was at least in part responsible for the agricultural wage differentials in England; and even a critic of this view had to agree that there was an apparent correlation between regional harvest wages and productivity.[32] A similar point has been made about the undernourishment of the Cornish miner.[33] As for differences between cultures, a labourer would need 2s. a day in England, but '5d. is deemed sufficient in Ireland and 3d. in Hindostan'; while high wages promoted exertion in England, Holland, or America, the author continued not without some exaggeration, 'even an Irishman is an example of the stimulating influence of good wages; in his own country he is notoriously lazy and negligent in the extreme; after crossing the channel he becomes a model of laboriousness and enterprise'.[34] Labour mobility, therefore, far from wiping out these cultural and economic differentials – as it ought to have done in a proper labour market – tended still further to confirm them.

In other occupations, even as late as the mid nineteenth century, when tramping and the railways had effected some levelling-out of unemployment and wage rates,[35] it was still one of the hardest tasks of the national unions established about that time to even out the rates within firms or towns, let alone over the country as a whole.[36] Even within the metropolis, Mayhew found the wages of parish rubbish-carters to range from 14s. to 20s. a week, according to the location of the city parishes in relation to the labour supplies from suburban harvesters. In Ashton in 1831, it was shown that work of the same kind, in the same town, varied from 3s. 4d. to 5s. per thousand hanks, 'and the highest sums were frequently given where the oldest machinery was employed, because the union had there accidentally acquired the greatest power'.[37] In Nottingham, the earnings of lace-machine hands varied from 15s. to 30s. a week; in 1819 carpenters' wages were 31s. 6d. in London, 25s. in Manchester, and 14s. in Glasgow, and masons' wages were 31s. 6d., 22s., and 15s. respectively.[38] As late as 1867 it was expressed as a pious wish of the trade unions that taking into account the cost of living 'and other local advantages and disadvantages, the pay of all workers of equal standing in a given trade shall be equivalent, wherever they may be employed', and the unions were only beginning to learn the 'rules of the game' of demanding what the trade would bear. Masons' wages were still varying, in different parts of the country, between 4½d. and 7⅜d. an hour, bricklayers' between 4½d. and 8d., and carpenters' between 4⅝d. and 8d.[39]

The reasons for this are many, and most are not difficult to find.

Adam Smith had noted the many non-pecuniary considerations which had to be eliminated before wage payments could be compared,[40] but beyond this there were frictions impeding mobility, and there were other factors powerful enough to impose their own logic on the labour market irrespective of wage rates. In fact, goods moved much more freely than labour. Factory employment was hated, long-distance migration was eschewed, and family income – rather than the individual income – often became the operative quantity;[41] nor were employers always certain whether to offer exceptionally high wages or relatively lower rates, in order to draw the whole family into employment. Much labour still migrated seasonally; workers could not be sure if a boom was short-lived or portended a secular trend, so that 'over short periods . . . the supply of industrial labour . . . was inelastic'.[42] The notion of 'skilled' work, the incidence of apprenticeship, and the power of trade unions were all in flux and were uncertain at any given time. If even in the mid twentieth century conventional and institutional elements enter largely into wages,[43] they must have exerted very great influence in the eighteenth.

It is clear that the vast sectoral shifts in employment and the absorption of millions of additional workers between 1750 and 1850 took place in a multitude of related markets, some only very tenuously related, rather than in a single labour market.

II. *Population Increase and Migration*

The population increase, adding these millions of hands to the labour force, was clearly one of the central features of the British industrial revolution: it would be surprising indeed if it did not form an important part of the mechanism by which that revolution was accomplished. There may be much controversy about the exact cause of the population increase which accompanied industrialization before 1801 and about its causation,[44] but there is near unanimity on at least two issues: one is that the 1780s mark a stepping-up in the rate of growth, and the other that most explanations of the increase – whether centred on a rising birth-rate or a falling death-rate – ultimately derive it from the demand for labour. Basically, no one has been inclined to dispute Arthur Young's observations:

The hands, it is said, leave certain villages and go to towns. Why? Because there is not employment in one case, and there is in another – their going to the town, proves that they go to employment – they go to that very circumstance which is to increase their number. They go, because they are demanded; that demand it is true takes, but then it feeds them.

Let any person go to Glasgow, and its neighbourhood, to Birmingham, to Sheffield, or to Manchester, according to some writers, every cause of depopulation has acted powerfully against such places: how then have they increased their people? Why, by emigrations from the country. It would be very difficult for any person to show me a depopulation in the country comparable to the increase of towns, not to speak of counter tracts in the country that have doubled and trebled their people: But why have not these emigrations been to other towns, to York, to Winchester, to Canterbury, &c.? Because employment does not abound in those places – and therefore they do not increase. Does not this prove that in every light you view it, it is employment which creates population? A position impossible to be disproved; and which, if allowed, throws the enquiry concerning the depopulation of the kingdom into an examination of the decline or increase of employment.[45]

The explanation in terms of a rising birth-rate is often based on earlier marriage, or on the earlier possibility of children's earnings opened up by the new industry; that in terms of a falling death-rate, especially in the first years of life, is based on the new power of society to counteract the rising mortality which is the traditional response to a rising birth-rate, so that now more of the newly born were able to survive.[46] There may, indeed, have been a two-phase acceleration. The first, associated with a turning point around 1740, depended mainly (after the usual lag) on a higher survival rate based on better nutrition; the second, beginning in the 1780s, reflected the earlier age of marriage and the greater recklessness of the early stages of industrialization. Explanations in purely medical terms – such as the conquest of smallpox by inoculation, or the national development of resistance to diseases, or a weakening of the attacking viruses – would require a truly remarkable historical coincidence;[47] medical historians have firmly ruled out improved medical knowledge as an explanation,[48] though their views have recently been challenged,[49] and improved medical care and attention, coupled with the containment of certain killers, may have contributed to better survival or at least may have counteracted the fatally adverse effects of urbanization in the first half of the nineteenth century.

The idea that the sharp population increase is itself one of the responses to industrialization is supported by the fact that the industrial counties like Warwickshire, Cheshire, Lancashire, and the West Riding actually showed a greater natural increase (and a lower average age at marriage) than the purely agricultural counties, quite apart from the effects of internal migration.[50] This itself might help to account for the labour abundance of the industrial revolution, but before jumping to the conclusion of a simple model relating population to industrialization it is well to remember that the socio-medical factors could not be limited to the strictly industrial areas but had necessarily to spill over into the agricultural areas or those with stagnating industries, where they led to such phenomena as the Speenhamland system and the Malthusian alternatives following upon a sharp population increase – starvation or emigration.

According to the Lewis model there should now have ensued an adequate migration from the latter areas, called for convenience the South, to the industrializing North. But the striking fact was that this migration did not take place. There was a substantial movement into London. There was also migration from the countryside into the towns and the industrial and mining villages, but it was all short-distance migration.[51] When the Southern villager finally decided to emigrate, he was more likely to turn his steps to the United States or to Canada than to Lancashire.

We see [wrote John Barton], in point of fact, that the fluctuations of manufacturing labour scarcely affect in any sensible degree the rate of husbandry wages in their immediate neighbourhood; much less is it to be supposed that this effect should be perceptible in distant parts of the kingdom: that a rise in the earnings of the Lancashire weavers, for instance, should induce a farmer's man in Sussex to migrate to the north for the sake of bettering his circumstances.[52]

[If the Corn Laws were to be repealed], is it supposed, then, that the ploughmen no longer wanted in Sussex might travel to Manchester, and there find employment as cotton-spinners? Surely such a proposition is too absurd to require serious refutation. The slightest attention to facts might show that a district overburdened with population is scarcely ever relieved, unless by the cruel process of extermination. Not one in a thousand of the inhabitants of the agricultural districts would migrate to the manufacturing counties – nor probably one in a hundred of their grand-children, or great-grand-children. 'Of all commodities', observes Adam Smith, 'the most difficult to transport is men.' And I may add, that of all men, the most difficult of transport is an agricultural labourer.[53]

Even in the Northern areas, parishes not in easy communication with the rising industrial districts, like Gisburn, Sedbergh, Pately Bridge, and Kettlewell in the West Riding, had 'a genuine labour surplus and the working population was sustained by practices similar to those found in the south'. In Glamorgan, conversely, there was a labour shortage into the 1830s and 1840s because of the relative inaccessibility of the industrial valleys even to potential short-distance migrants.[54]

Just as the mills' recruiting agents seem to have limited themselves to nearby communities after the falling-off of the supply of paupers from city workhouses, such mobility as there was in the Southern counties appears to have been mainly local also:[55] if it went further afield, it was to London or overseas. 'Yes, wages were low then, but few 'ad the 'eart to leave Heyshott [Sussex]', recalled a villager; 'they was afeared of them outlandish parts.' 'I've done all sorts of work in my time,' recalled another, 'movin' about from place to place, just where I could get the most ... Sometimes I even went as far as Lunnon, grass-mowin', to Wandsworth and Wimbledon.' One man recollected that his father, about the 1840s, 'made his escape to that goal of every countryman – London'; another, one of a large family from East Anglia, remembered that 'two of my brothers went to America because my father did not know what to do with them'; a third, from Wiltshire, reported that 'there was a surplus of labour, and few outlets beyond the village of their birth. A few drifted into the towns, and the recruiting sergeant periodically at fairs selected some of the best lads. The girls made excellent domestic servants.'[56] Few seemed to view the Northern industries as possible destinations.

The latter, in turn, when they needed more labour than their vicinity could supply, drew on the Irish, as did the Scottish lowlands, which also drew on the expelled Highlanders. However, in the main the urban manufacturers depended on labour from their near neighbourhood, even though wages were already higher there and labour was in relatively short supply, so that this process of recruitment itself drove up wages even further. They did not, as the Lewis model would have led one to believe, go for labour from the overpopulated and low-wage agricultural South.[57] Moreover, at a time when some parts of the home economy were avaricious for labour, a substantial emigration from other parts of Great Britain took place, some of it even subsidized by the authorities. These complex divergences from the simple model are significant.

Why did urban industry fail to use a large part of the English countryside as its natural recruiting ground? There were several reasons. One was the sheer technical difficulty of transport. For a man of Kent or a man from Gloucestershire, it was easier to take ship from London or Bristol respectively than to take the high road to Manchester or Leeds. When the railways finally removed this obstacle, they inhibited cross-country movement by themselves becoming the main magnet for rural labour, as well as drawing manpower from Ireland and Scotland and from other transport undertakings.[58]

Secondly, there was ignorance and fear of the novel industrial employment and a consequent reluctance to face a new occupation as well as a new environment: to that extent, emigration to rural Canada might leave a countryman in more familiar surroundings than migration to Manchester. If experience of internal British migration in the twentieth century is any guide, workers are attracted by the availability of work rather than by pay differentials, which in the case of family earnings are in any case hard to establish, so that higher prospective pay would not exert an effective pull over long distances. Besides, the pay, even if higher, might well be less certain: 'North and South have each gotten their own troubles,' observed Higgins in Mrs Gaskell's *North and South*.[59] 'If work's sure and steady theer, labour's paid at starvation prices; while here we'n rucks o' money coming in one quarter, and ne'er a farthing th'next.' Moreover, higher wages might soon be swallowed up in higher prices (above all, higher rents), and it is not impossible that the overcrowding and lack of amenities in the towns, which we now know to have gravely increased mortality over that of comparable classes in the countryside, were not unknown to contemporaries as adverse urban factors also.[60]

Thirdly, there was the Poor Law. The role of the Settlement Acts has continued to be the subject of debate to the present day.[61] They clearly prevented neither urbanization nor migration, yet their nuisance value should not be underrated. Pitt declared in 1796 that

The poor laws of this country . . . had constituted a fetter to the circulation of labour . . . the laws of settlement prevented the workman from going to that market where he could dispose of his industry to the greatest advantage, and the capitalist, from employing the person who was qualified to procure him the best return for his advances.[62]

Complaints may be found in plenty, coming from agriculturists who deplored the Poor Law's effects on the land, industrialists in such towns as Stockport who deplored the periodic dispersal of a skilled labour force, and Poor Law administrators who spent considerable sums on removals and litigation arising from settlement cases in all the major towns. In London, Mayhew declared, the failure of orphans and runaways from other areas to get relief drove them into the ranks of the criminal and submerged classes.[63] Certainly, the Scots had no doubt that their freedom from the restraints of Settlement increased the mobility of labour in their country.[64]

Yet it is not without significance that the Poor Law Commission of 1832–4 paid virtually no attention to the Settlement Acts and certainly did not propose to make them less restrictive. Even more strikingly, with all the economic expertise and all the massive information at its command, it totally failed to relate the rural unemployment to the potential industrial demand for labour. At no point did it seem to have occurred to its members that one way of solving the apparent idleness and wastefulness in the Southern rural communities would be to transfer labour to the mills and mines in the North, where it could find employment, increase its marginal product, and incidentally lower the bargaining power of the existing industrial labour force. Instead, the new law was to set all the labourers to work in their own villages or, if that failed, would force them to emigrate altogether.

One reason for this curious failure was that it was in the interest of the landlords and farmers to keep the labour reserve on the land for the harvest weeks, and this became increasingly critical as the reduction in part-time rural industries in many districts removed some of the traditional harvest labour reserve. Indeed, Speenhamland could be taken to be an alternative to declining cottage and rural industry. Of course, relief payments were a burden for the rest of the year, but the alternative was worse. The Poor Law, in John Barton's words, gave 'a sort of monopoly, or at least a right of pre-emption, of the services of the labourer, to the employer of labour in the parish where he happens to be settled'.[65] In the same strain, John Christian Curwen remarked rather naively about the Irish:

If it had not been that a great number of these people had been resident in Cumberland during the war, it would have been impossible to bring into cultivation the 300,000 acres which have been cultivated; therefore, to a certain amount, I consider the residence of the Irish to be an advantage to us and that it is only bringing in hands when we do not want them, that an inconvenience arises.[66]

The failure to relate labour surplus and deficit areas is more surprising in the case of those familiar with the needs of industry and commerce, rather than agriculture, particularly since the idea, besides being obvious, had been discussed many times since Patrick Colquhoun derived it in 1806 from the earlier practice of sending Southern pauper children into the Northern mills.[67] The First Report of the Factories Commission of 1833 had been most explicit: it accused the Poor Law of being

an obstruction . . to the circulation of labour . . . The fact that the general wages of children and youths in the manufacturing towns are double the wages of children and youths in the agricultural districts, whilst in the latter the workhouses are full of unemployed persons, affords an indication of the working of the system . . . The present administration of the poor laws, and in some degree the state of the law itself, frequently operate most mischievously, by indisposing workmen to follow the demands of employment into new districts, and also by weakening the motives to seek new employments when old ones have altogether ceased . . . We trust . . . that the present system of the poor laws will not be allowed by parliament to remain a barrier to the wholesome circulation of labour.[68]

As chance would have it, almost as soon as the New Poor Law was enacted in 1834, with its emphasis on forcing labour into employment at its existing location, there began one of the most rapid phases of industrial expansion in nineteenth-century Britain, leading in some areas, particularly in Lancashire, to an unexampled shortage of labour. Three of the leading cotton-spinners, Edmund Ashworth, Robert Hyde Greg, and Henry Ashworth, seeing their mills stand idle for want of labour and finding their usual recruiting grounds barren, approached the Poor Law Commissioners between June 1834 and February 1835 with a request to use their facilities to transfer docile surplus labour from the South to the Northern mills: 'English labourers are much preferred to the Irish', as Greg put it in his letter of 17 September 1834 to Chadwick, 'and justly so. We cannot do with refuse population, and insubordinate paupers. Hard working men, and widows with families, would be in demand.'

The Commissioners took up the suggestion with alacrity. They were encouraged by J. P. Kay, who reported on 22 July 1835 that

Irish labour has certainly (under the circumstance of the extraordinary extension of trade, and a deficiency of supply from the English counties) been absolutely necessary to maintain the commercial position of the cotton manufacture of England amongst its foreign rivals, but it has not been an unmingled benefit. With the deepest and most sincere commiseration of the sufferings of that gallant but degraded race, I cannot but consider the extent to which the immigration of the Irish has proceeded in the cotton district, an evil, as far as the manners, habits and domestic comfort of the people are concerned . . . The English are more steady, cleanly, skilful labourers, and are more faithful in the fulfilment of contracts made between master and servant . . . The unwillingness of hand-loom weavers to enter the mills and manufactories, is known to the whole trade. This arises from their having acquired habits which render the occupation in mills disgusting to them, on account of its uniformity and of the strictness of its discipline. They are unwilling to surrender their imaginary independence, and prefer being enslaved by poverty, to the confinement and unvarying routine of factory employment.[69]

The choice therefore was between employing more Irish and employing Southern agricultural labourers.

Edwin Chadwick, Secretary of the Commission, circularized manufacturers on 2 March 1835, asking them to submit lists of vacancies and promising the Commissioners' help in filling them by the supply of Southern paupers, and in their first Report the Commissioners stated that they 'felt it [their] duty to the pauperized labourers themselves to direct them to the sources of the highest wages; and we believe that this course of proceeding will be conducive to the most enlarged public interests'.[70] Two offices were set up, in Leeds and Manchester, and recruiting went under way in the middle of 1835.

Opinions differ on the degree of coercion used to move pauper families to the North, on the hardships endured by them on the journey, and on the difficulties they faced on arrival in an unfamiliar environment. But there can be no doubt that the scheme as a whole turned out to be a resounding failure. Only some three thousand were moved altogether (some higher official figures are suspect); a severe slump broke out soon after they arrived; and in the ensuing scramble the guarantees of three years' employment were often not kept, and the migrants were turned loose, generally to beg their way back to the homes they knew.[71] The failure of this official scheme illustrates some of the causes of the absence of any voluntary migration of any magnitude in this period.

There were certain select skilled trades which had no difficulty in following market demand across the country; but without doubt the largest and most significant migration of labour was that of the Irish – and to a much lesser extent that of the Scots, who moved much more freely over very long distances, even within the United Kingdom. The Irish in particular – much the largest single migrant group – form a crucial element in the response of labour to the industrial revolution. Up to around 1820, immigrants both to England and to Scotland were mostly seasonal and, in the absence of a Poor Law in Ireland, were often able to use the English Poor Law to get free transport part of the way home. This immigration, it should be noted, was into agriculture, the losing sector, not into industry, though it did allow England and Scotland to convert some of their own part-time agriculturalists, tied down as harvest labour reserve, into full-time industrial workers.

The main effect of the Irish incursion was to level out the peak labour demand at harvest time, and to reduce the chance of the poorly paid Southern labourer to exploit the one annual occasion when the market was in his favour.

It is fortunate for corn counties, that the operation of the harvest is aided by Irish labourers. Were it not for these seasonal and able assistants, the work would not be performed in time, and the workmen of the country would know no bound to their demands, both as to price and as to beer.[72]

This annual influx continued when the wartime labour shortage turned into the post-war labour surplus, though in times of real distress migrant Irish harvest workers were liable to be met by much hostility on the part of the local labourers.[73] The number of migrant Irish harvesters has been estimated at 22,000 in 1810, rising to 63,400 in 1840 and to a peak of 75,000 in 1845, when they formed about half the migrant harvest labour force.[74] Significantly, however, they did not settle on the land as regular labourers, even in the counties which took the main Irish immigration, such as Lancashire.[75]

After 1820 there were, in addition to the seasonal migrants, Irish arrivals who came to settle – first in a trickle and later, but even before the famine, in a flood. As fares were progressively lowered by the vigorous competition between the steamship companies, even the poorest could raise enough cash to cross the Irish sea. Most of them had been peasants, but even those who had been artisans at home could not find employment as such. They supplied the unskilled element of the building labour force (this was also, to some extent, a seasonal occupation) and of the canal, dock, and railway builders, particularly in those parts of the country where industrial development had reduced the local labour supply. They also provided the unskilled element in irregular or unpleasant jobs, in dock and road transport, in chemical and textile industries, in domestic service, and in a substratum of street cleaners, petty traders, and hucksters.[76] They were everywhere to be found among the poorest and among the least regularly employed, bearing much of the shock of trade fluctuation or technological unemployment. Thus in 1837, among 3,072 persons who were given work by the Glasgow Relief Committee 2,884 were weavers, and among those no fewer than 1,103 were Irish.[77] They were highly concentrated geographically: according to the Census of 1841, about three-quarters of the 419,000 resident in Great Britain lived in four areas only – the London region, the Glasgow region, the West Riding, and Lancashire/Cheshire; and the half-million or so who flocked in in the famine decade of the 1840s made for much the same areas. They were, in many aspects, the mobile shock troops of the industrial revolution, whose role consisted in allowing the key areas to grow without distorting the labour market unduly, and in keeping down the marginal return to labour at critical points in place and in time, particularly at the top of booms.

As the Rev. A. Campbell of Liverpool put it in 1854,

In the present state of the labour market English labour would be almost unpurchasable if it were not for the competition of Irish labour . . . we are very frequently able to put on the screw of Irish competition.[78]

This was echoed by the *National Reformer*:

The recent enormous, and still continued, immigration of Irish poor into England is operating fearfully upon the condition of the poorer classes of the latter country. The Irish beggar is eating up the rates and the soup, which the English pauper regarded as his vested interests; and the Irish able-bodied labourer is everywhere reducing the wages of the like class of persons in England, through the unequal competition of cheap against dear labour.[79]

Given the appalling and indescribable poverty of the inhabitants of
Ireland, 'a people more wretched than those of any civilised country'[80]
right on the doorstep of Britain, their concept of 'subsistence' and
the minimum wage acceptable particularly to recent immigrants were
such as to rule out any comparison with wages normally paid in
England or Scotland.

> The Irish weavers are a little in advance in their career down hill, for they are
> the main cause of pulling the Scots down after them ... when a manu-
> facturer desires to lower his wages, it is ten to one but the Irish are the first to
> accept his terms.[81]

As the *National Reformer* hinted, the Irish added an exogenous element
not only to the labour market but also to the Poor Law administration,
and this was not without influence on the great Poor Law debate. As
we have noted, their non-settlement gave the Irish greater freedom of
movement than was possessed by the English poor, and in years of
distress they could choose townships with more generous relief procedures – such as Manchester, for example – as against surrounding
towns.[82] But beyond this it was alleged that not only would there be no
labour redundancy 'sensibly and permanently felt in England and
Scotland, were it not for the hordes of Irish who flock to either country
for employment, and obtain it by underselling the inhabitants of both
in their own market for labour', but they destroyed any chance of
limiting population *via* the Poor Law, and indeed burdened the land in
England with a Poor Rate which might be much lighter, were it not
for the labourers thrown out of work by Irish competition.[83] It was the
old dilemma of the propertied classes, of having to maintain in slack
times the labour surplus which benefited them by pulling down wages
in boom times.

Whatever the indirect pressure on the poor rates caused by the Irish,
their pressure on capital resources was likely to have been small.
Migrants drifting into building, hand-loom weaving, and domestic
service made little demand on capital formation for their employment,
nor did they require a great deal for their housing. When the numbers
rose to a flood from 1846, it was fortunate, and perhaps not entirely
coincidental, that they could be matched with the supreme effort of
saving and investment represented by the building of the railways.

As a conspicuous alien element, sometimes deliberately used as strike-
breakers,[84] at other times leading the rebellious spirits, the Irish were
often hated and attacked, but they were basically acceptable because
their vigorous and undisciplined labour provided a much-needed
component of the labour force and allowed some British workers who

would otherwise have been on the bottom rung of the social ladder to take up a superior position.

The migration of the expelled Highlanders to the Scottish industrial Lowlands was of a similar nature, causing similar friction and resentment, but on a much smaller scale. By contrast, the Scots moving to England were generally men like mechanics or farmers who came to obtain the full value of their skills rather than to escape starvation.

The role of Ireland in the British industrial revolution was not, of course, limited to its function as a labour reservoir. In the critical first half of the nineteenth century, the exporting of food, such as grain, butter, pork, and bacon, to feed the growing population of Britain while the increased numbers in Ireland were progressively reduced to a potato diet, not only was of great significance by itself but also helped to reduce the demand for agricultural labour in Britain and to counteract a possible fall in the returns from British acres.[85] Moreover, a good proportion of these food exports was unrequited, representing ultimately the rent 'claims' by British residents on Irish land. This free gift – which a crude calculation reveals to have been of the order of $1-1\frac{1}{2}$ per cent of the British GNP[86] – gains in importance when it is viewed not so much as an aid to consumption but, since most of it went to rich individuals, as an aid to capital formation in Britain. Ireland may therefore be said to have contributed not only the labour but also some of the capital to employ it and some of the food to maintain it.

Nevertheless, Ireland functioned predominantly as a labour reservoir, and this role was not lost on contemporaries. Thus Burness, the astute former land steward to the Duke of Manchester, calculated in 1848 that Irish agriculture, employing one million labourers, could in addition to the labour already exported free half that number for manufacture if the output of the remainder could be raised by suitable incentives.[87] This disguised unemployment on Irish soil corresponds to the agricultural sector in the Lewis model, and Irish labour became an integral part of British industrialization; but it should be noted that, as a result, the British economy in that phase was a triple rather than a dual economy, with British agriculture playing an independent part between the industrializing and the (Irish) 'agricultural' sectors. In turn, the labour supply from British agriculture could be divided into two parts, with several shades in between, the fairly inelastic supply from the North being drawn on heavily by the industrial sector, while the apparently elastic supply from the South was by-passed and used, at most, to populate London and some of the colonies. Even at this level of generalization, therefore, the actual movements are seen to have been far more complex than those represented by a two-sector model.

III.   *Movements and Counter-Movements*

The general evolution of a much-enlarged 'industrial' sector is usually assumed to have been accompanied by other changes working, in a subordinate way, in the same direction. Among them are the movement from the countryside to the town; the destruction of old skills and the creation of a fairly undifferentiated proletariat; the increasing employment of women and children; the conversion of part-time workers into full-time ones; and the change from domestic manufacture to factory industry. This assumption is basically correct, but closer inspection reveals that each of these changes represented not a simple one-way movement, but the net effect of complex and multidirectional developments. We shall examine each of them in turn.

One of the best-documented movements is that from rural to urban communities, generally from the villages into the nearby towns. In the years 1820–50 in particular, this move was one from low-mortality to high-mortality areas. According to the Census figures of 1841 and 1851, around half the population in most industrial cities were born elsewhere, mostly in the surrounding counties, and a further proportion was made up of the young children of immigrant families.

Nevertheless, even here the movement was by no means simple and one-directional. The growth of towns, it has often been remarked, was seldom the result of a pure inflow but was the net result of a two-way movement.[88]

The absorption of population by towns from their hinterland of ten to twenty miles' radius antedates the industrial revolution. Where some figures exist, as for Norwich and Sheffield,[89] let alone London, they show that earlier types of industry could attract new citizens at a faster rate than urban conditions could kill them off. Further, agriculture and rural Britain did not experience any net loss of population, and it is only the surplus or additional numbers which went to swell the towns.[90] But behind this statistical fact there is hidden a variety of movements. Much of the new agriculture required more labour rather than less. Over long periods, industrialization in such trades as textiles and metals implied greater specialization rather than migration, as rural domestic workers increasingly dropped their agricultural by-employment and turned from part-time to full-time industrial work.[91] Thus, despite the enormous development of the cotton industry, the proportion of textile workers among bridegrooms in Walton-le-Dale, Lancashire, between 1705–14 and 1809–12 rose only from 55 per cent to 64 per cent.[92] In such conditions, development meant an expansion rather than a contraction of the rural population. Before 1800 even the large-scale new industries such as coal-mining, iron-making, copper-smelting, and water-driven cotton-spinning [93] were mainly rural, so that at times, as in the case of the parish apprentices, development meant movement from the towns to the villages. Other industries left the towns – and London in particular – for the countryside, in search of cheap and docile labour, lower rents, more space, or fewer restrictions, or for other reasons. These industries included silk-weaving, framework knitting, boot- and shoemaking, papermaking, and printing.[94] The pull to the countryside was, to some extent, true of the railway-building period also.

Many rural workers who were attracted into the towns, particularly young men or young couples with growing families, did not settle easily or quickly. Out of their ranks were recruited those drifting and nomadic workers who formed, with the Irish, the shock troops and buffers of an erratic and ill-organized labour market and who were described with such compassion by Faucher:

The migrators to Manchester are whole families, who wander from town to town, from factory to factory, seeking work, and who have no settled home. These unfortunate operatives live in furnished rooms, where several families are often crowded together in a single bedroom, at the rate of threepence each for bedding.[95]

Faucher goes on to quote an enumeration of the Manchester Statistical Society, according to which, out of 169,000 inhabitants in Manchester and Salford in 1836, 12,500 lived in lodging-houses. Some of these one-roomed lodgings, like those taken by William Chambers in Edinburgh in 1814–15,[96] were occupied by country lads who had good hopes of making their way in the city; but others housed the migrants and drifters, mainly on a temporary basis.

A representative view of the living conditions of that type of labour may be obtained from an inquiry conducted in some central parishes of London in about 1840. The total population of the area had been c. 48,000 in 1831, but the statistics cover what are described as the working classes only – 16,176 persons. They formed 5,294 families, of whom 3,852 lived in single rooms and 181 in lodging houses; only 1,053 families had two rooms, and only 208 had three or more. Of the 5,031 male main breadwinners, 1,718 were classed as labourers, and 431 were in the building trades. Of the 4,982 women, 929 were employed in domestic work, 420 in needlework, and 264 as hawkers; the rest were listed as not employed. Most significant, however, were their origins. Of 5,366 families, only 1,430 (or under 27 per cent) were Londoners. 2,624 came from the English provinces, 598 from Ireland, and 320 from Scotland, Wales, and elsewhere. There was no information about the remaining 394 families.[97]

There is much evidence that in periods of local or national slump many of these families returned to their villages, even if they were not compulsorily repatriated under the Poor Law. In the distressed years 1841–3, 15,365 persons were removed from the industrial towns of Lancashire, Yorkshire, and Cheshire to their (generally rural) places of settlement.[98] In the slump of 1825–6, Somerville described how 'labourers returned to the country [from Edinburgh] as well as the skilled artisan; and while fifteen months before I had been made a ploughman, men being so scarce, I could with difficulty get work of any kind now'. This illustrates, incidentally, that a slump could mean not only widespread unemployment but also widespread demotion. In the slump of 1837 it was estimated that at least one-third of the persons who had migrated to the towns in the boom had returned home. In 1847, when the slump was accompanied by massive Irish immigration, the ebb-tide back to the land flowed even more strongly.[99]

In these various ways, industrialization included a flow of labour out of the towns as well as into them, and the land – or that part of it which yielded up any labour at all – was not simply a source of supply but an integral part of a complex pattern of movements. It should also be borne in mind that the simple statistics of urbanization include innumerable cases in which no migration and no outward change took place, but in which total population growth turned villages, or strings of neighbouring villages, into towns.

It was only well after 1800 that the industrial town became the typical place of the new employment. It possessed external economies, a competitive environment, and above all a flexible labour supply, including an industrial reserve army of Irish, unemployed, and other submerged groups, for whom the employer was not responsible in any way except when he wanted their services. The rate of growth, wholly unplanned, of cities like Manchester (17,000 in 1760 to 180,000 in 1830), Liverpool (25,000 to 165,000), Birmingham (30,000 to 140,000), or Leeds (14,000 to 120,000)[100] has never been repeated and could probably not have taken place in any other social context.

A second aspect of the labour supply in which changes are associated with industrialization is the element of skill. Skill in the context of a fundamentally changing technology is not easy to define. Traditionally it involved manual dexterity, acquired after many years of practice, but it also included knowledge and judgement of processes and materials. Additionally, in the new conditions of machine technology, it might embrace a sense of responsibility, some reliability in timing of attendance and speed of work, a degree of literacy and other abstract (e.g. mathematical) knowledge. It is the very many-sidedness of the concept which makes it impossible to speak of a one-way change. Some skills were driven out and made redundant; others were newly created; others saw their rise and fall within this period; and the status and role of the skilled workers as such changed also.

Skilled labour normally received higher wages and, usually though not always, higher status. Coal-hewers, for example, enjoyed little prestige. The privileges of skill were protected by several separate, though interrelated, factors. Some of them were of a kind which are found in most ages: natural talent; a predisposition to hard, sustained, or responsible work; and years of training or experience. In some cases a strong trade union also helped to maintain a high wage differential. But there were other factors which were of particular significance in this period. The traditional element, according to which some occupations were paid at a higher rate, was to some extent broken down, especially in the textile trades; against this, new differentials were created by growth in other occupations rapid enough to keep demand for labour ahead of supply, irrespective of the skill involved, as in the early decades of machine spinning and in the case of the engineers; and differentials might be extended where expanding technological and managerial knowledge was kept in the hands of the wage earner, as in shipbuilding or ironworking. Skill and its protection thus depended on an amalgam of economic, social, technological, and political factors.

What, then, was the role of skill in the British industrial revolution? It has sometimes been argued that industrialization in Britain destroyed skills and turned the labour force into an undifferentiated proletariat dully serving the machine which had become its master. A parallel change in status was the decline of self-employed craftsmen and their conversion into wage-workers. The displaced skilled man looking for an unskilled labouring job is a familiar figure of the age.[101]

The old standard trades [wrote the London *Phalanx* in October 1842] remain almost in the same condition in which they were 40 or 50 years ago; but whenever steam-power and machinery has interfered with human labour, there misery has been the consequence to those immediately engaged in the process of production . . . Those who provide the staple materials of food and clothing, viz. the agricultural labourers, the spinners and the weavers, are now in the lowest physical condition.[102]

The simultaneous collapse of status and skill is, in fact, perhaps best documented in the textile industries. The Lancashire muslin-weaver of the 1780s, of the type of Samuel Bamford's father (even if remembered romantically and stated to be untypical), who 'was considerably imbued with book knowledge, particularly of a religious kind; wrote

a good hand; understood arithmetic; had some acquaintance with
astronomy; was a vocal and instrumental musician, singing from the
book and playing the flute . . .', or the well-known type of independent
Yorkshire weavers, 'with their 50 or 100 or 200 *l.*, who were able
to make their cloth at home, and go to sell it in the market', or the
Kirkintilloch hand weaver who 'could ask from eighteen to twenty
shillings a week, and that working ten hours a day, with now and then
a holiday for digging in his garden, rambling in the country, or some
merry-making; and the old race of weavers were the best educated,
most reading, and most respectable of all the operatives of the north'[103]
– all these were among the aristocracy of labour of their day. But within
two or three decades, the formerly respected and privileged occupations of weaving, framework knitting, or calico-printing had been
reduced to virtual unskilled status, to be entered by any untrained
outsider.[104]

Nothing is more striking than the differences in 'morals and intelligence' between the older and younger generations of weavers noted
in the hand-loom weavers' inquiry of 1839.[105] An apparently safe 'skill'
could then very quickly become precarious.

It has been stated, that the trade of a Handloom Weaver can be learned in a
few weeks; so can the trade of a carpenter, if learning to saw a piece of wood
constitutes a carpenter; but to learn to be a good and practical silk weaver it
will take many years. It is true, persons may soon learn to make the lowest
sort of work, by having an experienced hand to superintend it; and it is on
that account that persons can become weavers with apparent facility; because
when they have learned to make one sort, they can, with further instruction,
learn to make another, and so on; so that, in the course of years, and by the
instructions of the experienced, they become practical workmen.[106]

Those who were at that time attempting to classify industrial
society drew a very sharp distinction between the skilled and apprenticed artisan, with his reasonable and secure income, and the mill
hand, overworked, always on the verge of starvation, and buffeted by
every wind of trade.[107] Indeed, in 1833 one of the Factory Commissioners thought it most inappropriate that in their demand for a ten-
hour day the mill-hands should compare themselves to

the small class, comparatively speaking, of labouring artisans, such as carpenters, stonemasons, bricklayers, etc. who they say work only from six to
six; a class, however, in this respect distinguished from the operatives, that
their work is done entirely by hand labour, and after service of apprenticeship, accompanied with some outlay; but what do they think of the numerous
classes of domestic operatives, the framework-knitters, the hand-loom
weavers, the wool combers, the lace-manufacturers, and a variety of others,

who work, and work hard, from twelve to fifteen hours a day to earn a bare subsistence; and this frequently from a very early age, and in a state of confinement which may be truly called injurious to the health?[108]

Trades not directly affected by mechanization, particularly the finishing of consumer goods, offered what looked like a haven of refuge, and in these there was likely to occur a more than proportionate and uncontrolled increase in the labour supply. The inrush of young men badly trained in the countryside or in small towns, and the rearing of 'colts' or young men not properly apprenticed and with limited skills only, might depress all or part of a formerly privileged trade, as in the 'slop' shops and sweated trades.[109]

Tailoring in London, particularly after the disastrous strike of 1834, was a well-attested example. Elsewhere, as in shoemaking, hosiery, or knitting, formerly despised provincial machine work might capture larger markets and offer better conditions to its labour, while the old metropolitan crafts sank into a hopeless depression. The old, stable world – a world in which 'tradesmen' had their fixed and secure position in society, and in which institutions like the Lincoln Bluecoats (charity) School could, as late as 1802–28, safely send out twenty-six boys to be apprenticed to cordwainers, curriers and leather dressers, nineteen to joiners, fifteen to blacksmiths, eight to wheelwrights, and so on through a list of 110 names – was crumbling.[110] Neither the seven-year apprenticeship nor the subsequent independence could be taken for granted.

But it has also been maintained, on the contrary, that some of the benefits of the new age were transmitted to labour in the form of new skills, a higher proportion of skilled work, and widening horizons,[111] symbolized by the audiences of intelligent and interested mechanics at the Andersonian Institution in Glasgow and the early membership of the Mechanics' Institutes. The engineers were the most successful among the newcomers in raising themselves to an accepted high level, maintained – at least in the large cities like London – by tough rules restricting entrance, which emphasized proper training and skill.[112] While in this they followed the practices of some of the established trades, like those in building, the latter for their part found it hard to survive the rapid growth and influx of labour from the provinces and underwent a temporary decline before again re-establishing themselves as privileged skilled trades in the second half of the nineteenth century.

Both views are correct, and examples of both declining and rising skill can be found. By the end of the period there were numerous trades in which the trade unions had rules on apprenticeship and limitation of numbers but could not enforce them,[113] while elsewhere new trades established and enforced their apprenticeship rules and limitations with great effectiveness. Some historians have held that the true difference between apprenticed skill and the 'undifferentiated mass of unskilled labour' existed only up to the early nineteenth century, representing the particular shortage of skill in a generally surplus-labour economy, while at the end of the century there was 'a whole spectrum of degrees of skill'. Some, indeed, see the true period of the 'labour aristocracy' to be pre-industrial England, and their view may be coloured by the fact that a very large part of the skilled crafts of the day, among building workers, furniture, glass, or printing workers, and the like, was deployed in luxury trades for the rich in which skill mattered much and cost mattered little, rather than in making mass-produced manufactured articles for the masses.[114] Others saw the aristocracy of labour, based on skill, developing only in the second half of the century and reaching its high point of privilege some time near its end.[115]

Again, both are right. The practices of the traditional 'aristocracy' are well described by Somerville in his reminiscences as a mason's labourer. The labourers were not allowed into the same room in the public house as the masons, and if there was only one room the labourers had to drink out of doors; for speaking out of turn, Somerville was ordered by the mason to be beaten by the apprentices; and even his friend, a mason, opined that 'building could not be carried on if labourers were to have equal rights with masons'. There were then social distinctions not only in the upper classes but

also between the artisan who has long tails to his coat, and the humbler labourer who has short tails to his coat; between the engine-maker, who is a free member of his trade, and the blacksmith, who has not been apprenticed to engine-making ... No matter how high the ability of the blacksmith may be, nor how willing the master mechanic may be to promote him and make use of his superior abilities, he is doomed to remain a blacksmith; he cannot pass the boundary which rigorously excludes him from rising above the level of the blacksmith class.[116]

In the course of the first half of the nineteenth century, contemporaries were well aware of the gap between the aristocracy and the rest, and Sir Archibald Alison referred to the trade combination of 1838 as 'just a system of the aristocracy of skilled labour against the mass of unskilled labour', while Ernest Jones criticized the skilled building workers for not coming to the aid of the less skilled: 'The aristocracy of 30s. per week looked down upon 7s. per week, saying "we are safe". Our *skilled* labour can never become a drug.'[117] Here were the origins of that more modern, Victorian 'aristocracy' which was based largely on strong national trade-union organization.

The repeal in 1814 of the apprenticeship clauses of the Statute of Apprentices, following the fruitless attempt by some London trade unions to invoke them in their favour, marked the end of the old era, represented typically by the independent craftsman–shopkeeper or the subcontracting artisan.[118] For the next decades, the status of skill was uncertain. In the 1830s, Marx noted, mechanics and other skilled artisans were expressly excluded from the Factory Acts but included in the statistics derived from them.[119] The rise of the Amalgamated Society of Engineers in 1851 marked the beginning of the new era, when skill was defined and protected not so much by a temporary excess in demand or by arcane knowledge as by using a new type of organization to conduct collective bargaining with the employer. It is not even possible to say with any certainty whether the proportion of skilled and semi-skilled workers as a whole rose or fell in this period; all one can say is that the nature of skill and the sources of privilege were different in the new conditions, both within the factory and without.

Similarly complex is the evidence relating to the employment of women and children. In one conventional view, they were among the groups detached by the process of industrialization from the disguised unemployment or part-employment in homes and farms in order to enter the labour market as an additional element. Labourers in the early spinning mills, for example, were recruited in this way, and the workhouses were raided for them; when cotton power-loom weaving became predominant from 1820 on, women and children took over weaving also from the men. By 1839, of 420,000 cotton factory workers 193,000 were aged under eighteen years; only 97,000 were adult males; and the rest were adult females. In the other textiles the proportions were higher still: thus in 1844, when females represented about 56 per cent of the labour force in cotton mills, they formed around 70 per cent in woollen, silk, and flax mills. They were also to be found, in many cases in growing numbers, in such less obvious occupations as coal-mining, nailmaking, and file-making, and in agricultural gangs.[120]

Yet women and children were employed perhaps even more widely, though usually far less intensively, before industrialization – in agriculture, in domestic work, and elsewhere. The industrial revolution merely increased and regularized their work, and it did so both in the mills and in the home. It was this aspect – that of taking the woman away from the home altogether – rather than her employment as such which led to the widespread observation that the factory system was associated with a disruption of family life and a decline in the domestic virtues.[121] In some areas, as in the Cornish mining districts, the absorption of female and child labour proceeded in two stages. In the first, mining expansion turned the part-time farmer into a full-time miner and increased the domestic and farming activities of his wife and children; in the second, further intensification required that the wife and children drop domestic and farm work and also engage in work on metals, mainly on the surface, dressing and preparing the ores.[122] It is significant that the proportion of children in employment did not fall with the 1833 Act,[123] since they continued to be eagerly employed both inside and outside the mills.[124] The strikingly low wage level for both women and children – estimated, perhaps even generously, by Kuczynski at 30–50 per cent of the male wage for women and 5–25 per cent for children[125] – seems to suggest that the demand did not press on the supply any harder than in the case of the men, though in some textile districts there were periods when men could find employment only if they brought with them women and child labour,[126] and in a few, men could find no work at all and had to be kept by their families.

Yet another aspect of the conventional view is that industrialization increased the rate of participation of all types of workers by turning part-time work into full-time work, by creating specialization within specific industries, and by transferring workers out of disguised unemployment in agriculture into full employment in industry or agriculture.[127] This is usually held to be one of the major sources of the easy labour supply which characterizes the Industrial Revolution. But here, too, the movement was not all one way. For while the participation ratio for some was increased, industrialization and urbanization created their own part-employment and unemployment. There was casual labour and seasonal labour, and there were the trade slumps affecting growing numbers as the share of market-oriented (and overseas-oriented) industries increased. A study purporting to show the typical wage level of Leeds in 1839 assumed nine months' average work a year for such trades as cloth pressers, slubbers, woollen piecers and fillers, dyers, paper-stainers, wood-sawyers, painters, plasterers, and bricklayers, and ten months' work for wool-sorters, weavers, woolcombers, shoemakers, wood-turners, hatters, wheelwrights, plumbers, and masons.[128] Building workers had always faced slack times in the winter, but what was new was that now there was no plot of land of their own, no agricultural economy to fall back on. Visitors from more traditional economies noted with surprise what Englishmen had come to take for granted, that 'not one of all the many thousand English factory workers has a square yard of land on which to grow food if he is out of work and draws no wages'.[129]

It was only superficially true, as some economists alleged, that the underemployment reflected by such less-than-full-time work represented an over-supply of labour.[130] Among the poorest and weakest workers it was the other way round. Precisely because among the London tailors one-third were only part-employed and a further third were wholly unemployed, their poverty forced them to send their wives out to work and thus to overstock the labour market even more.[131] In the sweated trades, in general, it was precisely because excessive hours were being worked that the labour market seemed overstocked: if labour had been strong enough to limit hours, the ensuing labour shortage would have strengthened its hand to limit hours further – a concept not unfamiliar to the trade unions pressing for factory legislation.[132] A recent study of changes in the hours of labour since the eighteenth century had as one of its most striking findings the close correlation between short hours and high wages, and vice versa.[133] The choice between income and leisure is largely an unreal one, invented by economists: labour in a strong position gained both, just as the large majority of workers in the industrial revolution lost out on both counts. Among the hangers-on of urban life – the porters, gardeners, casual workers, and labourers – the bane of seasonal unemployment in the winter was obvious enough to draw sympathy even from the Poor Law Commissioners.

Those who have not been accustomed to observe them [wrote William Pulteney Alison], are not aware how much reduction of comfort the family of the labouring man, disabled or deprived of employment, may undergo, and not only life be preserved, but the capacity for occasional and precarious employment continue. Their better clothes may be pawned, their furniture and bedclothes may be sold . . . two or more families may be crowded into a single room, and struggle to pay the rent among them . . . They gather cinders in the street late at night and early in the morning, they beg for bread . . . Three meals in the week will support life for many weeks . . . Thus, almost without visible means of subsistence, many of the poorest families in this and other great towns manage to pass the winter, while in summer they find precarious and desultory employment in fields and gardens.[134]

Mayhew estimated 'conservatively' that 125,000 families' income depended on the weather, 450,000 on seasonal fluctuations, and 150,000 on trading booms, making a total of 725,000 families or 3 million people. In any given trade, in London at least, one-third of the workers would be fully employed, one-third part-employed, and one-third unemployed – a total employment rate of 50 per cent – in the mid nineteenth century.[135]

Mayhew may have been exaggerating for normal years; but in slack times, especially in general trade slumps, the effects might be far worse than in former bad years of harvest failure. They were greatest in such vulnerable industries as ironmaking, a capital-goods industry, or cotton, which depended on exports. At times, unemployment rates of two-thirds were not unknown.[136]

In 1811, of perhaps 10,000 Spitalfields weavers it was found that 2,852 were unemployed and something like an equal number half-employed. In 1812, there were 'a considerable number out of work' in Stockport, others 'only partly employed . . . Never before saw the labour poor looking so ill, or appearing so ragged; many miserably wretched; a few nearly in a starving state.' In Bolton, 'in a population of 17,000 there are 3,000 paupers, notwithstanding *great numbers* have removed to seek for employment'. In Mansfield, 'Vast numbers experience great distress; many utterly unable to procure the common necessaries of life, many who had lived far above want, now in *very, very* abject poverty.' And so it went on, through large industrial towns and small, down to a little settlement like Disley near Stockport, where 'the writer has not heard of any place inclosing more indigence and perishing want; many families have sought sustenance from boiled nettles and wild greens, without salt'. At least one observer thought 'that the awful period is arrived, when there exists a greater amount and variety of individual distress arising from the want of provisions, than I believe has been heard of for many centuries'.[137]

It is this comparison with earlier periods which is so difficult to make. There had been years of unemployment and distress before, resulting from wars, bad harvests, interruptions of overseas trade, or the secular decline of individual industries. But it may be doubted if these were as regular and persistent as the cyclical unemployment now super-imposed on the evils of casual work and structural unemployment; and above all it is most unlikely that in the past there had ever been such a large proportion of the population exclusively dependent on income from market-oriented industry.

As late as 1819, it would still cause surprise in Paisley that relief was given for no better reason than 'that they could get no work'.[138] But in 1831–2, it was found that of 2,047 [*sic*] looms in Leeds, 434 were fully employed, 1,025 partially employed, and 587 standing idle; in Macclesfield, there had been 10,229 engaged in silk-throwing in 1824, but employment was only 3,762 in 1832, working but four days a week; and in Leeds, out of a population estimated at 71,602, 25,496 individuals were on relief.[139]

Over the period 1834–41 as a whole, it was estimated in the factory districts that although the nominal working day was twelve hours, the average, taking into account short time because of the slump, was only ten hours a day.[140] But this was totally put in the shade by the distress of 1841–2. It was found then that in a town like Leeds, 20,000 people subsisted on an average income of $11\frac{1}{4}d$. per head per week; in Paisley,

14,657 were on the roll of unemployed men, or nearly one-third of the *total* population; while in Stockport, an investigation of 2,965 houses showed that of 8,218 people seeking employment, only 1,204 were fully employed, 2,866 partially employed, and 4,148 totally out of work. In Bolton, of 8,124 operatives in cotton mills, 5,061 were on short time or were unemployed; and of 2,110 ironfounders, 785 were out of work, and the rest were on short time.[141]

In 1847, the same kind of statistics once more emerged from the manufacturing districts. In the cotton towns around Manchester, for example, of 382 mills only 126 were in full work, 212 were on short time, and 44 had stopped altogether. Of 71,215 hands usually employed by them, 10,141 were totally idle, and 26,510 were on half time.[142]

Unfortunately, the scattered nature of the statistics and the variations in the methods of calculation make it impossible to derive a meaningful national series on cyclical underemployment, even with the aid of occasional statistics of reductions in payrolls, or spindles or blast furnaces idle, which might be used to lend meaning to such terms as 'short-time work' or 'partial employment'. However, in view of the fact that in the trough of the depression, employment in the industrial centres ran at about one-half of labour capacity only, and in the worst cycles at one-third, an estimate of a loss of employment of 15–20 per cent of capacity averaged over good and bad years together does not seem too pessimistic.

To this must be added those sectors which as a matter of regular practice created underemployment by holding on to an excessive pool of labour. Some industries collected a penumbra of attached workers, like the 'grass hands' in printing, 'hanging round the offices . . . till a call came from this or that newspaper for temporary help'.[143] Casual labour was found particularly in the docks – where according to Mayhew employment might vary by 7,000 out of 20,000 daily in London – and in urban carting, portering, and other transport. Part-time employment remained the rule even in modernized agriculture, where additional labour had to be drawn out of 'unemployment' from the towns and the homes and from Ireland, for the weeks of the harvest. Further, more rapid technical change led to an increase of that structural unemployment which left displaced workers seeking new jobs for long periods before falling back on some unskilled jobs in unfamiliar industries.[144] Finally, there were part-time domestic industries, such as spinning or lace-making, which formerly employed agricultural part-time labour, especially women, but were now taken over by the factory, and created new rural underemployment.[145]

The balance is thus difficult to strike. Old-type underemployment before 1800 gave place to new-type underemployment after that date. The new type, however, was of a kind to increase the availability of a willing labour supply.

Finally, domestic work itself is usually pictured as a victim of industrialization, or as an earlier stage in industrial development, to be replaced in due course by the factory. On the contrary, in fact, it was often a product of industrialization,[146] though in the process it was being changed in a fundamental sense, turning from a family-based occupation – allowing some degree of independence, and integrated with the domestic duties of the housewife, with a small plot of land, or with the harvest cycle of the surrounding countryside – into full-time dependence on a factory or on a warehouse. Thus the large numbers of domestic weavers and of stocking-knitters *c.* 1790–1830 had been called forth precisely by the success of the spinning mill; and when, in turn, weaving became mechanized, domestic tailoring and dressmaking were greatly enlarged as a result, particularly in London. Both these waves of massive new employment opportunities resulted from the mechanization (and consequent cheapening) of an earlier stage in the productive process, which conforms to a very common pattern in the process of industrialization. It should be noted that both our examples – the hand-loom weaving of the 1790s and the tailoring and dressmaking of the 1830s and 1840s – drew their labour mainly from outside the industrial sphere itself,[147] so that the machine, which was basically labour-saving and therefore restrained the demand for labour within the mills, may be said to have had a more powerful effect in increasing the demand for and the extent of domestic labour than of factory labour.

The kind of division of labour which requires no elaborate new machinery, described by Adam Smith at the beginning of the industrial revolution and realized by entrepreneurs of genius like Boulton and Wedgwood inside their works, turned out also to offer very large opportunities for domestic work outside the factory. The more it led to sweating, to under-payment, and overwork, and the more easily it permitted large fluctuations in output without overhead costs to the employer, the more tenacious it became in the face of competition by improved machine technology. The dressmakers and milliners and cabinet-makers of London, the cutlers and nailmakers and straw-hat-makers and finishers of machine-made lace in the provinces, had by 1850 greatly expanded in numbers since the rise of the factory system and in some periods were multiplying faster than the factory population itself. Even when a new technology was introduced, as in cotton power-loom weaving in the 1820s and 1830s, domestic outwork might survive for long, and even be strengthened for a transitional time as the

buffer between high and low demand, before it was finally sup-
planted.[148] Conversely, at least in the early decades, the mills were
filled not by former domestic workers but by an influx of agricultural
workers, labourers, and paupers, together with a few necessary skilled
mechanics.

This brief survey has shown that the pattern of changes in the labour
market in the course of the industrial revolution was a much more
complex one than a mere measurement of net changes would show.
Movements in one direction – from the villages to the towns, from
part-time to full-time work, from domestic employment to factory
work – were often alternating with, or accompanied by, movements in
the opposite direction. At other times, a movement leading to an
ultimate net change might involve several intermediate moves, each
creating new conditions and new reactions in the labour market: thus
it might be the Irish migrant who freed an English labourer's wife from
part-time harvest work and permitted her to seek work, with her
family, in an urban mill, which in turn added her husband to the town's
labour force. Finally, it is important to stress at this point that the
apparent retention, or re-creation, of a traditional institution generally
hid a basic change in character. Thus child labour before industrialization was not the same as child labour afterwards; the domestic system,
when it represented the most advanced technology, was not the same as
domestic industry as an adjunct to the factory, which included the
worst exploited and sweated labour; and the skilled craftsmen of the
eighteenth century played a different role from that of the typical
skilled artisan of the later nineteenth.

IV. Case Studies of Four Typical Industries

Perhaps the point and counterpoint of the labour supply accompanying the main theme of industrialization is best illustrated by some
concrete examples. We have chosen four – the cotton industry, building, coal-mining, and agriculture – which between them cover a
broadly representative share of the labour market.

The cotton industry saw what were perhaps the most spectacular, but
also the most erratic, changes in the demand and supply for labour. In
the mid eighteenth century it had been a rural or small-town industry,
employing mainly part-time female spinners and part-time male
weavers. As the demand for cotton goods expanded, the supply of
spinners – several of whom were needed to keep one loom going with
yarn – tended to be exhausted first, and this bottleneck was broken by
the invention of spinning machines, which became generally available

in the 1780s. It is with this decade that the modern era may be said to have started, and the industry's development from then on is best seen as a series of consecutive phases.

In the first phase, to *c.* 1792, the spinning output expanded largely by technological improvement. In so far as it absorbed additional labour, it did so mostly by employing women and children, drawn partly from the former domestic workers, but also from a variety of other backgrounds including the workhouses. Male workers were relatively few, mainly overseers and mechanics, and this allowed the bulk of the additional male labour force to flow into weaving, where the vastly increased demand had to be met – in the absence of any substantial rises in productivity – by an increase in numbers. Skilled weavers for fine work were drawn mainly from former weavers of cotton and other textiles; they never formed a high proportion. It was the coarse work, employing at least 75 per cent of the labour force, which could be quickly learned by almost anyone and which attracted a rapid influx of labour from outside. Demand for labour remained ahead of supply for some years, especially for fine work, 'masters wanting servants, not servants wanting masters; so the workman demands excessive wages, is insolent, abandon'd, and drunk half the week'.[149] and the high wages (or at least the full employment) of this 'golden age'[150] themselves helped to attract more men into the trade. A further attraction was the work offered to other members of the weaver's family in the other sections of the industry. In Lancashire, recruiting was also furthered by the contemporary depression in small farming, by an abundance of casual labour, and by the availability of weavers in silk, linen, or wool in the surrounding counties.[151] The isolated rural water mills in Scotland and in such areas as the Midlands found it harder to recruit hands, mainly because of limited employment opportunities for men, and relied more on the uneconomic parish apprentices; by the 1800s either they were modal population centres or they showed signs of failure.[152]

An industry as volatile as cotton could not hope to match up its labour supply exactly to the demand, and when the first phase was over, in the comparative stagnation of 1793-7, the balance swung the other way: the crisis of 1797 actually pushed the most mobile adult workers out of the industry and into enlistment.[153] The supply of hand-loom weavers, having risen from 108,000 in 1788 to 164,000 in 1801,[154] henceforth remained well ahead of demand; and in consequence their wages, especially in the easily learnt coarse branches, underwent a long and painful process of erosion.[155] As Davies Giddy noted in 1808 with great perception, the weavers' troubles arose 'because at one time [their wages] had been too high, a circumstance which induced more people to adopt this trade than there was a demand for, or than it could support'.[156]

In spinning, the second boom of 1797–1803 could tap a supply of drifting unskilled labour in the towns and of migratory artisans.[157] For the rest of the war years, the growing output, interrupted by crises, was met mainly by better equipment and faster working, and there seems to have been no great shortage of labour in spite of military recruitment. The easier supply conditions are also shown by the fact that this was the period when unfree apprentice labour could be almost wholly replaced by 'free' women and children. Conditions were thus particularly unfavourable for returning soldiers and displaced agricultural labourers in 1815–20, who were further handicapped by the rapid population rise in Lancashire. It was in this period that adult male labour was restricted to about 17 per cent in spinning, and the exploitation of the labour of children, who were dismissed when they reached adulthood and wanted a full wage, was perhaps at its highest. The family unit now played a major role as recruiting agent: families moved to textile areas specifically to obtain employment for all members, the earnings of children often compensating for the decline in the earnings of adults and making at least one witness before the Select Committee on the State of Children in the Manufactories in 1816 'believe that the wages of the cotton factory are greater for children than they are for most other sorts of labour'.[158] The extent to which the household budget in the factory districts depended on the interplay of the number of dependants, children's pay, and adult earnings is shown by the sample in Table 32.

Table 32. *Family Size and Earnings in Eight Households, 1841*

Household no.	Workers	Eaters	Weekly earnings ($£$ s. d.)	Daily average per head (d.)[a]
1	4	8	1 4 0	5·14
2	4	11	1 5 0	3·90
3	1	5	0 15 0	5·14
4	3	5	0 14 0	4·80
5	1	4	0 12 0	5·14
6	4	10	1 0 0	3·43
7	2	9	0 17 0	3·24
8	2	6	0 12 0	3·43

[a] Turned into decimals (the original has fractions and appears to be full of errors).

SOURCE. *McDouall's Chartist Journal and Trades' Advocate*, no. 27, 2 October 1841, p. 210. Cf. also W. Felkin, 'The Labouring Classes in the Township of Hyde, Cheshire', *Journal of the Royal Statistical Society*, 1 (1838–9), 417.

Up to this point, the revolution in the cotton industry had turned many children temporarily,[159] and some women and fewer men permanently, into a factory proletariat, but it had also expanded greatly the domestic employment of an almost equally large number of mostly adult workers in weaving. It was the outworker who acted as a buffer bearing the brunt of depressions, and whose declining status made him view improvements in machinery with particular fear.[160]

From 1820 until the 1840s the industry sustained a remarkably high rate of growth. Spinning was, on balance, still recruiting labour, particularly in the boom of 1834–6, in spite of the rapidly rising output per head, and trade unions were now helping to keep up male wages. But in weaving the spread of the power loom allowed the operative to produce between three and six times as much as on a hand loom,[161] and the rising speed of its working limited the demand. It is likely that in c. 1830–45 output per head actually rose faster in weaving than in spinning. Moreover, the demand was now for girls rather than for men, and while the hand-loom weaver of Manchester could find employment in other expanding industries, those in the weaving villages lingered on for some decades more at starvation wages, unless they were sturdy enough to take to labouring or energetic enough to switch to other fabrics, such as silks or woollens. The large influx of Irish labour tended to augment the problem in certain areas of Lancashire, Cheshire, and the West of Scotland.[162] This phenomenon of the long-drawn-out agony of the decline of the hand-loom weavers, whose numbers did not decrease as their wages were inexorably depressed even further below subsistence level, forms one of the best known and most puzzling episodes of the industrial revolution. It will be better understood if it is remembered that many weavers were now women, often part-time; others combined weaving with farming;[163] and still others clung to their spurious independence with the help of other members of the family working in the mills (a factor which helped to split up the old family economy of the spinning mill).[164] Also, in boom times there was still work to be had, and the superiority of the power loom was not immediately obvious. Moreover, many of the new entrants were Irish (including weavers working in Ireland for Scots masters),[165] and even those among them who had been experienced textile workers in their own country were content on immigration into England to accept lower wages. Because of the hostility shown them, few were able to contemplate entering any other industry.[166]

The reduction of child labour by the Factory Acts did not provide new employment opportunities for men. They continued to form 24–28 per cent of the labour force, and the place of the children excluded by the Acts was taken by women and young persons; meanwhile, the children gravitated to related employments like calico-printing, where by the 1840s they formed 50 per cent of the labour force, one-third of them being under thirteen years old.[167]

By 1850 the industry had become wholly a factory industry,[168] fairly capital-intensive and with falling wage costs. Family employment was still characteristic, and as a result the local labour force was able to show superior resilience and attachment to the industry in depressions, even though wages were not high, apart from the small proportion of skilled men. Seventy years – in which output increased a hundredfold but the numbers engaged probably did not change very greatly – had seen the mushroom growth and massive rundown of a large male labour force in weaving. The industry's particular characteristic, however, was its ability to by-pass reliance on male labour, both in its labour-intensive phase and in the later phases of its development, avoiding in this way acute competition for labour with other sectors, even in boom years in boom towns.

Our second example, the building trades, represent perhaps the opposite extreme, an industry which saw virtually no technical change at all. Unlike cotton, building was entirely a home-market industry, but as such it was somewhat exceptional in that the demand for its products was growing faster than the population as long as population growth was accelerating. It formed the largest trade group for men in the country outside agriculture, and Clapham estimated the numbers employed in Great Britain in 1831, including apprentices and labourers, at 350,000 to 400,000, all men and boys.[169] Given an absence of technical innovation, the more-than-proportionate increase in demand for housing should have led to a more-than-proportionate increase in the labour force, and with it a need to attract labour from elsewhere by means of a favourable wage level. This was particularly so in London, which enjoyed an unusually high wage differential.[170] In the second half of the century, when census figures can be used in proof, there was a substantial increase of the proportion of building labour in the total occupied population,[171] and although no figures exist for earlier decades, it seems highly probable that the same relationship obtained then.

No very close correlation can, however, be established. This is partly because building showed substantial cyclical swings in activity.[172] But partly the reason seems to lie in the wasteful and archaic nature of the industry itself, which permitted substantial increases in productivity, at least for long runs of work, by better organization, even without an improved technology. Thus the censuses of 1831, 1841, and 1851 show no larger proportion of building labour among total labour, or among total population, in the rapidly growing industrial cities than in the older, stagnant towns in which housing figures registered hardly any increases. The explanations for this paradox may be complex and cannot be pursued here but are likely to include a different range of activities subsumed under such categories as 'carpenters' in old towns and in new, the differing incidence of repair work, a different complement of labourers and carters for each craftsman, and the speed-up associated with all the new industrial cities. But the better organization and utilization of labour in large-scale new domestic building together with such aids as cranes and the 'temporary iron rails... employed on construction works to transport materials, to remove earth from excavations, and to carry soil for the construction of terraces'[173] undoubtedly played a major part in this spatial contrast, which hides a form of temporal contrast between the traditional and the new. We may wonder even today at the speed of building large mills, when Benjamin Gott's mill of six stories, with over 100 windows on one side, took six weeks to erect, including roofing and flooring, and another, larger one, also of six stories, took three months in 1825; while a mill and engineering works which burnt down in Glasgow in 1814 had joiners and bricklayers working in the still-smoking ruins the next morning and was confidently expected to be in operation again in four to six weeks.[174]

Building was traditionally carried on by skilled, relatively well-paid craftsmen and their unskilled helpers, the latter receiving 60–70 per cent of the wage rates of the former.[175] While it was sometimes in the older, stagnating towns like Dublin that the skilled union could be most restrictive,[176] wages kept up best in the new industrial towns and in London, where the demand for building labour grew fastest. In 1816, skilled builders' wages in an old town like Tiverton were only 2s. a day, or half those of London.[177] This would be likely to set off a classical migration of skilled men as well as of labourers from the stagnant areas to the growth towns – a migration increasingly resisted by the localized trade unions in the reception areas in proportion as their power grew.

Organizationally, one section of the industry was transformed in this period, first by the large contractor of major public works or urban developments, and after 1815 by the master builder who maintained a permanent work force of skilled men, supplemented by the direct employment of others as occasion demanded.[178] It was as a reaction to these relatively new types of organization that the self-governing operative builders' guild arose in the heady days of Owenite influence in 1831–4. Its intention was to take contracts directly, by-passing the capitalist contractor; and, significantly, in September 1833 it expressed the hope that quarrymen, brickmakers, and labourers might in due course also be permitted to join 'as soon as they can be prepared with better habits and more knowledge to enable them to act for themselves assisted by the other branches'.[179] Even the former contractors were invited to 'consider yourselves as members of one great family'.[180] This attempt failed, and in the next three decades the scope of the large-scale builder and contractor expanded greatly, encouraged partly by the erection of public buildings, factories, and complete streets and squares in the large cities,[181] partly by railway works, and partly by the massive urban reconstruction schemes made necessary by the railways themselves.

The majority of workers, however, continued to be employed in a traditional manner by small master-craftsmen. The trade-union membership, even as late as the 1850s, probably did not exceed 10 per cent of those eligible, but it was strategically concentrated in London and the other major immigrant cities; and because of the genuine high skill involved, the survival of proper apprenticeship, and the favourable demand situation, the building craftsmen kept their status as 'aristocrats' of labour throughout the vicissitudes of this period. In the course of the second and third quarters of the nineteenth century, modern-type unions, managed with increasing skill and experience, were added to the prestige of the old-established crafts to regularize hours, reduce irregularity of work, and increase wages step by step, in spite of occasional relapses and in the teeth of a powerful body of employers. They were among the first to gain a sixty-hour week, and then to reduce their standard week below sixty hours in the 1850s.[182] T. S. Ashton noted the striking similarity in the wage movements of workers in the cotton industry – which saw enormous changes in technology – and in building – which saw virtually none (see Table 33).

Table 33. *Wages of Cotton and Building Workers, 1810–50*
(index: 1900 = 100)

	Cotton factory workers	Building workers
1810	58	57
1820	57	57
1831	52	53
1840	51	57
1850	51	58

SOURCE. T. S. Ashton, 'Some Statistics of the Industrial Revolution in Britain', *Manchester School*, XVI (1948). On the problem of paying similar wages in industries with very different changes in productivity, see Ashok V. Desai, *Real Wages in Germany, 1871–1913* (1968), 97–8.

Coal-mining was among the fastest-growing industries between 1750 and 1850. Its output increased well over tenfold in this period, but in contrast to cotton-spinning its productivity was not raised very greatly by any major technological breakthrough. The reason for this was that, as industrialization proceeded and annual output increased, the easy operations on shallow workings still prevalent in most districts *c*. 1750 [183] gave way increasingly to much more costly deep mining, spreading outward from the Northeast and the Northwest, so that whatever technological improvements were made did little more than to neutralize the natural cost increases. Consequently, the growth of coal output was achieved mainly by an increase in the labour force itself, and since this rate of growth was much higher than the natural rate of growth of the population at large, the industry – like building in London and some of the growth cities – was obliged as a condition of its existence to go on attracting labour out of other employments.

These apparent conditions of labour shortage, in marked contrast with the conditions of labour surplus assumed for the economy as a whole, should have provided a most favourable economic bargaining setting for the coal-miner. In practice, however, it did so only very intermittently. There were several reasons for this. One was the enormous extra-economic power wielded by the coal-owner. Unlike the German miner, or the man in the English non-ferrous metal mines, the British coal-miner had no medieval privileges on which to build a high status, and – such may be the power of social reality over the theoretical economic 'market' forces – his scarcity was perversely turned into a disadvantage rather than as advantage. In Scotland, because of the labour shortage in the pits, miners were made into serfs until 1799,[184] and in Northeastern England the normal yearly 'bond', together with a common state of indebtedness, made them only a degree less unfree.[185] Their social and geographical isolation became a further source of weakness as the coal-owners controlled the magistracy, while the company cottage was used to throttle independent trade-union action, blacklists of 'agitators' were widely maintained and used,[186] and educational facilities were even poorer than elsewhere. The influx of capital made matters worse rather than better: 'it was in the coal fields where technical progress was most marked that the extension of child labour was greatest'.[187]

How could labour be attracted into such an unusually oppressive social framework and into an occupation which appeared to most men to be dirty, lowly, and dangerous, enjoying only very erratic fortunes?[188] The most obvious source was the miner's own family, whose employment was encouraged by a form of subcontract in which the hewer himself was responsible for finding assistants to transport the coal from the face to the bottom of the shaft, or to the bank. Such recruitment may have been helped by the often-noted tendency of miners' families to be more fertile than the average.[189] Certainly, the marked isolation of the mining villages ensured that the miners' sons, and sometimes their daughters too, went into the pit as a matter of course. Since there was no formal apprenticeship, but instead a recognized progression to the skilled hewer's job,[190] the absorption of such new labour was easy. There was also some recruitment out of declining areas, such as the Derbyshire lead mines, and a movement of skilled men – specialist pit sinkers, and engineers, viewers, and overseers – from one coalfield to another.

These sources alone could not have sustained the kind of expansion of the labour force that was required. The relatively smooth absorption of additional labour into such an unattractive industry occurred thanks mainly to two factors. One was that the chief source of the additional influx was the agriculture of nearby areas, e.g. the Border country for the Northeast, and the Welsh Marches for Shropshire. Whatever the other comparative advantages, in terms of wages it was not difficult to trump the lowly earnings on the land. In some regions the miner remained partly an agriculturist for a time. In South Yorkshire and North Derbyshire, for example, 'the high proportion of very small holdings throughout the coalfield [suggests] that the collier, like the nailer and edge tool worker, was probably a landowner himself. It is certain that the majority of the miners were natives of the area in which they worked, as the Poor Law certificates . . . show only a thin trickle of movement into these [mining] parishes and in almost all cases, such migration was from a narrowly restricted region.'[191]

The second factor was more complex and rested on the unusually severe fluctuations of labour demand in the industry. The effective pull generally occurred in boom years, when mining wages were especially high, or at times when agricultural labour was made locally redundant. Thus in c. 1780–1800, when the demand for labour outran the supply in the Northeast, wages were raised, binding money and high premiums were paid, worker indebtedness was permitted or encouraged, 'play wages' were paid in temporary slack periods, and there were many complaints over the poaching of workers by rival firms. Similar conditions, at a much lower absolute wage level, applied to the South Wales coalfield in its period of expansion a little later. 'It was rapid adaptation of the ordinary labourers to colliery work which favoured the swift development of the Monmouthshire valleys in the first decades of the nineteenth century.'[192]

Coal-mining, however, was a notoriously fickle industry. Even in expansions the general upward trend could be temporarily interrupted, and there were some major slumps also. At such times, the glut of coal and of labour would be sudden and substantial, since supply was normally inflexible, and capacity could be closed down only at great expense, involving the idleness of a great deal of overhead capital. Thus the coal boom of the 1790s involved the creation of a canal network, with a lag of about ten years. The new areas opened up by it, in turn, used much newly recruited, formerly unskilled labour and less sophisticated techniques, and these ultimately helped to bring down wages and conditions from their boom levels, while even the period of high wages had not succeeded in raising the miner's status socially. By 1830, there were widespread complaints of excess capacity,[193] and the great strike in the Northeast in 1831 was successfully broken with the help of blackleg labour. The following twenty years saw another rapid expansion. Paradoxically once more, strikes were often responsible for a massive labour influx paid for by militant employers. Thus, 180 Irishmen were taken to the Marquis of Londonderry's Penshaw colliery in 1841, and one-half were reported to have settled there permanently; and in 1844 Harton recruited 'common labourers, blacksmiths, waggon-men, joiners and farm labourers' from Wales, Staffordshire and Nottinghamshire.[194] On the other hand, the coal-fields near the cities or other centres of employment, as in the Black Country, or far from any population reservoir, as the western extension of the South Wales field, became once more subject to acute labour shortages during the iron and railway booms.[195] Management in areas of alternative employment would share the experience of the Worsley Colliery which, having sacked numerous workers systematically in the slump of 1849, found itself desperately short of labour when trade picked up again in 1851.[196]

Thus the violent fluctuations in fortunes formed perhaps the most striking aspect of the industry and – in an industry as labour-intensive as mining – were reflected in equally violent fluctuations in rates and earnings, and in an unusually unstable and erratic trade-union development. The amplitude of these swings was increased by the common practice of skilled men to work to a 'stint' or 'darg' and – in good times, as wages rose – to work shorter hours, thus increasing the coal shortage even more. It was in these periods of voluntary stinting and rapid promotion of young men to skilled jobs that new unskilled labour could be introduced into the industry without running into objections by the unions. Thus it was said of Northumberland and Durham that at such times 'the boys of the hewers are insufficient to carry on the collieries and hence the boys of mechanics and labourers in the adjoining villages are generally employed, and hence in collieries families are eagerly sought after'.[197] By contrast, in slack times 'a collier rarely changes his occupation – one who has spent his infancy in the pits is fit for few if any other employments'. Even if made redundant, 'few of them entertained any thought of endeavouring to gain any livelihood by other means than their usual work'.[198]

Further, by the mid-century the structure of coal-mining adapted itself to some extent to a high growth rate, thus neutralizing the natural advantages for labour. This is shown by its age distribution even after the legislation of 1842 which limited the employment of women and children in the industry. According to the Census of 1851, there were 150,000 adult males and no fewer than 65,000 lads under 18 (besides 2,650 women) employed in coal-mining. But this structure of the labour force was ultimately connected with the sharp fluctuations in fortune, and between them they ensured that the excess demand for labour should not permanently raise wages much above the general level. For it was in booms that the additional labour was attracted by temporarily high earnings, and absorbed without friction; it was in slumps that wages were pulled down to something like the normal long-term level elsewhere. At the same time, the social powers of the mine-owners ensured that the miners' status should remain low.

Agriculture, the fourth sector to be examined, bears an altogether different relationship to the process of industrialization and to the labour market than do the industries examined so far; for it was, in one form or another, the main internal reservoir of labour which permitted a flexible expansion of the economy. In many ways, the whole character of the transformation of the economy took on its colouring from the way in which British agriculture was able to free labour for manufacture, transport, and other occupations.

Yet this process was not simple, either. Not even its statistical dimensions can be presented with any hope of clarity of meaning, still less reliable accuracy – though, in view of the importance of the issue, an attempt must be made.[199] According to the most authoritative recent estimate, the proportion of agriculture (together with forestry and fishing) in the total occupied population fell from 35·9 per cent in 1801 to 21·7 per cent in 1851.[200] The proportions in the middle of the eighteenth century are harder to come by; but taking the same authors' estimate that the agricultural population may have increased by about 25 per cent between 1750 and 1801,[201] and assuming that the total occupied population formed the same proportion of the total British population in 1750 as it did in 1801, 'agriculture' would have employed about 41 per cent of the occupied population in 1750. Other estimates, based on contemporary tabulations of shares of national income, which gave agriculture 56 per cent in 1688 (Gregory King) and 46 per cent in 1760 (Massie),[202] would put the 1750 figure nearer 50 per cent, particularly if it is assumed that output per head may have been lower in agriculture than elsewhere. In absolute figures, 'agriculture' might then have employed 1·35–1·6 million persons in 1750, 1·7 million in 1801, and 2·1 million in 1851.[203]

It is clear that the definitions used beg all the questions. Even leaving out of account the complication arising from the inclusion of 'fishing', the definition of an 'agricultural' population at a time when large numbers were engaged part-time in farming and part-time in industry, and when the changeover to greater specialization in one or the other was one of the most significant developments, was likely to be of very limited value. Similarly, when the economic roles of wives and children were in rapid flux, the concept of an 'occupied population' is likely to obscure more than it illuminates.

However, if we carry through the calculations for the purpose of arriving, at least, at an order of magnitude, we find that if agriculture had kept its share of 41 per cent it would have occupied about 2 million in 1801 instead of 1·7 million, and about 4 million in 1851 instead of 2·1 million, so that in some sense there had taken place a net 'transfer' of 300,000 by 1801, and 1,900,000 by 1851. These figures are the end-figures of a slowly accruing series and include the descendants of people who were born into industrial families but who had at some earlier stage left agriculture. The numbers of those who themselves transferred from agriculture to other occupations would of course be much smaller. The order of magnitude involved (see Table 7) may be derived from the calculations shown in Table 34. From the estimates of the total occupied population and the population occupied in agriculture for certain years we may interpolate year-by-year figures for these two series (T_t and A_t), and compare the yearly rate of increase in the total, $(T_t + 1)/T_t = \lambda_t$, with the actual agricultural rate of increase, the difference being the imputed emigration ($= e$) from agriculture, so that $(A_t + 1)/_t \lambda A_t = 1 - e_t$. The rate of emigration e is then applied to the annual agricultural population to give the actual numbers migrating every year, and these are summed for ten-year periods in the final column.[204] It will be seen that the net 'transfer' amounted to only 226,000 for 1751–1800 and 891,000 for 1801–51 – or just over 1,100,000 for the century as a whole, instead of 1,900,000 as suggested by the earlier calculation. Even then, the later T_t series, particularly for the 1840s, is unduly boosted by Irish immigration, which could not have added much to the A_t series. On the other hand, if the majority of Irish immigrants are counted as transferees from agriculture to other occupations, the number of the latter would be much higher.

Another way of measuring the net transfer is to assume that in the later periods the non-food-producers could not have borne any higher ratio to the actual agrarian population of their time than they did in 1750, i.e. 59:41. This would have limited the non-agrarian working population to 2·4 million in 1801 instead of the actual 3·1 million, and to 3·0 million in 1851 instead of the actual 7·6 million. In some sense, therefore, the increasing efficiency on the land and the ability to acquire the produce of foreign soils by the export of other goods and services, permitted another 700,000 to work in non-agrarian occupations in 1801 and 4,600,000 in 1851.

Table 34. *Emigration from Agriculture, 1751–1851*

Year	Estimate of total occupied population T_t (millions)	Estimate of numbers occupied in agriculture A_t (millions)	Decade	Average decennial emigration (e) per 1,000 in agriculture	Imputed total emigration in 10-year period
1751	3·3	1·35	1751–60	2·00	27,600
1761	—	—	1761–70	1·80	26,100
1771	—	—	1771–80	1·61	24,300
1781	4·0	1·55	1781–90	4·95	78,200
1791	—	—	1791–1800	4·18	69,400
1801	4·8	1·7	1801–10	7·87	137,700
1811	5·5	1·8	1811–20	11·90	214,200
1821	6·2	1·8	1821–30	14·90	267,500
1831	7·2	1·8	1831–40	9·96	184,300
1841	8·4	1·9	1841–50	4·38	87,600
1851	9·7	2·1			

SOURCE. Deane and Cole, *British Economic Growth, 1688–1959* (1962), Table 31, p. 143.

Neither of these two sets of counter-factual calculations may have much to recommend it in strict logic, but they help to illustrate some of the difficulties in the concept of the transfer of labour. Moreover, they also indicate the relatively minor role played by the actual movement of workers out of agriculture (as distinct from the compounded figure which includes their descendants) in comparison with the immense importance of the natural population increase itself: probably little more than 200,000 in 1750–1801, on the assumptions used above, compared with the 1,100,000 actual increase in the non-agrarian working population; and (say) 1,100,000 in the whole century 1750–1851, compared with the actual increase of 5,600,000 in the non-agrarian working population. In other words, on our assumptions, only about one-fifth of the additional working force in non-agrarian occupations was derived from direct transfer out of agriculture. Even then, many of these 'transfers' were not direct migrations but consisted of two separate movements – the emigration of agricultural labourers to the empty spaces overseas, and their 'replacement' by Irish immigrants into towns and industrial occupations.

The relative lightness of the pressure which the labour demand from industry exerted on the labour supply in agriculture is also illustrated by the fact that employment in 'agriculture' actually increased in this period – from perhaps 1,350,000 in 1750 to 1,700,000 in 1801, and to 2,100,000 in 1851. This figure includes farmers and peasants as well as wage-labourers, but since the numbers of landholders does not appear to have changed very much over 1750–1850, though their character was differentiated in many areas from peasant-type holders into either large farmers or part-industrial smallholders,[205] the changes represented mostly an increase in paid labour. The figures themselves should not be taken too literally and may, perhaps, represent little more than the transformation (in the statisticians' hands) of the work of members of the holder's family into what technically became paid wage labour. But they emphasize yet again that British agriculture in 1750–1850 bore no relation to a model which assumes mass disguised agrarian unemployment, out of which the stream manning the factories is fed. On the contrary, agriculture was itself transformed technically in line with industry and transport, and in a manner which makes it generally quite impossible to separate out the contributions of the different sectors. Thus the influence of road-building on enclosures and associated improvements, and the contrary influence of enclosures on road-building, would be difficult to separate out; and the agricultural labour freed by coal, reducing the demand for peat-cutters,[206] woodmen and horse-breeders, was quite substantial. In the process agriculture managed to feed a far larger urban population with a disproportionately small increase – but still an increase – in labour power, using not many more acres; and it was therefore in no position to release very great numbers into other occupations. This generalization hides the very different responses of agriculture in the North, and South, and Ireland, with important further variations within the regions.

It has sometimes been assumed that this industrialization by natural increase instead of by the massive siphoning off of labour from agriculture was a distinctive feature of the industrial revolution in Britain: a feature not matched elsewhere,[207] and one reflecting, perhaps, the leisurely progress of Britain as the pioneer, at a speed determined by the availability of resources rather than by the pressure of foreign competition or political demands. E. J. T. Collins has stressed the limited extent of labour demands from industry before the massive railway and urban building of the 1840s, since the industries growing fastest were those in which labour-saving devices were most highly developed; and in his view the social problem in agriculture in that era was to find employment and make work rather than to release labour.[208] However, Sir Arthur Lewis has recently extended his own model of the process of industrialization by showing that under conditions of rapid population increase there will be heavy unemployment and a labour surplus in the towns without trenching on the agricultural labour supply, since the additional population will be larger than even a fast-growing industry can absorb[209] – a picture which shows many essential similarities with the classic British model, though at lower absolute growth rates.

Ideally, an account of the agricultural labour market should pay great attention to the numerous local variations to be found in Britain. Unfortunately, space allows us to note only the striking differences between the industrial areas and the outskirts of London on the one hand, and the underdeveloped South and East (which were also the main wheat areas) on the other, and to treat the history in three main phases: the years of uneven development to the 1790s, the war years, and the crises and responses of the period c. 1815–50.

In the mid eighteenth century, agricultural labour was still far from conforming to a fully developed capitalistic model. Many workers were part-time, and had their own plots or domestic industry to fall back on; employment was in small numbers per farm, and there was a great deal of pay in kind, especially when living in; while the hours worked were uncertain but on the whole long and irregular, depending on the needs dictated by nature rather than on a labour contract. 'The custom of the time of course dictated that women take a large part in agricultural work . . . children too were set to work at an early age;[210] these groups were likely to have even less regular employment and pay. At least half the farms in the early eighteenth century 'could be worked with the labour of the farmer's family, no hired help being necessary except perhaps at harvest time'.[211] At such time, however, not only did the intensity of work increase sharply, but wages also rose to at least 50 per cent above normal, sufficient to attract out into the fields the whole of the labourer's family, as well as numerous urban artisans, their wives, and their children.[212] For the normal labourer, the additional harvest wage was a vital part of his income, and for that reason he was very sensitive to its loss. For example, in one survey of 1838, based on information provided by farmers in Norfolk and Suffolk, it was found that of a total wage roll of £19,130, £2,691 was made up of harvest wages, and £424 of the value of corn gleaned – or 14·1 per cent for wages, and 16·3 per cent for both combined.[213] In the second half of the eighteenth century, and in some regions well into the nineteenth, the effects of the rhythm of harvest work also still tended to spill over into much of the remainder of the labour market. As late as the 1830s, Somerville still left his Edinburgh job in the summers to make some money at the harvest, just as in the slump of 1826 craftsmen returned to the villages to find jobs. This 'two-way labour flow' for temporary reasons was superimposed on the multi-directional long-term migration.[214] Where there was no local reservoir of non-agricultural labour, or where it proved insufficient, regular seasonal migrations took place, frequently organized by contractors, particularly from Scotland, Wales, and Ireland, revealing a distinct difference in the degree of rural disguised unemployment in the different parts of the United Kingdom; there was also much short-distance migration during harvest time.

It was one of the achievements of the New Husbandry of the eighteenth century that it raised the output per worker on the land. It did this partly by more effective techniques; but it also increased the work load and intensity of independent holders, and of women and children in the village. By making some of them full-time, it made others redundant or (depending on the labour market) freed them for other work. The loss of commons lowered the reserve price of some labour; and the loss of domestic employment to the factory, and the nineteenth-century decline of cottage industry, freed other workers. In a period of accelerating population increase, the net result of all these tendencies was to create a potential surplus of labour in the villages.[215] The formerly disguised unemployment turned into something like an agricultural reserve army; it became more visible, and seasonal imbalances became more clearly marked.

In the Southern and Eastern counties, away from London, where there was no alternative employment, real wages therefore tended downward, to touch subsistence levels if they had not been there before, and stayed there. By contrast, in the areas in which quickening industrial development offered growing competition for rural labour, at wage rates which were traditionally higher, agricultural wages began to rise, to overtake 'Southern' agricultural wages, and soon to leave them far behind.[216] At first, this rise tended to be local or even temporary only, reflecting perhaps the digging of a canal or the expansion of a local firm. By the 1790s, however, the diffusion of higher agricultural wages was pretty general over all the industrial counties, though there were still local variations which usually reflected fairly precisely the pull of other local employment.[217] It should be emphasized that the pull was not merely from the factories but from a whole range of primary, secondary, and tertiary occupations, characteristic of the industrial revolution; it also came from the expanding opportunities for part-time work. Thus it was said of the farm worker in northern Lancashire, by no means a fully industrialized area, that he frequently combined his agricultural labours 'with handloom weaving, quarry work, iron ore mining (as in Furness), fishing or cockle gathering, or with canal excavation. He might make his winters more tolerable by obtaining work in the repair of the turnpike roads, or his family less poor by sending sons and daughters to work in a country cotton mill.'[218]

The war years saw a dramatic change in the fortunes of English agriculture. Agricultural labour also should have gained, since military recruitment reduced the supply just as the extension of canal-building, coal-mining, the reclaiming of wastes, and rising agricultural output itself all increased the demand. It was said that the harvest which formerly took three weeks could not now be finished in six.[219] Yet real wages in the agricultural areas did not benefit but, on the contrary, fell substantially,[220] and the reason was not wholly the normal time-lag of wages behind food prices during an inflation. For just as in mining the social power of the employer prevented the miner from raising his status, though it could not entirely prevent a rise in his income, so in agriculture – where the discrepancy in the non-economic power between capital and labour was even greater – agricultural labour was prevented from benefiting either in status or in income in the purely agricultural regions. Political repression, including prohibition of all forms of combination, was one method used. The Speenhamland system, which extended the pre-existing system of public subsidy for the war years, was another. It had the advantage, for the squires and farmers, of forcing the general public to contribute to the cost of their harvest labour reserve, and further of preserving the degraded status of the labourer and permitting a rapid scaling-down of costs when prices dropped after the war.[221] On the assumption that the demand for food was not totally inelastic, the artificially low costs of labour may also have helped to keep down unit costs and thus to extend cultivation to marginal lands during the war.

It was after 1815 that the last barriers broke and the agricultural depression ushered in the worst years for labour. These were the years of bitterness and revolt in the countryside,[222] the years of Cobbett's eloquence and of Malthusian argument. Output rose substantially, but both wages and employment, particularly in the winter, fell; industrial by-employment was further curtailed, and gang labour used women and children to replace men, where they were not being replaced by machines. Thus labour remained redundant except for harvest times,[223] and whatever absorption by other occupations occurred was more than counterbalanced by the continuing high rate of population growth. The New Poor Law merely brought into the open, but did not create, rural male unemployment, which could be as high as 60 per cent [224] – though it should be stressed that the Poor Law Commission Report gave a misleading impression of conditions on the land. In agriculture, too, a dual economy had developed, separating out those who had regular employment at subsistence wages, which were not lowered even when the market was depressed by surplus labour, from that surplus labour itself – employed intermittently, paid badly, and living on the mercy of the rates. It was one of the signs of deterioration in 1830–4 that the number of the latter was rising at the expense of the number of the former.[225] It was only the railway-building of the 1840s which seriously began to alter the labour surplus situation, and then only locally, fitfully, and temporarily.[226]

All this was true of the agricultural counties only; in the North there began a period of even faster growth in industry and communications, which stepped up the recruiting from the countryside, pulling agricultural wages up with it. Areas containing expanding collieries did particularly well. The differential between North and South now widened, according to Caird, to 37 per cent overall and 100 per cent in extreme cases; and it was found that in many Northern areas money wages had doubled between 1770 and 1850, while in some Southern areas they had not changed at all.[227] In 1850, labour was 'almost everywhere felt as a burden instead of a benefit to [the] employer' in the South, while in Lancashire 'native labour is so short that the farmers declare they could not get on at all without the aid of the Irish', and in Yorkshire 'the harvest could not be accomplished without the aid of the Irish'.[228] Not only were wages lower in the South: pauperism in 1850 was twice as high over the South as a whole as it was in the North, and several times as high in extreme cases.

It will be seen that the rural South exhibited, right up to the middle of the century, many of the features associated with an under-developed economy.[229] Low wages, low productivity, and overmanning were combined with a 'low wage' philosophy by the employing class. Mobility was fairly high seasonally and over very short distances, and the younger, more active men were drawn permanently from the farms into the towns or its railway building. But the power of ignorance and conservatism on the land, and the power of the landed classes, who wished to retain a labour surplus for the sake of the harvest and for the sake of the wage bargain, prevented any basic adjustment of supply to demand before 1850 (see above, pp. 107–11). In the social reality of the Southern English village, neither a trade union (such as had proved increasingly effective in the towns) nor the more traditional forms of direct protest were within the realm of the possible to allow agricultural workers even to make the most of their poor market opportunities: the prosecutions of 1830 and 1834 were sufficient proof of that. Other factors, too, could be perverted from their economic logic by the overweening control of the proprietors – as in the colliery villages. Thus the policy of limiting the number of cottages and allowing the existing ones to deteriorate was not punished by a falling-off in labour supply or by demands for higher compensatory wages but, on the contrary, led to even greater clamour for the few cottages, to greater overcrowding, and to a willingness to pay even higher rents.[230] Economic laws were not allowed to operate unhindered in the English village until it felt the pull of urban labour markets.

Thus the Southern agricultural labour reservoir, together with the Irish peasantry, undoubtedly forms part of the explanation of the general labour surplus economy in the decades to 1850. But this part was more complex, and less direct, than has often been allowed.

The four industries briefly discussed here were among the largest employers of labour and have been chosen to illustrate some of the main cross-currents of the labour supply. A larger number of examples would have shown still more idiosyncrasies and complexities in the shifts in labour and in labour utilization, set against the background of the ever-widening circles of industrialization and capitalistic employment for an ever-increasing proportion of the population.

The temporary counter-movements and periods of labour shortage in a world of labour surpluses; the geographical barriers to mobility; the extra-economic powers of social control; the irrational results of a joint supply of family labour which might leave the father idle while the children went out to work – these and numerous other instances brought out by a micro-study of single industries are not merely aberrations and frictions, to be ignored on a broad canvas, but are an integral part of the mechanism of British industrialization. In the absence of any exogenous pressure, the industrial revolution in Britain developed naturally and organically, and the availability of resources was therefore among its main determinants. Labour was one such resource, and it was transformed and transferred not by regimenting the old into the new according to some pre-existing master plan and by the shortest route, but as and when it became available, from the nearest, cheapest, and most convenient source, irrespective of whether the move would in the ultimate analysis prove to have been in a retrograde direction. By and large, this erratic, dovetailing, piecemeal kind of industrialization proved to be economical of labour; it eased industrial change, and to that extent it reduced the demand pressure on the labour market.

This need not necessarily mean that the labouring families were spared the drastic social changes known in other countries: probably the changes were as ruthless here as anywhere. It was rather that they were not as purposefully forward-looking to a known goal and reflected the many false starts and blind alleys associated with the pioneer economy. Moreover, they were imposed on an already advanced and complex economic and industrial fabric, and on a society enjoying a fairly high level of incomes, and therefore the movements of labour could be achieved not only by upward changes in the expanding sectors, but also by reductions of wages in the declining ones.[231] All this was in contrast both with more backward economies and with more purposeful later industrializing countries.

V. *Economic and Non-Economic Influences on the Labour Market*

It is time to return to the main outlines of the labour market and to reconsider it in the light of the last section. If we accept, as we must, the view of all observers that in general there was a plentiful labour supply or labour surplus for the period as a whole, and particularly *c.* 1814–50, the apparent difficulty – which all the economists' models were trying to solve in their different ways – is this: How could this easy labour supply be maintained at a time when new industries and occupations were voraciously absorbing labour at unprecedented rates? How did the industrial revolution manage to have its cake and eat it too?

Conventionally, part of the answer has been sought in the massive population increase which accompanied the process of industrialization (see above, pp. 105–8). The British population is estimated to have increased from around 7·4 million in 1750 to 8·9 million in 1781, 10·7 million in 1801, 16·4 million in 1831, and 20·9 million in 1851; the population of Ireland increased at a similarly rapid rate, from 3·1 million to 4·1, 5·2, 7·8, and 6.5 million in the same years respectively, having reached a peak of 8·3 million in the mid-1840s.[232] The total occupied population increased *pari passu*, from 4·8 million in Great Britain in 1801 to 9·7 million in 1851;[233] projected backwards at similar ratios, it must have numbered around 3·3 million in 1750. But the addition of 6·4 million to the occupied population of Great Britain, almost trebling it in a hundred years (or the addition of 5·6 million to the non-agrarian working population (see above, pp. 141–2), almost quadrupling it), does not by itself tell us much about the labour market, for the ratio of hands to mouths remained constant, and there is no reason to assume a drastic change in the ratio of producers to consumers. Changes of significance must be looked for in the variations between labour and the other factors of production, capital, and land; and it is in those terms that classical economics evaluated the effect of a population increase on the labour market. According to some observers, population was increasing too fast for circulating capital and was thus outrunning the supply of cash in the wages fund. In the case of land, diminishing returns brought into operation by the population increase, i.e. more and more people pressing on a virtually unchanging acreage, was alleged to have depressed real wages – though, perversely, it should also have led to an overwhelming demand for labour on the land, which clearly did not take place. Some 'colonizers' thought that there was a relative surplus of both capital and labour, and their solution was to combine both with overseas land; while Marx was outstanding among those who traced the weak bargaining position of labour to a disproportionate growth of capital, associated with a change in its organic and technical composition.

Plainly, there was not then, and there is not now, any agreement about the effect of a long-drawn-out population increase; nor is there much to be said for generalizations such as diminishing returns on land, or increasing returns on machinery, which leave out the vital factor of technological and market changes over time. The changes traced here took place over three generations, and most economic theories have not allowed sufficiently for the inevitable concomitant changes within such a time span. Bearing in mind the differing proportions of factor supplies and the changing technologies in the different industries over such a period, no simple formula can hope to describe them all.

Seen in this light, the large population increase helped to provide an 'abundant' labour supply not so much because there were now more potential workers – for the demand for labour also rose with the population – but because the growth factor eased the transition between one employment and another, which the industrial revolution made necessary. We noted above that because of this factor, only a relatively small exodus of agricultural labourers from the land sufficed to permit a massive and disproportionate increase in employment in industry (see p. 141 above). This applied, on a smaller scale, to every region and to every industry. In view of the erratic and multi-directional changes required, there appeared temporary and localized shortages, solved in part by attractive wage payments; but the overall mobility implied by the growing total labour supply made such effects rarer and weaker than they otherwise would have been. The dovetailing, the switching, and the marching and counter-marching thereby became cheaper and could be engineered mainly by a push, and only rarely by a pull.

Associated with the fact that the population change did not take place in an economic vacuum is a second factor – the fact that economic change itself did not take place in a political and social vacuum. We have seen how powerful this element was in certain special cases, as in Southern agriculture and in coal-mining, but it may also be generalized. First, both the property in the means of production and the economic initiative belonged to the owning classes, and change was, almost by definition, initiated by them and carried through only if it was in their favour. One of the most obvious reactions to a local labour shortage was a labour-saving invention, and in one sense it would be permissible to see the industrial revolution as a series of linked reactions to localized bottlenecks of labour, as well as of land and capital. The protests of skilled labour which was made redundant – or at the least was losing the benefit of its skill in the process – had no influence on the decision-making, though the social costs were real enough. In such cases, labour was defeated by economic attrition as well as by the use of the state's power. Its will to resist was sapped also by emphasizing the stigma that attached to those who opposed 'progress'. The use of social prejudice and social mores in the interests of those who made the economic decisions was, indeed, another important means of weakening the bargaining position of labour. One of the most interesting examples of this was the deliberate change in attitude towards the employment of women, independently and (as it were) in 'public' places, whenever a male labour shortage threatened.[234]

More significant, perhaps, than the broad social and economic powers of the employers was the fact that all these changes necessarily took place at a time when political power also came increasingly to be in the hands of the owning and entrepreneurial classes. The state apparatus of coercion was used, whenever necessary, and whenever economic and social forces alone could not have achieved it, to make sure that there was an overall abundance of labour, so that the market was rigged against labour.

In practice, economic and non-economic pressures could not always be easily separated. Thus the subversion of the traditional concept of mutuality (which involved rights as well as duties) inherent in apprenticeship, particularly the abuse of parish apprenticeship by cotton-mill-owners who employed the children as docile and cheap labour, clearly had elements of both; so had the use of Poor Law agents to procure labour for the cotton mills at times of labour shortage, after the passing of the New Poor Law. And working in the same direction, again, was the taxation system, which taxed the poor more heavily than the rich and transferred much of the resulting revenue to the latter. At times, however, the use of brute legal force clearly predominated. Among the most blatant pieces of class legislation designed to injure the bargaining power of labour were the Combination Acts of 1799 and 1800, the repeal of the justices' power to fix wages in 1813 and of the apprenticeship clauses in 1814, and the Poor Law Amendment Act of 1834.

The New Poor Law has in fact, placed in the hands of wealth a *perfectly despotic power over the labour of the people . . . that law deprives the poor of the Point of Resistance which by enabling the labourer to make terms, imposed a restraint upon employees . . .*

The New Poor Law has placed a screw in the hands of the masters, against which it is impossible for the workmen to bear up. The master, in fine, has the power of saying to the workman, *you must accept such wages as I choose to give*; for if you dare to refuse them, however inadequate or disproportionate to the value of your labour, the *New Poor Law has enacted that you shall starve.*

It is difficult to quarrel with these statements, by the *Standard* and by the *Morning Herald*,[235] as representing a major part of the intentions behind the new law and a considerable part of its effects, whatever the pious sentiments expressed when it was passed. There were numerous other measures passed with similar general tendencies, while many bills with opposite tendencies were rejected. It is not, however, without significance that the legislation of 1799–1800 and 1813–14, which in each case followed a temporary revival of labour organization, was passed without much public outcry, whereas the Poor Law of 1834 came perhaps nearer than any other Act of Parliament in the nineteenth century to provoking a civil war in Britain.

Beyond the actual law to be found in the Statute Books, there was its administration. It might seem surprising that, massively biased as the law was against the wage-earner, there was still need or room for its further misapplication by grossly partial Justices, to remove what protection the poorer citizen enjoyed as a nominal equal before the law, but there was. It is well known that the magistracy in the villages and in the mining districts, when faced with cases of poaching, breaches of contract, pay disputes, and the like, simply used the compulsion of the police power to enforce their selfish prejudices over the claims of other classes and of natural justice; but a glance at the pages of a journal like the *Poor Man's Guardian* will show that conditions were not very different in city magistrates' courts either – or indeed in the higher courts of the land. The staggering successes achieved in the 1840s by W. P. Roberts, the 'Miners' Advocate', in spite of all the odds against him of prejudiced judges, of coalmasters as magistrates, of lack of resources, illness, and overwork, were achieved merely by ensuring from time to time that the law as it stood was actually applied.[236] Similarly, much of the effectiveness of the trade unions at the time was due to their success in using as the thin end of the wedge one of the achievements of the preceding centuries: the fact that laws did not refer to men of property and status and men without, but simply to men, and slowly but inexorably this had to be recognized by the judiciary also as applying to wage-earners.

It is also important, though less easy, to bear in mind the pro-labour legislation that failed to reach the Statute Book, as well as the anti-labour legislation which succeeded. Nothing is more instructive than to trace the fate of the repeated attempts to provide, by legal encouragement, smallholdings for agricultural labourers, which had proved, wherever they were maintained by philanthropic landlords, to be highly beneficial to labourers and to the community. The causes of the failure are perhaps best given in Cobbett's language, describing the fatal opposition he encountered in his parish of Bishops Waltham when he attempted, during the post-war slump, to offer each married labourer an acre of waste land on condition that he would enclose it, cultivate it, and live on it: 'Budd said, that to give the labourers a bit of land would make them "sacy"; Chiddle said, that it would only make them "breed more children"; and Steel said, it would make them demand "higher wages".'[237] The social reality however was that farmers, landlords, and employers had votes, and labourers had not.

It would not be difficult to find other parallels, for example in the history of the factory legislation of that time. Perhaps most interesting is the attempt to deal with the trade unions, which helped to stabilize the labour market and carried out much that the middle classes were constantly urging labour to do for itself (including thrift, insurance, and the creation of self-respect), but which had one fatal flaw: they tended to raise wages. The period can show much legislation and proposed legislation about Savings Banks, Friendly Societies, and similar institutions that could relieve the middle classes of poor rates without strengthening the bargaining position of labour: perhaps the clearest such proposal is that for 'Employment Fund Societies' mooted by the Select Committee on Manufacturers' Employment[238] with precisely those aims in mind, and with the additional promise of a sounder actuarial base than the trade unions could offer. Among the most ingenious, however, must rank the battery of proposals put forward by the 'Society for Bettering the Conditions and Increasing the Comforts of the Poor,' which attempted to improve the lot of the lower-paid without affecting the labour market in their favour. This included the following: reducing the number of pence in the shilling to eight or ten, so that the lower-paid – whose pay was usually reckoned in pence – would obtain an increase in real income without raising prices or affecting other incomes; repeal of the Combination Acts; easing the Settlement Acts and constructing 'convenient movable houses', so that 'it is probable that a perambulatory population would originate, which would transfer itself expeditiously wherever wages rose, and thus keep them at a natural and even price all over the country'; reduction of taxes on food; improvement of hospitals for the aged and infirm; creation of better friendly societies; and the creation of a national system of teachers of domestic economy.[239] Except for the repeal of the Combination Acts over twenty years later, not one of these proposals was put into effect in the following decades, and several were altered in the reverse direction, unfavourably to labour.

Against this, the repeal of the Combination Acts in 1824, as modified in 1825, and the Factory Act of 1833 were the first important legal measures to favour labour's bargaining position. They were the first fruits of the power of labour to organize in new ways in the towns. But there were other causes also. Thus the 1824 repeal is usually represented as having been slipped past an unsuspecting House by a group of Radicals who believed trade unions to be ineffective,[240] and it can be argued that the Act of 1833 owed at least some of its success to the support of the large manufacturers, who wished to abolish some unfair competitive advantage held by the small ones; indeed, it is not impossible that large manufacturers, for the same reasons, may even have supported trade unions.[241] Furthermore, behind all these concessions stood the unreasoning fear of rebellion, on the part of 'the new ruling class of England, those whom late events have made the great men of England', as Edward Gibbon Wakefield wrote in 1833.

Even before the late change [i.e. the Reform Act], while the fears of the great men were urging them to bring about that change, while fires were blazing and mobs exacting higher wages in the south of England, a dread of the political evils likely to come from excessive numbers, induced the English government to form a Board of Emigration, with the avowed purpose of improving the conditions of the labouring class, by removing some of them to the colonies . . . for a country, situated like England . . . in which the subject orders, composing the bulk of the people, are in a state of gloomy discontent arising out of excessive numbers . . . for such a country, one chief end of colonization is to prevent tumults, to keep the peace, to maintain order, to uphold confidence in the security of property, to hinder interruptions of the regular course of industry and trade, to avert the terrible evils which, in a country like England, could not but follow any serious political convulsion.[242]

Nevertheless, the measures of 1824-5 and 1833 reflect above all the beginning of the new response of labour, adapting itself to the new conditions by trade-union association and by political pressure, in order to bend the wage bargain back in its favour.

There had, of course, been trade unions in the eighteenth century, and some even succeeded in surviving and in raising their money wages by strike action in the years of prohibition.[243] But essentially these were unions of exclusive, skilled groups which enjoyed some privileges, often of long standing.[244] The trade unions of employees in mills and mines, in large towns, or on great contracts were then only going through their embryonic stages. Many of their members were still badly educated, communications were poor, experience was lacking, over-enthusiasm was common, the barriers between the skilled and the unskilled were high, and the law was still hostile – frequently penalizing leading unionists, and encouraging others to embezzle the union funds with impunity. The first great peak of enthusiasm for trade unions and the ethos which they represented occurred in the early 1830s, and the unions reached maturity (in the sense of knowing how to play the market and how to secure permanency) only from about 1850 on.

Before 1850, the extent of the power of trade unions to influence wages was extremely uncertain. No doubt unions contributed to the frictions and rigidities of the market, and their role is perhaps best understood if we see it played out against a market which was neither very smooth nor highly responsive. On the contrary, the normal reaction was for pressures to be absorbed by elasticity in the system, by longer (or shorter) hours, by faster work, or by varying the length of the working day for part-time workers. Even in the 1830s, wages – except in cotton – did not move with trade cycles but at most reflected the movements of food prices.[245] The pressure would build up, however, and at some point, a crisis or a labour famine, or (particularly) a combination of both, would break through the barriers and set up new relationships. The trade cycle and earlier fluctuations thus not only shaped the industrial reserve army, as in the Marxian model,[246] but also played a vital part in the adaptation of the labour force, and at such critical points even a weak or ephemeral union might be in a position to influence events.

These were exceptional, even if important, cases. In general, over the period as a whole, the powers of trade unions and of the more traditional forms of rioting and intimidation were pathetically weak compared with the powers of legal coercion, political domination, and social pressure, coupled with the actions of employers' associations, which were used regularly and persistently to the detriment of labour.

Furthermore, a labour contract or wage bargain in which one side sets the conditions and gives the orders, while the other has merely the freedom to refuse to accept the terms but not the freedom to alter them, lends itself particularly to enhancing and snowballing the powers of the employer if he begins with a naturally strong position. The regular employment of women and children was one example of this, where it was induced by under-paying the adult male worker, for the competition of his wife and children was likely to depress his wages still further, and make him even more dependent on the labour of his family. Another example – one lying very near the heart of the complex issue of the adaptation of labour to the new system of working – was the increase in the speed and intensity of work.

The increase in the intensity of work that accompanied the industrial revolution did not necessarily mean that people worked 'harder' at any given task, though that might be included in the term; it might merely mean that they rested less between exertions, or had the job planned out so that its inherent rest periods or variations were eliminated. It is clear that in Adam Smith's classic example of a pin factory a vast increase in output was achieved very largely by keeping each worker at one constant, repetitive, high-speed task instead of allowing him the more leisurely method of moving between several tasks. In this some energy was no doubt wasted, but mental and physical recuperation were insensibly incorporated in the process also. This speed-up, described in *The Wealth of Nations*, was described from life[247] and was more typical in many industries, particularly before 1800, than the more spectacular introduction of complex machinery. Greater intensity often also included longer hours or fewer rest days. Like the employment of women and children, its introduction – by increasing, as it were, the labour supply while holding everything else constant, including the total wage bill – at the same time helped to lower wage costs in the future by weakening the labourer's bargaining position, so that a further increase in intensity became easier to enforce on the next occasion.

This was perhaps clearest in the case of the hand-loom weavers, as competition, first by the influx of new men and then by the spread of steam looms, drove down wages.[248] When the weavers were collected into hand-loom or 'dandy-loom' weavers' sheds in the 1830s and 1840s, the masters 'could control holidays and other absence from work and could enforce regular habits and prompt schedules'.[249] In the 1790s, Aikin had observed the Halifax weavers and had concluded that 'it appears evident, that the same number of hands regularly employed, will do more work by one third than when they depend on casual employ. One day in six is always lost to the head of a family by attending the mill, and another by attendance at the market.'[250] Fifty years later, by cutting out all other forms of lost time, the unremitting toil of weavers in supervised sheds allowed the masters to see that their output was doubled.

In turn, machine-loom working was markedly speeded up, from 7

pieces a week by one girl in 1823 to 20 pieces a week by two girls in
1833, and 22 in 1845 – the earlier two-loom working giving place to
three-loom and four-loom working at the same time.[251] There is no
suggestion here of a new technology which would have made labour
per loom any easier.

A similar process took place in spinning. The mule spinner, for
example, who walked 8 miles a day in 1815 walked 20 miles in 1832,
and even further – up to fourteen to thirty-two miles – in 1844, in spite
of the shorter hours. This was in part because 'since 1825, when Sir
John Hobhouse brought in his bill . . . the speed in cotton machinery
generally has been increasing, to speak within compass, one-fourth, or,
in other words, equivalent to an additional labour of three hours a
day'.[252] While the speed increased, so did the number of spindles
supervised by one person: from the 300 on each of a pair of mules, it had
risen by the early 1840s to 600, 1,000, and even 1,344. One man was
alleged to have worked 3,360 spindles, and another 2,400. 'It is said',
commented Dodd, 'that working these frames will break the strongest
constitution in six years.'[253]

Comparison with even the most advanced countries on the Continent
showed to what extent, at every stage, the exertions called forth by the
industrial revolution exceeded those of an earlier system. 'To reach
Manchester efficiency [in cotton-spinning] in Swiss factories', one Swiss
observer noted sadly in 1814, 'we should have to sack all our operatives and train up a new generation of apprentices.'[254] Even the
Belgians, working in the most advanced country on the Continent,
could not match the British cotton workers:

The energy of our operatives, the quickness of their hands, the heart-and-soul
interest which they take in the work they see about while they *are* about it (or
in other words, the quantity of work which their almost *ferocious* industry
can turn out in a given time) more than compensates the capitalist manufacturer for the superior wages *per day* which he gives. . . . It may be doubted
if that vigorous activity which characterises the English workman above *all
others* is to be found here [in Belgium].

Comparing the work of a British with a foreign [cotton-]spinner, the
average number of persons employed to spindles is – in France, one person to
fourteen spindles; in Russia, one to twenty-eight spindles; in Prussia, one to
thirty-seven; in Great Britain, one to seventy-four.[255]

Of course, it had taken time to reach that position; and 'even among
British manufacturers, confessedly the most industrious labourers in
Europe, those who work in their own houses are comparatively idle
and irregular, and yet they work under the stimulus of certain and
immediate gain'.[256] Conversely, within a few decades, Continental

factory workers would be induced to work at the same obsessive speed as the British.

Equally striking was the testimony of the railway engineers, who compared the prodigious efforts put in by the British navvies on the early railway lines constructed in France, with the much slower work of the native French, moving only a third or a quarter as much earth in a day as the British. But within a few years their exertion and their wages equalled those of the British. The same experience was met with in other countries.[257]

Similar examples may be found in all the other major sectors of the economy. In the traditional mining industries of Cornwall, work was intensified gradually by cutting out holidays, drinking days, and sports, by reducing the time wasted between shifts, and by abolishing 'St Mondays' or other off-days traditionally used to compensate for particularly heavy work. The Bank of England closed on forty-seven holidays in 1761. This was steadily and systematically reduced to eighteen in 1830 and a mere four in 1834: Good Friday, Christmas Day, the first of May, and the first of November. In retailing (as in many other industries) it was the opportunity provided by gas lighting which led to late opening and the consequent intensification of the assistants' labour; indeed, the role of improved lighting in lengthening the working day and allowing the employer to impose his control over the formerly predominant demands of the natural day and the seasons has not yet been fully acknowledged. Even in agriculture, it was alleged, the inducement of piecework payments could reduce the costs of excavating a trench from 8d. to 4d. a cubic yard in two years, and could increase the speed of harvesting threefold, though the corn might be badly hacked down in the process; and in the new circumstances farmers themselves 'have been obliged to be more industrious, and do the greater part of the labour themselves'.[258]

The same process even took place in traditional crafts which apparently underwent no technical change. The speed-up involved in new domestic building has been noted above (p. 134). The London coopers were obliged to work with more difficult materials at the old rates. And the London 'slop-work' shops, the 'slaughterhouses', employing non-union and partly skilled labour to produce at lowest prices, forced sections of the formerly highly regarded crafts of tailors, dressmakers, and milliners to work sixteen hours a day, seven days a week, and reduced, among cabinet-makers, the wage costs of 100 tables from 30s. to 5s., and the wage costs of mahogany desks from 10s. to 2s. 3d. a unit.[259]

Piecework, subcontract, the 'butty' system, and specialization – the latter often involving the subdivision of skills and the killing of the

joy of work – were all designed, in different ways, to increase speeds
or to intensify work in other respects. The piecework system, according to McCulloch,

gives the workmen an interest in being industrious, and makes them exert
themselves to execute the greatest quantity of work in the least space of time.
And, in consequence of its prevalence, this practice materially influences even
the day labourers; who, to avoid invidious comparisons, make exertions
unknown in other countries. Hence, a given number of hands in Great
Britain perform much more than is executed by the same number of hands
almost anywhere else.[260]

A less favourable view of the same phenomenon notes that

when liberally paid by the piece, [workmen] are tempted to overwork themselves, and to ruin their health and constitution in a few years. This is the case
of porters, coalheavers and many common labourers in London. A carpenter
is not supposed to last in his utmost vigour above eight years. The double
wages paid to country labourers during harvest, or to tailors during a general
mourning, are frequent sources of permanent injury, from the inducement
they offer to over-exertion.[261]

But in one respect McCulloch was surely right. The intensification
of work might have many particular reasons and points of origin; but
it was something which communicated itself, and became the norm,
through the whole of society. In a generalized way, it changed the
attitude of the worker to his job and that of the employer to his hands.
It represented a form of inner colonization, a way of drawing forth
labour whose existence had not been suspected – labour, moreover, that
was paid either at cut rates or not at all. It was a factor of production
that escaped the orthodox economists, though it was grasped by Marx
in his concept of 'absolute surplus value'. Yet it was a major factor in
filling the demand for labour in the industrial revolution without
driving up its price.

Beyond a certain point, the intensification of work was likely to
become a self-defeating process. If hours were lengthened and the
effort of each hour increased, there would come a point when real
wages would have to be raised to allow the worker to feed better, or
one or other of the two processes would have to be put in reverse.
Some examples of each course of action can be found, but in the end
the main change of the second half of the nineteenth century was to
keep the exertion at the new high level, but to reduce hours and raise
wages. In many cases, the reduction in hours was directly linked with
the speed-up.[262] This solution appeared to satisfy best both the needs of
capital, which began to find long hours increasingly uneconomic as it
had earlier found night work increasingly uneconomic with improved

technology and greater intensity of work, and the aspirations of labour, which reached out not merely for a higher income but for more leisure, now that its work had been turned into alienated drudgery.

The general reduction in hours of work, following their earlier extension to the humanly tolerable peak, began in some industries as early as the 1830s and was driven forward by the actions of both trade unions and factory inspectors. It reached different industries at different times, but it was everywhere a vital change affecting both the labour market and the quality of life for the majority of the population. It was, perhaps, the key to Victorian social history; but it should not be forgotten that, in origin, it was largely the consequence of the earlier intensification of labour.

Finally, a fourth factor might be mentioned which, in a generally unfavourable environment, contributed to weakening labour still further at times when it was weak, and reduced its bargaining power even at times when market conditions were in its favour. This factor is the disproportionate influence of the marginal unit, during the temporary conditions at the peak of the boom or at the worst trough of a slump, in a mobile and fluctuating market.

Thus in the French wars only the money wages of powerfully (and illegally) organized skilled trades rose to anything like the extent of the price level. The majority of workers found it impossible to enforce actively the substantial money-wage increases required to keep to the same real standards; and even if the market was in their favour, the Combination Acts and the repeal of legal protection in 1813–14 made it impossible for them to exploit that situation.[263] The resulting drop in real wages, to which workers had become accustomed in such sectors as agriculture, then persisted in many regions after the war, when heavy unemployment permitted employers to take the active step of *cutting* money wages in line with prices. This was the period in which Robert Owen recalled men begging for work at wages which he knew could not possible maintain them.[264] Again, in 1834–6, the great boom attracted much labour into the cotton-spinning mills and weaving sheds, while a real bottleneck developed in the supply of building labour, leading to mass absorption of labour there too. When the boom broke, this additional labour was stranded and helped to weaken labour's eroded bargaining position still further.[265]

This could be generalized: in booms, the better-off and privileged sections of labour were disarmed by massive absorptions of labour which at such times they were generally unable to prevent, while the underprivileged areas were not in a position to benefit fully from either the boom or the loss of labour; in slack times they were then both weakened and unable to resist dilution and wage cuts.[266] This sequence was broken only towards the middle of the century, when more comprehensive and national union organization, as well as the unprecedented demands of railway building,[267] began to differentiate the fate of different groups more permanently. The hitherto temporary loss of control by the stronger groups thus tended to have permanent consequences.

However, where the system worked the other way – where secular, cyclical, or technological factors might all combine at critical points to favour labour and thus to raise its rewards with similar, potentially more widespread effects – there was one final mechanism, in addition to all the social and political measures wielded against labour, to prevent its operation: the Irish immigrant. The range of occupations open to the Irish, particularly the first-generation immigrants, was in fact extremely limited, but it included occupations at the peak of their demand, with potential long-term effects on the whole wage level, like hand-loom weaving in the 1790s or railway work in the 1840s;[268] and these peaks were cut off either by the Irish themselves or by workers freed from their former jobs by Irish replacements. The addition to the labour force did not have to be very large at a critical point in time to act as the marginal unit and reduce the peak wage level, and with it the accepted level for years to come; and sometimes even the mere threat of the mobile Irish (or Highland) reserve might be enough to have the same effect.

The effect of the Irish in depressing British wage levels also worked in several other ways. By subsisting in overcrowded cellars or lodging-houses on a potato diet they lowered the accepted minimum subsistence level, and with it the whole spectrum of wages fanning out from it, and in fact taught the English labourer 'how to live upon a lower scale of diet, and of household comfort, than he was wont to do'.[269] As the recipients of charity, both privately and through the Poor Law, they reduced the funds available to English paupers and, above all, reduced the standards which it was thought fit to impose on the native poor. In the Northern towns, in particular, a scale that could be considered 'less eligible' than the standards of an Irish family at work represented a drastic cut in standards indeed. Finally, the Irish, by being mobile, prevented the emergence of local and temporary shortages and bottlenecks which could have raised the long-term accepted, and expected, wage levels.

The list is by no means exhaustive. But it covers the main factors which ensured that in spite of a high and rising demand for labour from industry, in spite of innumerable local and temporary bottlenecks in the labour supply, and in spite of great increases in the exertions of labour and in the value of the marginal product of labour, the general character of the labour market was that of surplus or at least of easy supply conditions.

VI. *Changes in the Standard of Living*

It now remains to see how far the share of labour in the total product changed as a result of these diverse influences, and how workers were affected as consumers in absolute terms. Unfortunately, no overall estimates of incomes and income shares are possible, even at the modest degree of accuracy of those available for the later decades in the century, and the partial information available has proved difficult to interpret.

It is generally agreed that total national income per head increased substantially in the period 1750–1850; it is also beyond dispute that the relative share of labour fell. A recent calculation concluded that a substantial share of national income, between 6 and 14 per cent, was transferred from labour to capital between 1790 and 1850 – assuming that in 1850 some 40 per cent of the national income was paid in wages.[270] Few indices are quite as striking in this period as the stagnation in *per capita* food consumption[271] and the increase in the numbers of domestic servants. What is not clear is whether the smaller share of a larger total represents an absolute rise or fall; nor is it clear how to evaluate a variety of non-pecuniary rewards and conditions, or how far to take them into account.

It may be granted that the standards of consumption of the lower-income-earners rose up to the 1760s or perhaps the 1770s, and that they began to rise sharply again towards the end of the 1840s. It is the years between, consisting of two periods separated by over twenty years of war, which are uncertain.[272] We have seen what complex internal adjustments of labour to the market were necessary in those years, and while many were achieved by means other than the purely economic one of differential payment, these clearly played a vital part. We would therefore expect different groups to have widely differing experiences. Thus it may be stated with confidence that those who moved from agriculture into manufacturing, mining, or transport improved their position, and so, to a lesser extent, did those who stayed in agriculture in the growth areas; but agricultural labour in rural districts was worse off at the end than at the beginning of the period. In any case, cheap coal gave some comforts to the poorer homes in the North and West which were lacking in the traditional wheat areas. Domestic workers who transferred to the factory raised their earnings;

those competing with factories had them reduced. Craftsmen in new skills, or those in increasing demand, raised their wage levels; those displaced by machines or forced into sweatshops, into manufactories, or into mass production lost out.[273] Labourers who felt at home in the changing, new, ruthless, competitive world might rise to become employers; but traditionalists among independent craftsmen could sink down to the proletariat. Taxation, if anything, took even more from the poor to give to the rich after 1815 than before 1793.

It is also certain that those whose wages went up worked much harder at the end of the period than at the beginning. Further, it is at least probable that women and children, by transferring from largely domestic to largely public employment, also worked much harder, and that the higher family money incomes, where indeed they were found at all, were generally achieved because of their work. The factories multiplied the social costs of the child work which had always existed, while they removed its positive aspects. Disguised unemployment – which before industrialization had often been, from the worker's point of view, simply a more leisurely way of life,[274] – now gave way to sharp bouts of massive and involuntary unemployment, which carries no compensations. Such years as 1816–19, 1826–7, 1830–1 and 1839–43, with their increasingly pervasive crises,[275] substantially weakened labour's general bargaining power and contributed to the need to send wives and children to work. The numbers and proportion of casual, inferior, and rootless labour of the kind found mainly in the cities (and merging into the criminal classes) certainly also increased. Again, nominally higher wages were often reduced by truck and by other chicanery.

Added to this were the problems of accepting the new work discipline and the new urban conditions of living, both of which were felt to be catastrophic declines from previous experiences. The valuation of urban amenities is a subjective matter, and their decline has been disputed; but statistics show beyond doubt that the state of the new towns appreciably shortened the life expectancy of those affected and increased their physical debility during those shorter years. Wherever comparisons can be made – either over time in any one city, or between industrial towns and the rest of the community at any one time – staggering differences in life expectancy appear, amounting in the worst decades to an average of twenty years of life expectancy lost by the average male urban wage-earner; and whatever horrors the English statistics showed, the Scottish were invariably even worse.[276] Nor is this surprising when we read the hair-raising accounts of housing and sanitary conditions which became the rule in London and the major towns, and which even today sicken and dismay the reader. If there had been slums before, the industrial revolution multiplied them, both absolutely and as a proportion of the total.[277]

Conditions within the factories have also been disputed, and there are those who today believe the defensive statements of the factory-owners, and of those who were financially dependent on them, to the effect that work in factories was carried out in pleasant and healthy or at least tolerable conditions. But again, measurements of air-space, and indeed the very buildings, survive and stir the imagination. And among those who had no axe to grind and who saw the mills and mines for the first time before they had time to become gradually inured to them, the horror was genuine and intelligible.[278] It was significant that at first only the riff-raff, the paupers, the displaced Highlanders and discharged soldiers went into the factories; and even later, many entered only as a last resort. As the first generation of the new proletariat was alienated from work and the family-based community, it sought solace in drink or in millennial religion, both of which made it harder for them to stand up to the new conditions by new methods. The confusion of movements in different directions within the labour market itself inhibited organization and solidarity, which, to be successful, require at least the feeling of a common destiny and firm roots in one milieu or another.

It took a generation – which was a lifetime in industrial Britain – to learn how to deal with industrialism, but in due course it was done. Workers learnt by bitter experience,[279] and after experimenting with all kinds of organization they ultimately evolved the most viable types of trade union.[280] New forms of mass agitation achieved some protective legislation. Hours began to be reduced, by Act of Parliament and by union power, so that the twelve-hour day became common in the 1820s, the eleven-hour day in the 1840s, and the ten-hour day thereafter.[281] Men came to accept the factory discipline; children were taught new skills; housewives learnt to make the best of urban shopping and cooking facilities.[282] Education, introduced in order to improve obedience, also promoted independent thought. Labour not only learnt the 'rules of the game' of capitalist society: it also helped to make its own rules. Town life and industrial change ultimately provided greater intellectual stimulus than rural or small-town life, or even the traditional crafts. The 'fork grinders of Sheffield . . . always confined to the same locality, following a dangerous occupation from boyhood to the grave, in the same slough of local interest, prejudice and passion, bear but a slight moral resemblance to the men of the engineering, building and other trades who are associated in their tens of thousands, who pass continually from shop to shop and from town to town, acquiring information by experience, and rubbing off or lessening stupid prejudices and personal animosity by constant contact with fresh faces, new ideas, and altered conditions of life'.[283]

The course of wages during the industrial revolution is uncertain. It is doubtful if real wages as a whole increased; and if they did, this gain had to be paid for by longer hours, by more intensive work, and by changes – generally felt to be for the worse – in working conditions. Our uncertainty stems largely from the fact that the movement was not all one way, but that, on the contrary, it reflected contradictory experiences of different groups of workers, in an expanding, industrial capitalism progressing by uneven development in what has recently been aptly called a 'syncopated' process.[284]

The observations of contemporaries were therefore correct. Throughout a period of nearly a century, wages remained somewhere near a level which had come to be accepted as subsistence. This betokens an economy operating essentially in conditions of abundant labour, and it is clear that an elastic labour supply at low cost and a transfer of income from labour to capital were two basic features of the British industrial revolution. This was a remarkable phenomenon in view of the vast expansion in the demand for labour and in output per head, which required massive, repeated, and complex internal shifts of labour. The labour market was rigged in such a way as to allow the labour supply to react sensitively to detailed attractions and repulsions while remaining in a state of overabundance as a whole. It was only when labour found its feet, in the second half of the nineteenth century, that a true labour market – one in which the supplier had at least a semblance of power – began slowly to emerge.

VII. *The Century since 1850*

About the middle of the nineteenth century there occurred a significant change in the development of the labour market in Britain. In the nature of things, no exact dating is possible, but the change was well on its way in the boom of 1845–6 and was largely completed in the boom years to 1857. Briefly, and in a greatly simplified way, it could be characterized as a change from a situation in which real wages remained constant, thus representing a falling share of a rising national income, into an economic system in which real wages rose in step with national income, thus remaining a constant share of a steadily rising total.

In superficial terms, it is not hard to see why this should have been so. An elementary model may make the basic difference clear. Suppose an economy using traditional methods in which a single major invention reduces the labour costs of making a certain product – say cotton yarn – by 90 per cent, thereby cutting total costs, including enlarged capital and other costs, by one-half. Three extreme solutions for dealing with the new situation may be imagined: (*a*) prices to the buyers of yarn (and therefore quantities produced) are left unchanged, entrepreneurs take the same profit rate as before, and all the benefits go to labour in higher wages; (*b*) prices to buyers (and quantities sold) remain constant as before, wages remain unchanged, and entrepreneurs pocket all the cost savings; or (*c*) the remuneration rates of factors of production remain the same, but selling prices are cut by fully one-half on (presumably) increased sales. Each of these improbable positions could be envisaged as the point of a triangle within which the actual solution must lie.[285] The problem is to find the actual locus of the distribution in relation to the three reference points.

Solution '*a*' is clearly the most unlikely. It is difficult to see why entrepreneurs should go to the trouble of venturing more capital and new methods without benefit to themselves; it is still more difficult to see how labour, hard pressed by the redundancies arising from the innovation, could hold its wage rates, let alone increase them, while everyone else was being sent away empty-handed. Solution '*b*' is somewhat more plausible. Certainly, unless we assume unlimited supplies of capital, the greater demand for capital will raise its price, if only slightly, to tempt resources away from hoards, from other uses, or from consumption. If a monopoly in the new method exists, say by the grant of a patent, solution '*b*' might be approached quite closely. Otherwise it will exert some pull, but not much.

In a competitive world, solution '*c*' will be the most powerful magnet, leading at once to sharp price reductions to the public, quickly followed by increases in quantities produced – increases which, depending on elasticities, may absorb part, or all, or even more than the total of the labour made redundant by the new device. This, in turn, will require much new capital, which may lead to an increase in its price and a move away from solution '*c*'. In a society with the features of eighteenth-century Britain, the upshot will be a point very near (*c*) – i.e. a sharp reduction in cotton yarn prices – but swinging to the (*b*)–(*c*) side, well away from the (*a*) apex of the triangle. The effects on real wages will be small; if, as in the case of cotton, the major portion of the output is exported, the contribution of lower cotton yarn prices to real wages will be negligible and may well (as the early cotton inventions did) benefit the foreign consumer of British exports much more than the workers in the cotton industry.

Now suppose a similar invention, not as an isolated event, but as part

of a stream of such cost-reducing innovations, including both capital-
and labour-saving examples, impacting upon a dynamic world in
constant process of adjusting to, but never quite catching up with,
earlier and similar disturbances. Competition will still tend to drive the
market towards the (c) apex, but in the supplies both of labour and of
capital each industry will have to meet the opportunity cost of other
progressing industries if it is to attract any additional quantities. In the
case of labour, there is now no longer an 'unlimited supply' available
outside the system; and since there is no reason to suppose that the flow
of innovation will affect the overall level of employment as such,
industries reducing costs in high-elasticity markets will have to attract
labour away from industries in which there are no cost-reducing
innovations, or in which reductions in labour cost lead to less-than-
proportionate increases in demand. In the case of capital, the nearer the
market had been to (b) in an earlier phase, the higher the capital
accumulation, and therefore the more effective the weakening of the
magnetic powers of point (b) in the following phase. But the general
tendency of drifting to (c) – i.e. the real cost reductions to consumers –
will now automatically raise real wages, unless the market is driven
even further away from point (a) than before. A constant location of
the market point over time will mean that labour shares fully in the
growth of national income by way of reductions in costs.

If we now introduce some of the complications of the real world,
and take the watershed around 1850 in Britain to represent in principle
a transition from a situation approximating to the first model to one
more akin to the second, it will be seen that the major differences
between two periods are: (i) an end of a totally elastic labour supply
from outside the system; (ii) a powerful force, outside the labour
market itself, raising real wages 'automatically' via real cost reductions;
and (iii) probably an easier supply of capital, reducing the chances of a
continued one-sided gain by capital. Further complications may easily
be introduced in the interest of greater realism: we may postulate
changes in the value of money, so that higher real wages have to be
fought for in terms of higher money wages rather than accruing at
constant money wages simply by falling prices; or we may investigate
the complex process by which wages in industries without technical
progress, or in those suffering reductions in demand, are kept fairly but
not wholly in step with wages in the favoured industries showing
drastic cost reductions or increases in demand. In our model the market
point may be located anywhere within the triangle, depending on
innumerable complex factors.

In point of fact, a large proportion of the economic literature published in the past century has been concerned with precisely this ques-

tion of its location. It is a debate into which we cannot enter here except to note that – in contrast with the presumptions on the phase of industrialization up to 1850, which were remarkably uniform among economists to the point of unanimity – there has been no agreement regarding the phase after *c.* 1850, covering the mature industrialized economy. Different theories have assumed wages to have formed a rising, constant, falling, or variable share of the national product, and real wages in the absolute sense to have taken an equally erratic course. Moreover, the concept of real wages, still more that of wages as a share of GNP, is itself a highly dubious one. For apart from the universal problem of defining 'real wages' and 'average wages' or earnings, particularly for a working force of changing composition, there is – as the economic structure redefined itself as mainly one of employers and employees – the additional difficulty of the changing ratio of wage-earners to all income-earners. In the phase of industrialization itself, the proportion of wage-earners in the population increased at the expense of peasants, independent handicraftsmen, and others. But in the mature economy the proportion fell, particularly in the last fifty years, when there occurred a dramatic rise in the numbers of white-collar workers, professional people, and other salary-earners.[286] If, say, in a given period the proportion of wage-earners among all occupied had fallen from 75 per cent to 60 per cent – a fall of one-fifth – and wages had fallen similarly by one-fifth from 40 per cent of all incomes to 32 per cent, would this constitute a proportional fall in wages, a constant share, or even a rise, in view of the fact that those promoted upwards into the salariat had been the better-paid section and that the remainder might have been expected to earn lower wages on average?

Bearing in mind the wide range of uncertainties, and the substantial increase in GNP and in GNP per head over this period, the stability of the share of wages shown by the available statistics is truly remarkable, as is the ratio of the wage levels to other income levels. In view of the ambiguities, no single indicator of these ratios would be adequate, and we therefore reproduce three of the most commonly used ratios here.

The simplest is the share of annual wage incomes in total incomes. Most wage statistics for the pre-1914 years are based on the work of A. L. Bowley, whose definition of wages excluded all salaries except those paid to shop assistants. The national income figures are those of Prest.[287] Various minor adjustments may be made to link the pre-1914 series with those of the war years and after. Table 35 is based on the series computed by Brown and Hart in 1952.

Although the annual figures show somewhat greater variations than the five-year averages, the extremes being a peak of 42·7 (1893) and a trough of 36·6 (1913), it is still evident that Keynes was right to stress that 'the stability of the proportion of the national dividend accruing to labour, irrespective . . . of the level of putput as a whole and of the phase of the trade cycle . . . is one of the most surprising, yet best-established, facts in the whole range of economic statistics, both for Great Britain and for the United States', and to reflect that 'the result

Table 35. *Shares of Wages and Wage-Earners, 1870–1950*

Annual averages	Wages as percentage of national income	Wage-earners as percentage of occupied population
1870–4	40·7	83·7
1875–9	41·5	82·7
1880–4	40·0	81·7
1885–9	40·1	80·8
1890–4	41·9	79·7
1895–9	40·7	78·7
1900–4	40·3	77·5
1905–9	38·0	75·9
1910–13	37·3	74·6
1924–9	41·1	72·7
1930–4	41·2	72·1
1935–9	39·4	71·6^a
1940–4	38·9	—
1945–50	41·3	66·3^b

^{a} Average 1935–8.
^{b} Provisional figures for 1948–50.

SOURCE. E. H. Phelps Brown and P. E. Hart, 'The Share of Wages in National Income', *Economic Journal*, LXII (1962), pp. 276–7, Table 1, Appendix.

remains a bit of a miracle'.[288] Bowley, who was equally struck by this stability, was led to the conclusion that 'the constancy of so many of the proportions and rates of movement . . . seems to point to a fixed system of causation and has the appearance of inevitableness'.[289]

It should be borne in mind that wage proportions vary greatly among different industries,[290] so that there must have been an uncanny compensatory industrial redistribution to arrive at such constancy. But what is perhaps even more 'miraculous' is that this stable share was paid to wage-earners, who formed a steadily declining proportion of the population and who therefore appeared to receive an increasing portion of the national dividend *per head* while taking a similar portion *as a group*. Clearly, the stability of around 40 per cent for wages depended in part on definitions of the terms 'wages' and 'salaries', and if a stable functional relationship is considered remarkable, this kind of stability

– which must be the result of compensatory movements, with fewer people receiving relatively more per head – is even more noteworthy.[291]

The share of 'income-earners' as a whole, far from remaining stable, was in fact rising sharply throughout this period at the expense both of rents and of profits and interest, as is shown in Table 36. The rising elements were salaries and employers' statutory insurance contributions.

Table 36. *Distribution of Total National Income and GNP, 1860–1968 (per cent)*

	Share of national income			Share of GNP			
Average for decade	Wages and salaries	Rents	Profits, interest, and mixed incomes	Wages	Forces' pay	Employers' contributions	Salaries
1860–9	48·5	13·7	38·9	38·7	—	—	6·5
1870–9	48·7	13·1	38·2	38·9	—	—	6·3
1880–9	48·2	14·0	37·9	38·6	—	—	7·6
1890–9	49·8	12·0	38·2	39·5	—	—	8·5
1900–9	48·4	11·4	40·2	38·0	—	—	9·7
1910–14	—	—	—	34·5	2·0	—	10·8
1920–9	59·7	6·6	33·7	38·0	1·7[a]	2·0[a]	16·6[a]
1930–9	62·0	8·7	29·2	37·4[b]	1·5[b]	2·5[b]	18·1[b]
1940–9	68·8	4·9	26·3	39·3[c]	3·6[c]	3·3[c]	19·1[c]
1950–9	72·4	4·9	22·7	39·3	2·1	4·2	20·6
1960–8	74·1	5·4	20·5	37·8[d]	1·6[d]	4·9[d]	23·1[d]

[a] 1921–9.
[b] 1930–8.
[c] 1946–9.
[d] 1960–3.

SOURCES

National income. Feinstein, 'Changes in the Distribution of National Income', in Marchal and Ducros (eds.), *Distribution of the National Income* (1968), based on Table 2, p. 119.
GNP. Deane and Cole, *British Economic Growth*, 245 and 247; for 1960 onwards, *National Income and Expenditure* (annual).

Although it might appear at first sight that labour alone also gained, since it formed a falling proportion of earners obtaining a stable share, this conclusion might well be misleading. For one thing, the additional non-wage-earners in the population consisted to a substantial extent of traditionally low-paid groups,[292] such as female clerks; and for another, a large proportion of the 'salaried' people were identical with the owners and partners of earlier decades, before the spread of the joint-stock form of organizing, whose income would then have come under the category of profit and interest. Even though, as Table 37 shows, there appears to have been a substantial shift of incomes from 'property' to 'labour' during the two world wars (the peacetime years between showing remarkable stability), it is not clear how much of this arose from an actual transfer and how much from a change in classification.

Table 37. *Distribution of GDP (per cent)*

	Labour	Property
1910–14	60·2	39·8
1921–4	70·6	29·4
1935–8	70·0	30·0
1946–9	74·3	25·7
1960–3	74·5	25·5

SOURCE. Feinstein, 'Changes in the Distribution of National Income', Table 5, p. 126.

It was to isolate this factor of numbers that Brown and Browne developed an elaborate alternative set of measurements for the share of labour in the British economy, as well as in four other economies. This measure, called the wage–income ratio, compares the total incomes of those employed with total incomes within industry – i.e. (generally) mining, manufacturing, transport, public utilities, and construction (see Table 38). Other sectors have been omitted because of the high

Table 38. *Wage–Income Ratios (annual averages)*

1871–4	61	1905–9	66
1875–9	70	1910–13	65
1880–4	71	1924–9	70
1885–9	72	1930–4	72
1890–4	70	1935–8	64
1895–9	65	1949–54	78
1900–4	64	1955–9	81

proportion of self-employed persons, for whom the wage element cannot be isolated. Although there are some exceptional years, such as 1873 (ratio = 54 per cent) and 1879 (79 per cent), the wage/income ratio, thus defined, remained remarkably stable over long periods, though it showed a substantial shift after the Second World War.[293]

Brown and Browne explain this long-term stability, both in Britain and in the other countries studied, in part by the stability of the other elements in the national income. Given the identity $S \equiv 1 - rk$, where S is the share of labour in the product, r the rate of profit, and k the capital–output ratio,[294] a profit rate of around 10 per cent and a capital–output ratio of 2·5 will produce a wage–income ratio of around 0·75, as $1 - (0 \cdot 10 \times 2 \cdot 5) = 0 \cdot 75$. However, it is not clear why the other two elements should be stable or move in a compensating way in the long period.

A third type of measure has been developed out of the Cobb–Douglas function and relates wages and salaries to total value added in manufacturing. By this measure also, though the ratios between different industries vary widely, the ratios for developed countries jointly and severally have stayed remarkably stable at 50 per cent over long periods.[295]

In the century of so since 1850 the national product, absolutely and per head, has multiplied several times over; and in that growth, drastic changes in the structure of industry and of the economy have taken place. Yet throughout that period wages, far from hovering around subsistence or any other fixed level, have clung like leeches to the upward curve of the national product, giving labour a closely proportionate share of the increase.

The result can be seen in the increase in real wages over the same period, shown in Table 39. These averages hide a multitude of relative internal changes, between industries, between occupations, and

Table 39. Index of Real Wages

Average of years	Average wages (not allowing for unemployment): Wood (1850 = 100)	Wages: Bowley (1914 = 100)	Average weekly real earnings of adult males in manufacturing: Min. of Labour (1958 = 100)	Approximate continuous series (1850 = 100)
1850–9	100	—	—	100
1860–9	111	—	—	111
1870–9	130	—	—	130
1880–9	146	—	—	146
1890–9	171	—	—	171
1900–9	196	100	—	196
1910–14	—	98	—	193
1924–9	—	115	—	225
1930–9	—	129[a]	66·2	253
1940–9	—	—	85·6	327
1950–9	—	—	93·9	359
1960–6	—	—	119·7	457

[a] 1930–6.

SOURCES. Based on Mitchell and Deane, *Abstract of British Historical Statistics* (1962), 343–5; London and Cambridge Economic Service and *The Times*, 'The British Economy: Key Statistics, 1902–1966', Table E.

between levels of skills. In the second half of the nineteenth century, the position of the labour 'aristocracy' was being strengthened very substantially in a number of major industries;[296] while in several of the same industries, the contrast with unskilled labourers and helpers increased, and there are indications that the gap between them may have widened.[297] Certainly, the remarkable similarity of a figure of around 30 per cent of the population (or, say, 40 per cent of the working-class population) living in poverty in widely different communities of London, York, and four provincial towns respectively in *c.* 1890, 1900, and 1912–13 – as found by Booth, Rowntree, Bowley, and their collaborators [298] – points to a widening gap between that submerged section and those in receipt of regular wages; though even here the uniformity is deceptive, the poverty being caused in varying proportions by unemployment, casual work, low pay, or the incapacity or death of the male breadwinner.

Yet, bearing in mind the complexities and uncertainties of definition, it is significant that the ratios of labourers' wages to those of the craftsmen they served in five major industries remained fairly constant between 1886 and 1913, averaging 60 per cent in the first year and 58·5 per cent in the last.[299] For the period since then, more detailed data exist, and they show the same noteworthy stability of the ratio:[300]

	1906	1960
Median earnings of unskilled as % of foremen and skilled (6 industries)	61·9	61·9
Median earnings of semi-skilled as % of foremen and skilled (5 industries)	75·7	73·3

Again, this represents not a simple immobility but the compensatory result of diverse movements in diverse directions. In particular, the two wars saw a substantial improvement in the relative position of the lower-paid, partly because over-full employment benefited them relatively more, partly because their particular form of machine-minding labour was in greatest demand, and partly, perhaps, because flat-rate wage increases favoured them marginally; yet it should be noted that the unskilled also gained in 1935–9, when heavy unemployment should have worked against them.[301] In the years after the wars and the post-war booms, however, these gains were whittled down again. It seems as if there were a force to rectify any disturbance of a traditional distribution pattern, no matter how caused.

Women's pay as a percentage of average pay remained stable also, averaging 63 per cent in 1913 and 64 per cent in 1960. The weighted average of women's *earnings* was 54 per cent in 1913–14 and the same in 1960. This result was partly based on the relative decline of the pay of some typical women's occupations, like clerical and professional work, and on the sharp rise in the remuneration of women in unskilled occupations from an absolute low of 10s. or 12s. a week pre-war, irrespective of the male rate, to a rate proportional to male earnings. The overall dispersion of men's pay was narrowed, while that for women was widened, between 1911 and 1958, so that again stability was obtained by compensatory movements.[302] Only the highest decile, and the very highest centiles within it, lost out relatively – but this may well be illusory, representing merely the greater need for, and greater skill at, successful tax evasion, rather than a genuine relative decline of the best-paid.

The substantial long-term increases in real wages since c. 1850 were accompanied by significant reductions in working hours. The trend to a shorter working week had begun before 1850, enforced by legislation for women and children in textile mills, but thereafter it became more widespread and was achieved as much by trade-union power as by Parliament. It may also be significant that it occurred in several brief periods of strong labour bargaining power, rather than in a slow and piecemeal progression; and since these reductions were not reversed (with the major exception of the miners after the defeat of 1926), there was, over a long period, a strong ratchet effect on the standard working week.

The first major reductions in hours were achieved in the boom years of 1871–4, which were marked by labour shortages, particularly in the capital-goods industries. The engineers won a nine-hour day, which became pretty nearly universal in the metal working trades; the textile hours were reduced from 60 to $56\frac{1}{2}$ to allow for the Saturday half-holiday (and were reduced further to $55\frac{1}{2}$ in 1902), and the London building trades, already working a $56\frac{1}{2}$-hour week, were reduced to $52\frac{1}{2}$–54 hours.

The re-awakening labour movement of the 1890s in Britain and abroad made the 8-hour day one of the central planks of its platform, but in Britain its success was limited to a few individual progressive firms rather than to whole industries which granted an eight- or eight-and-one-half-hour day.[303] The only major success was registered by the miners who after a lengthy struggle achieved a reduction of one hour per shift, belatedly, in 1909.[304] It was the immediate post-war years, 1919 and 1920, that saw the next substantial and general reduction in hours, to make the eight-hour day standard not only in those industries where nine hours had been worked before, but even in those, like steel-making, where twelve-hour shifts had still been common. A further slight reduction to a nominal seven- or seven-and-one-half-hour day followed after the Second World War, though actual hours of labour (including overtime) continued to average 46 to 48 a week. By that time a fortnight's annual holiday with pay had also become the norm.[305] The same time-span of a century also saw the enactment of compulsory schooling and the consequent elimination of, first, children under ten years of age, and ultimately all children under fifteen, from the work force, while the share of wage-earning families in the national income remained constant.

There is no obvious method of incorporating the fact of the reduction in hours into the concept of division of the national product between wages and other shares. On the face of it, it looks as though labour gained the whole of the increase in leisure while paying only its fractional share of the cost of lowered output, so that it gained at the expense of the other factors of production. In fact, the process was a much more complex one.

In the earlier decades of industrialization, the changeover to new processes had generally meant longer (or more regularly longer) hours, together with greater intensification of work, at roughly constant real wages. This crude method of achieving higher returns on capital, pursued by an unsophisticated entrepreneurial class, was bound to be self-defeating beyond a certain point. If one started with an over-tired, listless, and underfed proletariat – this stage was reached at different times in different industries, but the incidence bunched in the 1830s and 1840s – it was soon found by the experience of enlightened employers, and by others under compulsion of law, that higher returns could be achieved by shorter hours, by better pay and conditions, or by the substitution of adult for child labour. This discovery involved the shock of recognizing workers not merely as automatons with 'hands', but as human beings with a complexity of motives, abilities, and potential contributions to their firms. In place of the three simple variables – time of attendance, intensity of work, and wage, the first two to be kept as high, the other as low as possible – there was discovered a multiplicity of variables, relating to motives, skill, responsibility, and so on, and it was by no means clear at what combination of these the optimum results would be obtained.

Once the process had started, it acquired a logic and momentum of its own. Given more leisure and higher pay, workers could build up their trade unions; given the incentives, they could react more positively to monetary rewards, to status and responsibility, to invitations to loyalty and respectability. Every reduction in hours withdrew some labour from the market and in the long run strengthened labour's bargaining power for more pay, just as the surviving sweated trades spiralled in the opposite direction into ever worse conditions by weakness engendered by long hours and starvation. In this respect, also, the equilibrium position, which once had been fairly clearly definable, became wholly indeterminate. The framework of the labour market as a whole had changed radically, accompanied by all manner of variations, vagaries, and relapses in individual industries.

With the field wide open, what influence did in fact lift wages in general proportionately with national income? One approach to this long-term question might be an inquiry into the influences which have affected the short-term, cyclical variations in wages and wage shares of the national income. Broadly, two types of answers have been offered: those that seek to derive wage changes from the state of the demand for labour, and those that seek to derive them from the militancy or 'pushfulness' of the trade unions.

Among the former, the greatest success has been achieved by using unemployment as an indicator of the demand for labour, and thus linking wage changes with the rate of unemployment. The approach is particularly associated with Professor A. W. Phillips, and a considerable literature now exists on the 'Phillips relation',[306] which links the *rate of change* of wages with the *rate* of unemployment as well as the *rate of change* of unemployment. Thus for the first part of the period investigated, namely 1862–1913, Lipsey found that over 80·6 of all wage changes can be 'accounted for econometrically by changes in these two variables.[307]

What is perhaps most remarkable about Phillips's findings is that a single formula, without any 'shifts', can be used for the whole of the period covered by him, 1861–1957, even though it falls into three distinct phases, separated by the two world wars. From one point of view, the years to 1914 should be described as having moderate rates of unemployment, with strong cyclical characteristics; the years 1919–39 as suffering very heavy unemployment, with strong cyclical characteristics; and the years after 1945 as exhibiting very low unemployment on a weak cycle. As far as other relevant variables are concerned, the trade unions in period one would have to be described as weak, rising (after 1910) to moderate, in period two as starting strong and falling to moderate, and in period three as very strong. Price movements showed equally strong variations as between the three phases, although it may well be that it was precisely the compensatory movements of prices which kept the ratios similar in all three phases, despite the other massive secular shifts. Thus, if it could be assumed that the labour market had become in some way immune to the heavy unemployment of the 1920s and 1930s, leading to smaller wage cuts than similar rates of unemployment would have provoked before 1914, it was also the overall decline in world prices (particularly import prices) which kept real wages up to the 1862–1913 curve; and similarly, even if the economy might have become immune to the wage push of the very low unemployment rates of phase three after 1945, it was also world price rises which limited real wage increases, in an uncertain mixture of demand pull and cost push. Lipsey, indeed, re-working Phillips's figures, found that after 1918, contrary to Phillips's own deductions, wages reacted much more to prices than to unemployment rates or changes of rates.[308]

Phillips himself had allowed that price changes (at least beyond a minimum threshold) might act to disturb the relationship between unemployment and wages; and both Phillips and Lipsey recognized that trade-union power might also have some influence in this respect.[309] Moreover, the Phillips–Lipsey curve has a very peculiar slope. It is highly elastic at low levels of unemployment, indicating that as the economy approaches full employment a further increase in the demand for labour (as shown by a further reduction in unemployment) would lead to a disproportionately large increase in wages. At high unemployment, however, the curve is very inelastic, further reductions in employment opportunities leading to only very slight cuts in wages. This asymmetry or non-linear relationship is explained by Phillips by the mechanism of the labour market: 'when the demand for labour is high ... we should expect employers to bid wage rates up quite rapidly', whereas 'on the other hand it appears that workers are reluctant to offer their services at less than the prevailing rates when the demand for labour is low'.[310] It is difficult not to associate that reluctance with the attitude and power of the trade unions.[311]

Trade-union power is, in fact, the other major cause to which short-term wage changes have been attributed. It has found its most elegant expression in the work of A. G. Hines,[312] who related wage changes in his period (which is some thirty years shorter than the period covered by Phillips) to trade-union 'pushfulness', measured by the rate of change in union membership rather than by absolute numbers. However, for the period 1921–61, excluding the war years, Hines also found a correlation between the level of unionization and changes in wages.[313] Against this, he found that the level of unemployment made no 'significant contribution' to the rate of unionization except for the period 1893–1912.[314] It is particularly regrettable that the data did not allow him to push the analysis further back in time to see if this exception held good generally before 1914, even if it failed to explain the changes after 1919,[315] for the independence of the variable of union 'pushfulness' is clearly the weakest link in the chain of the argument. A priori, it does not seem plausible that accessions to trade union membership should have no connection with the state of the labour market, the success of other wage demands, or the recent history of wage changes in the industry concerned, even though they may also have exogenous causes, like political agitation, or may even be correlated with a learning process and thus may be a function of time.

It is not altogether surprising that the Hines formula does not hold unchanged for the whole period, and different slopes indicate certain shifts in the numerical value of the constants as between the three phases of the period which are separated by the two world wars. Again, empirically one would expect different reactions to accretions of union strength when these occur to weak unions as compared with strong ones, and expect similar accessions of members to count for far more among unions that have scarcely won recognition (typical for the 1890s) than they would count among unions that enjoy the prestige of having become part of the Establishment in the 1940s and 1950s. Certainly one would expect unions at the time of their effective creation or resuscitation to register more-than-normal, once-for-all wage gains for their members.[316] But if in the years before 1914 and especially before 1910, when trade-union membership was very unevenly distributed, high union density coincided in general with high wages, it was by no means clear which was cause and which was effect.[317]

Both the Phillips and the Hines theories have been criticized in detail as explanations of short-term, cyclical wage changes. From our point of view, attempting to find explanations for the behaviour of wages in the long run, the outstanding conclusion is the powerlessness of the factors which evidently weigh so heavily in the short run.[318] For the period of 1919–39, as compared with the long decades of peace before 1914, it could be argued that the two kinds of influences cancelled each other out: massive unemployment, showing a relatively low level of demand for labour, tended to lower relative wages, while substantial accretions to union strength, especially in the 1930s, pushed them up, leaving their share where it was. After 1945, however, both full employment and a high level of trade-union power ought to have worked in the same direction, yet they did not lead to a shift in the distribution of incomes but merely provided the steam behind the inflation in the economy. It is as if a force of gravity, or rather (to use an apter metaphor) a gyroscope, kept wages going in the same direction as national income, overriding any separate pulls affecting the demand and supply of labour.

It is noteworthy that all the most thorough of the studies of the long-term labour markets in the United Kingdom, like those of Brown and Browne or of Routh, in the end not only have to admit a variety of directly measurable influences on the share of wages, some being active and others permissive, but also have to fall back on some imponderable or other which either tends to beg the question or else throws the discussion back on to a further line where it cannot be pursued. Thus Brown and Browne had to admit the limitations of their analysis by concluding that (within certain tolerances themselves depending on such imponderables as employers' expectations of their future markets) 'the rate of rise of money wages depended on the vigour with which claims were pressed'.[319] Routh, covering a substantially shorter period in his empirical observations, quoted with approval a statement by Elliott Jacques that 'payment at the equitable level is intuitively experienced as fair relative to others . . . Deviations in payment below the equitable level are accompanied by feelings of dissatisfaction which become stronger the greater is the deviation'; and Routh added: 'There is something elemental in this attachment of a person to his level of income, measured in terms of its purchasing power . . . and in terms of the earnings of other occupations, that is not unlike the attachment of an animal to its young'.[320] The constancy of the wage share, and of the relationship of different wages to each other, may thus be explained by paths which economic science cannot tread.

We have observed many examples, and many more could be produced, showing that the apparent constancy of shares and apparent equilibrium in the labour market were due not so much to single natural (or metaphysical) causes, but to the complex balance of compensatory movements. The longer this phase lasts, however, and the more resilient the system is, the less plausible does it become to put these compensations down to a series of accidents, and the more are we obliged to assume the existence of Galbraithian countervailing power itself as an inherent characteristic of the system. Whether it be that the forces affecting the bargaining power of labour also affect the bargaining power of capital, so that in slumps and deflation both are weakened, and in booms and inflation both are strengthened; whether there is a sense of justice which is outraged by changes, and a past which imposes itself on economic reality far more than economic speculation has ever admitted; or whether the power of capital calls forth trade unionism, and trade unions call forth employers' federations, and the strengthening of each leads to a strengthening of the other, just as the use of political power by one leads to the use of political power by the other in classic countervailing manner: the outcome has been that shares have been broadly unchanged and the labour market broadly neutral and in balance, over more than a century.

The empirical data have shown a major switch in the behaviour of the labour market around the middle of the nineteenth century.[321] They are consistent with a view of the century before that turning point as a period of fundamental social transformation and realignment of classes, a period in which the wage-labouring class was being created in its modern and recognizable form, under conditions which put it at a sustained disadvantage and perhaps made that disadvantage a necessary engine of the transformation itself. Since that turning point much has changed, and wages, in terms of what they can buy, have increased four- or five-fold, keeping in step with national income per head. Yet the changes have been essentially of quantity, not of quality. The fundamental structure of society has not altered in the past century or so, and among the constancy of relationships one of the most remarkable has been the share of labour in the national product.

CHAPTER IV

Industrial Entrepreneurship and Management in Great Britain[1]

I. *Introduction*

Since the Second World War the effort to understand the process of economic growth has been a major preoccupation of the social scientist. During this quarter-century those economic historians investigating this complex phenomenon have tended to follow the lead of the late T. S. Ashton by according a critical significance to the entrepreneur;[2] and with their growing disenchantment with the strategic roles of natural resources and capital in economic development, economists too are increasingly promoting entrepreneurship and the supply of managerial ability to a position of greater and greater importance.[3] More and more attention is being given to the economic and social circumstances favourable to increasing the supply of entrepreneurs, and the investigation of these circumstances is becoming ever more sophisticated. Economic historians and sociologists

have identified a number of beliefs, attitudes, value systems, climates of opinion, and propensities which they have found to exert a favorable influence on the generation of enterprise and of developmental initiative. They have also stressed the role of minorities and of deviant behavior in the formation of entrepreneurial groups. [And] joining in the search, ... psychologists have recently undertaken to establish the dependence of development and of entrepreneurial activity on the presence of achievement motivation.[4]

These interrelated explorations leave the student of the phenomenon of entrepreneurship both stimulated and not a little bewildered. The arguments advanced by both sociologists and psychologists are often fascinating, but the majority of them are as yet imprecise, chronologically ill-fitting, and empirically insubstantial.[5] Furthermore, a full understanding of the origins, motivations, and practical consequences of entrepreneurial behaviour is made more difficult by the inclusive nature of the term 'entrepreneur' itself.[6] The following discussion will be clarified if Edith Penrose's definition is adopted as the most satisfactory of the many enunciated. Thus, throughout this essay the term 'entrepreneur' will be employed in a functional sense to refer to

individuals or groups within the firm [who are responsible for] the introduction and acceptance on behalf of the firm of new ideas, particularly with respect to products, location, and significant changes in technology [and for] the acquisition of new managerial personnel, fundamental changes in the administrative organisation of the firm, . . . the raising of capital, and [for] the making of plans for expansion, including the choice of methods of expansion.[7]

In contrast, managerial services, which until recent times have overwhelmingly been provided by the same individuals, relate to the execution of entrepreneurial ideas and proposals and to the supervision of existing day-to-day operations. Professor Penrose's definition has the very real merit of being applicable throughout the lengthy time span of this brief essay.

While it is unquestionable that during the industrial revolution the entrepreneur often 'fulfilled in one person the function of capitalist, financier, works manager, merchant and salesman',[8] it is necessary to emphasize that any definition that rests on these distinctive characteristics is applicable to a historical period now past. Such entrepreneurs may still be found in British industry, but they have survived only in small and medium-sized enterprises, which are relatively unimportant. Even in the pioneering days many entrepreneurs were divesting themselves of one or more of these functions, until as early as the opening decades of the nineteenth century the 'complete businessman' was already a rare phenomenon in some branches of industry. As the multipartnership and then the joint-stock company permeated different areas of economic activity, the proprietor's role was taken by a team of businessmen (albeit sometimes drawn entirely from his own family) making strategic decisions and running the enterprise. They no longer expected to finance their undertakings solely with funds of their own or those of relatives and friends borrowed on their own responsibility.[9] The function of the capitalist became a separate one. Subsequently, a second functional split occurred: those who made strategic decisions became differentiated from those whose role was to keep the concern running. The first may continue to be labelled 'entrepreneurs' – remembering that their role was substantially different from that of earlier entrepreneurs – while the latter are simply managers. Thus, however important it may be to examine the historical record in search of particular individuals who can be labelled 'entrepreneurs' in the period of the industrial revolution, thereafter, as Aitken has observed, it is 'the *association*, not the individual, that exhibits entrepreneurship'.[10] Because the inevitable corollary is that 'the nature of the organisation of a firm and the relationship between the individuals within it have often as important an influence on the competence and enterprise of management and on the kinds of decisions taken as do the inherent characteristics of the individuals themselves', considerable attention is devoted in this essay to the changing structure of the firm.[11]

II. *The Industrial Revolution, 1760–1830*

THE ENTREPRENEUR: ORIGINS AND MOTIVATION

During the classic period of the industrial revolution, it *is* realistic to think in terms of the individual entrepreneur, the man (or small group of men) of 'wit and resource'[12] who organized, managed, and controlled the affairs of a unit that combined the factors of production for the supply of goods and services.[13] It has been suggested that the mid eighteenth century saw a flowering of entrepreneurial personalities, that the acceleration in economic growth of this period was in part a function of a growing proportion of the total population possessing and exploiting entrepreneurial qualities.[14] Inquiries into the origins of these pioneers indicate, as T. S. Ashton showed, that they 'came from every social class and from all parts of the country',[15] and although subsequent investigations have increased our knowledge of the entrepreneurial class and its geographical, social, and occupational origins, it is still permissible only to affirm that the body of known industrialists contained representatives of every stratum of society, every county, and virtually every category of economic activity.[16] Recruits from 'the lower levels of the middle ranks'[17] – often with mercantile connections[18] – appear to have predominated; but until many more entrepreneurs are rescued from anonymity and obscurity, generalizations regarding the relative contributions of each group to the transformation of the economy will remain hazardous and potentially misleading.[19]

In the current state of knowledge, it would seem that Nonconformists comprised a 'disproportionately large share in the ranks of the entrepreneurs'.[20] Explanations of this apparent correlation between dissent and entrepreneurial activity in eighteenth-century Britain have emphasized certain fundamental precepts of dissenting doctrines that are conducive to capitalist enterprise, but the evidence is not fully convincing.[21] Nor has Ashton's 'simpler explanation' in terms of the better educational facilities available to middle-class dissenters remained unscathed, for it has been pointed out that the innovating and unique role of the Dissenting Academies has been exaggerated.[22] Psychologists have added a new and fascinating dimension to our understanding of entrepreneurial motivation by emphasizing the need for achievement and the attainment of higher status by innovational creativity, apparently operating through systems of child-rearing which are themselves significantly influenced by religious persuasion.[23] The suspicion remains that the overrepresentation of Nonconformists among the 'entrepreneurs who attained prominence' may be explicable not in terms of their religious precepts, their superior education, or their need for achievement, but because they belonged to extended kinship families that gave them access to credit, which permitted their firms, and their records, to survive while others, less well connected, went to the wall.

In the researches necessary to verify or refine such hypotheses, which undoubtedly promise to enlarge our comprehension of the social springs of economic growth, it may perhaps be permissible to plead for the investigation of the potential influence of family position on entrepreneurial attitudes. More is known about – or at least greater efforts have hitherto been made to discover and record – religious affiliations than the family positions of successful entrepreneurs. Yet there is some evidence that only eldest children – while perhaps neither better nor worse endowed than their siblings – tend to become, as a result of experience in their position, more capable than their brothers in dealing with situations demanding individual initiative.[24]

Be that as it may, the early entrepreneurs – whatever their geographical, occupational, or social origins – were similarly motivated. They sought to enrich themselves. Yet, as Perkin has observed, 'the limitless pursuit of wealth for its own sake is a rare phenomenon', and he quotes Adam Smith approvingly: ' "to what purpose is all the toil and bustle of the world? . . . it is our vanity which urges us on . . . it is not wealth that men desire, but the consideration and good opinion that wait upon riches" . . . The pursuit of wealth was the pursuit of social status, not merely for oneself but for one's family',[25] and this often meant the acquisition of a landed estate, the purchase or building of a great house, and the quest for political power on either the national or the local scene. It was always so, during and after the industrial revolution.[26] Only the relative attractiveness of land, the stately home, and the title of nobility or knighthood as symbols of social advancement appear to have varied over time; and those who have argued that this pursuit of non-economic ends inevitably involved a haemorrhage of entrepreneurial talent as the nineteenth century progressed[27] should perhaps balance this against what might be called the demonstration effect of conspicuous consumption or social elevation on the new men crowding in to emulate those who had already succeeded.

One cannot help believing that many new thrusting firms would not have come into existence, or small established companies grown, had not their founders or owners, or their socially ambitious wives, seen or been aware of the tangible results of commercial or industrial success. In one sense there was a need for the 'frenetically tangled French Gothic skylines' of the palaces of the cotton grandees, the Wagnerian retreat of Sir Titus Salt in the woods above Saltaire, or the enormous Old English house built for Sir H. W. Peek, and the metamorphosis of Mr. Edward

Strutt – who appears to have devoted much of his time to politics and government rather than to the direct management of the firm established by his grandfather – into Lord Belper.[28] These manifestations of success, supplemented by the knowledge of the vast fortunes left by several industrialists,[29] served to encourage the others.

THE ENTREPRENEUR: FUNCTION AND QUALITY

In performing his function, the early entrepreneur – whatever his origin, his motivation, or his position in the family – is frequently assumed to have exhibited qualities of leadership and to have been an innovator and risk-bearer. But how far did the early men of business in fact possess the qualities so often attributed to them?

Again, definitional problems arise. What is meant by innovation? Implicitly, and sometimes explicitly, nearly all those who have discussed the entrepreneur have been influenced by the work of Schumpeter.[30] It has been felt that ideally the entrepreneur should be a 'creative innovator' to warrant the appellation. If it be agreed that Schumpeter used 'innovation' to mean doing something that has never been done before anywhere, then the concept is of very little practical value, so rarely is it encountered historically. More useful is Redlich's idea of 'derivative innovation', bringing into a geographical area or into an industry something which has been done before but not in that region or in that sphere of economic activity.[31] Even this phenomenon is by no means common. The fact is that the vast majority of entrepreneurs appear to have been imitative, even (one might argue, especially) during the period of the industrial revolution, and the sooner the insistence on primary innovation as a necessary criterion of entrepreneurship is abandoned, the faster will the study of the entrepreneur's role and function approach historical reality. This is not to say that innovating entrepreneurs cannot be identified in both past and present – simply that such individuals constitute special cases. They were the leaders; the great army of entrepreneurs were followers, dependent for their prosperity, even for their survival, on good management rather than innovation.[32]

One distinguishing function common to all early entrepreneurs was that of risk-bearing. The essence of the sole proprietorship or small partnership as a method of economic organization is that the decision-maker has sole property rights over his instruments of production; and by the unification of ownership and management, the partners who carry the risk also make the decisions determining its extent. It is important to recognize that one of the legitimate functions of the owner-manager was that of reducing risk to a minimum. Only thus can the paradox of enterprise and caution existing simultaneously be resolved (see below, p. 189). Some opportunities for risk-shifting were very great in the late eighteenth and early nineteenth centuries, the most significant being manifest in a ruthless attitude towards the labour force, which could be taken on and laid off almost at will, especially when fixed costs were low, or in price- and output-fixing arrangements, the possibilities of which were enhanced by the existence of regional markets. But what was the type and degree of risk shouldered by the early entrepreneurs? In many of the comparisons between the entrepreneurs of the industrial revolution and those of, for example, the last quarter of the nineteenth century, there is an implicit assumption that whereas the former were ready to undertake the most hazardous operations, the latter were so overwhelmed by fear of loss, or so sunk in complacency, that innumerable opportunities were missed which would have been eagerly seized by their vigorous forebears.

Do the pioneers fully deserve their reputation for courage and adventurousness, progressive efficiency, organizational ability, and grasp of commercial opportunity, combined with the capacity to exploit it?[33] In a general sense, the economic historian's answer has tended to be in the affirmative, the underlying assumption being that there was some sort of correlation between the exploitation of these entrepreneurial qualities and the undeniable acceleration of economic growth that took place during the industrial revolution, coupled with a somewhat later rise in the standard of living for all save the *Lumpenproletariat*. What remains unresolved is the degree to which it was imperative that the early entrepreneurs should possess the characteristics attributed to them. In order to succeed, was it necessary for them to possess a blend of all these qualities, or merely some of them? Alternatively, would similarly endowed entrepreneurs have coped with the problems of the late Victorian economy more successfully than their successors are deemed to have done?

This is the sort of counter-factual question currently exercising the 'new' economic historians; such issues should be discussed, and if in so doing there is undue reliance on argument by example, at least this fundamental weakness is fully recognized.[34] More information will come, if it is ever to come, from a close study of the business records increasingly being tracked down and preserved throughout the United Kingdom. Any participant in this search can hardly avoid entertaining the suspicion that our current assessment of the early entrepreneurs has been built on a biased sample: that is, there is a possibility that the majority of the records that have been located and 'worked' for this period – and these, it must be admitted, are few in number – are predominantly those of concerns that were sufficiently successful to have created conditions favourable for untypical longevity[35] – hence the survival of their archives.

Furthermore, with what knowledge we do have of certain aspects of the resuscitated leading figures of the industrial revolution, there has been a temptation not only to reconstruct a composite 'complete business man'[36] possessing all, or nearly all, the virtues, but also to extrapolate these qualities to the many hundreds whose careers have warranted simply a mention – hardly more – in the county histories, the accounts of the local clergy and the past historians of regional industry. Yet it is possible that this procedure is illegitimate and that the majority of the manufacturers were literally 'plodding men of business', as Robert Owen described them.[37] It may also be extremely misleading. The stage armies of 'early cotton manufacturers' or 'ironmasters' are apt to be depicted as 'ants tirelessly maximising profits to lift the graph of economic growth', but this simile would seem to be inapplicable to, for example, the Leeds merchants and the merchant hosiers in the Midland counties.[38]

This is not to deny the revolutionary organizational changes introduced in the heroic years up to 1830, so comprehensively surveyed by Pollard,[39] but simply to suggest that it is conceivable that many who succeeded in the early years, with all their difficulties, may not have fared so well in later decades – that the ancestors of the much-criticized late Victorians were not, on the whole, superior entrepreneurs in every facet of business activity.

Consider the economic environment in which they played out their historical roles, and consider too the limited product markets they chose to exploit. However significant and interesting are the contributions of the ironmasters and engineers, the potters, the chemists and the brewers, one must agree with Hobsbawm that 'whoever says Industrial Revolution says cotton . . . the pace-maker of industrial change'.[40] It is unnecessary here to explain the predominance of cotton, since the reasons have been so brilliantly examined by David Landes; but fundamental to any understanding of the expansion of this and the other industries that experienced accelerated growth is that 'the home market for manufactures was growing, thanks to improving communications, increase in population, high and rising average income, a buying pattern favourable to solid, standardized, moderately priced products, and unhampered commercial enterprise'.[41]

The risks incurred by the early entrepreneurs must surely be assessed in the light of this buoyant domestic market, buttressed, particularly in cotton textiles, by a flourishing (sometimes almost insatiable) overseas demand. Indeed, the demand situation in foreign markets was perhaps never again to be so favourable. Britain became 'the workshop of the world' largely because of the monopolistic position of the pioneers, but the principal incentive inducing the entrepreneurs to embark on the transformation of manufacturing activity was the great potentiality possessed by the home market for profitable exploitation. This, as Eversley has emphasized, was the essential basis for export activity:

the home market could absorb stocks if exports ceased or diminished. Secondly, it provided the foundation for mass production, so that the cost per unit could be reduced to levels which made it feasible to export articles with a relatively unfavourable weight/value ratio, like pottery. Thirdly, it provided an outlet for the inevitable sub-standard qualities (this applies particularly to pottery, glass, and dyed and printed textiles).[42]

Overseas markets were undoubtedly critical in the continued expansion of the cotton industry after 1790;[43] but other sectors of the economy, even the pig iron trade and the Midlands nailing industry, were for long essentially home-based.[44] It was in serving the domestic market – less volatile, less hazardous than overseas markets – that new entrants to the ranks of the entrepreneurs could acquire their business acumen and skill.

This is not to deny that the entrepreneurs ran many risks – the number of recorded bankruptcies, particularly in the cotton trade and especially among exporters, is a sufficient indication that they did[45] – but to emphasize that the demand conditions for most manufactured goods were relatively favourable: the large number of business failures is not necessarily evidence of praiseworthy adventurousness (an interpretation denied to the Victorians) but may have been the consequence of sheer incompetence.

The names that have become famous – Arkwright, Oldknow, Strutt, Peel, Owen, M'Connel and Kennedy, Gott, Marshall in textiles; Crawshay, Lloyd, Reynolds, Roebuck, Walker, Wilkinson, Boulton, Watt, Bramah, Maudslay in iron and engineering; Minton, Spode, Wedgwood in pottery; Dundonald, Garbett, Keir, Macintosh, Tennant in chemicals; Whitbread, Thrale, Truman in brewing – were not typical manufacturers.[46] The majority of them conducted their operations on a scale much greater than their less well-known competitors; many of them owed their successful growth to some degree of monopoly power acquired through patent exploitation, the possession of some unique skill, the differentiation of their products.[47] And undoubtedly sheer chance played a part. Much depended on the demand situation in the first few years of the establishment of the partnership. So great were the profit potentials in the closing decades of the eighteenth century that entrepreneurs who, like George Newton and Thomas Chambers, fortuitously caught a rising market could often amass sufficient funds to enable their companies to weather the later economic storms.[48] Careful and unceasing application to business was clearly required; but the possession of all the entrepreneurial qualities was to little avail if luck went against the new manufacturer.

Take the case of M'Connel and Kennedy, whose historian has observed:

The most significant factor in the growth [of this firm] was that of time. The situation in the cotton trade in the 1790's was conducive to growth and expansion because of the stimulus provided by the recent technical innovations in spinning, particularly Crompton's mule, and the ready demand for the fine fabrics which could now be produced. Equally important was the fact that this boom of activity was in its early stages and the structure of the spinning trade was still fluid and flexible. All this meant that the young man with ability but not necessarily endowed with capital could begin business in the trade without being doomed to fail. Such was the opportunity open to M'Connel and Kennedy and taken by them and numerous others.[49]

The subsequent growth of this firm – whose high initial profits permitted rapid accumulation – was characterized by a policy of 'scrupulous caution'. This 'was manifest in the firm's search for security and stability in all aspects of its commercial life'. Furthermore, M'Connel and Kennedy apparently made no attempt to expand the market by creating demand, nor was there any attempt to monopolize or control the market in any way. Indeed, the market for fine yarn was large and was expanding throughout this period. When the home market was saturated, then yarn could easily be exported. Thus, except for periods of trade depression, 'there was enough business to remove ferocity from competition between spinners . . . lethal competition did not greatly affect the spinning trade until the 1830's'. Nevertheless, for all the factors operating in favour of M'Connel and Kennedy, the growth of their firm was a considerable personal achievement. The partners had had to recruit and organize a large labour force (the efficient employment of which demanded a sensible factory layout) and to co-ordinate the various stages of production. They also acquired a thorough knowledge of both cotton and yarn markets, though in this they were undoubtedly helped by the specialist assistance of middlemen.[50]

It is increasingly recognized that the bulk of the capital invested in the cotton industry during the first phase of industrialization (1770–95) came from merchants, that the fixed capital requirements were comparatively modest, and that credit could often be obtained for raw materials and machinery, while factory space and plant could be rented.[51] With respect to provision of capital, the major problems, particularly for the smaller manufacturers, were the financing of

expansion plans and the finding of means partially to insulate themselves from the shock of periodic financial crises or sudden contractions
in the market often associated with the events of the Napoleonic Wars.[52]
But it would appear probable that in some years (e.g. 1808–10) the
severity of these difficulties was exacerbated by feverish overproduction
– 'here as in England business is overdone, the Manchester houses have
manufactured enough yarn to serve the world for four or five years',
wrote one disappointed partner from Boston in 1809.[53] This error of
judgement is so often encountered in the literature that it can hardly
fail to diminish any estimate of the commercial acumen of the cotton
entrepreneurs, for all the difficulties encountered in obtaining the latest
'market intelligence'. It is therefore not surprising that the thoughtful
businessman proceeded with great care.[54] 'This was the key to the
policy of M'Connel and Kennedy and explains the caution amounting
to suspicion with which all potential customers were scrutinized before
doing business.'[55] Those – and they were the majority – who did not do
likewise ran the very real risk of bankruptcy, the route to which
was marked by a chronic shortage of working capital and trade
credit.

It now seems generally agreed that the acquisition of the necessary
capital was less difficult than the recruitment, organization, and control
of a labour force.[56] It is arguable that the problems of 'recruitment'
have also been somewhat overstated. M'Connel and Kennedy, for
example, do not seem to have encountered any difficulty in finding
workers, nor did John Marshall at Water Lane, Leeds; while North-
amptonshire boot and shoe manufacturers were able to expand output
by recruiting from an abundant labour supply released from the
county's declining craft industries, silk, woollens, and lace in particular.[57] Demographic factors were operating in favour of the early
manufacturers; the cotton industry and some branches of the metallurgical industries could tap a vast pool of unemployed or underemployed domestic workers acquainted with textile production and the
manufacture of iron wares; and in some cases many of the problems of
labour management could be virtually ignored 'as long as managerial
responsibility as well as the risks of managerial failure fell to the lot of
subcontractors'.[58] The major labour difficulties arose whenever the
organization of production involved the concentration of work within
the factory and necessitated making the hands respond to work incentives. Pollard and E. P. Thompson, among others, have described
how this problem was overcome; but in any assessment of the effectiveness with which this facet of the manufacturers' operations was conducted, it should not be forgotten that they probably derived some
advantage from the prior existence of 'an ethic of work performance

which had developed among the masses of workers out of the combined legacies of craftsmanship, the Puritan ethic and the rising ideology of individual striving and success',[59] buttressed by an inherent docility among the young and female sections of the labour force, whose compliance with oppressive rules and regulations was to some degree, particularly in the factory villages, secured by the fear of eviction and consequent homelessness.

In the early days, individual entrepreneurs in outlying districts undoubtedly experienced difficulties in the creation of a disciplined labour force. Nearly all manufacturers were initially hard-pressed to obtain skilled artisans either by external recruitment or by internal training; but the fact remains that if the industrialist paid good wages and provided reasonable conditions these problems could be and were overcome.[60] One should not confuse the very special needs of Wedgwood and Boulton & Watt with the labour requirements of the majority of cotton-masters, paper-makers, and brewers, particularly those whose scale of operations was relatively small.[61]

These remarks are not intended to disparage the pioneer entrepreneurs; their object is to emphasize the need for more detailed comparative investigations of the obstacles which confronted them in the context of the overall economic environment within which they operated. Fierce internal competition – mitigated by nebulous trade associations – there may indeed have been; yet M'Connel and Kennedy, for example, were apparently always able to find a ready market for their yarn, and in the export market Kirkman Finlay, for example, met with no foreign competition of any significance until after 1815.[62] When Wedgwood's showroom sales in London started falling off in the late 1760s, he suggested to his partner Bentley that the firm might make 'a gentle push in foreign markets'[63] – hardly the language of an embattled entrepreneur. It is hints such as these that have raised doubts concerning the relative magnitude of the difficulties confronting the entrepreneur of the industrial revolution.

Take the case of technological change. It has been argued that

The technology of cotton manufacture was fairly simple and so . . . was that of most of the rest of the changes which collectively made up the 'Industrial Revolution'. It required little scientific knowledge or technical skill beyond the scope of a practical mechanic of the early eighteenth century. It hardly even required steam power, for though cotton adopted the new steam engine rapidly, and to a greater extent than other industries (except mining and metallurgy), as late as 1838 one quarter of its power was still provided by water . . . It was simple because, by and large, the application of simple ideas and devices, often of ideas available for centuries, often by no means expensive, could produce striking results.[64]

Nevertheless, do not the early manufacturers exhibit considerable perspicacity in taking up the new machines and devices and in rapidly adopting even minor cost-reducing modifications? And was not considerable risk involved in their so doing?

Although these questions are difficult to resolve, most recent commentators have had little hesitation in asserting the achievements of the early entrepreneurs. Yet it is arguable that some qualification is required. Given the competitive conditions in many industries, particularly in times of market glut, entrepreneurs doubtless felt themselves to be under unremitting pressure to reduce relative costs. As Rosenberg has asked, since a firm exploring new techniques 'cannot explore in all directions, what are the forces which induce it to strike out in a particular direction?'[65] His answer is that most firms will seek a relatively short-term solution promising quick results, and that searching the technological horizon will lead them to attack the most restrictive constraint. But his 'primary point is that most mechanical productive processes throw off signals of a sort which are both compelling and fairly obvious; indeed, these processes when sufficiently complex and inter-dependent . . . create internal compulsions and pressure which, in turn, initiate exploratory activity in particular directions'.[66]

This notion of compulsive sequences, of imbalances in processes, is of course admirably illustrated by the major inventions in the early cotton industry.[67] But it operated too in the innumerable minor improvements and modifications of machinery, methods, and organization which are less dramatic and consequently less well documented in this and in other industries.[68] In the context of this essay, Rosenberg's convincing argument gives rise to the feeling that such were the 'signals' given off by the relatively primitive machines characteristic of the industrial revolution that those manufacturers who have been credited with considerable entrepreneurial skill in choosing to adopt or to develop certain new devices perhaps do not deserve such unqualified praise. This is so, firstly, because the technological horizon was so limited that the point of greatest restraint was fairly obvious[69] and, secondly, because in many instances obsolete or out-dated equipment could readily be sold to the small man eagerly entering trade, thus reducing the net cost of (and the disincentives to) change.[70] It follows that the risks involved in the adoption of technological improvement, during the classic period of the industrial revolution, were perhaps less than have hitherto been believed.

THE STRUCTURE OF ENTERPRISE

The foregoing discussion has been concerned with some tentative observations on the degree of risk shouldered by the early entrepreneurs. It is perhaps legitimate to regard the fundamental business unit of the industrial revolution, the individual proprietorship or the partnership, as partly the product of risk avoidance. By the unification of ownership and control, the entrepreneur was able to reduce the real or imagined dangers inherent in entrusting his business to a manager. The unprincipled and damaging conduct of some managers almost certainly inhibited the establishment of a managerial hierarchy when the growing size of firms more than justified some delegation of authority. And even if potential managers were apparently honest and sober, the assessment of their ability, wisdom, and integrity involved considerable uncertainty, and their employment necessitated avoidable expense.[71]

The offsetting disadvantage of owner-management was, of course, the restraint which it imposed on the scale of operation, a restraint deriving from the difficulties of delegation; but at this stage of Britain's economic evolution, the benefits outweighed this disadvantage. If, like Sir Ambrose Crowley, principals of manufacturing concerns had a profound lack of faith in individual managers, then the answer was to place the superintendence of a separate works or department under one admitted to the partnership, so that his energy was stimulated by his direct interest in the success of the business.[72] It is perhaps significant that for all the efforts of Boulton & Watt to introduce regularity, delegation, and division of functions, the most important managerial innovations at the Soho Foundry were introduced not by managers trained in these practices but by the sons of the senior partners.[73] Other partnerships could be given to those who could contribute necessary expertise[74] or additional capital if ploughed-back profits did not suffice to attain the desired rate of growth.[75] What is remarkable is the rapid expansion permitted by internal financing at this time.[76]

Equally fascinating is the kaleidoscopic nature of those partnerships which are well documented. Partnerships were formed, supplemented, or terminated where necessary; the principal entrepreneurs were associated with others in the same or related businesses; and the entire system was apparently very adaptable and extremely flexible.[77] Arkwright, as is well known, numbered among his partners John Smalley, Samuel Oldknow, David Dale, Samuel Need, the Strutts, Richard Arkwright jun., Thomas Walshman, John Cross, and others;[78] but equally if not more elaborate partnership systems were built up by James and Kirkman Finlay and the Peel family.[79] Conversely, an ambitious individual could associate himself with the fortunes of a whole range of enterprises in differing branches of manufacturing activity: Samuel Garbett is perhaps the prime example.[80]

Not until technological requirements made for an increase in size beyond that manageable by the partners, and capital requirements went beyond the resources of small, often related, groups of men, was it necessary to devise a new structure for the firm – not, in fact, until the second half of the nineteenth century.

III. *The Next Fifty Years*

If there is a paucity of scholarly business histories helpful in assessing the achievement of the early entrepreneurs, the decades immediately after 1830 are virtually barren. Even the future position is unpromising. Whereas the surviving records of the industrialists of the heroic period have been carefully preserved and studied, the overwhelming majority of those of the following decades either have been destroyed or have not yet attracted much attention. Analysis is thus either impossible or insubstantial: not until the legal requirements associated with the adoption of corporate status guarantee the retention of certain basic records is it possible even to begin to assess the role of the entrepreneur with any confidence. Even here, a qualification is required. Those documents that must be kept will only be preserved in the case of going concerns. When a firm fails, the disposition of the records is ordinarily the responsibility of the liquidator who, the liquidation having been completed, usually destroys the books. Hence, the economic historian tends to have at best a biased sample.

This is a grave misfortune. Many of the problems of the pioneers had been surmounted; relatively sophisticated managerial techniques had evolved; and the markets of the world, many growing in depth, long remained open to British exploitation. For many decades competition from domestic sources and from foreign manufacturers was of little significance. Such was the development of the home and overseas market – the former enjoying a remarkable buoyancy with the coming of the railway and gradually rising living standards – that the British entrepreneur had no great inducement to alter the basic economic structure painfully evolved in the pioneering period: textiles and iron remained supreme. Not without reason Samuel Smiles was able to write: 'Anybody who devotes himself to making money, body and soul, can scarcely fail to make himself rich. Very little brains will do.'[81]

But how well did the second generation cope? Marshall argued that rich old firms could thrive by their mere momentum, even if they lost the springs of energy and initiative. Men whose childhood had been passed in the hard days before the repeal of the corn laws; who had come to business early in the morning, and stayed late in the afternoon; who had been full of enterprise and resource, were not infrequently succeeded by sons who had been brought up to think life easy, and were content to let the main work of the business be carried on by salaried assistants on the lines laid down in a previous generation. But yet so strongly were such men supported by the general inflation of prices, that in most cases they made good profits and were satisfied with themselves. Thus an extra-ordinary combination of favourable conditions, induced undue self-complacency . . .[82]

Was Marshall's argument correct or fair? And if his criticism was well founded, to just how many firms was his denunciation applicable?

SCALE, STRUCTURE, AND CONTROL

We know all too little about the age structure of firms in this, or indeed any other, period of the nineteenth century. An honoured family name may well have been embalmed in a company's title – a reminder of past success and a symbol of quality and fair dealing – but the fact that a partnership ended with the death of any of its members meant that effective control may have passed into other hands, with the new senior partners hidden by the universal suffix '& Co'. What proportion of entrepreneurs at any point in time were, in fact, of the first or second or third generation?[83] With the ever-changing internal power structure of partnerships and the high rates of dissolution and liquidation, it is possible that the controlling interest in relatively few firms remained in the hands of their founders' immediate families beyond two generations.[84] We are perhaps too eager to generalize from the records of those that did, forgetting that our inadequate sample is far from random.

The foregoing remarks are about control. They should not be interpreted to mean that readily identifiable continuing firms failed to grow in size. And alongside those experiencing organic growth there were, with each decade, an increasing number of firms whose size at birth (measured in terms of capital employed) would have dwarfed their predecessors – so much so that it has been argued that by the 1840s pressures had built up within the British economy that were tending to militate against the long-standing dominance of non-corporate enterprise.[85] Foremost of these pressures was the growing capital requirements necessitated by the exploitation of new techniques. In itself, the raising of large capitals apparently did not constitute so much of a problem as that feature of the English law of partnership that made each contributor fully liable for the losses of the enterprise. The rule had developed that this liability extended to each partner's private property, 'to his last shilling and acre'.[86] This was the spectre confronting all those who participated in the affairs of large partnerships or unincorporated companies, and understandably there were relatively few willing to take the risk.

As a consequence of the Bubble Act of 1720, the creation of a joint-stock company with transferable shares and corporate status was possible only with the consent of the state (the usual enabling procedure came to be by an act of parliament). This consent was not easy to obtain and was always costly. Manufacturing and trading enterprises, in particular, were rarely approved.[87] It is true that illegal 'equitable companies' were formed. The majority of them were in the traditional fields of joint-stock activity. There were hardly any in manufacturing, save for the joint factories created by wool weavers in the West Riding in order to pool fulling, dyeing, and similar facilities.[88]

The state of the law, burdensome though it may have been, was not however the sole or even the most important explanation of the slow development of the corporation. The fact was that there appeared to be no great necessity to depart from the traditional organizational framework. The practice of self-financing, coupled with a growing reliance on an increasingly sensitive network of monetary intermediaries, was able to meet the capital requirements of most firms. The essential simplicity of so many of the productive processes, characterized as they were by a growth pattern involving simply the multiplication of units, rather than by radical re-organization, permitted continued direction by the single entrepreneur or by the small group of enterprises far bigger than had once been thought feasible. These factors enabled manufacturing and trading firms to grow without recourse to the joint-stock form.

When change did come, the initial impetus was provided by 'a group of middle class philanthropists, most of whom accepted the title of Christian Socialists',[89] who wished to create 'facilities to safe investments for the savings of the middle and working class',[90] and by London financial interests who sought profitable industrial outlets for potential investors.[91] No such impetus came from those who argued in terms of freedom of contract, nor from the industrialists themselves, whose voices were seldom heard in the discussions that preceded the Joint Stock Companies Acts of 1856 and 1862.[92]

The response of the industrialists to this legislation confirms their muted interest. By 1885 limited companies accounted for at most between 5 and 10 per cent of the total number of important business organizations, and only in shipping, iron and steel, and cotton could their influence be said to have been considerable.[93] Although the firms that were limited were by far the most important in their spheres of activity, judged by size of unit and amount of fixed capital, the vast majority of the manufacturing firms of the country continued to be family businesses in the mid-eighties.[94] Nevertheless, by the mid-sixties a legal structure existed in Great Britain which made possible fundamental changes in the structure of the individual enterprise. The way was open for the emergence of the corporate economy, even though few trod the path. In contrast with the expectations of the statesmen responsible for the early Company Acts, there developed the private company (legally unrecognized until 1907). Since many of the concerns adopting this form of organization had previously existed as partnerships or joint-stock companies, the object of private registration was to obtain limited liability while retaining the original management and maintaining the privacy of the post. Further growth was made possible, but only to the extent of the capital of the shareholders named in the Articles of Association; and the introduction of new entrepreneurial talent to the Board was inhibited.[95] Hence, entrepreneurs operated within organizations which show little alteration from those of their pioneering forebears. Certainly there was little movement towards the differentiation of management from ownership – towards the elongation of organizational hierarchies.[96]

By 1830, as Pollard has shown, whereas 'well-defined classes of managers had emerged in various specific industries',[97] a managerial class as such could hardly be said to have emerged, nor any theory of management practice. The problems of control were not ignored by the entrepreneur in his managerial capacity, but such was the unique nature of the manifold problems exercising the pioneers in each sphere of manufacturing and trading activity that generalization seemed either impossible or unrealistic. Even where certain precepts were of universal applicability, like those of William Brown of Dundee, they were unlikely to have been widely disseminated, even within their own localities or industries.[98] The fact is that the familial structure of business enterprise inhibited interest in any collective body of management thought and militated against its acceptance even on those rare occasions when publication was undertaken.[99] This is hardly surprising in an age when the majority of entrepreneurs were their own managers and when the sons or near relatives who were to succeed to the control of the firm learned the mysteries of the trade by experience within the family enterprise. And this was to continue to be the case until ownership and management were divorced or until the growth in the scale of the individual enterprise was to render the delegation of authority imperative – until, that is, the closing decades of the nineteenth century.[100] This is one element in the explanation of the disappearance of interest in 'methodical accounting and . . . the need of at least some specific training for the discharge of executive responsibilities'[101] among the pioneers of the industrial revolution and their successors.

THE QUALITY OF ENTREPRENEURSHIP

The absence of any dramatic change in scale of operations, the relatively slow enlargement of the labour force of individual enterprises, and the close coincidence of firm and plant, together with the fact that the majority of large companies were but 'private firms converted',[102] meant that the nature of entrepreneurship and the structure of the firm changed but little in the middle decades of the nineteenth century.[103] But what of the quality of entrepreneurship? Influenced no doubt by the relatively high rate of economic growth, burgeoning exports, and apparently rapid technological diffusion, historians have offered little or no retrospective criticism. Yet the decline of a number of hitherto leading firms can be traced to this period. The 'final phase' of Marshalls of Leeds set in during the mid-forties, although this once-great firm was destined to linger on for another forty years, by which time many of its leading competitors in flax-spinning had already gone: Benyons in 1861, John Morfitt and John Wilkinson a few years later, and others, including W. B. Holdsworth, soon to follow.[104]

The Ashworth cotton enterprises, built up between 1818 and 1834 by Henry and Edward Ashworth – 'among the most renowned of the men who followed the great inventors and . . . took the cotton industry forward by "assiduity, perseverance, attention to detail, minor improvement" '[105] – began their relative decline in the forties, when the partners' will to expand withered away before diversifying interests, growing internal tensions, and low profits and even losses. In 1846 George Binns Ashworth, Henry's son, noted that

in the New Eagley Weaving Shed there were no costings, no control of quality, no regular stock-takings; customers suffered from late delivery, and often the lengths of cloths were shorter than had been ordered. Owing to technical and managerial defects the looms now ran for hardly half the working day and total production was much below that of their competitors.[106]

Although this was perhaps the worst of the firm's periodic managerial lapses, things improved after 1847,[107] but the firm never regained its earlier technical pre-eminence: 'Fortunes now will only be made by intense plodding and keenness', noted George Binns Ashworth in his diary.[108]

One who failed to 'plod' was James Thompson of the Primrose Works, near Clitheroe. Perhaps the leading firm in the calico-printing trade, his exclusive and expensive prints – in the design of which he called upon 'the talent even of Royal Academicians' – were specifically manufactured 'for the upper hundreds, and not for the millions'. Heedless of warnings by the young Lyon Playfair, who became chemical manager of the works in 1841, that the business was doomed unless he changed the character of his products, Thompson refused to abandon his short runs. 'His products were known all over Europe for their high excellence, and he could not bear to lower . . . their quality.' 'It was a common saying of Thompson that "once you become a Calico printer there are but two courses before you – the Gazette or the grave".' In the event, he died a disappointed man, in 1850, but a few months before his famous works were closed.[109] Other calico printers had, however, attempted to produce for the million instead of for the few and to do so had cut their costs to the bone by the debasement of design and by trying to convert 'herds of Lancashire boors into drawers, cutters, printers, machine workers, etc.', at appallingly low wages. Not surprisingly the products were execrable and failures numerous. As John Dugdale, owner of the Lowerhouse Print Works, near Burnley, observed in 1847: 'If yo'll look back for th' last six years, yo'll find half o' th' Printers are brocken – an' half o' those that are left canno' break, for nobody'll trust 'em, and the rest get on as weel as they con.'[110]

Courtaulds got on very well. When Samuel III went into semi-retirement in the mid-1860s, the firm, now directed by George Courtauld III, Harry Taylor, and John Warren, enjoyed enormous incomes – the fruits of the efforts of an earlier generation – while allowing the firm to fall technically far behind other silk throwsters and manufacturers. Indeed, George III 'contributed virtually nothing but inertia to the family business'. Only a buoyant and inelastic demand for its main product, ritual mourning crape, coupled with falling raw silk prices, permitted the enterprise to make its handsome returns on capital at a time when its senior partner brought to the family firm none of 'those qualities of vigour, perception, intelligence, and enterprise' to which it owed its establishment by his uncle.[111]

In iron, Joshua Walker & Co. did not long survive the end of the Napoleonic Wars, its steel trade being formally wound up in 1829 and the iron trade finally wasting away by the early 1830s.[112] Other ironmasters fared little better. John Darwin, sometime associate of Peter Stubs, and one of the leading Sheffield industrialists, had gone bankrupt by 1828;[113] many vanished in the middle decades of the nineteenth century, among them Lloyd, Foster & Co. of Wednesbury, the first exploiters of hot-blast and, later, the Bessemer process in the Black Country.[114] Even the Coalbrookdale Company faltered, bereft of managerial guidance when Abraham and Alfred Darby retired (in 1849) and Francis Darby died (in 1850); it was sustained only by sheer momentum and a continuing demand for the products of its foundry.[115] And in South Wales, William Crawshay II, regarding his family as 'Iron Kings and Cyfarthfa as the crown they wore, wanted to dictate terms and force his own ideas upon the buyers'. The Guests of Dowlais 'might send agents to Russia to canvas for orders but Crawshay sat in his counting house and orders came [or failed to come] to him'.[116]

Though these examples could be multiplied, nothing can be proved by them. They are mentioned merely to indicate the desirability of additional research into the quality of entrepreneurship in the staple British industries during the decades following the heroic age of the industrial revolution, and to suggest the possibility that many more firms would have gone down in this period had they been confronted by the degree of competition encountered by their successors – that, in fact, a 'decline in entrepreneurship' can be selectively exemplified at almost every time and in almost every well-established branch of trade. The closing decades of the century possess no monopoly of this phenomenon.

Nevertheless, in one respect there *may* have been a difference between the pre-1870 and post-1870 decades. Latterly, whatever ingenious defences the new economic historians may be engineering to re-establish our faith in the quality of British entrepreneurship in cotton, coal, and iron and steel, there is no gainsaying the belated recognition of the growth and profit potential of motor cars, some branches of chemicals, electrical engineering, and the like. Few such significant failures to appreciate the *new* can be perceived in earlier years.[117]

Take the possibilities for entrepreneurial resource engendered by the 'boundless demand' associated with the coming of the railways.[118] The number of patents taken out relating to railway equipment in the middle decades of the century was enormous.[119] Everywhere, the engineers of the railway companies and freelance inventors developed their own devices to provide greater efficiency, safety, and comfort, and the manufacture of many of their gadgets were taken up by both railway companies and outside firms, some of which were literally brought into being to exploit railway patents. George Spencer & Co., for example, was created to work Spencer's own conical rubber buffer, draw, and bearing spring patents of 1852 and 1853 and those granted to P. R. Hodge, J. E. Coleman, and Richard Eaton. Similarly, John Brown of Sheffield, quickly perceiving the need for more powerful buffers as locomotive rolling stock outgrew plain wooden headstocks or horse-hair pads confined by metal bands, was already building his fortune on the manufacture of steel helical or volute buffer springs; as early as 1855 he was said to dispense no less than £5,000 annually in 'getting people to uphold' his product – a sales technique which, coupled with a willingness to provide long credits and even take payments in shares, made him Spencer's most formidable rival in the ensuing decades.[120]

Other firms owed their origins to success in the desperate scramble to gain sole licences to work the patents of the host of railway inventors. Forges and brass- and iron-foundries came into being or were expanded in order to make innumerable fittings for locomotives and carriages, signals and lights, which – since they had been specified for use in the construction of a particular locomotive or carriage design – the railway company workshop, locomotive builders, or carriage and wagon manufacturers had no option but to 'buy in'.[121] Indeed, the engine and rolling-stock works, spawned by the dozen in the middle decades of the century by the railway companies themselves and by outside initiatives, were the pioneers in the process whereby complicated machines and vehicles came to be assembled from a wide range of component parts of metal, wood, leather, glass, textile, and rubber, for the most part manufactured by a host of suppliers working to exact specifications and, in the case of moving parts, to very close tolerances.[122]

There was, in this instance, apparently no hesitation in taking up new things, adopting new production techniques, devising new modes of organization, and fashioning new and flexible marketing organizations and techniques.[123] Is this rapid appreciation of the new perhaps the only significant difference between the middle years of the nineteenth century and the two or three decades preceding the First World War? Or is this too an illusion, a consequence of the nonexistence of competitive economics elsewhere against which to measure the mid-Victorian achievement? Indeed, how does one measure entrepreneurial capacity? 'The answer,' as Saul has argued, 'may lie in a series of international comparisons';[124] but what if this technique is, as in the present case, inappropriate? Can one then employ the concept of export market shares? Hardly, in a period when Britain was virtually in a monopolistic position, enjoying the benefits of an early start. It might be possible to analyse deviations from what is apparently best practice in particular industries, though here one runs the real danger of equating 'best' with 'most recent'. This problem of investment will recur. It is enough to say that at this juncture there is insufficient information to assess mid-Victorian entrepreneurship in any meaningful sense.

Some firms which traced their origins to the industrial revolution were declining in relative importance, some disappearing altogether; others were crowding in to take their chances in both old and new fields of enterprise. There were many who shared with Josiah Mason, the maker of steel pens and pioneer of electro-plating, a 'quickness in seizing a new idea, . . . sagacity in realising the possibilities of development, and . . . courage in bringing it within the range of practical application',[125] though few shared his great success. Yet an economic historian is ill equipped to judge the technical feasibility of the thousands of inventions the specifications of which – often deliberately obscure in their wording – line the walls of the Patent Office. How can one estimate what profitable opportunities went unexploited? It is not enough to say what had been done; it is necessary to assess what might have been done and was not. Not until the Americans, the Germans, and the Belgians were in a position to undertake a range of manufacturing activities comparable with that of the British can innovative neglect even begin to be appraised, though one would guess that in the middle decades of the nineteenth century such cases were few in number.[126] What more can society ask of its entrepreneurs?

IV. *The Critical Period, 1870–1914?*

In the last quarter of the nineteenth century, Britain ceased to be the only workshop of the world, an inevitable corollary of the development of competing economies. But need Britain's supremacy, once so overwhelmingly clear and apparently permanent, have been lost so quickly? Recent critics have argued, essentially, that 'to an indefinable but considerable extent leadership was not wrested from Britain, but fell from her ineffectual grasp',[127] a condemnation of British entrepreneurship most eloquently expressed by D. S. Landes in an earlier volume of this series.[128] The general validity of this charge will be discussed later.

THE STRUCTURE OF BUSINESS ENTERPRISE

First it is desirable to examine one of its constituent elements, that relating to the age and structure of the firm. As Landes puts it:

In many firms, the grandfather who started the business and built it by unremitting application and by thrift bordering on miserliness had long died; the father who took over a solid enterprise and, starting with larger ambitions, raised it to undreamed-of heights, had passed on the reins; now it was the turn of the third generation, the children of affluence, tired of the tedium of trade and flushed with the bucolic aspirations of the country gentleman . . . Many of them retired and forced the conversion of their firms into joint-stock companies. Others stayed on and went through the motions of entrepreneurship between the long weekends; they worked at play and played at work. Some of them were wise enough to leave the management of their enterprises to professionals . . . Yet such an arrangement is at best a poor substitute for interested ownership; at its worst, it is an invitation to conflict of interests and misfeasance . . .

Nor were corporate enterprises significantly better. For one thing, family considerations often determined their selection of managing personnel. For another, such scanty and impressionistic evidence as we have indicates that private and public companies alike recruited too many of their executives from the counting room rather than from the shop. And such production men as were elevated to high responsibility were more likely than not to be 'practical' people who had learned on the job and had a vested interest in the established way of doing things.[129]

On the third-generation question, it is possible that economic historians have been too strongly influenced by Rimmer's salutary story of Marshalls of Leeds, a firm which had been the world's leading concern in flax-spinning in the early decades of the nineteenth century but which, by the 1880s, had passed into receivership, after the founder's sons had neglected the business and their own sons in turn despised it. Other cases undoubtedly exist – one such was the business established by Benjamin Gott[130] – but they are suspiciously hard to find, certainly in this classic form. Nevertheless, some empirical support for the 'Buddenbrooks syndrome' has been provided, albeit in a qualified manner, by T. J. Byres, R. A. Church, and D. C. Coleman,[131] the last of whom has rightly drawn attention to the existence of equally significant exceptions[132] and to the fact that 'if one castigates successful mid-Victorian businessmen for quitting their offices and factories, one is only blaming them for following a long-established English custom'.[133] It may be salutary to remember the gloom and despondency suffered by Kirkman Finlay, who confided in his diary in 1831:

In 1819, I had a fortune which would have allowed me to spend £5 to £6,000 yearly, and since that period my profits have amounted to a sum which had all been accumulated would have put me in possession now of £180,000 to £200,000. But what had been my conduct? By a purchase of the lands of Achenwillan in 1819 p.£14,050 a commencement was made for the most wild and inconsiderate outlay. I was induced to make an addition to the House and my own pride and vanity, and the selfish conduct of the Architect, who considered only how his own reputation could be advanced, led me to a very large and expensive building, filled my mind with new and extravagant ideas and induced me to purchase more land, and to expend upon the property an immense and most imprudently large sum of money.[134]

There was nothing new about the diversion of entrepreneurial energies from the firm into manifold non-business activities in the closing decades of the nineteenth century,[135] nor was it a peculiarity of the second or third generation: it was not Robert Owen III who put his dreams to the test in New Harmony, or Richard Arkwright jun. who 'exchanged the company of mechanics for that of the Derbyshire gentry', or George Crosfield who frittered away the profits of his father's soapery in 'an extraordinary catalogue of speculative investments'.[136]

Indeed, just how many firms remained under the control of the same family for three generations? And of those, what proportion fell into the palsied hands of that third generation in the period under discussion? In mechanical engineering, 'few firms were born before 1850 and the third generation was not reached until after 1914'.[137] And taking an industry – woollen textiles – which can claim the necessary antiquity, the population of firms underwent such drastic changes during the years 1870–1914 that at the end of that period 'few could trace their origins back before its beginning'.[138] Furthermore, the work of E. M. Sigsworth and Janet Blackman suggests that

while woollen manufacturing firms (31 per cent of whom in 1912 had origins ante-dating 1870) were successful in meeting foreign competition, worsted manufacturing firms, only 8 per cent of whom originated before 1870, signally failed to do so, i.e., in this case firms of recent origin were less successful than firms of greater antiquity.

Equally apposite is Sigsworth's observation that

two of the few full scale histories of British wool textile firms would suggest that the third and fourth generations of a family were able to continue the business without too much hardship, one being especially prominent in the extent to which it acquired landed estates and allied its members with titled families. It should presumably have promptly bled to death.[139]

The third-generation argument remains unproven and will remain so until more data are available on the longevity of firms; but what of the related question of corporate control? Were the age-old critics of the joint-stock company form (with or without limited liability) correct in their belief that this was not an appropriate organization for manufacturing activity?[140] – that there was an inverse relationship between the vigour of enterprise and the growth of the joint-stock company? The argument, especially in the light of American experience, seems highly implausible.

If there was any connection between entrepreneurial decline and the form of business enterprise, it is much more likely to have operated through a reluctance to make radical changes in company structure in response to changing environmental conditions. The fact is that company registration after the codifying Act of 1862 served all too frequently to give the appearance of change while maintaining essential continuity. After a number of conspicuous 'limitations' of private firms in the early years, involving the creation of really public companies with freely transferable shares (for example, Palmer's Iron and Shipbuilding Company and Bolckow Vaughan & Co.), 'a large and increasing proportion of the companies formed under the Acts [were] private companies', the number of whose members generally did 'not exceed twenty, and very commonly [was] not above seven'; and of these, four, five, or even six might be 'dummies'.[141]

It would appear that the experience of Thomas Vickers was not untypical. In giving evidence to the 1886 Committee on Trade and Industry, he said that 'it has been an advantage to my company to be a Limited Liability Company – because I have always had as much power as a director of this company as I had as a partner and the resources of the company are greater than the resources of the old partnership'.[142] Indeed, the witnesses from the Northern industries constantly reiterated that the direction and management of their concerns were usually identical with those of the former partnerships.[143] The adoption of corporate status with limited liability usually meant that the technical ownership of many businesses, while sometimes in more hands, had not yet changed the groups of leading entrepreneurs.[144]

And if this verdict is correct in the case of limited companies, how much truer is it of 'the vast majority' of manufacturing concerns which remained family businesses in the mid-1880s, comprising

all, or nearly all, the wool firms; outside Oldham, nearly all the cotton firms; and the same in linen, silk, jute, lace and hosiery. Most of the smaller, and some of the largest, engineering firms, and nearly all the cutlery and pottery firms, were still private. Brewing was a family affair. So, with certain outstanding exceptions, were the Birmingham trades and a great, perhaps the major, part of the shipbuilding industry. In housebuilding and the associated trades there were very few limited companies; few in the clothing trades; few in the food trades . . . Add the many scores of thousands of retail businesses, 'unlimited almost to a shop'.[145]

There is, then, little evidence of any significant divorce of control from ownership in the two or three decades following the Act of 1862. Undoubtedly, scattered cases exist in addition to the Oldham Limiteds. Palmer's Shipbuilding Co., where in the 1860s perhaps only 25 of the 300 shareholders attended the annual meeting, was one.[146] And a growing lack of interest on the part of those shareholders who were slowly building up diversified equity portfolios or were geographically dispersed was reported to the Select Committee on the Company Acts of 1862 and 1867.[147] The increasing practice of 'proxy' voting too was encouraging a loosening of ownership for control, but, as Jefferys repeatedly shows, it must not be assumed that these developments were widespread, certainly not before the mid-1880s.

Not until the second half of the 1880s can there be discerned any marked divorce of ownership from control. It is perhaps in the quarter-century preceding the First World War that the roots of British 'managerial capitalism' can be perceived. Certainly, by the twentieth century 'the functions of ownership of the capital and control of its use were being separated. The right hand did not know, was losing the power to know, and often did not want to know, what the left hand was doing.'[148] This was a consequence of a number of interrelated developments. A growing number of shareholders were spreading their investments in order to enjoy a regular income. They might spread their savings over some thirty companies; indeed, they were advised by financial journalists 'not to carry all their eggs in one basket'. The corollary was that so long as the flow of dividends was uninterrupted, such rentier investors displayed little real interest in the conduct of those companies whose equity they owned. And if, on occasion, they did raise their voices at the annual general meeting, they were often frightened by the directors into agreeing to remain in darkness by the argument that the publication of any light on the subject of profits might lead to competition and labour troubles, or were bludgeoned into quiescence by a recital of past profits, the continuance of which was seriously threatened by any revelation of 'intimate business details'.[149] And whereas the passivity of the wealthy rentier could usually be ensured by such tactics, there were others, widows and orphans, clergymen, if not perhaps the great majority of the lower-middle-class investors – increasingly numbered among the shareholders of the public companies – whose *desire* for knowledge concerning the companies in which they had been advised to invest hardly extended beyond the names of their firms.[150]

Boards of directors were thus free to control the destinies of their companies. Indeed, for many decades there was little reason to question this arrangement, since the directors were usually the largest shareholders. The merger movement at the turn of the century was characterized by the great extent to which the vendors of the constituent companies retained the new equity in their own hands.[151] Nevertheless, an increasing proportion of the larger firms were controlled by directors whose total shareholdings represented a minority of the equity capital and whose holdings grew relatively smaller.[152] 'The effect was that [such] companies tended to develop a momentum of [their] own. Even when [the profits of such a company] were nil, owing to the lack of effective control being exercised by the owners of the capital, the company could go on existing'.[153] And there were strong reasons why it should continue. Drawing fees and other perquisites from the company, those directors whose sole purpose was 'ornamental', or who had acquired their seats to cement alliances with other firms with which a formal connection was desirable, had every incentive to support the man or group of men among their colleagues who provided the main motive power of the concern.

Thus, by the First World War, the policies of a number of home 'industrials' – in iron and steel, shipbuilding, engineering, textiles, chemicals, brewing, and foodstuffs – were controlled by groups of shareholders owning a minority of the voting capital. A partial divorce of ownership from control had taken place. The proportion of firms in which this development was taking place was probably small, but it is almost certain that it affected some of the biggest enterprises in each industrial group. What is perhaps remarkable is the enormous number of private companies[154] where there largely continued the complete marriage of ownership and control characteristic of the classical entrepreneur.

This brief discussion of the developing structure of the firm does little to weaken the force of Landes's argument that the management of corporate enterprises was not 'significantly better' than the family firm. All that has been shown is the tenacity of the older firm of business organization, for the private joint-stock company was simply the partnership writ large. And where a firm was ostensibly a *public* limited-liability company, such was the distribution of power that the vast majority of them behaved in a manner indistinguishable from their legally unrecognized competitors. Thus, 'leadership by inheritance applied in a great range of industrial activities: in steel, coal and brewing, "as well as in pottery, carpets, boots and shoes, cocoa . . . sugar and the older branches of engineering" '.[155] All too frequently the channels of advancement for the professional manager were blocked by family control, and where exceptions were made it appears to have been accountants rather than production staff who were promoted to the board,[156] perhaps because whereas those at the top were confident that they fully understood manufacturing methods, they often acknowledged, even boasted about, their complete ignorance of balance-sheets and accounts.

Nor did the establishment of the giant concerns produced by multifirm mergers in the period 1885–1905 create any irresistible pressure for internal organizational changes that might have made the recruitment of professional executives imperative.[157] The fact that the majority of them were single-product companies,[158] involving little integration and even less diversification, and that they were inspired by defensive motives rather than by a desire for greater efficiency meant that centralized management was still possible, if not appropriate. Thus those who came out on top during the course of the internecine wars of vendor–directors of the new combinations could continue to conduct the affairs of the merged companies as if all that had happened was that what had hitherto been their own particular firms had grown larger by the multiplication of units, a state of affairs that had deep historical roots. There was then no necessity to restructure the enterprises and little or no need for professional experts in different functions. This is not, of course, to deny that these mammoth concerns would not have been infinitely more efficient and longer-lived had restructuring taken place, but that it did not do so should be no cause for surprise: this was

Table 40. *Analysis of Large Mergers^a by Type, 1880–1918*

Type of merger	Number of large mergers		Number of firms disappearing in large mergers		Value of firms disappearing in large mergers	
	No.	% of total	No.	% of total	£m	% of total
Horizontal	64	87	643	98	116	92
Vertical	9	12	11	2	10	8
Diversifying	1	1	1	0	0·6	0
Total	74	100	655	100	126·6	100

^{a} Large merger: arbitrarily defined as one in which the firm(s) disappearing were valued at £250,000 or more up to 1899, and at £500,000 or more from 1900 onwards.

SOURCE. Leslie Hannah, 'Mergers in British Manufacturing Industry, 1880–1918', *Oxford Economic Papers*, n.s., XXVI (1974), 11.

not the prime reason for their initial creation. Their object was to achieve a significant degree of monopoly power in order to give effective sanction to the attempt to increase prices, and sufficiently to control the level of output of the constituent parts to effect this. 'They were,' as Peter Mathias has observed, 'more in the nature of an existing trade association given a single legal entity than they were effective operational units in a management sense.'[159]

AN ASSESSMENT OF PERFORMANCE

It is one thing to hunt the entrepreneur, quite another to assess his performance. Perhaps the high-water mark of the critical school was reached with the publication of volume VI of this *History*, when David Landes summarized the weaknesses of late-Victorian British enterprise which, he argued, reflected a

combination of amateurism and complacency. Her merchants, who had once seized the markets of the world, took them for granted; the consular reports are full of the incompetence of British exporters, their refusal to suit their goods to the tastes and pockets of the client, their unwillingness to try new products in new areas . . . Similarly, the British manufacturer was notorious for his indifference to style, his conservatism in the face of new techniques, his reluctance to abandon the individuality of tradition for the conformity implicit in mass production.[160]

Since this was written (apparently between 1958 and 1962), the tide has ebbed.[161] H. J. Habakkuk's stimulating essay *American and British Technology in the Nineteenth Century* drew attention to the possibility that British entrepreneurial deficiencies could be explained as a consequence of a slow rate of market growth – that, in fact, the well-attested lack of adventurousness in many branches of British industry was a logical response to demand conditions rather than evidence of waning entrepreneurship.[162] Shortly after this, Charles Wilson made a strong plea for an extension of the study of manufacturing activity beyond the frontiers of 'pig iron and cotton stockings' to new industries: soap, patent medicines, mass-produced foodstuffs, and light engineering – 'the production of vigorous and ingenious entrepreneurs as dynamic as any of their predecessors'.[163] Meanwhile, the authors marshalled by D. H. Aldcroft to examine a number of major British industries in an endeavour to refine his own earlier critical evaluation of 'the British entrepreneur'[164] were searching government reports, official commissions, and trade journals to discover (perhaps to the editor's – or to their own – surprise?) that really hard evidence of entrepreneurial failure was remarkably elusive, that generalization on this score was hazardous, and that, while some 'patchiness' was apparent, British industry appears to have been both competitive and efficient in the closing decades of the nineteenth century.[165]

Other recent studies have reached similar conclusions,[166] and if their authors have discussed deficiencies, technological lags, and gaps between the best and the average practice, much of the lost ground was being made up in the years preceding the First World War.[167] Meanwhile, the proponents of the new economic history, eschewing peripheral industries, have returned to the nineteenth-century staples. Although the Lancashire cotton industry 'continued to produce yarns and, to a lesser extent, piece goods more cheaply than the American industry throughout the period',[168] Britain's 'lag in ring spinning has usually been taken as a sign of technological conservatism, not to say backwardness'.[169] Yet Sandberg's careful examination of this contention concludes that 'under the conditions then prevailing with regard to factor costs, as well as the technical capabilities of the ring spindles then being built, the British may well have been acting rationally'.[170] While D. M. McCloskey, after an intensive study of the performance of the British iron and steel industry[171] – an industry 'which has to a special degree encouraged generalizations concerning the economy as a whole'[172] – has demonstrated, with a wealth of statistical data and an armoury of economic techniques, not only that the slow adoption of the basic steel-making process (which has been called 'the most notable single instance of entrepreneurial failure') and the much-criticized neglect of phosphoric Lincolnshire ores were a rational response in a competitive market to the location of the ores and a proper appreciation of the technological processes, but also that the British ironmasters and steelmakers exploited the potentialities of world technology before the First World War as well as – if not better than – their much-lauded American competitors. 'Late Victorian entrepreneurs in iron and steel did not fail. By any cogent measure of performance, in fact, they did very well indeed.'[173] From this, McCloskey has turned to a briefer examination of the British coal industry, from which he emerges with the finding that 'the case for a failure of masters and men in British coal mining before 1913 ... is vulnerable to a most damaging criticism: there was clearly no failure of productivity'.[174] Of all the recent reassessments employing the methodology of cost–benefit analysis, only the work of Peter H. Lindert and Keith Trace has clearly demonstrated entrepreneurial deficiencies – namely, among those producers who clung to the Leblanc process long after the superiority of the ammonia process (patented by Solvay) was apparent.[175]

All in all, the hypothesis of entrepreneurial failure in the late-Victorian economy has recently taken 'quite a beating'.[176] But doubts remain. So much depends on what yardsticks are traced for the measurement of success or failure: international comparisons of productivity? the rapidity of technological diffusion? adaptation to change? profitability? So much of the argument has turned upon a consideration of aggregative measures. So little attention has been given to marketing methods and techniques – an omission which, given contemporary anxieties concerning competition both at home and overseas, represents a major weakness in the current debate.[177]

It was perhaps this element in the overall situation that initially undermined the present writer's confidence in Landes's overall condemnation of British enterprise. Admittedly, the consular reports[178] are full of criticism, but it should be remembered that consular officials were paid to point out the inadequacies of the British selling effort: they are largely silent on the successes.[179] There is, however, a verisimilitude about some of the complaints that it would be foolish to deny; but for every salesman trying to force his goods into the unwilling hands of a protesting customer, passively displaying his inappropriate wares, or being thwarted by multi-lingual, thrusting German representatives or brash, indefatigable Yankee drummers,[180] there was a British manufacturer falling over himself to produce goods to the most perverse specifications in order to satisfy the customers' often unreasonable demands. How else can the multiplicity of shapes and sections offered by the British steelmakers be explained?[181] or the great diversity of locomotives, carriages, and wagons offered by the builders of engines and rolling stock be understood?[182] or the row after row of pattern books of the constituent firms of the United Turkey Red Company be appreciated?[183] Indeed, by ever-increasing specialization designed to exploit marginal differences in quality, and by creating the impression that the differences were greater than they were in reality, many British firms were able to secure a degree of oligopoly power in overseas (and domestic) markets that resulted in high unit profits.[184] This may have produced poor productivity figures, but for individual concerns it was often good business.[185]

Undoubtedly, the key to an understanding of the role of the entrepreneur, and hence to a proper assessment of his performance, lies in the analysis of the business records increasingly being located and calendared – so often is it necessary to seek a reconciliation between the actual behaviour of businessmen and the implications of 'the new economic history'. As H. W. Richardson has suggested, 'what makes a progressive entrepreneur is how he acts in a *given set of conditions*',[186] and to discover these conditions, which are often highly specific and extremely complex, it is imperative to examine the surviving letter books, bundles of incoming correspondence, agents' reports, and internal memoranda of individual firms, and to compare the findings with those derived from the records of similar firms in the same line of business operating in the same markets. Such investigations will doubtless reveal a spectrum of leading and lagging firms, and whether or not an industry evinces flagging entrepreneurship will depend upon the relative economic weight of the leaders and the laggards.

However, such a procedure promises to permit only a more accurate assessment of enterprises that were implemented. What it cannot show is where some new and potentially profitable avenues of enterprise were apparently either neglected or ignored.[187] It has been argued that the reason for this failure was 'the absence of a scientific education among the young in all grades and conditions in this country . . . Other contributory causes have doubtless led to our inability to maintain preeminence in the world of industry. But our educational system, or want of system, is the root cause.'[188] But here the sinner was not so much the British industrialist as society at large.[189] Furthermore, the emphasis on specific and neglected innovations tends to obscure the very real structural changes transforming the late-Victorian economy.[190] The trade, transport, professional, and service sectors were growing faster than the industrial sectors in the period 1870–1914; surely this is a manifestation of entrepreneurial perspicacity?

Was it then a critical period of entrepreneurship? The answer is No. It was simply that with the development of competitive economies, British entrepreneurial errors and hesitations – always present, even in the period of the classic industrial revolution – became more apparent, and the belabouring of the businessmen who seemed inadequate in their resources mollified the frustrations of those who believed that British industrial supremacy before the mid-1870s was somehow normal, and her accelerating relative decline thereafter abnormal. Rather, it was that the whole complex of circumstances that produced British pre-eminence before 1873 was fortuitous. To see the course of British economic development in the eighteenth and nineteenth centuries in terms of the dissipation of an initial fund of entrepreneurship is untenable.

V. The Inter-War Years

INSTITUTIONAL CHANGE AND THE LOCATION OF ENTREPRENEURSHIP

The developments in industrial ownership and control apparent in the decades preceding the First World War accelerated in the inter-war period. The virtual disappearance of the sole proprietorship or small partnership in manufacturing organization coincided with a marked increase in the number of private limited-liability companies, which by 1938 outnumbered the public companies by ten to one. Yet with all this numerical increase, the economic significance of private companies was decreasing: their aggregate capital was only £1,900 million compared with the £4,100 million of the public companies.[191]

More important, the two decades between the wars saw an enormous increase in the number and variety of companies characterized by some degree of separation of ownership from control. In the majority of the larger companies the proportion of the shares held by any single holder (or, indeed, by the board of directors jointly) had become relatively insignificant, and some enterprises numbered their shareholders by thousands, even tens of thousands.[192] Nevertheless, P. S. Florence's 1947 analysis of twenty joint-stock companies indicated that in the mid-1930s 'the *partial* divorce of ownership from control [seemed] characteristic of large companies'.[193]

But there seems little doubt that the inter-war period saw a steady diminution in the powers of the shareholders in the larger – and therefore economically most significant – companies. In a 'realistic structural analysis of the actual shareholders and the distribution of shares among them', Florence showed that 'the voting rights of shares [tended] to be more unequal in the larger than the smaller English companies'.[194] But he argued that

> the main reason . . . for denying that shareholders as a whole wield top powers in the government of companies and corporations [lay] in their situation and behaviour. To start with, there [were] too many of them for effective deliberation and decision . . . It may be estimated with some confidence that the bulk of industrial transactions . . . in Britain [were] conducted by companies . . . of 2,000 shareholders or more . . . an effective general meeting [was] obviously impossible.[195]

Equally significant is the fact that the great majority of persons holding shares sought no active role in company government. A large number of them were children or very old people; nearly half were women, many of them shy (or positively frightened) of business; and even those shareholders (undoubtedly the minority) who were capable of participating in the affairs of their companies chose not to do so, since the bulk of them had diversified portfolios, and hence their holdings in any one company were very small – certainly too small to influence the Board's decisions. Such shareholders were, moreover, often merely transient speculators, having no sustained interest in the company's affairs.[196]

Such a situation was, and is, conducive to allowing the control of the largest companies to reside in the hands of the larger shareholders. Florence has argued that when the twenty largest shareholders own at least 20 per cent of the voting stock among them, they possess real control of the company with little fear of any strong opposition, so rapidly does the percentage of voting power owned by smaller holders taper off.[197] This is especially so where the twenty largest shareholders are linked by family and other connections, and where a significant proportion are directors. An outstanding – if somewhat exceptional – example of family control through large shareholdings in the mid-thirties was Tate and Lyle Limited, where in 1935 six members of the Tate family were among the twenty largest shareholders, holding among them 27·4 per cent of all voting stock and six directorships, and three members of the Lyle family holding among them 15·2 per cent of all voting shares and two directorships. Other examples of relatively concentrated ownership, much of it by connected persons, were found in brewing, foodstuffs, and distribution.

Indeed, such a large proportion (58 per cent) of the 82 largest British industrial companies analysed were characterized in 1935 by a dominant ownership interest, and so few (9 per cent) by no discernible dominance of ownership interest (33 per cent were marginal cases), that Florence believed that any proclamation of the managerial revolution in the Britain of the mid-thirties was quite unjustified.[198] Instead, in the largest companies there appears to have been very many cases where control was exercised by virtue of partial ownership. Where ownership was so distributed that a small coherent group of shareholders could have control through the ownership of but a minority of the capital, there has, in fact, been little departure from the case of the classic entrepreneur. If to this economically significant group be added the enormous number of private companies and small and medium-sized public companies where the same is true, the slow growth of managerial capitalism is apparent. Nevertheless, there were great companies where almost complete divorce of control from ownership had taken place: cases such as Dunlop Rubber, Liebigs Meat Extract Co., Rylands (Textiles), where there was little concentration in shareholding, or cases such as Associated Electrical Industries, Birmingham Small Arms, British Aluminium, English Sewing Cotton, and ICI, where the directors owned but a minute percentage of the shares.[199]

There is no question that many boards of directors in British firms in the inter-war period contained members who regarded 'balance sheets with dread and [found] themselves unable to grasp the principles upon which they were compiled'. Such were the guinea-pig or decorative directors whose role had been the subject of complaints since the latter part of the nineteenth century. According to Horace Samuel, in 1932 there were 562 directorships held by English peers not distinguished before their elevation to the peerage as captains of industry or as active members of City firms, or in other ways known as executive members of industrial undertakings.[200] Conversely, by the mid-thirties many directors owed their positions not to their share holdings or their family connections, or to their 'drawing power', but to their valuable specialized knowledge, gained sometimes in the employment of the firm and sometimes in the course of their professional training.[201]

The presence of an increasing number of accountants, lawyers, and technicians in the boardroom is a reflection of managerial innovations necessitated by the increase in the size of the major large-scale firms. Whereas the merger movement at the turn of the century had so often resulted in large, cumbersome, and inefficient boards of directors,[202] many of the very large enterprises that emerged as a result of the intensive merger wave of the 1920s began – albeit feebly – to grapple with the fundamental problems of management that were an inevitable corollary of growth.[203] One of the most successful companies to do so was ICI, which, at the time of its formation in 1926, was the largest company formed by merger in British manufacturing industry, being an amalgamation of four companies (Nobel, Brunner Mond, The British Dyestuffs Corporation, and the United Alkali Co. – themselves the products of previous mergers) having a total market value of over £60 million.[204] By adopting a managerial structure characterized by a central office responsible for purchasing, personnel, publicity, legal, taxation, and investment matters, and some devolution of responsibility to the manufacturing units – a structure that had been evolved by Nobels in the quinquennium before 1926 – ICI inherited the germs of a financially centralized group with decentralized divisional management. That is, it adopted a managerial structure which the pioneering work of Alfred D. Chandler has shown was rapidly evolving in the United States in the 1920s and early 1930s and which was to become the standard form of internal organization for an enterprise that had embarked on a strategy of product diversification and overseas expansion.[205]

Although ICI appears to have advanced further than most British firms towards a structure of decentralized divisions in the inter-war years, some other companies[206] – particularly those whose rapid growth threatened to outrun their managerial resources, unless radical organizational changes were adopted – took up certain elements of what was to become known as the multi-divisional structure.[207] Despite the fact that there was considerable variation between companies, and within the same company at different points in time, the increasing number of growing concerns which moved hesitantly in this direction – often limiting themselves to sequential acquisitions[208] in order to postpone the inevitable internal reorganization – had to recruit functional specialists in personnel, finance, accounting, and technical matters. Some of these could be trained within the firm; others were recruited from the civil service (particularly the Inland Revenue) and, where men experienced in bureaucratic production and large-scale administrative control were required, from the armed forces. Of particular importance were accountants, 'for it was particularly through developments in accounting that the introduction of new methods for the oversight and assessment of subsidiaries was encouraged and facilitated'.[209]

But the mergers brought with them more than managerial innovation. They were the primary cause of the increasing concentration of British industry. This subject has been touched upon in the discussion of the four decades before the First World War,[210] but not until the pioneering work of Leak and Maizels was it possible to say anything precise about the degree of concentration that had occurred. Using data collected for the 1935 Census of Production, they calculated that the 135 largest business units (i.e. those employing 5,000 or more persons) employed nearly a quarter of all those enumerated and were responsible for a similar proportion of total gross output.[211] Among the fifteen main trade groups there were five in which the three largest units employed 39 per cent of the labour force or more, and when trades were further subdivided there were no fewer than thirty-three subdivisions (or over 10 per cent of the total number) in which the largest three enterprises accounted for over 70 per cent of the total employment. Of these trades or subdivisions of trades, eight were in the 'chemical and allied trades' group; six in the 'engineering, shipbuilding, and vehicles' group; five in the 'food, drink, and tobacco' group; and five in the 'miscellaneous' groups.[212]

The subsequent work of Hart and Prais makes it clear that the concentration of industry in the United Kingdom had tended to increase markedly since the turn of the century, particularly among those enterprises whose establishment dates back to that period; this is basically because during the first fifty years of this century firms expanded largely by internal growth, and each increment of growth appears to have been associated with a decrease in the probability of 'death'. Essentially, increase in size apparently made for continued survival and hence the likelihood of growing concentration.[213] Now it is among these surviving firms that the divorce of ownership from control is likely to have gone furthest; 'mere age has an important influence on the distribution of ownership. If Tate and Lyle had been a company as long as the Bleachers' Association, fewer Tates and Lyles would probably be found among the shareholders and there would be a much wider distribution of stock.'[214] The indications are that by the eve of the Second World War entrepreneurship in the most important concerns in each branch of industry was increasingly located among salaried managers, however pertinacious may have been the grip of the classical entrepreneur lower down the scale.[215] (The possible implications of this tendency will be considered in section VI below, on the post-war years.)

ENTREPRENEURIAL PERFORMANCE: A PROVISIONAL ASSESSMENT

To assess the performance of British entrepreneurship in the inter-war years is difficult, if not – in the absence, so far, of much of the data necessary for such an exercise – impossible. The majority of scholarly business histories of British firms effectively end at about 1914,[216] but even had the histories we have analysed been brought nearer to the present, the scarcity of such studies would inhibit generalization. Such information as is available on, say, productivity and the adoption of the latest technological knowledge would, on balance, seem to indicate that Britain increasingly lagged behind her major competitors.[217] These findings have led to a belief that some part of the explanation must be sought in entrepreneurial imperfections.[218] So it may prove.

The verdict of Professor Coleman on Courtaulds may, as he suggests, have a more general applicability:

If in reality its technical dynamism was poor, its management weaker than it should have been, and its organization inappropriate to its required function, these defects were overshadowed by its practical achievements and its solid financial position. Though it no longer had the vigour of Samuel Courtauld III or of Henry Tetley, it had other and less dramatic virtues. In certain ways Courtaulds Ltd still had some Victorian qualities about it, with the strengths and weaknesses which belonged to that practical and earnest era. And in that it probably resembled more than we sometimes care to admit a good deal of British industry before the Second World War.[219]

The fact is, of course, that entrepreneurial behaviour must be assessed within the context of the firm. There has been all too much criticism based upon social and/or general economic factors. As Richardson has emphasized,

If innovations do not yield reductions in average unit costs, then it would be irrational for a businessman to introduce them even if the innovations would benefit the future growth of the economy. The individual businessman cannot be expected to estimate external economies. The net social returns from investment in innovations may be higher than the private returns, with the result that a capitalistic environment may produce a rate of innovation well below the social optimum.[220]

But if social considerations are to be regarded as relevant, then in the inter-war period not the least one could ask of those providing entrepreneurial services was that they kept their firms or their plant in existence, providing employment if not profits. Certainly, John Craig of Colvilles Ltd – one of the leaders of the 'inferior'[221] British iron and steel industry – was so motivated, as was his successor, Sir Andrew McCance.[222] The question resolves itself into asking whether growth is to be achieved at any price.[223] The trouble is that when one studies the records of individual firms in detail, one can so often see that the decisions arrived at *appear* to have been the most rational at the time with regard both to profitability and to social considerations for the foreseeable future.[224]

The difficulty lies in assessing the 'term' of these criteria. What may be most profitable, or most conducive to survival in bad times, or most socially desirable for the next few years may produce almost diametrically opposite results in the longer term. By tinkering with existing plant, for example, the firm may overcome immediate difficulties, only to collapse entirely within a decade, squeezed out by more radical competitors both at home and overseas; and what then of employment considerations and the well-being of the dependent community? The problem is that the outsider, confronted with the identical data considered by the board or the partners, can rarely fault the contemporary decision in terms of the relevant time horizon. Only with hindsight can one perceive what might have been, and perhaps the greatest failure of the British entrepreneur – if indeed there was a failure – was his frequent lack of appreciation of future possibilities, one of the reasons being rooted in the paucity of technical expertise in the boardrooms.[225] It is conceivable that the fundamental difference between British and – for example – American entrepreneurs lies in their different time horizons, coupled with a greater ruthlessness on the latter's part.[226]

But it may be that the poor response from British firms to organizational challenges – frequently made manifest in what was, perhaps, an unjustified belief in the continued efficiency of the holding-company form – was in itself a cause of relative stagnation. Because otherwise progressive firms feared the managerial stresses involved in diversification, many opportunities which might have been exploited had the company possessed a variant of the multi-divisional structure were ignored or rejected or – even more unfortunately for long-term economic growth – taken up unsuccessfully, so inhibiting further change. Thus, as Hannah has emphasized, Vickers failed in their postwar strategy of diversifying into railway and electrical equipment – by the acquisition in 1919 of the Metropolitan Amalgamated Railway Carriage and Wagon Company (which itself had taken over British Westinghouse in 1917) – and expanding their automobile subsidiary, Wolseley. After calamitous losses in 1923–5, Wolseley went into receivership and was sold to William Morris; in 1928 Vickers' electrical manufacturing interest returned to American control, a major holding having been bought by the International General Electric Company of the United States; and the Metropolitan Co. passed into the hands of the Metropolitan–Cammell Carriage, Wagon & Finance Company, whose ordinary share capital was held jointly by Vickers and Cammell Laird. 'It is,' Hannah observes, 'difficult to resist the conclusion that Vickers' strategy of diversification had been too ambitious and its managerial response to the problems of diversification quite inadequate.'[227]

Other firms contemplating diversification were perhaps dissuaded from so doing by the example of Vickers, simply because they were reluctant radically to alter their internal organizations.[228] Thus structure shaped strategy, and if one criticizes British industrialists for their policies during the inter-war period one is, in effect, frequently condemning not their conservative decisions – to have been more ambitious while operating within the traditional framework of control would often have courted disaster – but their failure to appreciate the need for fundamental organizational innovation. This would have permitted more flexible policies and may even have produced superior lines of communication between board and top management whereby the executives were supplied with both more and better information.[229]

There is considerable evidence that British industry was and is over-manned, and this in turn may be a consequence of the fact that industrialists have had to operate with a work force which, as Hobsbawm puts it, had learned 'the rules of the game' for some decades before the First World War.[230] It is also plausible to argue that the changing structure of the firm was conducive to a greater sensitivity towards the demands and rights of the workers. As the small, internally financed family firm gradually gave way to the public company, enterprises increasingly offered less resistance to trade unions and collective bargaining, because such giving way would no longer expose them to the ruin which might have overcome the small firm earlier in the nineteenth century. 'There was also under these conditions much less resentment of factory legislation as an infraction of the employers' personal rights, for a company could less easily plead to be the embodiment of the virtues of individual self-reliance.'[231] There is little doubt that many businessmen believed, with Samuel Courtauld, that 'the highest rate of profit should not be the over-ruling consideration'.[232]

This may go some way to explain Britain's apparently flagging entrepreneurial performance. It in no way excuses many clear and, in some cases, remediable weaknesses: the notorious failures to provide proper information on which decisions might be made;[233] the obvious departures from the best international practice; the irrational policies of 'keeping the scientists in their place';[234] the continued general indifference to – even outright hostility towards – Taylorism and scientific management, long after its more obvious merits had been demonstrated by such advocates as Edward Cadbury, B. Seebohm Rowntree, and Hans and G. C. Reynold;[235] the occasional mad scrambles into ill-considered diversification;[236] the increasing perversities of some industrial leaders – 'the tragic story of the later years of the Morris empire illustrates at every step the ravages of an eccentric dictator';[237] and the tardiness with which merged concerns were properly integrated.[238]

This last weakness echoes similar failings of the closing years of the nineteenth century.[239] Indeed, it is possible to list a comprehensive range of criticisms of the inter-war entrepreneur which is already historically familiar. Whether these deficiencies had a greater or lesser aggregative impact on the national economy than those of earlier periods there is as yet no way of knowing, nor is it yet possible to assess the typicality of the documented examples. They simply illustrate the hypothesis that there is no justification for singling out any epoch for either unalloyed praise or unqualified denunciation of its entrepreneurial behaviour. There will always be business leaders whose performance lags behind the best or even the average, but prima facie cases of inefficiency deserve careful investigation before condemnation is fully justified. All too many entrepreneurs, like J. D. Rockefeller, have believed in the policy of keeping silent under attack, giving rise to the belief, as T. S. Ashton pointed out, that they 'must have a good deal to be silent about'.[240]

Because many leading industrialists in the immediate past have consciously chosen not to explain their actions, certainly not to the public, several apparently erroneous decisions seem to have been based on sheer prejudice instead of the rational calculation revealed by company records and the oral evidence of those who participated in the decision-making process.[241]

Few entrepreneurs of the inter-war period have been so heartily castigated as the coal-masters, yet in one of the rare industrial studies specifically devoted to an examination of their performance, it has been contended that 'although there were certain evident weaknesses on the supply side of the industry, these and the subsequent decline of coal mining owed little to entrepreneurial failings; that the entrepreneur reached decisions regarding plant size, investment and wages policy that were both rational and justified; and that while, with the benefit of hindsight, it might be argued that in certain instances more vigorous and decisive policies could have been adopted, it would be unreasonable to expect these to have done more than mitigate the deleterious effects of demand-side forces.'[242] A similar general verdict might well be brought in on the entrepreneurs of other industries, however stupid or irresponsible might have been the behaviour of those who led, or failed to lead, certain individual enterprises.

VI. *Recent Developments, 1945–70*

MERGERS AND CONCENTRATION

Since 1945 the trends in industrial ownership and management apparent during the two preceding periods have continued,[243] slowly at first (certainly until the mid-fifties), then rapidly accelerating. Indeed, the movement towards increasing concentration in British industry may even have suffered a reversal during the war and the immediate post-war years, though the long-term trend reasserted itself thereafter. Despite the difficulties of making comparisons of concentration over time,[244] it would appear that between 1935 and 1968 a trend towards larger plants was paralleled by a trend towards larger enterprises,[245] and that the concentration ratios (whether measured by sales, employment, or gross output) of the majority of industries was growing. By 1958 it was already apparent that 'the extent to which many industries [were] dominated by a few "giant" enterprises [seemed] to be increasing', and since that time industry has experienced a massive wave of mergers, which has accelerated what appears to be a natural tendency towards increasing concentration.[246] The number of companies acquired may have fallen off between 1965 and 1967, but the value of those companies increased markedly (see Table 41). Indeed, whereas in the first half of

Table 41. *Merger Activity: Acquisitions by Quoted Companies in Manufacturing, Distribution, and Services, 1954–68*

	Number	Value ($£$m)
1954	275	105
1955	294	89
1956	246	131
1957	301	136
1958	341	120
1959	559	307
1960	736	338
1961	632	368
1962	636	358
1963	885	332
1964	939	502
1965	995	507
1966	805	447
1967	763	822
1968	942	1,774

SOURCE. P. E. Hart, M. A. Utton, and G. Walshe, *Mergers and Concentration in British Industry* (Cambridge, 1973), 3.

the century there is some evidence that growth in size tended to produce immortality in firms (see above, p. 215), in the last twenty years life at all but the very top has become somewhat less secure.[247] Moreover, it is clear that the degree of concentration for many trades was increasing very rapidly during the sixties (Table 42), and that the structure of

Table 42. *Average Level of Five-Firm Concentration Ratios in Manufacturing, 1935–74 (per cent)*

1935	52·0	1963	63·5
1951	55·8	1968	69·0
1958	58·7	1974	c. 76·0

SOURCE. Estimates by S. Aaronovitch and M. C. Sawyer, 'The Concentration of British Manufacturing', *Lloyds Bank Review*, no. 114 (October 1974), 15–16.

many British industries is currently undergoing widespread transformation. The importance of the hundred leading companies is remarkable. In 1970 they probably accounted for about 45 per cent of manufacturing net output in Britain (Table 43), about 50 per cent of all profits in

Table 43. *Share of the Largest Manufacturing Enterprises in Net Output, 1935–70 (per cent)*

1935	24	1963	38
1949	21	1968	42
1953	26	1970	(45)[a]
1958	33		

[a] 1970 figure is a provisional estimate.

SOURCE. S. J. Prais, 'A New Look at the Growth of Industrial Concentration', *Oxford Economic Papers*, n.s., XXVI (1974), 283.

manufacturing, building, and distribution, a considerably higher proportion of total assets, and about one-third of total employment of all industrial and commercial companies.[248]

OWNERSHIP AND CONTROL

In the post-1945 period there has been considerable discussion of the democratization of company holdings,[249] and many firms – particularly those perturbed by the threat of nationalization or governmental interference – have made much of graphical illustrations which purport to show that their capital is owned by very large, and growing, numbers of individuals and institutions.[250] This increasing democratization has clearly involved increasing separation of ownership from control,[251] but it should not be overstated, certainly not before the early 1950s when a significant number (perhaps a third) of large companies was still owner-controlled. Nevertheless, there is little question that in the larger companies the proportion of total votes held by the largest shareholders fell between 1936 to 1951 from 30 per cent to 19 per cent, and that over the same period there was a diminution in both the proportion of shares held by the directors and the number of directors among the twenty largest shareholders.[252] By 1968–9, the chairmen of the top hundred British industrial companies controlled only $2\frac{1}{2}$ per cent, and the entire boards of directors only $7\frac{1}{2}$ per cent, of the equity of those companies.[253] Moreover, it has been estimated that between 1957 and 1969 the beneficial holdings of persons, executors, and trustees fell from 65·8 per cent to 47·4 per cent of total holdings. That is, while the total *number* of individual shareholders has been increasing, the importance of individual holders of ordinary shares in terms of the relative *value* of their holdings compared with total holdings has been declining.[254]

Increasingly since 1945 professional directors and managers have displaced owner–managers. This trend is associated with the merger movement, which, in creating larger firms, has inevitably meant a diminution of shareholders' control through the dispersion of ownership;[255] with the supercession of the holding company in which the operating subsidiaries were long supervised by family firms; and with the increasing age of the existing public companies.[256] As early as 1951, Copeman believed that it was likely that 'an overwhelming majority of the existing public companies had been registered as public for more than one generation' and that, however large a proportion of the shares had originally been held by the original, often family-linked, owners, in subsequent years some of the large shareholders were undoubtedly obliged to sell some of their shares, particularly to meet estate duty.[257] Thus the sheer passage of time usually sees the fragmentation of large holdings.

Within the decade following Florence's analysis of 1951, it is probable that many firms then categorized as owner-controlled – for example, Associated Electrical Industries, the Bristol Aeroplane Company, J. and J. Coleman, and Bovril – ceased to qualify for inclusion in this group. Furthermore, 'several other firms, possibly as many as eight, had in the meantime grown to qualify for inclusion among the "largest" companies, but the relative numbers of owner-controlled firms among them was, if anything, smaller than in Florence's older sample'. Moreover, the trends in ownership evident in the largest firms are apparent in the next size category – the 'medium large' concerns with capitals between £1 million and £3 million – where the number of companies with concentrated ownership was getting smaller and was probably a minority by the mid-sixties, when only among companies smaller still (£0·2 million to £1 million) was control by owners still characteristic of the majority of enterprises.[258]

The reduction in the number of firms marked by a concentration of ownership, however, probably underestimates the degree to which shifts in the location of effective company rule have taken place in postwar Britain. That is, it is possible that the number of cases where potentialities for owner rule exist not only are becoming relatively fewer but are being less exploited. Such have been the competitive pressures in British industry since the mid-fifties that more and more firms characterized by concentrated, often family-linked, shareholding have been inclined – even forced – to entrust the control of their businesses to the most capable executives, irrespective of the latter's share in ownership or their absence of familial connections.[259] What is as yet obscure is how far the increasingly important institutional owners (themselves manager-controlled) exercise their growing power both over appointments to the board and in decision-making. Although in the past they seem to have been generally passive – not to say complacent – there is some evidence that they are increasingly prepared to 'intervene'; and with the formation in 1973 of the Institutional Shareholders Committee – which represents upwards of one-third of all ordinary shares – the institutions 'have the potential to exercise control over most of the large companies, if they choose to do so'. But because the new joint committee intends to work 'directly and without publicity', the economic historian is unlikely for many years to be in a position to gather empirical data on this question.[260]

The possible implications of the growing importance of managerial control will be considered later; at this point it is necessary simply to emphasize the acceleration in the growth of entrepreneurial power of professional executives throughout every branch of industrial activity and briefly to indicate the genesis of such leaders of industry. It is often alleged that some, perhaps almost a majority by the fifties, had 'come up from the ranks', but considerable caution is required in analysing and comparing the figures given by the various authorities because of confusion between directors, 'top management officials', and departmental and other managers.[261] Our concern is with entrepreneurial services, and these are provided by directors and chief executives. When only the recruitment to these two groups is considered, the proportion of those among them who started 'at the bottom' is not only very small but likely to decline as educational qualifications for managerial and executive positions slowly rise.[262] A larger number come from outside the firm altogether – scientists or technicians brought in from other firms or from universities.

The federated board of Imperial Chemical Industries and to a smaller extent the boards of firms like Shell or Unilever had come to contain scientists and engineers and themselves became recruiting grounds for other firms on a look-out for scientifically oriented directors. By 1964 erstwhile research scientists and engineers had come to occupy commanding positions in some of the largest firms in man-made fibres, for example, Courtauld, or heavy electrical engineering, such as the English Electric, or in aircraft groups, such as Hawker Siddeley and the British Aircraft Corporation.

Others were entrants from the Civil Service or from the professions, most significantly the accountants.[263]

This type of recruitment, relatively rare before 1939, is perhaps less remarkable than the high proportion of directors who have no formal qualifications at all.[264] Although the proportion of non-qualified directors is inversely related to the size of the firm, 'the striking feature' of the 1959 survey conducted by the Institute of Directors was 'the relatively small proportion [of directors] with a university degree and the high number who think that experience alone qualifies them for a directorship . . . [it would seem that] . . . business is not learned at school but depends largely on training on the job. The professional, academic man as yet plays a minor part in industry.'[265] The overall impression given by the various studies of top management recruitment, as Nichols found, is that 'directors are predominantly recruited from the top two social classes and that a substantial proportion of them had fathers who were themselves in business; probably about half of them have been to a public school and where they have been to a University at all there is a strong tendency to have been to Oxford or Cambridge', where, moreover, they are most likely to have taken an arts degree.[266] It is, as yet, too early to assess the impact on British management of the somewhat feverishly created business schools and the postgraduate business courses mounted in British universities, which fly in the face of the long-held belief that managerial principles cannot be taught. Certainly, the omens are not encouraging.[267]

In those firms still characterized by some degree of family ownership – Pilkington's, Wimpey, John Laing, Rowntree's, Cadbury's, Weir's, and innumerable brewing firms, Guinness's and Whitbread's among them[268] – men bearing the firm's name continue to occupy directoral seats or to be promoted to the board, though it would appear that increasingly the mere possession of a family connection is not enough to qualify.[269] The name has to be supported by professional expertise. In this, the 'close' firms are similar to the others. Everywhere the number of university graduates and those professionally qualified is increasing, albeit slowly; and if the proportion of graduates on boards of directors is lower and is growing less rapidly than among top managers, it might be expected that in time – as top management ascend to the commanding heights of the board to fill vacancies created by the death or retirement of those who began the ascent to the top in the inter-war years – the non-graduate director and executive will become increasingly rare.

This brief discussion of top management recruitment and the growing importance of what has been termed the 'non-propertied director' must not be allowed to obscure the fact that most small and medium-sized firms continue to be run as they have been since the earliest days of the industrial revolution. Indeed, the ownership and control of the overwhelming majority of unquoted companies is essentially unchanged. Private companies constituted no less than 98 per cent of all companies in 1961 and accounted for 39 per cent of civil employees (of whom over a third, 38 per cent, was in manufacturing and allied industries) and 40 per cent of the total profits generated by all enterprises. In such concerns – and some of them are very large by any standards – entrepreneurial power remains with the owner–manager: with the Ferrantis in electrical engineering, the McAlpines and Wates in construction, the Sainsburys in retailing, the Lithgows and Yarrows in shipbuilding, the Clarks in footwear.[270]

INTERNAL ORGANIZATION AND MANAGEMENT

If considerable vestiges of age-old ownership and control patterns can still be discerned in the British manufacturing sector, so too can Victorian organizational structures. The essential elements of the multi-divisional structure which by the 1940s had become the dominant form of organization in the United States have been detected in inter-war Britain (see above, pp. 213–14). But Derek Channon has shown clearly that by 1950 only about a dozen among the largest British firms had adopted such a structure, and of these eight were 'foreign owned, mainly with U.S. parents [e.g. Vauxhall and Ford], and one of the indigenous companies was Unilever, the multinational, Anglo-Dutch concern'.[271] The overwhelming majority of the largest British industrial undertakings were loose-knit, decentralized holding companies in which each major function – manufacturing, sales, purchasing, finance, or research – was managed through its own department. Significant changes have taken place in the last twenty-five years. The merger movement is partly responsible. In the years immediately following the end of the Second World War most of the largest industrial enterprises in Britain were essentially either single-product or dominant-product companies, the latter possessing the distinguishing feature of concentrating on one major product line which accounted for 70 per cent or more of their total sales.[272] Such companies could grapple with the managerial problems associated with growth. They had been doing so – with varying degrees of success – for decades. But increasing diversification in the period 1950–70 – achieved either by merger or internal development – not only brought about a decline in the number of single- and dominant-product companies but also compelled major organizational changes in order to cope with the ever-increasing complexity of managing these diversified enterprises. Only by adopting some variant of the multi-divisional structure could the necessary control and planning procedures be properly instituted. Without such structural change, many of the major firms, increasingly producing an ever-widening range of tenuously related products, were probably doomed to linger or even to die. Indeed, it was frequently only some potentially lethal financial crisis that induced structural change. Only then would a board not only call in management consultants – such as the American firm of McKinsey & Co. – but even accept their advice.[273] Conversely, and much more rarely, some firms (for example, Tate and Lyle, Associated Portland Cement, and the Burton Group) felt constrained to modify their structure to a multi-divisional form for the express purpose of diversifying.[274]

Despite the fact that nearly three-quarters of the firms studied by Channon had adopted the multi-divisional form by 1970 (as compared with 86 per cent in the United States), their structures were 'less clearly defined and articulated than those of American firms. The duties and functions of the general office and the divisions . . . [were] less clearly spelled out. Individual authority and responsibility . . . [were] not as sharply pinpointed.' British firms continue to use more committees and boards in managing day-to-day operations than their American counterparts. The distinction between policy and operations is often blurred. 'By 1970 few British firms had gone beyond financial performance as the criterion used in monitoring and evaluating the performance of the divisions . . . relatively few firms had formal planning offices.'[275] In Britain, it was only in technologically advanced diversified firms in the chemical, pharmaceutical, electrical, and electronic industries that Channon found control and planning procedures which were as sophisticated and clearly defined as those in the large multi-divisional American firms, a contrast which Chandler explains by the fact that in Britain the multi-divisional structure 'has come only recently and [has grown] out of the holding company form; whereas in the United States, it came earlier . . . and grew out of the functionally departmentalized structure'. Nevertheless, despite its relative immaturity in Britain, the multi-divisional organization – with its sophisticated machinery for co-ordinating, evaluating, and planning capital-intensive, technologically complex industrial activity – has necessitated the employment of an increasing number of full-time career managers who had no connection with the owners of the enterprise; and as this class grew, so too did the number of specialized management consultants, courses, journals, and associations – 'the essential paraphernalia of a new professional class'.[276]

THE POSSIBLE IMPLICATIONS OF MANAGERIAL CONTROL

In the past few years it has increasingly been assumed by the managerial economists that whereas the owner–manager aims at maximizing profits – the supposed goal of the classical entrepreneur – the professional director or top manager in enterprises characterized by a marked degree of separation of ownership from control pursues objectives conducive to the executives' own material welfare and psychological satisfaction: self-interested objectives, the attainment of which will be congruent with a firm's profit maximization only in special cases. Indeed, it has been said that 'the managerial revolution is quite fatal to long-run profit maximisation'.[277] Instead, Marris, for example, takes as 'working assumptions . . . that in addition to "narrow" economic rewards, such as salary, bonus, stock options . . . and the like, executives desire power, status, opportunity for creative satisfaction, opportunity for group-belonging and security' – aims which are mostly likely to be achieved with the growth of the enterprise.[278]

It is not possible to pursue this argument here,[279] but it behoves economic and business historians to devote more attention to this theme, for it has important implications for business policy and the understanding of industrial structure and modern economic growth. If it is true that the growth of the enterprise is the principal objective of the large management-controlled company, then the distribution of the earnings of such companies will be carried out in a manner that minimizes payments to shareholders and maximizes the retention of funds within the firm.[280] Such a policy, if successfully pursued, is conducive to further growth and, possibly, to the greater concentration of industry. Furthermore, if the demand conditions are not favourable to an expansion of the firm's existing products, then diversification is encouraged, either by merger or by the addition of new lines or services, the exploitation of which may have been suggested by the activities of the industrial research establishments that are increasingly characteristic of the larger companies. Further empirical studies at the level of the individual firm are needed to support or refute this type of hypothesis.[281]

So, too, is there a need to investigate whether managers in large enterprises characterized by a divorce of ownership from control act more in accordance with conceptions of social responsibility and of service to the community than does the owner–entrepreneur. Some managerialists have argued that since managers are under no imperative necessity to maximize the returns to ownership, they are better able to pursue policies which reflect social objectives.[282] The empirical basis for this belief is weak. Suffice it here to emphasize that the social responsibilities of business men were recognized, particularly by those entrepreneurs with strong religious affiliations, long before the evolution of modern management, and certainly before the development of a managerial ideology.[283]

So far the evidence – such as it is – suggests that in modern capitalist society there are economic, social, and technological constraints operating on business enterprise – not the least important being government intervention – which tend to minimize the behavioural differences between entrepreneurs and salaried managers.[284] This is a subject worthy of more research. Certainly it would appear plausible that the maximization of growth (if that proves to be the principal objective of the executive) implies policies virtually identical with those aimed at profit-maximization.[285] Only one thing is certain: from many large joint-stock companies, the entrepreneur as such has essentially disappeared. There are those who provide entrepreneurial services, but there is, in the majority of cases, no one person who can be said to be 'the entrepreneur'.[286]

SOME OBSERVATIONS ON THE POST-1945 PERIOD

For earlier periods, some tentative assessments have been made of the quality of entrepreneurial performance in the British economy; in conclusion one or two observations on the period since the Second World War may draw attention to themes deserving further investigation.

On the basis of productivity figures – to employ one of the many possible yardsticks – British entrepreneurial performance has improved since 1945.[287] British management techniques now appear to show little or no significant differences from those encountered in the USA or Germany at either the larger or smaller size level.[288] The structure of British industry has become as concentrated as in the United States – it is now probably the most concentrated in the world; and in a situation in which the largest hundred companies account for about half of all profits, an even larger proportion of total assets,[289] and about one-third of total employment, and when those companies can call upon batteries of expert advice, it is not surprising that management techniques have received a healthy boost.

Yet, clearly, gross errors and major inadequacies can be and have been isolated. Government inquiries (often by the National Economic Development Office) have revealed a low degree of professionalism in some industries (for example, woollen textiles and shipbuilding), underdeveloped planning and control systems, a tendency to resist innovation, and many other deficiencies;[290] and the financial press frequently regales its readers with boardroom crises, childish mistakes (often resulting from an almost inconceivable neglect of statistical and operational information), inept use of resources, and singular naiveties.[291] Since business institutions are human institutions, it would be surprising were this not to be the case.[292] What is troublesome is the growing recognition of the absence of quantitative information on the economies of scale which have so often been used to justify massive industrial concentration,[293] and the possibility that major entrepreneurial error will be perpetrated without the earlier consequences of liquidation or some decline in relative position.[294] It will be increasingly difficult – because of the squid-like ability of the largest corporations to obscure all but the very greatest managerial breakdowns with a cloud of ink – to discover what went wrong, who made a mistake, and what were the long-term consequences for economic growth or social welfare.

Perhaps the most significant entrepreneurial activity in the past decade has been the merger movement itself, but one's confidence in the beneficial consequences of this movement – which, as the short-lived Industrial Reorganisation Corporation implied, would, by increasing concentration and rationalization, promote the greater efficiency and international competitiveness of British industry[295] – is severely shaken by a number of careful analyses which found, in Newbould's words, that many acquisitive firms appear not to have given much consideration to 'the economies of scale, the balance of costs, the relative profitability of internal and external growth, or other rationalities'.[296] The sheer speed with which many of the arrangements were formulated during the 1967–8 merger boom ruled out the possibility of adequate analysis of the problems involved. The verdict of the Monopolies Commission in 1969 on the proposed Unilever/Allied Breweries merger – that in both the technical and marketing fields 'there is a certain vagueness on the part of the two companies as to precisely what form the expected benefits will take and this in turn has led to some overstatement of what these benefits may amount to'[297] – almost certainly has a more general applicability. It is, therefore, hardly surprising that many successful bidding companies have experienced disappointing post-merger profitability and that a very high proportion of total acquisitions are adjudged to have been failures.[298] Although there are very great problems involved in attempting to evaluate the effect of mergers on efficiency, these findings are somewhat disconcerting. The frequent lack of adequate preliminary planning before a takeover does not inspire confidence in post-merger managerial activity. But perhaps too little time has elapsed to have permitted proper re-organization to have taken place in many cases. Certainly, the establishment and proper functioning of new management structures appropriate to a newly created diversified firm or conglomerate cannot be achieved rapidly. It may come out right in the end.

Meanwhile, the structure of British industry is undergoing a profound transformation, the long-term consequences of which are not yet clear. Maybe, as Bannock fears, the giant or mature corporation, for all its investment in research and development, lacks 'both the will and the ability to innovate in any important sense'[299] and will increasingly depend upon the acquisition of new ideas, new products, and new processes originated among the smaller companies, some of which have been established simply to exploit a single innovation and whose leadership and organizations continue to display all the characteristics of those of their classical forebears.[300]

CHAPTER V

Capital Investment and Economic Growth in France, 1820–1930[1]

I. *The General Argument*

Until quite recently, studies of capital formation in France were few in number and relatively cursory. This lacuna was of little importance: it seemed that the findings to be expected of such research were already well known. It was thought that the level of economic growth and of investment had remained below the level which technical advance made it possible to reach – or so it seemed from a comparison with the relevant figures for other countries or even with those for France during the earlier part of the nineteenth century. For of all the countries that underwent industrialization France was one of the few to experience an early and lasting break in development. François Perroux was the first to identify the problem.'About 1860', he writes, 'there appeared the first signs of a slowing-down of the economy; from 1880, this became a pronounced trend.' The rate of growth fell, and this falling-off had long-lasting effects on the economy, for during its early stages – the period 1892–1914 – the second phase of industrialization was 'much less vigorous than the first'.[2] Various arguments have been put forward to explain this deceleration. Two of them, related to the state of the economy, have gained general acceptance in the past.

Underinvestment, runs the argument, was connected, in the first place, to the shortness of the periods during which long-term planning was possible. At the very beginning of the nineteenth century, France already laboured under this disadvantage: the stagnation of agricultural productivity and the decline in international trade had paralysed industry throughout the thirty years of insecurity and of war which lasted until 1820. The resulting delay in the adoption of new techniques continued thereafter. Short-term economic fluctuations, together with political and military crises, made for frequent interruptions in growth and led to periodic cuts in expenditure on major structural work and on plant and machinery. Decisions about investment in certain key sectors, instead of being planned on a long-term basis, were taken piecemeal and in relation to programmes which were over-ambitious; and these investment programmes were generally abandoned before completion. Some large concerns, which were able from the outset to effect economies of scale and to operate against foreign competition, were successfully created; but they were too few in number. In 1926–9, at the end of the period under review, large-scale production units (comprising more than five hundred employees or more than one hundred hectares, depending on the sector) accounted for only 32 per cent of the work force in the transport sector (railways excluded), 19 per cent of wage-earners in industry, 17 per cent of those in the various branches of commerce, and 16 per cent of cultivated agricultural land. These, then, are the indications that full investment potential was not realized: on the one hand, programmes of public works which were never completed; on the other, the persistence, throughout the century, of two categories of production units – alongside the most up-to-date concerns, there continued to exist small farms geared to a closed economy, and antiquated workshops which had long since amortized their plant and machinery but were inefficient.

When considered in a long-term perspective, the pursuit of expansion was clearly related to technical advance in general, but also to the growth of the labour force and to the harnessing of new resources. It seems that the country suffered throughout from the consequences of its shortage of energy resources and of raw materials, and – later on in the period – from the effects of the levelling-off of population growth. The support that a market economy receives from a growth in population, from an increase in the percentage of the active working population, from the latter's movements between the various sectors of the economy, and from the consequent improvement in productivity, was lacking from as early as the 1860s. Was the profit-earning capacity of firms and businesses affected accordingly? Were the effects of the different levels of investment in plant and machinery reflected in, and reinforced by, the gap in profit margins? What does seem clear is that capital investment abroad was probably excessive: the interest it earned was one-third higher – some 4·75 per cent, as against the average of 3·55 per cent yielded during the period 1878–1911 by French bonds. According to H. Feis, the share of the country's wealth which was invested abroad during these years increased from 8 per cent to 15 per cent – the national income was cut annually by something like 2 per cent, and later 4 per cent, from the 1880s to the 1900s, and by 6 per cent during 1913–14.[3] In short, according to this analysis, and on the assumption that the level of savings did not fall despite the stagnation in incomes, it was not that capital was lacking but rather that capital was invested in sectors that were relatively unproductive for the economy, particularly because, as political criteria determined the choice of where to invest, capital was invested in countries which were underdeveloped, which could not give increasing export orders for France, and which could not meet the obligations imposed by their debts.

These cursory remarks appear to be corroborated by the existing series of figures for investment. Paradoxically, instead of progressing – as was the norm with countries undergoing industrialization – from some 5 or 6 per cent of the national income to 12 per cent and more, the level of capital formation in France declined during the last third of the nineteenth century. This development was already suggested by René Pupin, writing in 1916. For the four years 1853, 1878, 1903, and 1911 he compiled balance-sheets showing the total stock of fixed and transferable capital, taking care, in so doing, to eliminate appreciation (and depreciation) brought about by price fluctuations, and to deduct from the total of transferable securities those which represented claims on assets which already figured in the calculations. Pupin's findings showed a growth rate of capital investment of 0·91 per cent per annum in 1878–1903, as against 1·71 per cent and 1·34 per cent in the preceding and subsequent periods. It therefore seems clear that there was a halt in investment, which either accompanied or accentuated the reduction in the pace of growth, noted during the great depression. If we re-examine these figures and calculate the difference between the totals of successive inventories, we find that savings stagnated at 2,200 million francs per annum in 1853–78 and then at 2,040 million in 1878–1903. It was not until just before 1914 that savings increased again – the annual average between 1903 and 1911 was 3,500 million francs, at a time when private income totalled 32,000 million. This corresponds to a fall in the level of investment of some two-fifths by the end of the century – from 14·5 per cent of the national product to 8·5 per cent. The economic recovery that occurred after 1900 was financed by a level of investment lower than previous levels (Table 44).

Apart from some small corrections, these estimates have been accepted by many other writers. They have not been invalidated by more recently published estimates for the nineteenth century, except that T. J. Markovitch has identified not one period of recession but two, in 1815–34 and in 1865–94.[4] Moreover, several of the series of data computed for the inter-war period have confirmed the picture of stagnation that the figures suggest. It appears that net domestic capital formation remained at a relatively low level: 11·2 per cent of national product in 1927–30 – or 30,000 million current francs, when the national product was 304,000 million – according to the initial estimates of H. Lubell; or even only 7·0 per cent during these four years, according to S. Kuznets (in fact only 5·6 per cent if the calculations are based on fixed capital, excluding inventories). In other words, the progress of the economy appears to have been hindered, perhaps beginning in 1860 or 1880, by the shortage or the poor distribution of the nation's savings. To revert to an international comparison bearing on the last years of our period, the build-up of

Table 44. *Estimates of French Capital Formation as a Percentage of the National Product*

	First industrial-ization (pre–1840)	Railway Era (1840–80)	Great depression	Second industrial-ization (pre–1914)	Second industrial-ization (post-1920)
Pupin 1916[a]	—	14·5	8·5	11·9	—
Mayer 1949[a]	9·5	13·0	8·1	—	—
Lubell 1952:					
(A)[a]	—	—	—	—	16·1
(B)[b]	—	—	—	—	11·2
Kuznets 1956[b]	—	8·6	4·6	5·6	7·0[c]
Markovitch 1966:					
variant I[a]	17·9	19·0	19·5	21·1	20·6
variant III[a]	7·9	12·7	14·9	16·6	18·9
Michalet 1968[b]	—	5·6	7·0	7·1	—
Vincent 1972[a]	—	—	—	18·1	20·3

[a] Gross.
[b] Net.
[c] Kuznets gives the gross figure of 9·1 for the post-1920 period.

SOURCES. R. Pupin, *La Richesse française devant la guerre* (Paris, 1916); J. Mayer, 'La Croissance du revenu national français', *Cahiers de l'Institut de Science Économique Appliquée* (ISEA), ser. D 7 (1949); H. Lubell, *The French Investment Program: A Defense of the Monnet Plan* (Paris, 1952); S. Kuznets, 'International Differences in Capital Formation and Financing', in M. Abramovitz (ed.), *Capital Formation and Economic Growth* (New York, 1956); T. J. Markovitch, 'L'Industrie française de 1789 à 1964: Conclusions générales', *Cahiers de l'ISEA*, ser. AF 7, no. 179 (November 1966); C. A. Michalet, *Les Placements des épargnants français de 1815 à nos jours* (Paris, 1968); L. A. Vincent, 'Les Comptes nationaux', in A. Sauvy (ed.), *Histoire économique de la France dans l'entre-deux-guerres*, 3 vols. (Paris, 1965–72), III.

French productive capacity, during the phase of expansion which preceded the crisis of 1929, was apparently 'only 40 to 60 per cent of that of other industrialized countries'.[5]

Definitions vary from one author to another: with three exceptions – H. Lubell (column B), S. Kuznets, and C. A. Michalet – the figures relate to gross investment and include depreciation expenditure. The lowest series of figures, those of Kuznets, relate to internal net capital formation. His estimate of gross investment (GDCF) nonetheless remains below the others for the period 1927–30. It is 9·1 per cent of national product and falls to 8·4 per cent if capital reserves are omitted.

Thus, different lines of reasoning lead to the same conclusion. Nonetheless, is there really justification for the claim that there was a shortage of investment in France? Should one ascribe a determining role (positive before 1860, negative thereafter) to the mobilization of financial resources, the installation and renewal of fixed plant and machinery? Are economic expansion and technical progress predetermined by the amount of capital investment? In fact, given the doubts that surround the various numerical estimates – the growth of the national product (per capita) was more stable and more progressive than the first calculations suggested – and given the wide range of possible interactions with variables other than capital, the problem is essentially a statistical one. It comes down to deciding how much reliance can be placed on existing series of data, and whether it is possible to replace them. Historical estimates of capital formation are at best tentative. They lend themselves very badly to comparisons with other variables, other periods, and other countries. The oldest of the series in Table 44 reveals two anomalies which are the starting point for subsequent investigation: a level of investment in France (6·4 per cent for net investment between 1878 and 1930, according to Kuznets) on average lower than the one considered necessary in other countries for the development of an economy; and a break in the rhythm, which however is less pronounced in the recent series of data than in those compiled before 1960. Do we have here a reliable portrayal of the situation? Or does the root cause of these two phenomena lie in the accountancy definitions which have been used and in the methods of calculation?

The term 'capital formation' covers the sums added each year to the stock of domestic fixed reproducible assets: we have excluded both external investment (which is calculated separately) and inventories (for which we have no figures either for industry or commerce). Whether it is a matter of building a new or replacing old and worn-out assets, investment here comprises the full range of capital expenditure on all manner of buildings and artefacts such as factories, plant, machinery, and work premises, provided that the object is to increase their number and their quality; the same holds true for expenditure on improvements to cultivated land, to mines, etc. At first sight, it would seem that the data for capital expenditure cover a relatively wide range. However, as the criterion for net investment is an increase in productive capacity, we must exclude all expenditure on maintenance and repair work which, strictly speaking, neither increases the efficiency of the materials, plant, and machinery nor prolongs their life-span beyond the period envisaged when they were purchased.

This mode of reckoning seems valid, especially when it is a matter of modern equipment, with an ever-shortening life-span, which becomes obsolete even before it is worn out, and which consequently does not entail heavy repair and maintenance expenditure, but does require rapid amortization. In France, funds reserved for capital renewal, in fact, increased: in national terms, they apparently totalled 15 per cent in the 1860s (380 million francs, as against a gross investment of 2,530 million), rising to an average of 35 per cent in 1927–30, according to Lubell, and perhaps even to 41–6 per cent in 1913 and 1929.[6] But the same mode of reckoning, when applied to the past record of a country which had kept its traditional structures, may be somewhat arbitrary: it tends to understate the value of investment undertaken by those directly concerned (farmers during the slack season) or by specialist firms, on agricultural installations and equipment, on dwellings, or even on roads – these three accounted for some 60 to 70 per cent of investment at the beginning of the century, and the figure remained sizeable thereafter. There was virtually no end to the life-span of these items. They therefore required little or no amortization; they were kept in good condition by continual repair, and indeed they were gradually improved because of this continuous maintenance, for in the long run the initial construction was less important than later additional work. In other words, when assessing capital investment in accounting terms, in the one case we introduce technical obsolescence, in the form of amortization, and thus increase the aggregate investment. But in the other case, even if maintenance costs are heavier and more important, they are excluded from the calculation and thus reduce the figure for capital investment.

The choice of method used to calculate results materially affects them. For instance, by one method we can reconstruct the annual flow of investment, in current and in constant prices, and then deduce from it successive estimates for the stocks of equipment, by cumulating past outlays, revalued at the replacement cost at a base year. Or else, by a reverse method, we can calculate directly the stock of material assets at various dates: this we can do either by ascribing an average age and price to the various assets and by adding up the results thus obtained, or by capitalizing the income they yield. All that then remains is to deduce the annual average increase in the stock, as Pupin did. But there is a strong likelihood that this second method, which was used in compiling the older series of data, tends to give results that are too low, because it takes into consideration only the healthy and flourishing sector of the economy. The real estate sector is the classic example of this: if only the net increase in the number of dwelling units is taken into account, then the figure for expenditure on buildings completed annually must be below the sum effectively spent, because buildings constructed to re-place those which have been demolished will not be included in the calculations.[7] Similarly, there is a danger, when compiling figures for the stock of capital assets, of omitting items purchased in error, sales-promotion schemes which proved abortive, and undertakings which were abandoned or which made losses. These last sometimes immobilized large sums, even after they had stopped producing income. For 1898, for example, this second method of calculation would lead one to omit figures for investment in three-quarters of all mining works, because a mere 446 out of a total of 1,832 mines were actually in production – 216 showed a profit, and 230 a loss. Besides, it is possible to put a price on the various assets, on the basis of figures recorded in company balance-sheets or in insurance policies. Attempting to assess the market value of these same assets is a much more hazardous task. For example, apart from material assets these values include the costs occasioned by transport changes and their entry into service, which can hardly be considered as operating costs, as they are not recurrent; and professional and legal fees, commissions, and the cost of financing – particularly interest payments made by the railway companies during the period of construction, which accounted on average for 11·3 per cent of railway investment between 1855 and 1896 (after deduction of sums spent on purchasing land). Of course, we could always upgrade the level of capital expenditure thus computed, by applying adjustment ratios. But this would introduce a measure of uncertainty which would prove very difficult to evaluate, because of the paucity of French documentation. Pupin and the writers who have followed his figures have not applied such ratios: this casts some doubt on the correctness of their figures.

To circumvent these difficulties, without exceeding the bounds of the possible as determined by the state of the sources, it seemed advisable to compile new series of data, using different methods. Subsequent comparisons between the different series would lend greater conviction to some of the findings. These new series comprise: (1) a series indicating the volume of investment, which strictly speaking is a commodity-flow index, compiled on an annual basis; (2) estimates of the level of gross capital formation, which are computed from figures for expenditure recorded in current prices, either as they appeared from estimates made for various sectors or as they were recorded by the railway companies, the public works services, and the like; (3) a summary of the findings of contemporary surveys and assessments, relating to the value and the structure of the stock of capital assets.[8] With such data, it should be possible to make a valid assessment of the level of investment, to chart its course during a long time-span, and to determine the reasons for the course it took. To simplify matters, we have divided our remarks about these series into two sections. The first relates to infrastructural expenditure, embracing construction work taken in its broadest sense, and public works; the other relates to investment in

tangible assets, comprising plant, machinery, and the various categories of equipment, all of which grew greatly in importance throughout the century. This comes down to a distinction between assets which
are inherited from the past, and those which are modern. This method
should also prove more helpful in identifying the regenerating forces
in the economy.

II. *Infrastructure Investment*

Looking at the period as a whole, our series of data tend to confirm
the broad outline of development suggested earlier: internal investment was remarkably stable for much of the nineteenth century. After
1880, largely as a result of the great depression, it suffered from the
consequences of a worsening economic climate. The annual rate of
growth of capital assets fell from an average of 2·0 per cent
between 1820 and 1884 to 1·2 per cent between 1874 and 1938. The
various series of data all agree on this. The sole difference among them
is a variation in the degree of the slope during the initial and terminal
periods, depending on whether the series of data on capital expenditure
were calculated in current or constant values (cf. Fig. 1). This difference,
however, does not put the results in doubt: it is simply due to a varia-

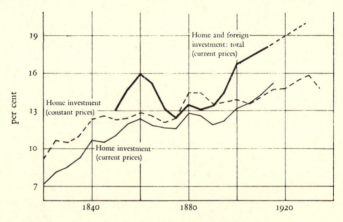

Fig. 1. Levels of Capital Formation, 1820–1935 (annual averages): Gross Investment
as a Percentage of the National Product

NOTE. Levels of investment – i.e. capital formation in relation to the national
product – are calculated in decennial averages (the figure for 1820 represents the
period 1815–25, and so forth). Those in constant prices are on a base 1908–12 = 100.

SOURCE. Cf. Tables 44, 45, and 60; the levels of aggregate investment, in current
prices, for 1913 and 1929 are taken from L. A. Vincent, 'Les Comptes nationaux', in
A. Sauvy (ed.), *Histoire économique de la France dans l'entre-deux-guerres*, III (Paris, 1972).

Table 45. *Capital Investment and National Product, 1810–1938 (decennial averages)*

	National product (thousand million 1910 francs)	Gross domestic capital formation (thousand million 1910 francs)	Share of national product invested (per cent)		National product (thousand million current francs)	Capital investment (thousand million current francs)		Share of national product invested (per cent)		
			Variant 1	Variant 2		Home	Abroad	Home	Abroad	Total
1810–19	9·75[a]	0·80[a]	8·2[a]	—	8·14	0·58	—	7·1	—	—
1820–9	11·23	1·20	10·7	—	9·02	0·74	—	8·2	—	—
1830–9	12·45	1·38	11·1	—	10·24	0·95	—	9·3	—	—
1840–9	14·65	1·84	12·5	—	12·28	1·29	0·41	10·5	2·7	14·7
1850–9	17·05	2·16	12·4	—	15·20	1·83	0·66	12·0	3·4	15·2
1860–9	21·19	2·68	12·6	—	19·13	2·27	0·18	11·8	0·8	12·5
1870–9	22·64	2·82	12·4	—	22·09	2·57	0·16	11·7	0·6	13·1
1880–9	25·32	3·65	14·4	—	24·97	3·11	0·64	12·5	2·4	14·5
1890–9	27·53	3·77	13·7	13·6[b]	26·96	3·27	1·20	12·1	3·8	17·3
1900–9	30·91	4·19	13·6	13·8	31·24	4·21	1·14	13·5	3·0	18·2
1910–13	31·81[c]	4·69[c]	14·7[c]	15·6	37·45	5·68	—	15·2	—	—
1920–9	39·54	6·09	15·2	15·5	—	—	—	—	—	—
1930–8	44·20	6·55	14·8	15·8	—	—	—	—	—	—

[a] 1815–19. [b] 1896–9. [c] 1910–19.

NOTE. Indices of the volume of investment and of the aggregate product (see Table 60 below) were used for the calculations given in constant francs (first three columns above), on a base of 34,600 million francs for the national product and 4,925 million francs for gross annual investment in 1905–13.

SOURCES. Appendix, Table 60 below; and J. Berthet *et al.*, 'Sources et origines de la croissance française' (first draft, mimeographed: Paris, June 1965), Tables 1 and 3, pp. 161–4, for the share of income invested, variant 2 (fourth column above).

tion in the cost and in the nature of the plant and equipment. Between 1820 and 1860, price rises of 45–55 per cent were recorded for some construction materials – they had remained abnormally low during the post-Napoleonic period – and wages rose by one-fifth: this suffices to explain the quicker rate of increase of the series based on current values. The same gap appears between 1890 and 1930, despite the relative price stability of the period, because prices of machinery and of electrical equipment apparently fell by a quarter (reckoned in pre-1928 'francs of Germinal'), whereas prices in the building industry and in the public works sector remained at the same level. But during this period, capital equipment – which is relatively more costly than ordinary public-works projects – accounted for a larger share of invest-ment expenditure; changing the weighting has the effect of increasing average prices and current values.

A problem does arise, however, in deciding on the chronological framework to be adopted when studying investment. Contrary to our expectations, we can discern neither short-term cycles nor long-term movements. Perhaps short-term cycles – of some seven to ten years – are not apparent because they were more closely connected to the variation in stocks than to that of production and the formation of capital; but long-term movements, which it was believed originated in a relative abundance of precious metals, were thought to affect prices, profits, and investment. In fact, what we find is seven cycles, lasting some twenty years each. They stimulated and then retarded the growth of the economy but did not interrupt it, reaching their respective peaks in 1826, 1846, 1869, 1882, 1900 (the fluctuation here was barely per-ceptible), 1913, and 1930 (see Table 46). The seeming absence of true long-term trends leads us at least to exclude them as a possible causal variable when we analyse investment, and it perhaps strengthens doubts about their very existence, in practice if not in theory.

There are in fact no signs of such movements in the French series of data for money stocks and for prices. And their influence on capital expenditure remains problematical. As a result of the findings of F. Simiand, it has been said that entrepreneurs only invested when forced to – that they were no more encouraged to do so when prices and pro-fits were rising, i.e. in 1848–73 and 1895–1913 (A phases), than they had been in the past; and conversely, that they were forced to do so during intermediate periods (B phases), when falling prices and the partial dismissal of the work force obliged them to mechanize so as to avoid a fall in production and the consequent greater burden of overheads. According to this view, investment only increased in order to protect profits. But as Figure 2 shows, there is no correlation (negative or positive) between the cycles and Simiand's A and B phases, because

Table 46. *Amplitude and Duration of Investment Cycles, 1820–1938*

Cycle	Duration (years)	Industrial production				Capital formation				Investment in basic industries			
		Peak year	Trough year	% growth per annum P–P^a	% growth per annum T–T^a	Peak year	Trough year	% growth per annum P–P	% growth per annum T–T	Peak year	Trough year	% growth per annum P–P	% growth per annum T–T
I	—	1826	1831	—	—	1825	1831	—	—	1825	1831	—	—
II	20–21	1836	1838	1·29	1·73	1839	1842	1·72	4·48	1840	1842	1·92	4·82
		1846	1848	1·98	1·93	1846	1850	1·93	1·97	1846	1850	2·00	1·86
		—	—	—	—	1857	1859	1·87	4·78	1858	1859	1·25	4·67
III	23	1869	1871	1·62	1·42	1869	1871	1·56	1·12	1869	1871	1·54	0·67
		1876	1878	0·89	3·38	—	—	—	—	—	—	—	—
IV	13	1882	1885	1·60 (1·12)	2·25 (1·46)^a	1882	1886	3·01	3·65	1882	1886	2·48	4·39
V	17–18	1892	1895	0·77	1·13	1891	1893	−1·22	1·20	1891	1893	−2·32	−0·14
		1900	1902	1·08 (0·74)	1·40 (0·96)	1900	1905	0·26	0·89	1899	1904	−0·60	0·21
VI	12–14	1912	1919	2·81 (2·04)	−1·08 (−0·76)	1913	1918	2·27	−0·74	1913	1918	1·17	−2·79
VII	17–18	1930	1935	1·91 (1·38)	3·18 (3·48)	1930	1935	2·58	3·12	1930	1938	1·76	2·15

NOTE. Minor setbacks of less than two years' duration are not transcribed. The amplitude of cycles was calculated on a percentage basis, as an annual rate of growth, from the preceding major peak to the following minor and major ones (P–P), and from trough to trough (T–T).
^a Figures in parentheses relate to the growth of the national product: the phases of its development do not coincide precisely with those of industrial production.

SOURCE. Appendix, Table 60 below.

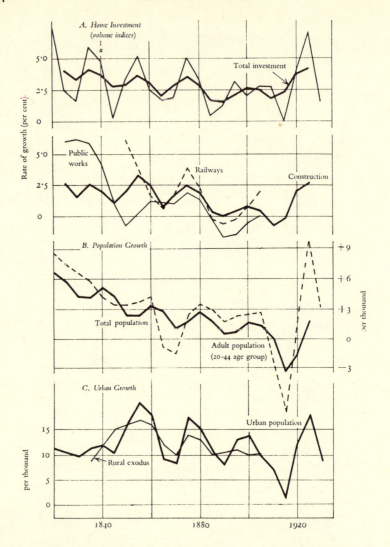

Fig. 2. Population and Gross Capital Formation, 1820–1935 (annual averages)

NOTE. The growth in the volume of investment is assessed every ten years for the series labelled *a* (the 1820 figure thus represents growth during the period from 1813–17 to 1823–7, and so forth). The rates for all other investment data – total home investment, and investment in the various sectors (public works, railways, and construction) – are calculated for a twenty-year period (the 1825 rate is therefore the mean of the three ten-year averages 1820, 1825, and 1830 – i.e. the period 1815–35).

Figures for population are likewise compiled on a ten-year base. Thus, of the figures for the growth rate of the total population and that of the urban population (i.e. in towns of more than 3,000 inhabitants), those for 1821 in fact cover the period

1816–26. The annual number of rural migrants is related to the average figure for the corresponding urban population.

SOURCES. Tables 44, 45, and 60; for population data, *Annuaire Statistique* for 1966; J. Bourgeois-Pichat, 'Evolution générale de la population française depuis le XVIIIe siècle', *Population*, VI, 4 (1951), 661–2; M. Lévy-Leboyer, 'La Décélération de l'économie française dans la seconde moitié du XIXe siècle', *Revue d'Histoire Economique et Soicale*, XLIX, 4 (1971), 506; P. Merlin, *L'Exode rural* (Paris, 1971); G. Dupeux, 'La Croissance urbaine en France au XIXe siècle', *Revue d'Histoire Economique et Sociale*, LIII, 4 (1975).

profits and capital expenditure were related not to the long-term movement of prices but to economic growth itself. For example, the depression at the end of the century, which corresponds to a B phase, was a period of reduced activity and therefore of reduced investment. Between 1885 and 1900, total annual investment, reckoned in 1910 francs, remained at an average low of 3,620 million francs or 13·6 per cent of the national product, compared with 3,980 million francs, or 15·4 per cent, in 1880–84.

On the other hand, the dynamic role which is ascribed to technical advance in descriptions of long-term trends does appear to be valid. Some innovations had an effect, albeit an irregular one, on investment, particularly on infrastructural expenditure; they brought about fundamental changes in the economy and periodically led to rises in prices and in incomes, until the application of new productive capacity caused changes in profit margins and in expectations, and induced a change in the trend of the economy. This view, however, does have two disadvantages. First, it ascribes to certain innovations the power to stimulate growth during very long periods – each stage of technical advance corresponding to one of the Kondratief cycles. This appears unlikely in France, where production methods changed little and the time-span of the cycles was relatively short. At most, it is possible that technical advance occurred at the same time that a cycle began (i.e. every twenty years), capital being first attracted to public works, which developed anew in the period 1820–40, then to railway construction in the period 1840–60, and then to urban development in 1860–80 (Fig. 2). Public-works projects for infrastructure development accounted in all for some 71 per cent of fixed investment before 1880 and still accounted for 54 per cent in 1880–1913. Secondly, this theory, while emphasizing the dynamic aspects of technical advance, neglects its negative aspects. In particular, it fails to take into account the harmful effects which may well have resulted from poorly managed or over-committed investment, through the paralysing effect on the very sector which had hitherto been the mainspring of the economy. The reduced duration of the cycles during the period 1880–1920 stemmed from the reduction in investment in basic industries, for the rate of increase of the latter (calculated as the mean of cycles V, VI, and VII) fell to 0·78 per cent per annum, which is only half the figure for aggregate investment (Table 46). This reversal of trend appears even more characteristic of French economic development than the stability of profit or the irregularity of technical advance. What contribution to growth was made by investment in the basic industries, during the phase when they played a positive role? What is the explanation for the excess capacity of that sector at the end of the century? More specifically, why was the level of infrastructural expenditure attained in 1882 not reached again until 1926 – or indeed, given the pause attendant on the monetary crisis of the period, until 1929?

A. THE BUILDING INDUSTRY

In the 1860s the construction industry still employed one-fifth of the industrial work force, and its output represented a quarter of the value added by all industrial firms. The building industry was consequently an independent source of income for a large fraction of the work force and was a potential spur to growth. But it is difficult to see how it could have acted on the twenty-year cycles, which emerge from the various series of data about capital formation because, as the population declined throughout the century, it seems natural to expect that the pressure on housing was weak. Furthermore, building contractors, because of the loose organizational structure of their firms, were able to adapt quickly to changes in demand, and thus to react to economic trends, rather than influencing them. What then was the role of this sector, and what effect did it have on investment?

If we look at demand, two factors at least could well have imposed on the building industry a distinctive pattern which subsequently spread to the rest of the economy. One factor is changes in the size of the population itself. Although the rate of natural increase fell steadily, it is well known that after the Napoleonic wars an increase in the birth rate, following as it did a long period of high death rates and low birth rates, led to quite a sharp increase in the total population. This was subsequently reflected in successive twenty-year figures: there was a net annual surplus of 202,350 inhabitants (5·6 per cent of the population) in the ten years centred on 1821; there were further peaks in 1841 (174,800, or 5·1 per cent), in 1861 (122,250 or 3·3 per cent), and again – with the war of 1870-1 shortening the period by five years and then prompting a further increase – in 1876 (122,400 or 3·3 per cent), and so on. In terms of buildings under construction, this growth was reflected in an increase in the pressure of demand, which appears at twenty-year intervals on the curve of growth described by the age-group between twenty- and forty-four – if not in 1841, then at least in 1861 and 1881 (Fig. 2, part B).

In fact, the cycle in the building industry does not coincide with the population cycle: it peaked in 1856 and 1876 (i.e. in the ten-year periods centred on those dates); and the range of its fluctuations was greater. We must therefore take into consideration, as the second factor, changes in population through migration. There had always existed a surplus rural population: unable to make a living from agriculture, its members had had to follow the pattern of demographic trends, and they periodically moved to the towns, either to seek supplementary income on a temporary basis, or to escape starvation. At the beginning of the century these additions did not act as a spur to the building industry, because during the post-Napoleonic depression the number of dwellings dating from the *ancien régime* was probably still considerable, and the possibilities of employment in the towns were uncertain. During crises, indeed, migrant workers returned to the countryside – for instance, Paris lost almost 150,000 inhabitants in 1806–11 and in 1826–31 for this reason. With time, however, the rural exodus changed in character. First, it became no longer temporary but definitive. With the sharpening of agricultural competition between different regions, the de-industrialization of the countryside, the territorial losses incurred in 1871, and so forth, migrant workers left the country to settle in the towns permanently. And their numbers increased substantially, especially in 1856 and 1876, after the series of disastrous harvests which marked the period 1845–56, and after the wine and cereals crises of the late 1870s (Fig. 2, part C). The numbers of country-dwellers who left for the towns is put at 135,000 per annum between 1851 and 1856, and at 165,000 in 1876–81, i.e. respectively 36 and 54 per cent more than the net surplus in births during these periods. The Parisian region absorbed 45 per cent of the total number of migrants during this period: the average number of arrivals exceeded 50,000 per annum in the 1850s and the 1870s and constituted almost nine-tenths of the region's population increase. These migrations and the novel phenomenon of urban congestion were chiefly responsible for the very substantial amplitude and the periodicity of the cycle in the building industry.

After 1880 the pressure of demand was maintained, although clearly at a lower level, and the same intervals (in relation to the cycles) were observed. Natural population increase reached a peak in the ten years centred on 1901 and in 1926; its growth rate, however, was now only 1·8–1·9 per cent (the annual surpluses were in the region of 75,000 in both cases). Also, after a drop at the end of the century, movements of population grew once again, spurred on by the 1914–18 war. The average annual number of migrants was 140,000 from 1906 to 1926, which is 18,000 more than during the peak period of 1896–1906; and this number was swollen by migrants from abroad, because there were always more immigrants entering France than emigrants leaving – the balance increased by 28,350 per annum between 1891 and 1901, and by an average of 195,300 in 1921–31 (235,500 per annum if we refer to the gross figures).[9] As a consequence of this population growth, as has already been shown, in the 1920s cycle, there was another upturn in the building sector: investment in real estate once again touched 1855 and 1875 levels (Fig. 2, part A). But this occurred only after a very long and very severe depression, which is not fully explained by the long decline in the population and the slowing-down of the rural exodus. Thus we must also consider, as an alternative explanation, the possibility that too many dwellings were built during the period 1860–80 and that they subsequently depressed the market for new housing.

There may seem something paradoxical about this view that supply exceeded demand at the end of the century. Building firms were, after all, small in size – in 1851–66 there were 1·27–1·44 wage-earners for each employer.[10] They operated on short-term credit and could hardly afford to take any risks. At first sight, then, they do not appear a likely cause of such an imbalance. Nonetheless, the industry received at regular intervals an influx of capital seeking long-term investment: this might take the form of subscriptions to shares, or of mortgage loans intended to finance property development companies and to facilitate private home-buying. Indeed, from the early nineteenth century there was overinvestment in the later stages of each cycle; but no major catastrophe occurred, as the capital was released in the next upswing. In the middle of the century, however, the braking mechanism of the market doubtless worked less well, because demand reached an unprecedented scale, and above all because promoters were less sensitive to variation in costs – they hoped to make quick killings on appreciating land values. They also received aid from the state, from municipal authorities, and from specialized concerns like the Caisse des Grands Travaux, founded in November 1858 by the prefect Haussmann, and from the new deposit banks. The rise in money-lending rates, instead of stopping such initiatives, simply led many businesses to alter their methods. Some moved their construction teams to work in the suburbs, where plots of land were more plentiful; they used materials which were less expensive than stone, and they cut down on the foundations, the number of storeys, etc. Others chose to apply themselves to overcoming the problems of the congestion of city centres: instead of the traditional individual houses, they proposed blocks of buildings over-looking main roads or boulevards, whose outer shells were already completely finished – the Crédit Mobilier, for instance, ruined itself by building up districts which subsequently failed to attract residents. In addition, especially after 1870, they adapted existing buildings (in Paris, the percentage of buildings with more than five storeys almost doubled (from 26 per cent to 47 per cent) between 1861 and 1926); they increased the number of units within each house, and raised the quality of the construction and of the buildings – rental values increased by some 190 per cent between 1851–3 and 1887–9, and a third of the increase was already being attributed to 'rising standards of comfort'.[11] The major cities – barely eleven had more than 90,000 inhabitants in 1881 – were overbuilt.

In a sector where it was normal to invest at long term for up to one hundred years, the imbalance between supply and demand might well continue and might be reflected in a large number of unoccupied dwellings. In Paris, there had been previous occasions when the rate of such vacancies was high: it appears that after the events of 1848, 60 per cent of lodgings were unoccupied in three districts of the town, as against 12 per cent and 19 per cent in 1853–9; 54,000 dwellings were uninhabited in 1871 (compared with 19,000 the previous year), which then represented some 9 per cent of all Parisian dwellings, and indeed 15 per cent of its rented accommodation. From 1883, however, because of the overbuilding, this characteristic became permanent. It has been calculated that each year there were some 70,000 to 90,000 vacant dwellings in the capital, i.e. a tenth of the total, whereas the figure for France as a whole was between 5 and 7 per cent (in 1887–9 there were 612,000 unoccupied houses out of a total of 8·91 million; in 1914, 500,000 out of 9·44 million). Not until the turn of the century did the number of vacant dwellings in Paris fall below 25,000; on the eve of the First World War it was only 6,000. In social terms, this had two consequences. In Paris, a fall in rents occurred from 1885, being relatively sharper in richer districts and for large flats. With the slowing-down in the rate of development, in sales of land, in the starting of new building sites, and in the number of newly completed buildings, the eventual return to some kind of balance between supply and demand was foreseeable. But the process must have been slow, because demand – and consequently the prices and rents for 'middle-class homes', of which there were many in the capital – did not recover before 1905. Thus, the number of residential buildings in Paris, which was 68,100, remained stable at 10–15 per cent of the total stock; it subsequently reached 82,000 in 1921 and 95,000 in 1931. One might also expect that the 1890s cycle (cycle V in Table 46) would have been favourably affected, at the working-class level, by the fall in the cost of food, by the greater prominence given in the family budget to housing, by the spread and electrification of urban transport, and indeed ultimately by the fragmenting of families. In fact, it showed few signs of this. In the Parisian suburbs, which were comparatively inexpensive in relation to the city centre, the number of houses only rose from 51,000 to 87,000 between 1881 and 1901. Here again, it was not until the 1920s that the number rose substantially – to over 150,000 and later to over 250,000, which was 73 per cent of the region's housing facilities.[12]

A more favourable trend undoubtedly existed in the East, the Southeast, and the South. The building industry benefited from the considerable demand in the new industrial or residential areas, where migrant workers arrived to find that no accommodation existed for them. But the industry's output stagnated in Paris and in the other ten or so large towns where urbanization had first begun. This slackening in pace reflected that of the rural exodus and was bound to last: the building industry depends on transient labour and employs migrant workers. Given also that the recovery of 1905–13 proved short-lived and that inflation and the rent freeze, after the war, delayed the building cycle until 1929 – 604,000 dwellings were built in 1929–32, i.e. as many as during the ten preceding years – one may conclude that an element was lacking in the economy after 1880. The building sector lost the role it had traditionally occupied in the economy. It had become more vulnerable, and because it was unable to resist the deflationary measures of the time, it may have accentuated the depression of the 1930s – barely 71,000 dwellings were built per year in 1936–9, i.e. less than 0.4 per cent of the existing number.

B. THE PUBLIC WORKS SECTOR

It would seem that the railways, and the transport system in general – because of the volume of capital investment and the control exercised by the government throughout the period in this sector – ought to have played a role in the economy comparable to that of the building industry, and indeed might perhaps have made up for the deficiencies of the latter. Work on the basic installations was supervised by a central authority. Programmes were devised on a national scale by engineers of the Ponts et Chaussées (the Highways Department), right through from the first plans for building canals and railways – the plans Becquey in 1822 and Legrand in 1838 – to those launched by E. Krantz in 1872–4 and by Freycinet in 1878, which were debated in parliament. The capital involved was considerable: at the beginning of the century it represented one-fifth, and from 1840 one-half, of all property investment. The bulk was provided or guaranteed by public authorities, who also supervised its distribution, in successive stages, so as to ensure that construction work advanced steadily. In all, 330 bridges and 2,900 km of canals – i.e. a third of the operational waterways in 1850 – were built by the Restoration and July Monarchies. Laws of 1831 and 1836 ensured that the road network developed also, with 48,000 km of major highways being built or renovated, 60,000 km of local roads opened, and isolated villages thus brought into contact with the rest of the nation. Finally, railway development – following the period in the 1820s when it was left to private initiative, in Saint Etienne, Alais, Mulhouse, etc. – received a decisive impetus in 1837 with the creation of a special fund to finance major projects, and with the adoption of the first experiments in mixed financing in 1839–42. With these developments, the authorities could compel the contracting companies to proceed with the completion of the main-line network on a step-by-step basis. As to the secondary network, which would ultimately account for 50,000 km out of a total of 90,000 km of track, its construction was left in 1865 to the discretion of local authorities, but its financial management was placed under the control of the Ministry of Finance by two laws passed in 1873 and 1880.[13]

Therefore, it was thanks to the support given by the state that this sector was spared from the bankruptcies, and almost spared from the technical failures, which it frequently experienced abroad. The six major railway companies developed under the protection of their regional monopolies; and the local railway companies, when they made losses, were assisted, reorganized, or even taken over, without any interruption of their building programmes. In this sector, the growth rate of investment during the nineteenth century was all of 5·35 per cent per annum, as against 1·22 per cent for investment in conventional means of transport. Furthermore, the division of funds for investment between the two categories of transport was of benefit to both. The road network, which required regular maintenance (costing on average 170 million francs in the 1870s, i.e. a third of all expenditure on public works), was extended in conjunction with the railway network. Expenditure on waterways, by contrast, was periodically cut back. For instance, in the 1850s it was reduced, and priority was given to hastening the completion of the principal railway lines. Expenditure on port and harbour installations was reduced from 16·5 million francs per annum to 10·9 million over a five-year period between 1845 and 1855, and canal construction from 48·3 million francs to 17·9 million between 1840 and 1860. In short, the government sought to stimulate investment in transport infrastructure. But it also knew how to regulate it,

Table 47. *Infrastructure and Construction: Total Annual Expenditure, 1815–1913 (million francs, current prices)*

	Public works (railways excluded)					Railways			Public works (including railways)		Maintenance costs as % of total
	Ports	Canals	Roads	Total	New expenditure	Total expenditure	New expenditure	Additional expenditure	Total expenditure	New expenditure	
1815–19	1·7	5·0	58·2	64·9	13·8	—	—	—	64·9	13·8	78·7
1820–9	3·3	19·1	65·0	84·5	34·7	—	—	—	87·5	35·1	59·9
1830–9	7·3	28·5	110·3	146·1	79·0	7·6	7·2	1·6	153·7	85·2	43·9
1840–9	15·5	40·7	170·6	226·8	125·7	87·1	84·5	15·1	313·9	210·2	33·0
1850–9	12·6	19·0	176·8	208·4	77·1	233·2	215·0	54·0	441·6	292·1	33·9
1860–9	20·8	30·0	220·7	271·5	100·5	272·5	227·5	82·0	543·5	328·0	39·7
1870–9	23·0	28·2	223·7	274·9	75·3	233·2	158·1	51·0	508·1	233·4	54·1
1880–9	45·1	54·5	243·9	343·5	127·1	354·5	262·3	87·0	698·0	389·4	44·2
1890–9	26·4	27·1	231·9	285·4	76·1	262·9	164·0	48·0	548·3	240·1	56·2
1900–9	33·4	25·9	234·2	293·5	82·0	338·5	214·3	22·0	632·0	296·3	53·1
1910–13	49·4	38·5	249·0	336·9	110·3	543·1	372·4	38·0	880·0	481·7	45·3

NOTE. New expenditure corresponds to total expenditure less maintenance costs. Additional expenditure, omitted from the calculations, is itemized in the Appendix.

SOURCE. Appendix, Table 54 below.

by imposing priorities where necessary. This can be interpreted as a move towards an anti-cyclical policy (see Table 47).

The public works sector was therefore affected by external, almost artificial, factors. Nonetheless, it was not untouched by the cyclical fluctuations noted elsewhere. The periods of its cycles, for example, tally with those of the house-building sector: expenditure (in current francs) peaked in 1847, 1862 (but 1869 if we refer to the index of the volume of investment), 1883, 1900, and 1913 (Fig. 3). The volume of

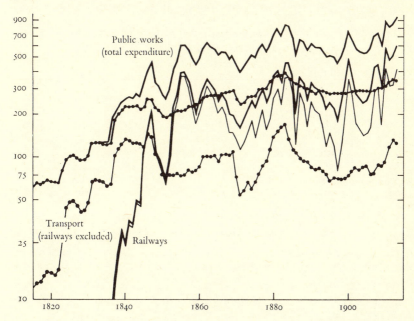

Fig. 3. Infrastructure and Construction: Annual Expenditure, 1815–1913 (million francs, current prices)

NOTE. Total expenditure is represented by thick lines; new expenditure (i.e. excluding maintenance costs) is represented by thin lines.

SOURCE. Tables 47 and 54.

the cycles was particularly large during the period of take-off (the growth rate of investment reached 5·4 per cent per annum during the phase of expansion between 1826 and 1847); it was only middling during cycles III and IV (1·18 per cent per annum), was negative at the end of the century (despite the recovery in the economy, the peak of cycle V, at − 1·56 per cent per annum, was below that of the preceding cycle) and was once again high in 1900–13 (+ 1·22 per cent), as was also the case in the building sector. The indices of railway investment, in fact, show the same phases and similar variations in size as appear in the latter: $+1.58$ per cent per annum, then -0.68 per cent, between 1847 and 1893; only the slope is slightly more marked (about $+1.72$ per cent) on the eve of the war. The state, it therefore seems, inherited the traditions and skilled engineers of the *ancien régime*, was responsible for the important public works programmes that were undertaken, but lacked the necessary means to ensure the completion of the work. After 1872, public expenditure on transport and on urban development did not exceed 1 per cent of the national income, except during post-war periods (Table 48). The contribution of the state also appears small

Table 48. *Public Expenditure Allotted to Interest Payments on the National Debt and to Public Works, 1872–1932*

	In millions of francs		As % of budget		As % of national product		
	National debt	Public works	National debt	Public works	National debt	Public works	Total expenditure
1872	1,030	106	38·4	3·8	3·6	0·4	9·7
1880	984	398	34·2	11·2	3·6	1·5	13·1
1890	1,264	174	36·8	4·8	4·4	0·6	12·5
1900	930	150	28·4	4·2	2·9	0·5	11·0
1912	827	205	20·7	4·8	1·6	0·4	8·4
1920	8,875	3,725	22·7	4·9	4·9	2·1	21·8
1932	11,142	5,579	19·0	9·6	3·9	2·0	21·5

NOTE. Figures for expenditure by local authorities – which represented 3·2 per cent of the national product in 1880 and 10·7 per cent in 1932 – are not included in this table.

SOURCE. G. Terny et al., *L'Evolution de longue période des dépenses publiques françaises* (Paris, 1974), part 3, pp. 155–8.

when calculated in comparison with the aggregate total of fixed investment: in 1863, a period when public expenditure still appeared the decisive factor, it accounted for only 8·25 per cent, i.e. 213 million francs out of a total investment of 2,580 million francs.[14] In 1872 and 1880, when the recovery in the economy coincided with the application of the Freycinet plan, it still amounted to 4·4 per cent and 13·1 per cent respectively. But thereafter it fell to 5·7 per cent, 4·1 per cent, and 4·2 per cent in 1890, 1900, and 1912. This may have been because the state was hampered by the narrowness and rigidity of the fiscal system and by the financial burdens which the wars had placed upon it – for more than fifty years, state expenditure on paying the obligations of the national debt was five or six times more than the sum allotted to public investment.

Throughout the period, in fact, decisions concerning the public works sector were taken not freely but in response to economic pressures. First of all, they were governed by variations in the flow of traffic: these variations were of two kinds. In the first place, on several occasions it was a question of responding to a recovery and increase in traffic, once at the beginning of the century (when the volume of passenger and goods traffic increased by more than 4 per cent per annum between 1820 and 1860) and again in the 1870s (when railway traffic grew again, by 4·6 per cent per annum). Then, following the end of the great depression, there was a steadier, more lasting increase – goods traffic by rail, after falling by 1·50 per cent in the 1880s, developed between 1890 and 1910 at the rate of 3·20 per cent per annum.[15] Secondly, after the war of 1870 it was a matter of reorganizing a communications system which was disorientated by territorial losses and the severing of the link with the Rhine. Allowing, then, for some ten years' delay for public works programmes to get fully under way, it seems that there were three major cycles. The first corresponds to the renovation and extension of the existing network of conventional means of transport; the second, to the building of the railways in the 1850s; and the third, to their modernization, with the recovery in trade at the beginning of the twentieth century. And there was a further, more artificial, cycle in the late 1870s. This stemmed from certain decisions by parliament: first, that 9,000 km of waterways should be constructed or improved; second, that the state should complete the network of 2,615 km brought into being by the merger of local railway companies in western France; and third, that it should build a further 10,000 km of main-line track, to add to the existing 22,000 km. The construction of this was ultimately, in 1883, to be entrusted to the existing private companies. The scale of this programme, with the almost immediate opening of some hundred building sites, marks out this final cycle as comprising a greater mass of investment capital than was shown in all the previous series of data. By August 1881, within two years of the enactment of the Freycinet plan, a programme of 9,615 km of new railway track had been declared to be in the public interest, and work had been started on half this length. But the unusual character of this cycle must not blind us to the link which existed, here as in every cycle, between infrastructure investment and general economic trends (Fig. 2).

A second factor, related to the way in which railways were built and to the life-span of the materials used, also deserves mention, because it led the companies to invest twice over before the end of the usual period of amortization, and thus it modified the normal course of a cycle. There were two reasons for the very high level of activity in railway construction in the 1850s. The first was the inexperience of the railway engineers. With no precedents on which to rely, they were unable to anticipate many problems, particularly the rapid wear and tear on the materials in consequence of the rapid increase in the traffic once the network entered service. Calculated in terms of units per km, passenger and goods traffic transported by rail increased by 11·6 per cent per annum between 1851–3 and 1867–9. Furthermore, early construction work was done on the cheap: this may have been because of a lack of funds, or because of the fear of being unable to recoup the cost of materials in the brief periods stipulated in the subcontracting agreements. When, from 1852, their lease was extended (from 46 to 99 years) and traffic built up, the companies found they had not only to lay new tracks, as specified in the contracts, but also to rebuild embankments and stations, to devise supplementary lines to make up for the failings of the existing network, and to order rails and equipment in advance of when they were needed, so as to forestall price increases.[16] As a result, the period 1854–6 led to an exceptionally high level of railway investment (the highest of the century, in current prices). This was followed by a minor cycle which corresponded to the beginning of construction work on the second network in 1859. During this period railway investment probably developed independently of investment in other categories. The railway cycle preceded the normal investment cycle; and it had two peaks, in 1856 and 1862, unlike the other series.

The first railway equipment used was technically of poor quality. The rails, made of iron, had to be replaced every ten or twelve years, and often less. Because of its price, steel was kept for the points and for parts subject to great wear and tear. As early as the 1860s, for every 800 km of line opened annually, an average of 1,275 km had to be replaced annually (i.e. 9·5 per cent of the 13,440 km of track then in service). Maintenance costs threatened to run higher than construction costs. This was why measures were taken to speed up the application of the Bessemer process, patented in 1856 and put to trial use from 1863 onwards. This process made it possible to use the new material and led to a rapid fall in its price. The total cost of the purchase of iron rails during this period was in the region of 40–45 million francs per annum: if the same quantity of steel rails had been bought, they would have cost 175 million francs per annum in 1863–4, half that sum in 1865–9, and 70 million in 1870–9 – on the assumption that construction and replacement were maintained at the same pace. Without even waiting for the stabilization of prices – which took place in 1883 – the companies re-equipped the whole network as early as 1874–6 and 1878–82; for however dear they might be in initial capital costs, steel rails, which were stronger and more resistant than iron rails, were a better investment. A survey conducted in 1887 showed that after fifteen years of using steel rails, the rate of replacement on the network had fallen substantially – on control samples of track, barely 6 per cent, and sometimes only 2 per cent, of steel rails had been replaced during the period, whereas the corresponding figure for iron rails was 79 per cent.[17]

Therefore, to the reasons already adduced to explain the cycle of the 1870s we should add the change in construction materials and in the periods allowed for depreciation. The average life-span of the network could thus be prolonged, without any loss of efficiency. The average production of 233,000 tons of rails per annum between 1860 and 1879 rose to more than 360,000 tons per annum between 1880 and 1885. Steel rails accounted for one-third of the production in 1870–2, two-thirds in 1873–7, and more than nine-tenths in 1878–85. Thereafter, the advantages of steel were brought home. For the next twenty years – a period corresponding to twice the normal life-span of the former iron rails – steelworks turned out an average of only 220,000 tons of rail per annum. If we assume that steelworks were equipped to maintain production at 1883 levels, then some 43 per cent of their capacity remained unused until 1898. Consequently, overinvestment contributed to deepening the depression that followed.

In short, there were two major causes of development in the public works sector. One, which lasted throughout, was linked to the development of the transport system. Here, investment followed the pattern of the twenty- to twenty-five-year cycles which marked the building industry and the economy as a whole. The other operated only during certain periods and stemmed from the rapid wear and tear on materials and from technical change. Because of it, the range of the fluctuations increased on two occasions, with the early replacement of some railway equipment in 1854–6, and more specifically of the railway track in 1878–82. It was therefore maintenance work which strengthened the accelerated pace of railway construction work, and which led to the phased appearance of investment in the transport sector.

C. EXCESS CAPACITY

These various factors, however, do not fully explain the slowing-down of the economy at the end of the nineteenth century. In none of the sectors was the high level that was reached in 1880–4 subsequently maintained. Output in the building industry during the next twenty-seven years fell off by an average of two-fifths; work on the railways fell by a comparable amount during the same period. What is more, the economic recovery that began in other Western European countries at the turn of the century was not sufficient in France to bring about a return to previous peaks. At their highest, in 1898–1901, the indices (see Fig. 3) remained some 6 to 11 per cent below earlier maximum levels. Signs of improvement did not appear until the four years before the war: in both sectors the level of capital formation during these years was 12·5 per cent higher than the 1882–4 level – although the level for conventional means of transport (roads, ports, and canals) still remained some 25 per cent lower (see Table 60, pp. 292–5). Profits, during the period after 1880, felt the effects of the reduced growth rate of the economy. In the Paris building industry, the ratio between rents and costs – which, as a measure of the profitability of houses built for the middle-class market, evidently leaves much to be desired – fell by a third: the index declined from 149·1 in 1875–9 to 100·0 in 1908–12 (98·7 in 1910–14). After the war it plummeted, following the rent freeze and the rise in the price of construction work proper, which doubled in relation to the cost of land (Table 49). In the railway sector, the situation was less clear-cut. The dividend paid out by the major companies undoubtedly fell: on the basis of the extreme limits of the fluctuation, the annual rate of return on their stock fell from 8·09 per cent in 1864 to 3·08 per cent in 1898 (last column of Table 49). This, however, gives an incomplete picture of the situation. During this period 90 per cent of the companies' capital came from debentures and subsidies; also, no analysis of operating costs and investment has been made on the basis of the companies' books. Nonetheless, the ratio between tariffs and costs – indicated in Table 49 in centimes per unit-km – shows a similar drop. The fall was of the order of 35–40 per cent: the ratio reached 2·49 in 1850–69 (having been 2·89 in 1849) but was down to 1·86 in 1870–99 and to 1·55 in 1900–29.

The factor which remains an enigma during the period 1880–1910 is the apparent lack of reaction from industrialists. F. Simiand maintained that profits continued or increased during a depression because manufacturers were then forced to innovate and invest so as to compensate for the increase in constant costs. Why did this not happen during this period? In the building industry, the dispersed nature of the work and the very small size of the firms suggest that the fall in demand led to the break-up of many firms and brought technological advance to a halt. In this sector, the work force totalled 720,000 to 730,000 in 1851. Thereafter it fell, if not in absolute terms – in the building and public works sector, it comprised 820,000 persons in 1896 – then at least in relative terms, from 17·5 per cent of the industrial labour force to 12·0 per cent. Average productivity does not appear to have varied, except in related branches. In the second half of the century, for every 100 houses completed (with 1·52–1·75 storeys per house), there were 12·7 workers, and later 10·9.[18] In the railway sector, however, the situation was very different. The companies were compelled to press on with their con-

Table 49. *Profits and Volume of Investment in Basic Sectors, 1850–1929*

	Construction work in Paris, indices (base: 1908–12 = 100)						Compagnie du Chemin de Fer du Nord				
	Rents of middle-class homes	Cost of land	Cost of construction	Rent–cost ratio (per cent)	Volume of construction	Cheap rents	Tariff	Costs	Tariff–cost ratio (G/H)	Traffic (thousands of unit-km)	Yield on railway stocks (per cent)
							(centimes per unit-km)				
	A	B	C	D	E	F	G	H	I	J	K
1850–9	—	—	—	—	—	53·4	7·68	2·82	2·72	568	6·14
1860–9	80·9	42·1	61·5	132·3	176·9	75·8	6·33	2·80	2·26	1,124	6·85
1870–9	91·7	43·4	62·4	146·9	125·5	84·2	5·61	3·00	1·87	1,878	5·79
1880–9	102·9	48·7	80·3	128·2	171·1	94·6	5·26	2·73	1·93	2,859	4·23
1890–9	99·8	72·6	82·7	120·7	131·6	—	4·48	2·51	1·78	4,102	3·59
1900–9	98·8	82·8	92·2	107·2	99·6	96·4	3·81	2·35	1·62	5,934	3·90
1910–19	105·5	96·1	197·3	53·5	66·5	104·5	3·60	2·42	1·49	7,875	4·47
1920–9	199·8	263·5	526·9	379	76·1	225·0	17·20	11·22	1·53	9,950	5·84

SOURCES. Columns A, C, D, E: F. Marnata, *Les Loyers des bourgeois de Paris, 1860–1958* (Paris, 1961). Columns B, F: M. Halbwachs, *Les Expropriations et le prix des terrains à Paris, 1860–1900* (Paris, 1909); indices for cheap rents are calculated from figures in the *Annuaire Statistique* for 1966, p. 404. Columns G, H: F. Caron, *Histoire de l'exploitation d'un grand réseau: La Compagnie du Chemin de Fer du Nord, 1846–1937* (Paris, and The Hague, 1973), 295, 481, and 488. Column K: J. Denuc, 'Dividendes, valeur mobilière et taux de capitalisation des valeurs mobilières françaises', *Bulletin Statistique Générale de la France*, XIII, 4 (1934), 732.

struction work and to keep on the same work force, comprising some 240,000 to 250,000 wage-earners. They benefited from a central organization and financial assistance from the state. It is less easy, then, to understand why investment was not maintained so as to protect the effectiveness of capital. Why were the policies of the companies and of the state reversed (the extraordinary budget for the public works programme being abolished in 1888)? Or, limiting ourselves to quantifiable data, why was it that the aggregate productivity of the railways (comprising both infrastructure work and railway equipment) increased in 1855–67 and in 1900–13 at the respective rates of 1·93 and 1·73 per cent per annum, yet stagnated during the intervening period of some thirty years, at −0·06 per cent per annum in 1867–81 and +0·85 per cent in 1881–1900?

The first of the probable reasons for this reversal of trends was the inevitable variation in the intensity of the traffic using the network. It has often been pointed out that there exists a time-lag in railway development, between capital investment and the actual putting into service of railway equipment. Problems resulting from the internal organization of the companies, and the slowness inherent in the creation of markets, brought about the accumulation of reserves of latent productivity, which took time to realize. On the other hand, once a certain level of capital-intensity was reached, marginal productivity figures must have fallen. This was the case from the 1860s onwards. Before then, the railways offered clear-cut advantages on the score of both prices and services. Their market developed primarily at the expense of other means of transport. The railway cut the tariff for passenger traffic to some 7 centimes per km, compared to the 11–16 centimes previously charged by road transport. Similarly, in 1845–54 freight charges for goods traffic were reduced from the 23–28 centimes per ton/km charged for ordinary road haulage to 10·6 centimes by rail; and thereafter, while road-haulage rates remained unchanged, rail charges for goods traffic fell still further, to 8–9 centimes in 1860 and to 7·5 centimes in 1870.[19] Canals charged lower prices than the railways (for inferior services) – in the late 1860s canal charges ranged from 4 centimes to 1·75 centimes per ton/km. But even they lost much traffic to the railways and entered a period of stagnation. The volume of traffic transported by the waterways remained at an average of 1,900 million tons per km between 1860 and 1869, which was some 5 per cent lower than the figures for 1850–9. During this same period, from 1855 to 1867, rail traffic increased by 10·4 per cent per annum, which was a higher rate than the 8·12 per cent per annum rate of investment. Throughout this period, therefore, the railway network assumed an ever-increasing burden of traffic and improved its productivity.

Thereafter, the rate of increase in rail traffic fell to an average of 4 per cent per annum. This may have been because of a levelling-off or standardizing of the rates charged for the same service by different types of transport; or because the market was saturated, so that expansion could no longer come about merely through the displacement of other means of transport; or because the long-term deceleration in economic growth had begun. In fact, in 1867–9 the first signs appeared that the increase in the traffic was reaching its limits. Indeed, there were relatively severe falls in 1870–1 and in 1874–7. These developments, which at the time were novel, and the over-rapid recovery, during the cycle which peaked in 1882, were the reasons why investment – particularly in the replacement of rails and of rolling stock – was at first delayed and then concentrated within a few years, and why technical innovations were then introduced but failed to gain widespread application. To sum up, during the first period, the employment of capital lagged behind its investment. But following the slowing-down in the pace of construction which occurred between 1871 and 1876, the gap between the two disappeared. Consequently, because the volume of investment was too large between 1876 and 1883, for so short a period, a crisis of excess capacity resulted. The rate of growth of productivity of capital could not be maintained: from an average of 2·04 per cent per annum in the period 1855–67, it fell to 1·0 per cent between 1867 and 1881. In the aftermath of the depression of 1881–3, the worst of the century, it collapsed to −4·3 per cent per annum (Fig. 4). In terms of

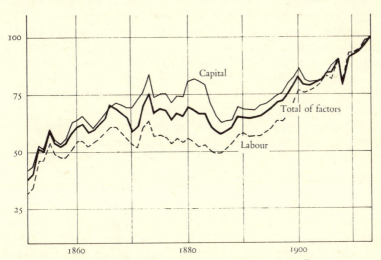

Fig. 4. Indices of Productivity in the Railway Sector, 1850–1913 (base: 1913 = 100)

SOURCE. Appendix, below.

financial return, the profitability of the new construction work – as measured by the (ten-year) growth of the net product as a percentage of new investment expenditure (less maintenance expenditure) during the period – fell likewise. On a base of 1854–63 = 100, the index rose to 144·8 in 1864–73 (for the war weighed less heavily on revenue than on capital expenditure), but it then fell to 85·1 in 1874–83, despite the prosperity then prevailing, and to 31·5 in 1884–93.[20] With the fall in the return on capital, a fall in the level of investment was bound to ensue.

A very different explanation for this fall is suggested by a second set of factors which relate to the geography of the country. The transport system depended on raw materials for a good part of its traffic, and in the middle of the century the railway companies sought to secure a monopoly of this freight. France was not well endowed with raw materials: their shortage was perhaps particularly felt at the end of the century, when structural crises hit the textile industry in the 1860s, the output of basic industries in 1874–7, and cereal and wine output from 1879 onwards, and so forth. Moreover, there was no interdependence between the different transport systems. For example, the pattern of coal imports made the coasting trade a small, but rival, alternative to the railway. On various occasions the government took measures to encourage the transport of heavy merchandise by the canals – not so much by investments aimed at improving canal services, but by fiscal relief (1872) or the reduction and abolition of dues (1880). These measures had a social purpose – it was more a matter of saving inland navigation than of improving the general transport system.

Another drawback in the long run was the lack of urban markets which alone might have made the railway networks economically viable. Industrialization had come about through the decentralization of labour to the countryside and the small towns. As a result, the population was still 74 per cent rural in 1880. Paris, of course, had the appearance of a major metropolis, with 2·27 million inhabitants, or 23 per cent of France's urban population, and 60 per cent more than the other six major conurbations put together. But Paris was an exception. Urbanization was marked less by the growth in the size of towns than by their dispersion. Omitting the group of seven large cities, the number of towns increased from 450 to 700 between 1820 and 1880, but the population of each town did not vary much from the average figure of 7,500 inhabitants.[21] This argument, then, comes down to maintaining that what the railways lacked were modern towns and their traffic. Yet this handicap had existed for a long time. Perhaps the question should be put the other way round: instead of extending the railway network, which they knew to be deficient, and adapting it to a decentralized industrial structure, should not the authorities have used it to bring industries together, to relocate the work force and give it more productive employment? After 1860, the railway penetrated to remote regions – the length of track in operation quintupled by 1914. Yet the gain in the extension of the track was more than offset by the loss in traffic. The annual increase in freight (reckoned in tons per km) was no more than 1·6 per cent after 1883; and there was no further increase in the distances travelled (reckoned in km per ton). Examined in this light, the railway helped in the formation of the national market. But at a later stage, because the network was overextended, it probably helped to immobilize the economy and retard its growth.

In response to these underlying trends, the railway companies also altered their policy. Yet, in so doing, they probably added a third factor to the crisis. In the past, the proliferation of lines and stations had multiplied the number of jobs. An abundant work force had simplified the situation for employers: many country-dwellers wanted to give up working the land without leaving the countryside; artisans could find jobs on the railway where they could use their skills; and so on. The railways had 30,000 employees in the middle of the century, four times that number in 1867, and eight times in 1883. Yet this uncomplicated employment policy was gradually threatened – in the 1860s, by price and wage increases (wages representing 45 per cent of all expenditure and up to 85 per cent of operating costs); in 1867–81, by the falling return on capital, even though the latter still made up for the fall in the productivity of the work force; and in 1881–6, by the change in the structure of costs. In the Northern Railway Company, owing to the increase in the wages bill, operating costs rose from 39·7 per cent of revenue in 1857–66 to 54·9 per cent in 1867–83, while gross profits fell from 37·1 per cent to 18·0 per cent. The solutions adopted by the companies are well known. They led to a rationalization of the use of lines and stations through greater specialization, and to better management of the rolling stock through an increase in the power and eventually in the speed of the locomotives and in the carrying capacity of the wagons. So far as the labour force was concerned, the innovations led to the widespread use of air-brakes, of the block system of signalling, of electricity at stations, so that the more menial jobs were abolished without any overall reduction in the number of employees, and so forth.[22] The period of heavy investment was over: the task now was to improve working conditions through methods which required little capital, and to obtain, as the director of one company put it, 'the maximum return with the maximum effort and the minimum of material inputs'. It would seem that this aim was attained, because the productivity of the work force improved. Indeed, throughout the various networks its growth was sufficient to make up for the failings of the other factors. According to J. Dessirer, the annual growth of labour productivity was o·1 per cent in 1860–80, and 2·5 per cent in 1880–1930. According to the calculations given in Table 50, it was, on average, about 2 per cent per annum from 1886 to 1913.[23]

Such a policy, of course, entailed a certain sacrifice of capital expenditure, as the sector adjusted to a period of stagnation. From the 1880s onwards, the government, which supervised the companies' financial management and their scale of charges, urged them to make economies, which they themselves wanted to do. Increased maintenance, instead of replacement, was the policy adopted towards major construction works nearing the end of their normal life-span. Figures for the maintenance costs of the Compagnie du Chemin de Fer de l'Est show that spending on buildings and earthworks increased – by 24 per cent before 1886 and 36 per cent thereafter. The working life of the locomotives of the Compagnie du Chemin de Fer du Nord, which in 1885 was some twenty to twenty-five years, was prolonged to thirty years by 1877, even though the distances they travelled daily were increased by some 50 per cent.[24] The railways were therefore ill prepared for the renewed demand for transport which was felt sporadically in the late 1890s and then continuously from 1904 to 1932.

The companies were in fact subject to two kinds of pressure. Because their operations were so labour-intensive, they developed a comprehensive social policy aimed at maintaining a stable work force and improving the level of technical skills. However, a combination of factors – the increase in traffic, the run-down state of some of the equipment, and (from 1894 onwards) the reduction in the hours of work which was stipulated by law – forced the railway companies to cover their extra labour requirements by employing workers whose standards were often low. An extra 100,000 workers were taken on before 1913, and another 180,000 in 1922. The total work force consequently doubled, and railway employers were forced to grant wage increases, often quite large ones, and to make social-welfare provisions more widespread. Some companies had to devote a large share of their financial reserves to this – up to 70 per cent between 1887 and 1913, in the case of the Northern Railway Company. The fall in construction and repair work does not mean that the railways stopped ordering equipment from industry during the period 1880–1900. For example, increased wear and tear on the tracks, brought about by the increase in train loads, led to major rebuilding works from the 1890s onwards, as well as the re-bedding of much track (by 1913, 29 per cent of the rails had been relaid). But the firms engaged in producing and processing metals had to readjust to the changed circumstances. Railway companies

Table 50. *Inputs, Output, and Total Factor Productivity in Railways, 1855–1913 (base: 1908–13 = 100)*

	Inputs				Output	Productivity per unit				Years	Growth rates (% p.a.)			
	Capital	Energy	Labour	Total		Capital	Energy	Labour	Total		Capital	Energy	Labour	All inputs
1855	13·2	8·4	14·3	13·2	7·9	59·8	93·2	55·3	59·6	—	—	—	—	—
1867	33·7	16·8	39·0	34·1	25·8	76·3	152·6	66·0	75·4	12	+2·04	+4·19	+1·48	+1·93
1881	50·9	31·7	75·4	59·8	44·7	87·7	140·9	59·3	74·7	14	+1·00	−0·57	−0·67	−0·06
1886	59·8	34·3	77·3	66·0	42·5	71·1	124·1	55·0	64·5	5	−3·52	−2·29	−1·51	−2·60
1900	81·7	64·1	89·3	83·9	73·5	90·0	114·6	82·3	87·7	14	+1·70	−0·53	+2·92	+2·22
1913	108·5	99·3	106·4	106·8	117·2	108·0	118·1	110·1	109·7	13	+1·41	+0·25	+2·26	+1·73

SOURCE. Appendix, below.

had taken 11 per cent of their production in 1855–64 and 7·3 per cent in 1875–84, but they took only 5·9 per cent between 1885 and 1913. In 1878–83, five firms supplied more than 90 per cent of the orders for locomotives: machine-builders like these subsequently underwent a severe crisis, which was aggravated in export markets by foreign competition. As investment began to pick up, therefore, the situation with respect to both prices and delays was very difficult. First, rolling stock was increased and, after 1923, modernized without prejudice to the total figure (in 1937, 34 per cent of the locomotives and 60 per cent of the wagons were under seventeen years of age). Secondly, infrastructure work was renewed – it accounted for only 59 per cent of capital expenditure in 1935, compared with 68 per cent in 1923 and 74 per cent in 1913.[25]

Given the depleted state of the reserves, which in any event could not have covered the total cost of the new investment, these rebuilding programmes were financed by recourse to the market. The indebtedness of the railway companies, which totalled some 18,700 million francs in 1913, rose to some 35,000 million (in current francs) in 1923 and to 82,800 million in 1935, without taking into account share capital of 1,460 million francs at the outbreak of the war. A total of 78,400 million francs of debentures and preference shares covered 95 per cent of liabilities.[26]

In a long-term perspective, this policy throws light on the role that investment in the basic industries occupied in the nation's savings. From 1850 to 1880, this sector – comprising the building industry, railways, and traditional means of transport – absorbed 1,630 million francs per annum (or, if we exclude railway equipment which ought to be entered under the heading 'investment in plant and machinery', 1,550 million francs). This represents 73·7 per cent of internal investment, or 65·1 per cent of all investment if we include investment abroad. Because of the crisis of excess capacity at the end of the century, investment in this sector remained important in absolute terms – it totalled some 2,102 million francs in 1880–9 and 1,976 million in 1890–9 – but it fell in relative terms to 67·7 per cent and 60·4 per cent of internal capital expenditure. The change in the structure of investment, which was inevitable, accelerated. This explains the diversion of capital to investment abroad, since during this period foreign investment increased, as a percentage of total savings invested, from 4·9 per cent in 1880–9 to 16·3 per cent and 22·2 per cent in the 1890s and 1900s. But the cause must not be confused with the effects. In the last third of the nineteenth century the outflow of funds into foreign ventures had no impact on infrastructure work; and it did not slow down investment in plant and machinery, which was to play a major role in the second industrial revolution. Such investment increased throughout the period, accounting for 37·1 per cent of domestic capital investment in 1880–9, 38·5 per cent in 1895–1904, and 47·8 per cent in 1910–13 (see Fig. 5). On the other hand, the renewal of railway (and housing) development, given this sector's unpreparedness after 1904, had harmful consequences: these hit particularly hard because the rise in costs and in wages, when compared with delays in the attendant price-rises, reduced the possibilities of self-financing for firms in general.

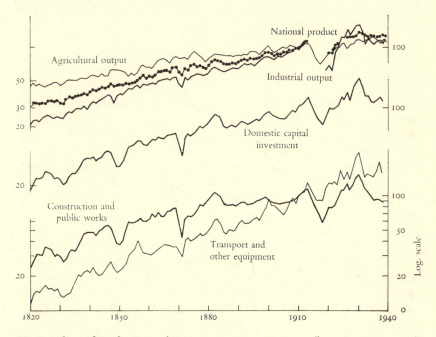

Fig. 5. Indices of Production and Home Investment, 1820–1938 (base: 1908–12 = 100)
SOURCE. Table 60.

Seen in this light, investment in the basic sector after the turn of the century played a useful role. Once again the nation's savings centred on infrastructure. From 1910, there was a marked fall in investment abroad. Yet it may have attracted too large a share of the capital available. From 1910 to 1927, the railways accounted for 19·3 per cent of all private borrowing – it was not until 1928–31 that their share fell to 9·6 per cent – and they contributed to the rise in interest rates. Loans in this sector were raised at 4·25 per cent in 1880–1900 and at 4·94 per cent in 1900–13, but at 8·52 per cent in 1919–30 (and up to 12·6 per cent in 1925–6). Investment in the basic sector undoubtedly contributed to the first industrialization of France. But from the 1880s onwards,

it no longer played a regulating role. When the infrastructure investment was at too low a level, it encouraged an excessive capital outflow;
and when at too high level, it brought about a corresponding lag in
industrial development.

III.   Industrial investment[27]

In the medium term, the pattern of the cycles of industrial investment closely resembled that of investment in the infrastructure, but the
amplitude of each cycle and above all the general aspect of the long-
term curve differed markedly. Before 1885, the amplitude of the cycles
of investment in industrial plant and machinery was smaller than that
of investment, which in this essay we have classified as that of the 'basic
sector'. Thereafter, it was greater. In the long term, the pace of industrial investment quickened, unlike that of both investment in the basic
sector and industrial production itself. The rate of growth of industrial
investment was 2·1 per cent from 1820–4 to 1865–9, and 2·8 per cent
from 1865–9 to 1910–13. The concave curve of industrial investment
stands out against the convex curve of investment in the basic sector.

Thus, French industry tended to become increasingly capitalistic. A
comparison between the phasing of growth in production and that in
industrial investment suggests that there were three phases in French
industrial development:

In the 1820s and 1830s and the early 1840s, growth was 'dualistic':
alongside highly capitalized sectors, there developed sectors based on a
work force which continued to be plentiful and cheap. This was not a
survival from times past but reflected a definite growth in the number
of workers in domestic and artisan industries. In addition, factories
themselves continued to use labour-intensive methods. The two sharp
spurts in investment which occurred in the late 1820s and the 1830s
were concentrated in particular industries: in the 1820s large metallurgical works, based on English models, and the major spinning-mills
were established; in the 1830s investment was concentrated in the coal-
mining industry and, as in the previous decade, in metallurgy and
cotton. Industrial growth continued to be based on an increase in the
labour force. From Toutain's figures (which are open to question) it
seems that the annual mean increase in the growth of the active industrial population totalled 46,000 from the Empire to the early 1840s.

Between the 1840s and the 1860s this increase fell to 32,000 per
annum. Nonetheless, the growth of industrial production accelerated
during this period, according to François Crouzet: he believes that the
'key period' in the industrialization of France was the last years of
the July Monarchy, and 'the authoritarian Empire' – the first half of

the Second Empire.[28] According to Lévy-Leboyer, industrial growth developed at the rate of 2·98 per cent per annum from 1815 to 1845, and at 2·56 per cent from 1845 to 1865.[29] He suggests, therefore, that the fall in the growth rate was very slight. One might have expected that there would be a change in the relative weight of the components of growth, with capital increasing relative to other factors; yet the evidence, far from indicating an acceleration in the growth of industrial investment, appears to show the reverse.

It therefore seems that the increased productivity of labour stemmed mainly from a more efficient deployment of labour. Between the 1840s and the 1860s the balance between the rural and urban components of the work force was disturbed, for this was the period when, as we have seen, the rural exodus increased, reaching its peak in the 1850s. The situation, then, was as much due to a reorganization of the pattern and methods of labour as to a growing relative recourse to capital. Indeed, the small contribution of capital investment to growth which is evident in the earlier period continued from the 1840s to the 1860s. The 100,163 industrial concerns covered in a survey of 1861–5 used the different sources of energy in the following proportions: water-mills, 60 per cent; windmills, 8 per cent; horse-driven mills, 1 per cent; steam-powered mills, 31 per cent.

A total of 320,000 horsepower was in service in 1869. This was only a tenth of the figure for 1913; yet the index of industrial production in 1865–9 stood at 41·7 according to Crouzet, and at 34·5 according to Lévy-Leboyer. In 1878, the steam power capacity in industry was still only a fifth of the figure for the railways.

In the 1870s and 1880s, industrial growth slowed markedly (to a figure of 1·5 per cent per annum from 1870 to 1896, according to E. Malinvaud). The slowdown in production was not accompanied by an equivalent slowdown in the growth of investment. Indeed, the latter even increased, up to 1883. The volume of investment then fell from 1884 to 1889 (the index for 1885–9 was 44·5, as against an index of 50 for 1880–4), but growth subsequently picked up. Overall, from 1865–9 to 1880–4 the annual average growth in production was 1·5 per cent and that of investment was 3·3. For the period from 1865–9 to 1890–4, the figures are 1·5 per cent and 2·4 per cent respectively. Thus, industrial production tended to become more capitalistic at a time when its rate of growth was falling.

Furthermore, census returns show that the active industrial population remained stationary in these years at approximately 4·4 million. How, then, can one account for the increased investment programme? There are two conventional explanations: on the one hand, the changing relative costs of the various factors of production; on the other, increased competition. Both made for increased productivity. On the first point, a comparison between the index of nominal wages and that of prices of heavy industrial products multiplied by an index of interest rates (base: 1908–12 = 100) gives the following figures:

	Wages	Prices of heavy industrial products
1855–9	68·0	166
1885–9	105·3	66
1890–4	109·3	64

On the second point, we believe that it was not before the 1860s, with the spread of the railway, that competition increased at the inter-regional and international levels. This competition undoubtedly stimulated growth in certain industries. Wherever there existed 'advanced' techniques, which required considerable capital, firms intent on growth had to adopt them.

In most sectors during the period 1877–83, large factories were built (in the metallurgical, cement, textile, and chemical industries) whose methods economized on labour per unit of output, but which required considerable outlays on capital. This investment programme occurred at a time when the market was about to become very depressed, because of the fall in agricultural earnings, the stagnation of exports, and the fall of investment in the 'basic' sector. The excess capacity which resulted led to the fall in rates of growth during the late 1880s, a period when a large number of new industrial techniques first appeared in the world economy.

From the early 1890s onwards, the curve of industrial investment became sharply distinct from that of investment in the 'basic' sector. The growth rate of the former was 3·3 per cent from 1890–4 to 1910–13, 3·7 per cent from 1900–04 to 1910–13, and 5·2 per cent from 1905–9 to 1910–13. During this period the growth rate of industrial investment is thus paralleled by that of industrial production. First, production had grown more rapidly than investment; then, the reverse was the case; now, each developed in conjunction with the other. The annual mean increase in the horsepower installed in industry rose from 73,350 in the period 1883–1903 to 141,800 in the period 1903–13. According to Malinvaud, the rate of investment was 13·4 per cent in 1896 and 16·8 per cent in 1913. The increase was concentrated in industrial plant and machinery, a sector in which investment more than doubled between 1905 and 1913. The index for imports of machinery, computed by A. Aftalion, rose from 30 in 1895 to 100 in 1910; and the volume of capital investment steadily increased in all sectors of the economy. Aftalion identified the same trend in the clothing industry in 1903.

Changes in relative factor costs, however, played a less helpful role in encouraging capital-intensification than in previous periods. Between 1895–9 and 1900–14, the wage index rose by 1·1 per cent, the index of prices in heavy industry by 1·2 per cent, and that of the latter multiplied by interest rates by 2·3 per cent. The effect of this change in the relationship between the costs of the various factors was more than compensated for by the fact that investment made it possible to adopt new techniques which brought increased or improved productivity.

French industrialization had long depended heavily on agricultural prosperity and on decisions relating to investment in the basic sector. This trend now ended: indeed, the reverse occurred. Thus, there were two distinct periods in the history of capital formation in France. During the first two-thirds of the nineteenth century, the dynamic element in investment was investment in the basic sector: industrial investment merely followed suit. In the last years of the nineteenth century, and especially during the first decade of the twentieth century, investment in the basic sector – depressed since the 1880s – finally recovered under the stimulus of industrial investment. An important role in this recovery was played by new innovations such as the motor-car, which stimulated new industries remarkable for their new production methods. Such innovations, based upon consumer durable, led to a new pattern of production and consumption.

In this brief chapter we cannot give detailed consideration to the various problems posed by the history of industrial finance. We shall therefore limit ourselves to a brief consideration of companies' internal and external financing.

A. EXTERNAL FINANCING

The process of industrial capital formation was markedly different from the formation of capital in the various communications networks. The latter were financed, in the main, by the issue of debentures, a type of security which closely resembled government bonds, since it was guaranteed by the state. Industrial investment, by contrast, always maintained a more personal character.

Industrial entrepreneurs came from all classes of society, but a particularly large number emerged from the ranks of artisans and middle-class businessmen. The former prevailed in machine industries, the latter in textiles. The metallurgical industry of the nineteenth century was in some ways a continuation of the older business style of the traditional ironmasters, but it also saw the advent of a new race of men, iron-merchants or businessmen. In short, industrial capital in nineteenth-century France came from a wide variety of sources. The industrialists of Alsace and Nevers in the first part of the century, and the industrialists of Lorraine and Grenoble in the second, discovered how to attract local resources of capital. There was considerable exchange betwen industries. In the North, textile manufacturers substantially financed the great expansion of the coal industry; in the Alpine region, at the end of the century, much of the finance for the electrochemical and the electrometallurgical industries came from local resources, which had earlier financed the cement and paper industries. The example of the car industry illustrates this trend well. By and large, car firms were created either by lower-middle-class business-men, such as Renault and Panhard, who had recently specialized in the production of finished articles, or by 'mechanically minded' artisans like Berliet. The capital needed to launch the concern was found relatively easily from within a narrow circle of friends or relatives.

Until 1863, the formation of a limited liability company (*société anonyme*) required the approval of the state: and the Conseil d'Etat, the body which examined applications, rarely gave the necessary authoriza-tion. Between 1819 and 1867, 660 such companies were formed, only eighty of which were active in the industrial sector. In fact, the most usual legal form adopted by private business was the limited partnership (*société en commandite*). Between 1840 and 1859, an annual average of 218 limited partnerships and 14 limited liability companies were formed in France. It is therefore clear, as C. F. Freedeman has argued, that French company law did not hinder industrial development: the limited partnership was a suitable framework for the development of the limitation of individual liability. Indeed, this framework did not exist in other countries, not even in England.

The law of 1867 removed all remaining obstacles. It is surprising that, although documentary evidence exists, no serious study has yet been made of the companies created in France during the nineteenth century. To quote some of the data for the period of the Third Republic: 181,000 companies were formed; 120,000 of these were general partner-ship (*sociétés en nom collectif*), 30,600 were limited partnerships with no share capital (*sociétés en commandite simple*), and 31,200 were joint-stock companies (*sociétés par action*) of which 20,800 were limited liability companies (*sociétés anonymes*). Joint-stock companies accounted for 14 per cent of the companies formed between 1879 and 1883, and for 17 per cent of those formed between 1909 and 1913. We know the figures for the total capital of joint-stock companies from 1889 onwards: the annual mean for five-year periods is as follows:

1889–93:	559 million francs	1904–8:	691 million francs
1894–8:	664 million francs	1909–13:	1,072 million francs
1899–1903:	1,169 million francs		

Table 51. *Sectoral Distribution of Industrial Capital, 1898*

	Number of companies		Nominal value of shares		Nominal value of quoted companies		Quoted stock of quoted companies	
	No.	% of total	Francs (m)	% of total	Francs (m)	% of total	Francs (m)	% of total
Mines and quarries	366	14·0	752·2	25·1	702·5	24·7	1,731·5	35·1
Food industry	689	26·3	327·2	11·0	308·5	10·8	594·2	12·1
Chemicals	496	19·0	514·6	17·2	497·1	17·5	899·0	18·2
Metals	437	16·7	754·0	25·2	729·6	25·6	963·3	19·5
Manufacturing industry	634	24·0	644·5	21·5	611·0	21·4	741·8	15·1
Total	2,622	100·0	2,992·5	100·0	2,848·7	100·0	4,929·8	100·0

SOURCE. *Annuaire Statistique* for 1901.

These figures highlight the importance of the period 1899–1903, during which the initial capital was assembled for the companies which would be the mainspring of the intensive industrialization of 1906–29.

The *Annuaire statistique* of 1901 contains a breakdown of the capital of joint-stock companies in 1898. 6,325 joint-stock companies were then operating in France, with a total nominal capital of 13,500 million francs. Industrial companies accounted for only 22 per cent of that total capital; but they accounted for 34 per cent of the quoted stock of companies listed on the Stock Exchange – the nominal capital of the latter was 12,900 million francs, and the quoted capital 14,400 million. This shows that for industrial companies in comparison with the sum total of all companies the gap between the nominal capital and the quoted capital was much greater: 73 per cent more compared to 11·6 per cent more. Industrial capital was distributed between the different sectors: cf. Table 51.

From the 1840s onwards – 'once the battle for the railway contracts was over' – the leading investment banks moved into industrial investment. Their names figured among the limited partners of the many companies engaged in metallurgy and machinery which were launched in the 1840s and 1850s. By 1914, in addition to their substantial holdings in foreign securities, the majority of investment banks controlled blocks of shares in the metallurgical and electrical industries, which, indeed, they had helped to create. The major deposit banks, created in the 1860s, did not particularly promote such investment, except during certain boom periods for investment such as the 1870s and the years from 1908 to 1914. In short, the French banking system does not seem to have played a *direct* role in encouraging industrial investment. Yet the creation of this system was itself a vital element in capital formation. Through its encouragement of discount facilities and short-term credit, it brought about a transfer of capital and therefore a better use of companies' indigenous resources. In short, it encouraged self-financing.

B. INTERNAL FINANCING

Three fundamental aspects of the industrial economy are highlighted by firms' self-financing during the nineteenth century.

In contrast to the railway sector, in manufacturing industry internal financing was preferred to other ways of raising finance. This preference was general, whatever the particular legal form of a company might be. Nevertheless, it appeared more marked in the case of the straightforward family firm and in that of the very large firm whose capital was entirely or largely depersonalized. In the case of limited partnerships or limited liability companies, in which control was vested in the hands of a small number of families, the sleeping partners or the small number of shareholders could exercise sufficient pressure to force the managing director or the board of directors to increase the share of income which was distributed as a dividend. In 1897, the director of the large Vicoigne-Noeux mining company in northern France deplored the tendency to 'distribute exaggerated dividends', adding, 'our firm has somewhat overdone this'. This feeling of guilt is itself revealing: any increase in the amount of profit distributed to a company's investors was considered inimical to good management. An industrial company ought to form 'war reserves' and to reinvest the greatest possible share of its profits. Boards of directors were never prouder than when they were able to tell their shareholders that the anticipated investment would be amortized within a record number of years.

The development of internal financing was also made possible by a transfer of surpluses to capital expenditure, which itself was made possible by the technological innovations of the nineteenth century. The transport system ensured rapid and secure deliveries, which allowed firms to substantially reduce the size of their stocks of items, such as coal, which they had formerly to lay in at the beginning of winter in anticipation of the temporary closure of the canals. The development of short-term credit and of discount facilities had similar effects. Above all, advances in production methods made for savings in labour and raw materials. This allowed a transfer of resources towards capital expenditure; but, secondly, they soon made for savings in capital. Thus there were two contradictory trends, which explain why, despite the increase in investment, the capital–output ratio remained stable. On the one hand, technological advance favoured the substitution of capital for labour, while the increase in the productivity of capital led to a reduced need for capital. The growth in the productivity of capital, like the growth in the productivity of labour, increased the financing capacity of firms.

Research has not yet advanced sufficiently for us to assess the respective contributions of internal and external financing to the development of industrial firms. There is no doubt that the investment of the 1870s was in large measure financed by the reserves formed during the 1850s and 1860s, a period when profits were high. (These profits were due to a substantial reduction in costs at a time when the fall in prices was levelling off or slowing-down.) In the 1890s and 1900s, the capital reserves for both internal and external financing increased. Most of the commentators writing on the eve of the First World War stressed the importance of the reinvestment of profits. Lescure stated that half the profits were put into the reserves, and C. Colson maintained that French companies 'devote a *considerable* amount of their profits to building up their plant instead of increasing their dividends' and so 'avoid having to issue new stock'. G. F. Teneul reckoned that, during the period 1890–1913, something like 50 per cent of profits were reinvested. There is not necessarily any contradiction between these remarks and the notion that firms raised increasingly large sums by external financing. According to Malinvaud, gross issues of stock floated by French companies on the money market represented 2·1 per cent of the gross internal product in 1896, 3·9 per cent in 1900, and 6 per cent in 1913. L. A. Vincent has suggested that the capital of French firms in 1913 was distributed as follows:

Gross formation of fixed capital assets:	6,600 million francs
of which the reserve formed:	3,000 million francs
Gross undistributed income of companies:	4,200 million francs
Financing of investment by individual firms:	1,100 million francs
Net loans:	1,300 million francs

Thus 40 per cent of a net investment of 3,300 million francs was financed by loans. In the years preceding the war, the proportion represented by loans increased. F. Marnata has compiled a balance-sheet summarizing issues floated on the Stock Exchange during the period 1892–1911. The figures for industrial stock are presented in Table 52. The industrial sector generally accounted for more than two-fifths of all issues after 1897, and two-thirds of the issues of shares. It was allowed access to the debenture market, but less so than the banking and transport sectors.

Table 52. *Issues Floated on the Stock Exchange, 1892–1911*
(million francs)

	Shares and debentures			Shares		
	Total (A)	Industrial (B)	(B):(A)%	Total (C)	Industrial (D)	(C):(D)%
1892–6	543	188	34·7	176	67·6	55·5
1897–1901	941	409	43·5	470	214·2	62·6
1902–6	710	299	42·1	369	248·3	67·3
1907–11	1,444	605	41·9	616	410·8	66·7

SOURCE. F. Marnata, *La Bourse et le financement des investissements* (Paris, 1973).

Total French investment increased from 5,000 million francs in 1830 to 122,000 million in 1913, i.e. 3·4 times the rate of growth of national income and five times that of the amount of money in circulation. The annual mean increase was 200 million francs between 1830 and 1850, 1,560 million francs between 1850 and 1880, and 2,000 million francs between 1880 and 1913. These investment trends were reflected in analysis of inherited wealth: movable assets increased from 32·8 per cent of the total in 1851–5 to 44·2 per cent in 1861–5 and 58·6 per cent in 1911–15. Of these assets, transferable securities did not make their real breakthrough until after the Second Empire: they accounted for 6·9 per cent of movable assets in 1851–5, 8·6 per cent in 1871–5, 17 per cent in 1881–5, 32 per cent in 1891–5, and 39·1 per cent on the eve of the First World War. Until the 1880s, the dominant investment was in *rentes* (government securities). The greatest increase in the national debt occurred between 1850 and 1880, when it rose from 4,700 million francs in 1830 to 5,400 million in 1850, and by 1880 to 21,600 million. Its subsequent growth was more moderate: in 1913, it totalled 33,000 million. *Rentes* were largely replaced by investment in the railways, in the form of either shares or debentures; but, in the years immediately preceding the war, industrial securities tended to outstrip the latter in importance.

APPENDIX

This chapter seeks to assess the contribution of capital to growth, by measuring the variation in the volume of investment, and this volume as a proportion of the national product, and to clarify the role of plant and machinery as the dynamic factor in the sequence of cyclical fluctuations. To realize these aims we need to tabulate returns, itemizing annual gross investment, i.e. capital expenditure which was intended to replace and increase the stock of domestic reproducible fixed assets. Unfortunately, no such series of data exist, except for those devised – for the twentieth century only – by H. Lubell, by J. J. Carré *et al.*, and by J. Mairesse.[30] We have therefore tried to extrapolate backward from their findings. Yet, clearly, the data thus obtained for the past – which are inevitably approximate – cannot be put on a par with the statistical series which were computed and cross-checked from contemporary documents.

The French documents present three major difficulties. One method of calculating the total of a given stock of capital investment is to capitalize the yield of that stock. However, as the reform of the tax system only came into effect in 1916, fiscal returns provide very little in the way of useful data about individual earnings. The only precise data relate to rents and to built-up land. On three occasions during the nineteenth century, government departments published the total number of landed properties, their rateable value, and their market value: there were 7·44 million houses in 1851–3 (which brought in a net income of 677 million francs); 8·91 million in 1887–9 (when the income was some 1,950 million francs); and 9·17 million in 1899–1900 (with an income of 2,200 million francs). Unfortunately, comparisons between these three sets of data are not as fruitful as one might expect, because the figures do not relate to precisely the same items at different times. By 1887–9, the tax had changed from a tax assessed by the local authority to a coefficient tax – it was only after this change that the valuations became accurate. The geographic basis of the surveys varied; public buildings and non-residential farm buildings were not recorded in the inventories; and on several occasions the authorities changed the definition of 'works' (*usines*), which were taxed separately. This affected the aggregations because *usines* benefited from a deduction of 40 per cent of their gross income to cover maintenance and the amortization of their plant and fittings, as against the 25 per cent deduction which houses were allowed. Even if we assume that the selected rates of capitalization hold good for both income and capital, the fact remains that the official data are discontinuous and relate to different things, and that they cannot really be considered together.

A second method seems to avoid these difficulties. Once we have a detailed estimate of the stock of capital investment for a given year, it is possible to compile an inventory of actual new investment, by each year adding to the stock the new plant and equipment, and by subtracting those which have come to the end of their life-span or which are entered as scrap. But here again, while this method has been applied successfully elsewhere, it does not appear well suited to the French case, because of the paucity of the data. It would first be necessary to assess the stock for the base year; yet inventories of plant and equipment, and of their prices, are lacking. Besides, the definition of reproducible capital would require us to omit items which are often not entered separately in the statistics – for example, in the figures for built-up land, the value of the land forming the site is often not distinguished from that of the buildings themselves. Furthermore, how can we add the annual totals for investment to the figure for the base year, when the whole aim of this study is to ascertain the precise total? We could of course limit ourselves to partial estimates, e.g. attempting to reconstruct the development of the power supply, for which M. Huber gave details in 1906. But even here, there are many gaps in the evidence. For instance, we know nothing about the construction of water-driven mills, which (according to C. Dupin)[31] provided 67 per cent of the power-supply in 1827 and still provided 22 per cent in 1906, nor about that of horse-driven mills and windmills, which provided 11 per cent in 1827 and 5 per cent in 1906. Or, if we look at the other end of the production process, the ways in which worn-out or out-moded plant and equipment were dispensed with presupposes information about their life-span. The little fragmentary evidence that we do have – for instance, the fact that the average age of merchant ships in 1913 may be reckoned at 14·7 years (15·2 years for sailing-ships, 14·5 for steamships) – only serves to highlight how much we do not know. In short, this method appears over-ambitious given the lack of information concerning capital, investment, and the scrapping of plant and equipment.

The prices of plant and machinery are the source of one final difficulty. The archives of insurance companies and the bookkeeping accounts of firms have not been investigated in this connection. Consequently, the historian working on France does not have reliable series of data for the prices of plant and equipment and of public works. Yet these are necessary for both of the methods which we have just reviewed, because throughout the period comparisons are made in relation to the replacement cost in the base year. To get round the difficulty, limited sets of prices for selected sectors were devised. Table 53 gives summaries of the findings for three sectors: building and public works (this series was devised by allowing 45 per cent for wages, 35 per cent for building materials, and 20 per cent for various items, given here in wholesale prices); material required for the permanent way of the railways (10 per cent for wages (on the basis of the accounts of the Cie du Nord), 35 per cent for building materials, 40 per cent for rails, and 15 per cent for other ancillary track items); and finally, railway rolling stock (40 per cent for locomotives, 30 per cent for wagons, and 30 per cent for driving-axles, wheel-housings, etc.). It would, however, be unwise to use a series *in toto* (e.g., the last column of Table 53 was devised by adopting the adjusted, weighted factors of the inter-war years), because the base of the different series of data is narrow, and we have no way of cross-checking.

Our choice of method was therefore determined by the gaps in the evidence. Instead of trying to trace the pattern of the annual change in the total stock of fixed capital we limited ourselves to devising series of data which cover investment in six sectors of the economy. We used methods comparable to those employed in calculating commodity-flow indices or price indices – for frequently the weighting had to be adjusted to allow for the degree to which sub-series of data were representative or, indeed, reliable. We then integrated the findings to obtain a series of data which would be indicative of capital investment. In order to shorten and simplify our account of this, we have here summarized the various calculations in the form of decennial tables – 1825–34, 1835–44, etc. (the text refers to the mean for 1820–9, 1830–9, etc.). However, except for Table 56, which brings together the findings for the major items in capital formation (expressed in current values) and which supplies the weighting factors used in calculating the final index of investment, the base series employed are annual, and they are presented as such in Table 60, where the aggregate series of production and investment are listed together.

A. COMPONENT SERIES OF DATA

Ideally, it would have been preferable first to establish indices of production for each sector, by assessing the consumption of raw materials and the degree of technical complexity or even by deflating an index of the output figures – for example, that of the engineering industries – next to calculate the amount retained for fixed plant and equipment, and the balance between imports and exports; and finally to deduce from these figures how much was invested annually. This was the procedure adopted by J. J. Carré *et al.* Unfortunately, the sources made it impossible for us to follow suit. We therefore adopted different methods for each sector.

Table 53. *Indices of Prices of Materials and Equipment, 1815–1913 (annual averages: base: 1908–12 = 100)*

| | Stone, etc. | Wood | Metals | Machinery | Railway plant and equipment | | Whole-sale prices | Wages | Construction, public works | Railway infra-structure | Total |
| | | | | | Fixed capital | Rolling stock | | | | | |
	1	2	3	4	5	6	7	8	9	10	11
1815–24	47·4	49·9	217·4	—	—	—	118·1	46·2	70·8	—	92·6
1825–34	48·8	51·5	198·9	—	—	—	98·3	49·6	67·8	201·2	87·9
1835–44	53·0	54·4	162·9	—	—	—	96·1	44·7	64·3	151·9	81·6
1845–54	54·0	55·5	153·2	143·8	207·5	124·4	94·6	43·8	63·3	146·6	79·3
1855–64	62·2	80·6	138·5	135·4	172·6	122·8	112·7	53·2	75·4	133·8	90·8
1865–74	69·0	84·4	115·6	113·6	139·6	109·8	109·8	63·2	79·6	115·7	90·3
1875–84	77·3	64·4	98·7	98·0	115·7	100·9	100·9	76·2	81·1	101·8	86·7
1885–94	83·9	64·6	71·4	90·7	77·4	90·2	90·2	83·1	81·9	80·9	84·1
1895–1904	90·4	80·1	78·2	98·9	86·2	84·7	85·3	89·6	87·6	89·3	88·2
1905–14	97·5	98·0	88·3	108·8	101·0	92·9	99·5	98·8	98·4	100·8	99·8

SOURCES. Columns 1–4 and 7: M. Lévy-Leboyer, 'L'Héritage de Simiand: prix, profit et termes de l'échange au XIXe siècle', *Revue Historique*, 493 (1970), and Lévy-Leboyer, 'La Décélération de l'économie française'; Columns 5 and 6: Caron, *Histoire d'un grand réseau*.

(a) The Building Industry

Figures for the consumption of building materials, which were preserved in city toll records, were used to compute the index: these figures were taken from L. Chevalier, R. Laurent, and G. Désert.[32] We have slightly modified the data, however, in the following respects. (1) After 1860, in the towns, a wider range of materials was used, whereas wood continued to be one of the major building materials in the countryside. We therefore used the series of data listed by M. Merger and J. Gaillard,[33] and those relating to the consumption of materials in the *Annuaire Statistique*. (2) The series of figures for Paris was altered in relation to the town's population movements, so as to allow for the incorporation of suburban communes in 1855–60; and the aggregate national index was increased by 4·6 per cent in 1871 in order to compensate for the loss of territory. (3) A standard of living index, equivalent to 0·5 per cent, and after 1860 to 1 per cent, was included in the final series. (4) At the beginning of the twentieth century, our index was progressively replaced by that of Carré *et al.*[34]

(b) Roads, Ports, and Canals

The various figures for capital investment in traditional means of transport – urban highways excepted – were calculated (in current francs) by adding together new expenditure (designated as 'extraordinary') and ordinary expenditure (maintenance and replacement). They have been grouped under four headings: (1) National roads, as recorded in the budgets of the Ministry of Public Works, reproduced in the various *Annuaires Statistiques*. (2) Departmental roads, as listed by F. Lucas,[35] and in the *Annuaire Statistique* for the period after 1870. Figures for expenditure on maintenance are missing for 1870–5 and for 1888–9; we have therefore interpolated them by applying to this road network the mean annual costs per km. (3) The necessary data for local roads are contained in the same documents. Figures for building costs before 1870 are taken from A. de Foville and C. Colson.[36] Maintenance costs were calculated by multiplying the number of kilometres by the mean annual expenditure: the latter was obtained by taking Lucas's figures for 1860, and adjusting these for other years by means of the index of the cost of public works (column 9 of Table 53). (4) Lucas gives the figures for expenditure by the companies on canals, rivers, and ports. For expenditure by the state, we have used the figures given by the Ministry of Public Works in *Actes législatifs et dépenses concernant la navigation intérieure et maritime 1814–1912* (1902 and 1914), and in the two publications produced by the Sub-Department of Navigation, *Dépenses d'établissement et d'entretien* (1898 and 1912). Finally, as the various items of expenditure were expressed in current values, we deflated the figures by means of the annual price index summarized in column 9 of Table 53.

(c) Fixed Capital in Transport

As in the previous case, we have broken down fixed investment in the railways (i.e. the sum total of expenditure on track, rails, stations, bridges, etc.) into new construction works and expenditure on maintenance and replacement. Three items, however, were omitted: land purchases, the deficit on lines currently being laid, and financing charges. These three items (listed as 'Additional' in Table 54) – which together accounted for an average of 13

Table 54. *Investment in Fixed Capital, 1815–1914 (annual averages in millions of francs, current prices)*

	Roads, ports, and canals			Railways			
	New expenditure	Maintenance	Total	New expenditure	Maintenance	Total	Additional
1815–24	18·8	52·0	70·8	—	—	—	—
1825–34	54·8	65·4	120·2	0·6	—	0·7	0·2
1835–44	111·7	95·7	207·4	25·2	1·5	26·7	4·7
1845–54	99·1	116·7	215·8	134·9	5·7	140·6	22·7
1855–64	87·9	154·9	242·8	280·0	33·8	313·8	91·0
1865–74	82·9	184·2	267·1	164·7	52·9	217·6	57·4
1875–84	120·1	216·1	336·2	240·5	97·3	337·8	78·1
1885–94	91·8	212·3	304·1	205·0	89·7	294·7	72·2
1895–1904	75·6	210·8	286·4	175·3	107·3	282·6	25·7
1905–14	95·3	219·8	315·1	284·1	150·6	434·7	30·1

SOURCE. See text.

per cent of the total investment – were omitted from our breakdown because they do not tally with our definition of reproducible fixed assets. The sources used in compiling these data can be put under three headings. (1) The Ministry of Public Works published annual figures for new expenditure. The latter were brought together in the *Statistique des chemins de fer français: Documents principaux* (1887–1913), and SNCF, *Principaux résultats statistiques des chemins de fer français depuis leur origine, 1821–1890* (undated). To break down expenditure into rolling-stock and basic equipment we used the classifications (formula 'A') to which the Ministry required the companies to comply: these were published in the *Statistique annuelle des chemins de fer*. (2) For the period 1899–1912, maintenance costs are given by the Ministry of Public Works in *Comptes d'établissement des compagnies*, and in A. Picard, *Traité des chemins de fer*.[37] The outlay on maintenance during the earlier period was calculated on the basis of the balance-sheets of four of the major companies.[38] (3) To the figures published by Picard for total expenditure during the period up to 1845, we applied the breakdown which we had previously calculated for the period 1845–9 – having first subtracted the 13 per cent absorbed by financing costs. In this breakdown, 83 per cent was allotted to expenditure on basic equipment, and 17 per cent to that on plant and machinery. As in the previous case, we then deflated expenditure with the aid of the price series for basic equipment on the railways (column 10 of Table 53). This method seems preferable to one which consists of adding together the figures for the annual increase in the number of kilometres of rails, for it takes into account the complementary outlay which follows on from the time when the track was first laid.

(d) Means of Transport

We were unable to obtain data for all the items which come under this heading. For instance, the number of units of the traditional means of transport, such as small boats, wagons, and barges, cannot be determined. Instead, under the heading 'Traditional Means of Transport' we have listed the index of agricultural output, and the index, calculated by J. C. Toutain, of the volume of road traffic.[39] The two series of data listed by Toutain – the number of passengers and the number of horse-drawn wagons, expressed per day and per kilometre – were weighted on the assumption that freight charges were double the charge for passengers. The other series of data were calculated directly. (1) The series for investment in railway rolling stock was calculated from the same sources and by the same method as were used in calculating expenditure on basic equipment in the railways. We found in the same documents the figures, expressed in current prices, for outlay (expenditure on new items and on replacing existing stock), and maintenance costs, which we deflated by using the index of the corresponding prices (column 6 of Table 53). (2) For automobiles, the calculations are simplified because of the minimal role played by the motor vehicle industry before 1913. The annual increase in the number of motor vehicles (which is known for 1905, 1910, and 1914) was ascertained by assuming that the average life-span of a vehicle was nine years, and adding together the figures for the number of vehicles produced annually.[40] No distinction was made between private cars and utility vehicles, for the tax concession of 1898 led to a somewhat arbitrary increase in the share of the latter in relation to the total.[41] (3) Figures for the number of merchant vessels built or registered in France – in other words, the gross increase in the merchant fleet due to the purchase of French and foreign merchant vessels, less those which were exported – are expressed in net tonnage, both year by year and in summary form, in the *Tableaux du commerce et de la navigation de la France*. We used these figures as the basis for our calculations. But three adjustments were made to them. They were first converted into gross tonnage, because building costs are expressed only in the latter form. We assumed that the gross tonnage of sailing-ships was 1·25 times the net tonnage during the nineteenth century, 1·3 times in 1870, and up to 1·9 times in 1900; and that the gross tonnage of steamships was 1·82 times the net tonnage until the 1870s, 2·25 times in 1890, and 2·73 times in 1913. Furthermore, the price of sailing-ships was generally two-fifths lower than that of steamships. In order to calculate the index, their weight was reduced in proportion: only 60 per cent of the gross tonnage of sailing-ships was assessed in the final figure. Finally, expenditure on repair work and maintenance was assessed as some 3·5 per cent of the aggregate tonnage and was integrated into the index (column 2 of Table 55).

(e) Plant and Machinery

French consumption of metals provides a rough preliminary indication of how many machines were built. We have established two sets of figures. One shows metal production – cast iron, iron, steel, and non-ferrous metals – and is adjusted to allow for metal imports and exports; the other relates to the output of processed metals, i.e. foundry-pig, wire-drawing, tin-plate, sheet iron, etc.[42] The two series of data, entered as a composite item in Table 55 (column 6), should not be considered as representative of investment in machinery. In one respect they cover too much, for part of the data were included in previous indices; in another respect they are not comprehensive enough, for the value of the raw materials once they had become machines doubtless increased with the passage of time. We have therefore constructed additional series, which relate either to the cost of working stock or to investment in industrial plant, and integrated them into the final index.

The first of these additional series is an index of fixed steam-powered machinery. Annual figures for these machines exist from 1825, when their makers were required by law to submit them for inspection by the Department of Mines before they entered service. At first, only high-pressure machines were liable to these tests (in 1840, these were some 71 per cent of the total); but from May 1843, records of such tests exist for all categories, with some minor amendments in January 1865 and April 1880. These changes in the regulations led to breaks in the series: we therefore devised a second series, a control series, on the basis of the annual net increase in the stock of fixed machinery, measured in horsepower. We added to this the increment which was necessary to maintain the power supply at the level of the previous year and made the assumption, after investigation, that these machines were used for some twenty years during the first third of the century, and that their life-span subsequently increased to some thirty to thirty-three years. Steam partly replaced previous sources of energy, which led us to revise the trend in this series of data. We assumed that water-driven mills, windmills, etc., were the source of power for three-quarters of the factories in 1825, of half in 1855, of one-sixth in 1880, and of one-twentieth in 1900. Column 7 of Table 55 records the mean of the two series of figures, i.e. the figures from the inspection records and those showing the annual increase in the amount of fixed steam-powered machines. As additional evidence, we have also presented data, collected by A. Aftalion, showing imports of machinery and a series, devised by Markovitch, showing the output of machine tools.[43]

To trace the pattern of the investment policy followed by individual companies, we have produced three series of figures. We first examined the motor vehicle industry, drawing up a series based on the plant (the area covered and the number of machine tools) of the Renault and Citroën factories (1897–

Table 55. *Investment in Plant and Equipment: Indices of Volume (annual averages; base: 1908–12 = 100)*

	Transport sector				Plant and machinery					Other categories of equipment			
					Heavy plant		Machinery					Textile industries, etc.	
	Road transport	Ship-building	Railway equipment	Total	Output	Investment	Increase	Imports	Total	Increase	Imports	Various	Total
	1	2	3	4	5	6	7	8	9	10	11	12	13
1825–34	56·0	—	—	—	5·5	—	1·9	—	3·2	14·4	—	15·5	14·8
1835–44	73·8	19·6	4·8	25·6	9·9	9·0	5·2	—	6·2	25·1	—	23·1	25·0
1845–54	86·5	25·1	8·7	33·9	13·5	13·0	8·9	—	10·0	28·6	19·2	24·1	26·8
1855–64	93·4	38·8	27·5	43·1	25·1	25·5	17·5	3·4	19·8	37·6	26·2	31·3	36·0
1865–74	96·9	40·9	31·4	42·7	31·9	31·4	21·0	7·2	27·3	42·3	27·9	35·8	37·7
1875–84	99·3	56·0	54·6	59·0	45·4	41·0	33·9	24·7	33·2	61·2	49·5	48·5	50·5
1885–94	96·6	45·6	49·4	56·6	48·1	44·4	39·5	22·9	40·2	62·3	53·7	52·8	59·4
1895–1904	95·7	81·2	63·2	73·3	65·4	69·4	67·3	46·8	65·1	80·5	72·4	72·4	77·2
1905–13	99·7	102·1	91·2	94·9	97·0	97·8	99·2	95·2	98·2	94·9	96·2	96·2	95·3

SOURCE. See text.

1939 and 1919–27 respectively). The proportion of capital expenditure on these two categories of plant which emerged from the balance-sheets of the Renault factory for 1913 and 1920 was used in reaching the composite figure.[44] Turning to heavy industry, i.e. collieries and iron and steel mills, investment was assessed in current francs and then deflated. To the figure for output per sector we applied an annual coefficient obtained by establishing, on the basis of figures in the balance-sheets, how much of the gross receipts were reserved for capital expenditure. Data for the collieries of central France (nine companies over the years 1848–97) and for the Pas-de-Calais are taken from M. Gillet; data for a sample of the major metallurgical companies are taken from G. Thuillier's study of Fourchambault, and the works of J. Vial, B. Gille, J. Bouvier, and F. Furet.[45] The difference in the size of the annual variations notwithstanding, the results closely resemble those which were computed on the basis of figures for metal output. The three concluding series are expressed in annual terms in Table 60 (below). However, from 1895 onwards the last two series – 'plant and machinery', and 'other categories of equipment' – are included in the series for 'investment in plant and equipment' following J. J. Carré et al. and are therefore not listed separately.

(f) Other Categories of Equipment

Grouped under this heading are various unrelated series of data. To list them separately would have complicated matters. In fact, certain series are common to them all: the two sets of figures for wood consumption, listed by Marko-vitch and by M. Brosselin, and various series relating to investment in con-sumer industries, including textiles. For textiles, there exist comprehensive surveys. These enable us to divide the period in two, using different sources and methods for each. (1) For the period up to 1945, the extant series at the local level were used. We were able to reconstruct annual figures for looms in the Rhône and Loire regions and in Alsace; and, after Lévy-Leboyer, those for steam-engines (expressed in h.p.) employed in the textile mills of the Haut-Rhin, Nord, and Seine inférieure. These local series of data were merged together: in weighting them we used the estimates for investment capital compiled by J. Dollfus and, within the textile sector, a simplified table of value-added output. We also compiled a list of 'newly founded factories' – producers of chemicals, glass, and crystal (1811–35); sugar refineries, soap-works, tile-works, and brick-works (1823–35) – from the orders authorizing their creation, recorded in the Bulletin des lois and the Archives statistiques of 1837. (2) Because we lack more exact information for the period after 1840, we have tried to reconstruct the annual increase in plant and equipment in each sector by piecing together data from regional monographs (of which there are many) and from the Statistique générale de la France, which for the period 1872–86 contains detailed annual inventories of fixed plant and of the equipment installed; and by substituting the series on the consumption of raw materials for those on plant and equipment, when (as in the case of Lyonnais factories) figures for the latter are lacking. As for the earlier period, we gathered additional data relating to imports of equipment used in manufacturing textiles – this is summarized in column 11 of Table 55 – and to electricity consumption in the Alpine region, as recorded in studies by J. M. Jeanneney and C. A. Colliard and by H. Morsel.[46]

B. Aggregate Series

In devising composite series, we left aside the series resulting from the preceding calculations and reverted to the initial series of data, as expressed in current francs, or else calculated new series in current values, in order to obtain estimates (and the breakdown) of aggregate investment and of the national product.

(a) Capital Formation

We already have figures for infrastructure investment so far as the railways and other means of transport are concerned: these were the data which were deflated in order to obtain the various indices of the volume of public works. But we have yet to calculate capital investment in property development. The estimates made by government departments during the nineteenth century and again in 1909–10 and 1924–5 give some idea of the sums involved (their findings are summarized in the *Annuaire Statistique* of 1946). They show a net annual increase in investment in dwellings and country houses of 763 million francs between 1851–3 and 1887–9 (Zylberman puts the gross increase at 830 million francs per annum between 1850 and 1870) and of 640 million between 1880 and 1910; the increase in investment in factories was some 50 million francs per annum between 1852 and 1888, 72 million per annum in the 1890s, and 126 million per annum in 1900–10. Figures for the number of new constructions and of demolished buildings do not appear in the net estimate of the numbers of buildings – they may have accounted for some 40 per cent of gross annual expenditure. Allowing for these, for the growing number of accessories attendant on rising living standards, and for the increasing structural complexity of buildings, the authors of these estimates reckon that annual capital investment during the period 1900–13 was 1,500 million francs. With this as the base figure, we established a series expressed in current values by multiplying the index of the volume of the output of the building industry (column 4 of Table 60, below) by the index of the prices of the building industry (column 9 of Table 53). Expenditures on roadworks and on municipal services – water, gas, electricity, schools, hospitals, etc. – which have not yet been included in our calculations are included in the final series (column 1 of Table 56). We assumed that the expenditure they occasioned was equal to the annual increase in the loans raised by the authorities of the departments and communes, i.e. an average of 57·8 million francs per annum in 1886–9, 73·7 million per annum in 1890–9, 88·6 million per annum in 1900–9 (only a tenth of this sum, in fact, in 1901–2), and as much as 180·7 million per annum in 1910–13.

Figures do exist for investment in plant, machinery, and other equipment, but they are not complete. (1) We have figures for expenditure on the railways: the cost of the rolling stock was obtained from the accounts of the railway companies and from official documents. (2) We were also able to assess the cost of the gross annual increase in the merchant fleet. We first assumed that the purchase prices were the same as those charged by English dockyards;[47] we then added to these prices the supplementary outlay which was due to the scale of charges operated by French shipbuilders. This was some 50 to 55 per cent higher (bonuses included): the parliamentary commission headed by P. Doumer in 1903 allowed for a differential of this order.[48] These sets of figures relating to railways and merchant shipping are listed in columns 5 and 6 of Table 56. (3) There is no direct way of calculating the outlay on 'traditional means of transport'. But there are three sources of information which we can use. The first concerns road transport. According to Foville,[49] it was reckoned that for express vehicles, depreciation and maintenance were assessed at one-eighth of the turnover. Assuming that this proportion held good for the greater part of the period under study, we can use the figures for road transport[50] to obtain figures for this type of expenditure. It totalled some 100 million francs per annum about 1850, and 155 million at the beginning of the twentieth century. The second source of information relates to lighterage. Foville reckoned that the cost of maintenance and of replacement about 1855 accounted for 11 per cent of the sums invested on inland vessels, or 7 million francs per annum. According to Colson, in 1913 the cost (which was spread over thirty years) of amortizing the 16,000 ships which comprised the inland water fleet, at 12,500 francs each, added to their maintenance, most probably came to 11·5 million francs per annum, or 14 per cent of the turnover. Major repairs boosted this figure: consequently, we assessed the total gross investment at 20 per cent and related this figure to the figures for the units of water transport as calculated by Toutain. Finally, in order to ascertain how many motor vehicles were purchased, we multiplied the net increase in the stock (expressed in h.p.) by their mean price.[51] Purchases of motor vehicles totalled 2·7 million francs in 1902 and 19·0 million in 1908: with 15 per cent of the value of the stock added for maintenance and amortization, the gross figure for 1908 was 30 million francs. These three items were entered as one composite item in column 4 of Table 56.

The final heading – plant, machinery, and other types of equipment – covers figures which are much more tentative than those recorded under the previous headings: the series of data used in compiling it could not be weighted with precision, and writers of the period did not make independent estimates of their aggregate value. Until new research is carried out, the two following estimates may be of value. First of all, like many other writers, we divided investment into two parts: materials used in construction work (in which we included railway equipment, so as to be in line with other studies), and materials intended for other uses. We followed the general trend of the relationship between them as traced by Markovitch, i.e. taking the ratios 78–22 during the period 1820–60, 65–35 in 1860–90, and 53–47 in 1890–1913. Consequently, using data already collated we were able to estimate the aggregate investment in French capital equipment. Also, using the breakdown of the figures item by item, we subtracted the figure for investment in transport systems (both sea-going and inland) and thus obtained the figure

Table 56. *Summary of the Principal Elements in Capital Formation, 1815–1934 (annual averages; million current francs)*

	Investment in plant and equipment									Gross capital formation					
	Infrastructure			Transport (roads and waterways)	Merchant shipping	Railways	Other plant and machinery	Total	Home	Distribution between			GNP	Share of investment (%)	
	Construction	Transport	Total							Infrastructure	Plant and equipment	Total		Home	Total
	1	2	3	4	5	6	7	8	9	10	11	12	13	14	15
1815–24	374	71	445	58	25	—	83	166	611	72·8	27·2	—	8,530	7·2	—
1825–34	505	112	617	69	29	—	100	198	816	75·6	24·3	—	9,490	8·6	—
1835–44	687	222	909	86	23	7	143	269	1,178	77·2	22·8	—	11,150	10·6	—
1845–54	741	357	1,098	98	45	32	190	365	1,463	75·1	24·9	1,711	13,300	11·0	—
1855–64	990	557	1,547	114	70	85	337	606	2,153	71·9	28·1	2,781	17,300	12·4	15·9
1865–74	1,152	485	1,637	111	76	86	490	763	2,400	68·2	31·8	2,717	20,480	11·7	13·2
1875–84	1,232	674	1,906	108	100	140	903	1,124	3,030	62·9	37·1	3,171	23,680	12·8	13·4
1885–94	1,283	607	1,890	102	55	121	1,287	1,181	3,071	61·5	38·5	3,463	25,760	11·9	13·4
1895–1904	1,415	569	1,984	109	112	170	1,860	1,678	3,662	54·2	45·8	4,657	27,650	13·2	16·7
1905–13	1,848	709	2,557	140	130	236	—	2,366	4,923	51·9	48·1	6,172	34,580	14·2	17·8
1925–34	—	—	3,320	—	—	—	—	3,540	6,860	48·4	51·6	—	41,576	16·5	—

SOURCE. See text.

for plant and machinery. In fact, the results do not differ very much from those for Great Britain in 1907 published by A. Cairncross: £75·4 million for the various categories of equipment (shipbuilding included), or 50·3 per cent of gross investment. Using similar methods, C. Feinstein has analysed five of the categories which in our table are subsumed under the heading 'plant and machinery'. Converted into francs, these figures bear out our own, either in absolute terms or as a percentage of aggregate investment: plant, machinery, and other equipment in Great Britain absorbed 375 million francs in 1856–60, 915 million in 1875, 618–30 million in 1885–90, and as much as 1,850 million in 1900, before returning to the lower figures of 1,720 million and 1,420 million in 1905 and 1910 respectively. However, when compared with the set of figures listed by Mairesse, the relative increase in investment in working equipment which emerges from our set of figures appears a rather conservative estimate. According to Mairesse, this category of investment rose from 35·3 per cent to 50·3 per cent of gross capital formation between 1896 and 1914. We therefore devised a second series as a control: the index of the volume of equipment (columns 9 and 13 of Table 55) was multiplied by a price index, on the basis of an average outlay of 770 million francs per annum during the period 1820–1910. The mean of the two series is entered as the final set of figures for 'plant and machinery' (column 7 of Table 56).[52]

Figures for gross capital formation (columns 9 and 12 of Table 56) were obtained by adding up the figures for the different items, decade by decade (the respective percentages of investment in basic equipment and in working plant are listed in columns 10 and 11). Figures for investment abroad were added, also on a decennial basis.[53] The weighting factors, used in computing the volume of investment, were derived from Table 56. This table completes the data for 1820–9, 1830–9, etc., listed in Table 45. Column 1 of Table 56 includes municipal works; column 2 comprises basic equipment in both the railways and other transport systems; columns 12 and 15 include investment abroad. Columns 10 and 11 indicate the breakdown (expressed in percentages) of home investment.

(b) The National Product and Commodity Output Series

In order to make comparisons with the national product, expressed both in current values and in constant prices, series of data to which reference could be made were indispensable. Yet many doubts surround these figures. The five existing series of estimates of the national product (expressed in current values) frequently differ sharply from one another, partly because their several authors have not used the same definitions (Table 57). Rather than compile a new series, we have used the existing data: the figures (listed in Table 45 and in column 13 of Table 56) are simply the mean of the previous estimates, which we have corrected whenever we found contemporary data for the corresponding period – for example, the figures listed by J. Dutens and C. Dupin for the period 1815–40, by A. Cochut for the 1850s, by Zylberman for 1860, by Foville for 1865, by R. Pupin and F. Simiand for 1880, and by Colson for 1890. We have advanced the estimates of J. Mayer and F. Perroux

Table 57. *Estimates of National Product, 1790–1910*
(thousand million francs)

	Sauvy 1965–71	Mayer 1949	Perroux 1955	Toutain 1967	Markovitch 1966
1790	4·66	4·34	6·10	5·39	7·70
1810	6·27	5·76	8·29	7·42	9·76
1820	7·86	7·46	9·10	8·12	10·50
1830	8·81	—	10·27	9·64	12·60
1840	10·00	9·20	—	11·31	14·82
1850	11·41	10·38	13·59	13·17	17·41
1860	15·2	13·7	19·4	17·4	22·8
1870	18·8	—	22·2	19·6	26·5
1880	22·4	18·9	26·4	19·7	27·2
1890	25·0	—	—	19·4	27·3
1900	26·3	—	30·2	21·2	29·1
1910	33·2	—	38·2	28·1	38·0

SOURCES. A. Sauvy, 'Le Revenu des Français au XIXe siècle', *Population*, xx, 5 (1965), 517ff, and xxvii, 1 (1971), 139ff; Mayer, 'La Croissance du revenu national français'; F. Perroux, 'Prise de vue sur la croissance de l'économie française, 1780–1950', in S. Kuznets (ed.), *Income and Wealth*, ser. v (London, 1955); J. C. Toutain, 'Les Transports en France de 1830 à 1965', *Cahiers de l'ISEA*, ser. AF 9, no. 8 (September–October 1967); Markovitch, 'L'Industrie française'.

by five years: they actually apply to 1815, 1825, and 1835 instead of 1810, 1820, and 1830.

The annual indices of the volume of output (columns 1–3 of Table 60) are improved versions of series of data which we compiled several years ago. The data for agricultural production were published, in an abbreviated form, in 1971; and those for output as a whole appeared in 1968;[54] but at that time the base used in compiling them was too narrow. Because when we compiled these figures we lacked statistics for the output of the new industries, we increased the place assigned to modern textile industries – designated as an 'advanced-technology industry' (listed here as column 2 of Table 58) – in relation to total output. As a comparison between columns 2 and 6 will show, this exaggerated the trend of the series. The study of capital formation has led us to increase the number of series used to calculate the national product, so that in the new version (column 8), reproduced in Table 60, we have strengthened the existing series of data, eliminated the incomplete index for the 'advanced-technology industry', and added the series for mechanical engineering (column 6), which comprises the series for the consumption of wood and of metals, the two series for fixed plant, textile looms, and units of transport. The weightings used earlier[55] were again employed to calculate the two series for output as well as the series for commodity output – which is a composite series covering agriculture, industry, and transport.[56]

Such calculations are not necessary for the inter-war period: the studies of Vincent, Carré, and Mairesse, quoted above, contain the relevant data. The

Table 58. *Indices of Output, 1825–1934 (annual averages; base: 1908–12 = 100)*

	Textiles									
	advanced technology	general	Food	Chemicals, metallurgy	Mechanical engineering	Con-struction	Industry	Transport	Commodity output
Agriculture									
1	2	3	4	5	6	7	8	9	10
1825–34	57·7	13·3	26·9	22·2	5·7	13·3	31·3	24·9	7·8	33·8
1835–44	54·3	21·3	34·4	28·4	9·0	17·7	40·3	31·1	10·4	40·2
1845–54	59·7	31·3	41·6	33·2	12·2	21·7	41·9	38·5	14·8	46·6
1855–64	74·0	48·1	51·5	44·7	21·9	32·8	59·0	47·3	24·9	55·5
1865–74	79·1	55·9	57·8	49·5	30·5	34·8	61·3	51·6	34·9	63·3
1875–84	82·5	65·3	68·4	58·8	40·7	44·6	84·1	60·3	45·1	71·4
1885–94	84·6	78·8	78·4	70·5	49·4	43·6	79·7	66·6	57·1	74·4
1895–1904	92·9	92·0	88·5	83·0	69·2	64·1	88·0	77·7	75·5	84·2
1905–13	100·5	98·5	95·6	99·4	96·4	93·9	97·1	97·0	96·9	98·2
1915–19	78·5	—	—	—	—	—	—	64·6[a]	—	—
1920–4	97·1	—	—	—	—	—	—	88·9	—	102·1
1925–34	111·12	—	—	—	—	—	—	133·3	—	127·7

[a] 1919 only.

SOURCE. See text.

series used here – presented in Fig. 4, and summarized in Table 58 – are taken from those studies, with the exception of the data for agricultural output, which we compiled independently, and the data for industrial output, which are taken from the *Annuaire Statistique* (1946) and *Le Mouvement économique en France de 1929 à 1939* (1941).

(c) The Aggregate Productivity of Factors in the Railway Sector

The figures for the aggregate productivity of the railway sector are the findings of F. Caron. They relate to the network as a whole: main lines, branch lines, and tramways. The index of capital formation was computed from the cumulative figures for new expenditure, expressed in constant values, for the whole of the sector. The labour-force index was calculated from the figures of personnel of the main-line companies, of the branch-line companies, and of the tramways.[57] These figures were multiplied by the time-rates of the SNCF. The energy index corresponds, during the period 1881–1913, to the figures for fuel consumption recorded in the *Statistique minérale* (as corrected by a weight factor for the tramways). For the period before 1881, this index represents the number of kilometres covered, multiplied by the average fuel consumption per kilometre as given in the *Statistique annuelle de chemins de fer*. The weights used in calculating the aggregate index of the factors were: 8 for the various fuels, 49 for the capital, and 49 for the labour force. These figures were chosen on the basis of the distribution of costs in 1913. The cost of capital comprises the return on share capital and on debenture capital, the guarantee paid by the state, the interest on capital loans raised for construction work, and state subsidies.

Table 59. *Inputs and Output in the Railway Sector, 1855–1913 (annual averages; base: 1913 = 100)*

	Inputs				Output
	Capital	Energy	Labour	Total	
1855–64	19·6	12·1	22·8	20·3	11·9
1865–74	33·3	18·2	40·6	35·1	23·5
1875–84	45·0	28·9	63·9	51·8	34·5
1885–94	62·1	41·7	76·2	66·5	42·7
1895–1904	74·7	65·0	83·5	77·7	59·4
1905–13	90·3	95·6	91·4	91·4	82·9

SOURCE. See text.

Table 60. *Output and Fixed Investment, 1820–1913: Indices of Volume (base: 1908–12 = 100)*

	Output			Building and public works				Investment in plant and equipment				Investment
	Agriculture	Industry	Commodity output	Construction	Roads, Ports, canals	Railways	Total	Transport	Machinery	Other equipment	Total	Total
	1	2	3	4	5	6	7	8	9	10	11	12
1820	45·3	20·4	29·7	24·1	26·9	—	23·3	—	—	7·7	11·6	18·9
1821	48·3	22·5	32·2	28·8	27·3	—	26·8	—	—	12·9	14·0	21·6
1822	46·1	23·0	31·9	34·3	26·7	—	30·8	—	—	15·5	14·9	24·3
1823	47·1	22·3	32·0	32·6	31·8	—	30·5	—	—	12·7	14·2	24·1
1824	45·7	23·9	32·2	31·4	39·1	0·1	31·1	—	—	19·9	15·2	24·8
1825	44·8	24·4	32·6	38·2	38·8	0·1	36·1	—	—	24·1	16·8	28·0
1826	46·6	25·5	33·7	36·8	39·6	0·3	35·1	—	—	16·7	15·5	27·3
1827	47·6	24·7	33·6	35·5	39·0	0·3	34·0	—	—	18·0	15·8	26·7
1828	48·9	23·3	33·1	30·4	39·9	0·3	30·0	—	—	16·1	14·9	24·0
1829	48·9	24·4	33·7	31·2	42·7	0·5	31·1	—	—	16·8	15·4	24·8
1830	45·9	23·9	32·1	28·8	44·1	0·1	29·3	—	2·6	11·2	13·7	23·3
1831	47·3	23·4	32·1	23·2	55·3	0·1	26·4	—	2·5	9·1	13·1	21·1
1832	50·4	25·8	34·5	25·2	56·1	0·2	28·1	—	2·7	10·2	13·9	22·2
1833	51·7	27·0	36·2	30·7	55·2	0·9	32·5	—	3·7	9·7	14·1	25·3
1834	51·5	26·8	36·1	33·1	54·5	1·2	34·3	—	4·4	15·8	16·0	26·8
1835	51·5	28·5	36·8	32·1	51·9	1·1	33·1	—	5·2	26·6	18·1	26·5
1836	51·5	29·0	37·4	36·0	53·3	3·6	36·5	—	6·0	31·9	20·5	29·0
1837	52·9	28·7	38·2	38·0	76·8	7·8	41·7	23·1	4·4	24·8	19·8	31·8
1838	52·7	30·4	39·3	43·0	82·8	13·0	46·9	24·8	4·6	37·8	21·8	35·6
1839	52·7	28·5	38·6	43·7	85·9	19·8	48·2	27·3	5·6	27·4	22·3	36·5

Year												
1840	36·1	21·5	21·7	5·5	26·1	48·1	17·6	91·4	42·8	40·7	31·2	55·5
1841	37·1	23·8	19·3	7·7	29·9	47·9	24·5	91·2	42·1	42·3	32·9	56·7
1842	34·2	21·8	19·2	6·8	26·5	44·3	24·1	91·7	37·6	41·7	32·5	55·8
1843	36·1	20·3	17·2	8·2	23·3	49·1	35·6	94·7	42·3	42·7	34·3	55·5
1844	37·2	20·9	24·4	8·2	23·9	50·5	35·8	88·9	45·0	44·4	35·1	57·8
1845	40·9	22·4	26·6	10·1	25·6	54·7	56·1	104·1	46·3	44·2	36·2	55·7
1846	41·8	24·6	28·4	10·5	29·5	55·1	56·9	99·2	47·6	44·9	37·8	55·4
1847	40·7	26·4	28·6	9·8	32·0	52·2	59·0	97·4	45·2	47·6	36·9	62·7
1848	34·6	23·2	23·1	7·7	28·8	44·1	42·5	96·6	35·2	45·1	32·4	63·5
1849	30·7	21·6	21·8	5·1	27·5	38·2	41·0	93·2	28·6	45·9	37·2	62·3
1850	30·6	22·1	19·4	8·1	28·1	37·5	37·8	82·1	29·9	46·8	38·9	62·3
1851	33·0	23·5	21·3	7·8	30·2	40·8	39·2	83·0	33·8	46·6	38·1	61·5
1852	39·4	25·3	28·3	9·1	30·9	51·0	48·3	83·6	45·8	48·3	41·2	59·7
1853	45·7	30·3	35·8	14·5	35·4	58·3	59·0	80·3	54·3	48·1	43·7	55·6
1854	46·5	32·7	34·8	17·4	39·1	57·7	58·6	76·7	52·1	48·3	42·6	58·3
1855	47·3	33·8	31·8	17·8	42·9	58·4	66·9	73·9	54·0	49·2	45·0	56·1
1856	51·3	40·0	36·7	20·4	51·3	60·5	70·5	75·3	56·9	51·3	46·1	59·2
1857	51·3	35·7	33·7	19·1	44·7	64·0	69·3	80·1	60·3	53·9	43·9	66·6
1858	47·1	32·0	36·6	17·1	36·9	59·5	61·9	83·3	55·6	56·2	47·0	69·7
1859	46·6	31·3	38·5	18·3	33·9	59·2	58·7	82·8	54·3	53·8	46·3	66·2
1860	48·5	31·0	38·3	16·9	35·0	62·9	63·6	88·6	58·2	55·5	47·8	66·8
1861	52·3	30·8	35·5	19·7	35·9	69·8	72·3	97·9	64·3	55·1	48·1	64·9
1862	50·7	32·2	32·6	21·1	39·3	65·8	72·8	96·1	58·7	57·1	47·1	71·7
1863	54·3	33·7	38·3	23·8	39·5	71·2	74·9	100·3	65·3	61·2	50·3	76·4
1864	53·6	35·5	37·7	23·6	41·6	66·1	71·1	98·8	62·3	61·6	51·2	77·4

Table 60 (cont.). Output and Fixed Investment, 1820–1913

| | Output | | | Building and public works | | | | Investment in working stock | | | | Investment |
	Agri-culture	Industry	Com-modity output	Construc-tion	Roads, Ports, canals	Rail-ways	Total	Trans-port	Machin-ery	Other equip-ment	Total	Total
	1	2	3	4	5	6	7	8	9	10	11	12
1865	78·8	51·1	62·4	59·4	99·5	66·0	66·1	43·2	23·9	41·4	37·6	53·3
1866	76·0	52·4	62·7	67·4	101·1	72·6	72·5	45·1	23·9	38·0	37·5	56·8
1867	72·5	51·1	60·9	68·9	104·0	72·5	73·9	43·3	22·9	40·5	37·3	57·4
1868	79·3	53·8	65·5	74·3	104·1	71·6	77·6	40·0	23·7	39·0	35·8	58·8
1869	82·2	54·7	67·3	74·1	108·8	72·4	78·2	41·4	21·6	39·4	35·9	59·2
1870	79·7	48·0	60·8	50·8	94·2	54·3	57·1	40·3	21·5	23·8	32·6	48·2
1871	78·6	44·8	57·2	34·1	83·8	42·4	43·0	38·8	14·4	24·5	29·9	38·6
1872	80·8	53·7	64·7	59·7	83·4	56·8	63·3	47·1	24·8	41·5	40·6	55·3
1873	77·3	51·7	62·3	63·3	87·5	58·0	66·5	43·4	27·0	47·0	42·8	58·1
1874	86·0	54·8	69·3	61·0	91·1	61·3	65·8	44·3	27·3	42·1	40·3	56·5
1875	90·2	56·2	70·6	63·4	95·3	62·9	68·3	43·4	27·1	46·0	41·7	58·8
1876	83·2	58·2	68·5	67·3	108·7	71·9	74·3	44·9	29·1	48·7	43·8	63·1
1877	82·0	57·2	69·3	77·6	109·4	81·0	83·4	49·8	32·0	54·3	46·5	67·7
1878	78·7	56·5	67·1	74·4	112·1	75·6	80·7	49·9	28·0	51·2	44·9	65·2
1879	73·7	57·1	64·9	77·9	124·5	82·3	86·0	51·9	31·0	46·2	46·4	68·6
1880	78·2	59·5	69·7	88·1	124·1	91·6	93·1	57·1	32·7	49·5	49·6	73·5
1881	83·3	64·9	75·1	97·7	126·9	98·3	101·2	62·1	37·3	51·7	55·1	80·4
1882	85·9	67·2	77·9	106·2	128·3	99·2	107·5	78·8	39·0	54·8	61·9	87·0
1883	85·7	64·6	76·3	96·9	134·8	101·7	102·3	77·8	40·0	55·9	62·3	84·3
1884	84·4	62·0	74·2	91·4	127·5	97·8	96·8	74·1	35·7	47·0	57·1	78·9
1885	84·2	61·2	71·7	78·6	124·7	86·5	85·8	58·0	30·6	46·1	48·0	68·8

Year	1	2	3	4	5	6	7	8	9	10	11	12
1886	83·3	62·5	71·1	76·0	124·1	74·4	82·0	52·0	31·3	51·6	46·7	66·1
1887	83·5	63·4	71·6	75·0	120·5	85·8	82·5	59·6	32·9	52·3	50·5	68·1
1888	82·2	65·9	72·6	78·1	116·6	84·2	83·9	60·8	33·0	45·5	49·3	68·3
1889	83·7	64·6	72·1	75·1	112·6	77·3	80·2	57·0	35·7	45·3	50·2	66·7
1890	84·4	65·5	74·1	80·1	108·2	83·7	84·0	62·7	39·7	64·2	56·7	71·7
1891	83·7	68·9	75·9	86·0	105·6	84·5	87·9	60·0	44·5	73·6	60·1	75·4
1892	86·0	72·6	78·5	85·5	105·9	82·6	87·3	52·9	45·9	66·2	56·9	73·6
1893	85·0	69·7	76·4	80·3	104·6	79·5	83·0	52·5	44·5	68·6	56·8	71·2
1894	90·4	71·8	79·7	82·5	103·9	79·0	84·4	50·7	42·8	80·1	58·6	72·8
1895	91·1	68·5	78·2	83·8	101·5	80·8	85·2	54·7		65·1	62·8	75·0
1896	88·7	71·5	79·4	88·6	103·8	81·9	89·2	55·4		67·6	64·9	78·3
1897	84·7	75·7	80·3	90·2	102·0	80·3	90·0	59·1		61·5	61·0	77·0
1898	91·2	78·8	84·6	94·6	100·4	84·5	93·8	68·4		69·2	69·0	82·6
1899	97·9	81·4	88·9	99·1	92·7	93·0	97·2	74·1		77·8	77·0	88·1
1900	101·1	81·5	89·1	89·1	95·2	91·1	90·3	95·1		99·1	92·6	91·3
1901	94·0	78·8	86·2	84·7	97·6	85·1	86·7	87·4		77·1	82·3	84·7
1902	90·1	77·5	82·8	83·7	101·7	80·7	86·0	86·2		74·9	80·6	83·6
1903	93·3	82·2	86·0	82·9	100·4	79·8	85·1	73·5		79·8	76·7	81·3
1904	96·8	81·2	86·8	83·2	101·0	78·3	85·1	79·3		64·6	72·0	79·2
1905	98·9	83·9	89·0	85·0	99·8	79·6	86·4	68·6		67·5	68·1	78·3
1906	97·4	86·2	89·9	85·9	94·6	80·8	86·4	64·9		78·9	75·8	81·7
1907	102·6	90·3	93·8	85·7	92·7	89·0	87·2	81·6		90·2	88·3	88·0
1908	100·2	90·7	93·9	88·1	100·3	91·1	90·4	100·1		94·1	95·4	93·1
1909	99·5	94·8	96·3	92·3	98·0	85·6	92·1	74·8		90·8	87·3	89·9
1910	92·5	97·8	96·2	99·2	96·0	104·0	99·5	106·0		101·3	102·3	100·8
1911	99·7	102·5	102·0	106·1	102·3	105·7	105·3	99·1		108·2	106·2	105·7
1912	106·3	113·7	110·7	114·3	103·4	113·6	112·0	120·0		105·5	108·7	110·5
1913	107·6	113·2	111·6	117·1	100·6	118·4	114·1	138·6		127·9	120·3	121·3

SOURCE. See text.

CHAPTER VI

Labour in the French Economy since the Revolution

I. *Introduction*

Even though neglected by historians since E. Levasseur and a few other precursors, the demographic analysis of the labour force has been the subject of much contemporary attention, and it is not surprising that the failings of historians have been redeemed by demographers and economists. One fundamental demographic fact is apparent, however: the weakness of French population growth from the 1800s until the 1940s. With its 28·3 million inhabitants at the end of the eighteenth century, France was the 'China of Europe', accounting for 15 to 16 per cent of its population, while Napoleon's military success was based largely on her big battalions. But this population growth was checked very early and slowed down after 1850, when it reached 35·7 million. In 1911, France's 39·6 million inhabitants made up only 9 per cent of the European total, and the density of her population was the lowest on the continent, at a level in 1846 that Great Britain had reached in 1775. The population increased by only 14 per cent in 60 years or so, as against 78 per cent in Great Britain, 64 per cent in the Netherlands, 56 per cent in Belgium, and 57 per cent in Germany. The nineteenth century, long considered the period of decisive transformation, was in fact one of stagnation, and a catastrophe intervened after the First World War before a spectacular reversal of the situation, in a twentieth century which, beneath superficially confused trends, was to prove an epoch of real change. Only this later transformation revealed how modest was that trend which had previously been seen as a revolution, and the change naturally posed certain questions about the relations between economy and society. Was economic malthusianism the other face of demographic malthusianism? Was not the relative decline of France above all a demographic decline – the result of a shortage of labour? The question remains a critical one, even if it does not exhaust the problem.

II. *A Static Nineteenth Century?*

A. THE WEAKENING OF NATURAL GROWTH

Just as the industrial revolution was developing in Britain, the birth rate in France began a long-term decline. Diminishing fecundity and voluntary birth control before 1789 explained this initially, but the French Revolution, resolutely 'populationist' though it was, accelerated the movement. The notion that 'population grows with liberty' held sway. The Constitution of 1791, which emphasized the authority of heads of families, and Robespierre, who declared in 1793 that 'parents are the true citizens', were in direct descent from the thinking of the Encyclopaedia, which defined marriage as 'the voluntary marital union of man and woman contracted by free persons for the purpose of having children'. The new taxes of 1790, which relieved families, conscription, which applied only to bachelors, and the decree of 8 June 1796, which created pregnancy and suckling allowances, were part of a latent policy of encouraging the birth rate. Political revolution was to make way for demographic revolution and an increase in prosperity in a France which, everyone was agreed, was insufficiently populated.

Facts belied this ambition, however, for there was a sharp slump in the birth rate during the Revolution and Empire. The calculations of J. Bourgeois-Pichat show a decline for the whole country from 35·9 per thousand in 1791–5 to 31·6 per thousand in 1811–15. In Languedoc the birth rate fell from 37 or 38 per thousand in 1785–9 to 32 or 33 per thousand in 1802–6. At Meulan, a medium-sized town near Paris, only 16 per cent of the couples who married between 1765 and 1789 had two children or less; for couples marrying during the Revolution and the Empire, the figure rose to 40 per cent. Social changes were more decisive than declared principles and worked against them. Some families were broken up by the institution of divorce (the law of 9 September 1792, completed in 1793 and 1794). Equal rights stimulated that 'social capillarity' of which Arsène Dumont would speak a century later, but this social mobility could be achieved only by limiting the size of the family. The suppression of some customary rights in the countryside, which diminished the resources of the traditionally prolific landless labourers; the loosening grip of religious habits; and increased geographical mobility, which permitted the diffusion of 'evil secrets', also contributed to reduce the birth rate.

The political restoration was not accompanied by a demographic restoration. The mean annual number of births increased at a reduced rate until the middle of the Second Empire, reaching a maximum of 1,004,900 births in the period 1861–5. This was not to be repeated, for the gross birth rates reached a climax as early as 1816–20, at 32·9 per thousand, itself a clear drop from the end of the eighteenth century. After this, rates declined steadily. France was a 'pilot' nation in this respect, with the lowest birth rate in Europe under the July monarchy: 28·1 per thousand in 1841–5, 26·1 per thousand in 1851–6. The crisis of 1846–51 reduced the number of births in 1847 to 901,000, the poorest year of the century. If there was a recovery after 1851, it was short and slight. The trend of the Second Empire was stable, but with a gradual decline and a birth rate of between 26·5 and 26·9 per thousand until 1868; the level of 1851 (27 per thousand) was touched again only once, in 1859. Subsequently, the decline set in again. The level of a 25 per thousand birth rate collapsed in 1886–90, that of 900,000 annual births in 1896–1900. On the eve of the First World War, the gross birth rate dropped to 20·2 per thousand (1906–11), 5·5 percentage points below the 1876–80 level, 12·5 per thousand below the level of the beginning of the century. The decline in births, in number and in rate, can be explained largely by the generalization of malthusian practices; the gross reproduction rate fell from 1·99 in about 1810–20 to 1·23 in 1910, and the net rate from 1·08 to 0·95.

The gross death rate, in contrast, remained more or less constant, at about 25 per thousand, during the whole Restoration period. If a decline did set in after 1845, it was moderate under the July monarchy and even until the end of the century. The health of Frenchmen, in fact, scarcely improved. Successive regimes devoted very little attention to it. There was no progress in hospitals or qualified medical staff. The general lack of hygiene, a poor and unbalanced diet which still caused deficiency illnesses like goitre in backward regions and the suffering of the industrial proletariat made the population always extremely fragile. The great scourges of another era had ceased, but epidemics were no less deadly. Cholera pushed the gross death rate up to 28·5 per thousand in 1832 and 27·8 per thousand in 1833, claiming 100,000 victims in 1849 in a nation weakened by the serious crisis of 1846–7, and 145,000 in 1854, which explained the new record of 993,000 deaths. Diphtheria caused 8,500 deaths in 1855–7, smallpox nearly 18,000 between 1869 and 1875. Around 1850, tuberculosis was at the root of about 10 per cent of all deaths, and in the working-class towns of Lille, half the populace was wiped out before reaching the age of 24.

The gross mortality rate remained at about 22 per thousand in the period 1890–5, as against 24·4 per thousand in 1866–70. The Franco-Prussian war pushed up the number of deaths to 1,271,000 in 1871, and that was in a country whose eastern territories had been amputated. No decline set in until after 1895, with the widening application of Pasteur's discoveries, the doubling of the medical corps, and above all the laws of 1893 which established free medical help, and that of 1902 for 'the protection of national health', which made anti-smallpox vaccination compulsory. Most significant was the net decline in infant mortality – to 106 per thousand in 1912. As for the gross rate, that dropped beneath 20 per thousand with the new century, to 19·6 per thousand between 1901 and 1905, and to 18·3 per thousand on the eve of the First World

War. In about thirty years, life expectancy at birth had increased three times as fast as it had in the previous sixty-five years, as Table 61 shows.

The reversal was nevertheless too late and too slight to change the general trend in French population growth. An initial warning during the mid-century crisis cut back the natural surplus to very little: no more than 52,000 in 1847 and 12,000 in 1849, as against 245,000 in 1845. After 1870 the trend increased, with the mean surplus dropping to less

Table 61. *Life Expectancy at Birth (years), c. 1817–1913*

	Men		Women	
c. 1817	38·3		40·8	
c. 1881	40·8		43·4	
gain 1817–81		2·5		2·6
1913	48·5		52·4	
gain 1881–1913		7·7		9·0

than 100,000 in the 1880s. Between 1891 and 1895, for the first time in any five-year period, deaths had the edge over births. The phenomenon was to become no exception, repeating itself in 1891, 1892, 1895, 1900, 1907, and 1911. The total population was almost stationary, increasing by only 0·12 per cent a year during the first decade of the twentieth century, when all the other great industrial powers were advancing at a rate of 1·0 per cent. Even worse, the level of the net rate of reproduction sent France into a phase of virtual depopulation.

B. THE CALL FOR IMMIGRATION

These weaknesses of French population growth in the nineteenth century were masked by the already important and regular contribution of immigration. As the century progressed, the number of arrivals rose to a high figure, but it is difficult to measure the precise trends, because immigration was a spontaneous affair, independent of official policy or controls. Immigration was not something completely new: its roots were in the *ancien régime*, but it then involved only small numbers of specialists, whether Dutch shipwrights, German miners and metal-workers, or Italians skilled in luxury manufactures like silk. This was still the shape of things for the first half of the nineteenth century, and indeed, the technical transformation of the French iron and steel industry was achieved largely with the help of skilled foreign workers. The presence of numerous Belgians and Germans was noted in the Moselle region about 1819. Fourchambault (Nièvre) employed some thirty Englishmen in 1825, and there were Englishmen at Le Creusot in 1828, at St-Julien-en-Jarret in the Forez mountains, and at Decazeville in 1830. Jacob Holtzer organized his Unieux workshops with Germans from the Ruhr; Alais had a colony of Belgians and Piedmontese. In the middle years of the century Paris sheltered thousands of Germans exiled from their fatherland by the pressure of population, the crisis of the political regimes, and by political persecution after the failure of the Revolutions of 1848. It is possible that in some sectors this influx of specialists continued till the end of the century: around 1880, natives of Baden and Württemberg were working at Pont-Salomon (Haute-Loire), there were Italian glassblowers at Rive de Gier (Loire), and German brewers in the Lyons area. But by that time they were a marginal contribution, vestiges of a kind of immigration which involved only modest numbers: in 1851 there were just under 380,000 foreigners in France, less than 1 per cent of the total population.

The nature and rhythm of immigration changed under the Second Empire. By 1872 the number of foreigners had doubled, both in absolute terms (to 741,000 individuals) and relative to the total population (2 per cent). By 1911 there were 1,160,000 aliens or 2·8 per cent of the total (3·3 per cent if naturalized citizens are included). The rate was then steady until 1891 and slowed thereafter, but account must be taken of the greater number of immigrants of French nationality. It seems rather that, in the short term, the level of immigration corresponded broadly with the rate of French economic growth, following the great expansion of 1851–72, and the depression of the 1880s. The importance of temporary, seasonal, and even daily immigration, facilitated by improved means of transport, must also be considered. In 1913, between 50,000 and 60,000 Belgians alone were crossing the frontier daily, with 100,000 coming to work during the wheat and sugar-beet harvests.

For a long time, this trickle of immigrants passed unnoticed. For the most part, it involved only France's neighbours, and this just increased old currents of population exchange, even though a one-way system had now developed. The adjacent countries, in fact, provided 78 per cent of foreign immigrants in 1851, and 83 per cent in 1911. There was, nevertheless, a changing balance between these countries. The Belgians, clearly in the lead in the mid-century with 33 per cent, dropped back to second place with 25 per cent on the eve of the First World War. At that point the Italians had taken over, with 36 per cent as against 16 per cent in 1851. The decline in the contribution from Germany, now in process of industrialization, was understandable: numbers fell from one in six immigrants in 1851 to less than one in ten in 1911, which was on a par with the Spaniards, whose proportion was rising slowly. The Italians and Belgians took an even more pronounced lead, providing 419,000 individuals in 1851, and 287,000 in 1911 – that is three out of five as against one out of two foreigners. The geography of the immigrant populations could still be traced by proximity to these two reservoirs. The West and Centre remained inviolate of any significant settlement, which concentrated in the North, the East, and the South-east, making up 16 per cent of the population of the Bouches-du-Rhône, and 14 per cent of that of the Var, at its highest points.

Integration into the French nation was made easier by common linguistic roots and was accelerated by the greater number of mixed marriages and above all, after 1890, of naturalizations. These were encouraged by the law of 1889: French nationality was accorded auto-matically to the children of foreigners themselves born in France, a procedure which was optional when the parents were born abroad. In all, there were about a million naturalizations between 1872 and 1911. There is no doubt that immigrants provoked a certain suspicion: the history of the nascent labour movement was marked by numerous strikes, and some violence, in the North and especially the Southeast, in campaigns for their expulsion. Between 1883 and 1914 there were no fewer than fifty bills aimed at reducing their number: in 1899 Millerand even conceded a *numerus clausus* on foreigners in state employment and local collectives. But the anti-Italian riots which followed the assassina-tion of President Carnot at Lyons in 1894 demonstrated the complexity of the resistance, inspired less by fear of competition for employment than by political motives, xenophobia, and even racialism, with all the irrationality which that implied.

In the labour market, as a member of parliament observed in 1904, foreigners took up those jobs that Frenchmen refused. In 1911 they made up 6·4 per cent of the working population, but half of all labourers, stevedores, quarrymen, navvies, and masons were im-migrants. Shortly before the First World War an organized policy of immigration developed among employers. The agricultural em-ployers' union brought about 20,000 foreigners, with work permits, into Lorraine, Champagne, and Burgundy. After 1900 the ironmasters set up recruiting agents at the frontiers, and their committee, established in 1911, started a combined recruiting service which negotiated an agreement with Italy and settled 7,000 Italians in the East, chiefly in the basins of Briey and Longwy.

This new kind of selective immigration offered future economic benefits by mitigating the effects of demographic stagnation among Frenchmen themselves. Between 1851 and 1911 the number of foreigners tripled, whereas the total population of the country in-creased by only a fifth. In addition, those coming into the country were in general young people, with proportionately more in this age-group than was the case for the French population as a whole. Table 62 (after Mauco) gives age-distribution figures for 1911.

The result was twofold. In the first place, despite the proportion of bachelors and the majority of males, births were abundant, since the fertility of foreign couples was higher than that of the French: the average family size was 3·7 children instead of 2·6. The small numbers of elderly people reduced the death rate and ensured a constant natural

Table 62. *Age Distribution of Active French and Foreign Populations (per cent), 1911*

Age-group	Foreign	French
Under 20	14	13·9
20–39	52	42
40–59	27	31
60 and Over	6·4	11·9
Unknown	0·2	0·5

SOURCE. G. Mauco, *Les Migrations ouvrières en France au début du XXe Siècle* (Paris, 1932).

surplus. In the second place, the proportion of active persons was clearly higher, being 58 per cent of the immigrant population in 1911 and even 61 per cent in the case of the Italians, against 52 per cent for the French. This was determined largely by the greater proportion of the potentially active population (those aged twenty to fifty-nine – a minimum definition, because work was carried on beyond the age of sixty), which was 79 per cent as against 73 per cent, or for the most productive group among the working population (between twenty and thirty-nine years) 52 per cent for immigrants against 42 per cent for the French.

C. AN EXPANDING WORK FORCE

No doubt the malthusian behaviour of the French explains the overall ageing of the population, characterized by a relative decline in the numbers of the younger cohorts and a growth in those of the older ones. This development may be summed up at three key dates, as shown in Table 63. The younger age-group contracted by 10 per cent, while the elderly bracket gained 5·5 per cent. Yet J. C. Toutain has

Table 63. *High and Low Age-Groups as Percentages of the Total Population, 1776–1911*

	0–19 years	60 years and over
1776	4·4	7·1
1851	36·1	10·1
1911	33·8	12·6

pointed out that this trend coexisted with an extraordinary stability of the population of working age, from fifteen to sixty-nine years, considered as a percentage of the whole. The figures of J. Bourgeois-Pichat establish this proportion at 64·1 to 66·0 per cent between 1776 and 1861, and 68·3 to 69·1 per cent between 1851 and 1911. For the age-group fifteen to sixty-five, the proportion was maintained between 61·5 and 63·3 per cent for the first half of the nineteenth century. Support for this comes from the remarks of Fourastié, who established that the rise in the average age of the male working population was slight, from twenty-four at the time of Napoleon I to twenty-six at the beginning of the II Empire and twenty-eight in 1901. And here one must take account of compulsory education to the age of fourteen, which, by reducing child labour, obviously pushed up the average.

All these results reflect a solid increase in the absolute size of the potentially active population, which over the whole century grew faster than the total population of France. The figures of J. Bourgeois-Pichat are shown in Table 64.

Table 64. *Total Population and Potential Active Population* (*thousands*), *1776–1911*

	Total population	Potential active population (15–69 years)		
		Men	Women	Total
1776	25,612	8,079	8,432	16,502
1851	35,902	11,891	11,954	23,845
1911	39,193	13,342	13,834	27,176

Between 1776 and 1911 the potentially active population increased by 64·7 per cent, while the total increased by only 40·2 per cent. In the period 1776–1851 the figures were 44 per cent as against 40 per cent, and between 1851 and 1911 they were 14 per cent as against 9·1 per cent. It does not seem that the demographic deceleration contributed heavily to decreasing the size of the work force, even if the long-term trend was in this direction.

D. A NATION OF PEASANTS?

The size and distribution of the active population is difficult to determine before 1851, when for the first time a mere head count was accompanied by an occupational census. Methods were still summary, and more reliable data were not forthcoming before 1866. Even subsequently, uncertainty over definitions of economic activities, principles of classification, and even the means of collecting information make comparisons between censuses difficult. Numerous adjustments have to be made, and all results are necessarily subject to a margin of error.

Error is even more likely in those calculations which concern the documentary evidence about the active population in the first half of the nineteenth century, whether contemporary or modern. In the 'Table of the French Population' which appeared in 1780, the Abbé d'Expilly estimated the number of active males at 7,583,000. Others have given a figure of 6,200,000 – say, 22 to 30 per cent of the total population – and today Markovitch has pushed this up to 37 per cent, or about 10 million active people. The preponderance of agriculture was overwhelming, estimated by Markovitch as occupying 3·9 million men or 55 per cent of the whole as against 1·6 million artisans and industrial workers and 1·8 million servants, to which 1·6 million women must be added. Here he is closer to agreement with d'Expilly, who spoke of 50 per cent of the population as being engaged in agriculture, taking only men into account, which represents a figure of 3·8 to 4 millions. For artisans and industrial workers, d'Expilly calculated a total of 2·5 millions, but his classification contains difficulties; in 1789 Lavoisier suggested a figure of 1·8 million. A poll of the occupational origins of soldiers in the army between 1804 and 1815 puts the role of the primary sector at 71·6 per cent and reduces that of secondary industries to 20·9 per cent, with 3·5 per cent for commerce and transport. But suspicion is cast on this document by the ridiculously small number of servants. All in all, only general impressions can be drawn before 1851, when agriculture employed 56·9 per cent of men and industry 27·6 per cent, which implies that the agricultural population remained extremely stable, in percentage terms, during the first half of the nineteenth century. J. C. Toutain maintains that it progressed at the same rate as the total population, which presupposes the absence of any profound change in the structure of economic activity.

We know that, despite the quick recovery of French industry after the Napoleonic wars and its ability to seize those markets of quality goods abandoned by the British, the quarter-century after 1815 was probably a period of only moderate growth. The most dynamic sectors of industry – mines and iron and steel – made only moderate demands on the labour market in this period. Textiles were still the largest industrial employer, and dispersion, often in the countryside, remained the order of the day. The early stages of industrialization did not set up a massive demand for manpower, and between 1801 and 1851 there were no substantial concentrations of the population in particular *départements*, with the exception of the Rhône. From the limited nature of geographical mobility, it may be assumed that professional migration was on a small scale. The agricultural population's regular surplus served all new needs and was not itself threatened, while the archaic character of the crisis of 1845–7 showed that the economy was still largely traditional as far as its occupational structure was concerned.

F. Crouzet has recently demonstrated the accelerated economic growth, at least in terms of production series, from the 1840s until the 1870s – statistics which corroborate the old impression of rapid development corresponding roughly to the Second Empire. There does not, however, seem to have been a simultaneous burst of activity on all fronts, even though an unprecedented peak occurred in 1876. The relative stability of the distribution of the population between sectors is also evident, as Table 65 shows.

Table 65. *Sectoral Distribution of Population (per cent), 1856 and 1876*

	Primary	Secondary	Tertiary
1856	51·7	26·8	21·4
1876	48·8	27·3	22·8

An attempt at an overall calculation, for both sexes, reveals an increase in the active population from 7,275,000 in 1851 to 7,961,000 in 1876. The number of workers in industry rose from 3,793,000 in 1856 to 4,469,000 – still a modest figure: recently, Georges Duveau had cause to speculate whether, paradoxically, the working classes shrank in numbers under the Second Empire. Did the natural surplus of the rural population suffice to meet the demands of industry? At any rate, there is much evidence to contradict the idea of a general crisis in the countryside following the crisis years of 1845–51. A rural exodus may have been a reality in Picardy, Normandy, Perche, the north bank of the Garonne, upper Languedoc, and Gascony, but it was a response to the liquidation of rural industry rather than to a crisis in agriculture, which in fact prospered under Napoleon III. If the expansion of the rural population slowed down in the Bordelais, in Brittany, and in Coastal Languedoc, it retained all its vigour in Provence, the Lyons region, the plains of the Rhône and the Massif Central, and in the North.

It was not until the 1880s that a change took place and rural depopulation became general, with poor grain harvests and then phylloxera, despite the system of protection that had been established. The departure of agricultural workers from the land was therefore contemporary with the grave structural crisis which struck French industry, and then with recovery during the '*belle époque*', which (as Crouzet shows) was more modest than has long been supposed, even when incorporating particularly dynamic new sectors of industry into the figures of production. After a small decline, the proportion of the active population rose to 49·6 per cent in 1896 and continued upwards to 53·4 per cent in 1911. After 1886 the proportion of those engaged in agriculture fell, with the figure for 1911 (41·2 per cent) being 5·4 per cent below that for 1881, after a period of thirty years, whereas the drop had been only 4·8 per cent for the half-century before that. Yet, while this change of rhythm should be appreciated, it must be put in its context. In 1911, four Frenchmen in ten still worked on the land – perhaps 8,625,000, which was 1,039,000 more than in 1856. Until 1921, moreover, there was always a correlation between the growth of the total population and the growth of the active agricultural population. It seems, too, that this correspondence was even closer than it had been between the revolutionary period and the mid-century, despite the exodus of 40,000 peasants a year to other sectors between 1900 and 1913. The parallel between the two growth rates is perhaps the most characteristic aspect of the occupational evolution of the French people until the First World War. The development of the other sectors may be compared in Table 66.

The active industrial population was expanding three times faster than the total population, but it still represented only one worker in three in 1911. Hard on its heels came the service sector, precociously increasing by 7·7 per cent, as against 2·9 per cent for industry, in just over half a century. On the eve of the war, the two sectors were almost level, in both relative and absolute terms – with 6,223,000 employed in the secondary sector and no fewer than 6,083,000 in the tertiary. It seems as if industrialization was short-circuited by the proliferation of the services.

Table 66. *Sectoral Distribution of Active Population (per cent),*
1881–1911

	Agriculture	Industry	Services
1881	47·5	26·7	24·9
1891	44·6	27·9	26·8
1911	41·2	29·7	29·1

The rigidity of the socio-professional classifications in the various censuses is constraining. It is impossible to answer questions about the mobilization of the 'reserve army of labour' described by Marx for Britain, because the floating population was not well covered by the censuses. Only hypotheses are therefore possible.

There is no doubt as to the existence of these floating masses at the end of the eighteenth century, in a country where the population was rising fast. These are the 'lower classes' which François Furet rightly defines by the precariousness of their conditions and employment.

How many were there? Some commentators give a figure of 1,250,000; contemporaries like d'Aubry, who includes them with the poor, say 2,400,000. In any case account has to be taken of several hundred thousand of these 'temporary migrants' at the beginning of the nineteenth century, among whom the Limousin building workers were only a small element. The likelihood is that this floating mass of the underemployed was to be found in urban employment as well as in agriculture. Identifying them is made even more difficult by the regular presence of migration and exchange between economic sectors, and especially between regions. Geographical mobility was probably greater in nineteenth-century France than has long been believed.

It seems that France was still an aggregate of regional *pays*, changing at very different paces, despite the early date of political unification, and that the labour force was divided into stable sectors before the 1880s, or even at the beginning of the twentieth century. We have seen that there was no early migration of workers from agriculture on a large scale. Hence the originality of the French 'reserve army' – a function of the pattern of industrialization in France, which was essentially a rural phenomenon. It will not do to generalize about the decline of dispersed rural industries after 1850. A more accurate hypothesis is that of successive cycles, with one sector succeeding another. In Picardy, wool and linen-weaving took over from the declining spinning industry after 1830, and were in turn replaced by sugar-refining: agricultural workers increased in numbers here until 1872, concurrently with the expansion of sugar beet. In the Lyonnais and Beaujolais, recent research shows that cotton and silk manufacture advanced as linen declined. The picture was similar in the Dauphiné, where silk mills were being set up in the villages until 1876, and around La Tour Du Pin (Rhône) where hat-making and even iron-ore-mining continued. The same pattern can be found in the establishment of the iron and steel industry, at least before its domination by the centres of the North and East. It developed at Fourchambault, close to Nevers, where there was a pool of workers long experienced in the iron trade, and at Saint Etienne, with an old tradition of ironmongery and edged-tool-making. The great railway yards of the July Monarchy and the Second Empire did not cause the uprooting that Le Play and his disciples denounced; in fact, they brought together navvies from afar and gave work to unemployed industrial workers and peasants during the slack season. One can only be struck by the stability of the industrial map of France in the nineteenth century, which reproduced the old divisions of town and country. There was no question of an early mobilization of a 'reserve army of labour', which would have brought substantial geographical displacement in its wake.

The decline in numbers of those working in industry in short periods of crisis – and even more during the long depression of the 1830s – revealed a certain migration between industry and agriculture. The demand for labour in agriculture remained constant during the whole nineteenth century. At Decazeville there was complaint as late as 1865 about the competition for labour imposed by the harvest. In the mines of Rive-de-Gier and Saint Etienne a return to the soil was natural in time of slump. Even in Lyons, the silk-weavers preserved a tenuous but permanent lifeline to the villages. The links established by the silk industry between the Dauphiné and the Vivarais were particularly interesting. Originally, the silk mills of the Vivarais had sought their female labour force from as far away as the Alps; at the end of the nineteenth century, the direction was reversed, and the movement was from places like Aubenas and Chomérac to the mills of the Isère. But in both cases several tens of thousands of young women, who would return to the land after a few years, took industrial employment. At La Voulte and Pouzin, on the Middle Rhône, the disappearance of the blast furnaces in the 1880s resulted in a complete reabsorption of 2,000 iron-workers into agriculture without any local exodus. Even the hydro-electric plants of the great Alpine valleys had the same reasons for complaint in 1906–10 as had Decazeville half a century earlier.

Other modes of recruitment to industrial centres had to be effected by other means, often dictated by the nature of local economic activity. Here the continuing predominance of the textile industries was important. Textiles employed half the active industrial population in 1789 and 1856, while in 1911 the same industries still employed the high proportion of 41·7 per cent, or about 2,590,000 people – 800,000 more than half a century before. The absolute maximum of 2,610,000 workers was reached only in 1906. At the beginning of the twentieth century women made up 68 per cent of that number, and female textile workers alone composed 67 per cent of the total female industrial labour force. In many cases, wives and daughters of peasants or of workers in other industries must have been employed, so that the development of the largest French industry did not destroy the existing socio-professional structure.

Other industries, however, expanded at a faster rate. In the two leading sectors, metallurgy employed 8·9 per cent of the work force in 1856, and 15·7 per cent in 1911 (a rise from 337,000 workers to 947,000); while miners, though their proportion of the total rose only from 5·1 to 5·6 per cent, increased their numbers from 199,000 to 349,000. It appears that until the 1880s most recruitment was local, explained by the extremely prolific working-class population: hence those hosts of children whose presence in the factories so impressed the observers of the 1840s, and who still made up 10 per cent of the labour force in great enterprises like Anzin, Bessèges, Montlucon, and Le Creusot in 1867, and 7 per cent of the numbers at Commentry, Aubin, Alais, and Decazeville. The protective laws of 21 March 1841, 19 May 1874, and 2 November 1891 were ineffective in reducing these numbers before the introduction of compulsory elementary education. At Saint Etienne in 1834, 59 per cent of the workers were born in the commune, following a dramatic increase in their numbers. At Carmaux, of 448 young people taken on between 1892 and 1900, 404 were miners' sons, while between 1848 and 1914, 73·6 per cent of the miners were born in the three communes of the area. In the North, Philippe Ariès has pointed out that the mining region drew the bulk of its labour from industrial Flanders and that, until 1891, expansion was sustained by the mining community itself. Only after this date was the local monopoly of labour supply broken by arrivals from the countryside.

The tertiary sector was also dynamic, though its long-term evolution masks certain internal transformations. Domestic service declined from 31·8 per cent of this sector in 1856 to 14·6 per cent in 1911, but the slowness of that decline until 1881 (27·9 per cent) reinforces what has been said about the persistence of a floating population, especially as the word 'domestic' often implied the existence of underemployment. At the same time, the proportion of those in transport doubled (from 7·4 to 14·8 per cent), and there was growth in the public services (from 18·9 to 21·5 per cent) and commerce and banking (from 31·3 to 38·5 per cent) – a slower but no less significant rate of expansion. It is possible, in fact, that the rural population, located in the countryside but not necessarily employed in agriculture, moved into the services rather than into industry. In Lyons and Nancy, at the end of the century, such rural migrants became railwaymen and business clerks; in Paris, in the years 1840–60, they replenished the ranks of domestic servants; in Marseilles during the Second Empire, they became shopkeepers. This meant that in the last quarter of the century, industry had to draw directly on recruits from Italy. Such a refusal to accept industrial employment continued to some extent into the twentieth century: in contemporary Auxerre, for example, it is the grandsons of the peasants who became factory workers, a generation after the initial break with the land.

E. LITERACY AND THE QUALIFICATIONS OF THE LABOUR FORCE

The question of the qualifications of the labour force in the nineteenth century has not yet been the subject of detailed research. At most, some general notions have been deduced from what is known about the needs of an economy undergoing technological change. Research into prevailing levels of general knowledge and thus of capacities of responding to these new demands has been virtually nonexistent since the work of Emile Levasseur.

Literacy is the most basic consideration, conditioning everything else. Some progress was made in the eighteenth century but, as in so many other fields, the French Revolution belied its own principles by closing numerous 'little schools'. There is no firm evidence for the nineteenth century before 1825–30, at which point between 48 per cent and 52 per cent of conscripts to the army could not read, while one in every two men and three in every four women still signed the state marriage register with a cross. The low level of literacy, probably stable since the end of the eighteenth century, may be explained by the inadequacy of primary education. There is little doubt that the number of children at school increased after 1815. Cuvier and Montalivet suggest an increase among boys from 865,000 or 920,000 to 1,200,000 by the 1830s, while 500,000 girls were then receiving a regular education. But this level represents only a recovery, the figures being based on the mobilization or marriage of children who had been at school since the beginning of the Restoration. Even so, in 1821, 1,800,000 boys between the ages of five and fourteen, and 2,500,000 girls, had never set foot inside a school. Even these figures are deceptive, because they take no account of seasonal variations in school attendance, which was high only during the winter. The upward trend of the figures, moreover, cannot conceal the inadequacy of the primary schools; the law of 29 February 1816, which obliged every commune to maintain one, was a failure, and initiatives were too rare and too dispersed.

The Guizot law of 28 June 1833 was much more important, making the obligation on communes effective. This measure was backed up by the establishment of a system of primary-school inspection between 1835 and 1845. The Falloux law of 15 March 1840 then provided the incentive for much expansion in the private sector, and the legislation of the Second Empire consolidated the organization of the primary-school teachers (instituteurs). The Ministry of Victor Duruy sketched out a system of subventions which was later to prove decisive, and the law of 10 April 1867 gave financial support to the communes. In 1872 primary education was free for 57 per cent of the children attending such schools, as against 41 per cent in 1866.

Between Guizot's time and the 1880s the greatest novelty was the education of girls: numbers of girls at school rose not only in absolute terms but as a percentage of the whole. Trends in school attendance are shown in Table 67.

At the end of the Second Empire the illiteracy rate among conscripts was no higher than 25 per cent, and no higher than 17 per cent on average between 1870 and 1880. The change is clear, but the pace remained slow. There was resistance to the development of primary education, not so much because of the meanness of municipalities (for in 1863 there were only 818 communes without schools, as against 3,217 in 1847 and 10,400 in 1832) as because of psychological barriers, a certain inertia in rural society, a reluctance on the part of the urban and labouring classes to deprive themselves of the earnings of their children in sending them to school.

Table 67. *School Attendance of Children Aged 5–14, 1832–81*

	Pupils in primary schools (thousands)			Rate of school attendance (per cent)		
	Boys	Girls	Total	Boys	Girls	Total
1832	1,600	800	2,400	48	25	37
1851	1,794	1,528	3,322	55	48	51
1881	2,568	2,464	5,032	78	76	77

The legislation inspired by Jules Ferry completed the edifice of primary instruction. The law of 16 June 1881 made it a public service and entirely free; that of 28 March 1882 imposed compulsory attendance. Several years later, by the finance law of 1889, the state took over the payment of primary-school teachers. These different measures did not suddenly push up the number of children at school – in 1891 primary schools were educating 2,824,000 boys and 2,742,000 girls – but the rate of attendance rose to an average of 83 per cent in that year, and to 85 per cent in 1911 (a slight decline, strangely enough, on the 1906 level of 86 per cent). It is difficult to explain this. Was it the result of the conflicts between church and state, which involved the closing-down of some schools run by Catholic religious orders? Or of the lowering of the minimum school age, which demonstrated the weakness of nursery schools? Or was it a sign of the very success of an education policy which had now reached saturation point?

By the eve of the First World War, illiteracy was clearly on the retreat. Over 6,500,000 children were at school, 3,325,000 boys and 3,287,000 girls. Nineteen out of twenty conscripts could now write, and the percentage of crosses on marriage registers had shrunk to a negligible 1·6 per cent for men and 2·7 per cent for women. The decline had been a slow one during the nineteenth century, but it had been continuous, and France had now overcome her backwardness compared with other industrialized countries of Europe. As early as 1880, 90·9 per cent of Dutch conscripts, 98·7 per cent of German ones, and 97·9 per cent of Swiss could write, as against 87·7 per cent of French. Illiteracy was not eliminated, but (as J. C. Toutain has pointed out) its decline had a cumulative effect which was fundamental for the economy. Now 23 million Frenchmen had an elementary education which made them capable of undertaking complex tasks, compared with only 6 million at the end of the eighteenth century.

Was this the basic intention of all those laws, from Guizot to Ferry, which waged war on illiteracy? The first writers to examine the question – the Baron Dupin in 1826 and 1848, and the Comte D'Angeville under the July Monarchy – had been struck by the correlation between literacy and economic growth. Their maps illustrate the contrast between an unchanging France south of a line from Mont-St-Michel to Lake Geneva and a northern France in turbulence. In the 1830s, the distribution of steam engines corresponded with the map of primary education, showing progress in literacy in the North, Northeast, Champagne, and Alsace, which were also the economically dynamic regions, and stagnation in the illiterate parts, the Massif Central, Aquitaine, and Brittany. The only exceptions in the South were the Rhône–Loire crescent and the region around Marseilles. It was a double-edged division which dated back to the end of the *ancien régime* and which persisted until the 1850s, judging by the correlation between illiteracy rates and the distribution of workers in heavy industry, revealed for the first time in the census returns of 1851. But the line was penetrated in the Second Empire by a breakthrough of literacy in the Southeast and had dissolved by the end of the century.

The republican legend of Jules Ferry, then, masked an economic *arrière-pensée*, that of dispensing the minimum amount of instruction to endow the labour force with those capabilities necessary for economic growth. There are probably very few considerations which are purely technical, but in the opinion of Pierre Vilar this was an unconscious and unorganized reply to the necessity of having at least a literate population in an economy which had reached a certain stage of development. Formulated in these terms, the hypothesis might be as valid for Guizot and Victor Duruy. Yet it is surprising to observe that, even if the North–South opposition had disappeared by 1911, the industrialized departments of the Nord, the Pas-de-Calais, the Aisne, and the Somme were then below the national literacy average. The question is more complex than it first appears, but there has been no monograph to elucidate the problem in the specific terms that a regional study would make possible.

Georges Dupeux has stressed the almost total lack of practical considerations in this expanding field of primary education. A sole exception was for the agricultural context provided by the rural *instituteurs* – but then this worked against the trend of the changing labour force. It sprang from the nascent myth of the peasant, which only underlined prevailing ignorance of economic realities and the alternatives that they imposed. Such a lack of practical orientation was all the more paradoxical, as France had played a leading role in the formation of higher technical cadres. The way had been opened at the end of the *ancien régime* with the foundation by the monarchy of the School of Engineering in 1749, the School of Bridges and Highways in 1747, and the School of Mines in 1783. The revolutionary assemblies followed suit, and the decisive creation of the Ecole Polytechnique (22 October 1794) guaranteed for several decades the quality of a technical and economic elite. The Conservatoire National des Arts et Métiers, born at the same time, was less prestigious but played an important role, for among its alumni were Jacquard, Eugène Schneider, Nicolas Koechlin, and Emile Dollfüss – all prominent entrepreneurs. In 1817 a second School of Mines was established at Saint Etienne, while the Ecole Centrale des Arts et Manufactures was founded at Paris in 1829.

This original system of *grandes écoles* of engineering rested on a system of secondary education – that 'all-powerful empire of the middle term' of which Lucien Febvre spoke – which was organized very early. It, too, flowed from the colleges of the *ancien régime*, a tight network in its own right, to which the *'écoles centrales'* founded by the Revolution Convention added a syllabus of exact sciences, before they were themselves absorbed in the *lycées* of Napoleon, and the whole group set in the framework of a monopolistic 'state university'. The Falloux law of 1850, which broke the monopoly, provoked a new surge in secondary education by allowing the parallel development of private Catholic schools. Altogether, the number of pupils at secondary schools rose from 80,000 in about 1815 to 110,000 in 1853.

Between 1832 and 1870, the Central School of Arts and Manufactures produced 3,000 engineers, and served as a model for most of the industrialized countries. Until 1864, a quarter of its students came from abroad. Conversely, the quality of French technicians astonished southeastern Europe, Italy, the Near East, and even Belgium. The system of *grandes écoles* expanded, enriched in 1826 by the Ecole des Eaux et Forêts at Nancy, the Ecole des Arts Industriels at Lille in 1854, the Ecole Centrale Lyonnaise in 1857, and the National Institute of Agronomy, reconstituted in 1876 after a fruitless attempt between 1848 and 1855. Finally, the training of the lower grades of staff, who might today be called 'production engineers', was assured to an even greater extent by the development of 'Ecoles d'Arts et Métiers', of which the first was established at Châlons-sur-Marne in 1806 and the second at

Angers in 1811 (both reorganized in 1832), with a third at Aix-en-
Provence in 1841. Each had room for 300 pupils. There is no doubt that
in the 1860s France had the best system of higher technical and scientific
education in Europe. But while the officers of the industrial army were
being formed, the rank and file were completely ignored.

The decline of apprenticeship had in fact been continuous since the
beginning of the nineteenth century. Both social and economic factors
can explain this. To begin with, the dynamic sectors of industry did not
need large numbers of skilled workers with a professional training, but
sought instead brute physical strength for repetitive activity. New techniques were simple: in the iron industry of the Bourbonnais in the
1850s it took two weeks to grasp the essentials of lighting a blast furnace
and mixing the ore. In the textile industry, mechanization was giving
birth to a multitude of preparatory and finishing operations, which did
not demand great skill. Yet this was at a time when increasing concentration in factories would demand a certain upgrading in the skills
acquired in the small workshop. In the second place, apprenticeship was
expensive – for the master, who had to lend his time and talent, and
who increasingly regarded his apprentice as a workman to whom he
allocated menial tasks, and for the parents, who would have to pay the
master no small sum – which put the status of apprenticeship beyond
the purses of the industrial proletariat. Finally, in the artisan trades
themselves, except in a few cases like carpentry, the decline of *compagnonnage* (artisan brotherhoods) entailed the decline of professional
training. Even when it existed formally, apprenticeship was usually
lacking in substance.

The few measures taken to improve the situation seem to have been
ineffectual. Catholic organizations such as the Friends of Childhood
(1828) and the Society for the Protection of Apprentices (1867) found
good employers and provided subsidies and school clothes, but this was
an aspect of private charity, not a real and successful attempt to improve
apprenticeship. The actions of the state were hesitant and without
effect, despite the influence of working-class writers such as Joseph
Benoit and Corbon under the Second Republic, who sought to promote
an education which was both humane and professional. The law of
22 February 1851 – which made contracts compulsory, whether by
public or private agreement – required guarantees from employers
regarding morality and education, fixed the working day, and defined
the competence of arbitration boards (*conseils de prud'hommes*) in the
event of industrial disputes. However, it remained a dead letter. No
practical measures were taken as a result of the inquiry of 1863, which
followed the commercial treaties. The prizes created by the city of Paris
under the Second Empire had no effect. The Inquiry on Labour in 1848

had already demonstrated the obsolescence of the practice of contract in Paris, and by 1860 five workers in six started work without having received the least professional training.

There was no compensation to be found in an education outside the workshop for the decline of apprenticeship inside it. Not that the former was completely non-existent, though by and large a trade was learned empirically, on the job or in the family. This was what happened in the iron and steel industry in the 1850s, and the system continued in some branches of the weaving trades and small dispersed metalworking workshops until the beginning of the twentieth century. In certain large factories, apprenticeship was already being divorced from the workshop and organized in a school of the concern itself. This was the shape of things in the iron and steel industry about 1860, at Hayange, Alais, Terrenoire, Pont-Salomon, and also in printing-works like Chaix, at Paris. The system reached its apogee at Le Creusot, perfected by the Schneider family over the course of the century. As early as 1838 they had organized a school which provided both primary education and professional training adapted to the various needs of their factories, for which a small deduction was made from the wages of the apprentice's parents. Free places were instituted in 1873; and in 1882, although the 'normal' classes at primary level were handed over to the state, the 'special' schools in which mathematics, physics, chemistry, technology, and technical drawing were taught were retained and improved. In 1899 the edifice was crowned by a 'higher course' which prepared for the *grandes écoles*. Within the system, a rigorous process of selection set up a complete career structure, with access to careers at all levels of qualification. In this way the Schneiders trained their labourers, workmen, clerks of varying status, executives, and even their own engineers. The system was to survive to a large extent right up to the present, with consequences far greater than the purely economic ones. Yet despite local success, such a movement was not the spin-off from any national project. Only a minority of workers were affected, and they were often narrowly specialized and bound to a single establishment.

Outside these professional schools within factories, private or official initiatives were rare and fragmentary. The level of courses in applied science taught since 1819 in the Conservatoire des Arts et Métiers was too high for the needs of the working masses. The effect of those organized in a certain number of towns such as Reims, Bordeaux, Metz, and Montauban under the July Monarchy was weak, just as it was in the evening classes for adults set up by Victor Duruy, for it was scarcely possible to attend them after a long and hard day's work. Private organizations, like the Association Polytechnique (1830), from which sprang the Association Philotechnique in 1848, ran 322 courses under the Second Empire; but no real solution was provided by the Industrial Society of Nantes founded in 1832, the School of Saint Nicolas opened in Paris in 1827, or similar bodies founded under Napoleon III by chambers of commerce or municipalities. The Martinière school at Lyons – one of the most important, with 600 day-boys – remained fee-paying. In 1859 Corbon wrote that 'there is a much greater lack of professional education amongst the children of the working classes than amongst youth destined for the liberal professions'. Ten years later, his judgement would be just as pertinent.

The Third Republic began a phase which was much more fertile, at least for new foundations. Schools of apprenticeship proliferated right from its earliest years, particularly in Paris giving general practical instruction and also specialist training for metalworkers such as fitters, which was demanded by the development of mechanical engineering. In the 1880s, under the influence of senators of working-class origin such as Tolain and Corbon, manual schools of apprenticeship founded by local authorities were put on a parity with the state primary schools and subordinated to the Ministry of Commerce. Parallel to this, the Ministry of Public Instruction established Higher Primary Schools (EPS), which were designed to provide a complete primary education and to prepare for a subsequent professional training, following the model of the Vierzon (1881). In 1892 there was a basic restructuring. The EPS maintained their general function, while the more specialized of them fused with the apprenticeship schools in a new model, the Practical Schools of Commerce and Industry (EPCI). These were endowed with a special staff of teachers, trained after 1891 at the Ecole des Arts et Métiers at Châlons-sur-Marne, at the Higher School of Business Studies (HEC), at the Lyons Higher School of Commerce, and after 1912 at a special institution which was to become in 1934 the Higher Normal School of Technical Education. Besides this unified network of the EPCI, there remained the professional schools of the municipality of Paris, and four 'national professional schools' created in 1881-2 at Vierzon, Voiron, Armentières, and Nantes, rather like model EPS. Lastly the trade unions, which were agitating throughout the 1890s, resumed the teaching tradition of *compagnonnage*. At the outset, about 15,000 workers followed their courses in Paris alone. In 1905, there were about 408 unions with such projects, as well as some employers' organizations, catering for 95,000 'students'.

The crisis of apprenticeship, however, had not been in any way alleviated on the eve of the First World War. The establishment of a coherent system had come too late to have results, and those results did not really affect the mass of workers. Attendance at professional courses run by the unions or employers was greatly overestimated, with no sanctions against absenteeism. It would be interesting to know the content of these courses in detail and to measure their effectiveness. The number of pupils at the EPCI grew rapidly, from 1,717 in 1893 to 14,766 in 1912 (including 2,757 girls), but the modesty of these numbers in comparison to the total of those completing elementary education is patent. The idea of apprenticeship seemed to have been abandoned. The working-men's congress at Lyons noted in 1894 that it was 'confined in many cases to the home', and 95 per cent of the contracts passed in 1905 were verbal. The growing sophistication of mechanization had killed apprenticeship, but it also demanded enhanced qualifications in the worker. The leaders of the labour movement, now organized, had not yet caught up with this new requirement: Merrheim, one of the metalworkers' leaders, still spoke of the 'brute force' of the machine opposing the 'harmonious and creative thought' of the producer. The Higher Council of Labour, set up in 1891, discussed the question in 1901–2, reflecting a revived interest in the subject, but confined itself to passing resolutions.

While attempts to train the mass of the labour force were not succeeding, the system which had trained the engineers and higher cadres of the economy was being thrown out of gear. This was not for want of new foundations in the tradition of the *grandes écoles* of the nineteenth century. Progress was particularly striking in the tertiary sector, with the reorganization by the Paris Chamber of Commerce in 1869 of a Higher School of Commerce which had stagnated since 1820, and the creation of similar establishments at Le Havre (1871), Lyons and Bordeaux (1874), and Marseilles (1872), and especially the Ecole des Hautes Etudes Commerciales (1881). After 1871, the Free School of Political Sciences, the work of Emile Boutmy, was training the administrative bureaucratic class and the top personnel of business management. The teaching of 'Arts et Métiers' was helped with new schools at Lille (1881), Cluny (1901), and Paris (1906), and the training of engineers was being adapted to the technological innovations of the 'second industrial revolution' with the Chemical Institutes of Nancy (1890) and Lyons and the Electrical Institute of Grenoble (1892). Even so, as Rondo Cameron has pointed out, the export of technicians was rare after 1870, while the demand for highly qualified personnel was growing in France and in Europe generally.

The main problem was the ossification of the secondary-school system, which, as we have seen, formed the reservoir of the *grandes écoles*. Throughout the century this maintained an elitist character, being confined to a privileged minority. It was expensive, and those with scholarships formed on average only 8 per cent of the total.

Numbers did rise, at a rate of about 1·5 per cent per annum, from 110,000 in 1853 to roughly 190,000 in 1890 – with a rapid increase after 1880, which can be ascribed essentially to the development of *lycées* for girls. If these are excluded together with the primary classes of the secondary schools, which were also flourishing, the progress of secondary education appears much less considerable. The percentage of those at school, taking both sexes and considering them as a fraction of the total population in the age-groups from ten to nineteen, demonstrates that mediocrity even more convincingly: the rate rose from 2·9 per cent in 1898 to 3·8 per cent on the eve of the First World War, having been 1·7 per cent in 1853 and 1·6 per cent in 1815. Boys' *lycées* reached a ceiling of about 90,000 pupils in the 1880s and had less than 100,000 in the 1900s. Many of these pupils never completed their studies, and the science *baccalauréat*, gained by an increasing number of candidates in the first half of the nineteenth century, was awarded at a slower rate after 1850: 2,000 were gained in that year, with no more than 2,200 in 1866, 2,700 in 1876, just over 3,000 in 1880, and perhaps only 2,500 in 1913. The absolute decline in this field explains the lack of promotion in the *grandes écoles* for engineers. The expansion of higher education as such in the Faculties after 1900 was itself followed by stagnation and could not compensate for the drying-up of the traditional channels of training.

Just as illiteracy was being eliminated, attempts to give a professional training to the French labour force as a whole faltered. Worse, in the qualification of higher cadres – a field in which France had excelled for so long – there was now decline. Evidently, rigidity existed in the education system elsewhere than at the primary level. The ruling classes were indifferent to the needs of the economy and failed to understand its dynamic. Moreover, the French economy never really suffered from a shortage of labour. Everything combined to bring about a general downgrading of the French work force at all levels on the eve of the First World War. At the same time a barrier remained between the captains of industry and commerce, well supported by official policy even if their numbers and standards were declining, and the mass of workers, who with very few exceptions began their working lives without training. One cannot but be impressed, with Georges Dupeux, by the extraordinary time-lag between the needs being generated by the process of economic development and the educational response. This portended danger in the falling productivity of French workers in essential sectors, a phenomenon difficult to perceive but suspected by everyone – sensitive contemporaries, contemporary historians, and economists.

III. *The Uncertainty of the Inter-War Period*

A. THE CRISIS OF FRENCH DEMOGRAPHY

The 1914–18 period marked no fundamental change in the long-term trends of birth rate and death rate, but war losses aggravated the problems that had beset France in the nineteenth century and turned them into a demographic crisis. On the eve of 1939, as Jean Giraudoux commented, 'the Frenchman has become a rarity'.

Military losses were in fact considerable, with 1·4 million killed or missing. Civilians suffered less, despite privations behind the front. Only the year 1918 witnessed a sudden rise in the death rate (to 24·6 per thousand) as Spanish influenza swept over an enfeebled population. Much more serious for the demographic balance was the decline in the birth rate. This resulted in the first place from a heavy fall in the number of marriages – 45 per thousand in 1915 as against 149 per thousand in 1913 – and secondly from a decline in fecundity among couples separated by the summons of men to the front. There were no more than 313,000 births in 1916, or 9·5 per thousand, and the 1915 figure (11·6 per thousand) and that for 1917 (10·5 per thousand) were hardly better. It has been calculated that for the whole civilian population of the seventy-seven *départements* not invaded, the excess of 1·3 million deaths between January 1914 and December 1917 amounted to one-thirtieth of the total population. Lastly, losses from the war gravely mortgaged the future, for the fighting decimated those in the child-bearing age-group (29·2 per cent of that of 1914, 27·8 per cent of that of 1915), and the absence of births in the four war years projected another foreseeable decline in the birth rate into the 1930s.

The post-war demographic recovery, a well-known reaction to the end of hostilities, was ephemeral. The upswing in marriages and births exhausted itself, and the birth rate turned down again. By 1921–5 it was below the level of 1906–10, standing at 19·3 per thousand, and falling to 18·2 per thousand between 1926 and 1930, which expressed a new slump in fecundity within marriage. The trough was reached in the years 1929–30, with the advent of the depleted cohorts to marriageable age, reinforced by the Great Depression and the fear of unemployment, which made marriage a less attractive prospect. If one considers the mass of men between eighteen and fifty-nine and women between fifteen and forty-nine – i.e. of marriageable age – the percentage actually married in 1938 was respectively only 79·1 per cent for men and 70·5 per cent for women, as against 87·1 per cent and 79·2 per cent in 1930. The first measures to promote births – whether the law of 31 July 1920, which prohibited birth control propaganda and abortion, or that of 11 March 1932, which made compensation funds compulsory in the various professions – had no demographic effect. In 1938 there were only 612,000 births, corresponding to a gross birth rate of 14·6 per thousand – the lowest in the world.

France also held the record for the most slowly declining death rate after 1920. Between 1926 and 1930 it fell only to 16·8 per thousand, whereas it had stood at 19·1 per thousand between 1906 and 1910; and after the Depression it stagnated until the war, at 15·7 per thousand in 1931–5, despite the more rapid decline in infant mortality (95 per thousand in 1921–5, 66 per thousand in 1938).

Between 1920 and 1930, then, the natural increase in numbers remained at an extremely low level: an average of 84,000 a year in 1921–5, and 58,000 a year in 1926–30. The mere replacement of the population was not assured, with the net rate of reproduction hovering around 92, dropping to 90, and then to 88 on the eve of the Second World War. The deficit reappeared in 1929 (minus 9,000 persons) and became a permanent feature in 1930 and 1935–7. By 1938, therefore, the French population had increased by a mere 5·9 per cent over its 1921 figure – from 39,210,000 to 41,507,000, which was practically the same figure as that for 1911, despite the recovery of Alsace–Lorraine. This overall progression, however, masks an absolute decline just after the economic crisis, for the census of 1931 counted 41,815,000 people. For the first time there was a deficit not only in the natural increase in numbers but in the size of the total population itself. The crisis would appear even greater if no account were taken of immigration, which made an enormous leap in the 1920s and 30s, encouraged by official policy.

B. MASSIVE AND ORGANIZED IMMIGRATION

The general mobilization of French workers and the necessities of total war made necessary a massive influx of foreign labour between 1914 and 1918. After 1915, an Office of Agricultural Labour and the Ministry of Armaments brought in more than 225,000 foreign workers, of whom about 100,000 were Spaniards, 15,000 Portuguese, and 16,000 Greeks. 150,000 were settled on the land; 75,000 went into industry. The European labour reservoir was inadequate, however, so recourse had to be made to exotic immigrants, drawn from the colonial empire and even from China. In three years their numbers were as large as those of the European immigrants (223,000), which included 79,000 Algerians among 132,000 North Africans. At the time of the armistice in November 1918, there were about half a million immigrant workers in France, who made up one-fifth of the labour force in the arms factories.

The return of peace posed the question of the labour force in a new way. The military and civilian losses, the falling birth rate, the application of the Eight Hour Law, voted in 1910 (which created a loss equivalent to 900,000 labour units), shortened the supply at the very moment when the reconstruction of the invaded regions had to take place. Partial measures such as the lengthening of working life, the general (and short-lived) increase in the work-rate, and the mobilization of women could not compensate for a deficit estimated at 3 million individuals. Even more than in the nineteenth century, then, the French economy was in a markedly depressed state. The Agricultural Labour Service (1915) and the Ministry of Labour Foreign Labour Service (1917) continued after the war to develop the necessary immigration. A Labour Council was created in 1920 along with an Inter-ministerial Immigration Commission, which prospected in the European labour markets and signed a series of agreements in the 1920s, particularly with France's client states in central and southern Europe. Departments of state thus backed up such private activities of employers as the Committee of Forges and Mines of the East, and the Committee of Coal Mines, which explored Poland and Westphalia and established veritable recruitment networks there.

This new policy was a success. Between 1921 and 1930 there were 1,915,678 'controlled' immigrants, 1,147,514 going into industry, and 768,000 going into agriculture. The influx was irregular, with low points coinciding with the crisis of 1921 (81,820) and with the monetary stabilization of the Poincaré Ministry in 1927 (64,327), reductions which affected the industrial labour force above all (25,998 went into industry in 1921; 131,013 in 1922). The connection between the economic context and the net balance of arrivals and departures of migrants is even clearer, the latter flow being negative (minus 25,657) in 1927, and positive with record levels in 1923 and 1924, when the number of immigrants reached 271,976 and 263,097 respectively. This type of injection of a labour force to suit demands established a new and exceptional elasticity in the labour market, made economic recovery possible and diminished the risk of unemployment.

Foreign workers and their families, numbering 1,532,000 in 1921 (already an advance of 382,000 on the pre-war years), rose to 2,500,000 in 1926 and to 2,715,000 in 1931. Their percentage of the resident population almost doubled in a decade, from 3·9 per cent in 1921 to 7·5 per cent in 1931. The period of accelerated immigration was mostly between 1921 and 1926, when 1,050,000 arrivals pushed up the immigrant population by 66 per cent (after taking account of naturalizations). France thus became the second-highest population-importing country in the world after the United States, and even here she had the edge in relative terms, gaining 5·12 immigrants per thousand inhabitants as against 4·92 in America. The Great Depression of 1929 precipitated a decline in this influx: in 1936 there were 2,198,000 foreigners in France, 517,000 fewer than at the last census. In fact, one result of the economic slump was discrimination against non-nationals, whose qualifications were very low. But it seems that there were relatively few departures, so that the fall in this number may be attributed largely to naturalization. Just before the Second War, however, when the enforcement of the forty-hour week had contributed to a depression, a new wave of arrivals was swelled by refugees from Nazi Germany and its conquests in Southeast Europe, and then from the defeated Spanish Republic.

If we exclude immigrants who left their countries for political reasons, we can see a radical change in the distribution of immigrants by nationality. Proximity was still an important factor. Between 1920 and 1931 one arrival in three came from across the Alps, and the number of Italians in France rose from 450,960 to 760,116 between 1921 and 1926, though the ratio to the indigenous population remained steady at 30 and 31 per cent respectively, having dropped from the 36 per cent level of 1911. The Belgians were the second-largest national group after the First War with 23 per cent, but only 13 per cent in 1926, declining in absolute terms from 349,000 to 327,000. They were level with the Spaniards – whose proportion fell in the same period from 17 to 13 per cent, despite a numerical increase of 58,000 – and with the Poles. The rising number of Poles was perhaps the most remarkable feature in a picture which showed a relative increase in Slavic and exotic peoples. Between 1920 and 1931, one foreigner in five who moved into France was Polish: in all, 411,600 Poles crossed the frontier in those years. In 1911 they were scarcely 33,000, just 47,000 in 1921 (3 per cent of the foreign population), but 309,000 in 1926 (13 per cent) and 423,000 in 1936 (19 per cent). They now constituted the second-largest national group in France, far ahead of the Spaniards (254,000: 11 per cent) and the Belgians (195,000: 8·9 per cent). They were exceeded only by the Italians, though these had declined in absolute numbers by 721,000, and their proportion of all resident aliens was steady at 32 per cent. Immigration from North Africa was far behind at that time – a modest 3·3 per cent.

Within the country, the rising pressure of foreign workers produced a greater dispersion of settlement geographically, extending far beyond the frontier regions. The majority were still concentrated in these areas, but important nuclei formed in the mining and metallurgical regions of the Centre and West, and in the depopulated agricultural regions of the Southwest, Normandy, Burgundy, and Champagne.

These groups, though embedded in the national life, tended to preserve their cultural originality, and this resistance to assimilation provoked a certain xenophobia, which flourished on myths of criminality, lack of hygiene, and political subversiveness – prejudices that were reflected in G. Mauco's *Les Etrangers en France*, which appeared in 1932. This resentment was less a characteristic of the industrial working classes, who did not contest the laborious jobs taken up by the immigrants, than of the tertiary sector – whether commercial employees (28 per cent of waiters were foreign in 1928) or of the liberal professions, in which the number of foreigners increased especially after 1937, in the era of political and racial persecution.

C. CHANGES IN THE ACTIVE POPULATION

The age pyramid of 1921 illustrates the threats overshadowing the French labour force. Unlike the profile in the nineteenth century, it has two kinks, which were to deepen progressively and still appear marked in 1936. The first is in the age-groups from twenty to thirty-nine years, representing the wartime losses uncompensated by immigration. The most productive age-groups had been hit to the extent of 100 in every thousand active males. In this respect, France was the most seriously affected of all the European nations, with the one exception of Rumania. The second kink in the curve is at the base of the pyramid affecting both sexes, created by the absence of births in the war years. This was to compromise the renewal of the active population for the future, especially as the disappearance of young men at the age of maximum fertility made it difficult to envisage any compensation. The effects that this had on the birth rate have been considered. In addition, the presence of over a million war wounded meant the lowering of the work efficiency of a large number of survivors.

The full effects on the potential active population, between fifteen and sixty-nine years of age, were not evident at once. For though the lower age-groups were thinned out, they continued to increase gradually, following the trend of the nineteenth century. The 1936 figure of 28,549,000 people was an advance of 2·4 per cent or 671,000 people on 1921 – a comparison with 1911 would be misleading because of the recovery of Alsace–Lorraine in the meantime. Yet in the same period (1921–36) the total population increased by 6·1 per cent, so that, while the potential active population rose from 71·6 to 71·9 per cent of the total between 1921 and 1926, it declined between 1931 and 1936 from 71·3 to 69·2 per cent, and if only the most productive age groups, between twenty and sixty-four, are considered, there was an absolute decline of 180,000 between the last two censuses.

To a great extent, this decline explains the decline in the active population itself, though this was accentuated by the Great Depression and its long-term effects. The development may be summed up in Table 68 (drawn from Alfred Sauvy). The rise in the active population in the immediate post-war period was linked to the need for higher

Table 68. *Active Population, 1911–36*

	Total active population (thousands)	Active population as proportion of total population (per cent)	
		Men	Both sexes
1911	—	68·6	53·4
1921	20,757	71·1	56
1931	21,091	68·9	52·4
1936	19,874	65·4	49·2

productivity and the campaign of national defence. But the decline set in early, to a point which was lower even than the 1911 figure, and this was exacerbated by the crisis of the 1930s. The explanation can be found in a contraction of the active population at both its upper and lower extremes of age: various social welfare measures, such as pensions, encouraged workers to retire sooner, while the development of education delayed the young in taking up employment. In the 1930s this trend was to get worse, as unemployment and the absence of occupational outlets encouraged students to prolong their studies.

The proportion of under-twenties in the active population fell from 15·4 per cent in 1911 to 15·1 per cent in 1926 and 10·2 per cent in 1936. On the eve of the Second World War, fewer than 62 per cent of young men between the ages of fifteen and nineteen were working, as against 70 per cent some twenty years earlier. For those under fifteen, the proportion fell from 54 per cent to 34·5 per cent between 1926 and 1936. In the same period, however, the proportion of adults in work declined only from 90·7 per cent to 87·7 per cent. The overall distribution by sexes stayed more or less constant, men and women suffering in equal proportions the effects of the economic situation. The parallel decline in their activity emerges from Table 69.

Table 69. *Rate of Employment (per thousand persons), 1921–36*

	Men	Women
1921	711	423
1926	702	375
1931	689	371
1936	654	342

It is within this general framework that an important redistribution was taking place between the sectors, as shown in Table 70. The great new development was obviously the more rapid decline in agricultural activities. For the first time there was an absolute decline in the number of peasants, from 9,014,000 in 1921 to 7,694,000 in 1931 and 7,171,000 in 1936. Never had the rural exodus reached the level that it did between

Table 70. *Sectoral Distribution of the Active Population of Both Sexes*
(per cent), 1921–36

	Primary	Secondary	Tertiary
1921	43	29	28
1931	37	33	30
1936	37	30	33

the end of the First War and the Great Depression. In this decade the proportion of the rural population fell from 53·7 per cent to 48·8 per cent, and this was more significant than the decline in the nineteenth century, with the disappearance of industries dispersed in the countryside. Migration from the countryside affected 290,000 people a year, and though the crisis of the 1930s marginally checked this development, trimming the rate to 200,000 a year, it certainly did not interrupt it.

Table 71. *Workers in Main Sectors of Industrial Activity (thousands*
and as percentages of the whole), 1921–36

	1921		1931		1936	
	thousands	per cent	thousands	per cent	thousands	per cent
Extractive/energy	404	6·3	565	7·8	462	7·5
Metallurgical	1,369	21·5	1,641	22·8	1,408	22·8
Textile	2,190	34·4	2,140	29·7	1,766	28·6
Chemical	166	2·6	214	3	184	3
Building	837	13·1	1,091	15·2	871	14·1
Timber	649	10·2	649	8·5	525	9
Food-processing	508	8	584	8·1	587	9·5

The industrial sector gained, but what is striking was its relative stability in the medium term. In fact, the trend (when analysed more precisely) reflects a speeding-up of changes already outlined for the nineteenth century and the continuing importance of a certain tradition. For employment in the main sectors, the figures are presented in Table 71 (after J. C. Toutain). Textiles declined steadily, in both absolute and relative terms, continuing a trend which had set in before the war. These industries still employed three workers in ten, but the Depression did not reverse the trend but rather accelerated the decline. The metallurgical industries were different, expanding in numbers but remaining steady in percentage terms, though far above the 1911 figure of 15·2 per cent. These two examples illustrate both the genuine structural changes in industry and the sluggishness induced by the Depression. The development of the timber industries, which were giving way in numbers and in ranking, was characteristic of a traditional sector, and yet it employed three times as many then as did the chemical industries, which, though they had doubled since 1906, employed less than 200,000 men in 1936.

The transfers of labour among the various branches of industry were complex. It is probable, if not certain, that it was immigrant labour which supplied most of the needs of the most modern and dynamic sectors. Certainly there were few foreigners in the traditional activities – fewer than 5 per cent in textiles and clothing, with the exception of the Lille conglomeration. But in the Lyons region, 69 per cent of the workers in the main artificial silk factories, where production was booming, were immigrants around 1927. There were only 16 per cent of foreigners in the traditional chemical industries, but in the Alps, where electrotechnical industries established before 1914 had radically changed the geography of settlement, foreigners made up 56 per cent of the chemical workers, and 45 per cent of those in metallurgy, with a peak of 65 per cent in the factories of the Haute-Maurienne. Saint-Alban, the great aluminium complex in the Hautes-Alpes, employed as many as fifteen nationalities, while Ugine, in Savoy, was a true racial mosaic.

Besides this, strong contingents of immigrants were found in the most arduous jobs – much more than before 1914. An inquiry by poll in 1927 showed that they constituted a third of the building workers, 22 per cent of the glass workers, 33 per cent of the workers in iron and steel, and up to 42 per cent of the workers in some of the large factories near the frontier, like those of Wendel at Joeuf and Hagondange. In the iron basin of Briey and de Longwy, they provided 79 to 81 per cent of the labour force, while in the coal pits two in every five miners were foreign, and one in four was Polish.

Immigrants helped to guarantee the socio-professional promotion of Frenchmen, who could move directly into the tertiary sector, which had higher status than the industrial sector. The industrial sector achieved an absolute peak in 1931, with 7,192,000 workers, an advance of 821,000 on 1921 and of 969,000 on 1911; but this primacy was lost by 1936, with the total falling to 6,181,000. A consequence of the crisis, without question, was that while the industrial sector lost three percentage points, agriculture stayed level in the same period (1931–6), and those gains were picked up by the services sector, which expanded without interruption from 5,174,000 in 1926 to 6,876,000 in 1936. Excepting domestic servants, who were growing scarcer, and transport workers, whose numbers stayed constant while their proportions declined, all parts of the tertiary sector developed at roughly the same pace. In general, this meant a rise in the numbers of women employed in services, from 39·3 per cent to 39·7 per cent between 1931 and 1936, while between 1921 and 1936 their numbers in industry fell from 32 per cent to 27·7 per cent.

D. THE PROBLEM OF PROFESSIONAL TRAINING

Primary education was definitively organized at the end of the nineteenth century and thereafter underwent no major change, apart from the raising of the school-leaving age from thirteen to fourteen, in the summer of 1936, by the Popular Front minister Jean Zay. Once saturation point had been reached, which happened early, the fluctuation of overall numbers was not of great significance. Ups and downs in the short term reflected – with a delay of a few years – the changing birth rate the 'hollow ranks' of the years 1914–18, and then, after a recovery, the long-term decline. Much more important was the falling rate of school attendance of children between the ages of five and fourteen, which stood at 73 per cent after the armistice and at 77 per cent in 1936 – a clear retreat on the pre-1914 levels, as if the problems wrought by the war and its aftermath, political instability, and an economy of more or less latent stagnation after 1930 were responsible.

The growth of illiteracy among conscripts was also marked: 94 per thousand of them could not write in 1926 (as many as in 1891) and 62 per thousand in 1931 (which was more than in 1911). This growth must have been reinforced, for the whole population at all ages, by the proportion of immigrants now a part of the national labour force. All in all, foreigners accounted for about 16 per cent of illiterates in France. This is demonstrated by Table 72 (after a table drawn up by Henri Ulmer in 1931). By integrating all the generations, these figures show

Table 72. *Illiterates over Ten Years Old, as a Proportion of the Population (per thousand), 1931*

	Men	Women
French	37	52
Naturalized	74	100
Foreigners	162	163
Combined	48	57

the persistence of the trend towards the elimination of illiteracy among French nationals, because before the 1914 war the proportion of illiterates was 94 per thousand men and 139 per thousand women. But this trend was much less evident in the case of foreigners, whose pre-war illiteracy rates were 183 and 208 for men and women respectively; the decline in illiteracy among foreign males was particularly slow. The recent falling-off in the school population had hardly any effect on the cumulative mass of the literate generations, but there was neverthe-less a worrying reversal of the trend and a threat, in the long term, of a fundamental fall in the qualifications of the work force.

Secondary and higher education presented quite a different picture, but their expansion was still conditioned by the frailty of the primary-education system. The finance law of 1928 made education free from the *sixième* (age eleven) to the *troisième* (age 14–15), and this principle was extended in 1930 to *lycée* and college classes at all levels. The com-petitive examination for scholarships was unified and reorganized in 1927, and the examination to enter secondary education (class 6) was created in 1934. The number of pupils rose from 260,000 in 1920–1 to 469,000 in 1935–6, and the school-going population (between fourteen and nineteen years) more than doubled, from 3·8 per cent of their age-group to 8·1 per cent. Taking into account the Higher Primary Schools and the complementary courses, which had tripled in size, it may be calculated that 714,000 adolescents pursued a general education beyond the minimum school-leaving age, as against fewer than 400,000 just after the First World War. Qualifications still have to be made, for most of those at *lycées* and colleges never completed their seven years of secondary studies. In 1935–6, 12,299 *baccalauréats* were awarded, only 21 per cent more than in 1920–1 (10,144). In higher education, the number of students almost doubled – from 36,000 to 63,000, i.e. from 0·66 per cent to 1·21 per cent of young people between the ages of fifteen and twenty-four – yet there also the level remained low. The *grandes écoles* were still playing their essential part in training the higher staff of the economy, but if the seven principal ones – including the Polytechnique, the Ecole Centrale, the INA, and the School of Mines – are considered, graduations were decreasing in number. In 1936 they produced 5,800 engineers, as against 6,300 in 1920. There is also the impression of stagnation in the national professional schools and in the Ecoles d'Arts et Métiers, which offered 8,500 and 1,600 places respectively in 1937–8.

In the field of technical education, the ECPI continued to expand steadily, but the complexity of the system makes exact measurement impossible. According to J. P. Guinot, the number of pupils rose from 18,000 to about 46,000 between 1919 and 1938, with a marked increase in technical education for girls: they made up about a quarter of the total on the eve of the Second War. According to A. Prost, who included other establishments of the same kind and status, numbers rose from 15,000 to 56,000. More and more they afforded a general preparation, moving closer to the conventional secondary system, a trend confirmed by the creation in 1920 of an Under-Secretariat of Technical Education, which split this field off from the Ministry of Commerce to attach it to the Ministry of Public Instruction.

The inadequacy of the professional training of the mass of workers has been pointed out for the period before 1914. The spate of government initiatives in the inter-war years revealed at once the pressure of necessity and an increasing awareness of it. Here again, the presence of an immigrant labour force underscored the issue, for while the introduction of specialists in the 1920s, notably thousands of metalworkers from Central Europe, demonstrated the inadequate numbers of French nationals, the arrival of a mass of totally unskilled labourers made training an absolute priority. For among the Mediterranean and Slavic peoples who made up the bulk of the immigrants, it was estimated that only one in four had a minimum of technical instruction, and improving upon the latter was a precondition of reducing instability in business and the professions, and in the settlement of immigrants.

It was largely in answer to problems outstanding in the 1900s that the Astier law sought to reorganize professional training as a whole and to make it a responsibility of the state. The scheme emerged directly from discussions of the Higher Council of Labour in 1901–2, taking shape in 1905, presented as a bill in 1913, to be voted only on 25 July 1919, at a particularly propitious time, when there was a general scarcity of labour in the months after the armistice. Aware of the inadequacy (or absence) of training on the job, the law made post-school education compulsory up to eighteen years of age. Municipalities were required to open free professional courses, and each adolescent was to receive four hours' teaching a week – a hundred hours a year – in order to gain the Certificate of Professional Aptitude (CAP), which was created in 1911. This was the legal framework which had to be realized in practice.

This was to take place first of all in 'trade schools' set up by the Chambers of Commerce and various professional associations. The city of Paris made a substantial effort to the extent of recruiting 2,500 in 1935. The second focus was to be 'professional courses', organized since the nineteenth century by corporate groups and local organizations. These were in the lead by a long way, absorbing about half the government subsidies in 1938–9, while 20 per cent went to the employers' organizations, 8 per cent to the workers' unions, and the rest to

private institutions. This type of education seemed to answer fairly well
to practical needs: without sacrificing general instruction completely –
though this took up less room – it mixed theoretical formation and
workshop practice in about equal proportions.

Yet it did not solve the seemingly eternal problem of apprenticeship,
present at least since 1840 and coming periodically to the front of the
stage. It was not that successive governments took refuge in immobility. The Finance Law of 1875 was a significant step in the quest
for a solution. It laid an apprenticeship tax of 0·2 per cent on the wages
paid by businesses, from which there was no dispensation unless they
took the organization of apprenticeship in hand themselves. The
encouragement was twofold, for it provided the Treasury with new
resources while creating an incentive to employers to avoid payment.
At the same time, apprenticeship was to be surveyed by the Chambers
of Trade (26 July 1925), which were to regulate and enforce contracts.
Various measures intervened subsequently to perfect the system,
notably in 1928, when the written contract became compulsory and
businesses were required to provide a professional education for their
workers outside the factory as well as within it. It seems, however, that
these measures settled nothing. Numbers attending professional courses
of all types levelled out in 1927–32 at between 165,000 and 170,000
pupils, slumped after the crisis to 133,000, and climbed back with
difficulty to a little more than 160,000 in 1934–5. This was a long way
from the rapid and massive development that might have been
expected. And as with the other sorts of education, wastage was considerable. The number of CAPs rose from fewer than 5,500 per annum
in 1927–8 to an approximate average of 4,000 between 1931 and 1935,
but this bore no relation to the total number of apprentices.

The aftermath of the Great Depression demonstrated the persisting
inadequacy of professional training. A paradoxical situation was present
with the coexistence of widespread unemployment and a shortage of
skilled labour. The technical deficiencies of the majority of the unemployed prevented their transfer to sectors which were demanding
labour and made desperately obvious the rigidity of the labour market,
which seemed to have escaped the notice of observers in the relative
prosperity of the preceding decade. The failings of the Astier law, whose
wide rulings were backed up by unconvincing sanctions, became apparent. Employers dug themselves in, refusing to organize even the practical part of apprenticeship at the factory, while the psychological
effects of the tax – far from what was anticipated – meant that it became
a quick way of evading any obligations to encourage apprenticeship.
Lastly, attendance at professional courses met the same resistances as had
existed for the whole of the nineteenth century: six times out of ten,

they took place after the working day, and in only one case in ten did they encroach upon working time itself.

The problem worsened after 1937, with economic recovery supported, especially in the metallurgical industry, by the policy of rearmament. Numbers at the various professional courses leapt to 208,000 in 1938. A project of 1935 to re-educate the employed adult was resumed and gave rise to ten regional centres in 1937. But again the evasions of employers matched their protests, and only a few thousand individuals were trained. It took the exigencies of national defence to secure the decree of 21 September 1939 which installed a series of centres of professional training for both adults and adolescents whose technical expertise was insufficient, and the Walter and Paulin law of 10 March 1937 which extended apprenticeship requirements to workshops. The decree/law of 24 May 1938 took up a few previous clauses, making theoretical professional education compulsory for all adolescents between fourteen and seventeen, and required that businesses with fewer than five workers which were not affiliated to a Chamber of Trades take on a certain number of apprentices. A general law like the Astier law demonstrated both the persistence of efforts to overcome the problem and the persistence of the problem itself.

IV. A New France: A Late Entry into the Industrial Era

A. THE REORGANIZATION OF THE LABOUR FORCE

(1) The Situation at the End of the War

The impact of the Second World War on the French population was slight, if we compare it with that of the First War. Military losses were small, no more than 200,000 men being killed or missing in combat; civilian losses, on the other hand, rose to 400,000. Altogether, however, losses did not exceed 600,000, though to this must be added 320,000 foreigners returning to their own countries and Frenchmen settled elsewhere.

It is true that these losses meant a rise in the gross death rate, from 15·5 per thousand in 1939 to 18·3 per thousand in 1940 and 17·6 per thousand in 1944. Above all, the old scourge of infant mortality, which had dropped to 65 per thousand in 1936–9, returned with all its former savagery, not falling beneath 70 per thousand and pushed up to peaks of 90 per thousand in 1940 and 105 per thousand in 1945, as a result of summer diarrhoea, which had been absent since 1930. The prolonged captivity of a million prisoners in Germany, together with the arrival at marriageable age of some of those sparse generations of the 1914–18 period, cut back the number of marriages considerably, from 274,000 in 1938 to 170,000 (in eighty-seven *départements*) in 1940 and 199,000 in 1944. The total deficit was about 1·5 million people. At the end of the war, the census of 1946 revealed a population of 40,503,000 inhabitants, slightly below that of 1901, and the lowest density in Europe with the exception of Spain. At the same time, the population had aged. Those over sixty-nine years old now constituted nearly 11 per cent of the total, compared with 9·8 per cent in 1936; and children under fifteen were 21·8 per cent as against 24·7 per cent.

Just at this point, when the task of reconstruction was enormous, a rapid fall in the potential active population along with an increase in the burden of the unproductive element could be predicted. But one totally new factor, masked by the fall in the absolute number of births in the first years of the war, was to make predictions for the future uncertain: that was the reversal of the trend of declining fecundity. For, despite the storms weathered by nuptiality, and the arrival of the 'hollow ranks' of the First War at the age of greatest fertility, there was a rapid recovery in the number of births after 1942, and the average of the years 1943–4 (630,000, as against 530,000 in 1940–1) was about 15,000 higher than the pre-war average. Between 1940 and 1944, 590,000 children a year were born; if behaviour patterns had been the same as in 1914–18, there would have been only 410,000 births. This was the result of a clear rise in fertility among non-separated couples, the sign of a deep psychological change in attitudes to life, coming in the immediate post-war era, and was assisted by the demographic policy of the state. The decree/laws of 1938 extended family allowances to new categories of people and scaled them up. The family code of 29 July 1939 gave them to all wage-earners after the second child and completed several other partial measures. The creation of a Ministry of the Family in June 1940 testified to a growing awareness of the French demographic problem and the will to set it right, following as it did the establishment of a High Consultative Committee on the population in 1939. For the moment, the consequences passed unnoticed, but they would soon become fully apparent.

The restored Republic did not change direction, founding a Ministry of Public Health and Population in 1946, starting pre-natal allowances, and indirectly encouraging births by taking the size of the family into account in assessing income tax. At the same time the return of peace brought the usual burst of marriages (376,000 in 1945, 517,000 in 1946) and of births (840,000 in 1946). The return to normal conditions was to prove that it was not just a temporary expansion, but for the time being recourse had to be made to other reservoirs to re-establish the work force.

(2) *The Continued Need for Immigration*

France was suffering from a tragic shortage of labour after the liberation, made worse by the repatriation of 500,000 German prisoners, together with Czech and above all Polish workers reclaimed by their respective governments. To reconstruct the national economy, to equalize the burdens falling on an aged population, and to guarantee the growth of basic sectors like agriculture, mining, iron, and steel, Alfred Sauvy preached the necessity of large-scale immigration, which he wished to see at not less than 5·3 million people. It was not merely fortuitous that his article appeared in the first number of *Population*, a journal which symbolized the nation's realization of her demographic problems. Government circles echoed the opinion, talking of 4 million, and set up an Interministerial Commission on Immigration in November 1945, responsible for drawing up the plan. On 30 March 1946 a National Office of Immigration (ONI) was created to execute it and began prospecting the labour markets. After a number of partial measures, an agreement was signed with Italy (30 November 1946) and then with the British and American authorities of occupied Germany (15 December 1947 and 1 February 1948). In the interim, a clandestine immigration – for the most part from across the Alps, as always – was allowed to develop.

The statistics of the ONI make it possible to follow the rhythm of arrivals, but only roughly, because some few escaped its attention. Until 1950, despite official intentions, policy remained timid, for fear of a resurgence of unemployment among French nationals. Between 1946 and 1950, only 214,715 immigrants were registered, and although to this must be added about a hundred thousand Algerians – then considered French – and clandestine arrivals, things were a long way from the original forecasts. Then in the middle of 1947, after the most feverish period of reconstruction, a certain saturation of the French labour market set in. The general slowing-down of activity continued until the summer of 1950. The working week shortened, and the unions feared too great a flexibility in the offer of jobs. After a recovery from the summer of 1950 until the end of 1952, there was a new restriction of immigrants under Pinay. Between 1950 and 1955, the ONI registered only 110,851 permanent arrivals – about 18,500 a year, still far below the annual contingent of 100,000 in terms of which Sauvy was thinking. The increase during the years 1946–9 – 53,500 arrivals a year, or 214,175 altogether – began to look unrepresentative, the result of the exceptional needs of reconstruction.

A new period opened in 1955–6, with a rapid increase in immigration, made all the more decisive by the restrictive policy of previous years. The increase continued until 1964, checked only in 1959–60, which reflected the financial retrenchment of the time. A first peak came in 1956, explained by the effects of the revolt in Algeria upon the domestic labour force, before the high point of 1964, when 153,731 foreigners came into France to seek permanent work; the annual average rose to nearly 90,500 between 1956 and 1964. After that, despite an average figure of 130,000 until 1967, the curve turned downwards. The arrival of seasonal workers also increased after 1946, the regularity being explained by an agricultural demand which was less tied to the fluctuations of the economy and was stepped up by the rural exodus and the expansion of new types of cultivation, such as rice in the Carmargue, which were hungry for labour. The annual average rose from 18,200 between 1946 and 1949 to 104,600 between 1960 and 1964. Altogether in the period 1946–64 the ONI brought into France 1,139,093 permanent immigrants and 1,003,616 seasonal ones.

To these foreigners must be added the Algerians, who were counted as indigenous labour until 1962. Making allowances for those who returned, a net figure of 456,000 individuals may be calculated for 1946–64. The decolonization of North Africa brought about a repatriation of about 450,000 from Algeria and Morocco between 1954 and 1961, and 600,000 'pieds noirs' in 1962. It was their arrival which pushed the number of immigrants up to a record of over 860,000. Finally, in the last few years, immigrants from the overseas *départements* (DOM – Martinique, Guadaloupe) and the overseas territories (TOM) have multiplied. The net figure for immigrants since the end of the war, according to B. Granotier, would thus stand at 3,177,000. The census of 1968 revealed 2,664,000 foreigners on French soil, and to this must be added 200,000 from the DOM and TOM, and Algerian Muslims who opted for French nationality after the independence of their country. Against 1,744,000 immigrants in 1946, 1,755,000 in 1954, and 1,815,000 in 1962, the number of naturalized Frenchmen rose at the same dates from 853,000 to 1,068,000 and 1,266,700.

The main reservoir until 1956 was Italy, providing 66 per cent of the permanent immigrant arrivals counted by the ONI between 1946 and 1951 and 78 per cent of those between 1952 and 1956, when a maximum of 80 per cent was reached. For the first ten years after the liberation, one foreign worker in three was of Transalpine origin (28·9 per cent in 1946 and in 1956). After 1957, however, the economic development of Italy herself restricted this flow. In 1958 Italians made up only 48 per cent of the arrivals, and in 1968 there was only one Italian in every five foreigners (22·72 per cent). Leaving aside the ever-increasing number of North Africans, especially from Algeria, the lead was taken at first by the Spaniards (13 per cent of permanent immigrants in 1956, 33 per cent in 1959) and then by the Portuguese, whose proportion rose from 2 per cent to 7·5 per cent, and whose numbers rose sixfold between 1961 (6,716) and 1964 (43,751). Comparing the results of the Censuses of 1962 and 1968 throws light on these changes (Table 73).

Table 73. *Permanent Foreign Workers: Nationalities as Percentages of the Total, 1962 and 1968*

	Actively employed		With family	
	1962	1968	1962	1968
Italians	27·42	20·8	28·90	22·72
Spaniards	20·41	22·80	20·41	22·80
Portuguese	2·73	2·73	14·50	14·50
Algerians	20·22	24·0	16·15	22·88

In 1968, the Italian, Spanish, and Algerian national groups were roughly the same numerically. Algerians made up a greater percentage of the active population than they did of all foreigners together, for there were more males and bachelors among them, while the Italian proportion was lower because they had been in France longer or had come with their families. Altogether, the Mediterranean countries provided the vast majority of immigrants, especially if one counts Moroccans and Tunisians (5·75 per cent in 1968) – the Mediterranean accounted for eight immigrants in ten. The geography of labour reservoirs had changed completely since the inter-war days: traditional classes of immigrants were becoming rare. The Poles, above all, who had played a fundamental part in supplementing the labour force between the wars, had been thinned out by departures and naturalizations: having made up nearly a quarter of the foreign labour force in 1946 (24·2 per cent), they were down to 8·16 per cent in 1962 and 5·09 per cent in 1968. The overall qualifications of these workers were extremely low, quite apart from the linguistic handicap and frequent illiteracy. Between 1960 and 1967, 57 per cent of the new arrivals were unskilled labourers, and 31 per cent were mechanics and specialized labourers, while only 9·5 per cent had a genuine professional qualification. Of the Algerians, according to an inquiry of 1952, 4·3 per cent were in the last category and 72 per cent in the first.

In the post-war years these workers were moved towards those sectors whose recovery was a precondition of renewed growth. Between 1946 and 1951 agriculture absorbed 29 per cent of the foreign labour force (not counting seasonal workers), building and public works 14 per cent, iron and steel 10 per cent, and the mines 10 per cent. It was the immigrant workers who were largely responsible for winning the battle of coal, for coal-mining claimed 90 per cent of new arrivals between 1946 and 1949. This industry employed only 5·4 per cent of all foreign workers in 1962 and only 1·7 per cent in 1968; likewise, agriculture was employing only 13·77 per cent of foreign labourers in 1968. To a large extent this reflects the changing structure of the French economy, in which coal was becoming less important and agriculture more mechanized. It was the building industry which employed the largest contingent of immigrants, despite a temporary decline in 1959–60. The census of 1968 showed that it occupied 34·3 per cent of foreigners, as against 32·5 per cent in 1962 – more than one in three. The iron and steel industry was still employing about 10·4 per cent of foreign workers, and domestic services 12·39 per cent. Frenchmen from overseas – West Indians and those from Réunion – tended to monopolize the poorly qualified jobs in the public services, for example as railway staff and hospital porters. Immigrants were important in the tertiary sector as well as in industry. Their geographical distribution reflects these occupational preferences. 54·7 per cent of them (and 72·9 per cent of Algerians) were concentrated in the four great industrial regions – the North, Lorraine, Rhône–Alpes, and the Paris region, the last employing more than one in four (27·5 per cent) and four active Algerians in ten (41·6 per cent).

Even more than before 1939, immigrants did those jobs which were despised by the national labour force, which was more and more demanding about conditions of work. Indirectly, this fact guaranteed the socio-professional promotion of Frenchmen and of the immigrants who had arrived earliest. It is instructive, for example, to trace the decreasing proportion of Italians in building and public works, from 85–93 per cent in 1950–6 to only 53 per cent in 1960. In the opinion of B. Granotier, immigrants were the new reserve army in the post-Keynesian economy of full employment, in which unemployment was rarely over 2 or 3 per cent. At the same time, foreign labour allowed France to survive the critical phase of demographic renewal, and to sustain a transformation – until then unknown – of the active population.

(3) The Renewal of the French Population

The new attitude to life of French people, which had begun under the Occupation, continued in the post-war years. The rise in fertility was still the essential factor, with the gross birth rate remaining high at 21 per thousand between 1946 and 1950, 19 per thousand in 1951–5, and 18·2 per thousand in 1956–60. The concrete results were an annual average number of 828,000 births, with a maximum of 860,000. It was a return to the level of the 1920, but now all social milieus were affected. The change coming to the industrial regions was particularly important, above all in the towns, which for so long had proved malthusian traps. For every hundred couples married after 1945 there were 235 to 240 children, as against 198 around 1925. The explanation of this reversal is no doubt complex. Not only were material factors important – such as full employment and the establishment of a social security system which guarded against ill health and accident – but even such psychological reasons, hardly explored till now, as the new value set on marriage by 'Women's Liberation' and the rediscovery of the family as the basic unit of leisure.

The death rate declined in part for much the same reasons, and it declined faster than in most industrialized European countries. The gross death rate of 13 per thousand in 1946–50 dropped to 11·6 per thousand in 1956–60 and to around 11 per thousand after 1968. The decline in infant mortality, an area where France had long been backward, was largely responsible. Only 17 children died for every thousand births in 1967, as against 63 in 1946–50, 71 on the eve of the war, and 82 in 1931–2. Life expectancy increased by six years for men and eight for women between 1946–9 and 1966, passing respectively from 61·9 to 68·2 years and from 67·4 to 75·4 years (the increases compared with the year 1939 were 12·3 and 13·8 years). As far as the birth rate was concerned, the French population had returned by and large to the behaviour patterns of the 1920s. It remained largely malthusian, and there is evidence of a return to the limitation of births by contraceptive methods: in 1968 the gross birth rate fell to 16 per thousand, while the death rate remained more or less stationary. Nevertheless, the natural surpluses were positive, and greatly so, after 1946. The annual maxima of the Second Empire were not recovered, but at that time only 650,000 children survived to twenty years of age; after 1946, for 800,000 born a year, 770,000 survived. If France gained nearly ten million inhabitants between 1946 and 1969 – that is to say, as many as she gained between 1801 and 1946, and twice as many as between 1851 and 1946, for after the war the population grew from 40,503,000 to 49,800,000 – it was above all because of the recurrence and expansion of the natural surplus.

Yet it would be false to think that the potential labour force multiplied as well. The 'bulge' of the generations born after 1945 did not arrive on the labour market until after 1962. In fact the population of working age (between fifteen and sixty-nine) fell from 71·6 per cent of the total in 1946 – which was the same as that of 1921 – to 68·7 per cent in 1951, the same level as in 1891, according to J. C. Toutain. This broad definition of fifty-five years of active life is interesting, as it makes possible a comparison with the nineteenth century, when it was more or less the reality; but one would be closer to the present-day state of affairs in taking only the age-groups between twenty and sixty-five, which corresponds to the development of universal schooling and retirement. A better measure of the situation for the post-war period, made possible by the calculations of M. Parodi, is therefore as shown in Table 74. This shows the increasing proportion both of children and

Table 74. *Age Distribution of the Total Population (per cent), 1946–65*

	Under 20	20–64	65 and over
1946	29·5	59·4	11·1
1954	30·7	57·8	11·4
1965	33·9	54·1	12·0

adolescents and of the elderly – for the most part unproductive – and the relative decline in the population of working age. Reckoned against a base of 100 in 1946, the active population increased to 104 in 1954, 107 in 1962, and 112 in 1968, while in the same period the total population of France increased to 107, 116, and 124 – twice as fast a progression. In retrospect, one must appreciate the perception of Alfred Sauvy, that it was immigration – at least in part, for there were factors other than those relating to the sheer numbers of men – which satisfied the need for labour during the difficult period of the renewal of the French population. In 1962, for example, 67 per cent of the foreigners in France were between twenty and sixty-four years old, as against 55 per cent of Frenchmen.

B. THE POPULATION OF AN INDUSTRIALIZED COUNTRY

The background is provided by a lag between those in active employment and the potential labour force. There was, indeed, an increase of 702,000 workers between 1946 and 1968, and the active labour force rose in twenty-two years from 19·3 million to 20 million people. But this was a phenomenon of the 1960s alone, for there was a decline in the working population from the war until 1954 (18,950,000 people), which was not recovered by 1962 (19,056,000). The advent of 950,000 new workers between 1962 and 1968 was thus in part a catching-up process, and though it was a percentage increase of 4·8, the lag remained because if it had followed the demographic evolution it would have been 7·8 per cent. Taking the index on a base of 100 in 1946, we have 98 for 1954, 99 for 1962, and 104 for 1968. Alfred Nizard has summed up the disparity for the period 1946–68 as follows:

rate of increase of total population: +24 per cent
rate of increase of potential active population (20 to 64 years): +12 per cent
rate of increase of employed active population: +4 per cent

Finally, the development of the 1960s seems exceptional – even accidental – as a result of the repatriation of Frenchmen from North Africa. The arrival of the post-1945 'bulge' would only have moderated a trend, not broken it.

One of the fundamental reasons for the declining working population was obviously the new age structure of the French population. But the difference between the development of the potential labour force and the number actively employed proves that there is another factor. In the first place, there was the longer time spent in institutions of education. This was all the more evident after the war. For in the period 1936–46 the proportion of youths between fifteen and twenty in active employment had risen from 62 per cent to 67 per cent, reaching 13·2 per cent of the total active population (an increase of 3 per cent). After the war, these rates of economic activity, taken up to twenty-five years of age – for the development of higher education made the twenty-year dividing-line irrelevant – moved in the opposite direction to the rates of school attendance, which (as we shall see) increased rapidly. A second factor was the generalization of retirement. This can best be demonstrated not by age-group percentages but by a synthesis of these two trends, illustrating the decline in the average active life as shown in Table 75 (after A. Nizard).

Table 75. *Mean Active Life (in years), 1954–68*

	Men	Women
1954	43	25·0
1962	41·7	21·8
1968	39·5	21·6

Table 76. *Employed Population (number of persons, and indexes on base 1946 = 100), 1946–68*

	Men		Women	
	Thousands	Index	Thousands	Index
1946	12,405	100	6,895	100
1954	12,412	100	6,535	95
1962	12,478	101	6,578	95
1968	13,078	105	6,954	100

An analysis of the development by sexes (Table 76) shows another big change: the decline in female labour. For, despite exceptional circumstances, the number of women in work in 1968 was scarcely higher than in 1946, after fifteen years of marked fall. For the age-group between twenty and sixty-four, 445 women per thousand were working

after the war, only 438 in 1962, and 454 in 1968. This was an unexpected trend since it is certain that after 1954 jobs for women multiplied, essentially in the service sector. The explanation appears to be
that until 1962 the enrolment of women in other sectors was unable to
balance the effects of the rural exodus and the decline in rural employment. The levelling-out of that migration explains, in part, the rising
employment of women since 1962.

Here we touch on the second characteristic failure of the post-war
economy, the collapse of the pre-eminence of agriculture. Between
1946 and 1968 its labour force fell by half, from 6·2 million to 3·1
million – the fall was 56 per cent in the case of men and 47 per cent in
the case of women. The war had largely checked the rural exodus and
the desertion of the fields, but the return of peace released both these
forces again. In 1975 there were only four people engaged in agriculture for every twenty-five industrial workers, whereas a quarter of a
century ago the balance was more than one to three. The changing
balance of the three major sectors is recorded in Table 77.

Table 77. *Sectoral Distribution of the Active Population (per cent),*
1946–68

	Primary	Secondary	Tertiary
1946	36·46	29·26	34·28
1954	27·69	36·37	35·94
1962	20·60	39·07	40·33
1968	15·62	40·21	44·17

Industry has been growing at a much faster rate than before the war.
Within this general pattern, the population working in mines and
quarries fell from an index of 100 in 1946 to 64 in 1968, because of the
progressive closure of pits. But the index for the building industry
rose from 100 to 192, with a tendency to accelerate. Rates were more
modest in manufacturing industries, from 100 to 118 when considered
together, with a certain slowing-down since 1962 (numbers increased
6·1 per cent in 1954–62, and only 3·4 per cent in 1962–8). A closer look
shows that this was largely because the leading sectors here – engineering, chemicals, and electrical constructions – augmented their manpower in those two periods by 25 per cent and 8 per cent respectively.
The main growth, then, came in the sophisticated manufactures aimed
directly at the consumer, such as glass, books, and mechanical and
electrical repairs. Finally, decline was both considerable and constant in
the textile industry, which had for so long been prominent. The general
picture is that between 1946 and 1954 the industrial sector overtook
agriculture to become the principal employer.

Its triumph was short-lived, however. Since 1962, the service industries have squeezed into first place and increased their lead. Growth
rates have, in fact, been greatest here, with the exceptions of transport –
which declined between 1946 and 1954 during the improvement of the
railways and has progressed marginally since (the rate in 1968 was 84
per cent of that in 1946) – and of domestic service, which continued
its former decline. The banking, commerce, and insurance complex
increased by 30 per cent in twenty-two years, no doubt with internal
disparities, but swollen by the increase of sales staff in the big stores
(rising 50 per cent from 1954 to 1968) and of bank employees (rising
70 per cent). A similar expansion took place in public administration,
where employees increased by 63 per cent, and in specialized concerns
which were taking over work from the liberal professions for the
benefit of individuals (up by 53 per cent) or of business (142 per cent).
In this way, changes sketched out after 1921, developing slowly over a
long time, have now changed the face of the French working population and destroyed the myth and reality of an old country of peasants.
Such changes are not without problems, but these do not fall within the
present study.

C. THE SCHOOL EXPLOSION AND ITS CONSEQUENCES

The great expansion of numbers at school has been the major feature of
post-war education and has invited the epithet 'school explosion'.
Successive waves engulfed the different levels. Primary schools were the
first to be submerged by an inflow of 1·8 million new pupils between
1951 and 1959, which pushed up their total attendance from 5,120,000
in 1945–50 to 8,212,000 in 1963–4. In the same period, the volume of
pupils in *lycées* and colleges tripled; complementary courses which
corresponded to their lower forms bounded from 163,000 to 875,000;
and, overall, secondary education expanded in the period 1945–64 from
507,000 to 1,371,000 pupils. Faculties and *grandes écoles* had risen from
129,000 to 308,000 students in 1963, and had 440,000 students by 1967.

This was without doubt the result of the rising birth rate after the
war. The tide really began to flow after 1951, when the post-1945
generations arrived at school age, and the chronology of the movement
followed through the levels of schooling. Yet the demographic wave
had to coincide with a changed mentality on the part of the parents,
experiencing a general rise in the standard of living and making positive
efforts to send their children to school. The rate of growth of secondary
education, for example, far surpassed the growth of the new generations and was part of a movement going back to the 1930s, when
attendance at day schools was made free. The rates of school attendance

speak for themselves. At the primary level, of all children between five and fourteen, 87 per cent and 86 per cent went to school in 1951 and 1956, respectively – about 10 per cent more than in 1936. In the secondary system, among adolescents between the ages of ten and nineteen, about 19 per cent attended *lycées* in 1958–9, twice as many as before the war; and this rises to 26·9 per cent when complementary courses and modern colleges (the old EPS) are counted, as against 12·4 per cent in 1935–6.

Changes in attitudes were certainly integral with the profound structural changes in the country's active population, which happened in less than two decades, with a rapidity inconceivable in the nineteenth century. The pressure of necessity was felt in a more direct way than at the time of Jules Ferry, and the ordinance of 6 January 1959 which raised the minimum school-leaving age to fifteen endorsed an existing situation rather than establishing a new norm. As A. Prost has remarked, the school was responding to the demands of an economy now in greater need of brains than of brawn.

The backwardness was even more manifest when it came to the institutions and content of the education system. Only technical education seems to have evolved, in confused fashion, in response to immediate needs. It offered a hierarchy of establishments and syllabuses closely tied to qualifications. At the elementary level there was apprenticeship, still controlled by the Chambers of Trades and still beset by traditional vices. The figure of 382,000 apprentices recorded in the census of 1946 was a considerable overestimate which doubtless concealed an element of cheap labour. An inquiry by the Ministry of Labour in 1951, based upon contract signatures, reduced the number of apprentices to about 235,000. Artisans followed professional courses, and skilled workmen were trained by Apprenticeship Centres organized by the Vichy regime, originating in the pre-war Centres of Professional Training, consecrated by the law of 21 February 1949 and provided with masters themselves trained in National Normal Schools of Apprenticeships (ENNA). The final qualification in both cases, awarded at the age of 18 after three years of study, was the CAP. One degree higher came the technical colleges, formed from the old EPCI or from practical sections of the EPS, which after four years' study produced masters armed with the Certificate of Industrial or Commercial Education. Finally, at the top, there were the National Professional Schools (ENP) which prepared students for the Higher Industrial or Commercial Certificate. The intake to these different levels tended to reflect the social hierarchy. The system, indeed, had the merit of coherence, but its results were limited. In 1951, nearly one boy in three (32·8 per cent) entered active life immediately after the term of compulsory education, without professional training. Of both boys and girls, 21·3 per cent (24·3 per cent of boys only) went into apprentice-ship, but only 12·6 per cent benefited from any other kind of technical education. It must be added for the sake of clarity that 20·7 per cent of the others went to *lycées* or classical and modern colleges.

Nevertheless, the ability needed at a technical level made more and more outdated the existence of two parallel orders of education, quite separate beyond the period of compulsory schooling. The idea of the comprehensive school (*école unique*) was not new and made possible a better orientation and a wider choice. The Vichy regime outlined this fusion in the primary school by introducing practical workshop lessons in the last years of school. This, paradoxically, was taking up ideas already developed under the Popular Front. After the liberation, the Langevin–Wallon Commission worked on a reorganization of the *école unique* and of its study content and methods, but its conclusions came to nothing under the Fourth Republic. The project of M. Billières, the Minister of National Education, which timidly resumed some aspects of this enterprise, fell through in 1956. The Berthouin reform of 1959, setting up a 'cycle of observation' of two years for all children, opened the way for M. Fouchet's colleges of secondary education, which formed a bridge between the primary education of the *lycées* and colleges of all types and the urban Colleges of General Education (CEG), which had developed from the complementary courses of the primary schools.

Even as these were being set up, the problem of technical training remained unresolved. In 1962, the proportion of the labour force with technical and professional education was 11·8 per cent in the case of male employees and 12·4 per cent for male workers (and for women 18 and 4·8 per cent respectively). There were, naturally, big differences between one sector and the next, but the proportion of 26·3 per cent of electrical workers with diplomas and that of 22·2 per cent in metallurgy were exceptional. In chemistry the figure was only 11·6 per cent, in the building trade 10·4 per cent, falling to 8·6 per cent in textiles and cloth-ing, and 7 per cent in the extractive industries. In 1959, just before the extension of compulsory schooling, one in four children left school at fourteen with no intention of returning, and one in two had left at seventeen.

Once again, one can say with A. Prost that adaptation to current reality came too late to be effective. It is possible to ask whether material resources were adequate to deal both with expensive reforms and with the growing number of those at school. Resources were strained despite the fact that between 1952 and 1965 the education budget increased 376 per cent – from 7·21 per cent to 17 per cent of the central government budget, and from 2·019 per cent to 4·622 per cent of the national income. At the same time, the idea that education expenditure should be considered as investment came up against strong resistance and increased the tension between the desire to maintain a general humanistic education, now extended to the greatest number, and the desire to make the school system directly tributary to the needs of economic growth, which would dictate greater specialization. The latter side of the argument grew stronger and stronger, while planning requirements, seeking to forecast the needs of labour at all levels of qualification, tended to define the quantitative and qualitative norms of the changing school system.

One certain sign of the persistent inability to adapt was a new burgeoning of institutions directly useful to the employers of labour. The Chambers of Trades underlined their resistance to compulsory schooling up to 16, in order to be able to syphon off unqualified youth for the artisan employment. The Ministry of Agriculture developed its own *lycées* and colleges after 1960. Most large private businesses developed internal courses for training and promotion and their own schools for staff, narrowly specialized like their predecessors in the nineteenth century. Initiatives were often lost by the public education system for the creation of new techniques, above all in the tertiary sector, in such areas as public relations, secretarial courses, and interpreting. The state realized its own inadequacies and tried to mitigate them by a policy of co-operation with these establishments. Because of its economic importance, as well as its political and ideological implications, education was to remain one of the most thorny problems of contemporary French life.

V. *Conclusion*

The timidity of growth and resistance to change of the French economy before 1939 were reflected in the history of the labour force and its distribution. The permanence of the broad classifications was the main feature. The size of the total active population hardly increased in a century and a half. That of the female labour force – one woman for every two men, everywhere except on the land – remained stable. Industrial workers made up one-third of the work force in 1946 and in 1856. The original 'reserve army' survived until perhaps 1930, when Alfred Sauvy could detect it in the pattern of underemployment. Above all, agriculture continued to employ the greatest number of hands. Must it not be correct to seek the real source of changes – or their absence – here? Did not the torpor of the peasant world, safe in prosperity and then in protection, overwhelm the dynamism of certain industrial sectors? Rather than speaking of waves of expansion in an industrial labour force, should one not talk of periodic contractions of the agricultural population, contemporaneous with the transfer of labour between sectors? It is a provisional hypothesis, but one which has to be verified against the chronological 'lag' in the development of the various 'nations' within France.

Should we explain the slowness of French industrialization in the nineteenth century by an overall shortage of labour, consequent especially on the inadequate surplus flowing from the land combined with the refusal of the French to multiply? There is too much evidence not to see the close correlation between demographic and economic malthusianism. Yet there is nothing to prove that nineteenth-century France lacked labour. Complaints were very rare and occurred only at exceptional moments of full employment, or in sectors with the most rigorous conditions, such as the mines. As it happened, immigration became a permanent feature of the economy after 1850, and for over a century France was succoured by the surplus of the Italian population. After that, the size of the population of working age remained more or less constant. Should one admire this stability, persisting despite the weakness of the natural rate of growth of population, or deplore the deep and general immobility which it signified, because the enormous influx of foreigners was unable to shatter it? It is here that we came across the phenomenon of malthusianism so dear to Pierre Chaunu. The demographic trough at the end of the nineteenth century and the beginning of the twentieth was in a France of small producers, in which the peasants, with their privileged position, concerned only about the future of their children, limited the horizon of development. The malthusian curse was manifold, and its fear of change was illustrated by the inability to pass from artisan to industrial worker in professional training, and in the sluggishness to develop the minimum of education that the new sectors of the economy required. Even if it did not result in the numerical decline of the labour force, it had its revenge by reducing its quality by a disqualification which was serious for productivity – problems which were still unresolved on the eve of the Second World War.

It becomes apparent that one cause of the slow industrialization and economic growth of France in the nineteenth century and until 1939 – a sluggishness in population growth which brought no real shortage of labour in its wake – was a reflection of a general timidity and malthusianism, and it would be hazardous to posit any simple causal relations between them. The analysis is justified a posteriori by the situation in France after 1945, for the 'take-off' into sustained growth was not assured by the expansion of the labour force; the larger post-war generations did not arrive on the labour market until the mid-1960s, and the call for immigration was never so strong nor so conscious. But the rapid recovery of the birth rate coincides with an increase in productivity, of which the developments in the general and technical educational apparatus, despite their weaknesses, were an infallible sign. This rising productivity alone guaranteed the acceleration of growth, both by maintaining the length of the working day and by improving the quality of work, at a time when the expansion of education was lowering the participation ratio and the size of the labour force remained largely unchanged (1946–62). There was a marked and rapid deployment towards the most active sectors, and henceforth industrial growth would shift the population away from agriculture. If the growth of the French population was one, and perhaps the main, support of economic growth after 1945–6, it was by the mechanism of increasing the number of its non-active members, by a rise in the level and style of living which created new consumer needs on the national market and so stimulated production indirectly, rather than directly by furnishing a larger labour force. In short, population change was important mainly for its effects upon the level of demand rather than upon the supply of labour, which, paradoxically, remained stable in a completely different economic context. The rise in productivity demonstrates the totality and complexity of the malthusian phenomenon and of the way it was broken. It is the task of the impassive language of statistics to understand the psychological and emotional implications which are the very tissue of the history of men.

CHAPTER VII

Entrepreneurship and Management in France in the Nineteenth Century

I. *The Background*

Just after the Second World War, American economic historians launched a debate, which has remained inconclusive, on the causes of lags in the rate of growth of the French economy during the process of industrialization in the nineteenth century. Seeing a country impoverished by persistent depression in the 1930s and weakened by the German occupation, they sought other than specifically contemporary factors to explain the lag experienced by France in comparison with other European nations, particularly the two main belligerent powers of western Europe, Britain and Germany, who had led a titanic struggle for five years. If France had been retarded in her economic development, how was this to be explained?

Awareness of this supposed lag was certainly not new, for the industrial superiority of Britain and Germany – not to mention that of the United States – had long since been recognized. In the nineteenth century, scholars and economists had already noted this difference and tried to explain it. In 1819, the chemist and government minister Chaptal, who in addition to having an advanced scientific training was a strong and intelligent administrator, noted, 'If we have not made as extensive use of machinery [as in England], it is because manual labour here costs less and because the low price of fuel in England allows them to use steam-engines with advantage everywhere.'[1] Richard Cobden could also remark:

whilst the indigenous coal and iron in England have attracted to her shores the raw materials of her industry, and given her almost an European monopoly of the great primary elements of steam power, France on the contrary, relying on her ingenuity only to sustain a competition with England, is compelled to purchase a proportion of hers from their great rival.[2]

LACK OF ENTREPRENEURSHIP?[3]

These interpretations remained impressionistic, and what is new is the attempt to find something beyond traditional explanations, such as the English commercial genius, American adventurism, or German aggressiveness. The debate finally centred on factors of production in their widest sense, including three main elements: the availability of energy, the spirit of enterprise, and the cleavages in French society.

For Shepard B. Clough,[4] the deficiency in coal production explained the lag suffered by the French economy with respect to its two neighbours, Germany and Great Britain, who enjoyed the greatest advantage in this field. In 1800, France produced 1 million tons of coal as against 10 million in Great Britain and 1 million in Germany. In 1850 the gap in coal production between France and Great Britain was the same (5 million tons as against 49 million tons), while Germany had attained a production of 6·7 million tons. By 1913 coal production was respectively 290 million tons for Great Britain, 190 million for Germany, and 40 million for France. Producing less coal, France could only be at a disadvantage in the production of energy in an economy based on steam power. But this argument ignored the importance of water power, fundamental for French industry in the nineteenth century; moreover, it simply translates a statistical observation into an economic explanation of a global nature.

The theses of J. E. Sawyer and David Landes were both founded on a sociological analysis strongly influenced by the work of Talcott Parsons.[5] For Sawyer, French society was vitiated by internal tensions which hindered its development and retarded industrialization. Thus, in Sawyer's view, France carried forward into the nineteenth and twentieth centuries two sets of institutions, two sets of attitudes, whose contradictions had never been satisfactorily resolved, to be called, for convenience, the 'traditional' and the 'bourgeois' . . . To these had been added a third major institutional order – the 'industrial' – which has major conflicts with both the previous orders and which has not been fully accepted by the various groups necessary to its successful functioning. A series of conflicts resulted with repercussions on the economy. France carried forward into the age of industrialism elements of two distinct orders whose industrial conflicts may be summarized somewhat schematically: the political patterns of traditional authority, Church, and army as against the liberal democracy of the Revolution and Republic; the economic patterns of traditional agriculture, craftsmanship, and corporation as against bourgeois capitalism's rationalistic exchange economy; the social patterns of traditional hierarchy, status, and organism as against bourgeois individualism, equality, and opportunity.[6]

From this general overview, Sawyer drew some precise conclusions about the attitude of the businessman, always hostile to innovation because incapable of overcoming the traditionalist forces opposed to immediate change. Representative of the bourgeois spirit, he had become more attached to security than to taking risks. Moreover, why would he have chosen to take risks when his social status remained inferior to that of his German or American counterpart? A consequence of this mentality was the proliferation of *small* businesses, *small* trades, *small* rural enterprise, all organized on a family basis and poorly adapted to economic progress. 'France has clung to such small-scale and uneconomic methods that costs are high and the return is low . . . The tertiary industries show perhaps the most striking pattern of small, inefficient units retarding the flow of trade and the growth of industrialism.' Finally, France had only a few entrepreneurs of the type studied by Schumpeter in the United States; on the other hand, what the French economy knew was 'primarily a Weberian entrepreneur, engaged in a rational process of increasing his wealth through compound interest, saving and reinvesting.' In short, social tensions had killed the spirit of enterprise.

The approach of David Landes derived directly from the data of the behavioural sciences, in full development at the time he was writing in the United States. In contrast to Sawyer, he mounted a direct attack against the French entrepreneur, who became the unique central figure of his argument. For Landes, the French entrepreneur had certain fundamental characteristics which had hardly changed during the whole industrial revolution. 'To begin with, the average French entrepreneur was a small businessman acting for himself or at most on behalf of a handful of partners.' From that resulted the reduced size of French enterprises, with the exception of certain well-defined sectors like metallurgy and ground transportation towards the middle of the nineteenth century. 'In the second place, the French businessman was a fundamentally conservative man, with a firm distaste for the new and the unknown.' To deduce from that that French industry was unreceptive to innovation is only a step. 'A third major characteristic of the French entrepreneur was his independence: the typical firm was pretty much self-sufficient.' By virtue of this independence, the French entrepreneur could maintain a high rate of profit, but less for enlarging his business than purely and simply for accumulating money. Taking everything into account, 'cautious management, obsolescent plants, and high profits are not a combination designed to flourish in a world of cut-throat competition'.[7]

This mentality of the entrepreneur could be explained by the strong influence of the family on the firm. In fact, French enterprises have always had, and retain, the effects of the family, with both its good qualities and its faults. Under the circumstances, it was the faults which were most striking: pettiness, caution, a taste for secrecy, even in the case of large enterprises. Thus, when the metallurgical firm of Wendel had to appeal, for the first time, to the financial market in 1908, it preferred raising money on the German market at the rate of 4·5 per cent rather than on the French at 4 per cent in order not to make public its balance-sheets and statutes. Limited in his ambitions, the entrepreneur opted for a policy favouring quality rather than mass production, condemning himself to voluntary restrictions which were absent in other large industrial countries.

All this allows Landes to conclude:

Even if it is true that the average French entrepreneur has lacked drive, initiative, and imagination – and the evidence indicates that he has – the question still remains of to what extent it reflects severe, external handicaps with which he has been unable to cope . . . Many observers of the present day, from the impatiently chauvinistic American tourist to the leading figures of French commerce and industry, are inclined to give it (the French entrepreneurial psychology) first priority on the list of France's economic problems.

This thesis has been discussed very little in France, where economists are not very attracted by the study of business and entrepreneurship, because their training inclines them more towards macro-economics, but it has been accepted in Anglo-Saxon countries because of its simplicity and explanatory power. Several divergent opinions have nevertheless questioned the hypothesis as being ingenious but too restricted. Some, like Rondo Cameron, consider that France's contribution has been essential to the development of Europe and explain it, in part at least, by the spirit of enterprise. Apart from the rate of growth in France itself, Cameron considers the French contribution to European development very important in three fields: the organization of banks; the development of railways; and the stimulation of new industries, among which were glass (for example, Saint-Gobain), mining, and metallurgy.[8] French businessmen energetically helped to diffuse the new technology and exported capital, sometimes at great risk, to those countries least advanced economically. This argument deserves attention, but it does not follow that these entrepreneurs were as dynamic in France itself, for profits could have been higher outside the country than within.

As for the internal market, Cameron expressly denies that the causes of economic stagnation should be sought 'directly in the capacities, habits and attitudes of the French people, including, of course, the entrepreneurial groups . . . The deficiency of aggregate demand for the products of industry . . . and average high costs of production in certain key industries that prevailed elsewhere constituted the major obstacles to industrial development.'[9]

On the other hand, certain Marxist historians, like Tom Kemp, have turned the argument around, maintaining that the businessman was only a reflection of his environment and that entrepreneurship was negligible as an independent variable. 'Entrepreneurs seem to have been influenced by the existing environment and to have absorbed its prevailing ethos: they preferred, it is frequently argued, security to risk-taking, they clung too long to obsolete methods, they looked to the government to protect them from foreign competition and retired early to live on their *rentes*.'[10] There were numerous exceptions to this stereotyped portrait, in sectors as varied as the creation of department stores or aviation, which leads Kemp to conclude: 'The characteristics of nineteenth-century development can hardly be explained from the character of the businessman, rather does the businessman reflect by his behaviour environmental conditions to which not only the actions of himself and his fellows but also those of other members of the society contribute.'

Returning to the question of entrepreneurship in more recent articles, and bearing in mind criticisms which had been made, Landes added nuances to his interpretation by admitting that the spirit of enterprise, intimately linked to economic growth, had acted as both a brake and a stimulus, depending upon individuals and periods. 'The variation in rates of growth – the spurts of 1850–70, 1896–1913, and 1952, for example – far from demonstrating the unimportance of the entrepreneurial factor, are evidence of its powerful influence. All of these spurts are closely associated with changes in the quality of enterprise.'[11] According to Landes, these spurts were due to changes in the economic environment, to phases in the expansion of heavy industry as well as to the pressure of competition, but fundamentally they reflected a change in the mentality of the entrepreneur, as was the case with the Saint-Simonian influence in the middle of the nineteenth century. He concludes: 'Entrepreneurship, in short, has been a major influence on French economic growth both for better and worse.'

Only a deeper analysis of the structure of business and its evolution can bring an answer to this debate.

II. *The Structure of French Enterprise*

The main argument of those who maintain that French business was less dynamic than its foreign competitors is therefore its family character. According to them, the family was not only a social unit but also a unit of production, providing the framework of economic activities. From this stemmed both a constraint on the means of production and a certain narrowness of horizons. A family enterprise could not pretend to rival firms which drew on a vast financial market and conducted an aggressive commercial policy.

That French business was essentially a family affair is a result of contemporary legislation, particularly the Code de Commerce of 1807. Like all the Napoleonic codes, it was a synthesis of the legacy of the *ancien régime* and the more recent contributions of the Revolutionary period. For commercial firms the code was markedly conservative, for it 'merely maintained or developed certain old rules without taking into account the fact that the disappearance of the professional organization had created a gap in our law'.[12] The principal merit of this code was that it classified commercial firms rigorously into three types.

The *simple partnership* company, or family firm, was an association between two or more persons who were in business and whose names appeared on the legal documents of the firm. It was characterized by the total responsibility of all its associates as a matter of personal liability for the obligations of the business whatever their commitment in the firm. This kind of firm corresponded perfectly to a family set-up, since members of the same family could become associated in business, which explains the custom of giving the family name to the firm or business association. Such companies could be formed without any legal restrictions and were simply required to deposit a copy of their statutes at the registry of the Chamber of Commerce where they resided. They were very popular throughout the nineteenth century, and even in the twentieth in various branches of activity, whether industry, banking, or commerce.

The company of *limited partnership* was formed among legally liable associates responsible for managing the enterprise and other associates who were simply creditors and 'sleeping partners'. The former conducted the management of the company, with all the consequences which that implied, while the latter were liable only to the amount of the funds they contributed. These firms could be established freely, with the single stipulation that they had to register, giving the names of the directors responsible for management but not of the sleeping partners. The limited partnership consisted either in putting up money or in creating negotiable and transferable stocks which permitted the exigencies of family businesses to be equated with large-scale capital requirements. This type of company was therefore preferred by businesses above a certain size, which had outgrown the financial resources of the family.

The *joint-stock* company was an association of capital founded for a definite purpose, embodied in the name of the firm and giving the object of the enterprise. The capital was represented by stocks of nominal value. What distinguished this type of company was the close control kept by the state. In order to be formed, such a company had to submit its statutes to the Conseil d'Etat, which granted permission in the form of an ordinance or a decree. The enterprise then had to deposit every six months a financial statement with the Préfet, the local court, and the Conseil d'Etat. By these means the legislators sought to hinder the spread of such firms, which were considered as hazardous and speculative. As a contemporary specialist in commercial law noted:

To obtain the approval of the Conseil d'Etat . . . one must have collected the firm's capital. This is a formal obligation. But in order to make capitalists subscribe to the firm's capital, one must already have the approval of the Conseil d'Etat. This is a moral necessity. Thus the founders of a company are caught in a vicious circle. What, then, is the joint-stock company in France? A form reserved by privilege to certain extraordinary business enterprises, outstanding for their brilliancy and uncommon size . . . Businesses of this sort are rare and, by the fact of their rarity, are of secondary interest for the country.[13]

In fact, businessmen turned to the joint-stock company only in exceptional cases. Normally, 'the preference of capitalists went to two kinds of firms: the simple partnership, as long as the size of the enterprise allowed it to rest on family funds, and the limited partnership, in the opposite case.'[14]

During the whole of the nineteenth century, the simple partnership was the most popular form among businessmen. While we do not have overall statistics, we can at least cite some approximate figures. Out of some 2,600 companies created in 1847, 1,952 were simple partnerships (75 per cent), 647 were limited partnerships or limited partnerships with shares (25 per cent), and 14 were joint-stock companies. From 1848 to 1867, the Ministry of Justice recorded about 67,500 companies formed, of which 52,800 were simple partnerships (78 per cent), 14,400 limited partnerships (21 per cent), and 307 joint-stock companies. It would be interesting to know the capital of each of these three groups, but on this point there are no data.

Because of the liberty it enjoyed, the discretion surrounding it, and the flexibility which characterized it, the simple partnership company was the most popular. But the legal form covered many types of enterprise. Sometimes it related to a small business enterprise like the firm Méquillet–Noblot, a cotton-spinning mill in eastern France, which was created in 1802 by three associates – the father, his son, and a cousin – each contributing 15,000 francs, and which kept the same form through numerous dissolutions and reorganizations until 1901, when its capital was 3 million francs. On other occasions this legal form was adopted by more important enterprises, such as Thierry–Mieg et Cie at Mulhouse, because it allowed the family character of the business to be maintained.

The large business enterprises of the time were, for the most part, limited partnerships. When Boigues in 1819 created the Fourchambault company – one of the most modern metallurgical firms – he was financed by two iron merchants, Labbé and Paillot, who together contributed 150,000 francs, a sum equal to that which he himself put into the company. In 1821 a further contribution of 500,000 francs brought the capital up to 800,000 francs. Then Boigues paid off each of his partners by delivering iron to them and remained the only principal in the business. Since no stock had been created at the outset, it is difficult to determine whether, at this moment, the company was still a limited partnership or simply a simple partnership between Boigues and his son-in-law Martin. One often finds confusion between the limited partnership and the simple partnership because of the fact that a company may have characteristics of both types.

Several industrial companies inherited from the *ancien régime* were, in fact, limited partnerships with share capital, such as the mining company of Anzin or the glassworks of Saint-Gobain. New businesses looking for capital funds often adopted this juridicial framework: for example, the Société des Forges d'Audincourt, the Allevard ironworks in Dauphiné at the time of their reorganization in 1842, or the forges of Creusot. After a series of mishaps this last company was bought up in 1836 by the banker Seillière, the Schneider brothers (two of his former 'employees'), and the father-in-law of one of them, Boigues (already the owner of Fourchambault). A limited partnership with share capital was thus formed between the four buyers and a local ironmaster, with a capital of 4 million francs divided into eighty shares of 50,000 francs each, fifty of which were reserved for the founders. The juridical framework has not varied down to the middle of the twentieth century, and this was equally the case with other great iron magnates, like the Wendels in Lorraine or the Krupps in the Ruhr. All these businesses have kept their family character, which has in no way hindered their development. In 1849 the capital of Creusot grew to 22·5 million francs; and in 1872 that of the firm of Les Petits-Fils de François de Wendel was 30 million francs, while at the death of its founder in 1825 it had been valued at 4 million. The family framework in no way acted as a brake upon the growth of these businesses. By comparison, the limited partnership companies in textiles were quite modest in size: the most important had a capital of 1 to 2 million francs towards the middle of the nineteenth century.

However, certain of these limited partnership companies preferred changing their status to joint-stock companies at a time when they needed more capital. Such was the case for the Audincourt ironworks in 1824, the mines of Grand'Combe (created in 1837) in 1855, and many others, not to mention the analogous transformations of the Anzin mines and the venerable Saint-Gobain glassworks. Nothing, however, was done legally to favour such a transformation, since the joint-stock company stayed under strict controls until 1867, and all the efforts of the government were designed to discourage it. On this subject there is an illuminating text on the official reticence shown towards large industrial enterprises – the report of the Mining Council on the transformation of the Imphy ironworks into a joint-stock company.[15] In his remarks the writer of the report aimed to highlight the lack of guarantees with respect to the shareholders, and thus the risk of their being defrauded. In affairs of this sort, he noted, inventories were often overvalued in an artificial way. 'I shall propose that the Council adopt an article to add to the statutes, establishing rules according to which accurate valuations will have to be made in the inventories.' Moreover, the writer feared a lack of cash and as a consequence asked that a reserve fund be established, to be taken out of profits, according to the nature of the enterprise. In his conclusions, he insisted on the necessity of controlling such companies in order to protect the rights of stockholders and third parties. 'Joint-stock companies... ought to be subject to all precautionary measures tending to keep their capital intact and to ensure the survival of the business enterprise, and therefore the rights of third parties and those of shareholders.' To objections that these restrictive conditions would make it more difficult to bring capital together came the reply, 'That may be, but if, as a result, fewer joint-stock companies are created, they will certainly be stronger, and I am entirely convinced that the flow of capital into this type of enterprise will be much greater when it has been seen to prosper.' Thus it was to favour the creating of joint-stock companies that the government had to be so strict towards them. It is not certain, in any case, as Maurice Lévy-Leboyer says, that the Conseil d'Etat sought above all to increase its own powers 'without respect for the companies which it discredited or for the economy whose expansion it hindered'.[16]

It is nonetheless true that between 1815 and 1867 – the best-known period because of the control exercised by the Conseil d'Etat – few joint-stock companies were created. Only some 635 were authorized, divided in the following way:[17] 145 insurance companies (23 per cent), of which 95 per cent were in marine insurance; 26 banks (4 per cent); 194 transport companies (31 per cent), of which 66 were railway companies; 135 industrial companies, made up of 60 metallurgical and mining companies (9 per cent), 58 chemical companies (9 per cent) including city gas and light companies, and 17 textile companies (3 per cent); and 135 other non-industrial enterprises (21 per cent), in such various fields as public services, agricultural or colonial firms, purely local businesses for the construction of a bridge, etc.

Of the three most important groups – insurance, transportation, and industrial production – the second was clearly superior in numbers and still more so from the point of view of total capital funds, since in itself it represented about 85 per cent of undertakings. Industrial enterprises were ill at ease within the legal framework of the joint-stock company, which became too rigid because of the immobility it imposed upon capital in buildings and materials. Certain of these companies were legacies from the *ancien régime*, like the Anzin mines or the company of Saint-Gobain, the first with a capital of nearly 50 million francs around 1840, the other with 8·6 million francs in 1830 – a considerable figure for the time. Others, on the contrary, were small, almost marginal affairs in little-industrialized regions or in new and often speculative sectors: English-type ironworks, steel mills, linen-weaving by mechanical processes, soda or sulphur chemicals. Such companies had also been created where family traditions were insufficiently strong to sustain an industrial enterprise.

Virtually all joint-stock companies of the first half of the nineteenth century were alike in having little capital – in general less than 10 million francs each, divided into a small number of shares of high value. An extreme case was that of the Baccarat Company, founded in 1824 for the manufacture of glass and crystal with a capital of 1 million francs divided into eight shares of 125,000 francs each. In most cases, the value of stocks ranged between 1,000 and 5,000 francs (£40 and £250), more rarely between 10,000 and 25,000 francs (£400 and £10,000). For industrial companies, the number of shares issued was not very high (eighty in Vizille in 1825; 160 in the Imphy ironworks in 1829; 1,200 in the coal mines and foundries of Aveyron in 1826; 2,000 in the Compagnie des Salines et Mines de Sel de l'Est), which permitted a limited group, very often a family, to take over control of the business, often in the manner of a disguised limited partnership.

The large capitalist enterprise made its appearance with transport companies. If one very often associates it with railways, it is well to note that the device was first used for constructing canals. Between 1820 and 1830 there was intense activity in projecting canals in France equivalent to the canal mania in England at the end of the eighteenth century, or in the United States with the Erie Canal, at the same time as in France. The Compagnie du Canal de Bourgogne assembled a capital of 25 million francs in 1822, imitated the following year by the Compagnie des Quatre Canaux. These two companies were intended to raise loans for canal construction, not to construct the actual canals, and thus their operations were purely financial. When the banker Jacques Laffitte wanted to form a large financial bank with resources of 100 million francs, he encountered the veto of the Conseil d'Etat, which considered the sum too large, and the project failed.

After 1840, railway construction popularized joint-stock companies and disarmed the opposition which they had excited up to that date. Furthermore, the new governing group of the *bourgeoisie orléaniste* had a decidedly more favourable attitude to the development of business than their predecessors of the Restoration. Capital funds of from 20 to 40 million francs then became current, and the number of stocks issued augmented (80 million francs for the Société du Chemin de Fer de Paris à Orleans in 1838; 66 million for the Compagnie du Chemin de Fer, 1845). The unit value of these shares was almost always 500 francs (£20), which made them accessible to a greater number of subscribers. The decisive step was taken in 1845 when James de Rothschild merged several enterprises interested in the construction of railways into the Compagnie du Chemin de Fer du Nord, setting the capital at 200 million francs, divided into 400,000 shares of 500 francs. Only the Compagnie des Chemins de Fer de Paris à Lyon et à la Mediterranée (the PLM) went above this figure, attaining a capital of 400 million francs after mergers in 1857.

Impelled by the new needs of the railways, joint-stock companies thus mobilized considerable funds by 1850. If the main purpose of such companies was the construction of means of transportation, their activities still remained essentially financial – the collection and management of funds furnished by a restricted, well-to-do clientele. At the same time, industrial enterprises remained faithful to their traditional legal framework. It is true that, after 1850, several metallurgical companies adopted the form of joint-stock companies, but these were almost always transformations of already existing businesses, not new creations. Such was the case of the Forges de Denain–Anzin (a merger between the ironworks of Denain and the ironworks and rolling mills of Anzin), the Hauts Fourneaux de Maubeuge, the Compagnie des Forges de Châtillon–Commentry, the Aciéries d'Imphy et Saint-Seurin. A typical example is the merger of the ironworks in Franche-Comté, under the name of the Société des Hauts-Fourneaux, Fonderies et Forges de Franche-Comté, with a capital of 12 million francs in 24,000 shares. In fact, nine small companies had decided to make a joint effort to save an industry menaced by technical progress and the competition of better-placed businesses. But neither the textile nor the chemical industry was touched by the extension of the joint-stock company.

The general spread of joint-stock companies into other than industrial sectors and the issue of a greater number of shares of progressively smaller denominations led gradually to the abandonment of legal restraints. The law of 23 May 1863 created a new category of companies, companies of limited responsibility, inspired by English limited liability companies. These could be founded freely so long as their capital did not surpass 20 million francs, with the legal advantage that the liabilities of the directors did not go beyond their contributions to the authorized capital funds. Another law, of 24 July 1867, also following the example of what had happened in England, gave a real general status to joint-stock companies. In return for complete freedom of creation, it imposed some simple rules for management: the establishment of an administrative council, the obligation to hold an annual general meeting, the verification of the accounts by regularly designated commissioners, the provision of annual reserves.

This legislative transformation certainly gave more freedom of movement to business enterprises, without, however, revolutionizing their make-up. Limited liability companies had little immediate success, with only 338 creations in the five years following the law. Joint-stock companies multiplied, owing to the removal of controls, but the absence of the legal requirement of authorization deprives us of an essential historical source, so that it is difficult to follow their evolution after 1867. From a dozen a year the number created passed to a hundred, often in addition to conversions of companies already established under a different form. As affairs developed, businesses found it convenient to convert to the new company form in order to profit from the liberal dispositions of the law and eventually to be able to have recourse to the financial market. A typical case, among others, is that of the chemical company of Kuhlmann, in northern France, which was first a limited partnership company (1825) and was then transformed in 1854 into a limited partnership with shares and became a joint-stock company in 1870. Another typical case, in metallurgy, was that of the Compagnie des Forges d'Allevard, first a family enterprise, then a limited partnership with shares in 1842, and finally a joint-stock company in 1906. 'The limited partnership no longer responded to the needs of the time, and a more liberal form of organization for enterprise was indispensable.'[18]

III. *The Scale of Business Enterprise*

One of the most common current criteria of economic development is the size of enterprises, which can be measured in different ways, by number of workers, capital involved, or turnover. If this sort of information is regularly available in the twentieth century, it is less so for nineteenth-century France, because the majority of enterprises did not feel any necessity to communicate such knowledge and were not obliged by the state to do so. Hence, one must stick to the figures of official inquiries or statistics, but here too the data are hardly sufficient. It is well to recall, moreover, that one of the arguments used by those who rationalize French inferiority in matters of industrial production is the extreme dispersion of businesses as a consequence of their family-type organization. Thus, apropos of France (and of Germany), David Landes notes, 'the less efficient, smaller *fabriques* proved surprisingly tenacious; it took a cotton famine, tariff changes, and the Great Depression of 1873–96 to kill even the weakest of them off'.[19] The small enterprise is thus thought to be unprofitable and an obstacle to progress.

That there were in the nineteenth century a majority of small business enterprises in France can be readily seen from available statistics. According to the *Enquête parlementaire sur le travail* of 1848, one finds in small or middle-sized towns a majority of small businesses, and only certain large towns, such as Paris, Lille, Lyon, or Mulhouse, had large workshops, with a labour force of a few dozen or a few hundred workers. According to Paris statistics of 1851, 32,000 employers worked alone or with only one helper, while 7,000 had ten or more workers. From the census of 1851, one finds an average of eleven workers per business in the *grande industrie* against two in the *petite industrie* (124,000 employers with 1,300,000 workers for the first category; 1,550,000 *maîtres* with 2,800,000 workers for the second). This explains the fact that an alert economist like Charles de Laboulaye still considered big industrial enterprises to be 'artificial' in 1849.

This situation changed very slowly. In the 1866 census the distribution was as follows:[20]

working population	4,715,805
number of employers	1,661,584
number of salaried employees	116,068
number of workers	2,938,153

If we consider that the number of employers corresponds, in general, to the number of businesses, the average number of workers per business would be two. A survey of 1872 shows the results in a slightly different way:[21]

	Employers	Workers
Extractive industries	14,717	164,819
Factories and manufactures	183,227	1,112,000
Small industries	596,776	1,060,444
Total	794,720	2,337,263

In extractive industries (mines and quarries), the average was 11.5 workers per enterprise, but it fell to 6.1 in the second category. The *Recensement des industries* of 1896 gives still another presentation: of each 100 industrial establishments, 83 employ from one to four wage-earners, 13 employ from five to fifty wage-earners, and 4 employ more than fifty wage-earners and provide work for 40 per cent of all workers.

It is difficult to compare all these data on the size of enterprises, shown in terms of numbers of workers, because of the diversity of criteria used. The impression is naturally that of a multiplication of small businesses, but they have less significance in terms of economic development, in the sense that they did not generate progress. In any case it is not at the level of overall content that we can judge the reality of an enterprise. It is more precise to say that large and small enterprises co-existed, with a tendency towards concentration which swung the balance slowly in favour of the former.

The textile industry shows a great variety of enterprises, from the small workshop with a few weavers and fabric-printers to the large integrated enterprise. The first was especially widespread in regions with a long industrial tradition, where local production ensured or had ensured the supply of fibres – as in Brittany, Normandy, Maine, Champagne, and Picardy. There businesses kept their artisan character without integrating trading functions, business transactions being assured by factors or independent merchant firms. The most typical case is that of the Lyons silk-weavers (who wove the silk in their work-shops) or the ribbon-makers of Saint Etienne, both working for merchant firms in Lyons. This dissociation between manufacturing and trade persisted during the nineteenth century, at least for high-quality articles, for which mass production made little sense. On the other hand, in the fields of standardized items, the small-scale artisan enterprise regressed noticeably during the nineteenth century, either dying a natural death or expanding into an integrated firm.

The evolution of the textile industry reveals two traits: one tendency towards specialization, and another towards increasing scale. The firm of the first half of the nineteenth century was very often completely integrated from spinning to printing to finishing, covering all the manufacturing operations and controlling its raw material supplies and sales, especially in Alsace. Thus, at the mid-century, the firm of Dollfus–Mieg of Mulhouse owned a printing-works, a bleaching-house, and a spinning-works installed between 1812 and 1852 (with 650 power looms, installed in 1832); the firm employed 2,500 workers and employees and had a turnover of 13 million francs. But integrated businesses then became less common, for between 1830 and 1860 spinning, printing, and weaving developed separately. Maurice Lévy-

Leboyer attributes this separation of the different branches of textile manufacturing to the crisis of 1827–8, which disclosed conflicts of interest among manufacturers.[22] Spinners and weavers preferred jobbing work, to avoid dependence upon the cotton-printer. From there, it seems that the printing of cloth became a speciality *sui generis* and remained separated from spinning and weaving, which remained often, but not always, associated in the same firm. Thus, in the North, firms more often specialized either in spinning or in weaving. The house of Motte–Bossut, for example, built a spinning-mill of 18,000 spindles in 1843, which expanded to 70,000 spindles by 1860 and earned it the name of *filature monstre*. At this point specialization prevailed over integration.

The second aspect of this evolution was the slow but steady increase in the scale of enterprise and the growth of firms. This is a commonplace observation for the nineteenth century and does not need to be elaborated. Even though important, firms in the textile industry remained modest in size compared with those in mining or metallurgy. Dollfus–Mieg, with its 3,000 wage-earners in 1867, was an exception in this industry, and businesses employing a thousand workers were considered large. In Normandy, in 1860, the largest spinning-mill, La Foudre, employed 600 to 700 persons, making its owner, Pouyer-Quertier, the largest cotton industrialist of the region.

Metallurgical and mining enterprises were far ahead in scale of operations, although even here very great differences existed. In coal-mining the powerful Compagnie d'Anzin, which still supplied half of the coal production of the North in 1850 and was the prototype of the modern capitalist company, has to be contrasted with many small and middle-sized enterprises.[23] The Blanzy mines in Burgundy employed a hundred miners in 1811 and extracted less than 10,000 tons of coal; in 1850, with an effective underground and surface work force of 1,500 people, they extracted 160,000 tons and had a turnover of 1·3 million francs. In 1897 the labour force had fallen to 8,000 persons, output to 1,400,000 tons, and the turnover to 15 million francs. In the Carmaux mines (Tarn), the evolution was as follows:

	Quantity extracted (tons)	Turnover (fr.)	Number of workers
1811	9,690	216,000	225
1850	52,700	734,000	551
1875	273,800	5,552,000	1,526
1897	470,000	5,850,000	2,462

It was certainly in metallurgy and mechanical construction that the modern capitalist enterprise had progressed most since the beginning of the nineteenth century. At this time, we still find many small artisan businesses, dispersed according to the location of ore deposits and fuel resources (particularly forests). There were about forty blast furnaces in Franche-Comté and as many ironworks, but none of these enterprises employed more than a few workers, and their capital funds were minimal. Large enterprises were rare, except for Le Creusot, Indret, and certain other establishments founded often with the support of the state. The phenomenon which characterized metallurgy was the merging of groups of small isolated firms in a locality. In the North of Burgundy partial concentrations were effected from the first years of the nineteenth century, to be followed (albeit ineffectively) by Marshal Marmont. The trend was taken up again by various capitalists and was crowned in 1845 by the merger of the factories of Chatillonnais and of Bourbonnais. Thus the Compagnie de Chatillon–Commentry was born, with a capital of 20 million francs, grouping thirty-seven blast furnaces and fifty-six ironworks, with additional rented establishments (thirteen furnaces and twenty-six small ironworks), and an effective labour force of about 1,300 workers.[24] At the end of the century, Chatillon–Commentry had a turnover of 35 to 40 million francs, owned its own collieries, and was among the leading metallurgical companies. While the fusion of the ironworks of Franche-Comté into one business in 1854 was not crowned by success, that of the steel mills and ironworks of the Loire in the same year into the Compagnie de la Marine et des Chemins de Fer was. It was a consequence of the merger of the ironworks of Pétin–Gaudet with the Jackson steel mills, to which were added the locomotive construction shops of Parent–Schacken in Paris and in central France (Berry). Apart from coal production, this enterprise was integrated from the start, producing castings and rolled iron. From 1862 onwards, it pursued a systematic policy of purchasing mineral concessions. By the end of the century, while it had not attained the size of Le Creusot, it was still among the giants of metallurgy and regularly distributed substantial dividends.

It can thus be seen that the large industrial enterprise was present in all sectors of production. It remains to assess its relative importance in the French economy at the end of the nineteenth century. B. Gille has drawn up a table of the thirty largest French businesses in 1881, according to their capital.[25] By far the most important group was in transport, occupying the first five places and including in all nine companies (six of which were railway companies, two shipping companies, and one an urban transport enterprise), with a total capital of 1,450 million francs or 60 per cent of the total. Next came mining companies, all in coal, with five enterprises and a total capital of 331 million francs or 14 per cent of the total. The largest industrial enterprise in France, the Anzin mines, with 135 million francs in capital, was in this group. Next, in decreasing order, came gas companies (six enterprises, 188 million francs in capital) and water companies (three firms, 130 million francs in capital); then come two industrial groups, metallurgy (with four firms and 93 million francs in capital; but the most important metallurgical firm, Le Creusot, was only eighteenth in rank), and the chemical industry (represented only by the Compagnie de Saint-Gobain, with a capital of 80 million). No textile firm appears on this list, only one business in the then experimental field of electricity, and only one in the food industries.

At the heart of French capitalism, at the end of the nineteenth century, industrial enterprises were largely outdistanced in scale by transportation companies and public utilities.

IV. *Financing Industrial Enterprise*

Given that the great majority of industrial firms were and remained family enterprises, one must ask how they were financed. Here one has to face another aspect of the argument that the family framework was too narrow to assure business growth and thus caused a lag in the development of French industry.

There is still too little information for a satisfactory answer to be given to the question. Business history is so little developed that information is fragmentary and we must rely on a few isolated examples, more numerous in metallurgy than elsewhere. A glance at the particular conditions of French commerce for most of the nineteenth century shows a market closely protected by high tariffs, whose effects were to diminish the pressure of foreign competition and to leave producers almost in command of their prices. Added to the effect of national protection was a regional protection, at least down to 1850–60, which arose from imperfect internal communications before the railway era. Industrialists often complained of this disadvantage, omitting to add that its counterpart was a certain freedom from competition from producers in other regions.

Three means of financing were used: family sources, retention of profits, and recourse to banks.

Family funds explain the origins of most businesses. They often came from inheritance, being passed on from generation to generation, as was the case of de Wendel, at Hayange in Lorraine, going back to 1704, or of the Gouvys, also in Lorraine, established in 1751.[26] Inheritance was the principal way of coming into the ownership of a metallurgical enterprise, and that was the case in all sectors of production. Even in large enterprises family continuity was usually assured, and with it the continuity of the family inheritance – the business. Thus, the continuity of Le Creusot followed the genealogy of its founders, Adolphe and Eugène Schneider. The latter was solely responsible from 1845, after the death of his brother, down to 1875. He was followed by his son, Henri, from 1875 to 1898; then his grandson, Eugène II, who directed the business during nearly half a century (1898–1942); and finally by his great-grandson, Charles, who died in 1960. Such continuity of succession was exceptional, but at the back of the business there was nearly always a family inheritance. In metallurgy, it was often an estate which supplied the primary materials necessary to manufacture iron, whether wood or minerals. In Lorraine, Champagne, and Franche-Comté, at the end of the eighteenth century, a certain number of landlords, more than half of whom belonged to the nobility, became ironmasters. They succeeded in making their small enterprises work in conjunction with the revenues from their estates. Such a practice could succeed as long as technology remained elementary and investments were not too heavy, but as these conditions changed these marginal family enterprises disappeared in the course of the nineteenth century. Some sought survival by mergers, as with the Forges de Franche-Comté in 1854, or the Forges de Châtillon–Commentry in Burgundy and Bourbonnais in 1846. Mergers naturally made such an enterprise lose its family character.

More interesting was the pooling of family funds to establish a business. We have already noted this for the textile industry, where money might be furnished by a father and his children, by a father and his son-in-law, or sometimes by cousins or friends. These associates almost always had some experience in industry, not as manufacturers but as merchants. Several textile houses were founded or taken over by merchants who had accumulated a certain capital which they then used to buy a business. In metallurgy this role was assumed by iron merchants to take advantage of trends in the iron market. The case of Riant was typical. He was already interested in various mines and ironworks in the centre of France, before he founded the Aubin ironworks in 1845.[27] Sometimes the merchant–manufacturer, after having served as intermediary between the landlord and the labour force, decided to go into business on his own account. In other cases, a small firm grew by adding new manufacturing commitments. At the end of the eighteenth century, the Alsatian textile industry began with the printing of materials bought elsewhere. When spinning was mechanized at the beginning of the nineteenth century, printing enterprises grew with the construction of spinning mills, and 20 or 30 years later this was followed by power-loom weaving. The fortune of the Mahieu family in Armentières (Nord) had as its starting point in 1831 a small dyeshop, which was extended in 1845 by the addition of power looms. On the same pattern, a forge or a mill could become the starting point for a metallurgical enterprise.

A particularly favourable circumstance in France had been the sale of property under the Revolution. The abbeys and the properties of emigrants were sometimes bought up at a low price by capitalists and converted into factories under very favourable conditions. In this case, successful speculation was at the origin of a business.

The amount of capital required naturally varied greatly. According to Jean Vial, at the beginning of the nineteenth century, a catalan forge would be valued at 25,000 to 35,000 francs, or, exceptionally, 60,000 francs for a modernized one; a charcoal-fuel blast furnace from 50,000 to 100,000 francs, a coke blast furnace twice as much;[28] a rolling mill or a steam engine from 10,000 to 20,000 francs. An integrated iron factory would be worth at this time from 60,000 to 600,000 francs, and its cost was to grow with subsequent improvements. Thus, around 1840, an English-type factory was valued at at least 1·2 million francs, and sometimes at twice this figure. Investments have a tendency to increase with time as machines are improved. In textiles, the initial capital funds were markedly inferior: in one such business, created in 1802 in eastern France to spin cotton, each of three partners brought in 18,000 francs. In Lille in 1833, the two founders of a spinning factory put 12,000 francs between them into the new business. Naturally, one can find more highly capitalized textile firms, but they usually resulted either from the purchase of a former enterprise or from the greater capital requirements of new innovations, such as mechanical carding or printing with multicoloured rollers.

Such financial means were within reach of individuals or small groups of individuals, so that the establishment of a family business in these industries did not pose important financial problems. This does not imply that only small businesses could be sustained in this way. A textile business could be enlarged without considerable new investment coming at one time, by adding new machines gradually. This was no longer true in metallurgy. It has to be remembered that Le Creusot was bought in 1835 for 2,680,000 francs and that the joint capital of the firm created in 1836 was 4,000,000 francs. This level of capitalization was beyond the possibilities of a family's resources, even if the business was a family one like Le Creusot. Great diversity is shown in the original funding of businesses, but their subsequent financial management was always based on retained profits (autofinancement). 'Ploughback' was the classic means of sustaining the growth of business enterprises, at least in their early years, when the cost of technical innovations was not too high and could be attained by limited means. 'It seems,' writes Jean Bouvier,[29] 'that industrial development *in its beginning* was largely able to finance itself, both for the original establishment of businesses and for their expansion. Industry bred industry, industrial savings [*autofinancement*] bred investment. This was the essential process in the first phase of French industrial development from 1820 to 1850.' It still characterized financing after 1850, at least in sectors little touched by innovation.

A good example of the process is furnished by the Fourchambault ironworks, studied by Guy Thuillier. In three years, from 1821 to 1824, its capital doubled from 800,000 to 1,600,000 francs. From 1824 to 1835, by the same process, its total capital reached 4 million francs, to which one must add outside participation amounting to another million francs. This presupposes high profits: 300,000 francs in 1834–5, and 400,000 in 1836, for the single factory of Fourchambault, without counting the returns from other activities. In all, for these years, Dufaud gained a net profit of nearly 1·2 million francs. Thanks to these profits, investment was extended to other metallurgical factories, iron mines, coke ovens, and the manufacturing of hardware. Finally, in 1836, the director of Fourchambault participated in the creation of the new company of Le Creusot.

The size of the gains in this case was explained by the audacity of the entrepreneurs, Louis Boigues and Achille Dufaud, and the strength of their management. Dufaud had journeyed to Britain in 1823 to study new British processes of manufacturing, but also management methods and the control of costs. He greatly admired the Crawshay factory at Cyfarthfa in Wales and often referred to it. Thus, à propos of the importance of accounting, he wrote, 'I see that everything at Cyfarthfa is undertaken in such a way that one knows exactly the cost of things. We absolutely must do the same thing as soon as possible . . . The difference in administration between Cyfarthfa and other ironworks is such that this factory earns while others lose.' To make profits, one had to economize wherever possible: 'We waste an enormous quantity of grease, because those responsible for this task do not take care. At Cyfarthfa one saves 3,000 francs a year on this item. In order to do that, one must operate a whole week with good Russian grease, see what is strictly essential and deliver daily what is necessary, weighing it . . .'[30]

The extent of profits, and hence the possibilities for new investment, depended also on the quantities produced, and this is a familiar theme in Dufaud's correspondence. On this account also he profoundly admired Britain, and he meant to profit from the technical advances made by his enterprise, which was one of the first to have introduced new metallurgical techniques from across the Channel. 'You will be more convinced than ever, like me,' he wrote, 'that we can make high profits only by means of a large output, and this must be done right away. We only have five or six good years before us. Competition is mounting on all sides and Saint Etienne will kill us one day, but by then we ought to be rich.' He added these characteristic sentences: 'I am more and more convinced of the necessity for us to double our production immediately . . . For our fortune is truly at stake, and we must press . . . we must hasten and use the present . . .'[31] Dufaud was convinced, contrary to other ironmasters, that the future lay in the quantity and the cheapness of his products, as in England, and that one had to profit from a head start to accumulate profits rapidly.

Such a policy was seen to be successful at the business level. Between 1839 and 1847, Fourchambault's profits rose to 7·5 million francs, and at least half was reinvested in technical improvements and innovations, with no recourse to the financial market. To anticipate the future, one must invest even during depression periods; for example, a million francs was put into the business in 1847. In these hard years, when the price of iron fell, profits were maintained by a retrenchment of general expenses, of the order of 43 per cent in the 1840s, and by a reduction in the cost of raw materials (of much lesser importance), which followed the development of the railways. This did not prevent Fourchambault from being in deficit in 1848 and from appealing to the Bank of France for two loans of 0·9 million and 1·5 million francs.

Until then, *autofinancement* had accounted for the growth of this enterprise. The lack of assets after 1856 explains its decadence, and the absence of new investment – or rather the poor utilization of investment – its subsequent decline.

In metallurgy the practice of *autofinancement* became general and was evidence of a new spirit of enterprise: profit was sought no longer as an end in itself, but for the growth of assets which 'gratified the original stockholders, who were always anxious to preserve and enhance the value of their initial holdings'.[32] From its origin in 1854 until 1869, the Aciéries de la Marine had financed new investment to a figure of 11·2 million francs, of which 6·4 million francs had been drawn from profits. At the firm of Wendel, capital growth showed the power of *autofinancement:* the figures were 2 million francs in 1830, 7·3 million in 1840, 10·8 million in 1848, 23 million in 1860, and 30 million in 1869. Capital had thus grown by 311 per cent from 1840 to 1869.[33] At the Forges de Châtillon–Commentry, between 1861 and 1869, investments increased by just under 5 million francs, drawn solely from *autofinancement*. The same policy was followed by Eugène Schneider at Le Creusot, but in 1863 he had to dip into working capital to promote investment in fixed capital, raising the total from 14 to 18 million francs by the issue of 8,000 shares of 500 francs each.

The policy of *autofinancement* postulated a high rate of profit. According to a study made by Jean Bouvier,[34] limited mainly to the years 1860–1914 because of the lack of information for the preceding period, almost all metallurgical enterprises experienced a large increase in their rate of profit in these years: there was an initial increase between 1860 and 1880 (the exact dates varying according to the firm), then a decline during the depression of the 1880s, and finally a vigorous rise from the turn of the century onwards, carrying profits to their highest level known on the eve of the First World War. This was indeed the *belle époque* for all these enterprises. A graph of the gross product, retained profits, and net revenue of the coal companies of the Pas de Calais reveals a similar trend and shows that *autofinancement* reached its greatest height between 1900 and 1912.[35] The Compagnie métallurgique d'Allevard furnishes a precise example for the same period. Between 1872 and 1914, distributed profits represented a yearly average of 4·70 per cent of turnover, while the rate of annual profit was 25·11 per cent of turnover. With respect to capital, distributed profits represented 2·84 per cent of assets and the total rate of profit 15·9 per cent (as an annual average). This illustrates the large margin available for investment in a business without outside help.[36]

Resorting to banks or other modes of external financing developed gradually and unequally, according to region, type of business, and the type of advance required. It is still too early to give specific or even general conclusions in this field, in spite of recent interest in these questions.[37]

The position of businessmen in relation to bank finance is well known.

One is generally suspicious of banks, fearing changes of mood and especially panics at a moment of crisis. At the least sign of a tightening up of monetary facilities, banks – and especially private banks – abruptly restrict credit and hasten to call in their advances. This policy naturally obliges industrialists and merchants to throw a part of their stocks onto a declining market and thus provoke a fall in prices.[38]

The central districts of France reflected the same picture: 'Nivernais bankers engage little in ironworks,' it was reported; 'the only example known is that of the manufacture of Pont-Saint-Ours . . . The Nivernais bank played hardly any role in the development of industry: on the other hand, it financed agricultural expansion and the equipment of large estates . . . Bank operations were founded on the basis of land.'[39] Thus it seems that there were few ties, at least at the beginning of the nineteenth century, between banks and industrial enterprises. The suspicion between banker and industrialist was twofold: the bankers were cautious of the industrialists because the former feared long-term commitments which were not thought profitable on a short-term basis, while the industrialists considered the bankers too rapacious. Nevertheless, the two sectors were never completely closed to each other, and over time a sort of osmosis developed.

External financial intervention first occurred in forming or buying businesses. The classic example is that of the Creusot ironworks, bought in 1836 by the two Schneider brothers, helped by the Seillière bank, with which they were already closely connected. Since the eighteenth century, Alsatian industrialists had shown an astonishing aptitude for borrowing, and this became even more prominent in the nineteenth century. It is true that family relations and a proximity to the Swiss financial market gave them an advantage over entrepreneurs in other regions of France.[40] The Merian brothers were particularly active in this field, buying up businesses in difficulty and placing their agents in others. They financed two of the most important businesses in Mulhouse – Dollfus–Mieg et Cie, which was said to have received 'several million' francs, and Nicolas Koechlin et Cie, who, returning from a visit to England, negotiated a loan of 1,220,000 francs at 8 per cent in Basle on 1 January 1812, followed four years later by a new appeal for 1,440,000 francs at 6 per cent. In both cases the Merian brothers led the underwriters with offers of 680,000 and 945,000 francs. Following this, Strasbourg bankers participated in launching mechanical engineering companies, such as the workshops of Risler frères et Dixon. Then, as the enterprises grew, they became capable of sustaining their own investment requirements, and bankers no longer intervened except in rare cases. After 1830 Nicholas Schlumberger and André Koechlin, local manufacturers, themselves equipped new factories and sometimes even opened credits for their clients. In this case, the bank had only acted as an intermediary in launching a business.

The bank could act in another way as a financial intermediary, by guaranteeing discounts on commercial securities or short-term loans. This was frequently the case when capital had been locked up in buildings or the purchase of materials and, in consequence, a firm experienced a shortage of working capital, particularly for buying its raw materials. In such a situation it was common for a firm to discount or rediscount commercial securities with a bank. Thus the banks of Basle discounted the bills of their Mulhouse neighbours, as well as the banks of Strasbourg. But when a crisis came, the banks refused accommodation and a financial panic followed. This was what happened in the Mulhouse enterprises in 1827-8. Because of overproduction, the market for fabrics collapsed at the end of 1827, which led the banks of

Basle to cease discounting on securities and the Bank of France to limit its rediscounts. As soon as the panic reached Mulhouse, several firms were forced into liquidation. Enormous quantities of material were then thrown onto the market at a low price by large houses seeking cash. The day was saved only by the intervention of the Parisian banker Jacques Laffitte, who succeeded in obtaining help from a bankers' syndicate which immediately opened a credit of 5 million francs. Once this panic was over, Mulhouse industrialists became more prudent in seeking to ameliorate their sales and to accelerate the speed of turn-over of working capital.[41] More and more, banks, particularly local bankers, supported industrialists in their short-term financial needs, without becoming deeply involved in their business. But given the small resources of local banks, the possibility of help was limited, at least until the first *caisses* (commercial banks) appeared in the 1840s, inspired by the example of Jacques Laffitte. And it was scarcely before 1860, at the earliest, that Parisian or local banks began to have sufficient resources to play a more active role. 'The banks hardly have any capital and need none, except to guarantee themselves against possible losses and thus justify public confidence. Their role is limited to that of furnishing more or less short-term credit to manufacturers during the winter, to the farmers during the summer, and to the import trade during the intermediary months.'[42] This situation, which characterized the 1830s, changed but slowly, as far as the banking system's relation-ship to the average entrepreneur was concerned. Banks were flexible enough in short-term lending, but less so for middle- and long-term arrangements. They were afraid to tie up their own capital or diminish their liquid assets, because the depositors could suddenly reclaim their funds. The banks were often family affairs themselves, which only risked lending when they had intimate knowledge of local circum-stances. This state of affairs continued down to the formation of large banking companies between 1860 and 1870. Thus, the firm of André & Cottier refused to open a credit for an entrepreneur from Nantes interested in the ironworks of Basse–Indre in 1825,[43] fearing that it would only increase its commitments. Such examples were frequent at the beginning of the nineteenth century. From 1835–40 onwards, it seems that the attitude of banks becomes a little more flexible. The Seillière bank – which had participated, as we have seen, in the purchase of Le Creusot – opened a drawing account for Schneider regularly from 1836. The advances were high: 1,682,000 francs in 1838 and 837,000 francs in 1844. It is true that the Seillière bankers themselves were owners of the Bazeille ironworks in the Ardennes and that they made advances to other ironmasters at Hayange and at Montchanin. It is also true that Le Creusot was a heavily capitalized business which had already failed several times and required considerable working capital. For this reason, the support of several banks was necessary, which explains the presence of the Périer bank among the creditors of Le Creusot, with an advance of a million francs.

When the banks opened credits for business firms during these years, industrial enterprises were rarely involved, because they had been warned by experience. Between 1823 and 1830 Jacques Laffitte had often procured considerable credits for his spinners, drapers, and textile printers, who remained debtors at his downfall in 1830. This is why his Caisse générale du Commerce et de l'Industrie applied a different policy between 1837 and 1846, when it excluded industrial enterprises in favour of public utilities.[44] The Péreire brothers were to follow the same policy with the Crédit Mobilier. Important credits provided by this establishment went especially to railways, shipping companies, urban transport, and public utilities (water and gas), but industrial enterprises received little: the lesson of Jacques Laffitte had not been forgotten. In this sense, Landes's comment on the similarities between the 'old' and the 'new' is correct: not only does one find the same people in both, but their techniques in respect to business did not differ.[45] There was no noticeable break in continuity in their attitude to the financing of industrial enterprise.

After 1860, however, apart from the Crédit Mobilier, the new banks adopted a less restrictive attitude towards granting credits to industry. Jean Bouvier has underlined the personal ties between the Crédit Lyonnais and the metallurgical concerns of the Lyons region. Henri Germain, a director, and numerous executives of the bank were also to be found in the administrative counsels of mines or ironworks of Le Creusot, Chatillon–Commentry, and Firminy. And yet, while the deposit banks multiplied guarantees and safeguards for its large industrial credits, large-scale industry remained reticent in accepting bank credits.[46] And when a firm did commit itself to a bank in this way, it often found itself a loser, as in the unfortunate Fuchsine affair. This manufacturer of artificial dyes, established in Lyons in 1863, had issued 8,000 shares at 500 francs each, 3,000 of which were bought by the Crédit Lyonnais, which had opened a running account for the company and also made it cash advances. Business was bad, to such an extent that in 1870 the Crédit Lyonnais had to accept the liquidation of the firm with heavy losses. Following this failure, Henri Germain adopted the principle of never again participating directly in industrial financing and put the bank's capital into more profitable outlets, without excessive long-term commitments. He showed a preference for state loans.[47]

This particular failure in no way implied a general renunciation of relationships between industrial enterprises and banks. In the development of industrial concerns, a moment comes when 'the uncommon volume of investments as well as the unusual duration of fixed plant and equipment leads large firms to resort more and more to bank support'.[48] If the Crédit Lyonnais abandoned the 'worm-eaten branches of industry', other banks replaced it. Thus, the Société Générale, founded in 1864 by leading businessmen (among whom were iron magnates like Talabot and Eugène Schneider), adopted a liberal credit policy towards industrial firms. One of the first requests for credit was made by the Forges de Denain–Anzin, which needed 3 million francs to finish the construction of a Bessemer steel mill. The operation could not be conducted on this basis, but finally a reduced credit of 400,000 francs was opened for the firm.[49] Other credits were opened for metallurgical firms in the same years. But, according to Gille, it was less a question of joint participation or mergers between banks and industrial enterprise than of ad hoc financial support. Personal connections also existed between certain banks and industries, but at this time they did not necessarily imply stable and permanent financial links.

At least banks could help businesses as public intermediaries and underwriters, when issuing bonds or shares. In this case, the bank acted indirectly, but not without playing an important role. The company of Denain–Anzin had sought the support of the Société Générale in 1865 for issuing bonds, which had to be deferred until a later date because of the opposition of shareholders. Previously, the bank Charles Gautier of Lyons had sold some bonds of Commentry–Fourchambault. By the same token, the bank Charpenay of Grenoble became the exclusive agent of the Allevard enterprise when it decided to increase its capital in 1907 and, in consequence, enjoyed a quasi-monopoly of the issue of scrip and its placement under very advantageous conditions.[50] These two examples indicate the preponderant role played by local banks rather than national establishments in such business. In general, however, as P. Léon has maintained, one must not exaggerate the role of this external financing.

The introduction of technical innovations in industrial concerns posed the most severe financial problems, as was shown by the adoption of the Bessemer process in metallurgy. The formation of entirely new industries, such as electro-metallurgy or electro-chemistry, at the end of the nineteenth century, saw the convergence of the whole range of methods of financing.[51] In the French Alps, which was the centre of these new industries, the initial capital was furnished by inventors or their friends or relatives, but such contributions were, naturally, much smaller that total requirements. Thus, in the second stage, industrialists interested in the new products moved in, and subsequently, consolidating short-term credits, the banks gave support and attracted speculative capital in their turn. Once sure of the profitability of the business, Parisian banks took over. At this stage, banks developed a series of controls over the enterprises they were supporting: more rigorous accounting, patent protection for manufacturing technology, careful studies of production costs, and the like.

Can one say that these conditions of financing retarded the development of French enterprise and can explain the relatively slow development of the French economy? Nothing yet permits us to give a definite answer. There are too few studies to allow generalization to be made with confidence. One should also know what the entrepreneurs themselves thought of this question, but they hardly made known their ideas on the issue. From the comparative studies made in the last ten years, however, it can clearly be seen that French enterprises were financed in exactly the same manner as their counterparts in other capitalist countries. When their own capital proved inadequate, supplementation was assured by means of external financing, to the extent that profitability allowed in a market context. Technical innovations, which constitute the best means of testing the efficacy of financing, had been rapidly adopted in French enterprises, where they could be profitably employed, even when associated with very costly investment. The Bessemer process, aluminium metallurgy, and the electro-chemical industry are relevant examples. It is possible that investors were inclined to prefer more profitable placements, such as loans to foreign states, real estate speculation (the reconstruction of Paris at the time of Haussmann), or railway construction. But that raises a different problem, which goes beyond the framework of the productive enterprise – namely that returns were higher in non-industrial sectors.

In the present state of our knowledge, it does not seem that French enterprise was handicapped by the shortage of finance. If there were constraints upon the more rapid development of French industry, this was not their origin.

V. Business Management

The information we have in this field is scarce. First of all, entrepreneurs did not divulge their ways of managing their affairs. Secondly, the notion of *management* as a specialized function is too recent to be applied to French businesses of the nineteenth century. Thus we must limit ourselves to a few general remarks and confine the discussions to certain well-known firms.

One of the first problems to be posed was that of the division of responsibilities, or in other words the location of power in the enterprise. Who directed it, and if – as was increasingly the case – power was shared among several groups, how were different functions allocated to each? The question was not posed in small businesses where the boss considered himself the sole head and did not share control. Neither technology, where it was traditional, nor the management of limited capitals required special competence, so that effective management lay within the reach of a single man. He directed his business as a proprietor, just as he would have managed his estate or rented properties. Such was the case of the original ironmasters of Burgundy, Franche-Comté, or Berry, who often owned woods and mines. For them there was no question of calculating costs, since they themselves furnished the raw materials. They were called, moreover, *propriétaires–exploitants*, in the same sense that one designated owner-occupiers in agriculture. Far from being just a residual category, they were still numerous in the middle of the nineteenth century. In the Haute-Marne, for example, out of 110 metallurgical establishments, seventy-two belonged to this type in 1863. For them, there were no difficulties in management techniques: what counted was the overall state of receipts and expenses seen in a concrete manner in the cash flow of the business.[52] The next stage of sophistication was the establishment of an annual or semi-annual budget, which was important because it allowed an assessment of net profits. But accounting rules were then so simple that professional accountants were not required. Every entrepreneur had his own accounting conventions, in some degree, which makes it difficult to understand and compare these budgets.

The management of these businesses remained paternalistic – or militaristic – in style, to the extent that power was concentrated in the hands of a single person or persons of the same family and was exercised over employees who, very often, except in large agglomerations, also succeeded one another, in hereditary manner, in the same jobs. Examples are not lacking of these autocratic types of business. At the Allevard ironworks, a business of average size, Eugène Charrière held quasi-monarchical power during nearly half a century from 1842 until his death in 1885. The statutes of 1842 which had given him powers of control had also created a supervising committee of five members to restrain him. But in fact he remained the absolute master, for the legal arrangements gave him maximum power with a minimum of control. Until his death he led the business with an iron hand, in no way sharing his authority.

The appearance of large-scale businesses posed entirely new problems, to the extent that their mere size postulated a division of power at the top, the definition of policy and its execution at various levels. Alfred D. Chandler has shown how American big business modelled itself on railway companies, which were the first business organizations to adopt management techniques heralding those of today.[53] In this respect, French experience seems identical, judging by recent work on the Compagnie du Chemin de Fer du Nord.[54] Founded in 1845, it was the prototype of the large railway companies, on which other large companies in different branches of business modelled themselves. What characterized the locus of power in such a company at the beginning was its extreme concentration in the hands of a *comité de direction*, composed of four members, appointed by the Administrative Council, which itself was elected by a general meeting of stockholders. In the beginning, this committee had power of decision in all domains, financial as well as technical. The engineers submitted reports twice a week of the progress or functioning of their sections and the decisions which they had been led to take. The Administrative Council was reduced to a sort of accounting agency. Other bodies grew up beside this executive committee, among others a *commission de comptabilité*, whose responsibility was essentially to define accounting techniques and the financial policy of the enterprise. Significantly, many future directors of the company were to be found among the members of this commission, which made strict rules for the keeping of accounts by the different divisions of the enterprise. It marked a first attempt at specialization in the centre of an administration which was still very little specialized. In the operating divisions themselves the power of decision was still very limited, even on a regional basis, and the dominant chain of command simply derived from the authority which was exercised from the higher echelons. Thus the beginning of specialization can be discerned within a structure which can be described without hesitation as military, since the operative principle was that of authoritarian 'command'.

This organization, which was very rigid in the beginning, evolved towards greater flexibility and decentralization at the decision-making level, but not without difficulty. In 1860, railway companies can still be compared to autocratic regimes, and Walras affirmed in 1874 that 'all the conduct of these businesses was concentrated in the hands of a few directors and heads of sections concerned with the success of the organization just from their own position within it'.[55] The influence of the Administrative Council, already limited, tended to decline still more because of the way its members were recruited: seats became hereditary fiefs of the families who had been on the board from the beginning, the Rothschilds, the Kuhlmanns, the Agaches, and others. The executive committee kept its hold by changing its composition: it recruited members especially from among former high civil servants, particularly members of the Conseil d'Etat, who had been experts on transportation questions before entering the service of the company. These became managers, who were concerned above all else with the external policies of the company – that is to say, relations with public authorities and rival companies.

Internal management passed more and more into the hands of engineers, who maintained liaison after 1867 through periodic conferences, in close relation with the executive committee. They deployed investment in accordance with the real needs of the different operating sections, and if the executive committee kept its formal powers of decision in this field, it became limited to restraining or phasing out investment demands. In fact the power of the engineers grew at the expense of the administrators. Moreover a certain decentralization can be observed. Each service tended to specialize and develop its own autonomy, communication between the various sections being conducted via joint commissions or conferences, where there was always at least one member of the executive committee present. Each section eventually became a quasi-autonomous cell within the framework of the company. A similar trend developed on a geographical basis, with the regions becoming organized in four *inspections générales* (Lille, Boulogne, Amiens, and Arras), in addition to Paris. Thus an administrative equilibrium was achieved among the various sectors, on the basis of a growing complexity of functions. As in industry, the beneficiaries were the engineers, whose technical knowledge was indispensable for good management. For this reason, traditional links grew up with the institutions concerned with the training of engineers. François Caron notes that the Compagnie du Nord hired recruits especially from the Ecole des Ponts et Chaussées and the Ecole Centrale, while the 'administrators' came from the Ecole des Sciences Politiques.

The advantage of this organization's giving pre-eminence to engineers was that it maintained contact with operational realities, was more sensitive to general needs, and limited the extension of paper-work and bureaucracy. It in no way changed the rigorous discipline demanded of the personnel of the company, which continued to make railway organization resemble a military system until the appearance of trade unions in the first years of the twentieth century.

This complexity of railway companies had no equivalent in the industrial enterprises of the nineteenth century, although one finds analogous problems in the sharing of power among shareholders (or their representatives), the director(s), and the engineers. While the principle of a 'general assembly of shareholders' was respected where it was authorized in the prospectus, its role was limited to little more than registering share-ownership. Small shareholders were not always represented on this body, for a minimum holding of shares was necessary to allow participation, and the number of votes was usually proportional to the number of shares held. The agenda of the meetings, moreover, remained at the discretion of the 'administrative council', who held the legal authority, being 'invested with the broadest powers for the administration of the company'.[56] Whom did this council represent? Very often it was the founders of the company, who succeeded in adding a few personalities representing the world of finance, banking, or public administration. Thus, one notices that the provisional administrators who appointed themselves when the company was established were confirmed in office by the general assembly and remained in the council permanently thereafter. The general policies of the firm thus came to be controlled by a self-perpetuating oligarchy, because the functions of administrators on the council were, in general, concerned with long-term issues and were linked to the possession of a certain minimum number of shares (usually fifty or a hundred). In important firms the council might delegate executive powers to a smaller committee, following the precedent established by railway companies. In this respect, it was rare for the executive committee and the council to have their headquarters in the same place as the site of manufacturing operations: the general head office was usually located in a city of some importance, such as Paris, Lyons, Saint-Etienne, or Lille, where contacts could be maintained with banks, local stock exchanges, and the government.

This physical separation between head office and operating plants posed a problem for the local management of workshops and the links between them and the administration of the company. The distance of plants from the decision-making centre imposed serious delays, as was the case in Decazeville (Aveyron), where 'the central administration in Paris was completely apathetic and the local management in Decazeville completely anarchic'. It is true that Decazeville was a long way from the capital, with difficult communications. These directors and managers responsible for control were either public administrators, often former members of the Conseil d'Etat, ministerial officers (i.e. notaries), former civil servants of the prefectorial administration (i.e. counsellors of the prefecture), or engineers from the *grandes écoles*, such as the Polytechnique, Centrale, Arts et Métiers, or Mines. To them fell the tasks of stimulating business, co-ordinating and controlling diverse operations, which became a heavy burden in large enterprises, to the point where sometimes several directors were required, each specialized in a particular aspect of the business. As in the Compagnie de Commentry, the official powers of these directors were very great, including the hiring or firing of personnel, signing agreements, establishing production programmes, and determining budgets.[57]

More and more technical tasks were given to engineers who, in fact, under pressure of events, became administrators. This was also the case with many middle-sized businesses, which, having been initially run by merchants or people of that rank, ended up in the hands of engineers. The example of the Allevard ironworks, studied by Pierre Léon, is significant in this respect.[58] After the long authoritarian reign of Eugène Charrière, a self-made man (1842–85), and then those of his son-in-law and his grandson (1885–1905), it was the engineers who took over, with Joseph Reynaud and Clausel de Coussergues, both from the Ecole Centrale.

Three linked trends may be observed in developments: division of power, specialization of function, and the growing status of technicians. There still remains to consider the more general issue of management techniques and the definition of company policy, in contrast to managerial structure. Very great variations existed here, according to temperament, financial assets, and knowledge of the economic milieu. In an era of great technical transformation like the nineteenth century, certain choices had to be made *ex ante* about the level, and nature, of investment, which would determine the future of the enterprise, without a guarantee of success *ex post facto*. Certain principles were defined and developed to meet such problems. First of all, it became the practice to create reserves by applying part of the profits (varying according to circumstances) to the remuneration of capital and devoting the rest to share or loan redemptions, to new investment, or to the provision of reserves to be used in case of difficulty. The minimum amount of reserve funds was often laid down in the articles governing the firm, although this obligation was far from being universally respected – as at Allevard, where the reserve fund was completely exhausted in 1852–3. The most difficult concept to articulate was that of amortization, which remained unknown at the beginning of the nineteenth century. It would be interesting to know at what moment this provision appeared in firms' budgets, and exactly what it signified. Sometimes amortization was understood as the writing-down of assets; at others as *autofinancement*. Thus, in the financial report of the Compagnie des Forges de Châtillon–Commentry in 1863, it was explained that 'the rule . . . is to charge all purchases or construction expenses, whatever their nature and their degree of utility, against annual profits. This rule has been strictly observed.'[59] In this case amortization concerned only the financing of new works, so that it did not correspond to the creation of redemption funds to provide a reserve for future capital expenditure. Like the railway companies, industrialists had become used to making provision for future contingencies by sharing surpluses between new investment (in buildings, plant, and machinery), the creation of reserves, and the distribution of a residual of profits. Henri Germain, a director of the Crédit Lyonnais and himself a former ironmaster, commented in 1874, 'Most industrial companies have perished less for not having earned enough than for having distributed too much.'[60] The tight legal controls over joint-stock companies before 1867 encouraged prudent financing in this respect.

Apart from these elementary principles of modern management, appropriate means had to be found to fulfil the objectives which a business had accepted for itself. Achille Dufaud learned about the use of coal in iron-smelting and -forging (les forges à l'anglaise) on a visit to England in 1823 and was determined to make this innovation as soon as he established his works at Fourchambault. Thanks to judicious investment and financial control, the enterprise prospered. When the Schneiders took over the Creusot enterprise in 1836, after a long series of failures in the preceding half-century, they give precedence to new investment (for example by utilizing the steam hammer, which was unique at that time in France) and thus managed to become established in a market considered by some as already too encumbered. On the other hand, Pétin and Gaudet, from Saint Etienne, pursued a policy of developing outlets to secure their market. Numerous businesses disappeared following erroneous forecasts and unprofitable investment, as was the case with dye manufacturers who had not appreciated the implications of the aniline revolution in Germany, or ironmasters who had made wrong decisions when steel was launched after 1855. The Compagnie des Forges de Franche-Comté provides an example of the latter. After a difficult merger in 1854, which induced over-capitalization, the company made a series of disastrous choices which condemned it to negligible profits and niggardly, ill-judged investment. Consequently, the business fell farther and farther behind better-managed firms.

Business management in the nineteenth century placed a new emphasis on sales outlets and marketing strategy. The new means of transport resulted in the unification of the internal market and the reduction of costs. Henceforth, regional markets, which had accounted for the success of local enterprises, ceased to offer protection. The industrialist, abandoning manufacturing expertise to the engineers and management techniques to the administrators, now turned to a search for markets. Thus new ties were created between the producer and the consumer. One example was the liaison between the Compagnie du Chemin de Fer du Nord, the ironworks of Denain–Anzin, and the mechanical construction enterprises which supplied some of the rolling stock. Deliberately planned commercial prospects became an essential policy for every firm which wanted to be considered well-managed. 'Industrialization,' writes Vial, 'is accompanied by a growing commercialization of business activity. Once new techniques have been mastered and consumers satisfied, business has to educate customers in new needs which it can supply.'[61] This is the ultimate stage, but certainly the most important one, in the management of the firm.

VI. Conclusions

The nature and evolution of French enterprise seems to be very similar, if not exactly analogous, to that in any capitalist country during the nineteenth century. The great majority of French businesses were family affairs, but this characteristic cannot explain a presumed lack of the spirit of enterprise, or the disintegration of firms. It is rather the contrary impression which emerges: certain family firms, such as Dollfus–Mieg, Motte–Bossut, Schneider, and Wendel, attained dimensions comparable to those of analogous foreign establishments and, by judicious investment, were able to remain in the mainstream of technical progress, if not indeed to lead it. This type of business was remarkable for the foresight and vigour of its directors, who imposed a successful policy of expansion by their personal efforts. Such leading business families in France also pursued success rather more discreetly than did the Carnegies and the Rockefellers, the Krupps, the Thyssens, and the Krugers.

The large enterprise emerged gradually during the nineteenth century, in the form of joint-stock companies or companies with transferable shares, under the stimulus and example of the railway companies created between 1845 (Cie du Nord) and 1857 (Cie du PLM). Numbers expanded greatly after their liberation from government tutelage in 1867. Businesses of this type were not absolutely the most dynamic, because they often lacked the stimulus that a man or a family with authority could confer upon them. The most dynamic companies were often those still centring on a family, such as the Cie du Nord and James de Rothschild, or the Forges de Denain–Anzin and Léon Talabot. The share of incorporated enterprise has not stopped growing in the economy, although the very large number of family businesses still surpass them in turnover. The company form of organization was responsible for developing the administrative devices which were gradually adopted by other businesses, in particular that of the family firm.

The rise of heavily capitalized companies revealed two trends. On the one hand, capital investment was increasingly critical for the fortunes of a business, and this was itself linked to the policies pursued by entrepreneurs and to the objectives they set for their firms. At the same time, the process of capital investment had its limits: in nineteenth-century France, industry attracted little personal rentier capital, which is to be explained by lack of information but also by the fact that the return on such investment remained lower than that on state bonds or on loans to foreign governments or public utility companies. Thus neither the family enterprise nor the entrepreneur should be blamed, but an understandable reticence on the part of the public. Businesses did find themselves obliged to establish a planned commercial policy in order to assure outlets for their products and justify their capital investment outlays. The marketing strategy of French business remains unexplored, apart from the well-known agreements made between ironmasters and railway companies. More and more sophisticated and complex relationships were developed between industrial producers and their customers and suppliers.

These characteristics of business development can be found in other capitalist countries and are not peculiar to France. It is not at the level of the enterprise or the entrepreneur that the problem of assumed lags in French industrial growth is to be explored. Any explanation has to be sought in terms of an overall analysis taking into account all the various factors lying behind supply and demand schedules. We also need to know more about the basic mechanisms of French economic development in the nineteenth century before such assumptions can be explained – or dismissed.

CHAPTER VIII

Capital Formation in Germany in the Nineteenth Century

I. *Introduction*

In the present state of our knowledge, any piece of economic history bearing the title 'Capital Formation in Germany in the Nineteenth Century' certainly deserves a sceptical reaction from its readers. Much basic research remains to be done before the quantitative information that title implies will be available. Recent specialized investigations into the question have stressed the difficulties in the way of obtaining a general picture, especially for the early part of the nineteenth century. German agricultural history, for example, has focused too strongly, according to one expert, on describing the experience in individual regions and branches.

The variations between individual groups of peasant farmers – differentiated according to tenure rights (and thus according to tax or debt burden), quality of the soil, size of enterprise, as well as other criteria – were so great that one may well assume that there were large variations in agricultural income and hence in the possibilities for capital formation. Individual investigations which are limited to a few farms or villages either can reflect and confirm the broad development trends that affected production techniques, marketing conditions, or consumption in *all* farms, or can reflect an exceptional situation.[1]

In a more general survey, Knut Borchardt's scepticism seemed to go still further, when he labelled any attempt to estimate the national wealth as more or less 'jesting', since short-run price variations would tend to dominate the few observations one could hope to make.[2]

The difficulties must be conceded. Yet two arguments speak for a preliminary attempt at synthesis here and now: first, serious and valuable attempts to measure German capital formation in the nineteenth century exist, notably Walter Hoffmann's, and they can be usefully exploited for the comparative purposes of the present volume; secondly, the practical and conceptual difficulties of converting heterogeneous historical data on production and prices into a standard, aggregate magnitude like 'capital formation' illuminate both the historical experience of industrialization as a process and the meaning of the concept of capital formation itself. From a preliminary statement of the problem, that is, we can discover what still needs to be learned about it and, equally important, what kinds of information we need not continue to look for.

This survey of German capital formation reflects at points the belief that there is no single 'correct' definition and/or measure of capital formation, but varying definitions and measures – the appropriateness of which depends on the questions asked and/or on the data available.[3] In general it builds on two different procedures. First, it takes the data of Hoffmann et al.[4] for the period 1850–1913 as the point of departure, comments upon them, modifies them where desirable, and for a number of magnitudes projects them back into the period 1820–50. Second, it presents independent estimates of capital formation in a number of key sectors for Prussia for the first half of the nineteenth century, following or projecting them, where possible, into the second half of the century and onto Germany as a whole. These findings can then be compared and perhaps reconciled with the data of Hoffmann et al. With very few exceptions the aim of this survey is descriptive rather than analytical. An 'explanation' of the data described and generated here will have to be part of a sequel to this chapter.

GERMAN INDUSTRIALIZATION: AN OVERVIEW

'Capital formation in nineteenth-century Germany' obviously does not refer to the description of an historical constant. Germany underwent rapid and far-reaching economic transformation during the nineteenth century, both caused by and accompanied by substantial changes in the size, and shifts in the structure, of its capital stock. Moreover, this transformation took place at an uneven pace. No discussion of Germany's capital formation during this period can safely overlook these changes and shifts. Before turning to the description of capital formation itself, therefore, it will be useful to sketch out the main lines of Germany's industrialization.

W. W. Rostow's stages-of-growth schema offers a crude approximation to the German experience.[5] He distinguishes between the period in which 'preconditions' were built (in this case, roughly 1800–50), a phase of explosive growth or 'take-off' (in this case, 1850–73), and the ensuing phase characterized by the spread of growth impulses throughout the entire economy (in this case, 1873–1913). Since this chapter goes no further than 1913, Rostow's phase of 'mass consumption' need not detain us. Within these broad Rostowian divisions it is necessary to distinguish between phases of general prosperity and those of depression and to identify important political disturbances, such as the Revolutions of 1848–9.

Oversimplifying somewhat, we may date the beginnings of the

'preconditions' period to the first decade of the nineteenth century. Napoleon's defeat of the Prussian army at Jena in 1806, and the intensified French influences and political and administrative reforms in Prussia which followed that defeat, brought important institutional changes in their train. Most important of those changes from a long-run point of view were the agrarian reforms: (1) the abolition of serfdom (1807); (2) the conversion of manorial land tenures into commercial relationships, with aristocratic landlords receiving the right to compensation for land moving into peasant possession (1807 and 1811); and (3) the related division of the common grazing lands (1816 and 1821).

Such reforms were initiated in Prussia and in nearly all the German states between 1800 and 1820, and since something like 70 per cent of Germany's population lived by agriculture at this time, they were bound to have important overall political and economic consequences. Our concern is with the *economic* consequences, but it is worth emphasizing that the long-run political ramifications of a reform programme which ensured for generations the survival of a landed aristocracy, very largely at the expense of the peasantry, may well have been the most significant historical results of these early-nineteenth-century changes.[6]

Turning to those economic consequences, we may ask whether agriculture was a 'leading sector' in Prussian industrialization. That question cannot be resolved easily, for the literature on the question of Prussian agricultural development is not without controversy.[7] Still, the following summary would probably find a consensus among the knowledgeable historians.

In the decades following 1806–16, considerable additional supplies of land, labour, and capital became or were made available for the agricultural sector. A substantial increase in the overall level of production took place as a result. Though there is some evidence of 'overproduction' during the early 1820s, taking the period 1820–50 as a whole, the terms of trade tended to favour agriculture – one reason for its expansion.[8] This expansion, however, does not seem to have sprung from technical progress, and productivity increase was probably very modest. In any case, it seems doubtful whether Prussian agriculture produced in this period any surplus which was made available to other sectors on a large scale. Prussia's grain exports to Great Britain and Holland in the 1820s and 1830s might seem to suggest that realization of an agricultural surplus was possible, but presumably this surplus was not due to large productivity increases; moreover, the question of what returns it brought to Prussia remains open.[9] Increased agricultural productivity during 1815–50 seems certain for Prussia – perhaps even more certain for Germany as a whole.[10] However, much more substantial increases in agricultural productivity in Prussia appear to have taken place in the 1850s and 1860s, accompanied also by a large increase in total production.[11] They took place, that is, during the 'take-off', when, as we know, the non-agricultural sectors were already growing substantially. The conclusion of this review of agriculture's role in early Prussian industrialization is therefore that agriculture was probably not an important 'leading sector' (I say 'probably' because more information is necessary before this issue can be settled). However, it is true that agriculture could play a significant permissive role – a point to which I shall return.

The rise in agricultural incomes during the first half of the nineteenth century helped Prussian industry to expand. However, not all of that rise directly benefited Prussian industry, because much of it went to buy foreign securities and foreign goods.[12] In fact, the German producers had great difficulty in holding their own against British competition within German markets themselves.[13] Nor could German industry easily solve its market problems by exporting abroad, for here it faced – in stable lines of expansion such as cottons, woollens, or metal wares – the competition of the more advanced economies, particularly that of Great Britain.

This reference to British competition is significant, not only because it identifies *relative* backwardness as an element in German industrialization but also because the comparison helps locate the factors retarding German industrial growth. German contemporaries themselves made much use of such comparison. It was common to point, as the Prussian statistician–economist Dieterici did in 1849, to the much greater efficiency of British cotton factories relative to German ones, and to explain this gap in terms of regional concentration, specialization, size of plant, transportation and marketing costs, and availability of capital.[14] Given the lack of such 'external economies' for individual German producers, and given the resultant cost disadvantage, investment in such lines of production was – by market criteria – a less attractive proposition for owners of capital than the purchase of real estate or government bonds.

The expansion of industrial investment thus depended on offsetting such disadvantages through state policy – measures such as protective tariffs, subsidies, and/or infrastructure investments. This took place to some extent before the 1840s, and industrial production grew – substantially in some consumption-goods branches (such as textiles) – as did the building sector. In fact, some historians see the 1830s as a significant turning point.[15] Nevertheless, it seems clear that the decisive breakthrough came in the 1840s, when government-subsidized railway-building exploded, so to speak, supplying the coal-, iron-, and

machinery-producing sectors with an expanding market and trans-
portation-using sectors with rapidly improving facilities. According to
recent research, the level of railway investment reached in 1846 was not
equalled again in Germany until 1859 – one indication of the strength
of this investment wave.[16]

The boom of the 1840s was incomplete and short-lived, however –
incomplete because of the limited extent to which consumer goods such
as textiles shared in it; and short-lived because of a crisis in agriculture in
1845–7, when poor grain harvests combined with a potato blight, and
partly because of the as-yet-limited capacity of domestic heavy industry
to supply domestic railway needs. This crisis led into the political
troubles of 1848–9, showing, as it were, how important the agricultural
sector could be in restraining growth initiated elsewhere. This episode
clearly illustrates the importance of the agricultural sector as a 'permissive' factor in the growth process.

It is owing to the crisis of 1847–9 that Rostow and others have taken
1850 as the beginning point for the 'take-off' of German industry. In
my view this is not quite correct, for the breakthrough in the transportation field in the 1840s was highly significant and was merely
continuing further in the 1850s. Nevertheless, there is sense in the
Rostowian periodization. During the 1850s, consumption goods
expanded at high rates along with producers' goods, whereas the
former had stagnated in the 1840s. Moreover, the railway-building of
the 1850s led – as the construction of the 1840s had not – to very
substantial investment activity and production expansion in the coal
and iron industries.[17] Perhaps this was a delayed response to the initial
investment wave of the 1840s; but the quantitative secondary results,
in any case, belonged to the 1850s.

In keeping with this chapter's special preoccupation with the so-
called 'preconditions' and 'take-off' phases, we need spend much less
space discussing the subsequent developments. Perhaps the following
chronology will suffice:

Period	Pattern of development
1800–30	War (to 1815) and recovery, with living standards of 1805–6 re-attained by around 1830.
1830–40	Noticeable growth of industry, especially textiles, after found-ing of Zollverein in 1833.
1840–50	First burst of heavy industrial growth sparked by railway-building and interrupted by harvest failures of 1846–7 and revolutions of 1848–9.
1850–73	The 'take-off' period with growth particularly marked in the heavy industries – coal and iron and railways – culminating in the boom following unification, 1870–3.

1873–95   A period called the 'Great Depression' era, ushered in by a financial crisis in 1873, and characterized by frequent business failures, falling prices, and relatively slow growth (at least until the mid-eighties). These features as well as industrialists' political power reflected in tariff protection for industry in 1879.

1896–1914 Two decades of very rapid growth (with some interruptions) and structural change, led by such new industries as chemicals, steel, and electricity, accompanied by market concentration, cartel-building on a large scale, and an export drive leading to Anglo-German trade rivalry.

This periodization is to some extent derived from and confirmed by quantitative studies of the German economy (see Table 78). To be sure,

Table 78. *German Growth Rates, 1850–1913 (per cent per annum)*

Period	Net product	Net product per capita	Industrial employment
1850–74	2·5	1·7	1·6
1875–91	1·9	1·0	2·3
1892–1913	3·2	1·7	2·1

SOURCE. Hoffmann *et al.*, *Wachstum der Wirtschaft*, 172ff and 454ff.

such estimates of period differences are sensitive to the choice of end-year (e.g. whether we begin period two with 1873 or 1875 makes some difference). Nevertheless, small differences in compound growth rates (like 0·1 per cent) are significant for period as long as the above ones. And our main source has commented explicitly on the coincidence of his turning points with those in earlier studies.[18]

II. *Agricultural Capital Formation*

Investment in agriculture dominated capital formation in Germany during most of the nineteenth century, and especially, as one might well imagine, during the 'preconditions' period before 1840. Of course, the data for the early period leave much to be desired, but their quality is good enough to document agriculture's predominant position. For 1850, Hoffmann *et al.* have estimated the value of the agricultural capital stock in Germany (in current prices) at about 16 billion marks, roughly half of the total. Average annual net investment in agriculture during the early 1850s they estimated at around 210 million marks – roughly 30 per cent of the average for the entire economy.[19] Henning has converted Hoffmann's data into values per unit of area of cultivated land for 1850, estimated the change from 1800 to 1850 (from roughly

360 to 700 marks per hectare), and concluded that only a fraction of the annual investment in agriculture during 1830–50 would have sufficed to absorb all of the savings opportunities being offered at this time by the banking system – such was the quantitative predominance of agriculture in this period.[20]

By the end of our period this was clearly no longer the case. The capital stock in agriculture in 1913 accounted for roughly one-fifth of the economy's total, while in 1910–13 average annual net investment amounted to 1,070 million marks (in current prices), or 15 per cent of the aggregate total.[21]

Both the early dominance of agricultural capital formation and its subsequent diminishing importance are thus clear. Nevertheless, some interesting questions remain: What did the time path of agricultural investment look like? How did the various components of the agricultural capital stock shift over the entire period? What importance did replacement investment have? To answer these questions, we look first at Prussian agriculture between roughly 1815 and 1850, and then turn to the overall German data as developed by Hoffmann et al.

A. PRUSSIAN AGRICULTURE, 1815–50

Agricultural capital formation included investment in buildings, in livestock, in land clearing and improvement, and in other inputs such as seed, fertilizer, and farm implements and machinery. In dealing with Prussian agriculture during the first half of the nineteenth century, we may regard investment in machinery as negligible. However, this does not mean that agriculture was not investing substantially. If we define investment to mean the flow of resources into the production of capital goods and include in it all expenditures essential to the maintenance and increase of the productive capacity, then agriculture was clearly a capital-intensive branch of production and its investment needs enormous.

Foremost among these needs were the expenditures on seed, the costs of maintaining livestock, and the investment in buildings.[22] Land clearing and improvement were not unimportant in the early nineteenth century, as the huge increases in cultivated land show. To a large extent, however, this represented more intensive use of grazing land and/or of land which had been only infrequently cultivated, and not the clearing, drainage, and preparation of hitherto waste or virgin lands – which cost so much, for example, in the United States at this time.[23] For this reason, and also because the labour necessary for such investment was in any case drawn from an underemployed work force, we have set its value equal to zero.[24] Our attention thus focuses on the other components.

The research which went into this chapter did not succeed in making a complete and/or completely reliable inventory of Prussian agricultural production and investment for the period 1815–50; but the most important branches, and presumably the general trends, have been captured. Table 79 presents the data on production and seed-corn reinvestment for the main crops.

Table 80 summarizes and extrapolates the data of Table 79. Before interpreting the results, some comments on the assumptions and estimating techniques which underlie them are in order. First they assume a constant ratio of seed to cultivated land. This follows what agricultural historians tell us about actual practice in this period.[25] Second, the land area allocated to each crop is based on estimates for 1805, 1816, 1843, and 1861 interpolated for the intervening years.[26] Interpolating at a constant rate over time implicitly rules out cyclical shifts in the acreage devoted to individual crops in response to yield and/or price changes. Thus yield declines on rye-growing land in the 1840s may have been smaller than our figures suggest, and so forth. Third, the wholesale prices used here are an arithmetic average of the prices quoted for Berlin and Königsberg (in Jacobs and Richter). These may be unrepresentative market prices for Prussia as a whole; moreover, they also refer to products sold in urban markets – which may have required a higher quality on the average than that portion which was consumed or reinvested in the farms themselves. Only further research can shed light on these uncertainties.

The results themselves are certainly fascinating enough to call for that further research – soon. We see here the crisis of the mid-forties. We see significant gains in production in the 1820s and 1830s. Most important, however, we see a very high proportion of agricultural crop output flowing back into reinvestment. Now if we were to apply the wastage and livestock feed ratios calculated for Germany for the post-1850 period to this crop production, the rate of investment would rise still further: wheat by 5 per cent, rye by 28 per cent, oats by 93 per cent, and barley by a large but imprecisely known proportion.[27] Such a procedure is probably not permissible, since these feed ratios reflect an agricultural sector already specializing in livestock production and importing its cereal requirements. This does not seem to have been true of Prussian agriculture during the first half of the nineteenth century, though some upward adjustments for loss and feed would surely be in order.

But even if we ignore that form of investment – as we do here – it is necessary to add most of the production of grass crops, hay, alfalfa, straw, and other feed-crops as well as turnips, etc. to gross capital formation. According to the standard work on Prussian agriculture,

Table 79. *Value of Production and Seed Input for Major Agricultural Crops in Prussia, 1816–64 (production in millions of marks, 1913 prices)*

	Wheat		Rye		Barley		Oats		Potatoes	
	Production	% seed	Production	% seed	Production	% seed	Production	% seed	Production	% seed
1816	73·5	18·3	288·8	25·0	140·7	22·1	254·6	21·9	57·9	19·4
1819	97·4	17·7	368·2	24·1	171·1	21·1	314·7	21·3	99·9	18·7
1822	91·3	17·3	340·9	23·3	136·4	20·4	276·2	20·7	141·5	18·4
1825	97·8	16·8	346·8	22·7	145·4	19·6	292·2	20·3	178·3	18·6
1828	109·7	16·2	478·2	21·9	197·6	18·7	401·8	19·8	155·5	25·9
1831	116·2	15·8	487·7	21·3	181·2	18·4	375·5	19·4	262·1	18·5
1834	124·1	15·3	467·1	20·7	181·3	17·9	390·7	19·1	302·2	18·5
1837	142·8	14·9	516·2	20·2	192·7	17·5	413·0	18·7	344·3	18·4
1840	137·5	14·7	558·8	19·6	194·3	17·1	427·8	18·4	381·6	18·5
1843	130·4	16·3	579·9	22·8	182·7	19·3	386·6	21·3	347·7	22·0
1846	113·1	18·4	334·2	31·7	149·6	22·4	293·5	25·3	317·5	26·7
1849	166·9	14·9	634·5	17·2	212·6	15·7	354·7	18·9	548·7	17·6
1852	155·6	15·0	510·6	20·3	166·4	18·4	301·1	22·6	511·1	19·3
1861	178·1	13·9	616·9	18·5	180·5	14·8	351·9	19·2	497·6	22·4
1864	200·9	—	717·2	—	204·7	—	423·3	—	682·7	17·1

SOURCES. Von Finckenstein, *Entwicklung der Landwirtschaft*, Tables 1–4, 14, 15, and 17a in Appendix; A. Jacobs and H. Richter, *Die Grosshandelspreise in Deutschland von 1792 bis 1934*, Sonderhefte des Instituts für Konjunkturforschung (Berlin, 1935), 52–7.

Table 80. *Agricultural Crop Production and Seed Reinvestment in Prussia, 1816–49 (production in millions of marks, 1913 prices)*

	(1) Value of 5-crop production	(2) % of crop reinvested as seed	(3) Value of (2)	(4) Estimated total crop production	(5) Estimated feed plus seed (absolute)	(6) Investment (%)
1816	815.5	22.5	183.5	1,890.9	1,171.7	61.0
1819	1,051.3	21.7	228.1	2,392.6	—	—
1822	986.3	20.9	206.1	2,238.4	1,274.1	56.9
1825	1,060.5	20.3	215.3	—	—	—
1828	1,342.8	20.8	279.3	—	—	—
1831	1,422.7	19.4	276.0	3,085.8	1,654.0	53.6
1834	1,465.4	19.1	279.9	—	—	—
1837	1,609.0	18.6	299.3	—	—	—
1840	1,700.0	18.4	312.8	3,513.2	1,746.9	49.7
1843	1,627.3	21.3	346.6	—	—	—
1846	1,207.9	26.5	320.1	—	—	—
1849	1,921.6	17.2	330.5	3,601.8	1,647.5	45.7

SOURCE. See text, and Appendix below.

these crops were of considerable importance as capital inputs used for the maintenance and increase of livestock. They are included in columns 4 and 5 of Table 80.[28]

Clearly, then, this branch of agricultural production was highly capital-intensive. It is interesting to reflect that because of this fact technical and/or organizational changes leading to increased productivity here tended to be 'capital-saving'. Henning has estimated an increase in yields in Germany's family farms (*Bauernwirtschaft*), during the period 1800–50, from between three- and fivefold to between four- and sevenfold.[29] Franz (citing Bittermann) reports an increase in grain yields in Germany of about one-third;[30] and our own data for Prussia reflect a similar, if somewhat smaller, shift. These increases, one recognizes in retrospect, were the only adequate reply to complaints about capital shortage in agriculture during this period; owing to the capital-intensive character of agricultural production, these complaints contained a great deal of substance, after all.[31] The spread of potato and turnip cultivation leading to the exploitation of low-quality land – which was the major development in Prussian agriculture during this period – may have provided food and feed, and hence the basis for population increase; but it also dragged down product per acre and tied up labour in agriculture itself.[32]

However, increased productivity in grain-growing – even if the increase had been substantial – would not necessarily have released capital to the non-agricultural sector, because increased livestock production would tend to absorb a large share of the resources 'freed'. This is already reflected in Table 80. What we do not yet see are the results of that investment. Table 81 attempts to summarize those results. The

Table 81. *Value of Livestock, Animal Production, and Feed Costs in Prussia, 1816–58 (million marks, current and 1913 prices)*

	Value of livestock		Animal production[a]		Feed costs[b]	
	Current prices	1913 prices	Current prices	1913 prices	Current prices	1913 prices
1816	706·8	1,441·8	249·2	366·6	808·5	975·0
1822	569·1	1,724·3	246·5	419·5	523·7	1,067·8
1831	763·4	2,061·2	292·1	479·0	1,007·0	1,377·1
1840	998·6	2,696·1	369·2	602·2	827·8	1,434·9
1849	1,186·8	2,895·8	428·6	725·8	672·8	1,451·2
1858	1,718·2	3,367·6	647·7	853·7	1,076·0	1,438·4

[a] Includes commodity production only, not labour services.
[b] Feed crops valued as stated in note 28.

SOURCE. See text, and Appendix below.

estimates, once again, are extremely rough ones which further research will have to improve upon.[33]

Table 81 reveals the same upward break in growth trends for livestock and animal production around 1850 that Table 79 shows for crop production. It also reflects the high capital requirements for maintenance demanded in agricultural production 1800–50, although efficiency in animal and livestock production increased throughout the period.

Before summarizing the overall efficiency of investment in Prussian agriculture during the 'preconditions' period, it will be necessary to add estimates of investment in buildings to complete the picture. These figures are derived from data and procedures discussed in the next

Table 82. *Capital Stock in Prussian Agriculture, 1816–49*
(millions of marks, current prices)[a]

	Buildings	Seed	Livestock	Total
1816	1,850·3	148·5	706·8	2,705·6
1822	2,009·1	110·9	569·1	2,689·1
1831	2,167·1	220·3	736·4	3,150·8
1840	2,411·3	226·7	998·6	3,636·6
1849	2,672·0	200·5	1,186·8	4,059·3

[a] Current prices are used because an index to deflate the value of the building stock is not readily available.

SOURCE. See text, and Appendix A below.

section. Tables 82 and 83 present these estimates and combine them with data on other elements of agricultural capital and on production, to produce overall measures of the burden and yield of this investment.[34]

These results are somewhat problematical because of the weaknesses in the underlying data and the speculative character of some of the estimating assumptions (e.g. the age structure of the building stock). Agriculture raises problems because so many intermediate products consumed in that sector were also produced there, as was an uncertain share of its capital. Table 82, in any case, presents estimates of the capital stock, and Table 83 estimates of gross product and of gross capital formation. Table 84 gives data on value added, while Table 85 finally presents 'guesstimates' of net investment.

These data will need careful inspection and, no doubt, some correction before they can serve as links to the presumably more reliable estimates of agricultural production and investment in the later period. The rate of investment seems low by comparison with what we know of agriculture later; and if Hoffmann's data for Germany in the 1850s are roughly representative of Prussia in the 1840s, a rather substantial upward correction for machinery investment is in order. Since the data

Table 83. *Agricultural Gross Product in Prussia, 1816–49 (millions of marks, 1913 prices)*

	(1)	(2)	(3)	(4)	(5)	(6)	(7)	(8)
					Gross investment			
	Total crop	Feed	Net crop (1) – (2)	Animal product	Animal stock increment	Seed plus seed increment	Building investment	Gross product
1816	1,890·9	975·0	915·9	366·6	47·1	190·9	59·0	1,579·5
1819	2,392·6	1,190·9	1,201·7	—	—	—	—	—
1822	2,218·4	1,067·8	1,150·6	419·5	56·7	209·1	57·3	1,893·2
1825	2,516·5	1,230·0	1,286·5	—	—	—	—	—
1828	2,986·2	1,383·8	1,602·4	—	—	—	—	—
1831	3,085·8	1,377·1	1,708·7	479·0	54·0	277·3	55·9	2,574·9
1834	3,053·6	1,286·7	1,766·9	—	—	—	—	—
1837	3,328·3	1,376·3	1,952·0	—	—	—	—	—
1840	3,513·5	1,434·9	2,078·6	602·2	46·4	324·1	64·2	3,115·5
1843	3,893·9	1,750·6	2,143·3	—	—	—	—	—
1846	3,053·3	1,400·6	1,652·7	—	—	—	—	—
1849	3,864·6	1,451·2	2,413·4	724·8	37·8	328·5	82·2	3,586·7

SOURCE. See text, and Appendix below.

are consistent in deviation with the rest of our estimates, however, they have been allowed to stand. Interesting in this connection are some comparisons of levels and rates of growth. Our figures imply for 1816 a per capita income in agriculture of around 190 marks (in 1913 prices),

Table 84. *Value Added in Prussian Agriculture, 1816–49*
(millions of marks, 1913 prices)

	(1) Gross product	(2) Seed[a]	(3) Building outlays[b]	(4) Value added	(5) Net value added[c]	(6) Net value added per head
1816	1,579·5	190·9	29·5	1,359·1	1,323·3	187·9
1822	1,893·2	209·1	28·7	1,655·4	1,616·0	206·9
1831	2,574·9	277·3	28·0	2,269·6	2,226·0	261·3
1840	3,115·5	324·1	32·1	2,759·3	2,714·1	297·9
1849	3,586·7	328·5	41·1	3,217·1	3,167·0	328·5

[a] Seed saved for following year's production.
[b] Assumes half of farm construction was purchased (= one-half of column 7 of Table 83).
[c] Column 4 minus depreciation charges estimated at 1·5 per cent of the building stock of Table 82.

whereas other sources suggest for the same date for Prussia as a whole 150 to 160 marks at the most.[35] For roughly the same point in time (1818), Kuczynski has collected agricultural wage rates which could imply a wage bill of around 870 million for the Prussian agricultural

Table 85. *Average Annual Net Investment in Prussian Agriculture,*
1816–49 (millions of marks, 1913 prices)

	Seed	Livestock	Buildings	Total	% share of output[a]
1816–22	7·6	47·1	31·8	86·5	5·9
1822–31	7·8	37·4	23·2	70·4	3·7
1831–40	4·1	70·5	35·0	109·6	4·4
1840–9	2·0	22·2	35·7	59·9	2·0

[a] Output: column 5 of Table 84 (net value added).

SOURCE. See text, and Appendix below.

sector as a whole.[36] This can be compared, in turn, with the sector's interest and debt burden – an annual charge in 1816 of between 16 and 20 million marks – and with its imputed rental income of roughly 58 million marks. Taken together, these figures suggest that agriculture was already a sector generating a surplus.[37] That is also the impression we get if we observe the sector's development over time. Between 1816

and 1849, for example, the agricultural population grew by an estimated 37 per cent, while net output more than doubled. The resultant
75 per cent increase in per capita output implies an average income of
around 326 to 329 marks per head in 1849 – well above that suggested
by the literature.[38] That means that these figures must be used with care
and that they probably require correction. For example, 1849 was an
exceptionally good harvest year, so that taking an average of (say)
1849–52 would probably lower the rate of growth from 1816 onwards.
A broadening of the price index basis to include secondary markets
would probably have a similar effect.[39] Should the values be anywhere
near the mark, they deserve two further comments. First, both output
and output per capita appear to have grown significantly faster than
capital (though only slightly more rapidly than one estimate of arable
land).[40] That may be a hint at the capital-saving character even of early
industrialization, Rostow notwithstanding. Second, the high per capita
product figure implies nothing about income distribution as between
classes and between individuals. The data do not contradict the considerable evidence on rural poverty in Prussia during the 1830s and
1840s.[41] Both points bear on the role of agriculture in Prussian and
German industrialization, and both deserve closer attention.

B. GERMAN AGRICULTURE, 1850–1913

Turning to German agricultural investment in the second half of the
nineteenth century, we may confine ourselves to a discussion (including
minor modifications) of the estimates of Hoffmann *et al.* Tables 86 and
87 set out the relevant data.

Table 86. *Average Annual Net Investment in German Agriculture,
1850–1913 (millions of marks, 1913 prices)*

	(1) Buildings	(2) Implements and machines	(3) Livestock	(4) Stocks	(5) Total	(6) Total as % of agricultural product
1850–9	190	50	40	—20	260	5·74
1860–9	200	60	120	60	440	8·42
1870–9	240	60	10	10	320	5·39
1880–9	190	60	80	10	340	4·89
1890–9	170	70	150	70	460	5·55
1900–9	310	130	160	40	640	6·61
1910–13	590	160	250	80	1,080	10·60

Table 87. *Average Annual Gross Product and Feed–Seed Investment in German Agriculture, 1850–1913 (marks)*

	(1) Total agricultural product	(2) Total crop product	(3) Ratio I[a]	(4) Ratio II[b]
			\[Feed–seed investment\]	
1850–9	6,038,245,376	2,917,095,424	24·50	50·70
1860–9	7,485,095,936	3,580,054,272	24·67	51·55
1870–9	8,461,959,168	3,943,022,080	23·79	51·08
1880–9	9,720,750,080	4,439,347,200	23·47	51·36
1890–9	11,516,305,408	5,153,574,912	23·05	51·50
1900–9	14,065,860,608	6,256,873,472	23·94	53·79
1910–13	15,475,908,608	6,801,432,576	25·74	58·70

[a] Feed–seed outlays as percentage of column 1.
[b] Feed–seed outlays as percentage of column 2.

SOURCE. Hoffmann *et al.*, *Wachstum der Wirtschaft*, Tables 50, 56, and 60.

Several conclusions may be drawn from these data.

(1) The expected secular rise in the level of annual net investment is confirmed.

(2) The growth in investment levels roughly kept pace with agriculture's gross product (in the conventional sense of the term). Thus the overall increase in the share of output going to investment in the German economy cannot be attributed to agriculture.

(3) Large fluctuations in agricultural net investment took place throughout the entire period and were remarkably dependent on fluctuations in stocks, which in turn were highly dependent on fluctuations in the harvest.[42] This suggests, once again, the continued vulnerability of agriculture to natural forces, despite the considerable capital accumulation and technological progress of the period. What this must have meant for the economy as a whole can only be surmised, for a detailed empirical analysis has yet to be executed.

(4) In this connection one might note in addition (a) the relatively small importance of investment in machinery until around 1900 and (b) the considerable swings in investment in buildings and livestock. It seems to me that analyses 'explaining' agricultural investment as a whole should begin with these swings in its several components. Fig. 6 (p. 398) reproduces the investment values from Hoffmann *et al.* in graphic form.

Table 87 resumes the earlier discussion of agriculture's gross investment needs, this time for Germany as a whole. If resources devoted to the maintenance and increase (and/or improvement) of the productive capacity be regarded as capital formation, then it is clear that agriculture was a capital-intensive branch of production. Increases in productivity in crop production were in themselves capital-saving, but they tended to induce a relative increase in animal production, so that 'capital' in this real sense could not be released to the non-agricultural sectors. It is almost paradoxical to reflect that industrialization – i.e. the

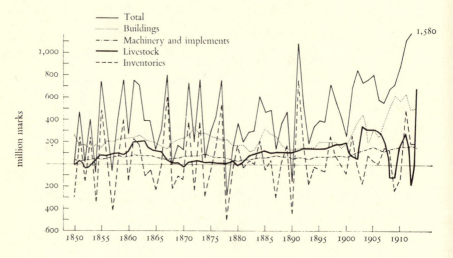

Fig. 6. Agricultural Investment and Its Components in Germany,
1850–1913 (1913 prices)

relative increase in industrial production – was itself capital-saving, since it meant a reduction in the overall importance of agricultural production. Because of the limited applicability of modern science and technology to agricultural production, interestingly, enormous amounts of resources had to be tied up there to secure the relatively modest net increases in product available for consumption and further investment which are recorded by our statistical coverage.[43] Even more significant in the light of modern-day concern with the ecological implications of industrial processes, however, is the fact that the disadvantages of agriculture relative to industry were related to the farmer's need to recycle its product and in general to his need to bow (so to speak) to natural, biological forces. This, it now appears, was an expensive necessity, whatever its positive aspects may have been.

III. *Investment in Buildings*

Throughout the nineteenth century, in Germany as in other countries, building absorbed the lion's share of resources flowing into capital formation. Hoffmann *et al.* have estimated for Germany as a whole during 1850–1913, a share fluctuating between roughly 45 per cent and 55 per cent. This share was, however, marked by distinct structural trends: agricultural buildings accounted in the 1850s for 55–60 per cent of the total stock, but over the years 1910–13 for barely one-fifth.[44] The corollaries to this shift were (1) the growing investment in industrial and commercial plant and equipment (between 1850 and 1913 this rose to around 700–800 million marks per year, or from roughly 10–12 per cent of total investment to more than 30 per cent: most of this relative increase, to be sure, was attributable to equipment); (2) increased investment in non-agricultural dwellings, whose share in total investment held its own and whose share in total capital increased to more than one-fourth of the total (in 1913 prices).[45] Table 88 provides a somewhat more detailed statement of the long-term trends.

Table 88. *Building Investment in Germany, 1850–1913 (annual averages in millions of marks, 1913 prices)*

	(1) Agricultural buildings	(2) Business plant	(3) Non-agricultural dwellings	(4) Public buildings	(5) Total
1851–9	180	50	190	40	460
1860–9	224	94	447	70	835
1870–9	236	222	734	121	1,313
1880–9	194	295	701	134	1,324
1890–9	167	576	1,321	161	2,223
1900–13	420	719	1,868	338	3,345

SOURCE. Hoffmann *et al.*, *Wachstum der Wirtschaft*, Tables 31 (column 1), 35 (column 1), and 41 (columns 3 and 4).

A. PRUSSIA, 1816 TO THE 1850S

The estimates of capital formation in buildings presented here cover roughly the period from 1816 to the 1850s and concentrate largely on developments in Prussia. They rely on three main data sources: (1) Hoffmann *et al.* for 1850 (and some post-1850) values, (2) fire insurance returns, and (3) the various buildings censuses. The Prussian building tax returns provide additional helpful information – though they are not quite as good a data source for the period before 1850 as Hoffmann *et al.* found them to be for the period 1850–1913. Our estimates combine these sources in a number of different ways, none of which can command the reader's full confidence. Indeed, the measurement of capital formation in building in Germany during the *first* half of the nineteenth century is a research problem which requires much more detailed attention than could be spared for the preparation of this chapter.[46]

Table 89. *Fire Insurance Values of Buildings in Prussia, 1800–67*
(millions of marks, current prices)

	Insurance value	Estimated non-insured value[a]
1800	1,444·2	722·1
1816	1,860·0	930·0
1819	1,866·0	931·0
1821	1,869·0	933·0
1828	2,124·0	1,062·0
1834	2,148·0	1,074·0
1840	2,865·0	954·0
1843	3,309·0	1,101·0
1849	3,690·0	1,230·0
1853	3,459·0	1,186·0
1858	3,834·0	1,278·0
1867	5,598·0	1,866·0

[a] According to F. W. von Reden, *Deutschland und das übrige Europa* (Wiesbaden, 1854), 240.

Table 89 shows the estimated value of buildings insured against fire through public fire insurance associations in Prussia from 1800 to 1867. Most writers have treated these statistics with great scepticism – though not always for the same reasons. The Prussian statistician Dieterici argued that the official figures understated both the true value of the stock of buildings at particular points in time *and* the growth of that stock (*a*) because a number of public buildings were not insured, (*b*) because many buildings were insured privately, through joint-stock companies like the Aachen–Munich or Gotha, and (*c*) because many buildings were only partially insured, to the value of 'that which is burnable'.[47]

On the other hand, Wilhelm von Reden, a reputable contemporary of Dieterici's, believed that the official statistics exaggerated the growth in the capital value of buildings in Prussia during this period, since they reflected increased insurance coverage rather than true investment. As he wrote, however, the existing stock of buildings remained larger than its officially insured portions suggested. His estimate of one-third of fire insurance values for non-insured buildings has been included in Table 89 (from 1840 on).[48]

As is usual in such controversies, both parties were right. In this case, Dieterici was writing at the end of the 1850s, when the joint-stock companies had in fact been making great progress in the fire insurance business, whereas von Reden was, in the main, looking back at the pre-1850 period. It does appear that the inroads of the private companies up to the 1850s were largely in the insuring of purely industrial buildings and mobile wealth (such as furnishings) against fire and not, by and large, in the main form of building capital – private residential structures.[49] On the other hand, though von Reden was probably correct in arguing that insurance was growing more rapidly than building activity, up to *c.* 1850, it may well be legitimate in trend analysis to focus exclusively on the portion to be insured (presumably more modern).[50] This question, however, must remain open for the moment.

Table 89 clearly reflects, in any case, two important probabilities: (1) Secular growth. According to the figures in the 'Insurance values' column, the capital in buildings almost doubled between 1816 and 1849 – in a period of falling prices – and even in per capita terms there was a substantial increase. (2) The sensitivity of the results to assumptions about little-known relationships. In this case, for example, including the estimated values for uninsured buildings (in Table 89) reduces the percentage rate of increase in per capita building capital in 1816–49 from 21 per cent to 7 per cent.

Table 90 offers a second measure of investment in building. Using the estimated stock values of 1816 (or 1849) as a point of departure, it is possible to estimate the growth *trend* by means of changes in the numbers of buildings reported in the various censuses, combined with data on urban population growth. The rationale for this procedure derives from sub-sample testing which showed that close relationships appear to exist between fire insurance values of buildings and the degree of urbanization on the one hand, and (especially in rural areas) between *number* of buildings and fire insurance values on the other.[51] It seems reasonable, therefore, to relate the growth in building values to an average of the growth rate (*a*) of the number of buildings and (*b*) of the urban population (defined as that portion of the population living in towns with at least 5,000 inhabitants).

This index of building investment suggests – as did Table 89 – substantial growth in the stock of buildings in Prussia during the first half of the nineteenth century and, in particular, a concentration of building activity in the 1830s and 1840s. Two comments are in order here, however. First, the numbers are sensitive to the assumptions about which published fire insurance values are most accurate or about the value of uninsured buildings. Though this may not affect the growth rates calculated, it does influence the absolute values and thus affects comparison with other sectors and periods. Second, Table 90 makes implicit use of the hypothesis that investment in buildings is a function of urbaniza-

Table 90. *Estimated Value of Capital in Buildings in Prussia, 1816–58*

	(1)	(2)	(3)	(4)	(5)
				Value (millions of marks, current prices)	
	Index numbers (1816 = 100)				
	Number of buildings	Urban population	Value of buildings	With 1849 value[a]	With 1816 value[a]
1816	100	100	100·0	2,754	2,790
1819	105	110	107·0	2,904	2,997
1822	109	117	113·0	3,051	3,153
1828	115	129	122·0	3,297	3,405
1831	117	134	125·5	3,396	3,501
1834	123	139	131·0	3,543	3,654
1840	132[b]	173	152·5	4,134	4,254
1843	137	191	164·0	4,476	4,575
1849	144	218	181·0	4,920	5,049
1858	155	279	217·0	5,904	6,054

[a] Based on fire insurance values for 1816 and 1849, plus estimated non-insured building values.
[b] Interpolated.

SOURCE. See text.

tion. This must be mentioned because such a hypothesis, while defensible, has not yet been discussed here. The main concern of this chapter is to construct reasonable measures of capital formation, not models explaining it; at times, however, this separation of purposes is extremely difficult to maintain.[52]

A third method for estimating the value of capital in buildings applies the estimated returns to real property calculated by Prussian tax officials in the late 1820s and early 1830s. We have taken the results as reported by two contemporary observers, Hansemann and von Viebahn, as the basis for our estimates.[53] Von Viebahn suggested that yearly rental values of buildings in the 1830s averaged about 3 per cent of their purchase prices, with other information suggesting that this figure may be slightly high.[54] For the estimates of Table 91, in any case, we have multiplied the rental values by a factor of 35 – implying rental values of around 2·8 per cent of capitalized value. These capitalized values, however, exclude non-residential farm buildings, and probably business plant as well.[55] We therefore follow Hoffmann *et al.* here in assuming that the value of residential and non-residential farm buildings were equal. Using the rental values of 1831 as bench-mark data, we then extrapolate values for the other years on the basis of a rate equal to the average of the rate of growth in number of buildings and urban population.

Table 91. *Capitalized Rental Values and Estimated Building Capital in Prussia, 1816–58 (millions of marks)*

	Rental values capitalized				Rental values capitalized		
	Dwellings	Other	Total		Dwellings	Other	Total
1816	1,368	807	2,175	1834	1,791	948	2,739
1819	1,470	852	2,322	1840	2,085	1,083	3,168
1822	1,545	882	2,427	1849	2,475	1,263	3,738
1828	1,668	918	2,586	1858	2,970	1,335	4,305
1831	1,710	924	2,634				

SOURCE. See text.

We thus have three alternative sets of numbers from which a 'best' estimate of building investment might be derived. Unfortunately, until a good deal more is known about fire insurance coverage or building rental values, etc. there can be no scientifically grounded choice of a 'best' estimate. Instead, we are reduced to the time-honoured practice of taking an average. The results of this exercise are displayed in Table 92. Now if we assume that normal depreciation of the building stock just equals the value of non-insured improvements and buildings not reflected in the series, and further assume that building values are original cost values, then our numbers represent net investment in current prices.[56] These current values can then be converted into constant prices by means of an index combining the cost of construction materials and construction workers' wages.[57]

The figures in Table 92 refer to *net* investment in buildings. Yet for some purposes, knowing the values of gross investment is just as important. Net investment is no doubt a better indicator of capacity growth, but gross investment better measures society's ability to abstain from consumption of its current output in the interest of the future. Unfortunately, information on building maintenance and replacement is neither abundant nor easily obtainable. For the purposes of this chapter we must be satisfied with the following superficial sketch of the problem.

Leopold Krug's masterly analysis of Prussia's economy around 1800 pointed to the annual charges upon the nation's 'real' surplus absorbed by the maintenance and insurance of its stock of buildings: 12 million talers (4 million marks) for maintenance and 2·4 million talers for fire and damage insurance – totalling roughly 2 per cent of the capitalized value.[58] About twenty-five years later David Hansemann estimated building maintenance charges at 50 per cent of the annual rents.[59] Now if the rental return of 3 per cent used earlier were correct, annual main-

Table 92. *Estimated Building Capital and Net Investment in Building in Prussia, 1800–58 (millions of marks)*

	Estimated building value		Average annual investment		Percentage rate of growth[a] (current prices)
			Current prices	1913 prices	
1800[b]	2,166[b]	1800–16	25·5	40·5	1·2
1816	2,574	1816–19	56·1	60·9	2·2
1819	2,742	1819–22	45·0	60·0	1·6
1822	2,877	1822–8	36·6	46·2	1·3
1828	3,096	1828–31	27·0	37·5	0·9
1831	3,137	1831–4	45·0	58·5	1·4
1834	3,312	1834–40	90·0	115·5	2·7
1840	3,852	1840–3	101·1	123·3	2·6
1843	4,155	1843–9	69·0	86·4	1·7
1849	4,569	1849–58	94·8	118·5	2·1
1858	5,421	—	—	—	—

[a] Cannot be calculated for 1913 constant prices.
[b] *Source.* L. Krug, *Betrachtungen über den Nationalreichtum der preussischen Staaten,* 2 vols. (Berlin, 1805; repr. Aalen, 1967).

tenance charges at this time (1828–31) would have amounted to roughly 1·5 per cent of the capitalized value of buildings, or some 46 million marks – much more than the estimated annual net investment. Prussian tax laws at this time granted an allowance for maintenance cost. If we regard this as including depreciation and maintenance charges, and if owners exploited the allowance to its maximum (50 per cent of rental values), then 1·5 per cent would be, in fact, a reasonable guess.[60]

B. SECTORAL DISTRIBUTION OF BUILDINGS

How was building investment distributed sectorally? Following Hoffmann *et al.*, we distinguish between four main building types: agricultural residential and non-residential buildings, non-agricultural dwellings, business plant, and public buildings. Three factors make our discussion somewhat easier: (1) the availability of the structural estimates of Hoffmann *et al.* for all of Germany from 1850; (2) the relatively small importance of both business and public buildings in the first half of the nineteenth century (suggested by Hoffmann's data for

1850); and (3) the existence of Prussian census data on the distribution of the *numbers* of buildings among different uses.

According to Hoffmann *et al* , the structure of building capital and investment in the early 1850s for Germany as a whole looked as follows.

(1) Capital stock in buildings at original cost prices in millions of marks:

Agricultural buildings	9,300
Non-agricultural dwellings	4,650
Business plant	1,560
Public buildings	1,210
Total buildings	16,720

(2) Average annual net investment in buildings in current prices in millions of marks, 1851–4

Agricultural buildings	135
Non-agricultural dwellings	203
Business plant	30
Public buildings	30
Total buildings	398

The pattern of building investment before 1850 in Prussia may have differed somewhat from this, but it is unlikely that the difference was a large one. What is important for our purposes is, above all, the relative unimportance of investment in business plant and public buildings – which may justify their treatment here as residuals.

We do not possess enough evidence to satisfactorily test Hoffmann's key assumptions that the value of agricultural residential buildings equalled both the value of agricultural non-residential buildings and that of non-agricultural dwellings. Some evidence suggesting the former equality is available,[61] but the latter seems clearly contradicted by the tendency of building values per capita to rise with population concentration, while population concentration – for which urbanization is one convenient indicator – is negatively related to the relative size of the agricultural population. It would therefore seem unwise to rely on Hoffmann *et al.* alone, and the estimates below turn to the building census material for help. These censuses give the number of buildings in different uses at different times and can be combined with urbanization data to estimate both the trends in growth and changes in structure.[62] If we can assume (as we did for Table 90) that the growth in the value of *all* buildings is equal to the average rates of growth of urban population and of total numbers of buildings, then it would seem reasonable to treat the value of farm buildings as related to their numbers alone. In

Table 93. *Value and Structure of Building Capital in Prussia, 1816–58*
(millions of marks)

	(1)	(2)	(3)	(4)	(5)	(6)	(7)
	Growth index			Value of buildings			
	Farm	Non-farm residen- tial	Farm residen- tial	Farm non- residen- tial	Non-farm residen- tial	Business plant	Public
1816	100	100	944	907	585		138
1819	105	110	—	—	—		—
1822	109	117	1,024	986	683		184
1828	115	129	—	—	—		—
1831	117	134	1,104	1,063	780		230
1834	122	139	1,150	1,107	813		242
1843	138	191	1,307	1,258	1,106		484
1849	145	218	1,361	1,311	1,268		629
1858	156	279	1,464	1,410	1,626	542	379

SOURCE. See text.

Table 93 we relate (*a*) the growth in the value of farm building to the rate of growth in the number of *all* buildings (column 1 of Table 90)[63] and (*b*) the growth of non-farm dwellings (values) to the growth rate of the urban population. We then adopt Hoffmann's proportions (for Germany as a whole) for 1858 and extrapolate them backwards by means of the index numbers (columns 1 and 2 of Table 90).

It appears that this procedure leads to partly absurd results, because the residual categories of business plant and public building show implausibly high rates of growth or, to state the matter differently, implausibly low values for the earlier years. One would expect a large increase in business plant because of industrialization, and because the figures for non-farm dwellings for the earlier years probably contained a more than negligible amount of business plant later reported exclusively as such. But even if we were to set business plant in 1816 equal to zero we would still get nearly a tripling in the value of public buildings of 1816–58 – surely implausible in the light of what we know about the relatively modest increases in government spending over the period.[64] Nevertheless, an easy solution is not to be found, and the figures of Table 93 have been allowed to stand.

C. BUILDING CAPITAL IN GERMANY BEFORE 1850

To what extent can this use of Prussian data be extended to Germany as a whole? For the purposes of this chapter a few rather superficial remarks and crude calculations must suffice. Fortunately, our speculations here can be aided by reference to the work of Hoffmann *et al.* We also have some crude pioneering contemporary attempts as guideposts. In 1854, for example, von Reden projected values derived from fire insurance data for Prussia to all of Germany by means of numbers of buildings per capita and per square kilometre.[65] He arrived at a total for Germany for 1849 (or 1850) of 5·07 million talers or 15·2 million marks. Hoffmann's estimate for 1850 is 16·7 million, or nearly 10 per cent higher.

This same von Reden, however, was very industrious in gathering and disseminating information on housing (and other forms of wealth) in all of the German states. It is possible to wring from von Reden's data estimates of the building capital stock for Württemberg, Baden, and Hannover for the early 1830s and the late 1840s. Those three states contained at the latter date an aggregate population of about 4·9 million (the rest of non-Prussian Germany, around 14·5 million). If fire insurance values in these countries accurately reflected actual building capital values, as Hoffmann *et al.* have claimed,[66] and if these states were representative of all Germany, then column 1 of Table 94 below gives a good

Table 94. *Estimates of Building Capital in Germany, 1830–50*

	(1) German values[a]		(2) Prussian values[b]		(3) (1) and (2) combined[c]		(4) Hoffmann values[d]	
	Per head	Total	Per head	Total	Per head	Total	Per head	Total
1816	—	—	222	5,553	—	—	374	9,352
1830–4	254	7,595	235	7,040	250	7,484	397	11,857
1849–50	458	16,396	277	9,916	376	13,455	466	16,700

[a] Per capita values as found in F. W. von Reden, *Finanz-Statistik*, 3 vols. (Darmstadt, 1856), I, part 2, section 1, extrapolated to all of Germany.
[b] Per capita values for Prussia as in Table 91, extrapolated for the entire German population and backwards by means of index in Table 89.
[c] Per capita values of column 1 extrapolated to non-Prussian population, plus Prussian totals as in Table 91.
[d] Hoffmann's 1850 values extrapolated backwards by means of index in Table 89.

rough idea of how the latter developed between the early 1830s and the late 1840s. Column 2 allows the Prussian values calculated here to prevail, column 3 combines them, and column 4 presents Hoffmann's estimate for 1850 and extrapolates it backwards through time. A substantial difference between Prussia and the rest of Germany for 1850 is not implausible, but the difference recorded here (between columns (1) and (2)) seems too large.[67] The relatively small difference between the values of columns (1) and (4) for 1849–50 is also worth noting.

D. INTERPRETING BUILDING INVESTMENT

Simply describing building investment in Prussia and Germany during the nineteenth century adequately requires enormous labour, and even the extensive computations which went into this chapter could do no more than establish a rough framework for further work. Nevertheless, while a description of the trends is difficult enough and must be a prerequisite for causal explanation, the latter excites most scientific interest. A causal model of the building investment described here will have to await further research, as will an adequate treatment of the impact of that investment; but a few words on the subject may be in order.

To begin with, it is necessary to limit the problem. As we have seen, public buildings did not become especially significant until quite late, so that their explanation and impact can be very largely ignored. Investment in business plant, on the other hand, was related to the components and causes of industrial capital formation. That means that the discussion of building investment should really focus on dwellings. In the nineteenth century, as we have seen, *non*-agricultural dwellings dominated the growth process, so it is with them that the analysis should begin. In lieu of an analysis, the following points are worth noting.

(1) Many historians of building activity would like to assign it a leading role in the process of industrialization in Germany. Thus, Knut Borchardt writes: 'Urban building was a leading sector in Germany's industrialization, stimulating not only the construction industry but also the building materials industry, the glass industry, the wood industry, the gas and waterworks, and from 1880 on, in addition, the electricity works and urban tramways. Without urban construction, the modern industries based on coal and steam could not have developed.'[68]

This statement calls our attention to the necessity of an explanation of building investment itself, for it seems to contradict the general view that such investment was largely *demand*-induced, the product of population growth, urbanization, and rising income levels working on and through rental values, with supply factors (such as the cost and/or availability of financing services) playing an increasing but (until 1913) still secondary role. The question requires further attention.

(2) Its treatment will have to begin with the fact that building investment in nineteenth-century Germany, as in other countries, displayed wide swings in volume over time. It must be possible to place these within the framework of a causal model. As Borchardt has argued, Hoffmann's data on investment in non-agricultural dwelling in Germany during 1850–1913 show wide swings which reflect not simply

general cycles of prosperity and depression but also the influence of credit and construction costs. Our data for Prussia for the earlier period show similar swings. In both cases, however, we are far from an adequate empirical identification of the turning points, let alone an explanation of the swings themselves.

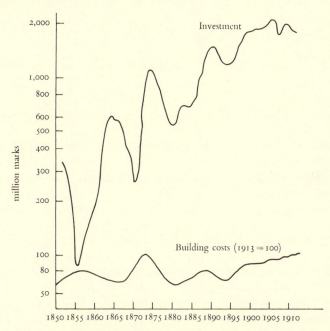

Fig. 7. Investment in Non-Agricultural Dwellings (1913 prices) and Building Costs in Germany, 1852–1912

(3) Throughout the nineteenth century, in Prussia and in Germany, investment in non-agricultural dwellings remained dominated by market forces. Most construction was done by private firms for private buyers. Moreover, as urbanization went on, the share of dwellings built for rental to non-owners grew disproportionately.[69] This meant that profit-maximization and market forces could have played a large and increasingly important role in the building investment process in the nineteenth century. It also meant that the weight of credit costs increased over time. Both developments have implications for further analysis of this type of capital formation. On the one hand, they suggest that an explanation relying on economic motivation and market forces should be able to account for a good portion of this investment and its fluctuations. On the other hand, in accounting for it we shall have to deal with the demand side (urbanization, etc.) and

also with the shifting importance of construction costs and credit conditions on the supply side. Of course, it is quite doubtful whether these influences can be so well identified as to permit a final judgement on the leading-sector thesis suggested by Borchardt; but that should remain one important goal of the further research necessary.

IV. *Investment in Social Overhead Capital*

The literature on modern economic development assigns a high priority to investment in 'social overhead capital'.[70] It is therefore important to include this in our survey of nineteenth-century German development. 'Social overhead capital' formation includes expenditures on transportation, communications, health, education, and scientific research facilities. Because of the uncertainty attached to the distribution of costs and benefits of such expenditures, they have historically tended to be very largely governmental expenditures in most countries. Since most countries have tended to treat government expenditures as consumption rather than investment, the official statistics have tended to understate capital formation historically – at least from the standpoint of students of economic development, who increasingly want to equate such expenditures with investment.

In fact, of course, the question is a difficult one, because many expenditures (education is a good example) contain elements of both consumption and investment, and their separation is extremely difficult if not impossible. Yet separation is essential because, on the one hand, treating all such expenditures as consumption will tend to understate the amounts of resources which societies were allocating to their future (i.e. were investing), while on the other hand, regarding them solely as investment might tend unduly to blur the distinction between consumption and investment: and, as Simon Kuznets has written, this distinction is necessary if we are not to believe that economic activity is production for production's sake.[71] Somewhere a line must be drawn.

Partly because of uncertainty with respect to this separation we concentrate in the following pages on investment in transportation facilities. To some extent, of course, this is justifiable in terms of the relatively small quantitative importance of some of the other categories of expenditure mentioned above. Public expenditures on health in Prussia around 1850 were absorbing no more than 0·4 per cent of the central government's budget. Research and development expenditures in the same period probably took an even smaller share of public funds, though it is not easy to ferret them out of the administrative and operating expenses of the various government branches.[72] Educational expenditures were quantitatively more significant, but they undoubtedly contain a large element of 'consumption'. For this reason, and because data on their total importance (including local expenditures) are in any case hard to assemble, they are excluded here. Finally, spending by the Prussian postal authority before 1850 – which might reasonably pass as 'communications investment' – will also be ignored here, though that authority carried out (at least before the advent of the railways in the 1840s) important shipping and communication functions. However, these expenditures, as well as the others just mentioned, will find a place in the quantitative summary of total investment at the end of the chapter, even if no explicit discussion of their role has been included here.

A. ROADS AND HIGHWAYS

All of the German states, and especially Prussia, devoted a considerable share of the public revenues to transportation improvements during the first half of the nineteenth century. According to one estimate, Prussia was spending around 9 per cent of its budget on transportation by mid-century.[73] Initially, at least, that meant spending on road-building and road maintenance. A quantitative evaluation of this investment which makes economic sense is not easy, for two reasons. (1) Most of the published estimates refer to kilometres built or in operation, rather than costs (and this procedure neglects investment in improving existing stretches, and also ignores differences in terrain). (2) Not all investment in roads was covered by the official figures – in particular the roads built by private companies, and also secondary road improvements. Nevertheless, some good pioneering research work has been done (notably by Gador and Borchard), and crude estimates are possible.[74]

Table 95 reproduces Borchard's figures for Prussia. This shows a respectable rate of growth in physical capacity, with average annual growth rates of 6 to 7 per cent – well above, for example, those of

Table 95. *Length of Prussian Road Network (kilometres)*

	Central government	Local government	Private	Total
1816	3,162	774		3,936[a]
1830	6,392	652	257	7,301
1845	10,636	1,362	1,015	13,013
1852	12,789	1,787	2,113	16,889

[a] Borchard gives total of 3,836.

SOURCE. Borchard, 'Staatsverbrauch und öffentliche Investitionen', 264.

population (of between 1·0 and 1·5 per cent). These figures, appro-priately modified, may be used as the basis for estimates of investment.[75]

Borchard's numbers suggest construction costs of between 6,000 and 6,500 talers per kilometre during the period 1816–51. Another source (Ungewitter) cites a cost spread between 20,000 and 80,000 talers per Prussian mile – roughly 2,700 to 10,000 talers per kilometre. Averaging this range would also yield construction costs of about 6,000 to 6,500 talers. These costs seem quite high by comparison with estimates for other German states (cited by Borchard), but perhaps the relatively high quality of the Prussian highways and/or difficulties of terrain explain the difference – in so far as the expenditure figures do not include some true maintenance costs.

Following these hints and assuming a cost increase comparable to that which characterizes the rest of the building industry, we derive the yearly totals of Table 96. Column 2 covers maintenance costs men-tioned in Prussian state budgets, also adjusted for cost changes, 1816–52. It should be pointed out that these high sums only partially burdened the state's budget, since well more than half of such current demands

Table 96. *Average Annual Investment in Roads and Highways in Prussia, 1817–53 (millions of marks)*

	(1) New investment	(2) Replace- ment	(3) Total	(4) New investment	(5) Replace- ment	(6) Total
	(current prices)			(1913 prices)		
1817–23	5·5	1·8	7·3	6·6	2·1	8·7
1824–30	6·5	2·7	9·2	8·6	3·6	12·2
1831–40	8·0	5·5	13·5	10·3	7·1	17·4
1841–50	7·9	7·8	15·7	9·8	9·7	19·5
1851–3	11·7	12·7	24·4	14·6	15·9	30·5

SOURCE. See text, and Appendix below.

were covered by usage fees (the so-called *Chausseengelder*).[76] What is interesting is not only the magnitude of the expenditures – amounting at times, for example, to more than a quarter of all of the building investment estimated in the previous section – but also their growth in the 1830s and 1840s. This growth took place at a time when the rail-roads were enjoying their first great burst of growth and seemed to be capturing all of the attention and support of governments. Roads and highways, it now seems, were essential complements to railway facili-ties. As Borchard has written, 'the extension of waterways, roads, and the emerging railways were complementary rather than competitive processes. The increase in public investments in the improvement of waterways and extension of the highway network in the second quarter of the nineteenth century may be viewed as proof of that complementarity.'[77]

B. WATERWAYS

Borchard's statement is an appropriate introduction to our next problem, investment in waterways. Estimating investment in waterways is made somewhat easier than for roads by the fact that governments virtually monopolized it; but this advantage is offset to some extent by the relatively greater difficulties here in distinguishing between new and replacement investment. Clearing a river bed from navigational impediments (such as logs, for instance) and thus effectively opening it to shipping was in a sense a net addition to a country's capital facilities; but if the operation was not repeated soon (say, in the following year), that facility became unusable. The Prussian government distinguished between new construction and maintenance expenditures on waterways, but maintenance expenditures do appear to have included some new construction spending, whereas some of the budgetary allocations for maintenance probably understated full costs, to the extent that (a) the collection of user fees covered some of such costs and (b) the wage bill of the government's construction department represented some of the fixed costs of the waterways as well. Furthermore, some capital spending on waterways by the Ministry of Public Works came out of a general construction fund and remains unidentified.[78]

For Table 97, in any case, we have adopted the official figures for 1849 and extrapolated the expenditure-per-kilometre relation backwards to 1816. We work with (a) a combination of the assumptions

Table 97. *Investment in Waterways in Prussia, 1816–50*
(marks, current prices)

	(1) Total investment	(2) New investment	(3) Replacement	(4) Total
		(annual averages)		
1816–20	8,832,810	318,312	1,448,238	1,766,550
1821–30	22,680,600	783,360	1,484,700	2,268,060
1831–40	33,531,690	1,577,280	1,775,889	3,353,169
1841–50	41,581,950	2,255,004	1,903,191	4,158,195

SOURCES. See text; and Borchard, 'Staatsverbrauch und öffentliche Investitionen', 225–59; von Reden, *Finanz-Statistik*, II, 398ff; Königliches Preussisches Statistisches Bureau, *Tabellen und amtliche Nachrichten für das Jahr 1849*, IV, 259.

that investment in river improvement had the same time path of development as had canals – for which relatively reliable observations exist[79] – and that the waterways network grew 20 kilometres per year, as another estimate[80] has suggested; and (b) the assumption that the official 1849 figure for physical capacity – 5,823 kilometres – is correct.

Table 97 reflects the conceptual difficulty (already alluded to) in distinguishing between replacement and net investment, thus confirming (so to speak) our continued emphasis on the former. It also reflects the market expansion of the 1840s, also noted above with respect to road and highway investment. Perhaps one can speak of a Prussian 'transportation revolution' in the 1840s, by no means confined to the more celebrated railways (to which we now turn).

C. RAILWAYS

Railways without a doubt played a central role in German and especially Prussian industrialization in the nineteenth century. For many students of German development, railways were the 'leading sector' *par excellence*, and there are many indications that for this reason the German 'take-off' really belongs to the 1840s.[81] Hoffmann's evidence for Germany as a whole suggests that both 'forward' and 'backward linkage' effects from railway-building were significant by the 1850s. For all of Germany for the period up to 1850, he shows a cumulated total investment worth around 970 million marks, and the share of railways in overall net capital formation, between the 1850s and the early 1870s, moving between 15 per cent and 25 per cent.[82] Fremdling's more recent and more precise treatment of the matter shows German railway investment in the 1850s and 1860s equal to roughly 60–70 per cent of that flowing into the entire manufacturing sector ('Gewerbe').[83] A slackening of this investment activity set in during the 1870s, but it speeded up again towards the end of the century, having an average level for 1900–13 of more than 500 million marks per year, or around 8 per cent of total net investment.

This is not the place for a full review of German, or even Prussian, railway history.[84] Nevertheless, a few important aspects deserve mention here. First, the development of Prussia's heavy industrial complex depended closely on the country's transport capacity. This is nowhere so clear as in a recent study of the Ruhr coal sector documenting the importance of the rail system as resource-user and service-provider.[85] That study cites rough input–output calculations for the early 1870s which suggest that railways took about half of the output of the iron industry, and the iron industry about one-third of Ruhr coal production, with the coal industry, in turn, supplying one-fourth of the railways' freight business. The importance of these interrelations comes out in the fact that the true 'take-off' of both iron and coal sectors in Prussia came in the 1850s, when railway-building began to draw mainly on domestic iron supplies – and thus, indirectly, on domestic coal as well – instead of on British and Belgian supplies as in the 1840s.[86] Moreover, the 1840s were marked by substantial reductions in freight charges, and these certainly contributed importantly to increased railway use.[87]

Second, government financing of railway construction played an important role in Prussia, and an even greater one in the other German states. According to the figures assembled by Borchard, up to 1850 the public purse supplied 137 million talers (411 million marks) or nearly 75 per cent of the funds for the largely state-owned railway system of the non-Prussian German states and, taking *all* German states (including Prussia), about half of all capital funds. In Prussia,[88] social and political backwardness necessitated a subsidy policy limited to outlays from current revenues, because resort to government borrowing on a large scale hinged on the support of the Prussian bourgeoisie and on constitutional reforms which were not forthcoming until the difficulties of 1847 and the Revolutions of 1848–9 had altered the situation.[89]

Table 98 reports the basic evidence on railroad capital formation in Prussia up to 1850, taken in large part from Fremdling's work. For the period 1850–1913 we also have Hoffmann's figures for Germany as a whole. The figures are comparable, since we follow Hoffmann *et al.* in that changes in the reported value of total capital invested are treated as net investment.[90]

Table 98 employs figures of the capital stock at original cost prices (*verwendetes Anlagekapital*) of those railways already at least partly in operation put together at the end of each year. Yearly differences represent net investment in current prices. The average lag between the start of construction and the partial opening of a line amounted to eighteen months, so that its net investment figure was allocated equally between the current and following years. To obtain constant values, we corrected Hoffmann *et al.* for the 1850–60 period according to Fremdling and extrapolated back to 1840.[91] The capital stock, calculated in 1913 prices (column 5 of Table 98), is derived by cumulating yearly net investment, assuming that the capital figure for 1840 represented the net investment of that year. The capital stock in current prices derives from capital stock in 1913 prices reflated by the price index, so that yearly differences are not net investment in current prices, but the capital stock at replacement cost. Replacement investment, however, has been set at a standard rate of 2 per cent of the capital stock, because although Prussia's railway company accounts included a 'maintenance and

Table 98. *Railway Investment in Prussia, 1840–60 (millions of marks)*

	(1)	(2)	(3)	(4)	(5)	(6)	(7)	(8)
	Current prices				1913 prices			
	Value of capital	Net investment	Replacement investment	Total investment (2) + (3)	Value of capital	Net investment	Replacement investment	Total investment (6) + (7)
1840	33·2	—	—	—	47·1	—	—	—
1841	50·3	18·8	1·0	19·8	75·1	28·0	1·5	29·5
1842	74·9	27·4	1·5	28·9	118·5	43·3	2·4	45·7
1843	95·4	24·0	1·9	25·9	158·2	39·7	3·2	42·9
1844	124·2	27·2	2·5	29·6	202·5	44·3	4·1	48·3
1845	222·7	81·5	4·5	85·9	319·2	116·7	6·4	123·1
1846	339·1	101·9	6·8	108·6	456·2	137·0	9·1	146·1
1847	411·6	63·7	8·2	71·9	539·7	83·5	10·8	94·3
1848	422·9	39·8	8·5	48·3	595·8	56·0	11·9	68·0
1849	414·1	29·3	8·3	37·6	641·2	45·4	12·8	58·2
1850	460·0	24·0	9·2	33·2	676·5	35·3	13·5	48·8
1851	499·3	38·8	10·0	48·8	733·5	57·0	14·7	71·6
1852	569·9	50·4	11·4	61·8	804·5	71·1	16·1	87·2
1853	685·9	36·2	13·7	49·9	849·3	44·8	17·0	61·8
1854	760·4	24·4	15·2	39·6	877·4	28·1	17·6	45·7
1855	828·7	74·0	16·6	90·6	963·4	86·0	19·3	105·3
1856	908·6	85·4	18·2	103·6	1,063·4	100·0	21·3	121·2
1857	963·6	50·2	19·3	69·4	1,121·8	58·4	22·4	80·8
1858	1,004·6	104·2	20·1	124·3	1,251·6	129·8	25·0	154·8
1859	1,115·0	148·1	22·3	170·4	1,443·2	191·6	28·9	220·5
1860	1,195·3	95·9	23·9	119·8	1,569·0	125·8	31·4	157·2

SOURCE. Fremdling, 'Eisenbahnen und Wirtschaftswachstum', 56.

replacement' item, it is difficult in fact to distinguish these outlays from other operating expenses or indeed from new investment. Moreover, there is some justification in the literature for such a figure.[92]

Two implications of the data of Table 98 should be emphasized. First, the concentration of growth in the 1840s confirms the periodization for Germany's industrialization suggested by Hoffmann, Spiethoff, Schumpeter, and others.[93] Estimated total net investment between 1835 and 1850 alone roughly equalled total gross investment on roads and highways for the entire period 1817–50, and more than 75 per cent of this was concentrated in the 1840s. Nevertheless, the table shows considerable growth in the 1850s as well, with absolute outlays well over those of the 1840s. Secondly, the railways realized large profits even as early as the 1840s, thanks to sharply rising sales of transportation services coupled to falling prices. Fremdling argues persuasively that this reflects a large latent demand for transportation, activated (so to speak) by the railways, and implies considerable growth in the economy beyond agricultural subsistence levels before 1840. More work on the nature and sources of this growth and 'latent demand' is, I think, a high priority for German economic history.

D. TRANSPORTATION INVESTMENT, GERMANY, 1850–1913

Space forbids a detailed discussion of transportation investment in Germany as a whole, both before and after 1850. Instead of venturing into this little-known field, we offer Tables 99 and 100, extracted from the work of Fremdling (for railway investment, 1835–50) and Hoffmann et al. (for transportation as a whole in Germany, 1850–1913).[94]

Table 99. *Railway Capital Formation in Germany, 1835–50*
(millions of marks)

	Kilometres in operation	Capital invested
1835	6	—
1840	462	58·8
1845	2,152	281·5
1850	5,875	891·4

SOURCE (capital invested). Fremdling, *op. cit.*, 56.

These tables surely underestimate the amount of resources Germany was using to maintain and expand her transportation system, because they exclude maintenance costs and also the entire 'floating capital' of the inland and high-seas merchant shipping fleet. However, with the aid of sources cited in Hoffmann et al. it should be possible to repair these defects soon.

Table 100. *Transportation Investment in Germany, 1850–1913*
(millions of marks, 1913 prices)

	(1) Railways	(2) Other	(3) Total	(4) Total net investment
1851–9	1,330	450	1,780	7,460
1860–9	2,390	648	3,038	15,100
1870–9	5,410	1,044	6,454	22,170
1880–9	2,390	1,227	3,617	26,470
1890–9	2,830	2,387	5,217	45,610
1900–13	7,400	5,098	12,498	91,680

SOURCE. Hoffmann *et al.*, *Wachstum der Wirtschaft*, Table 41, pp. 257–8, cols. 5–7.

V. *Industrial Capital Formation*

One of the best-known indicators of industrialization is the growth in the stock of industrial capital, and for nineteenth-century Germany there can be no doubt as to the secular trend. According to Hoffmann *et al.*, business investment (in '*Gewerbe*' – which was mostly industrial investment) grew from an annual rate of around 120–30 million marks in the early 1850s to over two billion marks in the 1900s, i.e. from roughly one-seventh to close to one-half of total net investment.[95] These figures, like some of the rest of our discussion, seem to suggest both (*a*) that analysis of capital formation and growth in the period 1850–1913 should focus on *industrial* investment and (*b*) that analysis of the *first* half of the nineteenth century might well concentrate on other forms of capital. Both points deserve some discussion, but since for the former fairly good data have been available for some time now,[96] we concentrate in the following remarks upon the early period.

Knut Borchardt's stimulating article on capital shortage in Germany in the first half of the nineteenth century concentrated on the adequacy of finance but at the same suggested quite strongly that industrial investment was of minor quantitative importance for this question. His most striking example showed Germany's largest industrial sector – the textile industries – to be absorbing only a small fraction of presumed savings during this period.[97] If those industries had had a combined capital stock worth 190 million talers (or 570 million marks) by 1850 (as Borchardt estimated) and had been increasing it at the virtually unbelievable rate of 10 per cent per year, then their peak demands (on savings) could have scarcely exceeded one-tenth of the capital Germans were investing at this time in buildings. In a later work treating all textile industries in the states of the Zollverein in 1846, Horst Blumberg came up with an estimated capital stock of 156 million talers (or 468 million marks), and since more than 130 million of this was *working capital*, this finding seemed to strongly support Borchardt's position.[98] Blumberg's numbers also show the combined capital stock increasing during 1846-61 at an annual rate of 3·2 per cent, or about 14-15 million marks per year.

Nevertheless, there are grounds for pursuing the question of pre-1850 industrial investment somewhat further. In the first place, authoritative sources such as Spiethoff and Hoffmann have attributed important increases in industrial capacity to this period. In the second place, aggregate quantitative unimportance may conceal significant shifts in the structure of industrial investment taking place in these years.

Table 101. *Estimated Value of Industrial Production of Twelve Commodities in Prussia, 1804–47 (millions of marks)*

	1804	1831	1842–3[a]	1846–7[b]
(1) Linen	30·0	75·0	79·2	84·6
(2) Wool	40·5	78·0	102·3	119·7
(3) Cotton	14·4	59·7	111·0	106·5
(4) Silk	8·4	42·3	45·0	55·5
All textiles (1)–(4)	93·3	255·0	337·5	366·3
(5) Metals	4·2	11·4	21·9	39·0
(6) Fuels	1·5	8·4	18·6	32·7
(7) Salt	1·1	4·8	15·4	4·2
Mining and Metals (5)–(7)	6·8	24·6	45·9	75·9
(8) Leather	11·4	25·8	32·1	30·0
(9) Tobacco	9·9	8·7	8·4	7·5
(10) Beer	9·3	16·5	18·6	18·9
(11) Wine	4·8	20·7	23·4	21·0
(12) Brandy	10·8	36·6	32·7	29·7
Total (1)–(12)	156·3	387·9	498·6	549·3
Total capital goods[c]	11·4	32·7	56·6	86·7

[a] Textiles data are for 1843; mining and metals for 1842. Dieterici, *Volkswohlstand*.
[b] Textiles data for 1846–7 from Blumberg, *Die deutsche Textilindustrie*, Appendix; G. Kirchhain, 'Das Wachstum der deutschen Baumwollindustrie im 19. Jahrhundert' (doctoral dissertation, University of Münster, 1971; privately published in photocopy); Hoffmann *et al.*, *Wachstum der Wirtschaft*, Table 7. Mining and metals for 1847 from Dieterici, *Handbuch der Statistik des preussischen Staates*, 342–6.
[c] Capital goods = lines 5 and 6, plus half of line 8.

The structure of industrial production offers a convenient starting point for discussing this question – not least of all because previous investigators such as Spiethoff and Hoffmann have also utilized these structural data to describe the pace of capital formation. The simplest procedure, once again, is to concentrate on Prussian data, working from the distinction between consumption goods and producers' goods.

Table 101 presents one set of estimates of value of industrial production.[99] We have, in all, twelve commodities, of which eight are clearly purely consumer goods, and the other four (salt, fuels, metals, and leather) only in part consumption articles. If we define 'capital-goods' production as the sum of all metal and fuels production plus one-half of leather production, then we can observe a steady relative increase in the importance of capital-goods production, with the largest jump in the 1840s – partly because stagnation overtook consumption-goods production in precisely these years used as benchmarks (1846–7) (see above). It is not possible, however, to detect in these figures the radical increases in industrial capacity associated with the 'take-off'. Applying 1913 prices to textiles, leather, and metals and fuels we obtain the results shown in Table 102: the expansion in producers' goods is

Table 102. *Production of Selected Industrial Commodities in Prussia, 1804–47 (millions of marks, 1913 prices)*

	1804	1831	1842–3	1846–7
(1) Linen	27·1	89·3	123·7	132·1
(2) Wool	34·3	61·4	91·3	99·8
(3) Cotton[a]	2·6	37·5	80·4	76·1
(4) Silk	5·4	38·8	33·1	42·4
All textiles (1)–(4)	69·4	227·0	328·5	350·4
(5) Metals[b]	1·9	11·5	23·5	27·3
(6) Fuels[c]	0·6	14·2	32·1	58·4
(7) Leather[d] × 0·5	7·6	19·8	26·7	28·3
Total (5)–(7)	10·1	45·5	82·3	114·0
Total (1)–(7)	79·5	272·5	410·8	464·4

[a] Data from Kirchhain, 'Wachstum der Baumwollindustrie', 128, weighting cotton goods three times as heavily as yarn, and interpolating from the following years: 1805, 1830, 1840, 1845, and 1850.
[b] From prices from Jacobs and Richter, *Grosshandelspreise in Deutschland*, 75.
[c] Hard coal prices; source as in note *b*.
[d] Average of cowhide and calfskin prices; source as in note *b*, p. 76.

clearly more pronounced when reckoned in constant prices. More work will be necessary here, particularly on the 1830s and 1840s; for the time being, however, it still seems justifiable to regard this entire period as a preparatory or 'preconditions' period, at least from the standpoint of the industrial productive capacity. This is particularly true when this period is viewed from the perspective of industrial growth between 1850 and 1913. Table 103 sets out some of the relevant data. A glance at the relatively low index numbers for columns 3, 5, and 6 tells us how much further these producers'-goods sectors were advancing during 1850–1913 than German industry as a whole. As a result, for example, by 1913, some 4 per cent of total gross product was being generated in mining alone, and in transportation half again as much.[100] By this time it was the capacity here which was determining growth in the economy as a whole.

Viewing industrial capital formation in terms of the production of 'capital goods' offers useful insights into the process of industrial investment and industrial growth generally. Indeed, in the long-run sense employed by Boehm-Bawerk, this is the true meaning of capital accumulation: the growth in production of means of production and, hence, an increasingly roundabout mode of production. Nevertheless, this approach can be misleading for analyses of capital formation. If one is also concerned with the short- and medium-term problems of financing capital formation one needs appropriate direct measures of the current sacrifice it requires. In open economies, moreover, the production of 'capital goods' could be exported in exchange for consumption goods, or vice versa; in addition, the production of consumption goods could be extremely capital-intensive, and that of capital goods labour-intensive. Production data alone, that is, do not necessarily provide the measure we need. The following discussion accordingly returns to the more conventional notions of capital formation employed earlier – as expenditures maintaining or increasing the capacity to produce, whatever the nature of the final product.

The aim here is to provide a crude measure of net (and gross) capital formation in the early stages of industrialization. For the sake of simplicity and comparison, we concentrate on Prussia.

Our starting point, however, is not Prussian but German industry. Several estimates of capital stock have been made for the combined German textiles industries, notably by Blumberg, Borchardt, and most recently Kirchhain.[101] With the help of data in Hoffmann et al., von Viebahn, and Dieterici, and some heroic assumptions (most notably the utilization of spindles and looms as bench-mark measures of capital), we derive the estimates of Table 104.[102]

According to Table 104, the textile industries accumulated capital at the respectable rate of between 2 and 3 per cent per year over the period – even, surprisingly, in the 1840s. Taking 1852 as a guide, we discover that the estimated 588 million marks represent roughly 11 per cent of the total industrial capital stock estimated by Hoffmann et al., whereas these industries employed more than 22 per cent of the industrial labour

Table 103. *Index of Industrial Growth in Selected Sectors in Germany, 1850–1913 (base: 1850 = 100)*

	(1) All textiles	(2) Foods and beverages	(3) Metals	(4) Construction	(5) Coal	(6) Transport	(7) Total production	(8) Total industry
1850	17·7	20·4	1·5	14·7	2·7	1·7	19·5	9·5
1860	25·7	25·3	3·2	16·0	6·5	3·8	23·9	12·7
1870	31·9	30·9	7·5	20·1	13·9	8·9	29·2	18·8
1880	40·1	41·6	13·9	29·0	24·7	16·1	36·5	26·1
1890	65·0	53·3	23·8	45·6	36·9	27·9	48·7	39·9
1900	72·8	74·6	47·5	61·0	57·5	50·1	68·4	61·4
1913	100·0	100·0	100·0	100·0	100·0	100·0	100·0	100·0

SOURCE. Hoffmann et al., *Wachstum der Wirtschaft*, 390–2, 338–42, and 451–2.

Table 104. *Capital Stock in German Textile Industries, 1820–52 (millions of marks, current prices)*

	Cotton			Wool			Linen			Silk (total)	Total
	Spinning	Weaving	Total	Spinning	Weaving	Total	Spinning	Weaving	Total		
1820	14·0	47·0	61·0	—	—	—	—	—	—	—	—
1830–1	15·0	62·0	77·0	38·0	43·0	81·0	7·0	122·0	129·0	18·0	305·0
1840	26·0	124·0	150·0	48·0	69·0	117·0	7·5	126·5	134·0	23·0	424·0
1846	27·0	139·0	166·0	62·0	76·0	138·0	8·0	135·0	143·0	45·0	492·0
1852	45·7	152·0	197·7	68·0	111·0	179·0	9·0	148·0	157·0	54·0	588·0

SOURCE. See text, and Appendix below.

force. This probably reflects not low capital intensity in textiles production but the exclusion here of certain finishing branches from the
capital figures and also the inclusion of part-time handicraft workers in
the employment figures. It is clear, however, that some estimating
problems remain to be clarified.

The next step is to convert these figures for Germany as a whole into
Prussian ones, which we do with the help of data on the regional distribution of spindles and looms among the German states.[103] Table 105

Table 105. *Capital Stock in Prussian Textile Industries and Total
Value of Products, 1830–52 (millions of marks)*

	(1)	(2)	(3)	(4)	(5)	(6) Total value of
	Cotton	Wool	Linen	Silk	Total	products
1830–1	33·7	48·6	46·7	16·6	145·6	255·0
1840	66·7	69·6	48·5	21·2	206·1	316·2
1846–7	74·1	83·3	51·8	41·5	250·7	366·3
1852	86·1	104·1	56·9	49·7	296·8	400·5

presents the desired distribution, along with estimated total value of
product (based on data from Tables 101 and 102). In the Prussian textile
industries, it seems, capital accumulation was proceeding faster than
production during the first half of the century, an interesting fact
(argued, incidentally, a long time ago – without statistical underpinning
– by Carl Brinkmann)[104] which requires further attention.

Unfortunately, it is impossible to give reliable estimates of production
and capital for the entire Prussian industrial sector. Instead, we can only
include the one other sector for which fairly good investment and
production data exist – coal mining. Two monographs on the Ruhr
coal sector, written at the University of Münster by Hans-Jürgen
Kinkel and Carl Holtfrerich, enable us to calculate investment and
capital stock for Prussian mining as a whole. For 1840 and 1852 fairly
reliable estimates are available for the value of invested capital in the
Ruhr's heavy industry; and, with the aid of statistics on steam horsepower, a machine price index, and production data, these can be
extrapolated to a number of other time points.[105] It is then possible to
relate these capital values to estimated coal production data (as is done
for textiles in Table 105) and, by means of these average capital–
production ratios, to estimate the total capital stock in all of the industries included in Tables 101 and 102 (and, by extrapolation, to get data
for 1852).[106]

From these data it is only a short further step to estimates of capital
formation for the industries concerned. The step is worth taking, I

think, because the sample of industries has a respectable size. Textiles and hard coal alone offered, as of 1846, around 25 per cent of all industrial employment in Germany, and the twelve products together accounted for around one-third. In Prussia, at mid-century, these industries offered 30 and 40 per cent of the total respectively. In taking

Table 106. *Estimated Stock of Industrial Capital in Prussia, 1830–52 (millions of marks)*

	Value of product			Capital		
	Textiles[a]	Coal	Twelve industries	Textiles	Coal	Twelve industries
1830–1	255·0	7·8	387·9	140·7	2·2	209·5
1840	316·2	19·7	470·1	198·4	8·1	286·8
1846–7	366·3	22·2	549·3	241·4	15·1	362·5
1852	400·5	25·2	616·6	285·9	30·6	456·3

[a] Includes substantial double counting from the point of view of aggregate national product, due to dis-integration of spinning and weaving production stages.

SOURCES. As for Tables 101–4, and Appendix below.

this step, we may usefully include depreciation charges (estimated by Kirchhain and Holtfrerich for cotton and Ruhr coal respectively), thus giving us numbers for both gross and net investment. It should be pointed out, however, that it is not easy to distinguish between net and gross investment in the rest of the textile industries with information now available. Most of the capital of these industries was *working capital*, which had to be replaced each year as well as enlarged with every enlargement in fixed plant and equipment; and the few depreciation rates we know about may refer either to total, or merely to fixed, investment.[107]

If these numbers reflect the true trend of industrial investment in Prussia between 1830 and 1850, then we may justifiably infer from them that that country was accumulating industrial capital at a respectable rate even before the 'take-off': roughly 4 per cent per year in the 1830s and even higher in the 1840s (in current prices – about half of that rate using 1913 prices). Even the lower rate is well above the country's population growth in these years. Agriculture, by comparison, was accumulating capital much more slowly, at a rate of less than 1·5 per cent per year (in current prices) during 1830–50 (see section II above). However, the absolute levels of industrial investment appear to have been quite modest by comparison with the other sectors of the economy. Between 1830 and 1849, for example, agricultural capital was growing, in absolute terms, by around four times as much as

Table 107. *Average Annual Investment in a Sample of Industries in Prussia, 1830–52 (millions of marks)*

	(Current prices) Textiles and Coal			(Current prices) 12 Industries			(1913 prices)[a] 12 Industries			Price index (1913 = 100)
	Net	Replacem't	Total	Net	Replacem't	Total	Net	Replacem't	Total	
1830/1–1840	6·63	3·37	10·0	8·1	4·8	12·9	4·7	2·8	7·5	173
1840–1846/7	7·70	4·88	12·58	11·6	6·3	17·9	5·8	3·1	8·9	202
1846/7–1852	10·90	6·75	17·65	17·1	8·3	25·4	8·55	4·15	12·7	200

[a] Deflating with investment goods price index in Hoffmann et al., *Wachstum der Wirtschaft*, 572–3.

SOURCE. As for Table 106.

industrial capital (in current prices); and in 1913 prices the value of average annual investment in agriculture ran at a level more than ten times the industrial level in the 1830s, and six times higher in the 1840s. A small change in agricultural productivity or a small change in acreage planted could have sufficed to 'finance' the relatively modest increase in industrial capacity taking place over the period – if a market had existed which could have induced such changes or transferred their results.[108]

VI. *Summary*

A survey as broad as this scarcely requires further summary. We may content ourselves with re-emphasis or identification of the following trends and/or features, many of which are reflected in Table 108.

Table 108. *Average Annual Net Investment in Prussia, 1816–49*
(millions of marks, 1913 prices)

	Agriculture	Non-agricultural buildings	Transport	Industry	Total
1816–22	86·5	28·7	7·0	2·8[a]	125·0
1822–31	70·4	18·7	8·8	5·1[a]	103·0
1830/1–1840	109·6	52·0	22·5	5·6	189·7
1840–9	59·9	69·2	73·7[b]	7·0	209·8

[a] 'Guesstimate' based on extrapolation of capital-product value trend 1830–49 to 1816 using value-of-product data.
[b] Railway investment in 1840 estimated at 15 million marks.

(1) The Prussian economy – the most important of the German economies – was clearly generating a surplus and converting it into real capital on a fairly substantial scale during the first half of the nineteenth century. Taking the 1816–49 period as a whole, the capital stock grew by about five billion marks (in 1913 prices). This sum must have represented an increase of something like 100 per cent over the level of 1816. That kind of accumulation was surely a new element in Prussian economic history. Interestingly, it seems to have been particularly concentrated in the period 1830–50, with the 1820s even showing some retreat. Nevertheless, although the figures reflect progress, they do not earn for the pre-1850 period as a whole any labels such as 'industrial revolution' or 'take-off'. By comparison with the investment increases of the 1850–1913 period, these early additions were quite modest. Whereas the level of investment in Prussia increased (in 1913 prices) by around 51 per cent between 1816/22 and 1840/49, in Germany as a whole between 1851/60 and 1881/90 it grew by more than 200 per cent! This was true self-sustaining growth.

(2) The main carrier of capital accumulation in Prussia before 1850 was clearly agricultural investment (including investment in buildings), although its predominance declined precisely in the decades of most rapid aggregate accumulation, 1830–50.[109] Agricultural investment, however, took place at shifting levels (and our averages capture only a part of the shifts). Perhaps the decline in the 1820s reflects the 'agrarian crisis' that historians have written about.[110] More interesting, however, is the large increase in the 1830s and its collapse in the 1840s. As we have argued above, this probably reflected the combination of productivity change and the relatively high capital requirements of agriculture: the poor harvests of the 1840s forced producers to channel their surplus into replacement investment or to consume it, and less remained for accumulation. In German agriculture after 1850 this weakness clearly diminished. Nevertheless, as we have seen (in section II), agriculture's capital requirements remained high in the period 1850–1913, and substantial fluctuations in investment activity related to them continued to take place. The real difference between the two eras lay in the power of the agricultural sector to influence the rest of the economy: by the end of the nineteenth century its size had diminished relative to other sectors, so that overall accumulation levels were clearly following other influences.

(3) The principal real form of capital accumulation was building investment (including agricultural buildings). This remained true throughout the nineteenth century, although by 1900 the share of machinery and equipment had increased considerably relative to that of buildings. The fact that this form of investment fluctuated substantially thus had significant consequences for the economy as a whole. In Prussia we find the whole of the relative decline in aggregate investment in the 1820s, and a large share of the expansion of the 1830s, attributable to building investment, and this continued growth in the 1840s helped considerably to offset the collapse of agricultural investment in those years. Throughout the nineteenth century, the phasing of building investment seems to have been somewhat different from the economy as a whole.

(4) Investment in social overhead capital became important in the 1830s and especially in the 1840s. Those accounts of Prussian and/or German industrialization that stress infrastructure investment and especially railway-building in the 1830s and 1840s would thus appear to be right (see pp. 411–17 above). This form of capital accumulation, one should add, continued to be important in Germany right up to 1913. Moreover, our survey has dealt only with part of the transportation investment and excluded from its measure of social overhead capital (among other things) shipping, health, education, and research expen-

ditures. If we were to add these to our estimates both absolute levels and growth trends would be enlarged.[111]

(5) Industrial investment grew very slowly in the first half of the nineteenth century – though it appears to have grown more rapidly than output, which is significant. Even in the 1840s our measure of industrial net capital formation amounted to less than 5 per cent of the aggregate total – and even the multiplier of 2·5 suggested above (pp. 424–5) would leave a small share (12·5 per cent). This changed radically in the 1850s, when the industrial capital stock began growing at a rate considerably above the overall average.[112] Taking these data as a point of departure, it is interesting to speculate on the connection between industrial investment and the availability of social overhead capital – in particular, the railways. To what extent was the former a delayed response to the latter, not only with respect to the 1850s and 1840s but for the century as a whole? This touches upon the old but still unsettled debate about balanced and unbalanced growth, and the relationship between aggregate investment, the structure of industrial investment, and the rate of economic growth.[113]

(6) Net capital formation – as conventionally defined – accounted for only a part of the resources tied up in maintaining and increasing Germany's productive capacity.[114] Agriculture, as we have seen, absorbed and tied up a great deal of capital as intermediate goods, and the same thing was true (albeit on a smaller scale) of transportation and industry as well. Much of the technological change and productivity advance we associate with industrialization was, in fact, directed at reducing those capital requirements. This kind of capital-saving has been often overlooked in accounts of industrialization and deserves closer attention.

APPENDIX

Our estimates of Prussian agricultural production and investment build mainly around the work of Graf von Finckenstein (for data on physical production) and Jacobs and Richter (for agricultural prices). For animal production (and livestock inventories), in addition, we have drawn on the work of E. Engel, as well as (for average weights of slaughtered animals and other miscellaneous points) W. Hoffmann et al. Agricultural building values were derived by extrapolation, using as a point of departure the figures for sectoral distribution of Hoffmann et al. (for Germany in 1850) and aggregate values as estimated in the text.[115] The basic data are set forth below.

In Table 109, the area of land under cereal production was estimated from

Table 109. *Area of Cultivated Land in Prussia, by Major Crops,*
1816–61 (tens of thousands of hectares)

	Wheat	Rye	Barley	Oats	Buck-wheat, etc.	All cereals	Pota-toes	Grand total
1816	37·8	216·1	108·1	145·9	32·4	540·3	9·0	1,254·2
1819	39·6	222·7	107·8	147·9	35·4	—	15·0	—
1822	41·4	229·3	107·5	151·9	38·4	—	21·0	—
1825	43·2	235·9	106·7	154·9	41·4	—	27·0	—
1828	45·0	242·5	106·4	157·9	44·4	—	33·0	—
1831	46·8	249·1	106·1	160·9	47·4	—	39·0	—
1834	48·6	255·7	105·8	163·9	50·4	—	45·0	—
1837	50·4	262·3	105·5	166·9	52·4	—	51·0	—
1840	52·6	269·6	105·2	170·9	59·2	657·6	57·0	1,411·4
1843	53·8	275·7	107·6	171·4	64·0	—	64·0	—
1846	55·0	281·7	109·9	171·8	68·7	687·1	69·1	—
1849	63·2	287·7	105·3	175·4	70·2	701·7	74·3	—
1852	64·5	293·7	107·5	179·1	71·6	716·4	79·3	—
1861	68·5	319·5	98·9	182·6	91·3	760·7	92·6	—

data presented by von Finckenstein,[116] giving his absolute hectarage estimates for each crop and all crops together for 1805–16 and 1861. Von Finckenstein's estimates of the total cereal-producing area for many of the intervening years had to be allocated to the different crops by interpolating the figures for 1805–16, 1843, and 1861. The amount of land under potato production derives similarly from von Finckenstein, though a separation of potato from other root crops had to be interpolated roughly by means of a key implying steadily diminishing rates of increased potato land.

Table 110. *Seed Inputs per Hectare of Cultivated Land, 1816–49*

	Bushels	Kilos
Wheat	4·6	190
Rye	5·4	208
Barley	5·3	183
Oats	10·5	231
Potatoes	—	2,000

For Table 110, the estimates for cereals derive from von Finckenstein (using conversion key for bushels to kilograms of Jacobs and Richter). Potato-land inputs derive from Hoffmann et al.[117] We have assumed (with von Finckenstein) that these inputs per hectare remained constant over the period.

Table 111 follows von Finckenstein's estimates of the nutritional or caloric value of these crops and sets them in relation to rye prices accordingly, feed crops receiving one-third of that price, and turnips being evaluated at potato prices.

In Table 112, straw prices are set at one-tenth of rye prices, analogous to the reasoning underlying Table 111.

Table 111. *Feed Crop Production in Prussia, 1816–58*

	Clover, hay, etc.			Turnips, beets, etc.			
	Physical production (thousand tons)	Current values	1913 values (millions of marks)	Physical production (thousand tons)	Current values (millions of marks)	Index	1913 values (millions of marks)
1816	18,130	799·5	975·0	—	—	—	—
1819	18,261	863·7	1,167·2	681	28·9	61	47·4
1822	18,390	500·2	1,020·8	1,363	46·9	50	93·8
1825	18,520	366·7	1,145·9	2,044	60·5	36	168·1
1828	18,649	708·7	1,288·4	2,725	72·5	38	190·8
1831	18,779	944·6	1,259·4	3,406	124·7	53	235·3
1834	18,908	606·7	1,145·0	4,088	127·5	45	283·3
1837	19,038	557·8	1,212·5	4,769	150·7	46	327·6
1840	19,167	736·0	1,247·4	5,450	183·7	49	374·9
1843	19,297	947·5	1,480·4	6,131	291·8	54	540·4
1846	19,428	1,107·4	1,165·6	6,813	314·8	67	469·9
1849	19,557	547·6	1,190·4	7,494	250·3	48	521·5
1852	—	—	—	—	—	—	—
1858	19,946	897·6	1,150·7	9,538	356·7	55	648·5

SOURCES

Physical Production: von Finckenstein, *Entwicklung der Landwirtschaft*, Table 14.
Prices: Jacobs and Richter, *Grosshandelspreise in Deutschland*, 52ff.

Table 112. *Straw Production in Prussia, 1816–61*

	Physical product (thousand tons)	Current values	1913 values
		(millions of marks)	
1816	6,192	82·4	100·4
1819	6,605	93·8	126·7
1822	7,024	57·6	117·5
1825	7,463	44·0	142·0
1828	7,921	90·3	164·2
1831	8,361	126·3	168·3
1834	8,828	84·8	159·9
1837	9,321	82·0	178·3
1840	9,810	112·8	191·2
1843	10,703	157·3	245·8
1846	11,662	199·4	209·9
1849	12,653	106·3	231·1
1858	15,858	214·1	274·5

SOURCE. As for Table 111.

Table 113. *Animal Production in Prussia, 1816–58*

A. Milk Production

	Cows (millions)	Milk per cow (kg)		Milk production (million kg)	Value of production (millions of marks)	
		A	B		Current prices	1913 prices
1816	2·15	640	1,382	2,681·1	134·1	209·5
1822	2·36	700	1,402	2,972·2	133·7	234·6
1831	2·52	790	1,442	3,273·3	157·1	253·6
1840	2·79	880	1,482	3,719·8	185·9	290·6
1849	3·08	970	1,522	4,215·9	193·9	328·7
1858	3·24	1,060	1,562	4,561·0	332·9	382·7

SOURCES

Milk per cow: A: von Finckenstein, *Entwicklung der Landwirtschaft*, 262–3 (1812–58 interpolated). B: Hoffmann *et al.*, *Wachstum der Wirtschaft*, 304 (1840–9 interpolated, 1816–22 extrapolated).

Milk production: Applies per-cow milk production of B above and the suggestion (in Hoffmann *et al.*, *op. cit.*) that 90 per cent of the stock of cows were milk-producers.

Value of production: valued with prices estimated for 1816–49 from the development of butter prices as in Jacobs and Richter, *Grosshandelspreise in Deutschland*, 58–9.

B. Beef Production

	No. of cattle	Slaughter weight (kg)	Percentage slaughtered	Physical production (million kg)	Values (million of marks)	
					Current	1913
1816	4·01	112	15	67·4	59·9	99·9
1822	4·25	121	14	72·0	46·1	112·4
1831	4·45	136	15	90·8	62·6	133·3
1840	4·98	155	15	115·8	78·7	171·2
1849	5·37	162	16	139·2	101·6	207·4
1858	5·49	180	16	158·1	148·6	265·4

SOURCES. Numbers from Engel, 'Die Viehhaltung im preussischen Staate'; slaughter weight from Hoffmann *et al.*, *Wachstum der Wirtschaft*; per cent slaughtered from von Finckenstein, *Entwicklung der Landwirtschaft*; prices from Jacobs and Richter, *Grosshandelspreise in Deutschland*.

Table 113 (cont.). *Animal Production in Prussia, 1816–58*

C. Pork Production

	No. of pigs (millions)	Slaughter weight (kg)	Percentage slaughtered	Physical production (million kg)	Value of product (millions of marks) Current prices	1913 prices
1816	1·49	36	37	19·8	19·0	32·8
1822	1·60	37	40	23·9	14·1	39·2
1831	1·74	43	41	31·0	20·5	51·2
1840	2·24	47	47	49·5	34·2	81·3
1849	2·47	58	55	78·8	56·0	129·9
1858	2·58	55	55	78·0	94·4	147·3

SOURCES. As for part B: numbers from Engel; slaughter weight from Hoffmann *et al.*; per cent slaughtered from von Finckenstein; prices from Jacobs and Richter.

D. Wool Production

	No. of sheep (millions)	Kg wool per sheep	(Prices (per kg) Current	1913	Values (millions of marks) Current	1913
1816	8·3	0·75	5·8	148	36·1	24·4
1822	10·04	0·77	6·8	158	52·6	33·3
1831	11·8	0·80	5·5	127	51·9	40·9
1840	16·3	0·83	5·2	119	70·4	59·1
1849	16·3	0·86	5·5	129	77·1	59·8
1858	15·4	0·88	5·3	123	71·8	58·3

SOURCES. As for part B: numbers from Engel; wool per sheep from von Finckenstein; prices from Jacobs and Richter.

Table 114. *Total Value of Animal Production in Prussia, 1816–58* (millions of marks)

	Current prices	1913 prices
1816	249·2	366·6
1822	246·5	419·5
1831	292·1	479·0
1840	369·2	602·2
1849	428·6	724·7
1858	647·7	853·7

SOURCES. Table 113 above.

The values in Table 115 bring our estimates closer in line with estimates of product levels found in the literature and also strengthen remarks in the text about the importance of gross investment in agricultural economies. The increase of 67 per cent in per capita product (from 157·8 to 262·8 million marks in 1913 prices), however, remains remarkably and suspiciously high.

Table 115. *Gross and Net Agricultural Product in Prussia, 1816–49, under Stronger Feed Assumptions (millions of marks, 1913 prices)*

	(1) Increments to yield of crop		Gross product		Net product	
	Potatoes	Oats	Minus (2)	Minus (1) and (2)	Minus (2)	Minus (1) and (2)
1816	6·9	254·6	1,338·1	1,331·2	1,117·7	1,110·8
1819	12·0	314·7	—	—	—	—
1822	17·0	276·2	1,652·9	1,635·9	1,415·1	1,398·1
1825	21·4	292·2	—	—	—	—
1828	18·7	401·8	—	—	—	—
1831	31·5	375·5	2,199·4	2,167·9	1,894·1	1,862·6
1834	36·3	390·7	—	—	—	—
1837	41·3	413·0	—	—	—	—
1840	45·8	427·8	2,687·6	2,641·8	2,331·4	2,285·6
1843	41·7	386·6	—	—	—	—
1846	38·1	293·5	—	—	—	—
1849	65·8	354·7	2,969·2	2,903·4	2,599·6	2,533·8

SOURCES. See text and this Appendix, and A. Meitzen, *Der Boden und die landwirtschaftlichen Verhältniss des preussischen Staates nach dem Gebietsumfange vor 1866*, 8 vols. (Berlin, 1868–1908), III, 386–7.

Table 96 above is based on Table 117.

The few quantitative statements on road investment have to be combined with the relatively reliable data on length of the network. These are converted into values by means of the per-kilometre rates of columns 5 and 6 of Table 117, taking the average length of the network (column 7) as the base. Investment costs follow the cost development path calculated for the building industry. For 1851–3 there are direct estimates. This table may overestimate both new and total investment to the extent that local and private road-building costs lagged behind those of the central government – for which we have direct estimates at *some* points. Gador gives figures on growth and costs.[118] These suggest an overall network growth of close to 16,000 kilometres – about 3,000 km more than we have estimated for the period 1816–52 – and (given Gador's smaller base) a percentage growth of 430 as opposed to our 350 per cent. His figures further imply construction costs close to ours (between 5,000 and 6,000 talers or 15,000–16,000 marks per kilometre) and replacement–maintenance costs of the same order of magnitude. Table 118 shows what investment levels our interpretation of Gador's data produces. (In the text we have adhered to our figures.)

Table 116. Number of Buildings in Prussia, 1816–67

Type of Buildings

	(1) Church buildings	(2) Government buildings	(3) Total public buildings	(4) Private dwellings	(5) Factory buildings	(6) Farm buildings	(7) Grand total
1816	16,412	33,768	50,180	1,537,204	79,401	1,325,605	2,992,390
1819	16,844	40,774	57,623	1,570,805	83,834	1,426,882	3,134,144
1822	16,848	44,894	61,742	1,606,790	87,070	1,496,991	3,252,593
1828	16,914	50,791	67,710	1,674,929	91,436	1,600,531	3,434,606
1831	16,881	53,546	70,427	1,699,035	91,131	1,648,941	3,509,534
1834	16,915	56,618	73,533	1,739,975	95,949	1,730,857	3,566,781
1843	16,688	59,465	76,733	1,874,472	110,161	2,028,107	4,012,740
1849	16,896	63,559	80,455	1,945,182	115,194	2,157,204	4,298,035
1852	17,217	65,306	82,523	1,996,368	115,244	2,230,834	4,424,969
1855	—	—	83,953	2,035,657	115,922	2,276,077	4,511,609
1858	17,567	69,176	86,743	2,069,925	118,327	2,348,928	4,623,923
1861	18,018	69,818	87,836	2,105,053	120,402	2,377,087	4,690,378
1867	17,854	89,047	106,901	2,167,021	294,703	2,861,215	5,430,713

SOURCES. Königliches Preussisches Statistisches Bureau, *Tabellen und Nachrichten für den preussischen Staat, 1849* (Berlin, 1855); *idem, Tabellen ... 1852* (Berlin, 1858); *idem, Preussische Statistik,* XVIII (Berlin, 1868).

Table 117. *Annual Investment in Roads and Highways in Prussia, 1817–53*

	Growth of network (km) (1)	Investment (million marks)		Total investment (million marks) (2) + (3) (4)	Investment per km (million marks)		Average length in operation (km) (7)
		New (2)	Replacement (3)		New (5)	Replacement (6)	
1817–23	2,385	5·5	1·8	7·3	16,000	351	5,000
1824–30	2,828	6·5	2·7	9·2	16,000	351	7,700
1831–40	4,454	8·0	5·5	13·5	18,000	500	11,000
1841–50	4,035	7·9	7·8	15·7	19,500	500	15,500
1851–3	1,665	11·7	12·7	24·4	21,000	708	18,000

Table 118. *Annual Investment in Roads and Highways in Prussia, 1816–53, after Gador's data*

	Growth of network (km) (1)	Investment (million marks)		Total investment (million marks) (2) + (3) (4)	Investment per km (million marks)		Average length in operation (km) (7)
		New (2)	replacement (3)		New (5)	Replacement (6)	
1816–31	4,317	4·4	2·7	7·1	15,285	441	6,026
1831–46	6,237	7·5	5·1	12·6	18,000	450	11,303
1846–53	8,216	22·9	9·3	32·2	19,500	500	18,529

Table 119. *Capital Stock in German Textile Industries, 1820–52 (millions of marks)*

	Cotton			Wool			Linen			Silk (total)	Grand total
	Spinning	Weaving	Total	Spinning	Weaving	Total	Spinning	Weaving	Total		
1820	14	47	61	—	—	—	—	—	—	—	—
1830–1	15	62	77	38	43	81	7	122	129	18	305
1840	26	124	150	48	69	117	7·5	126·5	134	23	424
1846–7	27	139	166	62	76	138	8	135	143	45	492
1852	45·7	152	197·7	68	111	179	9	148	157	54	588

Table 120. *Capital Stock in Prussian Textile Industries, 1830–52 (millions of marks)*

	Cotton				Wool				Linen				Silk		Total (cf. text)
	A	B	C	D	A	B	C	D	A	B	C	D	A+C	B+D	
1830	18	25	50	62	63	38	46	43	85	7	33	122	92	18	140·7
1840	18	26	50	124	63	48	46	69	85	7·5	33	126·5	92	23	198·4
1846–7	19	27	50	138	63	68	46	76	85	8	33	135	92	45	241·4
1852	22	45·7	50	152	62		46	111	85	9	33	148	92	54	285·9

Estimating industrial capital formation in Prussia in 1816–49 involves data and assumptions as follows.

(1) The capital stock in the German textile industries is estimated from bench-mark data given by Blumberg for the woollen and linen industries, from Kirchhain's data for cotton, and from Dieterici and von Viebahn for silk. Growth is extrapolated by means of data on the number of spindles and looms and (for silk) the production data of Hoffmann et al.:[119] see Table 119.

(2) Estimates of the Prussian share in total numbers of spindles and looms in Germany, from these sources, give the estimates of Prussian textile capital reported in Table 120.

(3) Average capital–output ratios are calculated using Dieterici's 1846 and 1861 value-of-product data.[120] These data then serve to estimate (a) the capital stock for earlier years, for which we have only Dieterici's output-

Table 121. *Estimated Steam Power and Capital Stock in Prussian Coal-Mining, 1830–55*

	Steam power (h.p.)		Capital (millions of marks)	
	Ruhr	Prussia	Ruhr	Prussia
1830–1	—	1·350	0·90	2·19
1837	—	2·354	—	2·81
1840	—	—	4·50	8·14
1843	—	6·930	—	13·48
1846	—	9·555	—	15·14
1849	—	13·695	—	29·69
1851	9·845	16·845	—	28·55
1852	11·569	18·490	18·75	30·56
1855	14·329	24·748	24·126	38·12

value data; (b) the value of product for 1816 and 1822, interpolating 1804 and 1831 data; and (c) the capital stock for the entire sample of twelve products covered by Dieterici, discussed in the text. The value-of-product data for coal derive from Dieterici and Holtfrerich.[121] The capital stock in coal-mining is derived from the data in Table 73 above, which extrapolates two estimates for the Ruhr to Prussia as a whole by means of data on the regional distribution of steam power and coal production.[122] The weighted averages of coal and textile capital–output ratios are then calculated and extrapolated to the entire sample of twelve products.

(4) Replacement investment is estimated using (a) for coal-mining, the estimated 4 per cent depreciation rate given by Holtfrerich; and (b) for all textiles, the 5 per cent of fixed capital depreciation rate cited by Kirchhain for cotton.[123] The share of fixed capital in total capital is taken from Kirchhain and from Blumberg.[124] Silk is taken to have the same depreciation rate as cotton.

Table 122. *Capital Stock, Total Value of Product, and Depreciation Charges in Selected Prussian Industries, 1804–52*
(millions of marks)

	Textiles and Coal				All twelve industries			
	Capital	Value of product	Capital output	Depreciation charge	Capital	Value of product	Capital output	Depreciation charge
1804	—	—	—	—	—	162·6	—	—
1816	—	—	—	—	99[a]	226[b]	0·44[a]	1·70
1822	—	—	—	—	132[a]	270[b]	0·49[a]	2·20
1830–1	142·9	262·8	0·54	2·44	209·5	387·9	0·54	3·56
1840	205·5	335·9	0·61	4·31	286·8	470·1	0·61	6·02
1846–7	256·5	388·5	0·66	4·63	362·5	549·3	0·66	5·60
1852	316·5	425·7	0·74	8·04	456·3	616·6	0·74	10·04

[a] Extrapolated ratio between capital and output value rates of change.
[b] Interpolated using value-of-product data for 1804 and 1831.

Table 123. *Capital Stock and Steam Power in Ruhr Coal, 1851–92*

	(1)	(2)	(3)	(4)	(5)
	Capital stock (talers)	Rate of h.p. growth (per cent)	Price index	Rate of price change (per cent)	((2) + (4))
1851	—		179·6	—	—
1852	6,250,000	17·5	175·4	−2	15·5
1853	7,218,750	12·8	168·5	−4	8·8
1854	7,854,000	0·4	171·1	2	2·4
1855	8,042,496	9·3	199·7	17	26·3
1856	10,157,672·45	23·4	211·6	6	29·4
1857	13,144,028·15	21·4	205·7	−3	18·4
1858	15,562,529·33	18·6	190·7	−7	11·6
1859	17,367,782·73	6·8	188·6	−1	5·8
1860	18,375,114·13	13·2	167·1	−11	2·2
1861	18,779,366·64	6·9	163·3	−2	4·9
1862	19,699,555·60	10·3	158·9	−3	7·3
1863	21,137,623·16	1·6	154·3	−3	−1·4
1864	21,433,549·89	4·4	159·7	4	8·4
1865	23,233,968·08	9·0	159·4	−0·19	8·8
1866	25,278,557·27	12·1	161·5	1	13·1
1867	28,590,048·27	8·7	163·3	1	9·7
1868	31,363,282·95	5·0	158·9	−3	2·0
1869	31,990,548·61	4·0	152·2	−4	—
1870	—	10·6	152·2	—	10·6
1871	35,381,546·76	11·8	148·8	−2	9·8
1872	38,848,938·35	12·9	151·4	2	14·9
1873	44,736,430·16	12·0	161·5	7	19·0
1874	53,118,541·89	15·5	196·1	21	36·5
1875	72,506,809·68	16·5	203·4	4	20·5
1876	87,370,705·67	4·5	168·7	−17	12·5
1877	98,292,043·87	8·0	149·3	−12	−4·0
1878	102,223,725·63	1·1	136·9	−8	−6·9
1879	109,277,162·70	2·0	132·5	−4	−1·0
1880	110,369,934·32	7·4	128·2	−3	4·4
1881	115,226,211·43	1·1	121·9	−5	−3·9
1882	119,720,033·68	5·6	132·6	9	14·6
1883	137,199,158·60	5·9	122·9	−7	−1·1
1884	138,708,349·34	7·4	129·5	5	12·4
1885	155,908,184·66	7·4	122·9	−5	2·4
1886	159,649,981·09	0·7	115·5	−6	−5·3
1887	168,111,430·09	−2·0	109·8	−5	−7·0
1888	179,879,230·20	4·0	113·4	3	7·0
1889	192,470,776·31	9·9	108·0	−5	4·9
1890	201,901,844·35	5·8	111·1	3	8·8
1891	219,669,206·65	8·7	121·7	10	18·7
1892	260,747,348·30	8·3	131·5	8	16·3

Table 124. *Population of Prussia and Germany, 1817–58 (thousands)*

	Prussia		
	Total	Agricultural	Germany
1816	10,349	7,040	—
1817	10,572	—	25,009
1822	11,664	7,810	26,851
1828	12,726	—	28,863
1831	—	8,520	—
1834	13,508	—	30,467
1840	14,929	9,110	32,621
1846	16,113	—	34,616
1849	—	9,620	—
1852	16,935	—	35,864
1858	17,740	—	36,831

SOURCES

Prussia: Königliches Preussisches Statistisches Bureau, *Jahrbuch für die amtliche Statistik des preussischen Staates*, v (1833), 73; and

Prussia, agricultural: Hoffmann *et al.*, *Wachstum der Wirtschaft*, Table 1, pp. 172–3 (includes Alsace-Lorraine).

Germany: Estimated on the basis of Hohorst, 'Bevölkerungsentwicklung und Wirtschaftswachstum', and urbanization data as used in Table 90 above.

CHAPTER IX

Labour in German Industrialization

I. *Size and Structure of the Labour Force*

The industrial revolution in Germany is generally dated from the 1840s. It exerted too localized an initial impact, however, to significantly relieve the pressure on subsistence caused by the rise in population from 15 million in 1750 to 35 million in 1850.[1] The heavy emigration that began in the 1840s reduced the annual rate of population growth from over 1 per cent between 1815 and 1843 to 0·7 per cent between 1843 and 1871. The spread of industrialization then permitted the rate of growth to recover to 1 per cent per annum between 1871 and 1890 and to rise to no less than 1·4 per cent per annum between 1890 and 1914, when the population reached 67 million.[2]

Food prices largely determined the timing of the migration of the one million emigrants who had left – mainly from the West and South – before 1860. Unprecedented peaks were recorded when rye prices soared in 1846–8 and again in 1853–5. Emigration from East Germany rose rapidly once land reclamation ground to a halt in the 1860s. The great boom of 1871–3 stimulated high internal migration in West Germany, but failed to divert most East Elbian migrants from American destinations. Both internal migration and emigration declined abruptly in the general slump from 1874 to 1878. The American recovery after 1879, coinciding with agricultural depression in East Germany, released a pent-up emigrant backlog. The emigration rate reached 4 per thousand between 1880 and 1885, when about a million emigrants left Germany. The strong German recovery of 1886–90, however, reduced the net emigration rate to 1·4 per thousand, while internal migration rose sharply. Emigration again increased somewhat when German depression coincided with American prosperity in 1891–3, but the surging recovery after 1894 turned Germany into a net immigrant country. Domestic demand for labour increased sufficiently after 1894 not only to absorb the most remote East German surpluses but to attract both seasonal and permanent immigrants, mainly Poles and Italians. The 1·2 million foreign workers in Germany on the eve of the First World War comprised at least 8 per cent of the agricultural, and 4 per cent of the non-agricultural, labour force.[3]

Internal migration reached massive proportions in the late nineteenth century. The occupational census of 1907 recorded 50 per cent of the population as internal migrants. This helps explain the growth of the urban proportion of the population from 20 per cent in 1850 to 60 per cent in 1910. No less than two-thirds of the labour force of the forty-two big cities with populations over 100,000 were classified as migrants in 1907.[4]

High internal migration caused marked changes in local age structures, raising the urban and reducing the rural proportions in the most active age groups. In national terms, however, it is the stability of the age structure before 1914, as recorded in Table 125, that is particularly

Table 125. *Age Structure of the German Population (per cent)*

	Under 14	14–64	65 and over
1852[a]	32·7	63·2	4·1
1911	32·1	63·0	5·0
1925	23·7	70·5	5·8
1939	21·6	70·2	7·7

[a] 1852 figures for Prussia only.

SOURCE. W. G. Hoffmann et al., *Das Wachstum der deutschen Wirtschaft seit der Mitte des 19. Jahrhunderts* (Berlin, 1965), 177.

striking. The experience of Saxony, the earliest industrialized state, recorded in Table 126, suggests that the age structure remained more or less steady from the early nineteenth century onwards.

Table 126. *Age Structure of the Population of Saxony (per cent)*

	Under 15	15–60	60 and over
1834	32·9	60·3	6·8
1890	33·7	59·2	7·1

SOURCE. K. H. Blaschke, 'Industrialisierung und Bevölkerung in Sachsen im Zeitraum von 1830 bis 1890', in *Raumordnung im 19. Jahrhundert* (part 1), Historische Raumforschung, 5 (Hanover, 1965), 91.

The stability of the age structure conceals, however, rapid changes in birth and death rates after 1890. Crude birth rate fluctuated around 37 per thousand in the century before 1890, but then fell from 36·5 in 1886–90 to 31·7 in 1906–10. Crude death rate, having fluctuated between 24 and 30 per thousand since the early nineteenth century, plunged from 24·4 in 1886–90 to 17·5 in 1906–10. Falling death rates, particularly as the decline was disproportionately concentrated among infants, sufficiently offset the fall in birth rate in the immediate pre-war decades to maintain a steady overall age structure. This was no longer the case after 1914. Crude death rate fell at only half the speed of crude birth rate between 1906–10 and 1936–9. These diverging rates of change reinforced the impact of the war and caused the first major shift in age structure, as Tables 125 and 126 indicate, for probably at least a century. Table 127 suggests that participation rates were primarily a function

Table 127. *Participation Rates (per cent)*

	Both sexes		Male		Female	
	Total	Excluding relatives assisting	Total	Excluding relatives assisting	Total	Excluding relatives assisting
1882	41·6	37·5	60·5	56·1	23·5	19·6
1895	42·4	38·7	60·1	57·6	24·3	20·5
1907	45·2	38·2	61·9	57·4	29·7	19·6
(1907)[a]	(45·7)	(38·9)	(61·4)	(57·8)	(30·5)	(20·5)
1925	51·3	42·6	68·0	63·7	35·6	22·8

[a] Figures in brackets for 1907 are following 1925 boundaries.

SOURCE. H. J. Platzer, 'Die Steigerung der Erwerbsziffer in Deutschland', *Jahrbücher für Nationalökonomie und Statistik*, CXXXV (1931), 330.

of age structure. The crude rates appear to have remained reasonably stable down to 1914. The big increase recorded in the occupation census of 1907 was largely spurious, reflecting the transfer of 'relatives assisting' – mainly members of farmers' families – from a 'dependent' to a 'gainfully occupied' category.

The demographic impact of the war and the subsequent territorial losses reduced the population from 67 million in 1913 to 63 million in 1925. Table 128 indicates that despite this fall, and also despite a slight

Table 128. *Size of Population and Labour Force (millions)*

	Population	Labour force	
		Total	Non-agricultural
1913	66·98	30·97	20·27
1925	63·17	31·03	21·25

SOURCE. Hoffmann *et al.*, *Das Wachstum der deutschen Wirtschaft*, 174 and 204–5.

decline in age-specific participation rates among males in the fourteen-to-forty age group between 1907 and 1925, the size of the labour force continued to increase after the First World War, owing to the marked change in the age structure of the population.

It is shown in Table 129 that age-specific participation rates among females rose somewhat in the eighteen-to-fifty age group between 1907 and 1925. This mainly reflected the change in the sex ratio as a result of the war, which, by increasing the number of single females in the particularly sensitive age group between twenty-five and thirty-five by

Table 129. *Age-Specific Participation Rates (per cent)*

	Male		Female	
	1907	1925	1907	1925
Under 14	1·8	1·7	1·4	1·3
14–16	77·4	72·4	58·0	52·0
16–18	89·1	88·9	73·1	72·1
18–20	93·3	93·6	74·1	77·4
20–25	95·5	95·0	62·0	67·8
25–30	97·6	97·2	40·5	48·1
30–40	97·7	97·5	34·7	39·5
40–50	96·2	96·8	37·1	38·1
50–60	90·5	92·4	37·7	37·3
60–65	71·2	79·7	30·7	31·9
65–70		61·6		23·7
Over 70	38·8	35·1	15·5	12·9

SOURCE. Platzer, 'Die Steigerung der Erwerbsziffer', 337.

nearly 20 per cent, compelled many potential wives to continue at work. The female proportion of the non-agricultural labour force, as indicated in Table 130, rose slowly in the half-century before 1939.

Table 131 records the changing sectoral distribution of the labour

Table 130. *Proportion of Women in Total Labour Force (per cent)*

	Industry	Trade and commerce
1882	18	19
1907	19	25
1925	22	30
1939	23	35

SOURCE. J. Kuczynski, *Die Geschichte der Lage der Arbeiter unter dem Kapitalismus*, XVIII, 204.

Table 131. *Sectoral Distribution of Labour Force (per cent)*

	Agriculture	Industry	Services
1852	55	25	20
1880	49	30	21
1910	36	37	27
1939	27	41	32

SOURCE. Hoffmann *et al.*, *Das Wachstum der deutschen Wirtschaft*, 202–4.

force. Tertiary functions were, of course, so little specialized in the pre-industrial economy that growth rates can prove somewhat deceptive. For what the figures are worth, however, the secondary and tertiary sectors appear to have experienced rather similar growth rates between 1850 and 1939. Services grew more rapidly than industry between the wars, but this largely reflects the Nazi impact on the bureaucracy and the armed forces. Intra-sectoral changes exerted more influence than inter-sectoral shifts on the distribution of the secondary and tertiary work forces. Within industry, as Table 132 indicates, the share of

Table 132. *Distribution of Industrial Labour Force (per cent)*

	1846	1913	1939
Coal and steel	3	11	7
Stones and clay	4	7	5
Metals and machines	9	22	30
Chemicals, gas, and water	—	3	6
Building	10	15	15
Textiles	22	10	10
Clothing	25	9	7
Leather	2	2	1
Food and drink	13	12	10
Timber	11	6	5
Paper and printing	1	5	5
Total	100	102	101

SOURCE. Calculated from Hoffmann *et al.*, *Das Wachstum der deutschen Wirtschaft*, 194–9 (1913 and 1939 totals due to rounding).

clothing and textiles fell from 47 per cent in 1846 to 17 per cent in 1939, while the share of metals and mining rose from 12 per cent to 37 per cent. Within the tertiary sector, as Table 133 indicates, the share of domestic service declined sharply.

Changing census definitions of skill complicate long-term comparisons of the skill structure of the labour force. The proportion of non-

Table 133. *Distribution of Tertiary Labour Force (as percentages of total labour force)*

	Transport	Trade, banking, insurance, catering	Domestic service	Other services (including defence)
1849–58	1·1	5·0	9·3	4·8
1910–13	3·6	11·0	5·2	7·2
1939	5·2	12·4	3·8	10·2

SOURCE. Hoffmann *et al.*, *Das Wachstum der deutschen Wirtschaft*, 35.

agricultural workers described in the returns as 'skilled' fell from 61 per cent to 59 per cent between 1895 and 1907 and then appears to have stabilized. The 1933 census – as shown in Table 134 – recorded males in industry as being 49 per cent skilled, 21 per cent semi-skilled, and 30 per cent unskilled. Although the introduction of a 'semi-skilled'

Table 134. *Skill Distribution of Male Work Force, 1933*

	Skilled		Semi-skilled		Others	
	Thousands	Per cent	Thousands	Per cent	Thousands	Per cent
Coal-mining	192	46	64	16	158	38
Stones and clays	76	27	66	23	138	50
Iron mines	58	30	80	42	54	28
Foundries	11	29	14	39	12	32
Iron, steel, and metal goods	127	60	47	22	37	18
Mechanical engineering	233	64	78	21	56	15
Electricity	56	56	24	24	20	20
Optical	25	67	7	14	5	15
Chemicals	33	25	18	14	80	61
Textiles	51	18	152	52	89	31
Paper	21	22	30	32	44	46
Mimeography (printing)	80	70	8	7	26	23
Leather	17	36	18	36	14	28
Rubber	4	20	6	29	10	51
Timber	128	54	42	18	65	28
Musical goods	5	49	3	28	2	24
Food and drink	251	61	46	11	113	28
Clothing	82	64	30	24	16	13
Building	342	58	54	9	193	33
Water, glass, and electricity	41	43	31	33	23	24
Laundry	41	82	4	8	5	10
Total	1,874	48·6	821	21·3	1,160	30·1

SOURCE. Kaiserliche Statistische Amt, *Statistik des deutschen Reichs*, 2nd ser., CCCCLXII, section 3, part 10.

category precludes direct comparison with the 1907 returns, these figures hardly point to a decisive tendency. It may be that the 'semi-skilled' category came somewhat closer, as wage differentials seem to imply, to 'unskilled' than to 'skilled'. Nevertheless, scattered data on individual industries and firms reinforces the impression of stability in the skill structure from at least the early twentieth century. Table 135 suggests a tendency towards stability in the important 'mechanical engineering sector, while in the electricity industry Siemens's skill quotient was the same in 1930 as in 1914.[5]

Despite the uncertainties concerning the quality of the data, the available evidence scarcely sustains the cataclysmic visions of the massive technological obsolescence of skilled workers which many of the investigators in the 'Auslese und Anpassung' inquiry, generalizing impressionistically from spectacular but extreme instances, considered the dominant tendency on the eve of the First World War.[6]

Table 135. *Skill Structure in Mechanical Engineering (per cent)*

	Skilled	Semi-skilled	Unskilled	Apprentices and others
1914	50·9	20·2	14·7	14·2
1920	44·3	18·7	16·5	20·5
1925	49·4	19·1	12·7	18·8
1933	64[a]	21	15	—[a]

[a] 'Skilled' figure for 1933 includes apprentices.

SOURCE. J. Kuczynski, *Die Geschichte der Lage der Arbeiter*, v, 173.

It seems probable that the overall level of skill was influenced more by changes in the industrial structure than by changes in skill quotients within individual industries. The increase between 1846 and 1939 in the relative importance of metals, dominated by skilled labour, and the decline in the relative importance of textiles, with its lower proportion of skilled workers, exerted particular influence in this respect.

Table 136. *Numbers of White-Collar and Blue-Collar Workers (millions)*

	White-collar	Blue-collar
1882	1·2	9·8
1895	2·1	11·3
1907	3·3	13·5
1925	5·5	16·2
1933	5·6	16·4
1939	7·7	17·5

SOURCE. J. Kuczynski, *Die Geschichte der Lage der Arbeiter*, v, 37.

Discussions of skill structures must not ignore the rise of a white-collar sector. The proportion of white-collar workers in the non-agricultural labour force rose from 12 per cent to 27 per cent between 1882 and 1939. Table 136 reflects a sevenfold increase in the absolute number of white-collar workers, compared with a doubling in the number of blue-collar workers.

The relative growth of the white-collar sector was one of the factors encouraging a rise in the female proportion of the labour force, for women flocked into white-collar employment. The growth of the white-collar sector reflects in turn the increase in the average size of firms, for the proportions of white-collar workers vary directly in most industries with size of firm. The proportion of the industrial labour force working in concerns employing more than fifty people rose from 26 per cent in 1882 to 46 per cent in 1907.[7]

II. *Recruitment*

Net annual labour supply to the non-agricultural sector rose from about 100,000 in 1850 to about 400,000 in 1913. Net entry rates to individual industries naturally fluctuated according to their sensitivity to cyclical influences. Numbers in commerce, banking, and insurance rose fairly steadily, relatively unaffected by the trade cycle. Transport proved more vulnerable to cyclical factors than commerce, but less sensitive than industry. Fortunes fluctuated within the five major industries. Employment in food and drink may, if anything, have moved in a contra-cyclical or at least an acyclical direction. Clothing and textiles proved exceptionally sensitive to cyclical influences before 1860, but then became progressively impervious to cycles as the income elasticity of demand for clothing fell with gradually rising living standards. The remaining big three industrial sectors – construction, engineering, and coal-mining – increasingly bore the brunt of fluctuations in entry rates. Net employment in the engineering sector, for instance, rose less than 1 per cent per annum between 1875 and 1885, then bounded up by 7 per cent per annum between 1885 and 1890, stagnated until 1895, and then recorded an 8 per cent annual rate of increase between 1895 and 1900. The collieries experienced notoriously severe fluctuations.[8]

The most striking short-term changes in entry rates to individual industries were recorded during the First World War. In Prussian firms employing more than ten workers, the labour force increased by 25 per cent per annum in chemicals and by about 15 per cent per annum in engineering. Krupp's work force rose from 34,000 in October 1914 to more than 100,000 in October 1918, and Thyssen's work force in Mülheim from 3,000 to 27,000. The abruptness and scale of the changes, particularly as the female proportion nearly doubled, far exceeded anything familiar from peacetime. The consequences for labour management – which might also cast helpful light on pre-war circumstances – have not been adequately investigated.[9]

Gross entry rates to individual industries, in peace or war, cannot be deduced from the available data. Annual wastage figures do not exist, and high levels of turnover complicate the translation of net into gross rates. In the most rapidly growing sectors, gross entry rates can hardly have been less than double the net rates and may have been as much as quadruple.

Unskilled labour was a surplus commodity until the end of the nineteenth century. Except in most unusual circumstances, employers could afford to wait for the unskilled to troop to them. The recruitment of foreign miners as domestic supplies dried up provided the main exception. The Concordia colliery, situated in the thinly populated Oberhausen district of the Ruhr, began to systematically recruit Silesian and Polish workers, unskilled and skilled, from as early as 1882. Some other large employers soon followed suit and dispatched agents to lure both unskilled and skilled recruits from foreign parts as well as distant German regions, by advancing travel costs and promising accommodation. A fair proportion of the 139,000 East Elbians working in the Ruhr coal mines in 1913 were apparently recruited in this manner.[10]

In sharp contrast to their general attitude towards unskilled labour, early industrial employers devoted close attention to the recruitment of skilled workers. Recognizing that their fate frequently depended on the ability of the craftsmen to push back the frontiers of their firm's technology, they scoured the market at home and abroad for promising prospects. The acquisition, transmission, and diffusion of skills created serious bottlenecks in early industrialization. There was nothing new in this. Skill shortages plagued the pre-industrial German economy. Virtually every innovation in the textile and iron industries depended heavily on imported labour. Migrants introduced the 'Dutch loom' to Wupper valley ribbon-makers in the late sixteenth century. Peter Wichelhausen, Barmen's leading merchant, recruited Dutch workers for his thimble factory in 1760. Wupper valley merchants imported French, Crefeld, and Hanau workers to initiate the locals into the mysteries of the silk manufacture in the 1770s. In the same decade, Prussian journeymen posed as innocent invalids seeking the solace of Saxon spas to secure access to the jealously guarded bleaching techniques. The Dresden woollen manufactory opened in 1679 with Dutch foremen, as did Naumann's tobacco manufactory in Bayreuth in 1797. Examples could easily be multiplied from the consumer-goods sector in general.[11]

Recurring bottlenecks due to shortages of skilled labour occurred in ironworks. The difficulty of ensuring the continuity of skilled labour supply probably contributed as much to the high mortality rates of pre-industrial and early industrial enterprises as did the difficulty in ensuring continuity in the quality of management. Swedish iron-workers imported into Brandenburg in 1664 insisted on confiding their craft secrets solely to their sons, rejecting a contract binding them to transmit their secrets to the locals 'so that in the event of their death the works will not come to a standstill'.[12]

As long as continental states, above all Holland, had been the main magnets for merchants in search of skills, suitable men could generally be recruited through correspondence agents. German businessmen possessed relatively few contacts with the industrial areas of England, however. When these superseded continental centres in the late eighteenth century as the main source of technological progress, the Germans were themselves compelled to venture in unprecedented numbers on the manufacturers' grand tour to acquire personally both machines and mechanics.

The hardness of German cast iron made English materials necessary for cylinders. Difficulties experienced with new machines were mainly due to the want of the necessary skill on the part of the workers. English workers proved as indispensable as English materials in breaking the crucial bottlenecks. Brügelmann had to hire an English mechanic to construct a spinning machine at his Cromford works in 1780 when none of the locals could persuade the machine which he had smuggled from Arkwright's factory to function. The Harthau cotton manufacturer, Karl Friedrich Bernhard, wisely secured the services of the mechanic Watson, the spinner Evans, and the iron-worker Moult not only to install but to supervise the functioning of the first mule in Saxony in 1799. Only the skill of British puddlers secured the successful introduction of Cort's process into Germany. Foreign workers continued to be imported with foreign processes later in the century. In 1861 Dundee workers were hired to teach the techniques of jute manufacture to the natives, and Ludwig Löwe brought American workers to operate his American machine tools in 1869.[13]

The significance of imported labour appears to have been out of all proportion to its size, but even its size – at least if interpreted to include until 1871 immigrants from other German as well as non-German states – was substantial. For example, only three of fifty-one skilled metal workers in the Haubold engineering works in Chemnitz in 1833 were locals: twenty-six came from the rest of Saxony, sixteen from other German states, and six from abroad.

Employers took great care to recruit key workers to solve specific problems of a once-for-all nature. But the lack of provision for systematic information concerning employment opportunities until the very end of the nineteenth century reflects employer confidence in the continuance of a generally elastic labour supply. Workers' memoirs reveal an absence of any systematic concept of formal recruiting procedures. The family, and wider kinship networks, acquired growing significance as a communications conduit as migration increased. Newspapers and trade journals were used to some extent for white-collar and skilled-labour recruitment as the century progressed, but their highly localized circulation restricted their appeal. Even compositors, the most literate and sophisticated group among skilled manual workers, depended far less on formal than informal information concerning employment opportunities. Kin and friends, in contrast to advertisements, could provide essential information on real, as distinct from nominal, working conditions. Notice boards on factory and building sites, in shop windows and municipal offices, advertised vacancies, while beer-house gossip further oriented potential applicants on job possibilities. Recruitment by foremen, subcontractors, or gang bosses naturally fostered a type of regional nepotism, encouraging the concentration of migrants from the same area – links in the information chain – in the same complex.[14]

Perhaps the most important economic consequence of this highly imperfect information market was the coincidence of severe labour shortage in West Germany with high emigration from East Germany between 1869 and 1873. The Elbe flowed into the Hudson rather than the Rhine, because the information network carried news of American labour markets quicker than news of West German labour markets to East Germany. It would be interesting to speculate on the course the *Gründerjahre* boom might have taken with more elastic supplies of labour.[15]

The first municipal labour bureau was established in Leipzig in 1860, but only an exiguous formal information system concerning vacancies existed until the creation of an information infrastructure through public and private labour exchanges, in the 1890s, at last began to generate a coherent information flow. The severe unemployment in the slump of 1891–3 stimulated state governments to encourage municipalities to establish or subsidize labour exchanges. Exchanges were consequently established or supported for the first time in Freiburg in 1892, Berlin in 1893, Cologne in 1894, Munich, Stuttgart, Frankfurt, and Strasbourg in 1895, and Nuremberg in 1896. Growing labour scarcity and increasing trade-union strength in the recovery after 1894 stimulated employers to establish their own exchanges. By 1907 over 700 local offices supplied regular returns to the Imperial Statistical Office.

By 1914 private and public registries each filled well over one million vacancies, accounting together for perhaps 30 per cent of the total. Employer exchanges disappeared in discredit after 1918, but by 1925 public exchanges alone probably filled about 40 per cent of total vacancies. It was left to the Nazis, however, to institute a national labour exchange system and to extend it to white-collar as well as blue-collar workers. The introduction in 1935 of work books recording the training and occupational history of 22 million workers created an unprecedented store of information concerning the quality of the labour force.[16]

Labour exchanges doubtless limited waste by reducing the length of time the unemployed spent seeking work. Trade-union spokesmen condemned the embryonic official exchanges in 1896 but soon came to appreciate their potential contribution to the unions' unemployment funds by shortening their members' out-of-work intervals. Indeed, the exchanges generally helped men still at work to find alternate employment without risking an idle interval. The exchanges were certainly the main public contribution to the smooth functioning of the labour market.[17]

Employers and their foremen did not, of course, generally employ patently unsuitable applicants. Although internal migration greatly increased in the course of the nineteenth century, the range of occupational types for which rural migrants were recruited tended to remain limited to 'dirty' or servile or inconvenient or out-of-door jobs. In 1907, for instance, rural-born workers accounted for over 60 per cent of the labour force in cities with populations over 100,000 in brickworks, breweries, and forges, and for 50–60 per cent in civil engineering, building, stones and clays, glassworks, catering, posts and telegraphs, railways, trams, haulage, and delivery services. At the opposite end of the occupational spectrum, the rural-born accounted for less than 20 per cent of goldsmiths and silversmiths, needle- and wireworkers, printers, precision instrument makers, photography workers, and carpet-makers and -weavers, and for less than 10 per cent of all technicians.[18]

Within the broad range of occupational types, therefore, migrant careers were largely determined before migration. Thus, rural-born workers comprised just over 50 per cent of city masons and carpenters, but only 25 per cent of painters, plumbers, and glaziers, for whom rural training opportunities were limited by the simpler aesthetics of rural housing. The occupational census data broadly confirm the conclusion, based on the more impressionistic 'Auslese und Anpassung' inquiry, that 'it is not the occupation, but the location, which changes'.[19]

III.   *Training*

If imported labour played an important role in the early stages of industrialization, the natives proved apt apprentices. Railway works continued to rely on England for some iron and steel after 1850, but they quickly dispensed with English labour. The fact that the major German locomotive concerns – Borsig in Berlin, Hartmann in Chemnitz, Egestorff in Hanover, Maffei in Munich, Henschel in Kassel, and Kessler in Karlsruhe – were located in cities partly reflected the importance their founders attached to existing pools of skilled artisans. The success and rapidity with which these pools were drawn upon testified to the adaptability of the artisanate to the needs of modern industry. The distinction conventionally posited between the industrial and artisan sectors by commentators like Max Weber, who drew disparaging attention to the dualistic structure of German industry by contrasting the myriad of sluggish small enterprises – in 1907 only 5 per cent employed more than five people – with a few thrusting giants, caricatures the quality of the artisan response to the challenge of industrialization.

The speed with which domestic spinning succumbed to factory competition after 1850 and the futile rearguard action waged by the handloom weavers until the end of the century have unduly influenced analysis of the artisan experience. Change has been customarily confused with decay, whereas in fact declining artisan occupations frequently fell victim not so much to modern factory competition as to rising artisan sectors. Tractor and motor repairmen, for instance, superseded the smiths and saddlers who had flourished during the great age of the horse in the nineteenth century. At the local level artisan fortunes often varied directly, not inversely, with the degree of industrialization, for factory and workshop proved more complementary than competitive in several sectors. Installation work created new markets for plumbers. Locksmiths found fresh employment in the repair of cables, and locksmith concerns employing ten workers proved competitive across a wide range of metal products in the early twentieth century.[20] The spread of electricity did not generally enable artisans to emulate the outworkers in the Solingen cutlery industry, who were enabled to recover and flourish in the face of factory competition when electricity provided the requisite power 'for drills, lathes, grindstones and polishing wheels' – as well as light, an important consideration in high-quality work. But in many instances electricity helped to counteract the advantages conferred by coal on concentrated concerns and allowed artisans to hold their own more comfortably.[21]

The proportion of artisans – defined as workers who had been awarded journeymen's certificates and were employed by firms of the type registered with the compulsory chambers of handicrafts after 1895 – no doubt fell in the course of the nineteenth century. The proportion, however, recovered from 27·3 per cent of the industrial labour force in 1895 to 33·6 per cent in 1939. Absolute numbers continued to increase even as the relative share declined in the second half of the nineteenth century, and the unprecedentedly rapid internal structural change reflects adaptation rather than collapse. The doubling in the proportion of journeymen to masters between 1816 and 1895 – it doubled again between 1895 and 1939 – points to the growing size of artisan concerns. Far from being the decaying sector of late nineteenth-century imagination and prognostication, the continuing vitality of the artisanate may have constituted a valuable asset for Germany in the economic stakes.[22]

The most significant contribution of the artisan sector lay in the supply of skills to industry. A few engineering firms established their own apprentice workshops in the 1850s, but by 1914 only about a hundred firms altogether had established similar workshops. This number did not increase significantly until after 1933. Even in the throes of the rationalization drive in the 1920s, large manufacturers were sufficiently satisfied with the quality of labour supply to restrict rationalization to the deployment of labour once it arrived in the factory. 400,000 of the 799,000 apprentices recorded in the 1895 occupational census were being trained in firms employing fewer than six workers, a further 172,000 in firms employing between six and twenty workers, and only 227,000 (about 30 per cent) in larger firms. In 1933, the share of firms employing more than twenty workers had fallen to 25 per cent. The abrupt reduction in the number of apprentices trained during the slump resulted in severe shortages of skilled labour from 1934, and provoked the Nazis to compel larger firms to adopt crash-course training schemes. By 1937 there were 836 apprentice workshops and 114 semi-skilled shops in operation, with another 404 and 113 respectively under construction. Despite Nazi efforts, however, the apprentice continued until the Second World War to generally receive his all-round training during his three years in the small workshops, before being recruited, and more finely honed, by the bigger firms. It was only Nazi pressure that persuaded the big employers to accept a skilled 'industrial worker's' certificate as the equivalent of the journeyman's.[23]

There was, then, no dual economy in the quality of labour. Workers' memoirs reveal little feeling of technical inferiority in moving from apprenticeships in small firms to employment in large ones. The familiar tendency to equate 'small' with 'bad' and 'big' with 'good' has little historical justification in this respect.

The craftsman's contribution has tended to be disparaged partly because of the presumed anachronistic influence of guilds on economic growth. However, discussion of the role of the guilds, in concentrating on their legal more than their economic impact, has clung too closely to the criteria of contemporary polemics. A desire to evade guild restrictions influenced some eighteenth-century businessmen to seek rural rather than urban locations, but guild regulations generally interfered more with personal convenience than with economic development. The Prussian industrial ordinance of 1849 reversed the trend towards liberalization contained in the code of 1845, but it did not prevent the unprecedentedly rapid growth of the 1850s, any more than Austria's gesture in abolishing guild regulations in 1859 accelerated her growth rate. Regulations varied considerably between states, without being obviously correlated with their rate of industrialization. Saxony's legislation, for instance, was frequently more restrictive than that of more agrarian states. The abolition of guild regulations in the North German Confederation in 1869, and throughout the empire in 1871, apparently signalled the demise of the guild spirit. A more sympathetic attitude re-emerged after 1890, however, as the abuses of the apprenticeship system under laissez-faire conditions roused resentment. In 1904, 500,000 artisans – perhaps one-eighth of the skilled labour force – belonged to guilds which, however archaic their rituals, did not noticeably inhibit the adaptation of their members to industrialization.[24]

There may be some truth in Clapham's contention that the inefficient implementation of the restrictive mid-century Prussian legislation modified its potentially constricting impact. The vociferous disputes about the legal privileges of artisan organisations can too easily distract attention, however, from the fact that on balance, the achievement of the guilds – in fostering commercial honesty, in adapting rapidly to the unprecedented demands for skill in the course of industrialization, and above all in encouraging high educational levels – entitles them to be considered positive rather than negative influences on the supply of skilled labour.

This reservoir of skilled labour stood Germany in good stead in the nineteenth century. It is possible, however, that its very quality may have helped to delay the adoption of assembly-line techniques and the conversion of production processes to techniques suitable for unskilled and semi-skilled workers. The shortage of skilled labour that contributed to the capital-intensity of American mechanization did not exist to anything like the same extent in Germany.

It was in education that the Germans sought a substitute for the 'spontaneous' technological originality of eighteenth-century England. Little of the ambitious educational legislation of the eighteenth century was translated into practice, but the impact of Napoleon added impetus to movements for reform. Forty-five teacher-training schools were established in Prussia between 1817 and 1842. By 1835, 80 per cent of children in Prussia were attending elementary schools. By 1850, illiteracy had virtually disappeared among younger age groups, except in the furthest recesses of East Germany.[25]

Unskilled and agricultural workers tended to resist compulsory and costly elementary education until after 1860, but artisan spokesmen generally displayed an avid thirst for knowledge and an acute awareness of the value of education. As early as 1841 the guilds of Cologne associated the diffusion of technical skill with book knowledge, and petitioned not only for universal free education but for the establishment of industrial libraries to spread familiarity with new techniques. Even the 'reactionary' Masters' Congress in Frankfurt in 1848 demanded universal free education, while the journeymen's congresses in Frankfurt and Berlin urged free adult as well as free child education.[26]

Some enlightened manufacturers supported Sunday schools. But the main motive force of this movement, which began in the late eighteenth century and became widespread by the 1830s, derived from artisan aspirations. The schools accordingly concentrated on practical subjects like German, arithmetic, drawing, geometry, physics, and geography.[27]

Little contact existed between the classical secondary schools or the universities on the one hand and industry on the other. But a parallel system of continuation schools, fostered by the artisan master's realization that to meet factory competition his apprentices needed further education, developed from the Sunday-school movement after 1830. Continuation schools suffered many legislative vicissitudes, but by the early twentieth century, six hours' attendance per week was generally compulsory for males until the age of eighteen. The number of students attending Prussian continuation schools rose from 58,000 in 1884 to 505,000 in 1913.[28]

Many employers welcomed the continuation schools, and some subsidized them. After 1890 recalcitrant businessmen were legally compelled by a series of measures to release their workers during normal hours for school attendance. An early hint of the application of cost-benefit thinking to educational investment can be detected in the 1904 decree forbidding continuation schools after 8 p.m. on the ground that the teachers would fail to hold the interest of the tired students and the schools 'will not give an adequate return for the money spent'. Without the widespread participation of artisan masters as teachers, the continuation schools could hardly have found the staff to cater for the demand. Voluntary attendance by an apparently significant proportion of journeymen and masters at schools adapted to their level further reinforced the educational orientation of industry, including small industry.[29]

Foremen and supervisors tended generally to be recruited from the better workers within existing firms, with ex-NCOs enjoying some preference. If few other employers emulated Hartmann of Chemnitz, who insisted from the 1860s that aspiring foremen in his engineering works attend the polytechnic, the training of foremen became gradually more systematized, and the first school in Europe for the training of foremen opened in Bochum in 1882. The coal industry had experimented with a formal training system much earlier. Schools for supervisors were established in Freiberg in Saxony in 1767, and in Berlin in 1770. By 1927 over a thousand students were attending the fifteen mining academies in Prussia and Saxony which helped forge some relation between theory and practice.[30]

At a more exalted level the technical high schools aspired to create a technological elite. These high schools – which achieved university status about 1900, after protracted wrangles – developed out of trade schools and polytechnics established earlier in the nineteenth century. The Prussian official Peter Beuth opened the Berliner Gewerbeschule in 1821, specifically to supply import substitutes for technical skills. Beuth, who was convinced that lack of skills rather than lack of capital constituted the main obstacle to Prussian industrialization, aimed to combine practical and theoretical instruction, to develop the school as a teacher-training centre in technical skills, and to provide refresher courses in rapidly changing basic technology for teachers in provincial schools. From the outset an intense industrial demand existed for the graduates, and the number of pupils rose from fifty-two in 1827 to 722 in 1875. The school became an institute in 1827 and an academy in 1866, when it could boast its superiority to anything England had to offer. With English observers already making the reverential journey to Charlottenburg, it could pride itself on the fact that it was no longer producing a mere import substitute but was proving highly competitive on export markets. The academy merged with the Berliner Bau-akademie in 1902 to become the Berliner Technische Hochschule. Karlsruhe boasted the first polytechnic in Germany, established in 1825. Reorganized by C. F. Nebenius in 1833, it became a model for several others.[31]

If relations between the technical educational system and industry were frequently troubled, they were usually intimate. Franz Reuleux – a pupil of Ferdinand Redtenbacher, the founder of applied mechanical engineering, at the Karlsruhe Polytechnic – became Director of the Berlin Trade Academy and Imperial Commissioner for World Exhibitions. Redtenbacher's successor at Karlsruhe, Franz Gasshoff, became a founder member of the influential Union of German Engineers in 1856 and drafted its important resolutions in 1865 and in 1875 on the principles and organization of technical education. Salaries were set sufficiently high to attract teachers from industry and to establish an interlocking network of businessmen and educators. Between 1890 and 1903 the number of students at the eleven technical universities rose from 5,000 to 17,000. This was roughly the saturation point. Numbers stagnated for the next decade, mainly because demand stabilized as industry sought more middle-grade supervisors, who did not require technical education at the level which the technical universities provided.[32]

When it came to commercial skills, German businessmen – in contrast to their heavy imports of technical skill – generally relied on domestic supplies. A scatter of private commercial schools catered for the eighteenth-century demand. Commercial clerks traditionally enjoyed high prestige because of their literacy. The rapid spread of literacy in the nineteenth century reduced their scarcity value and in some areas created a permanent buyer's market for the more common types of white-collar labour in the later nineteenth century. Continuation education for commerce lagged behind technical education, but the 15,000 students in Prussia in 1898 increased to 65,000 by 1910. Even then, commercial education developed to some extent as a status symbol, so great was the prestige attached to the formal qualifications; and the foundation of commercial high schools tended to precede the development of commercial subjects. These high schools were a parallel and subsequent development to the technical high schools, and commerce was developed as an academic subject partly to provide syllabuses for the six schools established between 1898 and 1914.[33]

The history of education for economic growth in Germany is rather more complicated and involves more preoccupation with status and other allegedly non-economic criteria than sometimes emerges from the literature. Nevertheless, there can be little doubt that the quality and range of its education constituted a major German asset in the struggle for economic supremacy in Europe. By 1900 the average German worker would have spent thirty-two hours a week for nine years in a primary school, compared with the English worker's twenty hours a week for seven years. In addition, the German worker would probably have averaged five hours a week at a continuation school for a further two to four years. As early as the 1860s, when theorists were rapidly superseding practical men in the engineering industry, even critical English observers emphasized the superior quality of both the general and the technical education enjoyed by German craftsmen. By 1914 observers might well contemplate with respect, if not affection, a society which had established not merely the finest university system but also the finest technical and commercial educational systems the world had yet seen.[34]

IV. *Adaptation*

The adaptation of labour to the needs of the new industrial system posed fresh problems for employers. The recruits had to be fashioned into malleable shape. Some missionary-minded entrepreneurs imagined themselves engaged in a historic struggle to mould a new man in their own image. Friedrich Harkort considered in 1844 that their inadequate industrial training constituted only one distinctive mark of the proletariat. Their other distinguishing features included the failure to conform to bourgeois hygienic, religious, educational, and marital conventions. Employers of this type deemed it their duty to instil a sense of discipline and deference, of sobriety and propriety, in the inchoate working masses. They must fashion a new tool out of the molten proletarian mass in the crucible of the factory. Hence the assault on personality reflected in the psycho-sadistic factory regulations of employers like the Brothers Stumm: 'every foreman and worker must behave in private life so as to bring honour to the house of the Stumm Brothers; they must expect their private lives will be kept under constant surveillance by their service chiefs'.[35]

It was partly in response to such psychic assault that a working-class consciousness emerged out of the search for identity of the pre-industrial craftsmen and sundry groups of unskilled workers. But most employers did not adopt such perfectionist standards. They were not crusaders. They were generally satisfied if they achieved partial success in creating a stable core of skilled workers which acquired a certain *esprit de corps* and around which the rest of the labour force revolved.

Turnover was the most persistent labour problem confronting employers. It naturally intensified with the increases in the size of the labour market and in the number of potential employers. In the early twentieth century, turnover in manufacturing industry fluctuated around 50 per cent per annum. It rarely fell below 25 per cent, even in such sedentary firms as Krupps, or in such isolated factories as the Ilseder Hütte. It was generally higher in new firms than in older ones, among females than males, among unskilled than skilled, and among blue-collar than white-collar workers. It reached a seasonal peak in spring and early summer and sank to a trough in December.[36]

Some turnover reflected the difficulty of pre-industrial labour in adapting to industrial requirements. However, its positive correlation with the trade cycle implies that turnover was more an index of hope than of despair. Turnover in the Ruhr coal mines, for instance, increased by 60 per cent between the cyclical trough of 1893 and the crest of 1900, then fell 25 per cent in the slump of 1901–2, rose 30 per cent to a new peak in 1907, and fell 15 per cent in the slump of 1908.

Turnover was an expression not only of the desire for improvement but also of the unprecedented opportunities – opportunities which would vitiate contrasts with putative pre-industrial 'stability'. 'Negative' reasons did predominate among the motives for changing jobs adduced by workers investigated by the 'Auslese und Anpassung' team, but 'the attempt to better myself' was the single most frequent reason cited. Even with the 'negative' cases, the fact that specific hard-headed reasons predominated – instead of the simple 'fed up with the job' alienation syndrome – implies the integration of even the dissatisfied worker into the general industrial milieu. The new industrial worker did not, except when he migrated in the final stages of a boom, have to make the best of a bad job by clinging to his first employer. Rapidity of turnover among first-year recruits points to the ease of finding alternative employment no less than to difficulty in adjusting to 'industrial society'. In fact, the main discipline required from many potential recruits was the patience to remain on the farm during industrial slumps until conditions improved sufficiently to be confident of finding work.[37]

Turnover served as a substitute for formal career guidance. It was heavily concentrated among single workers in their first year on the job. In 1906 about 60 per cent of all departures from Krupp occurred among workers who had been with the firm for less than six months. In the Upper Silesian factory inspectors' district, 80 per cent of departures were concentrated among first-year recruits. The labour force consisted of two more or less mutually exclusive groups, the sedentary and the mobile. This casts some doubt on Sombart's assertion that 'it appears that the modern worker seeks relief from his torment by frequent change of jobs: like the feverish patient on the bed he rolls from side to side'. Marriage steadied the patient, and he recuperated remarkably quickly from the initial infection. In industrial as in pre-industrial society, marriage – not the city or the factory – continued to mark the greatest discontinuity in the worker's life.[38]

Employers adopted a variety of stratagems to reduce turnover among their skilled workers. Krupp provided the best-known example of retention schemes, even if the Krupp approach was motivated more than most by the fear that rivals might acquire the firm's secrets by poaching skilled workers. Alfred Krupp actually demanded that the government impose an oath of secrecy on all workers. Krupp's schemes were subjected to some pressure in the 1880s by the extension of state welfare measures and by a court order in 1887 forbidding Krupp to deprive departing workers of the benefits of the funds to which they had contributed. Friedrich Alfred Krupp responded to the challenge by improving and extending the company's benefits well beyond the levels specified in state schemes. In 1900 12 per cent of the population of Essen lived in Krupp apartments, at rents 15 to 20 per cent below open-market rates for comparable accommodation. Despite the imposition of stringent directions on 'how to live in a flat', including the right of Krupp housing inspectors to enter the dwellings at any time, married Krupp workers flocked to queue for these apartments. Furthermore, about 50,000 registered purchasers could take advantage by 1913 of the subsidized prices of Krupp's consumer co-operative.[39]

Krupp's welfare expenditure exceeded 3 per cent of the wages bill as early as 1885. Only a small number of other firms could aspire to match the range, consistency, and cost of the Krupp arrangements, but many firms provided some benefits. Housing schemes, in particular, became increasingly popular. The provision of housing to retain skilled workers, especially in isolated locations, was a long-established custom. The Concordia colliery, on the then thinly populated mining frontier of the Ruhr, pioneered miners' houses in 1854. The pace of provision accelerated after 1900. The number of houses provided by mining companies rose from 26,000 in 1901 to 157,000 in 1927. These dwellings, mostly of the single-family type, let at subsidized rents, accommodated about two-fifths of the labour force in the Ruhr mines at that stage.[40]

The most intrinsically interesting schemes, if not the most influential, were pioneered by Zeiss of Jena, whose work force doubled to 5,000 between 1910 and 1913. These included bonus schemes, holidays, and high pensions, and they differed in fundamental inspiration from the Krupp approach by treating the workers as potential adults rather than as permanent dependents.[41]

It may be doubted whether retention schemes made as significant a contribution to the stability of the work force as the relatively low turnover figures of the model companies suggest. It is true that turnover was much lower among miners with company houses than among their workmates. However, as this largely involves a comparison between married and unmarried workers, it cannot be considered conclusive. Krupp's turnover in 1906–7 was only about 60 per cent of the average for the Düsseldorf district. But by no means all this relative stability can be attributed to welfare measures. Krupp paid the best wages in Essen and enjoyed a dominant position on the local labour market, accounting for over half the total employment in manufacturing industry in the city in 1913. Only limited alternatives existed for workers wishing to stay in Essen. The inducement of congenial retirement among other survivors in the company's old people's home can hardly have accounted for much of the gap between the turnover rates at Krupp and at other firms in the neighbourhood. It seems likely that welfare schemes made a greater contribution in fostering more intense loyalty among those who would have remained in the firm by choice than in actually retaining many more workers than would have otherwise been the case.[42]

Company welfare schemes may have contributed more to the energy and the punctuality of the labour force than to its stability. Company houses, built close to factory or mine, shortened the tiring journey to work, and deprived latecomers of the excuse of not knowing the time, when so many of their neighbours had clocked in punctually. The regular journey to work, as living and working quarters became separated in the course of industrialization, involved considerable adjustment of life styles. In the early nineteenth century, it was difficult for illiterate workers without clocks to guess how long before daybreak to start for work. Rural factories, to which workers had sometimes to travel considerable distances, were particularly vulnerable to miscalculations in this respect. Church bells were too erratically distributed to provide an adequate substitute for clock chimes. The preoccupation of the factory and mining regulations of the seventeenth and eighteenth centuries with the problem of punctuality reflects the pervasiveness of the problem. As industrialization proceeded, urban workers who frequently changed their jobs and their residence had to be induced to calculate the journey to work. The omnibus, tram, and train permitted – and compelled – somewhat more systematic concepts of time and distance. The frequency of fines for unpunctuality in early industrialization points to the seriousness of the problem, but it was a problem whose roots were as much technical as psychic, and one which strategically located company housing was partly designed to solve.[43]

Clock and machine are customarily held to have established a dual dominance over the industrial labour force. The dominance was far from absolute, however, even within the factory. Much early mechanization fostered instead of suppressing the personality of the skilled worker. The skilled man cherished his rapport with the machine, his main ally in demonstrating his quality to his workmates. 'A bad workman blames his tools,' but workers' memoirs suggest that the quality of the machine at their disposal greatly enhanced their job satisfaction – partly because satisfaction depended mainly on the status accorded them by their workmates, which in turn depended mainly on the calibre of their work. Their admiration for machines of high quality may have contributed to the apparently lower labour turnover in the largest and most mechanically sophisticated firms. Skilled workers remained acutely status-conscious, insisting on their own intricate structures of deference, derived largely from the complexity and challenge of their work. Many occupations clung to sartorial distinctions, and foremen and section leaders symbolized their status by asserting the coveted right to wear shirt and collar at work.[44]

Luddite activity, concentrated in the textile sector, was directed more against other abuses than against mechanization. Bouts of machine-breaking clustered in slumps – in Aachen in 1830, in Silesia in 1844, in Chemnitz in 1847. The opposition was less to machines than to efforts to introduce labour-saving devices during periods of high unemployment. Threats against machines were frequently tactical, used as a bargaining ploy by workers with little other negotiating strength. Aachen factory workers threatened textile machinery not because they opposed mechanization but in order to curtail the truck system. Workers rarely opposed capital-saving innovations. Most attacks on machines were perpetrated by domestic workers who felt their livelihood threatened by superior techniques. Factory workers themselves rarely assaulted machines. Even then, they were no more hostile to mechanization, in principle, than those who agitated against the employment of foreigners in slumps were xenophobes, than the lace workers who assaulted the girls employed on 'male' jobs in the Falckmann ribbon factory in Berlin in 1794 were misogynists, or than the peasants who hamstrung the cattle of land-grabbers were animal-haters.[45]

The unskilled could not establish the same rapport with their machines as the skilled, but their greatest problem was that of adapting not to mechanization but to men. Not the new machine, but the old Adam, grated most on the nerves of skilled and unskilled alike. Few workers had previously experienced the pressures of having to adapt to large numbers of new workmates. Family, kin, and reasonably sedentary neighbourhoods constituted a different type of working milieu from the frequently casual acquaintances of the factory. Personal relations played a more immediate role in shaping reactions to new situations than did the prominence of clock or machine. Revulsion against foremen or workmates looms far larger in workers' memoirs than revulsion against machines. New roles proved more disturbing than new tools. Disputes with foremen were the most frequent single recorded cause of resignation. As foremen generally enjoyed not only powers of hiring and firing, but also of determining wages – a power necessarily exercised more obtrusively as piece rates became more widespread – it was little wonder that 'the foreman's will is God's will'.[46]

In coal-mining, where 'the seam and the supervisor make the miner', mechanization bore relatively little responsibility for deteriorating labour conditions. Pick and shovel continued to dominate techniques at the coal face until the mechanization drive of the 1920s. Miners' complaints concentrated on the arbitrariness of supervisors' decisions with respect to allegedly inadequately filled wagons, the arbitrary allocation of extra shifts, the arbitrary imposition of disciplinary measures. The men found clear regulations more congenial than close personal relations, which subjected them to the arbitrary whims of foremen. After the strike of 1905 they hailed as a victory the substitution of a fixed scale of fines for the supervisors' prerogative, though the fines frequently exceeded the previous deductions. The 1903 Siemens strikes were partly provoked by worker resentment at the behaviour of foremen, and they led to severe restrictions in the latter's powers. Foremen were themselves condemned, however willingly, to a role conducive to schizophrenia, objects of suspicion to both workers and employers. However much a foreman's authority might be resented, he was still generally preferred to the proprietor himself. Fines seem to have been far more widely imposed in small concerns than in large ones, and – for what the figures are worth – turnover appears to have been lower in large firms than in small ones.[47]

Once they moved beyond the familiar circle of family and friends many migrants craved the relative anonymity of a large factory, where they might escape the scrimping proprietorial eye. Workers hated to be watched. Considerations of this sort presumably played an even more important role in the case of women. The progression in two generations from domestic service (which had the highest turnover rates of any occupation) to factory or office reflected the same urge for personal freedom, the silent revolt against authoritarianism.[48]

White-collar workers experienced somewhat different pressures as the size of firms grew. Their personal relations with the owner had been on a different basis from that of the manual worker, and they prized the personal relationship accordingly. They therefore experienced a sense of loss at the growing impersonality of bigger firms. The experience of the Siemens white-collar employees is exceptional in that their number grew unusually quickly and to an unusual size – from ten in 1860 to 360 in 1890 and to no fewer than 12,500 in 1912. They did not enjoy immunity, as their numbers grew, from the management's attempt to produce standardized personalities. In their case, however, the model most systematically applied was that of the civil servant, which the revised and restrictive service regulations, introduced in 1899, took as their exemplar. The Siemens case represents an extreme example of a general tendency. The increased size of firms brought few of the advantages to white-collar employees that it brought to manual workers. The technology was little better, and the sense of loss involved in the severing of the coveted contact with the owner was far greater.[49]

This primacy of personal over technical problems helps explain why foreign workers experienced the pressures of adaptation most severely. The Poles in the Ruhr are frequently cited to illustrate the difficulties encountered by novice labour adjusting to the machine. But the skilled British workers who came to instruct the natives in the first half of the nineteenth century frequently found considerable difficulty in adjusting – not (by definition) to the machine, but to Germany. Their problems arose because, *inter alia*, 'they are working with different people than they would be at home'. The culture gap between England and Germany yawned wider than that between industrial and 'pre-industrial' society. Poles and British alike, coming from opposite ends of the technological spectrum, had greater difficulty in adapting to Germans than to machines.[50]

The transition from pre-industrial to industrial work patterns probably proved less traumatic for participants than it appeared to many later observers. The idealized picture of the domestic worker proceeding at his convenience, stopping when and as he pleased, bears little relation to the relentless pressures imposed by sustained population growth from the mid eighteenth century. The spontaneous intervals of leisure in domestic industry, which whetted nostalgic fancies, became increasingly involuntary as population pressure took voluntary leisure – in so far as it ever existed – out of domestic manufacture. Conditions in Silesia, synonymous with misery by the 1840s, began to deteriorate as early as the 1780s, prior to the impact of serious factory competition. Domestic manufactures like the Berlin clothing and cigarette sweat-shops, or the Black Forest and Harz Mountains toy industries, where the famished children of the poor toiled to make dolls for the sated children of the rich, lingered into the twentieth century to rouse the horrified sympathy of observers weaned on the standards of industrial society. They did not represent corruptions of the domestic norm. They were the norm, now exposed in hideous mockery of the arcadian ideal by the revolution of rising expectations generated by industrialization.[51]

The exploitation of child labour in factories has outraged the sensitivities of later generations. It outraged fewer contemporaries, least of all the parents to whom the children provided indispensable assistance on the frame and the mule. Children proved useful in early textile factories not merely as cheap labour but because they were required to literally pick up the threads. Until the 1850s, when machines became more reliable and sophisticated, children played an active role in supplementing textile technology. Males supplied muscle power, women and children nimble fingers. 'The soft hand and the hard hand cannot be interchanged at pleasure' applied to industry no less than to crime.[52]

The factories inherited child labour from the domestic system. Indeed, between 1800 and 1846 child employment in domestic industry increased more rapidly than in factories, where between 10 and 20 per cent of the factory labour force were aged under fourteen. The transition to factory labour probably proved less irksome for children than for adults. The picture of the domestic worker taking time off 'when and as he pleased' could not apply, even in the most fictional reconstructions, to children. They took time off at home when and as their parents pleased, which doubtless rarely coincided with their own preferred schedule. Whereas adults, however relatively few were involved, had to discard certain conventions when transferring from the domestic sector to the factory, children may have found that becoming an adult, learning the conventions of adult behaviour, did not necessarily pose any more disagreeable task in factory than in domestic conditions. They did not spare much gratitude for the adults who made factory schooling compulsory. The children hated the schools at least as much as they hated the factory. Schoolwork was intrinsically just as boring, and corporal punishment was as brutal and was probably more resented for being inflicted by strangers instead of by kin.[53]

Children were concentrated in a few sectors. Agriculture – where their conditions remained unregulated throughout the nineteenth century, except by negative control through compulsory school attendance – was much the largest employer of children. Domestic industry, where hours did not begin to be regulated until 1891, was the second largest. Textiles, which accounted for two-thirds of child labour in 'factories' in 1846, came a long distance behind. The first Prussian legislation concerning child labour in 1839 forbade 'regular' employment of children under nine in factories and mines, and of illiterate children under sixteen. As no provisions for inspection were made, the law remained ineffective until 1853–4, when further legislation raised the age of exemption to twelve and instituted factory inspection at local option. Only when this legislation was further tightened and extended in 1878 did child labour finally become illegal in factories. Prussian legislation tended to anticipate that of other states. Saxony did not forbid child labour for children under ten until 1861, or for those under twelve until 1865.[54]

The changing demand pattern was probably at least as important as legislation in reducing the size of the factory child labour force in the 1850s. Legislation, at most, merely accelerated a decline in child labour which improved mechanization was already hastening in the late 1840s. The number of children in Prussian textile factories had fallen by about 30 per cent between 1846 and 1853, before legislation made any serious impact.[55]

Pre-industrial and early-industrial work rhythms did not diverge sharply. Agriculture may have required less sustained activity throughout the year than industry; but little respite could be found during the active agricultural seasons. The harvest demanded dawn-to-dusk exertion. The bulk of the textile, leather, and paper trades supplied seasonal markets and shared something of agriculture's rhythms. Pre-industrial techniques did not permit complete personal control of the pace of activity. The early factories did not, for their part, impose anything approaching conveyer-belt continuity of work. Industries initially dependent on water rather than steam power – nineteen out of twenty-five Saxon spinning mills relied exclusively on water as late as 1840 – were at the mercy of frost and drought. As the better water sites were occupied in the Harz Mountains, workers in the worse locations slaved round the clock when supplies of water were abundant and might remain idle for weeks when supplies failed. The unreliability of machines – and early spinning machines were notoriously liable to break down – frequently interrupted the working day. Before the railway regularized transport schedules, delays due to inadequate supplies of raw material were common.[56]

The widely held assumption that industrialization involved the mass migration of peasants into factories exaggerates the abruptness of the adjustment of working rhythms imposed by the industrialization process. The bulk of internal migration was short-distance in an occupational as well as a geographical sense. Two-thirds of internal migrants flocked into occupational types with which they were already familiar. The tendency to generalize from spectacular exceptions has tended to disguise the fact that 'farm to factory' represented a quite untypical migrant progression. 'From plough to pick' captures the essence of the first-generation redistribution process more accurately. Beneath the surface chaos, continuity rather than discontinuity of occupational type, defined in terms of work rhythms, characterized the employment structure of even first-generation rural–urban migrants. Despite the crudities at the margin, the process was more complex, more sophisticated, more economically rational, and more psychologically humane than the 'farm-to-factory' myth implies. Construction, catering, and transport, which drew a substantial proportion of rural migrants, involved broken or irregular hours and often also involved significant seasonal variations in work flow. Rural migrants concentrated disproportionately in occupations demanding intense but intermittent exertion, involving a loosening rather than a snapping of umbilical links with their rural origins. Most rural-born female migrants also sought urban sustenance in relatively familiar occupations, such as domestic service, food and drink, and laundry work. As late as 1907, 50 per cent of all rural-born female migrants were concentrated in domestic service.[57]

Long-distance migrants, particularly in the mining industry, constituted a special case. But long-distance migration became significant only towards the end of the nineteenth century. Local labour sufficed to satisfy the rising demand in the Ruhr in the 1850s. The boom of 1853–7 tempted migrants from further afield, but still from mainly within the Rhineland and Westphalia. These two provinces accounted for 79 per cent of the 69,000 migrants into the Ruhr towns between 1865 and 1870, compared with only 2·1 per cent from East Elbia. The trickle of Easterners gradually broadened into a stream, particularly as coal-mining expanded. In the Ruhr mines, 51,000 East Elbians accounted for 25 per cent of the labour force in 1900, 139,000 for 34 per cent in 1913. The newcomers concentrated into the newest and largest collieries in the northern sector of the coalfield. In Oberhausen, 85 per cent of the complement of the Ewald colliery and 71 per cent of the Graf Bismarck were Poles, whereas recruitment remained almost wholly local in the static southern sector – only 5 per cent of the labour force in the Werden area came from East Elbia.[58]

Long-distance migrants, whether Teuton or Slav, certainly felt sufficiently alien in the West to cling together, according not merely to ethnic but to local origins. Upper Silesians, for instance, accounted for 45 per cent of the East Elbian mining force in western Essen, but for only 3 per cent in eastern Essen. This concentration naturally focused attention on the newcomers. The conspicuous clustering of the Poles, whose numbers in the Ruhr rose from about 30,000 in 1890 to about 400,000 in 1913, provoked especially wild imputations – compounded by ethnic antipathies – of the contrariness of the immigrant's reaction to industrial society. There were special problems in this respect, but they seem to have been greatly exaggerated by hostile observers. Much of the evidence adduced to justify the soubriquet '*Zugvögel*' (migrant birds) for the Poles cannot survive scrutiny. When appropriate allowance is made for the age, sex, marital, and occupational structure of the Poles, their turnover rates may have been little higher than those of less conspicuous short-distance migrants.[59]

The jobs favoured by rural migrants served as virtual parachute occupations, which helped to break the fall from one type of society to another. They enabled the migrants to acquire an urban concept of time, but within a familiar if in many respects uncongenial framework, which preserved face-to-face structures of authority. They thus did some service as transition channels from rural to urban life, and not merely as dumping grounds for unfortunates who failed to find jobs in more attractive industrial sectors.[60]

The proportion of agricultural workers recruited directly into factory occupations was doubtless even smaller than the proportion of rural workers. The census statistics define as 'rural' all communities with fewer than 2,000 inhabitants. Many such communities contained some industry, particularly in the earlier nineteenth century. It seems

probable that a substantial proportion of rural migrants into factories
were drawn from a manufacturing background rather than from an
exclusively agricultural one. When Sombart claimed that the division
of labour took 'the greater part of skill' out of work and reduced it to the
level 'where every peasant girl could be taught quickly' he ignored the
fact that many peasant girls simply did not have hands that were suited
for work in factories where dexterity and finesse were the first requisites
for female workers. Employers accordingly took care to recruit precious
few peasant girls into factories. Factory work was more likely to be the
goal of second-generation female immigrants.[61]

The intractability of skilled labour in early industrialization reflected
not so much difficulties of adjustment to new work patterns – the
adjustment required was relatively limited at this stage – as the exploitation, in typical pre-industrial fashion, of a strong bargaining position by
workers at least partly conscious of their scarcity value. Even so, despite
the widening of differentials between themselves and unskilled workers
at this stage, the best skilled workers probably still earned well below
their real value. Had they experienced greater difficulty in adapting to
industrial requirements they might have fought more vigorously for
rewards commensurate with their contribution to the economy.

The worker's attitude to the factory depended very much on his
particular vantage point. Artisan masters cordially detested factories.
They themselves were generally too old, and too much in the habit of
giving orders to calmly contemplate taking them.[62] Journeymen
usually adopted a more positive attitude to factory employment. The
journeymen's congress in 1848 refused to support the demands of the
masters' congress, and bitterly resisted the attempt of the masters to
retain the restrictions on their freedom of movement and to forbid them
access to factory employment, to which they were drifting in increasing
numbers.[63]

The earliest factory workers were predominantly low-status women
and children, in the traditionally low-status textile industry. The spinning manufactory, often located in, and popularly associated with,
prisons and barracks, with 'pressed' orphan and pauper labour,
deservedly acquired a notorious reputation during the eighteenth
century. But this odium did not apply to engineering factories, dominated by adult male labour. The Berlin machine-builders were widely
accepted at their own valuation as the aristocrats of the labour force.
The valuation reflected not only their high wages but also the high
prestige attached to their technical virtuosity, which could be best displayed in factory employment. 'Pull' as well as 'push' factors helped to
create the early factory labour force.

As early as the mid eighteenth century, linen-weavers abandoned small masters in the Wupper Valley for the lure of the fleshpots – the coffee-breaks – with which owners seduced them into larger establishments. By 1830 domestic workers were attracted to Chemnitz factories not only by higher wages but by greater personal freedom than was common in the domestic system. However irksome factory discipline could be, factory employment generally offered freedom from interference – the Brothers Stumm notwithstanding – in private life. It was not only the better wages but also this greater personal freedom which attracted the journeymen weavers to the factories and deprived the masters of their customary services at Chemnitz.[64]

It is true that early-nineteenth-century bourgeois observers expressed horror at the ominous growth of a mass proletariat. Their observations would possess more objective value if the derogatory comments about the shoddy workmanship and wastrel ways of factory workers had not been previously directed at the domestic workers whom they now idealized as models of qualities which had earlier still been considered the monopoly of agricultural labour. Contemporary comment reveals more of bourgeois neuroses in the aftermath of the French Revolution than of working-class attitudes to the factory. Some workers certainly disliked factory work. But there is some evidence that the main object of their distaste was not the factory, but work.[65]

A trend can certainly be detected from self-controlled to collective work norms, from jobs where the worker to some extent set his own pace to jobs where the group set the pace, and then to detailed fixed specification by management, as occurred during rationalization in the 1920s. But the process, stretching over a century, was distinctly more gradual than a comparison of the initial and final stages might suggest. Indeed, the very bitterness of labour reactions to rationalization indicates the degree of control that many workers, even in large factories, still retained at that stage over their own work patterns.[66]

V. Income and Productivity

The most effective inducement to the worker to adapt to urban and industrial life was his income. Many employers disputed this. As late as 1901 Ruhr coal magnates argued that higher wages simply resulted in miners recruited from Eastern Europe doing less work. It is, however, difficult to find convincing evidence to support a belief in the existence of a backward-bending supply curve of labour since the eighteenth century. It applied to some extent in isolated communities where opportunities for expenditure or for improvement were objectively limited. But it did not generally apply, even in the eighteenth century, throughout most of Germany. Workers had already grasped the concept of material progress. There is ample evidence to suggest that wage increases were sought to permit material accumulation rather than greater leisure, and much turnover reflected the attractiveness of higher wages. Higher wages proved, in brief, an effective inducement to workers to change employment, except in the most unusual circumstances.[67]

Annual money wages probably rose marginally between 1800 and 1820, then rose by about 25 per cent by 1850, and by a further 50 per cent between 1850 and 1870. Hourly money wages may have risen somewhat less, for the length of the working day tended to increase in the second quarter of the century, and it did not begin to decline appreciably until about 1870. Annual real wages probably remained static over the seventy-year period, but this long-term stability conceals sharp changes in the short run as fluctuating food prices kept real wages gyrating.[68]

Between 1870 and 1914 annual and weekly money earnings trebled. Hourly money earnings quadrupled. Weekly real earnings rose about 50 per cent, and hourly real earnings nearly doubled. Real wages are generally assumed to have risen more rapidly between 1873 and 1896 than in the remainder of this pre-war period. Until more comprehensive data concerning retail prices become available, however, it seems premature to hazard dogmatic conclusions. It is a measure of the uncertainty still prevailing that Gerhard Bry felt able, only two years after publishing his invaluable inquiry into wages, to sharply modify his emphasis on the break about 1900 in the rising trend in real wages, solely on the basis of the implications of Albert Rees's upward revision of the American real-wage index when using retail prices instead of wholesale ones. Desai and Orsagh have modified J. Kuczynski's standard estimates – which suggested a sharp decline in the rate of increase in real wages in the immediate pre-war decade – mainly by revising Kuczynski's cost-of-living indices, though they still detect some retardation in the rate of growth from about the turn of the century.[69]

More research may carry this revision even further. The volume of contemporary complaints certainly suggests a widespread subjective sense of retardation in the upward movement of real wages after 1900. But this subjective feeling may not reflect objective developments. Trade-union propaganda greatly improved in the early twentieth century. Both the semi-skilled manual strata and the white-collar sector expanded, and workers became ever more keenly aware of status distinctions as inter-sectoral and intra-sectoral differentials narrowed. The fact that food prices rose in the pre-war decade after thirty years' experience of falling prices sharpened the sense of unprecedented change in the cost of living. White-collar workers were paid hardship bonuses as though they had been famished paupers after an eighteenth-century harvest failure. It is indicative of the changed level of expectations that many complaints concentrated on rising meat prices, and it would not be surprising if further research into local costs of living confirmed that the 'retardation of real wages' simply reflected a more rapidly rising trend of expectations rather than a retardation in the rate of increase in real incomes.[70]

Annual real earnings fluctuated wildly between 1914 and 1939 but were little higher at the end than at the beginning. Hourly real earnings exceeded 1913 levels by 20 per cent in 1939, but the reduction in the length of the working week nearly cancelled this increase.[71]

Total non-agricultural productivity changed little in the first half of the nineteenth century. Striking increases before 1840 were recorded only in mechanized sectors, particularly textiles. According to Hoffmann's calculations, productivity increased at an average annual rate of 1·7 per cent between 1850 and 1913. The sectoral rates in this period ranged between 0·6 per cent and 2·9 per cent, as follows:[72] trade and commerce, 0·6; agriculture, 1·2; industry, 1·8; mining, 2·0; transport, 2·9. Structural effects – the growing weight of sectors of higher productivity – accounted for about one-fifth of the average increase.[73]

Little short-term correlation existed between rates of increase in productivity and rates of increase in earnings. The distribution of earnings within the labour sector depended on a variety of rough-and-ready considerations, partly independent of productivity, at least in the short run. Demand elasticities, profit expectations, ease of entry, educational qualifications, status considerations, etc. influenced conventional levels of wages and salaries. This is not particularly surprising, since the measurement of productivity poses particular problems. Indeed, its measurement has not been carried far beyond the point where the major government inquiry into the economy despairingly abandoned it in 1930. The problems of measuring white-collar productivity, in particular, have proven even more intractable, and this precludes rigorous testing of Kocka's interesting hypothesis that the bureaucratic efficiency of the larger German enterprises, as a result of being modelled on the organization of the state ministries, constituted a German advantage against England in the competition race after 1895. Earnings and productivity often moved inversely in the short term. Productivity tended to be correlated inversely, earnings directly, with the trade cycle.[74]

Wage rates and earnings diverged increasingly as wage drift became more pronounced after about 1900, and this complicates the analysis of the response of labour incomes to the trade cycle. Bry found that between 1870 and 1933 wage rates generally lagged by about a year behind turning points in the cycle, while earnings lagged by only a few months. This, if anything, exaggerates the length of the lags. Bry emphasizes that in the *Gründerjahre* 'only a minor portion of the rise in wage rates took place during the expansion of 1870–72: the decisive rises occurred between 1872 and 1876, a period of contraction in general business'.[75]

The evidence, however, does not seem to warrant quite so firm a claim. Printers' rates rose sharply in 1871 and 1872 but did not rise after May 1873. Builders' hourly rates rose proportionately more sharply between 1871 and 1872 than in any later year. It is true that they did continue to rise, if more slowly, between 1873 and 1875. However, the building boom continued in most cities until 1875, two years after the general peak. The lag virtually disappears when builders' rates are related to the building cycle rather than to the general cycle. The failure of rates to conform to the 1903–4 recession recurs frequently in Bry's argument. As he notes himself, however, this recession was so mild that Spiethoff's index does not even register it. Some hesitation does in fact seem to be faintly discernible in quarterly earnings, but annual series are too insensitive to capture it. It is also possible, as Bry rightly recognizes, that data from individual firms, based on simple division of total payrolls by total labour force, may underrate the promptness of response to depression, because of the tendency to lay off unskilled men first, thus biasing average earnings upwards and masking the rapidity of the response to cyclical turning points.[76]

VI. *Trade Unions*

A number of national associations were founded as soon as the industrial code of the North German Federation effectively legalized trade unions in 1869. Total membership reached only 332,000 in 1895, less than 3 per cent of the non-agricultural labour force, but after that bounded up to over one million in 1900 and reached 3 million in 1914, about 15 per cent of non-agricultural workers. Membership fell to 1·2 million in 1916, but then surged in 1922 to a peak of 9·2 million, nearly 50 per cent of the non-agricultural labour force, before falling to 5·5 million, about 25 per cent of the work force, in 1929.[77]

Employers' organizations expanded a short step behind, and in response to, trade unions. Local employers' associations sprang up in 1872–3 to resist worker demands, only to wither away in the ensuing slump as labour became tractable once more. After the Crimmitschau textile strike in 1903, which provoked sympathetic support from employers throughout Germany, two national employers' associations emerged. One mainly represented light industry, the other heavy industry. They fused in 1913 to form the VDA (Union of German Employers' Associations). This initially represented industries employing 1·8 million workers. Its rate of expansion almost equalled that of the trade unions, and its coverage extended to about 8 million workers in 1920.[78]

Trade unions espoused the principle of collective bargaining, the natural result of the growth of large organizations. Some time elapsed, however, before the bulk of industrialists, particularly in the heavy-goods sector, were prepared to consider unions as equal bargaining partners. Employers' reactions were frequently irrational and were influenced more by a visceral response of outraged pride and prestige than by close calculation of profit rates. Wilhelm Siemens, for instance, conceded the justice of the collective demand of his foremen for a wage increase in 1872, but raged against their presumption in daring to think collectively. Several firms in heavy industry promoted tame 'yellow' unions but without much success, except for Siemens, who in 1913 employed 25,000 of the 111,000 workers who belonged to yellow unions.

Yet despite the hostility of the larger employers, collective bargaining achieved a definite role in labour relations by 1914, when 1·4 million workers – about 15 per cent of the industrial labour force – were covered by agreements. Many employers did gradually come to appreciate that they had an interest in strong trade unions which could keep their members in line, but heavy industry in general did not concede the principle of collective bargaining until the Stinnes–Legien agreement in 1918. By 1931, 12 million workers – about 75 per cent of the industrial labour force – were covered by collective agreements.[79]

The extent to which collective bargaining actually influenced wage levels remains debatable. The agreements frequently recorded results that would have been arrived at less systematically in response to market forces. Newly formed trade unions registered quick successes after 1869, but it is likely that these gains mainly reflected cyclical recovery. Unions proved powerless against market forces during the severe slump after 1873. The number of strikes fell from 285 in 1873 to only six in 1877. The unions had already proved ineffectual – a threat more to the employers' pride than to their pockets – before Bismarck's anti-socialist legislation restricted their freedom of action. Wages either stabilized or rose between 1879 and 1882, in the immediate aftermath of the anti-socialist legislation, reflecting the mild cyclical recovery from the trough of the mid-seventies. Trade-union membership actually fell immediately following the repeal of the Bismarckian legislation in

1890. Legislation was an irrelevance in the face of the slump of 1891–4. The rapid increase in trade-union membership after 1895 makes it more difficult to disentangle institutional influences from market forces. The proportion of wage increases won without strikes rose from 64 per cent in 1905 to 77 per cent in 1913. The readiness of both sides to negotiate settlements probably owed something to the realization that total conflict was likely to prove almost as costly to the victor as to the vanquished.[80]

The compulsory state arbitration established under Weimar reinforced the power of the market. It did not supplant it, contrary to some expectations. The arbitrators generally sought to assess the balance of market forces and delivered their verdicts accordingly. As trade unions were reluctant to accept wage cuts voluntarily after 1929, when massive unemployment eroded their bargaining power, about three-quarters of the workers covered by collective agreements were working under 'arbitration' awards in 1931, which in the existing market circumstances favoured the employers' case.[81]

Unions probably played a more important role in extracting concessions on hours and working conditions than in influencing wage levels. Individuals were often in a position to bargain about their wages, and wage movements had been common before the advent of trade unions at all. Hours were traditionally stickier than wages and required collective rather than individual bargaining. Ironically enough, the success of the unions in winning shorter hours, overtime rates, etc. widened the gap between wage rates and earnings and thus impaired the ability of the unions to resist reductions in earnings and deprived their success in negotiating minimum rates of some of its significance.[82]

Signs of increasing downward rigidity in wage rates can be detected at about the turn of the century. The depression of 1901–2 seems to have been the first in which rates failed to decline in accordance with the cycle. Earnings henceforth largely bore the brunt of contraction, as negotiated minimum wage rates continued in operation during slumps. The apparent lag in the great slump – when rates reached a peak in May 1930, thirteen months after the onset of the depression – reflects the fact that several contracts in building, metals, textiles, and coal did not expire until 1930. Earnings declined much more rapidly than wage rates in these sectors. Even at the trough of the great slump, however, the decline could not compare with the savage reductions in wages in early-nineteenth-century slumps, when it was not uncommon for rates to be slashed by 50 per cent, as in Chemnitz textiles in 1816. Twentieth-century workers experienced nothing comparable to the declines in money wages, much less in real wages, in 1829, 1842, and 1847. Both seasonal and annual fluctuations in wages became far less severe as industrialization progressed, and the greater consequent security represented a major improvement in the quality of working-class life.[83]

Collective bargaining probably led to a narrowing of regional and skill differentials. Flat-rate rises became increasingly national in scope. This again, however, at least partly reflected the objective growth of a national labour market by the early twentieth century.[84]

Trade unions influenced the style of wage negotiations more than their substance. They exerted a deterrent influence on potential extremists among employers, particularly perhaps by discouraging them from risking blatantly aggressive action during slumps, and they also reduced the number of strikes necessary to force concessions from employers during cyclical recoveries. They did not, however, supplant the market mechanism. Indeed, their success depended on the skill with which they exploited the market. By institutionalizing labour relations, they helped to integrate workers into industrial society. They fostered a work ethos and tutored their members in the norms of bourgeois respectability and responsibility. About one-third of the cases dealt with by the Labour Secretariats which the unions established after 1887 concerned problems of civil law, and another third treated issues of industrial law. In the 1880s, masons' spokesmen extolled the virtues of the citizen–worker, and in 1899 miners' leaders denounced absenteeism – then running at 2 to 3 per cent – as 'dishonourable'. Friedrich Harkort would have been pleased.[85]

Before 1850 labour conflict tended to be fiercest in the depths of a depression, as in Silesia in 1844. The 1850s and 60s were a transitional period, and from the late 1860s strikes tended to cluster in recovery and boom years. The change in strike activity from mere instinctive protest to the more calculated exploitation of the possibilities of cyclical movements provides the best index we have of the subjective adaptation of working-class mentalities to industrialization. Even the coal-miners, whose strike patterns continued to reflect something of a peasant-revolt syndrome – long periods of docility punctuated by short, fierce outbursts – acquired the wit to explode in boom years like 1872, 1889, and 1905. Between 1899 – when comprehensive statistics began to be collected – and 1933, the peak years for days lost through strikes were 1905, 1913, 1919, and 1923. The peak years for lockouts were 1910, 1924, and 1929, when more days were actually lost than through strikes. The total number of days lost was, however, small. The pre-war peak of 19 million days lost in 1905 represented less than two days per annum per industrial wage-earner. Even the peak post-war year, 1924, when 36 million days were lost, represented less than three days per industrial wage-earner. Obviously, the indirect effects of days lost could have significant consequences. Large numbers of other workers might be left involuntarily unemployed or underemployed as a result of the actions of workers or employers in key linkage sectors. The consequences of labour disputes were therefore more serious than emerges from a recitation of time directly lost.[86]

The concentration of labour conflict in recovery or boom years after about 1870 does not necessarily imply that the wage movements in those years were primarily attributable to industrial action. Decisions to strike or to lock out usually resulted from marginal differences of opinion. They depended to a large extent on expectations. Strikes clustered in recovery years even more than in boom years because at that stage employers' expectations tended to remain relatively pessimistic, whereas they were frequently over-optimistic at the peak and made concessions which they subsequently found they could not afford.[87]

The vast majority of disputes were settled without stoppages of work, primarily through the agency of the industrial courts. These institutions were merely embryonic in the Industrial Code of 1869 and only began to develop to a significant extent after 1890. The courts, composed of mutually agreed arbitrators, lacked compulsory powers, but they prevented many minor disputes from assuming more serious proportions. In 1904–5 the Berlin court alone dealt with 13,000 cases. It settled about half of these by agreement, and another quarter were settled out of court.[88]

Although trade unions did not raise wage levels directly and significantly, they probably exerted a subtle influence on the quality of employer thinking about labour costs. Even the employers' apologists conceded that the trade unions far surpassed employers in the quality of their investigation into labour problems, and trade-union pressures certainly compelled employers to think more systematically about cost structures than many seemed prepared to do on their own initiative.[89]

Few nineteenth-century businessmen conceded that higher wages or shorter hours might increase productivity. Their instinctive reaction to crises was to reduce wages and increase hours. This reaction was tempered only by the necessity to cling to their core workers who had to be retained at all costs. This consideration apart, employers in times of slump attempted to substitute cheaper labour for dearer. But the narrowing skill differentials in the early twentieth century, and the spread of minimum wage rates, restricted the range of potential options open to employers in slump conditions. There is ample evidence that wage increases provoked employers to make labour-saving investments. The rationalization drive of the 1920s was to some extent a belated response to the introduction of the compulsory eight-hour day in 1919. Though the eight-hour limit tended to be breached after 1924, em-

ployers were still compelled to confront the implications of the reduction in hours once the inflation ended in 1924.[90]

J. Kuczynski has argued vigorously that between 1860 and 1866 – the
first period he has investigated which records an increase in real wages
in the nineteenth century – employers accepted the logic of the
economy of higher wages and shifted from 'extensive' to 'intensive'
labour exploitation. The emphasis on labour-deepening in the course of
industrialization is a valuable one, but the attempt to attribute the shift
to this period is not altogether convincing. Kuczynski's argument
appears to overlook his own evidence that money wages rose steadily,
if slowly, in the first sixty years of the nineteenth century. Money
wages, the employers' prime concern, rose at a slower rate between
1860 and 1866 than between 1850 and 1856. Real wages rose in this
period not because of a change in the techniques of exploitation but
because of the unprecedented stability in the cost of living, the decisive
influence on short-term change. Instead of maintaining the rate of
increase of 1860–6, real wages fell slightly between 1866 and 1870 because prices rose. This can scarcely be taken to imply a reversion to
extensive from intensive exploitation. Indeed, the period 1861–6 fails
to maintain the rate of increase in real wages registered in 1857–61
compared with 1852–6.[91]

Employers' fears concerning the diseconomies of higher wages were
clearly unjustified in anything but the shortest of short terms. It is more
difficult to decide (in the absence of adequate micro-studies) to what
extent the employers' opposition to the economy of shorter hours was
justified. Circumstances varied widely between industries. The substitution of an eight-hour for a twelve-hour shift in the Upper Silesian
coalfield in 1889 led to a sharp but not quite proportionate increase
in hourly output. Changing geological conditions posed particularly
awkward problems in assessing in isolation the effects of innovation in
coal-mining. In the later nineteenth century, productivity tended to
stagnate or fall throughout European coalfields, and it may be that the
drastic reduction in hours in Silesia presented an even sharper fall in
productivity in that area. The imposition of the eight-hour day in 1919
might seem to provide an admirable opportunity for measuring the
economy of shorter hours in a wide range of industries. Unfortunately,
the peculiar conditions affecting productivity in 1917 and 1918 make
all calculations dubious. Rapid shifts in the sex, age, and skill structure
of the labour force and the sharp changes in nutrition between 1916 and
1924 make it virtually impossible to isolate the impact of the shorter
day.[92]

VII. *Wages*

A. WAGE DIFFERENTIALS

Skill differentials widened in the final quarter of the eighteenth century as population growth began to outstrip economic growth. In the century after 1770, differentials within the skilled sector probably widened even more strikingly than differentials between skilled and unskilled workers. Industrialization differentiated sharply between the types of skills required, increasing demand for some and condemning others to obsolescence. By multiplying the number of skills and of categories of workers, industrial growth disturbed the relative simplicity of the pre-industrial income structure. The increase in Krupp's labour force from ten workers in 1825 to 115 in 1845 brought an increase in the number of different wage rates from three to seventeen, and an expansion from a two-to-one to a five-to-one range in skill differentials. Differentials probably remained roughly stable between 1850 and 1895 and then narrowed appreciably until 1914. They narrowed slightly further in the course of the First World War and again during the inflation, before reverting to 1914 levels after 1925.[93]

It is difficult to guess to what extent changing skill differentials represented pure movements or merely indicate the changing skill content of jobs which remained nominally the same. Many unskilled jobs must have contained a semi-skilled quotient before firms began to distinguish semi-skilled from unskilled after about 1900. In Siemens in 1903–4, semi-skilled rates were 27 per cent higher than unskilled, while skilled rates in turn were 38 per cent higher than semi-skilled. The fluctuating differentials between foremen and skilled workers, ranging from 40 to 10 per cent in Siemens between 1866 and 1914, largely reflected the objective changes in the functions of foremen. Differentials between manual and white-collar workers also narrowed appreciably from the early twentieth century. In 1903 the average Siemens white-collar employee earned 2·26 times as much as the average manual worker, but in 1912 only 1·75 times as much. The speed of this movement may have been unrepresentative in that the size of the white-collar force in Siemens increased exceptionally rapidly in this period, and this doubtless involved heavy recruitment into the lower white-collar grades. Nevertheless, the direction if not the extent of the movement seems to be representative. The extent to which differentials narrowed throughout the whole wage structure between 1895 and 1914 has not perhaps been adequately appreciated.[94] Narrowing differentials owed something to rising living costs, which stimulated flat-rate increases, and something to the increased supply of skills from the rapidly expanding technical education system. If in 1914 the incomes of German skilled workers still compared unfavourably with British levels, German unskilled labour enjoyed relatively more favourable rates.[95]

Sex differentials remained roughly static between 1750 and 1914. Female employees' incomes generally fluctuated between one-third and one-half of the corresponding male wage in both blue-collar and white-collar occupations. Sex differentials were naturally narrower when workers were largely paid in kind, as remained the case in many rural areas until the second half of the nineteenth century. The shift from payment in kind to payment in cash therefore militated differentially against females.[96]

Differentials widened at the outset of the First World War. Male labour grew scarcer, and the reservoir of young females was swollen by an inflow of those deprived of immediate marriage opportunities. As it became clear that the war would continue and that female labour had a crucial role to play, differentials began to narrow. More important than slowly narrowing differentials was the adaptation of production processes to female labour, which presented opportunities for responsible work in what were previously male preserves. Sex differentials narrowed further during the great inflation, and their overall reduction between 1913 and 1925 amounted to about 15 per cent. From 1925 until 1939 sex differentials remained more or less static, with women generally earning three-fifths the corresponding male rates.[97]

Apprentices paid fees to masters in pre-industrial times. As industrialization progressed, and acute skill shortages developed, the bargaining position of apprentices improved. They could now earn a net income, and in boom periods they might hope to be promoted particularly quickly, as was the case with apprentice hewers in the Ruhr mines, who were frequently promoted to full status after only a year instead of the customary three years. Trade unions exerted themselves to maintain this improvement, partly to discourage employers from substituting cheap apprentices for adults. In 1930, Berlin building apprentices began at 10 per cent of the adult rate and reached 50 per cent in the final half-year of their three-year apprenticeship. Neither males nor females customarily attained full adult rates, however, until after their twentieth year. Manual workers' earnings generally reached a peak between the ages of twenty-five and forty and then declined appreciably. White-collar workers, on the other hand, generally reached maximum earnings in their forties and continued to enjoy this level long after the skilled workers' income had begun to fall. This difference in the flow of lifetime earnings – with all its implications for expectations, for security, and for life-styles – marked perhaps the most important single distinction between blue-collar and white-collar workers.[98]

Differentials between industries generally narrowed after the mid nineteenth century. It is, however, impossible to disentangle the specific industrial differential from the skill, sex, age, and regional influences. Comparable rates seem to have prevailed for the same occupation in different industries. Locksmiths employed outside the metal industry, for instance – in 1933 about one-third of the total – appear to have expected incomes comparable with those of their colleagues in the metal industry.[99]

B. METHODS OF PAYMENT

In the eighteenth century, craftsmen were employed at weekly or longer rates, unskilled labourers usually at day rates. As working hours tended to increase in early industrialization, and as employers' sense of responsibility for their workers in slack times weakened, day rates – which naturally facilitated summary dismissal – increasingly spread to skilled labour. They never extended, however, to white-collar workers, who remained particularly privileged in this respect. Once effective agitation for shorter hours began in the 1860s, employers rapidly grasped the virtues of hourly rates.[100]

In the eighteenth century most workers received substantial shares of their incomes in kind. Money payment became increasingly widespread as industrialization progressed; but a minority of employers continued to exploit the truck system to swindle their workers. If currency shortages sometimes made truck temporarily unavoidable, local officials agreed that workers' hostility to the system (expressed, for instance, during the Aachen revolt of 1830) was fully justified. However, it required further outbreaks in 1848 to persuade the Prussian and Saxon authorities to legislate against the system in 1849.[101]

Piece rates, which had long been familiar in the putting-out system, spread rapidly in mechanized industry and in construction in the late nineteenth century, as employers began to grope towards a clearer understanding of labour costs. By 1914 probably about half the industrial labour force worked mainly on piece rates. Trade-union leaders bitterly denounced piece work, but workers' attitudes were more ambivalent. Faster workers generally approved in principle; slower workers, or more careful ones, were less enthusiastic. In practice, even faster workers became involved in endless disputes, as employers abused the system by exploiting 'Stakhanovite' performances to intensify the pace and reduce rates. As foremen determined wages in all but the largest firms, workers felt exposed to arbitrary personal whims in the setting of rates. Over 50 per cent of the labour disputes in the Berlin metal industry in 1906 concerned piece rates. Even with good will, there were real difficulties in calculating fair rates in many occupations, especially engineering. Where feasible – as with hewers and haulers in coal, boilermakers, fitters, moulders, smelters, and cement, pottery, and sawmill workers – employers preferred to pay group piece rates, which the members of the teams divided among themselves at their own discretion.[102]

Few enduring innovations in payment techniques occurred after 1914. At the height of the hyper-inflation in 1923, wages were frequently paid in instalments during the course of the week in an effort to keep abreast of the inflationary upsurge. Many firms reverted to payment in kind, and contracts were negotiated, in effect, in real rather than money wages. Trade unions generally adopted a more flexible attitude towards piece rates after the First World War than before. As their membership now included the work forces of large factories in the heavy industries, where piece rates predominated, the unions had perforce to adopt the attitude of their members who would not tolerate a reversion to time rates. Indeed, piece rates came to be institutionalized in the collective agreements of the Weimar period and were usually set at about 15 per cent above the appropriate time rates.[103]

Standard rates, whether time or piece, ignored the 'extras' accruing to particular occupations. Catering and transport workers expected tips ranging apparently from 5 to 15 per cent of their basic wage. Christmas bonuses – perhaps a week's wage for manual workers, a month's for white-collar employees – had become common by 1914. Overtime came to be remunerated at time and a quarter after about 1890 – once hours were reduced sufficiently to make overtime a practicable proposition. Ironically, employers reacted less indignantly against demands for overtime rates by blue-collar than by white-collar workers: they considered such demands unworthy of 'loyal' employees. Nevertheless, 59 per cent of all white-collar workers in Berlin in 1907 received special rates for overtime.[104]

VIII. Hours and Conditions

Workers averaged a thirteen-hour day in the eighteenth century. This increased to fourteen hours in textile factories in the early nineteenth century and probably increased even more sharply outside factories. Between 1825 and 1850 hours generally tended to increase, though not usually to the textile levels. The average working week remained stable at about seventy-five hours between 1850 and 1870. It then fell to sixty-six by 1890 and to fifty-four by 1914. The chronology of change varied between industries until the uniformity of the eight-hour day was achieved in most industries in the legislation of 1918–19, but differences began to creep back after 1923, and more emphatically after 1933. White-collar workers enjoyed distinctly shorter hours than manual workers – generally an eight-hour day – from the mid nineteenth century. The relative reduction in the hours of manual workers represents a major improvement in their relative working conditions compared with white-collar workers. The longest hours of all occurred in agriculture and in self-employment. Agricultural labourers did not achieve a ten-hour day by law until the legislation of 1919. State governments began gradually and grudgingly to regulate children's hours from 1839, but struggles for factory acts do not loom large in the early history of the German working class. Wages remained sufficiently low until the late 1860s, when the first wave of reductions in hours occurred, to dominate workers' demands. Furthermore, the textile industry, with its exceptionally high proportion of women and children, did not play as prominent a role in German as in British industrialization. Hours for women were not legally regulated until the industrial ordinance of 1892, which imposed an eleven-hour daily maximum. Hours in domestic industry, as in agriculture, remained uncontrolled until after the First World War.[105]

As employers grew more sophisticated in the search for productivity growth in the course of the nineteenth century, they began to experiment with variations in hours, sometimes independently of trade-union pressure. Shift work became widespread after 1870, particularly in the capital-goods industries, which were increasingly dependent on the continuous use of fixed capital. 'English hours' – a shorter working day with a shorter break for lunch – acquired popularity among workers unable to return home as the journey to work lengthened, and as the spread of works' canteens afforded an opportunity for a warm midday meal, perhaps better cooked than that served up in primitive domestic conditions, and insulated from the nagging of wives and the whining of children. Short coffee breaks were found to increase productivity, particularly in the steel industry.[106]

Overtime flourished once the length of the basic working day fell. Workers quickly grasped the link between shorter hours and higher take-home pay from overtime. Demands for reductions in the length of the basic working day were partly disguised demands for higher wages, and overtime became a regular feature of most industries. In the boom year of 1911, 48 per cent of the 203,000 workers in the iron industry whose hours were investigated averaged three hours' overtime a week. Indeed, the reduction in the basic working week was to some extent illusory, for much overtime was compulsory. Sunday work, apparently widespread in the mid nineteenth century, had come to be considered unusual half a century later. It was, nonetheless, still sufficiently prevalent in the coal industry for its abolition to rank high on the list of demands of the Ruhr strikers in 1905. White-collar employees generally enjoyed a week's or a fortnight's paid holiday after about 1880. Blue-collar workers might snatch an occasional day or two at their own expense, but they did not in general enjoy paid leave until 1919.[107]

When conclusions are so ambiguous concerning the productivity offsets of reductions in hours even as recently as the 1960s, it can hardly be expected that remotely definitive conclusions can be deduced from the fragmentary and contradictory evidence concerning earlier periods. It seems reasonable to assume, however, that in most occupations reductions in the length of the working week, from the seventy-hour levels of the 1870s, led to complete or more-than-complete productivity offsets, either through increased effort on the part of less exhausted labour or through what Denison called 'induced improvement in the quality of management' in response to the new challenge. In the First World War, an increase in hours from a base of fifty-four apparently led to a decline, after a lag, in total output.[108]

The decline in the length of the working week may be of particular relevance for German investment patterns, and particularly for relative factor intensities. The length of the working week declined more sharply in Germany than in either Great Britain or the United States between 1871 and 1913. The relative rapidity of the decline in hours both before and after the First World War, combined with the rapid rise in money wages and the narrowing of skill differentials, may have contributed significantly to the employers' growing preference for capital-intensive investment.[109]

The reduction of hours was the most important single contribution to the improvement of the working conditions of manual labour. The gradual increase in the journey to work, however, partly whittled down the gains. By 1914 workers probably spent, on average, at least five hours a week commuting. In Mannheim, with a relatively small population of 80,000, about 40 per cent of the labour force in forty-seven factories whose journey to work was investigated in 1890 had to make a round trip of at least 6 km a day. High residential turnover suggests that many workers attempted to follow the job; it was a simple matter for single if not for married workers, and it was largely unavoidable in sectors like construction, where a man might work on several different building sites during the year.[110]

The normal conditions of pre-industrial and early industrial work included noise, dirt, heat, cold, and physical and psychic brutality. They were gradually improved, as industrialization progressed in the later nineteenth century, through a combination of enlightened self-interest on the part of employers and intense pressure on the part of workers. The great extent of new industrial building made it possible to incorporate into factory design such social advantages of the late start as better facilities for workers. By 1900 chest and lung diseases no longer flourished in nail-making, which early in the nineteenth century had taken place in almost hermetically sealed rooms. Women working in match factories were increasingly protected from exposure to phosphorus, which had inflicted hideous diseases on the facial bone structure of earlier generations of unfortunate women. Mining regulations in 1884 limited to six hours the period which miners were permitted to work underground daily in a temperature exceeding 29 °C. Physical working conditions improved sharply in the course of the century, until the time came when many workers enjoyed better conditions at work than at home, particularly as a growing proportion of dwellings came to be situated in tall tenement housing, and the house with a little garden attached – hitherto frequent if not usual – virtually disappeared among the working classes.[111]

Conditions continued to vary widely between occupations. The more 'agricultural' the industry, the more primitive were the general standards. The demands of the flour-workers' union in 1891 – a twelve-hour day, guaranteed Sunday rest, abolition of truck, state inspection of the mills, abolition of night work for apprentices, and the regulation of the number of apprentices – cast a lurid light on existing standards in the agricultural processing sector in the industrially advanced state of Saxony.[112]

The shorter hours may have increased the intensity of effort required from manual workers. Unfortunately, the intensity of labour is notoriously difficult to measure. Fatal accidents in Prussian coal-mining between 1821 and 1850 and non-fatal accidents in the Aachen coal field from 1814 to 1853 – the only specific figures for accidents available for the first half of the nineteenth century – record slightly falling rates. J. Kuczynski, to whose prodigious labours we are primarily indebted for disinterring the relevant data, advances plausible arguments for believing that the fatal-accident rates are biased downwards. It seems probable that adult accident rates remained more or less static over the period, while high child accident rates raised the overall incidence of factory accidents.[113]

In coal-mining, the fatality rate rose from 2·04 per thousand between 1852 and 1860 to 3·04 between 1876 and 1886, and then fell to 2·16 between 1892 and 1914. In industry as a whole, the rate fell from 0·70 per thousand between 1887 and 1893 to 0·63 between 1907 and 1914, and to 0·45 between 1924 and 1932, before rising steadily to 0·57 in 1937. Kuczynski staunchly maintains that the decline reflects an increase in the intensity of exploitation when account is taken of shorter hours and better protective measures. Valuable though Kuczynski's analysis is in this respect, it seems doubtful whether firm conclusions concerning intensity can be derived from these accident statistics. The figures probably understate the decline between 1887 and 1914. Double counting inflated the membership statistics of the accident-insurance fund until about 1900. Applied as a denominator in calculating accident rates, the membership data of the insurance fund tend to underrate the late-nineteenth-century figures. More significantly, perhaps, accidents to beginners must be distinguished from accidents to more experienced workers. If the propensity for fatal accidents was distinctly above average among newcomers, then one would expect rising rates due to the increasing weight of new recruits in the labour force. First-year workers do seem, in fact, to have been disproportionately vulnerable to accidents. Over 40 per cent of accidents in the Rhenish–Westphalian iron and steel association between 1895 and 1910 and in the Luxemburg iron and steel association between 1903 and 1910 occurred among first-year men. Accident rates rose 40 per cent between 1914 and 1918, at least partly because of the exceptional number of new recruits. Fatal-accident rates regularly increased when new machinery was installed and then fell again when workers had become familiar with it. Although new machines may often have required greater intensity, the problem in general seems to have been less one of intensity than of familiarity. Fatal-accident rates tended to decline in depression years like 1892, 1902, and 1929–33, despite the greater pressure on workers in fear of the sack in slumps, and this is presumably at least partly because of the steep fall in the recruitment of new workers. Rates rose correspondingly in recovery years. Some of the increase between 1933 and 1938, for instance, occurred partly because of the exceptionally heavy inflow of new workers.[114]

The health insurance statistics record a rise from 5·47 to 8·66 'sick' days per member between 1890 and 1913. There must be some doubt, however, as with the accident statistics, as to how far these data can be pressed to support deductions concerning increasing intensity of labour despite improved nutrition and shorter hours. There may have been double counting of membership in early years. Coverage was gradually extended to sectors of the population at greater risk than those originally included, and membership rose from 6·6 million in 1890 to 14·6 million in 1913. As the sick fund paid benefits for thirteen weeks, there was less necessity for injured workers to return to work as early as physically possible. Above all, the number of doctors rose at three times the rate of population growth between 1880 and 1914, so that the supply of medical services at last began to bear some relation to the potential demand.[115]

The worst complaint about work was the lack of it. Except in the case of the linen industry in the second quarter of the nineteenth century, the bulk of German unemployment was cyclical or seasonal and not technological or structural. Except in 1887, 1891–2, and 1901, trade-union unemployment figures, which were first calculated in 1887, never recorded more than 3 per cent unemployment before the First World War. This certainly underrates unemployment in crisis years. Unemployment in 1893 probably considerably exceeded the proportion recorded for the relatively favoured unionized stratum, which comprised at that date only 5 per cent of the industrial labour force. Trade-union membership rapidly increased in the following twenty years, but the most revealing, if imprecise, indication of the intensity of the employment cycle may be the checks to trade-union growth compared with the anticipated increase on trend. This criterion suggests a shortfall of nearly 10 per cent in both 1901 and 1908–9.[116] Unemployment, though underrated by the official figures, remained low between 1919 and 1922. It surged to 25 per cent immediately before the stabilization of the mark in November, 1923, and it subsequently did not fall below 8 per cent until the Nazi period.

The fact that emigration declined to a trickle after 1895 and that thereafter Germany was frequently a country of net immigration points to a tightening labour market before 1914. From 1849 until 1929 the severity of depressions appears to have declined fairly steadily. Unemployment may have reached 15 per cent in 1876–7, 10 per cent in 1892–3, and slightly less in 1901 and 1908. Not even the deep slump after 1873 registered declines in output as abrupt as the 40 per cent fall in Prussian cotton production between 1845 and 1846 or the 75 per cent reduction in the number of workers in the Berlin mechanical engineering industry between 1847 and 1848. It is true that workers in new firms, or in new industries, were more vulnerable to sharp swings of this sort than those in older-established industries. The motorcar industry, for instance, was particularly affected in 1907–8. The switch from overtime to short time further accentuated the swings of the cycle. The decline in hours worked was invariably greater than the figures of unemployed persons suggest. In the Magdeburg factory inspector's district in 1891, for instance, 13 per cent of workers were sacked, and about 20 per cent were put on short time. Ruhr miners worked about 8 per cent more shifts in the boom year of 1900 than in the trough of 1892. Nevertheless, the fact that, in general, depressions became milder and shorter after 1850 must not be overlooked in any assessment of changes in living standards. The great slump of 1929–32, which was unparalleled in intensity since at least the 1840s, formed the major exception to this general, if gradual, improvement. Unemployment began to increase in October 1927, accelerated after November 1928, and did not reach its peak until 1932, when about 8 million people – 40 per cent of the non-agricultural labour force – were unemployed.[117]

IX. *Epilogue*

The grim shadow of old age loomed over working-class lives throughout history. For manual workers, in 1914 no less than in 1800, old age began in their forties. But the fate of the old changed fundamentally between the two dates. In the vast majority of cases, a manual worker could still anticipate falling earnings once he had passed his physical peak. A small proportion were promoted to supervisory grades, but the earnings of a much higher proportion sank considerably. The possibility of a return to the land existed only for first-generation migrants, predominately in the building industry, but only those who had actually continued to take seasonal work in agriculture could hope to retire to farm jobs. The bulk of 'old' manual workers perforce became increasingly parasitic – but after the introduction of old-age insurance in 1889 the financial burden began to shift from their families to the state. By 1914 most workers could anticipate security, if not comfort, in their ultimate decline.[118]

'Old age' was generally reckoned to begin fifteen years later for white-collar employees than for manual workers. As late as 1937 about one-third of white-collar but only one-eighth of manual workers were aged over forty.[119]

The transfer to the state of some of the burden of supporting the aged partly relieved the family of one of its important traditional functions. Compulsory elementary education, the gradual spread of labour exchanges and career guidance in the schools, the expansion of trade schools, and the sheer rapidity of change in the occupational structure relieved the family of some responsibility for the provision of information for, and the occupational training of, its younger members. Nevertheless, even when due allowance is made for the growing institutional specialization of labour in this respect, parental advice probably remained the single most important influence in determining the children's initial job choice, and parental income certainly continued to determine the child's range of choice.

It remains unclear how far social mobility loosened inherited social bonds. Kaelble found that opportunities to move from the middle to the upper classes were proportionately far greater than the opportunities to move from the working to the middle classes. There is little doubt that the middle classes – as represented by their rearguard, the white-collar strata – laboured to widen the gulf protecting them from the working classes. Bismarck's first tentative steps in the direction of a welfare state provoked Berlin technicians to establish their own benefit funds to avoid the ignominy of participating in the same schemes as workers. The commercial white-collar sector extracted its own special insurance fund from the state in 1911, with the right to pay benefits to members unfit for work in their occupation instead of merely unfit for work in general. Nevertheless, the concern of white-collar workers about their status suggests a successful infiltration from below. Kaelble points out that even in the rapid early-twentieth-century expansion of the white-collar sector only about one-sixth of the new recruits came from working-class origins. This may have represented, however, up to one-fifth of the eligible children of skilled workers. By pre-industrial standards this probably marked an unprecedentedly high proportion crossing class demarcation lines. The skilled worker might despise, or affect to despise, the 'unproductive' white-collar pen-pusher as long as there was little opportunity for his children to join their ranks. As the rapid increase in white-collar numbers made it realistic for him to think of educating his children to the required standard he soon became convinced, if not quite as soon as his wife, that 'to be a white-collar worker is to be a somebody'.[120]

Social mobility within classes became more important with the growing complexity of the structure of the labour force. Both the white-collar and the blue-collar sectors contained wide ranges of social distinctions. Even the males in both sectors developed an insidious pecking order of almost feminine sensitivity. The relaxation of guild restrictions, and the growth of a semi-skilled stratum which seems to have been recruited at least as much from rising unskilled as from falling skilled workers after about 1880, increased the scope for upward mobility and softened the impact of downward mobility in the manual sector.

A woman's chances of picking her way up the social ladder may have depended more on her fate in the marriage market than on progress in her working career, though her choice of a husband would appear to have been usually rather rigorously restricted – if not perhaps quite as rigorously as in pre-industrial society – to her own social stratum.[121]

Whatever their subjective feeling about the propriety of their particular place on the social ladder at any given moment, few workers shared the illusions of the splendour-in-the-grass school of bourgeois searchers for a lost golden age of working-class bliss. Where workers waxed nostalgic it was with specific purpose, as when the striking Ruhr miners in 1889 lamented the loss of the eight-hour shift 'inherited from our fathers'. In principle, however, working-class spokesmen were prone to deride 'the good old days' and to complain that labour relations were the only aspect of economic life that had not been adequately modernized. The reluctance of the German worker to return to the land during urban slumps adequately expressed his opinion of bucolic delights. Industrialization provided the only feasible alternative to much heavier emigration after the 1840s. Later generations of workers were still sufficiently close to rural realities to appreciate that only economic growth, however high its social costs, saved them from paying the even higher price of economic stagnation.[122]

CHAPTER X

Entrepreneurs and Managers in German Industrialization

I. *Concepts and Scope*

The definitions used in this chapter have to meet two requirements. First, they must be applicable within the whole period under discussion. They must be flexible and broad enough to subsume the tremendous changes occurring within entrepreneurship and management from the late eighteenth century to the twentieth. However, they need *not* be so broad and abstract as to cover all types of entrepreneurs and managers in history. They should rather be framed with regard to characteristics of the German economy which remained constant through this whole period (without necessarily existing at other times and places) and which were, at the same time, of central importance for the development of entrepreneurship and management. Such a characteristic we find in the fact that this has been, and – for the larger part of Germany – still is, a period of industrialization structured according to capitalist principles. The general features of industrial capitalism which are most central for the study of entrepreneurship and management during the whole period are (*a*) a factory system which is characterized by power-generating and manufacturing machines, by large amounts of fixed capital, by maturing techniques on an increasingly scientific basis, by the separation between organizational and operative functions, and by contractual labour working under centralized managerial authority, not at home, according to elaborate patterns of labour division; and (*b*) largely independent and autonomous business enterprises on the basis of the private ownership and control of capital, which is used for the production of goods and services and their sale on the commercial market, according to the criteria of profitability; business enterprises relate to each other mainly through market mechanisms.[1]

Secondly, the definitions and concepts must be chosen with consideration for the purposes of this volume. In a book whose major aim is the description and explanation of economic growth in terms of growing and changing input factors (see chapter I above), the focus cannot be on the entrepreneurs and managers as social groups or holders of authority, but the central questions should be: to what extent and in what ways, on the basis of which motives, under which conditions, because of what causes, by which devices, and with what consequences and by-products (including social consequences and costs) did entrepreneurs and managers contribute to economic growth and development in Germany in the period of industrialization? While it will be impossible to answer these questions directly or in any even roughly quantifying way, it follows from this starting-point that the economic functions of entrepreneurs and managers – more precisely, the entrepreneurial and managerial functions within the firm and in the economy as a whole – should be the focus of discussion. As much as it seems necessary, desirable and possible, other phenomena (e.g. the social and ideological characteristics of businessmen, the structure of the firm, general factors of economic, social, and general history, etc.) will be brought into the picture; but they will mainly be treated as causes and conditions, manifestations and instruments, consequences and costs of the entrepreneurial and managerial activities and functions within the growing enterprises and the economy.

In view of these criteria, this chapter regards as entrepreneurial functions the taking of basic ('strategic') decisions which determine the objectives of the enterprise, its position in the market, and its relation to the economic and social environment at large, according to criteria in which profits and return on capital play a major role. These decisions include the mobilization and combination of the factors of production, especially decisions on investment, the allocation of funds, and the acquisition of new managerial personnel. Management functions consist of 'tactical' decisions with reference to the devices necessary to execute the entrepreneurial decisions, especially with reference to the internal structure of the enterprise and the day-to-day supervision of operations. It is part of managerial functions to decide about the relationship between parts of the enterprise and its functional organization in general; to ensure sufficient internal information and co-ordination; to establish the authority-structure within the enterprise and to control the employees. While innovation is only one aspect of entrepreneurship, management is not confined to routine but may be innovative too. Both spheres imply decision-making and authority-holding, though with respect to different areas of decision. Neither of them is identical with a third function necessary for the organization and survival of capitalist enterprises, that of providing for the necessary capital (i.e. making the basic or original investment decision) and bearing the ensuing risk. While this last function defines those who perform it as 'owners' – however fragmented and split-up the ownership may be – both the managerial and the entrepreneurial functions can be fulfilled by independent, self-employed persons as well as by salaried men.[2]

There is no doubt that, especially in the early period of industrialization, but also in most smaller firms today, the capitalist, entrepreneurial, and managerial functions were and are taken care of by the same person or the same small group of persons. Only in the large corporations of this century is there a clear tendency towards separating these three functions and vesting them in different groups of persons. One of the chief questions in the following discussion is that of what persons or groups of persons, in or outside the firms, performed these three functions in different types of enterprises at different stages of development, and how it influenced the functioning of the enterprise and the economy. We shall describe as an 'entrepreneur', a 'manager', or a 'capitalist' a person within whose activities the entrepreneurial, the managerial, or the capital-owning function dominates.

Given the importance of the production sectors within industrializing economies, this chapter concentrates on industrial entrepreneurs and managers within the extracting and manufacturing sectors of the economy. Entrepreneurs and managers within commerce and services are touched on only peripherally.

Whether entrepreneurial and managerial resources are independent facilitating factors or even strategic prerequisites for industrialization (or for economic growth in general) or whether they are mere responses appearing quasi-automatically as soon as they are demanded by the appearance of environmental factors (such as market opportunities, availability of factors of production, profit chances, inventions, etc.) is a much-debated question with different answers depending on the specialization of the authors, the general intellectual climate, scientific or non-scientific interests, and other factors.[3] To avoid a general discussion of these problems, the present chapter starts from these assumptions. Even if entrepreneurial and managerial supply (in all necessary respects) were highly elastic, and even if the appearance and availability of sufficiently qualified entrepreneurial and managerial services were a highly probable and quasi-automatic response to the appearance of certain environmental factors on the demand side (as some economists seem to think), even then it could be interesting to study entrepreneurship and management in the context of economic growth and development, in order to find out how these environmental factors affected economic change and why this happened in such a quasi-automatic way. Since it is beyond doubt that economic change (like social and historical change in general), although highly conditioned by environmental factors, does not occur without the interference of human actions based on perceptions, motives, and decisions, it is meaningful to study the orientation, decisions, and actions of the main economic actors – the entrepreneurs and managers. One should not expect, however, that these actors were wholly and correctly aware of the causes and conditions influencing them and of the effects which resulted from their decisions and actions (which were not necessarily what they intended). Studying the history of entrepreneurship and management in this sense would mean studying the points (or areas) of transmission through which environmental factors must have been channelled if they produced economic changes at all. After all, a market opportunity must be perceived as such and acted upon in a certain way if a combination of factors leading to economic growth is to be stimulated into effectiveness. As with all human perceptions, decisions, and actions, various factors – psychological, sociological, and historical – play a role in such a process of responding to a potential market opportunity. If the above-mentioned demand-centred line of thought, which treats entrepreneurial/managerial services as a dependent and passive factor, is correct in neglecting these psychological and sociological factors, it can do so for one of three reasons: because the relevant psychological and sociological factors are constants of human behaviour and consequently can be taken for granted; or because these factors (within the period under discussion) can be assumed to be effective frequently enough for it to be taken for granted that if one actor fails to respond in the expected way, another will take his place; or because the 'rules of the game', built into the economic system, compel the actors to behave in certain uniform ways if they do not want to be excluded completely. A study of entrepreneurship over long periods of time might try to determine which of these possibilities was the more realistic, and through what mechanisms and within what limits. Enough has been said to leave no doubt that the study of entrepreneurial and managerial history has to take sufficient account of the environmental (specifically, the economic) factors outside the entrepreneurs and managers, who were influenced by them, whether consciously or not, and who in turn influenced them by their actions. But, conversely, there should be no doubt that the full story cannot be understood without referring to entrepreneurship and management at least in the sense of links between input factors on one side and economic growth and development on the other.

It may be unnecessary, however, to fall back on such a minimal position of argument. Although they are not totally conclusive, there are good theoretical and empirical arguments pointing to the fact that historically and socially conditioned weaknesses of entrepreneurial and managerial resources may delay and hinder – if not prevent – the beginning of an industrialization process, while it seems that they may be (at least partly) taken for granted once industrialization is firmly under way.[4] But even in later periods of economic development, traditions, orientations, and behaviour patterns of entrepreneurs and managers – which cannot be explained in economic terms alone – seem to account

for some of the international differences in the process of industrialization, in terms of its forms, emphases, social and ideological consequences, and perhaps even speed.[5] While generalizations seem hazardous, the available evidence seems sufficient to justify interest in
entrepreneurial, managerial, and business history also from the point of
view of economic growth. Cautiously pursued and informed by pertinent theoretical models, it may deserve more interest from economic
historians than it at present receives.[6]

The following essay concentrates on the initial phases of industrialization – the 'industrial revolution' or the 'take-off'. In Germany, this
phase can be defined as the period between the 1830s or 1840s and the
beginning of the 'Great Depression' in 1873. It is true that there were
strong 'proto-industrial' traditions in some German regions dating
back into the eighteenth and seventeenth centuries (and even earlier).
Usually it is difficult if not impossible to draw a sharp line between
'proto-industrialization' and 'industrial revolution'; but it was not
before the middle third of the nineteenth century that the building of
the railways and the associated strong acceleration in the development
of manufacturing industries brought the first massive disposal of
permanent, fixed capital in the industrial sphere. Net investment grew
strongly as a percentage of GNP. Growth became self-sustained, with
only short-term interruptions, which is typical of industrializing
economies. Such growth was based on an increasingly integrated
market which was enlarged through the attainment of economic and
political unity (Customs Union, 1834; *Norddeutscher Bund*, 1866/7;
Foundation of the Empire, 1870/1), and through the expansion of the
means of transport (primarily the railways). The share of the business
and industrial sector in GNP notably increased. Within the industrial
sector (but above all in the supply of raw materials, and in the metalworking and textile industries), the modern factory system on private
capitalist lines was established. Germany began its breakthrough phase –
the 'great spurt' which is typical of the start of industrialization – about
half a century after England and two decades after France, but about
fifty years before Russia.[7]

The following inquiry concentrates on this period – the middle third
of the nineteenth century – and deals in detail with entrepreneurship
and management at that time (section III). But sharply defined periodization is impossible in the history of entrepreneurship, above all
because developments in the various branches did not happen at the
same time and because the development of a small group of large-scale
concerns was decades in advance with regard to entrepreneurial and
managerial practices compared with the small and medium-sized ones.
This makes every generalization in this subject difficult, and sharp

periodization futile. Much in section III therefore also applies to the last quarter of the nineteenth century and to the early twentieth. But a rough chronological arrangement is indispensable, in order to emphasize the trends of development and to consider in some degree the general economic and social framework in which German entrepreneurship and management developed.

Section II deals with general preconditions, and the precursors of industrial entrepreneurs in the eighteenth and early nineteenth centuries. Section III deals with the entrepreneurs and managers of the industrial revolution (second third of the nineteenth century). There is a discussion of their economic background and career patterns (III.A) and of the motives and qualifications that were typical of them (III.B). There is an attempt to describe and evaluate entrepreneurial and managerial performance during this period, concentrating on the tasks of financing, industrial accounting, and early labour relations, and on the beginnings of large-scale management (III.C). Section IV analyses some of the central alterations which entrepreneurship and management have undergone since the last third of the nineteenth century, during the rise of 'big business' and 'organized capitalism'.[8]

The approach which dominates in section IV differs slightly from the one which guides the discussions in section III. Whereas it is possible to see entrepreneurship and management to some extent as independent factors and initiating forces of economic development during the first phase of industrialization, the process of industrialization in its later stages had gathered so much independent weight and momentum that entrepreneurship and management can be seen more as influenced factors and consequences of development than as independent causal variables. Consequently, in section III entrepreneurs and managers are analysed at least partly as the subjects of change, though not neglecting the factors which formed, determined, and stimulated them; section IV, on the other hand, concentrates on overall structural changes in the corporations and the economy, on what they meant for the changing patterns of entrepreneurship and management, and on what the alterations in entrepreneurship and management meant for them. In this respect, the main points of interest will be the expansion, diversification, and integration of large-scale corporations (IV.A); the rise of cartels and associations (IV.B); the relations between banks and manufacturing industries (IV.C); the growing importance of the sciences in industry (IV.D); the rise and the limits of systematic management (IV.E); the division between ownership and control and the rise of salaried entrepreneurs (IV.F); and the changing patterns of entrepreneurship in later periods in general (IV.G).

II. *Preconditions*

A. CRAFTS – THE PUTTING-OUT SYSTEM – MANUFACTORIES

Unlike developments in many countries which began to industrialize only after the Second World War, the German industrial revolution of the middle third of the nineteenth century was based on a century's tradition of industry and commerce, which had developed slowly, with great regional variations, and made significant inroads into an otherwise primarily agricultural society. Although generally less developed than in West European countries, large-scale and long-distance trade on the one hand and industrial production on the other had gradually overcome the vast setback of the Thirty Years' War, particularly in the Rhineland and Westphalia, in Saxony, in Southwest Germany, and in Silesia. They had made such progress by the end of the eighteenth century – particularly in some branches of textile production, the production and working of metal, and mining – that works with steam power and machinery on the West European model had appeared, although they remained exceptions and were not so widespread that one could talk of a general economic 'take-off'. These developments encouraged technical progress, the appearance of funds which could be invested, and the creation of a work force; they also enabled a class of entrepreneurs and potential entrepreneurs to appear, which was to be a major advantage in the industrial revolution.

How far was there continuity between the entrepreneurs and managers of the industrial revolution on the one hand and those of the eighteenth and early nineteenth centuries on the other? To answer this question it is useful to distinguish three traditional types of industrial organization: craft industry (*Handwerk*), the putting-out system (*Verlag*), and the manufactory (*Manufaktur*).[9] The typical master craftsman of around 1800 – working usually alone or with a very small number of assistants and apprentices – knew nothing of elaborate financial calculations. He produced without machinery and with little division of labour, and he combined supervision and actual production in one person; he bought his own raw materials, and he sold his product at the local market to the consumer or sometimes to a trader. The putting-out system differed from this completely decentralized handicraft system in that it implied a centralized distribution, often with centralized buying of raw materials, in many cases a centralized ownership of the means of production, and – if advanced – even a co-ordinated division of labour; but it left production geographically decentralized. The workers in this system produced for a common, predetermined, large-scale receiver, the putter-out (*Verleger*), who did not consume the goods himself but sold them, usually beyond the local market and according to capitalist principles. He increasingly determined the nature, quantities, quality, and price of the goods. Sometimes he provided the craftsman with the raw materials or half-finished goods, and sometimes also the tools. Thus the independence of the craftsman turned into dependence on the putter-out; increasingly the latter came to influence the course of production itself and could structure the work processes, as in the decentralized production of needles. In the process, the craftsman turned into a specialized cottage worker.

By 'manufactory', on the other hand, we mean a large-scale plant with a division of labour, big enough – in contrast to craft industry – to have a clear functional division between the organization of production on the one hand and the execution of the job on the other, but differing from the factory in that it did not use machines, and from the putting-out system in that it was geographically centralized. In contrast to the crafts and putting-out systems, the manufactory system shows for the first time a separation between the home and the place of work, at least for the majority of the workers. In practice, however, these three types rarely appeared in their pure forms. There were many transitional stages between the craft and putting-out systems. Manufactory and putting-out were often linked, particularly when a part of the production process (e.g. dyeing, fulling, and the final working of the materials) was already geographically centralized, whereas part of it (e.g. the spinning and weaving) was still done by craftsmen or cottage workers.[10]

There can be no doubt that of those who ran these three types of business, the typical craftsman was the one who was most different from the industrialist, the capitalist entrepreneur of later times. He did not have the latter's specialization in non-operative activities, and he frequently lacked the industrialist's market- and profit-orientation. He was not responsible for the management of a large plant with machinery and an elaborate division of labour, nor had he to cope with a numerous labour force; normally he did not know how to handle and control large amounts of capital. He tended to stick to the old production and sales methods rather than changing them, and certainly he did not go in for radical and abrupt improvements, as long as the old methods were adequate to support him and maintain his well-being; this was particularly the case if he was a member of an organized guild, but it remained quite frequently true when – as in the late eighteenth and early nineteenth centuries – the guild regulations lost much of their former binding force. The profits of the craftsman were seldom so large that they would have driven him to expand, change, and innovate. Around 1800 at least half of all persons engaged in non-agricultural activities were working in a craft setting, mostly as independent men. There were roughly a million craft masters.[11] Nevertheless, the entrepreneurs of the industrial revolution were in general not recruited from among the owners of prospering craft shops. In general, the factory of the first phase of industrialization did not develop out of a former craftsman's workshop. We will examine later how the craftsman tradition was nonetheless of benefit to industry.

The relationship between the putting-out enterprises of the late eighteenth and early nineteenth centuries and the developing factory entrepreneurs was much more direct. The putters-out in the traditional centres of trade and industry, e.g. in Saxony, the Rhineland, and the Augsburg area, were mostly ex-shopkeepers or members of commercial families with traditions in large-scale and long-distance trade, supplemented by some craftsmen and a few officials. The majority of putters-out, thanks to their background as shopkeepers, had a notable experience of and orientation to the market. In branches which had to do with the large-scale sale of relatively homogeneous articles (e.g. cloth, ribbon, clocks, needles, knives, etc.), they could synchronize production with the changing demand in expanding and changing markets on a scale which was impossible for the traditional craftsman, restricted as he was to his locality. The advantages of such men were especially important in areas like textile production, in which the commercial orientation of output to changing demand was at least as important as the techniques of production themselves. These directors of decentralized but large-scale businesses, operating without large fixed capital – profit-orientated, frequently capable of proper written controls, often ready to experiment and less strongly bound to tradition than the average craftsman – made a contribution to industrial progress and social change long before the factory had appeared. Thus it was they who transformed the independent craftsman into the frequently exploited cottage worker. They raised productivity by increasingly subdividing the work. They decided on the differentiation and expansion of the areas of production, and contributed to the development of production techniques by tightening the controls on production and sometimes modernizing the tools – culminating in the distribution of small machines (e.g. spinning machines and later sewing machines) to the homes of the cottage workers.[12] The putter-out thus already fulfilled important functions of an industrial entrepreneur and made for innovations in the areas of production and distribution. On the other hand, he scarcely fulfilled the function of the industrial entrepreneur of later decades, since in decentralized large-scale business there was not yet much fixed capital, and the tools were still often owned by the actual producers.[13] Because production and the labour force were decentralized, he did not need to concern himself with managerial functions.

Even before mechanization called for centralization of production, some putters-out had begun to integrate work processes geographically, and had thus taken a further step towards becoming manufactory entrepreneurs. They did this for various reasons: in order to improve control and influence production more continuously, in view of changing demand – sometimes already dictated by fashion – and stronger competition, the need to improve quality, and the increasing cost of raw materials. They also sought to make themselves independent of suppliers and finishers such as the guilds or co-operatives of fullers or dyers, and to protect their production secrets more effectively or to break guild rules without disturbance. To a larger extent putters-out went over to centralized large plants when they began to use water-power and later steam-power for individual stages of production, or when they introduced machines. Normally some stages of production remained decentralized; the finishing processes were brought together first, in big, often multi-storied buildings, or in workrooms with up to several hundred workers.

B. MANUFACTORY ENTREPRENEURS AS PRECURSORS OF THE ENTREPRENEURS OF THE INDUSTRIAL REVOLUTION[14]

In so far as the individual putters-out became manufactory entrepreneurs – above all in textiles, the largest industrial sector, comprising more than 90 per cent of all putting-out enterprises – they changed their functions and became more like the factory entrepreneurs of the industrial revolution. Manufactory entrepreneurs, in contrast to the mere putters-out, had to mobilize and handle large amounts of fixed capital, in addition to their liquid and circulating capital. While the putter-out could devote himself to marketing, the general organization of his enterprise, and sometimes the supply of raw materials, the manufactory entrepreneur had in addition to control production itself.[15] Problems of work organization, technology, and personnel management had to be solved by the manufactory entrepreneur besides the business, general organizational, and financial functions which stood in the foreground for the putter-out. For many manufactory entrepreneurs of the seventeenth and eighteenth centuries, the functions of capitalist, entrepreneur, and manager were joined in one person; good examples are some of the leading members of the Krefeld Mennonite family of von der Leyen, with their silk manufactories, who in 1794 controlled a private capital of over 1·2 million talers.[16]

The manufactories, however, did not displace the putting-out system to any large extent; rather, this decentralized form of production maintained its clear predominance in the decades before the industrial revolution, particularly in the more advanced centres of industry, i.e. in areas (such as the Rhineland) where the chief impetus towards business and commercial modernization came from capitalists and private entrepreneurs rather than from the state.[17] On the other hand, by no means all manufactories of the late eighteenth and early nineteenth centuries emerged from putting-out enterprises. For centuries there had been firms producing and working up raw materials which understood the division of labour, which were concentrated in one place, and which integrated separate stages of production (such as the stages from the producing of iron ore via the furnace and the hammering process through to the making of weapons). They had been much larger than the usual craftsman's workshop, they had mechanized individual work processes early, and they often used simple forms of non-human energy – particularly water-power – for machinery.[18]

Beyond this, the seventeenth and eighteenth centuries increasingly saw the foundation of large-scale enterprises which were fully or partly centralized from the start in other sectors as well. In fact, it seems that in regions or branches of industry where there was no established craft and commercial structure which could have provided the basis of a putting-out system, founders were virtually forced to set up centralized manufacturing enterprises, integrating several functions and stages of production, as the only feasible way of establishing an enterprise in this field. This was true, for example, of the entrepreneurs who – on religious grounds, or in order to escape the resistance of the established guilds – left the town, with its business structure and its developed secondary industries, and set up in the countryside with imported workers.[19] It was also true of the aristocratic landowners, who at an early stage established large, highly diversified enterprises on their estates, in order to exploit their own or nearby natural resources.[20] If they wanted to establish an enterprise at all in an area without a business tradition, its operation would have to cover several stages of production and fulfil several functions which the entrepreneur in an area with a developed business structure would probably have left to a supplier, to an independent business unit of a related branch, and/or to a trader. On the other hand, an enterprise in an area with little competition could try out new product lines with relatively little danger, whereas in traditional areas of industry such a venture would have had to win its market with great difficulty, against established and experienced specialists. The situation was similar for the mercantilist industrial policies of the absolutist princes. Without sufficient reference to the actual economic risks of operating in areas without a developed industry, they often tried to establish industrial enterprises such as silk- or porcelain-manufacturing, or the production of arms, by founding firms or giving special privileges to private entrepreneurs. Thus the centralized and integrated large works (often with an associated putting-out enterprise), which the risk-taking private entrepreneur usually avoided because of its high capital-intensity, unless there were special reasons for him to become involved in it, was already – before the industrial revolution – both a consequence of relative backwardness and an attempt to make up for it. It is in keeping with this picture that most of the state-owned or strongly state-influenced enterprises were larger and more differentiated, but seldom more successful and sometimes even less viable, than the profit-orientated private enterprises.[21]

The manufactory entrepreneur of the second half of the eighteenth century resembled the later businessman of the industrial revolution not only because he often combined the functions of the capitalist, entrepreneur, and manager in one person, but also because he sometimes left either the function of the capitalist or that of the manager to other persons or institutions. The overwhelming mass of manufactory capital came from traders, craftsmen, several officials, and – above all in the mining and raw-materials industries – from noble landowners, from private individuals who then also made most of the more important entrepreneurial decisions, although often under strong state influence. But there were nonetheless many cases of manufactories being established with public finance. As long as they were not sold to private interests (and the officials usually tried to encourage this), such enterprises were run by public commissions and officials, or by leaseholders and delegated entrepreneurs, who often joined the civil service. A similar personal split between the ownership of capital and the function of the entrepreneur was evident in the case of manufactories which were run by private associations. Their number increased, at least in Saxony, during the eighteenth century.[22] On the other side there were a few entrepreneurs, especially in the backward areas subject to strong state influence, who were active in several related businesses and who doubtless delegated the daily management of such very disaggregated businesses – similar to the modern conglomerate – to specialists, normally craftsmen and ex-officials. Apart from their diverse international trade, the major Berlin entrepreneurs David Splitgerber and Gottfried Adolph Daum not only operated banking and transport concerns (as was common at the time) but also leased four state-owned metal works, founded the Spandauer Gewehr- und Waffenmanufaktur at the instigation of the king, and acquired a sugar refinery, a mirror manufactory, an ivory-comb manufactory, and a bone-meal manufactory. They could hardly heve exercised day-to-day control over these various concerns.[23] The same is true of the aristocratic entrepreneurs, who used their agricultural capital and their privileges, particularly in Silesia and Bohemia, to become active entrepreneurs, above all in the raw-materials industries, such as mining, metal-refining and metalworking, brick-making and glass-manufacturing, brewing and distilling. In most cases the management of their industrial, no less than their agricultural, concerns was left to middle-class managers, supervisors, and inspectors.[24]

The manufactory entrepreneurs and the putters-out of the eighteenth century, whether they were former merchants, craftsmen, officials, or landowners, shared a desire to free themselves from the established guilds of craftsmen and traders. It would be misleading to call them outsiders; many of them were too rich and too powerful for that. These traders, officials, better-off craftsmen, landowners, and free peasants were seldom recruits from the lower classes, coming mostly from the middle and higher classes in town or country. But there was often, if not always, a certain tension between them and the old-established men of business, and they were not always fully – or at least not immediately – integrated into the social structure of their area of operations. Some West German industrial entrepreneurs, e.g. in the Rhineland, had already in the eighteenth century achieved great wealth and social status and a distinct bourgeois self-confidence, but typically they made their way not in the old trading and commercial towns (such as Cologne, Düsseldorf, and Frankfurt) but rather in small towns and rural areas, where the corporations and guilds could create fewer difficulties for them. It is true that the metal industrialists, like Stumm and Hoesch, came from long-established and well-respected families which had long been engaged in metal-producing; but their businesses had frequently originated as agricultural sidelines, and there was a clear distinction between them and the guild industry of the towns.[25]

In areas with a strong policy of mercantilist encouragement to industry – and this normally also meant weaker initiative on the part of local private entrepreneurs – the power of attraction of the court was strong enough to persuade entrepreneurs to found their manufactories in the towns with royal residences and to concentrate their putting-out enterprises there. They did not have to escape to the country to avoid the opposition of the guilds: they got round them with the help of privileges from the prince. Political factors thus influenced the choice of site and often led to foundations which were not optimally conceived from an economic point of view, in terms of access to raw materials and markets, and which came into difficulties as soon as the political wind changed – in particular, when the mercantilist policy towards manufacturing was abandoned around 1800 by economically liberal officials.[26] It was also partly as a result of mercantilist policy that manufactory entrepreneurs did not belong to the long-settled, well-established core of the population in the region concerned. The manufacturing policy of the princes was often based on recruited immigrants with skills and experience from more advanced areas. Normally, entrepreneurs with capital and knowledge from Switzerland, France, and Holland were very much welcomed, but the number of indigenous persons among the privileged manufactory entrepreneurs seems to have increased in the late eighteenth century, just as elsewhere private local manufacturers became more willing to found enterprises and run them, without major privileges from the prince.[27]

Even in the more backward regions of Germany, there was no lack of people in the eighteenth century who tried to attain profit and wealth by running manufactories and putting-out enterprises, if they could get the necessary state concessions – although they frequently wanted financial help and special privileges, too. The number of requests for privileges and concessions usually ran beyond the number awarded. Among the petitioners were many '*Projektemacher*' (projectors) who had already tried many ventures and often failed, but who could frequently be useful for practical innovations; there were also pure charlatans who offered fantastic technical inventions and secrets to the court, and swindlers who distinguished themselves even in this doubtful company by their corruption and deceit. At that time business morality was weak, especially in the more backward regions. The officials granting the concessions tried to make their selection between applicants, often with insufficient information, without general guidelines, and sometimes themselves yielding to misguided, irrelevant, and occasionally even corrupt influences. Through this initial selection and later through controls, interventions, and subsidies, public officials exercised important entrepreneurial functions. It was not the profit-orientated entrepreneur, anxious to use any opportunity to gain success and riches, who was lacking; but there was frequently a shortage of people who combined profit-orientation with the necessary skill and ability to succeed in conditions of high risk.

The good manufactory entrepreneur was a many-sided, adroit, receptive empiricist, who required a broad knowledge. He needed an overall view of the possibilities governing sales and distribution and of the chief customers, markets, and fairs; he needed a basic knowledge of his products and the methods of production; he had to know about technical developments and perhaps be able to incorporate them. In ideal circumstances, he would have gained business and technical knowledge on journeys abroad and in work in certain famous large-scale works, like the Schülesche Textil-Manufaktur in Augsburg. Both for sales and for information about technical innovations, his personal contacts remained of the greatest importance, even decisive. This was also true of his ability to recruit and import some of the scarce skilled workers from more developed regions. He had to utilize a large number of non-guild workers and to give them some training and instil motivation, retain them for the firm, and control and discipline them. Noneconomic methods were also available to him for these purposes: he was sometimes allowed by the authorities to take 'hands' from the work-house, or to forbid his workers to change their place of work. Sometimes the manufactory entrepreneur – like the landlords – could use the machinery of the lower courts to control their workers. If there was not enough accommodation, particularly in rural areas, the entrepreneur built houses for his imported labour force; sometimes they even lived in the works itself. He tried to get legal privileges for his imported skilled labour (exemption from military service and from taxation) and normally exploited the local unskilled or semi-skilled, including many children, the more harshly for it. The general poverty of the time was shared by the less-qualified manufactory workers but not by many manufactory entrepreneurs, who in the Berlin of the last quarter of the eighteenth century exceeded many aristocrats in luxury and visible wealth and were quite different from the economical, reinvesting factory lords of the later industrial revolution. Finally, the good manufacturer needed a great deal of diplomatic and political skill in the mercantilist political system, and a talent for intrigue, corruption, and adaptability to authority. His contacts with the prince and his officials were of central importance in that state-influenced economic system, in which political decisions and political interests intervened directly in the processes of production and distribution. At least in the short term, it was not failure in the market which determined the bankruptcy of an enterprise, but the withdrawal of official support, privileges, tariff concessions, commissions, and subsidies. Often, losses would become dangerous only if a royal investigating commission noticed them. The policy of the authorities often had little relation to the market and was erratic and difficult to calculate. Although better protected from the vagaries of the market than the entrepreneur in the western provinces, who had to rely largely on himself, the manufacturer in Berlin or Munich bore a higher risk factor than they. Great riches, a title from the state, and the peerage were within his sights, as were poverty and misery in the event of failure.[28]

If the possibility of safely taking account of political factors is one prerequisite for a rational capitalist enterprise, as Max Weber has pointed out, the mercantilist politics of the absolutist princes created a particularly unpropitious context. The situation encouraged the appearance of flexible, active entrepreneurs, fighting with every means, ambitious and even daring, who nevertheless put more value on political than on economic considerations and were very far removed from the sober and rational behaviour of the entrepreneur of the industrial revolution. In view of the fluctuations of fortune, they happily became rentiers or estate-owners, once they had gathered enough wealth. As managers, these early businessmen remained wedded to the unsystematic methods more fitting for a small concern – even though, in highly developed Franconia, such firms had an average of forty-five workers and a maximum of up to 500, and needed fixed capital on a large scale. Without a good knowledge of bookkeeping and without the concept of depreciation, they were not able to value their buildings, equipment, tools, or machines in money terms as fixed capital, and thus were unable to test their profitability. The underestimation of the capital needs of a profitable large-scale enterprise seems to have been a distinct weakness of these entrepreneurs. Often the manufactory entrepreneurs of the eighteenth century did not even employ single-entry bookkeeping. Entrepreneurs often had no overall view of profitability and finance, considering that they had made a profit if there was money in the till at the end of the year. They had no idea about long-term planning of investments or the supply of raw materials. Without exact financial controls it was impossible for them to take daily decisions strictly on the criterion of profitability. Many entrepreneurs of the period also avoided the problem of directly controlling a great number of workers: internal subcontracting was common, and this meant that the chain of centralized authority often ended with the foremen or 'butty-masters' who alone were responsible for managing the operatives. Thus, in contrast to later factories, centralized control of the work force was frequently lacking. Manufactory entrepreneurs thus side-stepped problems of large-scale management which were here appearing for the first time, and which were to become typical of the later factory system too. Finally, most of the manufactory entrepreneurs seem at best to have adopted known technical advances, but seldom to have initiated them themselves. It is notable that the weaknesses and idiosyncrasies of eighteenth-century industrialists were the same as those common among entrepreneurs in the developing countries today: what is absent is not concern for profits, market-orientation, or an aptitude for political dealing, but abilities and motivations for rational, systematic, steady entrepreneurship and for innovatory control over the technological processes. In these respects these early entrepreneurs were quite different from the typical factory entrepreneur of the industrial revolution.[29]

The life expectancy of the average manufacturing venture was sharply limited by several factors: a shortage of entrepreneurial and managerial skills, with the great dependence of the concern on the personal abilities and contacts of its director; the shortage of capital of most of these concerns, which was a result of the unwillingness of propertied people to invest in the risky manufactories; and also the small chances which the relatively undeveloped and politically divided markets offered. Of 190 Bavarian manufactories, 50 per cent survived less than twenty years, and 22 per cent less than ten years. In industrially advanced Franconia, one-fourth of the manufactories whose date of foundation is known were brought down by difficulties in the first ten years, although 30 per cent were over fifty years old. Bankruptcies increased (although new foundations did also) between 1800 and 1830 – i.e. in the period of the breakthrough of economic liberalism.[30]

C. THE PROBLEM OF CONTINUITY

What did this manufactory tradition mean for entrepreneurial and managerial potential in the industrial revolution? Here it is important to differentiate clearly: in the economically advanced areas – above all the Rhineland – where the manufactories had arisen primarily from market-orientated decisions of private entrepreneurs and without strong state intervention, there was a marked continuity of the main branches of production – primarily the textile industry, but also ore- and metal-working, and paper production. Although here too, of course, many of the old concerns disappeared, and even more new ones were founded from scratch by new men, many factories and the men who ran them emerged here from the earlier manufactory system. The accumulated capital and experience of the putting-out and manufactory enterprises, their long-standing relations with the market, and the reservoir of qualified workers that they had gradually built up all show direct continuity with the industrialization of the nineteenth century. However, technical change, increasing competition, and adaptation to the changing market called for the right decisions at the right time, and this was by no means always successfully achieved. One can study in the long-established and highly skilled textile, paper, and metal works in Düren how putters-out and manufactory entrepreneurs successfully accomplished the adaptation, through the timely introduction of machinery and specialization under pressure of competition, and were able to preserve and develop their important position in the nineteenth century.[31] This kind of continuity was also great in iron-ore production and the ironworking industry, with its strong connections with the land. The 'Reidemeister' (putting-out entrepreneurs) of the Siegerland and Oberbergland ironworks and the owners of the metalworks – similar to manufactories – in the Hunsrück, in the Eifel, or on the Saar had names which were still well known in the mining industry of the nineteenth and twentieth centuries. In some of these cases the modernized blast-furnace plant of the nineteenth century grew fairly directly out of the works of earlier centuries. But in most cases the decline of the rural iron industry, beginning in the eighteenth century and continuing during industrialization, meant that the successors of these old ore-industry families had to move to new places and sometimes into different types of activity.[32]

In industrially advanced Saxony, too, one can see similar continuities, above all in the textile industry, even though here the stronger influence of the mercantilist state had created commercial and market conditions which disappeared with the end of mercantilism. When this happened, many manufactories ceased to be viable. Other factors, such as war, the continental blockade, and lack of flexibility on the part of older directors of enterprises in switching to potentially more successful branches of production (such as cotton) all played a part, so that only a minority of the manufactories existing in 1800 succeeded in changing over to mechanized production. The majority disappeared. Nevertheless, manufactory and putting-out entrepreneurs played a decisive role in the financing and direction of the new Saxon textile factories (at least in the cotton, carded-wool, and worsted industries). Their role was certainly more important than that of the craftsmen and pure merchants.[33]

Large-scale enterprises of the late eighteenth and early nineteenth centuries, founded by the state and run by officials, were able to survive best in mining, smelting, and the first stages of working up the raw materials. The heavy industrial concerns founded in Silesia by the ministers Heinitz and Reden under the *ancien régime* proved themselves to be the reverse of artificial, unprofitable creations of a mercantilist protectionist policy. At least until the mid nineteenth century the private Silesian enterprises did not compare with the state ventures in size or productive capacity. Through their exemplary innovations, through training the men who later became the principal entrepreneurs of private enterprise, and through the demand they stimulated, these state enterprises had a primarily beneficial effect on the development of Silesian heavy industry.[34]

Despite this, there was in general only a limited continuity between manufactories and manufactory entrepreneurs encouraged by mercantilism on the one hand, and developing private industry with its factories and entrepreneurs on the other. There was too great a contrast between conditions under the artificial umbrella of protection and absolutist interventionism and those of the free market economy of the industrial revolution for the old institutions, skills, and personalities to have been able to continue uninterrupted into the new era. In addition the wars, frontier changes, and political turbulence at the turn of the century destroyed works which might otherwise have been able to continue successfully and perhaps to convert to factory methods. In Bavaria only sixteen of all the manufactories working in 1833 succeeded in this adaptation – roughly one-tenth of those traceable between 1740 and 1833. The proportion of manufactories able to develop was only a little higher in Franconia (fifteen out of ninety-eight). The Berlin textile manufactories and putting-out enterprises, which received so much encouragement from the state, did not in general long survive the end of the mercantilist system, in contrast to the private enterprises in the Rhineland. New industries such as machine-building, clothing firms, and the like were founded in the Prussian capital during the industrial revolution, but this time on the basis of market-orientated commercial considerations, and not through a state policy of privilege.[35] The number of manufactory entrepreneurs in the *ancien régime* was in any case small – smaller than the number of putting-out entrepreneurs – and tiny in comparison with the number of artisans. Of these few, only a small minority succeeded in preserving their viability into the new era.

In all, therefore, there was only a limited continuity between the pre-industrial period and the industrial revolution, on the level of the institutions and their directors. The new factories were most likely to develop out of earlier putting-out enterprises, less likely to grow out of old manufactories, and still less likely to evolve out of old craftsmen's shops. This development was also more likely in the advanced West of Germany than in the areas of entrepreneurial backwardness and the regions where the mercantilist policy of encouragement of industry had been concentrated. Bearing in mind these differences and the need for further research, one can say that the directors of pre-industrial business enterprises did not normally develop into the heads of industrial enterprises.

In contrast to this discontinuity in the case of institutions and individual entrepreneurs, there was probably a far greater continuity in terms of the family and of society in general. Even when a manufactory entrepreneur, a master craftsman, or a putting-out entrepreneur failed to convert his business into a factory, it was often the case that his descendants did become factory-owners, perhaps in another place or in another line of business. This explains how many famous entrepreneurs of the industrial revolution, particularly in Western Germany, came from old families which even in the seventeenth and eighteenth centuries had been established in industrial or business activities: Stumm, Wendel, and Hoesch; Krupp, Poensgen, and Schöller are examples. These names stand for old and complex bourgeois business dynasties, often interrelated, and quite like aristocratic dynasties in their marriage policies, except that with them it was not so much a matter of increasing their territories as of increasing businesses, entrepreneurial skills, and capital. Fritz Redlich conjectured, partly for these reasons, that the whole modern economic expansion in Germany, as in other Western countries, was the work of a few hundred families. This view needs and deserves thorough investigation. If correct, it would be an indication of an interesting social-historical continuity in a period which saw changes which are correctly described as 'revolutionary'.

This view is supported by the fact that of the Berlin entrepreneurs of the industrial revolution only about one person in three had inherited his business from his father, while three-quarters were nonetheless the sons of entrepreneurs. Other investigations show clearly that most of the entrepreneurs of the industrial revolution were the sons of craftsmen, traders, and businessmen; a sizeable minority of them had civil servants as fathers, and some came from peasants' and landowners' families, but they rarely came from the propertyless lower classes.[36]

In conclusion, the discontinuity at the level of individual concerns and their directors is an indication of a rapid and major change in economic development. Very different forms of organization appeared, new qualifications were demanded which the established leaders of traditional industrial units could not easily provide. In addition, quite new industries gained in importance (railways, engineering, and heavy industry above all); they relegated the industrial sectors – which had been the most modern before the industrial revolution and in which institutional continuity was most possible (notably the textile industry) – to a relatively declining position. There were also similar alterations within the individual sectors: the relative importance of various locations changed; thus new institutions and new men replaced the old. But on the other hand these new men were not always so new. As the sons of independent traders, craftsmen, and businessmen, they profited from traditions created in the proto-industrial era, and found it easier than many others to gain access to capital, entrepreneurial motivation, knowledge, skills, and contacts. These assets were often handed down from one generation to another within entrepreneurial families. This not only indicates a limit to the chances of upward social mobility; it also shows the significance which early craft and commercial traditions, some reaching far into the past, had for the German industrial revolution.

D. SOME SOCIAL AND CULTURAL FACTORS

Connected with this pre-industrial economic tradition was the fact that in most of the German states there was a legal, social, and socio-cultural environment which did not hinder the emergence of native industrial entrepreneurs, and to some extent even encouraged them. In spite of major feudal survivals in a society which was modernizing without a revolution, there were not many effective legal obstacles in pre-1848 Germany which would have hindered individuals or particular social groups from pursuing particular economic activities. Limitations on business freedom existed, but more in the southern and southwestern states than in Prussia. Certainly the remnants of the state policy of concessions made difficulties for individuals who wanted to take up entrepreneurial activity – although less so than in the eighteenth century. These obstacles finally disappeared only in the last third of the century; but in practice such barriers could be overcome, and they were an expression rather than a cause of economic backwardness.[37]

In spite of the political complexity of Germany before 1870, no real barriers existed against geographical mobility on the part of entrepreneurs. It is true that in the traditional centres of industry businessmen seem to have had relatively little geographical mobility during the industrial revolution: the stability and permanence of the early entrepreneurs in the Rhineland and Westphalia has always been emphasized. On the other hand, the early entrepreneurs in areas without a strong and established business tradition were mostly immigrants. In Bremen they came primarily from the smaller towns of the North German interior. Very few of the Berlin entrepreneurs of the early period of industrialization originated in Berlin. Particularly in the 1830s and 40s, they tended to be immigrants, and some came from very distant provinces.[38]

In principle, it was also possible for a member of the lower classes to achieve a position as an independent entrepreneur, and in some cases this happened. At the same time, at that period there was no basic hostility towards business activity on the part of the German upper classes. For decades, it had been normal – with regional variations – to reward trading and industrial success with the grant of a noble title. Certainly such men, once integrated into the upper classes, usually, though not always, gave up their former activities and became landowners and rentiers. Nevertheless, the respect and high regard in which economic success was held under the mercantilist economic policy of the absolutist princes of the seventeenth and eighteenth centuries, and the high status given to the businessman during the Enlightenment as a far-sighted, rational, unprejudiced, and experienced member of the community helped to make business activity as such and economic success in general more acceptable to the upper classes, including the nobility.[39]

The entrepreneurs of the industrial revolution came from various regions and groups, even though people from Berlin, Bremen and Hamburg, the Rhineland, Saxony, Thuringia, and Westphalia were more strongly represented than others. Entrepreneurs came from villages and the countryside, although most of them were clearly of urban background. They belonged to all religious denominations, even if here the anomalies were most evident: of a sample of 370 well-known German entrepreneurs of the nineteenth century, 74 per cent were of Protestant faith, 16 per cent Roman Catholic, and 7 per cent Jewish, while the same groups represented 62, 36, and 1 per cent of the total population around 1900. Protestant over-representation among early entrepreneurs existed both in predominantly Catholic regions (like the Rhineland and Bavaria) and in predominantly Protestant regions (like Berlin and the central parts of Germany).[40] This seems to support part of the much-discussed Weber thesis which holds that certain aspects of the Protestant belief favoured the development of specific work ethics, achievement-orientation, ascetic life-styles, and the readiness to save and to plan ahead, and thus provide good ideological conditions for the emergence of a capitalist spirit and the development of an entrepreneurial class. The uneven distribution of entrepreneurs among the denominations may also point to certain anti-modern elements in the Catholic milieu which hindered mobility and strong individual striving while developing a sceptical or even hostile attitude against secularized liberalism, the new 'materialistic' spirit, and the dynamics of the developing capitalist system. In regions with a Catholic majority and good business opportunities, the Protestants' minority situation in itself may have helped this group to develop strong entrepreneurial talents. Here the traditional roads to wealth, respect, and power had been largely closed to them, which encouraged them to stick together as a group, in a way that was particularly well suited to the needs of longer-distance trade and the business activities which went with it. In some areas such as Berlin and Silesia, the same mechanism led to a similar result with respect to Jewish businessmen.[41] But it is important to note that Protestant over-representation among nineteenth-century entrepreneurs was not limited to regions with a Catholic majority.

In any case, access to the position of entrepreneur was open enough to keep the exercise of entrepreneurial functions from being restricted – as in some developing countries today – to social, ethnic, or religious minorities. But there were very clear counter-tendencies which restricted access to entrepreneurial positions and played a part in preventing the entrepreneurial potential of some social groups from being fully realized.[42] The specific role of women was so rigidly defined that there were practically no female entrepreneurs in the industrial revolution – in marked contrast to earlier centuries.[43] The significant under-representation of peasants, and the virtual exclusion of workers and the servant classes from access to entrepreneurial positions indicates that a lack of skills, motivation, information, and property were barriers which the members of the lower classes could not normally overcome.[44]

On the other hand, there were attitudes in the upper and upper middle classes which made it slightly less likely that their members would want to become businessmen. For the nobility, manual work – and for some of them (particularly in the West and Southwest) trade and industry in general – was a form of livelihood incompatible with their social position. But if the enterprise was primarily in one of the branches of industry connected with agriculture (such as mining, smelting, brickworks, etc.), or if it was linked with a state appointment, it became perfectly respectable for many aristocrats (for example in Silesia and Bohemia).[45]

More than in the USA, and probably also more than in Great Britain, the educated middle classes in relatively backward Germany adopted a disparaging attitude towards those in 'trade'. The more that *Bildung* (education) served as the basis of the middle class's conception of itself and its claim to respect, the more academics and officials looked down upon the frequently ill-educated small businessmen and petty-bourgeois industrialists of the mid-century. They rather despised these '*Kommis*' (petty traders), craftsmen, and financial dealers, who followed particular money-grubbing interests, while they themselves, without access to material wealth, carried out 'intellectual' (*geistig*) tasks and, in the case of officials, served the 'general' interest of the state. Holding such attitudes, they certainly did not encourage their sons to choose industrial or trading professions.[46]

Some of this distaste on the part of the educated middle classes survived into the twentieth century; but it had already been much weakened before the First World War. There were strong counter-pressures against it. In so far as industrial technology went hand in hand with the natural sciences from the mid nineteenth century onwards, it was possible for academics to find their way into industry with a justification in terms of scientific progress – a clearly 'intellectual' value.[47] It was also normal to endow the rhetoric of progress – with which bourgeois economic groups demanded the development of transport, trade, and industry – with nationalist overtones. The demand for 'industry for the fatherland' was heard in the individual states even before 1848. It served as an argument for a state policy which (particularly in Prussia) tried to spread technical knowledge through technical and business education, through the creation of business associations (*Vereine*), and through exhibitions and competitions. All these efforts sought to encourage entrepreneurial initiative and improvement on national/political grounds. The demand for strengthening 'industry for the fatherland' was soon linked with hopes for political unity, expressed through the political demands of liberal entrepreneurs before 1848 and in the emerging engineering associations of the 1850s and 60s. Later, after the wars of unity, in which modern industry and technology were for the first time conceived of as instruments of war and were celebrated as one of the causes of victory, this national – and soon nationalist – ideology of industrial progress and economic expansion was strengthened. It finally merged into the imperialist propaganda of the turn of the century.[48] In the course of these social and psychological changes, the feudal and upper-middle-class reservations about industry and trade weakened, particularly with regard to productive industry, and to activities which were scientifically interesting and of central importance to the nation's power and prestige.

But even before these changes in the second half of the century finally won through, the industrialist's profession had lost much of its stigma. In spite of some reservations in sections of the upper classes, the industrialist belonged to one of those occupations which were only to a limited extent conditioned by status and were in principle acceptable to all groups, although in varying degrees. After two centuries of absolutism, after the Enlightenment and the reforms of around 1800, the barriers of social position were lowered sufficiently to ensure that no major obstacles were put in the way of a realization of entrepreneurial potential. In addition, there was sufficient social mobility to ensure that in various situations – not least in state-sponsored business and technical societies – craftsmen and technicians, officials and businessmen, professors and *Projektemacher* could come into contact with one another and, on occasion, bring capital and technical knowledge, initiative, and business experience together for joint projects.[49]

In addition, the destruction of the old corporate world, which had already gone a long way by around 1830, facilitated the development of entrepreneurial attitudes in a more general way: in so far as the traditional expressions, symbols, and life-styles of the crumbling estatist (corporate) society became less strong and less widely accepted, greater scope was offered for individual choice in work and life, for new symbols of individual standing and individual success. The continuing disintegration of the traditional corporate order made it possible for a rather independent sphere of economic activities to appear; until then, economic activities had been incorporated parts of rather integrated systems and had been closely interrelated with social, political, and cultural dimensions.[50] Economic success now became possible without regard to, or even in defiance of, the inherited guild and class order; economic success could be demonstrated by 'conspicuous consumption' independently of criteria of social status.[51] The ability to change one's own fate through individual achievement and initiative became observable precisely in the period of breakthrough in the late eighteenth and early nineteenth centuries. Even without a revolution, much that was passed down from the past had lost its traditional legitimacy, the self-evident justification for its existence. It seems to be demonstrable in the contemporary social and economic literature that in Germany – albeit later and less strongly than in England – the pressure for change and innovation built up, and the spokesmen for the new values gained in respectability among the educated classes.[52] In a weaker form, and specifically on the economic level, this high regard for innovation and progress also won through in the public industrial and technical schools, which had been built up in Prussia after 1820 with the aim of encouraging industry on national political grounds.[53]

There are undoubtedly institutional, legal, and socio-cultural contexts which make the appearance of industrial enterprises impossible, or at best extremely difficult. In Germany such obstacles were so far overcome by the beginning of the nineteenth century that on this score nothing important stood in the way of industrialization.

III. *Entrepreneur and Manager in the Industrial Revolution*

A. ECONOMIC BACKGROUND AND CAREER PATTERNS

Who were the entrepreneurs of the industrial revolution in the middle third of the nineteenth century, and from what socio-economic backgrounds did they come? We will not inquire here into their social origins or the occupations of their fathers, but into the socio-economic position from which they began: the starting-point for their activities as entrepreneurs. We will also investigate the channels by which people entered entrepreneurial positions between the 1830s and the 1870s, the mechanisms which were involved in the process, and the positions which they achieved.[54]

It is striking that in the industrial revolution, as before, only the exceptional industrialist had started as a skilled or unskilled worker, a factory worker or labourer, a servant, or something similar. Apart from individual exceptions, and the craft apprentices (with whom we will deal separately), the urban lower classes lacked not only capital – as did many entrepreneurs from a craftsman's background – but also useful business and technical knowledge, information about opportunities, and often an education which would have passed on motivation and a spirit of enterprise.[55] It is also noticeable that only a few peasants, farm hands, and agricultural workers became industrial entrepreneurs. There were certainly exceptions, particularly in rural areas where industrialization started only after the mid-century.[56] But in general the emergence of an individual from a lower or middle agricultural milieu as an industrial or business entrepreneur was a rarity. The great majority of the people, therefore, took no part in the creation of the industrialist class. The permeability of the society of the time thus had very clear limits, even with regard to the by no means prestigious position of entrepreneur. In this, Germany was not very different from the English-speaking countries, where 'one-generational' chances for upward social mobility seem to have been only a little higher.[57]

The overwhelming majority of entrepreneurs of the industrial revolution came – in Germany just as in France, England, and the USA – from industrial and business trades and activities. This shows clearly how important it was to have had a century-old industrial business and trading tradition, in spite of the discontinuity in respect of institutions and individual persons which we have already mentioned. The circles from which the entrepreneurs of the industrial revolution primarily came had all, in one way or another, something to do with the craft or trading economy – whether as master craftsman or apprentice, as merchant, shopkeeper, or putter-out, as technician or son of the master of a workshop. The great majority of entrepreneurs brought some industrial, technical, or business knowledge with them, and many had financial means at their disposal, which they had gathered in industrial or business activities.

1. Entrepreneurs with a Background in Trading

If we concentrate at first on the most numerous group, the founders of independent firms, and leave the successors out of account for the moment, it is the traders and putters-out – who sometimes (at least until around 1850) also ran banking and transport concerns – who emerge as the group which played the most important role in the recruitment of early industrial entrepreneurs.[58] This was particularly true of that branch of industry in which the first factories appeared – the textile industries. The dominance of wholesale merchants and putters-out among early textile entrepreneurs is explained partly by the traditions of putting-out and manufactory which we have described, which were continued with the least interruption in this sector. It was also in the textile industry that mass consumption and long-distance trade developed earliest and most clearly, influenced by changes in demand induced by fashion. Great demands were made on business knowledge and abilities, while production itself presented no great technical problems. All this gave the putting-out merchant (who seems to have been particularly common among the textile factory-founders of the 1840s) and the textile trader (who later often became a factory-owner without the intermediate stage of putting-out) a clear preponderance over the craftsman. The fact that it was mostly the putters-out and merchants with special experience in trade in yarn and fabrics, and not just any shopkeeper, shows the great significance of specialized skills and abilities for this connection between traders and the emerging textile industry. In addition, the growing capital needs of firms in the worsted and cotton industries made it more difficult for the craftsman with little capital to rise to an entrepreneurial position in this branch, although he could enter with a trader into one of the partnerships which were so frequent in the textile industry.[59]

Ex-merchants also played the leading role in the development of the Berlin ready-made clothes industry after the 1830s. Here the impetus came from the retail trade, whereas normally it was the wholesale traders who were industrially active as suppliers of capital, silent partners, putters-out, and factory-owners. Under the strong influence of developments in fashion, and in constant conflict with the guilds of tailors, the ready-made clothing firms created a form of production which was partly centralized and partly decentralized.[60] Apart from the proprietors of chemist's shops, it was the merchants dealing in drugs, non-ferrous metals, and paints who became the founders of the German chemical industry.[61] Similarly, in the metalworking industry, merchants played a role in those regions which had a firm tradition of decentralized craft metalworks. As shown by the examples of the Remscheid family of Mannesmann and the many entrepreneurs in the small ironworks in Solingen, the conversion from craft to factory via the putting-out system was pushed forward by merchants in this field of production too. The foundation in 1819 of the 'Mechanische Werkstätte' in the citadel of Wetter on the Ruhr – one of the pioneering engineering enterprises – was the work of a tradesman (Friedrich Harkort), supported by a banker from Aachen and a technician from England.[62]

In mining as in the production and working of iron and steel, traders played a leading role as well. Franz Haniel and Matthias Stinnes are only the most obvious examples of the influence of the coal trade on the heavy industry that developed on the Rhine and Ruhr from 1808 onwards. The coal-trader Haniel brought his capital and his spirit of enterprise to a lower-Rhine smelting works, which until then had been scattered and unsuccessful. He formed the Gutehoffnungshütte with help from another trading family and a technician from one of the old smelting works. This firm soon extended its field of activities from the extraction of raw materials on the one hand to the production of goods (shipbuilding, the manufacture of railway equipment) on the other, and employed 2,000 men as early as 1843. Haniel was also one of the pioneers of vertical-shaft mining. Stinnes moved over from his coal-trading and his ship transport concern to the extraction of coal itself. He acquired, consolidated, and sank mines, and became – even under the state control of mining which was lifted in the Ruhr only in 1861 – one of the most important mining entrepreneurs in the Ruhr, employing some 1,000 men in his various enterprises at the time of his death in 1848. Friedrich Grillo who took over his father's iron and cloth shop in Essen in the same year, was one of the dominant organizers and large-scale entrepreneurs of the Ruhr coal industry, well versed in business, financial, and political affairs. It was merchants who, along with bankers, founded the large joint-stock mining companies after the 1850s. Friedrich Krupp, too, the pioneer of cast steel and the founder of the Krupp concern, was a trader who at first joined up with various technically qualified partners, but in vain, and finally went deeply enough into the technology of steel production to be able to make history as a pioneering industrial founding father. Similarly, in the history of the heavy industry of the Saar, old commercial interests from Saarbrücken were actively involved.

In all these cases there was a close technical link between the special field in which these traders had been active and the branch of industry which they entered. They therefore brought from the trading to the production sector not only capital, a general spirit of enterprise and initiative, and their organizational abilities, but also specific practical knowledge of their particular branch.[63]

Finally we must comment on the type of all-round entrepreneur, also coming primarily from trade, who played such a large role in the industrial revolution. Ludolf Camphausen (1803–90), the son of a Rhineland trader, can be taken as an example. He at first ran an oil and corn business, acquired an oil mill, opened a banking business with his brother, and was active in the local economic politics of Cologne. Like other traders and factory-owners with backgrounds in trade, he was one of the earliest railway entrepreneurs of the Rhineland, and one of the promoters of steam navigation on the Rhine. Alongside his entrepreneurial activities in many different projects only loosely connected with each other, in transport and industry, he played an important role in general politics and in 1848 led the first Liberal ministry in Prussia. Gustav von Mevissen (1815–99), the son of a Protestant putting-out and merchant family of the Krefeld textile trade, is another example of that kind of early entrepreneur who was active at once in trade, banking, transport, and industry, as well as in politics. He invested his own capital and deployed that of others – as a banker and with the legal device of the joint-stock company; he took entrepreneurial decisions of great significance and implemented them, but he rarely fulfilled managerial functions. Such many-sided entrepreneurs with daring and vision, showing great interest in profit and concern with general problems, were from the 1830s onwards the chief founders and first entrepreneurs of the railway companies, which from the first were founded as joint-stock companies. They formed and financed these pioneering, capital-intensive transport concerns, against much opposition, partly in order to profit directly from their investment, but also partly with the object of encouraging the development of their towns (and thus as an indirect encouragement to their other business and trading relations).[64] But these all-round entrepreneurs were not only to be found in connection with the railways. One thinks, for example, of the representative Berlin entrepreneur Wilhelm Herz (born 1823), the son of a corn dealer with an excellent education and a luxurious style of life, who maintained the wholesale trading business of his father, and also ran a seed-crushing mill as manager. In addition he worked as director of a coal company, built up a rubber-goods factory, and played a leading part in the foundation of the Berlin Schultheiss brewery.[65] Many more such examples might be found.[66]

Unlike the capitalists and speculators who merely invested here and there, these all-round entrepreneurs were active in directing their businesses. They were engaged in various economic sectors which in practice had little or nothing to do with each other. For this reason alone they could not integrate their concerns through a unified administrative structure and through unified management. In this respect this group of all-round entrepreneurs, who were gradually declining in numbers, differed from the later, more common business leaders, who held their empires together with a centralized management. Unlike most of the other entrepreneurs of the industrial revolution, they were not specialists in cloth, iron, or machine production, nor in distribution, supply, or labour management. They exercised all these entrepreneurial functions in the various branches, either together or with rapid change from one to another: as non-specialists such entrepreneurs did not stick to a single venture and explore it systematically, but looked to the main chance wherever opportunity offered; their lives showed a restless quest for success.[67]

The thesis has often been advanced that the craftsman or technically qualified entrepreneur was the leading type of entrepreneur in early German industrialization and that the businessman only gradually took over from the technician in the direction of the enterprise.[68] This thesis contains a certain amount of nostalgic romanticizing. It confirms the 'picture of the untiring small man who climbs from being the owner of a craftsman's shop to become director of a large enterprise'.[69] This view of the aims and concerns of the early entrepreneurs as being primarily in terms of the 'product' rather than the profit, reflects certain anti-commercial and anti-capitalist currents in German public opinion, which the industrial firms and their brochures took into account when they portrayed themselves as pioneers of technical development and the servants of industrial progress rather than as profit-orientated businesses – as 'producers' rather than as 'dealers'. There is certainly some truth in this picture of the early days of many large firms; also, it should be granted, the available evidence is not exhaustive. Finally, it should be noted that in most cases the merchant who was becoming an industrialist worked with a craftsman–technician as partner.[70] But nonetheless, as we have shown, the information available indicates the extremely strong and perhaps even dominant role of merchants and traders in the German industrial revolution.

2. Entrepreneurs with a Background in Crafts

The role of the ex-artisans among the early entrepreneurs should not be minimized. Overall, the entrepreneurs from an artisan background were probably more numerous than those with trading experience. The ex-artisan predominated in the small or medium-sized industrial branches and normally managed a distinctly smaller enterprise than the entrepreneur from a commercial background.[71] The transfer from craftsman to entrepreneur was undoubtedly one of the most important intra-generational modes of advancement in industrializing Germany, especially when one considers that these rising artisans were not normally the wealthiest but frequently stood on the edge of an artisan existence, the income from which was no longer adequate, or were craft apprentices not yet established, or sometimes proto-proletarians whose real position was in painful contrast to their petty-bourgeois aspirations.[72] The transfer from artisan to factory entrepreneur was also the most important avenue through which technical knowledge was brought into the emerging factory management of the industrial revolution.

Nowhere did the entrepreneur come more frequently from the artisan class than in the engineering branch, and the normally small-scale metalworking sector generally. The reasons for this were several: the great importance of technical knowledge in this field of production; the dominance, in the first decades of production, of individual products made to order rather than for general sale; and also the unwillingness of commercial capital to invest in this novel branch, which was considered extremely risky. Of thirty-two known Berlin engineering entrepreneurs up to 1870, twenty-five came direct from artisan work, and seven had had a technical- or high-school education; none came from commerce. In a sample of seventy-two entrepreneurs who between 1831 and 1850 founded engineering works in the German states, and whose jobs of origin could be ascertained, eleven had been traders, seventeen had enjoyed some sort of technical-school training (including some previous artisans), and thirty-three were craftsmen without any further technical training. Among these thirty-three craftsmen were ten locksmiths, five cabinet-makers, four smiths, four carpenters, two watchmakers, two casters, two printers, two clothiers, one cooper, and one 'worker'.[73] Here, as in other cases, there was a predominance of craftsmen with experience in the same branch, but there were also craftsmen from other branches.[74]

Frequently craftsmen founded their factories very soon after their '*Wanderjahre*', on which they had become acquainted with new processes or machines – mostly abroad in Western Europe – and had their ambitions aroused. Like most founders of nineteenth-century factories, they started their own businesses in their late twenties.[75] Johann Nikolaus Dreyse, the son of a master locksmith, on his return from his journeys which had taken him finally to Paris, founded in 1822 a small factory for buttons, nails, and window fittings with the help of a money-lender. After 1835, when he invented his needle gun, he devoted himself exclusively to this speciality and built a rapidly growing gun factory. In general, inventions and technical improvements of some sort, which were usually made by younger craftsmen, were frequently the impulse for the foundation of a factory. For example, Jacob Meyer (born 1813), the son of a Swabian farmer, learnt the craft of watchmaker with his uncle in Cologne and became concerned to find a better steel for the springs; he went to England and discovered a practicable steel after his return in 1836. Together with a trader and a money-lender, he soon built a factory for cast steel in Bochum, because it lay near the coal he needed. Out of this factory, after many financial difficulties, emerged the Bochumer Verein für Bergbau und Gussstahlfabrikation AG. Carl Gottlieb Haubold (1783–1856) had already learned the carpenter's trade when, at the age of twenty, he entered the repair workshop of a Chemnitz textile firm, got to know some English mechanics, and after some attempts in his own home (when he was about thirty) founded the first engineering works in Chemnitz. This factory developed with great difficulty and with a constant shortage of capital, but it was one of those 'nursery firms' in which – as with Egells or Borsig in Berlin – many future engineers learnt their trade.[76]

These examples could be continued easily. They appear to show that the craftsman who became an entrepreneur in the industrial revolution seldom achieved this through the gradual expansion of a craftsman's workshop in the same line of business as he was already running.[77] The factory-owner did not normally grow directly out of the master crafts- man: rather, the factory established by a former craftsman was estab- lished from the start in the form of a large works, as a manufactory or factory. The founder was most often an artisan at the start of his career who did not own his own workshop, or someone who had given up a previous job in order to find another. Often the founding of a business involved a change of locality,[78] sometimes even a change of trade. A break in their development or at least a certain distancing from tradition seems often to have preceded success as an industrial entre- preneur.[79]

On the other hand, there were many cases where craftsmen's shops developed continuously into small factories: but it usually took two or more generations and was a main route of inter-generational mobility. This development was not, therefore, very effective for the first phase of industrialization but became so in later decades. In fact, the trans- formation of craft enterprises into factories seems to have been more common in the last third of the nineteenth century and the early twentieth, when the appearance of a factory was not so 'revolutionary' as in the first phase of industrialization. Such transformations later took place frequently in branches of industry – such as building and food production – which had escaped, or almost escaped, conversion to the factory system in the middle third of the nineteenth century.[80]

The entrepreneur who came direct from artisan work, and very often formed a partnership with another craftsman or sometimes with a trader, usually started his enterprise with little capital and little experi- ence of industry. It appears that such new foundations usually grew very slowly, scarcely diversified, and frequently collapsed. In these enterprises there was no division of entrepreneurial and managerial functions between different people, and the director of the enterprise almost always owned the bulk of the capital. But in the 1860s and 70s, in some branches such as mechanical engineering, the number of cases increased in which firms founded by artisans had to use commercial or bank capital, because of their growing capital needs. By this time the merchants and bankers had mostly abandoned their cautious attitudes towards investment in engineering firms. The majority of the leading firms in the engineering industry were now refounded as joint-stock companies. The previous factory-owner normally retained an im- portant share of the capital and often held the position of technical director; but a business director was usually given equality or was even placed above him. Many small and medium-sized artisan's firms, however, remained in private hands, particularly if they could solve their capital and management problems on the basis of a large and actively participating family.[81]

3. *Technicians and Others*

A third starting position for the leap to the founding and direction of one's own enterprise was that of the technician. This covered people from various social circles (although mostly ex-artisans) with one of two career patterns. Either they were graduates from technical school or college who founded their factories soon after leaving the school; or they were technicians, with or without a technical education, who had been employed for some years in factories as foremen or in some other leading position and had gained much practical experience. Thus in 1805 Gottlieb Jacobi, a smelting-works inspector of many years' standing, after many previous schemes became one of the founders of the Hüttengewerkschaft out of which the Gutehoffnungshütte emerged. Some long-serving foremen in textile factories succeeded in founding their own factories. The craftsman's son August Borsig, after his carpenter's training, visited the state Berliner Gewerbe-Institut, founded in 1821 (out of which the Technische Hochschule Berlin–Charlottenburg developed in 1879). For thirteen years he worked as foreman and manager in the Berlin engineering factory of F. A. Egells, in which a great number of later factory-owners worked for long periods as technical staff. In 1837 Borsig founded an engineering works with fifty workers; in 1841 they built the first German locomotive; by 1848 he employed 300 workers, and the factory had in its turn become one of the most important practical training grounds of later factory-owners.[82]

As technical staff of many years' standing, these founders gained not only relevant empirical knowledge at the level of technical understanding, markets, and factory organization, but also acquired a certain amount of capital, because of their relatively high incomes and often with some financial help from their previous employers. As a result they could build their factories on a relatively large scale and, in general, could expand more quickly than the factories founded by craftsmen. In those decades it was clearly more important for the success of a factory-owner to have gathered empirical knowledge in one of the few big and highly qualified enterprises than to have graduated from a technical college. Nonetheless, the number of students from technical schools and colleges was notable even at that time. From a sample of one hundred technicians who left the Berlin Gewerbe-Institut between 1821 and 1850, thirty-nine became independent (as factory-owners or craftsmen)

– most of them, to be sure, in the small-scale building industry. Of the known textile technicians who graduated from this school, about one-third got independent positions; of the technicians in metalworking and machine-building, on the other hand, only 10 per cent did so. In all, the Berlin Gewerbe-Institut, a centre of the better technical education of the time, must have had an output of 1,000 students up to 1850. The proportion of entrepreneurs with a technical education increased in the decades of the industrial revolution.[83]

Apart from these major sources of recruits, no social group failed to produce at least a few entrepreneurs. There was the musician who moved in 1826 to Gummersbach and did not earn enough to keep his family. He first tried twice to set up as a shopkeeper and then opened a small wax-paper workshop, which developed, via the repair of their own vehicles, under the son's direction to be a medium-sized paper and boiler factory. There was the ex-officer Kulmiz, who around the mid-century not only was the leading railway entrepreneur in Silesia but also exploited mineral deposits, had here a glassworks and there a saw-making factory, and founded trading branches everywhere. Finally in 1858 he built Silesia's first big chemical factory, in Saarau. There were the state officials who ran the state mining works, and others who because of their reputations and their connections with the authorities were elected to the boards of developing railways. There was Francke, the Lord Mayor of Magdeburg, who like many local officials succeeded in ensuring the erection of a railway line which would include his town in its net. There was the theologian who became a paper manufacturer in Düren, and the doctor who in 1855 became co-founder of the Harpener Bergbau-Gesellschaft.[84]

Finally we must mention the aristocratic estate-owners, who – particularly in Silesia, but also in Bohemia, Saxony, and other states – in the late eighteenth and early nineteenth centuries created large, very highly diversified enterprises, usually centred in coal. These magnates from the families of Donnersmarck, Hohenlohe–Ingelfingen, Colonna, Ballestrem, Pless, Tiele–Winckler, Schaffgotsch, and others could utilize their aristocratic privileges and their agricultural capital when they began to industrialize on their own lands, often at the instigation of the state and on the model of state enterprise. Even after the reorganization of their properties in joint-stock companies in the 1850s, most of them continued to hold decisive influence in their companies. The most important of them was Count (from 1902, Prince) Guido Henckel von Donnersmarck (1830–1917), who in 1853 founded the Schlesische AG für Bergbau und Zinkhüttenbetrieb and soon collected in his vertically integrated empire coal and iron-ore mines and smelting and rolling mills both inside and outside Silesia. He also assembled paper, cellulose, artificial silk, fertilizer, potash, and cement works, and finally entered the building industry.[85]

So far we have dealt with the founders of firms among the entrepreneurs of the industrial revolution. But as industrialization advanced, an increasing proportion of entrepreneurs had inherited their concerns from their fathers. Their increasing significance in Berlin has been analysed (see Table 137).[86] While over the whole period only 14 per

Table 137. *Heirs and Founders of Enterprises among Berlin Entrepreneurs (per cent)*

Time of take-over or foundation of of enterprise	To 1835	1835–50	1851–73	Total
Heirs	14	28	57	35
Founders	86	72	43	65
Total	100	100	100	100
Number of cases	58	65	74	197

SOURCE. Kaelble, *Berliner Unternehmer*, 55f.

cent of the engineering industrialists can be classified as heirs, 60 per cent of the textile industrialists belong in this category. For the owners of private enterprises (including partnerships) it was a basic assumption that their offspring would inherit the works – not merely the ownership, but the practical direction of the concern. In some medium-sized industries, factory-owners regarded this so much as their duty that they founded extra factories – one for each son. On the other hand, cases of sons refusing to take over their inheritance in this early period were rare. Rather the reverse: Alfred Krupp is the best example for what was called the '*Suprematie der zweiten Generation*'.[87] How this was connected with their education and motivation will be discussed below.

Finally we must refer to the type of entrepreneur of whom there were not very many in the industrial revolution itself, but whose role grew: the commissioned, salaried entrepreneur. Some 3 per cent of almost two hundred Berlin entrepreneurs of that time fell into this category. Without large-scale capital, and without being bound to the owners by family ties they gained positions in which they combined managerial with, to some extent, entrepreneurial functions. They appeared most frequently in the tertiary sector, in banking, insurance, and railway companies. But they also played an important role in the mining industry from the start of industrialization. The Silesian magnates were only following an old tradition of agricultural management when they left the daily management of their industrial concerns, and also the less important entrepreneurial decisions, to bourgeois administrators and limited themselves to the major decision-making. The specialists from the state mining and smelting administration, in the mining industry which developed on the Ruhr from the late eighteenth century onwards, carried out functions which had both managerial and entrepreneurial elements. Thomas Mulvany from Ireland, and Louis Baare, the business-trained former railway official, embodied perfectly in the 1850s the type of commissioned entrepreneur, without capital, as directors of the Hibernia and Shamrock mining companies and the Bochumer Verein für Bergbau und Gussstahlfabrikation. When, in 1873, Berlin banking houses finally bought up the mines Mulvany directed, they bought Mulvany too. In this way trained lawyers found their way into positions as directors of enterprises, at first in railways and banking, but later in industry too. Textile experts with specialized training but no capital of their own also succeeded, at least in individual cases, in reaching important positions around the mid-century. Ferdinand Kaselowsky, for example, who came from the Berlin Gewerbe-Institut, founded several spinning factories at the commission of the state-run Seehandlung, and between 1854 and 1871 ran the Ravensberg Spinning Works, a state-supported model works in Bielefeld.[88]

B. MOTIVES AND QUALIFICATIONS

What made these people decide to take up entrepreneurial activity? Those who came from long-distance and wholesale trading were used to striving for profit and seeking economic success on the basis of new opportunities, although they were mostly well enough off to be able to satisfy the material needs of life either adequately or well. In long-distance and bulk trading, economic success had for long been an important determinant of social status and respect. Far-sightedness, dynamism, and readiness to innovate had been able to develop relatively early in this well-educated and widely travelled profession with its far-flung connections. The systematic and rational pursuit of aims and the weighing of chances were here most closely connected with entrepreneurial daring. Whether these entrepreneurial attitudes would be used for industrial enterprises or would remain limited to purely commercial activities depended on many individual and changing factors, but certainly on no factor more than the real and visible chances of the market, and the opportunity for profit. When Rhineland merchants went over to the centralization and the mechanization of the textile industry whilst Silesian linen merchants left such changes to the state on the grounds that it was too difficult,[89] this may have been a product of the bureaucratic traditions which existed in Silesia but not in the Rhineland; but it may just as well have been due to cautious and rational calculations: the Silesian market and particularly the Silesian transport network were underdeveloped and isolated in comparison with those of the Rhineland, and so the chances of economic success were small.

Other founders of firms, particularly those from an artisan background, were often motivated by their poor economic and social position, which – and this was the decisive factor – they perceived as burdensome but alterable. One must remember that real incomes dropped from the 1820s to about 1850, and they remained low even when they had begun to rise in the 1860s. Because of the generally low level of incomes, even minor economic down-turns created crisis situations for the lower and lower middle classes. In addition, in the business and industrial sector unemployment and underemployment were widespread. The prospects for an unestablished craft apprentice without property were at best very uncertain if not downright bad. There were not many chances for him to establish his position, especially if he was trying to start or to support a family. The struggle with actual or potential poverty was an elementary driving force behind many early entrepreneurs' energy, drudgery, and readiness to take risks which in today's conditions would be scarcely conceivable. Many would-be entrepreneurs went hopefully from one project to another, started, tried, failed but did not give up, and finally sometimes succeeded, with agonizing pains and with the help of the entire family, in creating a secure, prosperous, and respected independent position.[90] Although he was by no means the poorest of men, the army officer Werner Siemens, responsible for his family after the death of his parents, complained in 1846: 'If only damned money did not keep one in the dirt!' He tried with great vigour to bring himself and his family 'into a position free from worries', and he searched in the most diverse areas for financially profitable discoveries, until eventually he found one in the pointer telegraph.[91]

But more was, of course, necessary to lead such an endeavour to entrepreneurial success: technical and/or business talent, perhaps an invention, information about a new opportunity, knowledge, capital, luck, and above all real and recognized chances. But the contemporary pressure of material conditions – a pressure which in many examples of individual success was no longer accepted as fate, at least in the urban lower middle class – should not be underestimated as a driving force for entrepreneurial aspirations and activities in the cases of many founders. To this were frequently added a strong desire for independence, a marked stress on social status, and aspirations for power and dominance.

It is characteristic that in several known cases – though by no means all – technicians preferred an independent position as entrepreneur to a more secure, but in the long term probably less profitable and above all dependent, position as manager. Sons of entrepreneurs sometimes founded their own businesses rather than play the role of junior boss in the fathers' firms and wait for the inheritance.[92]

The striving for individual independence and a position as an industrialist was very easily regarded as rational in the spirit of the time. Did not the state try to arouse individual business activity through prizes and societies, in schools, and in the public at large through legal concessions and subsidies? Did not individual success also promise in the end to lead to the general good – at least in the liberal economic faith which had influenced many of the educated? In view of the well-known advantages of foreign competitors, did not technical and industrial success serve national ends? Such arguments played a demonstrable role, particularly with entrepreneurs whose activities were not motivated by material necessity. One should remember that the railways, the 'leading sector' of the German industrial revolution, were propagated and introduced as an instrument of a long-term development policy (for the benefit of one's own works, town, or country). Thus the most important decisions of the industrial revolution were in one sense political decisions of an increasingly self-confident, organized, and forward-looking bourgeoisie. There was a symbolic value as well as a political example and an educational effect when the first railway companies published the records of their board meetings, instead of holding them in mistrustful secrecy like the 'public' bureaucracy. Men like Mevissen, Camphausen, Hansemann, Siemens, Harkort, and List saw their entrepreneurial activity not only as a means to personal success, but also as a part of a national and civilizing mission.[93]

There were certainly social and psychological factors which worked in the other direction and made the utilization of capital and entrepreneurial efforts for industrial purposes more difficult. We have already referred to the relatively low prestige of the industrial entrepreneur at the beginning of the period of industrialization; this may have kept some merchants from attempting to promote industrial enterprises. Also, apprehension about the social consequences of industrialization – in particular the fear of bringing together a 'mob' and creating a proletariat – motivated some traders and capitalists to take a reserved attitude towards the growth of industry – the more so, as long as there were other, more normal and less risky, if perhaps more limited, possibilities for enterprise and investment in trade, agriculture, and the public debt.

Finally we must mention the high ethical and religious valuation placed on the concept of work, which legitimized economic achievement and success, even when these were no longer necessary for the satisfaction of immediate personal needs. Success in work not only ensured the support of one's family; it also formed the basis of pride in one's achievements, the individual's personal honour which, according to middle-class conceptions, was always indissolubly linked with honesty, quality, solidity, and diligence. For the frequently very Calvinist entrepreneurs of that time, it was also a pledge of the love of God for them. This conception of work and achievement legitimized the hard work and the thrift (in private life as well), the sense of order and sobriety, the rationality and the pleasure in making money. It thus legitimized motives and virtues whose objective function it was to secure a rational leadership of the firm and the profitability of the invested capital, to encourage the expansion of the concern through self-financing, and to subordinate the private life of the entrepreneur's family to this success of the enterprise. It rationalized a preoccupation with success and expansion which might otherwise have appeared senseless. Its favourable effect on the economic growth of the time is clear.[94]

It must be emphasized that the restless endeavour for profit and expansion was not necessarily a result of this religious and ethical justification and later was much less bound up with it. Even in the boom of the 1850s, and above all in the 'Gründerjahre' after 1870, contemporaries criticized the very widespread fever of speculation and striving for profit on the part of the public investing in shares. By the end of the industrial revolution (in the 1870s) the endeavour for profit independent of the work ethic had permeated down to the petty bourgeoisie. The ascetic frugality and simple style of living which the early entrepreneurs had observed in their private lives was also partly lost in the industrial revolution. In the boom of 1869–73, at the latest, textile industrialists in the Rhineland and elsewhere were known for their new wealth, luxury, and lavishness.[95]

On the other hand, the restless striving for achievement, success, and the expansion of the firm, for improvement and progress, remained dominant with a great number of entrepreneurs even when it no longer had a religious or ethical meaning and when its goal of providing for the industrialist's family had also long disappeared. The entrepreneurs of that time worked hard into old age. 'When one has so long been involved in so many concerns, as I have, there must always be something to do or one would dry up.'[96] Even without consciously basing their ideas on a religious work ethic, many founders, and heirs brought up in the same tradition, thought of themselves as being almost the servants of their business. They tried to ensure the concern's survival beyond their own deaths. 'I always thought of the factory as a child, and as a well-brought-up one that gives one pleasure by its behaviour. Who would not wish to concern himself as much as possible with it?' (A. Krupp).[97] Werner Siemens said in 1861 that he had worked on the fate of his business 'day and night', and emphasized 'this consideration is the most important for me in my attitude to every question'. Like many other founders and owner-entrepreneurs of that time, he justified this permanent concern with the business in terms of the family, with which most of these entrepreneurs felt themselves to be deeply and strongly bound up. They thus won a long-term perspective which made it easier for them to renounce short-term advantages if it would help the long-term success of the business. 'It is my main concern ... to found a lasting firm, which perhaps one day under the leadership of the young ones could become a world firm like Rothschild etc., and bring our name to the notice of the world! The individual must be willing to accept personal sacrifices for this great plan, if he thinks it a good one!'[98]

But even when such justifications in family terms for a man's unswerving endeavours were not available, most entrepreneurs followed a policy of constant expansion which virtually forced itself on them. This will be considered again below.

Their experience of England as an economically more advanced country did not only act as a spur to achievement and success on the part of many German entrepreneurs; the stimulation and knowledge which early entrepreneurs gained through journeys abroad and through contacts with skilled foreigners were at the same time one of their qualifications. The Western European countries which had started to industrialize earlier influenced the latecomer Germany in many ways, as is well known. These influences were themselves part of the reason that the industrialization of Germany did not exactly follow the English model. They were manifold and were of course not limited to the eastward flow of knowledge and experience which was a mark of European industrialization in the eighteenth and nineteenth centuries. But nonetheless, the transmission of technical and business knowledge, of entrepreneurial stimuli and vision, was undoubtedly one of the most important ways in which the economically more advanced Western Europe influenced the industrialization of Central and, later, Eastern Europe.

For the German industrial revolution, the most important exporter of know-how was Great Britain, more important than France or Belgium; the significance of the USA was small, because of its distance, but it grew towards the end of the nineteenth century and in the twentieth, to become more important than that of Britain. English experience was particularly influential for German engineering, steel, and textile industrialists. France and Belgium played a large role for the early travelling craftsmen, and also for bankers, while experience from the USA affected primarily some later technicians, engineers, and organizational experts. Of the methods by which this knowledge was transmitted, the most important was the foreign journeys of the entrepreneur or would-be entrepreneur, his son, or a leading employee. This was more important than migrations of foreign entrepreneurs and technicians (such as Cockerill, Mulvany, Thomas, Dobbs, and others), the recruitment of foreign workers, or the distribution of written information. At that time of primarily empirical methods of passing on knowledge, personal impressions and direct observation were irreplaceable. Up to 1870, almost every third entrepreneur in the Rhineland and Westphalia had been on business or study visits abroad. Entrepreneurs in the raw-materials and chemical industries were over-represented among the 'travelling' industrialists.

The 'Grand Tour', which was common in the aristocracy, meant that many Silesian magnates became acquainted with English methods and tried to copy them at home. The long educational stay with foreign business friends and the frequent business trips abroad were long-standing practices of the larger merchant, and he took them with him into industry. The craft apprentice who travelled abroad did not merely confront the reactionary German governments with political problems; he also brought home with him more advanced technology and entrepreneurial motivation. Finally from the late eighteenth century onwards the conscious 'technological journeys' – the study and information visits of officials and industrialists to the English Eldorado of technical and industrial progress – increased in number and significance. Around 1800 such journeys were often used at the same time as opportunities to buy new machines and tools. In the pre-1848 period they were frequently subsidized by state financing and recommendations. Not infrequently, they also turned into missions of industrial espionage, against English law, which up to 1825 forbade the emigration of skilled workers, and up to 1842 also the export of machinery. Innumerable impulses to imitate, adapt, and improve technical innovations came out of such travels, and their value can scarcely be exaggerated. This was not only true for the older industries such as textiles, mining, and metalworking. The emerging German coal-tar dye industry was also based in the 1850s and 1860s on English and French methods. This imitation was made easier by the imperfections of German patent law.[99]

One consequence of the advance made by English technology was that some branches of German industry tried to jump over the initial improvements and start immediately at a more advanced level. This led, in the early period, to businesses which in their fascination with the English example quite overlooked the fact that the German market and infrastructure were not at all adapted to such advanced forms of production. There were failures from this fact alone.[100] On the other hand, the importing of fascinating know-how beyond the actual needs of the time led to early initiatives being taken. Even though technological expertise ran ahead of requirements, this led in turn to efforts to resolve the other constraints which had been revealed.[101] Thus what in the short term and for the individual firm might have been a commercially mistaken decision could lead in the long run to a positive impetus for growth.[102]

This emphasis on advanced production technology, rather than the immediate market solution, was more typical of the technician-entrepreneur than of the entrepreneur with a background in trade; but Friedrich Krupp, Friedrich Harkort, and some early textile industrialists are examples which show that the demand for pioneering innovations in production technology could also come from entrepreneurs with a business background.

This early emphasis on advances in production and the size of the enterprise was supported by the rapid development of the German technical schools and higher education. Among the founders of the industrial revolution an empirical education was dominant: with some, a limited elementary-school education, craftsman's apprenticeship, and a period of travelling; with others, frequently a medium-to-high-level school education and some kind of business training. A growing minority of industrialists had in addition some practical experience on the industrial shop floor; they had worked in one of the 'nursery firms' (e.g. Egells or Borsig) or – in the case of second-generation industrialists – at least partly in their fathers' concerns. Empirical business training – in spite of some old and new commercial and evening schools – remained for decades closely wedded to the traditional pattern, but business and technical schools and colleges developed, particularly in response to state initiatives after the 1820s, which supplemented the empirical and technical training in craft and factory methods with a more scientifically based education. These schools certainly educated many more qualified technical employees than independent entrepreneurs, and undoubtedly had much more influence in the last third of the century than in the second; but even in the industrial revolution they left their mark on the education of industrialists. This seems to have been primarily the case in the education of second-generation industrialists.

The sons of entrepreneurs were exposed within the family to the values and norms of behaviour of their parents. The education of children in the closely united entrepreneurial families in the Rhineland was strict and religious and was directed towards the inculcation of the business and middle-class virtues. Great emphasis was placed on the exact fulfilling of duties at home and at school. Only the children of the smallest factory-owners, those emerging from the craftsman's position, had to content themselves with an elementary-school education, immediately followed by their practical apprenticeship, which was normally in their fathers' firms. Most factory-owners' sons, at least in the Rhineland, were privately educated and then went to the higher grade of school until the age of fifteen or sixteen. Their fathers did not have much sympathy for the humanistic grammar-school education, preferring the natural sciences and modern languages. The sons frequently received a practical training with the emphasis on either business or technical matters, normally in their family concerns, but often in some other highly respected firm in the same line. Before entering their fathers' firms, the sons normally then worked for some years abroad as employees. Increasingly this traditional education of the sons of industrialists was supplemented with attendance at a technical school or college.[103]

The increase both in general and in business and technical education is shown in a sample of 400 entrepreneurs from the Rhineland and Westphalia from 1790 to 1870 (Table 138). Forty-four of the sixty-

Table 138. *Education of Entrepreneurs in the Rhineland and Westphalia*
(per cent)

	1790–1810	1811–30	1831–50	1851–70	1790–1870
General education					
Elementary	72·8	58·3	31·4	19·2	43·5
Higher	27·2	41·7	68·6	80·8	56·5
Specialist education					
Exclusively empirical–practical	96·3	95·8	67·5	47·7	74·0
Business or technical school	0·9	2·8	16·8	14·6	9·3
Higher (academic) study	2·8	1·4	15·7	37·7	16·7
Numbers	109	72	89	130	400

SOURCE. Beau, *Das Leistungswissen*, 66–8. The group surveyed includes some very small craftsman-like entrepreneurs.

seven entrepreneurs with a higher (academic) education belonged to the mining industries. This reflects the relatively higher social origins of these industrialists, and also the frequency with which the education of the mining academy, founded in the eighteenth century, was used not only by the higher state mining officials (for whom it was compulsory) but also by the leading directors of the private mining companies. The great majority of the leaders of mining enterprises were '*Bergassessoren*', even into the twentieth century. Another twelve of the sixty-seven academically trained industrialists belonged to the chemical industry, the complicated technology of which acted as a draw to scientifically qualified managerial potential, particularly from the 1860s onwards. The academically trained entrepreneur played as yet no role in the textile or metalworking industries.

The proportion of students from technical schools was about the same – around 10 per cent – over the whole period, in the metalworking, chemical, and textile industries; before 1830 it had been virtually nil. The relatively large, and only slowly declining, proportion of mere empiricists in textiles and metalworking – 88 per cent and 85 per cent, respectively, of all the entrepreneurs in these branches of industry had neither a technical-school nor a high-school education – indicates the low social status and also the predominantly small- and medium-scale character of the metalworking industry (then only partly mechanized) and the not very sophisticated production methods in the textile industry.

If the empiricists and those with different types of school experience are lumped together, out of the 400 entrepreneurs those with a 'technical' training (212) outweighed those with a 'business' background (188). The predominance of technicians was particularly evident in the basic industries and metalworking. Businessmen rather than technicians predominated in the textile industry, and also in the chemical; but in the latter, after 1850 (in contrast to the years before), technically trained men came to the top.

To sum up: apart from the mining industries, in which long years of the tradition of the state mining officials' education had created a special situation, and leaving out the new tendencies in the very small chemical industry after 1850, the proportion of entrepreneurs in the industrial revolution with a technical-school or technical-college education was very small (10–15 per cent); but it increased considerably after 1830. This was partly a result of changing technology linked to the development of technical schools and colleges, and partly a result of the absolute and relative increase in the number of heirs of enterprises who had been educated in this way. There was no increase in theoretical *business* education parallel to this improvement in theoretical *technical* education: business expertise was still acquired primarily in practical experience. General management skills or business administration were not taught in the developing technical schools. After 1830 (though not before), most entrepreneurs had in addition a general education which went beyond the elementary-school level. By the end of the industrial revolution a better general education for the average entrepreneur had become the rule. With public opinion increasingly conscious of the importance of education, this brought increased respect and higher status to the businessman. As the proportion of second-generation owners of industrial firms increased among entrepreneurs, so the percentage grew of those who had been deliberately trained for this vocation. No decline in motivation seems to have accompanied this change. In all, therefore, it seems that the industrialists of 1870 were better trained for their activities than those of the previous generation.

C. ENTREPRENEURIAL AND MANAGERIAL PERFORMANCE: PROBLEMS, SOLUTIONS, AND DEFICIENCIES

1. *Financing*

Did the performance of the industrialists within their firms and for the economy as a whole therefore improve? The present state of research does not allow a definitive answer to this question: we can only make tentative observations, concentrating on the problems which the industrialists considered most significant at the time.

In recent years most economic historians have turned away from the old theory that shortage of capital (in the sense of an absolute shortage of available savings) retarded the German economy, and that for this reason the process of early industrialization in Germany differed from that in England. This thesis has at least been modified: the availability of savings for state loans, railway works, and other non-manufacturing purposes seems to indicate that it was not savings *per se* which were lacking, but primarily that there was an insufficient propensity to convert existing savings into industrial capital. It is not easy to know how far this unwillingness on the part of owners of potentially investible funds was a reflection of a situation in which market opportunities and the chances of profit in the industrial sector were, in fact, so small and/or so uncertain that rational economic decision-making shrank from the risk of industrial investment, or whether the actually existing opportunities were simply not exploited because of an unfavourable distribution of savings (principally held by anti-industrial groups – above all by large estate-owners) and because of caution, prejudices, and other non-economic barriers. The problem is to know the relative weightings of these (and other) factors.[104]

It is clear that the shortage of available capital was the major barrier explaining the failure of many people who would have liked to establish enterprises in the first years of industrialization and who evidently believed they saw opportunities for such enterprises. It is clear from the correspondence of the Berlin Gewerbe-Institut with its former students that the hopes of technical students for founding enterprises usually failed because of the lack of a partner with capital.[105] It is also known that, even for existing firms at this time, procuring sufficient capital was often one of the most pressing and difficult problems of the entrepreneur. An inquiry into bankruptcies in the decade after 1870 found that shortage of capital was the cause of the collapse in 12 per cent of the cases and was thus third in a list of twenty causes of bankruptcies (after lack of ability on the part of the entrepreneur and over-extension of the enterprise).[106]

Difficulties over the supply of capital varied from one branch of industry to another: it was, for example, easier up to 1850 to get commercial capital for textile enterprises than for novel, risky engineering works. This was true in spite of the fact that the latter cost less and, as pioneering concerns in the 1840s, were able to make vast – if fluctuating – profits, which were certainly above the average profit of a normal, well-established textile enterprise and in any case above the interest rate on state loans.[107] On the other hand, other firms rapidly went bankrupt. There were big opportunities for profit, but the risk was at least equally big. The known cases seem to indicate that the entrepreneur trying to find capital was usually more ready to take risks than the potential lender (who did exist, at least in principle). Generalizing from the famous (usually successful) examples, one would tend with hindsight to attribute greater economic rationality to the entrepreneurs; but the conclusion would easily look quite different if one could include in the picture the unknown firms which failed.

There were undoubtedly various factors which made it extremely difficult, if not quite impossible, for a potential capital investor to assess clearly the opportunities and risks of an industrial project. The novelty of the possibilities, the lack of established rules, the regional variations, the individuality of each case, and the rapidly changing market situation all meant that if he was not deeply familiar with local conditions and the industry concerned, it was very hazardous to calculate the opportunities rationally and coolly. One thinks, for example, of the very experienced early railway-builders, who greatly underestimated the capital needs of their projects, although they tried to carry out systematic valuations and estimates with the help of assistants and technical staff.[108] The investment potentialities were difficult to judge in individual cases, even if the general position was clear; and because it was impossible to analyse all cases in objective terms, credit was given on the basis of trust in the borrower personally, a trust based partly on economic considerations but partly on quite non-economic factors.

In fact, in the first decades of the industrial revolution, financing was done almost entirely on a personal basis. In the first place, the personal savings of the founder were supplemented by those of his family and closest friends, who put their money at his disposal on the basis of family loyalty and personal trust – not usually on the basis of a know-ledge of the market and production methods. The close unity and the solidarity of the middle-class families of the time played an important and useful role in the early financing of industry.[109]

Subsidies and advances on credit from the state remained extremely rare after 1830, in spite of the fact that entrepreneurs seeking help repeatedly applied for them because of the apparent lack of alternative sources of capital. The large estate-owners, too, held back from indus-trial investments until the 1850s. Trading capital may have been the most important source: it too found its way into industry via personal connections, either when the merchant himself became an industrial entrepreneur, or when he entered one of the very numerous partner-ships with a craftsman or technician or as a sleeping partner with an industrialist who was known to him personally. Long-term bank credits also existed before 1850, although not to the extent that later became common. Some private bankers in Cologne, Leipzig, Dresden, Augsburg, and Berlin were involved early in promoting industrial growth; up to 1870 they were probably more important as links between savings and investments than the joint-stock banks which appeared after 1850. But those local bankers usually confined their business connections to a limited area over which they could keep a close scrutiny, and in addition they were spread very unevenly over the country. The personal trust between industrialist and banker was decisive here too. Contacts and control mechanisms for supervising business in a distant locality were not sufficiently developed to dispense with reliance on personal relationships.[110]

In this situation, deliberately invoking relationships in private life was one of the decisive ways in which the early entrepreneurs sought to solve the problem of lack of capital. First of all they could achieve a high degree of self-financing by reducing personal consumption. Second, they cultivated close relationships with their extended families, perhaps with the help of carefully arranged marriages. Third, they shaped their private life to give an impression of solidity and honesty, in keeping with their position, so as to gain and keep personal credit-worthiness. The virtuous private and family life of the Rhineland industrialists of the industrial revolution was a piece of rational business policy, at a time when the individual was not yet eclipsed by the collective unity of the firm.

The anonymous, large-scale mobilization of capital through joint-stock companies played a more important role in the German industrial revolution than in the English. The joint-stock company as an institution limited risks for an individual investor and thus overcame an important barrier to private investment activity. It facilitated the collection and investment of small contributions and thus made widespread savings available for industry. It loosened the close geographical and personal links between the distribution of savings and that of entrepreneurial opportunities. The joint-stock company also created a series of mechanisms which made the risks of investment more calculable for the private individual and thus more attractive. It was associated, to an increasing extent, with the presence of investment banks. These institutions attracted savings and placed investments in a well-informed, prudent way. The combination of the joint-stock company and the investment bank thus created a strong mechanism for encouraging savings, which would otherwise not have been attracted to industrial investment, towards industry in need of capital. Legal controls over companies, which had been diminishing before 1870 but which increased thereafter, also minimized risks for investors.

Even in the 1840s the joint-stock company was called for as an instrument for economic development by business-orientated and broadly based entrepreneurs (like Mevissen and Camphausen) to encourage capital mobilization in a country where the availability of capital was limited.[111] Nevertheless the joint-stock company succeeded in the industrial field only slowly before 1850. The backward state of company law, and particularly the concessionary system, allowed state officials to curb the growth of such corporations. The number of proposals for new companies submitted by private applicants was larger than the number of concessions granted by the authorities. The bureaucracy watched the enlargement of private property and power with distrust. The authorities feared also that investments rising too quickly in the industrial sector would harm the interests of the large landowners. The liberal economic spirit of the time, which affected the administration and parts of the general public, conceded to the joint-stock companies only a very marginal and exceptional role: it was prepared to accept them as monopolistic and exceptional arrangements in particular cases where free competition was unable to achieve its desired ends without such an institutional form of enterprise, but it was opposed to them under normal conditions. Many entrepreneurs who championed the personal responsibility of the entrepreneur with private capital and financial methods based on personal connections regarded these companies with their financing experts and their salaried staff with great reserve. Finally, the distrust of the public at large was a further restraining influence until the new instrument was used from the mid-1830s onwards to finance the massive capital needs of the railways; it thus established itself in public opinion, partly with the help of state interest guarantees.[112]

Nevertheless, at least 33 million talers (or about 15 per cent of all share capital invested up to that time) were invested in Prussian industrial corporations before 1850, of which over 28 million were in the twenty-one mining companies.[113] Joint-stock companies played a major role in coal-mining, whose capital needs were greatly increased by the move from drift mining to deep-level pits (from the 1830s), and in the smelting industry. In the fifth decade of the century, specialized smelting works needed 200,000–300,000 talers as initial capital, purely mining concerns 500,000–750,000 talers, and combined blast furnace and puddling works one million talers. This level of capitalization was beyond the financial resources of most individual families. The introduction of the joint-stock company in Ruhr mining was also facilitated by a long tradition of separating ownership from control: beginning as early as the 1770s, the Prussian state mines administration had taken over the functions of entrepreneur and manager. The private participants (*Gewerken*) were limited to the provision of capital (often with very small and dispersed contributions), receiving the profits that came from it, and electing representatives who enjoyed only limited powers against the state mines' administration. The actual entrepreneurial and managerial work was done not by the owners but by state officials. This structure continued after 1851, when the Prussian state started to withdraw from the direction of the mines, and private capital became the basis of entrepreneurial decisions in place of the authority of the state.[114]

Otherwise the corporate form of organization remained rare, and its details unsettled. The statutes of early joint-stock companies varied markedly from each other. Some of them laid down that only shareholders could run the administration; this of course hindered a clear separation between ownership and control. The capital market was not yet really anonymous: without the ability to sell on the stock market, the distribution of shares and thus the financing of joint-stock companies remained very closely linked to personal relationships; potential shareholders were very closely scrutinized to decide if they were acceptable as participants. Thus the company could in some cases call in the shares of a deceased investor, if it did not want his heirs as successors. Nor did all shareholders by any means get the same voting rights. Local capital predominated; it was normally distributed within a small, observable circle of people who knew each other (merchants, bankers, factory-owners, and also military men, officials, men of private means, and other citizens). A fixed dividend was frequently guaranteed, which reflected the transition from fixed-interest loans to shares, with their attendant equity risk. Some statutes limited the life of the newly formed joint-stock companies in advance, and anticipated using eventual profits to redeem shares at their face value by lot. Thus one external shareholder after another would gradually withdraw, until the original owning family was left; they had decided to change the organization of the firm into a joint-stock company only in order to overcome a capital shortage which, it was hoped, would be temporary. In such cases this form of organization was clearly meant to be a transitional expedient. The new corporate form was reached only gradually: the motivation for the quest was capital shortage, and every step was a small innovation.[115]

From 1850 to 1870 the share capital invested in Prussian industry increased to about 165 million talers. This continued to constitute only about 15–16 per cent of all the share capital invested in the Prussian economy, because the capital invested in the railways grew proportionally faster during the same period. The great leap for industrial share capital came in 1870–4. In these five years the capital invested in Prussian industrial corporations amounted to almost 343 million talers, or 28 per cent of the total share capital invested in this period. The investments in industrial corporations in these five years were more than double the total for all the years up to 1870.[116] Whereas in 1850–70 some 69 per cent of all share capital invested in industry was in the mining sector, 16 per cent in textiles, 8·5 per cent in the metalworking and engineering industries, 5 per cent in the foodstuffs industry, and 2 per cent in the chemical industry, the proportions for the same sectors in 1870–4 were 38 per cent, 6·5 per cent, 22·5 per cent, 16 per cent, and 4·5 per cent respectively.

It is clear from these figures that the strong over-representation of the mining sector in the establishment of industrial joint-stock companies began to decline only around 1870. The increase in share capital resulted to a large extent from the transformation of existing enterprises into joint-stock companies, which thus created possibilities for the desired expansion and the adoption of rapidly advancing technology. Through subsequent selling, the shares were separated from their original owners and thus became 'anonymous'. From the mid-1850s onwards, the Cologne and Berlin stock exchanges dealt in mining shares from Rhineland and Westphalian companies; it was also at this time that the newspapers began to carry quotations of mining shares. The general sale of industrial shares became normal only after about 1870. Prospectuses and public advertising for capital were common in the mining industry from the 1850s onwards. A relatively broad spread of capital ownership was achieved – as in the railways earlier – but state control was not always effective. Non-Prussian capital (partly from France and

Belgium) contributed, on average, up to one-third of the effective capital involved in establishing the mining companies of the Rhineland and Westphalia in the 1850s. A supra-regional and to some extent international capital market had appeared.

Between 1851 and 1865 the Prussian state withdraw from its entrepreneurial and managerial role in the Ruhr; the 'principle of [state] direction' (*Direktionsprinzip*) came to an end. This raised the problem of how far decentralized ownership of shares should imply decentralized control – an issue which was strongly disputed in some AGMs around 1860. But appearances are deceptive. It is necessary to distinguish between two 'inner circles' among the shareholders. The 'founders' of companies – who normally took over large portfolios of equity capital, sat on the board, and were involved in basic entrepreneurial decisions – have been examined in a sample of forty-two Prussian mining companies founded in the 1850s: 30 per cent came from trade, 15 per cent from the state civil service; 11 per cent were bankers, and 9 per cent large landowners; 6 per cent signed themselves as owners of mines and metalworks, 5 per cent as factory-owners, and 3 per cent as rentiers. This group also included many outsiders and pure capitalists who came to the board meetings but whose main interests lay elsewhere. Within this group there was a smaller 'inner circle' of local people, who clearly took over the control which the state gave up in the 1860s. The members of this inner group were large shareholders, but they rarely owned the majority of the shares. They accumulated seats on the board and concentrated fully on the direction of the various mining enterprises in which they had influence; they were expert in the field and knew each other. They were mostly members of old commercial and entrepreneurial families (Stinnes, Grillo, Servaes, Haniel, *et al.*), who had preserved, consolidated, and usually greatly strengthened their leading positions in these businesses under conditions of incorporated enterprise and through all the refoundations and movements for concentration. Former leading officials of the state administration were next in importance to them, in entrepreneurial functions and power. Apart from these two groups, from the 1850s local, and soon thereafter Berlin, bankers appeared for the first time, representing the new share-dealing banks. In contrast to the old private banks, they insisted more strongly on their right to a voice in entrepreneurial decision-making. In the crisis after 1857 capital became once again in short supply, and these bankers increased their influence, especially the Berlin Disconto-Gesellschaft. The high point of their power came in the period of merger, regrouping and promotional activity of the early 1870s. Because of the extremely large capital requirements and the particular traditions of state capitalism, the corporate system of the following decades was already shaped in its essentials in the Ruhr area by the end of the first phase of industrialization.[117]

As we have seen, the share system also developed in other industries in the boom years around 1870. The great increase in the share of the metalworking industry (including engineering) and that of the food-stuffs industry in the total industrial share capital is particularly striking. This was to a large extent a result of the refounding of existing firms as companies, not new foundations, which often took place for speculative purposes. The far-reaching liberalization of company law governing share issues and the lifting of the state concessionary system abolished the remaining legal barriers; this facilitated a wave of company flota-tions and re-flotations which ended only with the crisis of 1873. For the directors of the large companies the capital-shortage problem was put in a new form: it was no longer solvable on a personal basis. But it must not be forgotten that the great majority of entrepreneurs – in some branches of trade, almost all – were not immediately affected by these changes. For them the problem of capital continued in its old form and was for a long time still solved on a personal basis in terms of thrift, family help, personal credit, and self-financing.

2. Accounting and Bookkeeping

Closely connected with the problem of the supply of capital was the problem of orderly accounting and bookkeeping. Werner Sombart regarded double-entry bookkeeping as the centrepiece of every capital-ist enterprise. 'When someone is deeply involved in double-entry bookkeeping, he forgets the quality of goods and services; he forgets all the organic limitations inherent in the principle of the satisfaction of needs (*Bedarfsdeckungsprinzip*); he is exclusively impressed by the single idea of profit; he can do nothing else if he wants to find his way about this system: he must see not boots or cargoes, flour or cotton, but only monetary values which increase or diminish.'[118] It may well be that Sombart overstated this case. Single-entry bookkeeping seems to have served some nineteenth-century industrial entrepreneurs rather well.[119] But at any rate the problem of bookkeeping and accounting caused perennial difficulties for many entrepreneurs throughout the nineteenth century, especially for smaller businessmen.

While the methods of double-entry bookkeeping had been developed in the late middle ages, and in principle were available to industrialists, they needed important modifications for their successful application to the capitalist factory for which there was no precedent. On the one hand, they had to be so modified that they could take into account the great quantities of fixed capital, which had not played a large role in the trader's business; the technique of depreciation provided the main answer to this problem. But on the other hand, double-entry book-keeping had to be extended and modified so that it allowed control to be maintained not only over the success of the whole enterprise but also – at least in large-scale concerns – over the success of individual production and trading processes, or at least of individual departments, so as to be able to identify and eliminate the areas of poor performance.

Industrial bookkeeping and accounting was developed in the first half of the nineteenth century on a trial-and-error basis, in the expanding factories, by men who are now forgotten. It is known that factory entrepreneurs, in contrast to artisans, were considered by the law to be traders and were therefore obliged from the eighteenth century onwards to keep 'trading books' in 'a commercial way'; and they had to meet certain legally specified requirements. For the 'open trading companies' (offene Handelsgesellschaften) – the usual legal form of the partnerships which predominated at the time – there was the additional duty of submitting annual inventories and profit-and-loss accounts.[120]

It is also established that accountancy was one of the most difficult barriers, especially for early entrepreneurs from an artisan background. It is reported in many such firms that bookkeepers, appointed a few years after the firm was founded, unearthed massive chaos, because the industrialist had long since lost all overall view and control. In other cases creditors who were asked to help out an entrepreneur with a craft or technical background who had got into difficulties insisted on a change in the accountancy methods, and often on the appointment of a qualified business director, before they would involve themselves financially. It is true that in the inquiry into 400 enterprises in the Rhineland and Westphalia during 1790–1870 which we have already mentioned, more than half were partnerships in which a technically skilled person and a businessman worked together, and only in seventy-eight cases did a technically skilled person control the concern alone. But in many cases only one of the persons actively directed the concern, while the other was a 'sleeping partner' and attended to other businesses. Even after 1870, lack of knowledge of accountancy was the most common failing in those bankruptcy cases which could be traced back to inadequacies in the firm's management. Frequently, for example, debits were entered on the balance-sheet not at the time of incurring the debts but only when they were called in; or outstanding debts were overvalued, or depreciation neglected. The result was an illusory estimate of success. In an investigation into the reasons for the collapse of enterprises after 1870, twenty-eight cases (17 per cent) were a result of the 'inability' of its entrepreneurs: in all twenty-eight cases they were entrepreneurs who had a technical or some other qualification but not a business one.[121] Even when there was a director versed in business methods or when a technician–entrepreneur had appointed a book-keeper, and there was a reasonably efficient accountancy system (normally on the basis of inventories), there were often no depreciation allowances or methods of apportioning overhead expenses more pre-cisely to particular branches of production and departments.[122] As late as 1878, an author with experience in the engineering industry wrote: 'Most factories do not have an exact reckoning of their individual products, because this seems too difficult in view of the multiplicity of the articles they produce, and they shy away from the cost of a some-what larger accounting staff.'[123] Practices varied considerably from one firm to another at the beginning. Manuals for factory bookkeeping existed at least from 1850, and appeared in increasing numbers from the 1860s onwards.[124] Accounting was made more effective at the latest when private companies or individual firms were turned into joint-stock companies, and shareholders or banks took controlling interests.

The more complex technology became, the more it became decisive for an entrepreneur with purely commercial experience to find a good technical director or foreman to whom he could leave the solution of technical problems. Complaints about the technical deficiencies of entrepreneurs with a business background were far rarer than com-plaints about the lack of business qualifications of technician–entre-preneurs, but they did exist. The businessman without technical qualifications could easily become dependent on his foreman. In the early years and in less capital-intensive industries – for example the Bremen docks – foremen drew the obvious conclusion, threw off their dependence on businessmen, and set up independently. The greater the necessary capital and the more important distribution and finance prob-lems became, the less likely was such an emancipation of the foreman/ technician from dependence on the businessman partner. The tendency to co-operative, functionalized management increased in the second half of the century, a fact which complicated managerial as well as tech-nical tasks in some degree, as operations expanded. In general and in the long term, the influence and power of the businessman relative to the technical expert seem to have increased in directorates which were in-creasingly organized along functional lines (as in the mining, engineer-ing, and electrical industries). But vast differences continued to exist from sector to sector and from firm to firm.[125]

3. Problems of Labour Relations

The impression given by the sources is that the problems of assembling a work force were more easily solved and less worrying for most entrepreneurs than were the problems of the shortage of capital.[126] Compared with the eighteenth and early nineteenth centuries, the efficiency of the labour market improved notably during the industrial revolution. The shortage of *qualified* workers for enterprises in fast-growing branches with advanced production technology (such as tool manufacture, engineering, or optical instruments) certainly created problems, especially in times of boom. It was also often not easy for the larger firms to find senior salaried staff who were qualified and loyal, honest, and sufficiently motivated.

In contrast to the craft workshop and the putting-out system, the factory necessitated the co-ordination, effective deployment, and disciplining of a large number of workers on a centralized basis. Much more than in manufactories, the factory entrepreneur had to ensure that the processes were carried out to a central plan, that they were adapted to the machine system, that they were done to a common rhythm and harmonized with each other. New forms of organization and systems of co-ordination, new relationships of subordination and co-operation, new incentives for motivation, and new controls had to be adopted. The problems of managing workers became even more acute in conflict. Passive resistance against factory discipline and exploitation was widespread among the first generation of factory workers. Those who came from a craft background frequently saw factory work as degrading, although it paid better. Those who came from a rural background – the majority – regarded the new factory system with its discipline and controls, its new rhythms of time and its splitting-up of work processes, as unnatural and coercive. The long hours and low wages meant harsh exploitation, and they were frequently felt as such. The widespread practice of many entrepreneurs of transferring their risk as far as possible to the workers and reacting to the strong and frequent market fluctuations with short-term mass sackings certainly did not arouse among the people concerned any affection for the factory system. Open protests, sometimes organized by social democrats, became frequent enough in the 1860s and 70s to create a special problem for the managers. But the older, more passive internal opposition also had dysfunctional consequences for the work processes: it reduced work satisfaction and, as at least some industrialists recognized, thus limited efficiency.

What methods did entrepreneurs use in the industrial revolution when faced with these problems? Direct instructions and orders on the basis of entrepreneurial authority stemming from ownership were the most usual. In the early factories, open harshness was common, with threats and the implementation of sanctions (corporal punishment, fines, sacking) in order to enforce obedience, if not loyalty. This was indicative of the lack of more effective, skilful techniques of control, and of the intensity of conflict within the plant. When it became impossible, in growing firms, to have direct instructions and controls on a person-to-person basis, and when at the same time in some firms production, sales, and bookkeeping demanded greater exactitude, the entrepreneurs began to issue detailed – often written – factory and works rules for the workshops, and rules of service for the office staff.[127] These frequently covered the behaviour of employees out of hours as well; chiefly, they regulated (with increasing exactitude) the duties of the employees whilst neglecting their rights. By bringing a bureaucratic impulse – though one varying greatly in strength – into the firm's organization and authority relationships, such written regulations could, in principle, serve to limit arbitrary use of personal power on the part of the foreman and workshop director; they spoke of positions and functions rather than of persons and thus strengthened the tendency to formalized organization. These methods of worker control were implicitly and explicitly based on old models from the civil service and the military. Ex-officials and former military men were common in the emerging industrial administrations. They brought with them the methods and structures, the spirit and even the language of the bureaucracy into the growing factories. 'Exactly specified organization, personal responsibility, and the strictest control must be implemented . . . I only want to have a deliberate order and organization, no charging blindly into the work, so that an expedient is only thought of when it is too late. Everyone should know what he has to do, and to whom he is responsible.'[128] A simple imitation of bureaucratic methods was, however, impossible: most works were too small, their operations too varying and unstable, their organization too bound up with personalities, and their orientation to profits and markets too strong. Other methods of personnel management went alongside the bureaucratic ones.

Material incentives, in the form of payment by results and profit-sharing, served to motivate the labour force. Piece-rate payment increased from the 1840s onwards. Profit-sharing was instituted by entrepreneurs in various forms, above all to salaried staff at decision-making level. This managerial device showed itself to be particularly useful when direct controls were difficult. 'I have always found it to be the greatest extravagance not to let those who are involved in the direction of businesses share in the result . . . In large and ramified businesses which one cannot personally supervise, one must allow an important part of the profits to one's deputies; that is one of the basic rules for the good running of large businesses.'[129]

Bureaucratic and financial methods of direction and control were supplemented by paternalistic ones. Here too, pre-industrial examples provided guidelines, this time from the handicraft and agrarian–feudal contexts. In smaller firms the entrepreneur himself cultivated personal contact with the workers; if they fell ill, he granted them support (even though limited), which he was not contractually obliged to do. Other employers gave Christmas presents and premiums to old employees. In some cases factory-owners built houses and even whole factory villages for their work force; many employers founded and financed accident and pension funds. Such measures aimed at a relationship between employer and employee which went beyond the purely contractual. Through such extra voluntary benefits the employer offered some limited care for the worker as a whole person, and he expected in return more than the performance fixed in the employment contract: he expected fidelity, loyalty, and identification with the firm. At the greatest extreme – as with Alfred Krupp and the Saarland mining industrialist Freiherr von Stumm – the paternal industrialist laid claim to a charitable control of the worker in every aspect of his personality, in both his work and his private life, to the extent of imposing a ban on the reading of particular newspapers and requiring the firm's permission to marry.

To some extent such paternalistic methods grew directly out of the pre-industrial period, particularly in small works with a craft tradition, in aristocratic large-scale enterprises with agrarian–feudal traditions, and in rural industry in general. This 'natural', unplanned paternalism seems to have declined with advanced industrialization. It contradicted the profit- and market-orientated principles of laissez-faire liberalism which won ground in the 1850s and 60s – though with many exceptions. It had only a limited place in the profit-orientated calculations of employers, according to which – as long as there was an adequate demand – there should be flexible reactions to changing order-book situations, and production should be at the lowest possible cost. But it never completely disappeared. Firms which needed highly qualified workers made particular use of paternalistic methods in the 1840s, 50s, and 60s in order to bind their employees to the concern and give them extra motivation. With some employers there were also ethical, religious, and social reforming motives. Others looked to educational measures which would raise the efficiency of the workers and turn them into good citizens. From the 1860s, large employers who enjoyed a relatively steady growth and who could afford it used paternalistic methods as a 'weapon in the struggle for the souls of the workers', as an instrument in the struggle against increasingly strong organized protests, against unions and social democracy.

These three methods of labour management combined in forms which varied very considerably from firm to firm, from sector to sector, from district to district, and from decade to decade. They were adequate for the recruitment, disposition, and disciplining of a work force which was also influenced through school, military service, state social policy, and state sanctions in a way which encouraged their efficiency at work and their subordination. But such methods did not suffice to prevent the appearance of a radical, hostile proletarian class consciousness and an ever-growing labour movement.[130]

4. Problems of Organization and Management

Most enterprises in the industrial revolution were small or medium-sized units which limited their business to one branch of activity (e.g. yarn and cloth production, engineering and tool production, or paper production) and were normally managed by individuals or partnerships where the functions of capitalist and entrepreneur were combined. In these concerns a style of management was dominant which was strongly modelled on the leading personality of the time and was stamped by this individual. There was no literature on the correct methods of directing and organizing industrial concerns during the industrial revolution; this first appeared after the 1870s.[131] Apart from informal exchanges of experiences between employers, and what the later employer learnt during his apprenticeship in other factories, each employer solved problems in his own way as they arose. Secretiveness was widespread, and not only with respect to technical inventions; employers were not exactly pleased to see their organizational innovations displayed to competitors, either. The individual features of these firms were strongly marked. With greater justification than in later decades, most factory-owners regarded the firm as purely their own achievement, subject to their direct control (enforceable at any time), and tightly bound up with their person and family. They considered a business as their 'empire', not as a formal organization whose identity and continuing functioning was secured, despite changes in the leading personnel. The direct contact maintained between the head of a firm and his employees, coupled with the fact that firms could be easily supervised, frequently made it possible to dispense with strict, consciously planned hierarchies allocating competence and functions. Carefully articulated control mechanisms and systematically organized information flows were rare. The directors of such enterprises worked through their regular presence and participation, through frequent interventions and encouragement, through direct orders and control. It is significant that the first book which gave a 'System of Rules for the Successful Running of Businesses' from a practical and scholarly viewpoint, in 1868, insisted: 'The best instruction is the oral one which the ever-present, ubiquitous, and all-seeing employer delivers personally, and which constantly offers an example to the employees.'[132] As in the earlier manufactories, the success of the concern was very much dependent on the work of the individual persons at the top.

Three tendencies explain the fact that this informal, individualistic system of management comprising the capitalist–entrepreneur–manager did not remain adequate in some enterprises and had to be supplemented by new management devices. Such tendencies emerged as early as the industrial revolution.

In the first place, a threshold seems to have been reached when the number of employees in a firm reached one or two hundred, after which these personal and direct methods of management were no longer adequate. Overall control and internal communications were endangered if new methods were not introduced. This problem was particularly pressing when the growth of the concern was combined with geographical decentralization. The creation of branches in other towns and abroad was not uncommon. The combination of growth with decentralization was clearest in the railways. Running the railways made the greatest demands on administration in terms of precision and continuity.

Secondly, even during the industrial revolution enterprises were combining and integrating the functions of production and distribution. German merchants who were interested in extractive and manufacturing industries did not normally restrict themselves to financing them and exercising indirect influence: they tended to become industrial entrepreneurs themselves. Industrial enterprises tried to do their own marketing rather than working through independent merchants. There were many exceptions, of course, especially in textiles and in all those branches which were dominated by small- and medium-sized firms (such as paper-manufacturing). But in general this tendency to functional integration was earlier and stronger in Germany than in England. It is not easy to explain this difference adequately, and more research needs to be done. The entrepreneurs of the time do not seem to have spoken much about such functional integration; it was self-evident, obvious, and necessary as far as they were concerned. Probably the trend was connected with the relative backwardness of German industry and its consequent relatively rapid development. Industry in Germany had less continuity with the pre-industrial structures than in England. In

the industries most important for German development (engineering
and the extractive industries), the early industrialists frequently had no
established, developed trading structure to utilize. In addition, the producers therefore took over the marketing, when it was a matter of
selling technically complicated products and the necessary specialists
could only be provided by the manufacturers themselves. Frequently,
early factory-owners seem also to have had a deep distrust of the independent distributor: a frequent motive of the manufacturer seems to
have been to make himself 'independent' of these people. It may be
that in Germany, with its limited commercial and economic bourgeois
traditions, a fundamental trust in the fair behaviour of the other in the
market – which is a precondition for an interdependent market relationship with functional specialization of individuals and institutions – was
insufficiently developed. To bring together as many functions as possible, from the provision of raw materials to final sales, was thus both an
expansive and a defensive wish.[133]

As a consequence of this early tendency to functional integration, the
need for different qualifications in the leadership of firms was put in a
particularly sharp form. Many early industrialists tried to direct production and distribution in detail themselves, with the help of only a
few 'officials' or salaried staff. This proved impossible in large enterprises, with the increasing complexity of the entrepreneur's functions.
Specialists were needed for the individual tasks, and specialized departments quickly appeared. Construction departments, for example, were
established in medium-sized engineering factories at the end of the
1850s. The departments employed engineers and were clearly differentiated from the shop floor and from management. The distribution
organization at the same time rose in importance, as mass production
for the market (and for stock) became increasingly important alongside
production to order. Separate technical marketing offices appeared, and
at the same time departmentalization of the shop floor developed and
called for new special co-ordination.[134] Such enterprises necessitated
departmental management with different functions, and thus new
methods of overall co-ordination.

Quite similar management problems were, finally, posed by the
tendency of some early entrepreneurs to bring a considerable number
of plants into their hands and to extend their business into several
different branches of production. This tendency was also apparent in
various forms in the first decades of industrialization, and this can also
frequently be explained as another consequence of the relative backwardness of German development. Among early engineering industrialists, for example, there was a rule of producing as many things as
possible, because the market was not developed sufficiently to allow a

narrow specialized enterprise to survive.[135] This motive undoubtedly receded with more advanced development, and in fact the trend towards specialization in the 1850s and 60s included the engineering industry. Similarly, most of the textile manufacturers, who had established their own machine workshops in the first decades of industrialization in order to meet their own needs, disposed of them as an adequate independent textile-machine industry developed. But nevertheless, examples of diversified production were tried out early in Germany, and to some extent they survived beyond the conditions which brought about their appearance.

Vertical integration appeared early – above all in the mining industry. Even in the 1820s and 30s the Gutehoffnungshütte in Oberhausen had developed into a multi-process enterprise, embracing different 'stages' from iron-ore production to heavy engineering, and its own distribution network. In addition it soon produced its own coal and developed the chemical by-products. This early diversification occurred primarily by means of establishing new plants, but firms already in existence were also taken over, incorporated, and developed. Again it was the relatively underdeveloped situation which forced the founders of firms to adopt these expedients, particularly in the early phases: badly developed transport facilities, the limited extent of the market, and uncertain, fickle trends in demand made it wise to diversify one's output. This was particularly true for the early pioneering entrepreneurs, who founded their firms on 'green field' sites, using a technology or a scale which ran beyond the limits of existing demand; capacity was thus installed which could only be utilized through a marked diversification. There was also, once again, the ultimately defensive motive of striving for 'independence'. Admittedly, only a minority of mining companies diversified in this consistent way before 1870, and in other branches – such as the textile industry – this trend did not exist at all.[136]

The growth of firms and their regional decentralization, their complexity and division of labour (which were encouraged by their functional integration), and their tendency to diversification all presented, in a minority of concerns, management problems which the normal single-unit enterprise did not experience. The problem was how to secure the necessary co-ordination, information, and effective power in an organization which was no longer controllable by one man and which had introduced specialization or decentralized management methods. Those concerned were aware of the problem. Many saw clearly that one person, however able, could not alone integrate the most diverse functions of an expanding large-scale enterprise, the different plants of a diversified concern, or the various parts of a conglomerate with several different branches. But the alternative solutions were not at all clear. In 1862 a tariff-union commission (*Zollverein*) reported that managerial difficulties were restricting the further expansion of large enterprises.[137] 'I have my hands more than full with projects . . . and am beginning to see that it is necessary to restrict oneself to a limited number, if any of them are to be quickly implemented', wrote the entrepreneur Mevissen, who had many interests, in 1845 – although he continued to find such restraint difficult.[138] With the 'railway king' Bethel Henry Strousberg (1823–84) we see clearly the difficulties of holding together a large diversified group of enterprises by individual personal management methods. This merchant, insurance agent, and journalist settled in Berlin in 1855 after a long stay in England. In the 1860s and early 70s he became the biggest, richest, and most spectacular German railway-builder. He not only developed new methods of financing and founding lines but also remained in control of some of those that he built. In addition he bought and founded several industrial enterprises in mining, smelting, and heavy machinery, for supplying goods necessary for railway-building. In order to make himself 'independent' of suppliers, Strousberg tried to create a highly diversified concern. He founded or bought up the different constituents of the whole but did not understand how to integrate them. He failed to build up a controlling organization. Without this he lost the overall view, remained limited to intuitive, spontaneous decisions, and lacked the necessary co-ordination. Partly for this reason, he went bankrupt in the depression of the early 1870s, wrote his autobiography in a Russian debtors' jail, and died in poverty.[139]

In general there were, at this period, two strategies for the solution of the management problems which arose with the growth and rising complexity of business: the family-based and the bureaucratic strategies.[140] As in Great Britain fifty years earlier, or in the developing countries today, it was difficult for German factory-owners around 1850 to find qualified and reliable officials and office staff to perform those tasks which the entrepreneur could not closely control himself. Under the constant threat of fraud, employers found loyalty and honesty even more important criteria in the selection of staff than training and ability. As far as possible, employers of the time put relatives and close friends into those positions which carried decision-making power and which were hard to control. Thus personal loyalty performed functions which were later fulfilled by direct and even bureaucratic controls, financial incentives, and professional ethics. Often the senior salaried employee of a company was the brother or cousin of the founder, and the first general manager his closest friend from school or military service. When diversification of production created new management problems, an entrepreneur usually responded by establishing an independent company for the production of the new article and putting a trusted (and not completely incompetent) cousin or son in charge of it. Thus family loyalty provided the control – albeit informal – necessary for the successful decentralization of responsibility and authority. The co-ordination of the international electrical manufacturing company and distributor Siemens & Halske provides another example of the practical use of family connections. The co-ordination of the three main Siemens branches in Germany, Russia, and Great Britain was primarily achieved by private correspondence and family trust among the three Siemens brothers. Werner (Berlin), Carl (St Petersburg), and William (London) each headed one of the branches without detailed interference from the other two. At a time when communications were difficult, the loyalty of the brothers provided a kind of co-ordination at the international level which probably could not have been achieved by any other means. The importance of these family ties is indicated by the disruption and conflicts which emerged when a brother left his branch or lost his influence for other reasons. The 'nepotism' of early industrialists not only was a function of their strong family feeling but also facilitated the growth and success of the enterprise. Of course, such personal methods of co-ordination achieved only a loose connection between the various parts of the concern. Much autonomy was left to subdivisions, whether organized on functional or geographical lines. But as long as this level of co-ordination was sufficient, family loyalty was the outstanding tool – both inexpensive and manageable – for achieving it. The closely knit family structures from which the early entrepreneurs came were much more an asset than a liability for the growth of the company and hence of the economy in the early stages of industrialization, both in respect of capital formation (discussed above) and in respect of the beginnings of large-scale management.[141]

An alternative strategy was the adaptation of bureaucratic models of organization (as they had been developed in public administration) to the needs of growing private companies. In some medium-sized and large German companies the division of labour and the patterns of hierarchy were elaborated in detail and written down. The delineations of responsibility, the channels of information, and the stress on specialized, interrelated knowledge were remarkable, though limited by the small size and rapid changes of the companies, by the market orientation of their activities, and by the unique character of many operations, which defied general orders and prescribed rules. Within such limits, bureaucratic models from outside the companies facilitated the development of early devices for systematic management, especially in companies where entrepreneurial and managerial functions had already been assigned to different groups of persons.

The best example is presented by the railways. Here the need for systematic management was strong, and large-scale decentralized business in corporate form was the rule. The question of how many former state officials, technically trained and experienced in managerial affairs, entered these new and attractive positions needs further investigation. The regulations they produced and the organizations they built closely resembled the structure and procedures of the public bureaucracy, long before the government took over the railways around 1880.[142]

The impact of bureaucracy on early German industrial organization certainly varied considerably from sector to sector and from company to company. Bureaucratic techniques were closely intermingled with and balanced by non-bureaucratic methods such as financial incentives and family co-operation. Sometimes they may have produced rigidities and inflexibility. But on the whole, the bureaucratic impact was beneficial in developing early large-scale management, thus facilitating the growth of companies and of the economy. It is in this context that one must understand the remark of Werner Siemens, who knew both German and English entrepreneurship from close observation and experience: 'The superiority of Prussian enterprises over English lies in good organization; this outweighs many major advantages of the English.'[143]

IV. The Rise of Big Business and Organized Capitalism

The depression of the 1870s marked the end of the boom of the *Gründerjahre*. Cyclical downswings were particularly long and deep in the 1870s and 90s. A long period of steady and rapid expansion started again in the mid-1890s and lasted, with short breaks in 1900–2 and 1907–9, until the First World War. Between 1873 and 1913 German GNP tripled. The secondary sector contributed disproportionately to this expansion. While in 1873 about one-third of the national wealth came from industry, crafts, and mining, by 1913 these sectors produced almost one-half. In the same period the proportion of all those employed in industry and crafts rose from about 30 per cent to about 38 per cent of the labour force – a clear indication of the disproportionately growing productivity of the secondary sector. The rate of growth of industrial production (not including mining) during 1870–1913 was 3·7 per cent. Industries which grew faster than average included gas, water, and electricity supply, paper, chemicals, metal-producing and -working (including the engineering and electro-technical industries), and quarrying; the consumer-goods industries grew less than the producer-goods industries, but in the decade before the First World War the rates of growth of both groups of industries became more similar. Mining, with yearly growth rates of 4·3 per cent (hard coal), 5·8 per cent (brown coal), and 5·0 per cent (iron ore), also expanded faster than average.[144]

In these four decades the latecomer Germany finally overcame her relative economic backwardness; she overtook in economic size and modernity all other continental states, and in some important respects (such as pig-iron and steel production, chemical and electrochemical production, maturity of industrial organization and partly even technology) she passed even Great Britain. This expansion of German industry, which induced great self-confidence and optimism, was accompanied by structural changes, which were strongly affected by entrepreneurial decisions and were, on the other hand, of great significance for the development of entrepreneurship and management. The main trends included the growth of large-scale business through internal expansion and mergers; the increasing separation of ownership and control; the diversification of large concerns through internal expansion or by mergers; the cartelization of German industry, and the rise of shareholding banks. The increasing complexity of large concerns occasioned by the rise of science in production, distribution, and management also influenced these central structural changes.[145]

A. EXPANSION AND DIVERSIFICATION

The trend towards big business continued strongly in these decades. Whereas in 1882, of 1,000 persons employed in industry and crafts, only 263 worked in plants with more than fifty employees, in 1907 the number was 455. In 1882, 7·2 per cent of all employees in industry and crafts worked in plants with over 1,000 employees; but by 1907 the proportion was 13·7 per cent. The mining industry, the engineering (including electrical engineering) industry, the chemical industry, and the textile industry (which was also adopting a big-business character in these decades) were leading this trend towards concentration. In each of these branches more than two-thirds of all employees worked in plants with over fifty people. The least concentrated were the clothing, food-stuffs, wood, and leather industries.[146]

These figures give only an indication of the increasing concentration of 'plants' (Betriebe), i.e. local units of production, rather than firms, which are units of ownership and administration. Several plants frequently belonged to one enterprise, which was decentralized in terms of physical plant but centrally owned and administered. The process of concentration among firms undoubtedly took place even faster, but there are no representative figures for this. An indication is offered by one comparison: when in 1893 the Coal Syndicate of the Rhineland and Westphalia was established, ninety-eight mines joined it, with an average quota of 342,650 tons each; by 1915 a group which in 1893 had not joined the syndicate, the so-called 'foundry mines' belonging to mixed concerns, had become members, but nonetheless the syndicate had only fifty-seven members, and an average quota which had risen to 1·6 million tons.[147]

The expansion of firms undoubtedly reflected in most cases the specific objectives of their directors, who wanted to expand and worked for expansion. But it is sometimes more difficult to understand their underlying motives, especially in the case of the salaried entrepreneurs of the large expanding concerns around 1900. Undoubtedly they did not have profit as their overriding goal – not even profit as a means of satisfying their personal needs, which were already adequately supplied. Rather, they strove for profits to finance expansion, as a symbol of success, which in their minds and in the view of their peers was measured mainly in terms of turnover and profits. They strove for expansion as a means to mark the extension of their power, for the pleasure they took in the size of their enterprises, for the enjoyment of power, and in the knowledge that they could thus make a name for themselves. Walther Rathenau, the second-in-command of the AEG, described this justification of the expansion motive for its own sake with particular insight:

In so far as large private owners still exist, they have long accustomed themselves to regard their corporate business as an independent entity. This entity does its own accounting, works, grows, makes agreements and alliances, multiplies from its own resources, lives as an aim in itself. The fact that it feeds its founder is, if not a side effect, at least not usually the main thing; an able businessman will tend to limit his own and his family's consumption more than is really necessary in order to provide the firm with greater means to strengthen itself and expand. The growth and the power of these creations is the reward of the founder; much more so than the profits. The desire to enjoy possession weakens ambition and the urge to achieve. It is these modes of thought which we find in the leaders of great companies.[148]

Such a future-oriented entrepreneurial policy, which could forgo short-term gains in favour of long-term success, was clearly different from the efforts of a speculative entrepreneur, to whom the enterprise as such was unimportant so long as he got a reasonable rate of return on his capital; but it did not differ very greatly, with its orientation to the future, from the policy of the classic family entrepreneur, who, even in earlier decades, had been ready to accept short-term disadvantages for the sake of continuity and security.[149] But while this at least gave a certain justification to entrepreneurial success in non-economic terms – e.g. in familial terms – the industrial leaders to whom Rathenau referred were in danger of striving for expansion for the sake of expansion, success for the sake of success. Probably many of them would have difficulty in justifying their drive for expansion and economic success – which after all included struggle, sacrifice, and dominance.

This striving for expansion for its own sake was more typical of the increasing numbers of salaried entrepreneurs without a stake in their own equity than of the heads of the medium-sized or large family concerns. In order to preserve control and independence in their concerns, these latter entrepreneurs tended frequently to limit expansion or at least not to realize all the growth that would have been possible if every market opportunity was fully exploited and if all outside financial sources were utilized. Nevertheless, it frequently happened that industrialists with this philosophy saw themselves forced to expand if they were not to run the risk of decline. This is illustrated by the example of the Siemens family enterprise.[150] At the beginning of the 1880s Werner Siemens tried to prevent the diversification of his firm (founded in 1847) into the new area of high-voltage current; he wanted to preserve his business for his sons at a size that could be controlled by one man, and to avoid the use of outside capital in order to remain the independent master of his own empire. This reluctance gave the salaried entrepreneur Emil Rathenau the chance to build up the AEG. After a few years this reluctance to expand also threatened other market opportunities for the Siemens concern, and they hurried to make up for the missed opportunities. In 1897 the firm was changed into a joint-stock company under pressure from the banks, but the family was able to preserve a majority of the shares and most of its influence. Siemens & Halske was now a family concern in corporate form. In the waves of mergers at the beginning of this century, this process was repeated twice more. The leadership of the Siemens enterprise sought cartel-like agreements, with the aim of subduing competition and securing prices, but they had little interest in mergers involving large increases of share capital, since these could easily have affected the dominance of the family. But faced with the aggressiveness of Rathenau's AEG, which aimed at expansion through acquisition and was not held back by dynastic family interests, Siemens & Halske soon found themselves compelled to seek the acquisition or control of other companies as well. Otherwise their powerful competitor AEG would have done this, which would have cost Siemens vital bank support: and in the long run the firm would have been threatened with the danger of finally being itself dominated and ultimately swallowed by the AEG. For the conservative firm of Siemens, therefore, expansion was necessary as a means of defence. They were aggressive because they felt themselves – with justification – to be threatened. It shows something of the straitjacket imposed by the market situation – and the secondary significance of the personal motives of industrialists in developed industrial capitalism – that two companies with such varying traditions, motives, and connections arrived at such similar expansionist policies.

But such near-inevitability, which – to put it in rather extreme terms – operated independently of the actors and their non-economic motives, could occur only under particular preconditions. One of these was high capital-intensity in the enterprises concerned, which prevented a move into small, alternative markets with less competition, and which compelled them on pain of bankruptcy to strive for continuous full utilization of capacity; another was the lack of major advantages in production or marketing (such as production secrets or strong patents) in one of the firms concerned; and finally there was the existence of sufficiently strong – or sufficiently numerous – aggressive competitors, who did not share this non-economic reluctance to attempt limitless expansion.[151] In sectors dominated by a large number of highly specialized, labour-intensive family concerns, a policy of 'measured growth' in the interests of preserving a controllable family empire was quite realizable in Germany.[152] In the capital-intensive sectors like mining, iron and steel, electro-engineering, and chemicals, where corporate ownership and control were often separated from each other and where the more aggressive salaried staff were dominant, the drive to expand was more influential than any such private considerations, which sometimes – though by no means always – tended towards a slower rate of growth.[153]

In the final analysis, this drive to expansion displays a basic characteristic of industrial concerns in a competitive market economy, namely their inherent pressures towards expansion, improvement, rationalization, and 'progress'. An enterprise courts disaster if it repeatedly refuses to exploit fallow or newly developed utilizable chances, unless its competitors should agree to forgo the same opportunities, which is very unlikely at a high stage of industrial capitalism, and which in any event did not happen in Imperial Germany.[154]

In mining, in the electrical engineering and chemical industries and to some extent in other sectors, expansion meant a broadening of the enterprise's activities to include new production programmes and new functions. There was great expansion and multiplication of the large, integrated, mixed concerns, especially in mining.[155] Such firms integrated all the various stages of production from the mining of coal and iron ore, via pig iron and steel production, through many stages of working the metal, and sometimes even to heavy engineering. They included the utilization of by-products and usually took over wholesale marketing.

Technical discoveries added to the impetus for diversification: the discovery of the use of blast-furnace gases as a source of energy induced and even compelled the foundries to join up with steelworks and rolling mills, which could thus be operated more cheaply, while on the other hand for rolling mills the incentive increased to merge with – or to establish – foundries. The aim of exploiting technical advantages through the combination of various stages of production and thus to introduce economies was a frequent motive for diversification. A further incentive was a concern to control several stages of production and thus to ensure their interdependence in the interests of improving quality. But by the turn of the century the purely business motive – which of course had not been altogether lacking in earlier decades – became even more important. At the start of the war, two of the largest concerns, Krupp and the Gelsenkirchener Bergwerks AG, had a share capital of 180 million marks each and employed 80,000 and 30,000 people respectively. In view of this order of magnitude, even the slightest upset in production meant massive losses; diversification into raw materials and transport allowed this risk to be minimized; diversification of this sort made it possible to calculate as fixed costs the charges which had hitherto been dependent on unforeseeable market changes; these strategies served the firms' repeatedly emphasized aim of seeking the greatest possible 'market independence'. Finally, vertical integration was encouraged by cartelization, which had been particularly effective since the mid-1890s in coal distribution. Not only did it make it easier to bypass the existing wholesalers; it also stimulated increasing link-ups between mines and foundries, since coal for the company's own consumption did not count as part of the cartel quota, and it stimulated expansion into areas as yet not sharply cartelized (e.g. steel production and development) through the restrictions on profits in other areas (such as iron ore). An important impetus for all these diversifications was usually fear of being overtaken by competitors and/or the desire to be independent. The merger movement was an expression of the continuing struggle of all against all.

In view of the vast increases in production of the existing concerns, diversification in the mining industry in the two decades before the war proceeded primarily through the incorporation of existing companies by stronger ones, particularly through takeovers and mergers, but scarcely at all through new foundations. The great significance of non-family-based corporations in the mining sector made these mergers easier.

Other stimuli were more effective in the electrical and chemical industries.[156] The availability of a pool of highly qualified and expensive technical know-how, which could be put to many uses, and of relevant methods and machinery called for the widest possible utilization, in view of the continuing new possibilities for their application. Diversification in this area meant primarily the deployment of know-how and technical expertise across the whole technical–industrial field (which in the electrical industry, for example, meant everything from telegraphs to power stations) and the foundation of the relevant new departments, branches, and subsidiaries. Only from the late 1890s onwards do we see expansion through acquisition and merger, and the annexation of existing units providing raw materials and semi-finished products. Already in the mid-1880s, the technical complexity of the finished products and services led the large electrical and chemical concerns to take over retailing through to the final consumer.

The tendencies to diversification remained much more limited in the less capital-intensive and more labour-intensive finishing industries.[157] The large engineering factories often offered a very broad production programme, in order to spread risk and to ensure an even level of employment. They believed that the market was too restricted for narrow specialization and that the buyers wanted if possible to obtain all their machines from a single producer. Nevertheless, with the development of the market, the proportion of narrowly specialized engineering works seems to have increased in comparison with the earlier period. In engineering, as in many other labour-intensive industries (such as many textile branches, the leather industry, the ceramics industry, etc.), production techniques, materials, or rapidly changing or specialized patterns of demand made the predominance of standardized procedures more difficult and made intensive and special demands on the firm's leadership. On these grounds, highly diversified combinations including industries of this type (besides raw materials and heavy machinery) were exceptional before the First World War. This shows that in the early twentieth century barriers were still partly effective which had proved so important in the mid nineteenth century against the integration of mines and foundries – the limits of the abilities of entrepreneurs and managers. Before 1914 the functions of a director of a mining concern and those of a director of a large engineering concern seemed too disparate for unified management: the one restricted himself to the highest-level co-ordination of the production and marketing of relatively homogeneous staple goods; the other was concerned with an

extremely diverse and changing production, with individual large contracts and their technology.

The producers tended increasingly – in spite of some examples to the
contrary – to take over the trading function. Not only the electrical and
chemical industries but also the sewing-machine and bicycle industries
built up their own distributive networks, in which business and technical skills were combined. Of 500 German exporting industrial concerns who were questioned in 1906, some 290 exported to South
America direct; only 150 of them made use of independent export
companies, and sixty did both. Lingerie manufacturers in Bielefeld not
only had their own weaving shops; around 1900 they also established
their own marketing organization with their own outlets and sales-
people. In most branches of the textile industry, where giant concerns
and vertical organization were far less advanced than in the mining
industry, independent traders played a far smaller role as links between
the various stages of production than in the contemporary English
textile industry. Sometimes there was an integration initiative in
reverse: retail furniture and clothing shops, and also wholesalers, set up
small production units, run partly on a putting-out basis, through direct
annexation or indirect control.[158]

The picture remains unclear in detail, since the available statistics do
not allow a representative investigation of diversification. But it seems
certain that the tendency to combine functions and stages of production
in one and the same firm increased in the decades before 1914; it also
seems clear that it was much more marked than in Great Britain. But
the variations from industry to industry were enormous. The process of
integration and diversification in the period before the First World
War did not lead to the establishment of conglomerates, i.e. mergers of
firms making products and services, or operating at different stages of
production, or pursuing functions which were not related to each other
either technically or in marketing terms. Conglomerates first appeared
in large numbers in the inflation of the First World War and the early
1920s, when the flight into commodities was a primary motive. Before
1914 the difficulties of the entrepreneurial and managerial tasks which
would result from a union of very heterogeneous branches normally
frightened entrepreneurs away from such mergers. In this respect the
diversifying entrepreneur of the early twentieth century was more
cautious than the all-round entrepreneur of the early nineteenth century.

B. CARTELS AND ASSOCIATIONS

While expansion and diversification extended the large concerns internally, their external relations changed in a way typical of the 'organized

capitalism' developing at the time. On the one hand, co-operation between large industrial concerns for the control of product markets and labour markets increased; on the other, the relations between industrial concerns and banks altered and became more intensified. This double alteration in the relations between large enterprises was partly brought about by the decisions and actions of entrepreneurs; in turn, these structural changes influenced the entrepreneurial and managerial tasks, the organization of management, and the leading personnel of large enterprises.

The disruptions to growth, and the fall in prices from 1873 to the mid-1890s, led to a rapid increase in the number of concerns co-operating in cartels, beginning in the 1880s. These cartels were mostly voluntary agreements between concerns which remained independent – usually firms in the same branch of production and the same stage of production – and they had the aim of establishing a common policy in the market. The agreements reached in these contracts were at first usually aimed purely at a common price policy; the cartel gained stability when it also regulated the quantities of production for each firm and the conditions of distribution. The most successful cartels of later years – such as the Coal Syndicate of the Rhineland and Westphalia of 1893, which controlled 80 to 90 per cent of the entire coal sales of the Ruhr and which served as a model for other organizations – in addition established joint marketing organizations and were called 'syndicates'.

'Born of necessity' in the struggle against falling prices and over-production, cartels continued to develop in the upswing conditions prevailing after the mid-1890s; they even increased thereafter. They served to limit competition, to stabilize prices and profits, and they tended towards a monopoly control of the market. In 1897 the legality of cartels was confirmed by the highest court of the Reich. Public opinion, which in Germany had never been very strongly in favour of liberal ideas current in 'Manchester' economics, had moved even further away from them following the depression of the 1870s. In general cartels were regarded fairly favourably, at least at first; only after the turn of the century were there protests against the price 'terrorism' conducted by them and against their 'unfair' practices aimed at outsiders and consumers.

This did not prevent a continuing increase in the numbers of cartels in Germany. According to the calculations of various writers, there were four cartels in 1875; 106 in 1890; 205 in 1896; 385 in 1905; 1,500 in 1925; and about 2,100 in 1930. Most were regional, unstable, and short-lived. Sectors of industry organized for homogeneous mass production were more ready to cartelize than sectors with heterogeneous output and short production runs. Apart from brick production, with about 130 (mostly local) cartels, in 1905 the basic iron and steel industries had the largest number of cartels (62), followed by chemicals (32), and the textile industry (31). It is estimated that in 1907 some 82 per cent of the production of hard coal, 100 per cent of potash, 48 per cent of cement, 50 per cent of crude steel, and 90 per cent of paper, but only 5 per cent of leather and linoleum production, 20 per cent of iron and steel manufactured goods, and 2 per cent of machines and implements were produced by firms in cartels. It is thought that cartelized production in 1907 was 25 per cent of the total output. During the First World War and the inter-war period this proportion increased and had doubled by 1938. Only after 1945, under the influence of the victorious powers and neo-liberal teachings, was cartelization banned in West Germany. Exceptions and evasion of the rules remained possible, but other forms of market control and above all co-operation in the form of mergers and integration became more important. Even before 1914, German firms were involved in about a hundred international cartels.

Cartelization on the one hand and diversification and mergers (combinations) on the other have to be seen in mutual dependence. Both mergers and cartels meant a step away from competitive capitalism (which had never existed in its pure form) to more 'organization' (which was also never perfect). Mergers, like cartels, either reduced the number of competitors or lessened the intensity of the competition. Both led to greater steadiness in production and prices. Mergers also led, however, to the appearance of large and integrated concerns with a central administration – however loose and decentralized the organization may have been. Such organizations could utilize the technical advantages of purposeful integration of the separate processes of production and hence could achieve economies of scale. They also reduced the number of independent concerns. On the other hand, apart from the question of output quotas, which were particularly common in mining and chemicals, in principle the cartel secured the continuing independence of its members and did not of itself lead to the appearance of large, complex, integrated enterprises, even though co-operation between cartel members could go a long way and meant in any case a reduction of each participant's autonomy of action. The cartel scarcely altered the production context itself at all. It encouraged rationalizations of production and administration at best indirectly, in that because prices were fixed this was sometimes the only remaining method of increasing profits; only rarely was specialization of output agreed between members of a cartel.

As we have mentioned, cartels frequently encouraged their members to diversify. However, the appearance of large integrated concerns posed great problems for the cartels of which they were members, in relation to any single branch of production. As can be seen with the problem of the 'foundry mines' in the Coal Syndicate of the Rhineland and Westphalia, the large combinations had the tendency and the power to evade limitations on output imposed by the cartel by processing products within their own organizations.[159]

Organized co-operation between firms with the aim of price control and control over the market went in parallel with increasingly organized co-operation of firms seeking to secure social and political interests. Under the influence of the slumps of the 1870s, 80s, and 90s, and stimulated by increasingly strong state intervention in the economic and social spheres (through tariff laws, social insurance, increases of state industrial activity, and the like), there grew up, from the 1870s onwards, powerful special-interest associations and industrial pressure groups. They represented the interests of industrialists *vis-à-vis* the state and public opinion. From the end of the century, the challenge of organized labour strengthened the co-operation of industrialists in employers' associations on the national level. The confrontations between workers and employers was thus – even before 1914, and increasingly thereafter – centred on a level higher than the individual firm.[160] This changed the relationships of industrialists with each other and with their environment and put new demands on the leaders of enterprises.

C. BANKS AND INDUSTRY

The development of large firms, combinations, and cartels was closely linked to the changing role of the banks in the industrial system of the German empire. The large corporate banks which had appeared in the third quarter of the century had first played a central role in the financing of industry in the boom of the 1850s and in the years around 1870. With the appearance of the depression they became more cautious with regard to involvement in industry; but from the beginning of the 1890s, the co-operation between banks and industrial concerns increased steadily. Among the banks, it was the large Berlin joint-stock banks which predominated: the Schaaffhausen'sche Bankverein (1848), the Disconto-Gesellschaft (1851), the (Darmstadt) Bank für Handel und Industrie (1853), the Berliner Handelsgesellschaft (1856), the Deutsche Bank (1870), and the Dresdner Bank (1872). They dominated the Berlin stock exchange and in the two decades before 1914 brought the older private, local, and provincial banks largely under their influence. Almost all of them soon controlled a network of minor branches and centres all over Germany and abroad. In 1904 each of them had a share capital of between 100 million and 180 million marks. One of their chief functions was the financing of industrial concerns through long-term credits and the issue of industrial shares. In contrast to the pre-1870 period they supplied their rapidly expanding industrial customers with borrowed money on an increasing scale, which in 1913 constituted three-fourths of their balances and was mostly supplied from deposits from a broad public withdrawable at short notice. The German corporate banks thus combined 'regular' banking business with industrial financing. They provided central conduits for the mobilization of scattered savings and channelled these by their own judgement to industrial enterprises, which in Germany depended on the capital market for their finance more than was the case in England. This particular context enables us to understand why independent merchants, the 'middlemen', generally played so small a role in industrial financing and industrial affairs in Germany, compared with their English counterparts: the strength of the 'mixed' banks, the relatively small significance of independent trade in the industrial economy, and the early integration of production and marketing in the large industrial concerns conditioned each other.

Long-term credit became the main basis of a bank's relations with industry, to the extent that expansions, mergers, and conversions from private to joint-stock companies became more important and more frequent than the foundation of new ones.[161] The issue of shares and bonds, which was done by the large banks for industrial concerns, was usually only the second step after co-operation had been established on the long-term credit basis. Direct, long-term participation of the banks in industrial shares declined in comparison to the 1850s and early 70s; speculation in industrial shares also became less important for banks than in earlier times. In contrast to industrial financing by the smaller private banks (which continued to play a role) the large corporate banks at the turn of the century increasingly went beyond purely financial intermediacy. They sought to monopolize the financial arrangements of 'their' industrial concerns and to service them in various ways 'from the cradle to the grave', by developing a comprehensive policy towards them and being prepared to accept short-term financial losses in order to secure their long-term co-operation. Whereas in earlier depressions the banks had withdrawn their investments from the industrial concerns, in 1900–2 for the first time they used the economic downswing to expand rather than to decrease their industrial engagements. As a consequence of this close union with industry, the banks now – in contrast to earlier decades – sought direct influence on production decisions. The banks had a say in all the important investment decisions of the companies which they helped to finance. They frequently even influenced the choice of persons to occupy the leading positions in industrial concerns and gave suggestions to help with all kinds of business transactions.[162]

The precondition which gave a handful of large Berlin-centred banks such an influence on a large number of big industrial enterprises was that the latter were organized as joint-stock companies. In fact the necessity of calling on the capital market – and that normally meant the banks – to finance current business or new investment was the main reason for a private concern to turn itself into a joint-stock company with the help of a bank. In 1873 the paid-in capital of all joint-stock companies was about 1,200 million marks; in 1913 it was ten times as much. According to Sombart's calculations, between 1886 and 1895 some 1,696 joint-stock companies were founded with a total capital of 1,686 million marks; in 1896–1905 the total was 2,015 companies with a capital of 3,100 million marks, and in 1906–13 1,467 companies with 2,087 million marks in capital. In most cases they were not new foundations but rather conversions of businesses previously privately owned. Of the joint-stock companies which existed in Prussia in 1902, only 9·3 per cent had been founded before 1870, 54·3 per cent between 1871 and 1895, and 36·4 per cent since 1895. Whereas in 1873 only some 30 per cent of the total share capital was in industrial shares, by 1903–4 some 50 per cent of all share capital was invested in the industrial sector (including mining). Mining absorbed more share capital than any other single industrial sector, but even so its proportion of total industrial share capital was only 29 per cent. While the secondary sector had increased its proportion of the total joint-stock capital, above all at the cost of the transport sector, the corporate form had spread itself relatively evenly in the various branches of industry. Of the 4,740 joint-stock companies in the German empire in 1903–4, 535 were operating in the brewing industry, 369 in engineering, 358 in the pottery industries, 327 in textiles, 297 in mining, 217 in the paper industry and in printing, 212 in sugar and alcohol production, 157 in chemicals, 140 in the precision-instrument industry, 137 in food production, 123 in electrical engineering, and 62 in the leather and rubber industries. There was no sector where the joint-stock company was not present, even if (with the exception of the mining industry) most of the firms – particularly the small and medium-sized ones – continued to be privately owned.[163]

It was the establishment of the joint-stock company which offered the banks the means of influencing industrial enterprises. The issue of shares and bonds was normally done with the help of the banks; it was the joint-stock companies which first gave a certain clarity to the published accounts of an industrial enterprise and thus facilitated the financial engagement of outside investors. But above all, the joint-stock company brought to the industrial concern an internal structure which allowed the banks (which were also organized in this form) to exercise a direct influence on its affairs. The supervisory board (*Aufsichtsrat*) elected by the annual general meeting of the shareholders (or their representatives) was obligatory by law from 1870 and was strengthened by a law of 1884. Its functions were not limited to the appointment and supervision of the executive board (*Vorstand*); it could also make or influence the most important strategic decisions – especially investment decisions – in its quarterly or monthly meetings. Before 1914 bank directors were the largest single group among the members of the supervisory boards of German joint-stock companies, occupying some 20 per cent of all places. In 1913–14 the Deutsche Bank had representatives in 186 other companies. Some leading bank directors accumulated up to forty-four seats on supervisory boards each before the First World War; around 1930 some acquired about a hundred. By threatening to withdraw credit and refuse share issues, and by all sorts of informal contacts, the supervisory board was the most important channel through which the large banks exercised direct and continuous influence on industrial production. The shareholders' AGM played a relatively peripheral role.[164]

The influence of the banks normally seems to have led to a stronger emphasis on financial and business considerations in the directorates of firms influenced by them. Representatives of banks concerned themselves with the improvement of accountancy methods and administration, with the aim of greater efficiency and profitability in companies which needed reform. The close involvement of a large bank – necessarily conceived with a long-term perspective – reduced the dependence of the industrial enterprise on the short-term fluctuations of the market. Through the influence of the banks the investment policy of the industrial concern was directed more to long-term expectations for the future and was less dependent on the momentary conditions prevailing in commodity markets and money markets. The support of a bank with strong capital reserves and an orientation to the future brought many subsequently profitable enterprises through long barren periods which otherwise they would not have been able to survive. Once they were deeply involved, banks would come to the rescue in their own interest, even if the company did not deserve help from a long-term perspective. Through the intervention of banks, the short- and medium-term connection between market success and a firm's chance of survival was somewhat relaxed. Banks preferred large companies to small ones and thus accelerated an already existing trend. They preferred the capital-goods industries, especially mining and the electrical industry; but here too they only strengthened existing trends, which they had not themselves created. For example, they facilitated industrial mergers, but the initiative here normally came from the industrial concerns themselves. In general the banks acted like large flywheels: they did not initiate movements, but they accelerated and increased the momentum behind existing trends.[165]

The degree of interdependence between banks and industrial concerns varied from sector to sector, from firm to firm, and from year to year. The influence of the banks was greater in mining than in the chemical industry, where they never played a major role. The family concern of Siemens never gave the Deutsche Bank as much influence as Rathenau's AEG allowed to the Berliner Handelsgesellschaft. A firm in financial difficulties was subject to great pressure from its bank; a secure and profitable large-scale concern, on the other hand, could dictate to the banks, who competed to run its financial affairs. One should also remember that there were broad areas of decision where conflicts between the representatives of banks and industry were not likely and where one cannot speak of the dependence of one on the other. In general the influence of the banks on industry seems to have reached its peak at the turn of the century, after which it declined. The tendency towards industrial mergers, which the banks themselves had encouraged, increased the power of the large industrial concerns, whose capital needs now often outran the capacity of a single bank and so forced the banks into co-operation and the formation of larger banking groups. The rate of self-financing in the large concerns was high. The Siemens–Schuckert concern, for example, invested some 512 million marks in the fifteen years after its foundation in 1903, of which about 50 per cent came from its own profits. It is estimated that, up to 1900, the chemical industry was able to finance between a third and a half of its total expansion from operating surpluses, and the iron industry some 20 to 25 per cent. In the inter-war period and especially after the Second World War the rate of self-financing increased markedly. This meant a relatively large and, in the long term, growing amount of independence from the capital market and banks for the firm concerned. Particularly in the electrical industry – though by no means exclusively there – the large industrial concerns annexed their own banks and thus reduced their dependence on the large banks.

In the leaderships of the large concerns, the bank directors often found themselves in a difficult position. The number of seats they had on the supervisory boards was certainly of some importance. But the complexity of the technical and business problems increased the relative importance of the members of the executive board, who had a better detailed knowledge of the concern and were more regularly present than the members of the supervisory board, who only met at long intervals and who could not gain a detailed understanding of each enterprise, if only because of the large number of members. In the long term the executive board gained in influence as against the supervisory board, whatever the law and the statutes said. In 1905 the general director of the Gelsenkirchener Bergwerks AG denied that the large banks dominated the mining industry: 'The influence of the large banks on the industry of the Rhineland and Westphalia has never been so limited as it now is . . . The large banks seek the favours of industry, not the reverse.' With all the variations between sectors and firms, these remarks indicate the general trend correctly, which was later continued during and after the war. Rudolf Hilferding, in his *Finanzkapital* of 1910, formulated his theory of the dominance of the banks over industry, which has been constantly repeated since then. But this theory was already basically outdated when it was formulated.[166]

D. THE INCREASING RELEVANCE OF THE SCIENCES

Alongside the expansion and diversification of firms, the rise of cartels and associations, and the more intensified relations between banks and industry, another central change was the rise of science as a force in production and marketing. This change posed new problems for the leaders of large concerns and offered new means of solving them. This was particularly true of the application of the natural sciences in the area of production technology. We must distinguish three separate trends.

As we have noticed, the academically educated entrepreneur played a significant role in the industrial revolution only in the extractive industries, thanks primarily to the state training of mining and foundry officials which had derived from the mercantilist period and outlived the withdrawal of the state from entrepreneurial activity in the mines. In the second place academically trained men were becoming increasingly important in engineering technology and related fields from the middle third of the century onwards; the business academies, polytechnics, and technical colleges provided academically trained engineers who were quite different from those with a practical training only. Students from these institutions, although still in the minority, were gaining more and more positions, in engineering and other firms, as the industrial revolution progressed. They gained access most easily to the drawing offices which were appearing from the 1850s onwards. But engineers only really began to replace the purely empirically trained directors in the workshops and production plants themselves from about 1890. From about the same time the technical colleges took more notice of practical requirements: the work of training the students through lectures, demonstrations, and practical exercises was now supplemented by courses in the schools' own technical laboratories – based not least on American examples and following the wishes of industry. In 1899 the technical colleges succeeded in gaining the right to grant doctorates and thus achieved equal standing with the universities, which traditionally had contemptuously ignored the application of science to technology and offered no suitable courses for its study.[167]

The third channel for the increasing impact of science on production technology lay in the industrial laboratories, which were established during the 1870s and 80s in the chemical and electrical industries in close contact with natural science and technology in the universities and technical colleges. The founders of the German coal-tar-dye industry, among whom there were already a large number of university chemists,[168] at first set about systematically improving existing methods and then (from about 1880) began systematic basic research within the firms themselves. After some experimentation with various forms of organization, the relatively independent research laboratory appeared, employing a growing number of graduates from universities and technical colleges. For example, in 1891 Bayer's laboratory in Elberfeld, under the direction of Carl Duisberg, was large enough to fill a three-storey building costing 1·5 million marks. Krupp had established a company chemical laboratory for the analysis of steel and raw materials in 1862. In a laboratory under the direction of a university physicist of doctoral level, Siemens & Halske had in 1872 institutionalized the technical and physical development work which had hitherto been done by the founder himself with a few helpers. The basics of electrical technology were first taught in a polytechnic in 1876, and as a specialization in technical colleges after 1882. The physics professor Ernst Abbé put the optical industry on a new scientific level for Carl Zeiss in the 1870s, and in 1882 he founded a glass-technology laboratory in the Zeiss works in Jena.[169]

These growing laboratories fundamentally changed the process of technical innovation. It was now planned as far as possible with functional divisions: research became a long-term process, financed with a high level of investment which often did not serve particular, specifically determined aims (such as the development of the electric light bulb) but was increasingly involved in the operations of the firm because of its unforeseeable but, in the long term, useful by-products. The case of the individual inventor who achieved results without a supporting institution and then either sold his idea to a firm or established his own concern to exploit it himself – often in a somewhat difficult partnership with a merchant or financier – became less important, though it still occurred frequently.[170]

The more important scientific technology became for the activities of a firm, the more likely it was that the academically trained directors of the research departments would take over entrepreneurial functions and would be integrated into the leadership of the concern. The examples of Carl Duisberg, Ernst Abbé, and later Carl Bosch demonstrate that this route could lead to the top positions, if the person concerned also had business, organizational, and general entrepreneurial abilities. But apart from leaders of companies' research departments, the proportion of technical-college graduates among the entrepreneurs increased in these years. One reason was that industrialists let their prospective heirs study at technical colleges, even if their later positions would not depend primarily on their academic training. Another was that it became more common for engineers with diplomas and (after the turn of the century) graduates with the prestigious title of 'Dr Ing.' to rise within the firm and, as members of the executive or supervisory board, to become salaried entrepreneurs. But this was not always the case: even in 1953 only some 31 per cent of the 12,000 members of boards and owners of businesses had academic degrees, a good third of which were from technical colleges.[171]

In contrast to the recruitment of public officials, higher school qualifications were not an indispensable requirement for access to the highest posts in even the largest firms; the nearest to this professional–bureaucratic model, before the war and particularly in the inter-war period, were the large chemical companies, on whose executive boards scientifically qualified engineers and scientists very clearly predominated. But even a large number of scientifically and technically educated board members by no means indicates that technical considerations had become more significant, relative to business aspects, than in earlier decades. It seems rather to have been typical that, even in such technologically outstanding industries as chemicals and the electrical industry, the influence of the marketing organization and thus the weight of business considerations were institutionalized and strengthened in the late nineteenth century.[172] The increase in the amount of scientific and technical expertise in German company leadership may have strengthened a belief in the significance of technology and in long-term opportunities for development; it did not make technical progress a self-justifying goal of companies.

The business functions in capitalist industrial enterprises were from the start conducted on a written, systematic, theoretical basis, although often rather inadequately, and earlier than were the functions concerned with production technology. From the beginning of the depression of the 1870s, great progress was made by companies in the area of marketing and accountancy. The takeover of wholesaling and – to some extent

– retailing functions by manufacturing companies in the fields of chemicals, electrical technology, and sewing machines, and in large parts of the raw-material industries, demanded the establishment of networks of local branches and agencies. After 1885 Felix Deutsch built up for the AEG a far-flung, international marketing system, combining business and technical experience for the sale of electro-technical products. The large chemical corporations owed much of their success after 1885 to shrewd, aggressive salesmanship, using new forms of advertising, in their wholesale marketing.[173] From the depression of the 1870s with its restricted profits, the cost-consciousness of industrialists clearly increased; in their specialist literature, which was becoming more common, more refined bookkeeping methods were developed.[174] The growing number of conversions of personal firms or private companies into joint-stock corporations increased the requirements of formal accounting, as did the growing participation in cartels and trade associations. But it seems that these advances were made not so much by managers with an academic training for business as by practical men who had, at best, a medium-level commercial-school education.

The commercial-school system at the beginning of the twentieth century cannot be compared to the well-developed technical-school system. This was particularly clear at the lower school levels: in 1910 in Prussia there were 1,877 state technical continuation schools (*gewerbliche Fortbildungsschulen*) with a total of 327,000 students, but only 501 commercial schools (*kaufmännische Fortbildungsschulen*) with 65,000 students.[175] Motivated more by ideas of professional prestige on the part of businessmen, chambers of commerce, and professors than by the proven needs of commercial practice, between 1898 and 1920 commercial colleges (*Handelshochschulen*) were founded in Cologne, Leipzig, Berlin, Frankfurt, Mannheim, and Munich. At first they taught political economy and general education, but from 1906 also 'company economics' (*Betriebswirtschaftslehre*) – a variety of business administration centred on commercial procedures. At the same time technical colleges began to offer, or to develop more intensively, lectures on commercial and organizational subjects and on law. The process of making such training academically respectable occurred much later in Germany than the introduction of academic status and science into technical training. The title of 'Diplom-Kaufmann' was only granted in 1913. Men with an academic business education were scarcely to be found among the heads of firms before 1914; the chances for promotion for persons with a mere practical training remained open much longer in the business than in the technical departments of companies. Even in 1954 only 17 per cent of managers finished their higher education with the title of 'Diplom-Kaufmann', 'Diplom-Volkswirt', or

'Dr. rer. pol.'; this was a smaller proportion than those with a legal qualification (19 per cent). In the last two decades the former group has certainly increased markedly, both absolutely and relative to the numbers of qualified engineers and lawyers.[176]

E. THE RISE AND LIMITS OF SYSTEMATIC MANAGEMENT

The expansion of firms through internal development and mergers; the trends towards organization through cartels and trade associations; the close links between industrial and banking concerns – all these meant that the tasks of the leaders of large enterprises were made more difficult. The areas to be supervised and controlled became larger and more complex; problems of information and co-ordination appeared, which were unknown to the directors of small or medium-sized firms. Family-based and personally transmitted methods of management were now inadequate and, in view of the great demands for co-ordination and effectiveness, could even be counter-productive. The development of systematic large-scale management responded to these new needs. It varied according to the various parts of the concern.

'Scientific management' first appeared in the workshops of large enterprises about the turn of the century. It stemmed partly from American stimuli: German entrepreneurs and engineers undertook study trips to the USA to get to know American techniques of organization; many books and articles concerned themselves with the shop-floor organization of American factories; and by 1907 at the latest the 'Taylor system' was being publicly discussed. But in part large German companies developed systematic factory organization independently and implemented recommendations similar to Taylor's before his had been brought to Germany. Older bureaucratic traditions, which at an early stage had led to written instructions, precision, and formalization, helped them in this. In the production departments of large engineering concerns a clear division was established between preparations for and control of production on the one side, and the execution of production on the other. Shop-floor offices appeared as mediating forces between the technical departments and the workshops; the power of the foreman decreased; there was increasing paperwork, and refined card-index and paper-slip systems were developed; standardization of output and mass production was generally demanded, although standardization between different firms began only in the First World War. New systems of worker motivation and controls were developed, and time studies and stop-watches appeared.[177]

Bureaucratic models were fully employed in the organization of the growing salaried staff departments. Written instructions and regulations systematically covered the functions carried out by the lower- and middle-ranking salaried employees in the technical and commercial offices as well as those in the general administration. Far-reaching division of labour and the most exact lines of competence, hierarchies of authority and formalized lines of information meant that private bureaucracies grew up which differed little from that of the public authorities.[178]

It was different with the overall directing organization. There were certainly trends after the turn of the century towards a theory and study of general business organization and management. In a number of publications, rules for correct management – based on experience and supposedly for general applicability without limitation to specific sectors – were formulated, and there were attempts to bring them together into a 'scientific' system. 'Organization' became a common catchword, though far from being as popular as the concept of 'scientific management' in the USA at the same time. For the first time independent organization consultants appeared; larger enterprises employed 'special officials' who were concerned primarily with building the organization and solving its problems.

But these trends remained very limited. The leaders of the largest companies seem not infrequently to have opposed too systematic an organization at the top in order to preserve their own room to manoeuvre. In spite of all their respect for technology and science, for systematic management and regular organization at the lower and middle levels, they regarded personal qualities such as creativity and dynamism, courage and originality, intuition and leadership as decisive at the very top of enterprise. Too much scientific management, according to many of them, would only inhibit the appearance of unteachable and unorganizable virtues. The impact of science on the functions of the firm reached production technology first, and the top level last.[179]

At the top of large firms before the First World War and later there was an intricate mixture of system and improvisation, bureaucratic and personal methods, fixed order and flexibility. This can be demonstrated by analysing the channels of information. Even at the beginning of the 1870s Alfred Krupp set himself the aim that in his 10,000-man concern in Essen nothing of significance should happen 'that was not known about and approved at the top level of management'. He demanded 'that one should be able to study and survey the factory's past and its probable future in the office of the central administration, without having to question the dead'. He reorganized the leadership structure, exactly defining the distribution of authority and functions, and provided for a management conference which met at least twice weekly.[180]

In the large corporations of the early twentieth century, periodic conferences submitted reports prepared in standardized form, increasingly supported with statistics and tables, to try to solve the problem of information. On the other hand, more precise analysis shows that the most important information (e.g. intelligence passing between the leading directors and the representatives of the firm's bank) was exchanged through informal channels, by private letters and at social occasions. The introduction of the telephone also facilitated the circumvention of formal lines of communication.

The normal form of managerial control with specialized functions in a medium-sized concern provided for a technical director and a business director: the latter was normally responsible for general administration and organization as well. In larger companies the number of active directors (executive board members) increased. They usually represented the individual, functionally defined departments – marketing, production, finance, and perhaps export, and also sometimes the 'political economy department' which specialized in the firm's public relations and its contacts with the authorities, social organizations, and interest-groups; or they were the managers of particular areas of production, or perhaps of geographically defined parts of the concern. Even before 1914, the functional specialization of these board members, who combined entrepreneurial with managerial functions, went so far that it was possible for one to move between quite different sectors of industry (e.g. from a powder factory to an electrical enterprise) while retaining his previous function (e.g. as financial director). The transfer of high officials from the civil service on to the boards of industrial concerns was common – not only to exploit their connections, but also for the execution of administrative tasks in the companies. The more specialized the board became, the more essential became the non-specialized 'generalists' – the general directors who were common on the executive boards of the time. The division of labour between the directors was laid down in writing, through exact regulations. On the other hand the system was changed when important people entered or left the company. It was not the specification of the job but the person who came first. The fixed divisions of competence between the various organs of the corporation were supplemented by, and to some extent subordinated to, a highly decentralized, loose system of standing and *ad hoc* committees. The leading people in particular short-circuited the correct channels when it suited them. Personal relationships between them and the 'leading personalities' of other institutions (e.g. banks) remained of the greatest importance, in spite of all the system-building and the introduction of bureaucracy.[181]

There has been little research into the techniques of management by which the large vertically integrated and diversified concerns were held together. It is clear, however, that it was management problems in particular which held back entrepreneurs from further expansion through combinations and diversifications, or which (as in the case of Strousberg) caused the collapse of bold combinations. The extent of the moves towards centralization or decentralization which were necessary for the establishment of a well-integrated administrative unity varied according to whether the large diversified concern developed mainly through the acquisition of existing specialized firms or through internal expansion. Management solutions undoubtedly varied markedly and followed no general plan. Partly integrated, if yet decentralized, firms developed from federations of companies (which were held together almost exclusively through mere capital and personal connections and agreements), by means of the centralization of individual functions (such as investment decisions in a central directorate, or marketing in a central sales office). The vertically integrated concerns, however, needed more interdependence, and the continuity of throughput from raw materials to final sale. One may presume that the vertically integrated, centralized, functionally departmentalized form of organization predominated in Germany as in the USA at the time.[182] But there were undoubtedly many variations and mixed structures which consisted of well-integrated concerns at the centre, but loose federations at the periphery. The degree of integration of foreign subsidiaries in the home company, for example, varied greatly from case to case. The legal forms also changed.

In at least one case – Siemens & Halske in Berlin – the decentralized multi-divisional structure which became typical for highly diversified concerns later on in the twentieth century was already developed before the First World War. They left most of the day-to-day decisions and affairs to the individual units (divisions), which produced different products, had their own management, production, accountancy, and marketing, produced differing products, and were to some extent also geographically separated from each other. On the other hand, an elaborate system of administration was established – with boards, committees, and offices – which provided for central control, decision-making, and administrative supervision at the top. Top managers were free to concentrate on basic policy, the allocation of capital equipment and personnel, external relations, legal matters, patents, overall organization, and – increasingly – labour management. The executive board, on which most of the division heads as well as the top officials with functionally defined activities were included, met regularly. There was a separate general office, which participated in the formulation and administration of the company's overall policies. Regular reports, statistics, charts, and a high degree of administrative standardization permitted effective surveys and controls. An increasing number of central staff departments fulfilled several functions for the whole concern. They specialized in activities necessary for the supervision, co-ordination, and standardization of construction, in research and development, in the purchase of raw materials for the whole concern, in the supervision of the marketing offices in the field, the organization of overseas exports, legal and economic matters, public relations, and central accounting. Finally, a flexible system of top committees was developed, in which various board members and other top officials came together at irregular intervals. In addition, the divisions were co-ordinated by the corporation's internal price system, which incorporated non-bureaucratic market elements into this essentially non-market organization, and provided limited competition between the plants and departments. The individual divisions, whose success or failure was identifiable in departmental accounts in terms of gains or losses according to centrally set prices, treated each other to some extent as if they were independent competitors. This system made it easier to locate inefficiencies and establish efficiency inducements.[183]

There were internal price systems and limited competition between individual departments in other corporations, too; managerial de-centralization seems to have been recognized and accepted as a necessity by the creators of the large concerns even before 1914.[184] But these issues have been ignored in almost all historical monographs on in-dividual firms, so that further generalizations about the management of large concerns and enterprises at that time are impossible.

F. THE SEPARATION BETWEEN OWNERSHIP OF CAPITAL AND CONTROL: THE SALARIED ENTREPRENEUR

In the large corporations of the early twentieth century the separation between owners of capital, entrepreneurs, and managers became more marked than before; the separation took many forms, however, and remained incomplete. Not all joint-stock corporations developed a clear separation between ownership of capital and entrepreneurial func-tions. The joint-stock company was often only the external form of a continuing family concern. Wilhelm von Siemens, for example, the son of the founder Werner Siemens, owned with his family the majority of the shares of the Siemens & Halske joint-stock company, which itself, with the help of a large number of personal and institu-tional contacts, was the dominating centre of an international concern which employed over 80,000 people in 1913. As both general director and member of the supervisory board, Wilhelm Siemens made the most important entrepreneurial decisions. Often, however, he involved some of the top staff from the firm – selected primarily by himself – and representatives of the banks concerned, though the latter were involved less and less.

In large corporations with widely dispersed capital ownership, however, the most important entrepreneurial and managerial decision-making lay in the hands of salaried personnel from industry and the banks. Emil Kirdorf (the general director of the Gelsenkirchener Bergwerks AG and architect of the Coal Syndicate of the Rhineland and Westphalia), Emil Rathenau (the founder and general director of the AEG), and Carl Fürstenberg (the director of the Berliner Handelsgesellschaft) are examples of powerful entrepreneurs who did not own much capital themselves. These salaried entrepreneurs, who were generally referred to at the time as 'managers' (and are so today, though not in the terminology of this chapter), have aroused the interest both of social scientists and of the public since the late nineteenth century; but on the German side there is a lack of empirical investigation which would permit a systematic understanding of this category of entrepreneurs, which remained much smaller in number than the owner–entrepreneurs.[185]

In the areas of mining and industry – though not in the banking and transport sectors – these salaried entrepreneurs had to put up with distrust and disdain from public opinion and from the large owner–entrepreneurs in the last quarter of the century. According to many writers, the absence of the tie of ownership must mean that the salaried entrepreneur would not work so intensively for his firm, since he would not carry the whole risk if the firm were to fail or receive the full benefit should it succeed. Even in the 1880s it was thought that the motivation to work and the effectiveness of the salaried director were lower than those of the traditional factory-owner. The former was also thought to be more likely to indulge in doubtful business practices than the latter. Owner–entrepreneurs were disdainful towards the employed director to the extent that they themselves saw their equity stake, and the risk that this carried, as the basis of their claim to economic gain and social status, even when they were convinced of the director's ability.[186] On the other hand social scientists with interests in reform, from Gustav Schmoller via James Burnham to modern advocates of a technocratic philosophy, have attached great positive expectations to the rise of salaried entrepreneurs. Such men were expected to be more motivated than were the traditional owner–entrepreneurs by ideas of the public good, and not influenced so much by criteria of private profit (in this respect they were thought to be similar to public officials). Because of their education they were thought to be particularly disposed to rational, objective, and systematic behaviour and thus seemed suitable people for solving or at least soothing social conflict and for holding leading positions in society and the state in general. The increase in both numbers and importance of salaried entrepreneurs seemed to indicate a basic social and political transformation of the capitalist system – which up to then had been based on the ownership of the means of production – and of the class structure which stemmed from it.[187] The more articulate members of this new group of entrepreneurs adopted such ideas, and used them to articulate their own image of themselves and to legitimize their claims to social status and power.[188]

Both the negative and the positive expectations associated with the rise of the salaried entrepreneur proved basically unfounded. More effective legal regulation, combined with growing ease of control as a result of improving transport and communication systems, as well as some tendencies towards professional ethics in groups of salaried entrepreneurs, posed no greater risk of dishonesty for the partner to an agreement, the customer, or the capital-lending public than did the traditional owner–entrepreneur. Around 1900 these accusations against corporations and their directors became muted. The relative disdain for this new category of entrepreneurs who did not own much of the equity in their firms gradually died down, but even after 1945 it had not quite disappeared from Germany.[189] It also became clear that, with the gradual transition from owner–entrepreneur to salaried entrepreneur, little had changed in the basic aims of the leadership of firms. The preservation of the concern, its profits, and its expansion remained, as we have seen, the dominant aims – not so much because the income of the salaried entrepreneur was directly linked with the financial success of the firm through bonuses, and not primarily because the salaried entrepreneur was frequently bound to 'his' concern through contractually obligatory investments (whether of money or shares), but rather because, as we have indicated, profit and expansion remained demands of the system, which could only be ignored at the risk of danger to the company, and consequently to the standing of the man at the top. In the capitalist system of the first two-thirds of the twentieth century, profits and the expansion and survival of the firm remained the major yardsticks of entrepreneurial success. Normally it was necessary to be successful by these criteria as a precondition for the fulfilment of other aims and desires which also motivated many salaried entrepreneurs: fame, social status, striving for power, the desire for position, job satisfaction, care of the labour force, or service to the general good (whatever may have been understood by this).

From the point of view of the relationships between management and labour, the change from independent to salaried entrepreneur also meant no significant change. One sort of entrepreneur showed no more desire than the other sort to share his power of decision-making with the workers; optimal utilization of the labour force was a paramount aim for both types of industrial leaders. The indisputable differences in labour relations which can be observed in these decades are better explained by the differences between the sectors of industry, the state of profits, the composition of the work force, and the differences between large and small concerns, than by differences between concerns which were directed by the owner and those which had a salaried entrepreneur at the top. Neither *in* the firm itself nor in the social conflicts *outside* the firm is there any support for the assertion that the salaried entrepreneurs formed a 'new class' which was objective, rational, neutral between interests, and predisposed to solve conflicts, a class which could have overcome the antagonisms of the private capitalist system.[190] One has only to think of Emil Kirdorf, or of Ewald Hilger, the general director of the Vereinigte Königshütte und Laurahütte in Silesia, or of the Krupp directors Joh. Friedrich Jencke and Alfred Hugenberg, who were among the most uncompromising defenders of the traditional 'master in one's own house' viewpoint in the first third of this century and carried out a more sharply anti-union and reactionary social policy than many owner–entrepreneurs.[191]

When all this is said, one can point to some changes which were indeed associated with the change from independent to salaried entrepreneur – a change which affected only a minority of normally large (and important) firms, while the great majority of small and medium-sized industrial concerns continued to be directed by owner–entrepreneurs. As we have noted, the entrepreneurial striving for expansion increased rather than diminished with the salaried entrepreneurs, since they were less concerned with non-economic motives (such as family considerations) than were the early factory masters. It is possible that the readiness to innovate increased at the top level of decision-making – which completely contradicts Joseph Schumpeter's gloomy forecast of increasing rigidity affecting entrepreneurial dynamism in the modern bureaucratic large-scale enterprise.[192] Salaried entrepreneurs may also have tended to emphasize considerations of long-term planning, to put long-range future benefits before short-term opportunities, and to pursue the maintenance and continuity of the firm as dominant aims. They reacted to the fact that in their large organizations the proportion of fixed capital had risen to the point where it was improbable that the business could be liquidated without losses, and that even the shortest interruption to production would inevitably be accompanied by large losses. This awareness increased the need to ensure a steady, continuous development of the concern, if necessary rejecting sudden, short-term gains.[193] In this they differed from the earlier entrepreneurs with many interests, speculators, and tycoons, but not from the founders, owners, and directors of the family enterprises which were so dominant in the industrial revolution.[194] The salaried entrepreneur's policy of preserving and expanding the concern (almost as an aim in itself), rather than simply maximizing profits in the short run, found its clearest expression in the tendency to restrict the distribution of dividends and premiums in favour of retaining profits for re-investment, and insisting on this priority against the shareholding interests represented in the AGM. This may have been one factor contributing to the long-term increase in the rate of self-financing in the inter-war period and after 1945.[195]

The salaried entrepreneur undoubtedly differed from the owner-entrepreneur in his recruitment and career, but there are insufficient systematic, representative studies to document this problem for the pre-war and inter-war periods.[196] Access to entrepreneurial positions was in principle now independent of the ownership of capital and thus open to a larger group of people than before. It was now less true than before that the entrepreneur had to be rich himself, or be the child of rich parents, or seek rich partners. It is not surprising that in this connection there was talk of the 'democratization' of access to entrepreneurial positions.[197] But against such 'democratization' was the fact that educational qualifications were a much more important precondition for successful salaried entrepreneurs than they were for independent entrepreneurs. The investigation of a sample of 1,300 known entrepreneurs in the period 1890–1930 showed that 52 per cent of the salaried entrepreneurs had an academic education, but only 37 per cent of the owner-entrepreneurs. For only 5 per cent of the salaried entrepreneurs, but for 10 per cent of the owner–entrepreneurs, was schooling limited to the elementary level. The rest had a higher-school education but no more advanced academic study.[198] When one remembers that access to higher education and even partly to the higher levels of school depended very much on the socio-economic status of the father, and that the proportion of working-class children in higher education was until recently (even in the post-1945 Federal Republic) less than 5 per cent, it will be clear that education must have largely replaced ownership as the barrier to advancement.[199]

It is also clear from the great importance of formal education for the salaried entrepreneur that advancement from worker to director was possible only in exceptional cases.[200] But beyond that little is known yet about the careers of salaried entrepreneurs at that time. It seems to have been increasingly common for staff who had college or university qualifications but were nevertheless starting at a relatively low management level to rise through the hierarchy to board level; in the first years they might well change companies several times, but as they became more senior this became exceptional. They usually reached their first entrepreneurial position not before their late thirties, ten years later on average than the owner–entrepreneurs of the same period. This quasi-bureaucratic method of advancement created the problem that the rising generation of entrepreneurs acquired specialized (technical and business) experience but was not prepared for the co-ordinating and generalist activities which the good entrepreneur – but not the good specialist – had to be able to deal with. This was undoubtedly a disadvantage as against the education of heirs (which we have outlined above), who continued to play a large role in private firms, and who were groomed from the beginning to take over the company and who increasingly combined an academic education with practical all-round experience in their fathers' concerns. To a certain extent, however, this specifically entrepreneurial training did play a role in the large corporations too – and not just in those which were a cover for a family concern like Krupp or Siemens. The general director often selected a 'young man' as his successor, frequently his son, a relative, or a close friend, and granted him a broad training in the company which was to prepare him to direct it later. This practice was a result of the awareness that a good specialist no more made a good entrepreneur, than an able bureaucrat normally made a successful politician. Such self-help by the leaders of concerns also reflected the fact that universities and technical colleges produced very good specialists but – apart from some introduction to the study of company economics – no good entrepreneurs as such. In so far as good entrepreneurs can be trained at all in the schools, the process began only gradually after the Second World War.

Other salaried entrepreneurs had gained their practical experience in independent positions and had become salaried men when their companies merged or became joint-stock companies. Others again at the end of the nineteenth century, came directly from the technical colleges and universities into leading positions in industry, particularly in the 'new industries' (such as the electrical and chemical industries). The influx of bank directors on to industrial supervisory boards has already been mentioned. Finally the higher civil servants must be noted: they brought their experience of officialdom, their special experience (normally legal), their contacts, and their knowledge of bureaucratic organization into better-paid positions in functionally specialized company management.

Family contacts, relatives, and informal personal contacts of all sorts continued to play an enormous role in the co-option of people into the highest positions, particularly when specialized knowledge and pro-motion from the ranks were not accepted as sufficient (though perhaps necessary) qualifications; but other qualities were demanded – sub-jectively felt 'entrepreneurial' abilities, which were difficult to measure. It is clear that the unbureaucratic methods of recruiting the highest personnel, which seem to have continued with modifications until today, restricted the power of the co-opting entrepreneur less than bureaucratic rules would have done; it is equally obvious that this power was utilized against would-be recruits from not fully acceptable social groups, and worked against the 'democratization' of access to the top positions. Such criteria for selection (which could not be specifically defined) and such informal and nepotistic methods of selection, for positions which did not call for specific formal qualifications, had in general a positive effect on achievement, principally because they formed only secondary criteria for selection, in addition to the criterion of practical suitability and aptitude, and not as substitutes for it. Walther Rathenau succeeded his father not merely because he was his son but also because he had exceptional and proven abilities. With the pressure of competition (which as we have noted changed but did not diminish in the period of organized capitalism) and in a context of large concerns, no enterprise could afford to practise nepotism at the cost of the criterion of ability. But it was certainly true that the larger the number of possible candidates with similar or apparently similar ability and formal qualifications, the more decisive became the personal and subjective preferences of the heads of firms.

In spite of the informal and unprofessional elements in the selection of salaried entrepreneurs, which should not be underestimated and were by no means dysfunctional, the selection of entrepreneurs became less dependent on ownership of the means of production; the rise of salaried entrepreneurs also helped to make specialists' knowledge – technical, business, legal, and organizational skills – available to the leadership of companies. Without the traditional link with ownership, achievement could be a more important criterion for selection than it was when property and direction went strictly together. This encouraged the trends towards professional, rational, and systematic entrepreneurship and management.

G. CHANGING PATTERNS OF ENTREPRENEURSHIP

So much for the split between ownership and entrepreneurship, its limits and consequences. Another issue which is to be clearly differ-entiated from this and which arose independently of it is the division between entrepreneurship and management. This remained limited even in the largest corporations of the time. It was certainly made easier by the relatively sharp split between the executive and the supervisory board, which was and is normal in German company law,[201] but which has no parallel in the Anglo-American system of boards of directors. The supervisory board – composed of the large shareholders, bank directors, representatives of connected concerns, representatives of suppliers and customers, former board members, people from public life, and to some extent outside specialists – restricted itself almost entirely to entrepreneurial decisions. In the day-to-day activities of most directors and executive board members, by contrast, entrepreneurial and managerial elements were mixed. This was partly a result of the fact that normally the directors of the most important individual departments and divisions were appointed to the executive board. But even before 1914 general directorial positions appeared which were later to be much more common (and even general directorates which worked collectively). These directorial positions were not concerned with the management of individual departments and plants but with strategic decisions for the whole enterprise, entrepreneurial functions in the purest form, separate from the routine management and from all purely specialist tasks. It seems that these pure 'generalists', who included both large shareholders (perhaps representatives of the controlling family) and top staff without much capital (who frequently came from the public administration), did not feel very happy in their rather abstract and not very specifically orientated activities: even in 1930 it was reported that the general director of one of the largest heavy industrial concerns in Germany always participated in the management of at least one of his plants, in order at least to preserve regular direct contact with the operations and not to lose his basis of experience completely.[202] On the other side, in the direction of the subdivisions of a decentralized enterprise the entrepreneurial and managerial functions remained closely linked.

The changes in the entrepreneurial function itself were more a result of the growth and increasing complexity of the concern and of changes in production and market structures, and less a result of the division between ownership and control as such, as it appeared in the joint-stock company with dispersed capital ownership. In addition to the increase in technical competence and greater continuity in the work and aims of the company direction, beyond the trend towards the removal of entrepreneurial functions from the functions of the manager, and apart from all the individual alterations which we have already described, two other major changes occurred. One followed from the rise of cartels and associations and from the intensification of relations between industry and the banks: skill in the exercise of influence and behaviour within and between formal organizations became ever more clearly a qualification which entrepreneurs had to have, in addition to effectiveness in the market and other traditional entrepreneurial abilities, if the concern was to be successful. The skilful influencing of a partner in an agreement over whom one had no formal authority; the appointment of a man one could trust to an important position in a syndicate; negotiating a merger agreement; or making a good personal impression on the director of a powerful bank – such moves as these could now be of more importance than a single technical innovation introduced at the right moment or a giant contract secured by underbidding a competitor. Such a competitive success in the market could even be harmful, if it precluded desirable long-term possibilities of agreement with one's competitor. Within large concerns, too, with their many very independent sub-units and their leaders who seemed to be largely responsible only to themselves, decision-making and implementation had many elements of a political process, consisting of 'give and take', the use of influence rather than formal authority, conflicts, and compromises. The salaried entrepreneur of those decades had to understand how to create a majority in critical general meetings, if necessary, how to control business agendas, and how to act in a quasi-parliamentary manner.[203] In all these functions other qualities were demanded of the director of a large concern than those of a typical factory master of the industrial revolution.

The other major change was that a separation, a diffusion of the operator's functions, appeared before 1914 and increased in later years. This was to some extent in contradiction to the process we have described of the creation of ever-larger units and the separation of entrepreneurial functions from managerial ones. We have already mentioned the tendencies to functional specialization of the directors controlling a firm, and decentralization of some entrepreneurial areas of competence in the multi-divisional, diversified corporation. We have also referred to the bank directors who, as outsiders, undertook important entrepreneurial functions, sometimes for a large number of firms in a section of industry in which they were specialists, and with the help of a staff of bank employees. But the diffusion went further. The cartels and their directors took over the most important functions of the associated firms in the areas of marketing and – sometimes – some control of production. Trade associations, interest groups, and employers' associations did the same with regard to many industrial questions, including the progressively more important problem of the concern's relationships with the general public, the state authorities, and the labour force. In the cartels, syndicates, and trade associations of all sorts there rapidly appeared groups of salaried people, about whom little is known, who came often from individual firms, often from legal practice, and sometimes from the state service, and who took over a certain area of entrepreneurial functions for a large group of firms.[204] Thus, even before the state authorities interfered directly in the process of financing, production, and distribution – which happened especially during the First World War, the early 1920s, the dictatorship of the Third Reich, and the Second World War – and before public officials once again, as in the mercantilist period, made important entrepreneurial decisions on a large scale, a far-reaching diffusion of the entrepreneurial functions had already taken place at the level of the large firm. Entrepreneurial functions were carried out not only in many different *loci* within the large decentralized concerns but also beyond the frontiers of the individual companies themselves.

Because of this it became possible for individual persons to exercise entrepreneurial functions (or some of them) for whole groups of concerns: the institution of the joint-stock company with its supervisory board, the trend to divide entrepreneurial from managerial functions, the role of the banks, and the trend to inter-company, interregional, and international amalgamations and co-operation enabled a network of large concerns and 'interlocking directorates' to appear. This allowed particularly effective individual entrepreneurs to accumulate decision-making positions and power, and it enabled them to collectively co-ordinate, albeit through decentralized channels, the apparently diffuse system. According to the statement of an insider (Walther Rathenau, the second-in-command of AEG), before the First World War there developed a top group of 300 to 400 leading entrepreneurs – active large shareholders and owners of businesses, directors in the areas of banking, industry, transport, and trade – who directed the entire economic life of Europe and America.[205]

This economic power elite was by no means clearly defined, nor was it a closed community; it remained unclearly focused and was open to new recruits from the ranks of the successful. The communications structure was partly formal (through encounters on supervisory boards, cartel meetings, etc.), but beyond this intensive exchanges took place on an informal basis and through a social cohesion. There were also sharp competitive struggles within this elite, which were not merely about orders and patents but frequently concerned with the survival of large enterprises. At the same time the elite was held together through a basic consensus about the rules of the game, and through ideological agreement. Like the earlier entrepreneurs of the industrial revolution, who had diverse interests (see above), these large entrepreneurs made decisions for many concerns at once but on a much larger scale, and in a different institutional setting. In contrast to their forerunners, they had at their disposal a developed institutional network of supervisory boards, sophisticated forms of inter-company co-operation, and banks, as well as new management techniques and methods of communication, and above all the support of an experienced, functionally organized apparatus of officials.

These trends towards organizing the entrepreneur's function, however, remained incomplete in at least two respects. The continuation of intense struggles, competition, bankruptcies, overinvestment, depressions, unexpected new developments, and growth for its own sake shows the limits of entrepreneurial planning and organization. In spite of all co-ordination between companies, the central investment decisions remained in the hands of entrepreneurs and groups of entrepreneurs, who made them in competition with other groups in accordance with profit-orientated, particularist aims, and necessarily without full knowledge of the overall situation and its future development. This process of growth and change remained somewhat chaotic and primitive, however much it was now being carried out by gigantic companies and permeated by far-reaching tendencies to organization.

The second limit to this trend towards organized management and entrepreneurship is that the great majority of enterprises before and after the First World War continued to employ fewer than a hundred people and were directed by people who were more like the entrepreneurs of the industrial revolution described in section IV. Little is known about this broad entrepreneurial 'infantry', out of which new blood for the offices of large units arose, and for that reason alone it cannot be treated here; nevertheless, the widespread concentration, in the literature, on systematic management and the larger enterprises may be partly justified, in that these large corporations embodied the trends of the future, comprised an increasing proportion of the total number of entrepreneurs, and had an impact on the whole economy which went far beyond that of the small and medium-sized entrepreneurs.

After the First World War a whole series of new factors entered the history of entrepreneurship and management. Entrepreneurs saw (and still see) themselves confronted with complicated problems of self-legitimation and with radical critics among the general public; while the intervention of public authorities has become more intensive and direct and is more decisive than ever for the economic success of a firm. Both these trends have led to an increase in the significance of entrepreneurial efforts in the areas of social and economic policies, which are usually carried out by specialist functionaries and departments both within and outside the company. New problems of employee management were posed by the breakthrough of the independent trade unions to achieving recognition as representatives of the workers' interests, a breakthrough which happened in Germany during the First World War and which proved irreversible, except under the Nazi dictatorship and, in a different way, in the DDR. After the Second World War, 'co-determination' brought the unions on to the supervisory boards and, to some extent, on to the executive boards of large West German concerns. Assembly lines, automation, and computers altered production and the administration of companies in ways inconceivable in 1920. New industries appeared, particularly in the fields of automobiles, the aerospace industry, and electronics. The multinational concern was generally victorious after the Second World War. We cannot examine these and other changes in more detail here.

On the other hand, the trends analysed in section IV have basically continued until today and have even become stronger. The growth, expansion, and diversification of companies have advanced even further; inter-firm mergers and co-operation have been strengthened, even though since the Second World War cartels have been forbidden by law. The links between industry and banks have not been loosened; in the inter-war period the relationship of mutual influence continued to move in favour of the large industrial entrepreneur. The application of science has continued to grow in significance for production, marketing, and company administration. The systematization of management has developed further along the lines recognizable before 1914. The division between ownership and managerial control has made further advances, and its effects on the overall economic situation have remained rather limited, as they had been before the First World War. The professionalization of management personnel has increased, in recent decades particularly in the area of business organization. Skilled behaviour inside formal organizations, the ability to negotiate, and political skills of all sorts are even more clearly necessary for today's good entrepreneur. Division of labour and diffusion of entrepreneurial functions, coupled with their co-ordination through 'generalists' and personal and institutional networks on an international scale, have become more clearly crystallized. One can say that in the brief decades between the end of the industrial revolution and the First World War there appeared central characteristics of management and entrepreneurship in organized capitalism which have continued to mark its development until today.

Labour and Capital in the Scandinavian Countries in the Nineteenth and Twentieth Centuries

I. *The Course of Development*

'Scandinavia' is an international term; it is hardly ever used by Scandinavians. In its strict sense, it means the three countries of Denmark, Norway, and Sweden, but in practice it inevitably includes Finland, not only for historical reasons but also because Finnish society, both generally and economically, is typically Scandinavian. Finland even managed to retain its Scandinavian characteristics through a century of Russian sovereignty (1809–1917). For the purposes of this paper, however, it may simplify things if the very interesting Finnish case is treated separately, after the sections on Scandinavia proper.

The combined population of Denmark, Norway, and Sweden was 4·1 million in 1800, 6·3 million in 1850, 9·7 million in 1900, and 14·6 million in 1950. Thus in 150 years it had more than trebled. It is impossible to give precise, or even imprecise, figures for the national product of the three countries during the earlier part of the period, though a recent and very tentative Danish estimate goes as far back as 1820. Comparisons are possible beginning in the 1860s. During the ninety years from 1860 to 1950 the Swedish national product increased by a factor of fourteen – perhaps a somewhat exaggerated calculation – and its Danish counterpart by a factor of ten, while the Norwegian figures show an eightfold increase during the somewhat shorter period 1865–1950. These figures must of course be treated with the greatest caution, since the definitions and the means of calculating the figures are different in the several countries. The general impression, however, is certainly true. The period after 1950 was marked by a more rapid growth in GNP than ever before, combined with a relatively slow increase in the population.

Before the respective contributions of labour and capital are discussed, something should be said about the general nature of this long-sustained growth and about the main stages in its progress.

At the beginning of the nineteenth century the Scandinavian countries were in many respects well integrated into Europe. They had relatively efficient systems of government and a well-organized administration, comparatively honest by the international standards of the time. Economically, however, they were rather backward. The agrarian sector greatly predominated, and there was much subsistence economy in both Sweden and Norway. But it should be remembered that the agrarian sector was not as purely agrarian as it seemed. Agricultural activities were often combined with other work. Much of the latter was in other sectors of primary production, such as fishing and forestry – fish was the biggest individual item in Norwegian exports as late as the middle of the century – but there was also considerable participation in handicrafts, commerce, and transportation. So when the official statistics show a decline in the agrarian sector during the century, some part of this reflects a more clear-cut division of labour and does not wholly represent a transition between different sectors.

Commerce, both internal and external, must have accounted for a quite modest share of the GNP, but high transport costs and the need for fairly extensive storage owing to the slowness of transportation, coupled with various risks and uncertainties, meant that more capital and labour were needed, relative to the volume of transactions. Both the merchants' profits and their economic experience provided important starting points for future growth. In Denmark, the country's strategic position at the entrance to the Baltic was exploited to give it an important role in intermediary trade.

International trade was insignificant in proportion to the national income, except in Norway, where specific import needs led to a greater dependence on the international sector; but it was important in a qualitative sense. It provided commodities and foreign currencies essential for military power and the general functioning of the royal governments; it contributed to the cultural development – not to mention the luxuries – of the richer and better-educated classes; and it helped to develop the higher types of industrial and commercial organization. Foreign trade also met more elementary needs: despite the dominance of the agrarian sector, both Sweden and, in particular, Norway were net importers of grain.

The pattern of exports was characteristic of Scandinavia's general position. These sparsely populated countries on the fringe of Western Europe furnished the more advanced nations with a variety of raw materials and foodstuffs (together with certain semi-finished products), such as Danish cereals and butter, Norwegian timber and fish, Swedish iron and copper. Swedish exports of wrought iron were backed by an industrial tradition and even some scientific knowledge, but the main reason for their competitiveness was, from the beginning, the low cost of fuel from the Swedish forests. Through its commercial links with the rest of Europe, Scandinavian economic life was naturally affected by the ups and downs of the European economies, but neither this nor the existence of some industrial (or proto-industrial) production for the home market was sufficient to modify the general outline of the picture.

During the first half of the nineteenth century the system was not reshaped but experienced a perceptible pressure on its peripheries and a considerable growth within the traditional framework. Population increased by slightly more than 50 per cent, thereby continuing a process which had begun in the eighteenth century, rather earlier in Sweden and Norway than in Denmark. As the relative positions of the economic sectors changed only slightly, this population growth would have been impossible, or would have brought catastrophe, had there not been vigorous expansion in the agrarian sector.

Agrarian statistics being fallible, the degree of agricultural expansion cannot be measured at all precisely, except possibly in the case of Denmark, but it was evidently sufficient to outweigh – and more than outweigh – the growth in population. At all events, Danish grain exports rose by at least 80 per cent between 1824–7 and 1844–7, while Norwegian grain imports fell. Sweden was no longer a net importer of cereals by the middle of the century, and during the following decades oats, surprisingly enough, became one of the country's leading export items.

This early and remarkable expansion was, naturally, labour-intensive: agriculture was flexible enough to offer employment to an ever-growing active population. In all three countries there was still room for land reclamation. It was particularly notable in Sweden, while it was on a smaller scale in Denmark than in either of the other two countries. At the same time labour productivity also rose, as a result of better organization and of a technical progress which seems to have been marked by a continuous series of small steps rather than by any sensational leaps forward.

In the main, the advances were made when the general agricultural depression of the 1820s was over. The thirties and forties also brought considerable growth to other parts of the economy: to the staple industries as well as to the import-substituting industries (e.g. the emerging factory system in textiles) and to such industries as brewing and distilling. On the whole, this period of preliminary expansion provides an interesting example of successful growth undertaken with limited resources, outwardly modest but full of future promise.

About 1850, the population of Sweden was greater than that of Denmark and Norway combined. As regards the general level of income, the available figures seem to show, firstly, that Denmark had a considerably higher GNP per capita than Sweden. This is what might have been expected, since Denmark's agriculture was far more advanced during a period when the economy was still mainly agricultural.

Secondly, it would seem that Norwegian GNP per capita was equivalent to that of Denmark. This is much more surprising, in view of the pronounced economic advantages which Denmark enjoyed. But it should be stressed that some of the statistics are little more than guesswork. If the Norwegian starting point had been somewhat lower, and if the Norwegian advance after 1850 had been slightly faster than is generally supposed, the story would be more readily understandable. Here, however, we are in the realm of speculation.

The great transition occurred sometime between the middle of the nineteenth century and the First World War. Swedish gross domestic product per capita (in fixed prices) may have trebled during the period 1860–1914; the exact figures are, however, still under discussion. Danish net factor income per capita was nearly two and a half times the 1860 level. Norwegian growth, although rather slower, was nonetheless significant.

Changes of such magnitude were naturally matched by profound structural change. To use a rather conventional measure, the section of the population employed in agriculture (in its widest sense) predominated at the beginning of the period but had fallen to less than half in all three countries by 1914. However, to understand what really happened it must be realized that changes within the different sectors were as important as the changing proportions between them. Both in structure and in aggregate growth, two distinct stages can be recognized: one, more transitional in character, from 1850 to 1895, centred on the expansion of the early 1870s; the other, decidedly more modern in development, belonging to the period 1895–1914.

Much of the growth was export-generated, the two sub-periods representing differing forms of adaptation to an international market. The demand for Scandinavian products during the 70s and 80s developed along traditional lines. It was chiefly directed towards a few staple commodities and other products representing a preliminary stage of industrialization. This applied to the rapidly expanding production of timber, battens, and boards in northern Sweden, generally regarded as the starting point of Swedish industrialization. In Norway, the remarkable expansion in shipping, which made Norway one of the leading seafaring nations, was typical of the last great period of the sailing ships. It was followed by difficult problems of adaptation as sail was gradually ousted by steam. Norwegian fisheries made great advances both technically and economically, without losing their traditional position as an important ancillary occupation for the rural population. Despite considerable modernization, the Swedish iron industry was still characterized by the relatively small size of its production units and – as compared with the leading steel-producing countries – by a decidedly old-fashioned concentration on small-scale quality production. In Denmark, cereal exports reached a peak in the 1870s to be followed, after a difficult period of reorientation, by the rising predominance of butter and other animal products.

There was, of course, no complete change in any of these features after the mid-nineties. In Denmark during the last pre-war decade 1904–14, the agricultural sector's share in the GFI even rose slightly, from 31 to 32 per cent. But Danish agriculture in these expansive years was not of the old traditional type. The most conspicuous change in the country's economy lay in the processing and export of agricultural products. The growing success of the tightly controlled, high-quality Danish butter exports on the international market was the result of technical and organizational progress, with some of the characteristics of an industrial revolution. At the same time, Danish engineering, as well as other types of manufacture (still chiefly producing for the home market), passed through a stage of restructuring and growth.

In Sweden, it was during this period that exports of iron ore, i.e. of a raw material in its crude state, became most significant. Swedish timber exports were stagnant after the 1890s, but wood-pulp production now expanded on a very large scale, surpassing Norwegian production, which until then had played a pioneering role. Production of paper and newsprint was rising in both countries; and in Sweden the engineering industry was developing vigorously, anticipating the outstanding role it was to play in the next period. The general pattern is clearly discernible: from timber to pulp, from iron to engineering, from less-processed to more highly-processed industrial products.

The most striking reorientation occurred in the Norwegian economy. Industrialization in Norway had lagged a little, but its breakthrough now took place with explosive force. General advances in the electro-technical field gave a new value to the enormous resources of water power in Norway. There was a sudden and very dramatic emergence of new hydro-electric power stations, and among the industries using the new sources of energy were – even at this early stage – important and technically advanced chemical establishments. During this period the Norwegian merchant fleet adopted steam to a much higher degree than before.

Another aspect of the great transition was that, with the general broadening of economic activity and the rise in consumption standards, the demands of the home market gained fresh importance and gave further stimulus to production. At last a new society was being built, involving heavier and more widespread investment. A characteristic feature of this expansion was that the additional capacity of the growing Swedish steel industry now served domestic needs instead of increasing exports; this was only partly outweighed by the fact that some of the steel was later exported in a more highly processed form, as engineering products.

None of the Scandinavian countries took part in the First World War. While they prospered during the early war years, their economies were hit severely by blockade and other difficulties during the later years, the net effect being to retard economic growth. Among the results of lasting benefit, however, was an enormous growth in the number of hydro-electric power stations in Sweden, and even more so in Norway, under the challenge of a difficult fuel situation.

In Scandinavia, as everywhere, the period between the wars was fraught with serious difficulties, some of which are discussed below. The depression of the early twenties was particularly severe in Sweden, but recovery was more successful there than in the other countries. Around the middle of the twenties, economic growth met with difficulties in Norway; but the following expansion was very satisfactory, the crisis of the early thirties was relatively mild with regard to economic growth – though not with regard to employment – and the net result of the period, in Norway as in Sweden, was among the most impressive in the world. Denmark, on the other hand, with its heavy dependence on agricultural exports, was hit in a very dramatic way by the adverse market for foodstuffs and raw materials during the thirties and did not recover as easily as the other two countries. The economic nationalism of the decade, and the resulting emphasis on bilateral agreements, had a negative effect on an economy like that of Denmark, with its relatively small differentiation in the export pattern and its pressing need for a more diversified pattern of production.

There was, however, substantial growth in all three countries, even if it was not as rapid, on the whole, as during the two dynamic decades before the war. In many ways the path of economic growth followed the pre-war pattern: the structural change that occurred, or was under way, during this period produced its most important results later, after the Second World War. The same was true of the profound changes in social and economic policies during the thirties. Their historical and psychological relevance was great – and the differences among the three countries were extremely interesting – but immediate economic consequences were nowhere remarkable.

However, the results and the problems of Scandinavian industrialization were both deepened and broadened during the twenties and thirties. Development in urbanization and road transport continued, with a steady growth in the role of manufacturing in the economy and a gradual development towards a more advanced technology. In the export pattern of Sweden, wood pulp and engineering products reached the dominant position that had been anticipated before the war. In Denmark, the choice between a vigorous and increasingly important role for manufacturing and the continued dominance of agricultural products in exports though not in total output, became ever more crucial. The economic policies of the twenties favoured the agriculturalists; the policy of the thirties reversed the trend. Though structural changes may not have been overwhelming, the period stands out as something of a watershed. The modernization of the Norwegian economy, so well under way just before the war, continued vigorously in several fields, particularly in electro-metallurgy, as in mining and metallurgy more generally. Norway's merchant fleet attained a new peak of efficiency once the enormous war losses had been made good, chiefly by modern vessels.

During the Second World War, Denmark and Norway were invaded and occupied. Sweden, on the other hand, remained at peace. Its economy developed, and though some serious problems had to be faced the period was one of widespread social and economic stability. By contrast, the other two countries had to suffer severe difficulties, particularly in the case of Norway.

After the war, all Scandinavia entered a period of more rapid growth, with a considerably higher investment ratio than ever before. Sweden has been conspicuous during the period as the most prosperous of the three countries, due to the foundations laid by the country's successful inter-war development and its relatively privileged position during the war. The post-war rate of growth was not, however, any more remarkable in Sweden than in the two other countries, nor did Sweden have the highest investment ratio. That honour belongs to Norway, which for several reasons – among them the practical one of having once again to recreate a modern merchant fleet – had one of the highest investment ratios anywhere.

As everywhere after the war, the full-employment policy, and the risks of inflation and general overheating associated with it, created a new series of problems and sometimes diverted public attention to economic balance and economic performance in the short run. The general rise in production and productivity was, however, combined with continuous structural change. In Denmark, the transformation to a more strongly pronounced industrial society and, at the same time, the need to preserve a suitable part of the country's agricultural superiority took a particularly dramatic and interesting form. But the Danish case, in a way, forms merely a late and fascinating part of the general Scandinavian story. After a century and a half, the three Scandinavian countries no longer hold their early position as producers and suppliers of raw materials and agricultural commodities on the European periphery. They passed through several stages along the road to industrialization and modernization leading forward from an extension and a refinement of their traditional raw-material-oriented role in the European economy. They at last reached a level where the really decisive factors were to be found not in natural resources – which could often be provided and receive the first stages of processing at lower cost in other parts of the world – but in the skill, the technical and commercial training, the inventiveness characteristic of advanced industrial countries.

We now turn to the constantly changing roles of labour and capital in the developments briefly described above.

II. *The Age of Industrialization* (1850–1914)

A. LABOUR, CAPITAL, AND THE AGRICULTURAL CONTEXT

Through the centuries the land of Scandinavia has, for the most part, been parcelled out into small farms, owner-occupied or tenanted. During the early nineteenth century, the progress of land reclamation and, especially in Denmark and Sweden, of a strong enclosure movement provided fresh opportunities for the energy and enterprise of many small farmers. At the same time, the new situation brought with it a certain tendency towards polarization: those with greater initiative and more cash could afford the transitional costs involved in improving their situation; others faced greater difficulties and had to abandon independent farming.

The number of farms – especially independent farms – could not increase in proportion to the increasing rural population. There was thus a very strong growth in the mass of agricultural labour, with or without small holdings of land but in any case dependent for their livelihood on work for others. In Sweden, around 1850, this labour force represented a higher proportion of the agricultural population than the farmers; but things were to change again soon enough, when the rural population began its secular decline. The actual proportion between the two groups may not, even around 1850, give the impression of any 'capitalistic' development of note, but the change in structure was considerable. It should be remembered that there were strong regional variations and that changes may therefore have been more advanced in some parts than in others.

The greater part of this restructuring meant a shift between different groups of small or middle-sized farming units. There was also, however, a class of big landowners, for some of whom the rural population explosion provided an opportunity to utilize new low-cost labour on their estates for more efficient farming. Some Danish landowners sold a high proportion of the property rights which had brought them rent and labour services in former times, and reorganized the use of their remaining properties.

The big landowners, some of them officials and intellectuals, sometimes pioneered new agricultural techniques. Recent Norwegian research seems to indicate, however, that the technological contributions of small farmers should not be underestimated. Careful study of new methods and implements in the different regions has shown that the winds of change were stronger than is generally supposed – even in the case of Norway, where agriculture was less advanced than in Denmark and Sweden – and that the cumulative effects of small investments by the little man must, in the end, have had an effect comparable to that of the more closely observed performances of a few enlightened gentlemen-farmers. In many cases – such as draining and new building – they invested in kind by direct use of their own or, in any case, locally available labour. In others new implements were bought gradually and for small sums (which were, however, by no means small to the buyers and may in the end have added up to a very respectable total).

Much of this agricultural investment could be achieved by self-financing. Credit opportunities were not readily available to the small farmer, especially in Norway and in Sweden. The market for long-term agricultural credit was primitive. Private lenders played a considerable role as providers of mortgage loans. In Denmark, the old landowning class took part in financing their lease-holders – the descendants of the former unfree peasantry – who wished to acquire the property rights to their land. Denmark, however, was generally more advanced in its agricultural economy than the other two countries.

Special organizations for agricultural credit, such as credit unions, were of no real significance before the end of the period, around 1850, and were not at first particularly interested in the small farmer. The savings banks were soon to play a significant role in agricultural finance, but they were still at an introductory stage. It is self-evident that the personal connections and the general credit-worthiness of the landowners and really big farmers must have given them a disproportionate advantage in a credit market of this kind. The total volume of mortgage loans in the countryside was, however, rising steeply during the period.

A new kind of agricultural society was developing, marked by a greater degree of individual enterprise, more effective market orientation, and a growing use of borrowed money. This – and the favourable price movements in agriculture – manifested themselves in the growing activity of the land market, where land prices rose and there was a good deal of speculative business.

In Denmark, profits from agriculture – at least from the big agricultural enterprises – became important for industrial finance. This was hardly the case in Sweden and Norway. But profits in another quarter – among grain merchants and other dealers in agricultural products – must have been considerable and may well have had significant indirect consequences.

It is, perhaps, unnecessary to repeat that not everyone in the agricultural sector devoted his efforts exclusively to agriculture. The Norwegian fisheries, where output rose in the thirties and forties, are a case in point. The small coastal farmer found it natural to invest in boats and gear – sometimes in collective forms – and leave home for an extensive fishing season each year. It has recently been shown how small the profits must have been at times for the individual participant. His main benefit may well have lain in the fact that the return from fishing met his need for liquid resources. Nevertheless, as with the purely agricultural products, the intermediaries in the Norwegian fish trade must have earned considerable profits.

The net result of the main agricultural changes – the rise of a new type of individualistic farmer and the growth of a class of agricultural labour – must have been an increase in labour productivity, even if a good deal of less productive labour must have remained on the land until the situation was changed by migration and mechanization.

B. INDUSTRIAL LABOUR

The history of labour and capital between 1850 and 1914 was marked by important structural changes, such as the emergence of an industrial labour force and the establishment of a modern credit system. But above all, labour and capital contributed to a decisive rate of economic growth. In the following pages we discuss first labour, then capital, and finally the relationship between them.

The active population – defined as those aged between fifteen and sixty-four – in Scandinavia is shown in Table 139: there was a total increase between 1850 and 1910 of 2·4 million, or more than 60 per cent. This was less than might have been expected from Scandinavia's natural increase in population, but considerable emigration occurred from all three countries during the period. The net loss totalled about two million people, most of them naturally belonging to the active age groups. Emigration figures were lowest in Denmark, which was still the most prosperous of the Scandinavian countries, with an expanding and flexible agricultural economy. Norway, with its many stubborn problems, had the highest rate of emigration.

In one aspect, the effect of Scandinavian emigration was positive: it facilitated a relatively swift adaptation to economic fluctuations. The main stream of emigrants left Scandinavia during and immediately before and after the eighties. During that period the active population in Sweden showed no increase at all, while in Norway there was even a moderate decrease. When prosperity returned, the population rose once more.

Table 139. *Active Population (between 15 and 64 years) in Sweden, Denmark, and Norway, 1850–1910 (millions)*

	Sweden	Denmark	Norway	Total
1850	2·2	0·9	0·8	3·9
1870	2·5	1·1	1·0	4·6
1890	2·8	1·3	1·1	5·2
1910	3·3	1·6	1·4	6·3

SOURCES

Sweden: P. Silenstam, *Arbetskraftsutbudets utveckling i Sverige 1870–1965* (Uppsala, 1970), 97.

Denmark: S. A. Hansen, *Økonomisk vaekst i Danmark*, 2 vols., II (Copenhagen, 1974), 201–3.

Norway: J. Bjerke, *Langtidslinjer i norsk økonomi 1865–1960* (Oslo, 1966), 26; Norway, Central Bureau of Statistics, *Historisk statistikk 1968*, Norges Offisielle Statistikk, XII: 245 (Oslo, 1969), 38.

Much of the pre-emigration population of Scandinavia, of course, provided labour of low productivity. Those who were least productive – or were least productively employed – were often incapable of emigrating, but some of them found fresh opportunities open to them once the emigrants had left. The retarded growth of the labour supply also meant a stronger bargaining position for the remaining labour force. So much is clear. But the loss in the quality of the labour force is difficult to assess, just as it is difficult to imagine what might have been achieved with a larger labour force. It may well be that the favourable light in which emigration is regarded nowadays – in itself a natural reaction to the earlier patriotic condemnation – is a shade too optimistic.

Emigration reflects not only the difficulties in the lives of people but also the flexibility of the population. In this respect it is part of a more general pattern – one, moreover, of fundamental importance for general growth. Internal migration also increased sharply and was even more of a mass movement than external migration. The net figures for urbanization in general or for the growth of capital cities like Copenhagen and Stockholm are impressive in themselves, but they do not fully measure the process. The annual migration gains of a city such as Stockholm represented the relatively moderate difference between much greater inflows and outflows of population. All over the country, the seasonal population movements of a more primitive society gradually changed, at lèast in many cases, into a pattern of more sharply defined movements. These movements had corresponding social consequences. There was always a population surplus seeking employment. Economic gains from migration were bought at the expense of serious slum problems in the big cities, and even among the more successful workers there were newcomers unaccustomed to town and factory life.

Migration from the countryside did not, however, lead to the abrupt end of an agrarian society. Denmark is exceptional in many respects, and it may seem natural that the Danish agrarian labour force around 1900 was far greater than that employed in manufacturing. But in Sweden, too, the numbers employed in the agrarian sector were greater.

The growth of the industrial working class was a complicated and gradual process: the conventional divisions often seem inadequate when applied to it. What happened implied not so much the expansion of manufacturing employment at the expense of primary production as the mobilization of resources and the rationalization of productive capacity over a broad spectrum. Certain cases of great typological interest illuminate something of the dynamics of the process, even though they may not always be particularly important in absolute terms.

Towards the end of the nineteenth century the Swedish sawmills employed thirty to forty thousand workers in the narrow statistical meaning of the word. This figure, however, does not express the most interesting aspect of the situation. Firstly, the qualitative meaning of the terms 'labour' and 'labour force' at the sawmills changed during the period. Seasonal variations were marked; they had a greater impact in the beginning of the period, but at no time before 1914 were they negligible. During much of the winter, work was slack or ceased completely, while the demand for labour rose dramatically towards the end of the shipping season. Casual labour, therefore, played an important, although gradually declining, role. Several different streams of workers flowed to the mills in the Northeast of Sweden, ranging from groups trudging up from the distant West of the country in the hope of long-term jobs to the additional workers from the immediate vicinity or from Finland, who took on marginal loading jobs in the summer. In such a situation, the difficulty of defining a 'real' or 'typical' industrial worker is obvious. How were the seasonal workers occupied during the rest of the year? And what was their total individual productivity?

Secondly – and this is what really mattered – employment at the sawmills was only a fraction of the total employment provided by the sawmill industry. Timber costs were the main element in total production costs, but timber costs consisted chiefly of wages for work in the forests, for transporting the timber to the river, and for floating it down to the mill. A Finnish writer has tried to calculate the ratio in 1912 of sawmill workers to the other kinds of labour needed to supply them with timber, etc.: he reckoned that eight other workers were needed to support every man in the sawmill. The figure would be equally valid for the traditional sawmill industry in Sweden and Norway.

The evolution of the labour force, the relationship between capital and labour, and the standards of the workers employed can, thus, be easily misunderstood if the term 'industry' is too rigorously defined. Compared with other industrial workers, the sawmill workers of the period were relatively well paid. Their wage level, however, was of no great significance to their employers. Forest and timber-transport workers, on the other hand, were members of the agrarian population, for whom the work was a by-employment and was evidently badly paid, resulting in significant savings in labour cost to the companies. The sawmills carried on the traditional organization of labour supply formerly prevailing in ironworks, where for every worker at the furnaces or forges there were several charcoal-burners and transport workers. In consequence, the industry's impact on the labour market was far greater than might be imagined from the direct number of in-dustrial workers in the conventional sense of the term.

There is a certain resemblance between the Swedish timber industry and the Danish production of butter and pork for export. In Denmark, as in Sweden, industrialization set in at the final stage, and that implied significant technical and organizational changes; but the export com-modities were, in the main, indigenous agricultural products, and the corresponding effects on employment were, of course, felt chiefly in the agricultural sector. In Norway, the fisheries, even in a fairly advanced state, retained much of their connection with the agricultural milieu and much of their traditional and seasonal character.

The great transition that accompanied Scandinavian industrialism in its more decisive form was not only quantitative, as represented by the growth of the industrial sector: it was also, to a high degree, structural in the sense that it was represented by growth within the industrial sector of more permanently functioning and less seasonally bound establishments, and of industries with a higher rate of manufacturing 'value added' relative to the raw-material content of the product. Simultaneously there was a change from the more handicraft type of establishments to bigger and more highly mechanized ones.

Industrial development from the 1890s onwards was important in all these respects. To what extent the gradual nature of the change made it easier for the workers to adapt themselves to their new tasks is difficult to assess. Many of them came from the countryside and had yet to be assimilated into industrial society. The fact that popular education was comparatively well advanced in Scandinavia may have made it easier for them to assimilate. The additional knowledge demanded by their work was chiefly acquired on the job. The same may also well have been true of engineers: the local tradition of relatively well-managed establishments, coupled with foreign travel and study abroad, was of fundamental importance to them. A good deal was done, though, to provide higher technical education at home, at any rate in Sweden and Denmark.

The class-consciousness which is linked with the worker's personal independence, and also with his performance in the factory, must also have developed very gradually. A Norwegian investigation shows that the political attitudes of the workers around 1900 varied from region to region. The growth of political cohesion among the workers would have been affected by the scattered nature of industry in Norway and Sweden and by the fact that so many of the factories were located away from the cities. This, together with the more advanced state of the Danish economy and the more 'European' situation of Denmark, may explain why labour movements developed earlier in Denmark than in the other two countries. The process was fairly well advanced throughout Scandinavia before the First World War. Industrial relations, too, were relatively well developed, but it is interesting to note that in 1914, partly as the result of a not very successful labour conflict in 1909 (the 'Great Strike'), only a minority of the workers in Swedish industry belonged to trade unions. It seems unlikely that the Swedish trade unions influenced wage levels to any great extent before the First World War, but they may well have affected other conditions of employment such as the length of the working day. In Denmark, estimates of the trade unions' impact are more positive, though serious comparative studies have yet to be made.

Given the strong economic growth during the period, a rise in real wages was almost inevitable. Industrial development was dynamic and heterogeneous, and generalized comparisons are therefore necessarily hazardous. But studies so far indicate a quite remarkable increase. Real hourly wages in the Swedish mining and manufacturing industries in 1914 are thought to have been nearly two and a half times higher than in 1870; in Denmark the difference was even more spectacular, manufacturing wages trebling during the period. Daily wages (and yearly wages for the fully occupied) rose at a rather slower rate, because the working day was shortened.

Rising living standards should have increased the quality of the work performed. It is probable that this really happened, but the fact that it did so is not quite self-evident. As British scholars have remarked, better wages cannot be expected to lead to better health and a significant advance in well-being until workers' housing is improved. The gradual nature and the flexibility of the developments described no doubt facilitated the solution of some of the problems involved, but housing is notorious for having been a frequent bottleneck.

The new industrial labour force was new in many respects. While retaining close links with rural society, it had few traditions of its own and was unaccustomed to the ways of its new society. It was sometimes overawed by established authority and sometimes antagonistic, while always groping for some new basis for stability. In view of all this, its performance is all the more remarkable.

C. INVESTMENT

It is now generally accepted that in a period of industrialization the demands on investment for the infrastructure – for transport, urbanization, new housing, and public services – are greater than those for direct industrial development. The traditional sectors of the economy would still dominate the scene, at least in the early stages of industrialization, and a considerable share of total investment would therefore go to them. With the pronounced agricultural background of the Scandinavian countries and the gradual nature of their development these general rules must naturally apply during their industrialization period.

This may be illustrated by a Swedish calculation – shown in Table 140 – of the percentage distribution of total investment (in fixed assets) during a few selected five-year periods. According to these calculations, agriculture, transport, and housing were responsible for 78 per cent of all Swedish investment during the period 1866–70, or five to six times the figure for industrial investment. Agriculture's share was, in fact, far

Table 140. *Distribution of Gross Investment in Fixed Assets in Sweden, 1866–1915 (per cent)*

	Agriculture	Manufacturing and mining	Transport	Housing	Public Services	Total
1866–70	28	14	19	31	8	100
1881–5	20	19	13	40	8	100
1896–1900	10	21[a]	17	42	10	100
1911–15	9	26[a]	19	31	15	100

[a] Including 1 per cent commerce.

SOURCE. L. Lundberg, *Kapitalbildningen i Sverige 1861–1965* (Uppsala, 1969), 142.

greater than that of manufacturing and mining throughout the 1870s, even including the early boom years. The fundamental change – which brought the share for industry up to more than twice the figure for agriculture – did not occur until the second half of the 1890s. The fluctuations in transport investment reflect the different stages of Swedish railway-building: this was at a peak in the 1870s – not represented in Table 140 – and, after some decline, took a fresh upward turn in the nineties. In track miles the Swedish railway system was larger than either the Danish or Norwegian systems, both absolutely and relative to population. For the Danes and Norwegians, investment in shipping and shipping facilities such as harbours and docks was, for geographical reasons, of greater relative importance. The role of housing in the Swedish figures should also be noted. These figures for housing seem suspiciously high, but the general circumstance behind them (i.e. the remarkable importance of residential building in the investment pattern of those days) can hardly be doubted. The distribution of Danish investment was rather similar to the Swedish, the dominant position of agriculture being particularly well marked.

Sweden's total gross investment in fixed assets (repairs and maintenance excluded) did not exceed 8 per cent of GNP in the sixties. It rose sharply to a little more than 11 per cent in the early seventies, declined in the depression, and was between 9·5 and 10 per cent in the eighties. Its share then declined a little more again in the early nineties, only to rise to as high as 12·5 per cent during the expansionary decade of 1896–1905. After that it was somewhat lower again. Throughout all these fluctuations, the general upward trend is clear.

The most reliable of the Danish calculations are made on a somewhat different basis from the Swedish ones, but comparisons between them are nonetheless meaningful. The investment rate seems to have been lower in Denmark than in Sweden during the earlier part of the period – especially around 1890 – but it rose very sharply during the nineties and was rather above the Swedish level before 1914. The Norwegian rate was, evidently, of the same general order as that of the other countries. It was remarkably high around 1890 – when the Danish figures were low – and also during the years immediately before the First World War. In Scandinavia, as everywhere, rates of investment measure not only the sacrifices which people were willing to make for the sake of future progress but also the ease with which the various goals could be attained in different countries.

The main sources of investment were internal, but an additional contribution from capital imports proved necessary in all three countries. Imported capital was responsible for about one-sixth of total Swedish investment during the period 1870–1910. It was especially important during the eighties, when it contributed nearly a quarter. In this way, foreign capital helped to maintain Swedish investment at a tolerable level during the difficult years of low prices. Capital imports were also of considerable importance during the economic fluctuations at the turn of the century.

Foreign long-term investments were almost exclusively in bonds: not those of manufacturing companies, which had no ready market outside Sweden, but bonds issued by the state, the municipalities, the railway companies – whose loans were guaranteed by the state – and the agricultural credit associations. As already mentioned, these were the fields where the need for capital was greatest, and they did not always promise easy returns. An investigation into Swedish railway finance has shown that from the crisis of the 1870s to the end of the century the financial situation of the private railways was often precarious. It was essential, therefore, that the government should not only build the strategic main lines of the system but also help by guaranteeing the loans which the private railway companies issued abroad. The effort demanded by railway-building in Scandinavia was, incidentally, particularly heavy, since the direct economic impact of railway construction on other industries was relatively small. Even in steel production, nearly all the rails required in Sweden were imported; they could have been produced within the country, but that type of production did not fit into the general pattern of the Swedish iron industry.

Denmark differed from Sweden in one respect. Because of its considerable agricultural exports and the favourable trend in the terms of trade, the country had a balance-of-payments surplus as late as the 1870s. During the 1880s, however, the currency reserve was gradually eroded, and during the 1890s the time had come for fresh imports of capital. This increased gradually and soon became very important: the total amount at the beginning of the war was one thousand million Danish kroner, equivalent to about a quarter of all investment during the period of capital imports. In both form and composition foreign credits were much the same in Denmark as in Sweden, with Denmark – as the most experienced country in the financial field – acting as something of a mentor to the other Scandinavian countries.

In Norway, capital imports were of particular importance during the great industrialization period from the 1890s to 1914, being responsible for perhaps as much as 20 per cent of investment. Capital imports differed in form from those of Denmark and Sweden, where direct foreign investment in productive enterprise was quantitatively a very restricted phenomenon – though from other points of view an important one. In Norway, where the banking system was more conservative and less well adapted for financing industrial investment, direct investment from abroad was of vital importance. Out of a total debt in 1913 of 863 million kroner, more than a third was invested in industrial enterprises. Approximately 40 per cent of the shares in Norwegian joint-stock companies were in foreign hands. Sectors of strategic importance for future growth were particularly favoured by foreign investors: as much as 80 per cent of the shares in the mining industry and a large proportion of the Norwegian hydro-electric power industry were foreign-owned.

Foreign capital and enterprise certainly contributed to rapid economic growth in Norway, an important example being the electro-chemical industry, where both large capital inputs and good contacts with the international markets were needed. On the other hand, the potential consequences of the influx of foreign capital caused a good deal of concern and aroused strong nationalist opposition. Restrictive measures were introduced from 1907 onwards, first in provisional form but later – during the war – by legislation of more permanent character.

Whatever the importance of foreign capital, Scandinavian investment (as already mentioned) was chiefly financed out of the savings of the domestic economy. The problem of their sources and the ways in which those were utilized is here discussed in connection with its microeconomic aspects – from the point of view of enterprises, industrial or otherwise.

In the pre-industrial era real capital increased slowly, and the most pressing financial need of the individual enterprise was for working capital, not for fixed capital. The staple industries of iron and timber were seasonal – their expenditures on raw materials were, to a great extent, concentrated into the part of the year when shipments to the foreign buyer were impossible, a circumstance which was bound to create financial difficulties. Under the old system the natural providers of credit were the buyers of the goods, the Swedish merchant paying in advance for the wrought iron of the Swedish ironworks and receiving payment in advance from the British merchant on whom he was able to draw as soon as the iron had been shipped from the Swedish port.

This traditional system operated with considerable effect; seasonal credit quite often developed into long-term credit and led to the financial dependence of the enterprise on the creditor. It should be stressed, however, that the system was not necessarily universal. The capitalists of the *ancien régime* had neither the unlimited resources nor the Machiavellian cunning to conquer the whole field systematically, and the pattern of financing was in fact quite varied. Different studies of the Swedish iron industry in the eighteenth century and the first half of the nineteenth suggest that at the end of each year about 50 per cent of the ironworks were net debtors of the merchants; among the other 50 per cent some were, in fact, large creditors. An investigation of the relations between Hamburg merchants and their Bergen suppliers of fish and other products in the early nineteenth century has produced much the same picture. There is a very interesting Danish parallel. The merchants of Jylland were dependent on seasonal credit from Hamburg. In the western part of the peninsula this often led the debtors into a continuously dependent position, while short-term credits in the eastern part were generally repaid in due time and thus retained their seasonal character.

Subject to such limitations the traditional system continued during the expansion of the Swedish timber industry in the 1850s and the decades immediately following. Seasonal credits from the buyers were also an important factor in the export of oats to Britain about this time. Soon, however, there emerged a growing differentiation between the commodity trade and the credit system. Towards the end of the century, the big Swedish timber firms agreed not to grant more than one month's credit to their foreign customers. The credit needs of Swedish timber exporters had to be met in other ways.

Short-term credits from abroad were, by then, utilized in some very different fields. In Sweden, the expanding commercial banks had various devices for getting short-term money from Germany and elsewhere, some of these short-term credits being continuously renewed. Some of the less experienced banks took considerable risks in this way.

The need for growing amounts of fixed capital during the industrialization period was naturally affected, and in some respects mitigated, by the gradual nature of the process. At an early stage, when resources and credit facilities were limited, it was sometimes possible to concentrate on types of production requiring relatively low investment. Forests for the timber industry of northern Sweden (or the right to exploit them, with certain restrictions, over an agreed period) could be acquired very cheaply from farmers who had no means of organizing an efficient timber industry of their own. The great distances involved made it possible to avoid much of the inter-company competition which would otherwise have forced prices to rise. The main reason why the country's iron industry operated in the nineteenth century with small and sometimes old-fashioned establishments may well have been that extension and modernization would have demanded more risk-taking and more outside capital than the firms could stand; their financial situation was rather poor during the greater part of the century. When Norwegian shipping had to adapt to steam, much ingenuity was used not only to seek out routes where sailing ships could still be run profitably but also to utilize small or second-hand steamers so that a reasonable share of the market could be retained without heavy investment.

One aspect of the structural change occurring towards the very end of the century was the need to intensify and extend the whole system of investment in a large number of fields. As regards the need for long-term capital, this could be met in three ways: by direct contributions of the owners, by ploughing back profits once the enterprise got going, and by borrowing.

In none of the Scandinavian countries have there yet been any systematic investigations to discover who were responsible for starting or developing enterprises and where their resources came from. Some answers to these questions can, however, be attempted. Some of the money for Danish manufactures came (as already mentioned) from successful agriculturalists. Both in Denmark and in the other two countries, merchant capital was certainly an important factor. It has been shown in several cases that merchant interests were behind the timber industry of northern Sweden, moving over from the import trade and from the shipping business, which met with changed conditions and became less profitable after the middle of the century. As industrialization advanced, new industries were sometimes created by industrialists in older fields. The somewhat risky iron and steel industry in Sweden was sometimes financed by savings from the less glamorous, but also less risky, consumer-goods industries. The full story, however, has yet to be written.

Nor do we know at all precisely the degree of risk involved in investment in industrial enterprises. In new fields, where experience was inadequate and fluctuations were great, many investments inevitably failed. Such misallocations of capital, however, were of two distinct types. In some cases they involved investment in enterprises which were not just temporarily embarrassed but permanently unprofitable. In others, the objectives were right, but the capital resources or the skill of the individual pioneers proved inadequate. From the point of view of the economy as a whole, the former case meant total loss. In the latter case – where it often happened that a new establishment, with or without a formal bankruptcy, was eventually acquired at a reduced price and could yield a profit on that outlay – the investment costs proved higher for the economy as a whole than for the successful individuals who reaped the ultimate profits, but in these cases the undue optimism of the pioneers may well have fulfilled a constructive purpose.

At what precise point the joint-stock system led to a real broadening of industrial ownership it is impossible to say. The early companies were often founded for purposes other than manufacturing, e.g. for trade or transport; and for many companies, changing to joint stock often meant no more than altering the form of existing partnerships, with their actual ownership left unchanged. As in so much else, the two

decades immediately preceding the First World War brought a fundamental change even in this respect. Issues of shares to the general public
became much more common. Organized business on the stock exchange – and organized speculation – attained wholly new dimensions.
A long series of mergers and industrial amalgamations also took place,
sometimes on such a scale, particularly in the consumer goods industries,
as to create monopolies or at least oligopolistic situations.

This is not the place to discuss in detail the changing forms of agricultural enterprise, but one aspect of the changes should be mentioned.
In the remarkable case of Danish agricultural production, with its transition to more or less industrialized forms of processing, developments
were facilitated by the rapid growth of agricultural co-operation.
Danish butter achieved an international reputation thanks to a series of
well-equipped and hygienically well-supervised co-operative dairies
where technical innovations could be applied and production methods
progressively developed without a break in the structure of agricultural
ownership. The Danish savings banks were very helpful in financing
this co-operative enterprise.

A high degree of industrial self-financing and a corresponding degree
of financial caution were essential during the early stages of expansion.
Professor Gårdlund shows in his work on Swedish industrial finance in
the period 1830–1913 that profits were treated very circumspectly by
the larger and more conscientiously run enterprises, the pioneers often
taking no more out of the enterprise than the essential minimum for
their own use and frequently holding dividends down quite drastically.
He also shows that in a sample of about twenty-five firms the firms'
own capital accounted for the greater part of the assets until the big leap
forward around 1900, when expansion was more rapid and the credit
system better developed.

The distribution among different types of long-term industrial credit
is illustrated, for three selected years, in Table 141. The figures under
'Others' include credit from private individuals; such creditors represent more than 40 per cent in 1850, as much as 25 per cent in 1880, but

Table 141. *Types of Long-Term Credit in a Sample of Swedish
Industrial Firms (per cent)*

	Bank loans	Bonds	Others	Total
1850	24	—	76	100
1880	25	26	49	100
1910	39	37	24	100

SOURCE. T. Gårdlund, *Svensk industrifinansiering under genombrottsskedet 1830–1913*
Stockholm, 1947), 80.

only 10 per cent in 1910. Their role is especially interesting from a historical point of view. In early-nineteenth-century Scandinavia, credit – even that given to industrial enterprises – was not, in the main, institutionalized. Much of the private loans and credits came, of course, from relatives or personal connections of the entrepreneurs, but a substantial part also came through such intermediaries as brokers and private financiers. Before the banking system's breakthrough it was difficult not only for the industrialists to get loans and credits but also for private owners of capital to find a profitable and secure form of investment for their money. Contacts were lacking in both directions. Some of the private intermediaries conducted an astonishingly extensive business. When Johan Holm of Stockholm, whose transactions had played an important role for several big industrial enterprises, went bankrupt in 1865, his deficiency ran to twenty million kronor. An old-established industrial firm, Stora Kopparberg of Falun, received deposits directly and paid interest on them. As late as the early 1890s about two million kronor of its outside capital – on formal notice of a few months, but in practice in more or less permanent loan – was provided in this way by private persons and different public or semi-public funds. Up to the end of the period, there was room for private initiative in the Scandinavian countries both in the credit business and in floating companies. Private financiers were quite influential, and it should not be forgotten that the heads of Danish and Swedish commercial banks with especially strong industrial interests, such as Tietgen and Glückstadt in Denmark and the Wallenberg family and Louis Fraenckel in Sweden, combined their banking activities with personal transactions in their own names.

The credits granted by the national banks of the Scandinavian countries at the very beginning of industrialization were generally on terms advantageous to the borrowers; but if the interest was modest, the volume was very restricted. To this extent these credits were more in the nature of grants for industrial and other activities.

In agriculture, savings banks soon became influential. Their share of the total volume of credit was remarkable at the turn of the century, especially in Denmark, where their deposits in 1899 were twice as large as those of the commercial banks. The difference was rapidly reduced but did not disappear until 1913–14, the commercial banks having acquired a small lead in the final year.

There were instances of commercial banking in eighteenth-century Sweden, but there is no continuous line of development from them to modern banking. The first nineteenth-century commercial bank in Sweden was founded in 1830 in the southern part of the country; it had a special interest in commerce and agriculture and had a few successors in provincial Sweden. The important stage of Scandinavian banking history starts, in all three countries, in the 1850s. The banks played an important role – and met with considerable economic difficulties – during the 1870s. The real breakthrough came, however, in the 1890s and in the period immediately following, when the expansion of banking and that of the economy in general exerted reciprocal influences. Swedish commercial bank lending more than quadrupled from 560 million kronor in 1895 to about 2,500 million in 1913–14. Lending by the Danish banks rose even more steeply to more than five times the 1895 figure, although in absolute terms the figures were lower than the Swedish ones. In Norway, the rate of growth at this stage was about the same as in Sweden and Denmark.

Of the many banks in Denmark, those of importance to industrialization were the big Copenhagen banks, especially Privatbanken (established in the 1850s) and Landmansbanken (established in the 1870s). They tended to be of the German type, actively engaged in industrial finance and with their own capital playing a considerable role relative to deposits. Privatbanken during the earlier part of the period, and Landmansbanken during the later part, enjoyed a leading position in the expansion of big business. They also played a significant role in the supply of foreign capital, i.e. by organizing the sale of Danish government bonds abroad.

Swedish banking was far more dispersed. Characteristically, the country's largest bank until the turn of the century was not a Stockholm bank, but one with its head office in Malmö in southern Sweden. In 1910 it merged with the Skandinaviska Kreditaktiebolaget, a Gothenburg–Stockholm bank which had just taken the lead by a small margin; the merged bank so formed was, of course, far bigger than any other in Sweden. Ever since its foundation in 1864 the Skandinaviska's contribution to industrial development had been outstanding. It was, however, more conservative than two of its competitors, Stockholm's Enskilda Bank (established in 1856) and Stockholm's Handelsbank (established in 1871). These two – of which Enskilda was the earlier – were specially organized for co-operation with big business. Structurally the Handelsbank, at the end of the period, was very much of the German type; in 1910, only 60 per cent of its lending was covered by deposits. In Norway, plans for a bank of the *crédit-mobilier* type had been put forward as early as 1851, but (as already pointed out) Norwegian banking did not specialize in direct industrial finance, being rather more traditionally oriented than the big Danish and Swedish banks.

The issue of industrial bonds in Scandinavia was an innovation dating from the second half of the nineteenth century. At first it tended to be organized by private bankers, but it gradually became an accepted part

of the commercial banks' business. Changes in the character of the bond
issues reflected the economic and financial growth during the period.
By the beginning of the twentieth century after great developments,
bonds issued under the auspices of the banks were considered absolutely
secure and found a ready market; from the banks' point of view the
profits were small but the difficulties involved were trifling. A few
decades earlier, the whole structure of industrial finance had been
different. In Sweden, at least, the bonds of industrial and other companies had not been at all easy to sell: the major part of the stock had
sometimes remained for years on the hands of the issuing banks, and the
issuers had still carried considerable risks; but in successful cases the
profits from these earlier bond issues could be correspondingly handsome. The change in the financial environment of industrial business
was certainly remarkable.

D. THE CAPITAL–LABOUR RELATIONSHIP

Formalized expressions of the capital–labour relationship are far more
precise and important for recent years than for the period up to 1914;
but two Swedish contributions deserve to be briefly mentioned at this
stage. In 1966, K. G. Jungenfeldt attempted to measure the wages/
income ratio in Sweden for the whole period 1870–1950, including in
the wage bill that part of entrepreneurial income which represents compensation for work performed. From 1870 to around 1895 the ratio of
wages to total income was approximately 70 per cent. Its assumed
tendency to change counter-cyclically – rising during slumps and falling
during booms – is not always discernible in the Swedish figures, partly
because agriculture's share in the economy was still very great and the
fluctuations of agriculture did not always keep in step with those of
industry. The expansionary years in the early 1870s were accompanied
by a rising, rather than a falling, wages/income ratio. From the mid-
1890s onward, however, the ratio was falling. On average for 1896–
1900 it was still 70 per cent, or even slightly more, but by 1912–16 it
had fallen to just below 60 per cent. It was then that industrialization
achieved its real breakthrough and provided increasingly important
investment opportunities.

  In absolute terms the real wages of the workers rose in the years
1896–1914, but the change in their respective share is interesting and
illustrates the fact that growth during the period was not without its
social and political tensions. The changing relationship and accompanying tensions were most pronounced in the years at the beginning of the
century, when the growth in real wages was in fact slower than either
before or after. When this is said, it should be pointed out that these

figures remain highly hypothetical, that they are meaningful chiefly for long-term development, and that they should not be taken – nor were they meant to be taken – quite literally.

Yngve Åberg has analysed the development of productivity in the Swedish economy during the period 1896–1955. According to his figures, production per person employed increased, on average, by 1 per cent per annum between 1871 and 1890, and by no less than 2·8 per cent per annum between 1891 and 1915. An important part of the total increase was, of course, the result of the re-allocation of labour: an increasing proportion of the labour force had been transferred to more productive employment in manufacturing. The most marked productivity increase during the earlier period was in public services and transport; during the latter period productivity grew fastest in manufacturing and mining, with an annual growth rate of 3·2 per cent.

Taking a modified production function of the Cobb–Douglas type, Åberg attempts to show the contributions to the rate of growth of production attributable to capital, to labour, and to the 'residual factor', which includes improvements in technique and organization. The role of capital, naturally, grew in relation to the role of labour, especially with the intensified industrialization from the mid-1890s onwards. It appears that the country's total capital stock in 1913 was two and a half times its 1895 figure, while the labour force had increased by no more than 15 per cent.

According to Åberg, labour's share of the increase of production during the whole period 1870–1913 was a modest 10 per cent, while capital's share reached a unique level of no less than 48 per cent. The size of the residual, though not exceeding 42 per cent, was certainly considerable. The result is what might have been expected; the share of capital relative to labour was rising, and was large even in relation to the residual, during a phase in the industrial revolution when the pace of technical change was still fairly moderate. An earlier and more laconically expressed Norwegian assessment is very similar. The contribution of capital to growth was becoming increasingly important; the residual was smaller than it was to become later – but, in the Norwegian case, it was clearly increasing during the period.

From whatever angle Scandinavian industrialization is studied, the constantly recurring impression is that of the distinctive character of the two decades after 1895. During this short period things really happened.

III.   *The First World War and the Inter-War Period*

A. LABOUR

During the period 1910–40 the active population of Scandinavia – those aged fifteen to sixty-four – increased from 6·3 million to 9·1 million, or by about 45 per cent. This was a much more vigorous growth rate than that of the rest of the population. Economic growth and the economic policies of the twenties and thirties were not expansive enough for all the additional labour to be absorbed. More Scandinavians were gainfully employed than ever before; but even so, unemployment was far more serious than before the First World War.

Comparisons are difficult because of the deficiencies of pre-war statistics, but there seems no doubt that, apart from different types of agricultural underemployment or hidden unemployment, large-scale unemployment in Scandinavia in the nineteenth and early twentieth centuries was mainly a short-term phenomenon. Open unemployment was largely confined to periods of slump. Between the wars, by contrast, the peaks of unemployment were exceptionally high, and even in good years the level of unemployment was well above both present and pre-1914 standards.

Both demographic development and the pattern of unemployment were somewhat different in each country. In Sweden, where the share of the active population before the war had been unusually great and the continued growth was slower than in Denmark and Norway, the highest unemployment rate of the inter-war period, 26·6 per cent, was registered as early as 1921. It was followed by another peak in the early thirties (23·3 per cent in 1933), but the unemployment rate of the good years was generally not higher than 10–12 per cent. In Norway, the active population increased dramatically during the thirties, and unemployment, which had reached a peak of 33·4 per cent in 1933, stood at 22 per cent as late as 1938 – even though that was a time of general economic prosperity. In the twenties the Norwegian unemployment problem had been at its most acute not in the beginning but in the middle of the decade, when both Norway and Denmark were making strenuous efforts – rather later than Sweden – to revert to the gold standard. Unemployment was less severe in Denmark than in Norway. The peaks were somewhat less pronounced (32 per cent during 1932, which proved the worst year), and recovery was rather more successful in respect of employment, though not in that of general economic growth. The general pattern in the two countries, however, was similar: in both there was more widespread unemployment at the end of the period than in Sweden.

The general situation certainly did not give labour a strong bargaining position. Nevertheless, wages seem to have risen somewhat more than might have been expected. In Norway real hourly industrial wages almost doubled during the years 1914–39. In Sweden the increase was more than 80 per cent; in Denmark it was a little less. Most of the increase occurred in the twenties. In the thirties the situation was dominated by unemployment. In Sweden the net increase in hourly wages during the period 1930–9 was only 7 per cent, while in Denmark there was no increase at all. In Norway the wages of those lucky enough to be employed rose more than in the two other countries – about 10 per cent. There was thus a telling contrast between Norway, with its more favourable movement of wages, and Denmark, with its stagnant wages and a more favourable employment situation. Generally, compared with the situation in 1914, the aggregate earnings of workers did not move quite as favourably as their hourly wage rates: firstly because all three countries had adopted the eight-hour day at the end of the war, and secondly because the hours worked per annum, even by those who were not permanently unemployed, were often reduced on account of the economic situation.

Thus the twenties and the thirties were hardly a glorious period in the history of the working class. Nevertheless the period saw the beginnings of certain developments which proved to be of great future significance.

In the first place there were changes in the quality of labour and in the rational utilization of labour supplies. The statutory shortening of the working day – in Scandinavia as elsewhere this was an extension and codification of a process which had been going on for a long time – had the effect of intensifying the employers' concern for labour efficiency. The long working days of the past had left a legacy of traditional small breaks and irregularities in the day's work. Changes in this respect became important subjects for negotiations between the two sides of industry in the early twenties. Despite the abundant supply of labour, the employers' interest in the more general aspects of labour efficiency was, of course, strongly accentuated by the financial difficulties of Scandinavian enterprise during the period. The interaction of shortened hours and increased efficiency has continued ever since and has been a source of tension between the two sides, but the improved quality of the workers' performance has certainly contributed to economic growth.

At the same time, there was a gradual change in the status of labour and in the workers' psychological attitude to society. Trade-union membership had increased strongly during the war; the proportion of unionized labour in the total labour force became great enough to make the unions really representative. Politically, the Social Democrats achieved a position of far greater influence than before the war. By 1939 there were Social Democratic governments – or at any rate governments headed by Social Democratic prime ministers – in all three countries. None of them enjoyed an absolute Social Democratic majority; their power and prestige depended to a large extent on political arrangements with the farmers' parties. This was a political constellation new to Scandinavia, and it put the working population in an entirely new position. The practical difficulties of reaching and maintaining this type of political unity were considerable and were more acutely felt in Denmark and Norway than in Sweden – the Danish agricultural crisis comes immediately to mind – but the resultant changes in all parts of Scandinavia were unmistakable. The new political attitude of the workers was especially interesting in Norway, where the growth of the labouring class had occurred relatively late, and where labour had been extremely radical in the twenties. One consequence of the new situation was that in both Sweden and Norway labour conflicts became insignificant in the late thirties. In Denmark, several labour conflicts were forbidden by special provisional legislation during the difficult years.

Still another change was to play an important part in the future. The principle of the government's responsibility for fuller employment, as one of the most important objects of economic and social policy, was taken more seriously in the debate than ever before. The effects of the new policies in this direction were not at first overridingly great – the monetary policies after the abandonment of the gold standard in 1931 may have meant more, in practice, for the employment situation – and policies were not equally up-to-date in the three countries. But the various social reforms introduced, and political initiatives taken, produced not only practical results but also a new feeling, perhaps especially in Sweden, that governments were doing something at last. The ground was thus prepared both theoretically and psychologically for the full-employment policies of the future.

B. INVESTMENT

The role of capital and incentives for investment were, of course, influenced by the dramatic fluctuations in the economy during the twenties and thirties. It has been demonstrated in the Swedish case that the counter-cyclical behaviour of the wages/income ratio was very pronounced during the depression of the early twenties. Under the difficult economic conditions, wage-earners received a larger share of the shrinking national income. The other side of the picture – or one part of it – is to be found in the long sequence of declining profits, outright losses, and actual or impending bankruptcies. The experiences of the depression had a strong and lasting impact on the minds of both workers and entrepreneurs even after the bad years had passed. During the whole period profits fluctuated, of course, not only from time to time but also from industry to industry. In Sweden, sawmills and steel-works – the traditional staple industries of the country – were run at a loss for a number of years.

This, and the difficult credit market in the twenties, induced even quite successful firms and industries to become more cautious about their investment policies. Investment was concentrated as much as possible on carefully planned rationalization schemes with specific capital-saving or labour-saving ends in view. Financially, industrial entrepreneurs were less prone to risk-taking than before. Sometimes this change of attitude was forced on them because the very existence of a firm was in jeopardy and its management was under the control of a bank. Gradually a new spirit of careful calculation and sound finance developed. It provided a good starting point for development in the period to follow, but it had also something to do, of course, with the incomplete utilization of existing resources, as expressed in the unemployment rate. In any event the highly speculative spirit apparent in all three countries during the war – and still very active during the last pre-war decade – had largely disappeared. The fascinating record of constructive operations and the adventurous risk-taking of Ivar Kreuger were sensational exceptions to the normal Swedish – and Scandinavian – way of doing business in the twenties.

The investment rate in Denmark and Norway was generally a little lower than it had been in the years before 1914, but a Norwegian increase in 1937–9 did at last bring the figures above the former peak. In Sweden, the rate was above the pre-war level for most of the twenties and thirties – in the late thirties considerably so. Characteristically, however, the sectors which had a really high investment rate throughout the period were housing and public works, particularly road-building. Swedish industrial investment showed no corresponding increase.

Scandinavian investment, such as it was, did not need contributions from abroad to anything like the pre-war extent. The peculiar conditions of the war years transformed the Scandinavian countries from debtor to creditor nations. Sweden maintained this position throughout the 1920s, being a net exporter of capital. Conditions were very different in the other two countries, but Denmark did not revert to its pre-war position as a large capital-importer. There were some more dramatic changes in Norway's balance of payments: the country lost its creditor position quite rapidly and used a good deal of foreign capital in the twenties, especially for rebuilding the merchant fleet. During the thirties, however, Norway once again reached the unaccustomed position of having a constantly favourable balance of payments.

The drastic short-term fluctuations and the many local variations can easily conceal the general trend in economic growth. The net record of the period, especially in Sweden and Norway, was very satisfactory if compared with the contemporary experience of most Western countries. But progress was different in type from the dramatic and pioneering performance of pre-war Scandinavia. Growth between the two depression periods was characterized rather by recovered continuity and gradual extension of the pre-existing structure.

These general impressions accord well with the conclusions of formalized macro-economic studies. The Swedish wages/income ratio, which had declined during the years of intensive pre-war industrialization, rose again after 1914 and continued to do so – and not only during the depression years, when a rise would have been expected in any case – until 1933. A moderate decline set in after that, but the level remained well above the immediate pre-war one. As regards production functions, there was no continued growth in the share of the 'residual', the 'technological factor', while labour's contribution showed a significant increase. In this respect, the Norwegian picture gives the same general impression.

Important structural changes occurred in the credit system in all three countries. As already mentioned, the great expansion during the period 1890–1914 was accompanied by enormous growth in commercial banking. This continued during the war years, with their inflation, expansionist tendencies, and increasing amount of speculative business. At the same time, there was a process of concentration, with several mergers between banks. The net result is easily exhibited in the Swedish case by a comparison between 1908, when the four biggest banks accounted for 28 per cent of the turnover, and 1924, when the share of the four biggest was 56 per cent. At the latter date, the two largest banks, Svenska Handelsbanken (the former Stockholms Handelsbank) and Skandinaviska Kreditaktiebolaget, had between them as much as 40 per cent of the total.

The results of the structural change persisted, and concentration has continued during the following decades. But the great gains of the war years, and the general influence of the banking system in these years, were never to return. The depression, the return to gold, and low prices in the twenties caused a serious reaction. There were bank crises and reconstruction problems – sometimes prolonged – in all three

Scandinavian countries. These were followed by a period of stagnation and stabilization, with a reduced share for the commercial banks in the total volume of credit in the respective countries. The savings banks, and during the thirties also some government-owned credit institutions or special credit facilities offered by the government, filled much of the gap.

The quantitative change in the credit market combined with qualitative changes of various kinds. In Sweden a number of important industrial enterprises which had got into difficulties during the crisis remained for a long time in the hands of the banks – in some cases throughout the inter-war period – and were gradually reorganized until they had regained their capacity for independent development. In 1924 the outstanding advances to big industrial enterprises which were 'bank-controlled' or 'bank-owned' amounted to no less than 850 million kronor, or 18 per cent of the total lending of Sweden's commercial banks. Although the amount was reduced soon afterwards, it was back at the same level in the early thirties. The banks were prohibited by law from retaining companies' shares for more than a transitional period. But the reconstruction in big business which they carried out during the transition was of great importance for the continuity and solidity of Swedish industrial enterprise. It exposed some of the banks themselves at high risks, but they had of course, in some cases, got involved through their own over-optimism and misjudgement.

The twenties were, naturally, a decade in which industrial credit and industrial risk capital were difficult to obtain: the companies had to learn financial planning and economy the hard way. The experience of the thirties might give the impression that they had learnt their lesson astonishingly well. Neither in Norway nor in Sweden were the improved credit facilities of the prosperous late thirties met by as high a level of demand from the industrial sector as might have been expected. Self-financing had greatly increased, and the banks had real difficulty in finding outlets for all their funds, even at the low interest rate prevailing. Part of the change was the result of successful recovery after the crisis, but there were other contributory factors as well – much of the current expansion was gradual and continuous rather than experimental and revolutionary, and much of it took place in established enterprises rather than through the creation of new ones.

Neither capital resources nor labour resources were utilized to the full. The contrast with the situation after the Second World War is striking. But, with all its weaknesses and limitations, the Scandinavian economy of the twenties and thirties provided a broad and remarkably solid base for continued development – development of a partly new type and in a partly different society.

IV. *The Contemporary Age: 1945-70*

The age groups between fifteen and sixty-four have increased more slowly since the end of the Second World War than in the twenties and thirties. With a larger proportion of the young at school and with greater aid for the aged, the percentage of gainfully employed males in the whole population fell. The fall was compensated to some extent by an increasing supply of female labour, but the overall result was a smaller increase in the gainfully employed population than in the active age groups as a whole.

On the other hand, the available labour force has been utilized far more fully than was the case between the wars. In the difficult years of the 1950s, Danish unemployment was as high as 8–10 per cent, but this was an exceptional case. The employment problems of the 1970s will not be discussed here; in this respect, as in all others, the following remarks apply chiefly to the period up to the mid-sixties.

During the twenties and thirties it had been difficult to find jobs for everyone; after the war the difficulty was to find people for the jobs. In Sweden – where wages were highest – immigration contributed significantly to the general expansion. During the period 1945–65, net average immigration (all ages included) was about ten thousand per annum. The immigrants generally took the less attractive jobs in factories and in the service sector – jobs with lower wages or, sometimes, with satisfactory wages but less comfortable working conditions.

Much has been said about the negative effects of an exceptional demand for labour, such as an exaggerated tendency for workers to change jobs. However that may be, employers had every incentive to get as much as possible out of the less abundant labour supply. The Scandinavian countries had their proper share in the post-war technological revolution, and labour productivity grew far more vigorously than before. The benefits of new technologies and improved organization were probably enhanced by the greater efficiency of better-educated workers. Real wages were, of course, rising. There were differences both in timing and in the net effect of these changes in the three countries, but in each the results were considerable: for instance, real hourly wages of factory workers in Sweden rose by 87 per cent during the period 1946–61.

There was also a significant rise in the wages/income ratio, although this might seem surprising in a period of unusual prosperity. The causes were chiefly structural: people moved from occupations with a low wages/income ratio to those with a higher one – for instance, in the service sector – while others gave up small private enterprises to become wage-earners. The wages/income ratio in manufacturing alone seems to have undergone little change during the period.

Industrial relations during the period were generally harmonious. Open conflicts were few, and centralized wage bargaining made considerable progress, while the general economic expansion (and in Denmark and Norway the need for co-ordinated recovery during the immediate post-war years) seemed to bring home the benefits of co-operation. If something of this conciliatory spirit evaporated after the first two post-war decades, the reason is to be found in some new problems or, at least, in a new awareness of them.

Among the notable structural changes after the war was the increasing number of office workers and the changing relationship, in status and other respects, between office workers and the complicated hierarchy of skills and occupations among workers still conventionally classified as manual. To the problems of the general wage level were more than ever added those of differences, in both wages and general conditions, between different groups of wage-earners: in several cases this occasioned a concern for solidarity between higher-paid and lower-paid groups. Environmental problems, problems of the power structure in firms and industrial establishments, problems of job tenure and security have claimed as much attention as wages. The background to this discussion has been political and sociological, but to some extent it has also reflected a new pattern of production.

If the increase in manpower was comparatively slow, the increase in capital was very impressive, most of all in Norway. The stock of real capital in this country more than doubled during the period 1945-60, rising from 69,000 to 147,000 million kroner in 1955 prices. The rapid rise to such a level, very soon after the war, was to a large extent the result of political decisions required by the vast amount of reconstruction needed in the country. The need was intensified, and the high figures were accentuated, by the high relative prices of investment goods in the post-war economy. Swedish and Danish investment ratios were less impressive but still very considerable. The whole economy had undergone a radical change since the thirties.

In all three countries there was an increase in the share of total investment directly applied to productive purposes. In Sweden between the two periods 1939-40 and 1961-5 the share of manufacturing and mining in total investment (net) rose from 23 per cent to 29 per cent, while the share of housing fell from 33 per cent to 22 per cent. Economic policy was often directed towards safeguarding an adequate supply of capital for housing, through public lending or various kinds of credit regulation. At times, of course, this kind of official intervention, or certain aspects of it, was resented by the banks and industrialists. The fact remains, however, that more capital was invested in industry than ever before.

Attempts to express the contribution of different factors in a production function give a picture very different from its counterpart of the twenties and thirties. Although an enormous amount of capital was made available, the dominant role was played not by capital but by the residual. In the case of Sweden the 'technological factor' accounts for nearly 60 per cent of the increase in production. The share of labour, on the other hand, was lower than it had been between the wars. In other words, the production function had become decidedly modern in form.

In Norway, with its heavy investment policy, domestic savings had to be supplemented by capital imports, over and above the imports to meet the needs of the immediate post-war years. Net capital imports during the period 1946–62 accounted for something like 14 per cent of the increase in Norwegian real capital during the same period. In Denmark the situation fluctuated more, but after the early 1960s Danish expansion came to be accompanied by significant imports of capital. In Sweden, on the other hand, neither imports nor exports of capital were of any great significance during the period.

As regards the sources of saving it has been shown that in Scandinavia, as in other Western economies, the private sector contributed less to total savings than had been the case between the wars. The most important general change, both in patterns of Scandinavian saving and in the credit system, was the increasing influence, both direct and indirect, of the public sector. In the Scandinavian system government-owned enterprise had a relatively smaller, and other methods a relatively greater, importance in this respect than in many other countries.

The decades after the Second World War were characterized by an often surprisingly harmonious combination of expansive private enterprise, more successful in many respects than ever before, and greatly increased government activity, alternately stimulating and damping down the economy, and standing at times in a competitive relationship to the private sector. The type of society and the solutions of the problems of capital and labour that will eventually emerge from the present mixed economy are difficult to predict. But whatever they prove to be, there is no doubt that the period briefly discussed in this section was one of modest preparation for more radical changes. The difference between the immediate post-war period and that of a few decades hence will certainly be even greater than the difference between, for instance, the thirties and the sixties of this century.

V. *Finland*

Finland's economic development in the nineteenth and twentieth centuries has followed the general Scandinavian pattern – evolving from a comparatively modest position and a predominantly agrarian economy, through the utilization of the country's natural resources by increasing exports of staple commodities and gradual industrialization, to an advanced level of modern industrial performance and a high standard of living. This development has been more continuous than might be imagined from the dramatic political history of the country. It should be stressed that Finland had a remarkable degree of independence during the period of Russian sovereignty (1809–1917). The so-called Grand Duchy of Finland had a separate administration and a legislative and a monetary system of its own, and commerce with Russia was technically regarded as a branch of foreign trade.

Compared with the other Scandinavian countries, however, the economic starting point was less advantageous, the great changes were more delayed, and the economic and political difficulties to be overcome proved much greater. Around 1800, none of the three sister countries was as overwhelmingly agrarian as Finland; and even a century later, before the First World War, two-thirds of the active population in Finland were employed in the agrarian sector. The proportion naturally declined between the wars, but only after the Second World War did it fall to much less than 50 per cent.

The industrial growth that was to transform Finnish society was generated to a high degree by foreign demand. Like Sweden and Norway, Finland had resources of fundamental importance in its forests, and it is still – relative to its size and population – unusually well endowed with forest areas. But under the more elementary conditions characterizing nineteenth-century Finland, expansion depended more exclusively on timber than was the case in Sweden, not to speak of Norway. Boards and deals, increasingly complemented towards the end of the pre-war period by pulp and newsprint, were the biggest single – and also the absolutely predominant – group of export commodities, undergoing vigorous expansion from the 1870s and becoming of outstanding importance by the late 1890s and the beginning of the new century. Up to 1914 the products of the forest industries represented 70 per cent of exports in value. The greatest consumer of Finnish sawmill products was, predictably, Great Britain.

The entire industrial sector, however, was still relatively insignificant, providing employment for only 10–15 per cent of the population. But outside the forest group, Finnish industries in the nineteenth century were not merely a case of import-substitution and production for a regional market. During about half a century, from the 1830s to the 1880s, Finland's affiliation with the Russian Empire meant a favoured position for the country in respect of customs, while the competitive power of Russian industry for much of the time remained unimpressive. The Russian market, therefore, offered interesting opportunities, particularly for Finnish textile mills, and a few establishments were, astonishingly, among the biggest industrial units in Scandinavia. The opportunities faded again with the passing of the eighties. Russia's customs policy became less generous as its own industrialization progressed. But the picture as a whole showed potentialities for industrial growth far beyond the staple industries. There was also considerable progress in the infrastructure, especially in railway-building, which was almost completely government-financed.

The independent Finnish republic (from 1917) did not enjoy the same opportunities for Russian trade as had pre-war Finland. The country's foreign trade thus had to depend on the sale of forest products to the West to an even greater extent than before. In 1939, the share of these products in total exports was over 80 per cent. At the same time, exports and industrial production as a whole advanced considerably, both in quantity and in quality. It was in this period that the country's pulp and paper industries made their real breakthrough. The exceptional and continuous demand for these goods was largely responsible for the fact that the transition from wartime inflation and post-war crisis in the early twenties was so relatively harmonious and that the effects of the depression of the early thirties were so short-lived, despite the country's many problems. The late thirties were a period of strong and successful growth.

During the Second World War Finland was faced with a series of difficulties, including serious territorial losses. After the war, however, the rapid rate of growth was resumed sooner than might have been expected. In the 1950s, for example, Finland had the fastest growth rate in Scandinavia, and national income per capita at the end of the decade was not far below Norway's. There was a great advance in industrial differentiation. In exports, the forest industries were still predominant, but even here, and particularly in industrial production as a whole, there were important new developments (e.g. in metals and engineering). Far-reaching structural changes were, of course, even more essential for the Finns than for the Danes.

The indemnities which had to be paid to the Soviet Union after the war helped, paradoxically, to prepare the way for such changes. The indemnities were to be paid in kind, and, of course, in commodities required by the Soviet Union. Given the state of Russian industry immediately after the war, this meant such products as ships and engineering products. Finnish initiative and capital equipment in these fields therefore had to be developed, and investments were made which would otherwise have been most unlikely in the post-war situation.

It is easily seen that several characteristics of the general Scandinavian experience appeared in a more dramatic form in Finland. More than the other Scandinavian countries, Finland experienced, over a long period, a continuous contrast between a ready supply of labour and a relative scarcity of capital.

The population of Finland grew from 830,000 in 1800 to just over four million in 1950. During the greater part of the nineteenth century, population growth was rather uneven: crop failures could still interrupt the curve. But from 1870 to the First World War, population growth was consistently stronger in Finland than in the rest of Scandinavia. Emigration became important rather later than in the other countries and did not become an important outlet until the turn of the century.

With the low degree of flexibility and the great size of the agricultural sector in Finland at that time, population pressure in this sector was naturally strong. Urbanization and industrialization were still too weak to provide more than a very partial solution. Thus the great social question facing the country was the problem of cottagers and agricultural workers. When Finland attained political independence, passing through a period of civil war immediately afterwards, earlier attempts at reform were broadened and intensified, the result being that the smallholders had a comparatively large stake in Finnish agriculture. Further changes of a similar kind were necessary after the Second World War, when population from the lost territories had to be resettled.

The many problems that had to be solved in the agricultural sector certainly retarded growth. Before the First World War, animal husbandry had expanded considerably (and rather profitably), while the production of cereals had to cope with serious difficulties, partly because of Russian competition. The risks inherent in this situation were demonstrated during the war, when Russian supplies were cut off and Finnish agriculture was not able to ensure self-sufficiency. Against this background grain production was strongly encouraged again after the war, and animal husbandry lost its favoured position, despite its considerable possibilities for profits and growth. However, even with these handicaps there was an impressive development of productivity and an improvement of quality in the agricultural field.

As the number of industrial workers remained comparatively low for a long time, and as the forest industries, with typical linkages to non-industrial employment, were of such importance in Finland, the emergence of a clearly differentiated and class-conscious population of industrial workers met with natural difficulties. Because of restricted Finnish resources and the relatively weak position of the workers, industrial wages were inevitably low before 1914, and not even the good years of the twenties and thirties led to any dramatic increases. An additional reason was that the development of the trade-union movement in Finland was delayed and even met with legal impediments during that period. The constructive achievements on the agrarian front – the great social problem of the day – had no equally successful counterpart in the field of industrial relations.

After the Second World War, Finnish workers achieved a greatly improved position in society – not only because they represented a bigger proportion of the total population than before. Both real wages and the wages/income ratio rose significantly, at the same time that the trade unions became an important social and political factor. In typical contrast to the situation in the thirties, the relationship between wage increases and inflationary pressure soon became one of the country's great economic problems. At the same time, employment opportunities did not develop as favourably as wages, in this period of general economic change and restructuring, and there was a not insignificant Finnish emigration, especially to Sweden.

Needless to say, before the First World War demand for capital was far greater in the agricultural sector and in house-building than in industry. The contribution of capital imports was smaller than might have been expected, and much smaller than in Sweden. The savings which served to finance the country's own investments were not easily made, and the techniques for assembling and utilizing existing capital resources were in some respects rather primitive. For instance, there was no market for industrial bonds in Finland. Against this background, the growth of commercial banks before 1914 is quite impressive.

Some of the difficulties mentioned above were to turn up in different forms later on. Situations in which foreign credits were extremely difficult to obtain have not been uncommon in the history of Finnish finance. Just after the First World War, it took some time before the young republic achieved the stability and security required to inspire general confidence in the international business world. Somewhat later, however, the great investments of the later 1920s included a fair amount of foreign capital, complementing the quite remarkable performance of the Finns themselves. The debts incurred during this period and during the new depression in the early thirties were repaid with exceptional promptness during the rest of the decade. This made a deep impression on the international financial world of the period. It also reflected, of course, the strong position of capital in Finnish society before 1939. General prosperity, coupled with relatively low wages, meant that the good years of the decade were very profitable to the owners of industrial enterprises. But seen in perspective, the continued strength of investment and the improved financial position of the Finnish economy of the late thirties provided an extremely valuable base for further development. Heavy investment took place in agriculture, in manufacturing, and also in other sectors, such as in the harnessing of the country's hydro-electric potentialities.

After the Second World War financial assistance from abroad – though not entirely absent – was again very restricted: there was, for example, no Marshall aid for the Finns. Under the influence of an expansive economic policy, however, the investment rate was extremely high. But the remarkable feat of achieving vigorous and constructive growth under somewhat unfavourable circumstances strained the country's resources and made it impossible to avoid considerable inflation. This, and the employment problem, were the dark spots in an impressive development which meant the definite transition to a modern economy for this resourceful latecomer among the Scandinavian countries.

NOTES

CHAPTER I

Introduction: *The Inputs for Growth*

1 For a contrary view, see J. Robinson, 'The Production Function and the Theory of Capital', *Review of Economic Studies*, XXI (1953-4), 81-106. The technical literature on this question is surveyed in G. C. Harcourt, 'Some Cambridge Controversies in the Theory of Capital', *Journal of Economic Literature*, VII (1969), 369-405.

2 See E. J. Hobsbawm and R. M. Hartwell, 'The Standard of Living during the Industrial Revolution: A Discussion', *Economic History Review*, 2nd ser., XVI (1963-4), 119-46, and references cited there, particularly the early work of the Hammonds and Clapham. See also M. W. Flinn, 'Trends in Real Wages, 1750-1850', *Economic History Review*, 2nd ser., XXVII (1974), 395-413.

3 Simon Kuznets, 'Quantitative Aspects of the Economic Growth of Nations: II', *Economic Development and Cultural Change*, V (1957), Supp. to no. 4.

4 W. A. Cole and Phyllis Deane, 'The Growth of National Incomes', in *CEHE*, VI (Cambridge, 1965), 1.

5 The relations between economic growth and welfare on the one hand and structural changes on the other are of great interest. They will be considered more fully in volume VIII of *CEHE*; we are now asking about the inputs that produce economic growth.

6 We have adopted the convention of treating housewives as consumers for two reasons. First, the measure was evolved for modern use, and we are merely trying to be consistent. Second, the activities of housewives represent a stable part of the economy that is normally not available for alternative uses, and excluding them does not affect the estimates of changes in output – that is, in economic growth. It should be noted, however, that in the Second World War, housewives were used as factory workers in many countries. This appeared as an increase in output rather than as a transfer of resources from one use to another.

7 Alexander Gerschenkron, *Economic Backwardness in Historical Perspective* (Cambridge, Mass., 1962), ch. 9; Ira O. Scott, Jr, 'The Gerschenkron Hypothesis of Index Number Bias', *Review of Economics and Statistics*, XXXIV (November 1952), 386-7.

8 It is a mathematical result that in an economy with no economies or diseconomies of scale (i.e. an economy in which a doubling of inputs produces a doubling of outputs, all other things being equal), output equals the sum of the quantities of each of the inputs multiplied by its marginal product. It follows from this that the rate of growth of output is the sum of the rates of growth of the inputs multiplied by the elasticity of output with respect to that input. It must be emphasized that this is a mathematical result; the rate of growth of output in actuality may or may not be equal to the sum just described. It all depends on whether all other things are in fact equal.

9 E. D. Domar, 'On the Measurement of Technological Change', *Economic Journal*, LXXI (1961), 709-29.

10 Many refinements of this process have been worked out and applied experimentally; they have somewhat different data needs. It would be out of place to discuss them here.

11 It should be clear that we are discussing voluntary abstention from work by workers. Involuntary unemployment is not a source of pleasure to most people. It should also be noted that idle land can be a source of pleasure to some people – conservationists, for example – but this is the exception rather than the general rule.

12 Taken from the discussion in Edward F. Denison, *Why Growth Rates Differ* (Washington, 1967), ch. 6.

13 G. E. Rudé, 'Prices, Wages and Popular Movements in Paris during the French Revolution', *Economic History Review*, 2nd ser., VI (1953–4), 248.

14 Denison, *Why Growth Rates Differ*, ch. 8.

15 We cannot estimate the return to education by time-series analysis – using our assumption that intelligence levels have not risen – since increases in educational levels have been associated with increases in other investment, urbanization, and industrialization, and it is impossible to disentangle their individual effects.

16 We are talking here of *net* national product and *net* investment. Owing to the difficulty of getting data on depreciation, it is often neglected, giving what are called gross national product and gross investment.

17 This extension involves the assumption that the marginal rates of transformation in the economy are constant over the relevant ranges, i.e. that the production-possibilities curve is flat. This assumption was used often by John Stuart Mill and others but is less favoured now. If we abandon the assumption, the extra consumption goods capable of being produced would be less than the investment forgone because the efficiency of resources would vary in different uses. The argument in the text would then only be approximately true.

18 A brief discussion of these problems can be found in J. W. Kendrick, 'Some Theoretical Aspects of Capital Measurement', *American Economic Association, Papers and Proceedings*, LI (1961), 102–11.

19 See P. M. Deane and W. A. Cole, *British Economic Growth, 1688–1959* (Cambridge, 1962), for a discussion of these matters in eighteenth-century Britain.

20 H. Chenery, 'Patterns of Industrial Growth', *American Economic Review*, L (1960), 647–9.

21 See section II above.

22 This is the typical result for the twentieth century. See R. M. Solow, 'Technical Change and the Aggregate Production Function', *Review of Economics and Statistics*, XXXIX (1957), 312–20.

23 See D. W. Jorgenson and Z. Griliches, 'The Explanation of Productivity Change', *Review of Economic Studies*, XXXIV (1967), 249–83; E. F. Denison, 'Some Major Issues in Productivity Analysis: A Review of Estimates by Jorgenson and Griliches', *Survey of Current Business*, XLIX (1969), 1–27.

24 J. Schmookler, *Invention and Economic Growth* (Cambridge, Mass., 1966).

CHAPTER II

Capital Formation in Great Britain

1 I wish to acknowledge my indebtedness to Phyllis Deane, John Ginarlis, and Brian Mitchell for their kindness in allowing me to use their unpublished work. I am also extremely grateful to these colleagues and to Stan Engerman, Roderick Floud, Donald McCloskey, Robin Matthews, Sidney Pollard, Michael Thompson, and Nick von Tunzelmann for their constructive comments on a first draft of this chapter. It is perhaps particularly necessary to say that they bear no responsibility for the weaknesses which remain in the present version.

2 The only exception to this is the inclusion of claims against foreign countries, i.e. investment abroad; see section V.

3 For a full discussion of the supply of capital, see the introduction to F. Crouzet (ed.) *Capital Formation in the Industrial Revolution* (1972), 39–64, and the studies quoted there, including the classic articles by Postan and Heaton. Crouzet's own article 'Capital Formation in Britain during the Industrial Revolution', in *ibid.*, 163–203, is an authoritative survey of the sources of industrial capital. Recent studies covering the supply of capital to housing, transport, and banking include C. W. Chalklin, *The Provincial Towns of Georgian England: A Study of the Building Process, 1740–1820* (1974), 157–248; M. C. Reed, 'Railways and the Growth of the Capital Market', and S. A. Broadbridge, 'The Sources of Railway Share Capital', both in M. C. Reed (ed.), *Railways in the Victorian Economy* (1969), 162–228; S. A. Broadbridge, *Studies in Railway Expansion and the Capital Market in England, 1825–1873* (1970); J. R. Ward, *The Finance of Canal Building in Eighteenth Century England* (1974); M. C. Reed, *Investment in Railways in Britain, 1820–1844* (1975); and B. L. Anderson and P. L. Cottrell, 'Another Victorian Capital Market: A Study of Banking and Bank Investors on Merseyside', *Economic History Review*, 2nd ser., XXVIII (1975), 598–615.

4 See also Crouzet (ed.), *Capital Formation*, 9–39 (editor's introduction), for a more extended survey.

5 A. D. Gayer, W. W. Rostow, and A. J. Schwartz, *The Growth and Fluctuation of the British Economy, 1790–1850* (1953).

6 The most detailed study by Miss Deane is 'Capital Formation in Britain before the Railway Age', *Economic Development and Cultural Change*, IX (1961), reprinted in Crouzet (ed.), *Capital Formation*, ch. 3. See also P. M. Deane and H. J. Habakkuk, 'The Take-Off in Britain', in W. W. Rostow (ed.), *The Economics of Take-Off into Sustained Growth* (1963); P. M. Deane and W. A. Cole, *British Economic Growth, 1688–1959* (1962; 2nd edn, 1967); and P. M. Deane, *The First Industrial Revolution* (1965).

7 Deane, 'Capital Formation before the Railway Age', 97 and 115. In her *First Industrial Revolution* (p. 154) there are references to the rate of 5 per cent at the beginning of the eighteenth century, but it would seem from the more detailed earlier study that this was a 'best rate', not a long-term average.

8 The first estimate is given by Deane in 'Capital Formation before the Railway Age', 117; the second in *First Industrial Revolution*, 154.

9 *First Industrial Revolution*, 153 and 156.

10 S. Pollard, 'The Growth and Distribution of Capital in Great Britain, *c.* 1770–1870', in *Third International Conference of Economic History*, Munich 1965 (Paris, 1968), I, p. 362.

11 P. M. Deane, 'New Estimates of Gross National Product for the United Kingdom, 1830–1914', *Review of Income and Wealth*, XIV (1968). Miss Deane has kindly provided details of the components underlying her published totals.

12 See Deane, 'New Estimates', 111.

13 Crouzet (ed.), *Capital Formation*, 25.

14 C. H. Feinstein, *National Income, Expenditure and Output of the United Kingdom, 1856–1965* (1972), 191–5.

15 R. Giffen, *The Growth of Capital* (1889).

16 Deane and Cole, *British Economic Growth*, 271; Pollard, 'Growth and Distribution of Capital', 336–41.

17 Feinstein, *National Income*, 198.

18 See further pp. 35–6 above.

19 See also J. C. Stamp, *British Incomes and Property* (1916), 376–81.

20 For further discussion of these issues see C. H. Feinstein, *Domestic Capital Formation in the United Kingdom, 1920–1938* (1965), 257–8.

21 See Giffen, *Growth of Capital*, 25, and Stamp, *British Incomes and Property*, 394.

22 In practice one would, of course, find actual retirements distributed around the assumed (average) working life.

23 Central Statistical Office, *National Accounts Statistics: Sources and Methods* (1968), referred to below as '*Sources and Methods*'.

24 Feinstein, *National Income*, 182 and 196.

25 For a detailed analysis of a difficult issue, see E. F. Denison, 'Theoretical Aspects of Quality Change, Capital Consumption and Net Capital Formation', in *Problems of Capital Formation, Studies in Income and Wealth*, 19 (1957).

26 The conceptual problems are further discussed in Feinstein, *Domestic Capital Formation*, 7–10. See also J. P. P. Higgins and S. Pollard, *Aspects of Capital Investment in Great Britain, 1750–1850* (1971), 6–7 and 27–8.

27 See, for example, Feinstein, *National Income*, 190.

28 The main sources for the wage series used for the three indices are: (i) for building, the Gilboy series as given in Deane and Cole, *British Economic Growth*, and A. L. Bowley, *J. R. Stat. Soc.*, LXIV (1901), 107–12; (ii) for agriculture, Bowley, *J. R. Stat. Soc.*, LXII (1899), 562 (a series for Great Britain obtained by combining Bowley's series for England and Wales (weight 6) and Scotland (1)); and (iii) for engineering, Bowley and Wood, *J. R. Stat. Soc.*, LXIX (1906), 190.

29 The index for materials covers three major commodities used in the capital-goods industries: timber, iron, and bricks. The series for timber is based on the prices of imported Memel fir for 1760–1807, and of Memel fir and Quebec yellow pine for 1802–50; duty is included, and the sources used were *Reports from the Select Committee on Timber Duties*, PP 1835, HC 519, App. 11, and T. Tooke and W. Newmarch, *A History of Prices* (1838–57) vols. II–VI. For iron the series used is the one given by W. S. Jevons, *J. R. Stat. Soc.*, XXVIII (1865), 316–17. For bricks the index is based on the prices paid by Greenwich Hospital and the Office of Works as given by Lord Beveridge, *Prices and Wages in England*, I (1939), 725–30 for 1760–1830, and on Laxton's *Builder's Price Books* from 1830 onwards.

30 The weights used to combine the component series for labour and materials were selected in the light of a few scraps of information and are very uncertain; see, e.g., K. Maywald, 'An Index of Building Costs in the United Kingdom, 1845–1938', *Economic History Review*, 2nd ser., VII (1954–5), 194.

31 For a rough adjustment to cover the capital stock in Ireland, see p. 78 above.

32 Further consideration of the coverage of the series for dwellings and of its relationship to the estimates for other types of building is provided in the Appendix, p. 94.

33 The Census enumeration for April 1861 is taken as the stock at the end of 1860, and similarly for earlier years. For 1851 a 'house' was defined for the purpose of the Census as 'all the space within the external and party walls of a building', and this definition was used at subsequent censuses; prior to 1851 the interpretation of the term was left to the discretion of the enumerators but appears to have been fairly consistent. We consider further the composition of the inhabited houses in the Appendix, pp. 95–6 above; the uninhabited ones consisted mainly of buildings used as offices, warehouses, etc. and left unoccupied at night.

34 For estimates of the population in the late eighteenth century we have taken Brownlee's figures as given by Deane and Cole, *British Economic Growth*, 6.

35 This is the ratio derived from a population of 9,193,000 inhabiting 1,576,000 houses.

36 R. Wall, 'Mean Household Size in England from Printed Sources' in P. Laslett (ed.), *Household and Family in Past Time* (1972), 159–66 and 196–8. The adoption of a ratio rising from 5·5 to 5·8 to derive the number of houses from estimates of the population for 1761–1801 is broadly in line with the ratios calculated from samples

by contemporaries who were attempting to make the reverse calculation, i.e. to estimate the population from very uncertain figures for the number of houses assessed to, and exempt from, Hearth Duty. For example, the Rev. J. Howlett used a ratio of $5\frac{2}{3}$ in 1786; Sir Francis Eden, writing in 1800 (still before the first Census), adopted $5\frac{1}{2}$. For a full account of the controversy, the methods, and the estimates see E. C. K. Gonner, 'The Population of England in the 18th Century', *J. R. Stat. Soc.*, LXXVI (1913). His best estimate, on this basis, of the number of houses in 1777 is 1,170,000, which may be compared with our estimate of 1,330,000 for 1780.

37 The series has been continued down to 1910 to provide more evidence on which to assess the validity of the assumed rates of demolition. The result of the rates adopted is that some 79 per cent of the end-1760 stock of dwellings are found to have been scrapped by 1860 (assuming also that it is always the oldest houses which are demolished); and some 95 per cent of the end-1810 stock are found to have been scrapped by 1910. Taking another view of the implied relationships, total new building (net inter-censal increase plus demolitions) over the century 1761–1860 accounts for 4·04m (93 per cent) of the 1860 stock of 4·35m dwellings; and for the century 1811–1910 the new building is estimated at 8·05m and accounts for almost all the end-1910 stock of 8·15m. It is also possible to check the estimates of new building derived in this way against the direct estimates compiled by Weber and Parry Lewis; see J. Parry Lewis, 'Indices of House-Building in Great Britain, 1851–1913', *Scottish Journal of Political Economy*, VIII (1961).

38 Despite the extensive work of recent years on the history of urban development there is still extremely little firm information on which to base a judgement about the rate of improvement in the size and quality of nineteenth-century housing. For a rare quantitative assessment see W. Beckerman, *The British Economy in 1975* (1965), 373–4 and 588, where it is estimated that the rate of change for a typical working-class house averaged a little under 1·0 per cent per annum between 1840 and 1905, with almost all the improvement occurring in the period 1840–80. See also W. G. Rimmer, 'Working Men's Cottages in Leeds 1770–1840', *Publications of the Thoresby Society*, XLVI (1963), 178–86; J. N. Tarn, *Working Class Housing in the Nineteenth Century* (1971); S. D. Chapman (ed.), *The History of Working-class Housing – A Symposium* (1971); E. Gauldie, *Cruel Habitations* (1974), 41–2. Some useful contemporary evidence is given in J. Hole. *The Homes of the Working Classes* (1866).

39 H. A. Shannon, 'Bricks – A Trade Index, 1785–1849', *Economica*, I (1934). See also A. K. Cairncross and B. Weber, 'Fluctuations in Building in Great Britain, 1785–1849', *Economic History Review*, 2nd ser., IX (1956). For the 1840s we have followed G. R. Hawke, *Railways and Economic Growth in England and Wales, 1840–1870* (1970), 212, in assuming that one-third of the brick output was used by the railways, and this is excluded.

40 For the builders' contribution to urban street improvements see, for example, C. W. Chalklin, *The Provincial Towns of Georgian England: A Study of the Building Process, 1740–1820* (1974); H. Hobhouse, *Thomas Cubitt, Master Builder* (1971); D. J. Olsen, *Town Planning in London* (1964).

41 See A. K. Cairncross, *Home and Foreign Investment, 1870–1913* (1953), 107–9, for the derivation of the 1907 estimate, and Feinstein, *National Income*, 186, for the indices of building costs and of changing size and quality of dwelling used for the extrapolation to the 1850s; see also *ibid.*, 195, for a further comment on the 1907 base.

42 The total numbers with annual value below £20 (including 185,000 residential shops, hotels, etc.) and with annual value of £20 or more (excluding the shops, etc.), are estimated in the Appendix, p. 94 above. The classification of those below £20 is based on information for 1851 given in two parliamentary returns (HC 630, 1849, and HC 2, 1851) summarized by W. Newmarch, 'On the Electoral Statistics of the

Counties and Boroughs in England and Wales', *J. R. Stat. Soc.*, XX, 1857, 187–9, 230, and 314–21, and on the Inhabited House Duty statistics for 1874–5 (Stamp, *British Incomes and Property*, 141). The classification of those of £20 and over is based on estimates by Stamp for 1860–1 (*ibid.*, 445) based on a parliamentary return, HC 428, 1863.

43 This would cover the very large number of small and squalid huts, cottages, and slum dwellings which housed so many families at the end of the eighteenth century (see e.g. J. H. Clapham, *An Economic History of Modern Britain*, 3 vols. (1926–38), I, pp. 27–41, or Gauldie, *Cruel Habitations*, 27–57), as well as the very worst of the urban houses built in the early nineteenth century.

44 This seems a reasonable average for much urban building in the first half of the nineteenth century. See e.g. the evidence of builders and surveyors from Liverpool, London, Manchester, and Birmingham, quoted in the *Report of the Select Committee on Building Regulation and Improvement of Boroughs*, PP. 1842, X, Q. 217–19, 530–54, 747, 1318–72, 1734. H. R. Aldridge, Secretary of the National Housing and Town Planning Council, writing in *The National Housing Manual* (1923), 100, stated that 'There are hundreds of thousands of cases in which the cubic capacity of the dwelling is not more than 3,000 cu. ft., and reckoning the cost of construction in the year 1840 as, on an average, $4\frac{1}{2}d.$ per cu. ft. the building cost will be seen to have been £64-10-0.' See also the studies listed in note 38 above.

45 J. H. Walsh, *A Manual of Domestic Economy* (1857), 7–160, provides a very well-informed discussion of mid-nineteenth-century housing standards and building costs for the middle and upper classes. He recommends the purchase or building of a house on roughly the following scale:

Annual income	£100	£250	£500	£1,000
House price	£150	£300	£800	£1,200

For further description of housing in this range see Hobhouse, *Thomas Cubitt*, 241–2, or the detailed specifications of actual houses built, given by S. Hemming, a Birmingham architect, in his *Designs for Villas, Parsonages and Other Houses* (n.d.). These plans are discussed by H.-R. Hitchcock, *Early Victorian Architecture in Britain* (1954), 427–30, and related to other housing of the 1840s and 50s. F. M. L. Thompson, *Hampstead: Building a Borough, 1650–1964* (1974), 245–95, is a particularly valuable analysis of the economic and social forces behind the expansion of house-building of this type (for examples of specific prices on different estates in fashionable Swiss Cottage and Belsize, see *ibid.*, 258, 266, 277, and 290); and H. J. Dyos, *Victorian Suburb* (1961), 96–109, documents a similar process providing homes for men of property in the South London suburbs of Camberwell, Peckham, and Dulwich.

46 We have excluded the shops, hotels, etc., but this top group still includes some residential premises which are not dwelling-houses in the usual sense, e.g. colleges and schools which were not exempt because not of a strictly charitable character (Stamp, *British Incomes and Property*, 107 and 112). However, it will also, and more appropriately, cover the most lavish of the outlays on domestic architecture in this period, ranging from the £320,000 which the Duke of Northumberland is reported to have spent on Alnwick Castle in the 1850s, or the modest sum of £40,000 for which Eaton Hall was built for Lord Grosvenor in 1804–12, down to the houses which Thomas Cubitt was building on the Grosvenor Estate in London, where the smaller houses were 'worth about £1,700 and those on to the King's Road, which sold for about £3,000 to £4,000 were built earlier in the middle 1840s and 1850-1, and seem to have found fairly ready sale amongst widows, spinsters, and the occasional naval captain'. See F. M. L. Thompson, *English Landed Society in the Nineteenth Century*, (1963), 87–93, for the castles and country houses; Hobhouse, *op. cit.*, 147, for

Cubitt's provision for the affluent in Belgravia. Mrs Hobhouse's valuable study contains many other examples of Cubitt's houses, at prices up to £15,000 (pp. 46, 49–50, 133–6, 145–6, 155, 163, and 330); similar houses elsewhere in Britain are described in A. J. Youngson, *The Making of Classical Edinburgh* (1966), and in two studies by W. Ison, *The Georgian Buildings of Bath* (1948) and *The Georgian Buildings of Bristol* (1952). See also Hitchcock, *Early Victorian Architecture*, chaps. 8 and 9.

47 The actual number of houses in 1860 was 4·35m, or 8·57 per cent more than the standardized number (as given on p. 44 above) of 4·00m. The same proportionate adjustment can be made to the price, i.e. we can value either 4·35m actual houses at an actual cost of £138, or 4·00m standardized houses at a standardized cost of £150.

48 Chalklin, *Provincial Towns*, 309. See also *ibid.*, 188–227, for numerous examples of actual house prices, ranging from £35 for back-to-backs erected in Birmingham in the 1770s to £3,000 for houses built in Great George Square in Liverpool in the early years of the nineteenth century.

49 Some schools and colleges may be covered by our estimates for dwellings – see note 46 above.

50 H. Beeke, *Observations on the Produce of the Income Tax* (1800), 184, estimated the value of all provincial and municipal buildings at £25m; P. Colquhoun, *A Treatise on the Wealth, Power and Resources of the British Empire* (1815), 55 and 58, put the value in 1812 at £22m.

51 See J. Summerson, *Georgian London* (1945; 2nd edn 1962), for an excellent survey of the major London buildings of the late eighteenth and early nineteenth centuries; and Hitchcock, *Early Victorian Architecture, op. cit.*, chaps. 9 and 10, for a full account of the most prominent public buildings of 1830–60.

52 See J. Simon, *English Sanitary Institutions* (1897), for an account of the evolution of administration and expenditure from ineffectual Commissioners for Town Improvement, Sewers, etc., to centralized local authorities. This occurred under the impetus of the cholera epidemic of 1831–3, the work of Edwin Chadwick and the Poor Law Commissioners, and the passing of the Public Health Act of 1848. See also B. Keith-Lucas, 'Some Influences Affecting the Development of Sanitary Legislation in England', *Economic History Review*, 2nd ser., VI (1953–4), 290–6.

53 See Stamp, *British Incomes and Property*, 49 and 515. We reduce these assessments by £2m in the 1850s (see Table 31, p. 96 above), and by a corresponding proportion in earlier decades, to exclude the rental of farmhouses; these were assessed with lands under Schedule A but are included with dwellings in the present estimates.

54 Beeke, *Observations on the Income Tax*, put the gross rent for England and Wales at £23m (p. 20) and added one-fifth for Scotland (p. 183) and £2·8m for tithes. This seems more consistent with the later Schedule A valuation than the £33m suggested for England and Wales (excluding tithes) in P. M. Deane, 'The Implications of Early National Income Estimates', *Economic Development and Cultural Change*, IV (1955), 29.

55 This is based on the estimates quoted by Giffen, *Growth of Capital*, 86–94, suggesting that the rent of land and houses in England Wales in the mid eighteenth century was about £20m, of which land accounted for some £15·5m. We have raised the rent of the land by one-fifth to cover Scotland and have added £2m for tithes.

56 R. J. Thompson, 'An Inquiry into the Rent of Agricultural Land in England and Wales during the Nineteenth Century', *J. R. Stat. Soc.*, LXX (1907); and E. M. Carus-Wilson (ed.), *Essays in Economic History*, III, 128–31, ('A Century of Land Values: England and Wales'), a reprint of a letter by Norton, Trist, and Gilbert, which was first published in *The Times*, 20 April 1889. See also G. E. Mingay, *English Landed Society in the Eighteenth Century* (1963), 20–3 and 51.

57 B. A. Holderness, 'Capital Formation in Agriculture' in Higgins and Pollard (eds.), *Aspects of Capital Investment*, 159–91; and Holderness, 'Landlord's Capital Formation in East Anglia, 1750–1870', *Economic History Review*, xxv (1972), 434–47. Other sources consulted in making these very tentative estimates include Pollard, 'Growth and Distribution of Capital', 341–8; F. M. L. Thompson, *English Landed Society*, 212–68; R. J. Thompson, 'An Inquiry', 602–5; Mingay, *English Landed Society*, 178–83; D. Spring, *The English Landed Estate in the Nineteenth Century* (1963), 47–9; and R. Perren, 'The Landlord and Agricultural Transformation, 1870–1900', *Agricultural History Review*, xviii (1970), 36–51.

58 An average life of 100 years is perhaps rather too long: it is intended to cover not only the farm buildings, for which a life of fifty to sixty years would perhaps be more appropriate, but also the more or less permanent improvements to the land.

59 See W. J. Harris, 'A Comparison of the Growth of Wealth in France and England, specially with reference to their Agriculture Systems', *J. R. Stat. Soc.*, lvii (1894), 555, and other sources quoted in note 159 below.

60 R. J. Thompson, 'An Inquiry', 609. The sources from which his estimate is derived suggest that although given in 1907 it might be taken as based broadly on costs in the mid nineteenth century and thus as comparable with the present estimates at 1851–60 prices; see also *ibid.*, 621.

61 See R. J. Thompson, *op. cit.*, 605–9; Holderness, 'Capital Formation in Agriculture', 167–70; and A. Pell, 'The Making of the Land in England', *Journal of the Royal Agricultural Society*, ser. 2, xxiii (1887), 355–74.

62 D. Ricardo, *On the Principles of Political Economy and Taxation*, first published 1817, reprinted in *The Works and Correspondence of David Ricardo*, ed. P. Sraffa, II vols. (1951–73), vol. i, p. 67.

63 The most carefully considered estimate appears to be that by R. J. Thompson, 'An Inquiry', 605–11, who puts the interest on permanent improvements at 42 per cent of the gross rent. J. R. McCulloch, *A Statistical Account of the British Empire* (1837), 535, suggested 50 per cent and later (4th edn (1854), 561) raised this to 55 per cent. The question was discussed by Sir Thomas Whittaker, *The Ownership, Tenure and Taxation of Land* (1914), 87–90, who quoted the view of J. H. Sabin, 'an experienced surveyor', that farm-houses and building represent three-sevenths (43 per cent) of the value of a farm, and the estimates of Thompson, McCulloch, and others, and concluded that the proportion was at least 50 per cent and probably more.

64 Giffen, *Growth of Capital*, 30, used thirty years' purchase for farm land (including improvements) and fifteen years' for buildings, for his valuations for 1865 and 1875. Twenty years' purchase thus seems appropriate for the combination of farm buildings and improvements to land.

65 In making the comparison some allowance must be made for the effect of depreciation on the estimate obtained by capitalization; cf. p. 34 above.

66 This is based on a rental of £20m capitalized at twenty-five years' purchase. See note 55 above for the rental; Mingay, *English Landed Society*, 38–9, and Giffen, *Growth of Capital*, 91, for the number of years' purchase. See also note 68 below.

67 E. J. Kerridge, *The Agricultural Revolution* (1967), provides a very detailed account of the floating of water meadows, fen drainage, and other improvements introduced in England before 1760. However, his critics have argued that these innovations were not widely disseminated (see e.g. J. Thirsk's review in *History*, lv (1970), 259–62); and other innovations, such as new crops, new systems of husbandry, and the use of fertilizers, would not have involved significant outlays on fixed capital.

68 Given that the number of years' purchase was lower for the buildings and improvements than for the land (cf. note 64 above), this implies that the former represented slightly more than 25 per cent of the *rental*.

69 The underlying assumptions are that the assets had a life of one hundred years and were accumulated at a rate which rose at a moderate pace of about 10 per cent per decade from 1661–70 to 1751–60.

70 This procedure effectively allows for any understatement in the assessments and for the fact that the annual values cover not only the buildings but also the land underlying them. Assuming that adjustment for these factors (upwards in the first case, downwards in the second) would be proportionally the same for dwellings and for trade premises, any correction of the annual values would produce a corresponding change in the multiplier (ratio of gross stock to annual value) without affecting the estimates of the gross stock of trade premises. The assumption of a common multiplier for dwellings and trade premises was standard practice in the work of Giffen, Stamp, and other authorities.

71 This is somewhat higher than the estimate of 15 years' purchase used in the mid nineteenth century by Giffen (*Growth of Capital*, 14 and 43–5) and others to estimate the value of the stock of buildings. As observed above (p. 34), however, our measure of the stock of capital is conceptually somewhat different from Giffen's: in particular, although it excludes site values it is explicitly valued before any allowance for depreciation.

72 The basis for this division is an analysis of the underlying gross annual values as given in the Appendix above (p. 96), with the further assumption that about 25 per cent of the trade premises consisted of lock-up shops (cf. Stamp, *British Incomes and Property*, 113–14 and 122–3). This calculation gives two parts of roughly equal value.

73 The series used for industrial production was Hoffmann's index, excluding building, and the level of output was taken as the average of the five years centred on the end of each decade. See W. Hoffmann, *British Industry, 1700–1950* (1955), 330. One half the stock (i.e. £230m) was spread, *pro rata* to the change in this series, over the eight decades from 1781–90 to 1851–60; and the same ratio was applied to the change in the index in the two previous decades to extend the estimates back to 1761–70.

74 See Hitchcock, *Early Victorian Architecture*, 396: 'The Early Victorians did not precisely invent commercial architecture; but its development was so considerable and so rapid that commercial architecture became for the first time a field of primary significance in the 40s. Within fifteen years from Victoria's accession monumental scale and monumental design . . . became accepted as proper for all commercial premises of any consequence.' See also *ibid.*, 375, where 'the first building designed expressly and solely for use as offices' is dated from 1823, and more generally chaps. 11 and 12. See also Summerson, *Georgian London*, 252–3.

75 On the relationship between residential building, shops, and public houses see Hobhouse, *Thomas Cubitt*, 154–5 and 213–15; Olsen, *Town Planning in London*, 120–5 and 164–6; F. M. L. Thompson, *Hampstead*, 257, 265, and 279; and Dyos, *Victorian Suburb*, 148. For a general account of retail shops in the first half of the nineteenth century, see D. Davis, *A History of Shopping* (1966), chap. 12.

76 Cf. note 69 above. We again assume that capital formation increased at a moderate rate of some 10 per cent per decade, but in this case over an eighty-year period from 1681 to 1760.

77 Estimates are currently being made for this period by S. D. Chapman, D. T. Jenkins, and others, based mainly on fire-insurance values; when completed this work will greatly increase our knowledge of capital accumulation in the early stages of industrialization. See e.g. S. D. Chapman, 'Fixed Capital Formation in the British Cotton Industry, 1770–1815', *Economic History Review*, 2nd ser., XXIII (1970); Chapman, 'Industrial Capital before the Industrial Revolution' in N. B. Harte and K. G. Ponting (eds.), *Textile History and Economic History: Essays in Honour of Miss*

Julia de Lacy Mann (1973), 113–37; and D. T. Jenkins, 'Early Factory Development in the West Riding of Yorkshire 1770–1800' in *ibid.*, 247–80, and *The West Riding Wool Textile Industry, 1770–1835: A Study of Fixed Capital Formation* (1975).

78 The following sources all support an estimate of between 60 and 70 per cent for the share of machinery, etc. in the total fixed capital of the textile industry: G. White, *A Practical Treatise on Weaving by Hand and Power Looms* (1846), 272; E. Baines, *History of the Cotton Manufacture in Great Britain* (1835), 414–15; S. J. Chapman and F. J. Marquis, 'The Recruiting of Employing Classes in the Cotton Industry', *J. R. Stat. Soc.*, LXXV (1911–12), 301; E. M. Sigsworth, *Black Dyke Mills* (1958), 171–3; and Feinstein, *Capital Formation*, 145 and 105–6.

79 Clapham, *Economic History*, II, 80–8, describes the varying rates at which hand spinning and weaving were gradually eliminated in each branch of the textile industry during the middle decades of the nineteenth century.

80 The 1861 Census of Population figure for Great Britain is 1,180,000, and the Factory Return gives 732,000; C. Booth, 'Occupations of the People of the United Kingdom', *J. R. Stat. Soc.*, XLIX (1886), 415–19; and PP 1862, LV, 629.

81 These very rough estimates of machinery per worker were adopted after general consideration of the extent of mechanization in different industries by 1861 as shown, for example, in Clapham, *op. cit.*, II, 33–7 and 74–99; and after calculation of the corresponding figures for machinery per worker relative to textiles in 1924, using Feinstein, *Capital Formation*, 102–37, and the 1924 Census of Production. For the clothing trades, the sewing machine had only just come on the scene in 1860: according to one well-informed source 'there were not more at the highest estimate than 25,000': N. Salamon, *The History of the Sewing Machine* (1863), 80. They sold for around £10 each.

82 Clapham, *op. cit.*, II, 33–5.

83 See note 73 above.

84 See also note 77 above, and Crouzet, *Capital Formation*, 35–9.

85 Eden, *Observations and Statements on Insurance*, quoted by D. Macpherson, *Annals of Commerce, Manufacturers, Fisheries and Navigation* (1805), IV, 549, and by Colquhoun, *Treatise*, 94 (see also note 153 below). This was the basis for Colquhoun's own estimate of £60m for 1812 (*Treatise*, 56) and was referred to again by P. de Pebrer, *Taxation, Revenue, Expenditure, Power, Statistics and Debt of the Whole British Empire* (1833), 345. Pebrer expressed the view that the stock of machinery had 'more than doubled' between 1803 and 1833, and this provides some support for the increase in the present estimates from £26m to £61m between 1800 and 1830.

86 The actual life is uncertain, but in view of the very rapid growth in the series the capital-formation estimates would not be much affected if a longer life of (say) fifty or sixty years was assumed.

87 *Minutes of Evidence of the Coal Industry Commission* (1919), vol. 1; PP 1919, XII, Q. 771, 864–5 and 884–5; and *Minutes of Evidence of the Royal Commission on the Coal Industry* (1925), vol. II, part A (1926), Q. 5215 and 5269–89.

88 G. H. Wood, 'Real Wages and the Standard of Comfort since 1850', *J. R. Stat. Soc.*, LXXII (1909), 93.

89 See Clapham, *Economic History*, I, pp. 432–8, for a summary of the changes in mining practice; also S. Pollard, *The Genesis of Modern Management* (1965), 62–75.

90 Deane and Cole, *British Economic Growth*, 216, extrapolated to 1760 using Hoffman, *British Industry*, 331.

91 Giffen, *Growth of Capital*, 43, valued mines and quarries in 1863 at only £21m, including circulating capital, but was later criticized by Stamp (*British Incomes and Property*, 391–2) for failing to realize that the profits being capitalized included royalties, on which the rate of return would be much lower. Giffen had used only four

years' purchase, whereas Stamp recommended nine and one-half years, which would raise the 1863 valuation to £51m. J. R. McCulloch, *Dictionary of Commerce* (1871), 312, suggested that the total capital employed in the coal trade might be moderately estimated at £20–5 million.

92 B. R. Mitchell, 'The Coming of the Railway and United Kingdom Economic Growth', *Journal of Economic History*, XXIV (1964); A. G. Kenwood, 'Railway Investment in Britain, 1825–75', *Economica*, XXXII (1965).

93 Kenwood does not include renewals in his estimates of capital expenditure (*op. cit.*, 322), and this might account for roughly half the difference between the two series in the 1850s: the remaining difference and also the much larger discrepancy in the boom years 1845–9 is as yet unexplained. See also Hawke, *Railways and Economic Growth*, 197–204.

94 The series is published for 1870–1912 in H. Pollins (ed.), *Britain's Railways* (1971), 112–13. The estimates for 1831–60 (still unpublished) were kindly provided by Dr Mitchell.

95 See Feinstein, *Capital Formation*, 7–10, for a more detailed discussion.

96 J. E. Ginarlis, 'Road and Waterway Investment in Britain, 1750–1850' (unpublished Ph.D. thesis, University of Sheffield, 1970). I am very grateful to Dr Ginarlis for generously allowing me to use material from his dissertation; he is, of course, not responsible for the way in which I have adjusted his estimates to accord with the conceptual approach adopted for this chapter.

97 See e.g. PP 1824, XX; PP 1836, XLVII; and PP 1859, XXIII.

98 See Ginarlis, *op. cit.*, 102–12, for a more complete description of the estimation procedure. The sample of account books covered about 5 per cent of the total turnpike mileage in 1822 (*ibid.*, 77).

99 See e.g. PP 1863, L, 551.

100 W. Albert, *The Turnpike Road System in England, 1663–1840* (1972), 188–97; W. J. Jackman, *The Development of Transportation in Modern England* (1916), chap. 4, especially pp. 283–302; S. and B. Webb, *The Story of the King's Highway* (1913), 144, 163, and 192; and H. J. Dyos and D. H. Aldcroft, *British Transport* (1969), 70–9.

101 The parliamentary returns show separately – as expenditure on 'Improvements' – amounts which represent some 15 per cent of Ginarlis' quasi-net expenditure in the 1830s ('Road and Waterway Investment', 115 and 136) but a large part of the expenditure on labour, materials, salaries of clerks and surveyors, etc. should also be classified as new work and improvements.

102 PP 1818, XVI; PP 1839, XLIV; PP 1841, XXXVII; PP 1849, XLVI; and PP 1852, XLIII.

103 See Ginarlis, *op. cit.*, 201–23.

104 Jackman, *op. cit.*, 283–302; Webb, *op. cit.*, 193–200. D. Grigg, *The Agricultural Revolution in South Lincolnshire* (1966), 44.

105 See e.g. PP 1863, L, 467.

106 Ginarlis, *op. cit.*, 238. The estimate covers only those bridges for which accounts were found, and it is known to be incomplete.

107 See note 28 above.

108 Ginarlis, *op. cit.*, 197 and 199. The breakdown of expenditure on turnpikes and other roads taken by Ginarlis from the published returns is the source for the relative weights given to labour and materials; see *ibid.*, 134 and 214.

109 This corresponds to eighty years' expenditure at an average level of roughly £100,000 per annum at current prices, i.e. about one-third the level suggested for the 1760s in Table 7.

110 The length of turnpikes in England and Wales at the end of the 1830s was about 22,000 miles: see Jackman, *Development of Transportation*, 234. A figure of

5,000 miles is given for Scotland in a *Return of the Number of Miles of Roads in Scotland, both Turnpikes and Commutation*, PP 1859, XXIII, 439.

111 *Select Committee on Turnpike Trusts and Tolls, 1836, Minutes of Evidence*, PP 1836, XIX, Q. 1441. Another witness quoted costs of £2,000 per mile, but this was not based on personal knowledge; see Q. 461. Our price index suggests that costs would not have altered much between the 1830s and 1850s.

112 H. Law and D. K. Clark, *Construction of Roads and Streets*, 8th edn (1914), 158 and 162.

113 105,000 miles in England and Wales and 10,000 in Scotland (using the sources given in note 110 above).

114 See Law and Clark, *op. cit.*, 135.

115 J. L. McAdam, *Remarks on the System of Road Making*, 5th edn (1822), 41–2; R. Devereux, *John Loudon McAdam* (1936), 123; see also *ibid.*, 125.

116 Farm wagons and carts are included in the series for agriculture, and carts and vans for goods transport are included in the present series if available for hire: others are implicitly covered in the estimates for the railways and manufacturing.

117 See S. Dowell, *A History of Taxation and Taxes in England*, vols. (1884), III, 40–58, 195–209, and 225–30, for a general account of the duties, and some figures for the number of carriages in the eighteenth century. The main statistical sources used for 1800–60 were a return of 1830, PP 1830, XXV (HC 686); *Return of the number of Stage Carriages, etc.*, PP 1865, XXXI (HC 309) 457; and *Report of the Commissioners of Inland Revenue, 1870*, vol. II, PP 1870, XX, 546–9, which contains useful retrospective tables.

118 The main source used was J. H. Walsh, *A Manual of Domestic Economy* (1857), 603. Walsh quotes prices for each of nineteen types of carriage, varying from dog-carts at £18–60 up to a 'town-made coach or landau' at £250–300. We have taken the following as average prices for the 1850s: £250 for a 4-wheel carriage drawn by two or more horses, £100 for a 4-wheel carriage drawn by one horse, and £40 for a 2-wheel carriage. In the light of these prices, but more uncertainly, an average price of £60 was taken for hackney carriages and of £200 for post-chaises. The stage-coaches and omnibuses were valued at £100 each: see T. C. Barker and M. Robbins, *A History of London Transport* (1963), vol. I, 6 and 39. For an interesting attempt to estimate the amount of capital invested in cabs, carriages, carts, etc. in the Metropolitan area in 1870 see F. A. Paget's 'Report on . . . Steam Road-Rolling', reproduced in Appendix II of Law and Clark, *Construction of Roads*, 473. The average prices used by Paget were rather lower than those we adopted, e.g. £30 for light carriages, £35 for hackney cabs, £60 for omnibuses, and £120 for carriages, broughams, etc. He added harnesses at £4 each.

119 PP 1870, XX, 547. Note also Colquhoun's estimate that value added in the manufacture of carriages, wagons, carts, and other vehicles about 1812 was £0·8m (Colquhoun, *Treatise*, 93).

120 Ginarlis, 'Road and Waterway Investment', 252–5. These estimates of the extent of inland waterways are some 500 miles less than those given by C. Hadfield, *The Canal Age* (1968), 208, since Ginarlis excludes rivers (such as the Severn) which did not require any capital outlays to be made navigable.

121 Hadfield, *op. cit.*, 211–12.

122 Ginarlis, *op. cit.*, Appendix E, gives quasi-net expenditure series for a sample of canals, and we have used those for which the initial construction years are available.

123 See p. 59 above.

124 The corresponding value at the current prices of each decade would be some £27m, and for the new work alone £22m. Hadfield, *op. cit.*, 49, estimated that it cost £20m to build 2,600 miles of Canals in England and Wales between 1760 and

1850. Deane and Cole, *British Economic Growth*, 138, put expenditure on construction and improvement in the period 1755–1835 at £20m.

125 G. B. Poole, *Statistics of British Commerce* (1852), 47.

126 D. Swann, 'The Pace and Progress of Port Investment in England, 1660–1830', *Yorkshire Bulletin of Economic and Social Research*, XII (1960), 38–42. See also A. G. Kenwood, 'Port Investments in England and Wales, 1851–1913', *Yorkshire Bulletin of Economic and Social Research*, XVII (1965), 157.

127 PP 1876, LXV, 541.

128 The problems of estimating capital formation in shipping have been meticulously examined by R. Craig, 'Capital Formation in Shipping', in Higgins and Pollard (eds.), *Aspects of Capital Investment*, 131–48. The present estimates neglect several of the refinements to which Craig has called attention, notably the allowance for foreign and colonial purchases and sales of second-hand ships, and it is to be hoped that his promised series will soon be available to replace those given here.

129 The series for ships built and first registered in Britain is given for 1787–1805 and 1814–18 in B. R. Mitchell, *Abstract of British Historical Statistics* (1962), 220–1. The missing years were obtained by interpolation on the basis of the corresponding series (*ibid.*, 220) for the tonnage built in Britain and the Empire. From 1814 onwards Mitchell has a series for the United Kingdom, and Ireland was excluded from this using statistics of the tonnage built in Ireland given in parliamentary returns, e.g. PP 1849, LII, 187.

130 The tonnage on the UK register is given in Mitchell, *Abstract*, 217. The assumed life of twenty-five years corresponds to the 4 per cent depreciation rate endorsed by Craig, *op. cit.*, 140.

131 *Ibid.*, 138, and R. S. Craig, 'British Shipping and British North American Shipbuilding', in H. E. S. Fisher (ed.), *The South West and the Sea*, Exeter Papers in Economic History, no. 1 (1968), 21–43. In emphasizing this, Craig echoes the British shipowners who found it extraordinary that the government had overlooked the fact that 'Ships are admitted to British registry, not only if built in the UK, but if constructed in any part of the British Empire, and also those built abroad if purchased by British subjects. In fact British-built ships frequently constitute less than a moiety of those annually admitted to registry.' Correspondence of General Shipowners' Society with the Secretary of State, PP 1859 (Session 2), XXVII, 553.

132 The returns of colonial-built vessels registered annually are PP 1843, LII (HC 74), 373–5 for 1821–41; PP 1847, LX (HC 309), 310 for 1842–6; and thereafter annually (e.g. for 1860 PP 1861, LVIII (HC 261), 18). The returns of the total colonial tonnage on the British register, also provided by the Registrar General of Shipping, Custom House, are PP 1843, LII, 376–8 for 1831 and 1841, and PP 1847, LX (HC 308), 151–3 for 1846. As an example of the discrepancies, the total colonial tonnage on the register at ports in Great Britain is given as 335,000 tons in 1841 and 424,000 in 1846, a net increase (i.e. before allowing for any ships wrecked, sold, etc.) of 89,000 tons, whereas the aggregate of the annual registrations for 1842–6 is only 40,000 tons.

133 See PP 1852, XLIX, 18.

134 For a detailed account of shipbuilding in British North America in the mid nineteenth century see F. W. Wallace, *Wooden Ships and Iron Men* (1924).

135 Given in annual returns (e.g., for 1860 PP 1861, LVII, 18). The figures for the decade seem reasonably accurate, and they can be checked against the United States statistics of tonnage sold to foreigners.

136 J. G. B. Hutchins, *The American Maritime Industries and Public Policy, 1878–1914* (1941), 300 and 401–2. The source is an 1870 Report of a Select Committee of the US Congress (Lynch Report). Hutchins observes that by 1860 prices 'were somewhat depressed by the rising output of iron sailing ships, which were then becoming

common and were priced at from £17 to £18 per gross ton'. A similar range of prices is given in the *Report from the Select Committee on Merchant Shipping* (*1860*), PP 1860, XIII, *Minutes of Evidence*, Q. 1059, 2456, and 2715–16. McCulloch, *Statistical Account* (1854 edn), II, 74, took an average of £13 per ton in the early 1850s.

137 K. Maywald, 'The Construction Costs and the Value of the British Merchant Fleet, 1850–1938', *Scottish Journal of Political Economy*, III (1956), 46–52, has an average for 1851–60 of £15 16s. per gross ton for the cost of hulls. However, this was obtained from the average value of the hulls of steamers exported in the period 1905–9, extrapolated by means of his index of shipbuilding costs, and cannot be taken as direct evidence of the cost of sailing vessels in the 1850s.

138 *Ibid.*, 50.

139 The adjustment was based on a parliamentary *Return of Steam Vessels Registered in the United Kingdom on or before 1st January 1861*, showing a gross tonnage of 686,000 against a net register tonnage of 441,000, i.e. a ratio of 1·55:1 (PP 1861, LVIII, 321).

140 See *Report from the Select Committee on Merchant Shipping* (*1844*), PP 1844, VII, *Minute of Evidence*, Q. 147, 295, and 1179, and p. 180; Hutchins, *op. cit.*, 205, 281, and 301; and D. C. North, 'The United States Balance of Payments, 1790–1860', *Trends in the American Economy in the Nineteenth Century*, Studies in Income and Wealth, 24 (1960), 598.

141 See notes 28 and 29 above.

142 Craig, 'Capital Formation in Shipping', 143; J. Phipps, *A Guide to the Commerce of Bengal* (1823), 139–40; Colquhoun, *Treatise*, 94; *Report from the Select Committee on Manufactures, Commerce and Shipping* (*1833*), PP 1833, VI, *Minutes of Evidence*, Q. 5844–52, 6481, 6580–2, and 6602–8; Hutchins, *op. cit.*, 153, 202, 205, and 299; W. S. Lindsay, *History of Merchant Shipping* (1876), III, 151.

143 R. Davis, *The Rise of the English Shipping Industry* (1962), p. 27, and Appendix A, pp. 403–6.

144 The assets which are omitted from a complete inventory of domestic reproducible tangible wealth are military assets (in the period covered by the present study these would consist largely of naval vessels and army barracks), consumer durables (mainly household furniture), and works of art, plate, etc. All these can be regarded as 'non-productive' assets.

145 See further Feinstein, *National Income*, 204–5.

146 See p. 72 above for the reasons for including coin and bullion with overseas assets.

147 The non-reproducible wealth omitted is the value of coal, iron ore, and other subsoil assets.

148 E.g. for cotton, see T. Ellison, *The Cotton Trade of Great Britain* (1886), Table 1; and for pig iron, see Cairncross, *Home and Foreign Investment*, 159.

149 Act 27 Vict. c. 18. Insurance of agricultural stock had been exempt from duty since 1833 and so does not affect the present calculations.

150 See *Report of the Commissioners of Inland Revenue*, PP 1870, XX, vol. I, 151, for the receipt of duty at the two rates; and vol. II, 132, for the value of property insured in Britain in 1860.

151 For discussion of the coverage of the fire insurance, see S. Brown, 'On the Progress of Fire Insurance in Great Britain', *Assurance Magazine*, VII (1858); *Revised Report on Fire Insurance Duties*, PP 1863, XXVI (by G. Coode); and C. Walford, 'On Fires and Fire Insurance', *J. R. Stat. Soc.*, XL (1877), 409.

152 *Revised Report on Fire Insurance Duties*, PP 1863, XXVI, 29.

153 Eden's paper was widely quoted but does not appear to have been published. His estimates of stock-in-hand were reproduced in the form quoted above (with details of the output of £76m) by Sir John Sinclair, *The History of the Public Revenue*

of the British Empire, 3rd edn (1804), III, 290–2, and by Walford, *op. cit.*, 403–4. Macpherson, *Annals*, IV, 549, has a slightly different version, with imports taken as £55m to give a total of £171m, and the estimate of £39m described as follows: 'of British and Foreign merchandise, besides what remains in the East India Co.'s warehouses uninsured there may be stated as on hand, and therefore insurable, £39,000,000'. This estimate was apparently misinterpreted by Colquhoun (*Treatise*, 55–7), who took the value of 'manufactured goods in progress to maturity and in a finished state' in 1812 as equal to Eden's estimate of the value of the annual output (i.e. £116m) and added £37m for foreign merchandise. He was followed in this by Lowe and Pebrer (see Bibliography) and later by Pollard, *Growth and Distribution of Capital*, 358.

154 For the inter-war period the sources are Feinstein, *Capital Formation*, 25, for the stocks (a very uncertain estimate), and *National Income*, p. 111, for final expenditure at market prices. For the post-war years the source is the estimates in Central Statistical Office, *National Income and Expenditure*. The implication of the above ratios is that the inter-war stock estimates may be understated; this is supported by other evidence, see Feinstein, *National Income*, 203, n. 2.

155 For a very strong statement of the extent of this decline in the ratio of stocks to turnover in the mid nineteenth century, see Coode's *Revised Report on Fire Insurance Duties* (see note 151 above), 29.

156 The GDP estimates for 1800–60 are taken from Deane and Cole, *British Economic Growth*, 166. To extrapolate to 1760 we used their indices of real output reweighted on an 1800 base (cf. *ibid.*, 79), and corrected this for the change in prices using the Schumpeter–Gilboy indices given in Mitchell, *Abstract*, 469. For this purpose it was assumed that the 1801 estimate of GDP corresponded to prices of 1795–9 rather than to the exceptionally inflated prices of 1801.

157 The price indices used were Schumpeter–Gilboy for 1760 to 1800, Gayer–Rostow–Schwartz for 1790–1850, and Rousseaux for 1840–60. Three-year averages centred on the selected dates were taken for 1760, 1830, and 1860, and for 1800 we took the average of the indices for 1795–9 (cf. note 156 above). All three indices are reproduced in Mitchell, *Abstract*, 468–73.

158 The same general price indices were used, but now taking annual averages per decade; the index is given in column 4 of Table 5 (p. 38 above).

159 The first detailed and comprehensive estimate of tenants' capital relates to 1874 and was made (together with an estimate for 1893) by R. E. Turnbull in 1896, see *Royal Commission on Agriculture (1896) Minutes of Evidence*, PP 1896, XVII, Appendix A, 541–2. There are also detailed estimates for 1893 by H. Rew, 'Farm Revenue and Capital', *Journal of the Royal Agricultural Society*, 3rd ser., VI (1895), 44–5, and for 1894 by Harris, *A Comparison*, 553–5. All these cover the whole United Kingdom, as does the continuous series compiled more recently for 1867–1938 by A. J. Boreham and J. R. Bellerby, 'Farm Occupiers' Capital in the United Kingdom before 1939', *Farm Economist*, VII, 6 (1953), 263. See also Stamp, *British Incomes and Property*, 386–8.

160 The estimates of acreage, yield, and production were based mainly on Deane and Cole, *op. cit.*, 62–6 (for 1760–1800); Eden, as quoted in Sinclair, *History of the Public Revenue*, III, 291 (for 1800); J. Middleton, *View of the Agriculture of Middlesex* (1807), 637–45 (for 1800); W. Stevenson, article on England in *Edinburgh Encyclopaedia*, ed. D. Brewster (editions of 1815 and 1830), 734–7 (for 1800 and 1830); McCulloch, *Statistical Account*, 1st edn (1837), I, pp. 528–37, and 4th edn (1854), 549–63 (for 1830 and 1860); J. Caird, *English Agriculture in 1850 and 1851* (1851), 522 (for 1860); P. G. Craigie, 'Statistics of Agricultural Production', *J. R. Stat. Soc.*, XLVI (1883), 1–44 (for 1800–60); and J. B. Lawes and J. H. Gilbert, 'Home Produce, Imports, Consumption and Price of Wheat, 1852/3 to 1891/2', *Journal of the Royal Agricultural Society*, 3rd ser., IV (1893), 132. All these sources were evaluated in

the light of the official statistics for 1867 onwards, summarized in Mitchell, *Abstract*, 78–90.

161 PP 1878–9, LXV, 438.

162 This is based on the ratio of the value of the output of these crops to the output of the main grains shown in the sources quoted in note 160 above; see particularly Eden and McCulloch.

163 Boreham and Bellerby, *op. cit.*, 262.

164 As a check on this method we applied the same procedure to Turnbull's estimate of £80m for the value of wheat, barley, oats, and rye produced in the UK in 1874. Adding 60 per cent and then taking 85 per cent of the total gives £109m, as compared with Turnbull's own estimate of £122m, compiled by valuing separately the capital invested in stocks of manures, lime, seed, corn, hay, and straw, and manual and horse labour in respect of growing crops, hop gardens, etc. (*R. C. on Agriculture*, *op. cit.* (see note 159 above), 541–5).

165 See especially Deane and Cole, *British Economic Growth*, 68–74 and 195; Stevenson in *Edinburgh Encyclopaedia*, 732; and McCulloch, *Statistical Account* (1854), I, pp. 493, 499, and 504–5.

166 These prices are based on those used by Turnbull for 1874 (*R. C. on Agriculture*, *op. cit.*, 542), adjusted to 1851–60 levels by means of Sauerbeck's indices for the wholesale price of beef, mutton, and pork and bacon: A. Sauerbeck, 'Prices of Commodities and the Precious Metals', *J. R. Stat. Soc.*, XLIX (1886), 643. The prices suggested by Braithwaite Poole (*Statistics of British Commerce*, 59) for 1851 included £9 for cattle, £1 5s. for sheep, and £2 10s. for pigs.

167 See Deane and Cole, *op. cit.*, 69–71, for a brief account of an issue on which there is still great uncertainty.

168 Turnbull (*R. C. on Agriculture*, *op. cit.*, 542) uses £25 for 1874. Other estimates include McCulloch, *op. cit.*, I, p. 493, who takes £12–15 for 1846; F. M. L. Thompson, in Higgins and Pollard, *op. cit.*, 186, who suggests £20 for the 1820s for farm horses; and Paget, 'Report on Road-Rolling', 473–4, who values cab, carriage, and wagon horses in the Metropolis in the early 1870s at an average of about £28.

169 For 1800–60 Rousseaux's index for agricultural product, extrapolated to 1760 by means of the Schumpeter–Gilboy index for consumer goods: from Mitchell, *Abstract*, 469–72.

170 A. Young, *Tour through the North of England* (1770) IV, 498; Stevenson, in *Edinburgh Encyclopaedia*, 773; McCulloch, *op. cit.*, 561; Boreham, in Boreham and Bellerby, 'Farm Occupiers' Capital', 263, and Turnbull, *R. C. on Agriculture*, *op. cit.*, 541, both adjusted by means of the Rousseaux price index for agricultural products and with implements, etc. excluded.

171 See the last column of Table 5, p. 38 above.

172 A. H. Imlah, *Economic Elements in the Pax Britannica* (1958), 70–2. No adjustment has been made for the fact that this series relates to the United Kingdom rather than Great Britain.

173 The same indices as for the last column in Table 5 above, but taking quinquennial averages.

174 See A. Carter, 'Dutch Foreign Investment, 1738–1800', *Economica*, XX (1953), 330–40, and Sinclair, *History of the Public Revenue*, III, Appendix V, p. 161. See also the notes by C. Wilson and A. Carter on 'Dutch Investment in Eighteenth Century England', *Economic History Review*, 2nd ser., XII (1960), 434–44.

175 In 1806 some £18·5m of national debt was exempted from tax on the ground that it was foreign-owned: C. K. Hobson, *The Export of Capital* (1914), 96. There were also foreign holdings in the Bank and the East India Company. See also Carter, *op. cit.*, 339–40, and Imlah, *op. cit.*, 66.

176 Beeke, *Observations on the Income Tax*, 185, reckoned that in about 1800 the inhabitants of Britain owned foreign possessions to the value of at least £100m, and this is consistent with – and may be derived from – the estimate of £5m given by William Pitt in 1798 (*Speeches*, III (1806), 317) for the net *income* received by British residents from property in the West Indies (£4m) and Ireland (£1m). It is impossible to reconcile these figures with Imlah's well-supported estimates beginning with a net credit of only £10m in 1815, even when allowance is made for the fact that Imlah's series is for the United Kingdom and so would not include investment in Ireland. It seems likely, therefore, that Pitt and Beeke overstated Britain's foreign holdings.

177 See especially Carter, *op. cit.*, 330-40.

178 Total net imports of gold and silver were deducted from the net balance on current account to obtain the estimates of net acquisition of overseas assets (Imlah, *op. cit.*, 44-6), and to the extent that these were used for industrial purposes they are automatically treated as equivalent to any other imported raw materials. This is the treatment adopted in the current UK national accounts: see *Sources and Methods*, 448.

179 Since the greater part of the monetary holdings consisted of coin in active circulation with the public rather than reserves at the Bank of England, it might be argued that net additions to the currency in the nineteenth century were not equivalent to overseas assets, but it would, of course, have been possible in principle (if not yet in practice) to replace the metallic currency by paper and so to make the gold and silver available for use as an international reserve.

180 See especially, W. S. Jevons's estimates for 1868, reprinted in *Investigations in Currency and Finance* (1909), 238-50; Newmarch's estimates for 1844 and 1856 in Tooke and Newmarch, *History of Prices*, VI, Appendix XXII, pp. 696-703; A. del Mar, *A History of the Precious Metals* (1880), 209-11; E. V. Morgan, *The Theory and Practice of Central Banking*, *1797-1913* (1943), 35; Colquhoun, *Treatise*, 55; and Beeke, *op. cit.*, 184. Useful information on the period after 1860 is given in W. E. Beach, *British International Gold Movements and Banking Policy, 1881-1913* (1935), 43-91.

181 See Mitchell, *Abstract*, 441-6.

182 See note 180 above. It is difficult to reconcile the present estimates for the increase in monetary holdings of gold and silver in the period 1815-60 with the estimates for net imports of gold and silver given by Imlah. For 1830-60, for example, the present estimates show an increase of £40m, and we would expect total net imports to be larger than this in order to allow for industrial consumption, but Imlah's total is in fact only £30m. It thus seems possible that Imlah may have understated the imports in the period before 1858 for which no official records are available: see Imlah, *Pax Britannica*, 44-6. If so, the series for the net acquisition of overseas assets may be slightly overstated.

183 The rentals are based on the Schedule A assessments of lands (see p. 48 above). Beeke, *op. cit.*, pp. 20 and 183 took thirty years' purchase of the net rental for about 1800, which would correspond to twenty-six years on the gross. See also Mingay, *English Landed Society*, 38-9. Thirty years' purchase of the gross rental was commonly adopted in the mid nineteenth century, e.g. Giffen, *Growth of Capital*, 13, 30, and 43 for 1865 and 1875, and Stamp, *British Incomes and Property*, 382.

184 The estimates in line 3 of Table 8 were adjusted to exclude the tenants' implements, etc., and converted to current prices by means of an index of prices for agricultural works and buildings based on the series used for column 2 of Table 5 above.

185 On the authority of Stamp, *op. cit.*, 24-5, who explicitly rejected the view taken by Giffen, *op. cit.*, 18.

186 There is a series for land prices given by Norton, Trist, and Gilbert, *op. cit.* (see note 56 above), but it is based on rather small samples and does not seem satisfactory.

187 G. Slater, *The English Peasantry and the Enclosure of Common Fields* (1907), 267; W. H. R. Curtler, *The Enclosure and Redistribution of Our Land* (1920), 138–9.

188 Taken together with the series shown above at current prices, these estimates imply that the price of unimproved land rose sharply relative to the general index of wholesale prices (see note 157 above), the value of land roughly doubling in real terms between 1800 and 1860.

189 H. W. Singer, 'An Index of Urban Land Rents and House Rents in England and Wales, 1845–1913', *Econometrica*, IX (1941), 223. Urban land rent is defined as the difference between income derived from the land when in use as an urban site and when used as agricultural land.

190 See Stamp, *op. cit.*, 220, for the gross assessment on railways, etc., and *ibid.*, 351–2, for support for a ratio of about 25 per cent of the gross profits for the site value of these properties.

191 We have previously used the gross rent of the non-residential buildings in making estimates of the gross capital stock but the multiplier adopted for that purpose specifically allowed for the land rent component so that there is no duplication in the estimates. See note 70 above.

192 This estimate may be compared with the figure of £45m obtained by cumulating the railway companies' annual expenditures on the acquisition of land from 1830 to 1860 as given by Mitchell, 'Coming of the Railway', 335. The present estimate would be expected to exceed the original cost of acquisition to the extent that it allows for increases in site values resulting, in part, from the presence of the railways.

193 See Feinstein, *National Income*, 184–9 and 195 n. 4.

194 *Ibid.*, 186.

195 See e.g. Maywald, 'Index of Building Costs', 192–3.

196 See Giffen, *Growth of Capital*, 63–71 and 163–5.

197 Feinstein, *Capital Formation*.

198 Using the notation given on p. 35 above we would have $G_{n-1} = G_n - I_n + R_n$.

199 See Feinstein, *National Income*, 196–200, for further details.

200 See *ibid.*, 198, where I began the description of the estimates of the capital stock for 1855–1920 by saying: 'Of all the series in the present book these almost certainly have the best claim for early revision' and ended by emphasizing that the estimates were provisional and were given 'with loud warnings as to their margins of error'.

201 Cf. *ibid.*, 200.

202 This has been apparent for some time: see *ibid.*, pp. 199–200, and the other references given there.

203 This is strongly suggested by the comparison on p. 77 above. There is no contradiction between this suggestion and the preceding statement that the earlier estimate of the stock of commercial buildings was too high, since that earlier estimate was *not* derived by cumulating estimates of capital formation: see Feinstein, *Capital Formation*, 187.

204 When the earlier estimates were made there was no information about the level of the stock of machinery, etc. in the mid nineteenth century, or of capital formation at earlier dates, and hence no basis on which to estimate scrapping. Adjustment to a level more appropriate in the light of the present estimates of capital formation before 1860 would *raise* the 1860 stock by about £500m.

205 As reflected, for example, in the decline in the area under cultivation in Great Britain from over 13m acres in 1870 to about 10m in 1913.

206 See Table 23 for details of the adjustments made. The estimates have not been corrected for the difference in underlying prices: 1860 for Giffen, 1851–60 for the present estimates. This would, however, have very little effect: see note 195 above.

207 See pp. 33–4 above.

208 See p. 72 above, where the unimproved value is derived as the difference between a capitalization of the gross rental at thirty years' purchase and the estimated value of buildings and improvements. There is nevertheless some discrepancy, partly because the number of years' purchase implicit in Giffen's estimate for Great Britain is higher than thirty, partly because Giffen's estimates include some £60m for farm-houses, whereas the present estimates include these (at a value of some £30m) with other dwellings in line 2a of Table 23. There are also small differences between the assessments to Schedule A used by Giffen ('On Recent Accumulations of Capital', 30) and the series used for the present estimate from Stamp, *British Incomes and Property*, 49.

209 See note 91 above.

210 See especially the comments by Craigie following the presentation of Giffen's estimate for 1875 ('On Recent Accumulations of Capital', 35–6), and the reply by Giffen (*Growth of Capital*, 15–20). See also Boreham and Bellerby, 'Farm Occupiers' Capital', 258–9.

211 See p. 34 above.

212 The assumption that the volume of capital expenditure on industrial and commercial building and on machinery was proportional to the movement in the index of industrial production (see pp. 51 and 56 above) is perhaps the most important exception.

213 Throughout this section we use the terms 'capital stock' or 'wealth' to refer to tangible assets as defined in sections IV and V, i.e. excluding military assets, subsoil wealth, consumer durables, plate, and works of art. All estimates are at 1851–60 replacement costs, and fixed assets are measured gross, i.e. before provision for depreciation.

214 The estimates are for real gross domestic product at constant factor cost and are, at best, broad orders of magnitude. The sources from which the series has been stitched together are listed in the notes to Table 25.

215 For further general discussion of the theoretical issues and an assessment of the empirical evidence available for a number of countries see S. Kuznets, *Modern Economic Growth* (1966), 63–85, and J. D. Gould, *Economic Growth in History* (1972), 115–42.

216 For the other measures of capital stock the corresponding capital–output ratios are as follows:

	Fixed capital/GDP	*National wealth/GNP*
1760	5·4	18·1
1800	5·2	14·8
1830	3·8	9·2
1860	3·6	7·1

217 Deane and Cole, *British Economic Growth*, 143.

218 Calculated from the labour-force data given in the text and the population figures in Table 25.

219 There are many refinements which should, in principle, be made but which are clearly not warranted where the reliability of the crude series is so poor. There is thus no attempt made to correct for such factors as changes in hours worked, improvements in the quality of the labour force, cyclical variation in utilization of the capital stock, etc.

220 Given the general nature of the present exercise, the audacity of these additional calculations may perhaps be overlooked. For a discussion of the procedure and its underlying assumptions see, for example, J. W. Kendrick, *Productivity Trends in the*

United States (1961), and the survey of the subsequent literature in M. I. Nadiri, 'Some Approaches to the Theory and Measurement of Total Factor Productivity – A Survey', *Journal of Economic Literature*, VIII (1970), 1137-77. For the weights used in calculating the combined inputs, see the notes to column 4 of Table 26.

221 Here, of course, we are ignoring all conceptual and statistical qualifications and are, in general, rounding the reported rates of growth.

222 As suggested, for example, in a well-known passage by W. A. Lewis, 'Economic Development with Unlimited Supplies of Labour', *Manchester School*, XXII (1954), 155, and by W. W. Rostow, *Stages of Economic Growth* (1960), 8, 20, 27, and 41-5. See also introduction to Crouzet (ed.), *Capital Formation*, 9-17, for further discussion of this hypothesis with reference to Britain, and more generally Gould, *Economic Growth in History*, 132-57, and S. Kuznets, 'Capital Formation in Modern Economic Growth' (1965), reprinted in his *Population, Capital and Growth* (1973), 121-64.

223 The level of the GDP series is very uncertain indeed. The estimate we have used would be raised by taking market prices rather than factor cost, or by adjusting for the higher level of capital formation indicated by the present estimates as compared with those by Deane included in the GDP estimate; it would be lowered by taking account of the fact that alternative estimates compiled from the income side lie well below those compiled from the expenditure side in the 1850s and 1860s, see Feinstein, *National Income*, 12-18. Strictly, for comparison with total investment (line 3 of Table 28) an estimate of GNP should be used, but the difference is small for most of the period covered. In the last two decades the figures for GNP would be £460m and £610m, and the ratios shown in line 7 would be reduced from 14 per cent to 13 per cent.

224 See, however, the last sentence of the preceding note.

225 Deane and Cole, *British Economic Growth*, 261. Cf. R. M. Hartwell, *The Industrial Revolution and Economic Growth* (1971), 174: 'On capital accumulation, the crucial fact is that there was at no time in the eighteenth century a marked rise in the rate of investment out of national income.'

226 For England and Wales little error is involved in treating all houses as separate dwellings up to 1860, since the construction of large flats and tenement blocks falls almost entirely in the latter part of the century: see (e.g.) K. M. Riley, 'An Estimate of the Age Distribution of the Dwelling Stock in Great Britain', *Urban Studies*, X (1973), 374. This is not true, however, for Scotland: see p. 43 above.

227 Census of Population, England and Wales, 1911, *General Report*, 24.

228 See Stamp, *British Incomes and Property*, 14, for the total, and *ibid.*, 119-20, for the farmhouses.

229 For a similar comparison for 1910 see *ibid.*, 125-8.

230 See *ibid.*, 140-1 for the houses of £20 or more, 118 for the residential shops under £20, and, 119-20 for the farmhouses. The figure for dwelling-houses under £20 is the residual and includes hotels, etc. under £20 which are not shown separately (*ibid.*, 114).

CHAPTER III

Labour in Great Britain

1 The research on which this paper is based has been financed by grants from the Nuffield Trust and the Institute of International Studies of the University of California, Berkeley, whose help is hereby gratefully acknowledged. I have derived much benefit

from the work of Mr I. A. Gribble and Mr Robert Glen, who acted as research assistants.

2 Edgar S. Furniss, *The Position of the Labourer in a System of Nationalism* (1920; repr. 1957), especially chaps. 5 and 7. This view has recently been challenged by R. C. Wiles, 'The Theory of Wages in Later English Mercantilism', *Economic History Review*, 2nd ser., XXI (1968).

3 A. W. Coats, 'The Classical Economists and the Labourer', in E. L. Jones and G. E. Mingay (eds.), *Land, Labour and Population in the Industrial Revolution* (1967).

4 Josiah Tucker, *Reflections on the Present Low Price of Coarse Wools* (1782), 42–6; Sir James Steuart, *An Inquiry into the Principles of Political Œconomy* (2 vols., 1767; repr. 1966), 67; Adam Smith, *Wealth of Nations*, ed. J. R. McCulloch (1863), 38; James Anderson, *Observations on the Means of Exciting a Spirit of National Industry* (1777), 350–1; and in general, Furniss, *op. cit.*, chap. 6, and A. W. Coats, 'Changing Attitudes to Labour in the Mid-Eighteenth Century', *Economic History Review*, 2nd ser., XI (1958).

5 T. R. Malthus, *Essay on the Principle of Population*, 2 vols. (3rd edn, 1806), II, 167; also II, 478.

6 Sydney H. Coontz, *Population Theories and the Economic Interpretation* (1961), 88ff; Harold Perkin, *The Origins of Modern English Society, 1780–1880* (1969), 241–4; T. R. Malthus, *Principles of Political Economy* (2nd edn, 1836; repr. 1936), 218ff.

7 H. L. Beales, 'The Historic Context of the Essay on Population', in D. V. Glass (ed.), *Introduction to Malthus* (1953); R. L. Meek, *Marx and Engels on Malthus* (1953), especially 24ff.

8 Susan Fairlie, 'The Corn Laws and British Wheat Production, 1829–76', *Economic History Review*, 2nd ser., XXII (1969).

9 John Barton, *Observations on the Condition of the Labouring Classes of Society* (1817, repr. 1934), especially 16–19 and 26–7; Barton, *An Inquiry into the Causes of the Progressive Depreciation of Agricultural Labour in Modern Times* (1820), 49–60, repr. in G. Sotiroff (ed.), *Economic Writings*, 2 vols. (1962–3); Barton, *In Defence of the Corn Laws* (1833), 67–70, repr. in Sotiroff (ed.), *op. cit.*; E. J. Hamilton, 'Profit Inflation and the Industrial Revolution, 1751–1800', *Quarterly Journal of Economics*, LVI (1942).

10 David Ricardo, *Principles of Political Economy and Taxation*, in *The Works and Correspondence of David Ricardo*, ed. P. Sraffa and M. H. Doss, 11 vols. (1951–73), vol. I; also *Notes on Malthus, ibid.*, vol. II, especially 438, 446, and 449, and *Correspondence, ibid.*, vol. VIII, 130 and 183–5 (9 November 1819, 4 May 1820); M. Blaug, *Ricardian Economics: A Historical Study* (1958), 75–7.

11 J. R. McCulloch, *A Treatise on the Circumstances which Determine the Rate of Wages and the Condition of the Labouring Classes* (2nd edn, 1854; repr. 1963), 34.

12 Blaug, *Ricardian Economics*, 28.

13 Edward R. Kittrell, 'The Development of the Theory of Colonization in English Classical Political Economy', in A. G. L. Shaw (ed.), *Great Britain and the Colonies, 1815–1865* (1970), 52; R. N. Ghosh, 'The Colonization Controversy: R. J. Wilmot-Horton and the Classical Economists', *ibid.*, 112–17.

14 Edward Gibbon Wakefield, *England and America*, 2 vols. (1833), repr. in *The Collected Works of Edward Gibbon Wakefield*, ed. M. F. Ll. Pritchard (1968), 518; B. Semmel, 'The Philosophic Radicals and Colonialism', in Shaw (ed.), *op. cit.*, 67; H. O. Pappé, 'Wakefield and Marx', *ibid.*, 204–5.

15 *Capital*, vol. I Everyman edn, 2 parts (1930; repr. 1957), 303–4.

16 'In almost all occupations there is in this country a superfluity of labourers.' *London Labour and the London Poor*, 4 vols. (1861), II, 300. Also evidence quoted in I. J. Prothero, 'London Chartists and the Trades', *Economic History Review*, 2nd ser., XXIV, 2 (1971), 217–18.

17 *Northern Star*, 7 June 1845, quoted in I. J. Prothero, 'Chartism in London', *Past and Present*, no. 44 (1969), 99. Also Joy MacAskill, 'The Chartist Land Plan', in Asa Briggs (ed.), *Chartist Studies* (1959), 307.

18 Engels, *Condition of the Working Class in England* (1845; repr. 1968), 78–85; Marx, *Capital*, I (Everyman edn), 469ff, 689, and 698ff; III (Chicago, 1909 edn), 247ff. Joan Robinson, *An Essay on Marxian Economics* (1942; repr. 1947), 29ff.

19 Engels to Bebel, 18–28 March 1875. Engels believed that the wage level had to hold a delicate balance: a mill hand's wage had to be higher than, say, an Irish wage; it had to be high enough to allow members of his family to survive, but low enough to force them to go out to work as soon as they were old enough (Engels, *op. cit.*, 77–8).

20 E.g. M. W. Reder, 'The Size Distribution of Earnings', in Jean Marchal and Bernard Ducros (ed.), *The Distribution of National Income* (1968).

21 W. Arthur Lewis, 'Economic Development with Unlimited Supplies of Labour', *Manchester School*, XXII (1954); also R. Nurske, *Capital Formation* (1953); John C. H. Fei and Gustav Ranis, *Development of the Labor Surplus Economy* (1964), especially 3 and 156–9.

22 C. P. Kindleberger, *Europe's Postwar Growth: The Role of Labor Supply* (1967).

23 According to a recent calculation, between 1801–11 and 1831–41 the real product per head of the occupied population rose by 2·2 per cent a year in manufacturing, mining, and building, but by only 1·1 per cent in agriculture, forestry, and fishing: P. Deane and W. A. Cole, *British Economic Growth, 1688–1959* (1962), 172. There is a good description of disguised unemployment on the land in Ireland in Malthus, *Principles*, 345–7. Also see John Law, *Money and Trade* (1705), 97ff.

24 This finds strong support from Sir James Steuart: the 'labouring inhabitants . . . desert agriculture, in favour of a more lucrative occupation to be found in the city. Scarcity of hands in the country raises the price of labour on one hand, while it diminishes the price of subsistence on the other.' *Op. cit.*, 64. H. J. Habakkuk, *American and British Technology in the Nineteenth Century* (1962).

25 E. L. Jones, 'The Agricultural Origin of Industry', *Past and Present*, no. 40 (1968). This view has a certain plausibility for the earliest stages only. Even by the 1790s the tables had been turned, and not only were agricultural wages high in areas like Lancashire, but the rents of part-time farmers–cotton workers had been driven up to a point at which they were in part paid out of wages. Cf. John Aikin, *A Description of the Country from Thirty to Forty Miles round Manchester* (1795), 244 and 247.

26 This is suggested by Mark Blaug, 'The Myth of the Old Poor Law and the Making of the New', *Journal of Economic History*, XXIII, 2 (1963), 154–5.

27 J. R. Hicks, *Value and Capital* (1946), 302.

28 Cf. G. D. H. Cole, *Studies in Class Structure* (1955), p. 31.

29 Cf. J. Kuczynski, *Die Geschichte der Lage der Arbeiter in Deutschland*, I, part I (1954), 89ff. E. H. Hunt, *Regional Wage Variations in Britain, 1850–1914* (1973).

30 Elizabeth W. Gilboy, *Wages in Eighteenth Century England* (1934); Peter Mathias, *The First Industrial Nation: The Economic History of Britain, 1700–1914* (1969), 220; J. H. Clapham, *Economic History of Modern Britain*, 3 vols. (1926–39, repr. 1964), vol. I, p. 466; A. L. Bowley, *Wages in the United Kingdom in the Nineteenth Century* (1900), table opp. p. 144.

31 Valerie Morgan, 'Agricultural Wage Rates in Late Eighteenth-Century Scotland', *Economic History Review*, 2nd ser., XXIV (1971).

32 E. H. Hunt, *Regional Wage Variations*, 204–18; also the same author's 'Labour Productivity in English Agriculture, 1850–1914', *Economic History Review*, 2nd ser., XX (1967), and 'Quantitative and Other Evidence in Agriculture, 1850–1914', *ibid.*,

XXIII (1970); Paul A. David, 'Labour Productivity in English Agriculture, 1850–1914: Some Quantitative Evidence on Regional Differences', *ibid.* XXIII (1970), 510–12.

33 James Sims, in the *Mining Almanack for 1849*, reprinted in Roger Burt, *Cornish Mining* (1969), 96.

34 [John Wade], *History of the Middle and Working Classes* (1833), 241–2.

35 E. J. Hobsbawm, 'The Tramping Artisan', in *Labouring Men* (1964).

36 Raymond Challinor and Brian Ripley, *The Miners' Association: A Trade Union in the Age of the Chartists* (1968), 54–5.

37 James Ward, *Workmen and Wages at Home and Abroad* (1868), 16.

38 G. R. Porter, *Progress of the Nation* (3rd edn, 1851), 210 and 443.

39 J. M. Ludlow and Lloyd Jones, *The Progress of the Working Class, 1832–1867* (1867), 236; National Association for the Promotion of Social Science, *Trades' Societies and Strikes* (1860), Report, p. xii; E. J. Hobsbawm, 'Customs, Wages and Work-Load in Nineteenth-Century Industry', in Asa Briggs and J. Saville (eds.), *Essays in Labour History* (1960), and *Labouring Men*, 319; Mayhew, *op. cit.*, II, 292 and 336; *Return of Wage Rates, 1830–1886* (PP 1887, C. 5172, LXXXIX); Thomas, Lord Brassey, *Work and Wages* (1894 edn, first published 1872), 9.

40 *Wealth of Nations*, book I, chaps. 8 and 10.

41 An investigation of 309 cottages in Lancashire showed that while the average wage per person to be supported was 5s. 8½d. a week, this was so because of the large number of dependents at work – 1,134 persons supporting a total of 2,000. In families with only one or two earners, even at similar wages, income might fall to 4s. and even 2s. a week. P. M. M'Douall, 'Statistics of the Parish of Ramsbottom, nr Bury, Lancashire', *Journal of the Royal Statistical Society*, I (1838–9), 537.

42 T. S. Ashton, *Economic Fluctuations in England, 1700–1800* (1955), 173–4.

43 Marchal and Ducros (eds.), *op. cit.*, *passim*; and Barbara Wootton, *The Social Foundations of Wage Policy* (1955).

44 Michael Drake (ed.), *Population in Industrialization* (1969).

45 Young, *Political Arithmetic* (1774), 63–4.

46 H. J. Habakkuk, *Population Growth and Economic Development Since 1750* (1971).

47 J. D. Chambers, *Population, Economy and Society in Pre-Industrial England* (1972).

48 T. McKeown and R. G. Brown, 'Medical Evidence Relating to English Population Changes in the Eighteenth Century', in D. V. Glass and D. E. Eversley (ed.), *Population in History* (1965).

49 E. M. Sigsworth, 'A Provincial Hospital in the Eighteenth and Early Nineteenth Centuries', *College of General Practitioners, Yorkshire Faculty Journal*, June 1966; and J. H. Woodward, 'Before Bacteriology – Deaths in Hospitals', *ibid.*, Autumn 1969.

50 Deane and Cole, *op. cit.*, 106–22; A. K. Cairncross, 'Internal Migration in Victorian England', *Manchester School*, XVII (1949), 79. This tendency was also noted in the Census of 1831, but see the opposing view of Clapham, *Economic History*, vol. I, p. 54.

51 A. Redford, *Labour Migration in England, 1800–1850* (2nd edn, 1964).

52 Barton, *Inquiry into the Depreciation of Agricultural Labour*, 61 (reprinted in Sotiroff (ed.), *Economic Writings*).

53 Barton, *In Defence of the Corn Laws*, 29 (reprinted in Sotiroff (ed.), *op. cit.*).

54 John V. Mosley, 'Poor Law Administration in England and Wales, 1830 to 1850, with Special Reference to the Problem of the Able-Bodied Labourer' (unpublished Ph.D. thesis, London, 1976); A. H. John, *The Industrial Development of South Wales, 1750–1850* (1950), 68.

55 [William Dodd], *The Labouring Classes of England* (1847), 14; P. E. Razzell, 'Statistics and English Historical Sociology', in R. M. Hartwell (ed.), *The Industrial Revolution* (1970).

56 Mrs Cobden Unwin (ed.), *The Hungry Forties: Life Under the Bread Tax* (1904), 33, 37, 89, 119, and 142–3.

57 Japan is another country in which the assumption of a static subsistence wage in agriculture was found to be too rigid. K. Ohkawa and R. Minami, 'The Phase of Unlimited Supplies of Labour', *Hitotsubashi Journal of Economics*, v, 1 (1964).

58 G. R. Hawke, *Railways and Economic Growth in England and Wales, 1840–1870* (1970), 277; P. W. Kingsford, *Victorian Railwaymen* (1970), 2–3.

59 *North and South* (Penguin edn, 1970), 382.

60 Cf. Statistical Society of Manchester, 'Report on the Condition of the Population in Three Parishes in Rutlandshire', *Journal of the Royal Statistical Society*, II (1839–40), 297–8; G. Dyer, *Complaints of the People of England* (1793), 73–4.

61 E.g. Philip Styles, 'The Evolution of the Law of Settlement', *University of Birmingham Historical Journal*, IX (1963); and James Stephen Taylor, 'The Mythology of the Old Poor Law', *Journal of Economic History*, XXIX (1969); Redford, *op. cit.*, 81–96.

62 *Parliamentary History*, XXXII, cols. 707–8 (12 February 1796).

63 E.g. *Lords Committees on Poor Laws* (PP 1818, v, 400), Evidence of P. M. James, p. 179, and John Carter, p. 186; *S.C. on Agriculture* (PP 1833, v), Report, p. 7, and Evidence of John Cooper, QQ. 9723–4 and 9754–5; *S.C. on Settlement and Poor Removal*, 6th Report (PP 1847, XI), Evidence of Henry Coppock, QQ. 5258ff., App. 2 and 3; Mayhew, *op. cit.*, vol. I, p. 423.

64 E.g. Thomas Chalmers, *The Christian and Civic Economy of Large Towns*, 3 vols. (1821–6), III, 60–1; W. P. Alison, *Reply to the Pamphlet Entitled Proposed Alteration of the Scottish Poor Law* (1840), 29ff.

65 Barton, *Condition of the Labouring Classes*, 64.

66 In evidence to *S.C. on the Poor Laws* (Sturges Bourne Committee), (PP 1817, VI. 462), 85–6.

67 Colquhoun, *Treatise on Indigence* (1806), 72 and 172; also pp. 187ff for a powerful indictment of the Settlement Acts.

68 The issue is discussed with great insight by Charles Wing, *Evils of the Factory System, Demonstrated by Parliamentary Evidence* (1837, repr. 1967), especially 353ff.

69 These and other details concerning the origins of the transfer scheme are contained in Appendices to the *First Report of the Poor Law Commissioners for England and Wales* (PP 1835, XXXV), especially pp. 293–9 and 323.

70 *Ibid.*, 165 and 132.

71 There are good accounts in Redford, *op. cit.*, 92ff; J. T. Ward, *The Factory Movement, 1830–1855* (1962); Dodd, *op. cit.*; *The Fleet Papers*, I/14, I/35, II/1, II/4, and II/6; Poor Law Commissioners Reports: *Second Report* (PP 1836, XXIX), esp. Appendices; *Third Report* (1837, XXXI), 174–6; *Fourth Report* (1837–8, XXVIII), 183–4; *Eighth Report* (1842, XIX), 153; *S.C. on the Act for the Regulation of Mills and Factories* (1840, X), *Third Report*, Evidence of Henry Ashworth, QQ. 4845–53 and 4865–8.

72 *Evans' and Ruffy's Farm Journal*, 7 September 1812, quoted in E. J. T. Collins, 'Harvest Technology and Labour Supply in Britain, 1790–1870' (unpublished Ph.D. thesis, Nottingham, 1970), 122.

73 Sir Francis Hill, *Georgian Lincoln* (1966), 192–3.

74 Collins, 'Harvest Technology' (thesis), 101 and 137.

75 Evidence of William Reed to *S.C. on Agriculture* (PP 1833, v), QQ. 3711–4.

76 J. H. Treble, 'The Place of the Irish Catholics in the Social Life of the North of England, 1829–51' (unpublished Ph.D. thesis, Leeds, 1968), 54ff; J. E. Handley, *The Irish in Scotland, 1798–1845* (2nd edn, 1945), 36ff.

77 C. R. Baird, 'On the Poorest Class of Operative in Glasgow in 1837', *Journal of the Royal Statistical Society*, I (1838–9), 168. Interestingly enough, about the same

proportion of Irish as of the whole group – just over one-half – described themselves as trade unionists.

78 Quoted in Redford, *op. cit.*, 162.

79 *National Reformer*, n.s., no. 32 (8 May 1847), 11.

80 Baron d'Haussez, *Great Britain in 1833* (1833), p. 232.

81 Hand-loom Weavers' Commission, *Assistant Commissioners' Reports* (J. C. Symons) (PP 1839, XLII), 19.

82 Evidence of William Welsby, permanent Overseer of the Poor in Manchester, to *Lords Committee on the Poor Laws*, 10 July 1817 (PP 1818, v (400)), 167–8.

83 *Quarterly Review*, vol. XLIII, no. 86 (October 1830), 244–5.

84 Challinor and Ripley, *op. cit.*, 164.

85 On the somewhat unrealistic assumption that British corn consumption remained unchanged throughout at 2·25 quarters per person per annum, Ireland provided 0·7 per cent of British consumption in 1785, 1·5 per cent in 1803, and 7·1 per cent in 1844.

86 McCulloch calculated that the British spent £9 per capita per annum on food, and the Irish £5. Rent remitted to absentee landlords he calculated at £6 million, while total national income for 1841 has been estimated at *c.* £450 million. J. R. McCulloch, *A Descriptive and Statistical Account of the British Empire*, 2 vols. (3rd edn, 1847), 521; Deane and Cole, *op. cit.*, 166.

87 W. Burness, *Essay on the Elements of British Industry* (1848), 55–6.

88 E.g. Cairncross, 'Internal Migration', 70. Cairncross here speaks mainly of the period from the 1840s to the 1870s.

89 J. K. Edwards, 'Norwich Bills of Mortality, 1707–1830', *Yorkshire Bulletin*, XXI, 2 (1969); E. J. Buckatzsch, 'Places of Origin of a Group of Immigrants into Sheffield, 1624–1799', *Economic History Review*, 2nd ser., II, 3 (1950).

90 J. D. Chambers, 'Enclosure and Labour Supply in the Industrial Revolution', *Economic History Review*, 2nd ser., v (1953).

91 F. F. Mendels, 'Proto-Industrialization: The First Phase of the Industrialization Process', *Journal of Economic History*, XXXII (1972), 254.

92 E. J. Buckatzsch, 'The Constancy of Local Populations and Migration in England before 1800', *Population Studies*, v, 1 (1951).

93 Cf. the descriptions of the rise in employment in remote Cheshire and Derbyshire villages, in Aikin, *op. cit.*, 458–505.

94 R. A. Church, 'Labour Supply and Innovation, 1800–1860: The Boot and Shoe Industry', *Business History*, XII, 1 (1970), 28.

95 Léon Faucher, *Manchester in 1844: Its Present Condition and Future Prospect* (1844), 63.

96 William Chambers, *Memoir of Robert Chambers with Autobiographical Reminiscences* (1872), 85.

97 Committee of the Statistical Society of London, 'State of the Working Classes in the Parishes of St Margaret and St John, Westminster', *Journal of the Royal Statistical Society*, III (1840–1), 17–19.

98 Redford, *op. cit.*, 124. Also see Charles Wood's speech of 15 Feburary 1843, in *Hansard*, 3rd ser., LXVI (1843), 671–2.

99 Alexander Somerville, *The Autobiography of a Working Man* (1848; repr. 1967), 66; Poor Law Commissioners, *Third Annual Report* (PP 1837, XXXI), 175; E. J. T. Collins, 'Harvest Technology and Labour Supply in Britain, 1790–1870', *Economic History Review*, 2nd ser., XXII, 3 (1969), 467.

100 A. F. Weber, *The Growth of Cities in the 19th Century* (1899).

101 Engels, *op. cit.*, 136–9; P. Gaskell, *Artisans and Machinery* (1836, repr. 1968), 356ff.

102 *Phalanx*, no. 62 (October 1842), 129.

103 Samuel Bamford, *Autobiography*, 2 vols. (1967 edn; first published 1839–41), I, pp. 1–2; Oastler's speech of 2 January 1832, *Leeds Intelligencer*, 5 January 1832; *Poor Man's Guardian*, no. 67 (22 September 1832), 544; Jelinger C. Symons, *Arts and Artisans at Home and Abroad* (Edinburgh, 1839), 146ff; Peter Laslett, *The World We Have Lost* (1971 edn; first published 1965), 209–10. This distinction has recently been resuscitated by R. S. Neale in his concept of the 'middling class' including shopkeepers and artisans but excluding operatives: 'Class and Class Consciousness in Early Nineteenth-Century England. Three Classes or Five', *Victorian Studies*, XII (1968–9).

104 G. Turnbull, *A History of Calico Printing in Great Britain* (1939); M. I. Thomis, *Politics and Society in Nottingham, 1785–1835* (1969), 18–19.

105 *Assistant Commissioners' Report* (PP 1839, XLII); J. C. Symons, *op. cit.*, p. 44.

106 Petition of the Spitalfields Broad Silk Handloom-Weavers to the Board of Trade, 30 November 1843: printed in *Fleet Papers*, IV/4 (27 January 1844), 76–7.

107 E.g. Eugène Buret, *De la misère des classes laborieuses en Angleterre et en France*, 2 vols. (1840), II, 22–30; Dodd, *Labouring Classes of England*, 9–11.

108 Quoted in Wing, *Evils of the Factory System*, 370.

109 Mayhew, *op. cit.*, II, 311, 317, and 333–5; III, 229 and 300–1; Godfrey Lushington, in Nat. Assn Social Science, *Trades' Societies and Strikes*, 270; also *ibid.*, 388.

110 F. Hill, *op. cit.*, 284.

111 Deane, *The First Industrial Revolution* (1965), 253.

112 William Pole, *The Life of Sir William Fairbairn, Bart* (1877), 89ff; [Thomas Wright], *Some Habits and Customs of the Working Classes, by a Journeyman Engineer* (1867; repr. 1967), 49–50 and 60.

113 Cf. the impressive list in George Howell, *The Conflicts of Capital and Labour* (1878), 246ff.

114 Habakkuk, *op. cit.*, 22, also 152; Henry Pelling, 'The Concept of Labour Aristocracy', in *Popular Politics and Society in Late Victorian Britain* (1968), 40–1 and 46–51; W. Fischer, 'Innerbetrieblicher und sozialer Status der frühen Fabrikarbeiterschaft', *Forschungen zur Sozial- und Wirtschaftsgeschichte*, VI (1964).

115 E. J. Hobsbawm, 'The Labour Aristocracy in Nineteenth Century Britain', in *Labouring Men*, 273ff.

116 Somerville, *Autobiography*, 97–9 and 120.

117 P. E. Razzell, *op. cit.*, 104–6; R. L. Hill, *Toryism and the People, 1832–46* (1929), 111; *Notes to the People*, II (1852; repr. 1967), 543.

118 T. K. Derry, 'The Repeal of the Apprenticeship Clause of the Statute of Apprentices', *Economic History Review*, III (1931–2).

119 Marx, *Capital*, I, p. 448.

120 *Children's Employment Commission Reports* (1842–3); Ivy Pinchbeck, *Women Workers and the Industrial Revolution, 1750–1850* (1930).

121 Léon Faucher, *Etudes sur l'Angleterre*, 2 vols. (2nd edn, 1856), vol. I, pp. 280–1: this passage was omitted from the English edition. Also Neil J. Smelser, *Social Change in the Industrial Revolution* (1959).

122 John G. Rule, 'Some Social Aspects of the Cornish Industrial Revolution', in Roger Burt (ed.), *Industry and Society in the South-West* (1970), 73.

123 Which, in the words of one manufacturer, 'saddled the British operative with an idle, unprofitable family until they were 9 years old'. J. T. Ward, *The Factory Movement*, 54.

124 R. C. O. Matthews, *Economic Fluctuations in Great Britain, 1833–1842* (1954), 146–8 and 221.

125 Kuczynski, *op. cit.*, XXIII, 130.

126 J. T. Ward, *op. cit.*, 144. Curiously, this echoes the traditional practice of the

'bondager', the additional female worker to be supplied by the agricultural worker of Northumberland, where farm labour may have become scarce because of the expansion of mining. Somerville, *op. cit.*, 20; *McDowell's Chartist Journal*, no. 4 (21 April 1841), 31; Dodd, *op. cit.*, 35; L. Hindmarsh, 'Condition of the Agricultural Labourers in the Northern Division of Northumberland', *Journal of the Royal Statistical Society*, 1 (1838–9), 405.

127 E.g. T. S. Ashton, *An Economic History of England: The Eighteenth Century* (1955), 202–3; Steuart, *An Inquiry into the Principles of Political Œconomy*, 88–9.

128 There is, of course, a large element of arbitrariness in these figures, and about half the trades enumerated were calculated to draw wages for eleven or twelve months in the year. Statistical Committee of the Leeds Town Council, 'Report upon the Condition of the Town of Leeds and of Its Inhabitants', *Journal of the Royal Statistical Society*, 11 (1839–40), 422.

129 H. C. Escher's letters from England, 1814, in W. O. Henderson (ed.), *Industrial Britain under the Regency: The Diaries of Escher, Bodmer, May and de Gallois* (1968), 35.

130 W. R. Greg, 'English Socialism' (1850), in *Mistaken Aims and Attainable Ideals of the Artisan Class* (1876), 206.

131 *Notes to the People*, 1, 19, p. 367.

132 This kind of reasoning was applied by Owenites and other Socialist economists to the export industries, and particularly to cotton: the frantic speed-up and longer hours, lowering costs, merely turned the terms of trade against Britain, and the ever larger quantities of cotton manufactures exported benefited the foreigners but brought no more real commodities into Britain. E.g. *The Crisis*, 111, 19 (4 January 1834). Cf. also the resolution of the Leicester framework knitters in 1817, which argued that 'to reduce the wages of the Mechanic of this Country so low that he cannot live by his labour, in order to undersell Foreign Manufacturers in a Foreign Market, is to gain one customer abroad, and lose two at home'. Quoted in E. P. Thompson, *The Making of the English Working Class* (1963), 206. Of course, rising productivity may offset the loss due to falling prices, but Kindleberger is mistaken in using, in the case of British textiles from 1750 to 1850, the selling prices abroad: the cost of imported cotton has to be deducted, and the fall in the values added has to be used in the comparison, and that price fall was much greater than the price fall of finished cotton goods. C. P. Kindleberger, *Foreign Trade and the National Economy* (1962), 113.

133 M. A. Bienefeld, *Working Hours in British Industry: An Economic History* (1972).

134 *Observations on the Management of the Poor in Scotland*, 2nd edn (1840), 49. Poor Law Commissioners, *Seventh Report* (PP 1841, XI), 238.

135 Mayhew, *op. cit.*, 11, 300; *ibid.*, 111, 301–12; and Buret, *op. cit.*, 11, 42.

136 Kuczynski, *op. cit.*, XXIII, 106–8, and XXIV, 42; E. J. Hobsbawm, 'The British Standard of Living, 1790–1850', *Economic History Review*, 2nd ser., X (1957), 53.

137 *The Philanthropist*, 11 (1812), 185 and 316–17; *ibid.*, 111 (1813), 142.

138 *Edinburgh Review*, XLI, 81 (October 1824), art. XI.

139 *Carpenter's Monthly Political Magazine*, October 1831, p. 76; *ibid.*, January 1832, p. 214; *ibid.*, May 1832, pp. 374–5.

140 Letter from W. Walker and W. Rand to Sir James Graham, November 1841, quoted in J. T. Ward, *op. cit.*, 234.

141 *London Phalanx*, no. 31, 30 October 1841; *ibid.*, no. 41, 8 January 1842; *ibid.*, no. 45, 5 February 1842; Faucher, *Manchester in 1844*, 143–4.

142 *National Reformer*, n.s., no. 32 (8 May 1847), p. 11.

143 W. E. Adams, *Memoirs of a Social Atom* (1903, ed. of 1968, New York), p. 333.

144 F. A. Walker, *The Wages Question* (1887), 81–3; Thompson, *English Working Class*, 248–50.

145 Pinchbeck, *op. cit.*, 132–40.

146 Engels, *Condition of the Working Class*, 140; Marx, *Capital*, vol. I, chap. 13, p. 8; J. R. McCulloch, *Descriptive and Statistical Account*, 670-2.

147 Or from independent handicraftsmen, like the London tailors.

148 For Coventry silk weavers, see John Prest, *The Industrial Revolution in Coventry* (1960), chaps. 3 and 4. For London workers, E. P. Thompson and Eileen Yeo, *The Unknown Mayhew* (1971).

149 C. Bruyn Andrews (ed.), *The Torrington Diaries*, 4 vols. (1935-8), III, 115. This refers to Rochdale in 1792.

150 William Radcliffe, *Origin of the New System of Manufacture* (1828), 63; Bamford, *Autobiography*, 175, 226, and 311; P. Gaskell, *The Manufacturing Population of England* (1833).

151 'There is abundant evidence that in the '90's, with the probable exception of the bad periods, linen, woollens, and also silk manufactures were either losing labour to the cotton industry or were going over to cotton themselves.' M. M. Edwards, *The Growth of the British Cotton Trade, 1780-1815* (1967), 33.

152 S. D. Chapman, 'The Transition to the Factory System in the Midland Cotton Industry', *Economic History Review*, 2nd ser., XVIII (1965). S. J. Chapman, *The Early Factory Masters* (1967), 173.

153 'The enlistment of young men for soldiers, always a prosperous business in times of commercial depression, was extremely prevalent.' E. Butterworth, *Historical Sketches of Oldham* (1856), 136.

154 S. J. Chapman, *Factory Masters*, 40.

155 For the decline as early as 1802-12, see Porter, *Progress of the Nation*, 184.

156 Quoted in Duncan Bythell, *The Handloom Weavers* (1969), 170.

157 'The great demand for labour was met by newcomers to the towns, by people from the surrounding districts, from Wales, Scotland and Ireland who were attracted by the prospects afforded by the new industry.' F. Collier, *The Family Economy of the Working Class in the Cotton Industry, 1784-1833* (1964).

158 House of Commons, *Report of the Minutes of Evidence taken before the Select Committee on the State of Children in the Manufactories of the United Kingdom* (PP 1816, III (397)), 338, evidence of Nathaniel Gould.

159 'There are few persons who have been more than thirty years in the cotton-mills; and this circumstance is ascribed by the masters and overlookers to the better wages in other employments, and the consequent secession of operatives when they attain full age and strength.' C. Turner Thackrah, *The Effects of Arts, Trades and Professions . . . on Health and Longevity* (1832), 145. An enumeration of 1839 for Stockport and Manchester showed that of 22,094 mill hands, only 143, or 0·6 per cent, were over forty-five years of age (Dodd, *op. cit.*, 128). Another enumeration of April 1844 showed that of 116,281 in Manchester and district, only 8,650, or 7·6 per cent, were over 40 (McCulloch, *Description and Statistical Account*, vol. I, p. 702).

160 Collier, *op. cit.*, 7.

161 Porter, *op. cit.*, 183-4.

162 Handley, *The Irish in Scotland*, 121; Treble, *op. cit.*, 14.

163 *S.C. on Agriculture* (PP 1833, v), evidence of William Reed, QQ. 3717-22.

164 An enumeration of the mid-forties showed that of 116,281 mill workers in the Manchester area, 10,721 were married women, and 18,780 were married men. Of 10,062 married women, the husbands of 5,314 worked in the mills, 3,929 worked in other trades, and 821 had no regular employment. McCulloch, *Descriptive and Statistical Account*, 702.

165 Jelinger C. Symons, *Arts and Artisans*, 143.

166 According to Hugh Logan, a large Glasgow cotton manufacturer, 'The Irish send for their relations or acquaintances, or town's people, and take them in as

lodgers, and train them to weaving, which is so easily acquired, that a person of ordinary acuteness can do common work in a very short time . . . This accounts for the fact that the absolute number of Irish handloom weavers . . . is constantly on the increase.' Quoted in Handley, *op. cit.*, 117. J. L. Hammond and B. Hammond, *The Skilled Labourer, 1760–1832* (1920 edn), chap. 5. For women workers, see Pinchbeck, *op. cit.*, 157ff.

167 Turnbull, *Calico Printing*, 202.

168 H. D. Fong, *The Triumph of the Factory System* (1932), 25.

169 Clapham, *Economic History*, vol. 1, pp. 71–2; he estimated cotton employment at 375,000 to 400,000 in 1831 and 450,000 in 1833–4, but the majority of these workers were women and children. According to the Census of 1841, building and road-building in England and Wales employed about 350,000 out of a total of 6,630,000.

170 Brassey, *Work and Wages*, 8–9.

171 Marian Bowley, *The British Building Industry: Some Studies in Response and Resistance to Change* (1966), 326; M. Bowley, *Innovations in Building Materials* (1960), 50.

172 J. Parry Lewis, *Building Cycles and Britain's Growth* (1965); Matthews, *Economic Fluctuations*, 115–17.

173 Report by Louis de Gallois on English railways, in Henderson (ed.), *Industrial Britain under the Regency*, 171.

174 J. C. Fischer, *Tagebücher* (1951), 296–9; Escher's letters from England in Henderson (ed.), *op. cit.*, letter 10 of 11 September 1814.

175 A. L. Bowley, 'The Statistics of Wages in the United Kingdom during the Last Hundred Years', *Journal of the Royal Statistical Society*, LXIII (1900), 300–10; A. L. Bowley, *Wages in the United Kingdom*, 82–3.

176 Esp. see *S.C. on Combination of Workmen, 1st and 2nd Reports* (PP 1837–8, VIII), and Nat. Assn Social Science, *Trades' Societies and Strikes*, 338–9, 409, and 428; A. Aspinall, *Early English Trade Unions* (1949), 2–4.

177 G. Steffen, *Studien zur Geschichte der englischen Lohnarbeiter*, 3 vols. (1901), II, 43.

178 E. W. Cooney, 'The Origins of the Victorian Master Builders', *Economic History Review*, 2nd ser., VIII (1955).

179 R. W. Postgate, *The Builders' History* (1923), 93; S. Webb and B. Webb, *History of Trade Unionism* (1902 edn), 111–17; G. D. H. Cole, *Attempts at General Union* (1953), 104–6; James Ward, *Workmen and Wages*, 109–17; reports in *Poor Man's Guardian*, 13 August and 17 September 1831; 1 March, 8 March, 14 April, 2 August, 23 August, 30 August, and 6 September 1834.

180 Quoted in G. D. H. Cole and A. W. Filson (eds.), *British Working-Class Movements: Select Documents, 1789–1875* (1965 edn; first published 1951), 268–70; also Max Morris (ed.), *From Cobbett to the Chartists, 1815–1848* (1948), 91.

181 W. G. Rimmer, 'Working-Men's Cottages in Leeds, 1770–1840', *Thoresby Society*, XLVI (1960), 184. C. W. Chalklin, *The Provincial Towns of Georgian England* (1974), 231 and 234.

182 G. Shaw Lefevre and Thomas R. Bennet, 'Account of the Strike and Lockout in the Building Trades of London in 1858–60', in Nat. Assn Social Science, *Trades' Societies and Strikes*; W. S. Hilton, *Foes to Tyranny: A History of the Amalgamated Union of Building Trade Workers* (1963), esp. 36–8, 61–3, and 71–85; Pelling, *op. cit.*, 41–4; Clapham, *op. cit.*, I, pp. 71–2, 162–6, and 593; Brassey, 'On the Rise of Wages in the Building Trades of London' (1878), in *Work and Wages*, 183–5.

183 J. H. Clapham, 'Work and Wages', in G. M. Young (ed.), *Early Victorian England*, 2 vols. (1934, repr. 1963), I, p. 48; J. E. Williams, *The Derbyshire Miners* (1962), 27; Clapham, *Economic History*, vol. 1, p. 433; A. J. Taylor, 'The Sub-Contract

System in the British Coal Industry', in L. S. Pressnell (ed.), *Studies in the Industrial Revolution* (1960), 217.

184 Baron F. Duckham, 'Serfdom in Eighteenth Century Scotland', *History*, LIV (1969).

185 Henry Louis, 'The Pitmen's Yearly Bond', *Transactions of the North of England Institute of Mining*, LXXX (1930); Hylton Scott, 'The Miners' Bond in Northumberland and Durham', *Proceedings of the Society of Antiquaries of Newcastle-upon-Tyne*, 4th ser., XI (1947); R. Feynes, *History of the Northumberland and Durham Miners* (1873; repr. 1923), 10.

186 Challinor and Ripley, *op. cit.*, 95 and 144.

187 T. S. Ashton and J. Sykes, *The British Coal Industry in the Eighteenth Century* (1929), 173.

188 J. B. Simpson, *Capital and Labour in Coal Mining* (1900), 26; Edward Hughes, *North Country Life in the Eighteenth Century*, 2 vols. (1952), vol. I, p. 251.

189 E.g. *Seventy-Fifth Annual Report of the Registrar-General of Births, Deaths and Marriages in England and Wales, 1912* (1914), Table xv.

190 J. R. Leifchild, *Our Coal and Our Pits* (1856), 182–3; J. M. Ludlow, 'Account of West Yorkshire Coal Strike and Lock-out of 1858', Nat. Assn Social Science, in *Trades' Societies and Strikes*, 14; J. R. McCulloch, *Descriptive and Statistical Account*, 602.

191 G. G. Hopkinson, 'The Development of Lead Mining and of the Coal and Iron Industries in North Derbyshire and South Yorkshire, 1700–1850' (unpublished Ph.D. thesis, Sheffield, 1958), 274; also 360–2.

192 John, *Industrial Development of South Wales*, 64.

193 E.g. Buddle's evidence before S.C., House of Lords, *Report on the State of the Coal Trade* (PP 1830).

194 J. W. House, *North-Eastern England: Population Movements and the Landscape since the Early 19th Century* (Newcastle-upon-Tyne, 1954, cyclostyled), 40.

195 John, *Industrial Development*, 69; *Children's Employment Commission* (1842), First Report, Mines, Appendix part 1, evidence of Dr Mitchell, p. 82.

196 F. C. Mather, *After the Canal Duke* (1970), 324–5.

197 *Children's Employment Commission*, First Report, Appendix 1, p. 530, evidence of Leifchild.

198 *Ibid.*, Appendix 2, pp. 371 and 47 respectively.

199 The writing of every major section of this essay was accompanied by attempts to arrive at some quantitative measures, but they had all to be scrapped since the range of possible errors was in each case far wider than the limits of significance.

200 Deane and Cole, *op. cit.*, 142.

201 That is, the percentage increase in the agricultural counties, taken as an indication of the increase in the agricultural population as such. *Ibid.*, 75.

202 S. Pollard and D. W. Crossley, *The Wealth of Britain, 1085–1966* (1968), 163.

203 The last two figures from Deane and Cole, *op. cit.*, 143.

204 The influence of other migration is ignored, and various tests showed that the complication of differential rates of natural increase in industry and agriculture, even if they could be established, would not greatly alter the picture. I am grateful to Professor J. M. Gani for advice and assistance in these calculations.

205 Aikin, *op. cit.*, 23 and 93; G. E. Mingay, 'The Size of Farms in the Eighteenth Century', *Economic History Review*, 2nd ser., XIV (1962).

206 A. J. Youngson, *The Making of Classical Edinburgh, 1750–1850* (1966), 32.

207 E.g. Mataji Umemura, 'Agriculture and Labour Supply in Japan in the Meiji Era', *The Developing Economies*, III, 3 (1965), 274.

208 This is the main conclusion of his doctoral thesis, 'Harvest Technology and Labour Supply'. According to Collins, the agricultural labour market was tight in the

war years and began to tighten again in 1834–51, developing pronounced labour shortages in 1852–70 (p. 150). Cf. also E. J. T. Collins, 'Labour Supply and Demand in European Agriculture, 1800–1880', in E. L. Jones and S. J. Woolf (eds.), *Agrarian Change and Economic Development* (1969); James Caird, *English Agriculture in 1850–51* (2nd edn, 1968), 472; and J. V. Mosley, *op. cit.*, 471.

209 Lewis, *Socialism and Economic Growth* (1971), 6.

210 J. D. Chambers, *Nottinghamshire in the Eighteenth Century* (2nd edn, 1965), 287.

211 J. D. Chambers and G. E. Mingay, *The Agricultural Revolution, 1750–1880* (1966), 18.

212 [John Arbuthnot], *An Inquiry into the Connection between the Present Price of Provisions and the Size of Farms. By a Farmer* (1773), 50; W. Hasbach, *A History of the English Agricultural Labourer* (1908), 86.

213 J. P. Kay, 'Earnings of Agricultural Labourers in Norfolk and Suffolk', *Journal of the Royal Statistical Society*, 1 (1838–9), 181; also Paul A. David, 'Labour Productivity'; and Hunt, 'Quantitative Evidence'.

214 Somerville, *op. cit.*, 107 and 66; Collins, 'Harvest Technology' (article in *EHR*), 467–9.

215 Chambers and Mingay, *op. cit.*, 220; E. C. K. Gonner, *Common Land and Enclosure* (2nd edn, 1965), 416.

216 J. E. Thorold Rogers, *Six Centuries of Work and Wages* (1894), 406; E. W. Gilboy, *Wages in Eighteenth-Century England.*

217 A. H. John, 'Farming in Wartime, 1793–1815', in Jones and Mingay (eds.), *Land, Labour and Population*, 33; Arthur Young, *A Farmer's Tour through the East of England*, 4 vols. (1771), vol. I, 321–9; W. Marshall, *A Review of the Reports to the Board of Agriculture for the Northern Department of England* (1808), 252.

218 J. D. Marshall, 'The Lancashire Rural Labourer in the Early Nineteenth Century', *Transactions of the Lancashire and Cheshire Antiquarian Society*, LXXI (1961), 91.

219 *Torrington Diaries*, II, 209; L. Simond, *Journal of a Tour and Residence in Great Britain during the Years 1810 and 1811*, 2 vols. (1815), II, 214.

220 John Barton, *Condition of the Labouring Classes* (1817), in Sotiroff (ed.), *Economic Writings*, 26; Barton, *Inquiry into the Depreciation of Agricultural Labour*, in *ibid.*, 111–12 and 125.

221 E.g. E. P. Thompson, *The Making of the English Working Class* (1963), 221; Rogers, *op. cit.*, 408; Hasbach, *op. cit.*, 185 and 190. J. Kuczynski, *Die Geschichte der Lage der Arbeiter unter dem Kapitalismus*, 40 vols. (1962–8), XXIII, 120.

222 E.g. J. L. Hammond and B. Hammond, *The Village Labourer, 1760/1832* (1912); G. E. Fussell and M. Compton, 'Agricultural Adjustment after the Napoleonic Wars', *Economic History*, IV (1939); E. J. Hobsbawm and George Rudé, *Captain Swing* (1969); A. J. Peacock, *Bread or Blood* (1965); L. P. Adams, *Agricultural Depression and Farm Relief in England, 1813–1852* (1932, repr. 1965).

223 E.g. see evidence to the Emigration Inquiry of 1826–7, quoted in Clapham, *Economic History*, vol. I, 64–5; and the evidence to the *S.C. on Agricultural Distress* (1836); *S.C. on Agriculture* (1833), Report, p. 9, and evidence, *passim*.

224 N. Gash, 'Rural Unemployment, 1815–1834', *Economic History Review*, VI (1935), 93. This figure was selective and should not be taken as representative, even of the worst-affected countries.

225 *S.C. on Agriculture* (1833), evidence, QQ. 187, 1107–9, 1116–25, 1130, 3851–2, 3863–9, 5240–2, 8517–22, 8561.

226 Poor Law Commissioners, *Eighth Annual Report* (PP 1842, XIX), 150–1 (by E. C. Tufnell); E. L. Jones, 'The Agricultural Labour Market in England', *Economic History Review*, 2nd ser., XVII (1964), 328; and p. 142 above; D. Brooke, 'Railway

Navvies on the Pennines, 1841–1871', *Journal of Transport History*, n.s., III (1975), 49; J. Burnett, *Useful Toil: Autobiographies of Working People from the 1820's to the 1920's* (1974), 55–64.

227 Perkin, *op. cit.*, 128; Steffen, *Studien*, III, 214–15; A. L. Bowley, 'The Statistics of Wages in the United Kingdom during the Last Hundred Years', *Journal of the Royal Statistical Society*, LXI (1898); Bowley, *Wages in the United Kingdom*; p. 103 above.

228 Caird, *English Agriculture in 1850–51*, 284, 289, and 512–16.

229 Hunt, 'Labour Productivity in English Agriculture'.

230 C. Edward Lester, *The Glory and Shame of England*, 2 vols. (1866), II, 313.

231 Steffen, *op. cit.*, vol. I, 50–1.

232 Deane and Cole, *op. cit.*, 6–9. Estimates of eighteenth-century populations vary, but within fairly narrow limits.

233 *Ibid.*, 143.

234 E.g. Colquhoun, *A Treatise on Indigence*, 165.

235 Quoted in *Fleet Papers*, III, 17 (29 April 1843), and III, 25 (24 June 1843).

236 E.g. Challinor and Ripley, *op. cit.*, 105–7.

237 *Cobbett's Twopenny Trash*, IV, 1 October 1830, p. 88.

238 PP 1830, X (590), pp. 226–33.

239 Reported anonymously (by William Taylor) in *Annual Review*, I (1802), 424.

240 Graham Wallas, *Francis Place, 1771–1854* (1908); W. E. S. Thomas, 'Francis Place and Working-Class History', *Historical Journal*, V (1962).

241 Webb and Webb, *History of Trade Unionism*, 125–6, footnote.

242 Wakefield, *England and America*, repr. in *Collected Works*, 518.

243 E.g. Cole and Filson, *British Working-Class Movements*, 20 and 109.

244 Webb and Webb, *op. cit.*, 38.

245 Matthews, *Economic Fluctuations*, p. 220.

246 Engels, *op. cit.*, 84; Marx, *Capital*, I, p. 696. Also Steffen, *op. cit.*, III, 243ff.

247 Cf. Sir George Head, *A Home Tour through the Manufacturing Districts of England in the Summer of 1835* (1968 edn), 82–3. Among the fastest workers in the Warrington pin factory, which had evidently done its best to make full use of the division of labour, the traveller noted particularly the 'small boys' and 'little girls'.

248 Bythell, *The Handloom Weavers*, 99, 105, and 122–8.

249 Smelser, *op. cit.*, 143.

250 Aikin, *op. cit.*, 565.

251 John Guest, *Compendious History of the Cotton Manufacture* (1823, repr. 1968), 35 and 340; Porter, *Progress of the Nation*, 183–4; Marx, *Capital*, vol. I, 444; F. Merttens, 'The Hours and Cost of Labour in the Cotton Industry at Home and Abroad', *Transactions of the Manchester Statistical Society*, 1893–4.

252 Wing, *op. cit.*, 402–4 and 424; J. T. Ward, *op. cit.*, 286.

253 Dodd, *op. cit.*, 123–4; *London Phalanx*, no. 55, 61 April 1842, p. 870.

254 H. C. Escher, in Henderson (ed.), *Industrial Britain*, 50.

255 James Ward, *op. cit.*, 169–72; Brassey, *Work and Wages*, 15 (quoting Factory Inspectors' Reports).

256 Quoted in John C. Cobden, *The White Slaves of England* (1853), 365. The reference is to the *Edinburgh Review*, but the original could not be found in what appears to be the article referred to in vol. 41, no. 82 (January 1825).

257 Joseph Devey, *The Life of Joseph Locke* (1962), 164–8; Brassey, *Work and Wages*, 11–13, 79–83, and 244–7.

258 J. G. Rule, 'Some Social Aspects', 75–81; R. W. Cooke-Taylor, *The Modern Factory System* (1841), 149; Burness, *op. cit.*, 64–5; Somerville, *op. cit.*, 114; *S.C. on*

Agriculture (1833), evidence of W. Woodward, Q. 1711. J. A. R. Pimlott, *The Englishman's Holiday: A Social History* (1947), 80–1.

259 *Poor Man's Guardian*, no. 143, 1 March 1834; Mayhew, *op. cit.*, II, 301, and III, 224–7.

260 McCulloch, *Descriptive and Statistical Account*, 649.

261 Wade, *History of the Middle and Working Classes*, 243.

262 See the example of the coal-miners, *Notes to the People*, I (1851; repr. 1967), 76.

263 Rogers, *Six Centuries of Work and Wages*, 494; Thompson, *Making of the Working Class*, 257.

264 *Life of Robert Owen, by Himself* (1920 edn), 321; Owen, *On the Employment of Children in Manufactories* (1818), repr. in *New View of Society*, ed. G. D. H. Cole (1927), 132; also *ibid.*, 158.

265 Habakkuk, *American and British Technology*, 186–7; Redford, *op. cit.*, 115–16; Hilton, *op. cit.*, 61–3; J. Parry Lewis, *op. cit.*, 76 and 81.

266 E.g. Somerville, *op. cit.*, 71.

267 J. R. T. Hughes, *Fluctuations in Trade, Industry and Finance* (1960), 188 and 197.

268 J. H. Treble, 'Irish Navvies in the North of England, 1830–1880', *Transport History*, VI (1973); Hunt, *Regional Wage Variations*, 295; C. Richardson, 'Irish Settlement in Mid-Nineteenth-Century Bradford', *Yorkshire Bulletin of Economic and Social Research*, XX (1968).

269 Faucher, *Manchester*, 29, footnote.

270 Perkin, *op. cit.*, 138–9. According to the same author, there was also a substantial shift towards the top end of incomes. In 1830, 15·7 per cent of national income went to the top 1·4 per cent of income-earners; in 1867, 16·2 per cent went to the top 0·07 per cent. Similarly, between these two years the share of the top 2 per cent of incomes rose from one-fifth of all national income to two-fifths. *Ibid.*, 418–19.

271 Statistics in B. R. Mitchell and Phyllis Deane, *Abstract of British Historical Statistics* (1962), and Susan Fairlie, 'The Corn Laws and British Wheat Production', 102.

272 For some statistics of real wages, see Kuczynski, *op. cit.*, XXIII, 115 and 169, and XXIV, 37; and Pollard and Crossley, *The Wealth of Britain*, 200ff.

273 W. H. Chaloner, *The Skilled Artisans during the Industrial Revolution, 1750–1850* (1969).

274 E. P. Thompson, 'Time, Work Discipline and Industrial Capitalism', *Past and Present*, no. 38 (1967).

275 Matthews, *op. cit.*, 223–4.

276 William Pulteney Alison, *Reply to Dr Chalmers' Objections* (1841), pp. v–vi; Wing, *op. cit.*, 446 and 453.

277 Richard A. Lewis, *Edwin Chadwick and the Public Health Movement, 1832–1854* (1952).

278 E.g. J. T. Ward, *The Factory Movement*, 204ff; also the same author's *The Factory System*, 2 vols. (1970).

279 Michael Vester, *Die Entstehung des Proletariats als Lernprozess* (1970).

280 W. H. Fraser, *Trade Unions and Society: The Struggle for Acceptance, 1850–1880* (1974).

281 Steffen, *op. cit.*, III, 81–9; Frederic Keeling, *Child Labour in the United Kingdom* (1914); p. xxv. Bienefeld, *Working Hours*, 82ff.

282 The significance of spending patterns is often underrated as against that of earnings. See Steffen, *op. cit.*, I, pp. 26ff, and II, p. 50; Thompson, *Making of the Working Class*, 316ff; Engels, *op. cit.*, 71ff.

283 Ludlow and Jones, *The Progress of the Working Class*, p. xi.

284 Perkin, *op. cit.*, 177; also 141.

285 In practice there will be further complications, in particular the tendency for labour to take its share partly in the form of shorter hours. Compare the following typical national averages, for cotton (F. Merttens, 'The Hours and Cost of Labour', 128):

	Operatives per thousand spindles	Product per year (lb)	Product per operative per hour (lb)	Hours per week	Average wage per week (s. d.)	Labour costs per lb (s. d.)
Spinning		per spindle				
1829–31	14·0	21·6	0·431	69	10/6	4/2
1859–61	8·16	30·0	1·176	60	12/6	2/1
Weaving		per loom				
1829–31	—	470	0·145	69	7/– to 9/6	9/0
1859–61	—	1627	1·027	60	11/10	2/9

286 C. H. Feinstein, 'Changes in the Distribution of the National Income in the United Kingdom since 1860', in Marchal and Ducros (eds.), *Distribution of the National Income*, Table 3, p. 120.

Numbers employed

	Wage-earners (million)	Salary-earners (million)	Ratio of wage-earners to salary-earners
1911	15·18	1·67	9·1
1924	13·01	2·85	4·6
1931	12·93	3·17	4·1
1938	15·04	3·84	3·9
1951	16·17	5·69	2·8
1961	16·27	6·93	2·3

287 A. L. Bowley, *Wages and Incomes since 1860* (1937); A. R. Prest, 'National Income of the United Kingdom, 1870–1946', *Economic Journal*, LVIII (1948). See also Deane and Cole, *op. cit.*, 241ff.

288 J. M. Keynes, 'Relative Movements of Real Wages and Output', *Economic Journal*, XLIX (1939), 48 and 49.

289 A. L. Bowley, *The Change in the Distribution of the National Income, 1880–1913* (1920), 27.

290 E.g. A. L. Bowley, *The Division of the Product of Industry* (1919), Table VI, pp. 44–6.

291 Brown and Hart do in fact explain the stability of the ratio by a series of compensatory movements, in particular the complementary movements of wages and profits in trade cycles such that in depressions wages-plus-profits fall as against more stable incomes, but wages rise at the expense of profits within the unstable sector, with the opposite movements in booms. *Op. cit.*, 265–6.

292 E.g. Brown and Hart, *op. cit.*, 256ff.

293 E. H. Phelps Brown and Margaret H. Browne, *A Century of Pay* (1968), Appendix 3, pp. 444–7.

294 *Ibid.*, 333–6.

295 P. J. Loftus, 'Labour's Share in Manufacturing', *Lloyd's Bank Review*, XCII (1969).

296 Hobsbawm, 'The Labour Aristocracy in Nineteenth-Century Britain', in *Labouring Men*.

297 Pollard and Crossley, *The Wealth of Britain*, 216 and 237–8; R. J. Harrison, *Before the Socialists* (1965), 30–1.

298 Charles Booth, *Life and Labour of the People in London*, 2 vols. (1889), and 17 vols. (1903); B. Seebohm Rowntree, *Poverty: a Study of Town Life* (1901); A. L. Bowley and A. R. Burnett-Hurst, *Livelihood and Poverty* (1915).

299 K. G. J. C. Knowles and D. J. Robertson, 'Differences between the Wages of Skilled and Unskilled Workers, 1880–1950', *Bulletin of the Oxford Institute of Statistics*, XIII (1951).

300 Guy Routh, *Occupation and Pay in Great Britain, 1906–1960* (1965), Table 46, p. 102. Unweighted averages are used.

301 *Ibid.*, 127 and 144.

302 *Ibid.*, pp. x, 101, 105, and 147.

303 Brian McCormick, 'Hours of Work in British Industry', *Industrial and Labour Relations Review*, XII (1959), 426.

304 B. McCormick and J. E. Williams, 'The Miners and the Eight-Hour Day, 1863–1910', *Economic History Review*, 2nd ser., XII (1959).

305 A. L. Bowley, *Wages and Incomes*, 25; Brown and Browne, *op. cit.*, 55–6, 103, 171–3, 184, 208–12, and 279–80; M. A. Bienefeld, *Working Hours*.

306 A. W. Phillips, 'The Relation between Unemployment and the Rate of Change of Money Wage Rates in the United Kingdom, 1861–1957', *Economica*, XXV, 100 (1958); R. G. Lipsey, 'The Relation between Unemployment and the Rate of Change of Money Wages in the United Kingdom, 1862–1957', *ibid.*, XXVII, 105 (1960); Bernard Corry and David Laidler, 'The Phillips Relation: A Theoretical Explanation', *ibid.*, XXXIV, 134 (1967); J. M. Holmes and D. J. Smyth, 'The Relation between Unemployment and Excess Demand for Labour: An Examination of the Theory of the Phillips Curve', *ibid.*, XXXVII, 148 (1970); J. Vanderkamp, 'The Phillips Relation: A Theoretical Explanation – A Comment', *ibid.*, XXXV, 138 (1968); J. F. Brothwell, 'The Theoretical Basis for the Phillips Curve', *Bulletin of Economic Research*, XXIV (1972).

307 Lipsey, *op. cit.*, 6.

308 *Ibid.*, 26. A recent study attempted to relate age changes to the dispersal of unemployment rates, i.e. the differences among different groups of workers: R. L. Thomas and P. M. Stoney, 'Unemployment Dispersion as a Determinant of Wage Inflation in the U.K., 1926–1966', *Manchester School*, XXYIX (1971).

309 Phillips, *op. cit.*, 291–2 and 298–9; Lipsey, *op. cit.*, 9.

310 Phillips, *op. cit.*, 1.

311 As is done by Brown and Browne, *op. cit.*, 73.

312 Hines, 'Trade Unions and Wage Inflation in the United Kingdom, 1893–1961', *Review of Economic Studies*, XXXI (1964); and Hines, 'Unemployment and the Rate of Change of Money Wage Rates in the United Kingdom 1862–1963: A Reappraisal', *Review of Economics and Statistics*, L, 1 (1968).

313 Hines, 'Trade Unions and Wage Inflation', 223.

314 *Ibid.*, 234.

315 In his second paper, Hines admitted some influence of unemployment on wage rates in the nineteenth century, but progressively less in the twentieth. 'Unemployment', 60 and 65.

316 S. Pollard, 'Trade Unions and the Labour Market, 1870–1914', *Yorkshire Bulletin of Economic and Social Research*, XVII (1965).

317 H. A. Clegg, Alan Fox, and A. F. Thompson, *A History of British Trade Unions since 1889*, vol. 1: *1889–1910* (1964), 482–3.

318 Claude Rondeau, reworking the Phillips and Hines data, inclined to the view that wages depended in the long term on the state of the labour market (unemployment), in the short term on institutional factors (management expectations and trade-union pushfulness). Rondeau, 'The Autonomous Influence of Institutional Determinants of the Movement of Money Wages in the United Kingdom, 1862–1938' (unpublished Ph.D. thesis, London, 1969), 104. Management expectations were linked with the profit rate. See N. Kaldor, 'Economic Growth and the Problem of Inflation, II', *Economica*, XXVI, 104 (1959); R. G. Lipsey and M. D. Stever, 'The Relations between Profits and Wage Rates', *ibid.*, XXVIII, 110 (1961).

319 Brown and Browne, *op. cit.*, 148–9. The classic study is Barbara Wootton, *The Social Foundations of Wage Policy*.

320 Routh, *op. cit.*, 152.

321 From some points of view, the transition period itself was lengthy and complex. Trade unions exercised only limited power before the 1890s, and it may not be without significance that cyclical movements of wage shares were still substantial up to that decade. Brown and Browne, *op. cit.*, 131.

CHAPTER IV

Industrial Entrepreneurship and Management in Great Britain

1 For reading and commenting on an earlier draft of this chapter, I am greatly indebted to Professor S. G. Checkland, Mr Anthony Slaven, and Professor Roy Church, and to my colleagues in the Economic History Department of the University of Aberdeen.

2 T. S. Ashton, *The Industrial Revolution* (Oxford, 1948), see particularly p. 161.

3 See, for example, A. O. Hirschman, *The Strategy of Economic Development* (New Haven, Conn., 1959), 1. It should be noted, however, that the importance given to the entrepreneur as a causal variable in the growth process is strongly conditioned by the particular scholar's major field of interest. See Peter Kilby's very useful essay 'Hunting the Heffalump', in Kilby (ed.), *Entrepreneurship and Economic Development* (New York, 1971), 1–40.

4 Hirschman, *Strategy of Economic Development*, 2. See also David C. McClelland, *The Achieving Society* (Princeton, 1961); E. E. Hagen, *On the Theory of Social Change* (London, 1964).

5 See Fritz Redlich's penetrating essay 'Economic Development, Entrepreneurship and Psychologism: A Social Scientist's Critique of McClelland's *Achieving Society*', *Explorations in Entrepreneurial History*, 2nd ser., I, 1 (Fall 1963), 10–35.

6 G. H. Evans jun., 'The Entrepreneur and Economic Theory: A Historical and Analytical Approach', *American Economic Review*, XXXIX, 3 (May 1949), 336–48.

7 E. Penrose, *The Theory of the Growth of the Firm* (Oxford, 1959), 30–1 n.

8 Charles Wilson, 'The Entrepreneur in the Industrial Revolution in Britain', *Explorations in Entrepreneurial History*, VII, 3 (February 1955), 132. The notion of the entrepreneur as typically the owner–manager – which historians have perhaps too readily taken over from the classical economists – is something of a simplification. Undoubtedly, many early entrepreneurs did conform to this 'ideal' and did perform

the entire range of roles suggested by Wilson, but probably more common were small – often family-linked – partnerships, reliant in varying degrees on capital provided by sleeping partners, while the active members concentrated on different entrepreneurial functions. Indeed, it would be surprising had this not been so, for there is some evidence that the successful performance of different entrepreneurial tasks calls for individuals with different personality structures. A general introduction to this complex question is suggested by John W. Atkinson and Bert F. Hoselitz, 'Entrepreneurship and Personality', *Explorations in Entrepreneurial History*, x, 3–4 (April 1958), 107–12.

9 Redlich, 'Economic Development, Entrepreneurship and Psychologism', 23.

10 H. G. J. Aitken, 'The Future of Entrepreneurial Research', *Explorations in Entrepreneurial History*, 2nd ser., I, 1 (Fall 1963), 5.

11 Penrose, *Theory of the Growth of the Firm*, 32n. The theoretical implications of this emphasis on the organizational structure of the firm have been examined by, for example, R. M. Cyert and J. G. March, *A Behavioural Theory of the Firm* (Englewood Cliffs, N.J., 1963).

12 Ashton, *Industrial Revolution*, 161.

13 Evans, 'The Entrepreneur and Economic Theory', 336.

14 M. Flinn, *Origins of the Industrial Revolution* (London, 1966), 81; cf. S. Pollard, *The Genesis of Modern Management* (London, 1965), 245: Pollard has argued that the level of total profits in this period was such as to indicate a monopolistic element in the provision of entrepreneurial services.

15 Ashton, *Industrial Revolution*, 16.

16 Recent notable studies include Hagen, *Theory of Social Change*, 294–309 (I am indebted to Professor Hagen for kindly sending me photocopies of the research notes on which his Appendix 'Characteristics of the Innovators', pp. 303–9, was based); S. D. Chapman, *The Early Factory Masters* (Newton Abbot, 1967) chaps. 5 and 6; M. M. Edwards, *The Growth of the British Cotton Trade, 1780–1815* (Manchester, 1967); Seymour Shapiro, *Capital and the Cotton Industry* (Ithaca, N.Y., 1967); Harold Perkin, *The Origins of Modern English Society, 1780–1880* (London, 1969), chap. 3; S. G. Checkland, *The Rise of Industrial Society in England, 1815–1885* (London, 1964), particularly chaps. 4 and 7, section 2; W. M. Mathew, 'The Origins and Occupations of Glasgow Students, 1740–1839', *Past and Present*, no. 33 (April 1966), 74–94.

17 Perkin, *op. cit.*, 82.

18 But see R. G. Wilson, *Gentlemen Merchants: The Merchant Community in Leeds, 1700–1830* (Manchester and New York, 1971), 2–4, 52–4, and 97–108.

19 If and when a systematic attempt is made to analyse more accurately than hitherto the geographical, social and occupational origins of the early entrepreneurs, the investigator would do well to consider the statistical requirements for such an exercise postulated by Ralph Andreano, 'A Note on the Horatio Alger Legend: Statistical Studies of the Nineteenth Century American Business Elite', in Louis P. Cain and Paul J. Uselding (eds.), *Business Enterprise and Economic Change* (Kent, Ohio, 1973), 227–46.

20 Flinn, *Origins of the Industrial Revolution*, 82, based on Hagen, *Theory of Social Change*, 305–8, and D. Bogue and J. Bennett, *History of Dissenters*, 4 vols. (London, 1808–12), III, 330.

21 See R. M. Hartwell, 'Business Management in England during the Period of Early Industrialization: Inducements and Obstacles', in R. M. Hartwell (ed.), *The Industrial Revolution* (Oxford, 1970), 34–5; Perkin, *Origins of Modern English Society*, 71–3. It should not be forgotten that there were elements of such dissenting doctrines that were inimical to capitalistic enterprise. S. G. Checkland has drawn attention to the fact that Thomas Gladstone, for example, experienced considerable difficulty over

this. His religion – he was a Calvinistic Evangelical – told him that too great a concern with business success would destroy him and his home. He therefore refused to go beyond the level of business activity that he had chosen. This balance is illustrated in his warnings to his son, John Gladstone, who was told to 'keep clear of Covetousness . . . a Vice which creeps into the Mind under the disguise of something else to reconcile us to the ugly form' (Checkland, *The Gladstones: A Family Biography, 1764–1851* (Cambridge, 1971), 3–9 and 407–9). See also the interesting observations by Barrie Trinder, *The Industrial Revolution in Shropshire* (London, 1973), 196–213.

22 N. Hans, *New Trends in Education in the Eighteenth Century* (London, 1951).

23 See McClelland, *The Achieving Society*, and Hagen, *Theory of Social Change*. These two studies have generated considerable debate. The best introduction is by M. W. Flinn, 'Social Theory and the Industrial Revolution', in Tom Burns and S. B. Saul (eds.), *Social Theory and Economic Change* (London, 1967). For highly critical views, see F. Redlich, 'Economic Development, Entrepreneurship and Psychologism'; M. Brewster Smith's review of McClelland in *History and Theory*, III (1964), 371–81; and A. Gershenkron's review of Hagen's study, *Economica*, n.s., XXXII (1965), 94. Perkin, *Origins of Modern English Society*, 71–3, has some interesting observations on this theme. See also note 35, below.

24 The idea of the potential influence of family position on career patterns was first suggested to the author by Mr J. P. Lees of the Department of Philosophy of the University of Nottingham. See, for example, J. P. Lees and A. H. Stewart, 'Family or Sibship Position and Scholastic Ability', *Sociological Review*, V, 1 (July 1957), and J. P. Lees, 'The Social Mobility of a Group of Eldest-Born and Intermediate Adult Males', *British Journal of Psychology*, General Section, XLIII, part 3 (1952), 210–21. See also Brian Sutton Smith and B. G. Rosenberg, *The Sibling* (New York, 1970), 67–79 and 152–4. McClelland, *The Achieving Society*, 373–6, touches on the subject of birth order but finds it 'one of those difficult variables which are difficult to generalise [upon] because family variations mean different things in different countries'. See also Havelock Ellis, *A Study of British Genius* (London, 1904), 115–20.

25 Perkin, *Origins of Modern English Society*, 83.

26 D. C. Coleman, 'Gentlemen and Players', *Economic History Review*, 2nd ser., XXVI (1973), 95ff. There are, of course, exceptions. For an interesting – if not necessarily typical – example, see W. E. Minchinton's study of the tinplate makers of West Wales, *The British Tinplate Industry: A History* (Oxford, 1957), 106–7.

27 H. J. Habakkuk, *American and British Technology in the Nineteenth Century* (Cambridge, 1962), 190–1.

28 R. E. Pumphrey, 'The Introduction of Industrialists into the British Peerage: A Study in Adaptation of a Social Institution', *American Historical Review*, LXV (1959), 10–11.

29 That considerable publicity was given to the value of 'Wills and Bequests' is indicated by W. D. Rubinstein in his 'British Millionaires, 1809–1949', *Bulletin of the Institute of Historical Research*, XLVIII (1974), 202–23. And see his 'Men of Property: Some Aspects of Occupation, Inheritance and Power among Top British Wealthholders', in Philip Stanworth and Anthony Giddens (eds.), *Elites and Power in British Society* (Cambridge, 1974), 144–69.

30 See particularly Joseph Schumpeter, *Capitalism, Socialism, and Democracy* (New York, 1950), 132.

31 Redlich, 'Economic Development, Entrepreneurship and Psychologism', 28, and Hagen, *Theory of Social Change*, 30ff. See also V. Ruttan, 'Usher and Schumpeter on Invention, Innovation and Technological Change', *Quarterly Journal of Economics*, LXXIII (November 1959), 596–606.

32 See Hartwell, 'Business Management in England', 32. Although the question

of risk has yet to be discussed, it might be mentioned at this stage that the demonstration that a particular line of activity or the pursuit of a certain policy could be profitable considerably reduced the subjective risk to potential imitators.

33 The last quality is that 'common characteristic' said by Charles Wilson to have been possessed by all the great entrepreneurs ('The Entrepreneur in the Industrial Revolution', 132). If these qualities of the pioneering businessman are emphasized here it is not that the author is unmindful of the very different picture painted by their contemporary and more recent detractors – 'in which initiative and enterprise were metamorphosed into greed and overreaching, personal driving force into lust for irresponsible power, abstinence and frugality became meanness, avarice, and a will to impose privation upon others, and self-control turned into a soulless lack of cultural values' (G. D. H. Cole, 'Self-Reliance and Social Legislation', *The Listener*, 20 May 1948) – but simply that these characteristics, so favourable to economic growth, are frequently deemed to have withered away by the closing decades of the century and so contributed to Britain's relative economic decline.

34 H. W. Richardson has recently issued a salutary warning against this technique. See his article 'Chemicals', in D. H. Aldcroft (ed.), *The Development of British Industry and Foreign Competition, 1875–1914* (London, 1968), 274–7.

35 Indeed, perhaps the overrepresentation of Nonconformists among the entrepreneurs that attained sufficient prominence to have been included in, for example, the Ashton/Hagen analysis is to be explained not in terms of their religious principles, their superior education, or their achievement norms, but because they belonged to extended kinship families that gave them access to credit which permitted their firms (and their records) to survive, while others, less well connected, went to the wall. It is not without significance that in his 'survey of 132 industrialists, selected for their *prominence* in manufacturing during the period 1750–1850' (emphasis added), Bendix found that about two-thirds came from families already established in business: Reinhard Bendix, *Work and Authority in Industry: Ideologies of Management in the Course of Industrialization* (New York, 1956), 24. Of the 132 families, twenty-one were taken from P. Mantoux, *The Industrial Revolution in the Eighteenth Century* (London, 1923); twenty-one from *Fortunes Made in Business*, 3 vols. (London, 1884–7), I and II; and the rest from the *Dictionary of National Biography*. See also R. G. Wilson, *Gentlemen Merchants*, 115.

36 The phrase is that of Mantoux (*op. cit.*, 386).

37 R. Owen, *The Life of Robert Owen, Written by Himself* (London, 1857), 31.

38 See R. G. Wilson, *Gentlemen Merchants*, 122, and S. D. Chapman, 'Enterprise and Innovation in the British Hosiery Industry, 1750–1850', *Textile History*, v (1974), 28–32.

39 Pollard, *The Genesis of Modern Management*.

40 E. J. Hobsbawm, *Industry and Empire* (Harmondsworth, 1969), 56; cf. J. A. Schumpeter, *Business Cycles*, 2 vols. (New York, 1939), I, pp. 270–1: 'English industrial history can, in the epoch under discussion [1787–1843], be resolved into the history of a single industry [cotton]'.

41 D. S. Landes, 'Technological Change and Development in Western Europe, 1750–1914', in *Cambridge Economic History*, VI, 285. See also D. E. C. Eversley, 'The Home Market and Economic Growth in England, 1750–1780', in E. L. Jones and G. Mingay (eds.), *Land, Labour and Population in the Industrial Revolution: Essays Presented to J. D. Chambers* (London, 1967); D. C. Coleman, *Courtaulds: An Economic and Social History*, 2 vols. (Oxford, 1969), I: *The Nineteenth Century, Silk and Crepe*, 23; and Neil McKendrick, 'Josiah Wedgwood and Cost Accounting in the Industrial Revolution', *Economic History Review*, 2nd ser., XXIII, 1 (April 1970), 54 and 63–4.

42 Eversley, 'The Home Market and Economic Growth', 234.

43 See Edwards, *Growth of the Cotton Trade*, 25–9.

44 This is clearly not so in the case of the woollen industry. See R. G. Wilson, *Gentlemen Merchants*, 42–4 and 116.

45 See Edwards, *Growth of the Cotton Trade*, 22–3; S. D. Chapman, *Early Factory Masters*, 213 and 240; C. H. Lee, *A Cotton Enterprise, 1795–1840: A History of M'Connel and Kennedy, Fine Cotton Spinners* (Manchester, 1972), 37–43; S. D. Chapman, 'James Longsdon (1745–1821), Farmer and Fustian Manufacturer: The Small Firm in the Early English Cotton Industry', *Textile History*, I, 3 (December 1970), 289–92; S. Shapiro, *Capital and the Cotton Industry*, 156; S. D. Chapman, 'Working Capital in the British Cotton Industry, 1770–1850', unpublished paper presented at Ealing Business History Conference, 1975 (I am grateful to Professor Chapman for permission to cite this paper).

46 It has been suggested elsewhere that it is not inconceivable that more representative were the Wilsons of Wilsontown Ironworks, the Needhams of Litton, the Austins of Wotton-under-Edge, William Lupton of Leeds, and John Cartwright of Retford; all of whose concerns suffered from serious entrepreneurial shortcomings coupled with gross mismanagement. P. L. Payne, *British Entrepreneurship in the Nineteenth Century* (London, 1974), 34.

47 See Pollard, *The Genesis of Modern Management*, 246; A. J. Robertson, 'Robert Owen, Cotton Spinner: New Lanark, 1800–1825', in S. Pollard and J. Salt (eds.), *Robert Owen, Prophet of the Poor* (London, 1971), 146–8; Eric Robinson, 'Eighteenth-Century Commerce and Fashion: Matthew Boulton's Marketing Techniques', *Economic History Review*, 2nd ser., XVI, 1 (August 1963), 39–60; Neil McKendrick, 'Josiah Wedgwood: An Eighteenth-Century Entrepreneur in Salesmanship and Marketing Techniques', *Economic History Review*, 2nd ser., XII, 3 (April 1960), 408–33; S. G. Checkland, *The Mines of Tharsis* (London, 1967), 89–91; R. G. Wilson, *Gentlemen Merchants*, 127.

48 There are many examples. For Newton, Chambers & Co. of the Thorncliffe Ironworks, see T. S. Ashton, *Iron and Steel in the Industrial Revolution*, 2nd edn (Manchester, 1951), 156–61; for the Pleasley Mill of Cowpe, Oldknow, Siddon & Co. (one of whose partners was Henry Hollins), see S. Pigott, *Hollins: A Study of Industry, 1784–1949* (Nottingham, 1949), 37–8, and F. A. Wells, *Hollins and Viyella: A Study in Business History* (Newton Abbot, 1968), 25–45; for J. C. Gotch, a Kettering footwear manufacturer, who was able to survive a very lean period following the Peace of Paris by virtue of high profits during the Napoleonic Wars, see R. A. Church, 'Messrs Gotch & Sons and the Rise of the Kettering Footwear Industry', *Business History*, VII, 2 (July 1966), 148. The firm of Stubs, Wood & Co., pin manufacturers, was able to keep going during the generally depressed years 1814–21 because of the profits earned during earlier decades by the parent firm, Peter Stubs & Co., filemakers: ' "I thank my stars that I had a father born before me or I am sure the pin concern would sink in its infancy", wrote William Stubs . . . in May 1815'. T. S. Ashton, 'The Records of a Pin Manufactory, 1814–21', *Economica*, V (1925), 291, and the same author's *An Eighteenth Century Industrialist* (Manchester, 1939); W. G. Rimmer, *Marshalls of Leeds, Flax Spinners, 1788–1886* (Cambridge, 1960), 69ff. See also S. D. Chapman, 'Working Capital', 18–19, for some figures of profitability in the cotton industry generally, *c.* 1780–1840. For the very high profits at the close of the Napoleonic Wars and the subsequent losses in the mid-1820s made by the Birleys' Charlton Mills, see Willard E. Stone, 'An Early English Cotton Mill Cost Accounting System: Charlton Mills, 1810–1889', *Accounting and Business Research*, no. 13 (Winter 1973), 71–2.

49 C. H. Lee, *A Cotton Enterprise*, 145. Cf. R. G. Wilson, *Gentlemen Merchants*, 93–7.

50 C. H. Lee, *op. cit.*, 42 and 149; and his 'M'Connel & Kennedy, Fine Cotton Spinners' (unpublished M.Litt. thesis, Cambridge, 1966), 186 and 191.

51 S. Pollard, 'Fixed Capital in the Industrial Revolution in Britain', *Journal of Economic History*, XXIV (1964); H. Heaton, 'Benjamin Gott and the Industrial Revolution in Yorkshire', *Economic History Review*, III, 1 (1931–2), 51–2; S. D. Chapman, 'Fixed Capital Formation in the British Cotton Industry, 1770–1815', *Economic History Review*, 2nd ser., XXIII, 2 (August 1970); M. M. Edwards, *Growth of the Cotton Trade*, chaps. 9 and 10; S. D. Chapman, 'James Longsdon', 281 and 285. Cf. R. G. Wilson, *Gentlemen Merchants*, 94 and 106–7. Is it possible that the low fixed/working capital ratios that apparently prevailed have been partly misinterpreted? It is generally assumed that the fixed capital requirements were modest, whereas it is conceivable that the relative significance attached to fixed capital by the early entrepreneurs was unduly modest, and that had they increased this component they would more rapidly have attained a greater efficiency. That is, despite the point made below, the early entrepreneurs' desire for high liquidity may exhibit a certain degree of economic irrationality. Or was it perhaps a manifestation of (as it is sometimes called in discussions of current African economic development) the 'trader's mentality', and as such rooted in the earlier mercantile activities of many of the early British industrialists?

52 The whole question of working capital in the British Cotton Industry at this time has been carefully investigated by S. D. Chapman, 'Working Capital', *passim*. Chapman concludes that 'financial anxieties were the most frequent and significant restraint on business leadership in the period' (p. 37).

53 John Longsdon to James Longsdon, 14 August 1809, quoted by S. D. Chapman, 'James Longsdon', 286–7. Cf. R. G. Wilson, *Gentlemen Merchants*, 126.

54 See, for example, C. H. Lee, *A Cotton Enterprise*, 28–37.

55 *Ibid.*, 42.

56 See S. Pollard, *The Genesis of Modern Management*, 160–208; the brilliant essay by E. P. Thompson, 'Time, Work-Discipline, and Industrial Capitalism', *Past and Present*, no. 38 (December 1967), and the same author's *The Making of the English Working Class* (London, 1963); Bendix, *Work and Authority in Industry*, especially 34–60; S. D. Chapman, *The Early Factory Masters*, 156–209.

57 C. H. Lee, *A Cotton Enterprise*, 114–15; Rimmer, *Marshalls of Leeds*, 34; R. A. Church, 'Labour Supply and Innovation, 1800–1860: The Boot and Shoe Industry', *Business History*, XII, 1 (January 1970), 28.

58 R. Bendix, 'A Study of Managerial Ideologies', *Economic Development and Cultural Change*, V, 2 (1957), 124, and his *Work and Authority in Industry*, 53–4 and 213. The subject is discussed cogently by Pollard, *The Genesis of Modern Management*, 38–47, where the treatment is supported by a wealth of sources concerning, *inter alia*, coal-mining, ironmaking and the metal trades, engineering, textiles (cotton, woollens, and lace), and pottery. For subcontracting in the match industry, printing, paper, and the boot and shoe industry, see David F. Schloss, *Methods of Industrial Remuneration* (London, 1898), 197–203. For the shoe industry, see Church, 'Messrs Gotch & Sons', 143–4.

59 Bendix, 'A Study of Managerial Ideologies', 124.

60 C. H. Lee, *A Cotton Enterprise*, 115ff; S. D. Chapman, 'James Longsdon', 285.

61 For Wedgwood, see Neil McKendrick, 'Josiah Wedgwood and Factory Discipline', *Historical Journal*, IV, 1 (1961), 30–55; for Boulton & Watt, see E. Roll, *An Early Experiment in Industrial Organisation, being a History of Boulton & Watt, 1775–1805* (London, 1930), especially 189–236.

62 C. H. Lee, *A Cotton Enterprise*, 7 and 149.

63 John Thomas, *The Rise of the Staffordshire Potteries* (Bath, 1971), 21.

64 E. J. Hobsbawm, *Industry and Empire*, 59–60.

65 Nathan Rosenberg, 'The Direction of Technological Change: Inducement Mechanisms and Focusing Devices', *Economic Development and Cultural Change*, XVIII, 1, part 1 (October 1969), 3.

66 *Ibid.*, 4.

67 See Mantoux, *Industrial Revolution*, 244–51.

68 See Richard L. Hills, *Power in the Industrial Revolution* (Manchester, 1970); and C. H. Lee, *A Cotton Enterprise*, 19–22.

69 See Rimmer, *Marshalls of Leeds*, 84; Klaus H. Wolff, 'Textile Bleaching and the Birth of the Chemical Industry', *Business History Review*, XLVIII (1974), 149–50.

70 See C. H. Lee, *A Cotton Enterprise*, 103–4. Cf. G. F. Rainnie (ed.), *The Woollen and Worsted Industry: An Economic Analysis* (Oxford, 1965), 52.

71 Robin Marris, *The Economic Theory of 'Managerial' Capitalism* (London, 1964), 3–4.

72 See Pollard, *The Genesis of Modern Management*, 150–1; S. D. Chapman, 'The Peels in the Early English Cotton Industry', *Business History*, XI, 2 (July 1969); John C. Logan, 'The Dumbarton Glass Works Company: A Study in Entrepreneurship', *Business History*, XIV, 1 (January 1972), 71–81.

73 Pollard, *The Genesis of Modern Management*, 251–2.

74 For example, a feature of the Scottish paper industry was the granting of partnership status, on a small scale, to the mill manager, who was primarily responsible for the technical aspects of the business. A. G. Thomson, *The Paper Industry in Scotland* (Edinburgh, 1974), 98.

75 For 'sleeping partners' in the cotton industry, see Edwards, *Growth of the Cotton Trade*, 194–8

76 See François Crouzet, 'Capital Formation in Great Britain during the Industrial Revolution', in F. Crouzet (ed.), *Capital Formation in the Industrial Revolution* (London, 1972), 198–203.

77 See Landes in *Cambridge Economic History*, VI, 304–5.

78 See Mantoux, *Industrial Revolution*, 232; R. S. Fitton and A. P. Wadsworth, *The Strutts and the Arkwrights, 1758–1830* (Manchester, 1958), 78. David Dale was himself involved in numerous partnerships. See Henry Hamilton, *An Economic History of Scotland in the Eighteenth Century* (Oxford, 1963), 171–2.

79 Anon., *James Finlay & Company Limited, Manufacturers and East India Merchants, 1750–1950* (Glasgow, 1951), pp. xvii, 4, 7, 10–12, 14–15, 22, and 30; S. D. Chapman, 'The Peels', especially 80–4.

80 See Landes in *Cambridge Economic History*, VI, 304, and R. H. Campbell, *Carron Company* (Edinburgh, 1961), 7–20, 115–16, and 144–8.

81 Aileen Smiles, *Samuel Smiles and his Surroundings* (London, 1956), 107.

82 Alfred Marshall, *Industry and Trade* (London, 1920), 91–2. Cf. Sydney J. Chapman, *The Lancashire Cotton Industry: A Study in Economic Development* (Manchester, 1904), 216–17.

83 This question has been raised by, for example, Eric M. Sigsworth, 'Some Problems in Business History, 1870–1914', in Charles J. Kennedy (ed.), *Papers of the Sixteenth Business History Conference* (Lincoln, Nebraska, 1969), 32–3; and S. B. Saul, 'The Market and Development of the Mechanical Engineering Industries in Britain, 1860–1914', *Economic History Review*, 2nd ser., XX, 1 (April 1967), 111.

84 In Oldham, for example, it was said that of 138 concerns in existence in the town in 1846, only four had been in the possession of the same firm or family before 1800. S. D. Chapman, 'Working Capital', 23. For examples from an earlier period, *c.* 1780–1840, see *ibid.*, 9; R. G. Wilson, *Gentlemen Merchants*, 115 and 131; J. de L. Mann, *The Cloth Industry in the West of England from 1640 to 1880* (Oxford, 1971), 194–5.

85 J. B. Jefferys, 'Trends in Business Organisation in Great Britain since 1856' (unpublished Ph.D. thesis, University of London, 1938), 8–9. See also D. S. Landes, 'The Structure of Enterprise in the Nineteenth Century', in Comité International des Sciences Historiques, XLe Congrès International des Sciences Historiques (Stockholm, 21–8 August, 1960), Rapports, v: Histoire contemporaine (Uppsala, 1960), 109ff.

86 H. A. Shannon, 'The Coming of General Limited Liability', Economic History, II (1931), 271.

87 Landes, 'The Structure of Enterprise', 110. See also Leone Levi, 'On Joint Stock Companies', Journal of the [Royal] Statistical Society, XXXIII, 1 (March 1870), 12–14 and 24–5.

88 J. H. Clapham, An Economic History of Modern Britain, 3 vols., 1: The Early Railway Age, 1820–1850 (Cambridge, 1939), 194–6.

89 J. Saville, 'Sleeping Partnerships and Limited Liability, 1850–1856', Economic History Review, 2nd ser., VIII, 3 (April 1956), 419.

90 The words are those of Robert Slaney in moving for a Select Committee on the subject, 6 April 1850. Hansard, cx, 422–6, quoted by Saville, 'Sleeping Partnerships', 420.

91 Jefferys, 'Trends in Business Organisation', 10.

92 Saville, 'Sleeping Partnerships', 432.

93 Jefferys, op. cit., 105.

94 J. H. Clapham, An Economic History of Modern Britain, 3 vols., III: Machines and National Rivalries (Cambridge, 1938), 203.

95 P. L. Payne, 'The Emergence of the Large-Scale Company in Great Britain, 1870–1914', Economic History Review, 2nd ser., xx, 3 (December 1967), 520; H. A. Shannon, 'The First Five Thousand Limited Companies and Their Duration', Economic History, II (1932), 408, n. 2.

96 John Child, British Management Thought (London, 1969), 14.

97 Pollard, The Genesis of Modern Management, 250; a recent case study is Baron F. Duckham, History of the Scottish Coal Industry, 1: 1700–1815 (Newton Abbot, 1970), 113–40.

98 Dennis Chapman, 'William Brown of Dundee, 1791–1864: Management in a Scottish Flax Mill', Explorations in Entrepreneurial History, IV, 3 (1952); L. J. Hume, 'Jeremy Bentham on Industrial Management', Yorkshire Bulletin of Economic and Social Research, XXII, 1 (May 1970).

99 Pollard, The Genesis of Modern Management, 254.

100 On the increase in scale – the measurement of which before the eighties is exceedingly difficult – see J. H. Clapham, Economic History, II, 114–22 and 138–9.

101 L. Urwick and E. F. L. Brech, The Making of Scientific Management, 2 vols., II: Management in British Industry (London, 1949), p. 13. And see Neil McKendrick, 'Josiah Wedgwood and Cost Accounting', 46; and Anthony Tillett, 'Industry and Management', in A. Tillett, T. Kempner, and Gordon Wills (eds.), Management Thinkers (London, 1970), 33–4.

102 Clapham, Economic History, II, 138–9.

103 Where Victorian business leaders adopted the joint-stock form to permit the family firm to 'go on for ever', while freeing their sons from attendance at the mill, the superintendence of the factory must sometimes have devolved upon the professional works manager, though well-authenticated examples are difficult to find. Only where entirely new businesses were created as companies – and initially they too were rare, save among the 'Oldham Limiteds' – was there much divorce of ownership from control and management. Tyson's study of the Sun Mill reveals the ruthlessness with which managers were sacked by shareholders when unsatisfactory results were achieved. Between 1858 and 1862, there were no fewer than five managers; between

1862 and 1899, eleven. R. E. Tyson, 'The Sun Mill Company Limited: A Study in Democratic Investment, 1858–1959' (unpublished M.A. thesis, University of Manchester, 1962).

104 Rimmer, *Marshalls of Leeds*, 199 and 229.

105 Rhodes Boyson, *The Ashworth Cotton Enterprise: The Rise and Fall of a Family Firm, 1818–1880* (Oxford, 1970), 14, quoting Godfrey W. Armitage, 'The Lancashire Cotton Trade from the Great Inventors to the Great Disasters' (paper read to the Manchester Literary and Philosophical Society, 21 February 1951), 6.

106 Boyson, *op. cit.*, 42.

107 For the subsequent history of this firm, divided into two separate enterprises after 1854, see *ibid.*, 64ff.

108 *Ibid.*, 31.

109 Sir Wemyss Reid, *Memoirs and Correspondence of Lyon Playfair* (London, 1900), 43–4 and 52–6; G. Turnbull, *A History of the Calico Printing Industry of Great Britain* (Altrincham, 1951), 78–81.

110 Quoted Turnbull, *op. cit.*, 73.

111 Coleman, *Courtaulds*, I, pp. 174–7 and 213.

112 A. H. John (ed.), *The Walker Family. Ironfounders and Lead Manufacturers, 1741–1893* (London, 1951), 29–31.

113 Ashton, *An Eighteenth Century Industrialist*, 41–2; Alan Birch, *The Economic History of the British Iron and Steel Industry, 1784–1879* (London, 1967), 161–2.

114 Birch, *op. cit.*, 156.

115 A. Raistrick, *Dynasty of Iron Founders* (Newton Abbot, 1970), 270.

116 J. P. Addis, *The Crawshay Dynasty: A Study in Industrial Organisation and Development, 1756–1867* (Cardiff, 1957), 120–6.

117 S. B. Saul has argued persuasively that even the implicit assumption that Britain lagged badly behind the Americans in the development of techniques of standardization and interchangeable parts is 'seriously misleading' (Saul, 'Mechanical Engineering Industries', 111). This erroneous assumption is presumably based on, for example, D. L. Burn, 'The Genesis of American Engineering Competition', *Economic History*, II (1931), 292–311, and J. E. Sawyer, 'The Social Basis of the American System of Manufacturing', *Journal of Economic History*, XIV, 4 (Fall 1954), 361–79.

118 The phrase is that of the biographer of John Brown of Sheffield, in *Fortunes Made in Business*, I, pp. 265ff. Sixty years later W. R. Morris had a vision of the mass market for cars: W. R. Morris (Lord Nuffield), 'Policies that Have Built the Morris Business', *Journal of Industrial Economics*, II, 3 (August 1954), 194–5.

119 Some of the more prominent inventions may best be understood by visiting the Science Museum in London and by consulting E. A. Forward, *Handbook of the Collections Illustrating Land Transport*, III: *Railway Locomotives and Rolling Stock*, part 2: *Descriptive Catalogue* (London, 1948).

120 P. L. Payne, *Rubber and Railways in the Nineteenth Century* (Liverpool, 1961), 2–3 and 73–4; *Fortunes Made in Business*, I, p. 255.

121 Payne, *Rubber and Railways*, 138–41.

122 G. C. Allen, *The Industrial Development of Birmingham and the Black Country* (London, 1929), 73–4 and 93; S. Timmins (ed.), *The Resources, Products and Industrial History of Birmingham and the Midland Hardware District* (London, 1866), 669–70; D. Bremner, *The Industries of Scotland: Their Rise, Progress and Present Condition* (London, 1869), 98–102; H. Hamilton Ellis, *Nineteenth Century Railway Carriages* (London, 1949); Saul, 'Mechanical Engineering Industries', 114–17.

123 On the speed with which some of the Sheffield firms (John Brown, Charles Cammells, Brown, Bayley and Dixon, Thomas Turton, Craven's Railway Wagon

Works – all heavily engaged in railway work) expanded between the 1840s and 1870s, see S. Pollard, *History of Labour in Sheffield* (Liverpool, 1959), 159–64. For Kitson's, see *Fortunes Made in Business*, III, 313–73. For the rapid conversion of the Kidderminster carpet industry to power-loom weaving, following the perfection of a power loom capable of weaving traditional and Tapestry Brussels carpets, see J. N. Bartlett, 'The Mechanisation of the Kidderminster Carpet Industry', *Business History*, IX, 1 (January 1967), 49–67.

124 S. B. Saul, 'Some Thoughts on the Papers and Discussions on the Performance of the Late Victorian Economy', in Donald M. McCloskey (ed.), *Essays on a Mature Economy: Britain after 1840*, Papers and Proceedings of the MSSB Conference on the New Economic History of Britain, 1840–1930 (London, 1971), 394.

125 *Fortunes Made in Business*, I, p. 151.

126 An alternative interpretation of the significance of taking up patents (as an illustration of the adoption of tactics designed to permit survival rather than innovation and growth) has been developed elsewhere: Payne, *British Entrepreneurship*, 41–5.

127 The words are those used by Orsagh of the British iron and steel industry, but they summarize the more general case. T. G. Orsagh, 'Progress in Iron and Steel: 1870–1913', *Comparative Studies in Society and History*, III (1960–1), 230.

128 Landes, in *Cambridge Economic History*, VI, 563–4.

129 *Ibid.* Cf. Sydney J. Chapman, *The Lancashire Cotton Industry*, 170–1, and Clifford Gulvin, who quotes a Hawick minister castigating the local tweed-makers in 1909:

> We [have] had many men chiefly in the founders of our businesses – men not afraid of very hard work, keeping pleasure in its place, sticking fast to their posts. In the second generation, however, we have often seen a different spirit; sometimes contempt for trades, an aping of the fine gentleman, an aspiring to be what they were not . . . love of ease, self-indulgence and lack of grit and backbone. They must work in the spirit of their fathers . . . study the technique of their business, bend their energies and talents in one direction.

(Gulvin, *The Tweedmakers: A History of the Scottish Fancy Woollen Industry, 1600–1914* (Newton Abbot, 1973), 150).

130 Gott's sons were responsible for some improvements to the equipment of Bean Ing and Armley, despite a growing devotion to the arts; their own children were interested in other matters. 'Thus the third generation ended what the first had begun . . .' (Heaton, 'Benjamin Gott', 65–6).

131 T. J. Byres, 'The Scottish Economy during the Great Depression, 1873–96', 2 vols. (unpublished B.Litt. thesis, University of Glasgow, 1962), II, 789–893, and 904–10, and his article 'Entrepreneurship in the Scottish Heavy Industries, 1870–1900' in P. L. Payne (ed.), *Studies in Scottish Business History* (London, 1969), 250–96; R. A. Church, *Kenricks in Hardware: A Family Business, 1791–1966* (Newton Abbot, 1969), and an earlier example, Gotch & Sons, the footwear manufacturers and country bankers, who perished in the hands of the third generation in 1857: R. A. Church, 'An Aspect of Family Enterprise in the Industrial Revolution', *Business History*, IV, 2 (June 1962), 120–5; Coleman, *Courtaulds*, I, pp. 270–1. A. J. Robertson cites the case of about a dozen cotton mills destroyed by fire in the early 1890s which were not rebuilt because 'the owners . . . had made large fortunes and the next generation were lacking both in commercial enterprise and the stimulus of need to rebuild them' ('The Decline of the Scottish Cotton Industry, 1860–1914', *Business History*, XII, 2 (July 1970), 125); and A. E. Musson has shown that the second and third generations of Peels, proprietors of the Soho Foundry, Ancoats, 'seem to have lived like gentlemen upon the fruits of the capital and industry of the first George Peel . . . [and to have]

devoted an excessive amount of their time to public and social activities, neglecting their business', which closed down *c.* 1887 ('An Early Engineering Firm: Peel, Williams and Co. of Manchester', *Business History*, III, 1 (December 1960), 18). Professor Checkland has suggested to me that there were doubtless, in addition, a number of provincial businessmen who owed their positions and wealth to firms established by their forebears who went on to 'greater things' in the metropolis and in international big business. This widening of horizons may have been detrimental to their family firms and may have involved the 'creaming' of the provinces. The career of Sir Charles Tennant exemplifies this point. He became increasingly detached from his inherited interest, St Rollox, to become a cosmopolitan and international businessman. See Checkland, *Mines of Tharsis*, 97–103 and 263–9.

132 As has Saul, 'Mechanical Engineering Industries', 111.

133 Coleman, *Courtaulds*, vol. I, p. 271. See also Perkin, *Origins of Modern English Society*, 83–9.

134 Quoted Anon., *James Finlay & Company Limited*, 127. On the houses built for nineteenth-century entrepreneurs, see the fascinating study by Mark Girouard, *The Victorian Country House* (Oxford, 1971).

135 Byres, 'Entrepreneurship in the Scottish Heavy Industries', provides numerous examples.

136 S. D. Chapman, *Early Factory Masters*, 62–72; A. E. Musson, *Enterprise in Soap and Chemicals: Joseph Crosfield and Sons Ltd, 1815–1965* (Manchester, 1965), 48.

137 Saul, 'Mechanical Engineering Industries', 111.

138 Sigsworth, 'Some Problems in Business History', 33. A similar situation existed in silk-spinning: see Sir Frank Warner, *The Silk Industry of the United Kingdom: Its Origin and Development* (London, 1921), 424.

139 E. M. Sigsworth and J. Blackman, 'The Woollen and Worsted Industries', in Aldcroft (ed.), *British Industry and Foreign Competition*, 130; E. M. Sigsworth, 'Some Problems in Business History', 32–3. The full-scale histories to which Sigsworth refers are his own *Black Dyke Mills* (Liverpool, 1958), and F. J. Glover, 'History of Messrs Wormalds and Walker Ltd, Dewsbury' (unpublished Ph.D. thesis, University of Leeds, 1959); see his article 'The Rise of the Heavy Woollen Trade of the West Riding of Yorkshire in the Nineteenth Century', *Business History*, IV, 1 (December 1961), 1–21.

140 The company promoter Chadwick argued before the Select Committee on the Company Acts of 1862 and 1867 that 'the nearer you can approach the management of a private concern the better . . .' (Q. 2007). cf. Adam Smith, *Wealth of Nations*, book V, part III, art. 1; B. C. Hunt, *The Development of the Business Corporation in Britain, 1800–1867* (Cambridge, Mass., 1936), 132; T. B. Napier, 'The History of Joint Stock and Limited Liability Companies', in *A Century of Law Reform* (London, 1901), 400. Joyce M. Bellamy has given details of two disastrous joint-stock ventures whose object was to develop Hull as a cotton town; both failed because of their 'inability to accumulate reserves with which to modernise their machinery and withstand periods of severe trade depression; a situation which arose principally from inefficient management, due mainly to the inexperience of almost all the directors and shareholders, who thus became dependent upon single individuals for managing the mills' (Bellamy, 'Cotton Manufacture in Kingston Upon Hull', *Business History*, IV, 2 (June 1962), 105).

141 Clapham, *Economic History*, III, 204–5; *Report of the Company Law Amendment Committee*, 1906 (Cd 3052), pp. 17–19; Payne, 'The Large-Scale Company', 526; on 'dummy shareholders', see *Report of the Departmental Committee appointed by the Board of Trade . . . under the Companies Acts, 1862 to 1890*, 1895 (C. 7779), pp. vii, viii, and xix; Statement I, p. 63.

142 Jefferys, 'Trends in Business Organisation', 403, quoting Q. 3440. The general advantages of incorporation as a private limited liability company are set out by D. A. Farnie, 'The English Cotton Industry, 1850–1896' (unpublished M.A. thesis, University of Manchester, 1953), 333.

143 Jefferys, *op. cit.*, 116.

144 *Ibid.*, 116 and 118; Roland Smith, 'The Lancashire Cotton Industry and the Great Depression, 1873–1896' (unpublished Ph.D. thesis, University of Birmingham, 1954), 133, for the case of Joshua Hoyle & Son. The case of Rylands & Sons Ltd – whose commercial operations were thought to be paralleled only by the most flourishing days of the East India Company – is discussed by Farnie, *op. cit.*, 200–5, and in his more detailed article 'John Rylands of Manchester', *Bulletin of the John Rylands University Library of Manchester*, LVI, 1 (Autumn 1973), 93–129. Although Rylands was incorporated in 1873, this remarkable firm retained the character of a private firm until 1920. The shares of Horrockses, Crewdson & Co. were also very tightly held. The tactics of Jesse Boot – who maintained autocratic control of his group of companies despite a growing number of shareholders – are carefully examined by S. D. Chapman, *Jesse Boot of Boots the Chemists* (London, 1974), 120–34.

145 Clapham, *Economic History*, III, 203; and the same author's *Woollen and Worsted Industries* (London, 1907), 152–3. See also D. C. Coleman, *The British Paper Industry, 1495–1860* (Oxford, 1958), 245–6; Bruce Lenman and Kathleen Donaldson, 'Partners' Incomes, Investment and Diversification in the Scottish Linen Area, 1850–1921', *Business History*, XIII, 1 (January 1971), 4 and 9. On the Oldham Limiteds see Roland Smith, 'The Lancashire Cotton Industry', 133ff, and his article 'An Oldham Limited Liability Company, 1875–1896', *Business History*, IV, 1 (December 1961), 34–53; Tyson, 'The Sun Mill Company'; G. W. Daniels, 'The Balance Sheets of Three Limited Companies in the Cotton Industry', *Manchester School*, III, 2 (1932); W. A. Thomas, *The Provincial Stock Exchange* (London, 1973), 145–68.

146 Jefferys, 'Trends in Business Organisation', 397.

147 Evidence of John Morris, Q. 975, quoted *ibid.*, 397.

148 *Ibid.*, 381.

149 Payne, 'The Large-Scale Company', 530. See also S. D. Chapman, *Jesse Boot*, 125 and 132–3.

150 Payne, *op. cit.*, 523. It was, indeed, not unknown for large multiple *directors* to forget their own companies. The case of Sir James Anderson – 'a director of no fewer than three companies of whose existence he had forgotten' – was given some prominence in the *Economist*, vol. XLII, 10 May 1884, p. 570.

151 Payne, *op. cit.*, 536; H. W. Macrosty, 'Business Aspects of British Trusts', *Economic Journal*, XII (1902), 354; Jefferys, 'Trends in Business Organisation', 451.

152 Their power was often enhanced by their own possession of founders' shares and the issue to the public of pre-ordinary voteless stock.

153 Jefferys, *op. cit.*, 439, quoting from the *Journal of the Institute of Bankers*, VII (1886), 511: 'So long as a business is conducted by those who own all the capital, it will only be extended as the prospect of greater profit offers an inducement to do so. But if the capital is supplied by the many and the management confined to a few, it may become in the interest of the few to carry it on although the many derive little or no profit from its operations.'

154 The respective numbers are as follows:

	Private	Public
1909	24,207	25,930
1911	33,455	21,104
1913	48,492	14,270

Committee on Industry and Trade (Balfour Committee), *Factors in Industrial and Commercial Efficiency* (London, 1927). Jefferys, *op. cit.*, 153–4, summarizes the major developments in the company system.

155 Payne, 'The Large-Scale Company', 538, quoting from C. P. Kindleberger, *Economic Growth in France and Britain, 1851–1950* (Cambridge, Mass., 1964), 124.

156 But, here again, more information is required, of the type provided by Charlotte Erickson, *British Industrialists: Steel and Hosiery, 1850–1950* (Cambridge, 1959).

157 For the merger movement at this time, see Payne, 'The Large-Scale Company' *passim.*; M. A. Utton, 'Some Features of the Early Merger Movements in British Manufacturing Industry', *Business History*, XIV, 1 (January 1972), 51–60; Leslie Hannah, 'Mergers in British Manufacturing Industry, 1880–1918', *Oxford Economic Papers*, n.s., XXVI (1974), 1–20. The classic study is that by H. W. Macrosty, *The Trust Movement in British Industry* (London, 1907).

158 That is, companies whose sales lay predominantly within a single product area.

159 Peter Mathias, 'Conflicts of Function in the Rise of Big Business: The British Experience', in Harold F. Williamson (ed.), *Evolution of International Management Structures* (Newark, N.J., 1975), 42.

160 Landes, in *Cambridge Economic History*, VI, 564.

161 See David S. Landes, *The Unbound Prometheus: Technological Change and Industrial Development in Western Europe from 1750 to the Present* (Cambridge, 1969), p. vii. To be sure, A. L. Levine in 1967 gave considerable weight to entrepreneurial failings: Levine, *Industrial Retardation in Britain, 1880–1914* (London, 1967).

162 Habakkuk, *American and British Technology*, 212–14.

163 C. Wilson, 'Economy and Society in Late Victoiran Britain', *Economic History Review*, 2nd ser., XVIII, 1 (August 1965), 194–5. And see W. Ashworth, *An Economic History of England, 1870–1939* (London, 1960), 78 and 241.

164 D. H. Aldcroft, 'The Entrepreneur and the British Economy, 1870–1914', *Economic History Review*, 2nd ser., XVII, 1 (August 1964), 113–34; and see his 'Technical Progress and British Enterprise, 1875–1914', *Business History*, VIII, 2 (July 1966), 122–39.

165 Aldcroft (ed.), *British Industry and Foreign Competitition.*

166 R. A. Church, 'The Effect of the American Export Invasion on the British Boot and Shoe Industry, 1885–1914', *Journal of Economic History*, XXVIII (1968), 223–54, and the same author's 'The British Leather Industry and Foreign Competition, 1870–1914', *Economic History Review*, 2nd ser., XXIV, 4 (November 1971), 543–70; A. E. Harrison, 'The Competitiveness of the British Cycle Industry, 1890–1914', *Economic History Review*, 2nd ser., XXII, 2 (August 1969), 287–303; Saul, 'Mechanical Engineering Industries', 111–30, and the same author's 'The Machine Tool Industry in Britain to 1914', *Business History*, X, 1 (January 1968), 22–41.

167 See Landes, in *Cambridge Economic History*, VI, 565, and S. B. Saul, 'The American Impact on British Industry, 1895–1914', *Business History*, III, 1 (January 1960), 28.

168 R. E. Tyson, 'The Cotton Industry', in Aldcroft (ed.), *British Industry and Foreign Competition*, 124–6.

169 Lars G. Sandberg, 'American Rings and English Mules: The Role of Economic Rationality', *Quarterly Journal of Economics*, LXXXIII, 1 (February 1969), 26.

170 *Ibid.*, 26. This is also Tyson's conclusion, though it is not argued as rigorously as Sandberg. See Tyson, *op. cit.*, p. 122. Sandberg's overall verdict is that 'By any reasonable standard, the years leading up to World War I [1870–1913] witnessed at least a creditable performance by the British cotton textile industry': *Lancashire in Decline* (Columbus, Ohio, 1974), 131.

171 D. M. McCloskey, 'Economic Maturity and Entrepreneurial Decline: British Iron and Steel; 1870–1913' (unpublished Ph.D. thesis, University of Chicago, 1970; later published under the same title, Cambridge, Mass., 1973). I am greatly indebted to Professor McCloskey for permitting me to read this thesis before its publication.

172 McCloskey, in a summary of his thesis, p. 1. In the thesis, p. 2 (cf. the published version, p. 3), McCloskey notes that 'An index of the dominance of the steel industry in the evidence for general entrepreneurial failure, perhaps, is that in an earlier statement of the hypothesis by Landes *a third of the footnotes* deal with the industry' (emphasis added). McCloskey is referring to chap. 3 of Landes's 'Entrepreneurship in Advanced Industrial Countries: The Anglo-German Rivalry', in *Entrepreneurship and Economic Growth*, papers presented at a Conference sponsored jointly by the Committee on Economic Growth of the Social Science Research Foundation and the Harvard University Research Center in Entrepreneurial History, Cambridge, Mass., 12–13 November 1954 (mimeographed).

173 McCloskey, 'Economic Maturity and Entrepreneurial Decline' (thesis), p. 142 (cf. published version, p. 127), For an illuminating case study of successful performance, see H. W. Richardson and J. M. Bass, 'The Profitability of Consett Iron Company before 1914', *Business History*, VII, 2 (July 1965), 71–93.

174 D. M. McCloskey, 'Industrial Differences in Productivity? Coal and Steel in America and Britain before World War I', in McCloskey (ed.), *Essays on a Mature Economy: Britain after 1840* (London, 1971), 295; see the discussion of this paper, *ibid.*, 303–9. Cf. A. J. Taylor, 'The Coal Industry', in Aldcroft (ed.), *British Industry and Foreign Competition*, 69. Some support for McCloskey's view is contained in A. Slaven, 'Earnings and Productivity in the Scottish Coal-Mining Industry during the Nineteenth Century: The Dixon Enterprises', in Payne (ed.), *Studies in Scottish Business History*, 217–49.

175 P. H. Lindert and K. Trace, 'Yardsticks for Victorian Entrepreneurs', in McCloskey (ed.), *Essays on a Mature Economy*, 239–74, and discussion, 275–83. See also Checkland, *Mines of Tharsis*, 143–50. The overthrow of the Leblanc process, from the early seventies onward, and the general development of the alkali industry thereafter, form a great part of the theme of the first volume of W. J. Reader's *Imperial Chemical Industries: A History*, I: *The Forerunners, 1870–1926* (Oxford, 1970).

176 S. B. Saul, 'Some Thoughts on the Papers and Discussions on the Performance of the Late Victorian Economy', in McCloskey (ed.), *Essays on a Mature Economy*, 393, though few would as yet go as far as McCloskey's verdict in his paper 'Did Victorian Britain Fail?', *Economic History Review*, 2nd ser., XXIII, 3 (December 1970), 459: 'There is, indeed, little left of the dismal picture of British failure painted by historians. The alternative is a picture of an economy not stagnating but growing as rapidly as permitted by the growth of its resources and the effective exploitation of the alternative technology.' Essentially, this argument is restated by McCloskey and Lars G. Sandberg in their article 'From Damnation to Redemption: Judgments on the Late Victorian Entrepreneur', *Explorations in Economic History*, IX, 1 (Fall 1971), 89–108. A new dimension has been added by C. K. Harley, 'Skilled Labour and the Choice of Technique in Edwardian Industry', *Explorations in Economic History*, XI (1974), 391–414.

177 The whole subject of Victorian advertising deserves more study. See Leonard de Vries, *Victorian Advertisements* (London, 1969); E. S. Turner, *The Shocking History of Advertising* (London, 1952).

178 Much use is made of this source by Ross Hoffman, *Great Britain and the German Trade Rivalry, 1875–1914* (Philadelphia, 1933).

179 It is to be regretted that in his contribution to *Cambridge Economic History*, VI, Landes departed from his earlier assessment of the consular reports:

> The consuls reporting were less interested in the aggregate of British exports, or even the total of exports to their own areas, than in the fortunes of specific commodities, the outcome of given contract negotiations, the success of a particular business man or syndicate. Their accounts tended to emphasise the unfavourable news, to become in the course of these decades a compendium of derogatory information on British trade.

D. S. Landes, 'Entrepreneurship in Advanced Industrial Countries', chap. 2, p. 26.

180 Duncan Burn's comment is interesting: 'It is highly probable that though German selling was more actively persistent than the British it was less tactful' (*The Economic History of Steelmaking, 1867–1939* (Cambridge, 1940), 295 n.).

181 See P. L. Payne, 'Iron and Steel Manufacturers', in Aldcroft (ed.), *British Industry and Foreign Competition*, 80–1; Ingvar Svennilson, *Growth and Stagnation in the European Economy* (Geneva, 1954), 125.

182 The Great Western Railway undertook to build its own locomotives after the failure of outside builders to meet the 'impossible specifications' laid down by the chief engineer. C. P. Kindleberger, 'Obsolescence and Technical Change', *Bulletin of the Oxford Institute of Statistics*, XXIII, 3 (December 1961), 290. See also Wray Vamplew, 'Scottish Railways and the Development of Scottish Locomotive Building in the Nineteenth Century', *Business History Review*, XLVI (1972), 336–8. During the period 1856–1900, Greenwood & Batley made 793 differently named machine tools, of which 457 were ordered only once during the period. R. Floud, 'Changes in the Productivity of Labour in the British Machine Tool Industry, 1856–1900', in McCloskey (ed.), *Essays on a Mature Economy*, 321.

183 As early as 1843, Hagues and Cook were producing no less than 172 different priced blankets, the bulk of which were designed for sale in the United States (Glover, 'The Heavy Woollen Trade', 7–8). Between 1841 and 1861, the number of different types of cloth made by John Foster & Son Ltd, increased from fourteen to seventy (E. M. Sigsworth, 'The West Riding Wool Textile Industry and the Great Exhibition', *Yorkshire Bulletin of Economic and Social Research*, IV, 1 (1952), 27); and a single Trowbridge manufacturer exhibited 150 varieties of trouserings and coatings in wool and silk mixtures at the Paris Exhibition of 1878 (Mann, *Cloth Industry in the West of England*, 215). In 1896 the shoemakers C. and J. Clark were offering 223 types of boots, 353 of shoes, and 144 of slippers (G. B. Sutton, 'The Marketing of Ready Made Footwear in the Nineteenth Century: A Study of the Firm of C. and J. Clark', *Business History*, IV, 2 (June 1964), 96–7); and at about the same time, Huntley & Palmers were producing over 400 varieties of biscuits (T. A. B. Corley, *Quaker Enterprise in Biscuits: Huntley & Palmers of Reading, 1822–1972* (London, 1972), 78).

184 This tactic is discussed in Payne, 'The Large-Scale Company', 524–5, and has been developed in his *British Entrepreneurship*, 41–5. For a case study, see Payne, *Rubber and Railways*, 95–113. See also Sutton, 'Marketing of Ready Made Footwear', 96–8.

185 Perhaps the most successful exponent of the production and sale of 'uniques' was Josiah Wedgwood, who catered to the demands of the fashionable as an integral part of his scheme to gain the custom of the world. The cost of this undoubtedly successful technique is indicated by his letter to Bentley, 'Defend me from particular orders and I can make you allmost double the quantity and accompanied with much greater variety and Elegance' (10 January 1770). See McKendrick, 'Josiah Wedgwood: An Eighteenth-Century Entrepreneur', 408–33; Hensleigh C. Wedgwood, 'Josiah

Wedgwood, Eighteenth-Century Manager', *Explorations in Entrepreneurial History*, 2nd ser., II, 3 (Spring/Summer 1965), 205–26 (from which the quotation is taken, 219); and McKendrick, 'Josiah Wedgwood and Cost Accounting', 53–7.

186 In his article 'Chemicals' in Aldcroft (ed.), *British Industry and Foreign Competition*, 276.

187 A formidable list of new inventions, ideas, and developments more quickly put to practical use by Americans and Europeans than by the British was compiled in 1916 by H. G. Gray (a member of the Mosely Educational Commission to the United States of America in 1903) and Samuel Turner: *Eclipse or Empire?* (London, 1916), part III, pp. 128–305.

188 *Ibid.*, 128. On this major theme, see Landes in *Cambridge Economic History*, VI, 566–75; D. C. Coleman, 'Gentlemen and Players', 101–5; D. H. Aldcroft, 'Investment in and Utilisation of Manpower: Great Britain and her Rivals, 1870–1914', in Barrie M. Ratcliffe, (ed.), *Great Britain and Her World, 1750–1914: Essays in Honour of W. O. Henderson* (Manchester, 1975), 287–307; and Paul L. Robertson, 'Technical Education in the British Shipbuilding and Marine Engineering Industries, 1863–1914', *Economic History Review*, 2nd ser., XXVII (1974), 222–35. See also Richardson, 'Chemicals', in Aldcroft (ed.), *op. cit.*, 301–6.

189 To adapt Richardson's wording, *ibid.*, 306.

190 For structural change, see W. Ashworth, 'Changes in the Industrial Structure, 1870–1914', *Yorkshire Bulletin of Economic and Social Research*, XVII, 1 (May 1965), 61–74.

191 S. Pollard, *The Development of the British Economy, 1914–1950* (London, 1962), 162; G. H. Copeman, *Leaders of British Industry: A Study of the Careers of more than a Thousand Public Company Directors* (London, 1955), 30–1. A. B. Levy, *Private Corporations and Their Control*, 2 vols. (London, 1950), I, pp. 224–9, gives the number of British public companies in 1938 as 14,355 (paid-up capital £4,097m); the private companies numbered 135,221 (paid-up capital £1,894m).

192 See P. Sargeant Florence, *The Logic of British and American Industry: A Realistic Analysis of Economic Structure and Government*, 2nd edn (London, 1961), 178; Committee on Industry and Trade, *Factors in Industrial and Commercial Efficiency*, 128–30; Hargreaves Parkinson, *Ownership of Industry* (London, 1951), *passim*; P. Sargeant Florence, 'The Statistical Analysis of Joint Stock Company Control', *Journal of the Royal Statistical Society*, CX, 1 (1947), 4.

193 Florence, 'Statistical Analysis', 12: 'Out of the twenty large companies investigated, twelve showed 20 per cent to 65 per cent of the votes owned by the largest twenty shareholders; only three companies less than 10 per cent.'

194 Among the eighty largest English trading companies Mr H. M. Davis traced the ratio of capital with full voting rights to total capital. The ratio was 100 per cent (i.e. equal rights) for only twenty-eight of the companies. For thirty-one companies, voting capital formed 61 to 99 per cent of total capital, for eighteen the ratio was 21 to 60 per cent, and for three it was 20 per cent or less. Clearly, the larger companies show a wide variety but, on the average, their votes are more unequally shared, conducing to at least *partial* divorce of control from ownership. Florence, 'Statistical Analysis', 13.

195 Florence, *Logic of Industry*, 178–9. Among Parkinson's thirty large British companies (twenty-seven of them industrial), two had 100,000 or more ordinary (and deferred ordinary) shareholders; another two had 50,000 to 100,000; four, 25,000 to 50,000; and fourteen, from 10,000 to 25,000. Parkinson, *Ownership of Industry*, 106–9. The analysis refers to the years 1941–2.

196 See Florence, *Logic of Industry*, 178–86; Parkinson, *op. cit.*, 99–101.

197 Florence, 'Statistical Analysis', 9; *Logic of Industry*, 186–203. Significantly, in

1935 most of the large shareholders had large holdings only in one company, whereas the small or medium investors were apt to practise multiple share-holding and spread their risks.

198 Florence, *Logic of Industry*, 203.

199 The complete list is impressive; see P. S. Florence, *Ownership, Control and Success of Large Companies* (London, 1961), Appendix A.I, pp. 196–217.

200 H. Samuel, *Shareholders' Money* (London, 1932), 114, quoted Florence, *Logic of Industry*, 206.

201 The sample of 463 British companies of all sizes in 1936 analysed by J. Siviter and W. Baldamus (at the University of Birmingham, under the direction of Professor Florence) traced among directors at least 127 accountants, fifty-eight lawyers, and eighty-eight men with some technical qualification. The proportion of accountants and technicians among the directors, though not that of lawyers, increased with the size of the company: Florence, 'Statistical Analysis', 12; *Logic of Industry*, 211.

202 See Payne, 'The Large-Scale Company', 536 and 539–40.

203 See the illuminating article by Leslie Hannah, 'Managerial Innovation and the Rise of the Large-Scale Company in Interwar Britain', *Economic History Review*, 2nd ser., XXVII (1974), 252–70.

204 For ICI generally, see the second volume of W. J. Reader's monumental history: *Imperial Chemical Industries: A History*, II: *The First Quarter Century, 1926–1952* (Oxford, 1975).

205 This is, in Chandler's own words, 'the central theme' of his classic study *Strategy and Structure: Chapters in the History of Industrial Enterprise* (Cambridge, Mass., 1962).

206 Hannah, 'Managerial Innovation', 264. Hannah's article forms the basis of this and the preceding paragraph.

207 For example, Turner and Newall and the Dunlop Rubber Co. Hannah briefly examines these two companies in his paper (delivered at a conference on management history in June 1975) 'Strategy and Structure in the Manufacturing Sector', in L. Hannah (ed.), *Management Strategy and Business Development: An Historical and Comparative Study* (London, 1976).

208 A phrase used by Hannah to emphasize the difference between the large multi-firm merger of the 1880s and 1890s and the more balanced merger pattern of the inter-war period. During this period, rather than 'seeking instantaneously to convert an industry into a monopoly [firms] were choosing instead the path of sequential acquisition of smaller competitors and selective mergers with large ones, thus spacing out their growth more evenly . . . and [lessening] the managerial stresses of merger' (Hannah, 'Managerial Innovation', 267).

209 *Ibid.*, 259. The pages of John Vaizey's *History of British Steel* (London, 1974) abound with accountants. Perhaps the most significant example of the accountant in business is Francis D'Arcy Cooper at Unilever. C. Wilson, *The History of Unilever: A Study of Economic Growth and Social Change*, 2 vols. (London, 1954), I, pp. 297–301; II, pp. 309–13.

210 Utton, 'Some Features of the Early Merger Movements', 53, gives some tentative market share estimates for 1888–1912.

211 H. Leak and A. Maizels, 'The Structure of British Industry', *Journal of the Royal Statistical Society*, CVIII, 1–2 (1945), 144–5. A business unit is defined as single firms or aggregates of firms 'owned or controlled by a single company . . . control being defined as ownership of more than half the capital (or voting power) of each firm'.

212 *Ibid.*, 144–5 and 160.

213 P. E. Hart and S. J. Prais, 'The Analysis of Business Concentration: A Statistical Approach', *Journal of the Royal Statistical Society*, ser. A, CXIX (1956), 168–75.

214 Sir Henry Clay, in the discussion of Florence, 'Statistical Analysis', 20. The Bleachers' Association was formed in 1900, Tate and Lyle in 1921.

215 With this movement there has been associated a vast expansion of the proportion of salaried (or administrative) to production workers. Bendix has labelled changes in this ratio – the 'A/P' ratio – as an index of bureaucratization, which, he notes, has proceeded farther in tertiary industries than in most manufacturing fields (*Work and Authority in Industry*, 211–20). For his British data Bendix relies on Seymour Melman, *Dynamic Factors in Industrial Productivity* (Oxford, 1956), who gives the A/P ratios for the United Kingdom as 1907, 8·6 per cent; 1924, 13·0 per cent; 1930, 13·7 per cent; 1935, 15·0 per cent; 1948, 20 per cent (p. 73). These ratios are significantly lower than those prevailing in the United States at roughly comparable dates (Bendix, *op. cit.*, 214), and the relatively low figure for 1907 may perhaps indicate the pertinacity of the hold that the owner–manager still had over a wide range of British industry. There was no necessity for a sophisticated administrative structure when, as Marshall wrote, 'the master's eye is everywhere; there is no shirking by his foremen, no divided responsibility, no sending half-understood messages backwards and forwards from one department to another' (quoted H. J. Habakkuk, *Industrial Organisation since the Industrial Revolution: The Fifteenth Fawley Foundation Lecture* (Southampton, 1968), 5). Personal supervision by the owner–manager still applies in, for example, the woollen and worsted industry: Rainnie (ed.), *The Woollen and Worsted Industry*, 50.

216 See P. L. Payne, 'The Uses of Business History: A Contribution to the Discussion', *Business History*, V, 1 (December 1962), 13 and 19.

217 Marvin Frankel's explanation for the slowness of British technological change, and the existence of much obsolete and obsolescent capital equipment in the inter-war period, is interrelatedness, the possibility that in a complex economy the renewal of one element in the productive process may involve a whole range of highly expensive consequential capital changes: 'Obsolescence and Technical Change in a Maturing Economy', *American Economic Review*, XLV, 3 (June 1955), 296–319. The records of many substantial concerns might be expected to shed empirical light on this concept as it affects the firm. As yet this has not (so far as I know) been attempted in a British context, though Kindleberger ('Obsolescence and Technical Change', 284–9) has examined the idea in relation to British railway rolling stock, and D. H. Aldcroft has looked at the question in general terms ('Technical Progress and British Enterprise', 123–7).

218 But see the spirited defence of John Jewkes, 'Is British Industry Inefficient?', *Manchester School*, XIV, 1 (1946), 1–16, who quotes Allyn Young (*Economic Journal*, XXXVIII (1928)): 'I know of no facts which prove or even indicate that British Industry, seen against the background of its own problems and possibilities, is less efficiently organised or less ably directed than American Industry or the industry of any other century.' His own conclusion is that 'to argue that, in the past, the British business man has egregiously failed or that our efficiency in the future will depend ultimately upon the power of the business man to raise himself to new starry heights of intelligence and energy is unscientific, unfair and dangerous' (p. 16). Jewkes is particularly critical of the concept of output per man-year as a measure of efficiency.

219 Coleman, *Courtaulds*, II, p. 243.

220 In Aldcroft (ed.), *British Industry and Foreign Competition*, 275.

221 The adjective is that of Landes, *Unbound Prometheus*, 467–8.

222 Constantly pressed to create a new integrated tidewater steelworks, the corollary of which would be the closing-down of many – if not all – of the plants in

central Lanarkshire, Sir John and Sir Andrew repeatedly directed attention to the 'social dislocation involved'. Sir John Craig refused to follow the advice of those who sought to close down the distant Glengarnock works, because of the disastrous social effect on this part of central Ayrshire. (A study of the Colville group is in progress.) The United Steel Company continued to invest capital at Workington, despite the unprofitability of the plant and its high cost because 'the Company was very conscious of its responsibility as an important employer of labour in one of the depressed areas with which public opinion was very concerned'. Similarly, the colliery at Stocksbridge was kept working for years at a loss because a section of the community depended upon it for employment. P. S. Andrews and E. Brunner, *Capital Development in Steel* (Oxford, 1952), 208 and 362–3.

223 Cf. Samuel Courtauld, who admired American technical achievements and on more than one occasion deplored the backwardness of much of English industry in comparison with the superior mechanization to be found in the United States of America, but doubted 'whether American ideals of living – purely materialistic as they are – will finally lead to a contented working nation anywhere when the excitement of constant expansion has come to an end'. Coleman, *Courtaulds*, II, 218.

224 K. A. Tucker has emphasized the necessity of establishing certain criteria by which to judge business performance objectively. He makes a number of interesting suggestions. 'Business History: Some Proposals for Aims and Methodology', *Business History*, XIV, 1 (January 1972), 1–16. See also Coleman, 'Gentlemen and Players', 92–5 and 109–16.

225 This, of course, is a matter of balance. It is arguable that both Rolls Royce and Upper Clyde Shipbuilders have recently gone to the wall because of a surfeit of technical expertise, in the sense of striving for engineering excellence irrespective of commercial considerations. (For a pithy account of the Rolls Royce crisis, see Anthony Sampson, *The New Anatomy of Britain* (London, 1971), 578–83.) The car firm of Napiers provides an inter-war example (see Charles Wilson and William Reader, *Men and Machines: A History of D. Napier & Son, Engineers, Ltd, 1808–1958* (London, 1958), 83–100), Talbot's an earlier one. S. B. Saul, 'The Motor Industry in Britain', *Business History*, V, 1 (December 1962), 41.

226 See the impact of William C. Lusk, an American of Scottish extraction, on Associated Electrical Industries in 1932: Robert Jones and Oliver Marriott, *Anatomy of a Merger: A History of G.E.C., A.E.I. and English Electric* (London, 1970), 152ff.

227 Hannah, 'Strategy and Structure'. Hannah's account is based on J. D. Scott, *Vickers: A History* (London, 1962), 166–8, and on his own researches in the Vickers archives.

228 This argument may be condemned as a mere hypothesis: one can only say that the presence of very comprehensive and catholic newspaper-cutting books among the archives of many Scottish firms is some evidence that directors kept a much closer eye on the affairs of their competitors and the activities of companies in related fields than the author, at least, had imagined.

229 Space constraints prohibit the elaboration of this argument. It has been put forward because the author believes it to be worthy of further inquiry. Some provocative ideas on the subject of information flows within the large firm have been suggested by B. W. E. Alford, 'The Chandler Thesis – Some General Observations', in Hannah (ed.), *Management Strategy and Business Development*.

230 E. J. Hobsbawm, 'Custom, Wages and Work-Load in Nineteenth-Century Industry', in *Labouring Men* (London, 1964), 344–70. See E. F. Denison, *Why Growth Rates Differ* (Washington, 1967), 293–5.

231 G. D. H. Cole, 'Self-Reliance and Social Legislation'.

232 Coleman, *Courtaulds*, II, 220; and Coleman, 'Gentlemen and Players'. Cf. C. P. Kindleberger, who has pointed out that 'Andrews and Brunner defend the United Steel Company's investment policies from the criticism of Burn and of Burnham and Hoskins in a variety of ways, but they do not claim that it made the largest possible amount of money over time' (Kindleberger, 'Obsolescence and Technical Change', 294, citing D. L. Burn, *Economic History of Steelmaking*, and T. H. Burnham and G. O. Hoskins, *Iron and Steel in Britain, 1870–1930* (London, 1943); see Andrews and Brunner, *Capital Development in Steel*, particularly pp. 361–4). W. E. Minchinton has emphasized that in the tinplate industry of West Wales the unremitting pursuit of profit was not generally recognized as the end of human endeavour (*The British Tinplate Industry*, 105–7).

233 See R. A. Church, *Kenricks in Hardware*, 212ff; and Wells, *Hollins and Viyella*, 160–1.

234 See Coleman, *Courtaulds*, II, 230.

235 See Child, *British Management Thought*, 103. The entire subject of scientific management deserves further study. E. H. Phelps Brown, *The Growth of British Industrial Relations* (London, 1965), 92–8; Levine, *Industrial Retardation in Britain*, 60–8; Urwick and Brech, *The Making of Scientific Management, passim*; Tillett, Kempner, and Wills, *Management Thinkers*, especially part 1, pp. 75–96, and part 3, might provide a starting point; but the literature is enormous. It is extremely well surveyed by Child (*British Management Thought*), although the economic historian has difficulty – in the absence of case studies that discuss this issue – in determining the precise influence of the thought of the few on the practice of the many.

236 The best-documented example is Lever Brothers' purchases in the years after the First World War. Of one of them Lord Leverhulme was to write, 'I have never myself understood why this business was purchased. I have never seen that it could be of any interest to Lever Brothers or associated companies.' See C. Wilson, *History of Unilever*, I, p. 260. See also Armstrong Whitworth's disastrous Newfoundland Paper Mills scheme: Scott, *Vickers*, 153–5.

237 G. Turner, *The Leyland Papers* (London, 1971), 88–90. See also the case of Sir Glyn H. West, of Armstrong Whitworth (Scott, *Vickers*, 153).

238 A prime example is that of AEI's failure to integrate British Thomson–Houston and Metropolitan Vickers. See Jones and Marriott, *Anatomy of a Merger*, 147ff.

239 See Payne, 'The Large-Scale Company', 528–36.

240 T. S. Ashton, 'Business History', *Business History*, I, 1 (December 1958), 1.

241 This is not to say that mistakes were not made, simply that decisions were based upon objective factual analysis of the data available *at the time*. These observations are based on the author's conversations with businessmen in the West of Scotland.

242 Neil K. Buxton, 'Entrepreneurial Efficiency in the British Coal Industry between the Wars', *Economic History Review*, 2nd ser., XXIII, 3 (December 1970), 477.

243 Admittedly, the picture has become more complex with expanding areas of public ownership but, as M. M. Postan has argued, it would appear that 'most state-owned undertakings conformed to ordinary business objectives and management merely because the motivation and behaviour of their personnel, their labour force and their managers, were also the same as in private business' (*An Economic History of Western Europe, 1945–1964* (London, 1967), 228). See also G. Bannock, *The Juggernauts: The Age of the Big Corporation* (London, 1971), 133–9.

244 Hart and Prais, 'Analysis of Business Concentration', 155 and 175; R. Evely and I. M. D. Little, *Concentration in British Industry* (Cambridge, 1960), 18–24; A. Armstrong and A. Silbertson, 'Size of Plant, Size of Enterprise and Concentration in

British Manufacturing Industry, 1935–58', *Journal of the Royal Statistical Society*, ser. A, CXXVIII, 3 (1965), 401 and 403; William Mennell, *Takeover. The Growth of Monopoly in Britain, 1951–61* (London, 1962), 38.

245 Mennell, *op. cit.*, 405. There is a very large literature on this subject. For the economic historian, the more important sources are: Randall Smith and Dennis Brooks, *Mergers Past and Present* (London, 1963); Sam Aaronovitch and Malcolm C. Sawyer, 'The Concentration of British Manufacturing', *Lloyds Bank Review*, no. 114 (October 1974), 14–23; Aaronovitch and Sawyer, *Big Business: Concentration and Mergers in the United Kingdom, Some Empirical and Theoretical Aspects* (London, 1975); K. D. George and A. Silberston, 'The Causes and Effects of Mergers', *Scottish Journal of Political Economy*, XXII (1975), 179–93; K. D. George, 'A Note on Changes in Industrial Concentration in the United Kingdom', *Economic Journal*, LXXXV (1975), 124–8; P. E. Hart, M. A. Utton, and G. Walshe, *Mergers and Concentration in British Industry* (Cambridge, 1973); G. D. Newbould, *Management and Merger Activity* (Liverpool, 1970); S. J. Prais, 'A New Look at the Growth of Industrial Concentration', *Oxford Economic Papers*, n.s., XXVI (1974), 273–88; Nicholas A. H. Stacey, *Mergers in Modern Business*, 2nd edn (London, 1970); M. A. Utton, 'The Effect of Mergers on Concentration: U.K. Manufacturing Industry, 1954–65', *Journal of Industrial Economics*, XX (1971–2), 42–58; G. Walshe, *Recent Trends in Monopoly in Great Britain* (Cambridge, 1974).

246 Prais, 'A New Look', 283–6.

247 G. Whittington, 'Changes in the Top 100 Quoted Manufacturing Companies in the United Kingdom, 1948–1968', *Journal of Industrial Economics*, XXI (1972–3), 17–34.

248 Bannock, *The Juggernauts*, 39; Utton, 'The Effect of Mergers', 44.

249 Postan, *Economic History*, 215 and 232ff; Mennell, *Takeover*, 127.

250 See, for example, 'Who Controls the Steel Industry?', *British Iron and Steel Federation, Steel Review*, October 1958.

251 The extremely low level of shareholder participation in the affairs of the largest companies during the 1960s has been demonstrated by K. Midgley, 'How Much Control do Shareholders Exercise?', *Lloyds Bank Review*, no. 114 (October 1974), 24–37.

252 Florence, *Ownership, Control and Success*, 185ff.

253 Andrew Lumsden, 'The Wealth and Power in Britain's Top Boardrooms', *The Times*, 9 September 1969, quoted Bannock, *The Juggernauts*, 5. Even these figures include the abnormal holdings 'of such relics of the old order as the Pilkington board, which held 70 per cent of the equity'.

254 J. Moyle, *The Pattern of Ordinary Share Ownership, 1957–1970* (Cambridge, 1971), quoted Midgley, 'How Much Control?', 25.

255 The increasing use of paper to finance mergers has itself diluted the ownership of large corporations. Bannock, *The Juggernauts*, 92.

256 John Child, *The Business Enterprise in Modern Industrial Society* (London, 1969), 45–51.

257 Copeman, *Leaders of British Industry*, 29–30. See above, p. 215. David Granick claims that in Great Britain 'dominant stock owning families have lost interest in exercising control, their funds have been reinvested into a wide sweep of companies in order to gain the financial safety which comes from diversification' (Granick, *The European Executive* (New York, 1962), 94).

258 Postan, *Economic History*, 252.

259 The potential benefits from this course of action may sometimes be reduced or unrealized if 'imported' executives became, as in the case of L. W. Archer at Morton Sundour Fabrics, a 'shuttlecock between the opposing views of the family

members'. See the interesting study by Jocelyn Morton, *Three Generations in a Family Textile Firm* (London, 1971); the quotation is from p. 466.

260 Midgley, 'How Much Control?', 28 and 36. Of all quoted securities in 1963, about one-quarter were held by institutional investors (insurance companies, investment trusts, unit trusts, and pension funds): J. G. Blease, 'Institutional Investors and the Stock Exchange'. *District Bank Review*, no. 151 (September 1964), 43. See also *The Guardian*, 6 October 1975; Derek F. Channon, *The Strategy and Structure of British Enterprise* (London, 1973), 234; and Richard Spiegelberg, *The City: Power Without Responsibility* (London, 1973), 47–60.

261 Copeman, *Leaders of British Industry*; Acton Society Trust, *Management Succession: The Recruitment, Selection, Training and Promotion of Managers* (London, 1956); R. V. Clements, *Managers: A Study of Their Careers in Industry* (London, 1958); I. C. McGivering, D. G. J. Matthews, and W. H. Scott, *Management in Britain* (Liverpool, 1960); Roy Lewis and Rosemary Stewart, *The Boss: The Life and Times of the British Business Man* (London, 1961); Granick, *The European Executive*; D. G. Clark, *The Industrial Manager: His Background and Career Pattern* (London, 1966); Theo Nichols, *Ownership, Control and Ideology* (London, 1969); G. Copeman, *The Chief Executive and Business Growth* (London, 1971); B. Taylor and K. Macmillan (eds.), *Top Management* (London, 1973).

262 For example, of those in managerial positions in Clement's sample who had started 'at the bottom', only 4 per cent had become directors, and 'the small proportion in top management shows that their chances of getting into the top ranks of management are very limited'. R. V. Clements, *Managers*, 79.

263 Postan, *Economic History*, 272–3.

264 D. P. Barritt, 'The Stated Qualifications of Directors of Larger Public Companies', *Journal of Industrial Economics*, v (1956–7), 220–4. See also Granick, *The European Executive*, part 5, chap. 18, for a discussion of the 'amateur' concept of management in Britain; David J. Hall and Gilles Amado-Fischgrund, 'Who are the Top Managers? 1: Chief Executives in Britain', in Taylor and MacMillan eds.), *Top Management*, 104–6.

265 *The Director*, 1959, p. 301, quoted Nichols, *Ownership, Control and Ideology*, 80.

266 Nichols, *op. cit.*, 80–3 and 117–18; Acton Society Trust, *Management Succession*, 28–9; Granick, *The European Executive*, 242ff; Erickson, *British Industrialists*, 37; Coleman, 'Gentlemen and Players', 105–9; Channon, *Strategy and Structure*, 43–6 and 216–17; Philip Stanworth and Anthony Giddens, 'An Economic Elite: A Demographic Profile of Company Chairmen', in Stanworth and Giddens (eds.), *Elites and Power*, 80–101. See also Hester Jenkins and D. Caradog Jones, 'Social Class of Cambridge University Alumni of the 18th and 19th Centuries', *British Journal of Sociology*, 1, 2 (June 1950), 99, 100–1, and 114.

267 A report prepared by the Confederation of British Industry and the British Institute of Management in 1971 accused the British business schools and their graduates of being 'arrogant and remote from reality'. Conversely, few of the fifty-three leading firms questioned had any planned policy for dealing with the business-school men. (*Sunday Times*, 4 July 1971). Another worrying aspect of this question is the persistent tendency in British industry to discount the value of longer comprehensive courses as compared with short specialized ones, and a stubborn belief that the management processes and problems in many firms were unique. Channon, *op. cit.*, 45. The argument is based upon National Economic Development Office, *Management Education in the 1970's* (London, 1970). See also G. Turner, *Business in Britain* (London, 1969), 92–100; Granick, *The European Executive*, 242 and 249; Sampson, *Anatomy of Britain*, 590–4.

268 See Mennell, *Takeover*, 137ff.

269 *Ibid.*, 137–40; Turner, *Business in Britain*, 221–39; T. C. Barker, 'A Family Firm Becomes a Public Company: Changes at Pilkington Brothers Limited in the Inter-War Years', in Hannah (ed.), *Management Strategy and Business Development*.

270 See A. J. Merritt and M. E. Lehr, *The Private Company Today* (London, 1971), 6, 15, and 67–71.

271 Channon, *Strategy and Structure*, 68–9.

272 *Ibid.*, 10.

273 McKinsey & Co. played a major role in the reorganization of major British Companies in the food, tobacco, chemical, pharmaceutical, oil, paper, metals, materials, machinery, engineering, and electrical industries. *Ibid.*, *passim*.

274 *Ibid.*, 77.

275 A. D. Chandler, commenting on Channon's findings in a paper entitled 'The Development of Modern Management Structures in the U.S. and U.K.', in Hannah (ed.), *Management Strategy and Business Development*.

276 *Ibid.* This brief treatment can do justice neither to the richness of the data provided by Channon nor to Chandler's provocative ideas. The papers delivered at the Management History Conference (see note 207 above) should be consulted.

277 P. J. D. Wiles, *Price, Cost and Output* (Oxford, 1961), 187.

278 Marris, *Economic Theory of 'Managerial' Capitalism*, 63; Penrose, *Theory of the Growth of the Firm*, especially 26–30; Bannock, *The Juggernauts*, 108–9; H. F. Lydall, 'The Growth of Manufacturing Firms', *Bulletin of the Oxford University Institute of Statistics*, xxi (1959), 85–111.

279 Ajit Singh provides a useful summary of the controversy in his *Take-overs: Their Relevance to the Stock Market and the Theory of the Firm* (Cambridge, 1971), 6–12. See also Fritz Machlup, 'Theories of the Firm: Marginalist, Behavioral, Managerial', *American Economic Review*, LVII, 1 (March 1967), 1–33.

280 This policy is subject to certain restraints. Clearly, if the retention ratios become too high then lower share prices relative to asset value result, and conditions favourable to take-over bids are created, the success of which might result in the replacement of the existing management. Furthermore, the potential shareholder must not be completely alienated, for fear that future growth necessitating a public issue would be impracticable. The problem is discussed by Marris, *Economic Theory*, 18–45. See also Singh, *Take-overs*, 11–12 and 80–81.

281 Florence, who examined the ratios of distributed to retained profits in his sample of large British companies, claimed to find a positive association between his measures of low ownership control and low dividend distribution; but Nichols, who reworked Florence's data for large companies in the sample (those with assets upwards of £3m), found that while the results were in the direction asserted by Florence, none reached a 5 per cent level of significance. Florence, *Ownership, Control and Success*, 190; Nichols, *Ownership, Control and Ideology*, 106–7.

282 This has long been the claim of management theorists, see, for example, C. B. Kaysen, 'The Social Significance of the Modern Corporation', *American Economic Review*, XLVII (1957), 311–19.

283 For recent studies of the attitudes of Quaker employers towards industrial relations and the management of labour during the present century, see John Child's *British Management Thought*, 36–40, 47–8, and 77, and his 'Quaker Employers and Industrial Relations', *Sociological Review*, XII, 3 (November 1964), 293–315. See also Elizabeth R. Pafford and John H. P. Pafford, *Employer and Employed: Ford Ayrton & Co. Ltd, Silk Spinners* (Edington, Wilts, 1974).

284 Child, *The Business Enterprise*, 51. Nichols has made an important point:

if we are concerned with the *motives* of present day directors (and not merely the *control potential* of large shareholders) it is possible that the *percentage* of ordinary capital owned by the board is not a very satisfactory measure. What is required is an estimate of the actual *wealth* which directors have at risk in their companies or, more precisely, of that proportion of their income which derives from share ownership – and not the percentage of *all* ordinary shares which they own.

Nichols, *Ownership, Control and Ideology*, 73; and see *ibid.*, 78 and 141. Copeman, *The Chief Executive*, has recently found that 'there were no apparent, significant differences in management techniques among the nations or between fast and slow growing firms, but that share ownership by the chief executive appeared to exercise a great influence on company performance and growth' (p. 329).

285 See Penrose, *Theory of the Growth of the Firm*, 26–30, and Wiles, *Price, Cost and Output*, 181–209.

286 Wiles, *op. cit.*, 186.

287 For industrial productivity, see E. H. Phelps Brown and Margaret H. Browne, *A Century of Pay* (London, 1968), p. 300, and Appendix 3, p. 447. This is not to say that better results could not have been achieved. See J. Johnston, 'The Productivity of Management Consultants', *Journal of the Royal Statistical Society*, ser. A, CXXVI, 2 (1963), 237–49. Those sceptics who emphasize the relative inferiority of British to American entrepreneurship might remember that the Americans too have some way to go to reach perfection. As Robert Dorfman has observed:

we must recognise the firm for what operations research has disclosed it to be: often fumbling, sluggish, timid, uncertain and perplexed by unsolvable problems. Since its discriminating power is low it responds only to gross stimuli; since its decision processes are uncertain the timing and vigor of its responses are unpredictable. It reacts in familiar ways to the familiar and avoids the novel as long as it dares.

(Dorfman, 'Operations Research', *American Economic Review*, L, 4 (September 1960), 622.)

288 Copeman, *The Chief Executive*, especially chap. 2.

289 It has recently been argued that by 1985 twenty-one companies could dominate the non-nationalized sector of the British economy, managing between them some 74 per cent of the sector's assets. G. D. Newbould and Andrew S. Jackson, *The Receding Ideal* (Liverpool, 1972), 130–48.

290 A point made by Channon, *Strategy and Structure*, 43–4.

291 The temptation to generalize from these 'exposures' should be resisted. In 1965 L. J. Tolley, Group Managing Director of Renold Ltd, observed 'The greatest enemies of British economic strength appear to me to be the British themselves and their Press in particular. I know of no other country which delights in exposing its weaknesses and faults and at the same time hiding its strengths.' Basil H. Tripp, *Renold Limited, 1956–67* (London, 1969), 166.

292 As Robert Heller observed, after drawing attention to the recently fallen idols Joseph Maxwell, John Bloom, Cecil King, and Cyril Lord: 'In management, wonders nearly always cease. The kissing has to stop because one day events surely expose any manager in all his nakedness for what he is: a fallible human being, trying, with the help of others, who are equally fallible, to cope with circumstances which constantly change their shape and definition' (*The Naked Manager* (London, 1972), 4). But again and again one is confronted with the problem of judging business or entrepreneurial or managerial success. What criteria are to be used? Heller's 'doubling profits in real

terms in [a] decade, at least maintaining return on shareholders' equity over the ten years and only having one off-year'? listing the available new technology and the timing of its adoption (and so falling into the possible error of emphasizing the technical rather than the economic best)? the rate of return on capital? the growth of the firm, measured by turnover, compared with movements in the gross national product? Just what tests are to be applied? See above, pp. 209 and 216.

293 The whole of Bannock's book *The Juggernauts* is basically a series of variations on this theme. Discussing the level of concentration in the manufacturing sector of British industry over the period 1958–63, Malcolm C. Sawyer has argued that (if the economies of scale have been measured accurately) concentration in 1963 was much higher than it needed to have been to exploit the economies of scale. 'Concentration in British Manufacturing Industry', *Oxford Economic Papers*, n.s., XXIII, 3 (November 1971), 374. See also A. Sutherland, *The Monopolies Commission in Action* (Cambridge, 1969), 52–70, and cf. K. D. George, 'Changes in British Industrial Concentration, 1951–58', *Journal of Industrial Economics*, XV, 3 (July 1967), 206–11. Moreover, as W. B. Reddaway has emphasized, 'Dr Singh's research [*Take-overs*, 161–5] into what happens *after* a take-over provides no support whatever for the idea that profitability is, on average, increased by applying better methods to the assets which have been taken into new management.' Reddaway, 'An Analysis of Take-overs', *Lloyds Bank Review*, no. 104 (April 1972), 19.

294 See Habakkuk, *Industrial Organisation since the Industrial Revolution*, 6.

295 Industrial Reorganisation Corporation, *First Report and Accounts*, December 1966–March 1968 (London, 1968), 5. See also W. G. McClelland, 'The Industrial Reorganisation Corporation, 1966–71: An Experimental Prod', *The Three Banks Review*, no. 94 (June 1972), 23–42.

296 Newbould, *Management and Merger Activity*, 113.

297 Monopolies Commission, *Report on the Proposed Merger of Unilever Limited and Allied Breweries Limited* (London, 1969), quoted J. M. Samuels, 'The Success or Failure of Mergers and Takeovers', in J. M. Samuels (ed.), *Readings on Mergers and Takeovers* (London, 1972), 10.

298 See, for example, the studies by G. D. Newbould, 'Implications of Financial Analyses of Takeovers', in Samuels (ed.), *op. cit.*, 12–24; John Kitching, 'Why Acquisitions are Abortive', *Management Today*, November 1974, 82–7 and 148; and M. A. Utton, 'On Measuring the Effects of Industrial Mergers', *Scottish Journal of Political Economy*, XXI (1974), 13–26.

299 Bannock, *The Juggernauts*, 189. Cf. E. Mansfield, 'The Speed of Response of Firms to New Techniques', *Quarterly Journal of Economics*, LXXVII, 2 (May 1963), 310; Charles Wilson, *Unilever, 1945–65: Challenge and Response in the Post-War Industrial Revolution* (London, 1968), 139. See also T. Levitt, *The Marketing Mode* (New York, 1969), chap. 5.

300 Harry Miller, *The Way of Enterprise: A Study of the Origins, Problems and Achievements in the Growth of Post-War British Firms* (London, 1963), and Philip Clarke, *Small Businesses: How They Survive and Succeed* (Newton Abbot, 1973) provide some very interesting post-war examples. See also the point made by Habakkuk, *Industrial Organisation since the Industrial Revolution*, 22, and the questions raised by Jocelyn Morton, *Three Generations*, 465. For a general study see Jonathan Boswell, *The Rise and Decline of Small Firms* (London, 1972). The standard work on this subject is the Bolton Report: *Report of the Committee of Inquiry on Small Firms*, Cmnd 4811 (London, 1971).

CHAPTER V

Capital Investment and Economic Growth in France, 1820–1930

1 This chapter has benefited from the collaboration of Professor François Caron, who wrote section III and contributed ideas, data, and calculations, more specifically on the transport sector; his own views have been presented independently in 'Investment Strategy in France', in H. Daems and H. van der Wee (eds.), *The Rise of Managerial Capitalism* (Louvain, 1974).

2 F. Perroux, 'Prise de vue sur la croissance de l'économie française, 1780–1950', in S. Kuznets (ed.), *Income and Wealth*, ser. v (London, 1955), 41–78.

3 H. Feis, *Europe: The World's Banker, 1870–1914* (New York, 1965), 36, 48.

4 According to the first variant of the series tabulated by Markovitch, 16·3 per cent of national income was invested in 1815–34 (but 22 per cent during the period 1803–12), and an average of 19·4 per cent in 1865–94 (as against 20·5 per cent in 1855–64). Markovitch's variant III also suggests that there were two phases, but they are shorter and less marked: 7·1 per cent instead of 8·1 per cent at the beginning of the century, and 13·8 per cent in 1865–74, i.e. the same figures as for the middle of the century. T. J. Markovitch, 'L'Industrie française de 1789 à 1964: Conclusions générales'.

5 Kuznets, 'International Differences in Capital Formation and Financing', in Abramovitz (ed.), *Capital Formation and Economic Growth*.

6 These estimates are taken from E. Zylberman, 'La Croissance et les comptes économiques de la France sous le Second Empire' (unpublished thesis, University of Paris, 1969), for 1860; Lubell, *The French Investment Program*, for 1927–30; and Vincent, 'Les Comptes nationaux', in Sauvy (ed.), *Histoire économique de la France*, III, 334, for 1913–29.

7 The tables published by the Direction Générale des Contributions Directes, itemizing the numbers of houses, are relatively detailed. They do not, however, state the number of lodgings per house (in 1887–9, there were three occupants per house in the countryside, four to six in the small towns, eight to nine in the major conurbations, and twenty-eight in Paris), nor do they list the number of floors, the number of amenities, etc. Nonetheless, the figures recorded in these tables can be used to check the variations between our figures, depending on whether they are gross or net.

Numbers of houses (thousands):	1871–4	1875–9	1880–4	1885–9	1890–3
Demolished	63·1	79·3	84·5	131·6	147·6
Built	106·4	120·0	122·8	180·0	186·3
Balance	43·3	40·7	38·3	48·4	38·7
Value of houses (thousand francs):					
Demolished	367·0	383·7	425·6	457·2	454·4
Built	1,204·5	1,096·0	1,338·0	1,773·5	1,305·3
Balance	837·5	712·3	912·4	1,316·3	850·9
Francs per house	19,340	17,500	23,820	27,190	21,980
Volume index:					
Gross	57·1	64·4	65·9	96·6	100·0
Net	111·8	105·1	98·9	125·0	100·0
Value index:					
Gross	92·3	84·0	102·5	135·9	100·0
Net	94·8	83·7	107·2	154·7	100·0

8 Only the series of data for the nineteenth century are the result of our own research and calculations. Beginning with L. A. Vincent, 'Evolution de la production intérieure brute en France de 1896 à 1938', *Etudes et Conjoncture*, XVII, 11 (1962), 900ff, we were able to use, for the twentieth century, the series of studies produced by the Institut National de Statistique et des Etudes Economiques (INSEE), including J. Berthet, J. J. Carré, P. Dubois, and E. Malinvaud, 'Sources et origines de la croissance française au milieu de XXe siècle' (first draft, mimeographed: Paris, June 1965; see also note 30 below), which we have relied on throughout this study. The sources and methods used in calculating both the existing and the new series of data are discussed in the Appendix below.

9 M. Huber, H. Bunlé, and F. Boverat, *La Population française*, rev. edn (Paris, 1965), 287.

10 G. Désert, 'Aperçus sur l'industrie française, du bâtiment au XIXe siècle', in J. P. Bardet, *et al.*, *Le Bâtiment: Enquête d'histoire économique, XIVe–XIXe siècles* (Paris and The Hague, 1971), 84–5.

11 M. E. Boutin, 'La Propriété bâtie', *Journal de la Société de Statistique de Paris*, July 1891, 19.

12 M. Halbwachs, *Les Expropriations et le prix des terrains à Paris, 1860–1900* (Paris, 1909); L. Flaus, 'Fluctuations de la construction urbaine, 1830–1940', *Journal de la Société de Statistique de Paris*, 1949; M. Duon, *Documents sur le problème des logements à Paris*, INSEE (Paris, 1946); [anon.], 'Evolution des conditions de logements depuis cent ans', *Etudes et Conjoncture*, October–November 1957; F. Marnata, *Les Loyers des bourgeois de Paris, 1860–1958* (Paris, 1961), 25 and 59–63; J. Gaillard, *Paris: La Ville, 1852–1870* (Lille and Paris, 1975), 156 n.28.

13 P. Dauzet, *Le Siècle des chemins de fer en France* (Paris, 1948); L. Girard, *La Politique des travaux publics du Second Empire* (Paris, 1952); F. Caron, *Histoire de l'exploitation d'un grand réseau: La Compagnie du Chemin de Fer du Nord, 1846–1937* (Paris and The Hague, 1973).

14 Zylberman, 'La Croissance et les comptes économiques', 406 and 456.

15 J. C. Toutain, 'Les Transports en France de 1830 à 1965', *Cahiers de l'ISEA*, ser. AF 9, no. 8 (September–October 1967).

16 Caron, *Histoire d'un grand réseau*, 80ff.

17 A. M. James, 'Sidérurgie et chemins de fer en France', *Cahiers de l'ISEA*, ser. T5, no. 158 (February 1965), 127ff. Two developments during the 1870s may have thrown out the forecasts for the growth of railway traffic: first, in 1870–3 (when the increase in traffic reached 14·5 per cent per annum) the building-up of new stock to take the place of stock which had run down during the war, at a time when the number of wagons and draught animals had fallen by 20 per cent; and second, in 1879–82 (when the rate of increase was 6·9 per cent), the boost to railway traffic which resulted from the bad harvests – for the railways profited from the transport of imported wheat – and from the freezing of the canals during the winter of 1879–80.

18 Désert, 'Aperçus sur l'industrie du bâtiment', 77. See also Mme Cahen, 'Evolution de la population active en France depuis cent ans', *Etudes et Conjoncture*, 'Economie française', no. 3 (May–June 1953), 230ff; L. A. Vincent, 'Population active, production et productivité dans 21 branches de l'économie française, 1896–1962', *Etudes et Conjoncture*, XX, 2 (February 1965), Table 1, p. 87.

19 Toutain, 'Les Transports en France', 285–96.

20 The increase in the product – for example, the mean of the period 1864–73 compared with that of the preceding ten years – was calculated from figures listed in the *Annuaire Statistique* for 1946, pp. 124–5. New expenditure (on basic equipment and working stock) was 333·5m francs per annum in 1854–63, 210·0m in 1864–73, 283·1m in 1874–83, and 293·3m in 1884–93.

21 Dupeux, 'La Croissance urbaine'.

22 The gross product fell to 1·41 million francs on receipts totalling 3·79 million in 1850–66, and to 0·87 million on receipts totalling 4·83 million in 1867–83: Caron *Histoire d'un grand réseau*, 223. Concerning technological advances, see *ibid.*, 337ff.

23 J. Dessirier, 'Chemin de fer et progrès technique', *Année Ferroviaire*, 1952, 21–79.

24 Société Nationale des Chemins de Fer Français (SNCF), 'Principales Statistiques des chemins de fer depuis 1821' (internal document, 1964).

25 P. Riboud, 'Les Grands Réseaux de chemin de fer français de 1848 à 1937', *Revue Générale des Chemins de Fer*, 1938, 49ff.

26 G. Gripon-Lamothe, *Historique de réseau des chemins de fer français* (Paris, 1904), 'Annexe', p. 518; Riboud, 'Les Grands Réseaux'.

27 Section III is contributed by Professor F. Caron.

28 F. Crouzet, 'Un Indice de la production industrielle française au XIXe siècle', *Annales*, XXV, 1 (January–February 1970), 56–99.

29 M. Lévy-Leboyer, 'La Croissance économique en France au XIXe siècle: Résultats préliminaires', *Annales*, XXIII, 4 (1968); however, see p. 289 above, where the author points out that the 1968 series is superseded by column 8 of Table 58.

30 Lubell, *The French Investment Program*; J. J. Carré, P. Dubois, and E. Malinvaud, *La Croissance française: Un Essai d'analyse économique causale de l'après-guerre* (Paris, 1972: the definitive version of Berthet *et al.*, 'Sources et origines', cited in note 8 above); J. Mairesse, *L'Evaluation du capital fixe productif: Méthode et résultat*, Collections de l'INSEE, ser. C, nos. 18–19 (Paris, 1972).

31 C. Dupin, *Les Forces productives de la France* (Paris, 1827).

32 L. Chevalier, *La Formation de la population parisienne au XIXe siècle* (Paris, 1950); R. Laurent, *L'Octroi de Dijon au XIXe siècle* (Paris, 1960); Désert, 'Aperçus sur l'industrie du bâtiment'.

33 M. Merger, 'La Consommation chaumontaise' (unpublished thesis, University of Dijon, 1970); Gaillard, *Paris: La Ville*.

34 Carré *et al.*, *La Croissance française*.

35 F. Lucas, *Etude sur les voies de communication* (Paris, 1873).

36 A. de Foville, *La France économique* (Paris, 1887); C. Colson, *Cours d'économie politique*, 1st edn (Paris, 1903) and later editions.

37 A. Picard, *Traité des chemins de fer* (Paris, 1887).

38 Archives Nationales, 65 AQ E 304, 461, 516, 542, 560, and 561.

39 Toutain, 'Les Transports en France'.

40 *Cote de la Bourse et de la Banque*, 23 October 1907; H. Schwarz, 'L'Industrie de l'automobile', *Journal Officiel: Documents Administratifs*, 26–7 August 1936.

41 L. Massénat-Deroche, *L'Automobile aux Etats-Unis et en Angleterre* (Paris, 1910).

42 The first series is based on the *Statistique de l'industrie minérale et des appareils à vapeur* (Paris, 1901) and the *Annuaire Statistique* for 1913 and 1946. The second is based on these sources and on J. Vial, *L'Industrialisation de la sidérurgie française, 1814–1864*, 2 vols. (Paris and The Hague, 1967).

43 A. Aftalion, *Les Crises périodiques de surproduction* (Paris, 1913); Markovitch, 'L'Industrie française'.

44 See P. Fridenson, *Histoire des usines Renault* (Paris, 1972).

45 J. Bouvier, F. Furet, and M. Gillet, *Le Mouvement du profit en France au XIXe siècle: Matériaux et études* (Paris and The Hague, 1965); G. Thuillier, *Georges Dufaud et les débuts du grand capitalisme dans la métallurgie, en Nivernaus, au XIXe siècle* (Paris, 1959); Vial, *L'Industrialisation ce la sidérurgie*; B. Gille, *La Sidérurgie française au XIXe siècle* (Paris, 1968).

46 For this paragraph, see: Markovitch, 'L'Industrie française'; M. Brosselin, 'Evaluation de la production intérieure de bois d'oeuvre, 1840–1912 (unpublished

thesis, University of Dijon, 1972); M. Lévy-Leboyer, *Les Banques européennes et l'industrialisation internationale dans la première moitié du XIXe siècle* (Paris, 1964); J. Dollfus, *De l'industrie cotonnière* (Paris, 1855); Aftalion, *Les Crises de surproduction*; J. M. Jeanneney and C. A. Colliard, *Economie et droit de l'électricité* (Grenoble, 1950); H. Morsel, 'Les Industries hydro-électriques de la région alpine', in Centre National de la Recherche Scientifique, *L'Industrialisation en Europe au XIXe siècle* (Lyons, 1970).

47 See K. Maywald, 'The Construction Costs and the Value of the British Merchant Fleet, 1850–1938', *Scottish Journal of Political Economy*, III, 1 (1956), 44ff.

48 E. Rousseau, 'Rapport d'examen des demandes des constructeurs et des armateurs', in *Commission Extra-parlementaire de la Marine Marchande* (Paris, 1903).

49 Foville, *La France économique*.

50 Toutain, 'Les Transports en France'.

51 Data assembled by Massénat-Deroche, *L'Automobile*. Cf. M. Flageollet, 'Les Débuts de l'industrie automobile française: Panhard et Levassor' (unpublished thesis, University of Paris (Nanterre), 1970); Fridenson, *Histoire des usines Renault*.

52 For this paragraph, see: A. K. Cairncross, *Home and Foreign Investment, 1870–1913* (Cambridge, 1953); C. H. Feinstein, 'Home and Foreign Investment: Some Aspects of Capital, Finance and Income in the United Kingdom, 1870–1914' (unpublished Ph.D. thesis, University of Cambridge, 1959); Mairesse, *L'Evaluation du capital*.

53 These figures were taken from M. Lévy-Leboyer, 'La Balance des paiements et l'exportation des capitaux français, 1820–1940', in *La Position internationale de la France: Aspects économiques et financiers, XIXe et XXe siècles* (Paris and the Hague, 1977).

54 Lévy-Leboyer, 'La Décélération de l'économie française', 485ff; and Lévy-Leboyer, 'La Croissance économique en France', 788ff.

55 Lévy-Leboyer, 'La Croissance économique en France'.

56 Data for transport are taken from an unpublished annual series prepared by J. C. Toutain and communicated by him to the author.

57 Respectively, from an internal document of SNCF; O. Piquet-Marchal, *Etude économique des chemins de fer d'intérêt local* (Paris, 1964); and Colson, *Cours d'économie politique*.

CHAPTER VII

Entrepreneurship and Management in France in the Nineteenth Century

1 Chaptal, *De l'industrie française*, 2 vols. (Paris, 1819), 31.

2 Richard Cobden, *Political Writings*, 2 vols. (London, 1867), vol. 1, p. 469.

3 Maurice Lévy-Leboyer, 'Le Patronat français a-t-il été malthusien', *Le Mouvement Social*, LXXXVIII (1974), 3–49, appeared too late to be used here.

4 Shepard B. Clough, 'Retardative Factors in French Economic Development in the 19th and 20th Centuries', *Journal of Economic History*, Supp. III (1946), 91–102.

5 Talcott Parsons, *The Structure of Social Action* (New York and London, 1936). Cf. also his *Essays in Sociological Theory*, 2nd edn (New York, 1958).

6 John E. Sawyer, 'Strains in the Social Structure of Modern France', in Edward Mead Earle (ed.), *Modern France: Problems of the Third and Fourth Republics* (Princeton, N.J., 1951), 297.

7 David S. Landes, 'French Entrepreneurship and Industrial Growth in the Nine-teenth Century', *Journal of Economic History*, IX (1949), 45–61. See also Landes, 'French Business and the Businessmen: A Social and Cultural Analysis', in Earle, *op. cit.*, 334–53.

8 Rondo E. Cameron, *France and the Economic Development of Europe, 1800–1914*, (Princeton, N.J., 1961), especially chap. 5 and part III.

9 R. E. Cameron, 'Economic Growth and Stagnation in France, 1815–1914', *Journal of Modern History*, XXX (1958–9), 11.

10 Tom Kemp, *Industrialization in Nineteenth Century Europe* (London, 1969), 66.

11 David S. Landes, 'New Model Entrepreneurship in France and Problems of Historical Explanation', *Explorations in Entrepreneurial History*, I (1963), 71.

12 Georges Ripert, *Aspects juridiques du capitalisme moderne*, 2nd edn (Paris, 1951), 23.

13 Charles Coquelin, 'Des sociétés commerciales en France et en Angleterre', *Revue des Deux-Mondes*, III (1843), 397–437.

14 Jean Lhomme, *La Grande Bourgeoisie au pouvoir (1830–1880)* (Paris, 1960), 173.

15 Guy Thuillier, *Aspects de l'économie nivernaise* (Paris, 1966), 500–3.

16 Maurice Lévy-Leboyer, *Les Banques européennes et l'industrialisation internationale dans la première moitié du XIXe siècle* (Paris, 1964), 702–3.

17 Claude Fohlen, 'Sociétés anonymes et développement capitaliste', *Histoire des Entreprises*, VI and VIII (1960–1).

18 Pierre Léon, 'Crises et adaptations de la métallurgie alpine: L'Usine d'Allevard, 1869–1914', *Cahiers d'Histoire*, 1963, 143.

19 David S. Landes, *The Unbound Prometheus: Technical Change and Industrial Development in Western Europe from 1750 to the Present* (Cambridge, 1969), 159.

20 Emile Levasseur, *Histoire des classes ouvrières en France depuis 1789 jusqu'à nos iours*, 2 vols. (Paris, 1867), II, 576.

21 *Journal Officiel*, 1875, p. 9434.

22 Lévy-Leboyer, *Les Banques européennes*, 475–6.

23 Marcel Gillet, 'L'Age du charbon et l'essor du bassin houiller du Nord et du Pas de Calais', in *Charbon et Sciences Humaines*, Proceedings of a colloquium held by the Faculty of Letters of the University of Lille in May 1963 (Paris, 1966). On the coal-mining companies, see Jean Bouvier, François Furet, and Marcel Gillet, *Le Mouvement du profit en France au XIXe siècle: Matériaux et études* (Paris and The Hague, 1965), 294–395.

24 Bertrand Gille, *La Sidérurgie française au XIXe siècle* (Paris and Geneva, 1968), especially chap. 6, 'Les origines d'une grande société métallurgique, Châtillon-Commentry'.

25 *Ibid.*, 295.

26 J. Vial, *L'Industrialisation de la sidérurgie française, 1814–1964*, 2 vols. (Paris and The Hague, 1967).

27 *Ibid.*, I, p. 174; and Lévy-Leboyer, *Les Banques européennes*, 331, 336, and 338.

28 Vial, *op. cit.*, I, pp. 168–9.

29 Jean Bouvier, 'Rapports entre systèmes bancaires et entreprises industrielles', in the colloquium *L'Industrialisation en Europe au XIXe siècle*, Lyons, 7–10 October 1970 (Paris, 1972), 10.

30 G. Thuillier, *Georges Dufaud et les débuts du grand capitalisme dans la métallurgie, en Nivernais, au XIXe siècle* (Paris, 1959), 39–40.

31 *Ibid.*, 42.

32 Gille, *La Sidérurgie française*, 263. See especially *ibid.*, cap. 12, which shows the consequences of technical progress for the self-financing of iron and steel firms.

33 *Ibid.*, 208–9. The increase of investment after 1860 is explained by the adoption

of the Bessemer converter, which obliged the ironmasters to work out a new financial and commercial policy.

34 Bouvier, Furet, and Gillet, *Le Mouvement du profit*, 165–91. See also statistical data and balance sheets, *ibid.*, 409–30.

35 *Ibid.*, 138–9.

36 Léon, 'Crises et adaptations', 146.

37 Rondo Cameron (ed.), *Banking in the Early Stages of Industrialization* (New York and Oxford, 1967); on a special point, outside France, Richard Tilly, *Financial Institutions and Industrialization in the Rhineland, 1815–1870* (Madison, Wisconsin, 1966).

38 B. Gille, 'Les Problèmes du crédit en Alsace et les milieux financiers parisiens (1825–1848)', *Revue d'Alsace*, XCV (1956), 232.

39 Guy Thuillier, 'Pour une histoire bancaire régionale: En Nivernais, de 1800 à 1880, *Annales ESC*, 1955, 498–502.

40 Lévy-Leboyer, *Les Banques européennes*, 450–1.

41 *Ibid.* for a detailed story of this crisis, which is typical of the relations between the banks and industry.

42 *Ibid.* The author quotes the opinion of a Councillor of State, Emile Vincens: 'One must be careful not to multiply banks unnecessarily, and not to establish between them rivalries or alliances. One does not let them exchange notes or be responsible for one another . . .They should be restricted to local discount and to the compensation of receipts and payments.' The government appears to have been very restrictive as far as the powers of the banks are concerned, but we do not know whether it was so in reality.

43 B. Gille, *La Banque et le crédit en France de 1815 à 1848* (Paris, 1959), 149–50.

44 *Ibid.*, 153, quotes, among the beneficiaries, builders of fortifications in Paris, paving and cleaning companies, and companies for building ports, bridges, and canals.

45 David S. Landes, 'Vieille banque et banque nouvelle: La Révolution financière du XIXe siècle', *Revue d'Histoire Moderne et Contemporaine*, III (1956), 204–22. Landes's thesis opposes that of R. Cameron, who considers the 'new' bank different from the 'old'.

46 Jean Bouvier, *Le Crédit Lyonnais de 1863 à 1882*, 2 vols. (Paris, 1961), I, pp. 111–12.

47 *Ibid.*, I, pp. 378–81. This did not prevent the Crédit Lyonnais from becoming involved in various local and regional businesses, but only for short-term loans.

48 Bouvier, 'Rapports entre systèmes bancaires', 10.

49 Gille, *La Sidérurgie française*, 188 and 245.

50 P. Léon, 'Crises et adaptations', 145–6.

51 Henri Morsel, 'L'Innovation technique dans les Alpes françaises du Nord de 1870 à 1921', *Bulletin du Centre d'Histoire Economique et Sociale de la Région Lyonnaise*, II (1970), 31–2.

52 J. Vial, *L'Industrialisation de la sidérurgie*, I, p. 390.

53 Alfred D. Chandler, *Strategy and Structure: Chapters in the History of Industrial Enterprise* (Cambridge, Mass., 1962).

54 François Caron, *Histoire de l'exploitation d'un grand réseau: La Compagnie du Chemin de Fer du Nord, 1846–1937* (Paris and The Hague, 1973).

55 Quoted *ibid.*, 284.

56 Vial, *L'Industrialisation de la sidérurgie*, I, p. 392.

57 *Ibid.*, I, p. 411, n. 6.

58 Léon, 'Crises et adaptations', already quoted.

59 Quoted from Bouvier, Furet, and Gillet, *Le Mouvement du profit*, 15.

60 *Ibid.*, 16.

61 Vial, *op. cit.*, I, pp. 440–1.

CHAPTER VIII

Capital Formation in Germany in the Nineteenth Century

1 F.-W. Henning, 'Kapitalbildungsmöglichkeiten der bäuerlichen Bevölkerung im 19. Jahrhundert', in W. Fischer (ed.), *Beiträge zum Wirtschaftswachstum und Wirtschaftsstruktur im 16. und 19. Jahrhundert* (Berlin, 1971), 58.

2 Knut Borchardt, 'Zur Frage des Kapitalmangels in der ersten Hälfte des 19. Jahrhunderts in Deutschland', *Jahrbücher für Nationalökonomie und Statistik*, XLXXIII (1961), reprinted in R. Braun *et al.* (eds.), *Industrielle Revolution: Wirtschaftliche Aspekte* (Cologne, 1972), 218.

3 J. Higgins and S. Pollard, *Aspects of Capital Investment in Great Britain, 1750–1850* (London, 1971), 6–8 and 27–32.

4 W. Hoffmann *et al.*, *Das Wachstum der deutschen Wirtschaft seit der Mitte des 19. Jahrhunderts* (Berlin, Heidelberg, and New York, 1965). See also Hoffmann's article in F. Lutz and D. C. Hague (eds.), *The Theory of Capital* (London, 1961).

5 This is not the place for a discussion of Rostow's 'stages', which have many serious defects. Nevertheless, they form a useful link between the history of Germany's industrialization and the general problem of economic development on a world-wide scale. That is true of the Marxist school also, of course, and Rostow's stages are in fact (as Rostow claims) an alternative interpretation. Cf. W. W. Rostow, *The Stages of Economic Growth* (Cambridge, 1960); W. W. Rostow (ed.), *The Economics of Take-Off into Self-Sustained Growth* (New York and London, 1963). Ironically, however, the distinctiveness of Rostow's schema lies in its emphasis on technology and an economic determinism it mistakenly attributes to Marxist doctrine (which really emphasizes the political 'controllability' of economic development). The trouble with most Marxist analysis of German development has been in its failure to make explicit connections with the problem of the less-developed countries and the literature dealing with them – something which Rostow's schema does try to do.

6 For brief discussions of the reforms, see Hans Mottek, *Wirtschaftsgeschichte Deutschlands: Ein Grundriss*, II (East Berlin, 1964); Friedrich Lütge, *Deutsche Sozial- und Wirtschaftsgeschichte*, 3rd edn (Berlin, Heidelberg, and New York, 1966), 433–45; E. Klein, *Geschichte der deutschen Landwirtschaft im Industriezeitalter* (Wiesbaden, 1973), 68–91; and also David Landes, 'Die Industrialisierung in Japan und Europa: Ein Vergleich', in Wolfram Fischer (ed.), *Wirtschafts- und sozialgeschichtliche Probleme der frühen Industrialisierung* (Berlin, 1968). This discussion should not imply that the reforms (often called the Stein–Hardenberg reforms) sprang full-blown from the heads of Prussian or German administrators or from the pressure of events of 1806–13 alone. They had significant antecedents and regionally differential results, which space forbids us to discuss here. For some of the relevant literature, see Richard Tilly, 'Soll und Haben: Recent German Economic History and the Problem of Economic Development', *Journal of Economic History*, XXIX (1969).

7 There has been controversy, for example, over the amount of arable land under production in Prussia during 1816–64. For differing views, compare S. von Ciriacy-Wantrup, *Agrarkrisen und Stockungsspannen: Zur Frage der langen 'Wellen' in der wirtschaftlichen Entwicklung* (Berlin, 1936), esp. 41–50; Graf M. W. von Finckenstein, *Die Entwicklung der Landwirtschaft in Preussen und Deutschland, 1800–1930* (Würzburg, 1960), e.g. 34 and 100.

8 This is true even when we exclude the years of great shortage 1846–7, and look at the period 1820–45 only. Klein, *Geschichte der Landwirtschaft*, 116–19, speaks of the 'golden age' of German agriculture from 1830 to 1870, built on a secular relative price increase.

9 See Martin Kutz, 'Die deutsch–britischen Handelsbeziehungen von 1790 bis zur Gründung des Zollvereins', *Vierteljahrschrift für Sozial- und Wirtschaftsgeschichte*, September 1969; or Susan Fairlie, 'The Nineteenth-Century Corn Laws Reconsidered', *Economic History Review*, 2nd ser., XVIII (1965).

10 G. Helling, 'Berechnung eines Index der Agrarproduktion in Deutschland im 19. Jahrhundert', *Jahrbuch für Wirtschaftsgeschichte*, no. 4 (1965); Klein, *Geschichte der Landwirtschaft*; G. Franz, 'Landwirtschaft, 1800–1850', in H. Aubin and W. Zorn (eds.), *Handbuch der deutschen Wirtschafts- und Sozialgeschichte*, II (Stuttgart, 1976), Tables 15 and 16; see also pp. 388–96 below.

11 See von Finckenstein, *Entwicklung der Landwirtschaft*, Table 14; and esp. pp. 396–8 below. Our Tables 79–84 and 109–15 below show significantly larger increases in crop and animal production for the 1850s and 1860s than in the earlier period (with growth rates in 1913 prices of close to 2 per cent per annum as compared with less than 1·5 per cent for the period 1816–49).

12 On export surpluses, Kutz, 'Handelsbeziehungen'; on capital exports, B. Brockhage, *Zur Entwicklung des preussisch–deutschen Kapitalexports*, part I: *Der Berliner Markt für ausländische Staatspapiere 1816 bis um 1840*, Staats- und sozialwissenschaftliche Forschungen, 148 (Leipzig, 1910); Borchardt, 'Frage des Kapitalmangels'.

13 Although the difficulties have often been exaggerated by Germans. See Richard Tilly, 'Los von England: Probleme des Nationalismus in der deutschen Wirtschaftsgeschichte', *Zeitschrift für die gesamte Staatswissenschaft*, CXXIV (1968); Kutz, 'Handelsbeziehungen'.

14 C. F. W. Dieterici (ed.), *Mitteilungen des statistischen Bureaus in Berlin*, II, 12–14 (1849).

15 Increased activity may be reflected in evidence on increased use of the joint-stock company, in the indicators of building activity discussed below, and in employment data. On the first, P. C. Martin, 'Frühindustrielles Gewerbe in der Rechtsform der AG', in Fischer (ed.), *Beiträge*; the second, pp. 399–410 below; the last, K. Kaufhold, 'Handwerk und Industrie, 1800–1850', in Aubin and Zorn (eds.), *Handbuch*, II.

16 W. Hoffmann ('The Take-Off in Germany', in Rostow (ed.), *The Economics of Take-Off*) thought that 1868 was the next big year; but Rainer Fremdling ('Eisenbahnen und deutsches Wirtschaftswachstum, 1840–79', unpublished dissertation, University of Münster, 1974, p. 60) has identified 1859. This railway investment is discussed further below.

17 M. Sering, *Geschichte der preussisch–deutschen Eisenzölle von 1818 bis zur Gegenwart*, Staats- und sozialwissenschaftliche Forschungen, 3 (Leipzig, 1882), 53ff; Fremdling, *op. cit.*

18 Hoffmann *et al.*, *Wachstum der Wirtschaft*, 13.

19 *Ibid.*, Table 42, pp. 259–60.

20 Henning, 'Kapitalbildungsmöglichkeiten', 76. Henning believes that virtually all of this increase in capital per hectare took place between 1830 and 1850, i.e. at the rate of 17 marks per hectare per year, whereas an increase of one mark per hectare – 6 per cent of the estimated average – would have exhausted those savings opportunities.

21 Hoffmann *et al.*, *op. cit.*, 260.

22 This was the ordering found true of all German agriculture before 1850 by Henning (*op. cit.*, 65). However, it seems to be based on a not wholly justifiable mingling of replacement investment and/or working capital and net fixed investment needs. See also Franz, 'Landwirtschaft'.

23 See on this point M. Primack, 'Land Clearing under Nineteenth-Century Techniques: Some Preliminary Calculations', *Journal of Economic History*, XXII (1962).

24 The reference to agricultural unemployment is from T. von der Goltz, *Geschichte*

der deutschen Landwirtschaft, 2 vols. (Stuttgart, 1903; reprinted Aalen, 1963), 222. There is much uncertainty as to the land area under cultivation in Prussia in 1800–50. According to von Ciriacy-Wantrup (*Agrarkrisen*, 42–50), the amount of land under cultivation grew from 9·9 million hectares to 12 million in 1802–49, and further to 14 million hectares by 1864. According to him, it is not likely that a large proportion of the increased share of cultivated land in 1802–61 (up to 51 per cent of the total area from 35 per cent) derived from previously unused waste lands. However, Franz ('Landwirtschaft', following G. Ipsen, 'Die preussische Bauernbefreiung als Landes-ausbau'), *Zeitschrift für Agrargeschichte und Agrarsoziologie*, II (1954) gives an increase of 5·2 million hectares (from 7·3 million to 12·5 million), or more than 70 per cent, in 1816–49.

25 Henning, 'Kapitalbildungsmöglichkeiten', 65; von Finckenstein, *Entwicklung der Landwirtschaft*, 215.

26 Using the numbers in von Finckenstein, *op. cit.*, 100, 230–3, 248, and 329.

27 Hoffmann *et al.*, *Wachstum der Wirtschaft*, 288–94.

28 The 'feed crops included here have been valued with fractions of grain prices as suggested by the 'cereal values' (based on nutritional content) used by von Finckenstein (*op. cit.*, 6). Turnips were valued with potato prices, and half of annual production was allocated to feed.

29 Henning, *op. cit.*, 65.

30 Franz, 'Landwirtschaft', Table 9 (weighting Franz's yields with average crop output data from our Table 31).

31 Von Ciriacy-Wantrup (*Agrarkrisen*, 71) pointed out that the inability of Prussian agricultural producers to divert a significant share of output into livestock feed before the 1830s reflected, just as it perpetuated, a capital-poor agriculture. He mentioned credit conditions as one significant dimension of the problem, and one possible solution.

32 The technology of agricultural production was not, to be sure, the only factor creating and holding large supplies of resources in agriculture. See Ipsen, 'Preussische Bauernbefreiung', and R. Koselleck, *Preussen zwischen Reform und Revolution: Allgemeines Landrecht, Verwaltung und soziale Bewegung* (Stuttgart, 1967); also Klein, *Geschichte der Landwirtschaft*, 90.

33 See the Appendix to this chapter for basic data and estimating procedures.

34 One serious deficiency in our data is the absence of reliable deflators for the building stock. Where estimates are given in 1913 prices, the building figures (maintenance, depreciation and rental income) are mere guesses (based on the building stock in current values).

35 G. Hohorst gives for Prussia a figure of 156 marks per head. His data are based on an estimating procedure linking income data of Hoffmann and Müller and others for the period 1850–1913 to employment structure and regional differences, and using these to extrapolate back to 1816. Most of the data and procedure are given in Gerd Hohorst, 'Bevölkerungsentwicklung und Wirtschaftswachstum in Preussen, 1816 bis 1914' (dissertation, University of Münster, 1974); and cf. W. Hoffmann and J. Müller, *Das deutsche Volkseinkommen 1851–1957* (Tübingen, 1959). But see below, Table 115, where fairly close agreement with Hohorst is reached. Dieterici's data on consumption per head lie far below this (at around 88–90 marks in 1913 prices): cf. C. F. W. Dieterici, *Der Volkswohlstand im preussischen Staat* (Berlin, 1846).

36 Jürgen Kuczynski, *Die Geschichte der Lage der Arbeiter unter dem Kapitalismus*, vol. 1 (East Berlin, 1961), Appendix II, pp. 355–72. This is a non-weighted average, excluding non-monetary compensation and assuming that 60 per cent of the agricultural population earned wages; but these facts are not obviously at variance with reality, nor is the assumption of 200 working days per year.

37 Von Finckenstein, *Entwicklung der Landwirtschaft*, pp. 109–20, and *ibid.*, Tables 65–8, pp. 385–8, treating agricultural debt. He argues that Landschaften financed a smaller share of debt of landed estates than other credit institutions, so we have doubled his figures and applied the highest annual interest rates to that sum. Hoffmann *et al.*, *Wachstum der Wirtschaft*, gives values higher than von Finckenstein's, so we have included in the text a higher and lower figure – the former referring to Hoffmann's estimates. Brockhage, *Zur Entwicklung: Der Berliner Markt* (a good older study still worth consulting) sees agriculture during the 1820s and 1830s in general as a surplus sector which was channelling funds on net balance into the Prussian capital market.

38 Hoffmann and Müller, *op. cit.*, give for 1851 a value of 248 marks in 1913 prices. Hohorst, *op. cit.*, estimates 252 marks per head for 1849.

39 Taking crop production figures for 1852 instead of 1849 produces a fall in gross product of 276 million marks (in 1913 prices) and in net output per head a fall of nearly 10 per cent (to about 300 marks). On the other hand, broadening the price basis for potatoes to include observations for Breslau and Cologne lowers the percentage growth of net output for 1816–49 from 139 per cent to 138 per cent, and per capita product in 1849 from 328·5 marks to 326.

40 Franz, 'Landwirtschaft', Table 8, follows Ipsen, 'Preussische Bauernbefreiung', in estimating a 70 per cent increase in arable land in Prussia in 1815–49.

41 Cf. Kuczynski, *Die Lage der Arbeiter*, 1 (1961); C. Jantke and D. Hilger, *Die Eigentumslosen, der deutsche Pauperismus und die Emzanzipationskrise in Darstellungen und Deutungen der zeitgenössischen Literatur* (Freiburg and Munich, 1965).

42 A correlation coefficient of $r = 0.91$ was found to characterize the relationship between annual changes in harvest returns (Hoffmann *et al.*, *op. cit.*, Table 50) and investment in stocks.

43 Hoffmann *et al.*, *op. cit.*, 37, shows annual increases in agricultural product per worker of 1·2 per cent during 1850–1913; whereas in industry and trade – despite its large, low-productivity service component – productivity rose by 1·8 per cent and in mining by 2 per cent. Interesting in this connection is William Parker's observation (applied to American agriculture) that the triumphs of modern science so celebrated by historians of industrialization came quite late and incompletely, as far as the biological processes governing agriculture were concerned. See W. N. Parker, 'Productivity Growth in American Grain Farming: An Analysis of Its 19th-Century Sources', in R. W. Fogel and Stanley I. Engerman (eds.), *The Reinterpretation of American Economic History* (New York, Evanston, San Francisco, and London, 1971), 181–2.

44 Hoffmann *et al.*, *op. cit.*

45 The share in total capital stock increased more than the share in investment because of the longevity of such capital. See *ibid.*, 253–4.

46 A study of the subject of capital formation in housing in Germany in the first half of the nineteenth century would be very desirable – and feasible.

47 C. F. W. Dieterici, *Handbuch der Statistik des preussischen Staates* (Berlin, 1861), 173–4.

48 F. W. von Reden, *Deutschland und das übrige Europa* (Wiesbaden, 1854), 240; von Reden, *Erwerbs- und Verkehrsstatistik des Königstaats Preussen* (Darmstadt, 1853), 40–6. A more recent examination of the question, however, suggests substantial over-insurance, at least for one part of Prussia (the Rhineland). See W. Zorn, 'Die wirtschaftliche Struktur der Rheinprovinz um 1820', *Vierteljahrschrift für Sozial- und Wirtschaftsgeschichte*, IV, 3 (1967), esp. 299 and 303–4.

49 See Prussia, Königliches Preussisches Statistisches Bureau, *Tabellen amtliche und Nachrichten für das Jahr 1849*, I–VI (Berlin, 1853). Also Hoffmann *et al.*, *Wachstum der Wirtschaft*, for the small amount of business plant in 1850 (and, *a fortiori*, in the pre-1850

years). Also the article 'Feuerversicherung' in *Handwörterbuch der Staatswissenschaften* (Jena, 1909).

50 For an analogous argument, see Simon Kuznets, *Modern Economic Growth: Rate, Structure, Spread* (New Haven, Conn., 1966), 20–6.

51 The sub-sample consisted of (a) some 100 towns and villages selected at random from the statistical returns edited by L. Krug and L. von Mützell (*Neues topographisch-statistisch-geographisches Wörterbuch des preussischen Staates*, 6 vols. (Halle, 1825)), for 1816 and 1821, and arrayed by size and degree of urbanization; (b) the thirteen counties of the Prussian district of Düsseldorf in 1834; (c) the five districts of the Rhineland as of 1828; and (d) data on building values and population size of cities (presumably closely related to urbanization), as reported by von Reden (*Erwerbs- und Verkehrs-statistik*, 40–6).

52 A true model of capital formation in the building sector would need to include, at a minimum, supply-side elements such as the cost of building (including interest rates) and the already available stock of buildings, as well as the demand side. Some discussion of this problem as it applies to the period 1850–1913 may be found below.

53 D. Hansemann, *Preussen und Frankreich* (Leipzig, 1833), 36–52; G. von Viebahn, *Statistik und Geographie des Regierungs-Bezirks Düsseldorf* (Düsseldorf, 1836), 153–4 and 245.

54 Hans-Jürgen Kinkel ('Kapitalbildung und Finanzierungsprobleme im Ruhrge-biet, 1830–1880', unpublished diploma thesis, University of Münster, 1968) has found many references to rental values for the Rhineland and Westphalia lying below the 3 per cent cited by von Viebahn. This is an open question; however, Hansemann (*op. cit.*, 52) estimated capital value of buildings at twenty times the value of taxable income (a 5 per cent return) but argued that half of the rental values represented maintenance costs (*ibid.*, 35).

55 Farm buildings in Prussia, like land, were taxed purely on an area basis.

56 Hoffmann *et al.*, *Wachstum der Wirtschaft*, 218–28.

57 The index was equally weighted for material and labour costs. It may be some-what distorted since it employs wages of construction workers, whereas for farm building, farm-labour wages might be more appropriate. The data come from: A. Jacobs and H. Richter, *Die Grosshandelspreise in Deutschland von 1792 bis 1934*, Sonder-hefte des Instituts für Konjunkturforschung (Berlin, 1935), 78; Kuczynski, *Die Lage der Arbeiter*, I, pp. 244–6, 251, and Appendixes I–III; *ibid.*, II, pp. 145ff; Gerhard Bry, *Wages in Germany, 1871–1945* (Princeton, 1960), Tables A-4 and A-12.

58 L. Krug, *Betrachtungen über den Nationalreichtum der preussischen Staaten*, 2 vols. (Berlin, 1805; reprinted Aalen, 1967), I, pp. 279ff. Krug called this capital 'dead capital', which had to be supported by real income flows ('*echte Nationalzinsen*') generated elsewhere – naturally in agriculture.

59 Hansemann, *Preussen und Frankreich*, 35.

60 Evidence on this in von Viebahn, *Statistik und Geographie*, 153–4. Kinkel ('Kapi-talbildung und Finanzierungsprobleme') also has scattered evidence to report.

61 From Kinkel, *op. cit.*

62 These census data are contained in the Appendix below, Table 116.

63 This assumes that some part of the increases in urban population work positively on the values of farm buildings.

64 Prussian government spending rose by about 65 per cent in 1821–56, and by around 90 per cent in 1821–66 (Richard Tilly, 'The Political Economy of Public Finance and Prussian Industrialization, 1815–1866', *Journal of Economic History*, XXVI (1966), 492).

65 Von Reden, *Deutschland und das übrige Europa*.

66 Hoffmann *et al.*, *Wachstum der Wirtschaft*.

67 Hoffmann and Müller, *Das deutsche Volkseinkommen*, 39–40 and 86–7, show a difference in average per capita income of less than 10 per cent between Prussia and non-Prussian Germany in 1851–5.

68 Knut Borchardt, *Hundert Jahre Rheinische Hypothekenbank* (Frankfurt, 1971), 114.

69 *Ibid.*, 115–16.

70 See A. Hirschman, *The Strategy of Economic Development* (New Haven, Conn., 1958); R. Jochimsen, *Theorie der Infrastruktur: Grundlagen der marktwirtschaftlichen Entwicklung* (Tübingen, 1966).

71 Kuznets, *Modern Economic Growth*, 20–6.

72 Karl Borchard, 'Staatsverbrauch und öffentliche Investitionen in Deutschland, 1780–1850' (doctoral dissertation, University of Göttingen, 1968), 169–70 and 180–1. Expenditures for industry, commerce, and public works rose from some 3 per cent of all expenditures in 1821 to nearly 10 per cent in 1850, but most of this spending was for transportation. Spending on 'culture', 'instruction', and 'health' rose from around 4 per cent of total spending in 1821 to 5 per cent (more than ten million marks) in 1850.

73 Borchard, *op. cit.*, 176–7 and 180.

74 I have drawn especially on *ibid.*, 260–8; F. H. Ungewitter, *Die preussische Monarchie* (Berlin, 1859), esp. 48–53; and F. W. von Reden, *Finanz-Statistik*, 3 vols. (Darmstadt, 1856), vol. II. I became aware of Gador's work too late to make it worth-while to alter my calculations. His study is informative, but his numbers are not radically different. R. Gador, 'Die Entwicklung des Strassenbaues in Preussen 1815–1875 unter besonderer Berücksichtigung des Aktienstrassenbaues' (unpublished dissertation, Free University of Berlin, 1966).

75 We employ for our calculations somewhat different numbers, following Ungewitter, *op. cit.*, 49ff, and Preussisches Statistisches Bureau, *Tabellen und amtliche Nachrichten für das Jahr 1849*, IV, 254, which show an increase in physical capacity of close to 380 per cent between 1816 and 1853, and a total figure for 1852 lying roughly 15–20 per cent above Borchard's figures.

76 Von Reden, *Finanz-Statistik*, II, part 2, p. 401. Cf. also Gador, *op. cit.*, 155.

77 Borchard, 'Staatsverbrauch und öffentliche Investititionen', 277.

78 Von Reden, *Finanz-Statistik*, II, part 2, pp. 398 and 400.

79 Borchard, *op. cit.*, 225–59.

80 U. Ritter, *Die Rolle des Staates in den Frühstadien der Industrialisierung: Die preussische Industrieförderung in der ersten Hälfte des 19. Jahrhunderts* (Berlin, 1961), 141.

81 See the first section of this chapter for some discussion of this question with references; in addition, Mottek, *Wirtschaftsgeschichte Deutschlands*, II, 150–6; Tilly, 'Political Economy'; and now Fremdling, 'Eisenbahnen und Wirtschaftswachstum', for this whole question. One old standard work on German railways, still useful, is E. Sax, *Die Eisenbahnen*, vol. III of *Die Verkehrsmittel in Volks- und Staatswirtschaft*, 2nd edn (Berlin, 1922).

82 Hoffmann *et al.*, *Wachstum der Wirtschaft*, 255; also Hoffmann, 'The Take-Off in Germany', graph p. 105, discussion 105–6.

83 Fremdling, *op. cit.*, 62.

84 German work comparable to that of Fogel or Fishlow for the United States is just beginning to appear. Rainer Fremdling's 1974 dissertation (*op. cit.*) plays an important role in the following discussion (my thanks are due to him for his assistance). For a special problem, see also H. Wagenblass, *Der Eisenbahnbau und das Wachstum der deutschen Eisen- und Maschinenbauindustrie, 1835 bis 1860* (Stuttgart, 1973).

85 C. Holtfrerich, *Quantitative Wirtschaftsgeschichte des Ruhrkohlenbergbaus im 19. Jahrhundert: Eine Führungssektoranalyse* (Dortmund, 1973), chap. 5; Fremdling, *op. cit.*, 332–48, has shown that Holtfrerich may have overestimated the railways' impact

because of his use of the fixed input–output coefficients. The large contribution which German railways made to the level of demand faced by the iron and coal industries distinguish the German case from those of Great Britain or the United States.

86 Holtfrerich, *op. cit.*; Sering, *Geschichte der Eisenzölle*, 53ff and Appendix 10.

87 The 1840s were marked by a huge fall in freight and passenger rates and a corresponding increase in railway revenues. Cf. Fremdling, *op. cit.*

88 Borchard, 'Staatsverbrauch und öffentlich Investitionen', 198 and 298.

89 Borchard writes (*ibid.*, 300–1):

> Summing up, we may say that Prussia, hindered by that unhappy link between constitutional reform and government borrowing, had to limit her support of railway expansion to spending out of current revenues; not until 1849 was she able to follow the example of the other German states and push railway-building in areas which private capital had avoided and/or to finance her support of private enterprises with public loans.

See also Tilly, 'Political Economy'. However, Fremdling's work suggests still another explanation of the Prussian subsidy policies: private capital was interested enough to obviate the need for subsidy.

90 Hoffmann *et al.*, *Wachstum der Wirtschaft*, 261.

91 *Ibid.*, 567; Fremdling, 'Eisenbahnen und Wirtschaftswachstum'.

92 Sax, *Die Eisenbahnen*, 274, applies a 2·5 per cent rate around 1900, and Fremdling think the 2 per cent rate appropriate for the earlier period.

93 Hoffmann, 'The Take-Off in Germany'; A. Spiethoff, *Die wirtschaftlichen Wechsellagen*, 2 vols. (Tübingen, 1955), I, pp. 113–17; J. Schumpeter, *Business Cycles: A Theoretical, Historical and Statistical Analysis of the Capitalist Process*, 2 vols. (New York, 1939), I, pp. 346–7 and 350–1.

94 The figures of Hoffmann *et al.* are not wholly comparable with those in our Table 50 above, nor even wholly unobjectionable, since the Hoffmann price index and employment data are faulty, especially for the 1850s. On this, see Fremdling, *op. cit.*

95 Hoffmann *et al.*, *op. cit.*, 259–60.

96 *Ibid.*; P. Jostock, 'The Long-Term Growth of National Income in Germany', *Studies in Income and Wealth*, ser. V (London, 1955); R. Wagenführ, *Die industrie-wirtschaftlichen Entwicklungstendenzen der deutschen und internationalen Industrieproduktion 1860 bis 1932*, Sonderhefte des Instituts für Konjunkturforschung, 31 (Berlin, 1933); Karl Helfferich, *Deutschlands Volkswohlstand, 1888–1913* (Berlin, 1913).

97 Borchardt, 'Frage des Kapitalmangels', 218.

98 H. Blumberg, *Die deutsche Textilindustrie in der industriellen Revolution* (East Berlin, 1965), 43–52.

99 The data are derived mainly from Dieterici, *Volkswohlstand*, and Dieterici, *Handbuch der Statistik*. It may be stretching the point somewhat to include wine and brandy among 'industrial' products.

100 Hoffmann *et al.*, *Wachstum der Wirtschaft*, 454–5. The transportation sector admittedly produced consumption as well as productive services. The reader is referred to this whole section of Hoffmann *et al.*, 335ff. Also relevant in this connection is W. Hoffmann, *Growth of Industrial Economies*, transl. W. O. Henderson and W. H. Chaloner (Manchester, 1958).

101 As cited in note *b* of Table 53 above.

102 See Appendix D below for further details.

103 Relying mainly on G. Kirchhain, 'Das Wachstum der deutschen Baumwoll-industrie im 19. Jahrhundert' (doctoral dissertation, University of Münster, 1971 (privately published in photocopy)), 115; Blumberg, *Deutsche Textilindustrie*, 386–7,

his Appendix; G. von Viebahn, *Statistik des zollvereinten und nördlichen Deutschlands*, 3 vols. (Berlin, 1962), III.

104 Carl Brinkmann, 'The Place of Germany in the Economic History of the Nineteenth Century', *Economic History Review*, 1933.

105 I follow here a suggestion of Holtfrerich's to the effect that steam horsepower plus machine price index changes give a good reflection of investment activity in mining. For 1852 and 1840 we have, as remarked in the text, the benchmark estimates (derived independently of steam-horsepower data) made by Kinkel ('Kapitalbildung und Finanzierungsprobleme'); Holtfrerich's work has been cited above (*Wirtschafts-geschichte des Ruhrukohlenbergbaus*).

106 One ought to avoid regarding the estimates as more than hints about orders of magnitude, because – to mention just one difficulty – the capital–output ratios will shift with the business cycle, and will be different in the coal industry from other industries.

107 Table 107 applies the combined cotton–coal depreciation rate to our sample of twelve industries. The replacement investment reflects this charge alone, and working capital being renewed every year – which would have amounted in 1852 to around 200 million marks for textiles alone – has not been treated as seed inputs in agriculture were treated earlier but has been excluded or, rather, referred to as part of the permanent capital stock.

108 Our work thus confirms previous impressions of the capital needs and resources in this stage of Prussian (and German) development.

109 Government subsidies to agriculture might be included in this investment: in 1850 such subsidies amounted to 4·2 million marks.

110 For this question consult von Ciriacy-Wantrup, *Agrarkrisen*, 17–102; von Finckenstein, *Entwicklung der Landwirtschaft*, 98–120; and A. Ucke, 'Die Agrarkrise in Preussen während der zwanziger Jahre dieses Jahrhunderts' (doctoral dissertation, University of Halle, 1887).

111 How much they would grow is an open question. In Prussia in 1850, public expenditures in the areas of health, education, and research amounted to about 10 million marks, or 5 per cent of estimated total net investment (and 5 per cent of total central-government spending). Borchard, 'Staatsverbrauch und öffentliche Investitionen', 200. Some of this spending surely represented consumption, however.

112 Taking the combined growth for textiles and coal during 1852–61 (in Prussia), we get an average annual rate of increase of 6·2 per cent, as against an estimated rate of increase for all capital of about 3·5 per cent (in current prices).

113 For an attempt to discuss the Hirschman thesis using the data of Hoffmann *et al.* (*Wachstum der Wirtschaft*), see D. Klement, *Strukturwandlungen des Kapitalstocks nach Anlagearten in Deutschland seit der Mitte des 19. Jahrhunderts* (Tübingen, 1967). More work is necessary here. For the thesis itself, Hirschman, *Strategy of Economic Development*. See also Fremdling, 'Eisenbahnen und Wirtschaftswachstum'.

114 In this study, the distinction between capital expenditures and capital costs could be only imperfectly followed, and we thus have only a very rough idea of what 'true' depreciation and maintenance costs – and hence true gross investment – amounted to. Actual expenditures may be an inadequate guide here. However, it is not clear that such expenditures necessarily and chronically understate true capital costs during industrialization, because certain capital expenditures may produce services which, in turn, generate capital-saving productivity increases.

115 Von Finckenstein, *Entwicklung der Landwirtschaft*; Jacobs and Richter, *Gross-handelspreise in Deutschland*; Ernst Engel, 'Die Viehhaltung im preussischen Staate in der Zeit von 1816 bis mit 1858', *Zeitschrift des Königlichen Preussischen Statistischen Bureaus*, I, 8 (1861); Hoffmann *et al.*, *Wachstum der Wirtschaft*.

116 Von Finckenstein, *op. cit.*, 100, 248, and 329.

117 *Ibid.*, 214–15; Jacobs and Richter, *op. cit.*, 16. Hoffmann *et al.*, *op. cit.*, 291.

118 Gador, 'Entwicklung des Strassenbaues', 70, 123, 130–1, 134–5, 137, and 143–4.

119 Blumberg, *Deutsche Textilindustrie*; Kirchhain, 'Wachstum der Baumwoll-industrie'; Dieterici, *Volkswohlstand*; Dieterici, *Handbuch der Statistik*; von Viebahn, *Statistik und Geographie*. Hoffmann *et al.*, *op. cit.*

120 Dieterici, *Volkswohlstand*; Dieterici, *Handbuch der Statistik*.

121 Dieterici, *Volkswohlstand*; Holtfrerich, *Wirtschaftsgeschichte des Ruhrkohlenberg-baus*.

122 Dieterici, *Volkswohlstand*; Dieterici, *Handbuch der Statistik*; Engel, *Zeitalter des Dampfes*.

123 Holtfrerich, *op. cit.*, 152; Kirchhain, *op. cit.*, 122.

124 Kirchhain, *op. cit.*, 109; Blumberg, *op. cit.*

CHAPTER IX

Labour in German Industrialization

1 All references to Germany relate to the boundaries of 1 September 1914, unless otherwise specified.

2 John E. Knodel, *The Decline of Fertility in Germany, 1871–1939* (Princeton, 1974), 32.

3 *Ibid.*, 190; J. Kuczynski, *Die Geschichte der Lage der Arbeiter unter dem Kapitalismus*, 38 vols. (East Berlin, 1961–), IV, 318–19; Germany, Kaiserliche Statistische Amt, *Statistik des deutschen Reichs*, 2nd ser., CCXI, 304 and 307.

4 W. Köllmann, 'Industrialisierung, Binnenwanderung und "Soziale Frage"': Entstehungsgeschichte der deutschen Industriegrossstadt im 19. Jahrhundert', *Viertel-jahrschrift für Sozial- und Wirtschaftsgeschichte*, XLV (1959).

5 J. Kocka, *Unternehmensverwaltung und Angestelltenschaft am Beispiel Siemens, 1847–1914* (Stuttgart, 1969), 337 n.7 and 338 n.11.

6 See, for example, the hysterical account in D. Lande, 'Arbeits- und Lohnverhält-nisse in der Berliner Maschinenindustrie zu Beginn des 20. Jahrhunderts', *Schriften des Vereins für Sozialpolitik*, CXXXIV (1910), 322ff.

7 L. von Bienkowski, 'Untersuchungen über Arbeitseignung und Leistungs-fähigkeit der Arbeiterschaft einer Kabelfabrik', *Schriften des Vereins für Sozialpolitik*, CXXXIV (1910), 4.

8 Estimated from W. G. Hoffmann *et al.*, *Das Wachstum der deutschen Wirtschaft seit der Mitte des 19. Jahrhunderts* (Berlin, 1965), 194ff; *Statistik des deutschen Reichs*, 2nd ser., CCXI, 80.

9 See the suggestive survey by F. Syrup, 'Die Beschaffung von Arbeitskräften für die Industrie während des Krieges', *Jahrbücher für Nationalökonomie und Statistik*, LII (1916).

10 L. Pieper, *Die Lage der Bergarbeiter im Ruhrrevier* (Stuttgart, 1903), 71–9.

11 K. Hinze, *Die Arbeiterfrage zu Beginn des modernen Kapitalismus in Brandenburg–Preussen* (Berlin, 1927; reprinted 1963), 186; R. Forberger, *Die Manufaktur in Sachsen vom Ende des 16. bis zum Anfang des 19. Jahrhunderts* (East Berlin, 1958), 61, 134, 225, 282, and 290; O. Reuter, *Die Manufaktur im fränkischen Raum* (Stuttgart, 1961), 85; H. Kisch, 'From Monopoly to Laissez Faire: The Early Growth of the Wupper Valley Textile Trades', *Journal of European Economic History*, I (1972), 318.

12 Hinze, *op. cit.*, 55–63.

13 I. Lange-Kothe, 'Die ersten Dampfmaschinen im Düsseldorfer Raum', *Düssel-*

dorfer Jahrbuch, v, 1 (1963), 303; R. Strauss, *Die Lage und die Bewegung der Chemnitzer Arbeiter in der ersten Hälfte des 19. Jahrhunderts* (East Berlin, 1960), 54–5 and 59; W. O. Henderson, *Britain and Industrial Europe, 1750–1870* (Liverpool, 1954; 2nd edn, Leicester, 1965), 146–54; A. Schröter and W. Becker, *Die deutsche Maschinenbauindustrie in der industriellen Revolution* (East Berlin, 1962), 76, 225, 227, and 237; H. Wagenblass, *Der Eisenbahnbau und das Wachstum der deutschen Eisen- und Maschinenbauindustrie, 1835 bis 1860* (Stuttgart, 1973), 13–15.

14 R. J., 'Erlebnisse eines Metalldrehers', *Thünen-Archiv*, II (1909), 732; H. Hinke, 'Auslese und Anpassung der Arbeiter im Buchdruckergewerbe mit besonderer Rücksichtnahme auf die Setzmaschine', *Schriften des Vereins für Sozialpolitik*, cxxxiv (1910), 85; C. Heiss, 'Auslese und Anpassung der Arbeiter in der Berliner Feinmechanik', *ibid.*, 228; Bienkowski, 'Untersuchungen über Arbeitseignung und Leistungsfähigkeit', 6.

15 The number of emigrants who left the rest of Germany between 1871 and 1874 would probably have increased the non-agricultural labour force of the Rhineland and Westphalia by about 10 per cent, at that stage.

16 W. H. Dawson, *The German Workman* (London, 1906), 1–8; W. H. Beveridge, 'Public Labour Exchanges in Germany', *Economic Journal*, xviii (1908); O. Weigert, 'Die Organisation des Arbeitsmarktes', in B. Harms (ed.), *Strukturwandlungen der deutschen Volkswirtschaft*, 2 vols. (Berlin, 1928), i, pp. 472ff; H. Kühne, 'Der Arbeitseinsatz im Vier Jahres Plan', *Jahrbücher für Nationalökonomie und Statistik*, cxlvii (1937), 694–5.

17 Dawson, *The German Workman*.

18 *Statistik des deutschen Reichs*, 2nd ser., ccxi, 231 and 268–9.

19 M. Bernays, 'Berufswahl und Berufsschicksal des modernen Industriearbeiters', *Archiv für Sozialwissenschaft und Sozialpolitik*, xxxv (1912), 140; K. Gaebel, 'Eine Lanze für die Ungelernten!', *Soziale Praxis*, xlv, 21 (23 May 1936), col. 594.

20 W. Fischer, 'Das deutsche Handwerk in der Frühphase der Industrialisierung', *Zeitschrift für die gesamte Staatswissenschaft*, cxx (1964); Fischer, 'Die Rolle des Kleingewerbes im wirtschaftlichen Wachstumsprozess in Deutschland, 1850–1914', in *Wirtschaftliche und soziale Probleme der gewerbliche Entwicklung im 15.–16. und 19. Jahrhundert* (Stuttgart, 1968).

21 G. I. H. Lloyd, 'Labour Organisation in the Cutlery Trade of Solingen', *Economic Journal*, xviii (1908), 376.

22 P. Voigt, 'Die Hauptergebnisse der neuesten deutschen Handwerksstatistik von 1895', *Schmollers Jahrbuch*, xxi (1897), 238; W. Fischer and P. Czada, 'Wandlungen in der deutschen Industriestruktur im 20. Jahrhundert', in G. A. Ritter (ed.), *Entstehung und Wandel der modernen Gesellschaft* (Berlin, 1970), 160; Fischer, 'Die Rolle des Kleingewerbes'.

23 Statistik des deutschen Reichs, 2nd ser., ccccLxii, section 3, part 11; W. Sombart, *Der moderne Kapitalismus*, 2nd edn, 3 vols. (Munich and Leipzig, 1916; reprinted Berlin, 1955), III, part 1, pp. 439–41; H. Studders, *Die Facharbeiterfrage in der Kriegswirtschaft* (Hamburg, 1938), 33 and 72–5.

24 P. H. Noyes, *Organization and Revolution: Working Class Associations in the German Revolutions of 1848–49* (Princeton, 1966), 29, 319–20, and 374.

25 U. P. Ritter, *Die Rolle des Staates in den Frühstadien der Industrialisierung* (Berlin, 1961), 18–21; K. H. Rau, *Grundsätze der Volkswirtschaftspolitik*, 5th edn (Leipzig, 1862), 46.

26 Noyes, *Organization and Revolution*, 35, 75, and 189; Strauss, *Die Lage und die Bewegung der Chemnitzer Arbeiter*, 38.

27 Strauss, *op. cit.*, 134–5; T. C. Banfield, *Industry of the Rhine*, 2 vols. (1846–8), II, p. 133.

28 M. E. Sadleir, *Continuation Schools in England and Elsewhere* (Manchester, 1908), 517ff; Kocka, *Unternehmensverwaltung und Angestelltenschaft*, 471 n.28.

29 P. W. Musgrave, *Technical Change: The Labour Force and Education* (Oxford, 1967), 111.

30 *Ibid.*, 90–1; Bienkowski, 'Untersuchungen über Arbeitseignung und Leistungsfähigkeit', 6.

31 W. O. Henderson, 'Peter Beuth and the Rise of Prussian Industry, 1810–1845', *Economic History Review*, 2nd ser., VIII (1955–6).

32 Musgrave, *op. cit.*, 66ff.

33 *Ibid.*, 125ff; Kocka, *op. cit.*, 471 n.24; G. Kotowski, 'Bildungswesen', in H. Herzfeld (ed.), *Berlin und die Provinz Brandenburg im 19. und 20. Jahrhundert* (Berlin, 1968), 547.

34 Schröter and Becker, *Die deutsche Maschinenbauindustrie*, 200; James Samuelson, *The German Working Man* (London, 1869), 10 and 105–7.

35 W. Köllmann, *Friedrich Harkort* (Hagen, 1965).

36 R. Ehrenberg, 'Schwäche und Stärkung neuzeitlicher Arbeitsgemeinschaften', *Archiv für exacte Wirtschaftsforschung*, III (1911), 450ff; F. Syrup, 'Studien über den industriellen Arbeiterwechsel, *ibid.*, IV (1912), 264ff.

37 Ehrenberg, *op. cit.*, 448–57; Pieper, *Die Lage der Bergarbeiter*, 125–6; Bienkowski, 'Untersuchungen über Arbeitseignung und Leistungsfähigkeit', 21; C. Heiss, 'Auslese und Anpassung', 141ff; E. Bernhard, 'Auslese und Anpassung der Arbeiterschaft', *Schmollers Jahrbuch*, XXXV (1911), 380.

38 Ehrenberg, *op. cit.*, 461 and 469; Sombart, *Der moderne Kapitalismus*, III, part 1, p. 442; Syrup, 'Studien über den industriellen Arbeiterwechsel'.

39 E. C. McCreary, 'Social Welfare and Business: The Krupp Welfare Program, 1860–1914', *Business History Review*, XLII, 1 (1968), 31ff.

40 R. A. Brady, *The Rationalization Movement in German Industry* (Berkeley, Calif., 1933), 81.

41 Dr Schnorbus, 'Einiges aus dem Zeisswerk, Jena', *Der Arbeiterfreund*, L (1912), 453ff.

42 Syrup, 'Studien über den industriellen Arbeiterwechsel', 294; Reports of the Gainsborough Commission, *Life and Labour in Germany* (London, 1906), 26ff.

43 Hinze, *Die Arbeiterfrage*, 197–8.

44 Bernays, 'Berufswahl und Berufsschicksal', 162; F. Wörishoffer, *Die soziale Lage der Fabrikarbeiter in Mannheim* (Karlsruhe, 1891), 55; W. Zimmermann, 'Zur sozialen Lage der Eisenbahner in Preussen', *Schriften des Vereins für Sozialpolitik*, XCIX (1902), 84; R. J., 'Erlebnisse eines Metalldrehers', 737ff, 748, 752, and 756.

45 P. C. Ludz (ed.), *Soziologie und Sozialgeschichte* (Opladen, 1973), 553ff; Hinze, *op. cit.*, 139.

46 P. Göhre, *Three Months in a Workshop* (London, 1895: translation of *Drei Monate Fabrikarbeiter* (Leipzig, 1891), 67–8.

47 Pieper, *Die Lage der Bergarbeiter*, 30, 67, and 93.

48 Bernays, *op. cit.*, 162.

49 Kocka, *Unternehmensverwaltung und Angestelltenschaft*, 484.

50 Henderson, *Britain and Industrial Europe*, 9, 146 n.33, and 148 n.40.

51 W. H. Dawson, *Industrial Germany* (London, 1912), 238ff.

52 K. H. Ludwig, 'Die Fabrikarbeit von Kindern im 19. Jahrhundert', *Vierteljahrschift für Sozial- und Wirtschaftsgeschichte*, LII (1965), 68; Lande, 'Arbeits- und Lohnverhältnisse', 458; Heiss, 'Auslese und Anpassung', 229; A. Thun, *Die Industrie am Niederrhein und ihre Arbeiter*, 2 vols. (Leipzig, 1879), I, p. 51.

53 J. Kuczynski, *Die Geschichte der Lage der Arbeiter unter dem Kapitalismus*, I, p. 231; *ibid.*, XVIII, 68; W. Brepohl, *Industrievolk im Wandel von der agraren zur industriellen*

Daseinform dargestellt am Ruhrgebiet (Tübingen, 1967), 97; Forberger, *Die Manufaktur in Sachsen*, 64.

54 L. Puppke, *Sozialpolitik und soziale Anschauungen frühindustrieller Unternehmer in Rheinland und Westfalen* (Cologne, 1966), 46ff.

55 Ludwig, *op. cit.*, 68 and 77–8.

56 Strauss, *Die Lage und die Bewegung der Chemnitzer Arbeiter*, 21–2 and 49–50.

57 *Statistik des deutschen Reichs*, 2nd ser., CCXI, 120.

58 Pieper, *Die Lage der Bergarbeiter*, 17–20.

59 *Ibid.*, 21; R. Heberle and F. Meyer, *Die Grossstädte im Strome der Binnenwanderung* (Leipzig, 1937), 157ff.

60 The implications of the discovery that unrest in early industrialization was largely fomented by local-born rather than immigrant workers deserve to be carefully pondered. R. Tilly, 'Popular Disturbances in Nineteenth Century Germany: A Preliminary Survey', *Journal of Social History*, IV (1970), 25.

61 Sombart, *Der moderne Kapitalismus*, III, part 1, pp. 430–1; Bernays, 'Berufswahl und Berufsschicksal', 140–1.

62 Strauss, *Die Lage und die Bewegung der Chemnitzer Arbeiter*, 130ff.

63 Noyes, *Organization and Revolution*.

64 Strauss, *op. cit.*, 23.

65 For the unreliability of images as guides to reality with reference to one major group, see John G. Gagliardo, *From Pariah to Patriot: The Changing Image of the German Peasant, 1770–1840* (Lexington, Kentucky, 1969).

66 Brady, *The Rationalization Movement*.

67 Piper, *Die Lage der Bergarbeiter*, 113. Pieper's data indicate intense eagerness to work overtime and low rates of absenteeism in the late nineteenth century (pp. 48 and 54).

68 See, e.g., J. Kuczynski, *Die Geschichte der Lage der Arbeiter unter dem Kapitalismus*, II, 152.

69 G. Bry, *Wages in Germany, 1871–1945* (Princeton, 1960); G. Bry and C. Boschan, 'Secular Trends and Recent Changes in Real Wages and Wage Differentials in Three Western Industrial Countries, the United States, Great Britain and Germany', in *Second International Conference of Economic History* (The Hague, 1965), 179–80; A. V. Desai, *Real Wages in Germany, 1871–1913* (Oxford, 1968), 36–7; T. J. Orsagh, 'Löhne in Deutschland, 1871–1913', *Zeitschrift für die gesamte Staatswissenschaft*, CXXV, 3 (1969), 476–83.

70 *Schriften des Vereins für Sozialpolitik*, CXLV, parts 1 and 2 (1914), contains several studies of local price movements.

71 Bry, *Wages in Germany*, 54ff and 233ff.

72 Fischer and Czada, 'Wandlungen in der deutschen Industriestruktur', 125.

73 Hoffmann *et al.*, *Das Wachstum der deutschen Wirtschaft*, 37.

74 *Enquete-Ausschuss: Verhandlungen und Berichte des Unterausschusses für Arbeitsleistung* (Berlin, 1930), IX, 1–2, 24ff, and 227; Hoffmann *et al.*, *Das Wachstum der deutschen Wirtschaft*, 24; T. W. Mason, 'Labour in the Third Reich, 1933–1939', *Past and Present*, no. 33 (April 1966), 132 and 140; Kocka, *Unternehmensverwaltung und Angestelltenschaft*, 275 and 478.

75 Bry, *op. cit.*, 135ff and 147.

76 *Ibid.*, Table A3 (pp. 333–4); p. 132 and n.16.

77 J. Kuczynski, *Die Geschichte der Lage der Arbeiter unter dem Kapitalismus*, IV, 400, based on Bry, *op. cit.*, 28ff.

78 Bry, *op. cit.*, 37ff.

79 *Ibid.*, 42 (for this and the preceding paragraph).

80 H. Kaelble and H. Volkmann, 'Konjunktur und Streik während des Übergangs

zum Organisierten Kapitalismus', *Zeitschrift für Wirtschafts- und Sozialwissenschaften*, XCII (1972), 532–4; V. Böhmert, 'Das neueste Heft der Untersuchungen über die Entlohnungsmethoden in der deutschen Eisen- und Maschinenindustrie', *Der Arbeiterfreund*, XLIX (1911), 295. Conclusions concerning the influence of unions in the earlier stages of unionization must remain conjectural in view of the impossibility of establishing the extent to which employers improved wages and conditions to forestall the formation of unions or to avert spontaneous strikes.

81 Bry, *Wages in Germany*, 43 and 301.

82 *Ibid.*, 163.

83 *Ibid.*, 153ff.

84 J. Kuczynski, *Die Geschichte der Lage der Arbeiter unter dem Kapitalismus*, I, Appendix 1, pp. 350ff.

85 Pieper, *Die Lage der Bergarbeiter*, 54; Dawson, *The German Workman*, 220 and 235; G. Adelmann, *Die soziale Betriebsverfassung des Ruhrbergbaus vom Anfang des 19. Jahrhunderts bis zum Ersten Weltkrieg* (Bonn, 1962), 118.

86 Bry, *Wages in Germany*, 143; J. Kuczynski, *op. cit.*, I, pp. 250 and 254; Kaelble and Volkmann, 'Konjunktur und Streik'.

87 For wide-ranging discussions of the issues glanced at in this paragraph, see Kaelble and Volkmann, *op. cit.*; P. N. Stearns, 'Measuring the Evolution of Strike Movements', *International Review of Social History*, XIX, 1 (1974); L. Schofer, 'Patterns of Worker Protest: Upper Silesia, 1865–1914', *Journal of Social History*, V, 4 (1972).

88 Dawson, *The German Workman*, 176–92.

89 Even such a strong defender of management's prerogatives as Ehrenberg conceded this point in his 'Schwäche und Stärkung'.

90 Adelmann, *Die soziale Betriebsverfassung*, 152; Kocka, *Unternehmensverwaltung und Angestelltenschaft*, 212 n.26.

91 J. Kuczynski, *Die Geschichte der Lage der Arbeiter unter dem Kapitalismus*.

92 Pieper, *Die Lage der Bergarbeiter*, 118–19.

93 Forberger, *Die Manufaktur in Sachsen*, 224; Reuter, *Die Manufaktur im fränkischen Raum*, 88; O. Wiedfeldt, *Statistische Studien zur Entwicklungsgeschichte der Berliner Industrie von 1720 bis 1890* (Leipzig, 1898), 70; Strauss, *Die Lage und die Bewegung der Chemnitzer Arbeiter*, 24; W. Fischer, 'Innerbetrieblicher und sozialer Status der frühen Fabrikarbeiterschaft', in F. Lütge (ed.), *Die wirtschaftliche Situation in Deutschland und Österreich um die Wende vom 18. zum 19. Jahrhundert* (Stuttgart, 1964), 211–13.

94 Kocka, *Unternehmensverwaltung und Angestelltenschaft*, 226ff, 346, and 492.

95 Forberger, *op. cit.*, 221; *Life and Labour in Germany*, pp. xix–xx.

96 J. Kuczynski, *Die Geschichte der Lage der Arbeiter unter dem Kapitalismus*, I, p. 261; *ibid.*, IV, 49ff and 363; Hinze, *Die Arbeiterfrage*, 140.

97 Bry, *Wages in Germany*, 93–101.

98 Pieper, *Die Lage der Bergarbeiter*, 66; Bernays, 'Berufswahl und Berufsschicksal', 143–4.

99 *Statistik des deutschen Reichs*, 2nd ser., CCCCLVIII, 56.

100 Kocka, *Unternehmensverwaltung und Angestelltenschaft*, 107–8.

101 Lloyd, 'Labour Organisation in the Cutlery Trade', 375; Puppke, *Sozialpolitik und soziale Anschauungen*, 43 n.161.

102 J. Kuczynski, *Die Geschichte der Lage der Arbeiter unter dem Kapitalismus*, XVIII, 36; Kocka, *op. cit.*, 66 and 68 n.110; Lande, 'Arbeits- und Lohnverhältnisse', 332ff, 345–7, and 406ff; Wörishoffer, *Die soziale Lage der Fabrikarbeiter*, 56; Bernays, *op. cit.*, 163ff; V. Böhmert, 'Die Lehre vom Arbeitslohn und von den Entlohnungsmethoden, mit besonderer Beziehung auf die deutsche Eisen- und Maschinenindustrie', *Der Arbeiterfreund*, XLVII (1909), 423ff.

103 Bry, *Wages in Germany*, n.5, p. 124.

104 P. Mombert, 'Die Arbeits- und Lohnverhältnisse der Angestellten der Düsseldorfer Strassenbahnen', *Schriften des Vereins für Sozialpolitik*, XCIX (1902); Dr Hampke, 'Die Verhältnisse der Angestellten und Arbeiter der Strassenverkehrsgewerbe in Posen', *ibid.*, 310–11; Pieper, *Die Lage der Bergarbeiter*, 53; Kocka, *Unternehmensverwaltung und Angestelltenschaft*, 350, 490 n.99.

105 J. Kuczynski, *op. cit.*, I, p. 265 n.; *ibid.*, XVIII, 40 and 76; Reuter, *Die Manufaktur im fränkischen Raum*, 94; Hinze, *Die Arbeiterfrage*, 197–8; Forberger, *Die Manufaktur in Sachsen*, 221; Strauss, *Die Lage und die Bewegung der Chemnitzer Arbeiter*, 33 and 66; Ludwig, 'Die Fabrikarbeit von Kindern im 19. Jahrhundert', 74; Schröter and Becker, *Die deutsche Maschinenbauindustrie*, 232; Puppke, *Sozialpolitik und soziale Anschauungen*, 48; Kocka, *op. cit.*, 480; Adelmann, *Die soziale Betriebsverfassung des Ruhrbergbaus*, 33; A. Günther, 'Die Arbeitszeit in der Grosseisenindustrie', *Soziale Praxis*, XXI, 46 (15 August 1912), cols. 1450–1. Hoffmann *et al.*, *Das Wachstum der deutschen Wirtschaft*, 213, gives somewhat different figures, which do not appear entirely plausible.

106 Hinke, 'Auslese und Anpassung', 93; Lande, 'Arbeits- und Lohnverhältnisse', 404–5; Göhre, *Three Months in a Workshop*, 33; Brady, *The Rationalization Movement*, 41.

107 Adelmann, *Die soziale Betriebsverfassung des Ruhrbergbaus*, 82, 120, and 183; Lande, *op. cit.*, 423; Günther, *op. cit.*; Kocka, *op. cit.*, 102 n.266.

108 S. E. Denison, *Why Growth Rates Differ* (Washington, D.C., 1967), 61ff; Lande, *op. cit.*, 406; Göhre, *op. cit.*, 58–75; *Economic Journal*, XXVII (March 1917), 125.

109 Bry, *Wages in Germany*, 275.

110 Wörishoffer, *Die soziale Lage der Fabrikarbeiter*, 75.

111 J. Kuczynski, *Die Geschichte der Lage der Arbeiter unter dem Kapitalismus*, XVIII, 76; Strauss, *Die Lage und die Bewegung der Chemnitzer Arbeiter*, 51; Puppke, *Sozialpolitik und soziale Anschauungen*, 36 n.115; Adelmann, *Die soziale Betriebsverfassung des Ruhrbergbaus*, 112 n.4, and 177; Göhre, *op. cit.*, 75; F. Decker, *Die betriebliche Sozialordnung der Dürener Industrie im 19. Jahrhundert* (Cologne, 1965), 147–52.

112 *Sozialpolitisches Centralblatt*, I (4 January 1892), 8.

113 J. Kuczynski, *op. cit.*, III, 368ff.

114 Adelmann, *Die soziale Betriebsverfassung des Ruhrbergbaus*, 41; Syrup, 'Studien über den industriellen Arbeiterwechsel', 538–42.

115 H. Kaelble, 'Sozialer Aufstieg in Deutschland, 1850–1914', *Vierteljahrschrift für Sozial- und Wirtschaftsgeschichte*, LX (1973), 49; W. von Geldern, 'Ärzte und Versicherungskassen', *Schmollers Jahrbuch*, XXXVI (1912), 701.

116 Bry, *Wages in Germany*, 32.

117 J. Kuczynski, *op. cit.*, I, pp. 233–4 and 237; Strauss, *Die Lage und die Bewegung der Chemnitzer Arbeiter*, 20; Adelmann, *Die soziale Betriebsverfassung des Ruhrbergbaus*, 64; Kocka, *Unternehmensverwaltung und Angestelltenschaft*, 268; F. Schumann, 'Die Arbeiter der Daimler-Motoren-Gesellschaft, Stuttgart–Untertürkheim', *Schriften des Vereins für Sozialpolitik*, CXXXV, I (1911), 16.

118 Bernays, 'Berufswahl und Berufsschicksal', 132 and 143–4; Pieper, *Die Lage der Bergarbeiter*, 16; Schumann, *op. cit.*, 113; Bernhard, 'Auslese und Anpassung', 376; Bienkowski, 'Untersuchungen über Arbeitseignung und Leistungsfähigkeit', 21; Heiss, 'Auslese und Anpassung', 231; *Statistik des deutschen Reichs*, 2nd ser., CCXI, 100 and 259; Max Morgenstern, 'Auslese und Anpassung der industrieller Arbeiterschaft, betrachtet bei den Offenbacher Lederwarenarbeitern', *Schriften des Vereins für Sozialpolitik*, CXXXV (1912), 37; unsigned report in *Soziale Praxis*, XXIV, 28 (8 April 1915), col. 657; W. Böhmert, 'Das Berufsschicksal der Arbeiter nach Überschreitung des vierzigsten Lebensjahres', *Der Arbeiterfreund*, LI (9113).

119 Kocka, *op. cit.*, 501 n.134; Kühne, 'Der Arbeitseinsatz im Vier Jahres Plan',

709; Lande, 'Arbeits- und Lohnverhältnisse', 387; E. Lederer, 'Umsichtung der Einkommen und des Bedarfs', in Harms (ed.), *Strukturwandlungen der deutschen Wirtschaft*, I, pp. 86ff.

120 Kaelble, 'Sozialer Aufstieg in Deutschland', 71; Kocka, *op. cit.*, 101, 476–7, 516ff, and 522 n.33; P. N. Stearns, 'The European Labor Movement and the Working Classes, 1890–1914', in H. Mitchell and P. N. Stearns, *Workers and Protest* (Ithaca, N.Y., 1971), 147; K. M. Bolte, *Deutsche Gesellschaft im Wandel* (Opladen, 1967), 47 and 55. H. Lamprecht, 'Über die soziale Herkunft der Handwerker', *Soziale Welt*, III (1951), emphasizes the wide range of local variations. D. Crew, 'Definitions of Modernity: Social Mobility in a German Town, 1880–1901', *Journal of Social History*, VII, 1 (Fall 1973), provides a valuable case study of Bochum.

121 Lamprecht, *op. cit.*, 47ff; S. M. Lipset and R. Bendix, *Social Mobility in Industrial Society* (Berkeley, Calif., 1964), 43.

122 Pieper, *Die Lage der Bergarbeiter*, 34ff; Dawson, *The German Workman*, 13 and 81; Adelmann, *Die soziale Betriebsverfassung des Ruhrbergbaus*, 62.

CHAPTER X

Entrepreneurs and Managers in German Industrialization

1 Cf. K. Marx, *Das Kapital*, 3 vols. (Berlin, 1962–4); J. Schumpter, 'Unternehmer', in *Handwörterbuch der Staatswissenschaften*, VIII (Jena, 1928), 476–87; Schumpeter, *Capitalism, Socialism, and Democracy* (New York, 1950); D. S. Landes (ed.), *The Rise of Capitalism* (New York and London, 1966), 1ff.

2 Cf. F. Redlich, *Der Unternehmer* (Göttingen, 1964), 97f (English translation in *American Journal of Economics and Sociology*, VIII (April 1949), 132); E. T. Penrose, *The Theory of the Growth of the Firm* (Oxford, 1959), 26ff, 31f, and 185; A. D. Chandler and F. Redlich, 'Recent Developments in American Business Administration and Their Conceptualization', *Business History Review*, XXXV (1961), 1–27, esp. 24ff; G. Turin, *Der Begriff des Unternehmers* (Zürich, 1947), 222.

For the history of the concepts 'entrepreneur' and 'manager', and for alternative definitions: Redlich, *Der Unternehmer*, 171–88; V. Jungfer, 'Wandlungen des Unternehmerbegriffs', in *Gestaltwandel der Unternehmung*, Nürnberger Hochschulwoche 1953 (Berlin, 1954), 108–28; E. Salin, 'Manager', in *Handwörterbuch der Sozialwissenschaften*, VII (Stuttgart, 1961), 107–13; H. Hartmann, 'Managers and Entrepreneurs: A Useful Distinction?', *Administrative Science Quarterly*, III (1958–9), 429–51; F. Rexhausen, *Der Unternehmer und die volkswirtschaftliche Entwicklung* (Berlin, 1960), 14–31; F. Harbison and C. A. Myers (eds.), *Management in the Industrial World* (New York, 1964), 8ff; P. Kilby, 'Hunting the Heffalump', in Kilby (ed.), *Entrepreneurship and Economic Development* (New York and London, 1971), 1–40.

3 Cf. D. S. Landes, *The Unbound Prometheus* (Cambridge, 1969), 355–7, 525–8, and the studies by Svennilson and Habakkuk quoted there; Kilby, *Entrepreneurship and Economic Development*, esp. 2–3 and 24ff, and the works quoted there in notes 3 and 35. A. O. Hirschman, *The Strategy of Economic Development* (New Haven, Conn., 1958), 1–7.

4 Cf. Max Weber's interesting argument at the end of his 'Die protestantische Ethik und der Geist des Kapitalismus' (1905), in *Gesammelte Aufsätze zur Religionssoziologie*, I, 5th edn (Tübingen, 1963), 204ff. After showing the beneficial effect which Calvinistic beliefs had on the socio-economic attitudes of early entrepreneurs and thus on the development of capitalism, Weber states that this original spirit has

now left the system which it once supported. 'Victorious capitalism does not need this support any more, since it rests on a mechanical basis.' Most of the evidence which shows socio-cultural traditions impeding or slowing down economic development stems from societies before or at the beginning of industrialization. Cf. R. Braun, 'Zur Einwirkung soziokultureller Umweltbedingungen auf das Unternehmerpotential und das Unternehmerverhalten', in W. Fischer (ed.), *Wirtschafts- und sozialgeschichtliche Probleme der frühen Industrialisierung* (Berlin, 1968), 248ff; Kilby, *Entrepreneurship and Economic Development*, 29–40; Hirschman, *The Strategy of Economic Development*, 14–28; Harbison and Myers, *Management in the Industrial World*, 87ff.

5 Cf. the comparative study by K. Wiedenfeld, *Das Persönliche im modernen Unternehmertum* (Leipzig, 1911); D. S. Landes, 'Entrepreneurship in Advanced Industrial Countries: The Anglo-German Rivalry', in *Entrepreneurship and Economic Growth* (Cambridge, Mass., 1954); T. C. Cochran, 'The Entrepreneur in Economic Change', *Explorations in Entrepreneurial History*, 2nd ser., III (1965–6), 25–38; J. E. Sawyer, 'The Social Basis of the American System of Manufacturing', *Journal of Economic History*, XIV (1954), 361–79; D. Granick, *The European Executive* (New York, 1962). See also A. Gerschenkron, 'Social Attitudes, Entrepreneurship, and Economic Development', *Explorations in Entrepreneurial History*, VI (1953–4), 1–19 (as a warning against overdoing this approach), and the ensuing comments by Sawyer and Landes in the same journal, VI and VII (1953–5).

6 For a critical review of the present state of business and entrepreneurial history in Germany, see H. Jaeger, 'Business History in Germany: A Survey of Recent Developments', *Business History Review*, XLVIII (1974), 28–48. The most recent general summaries of German economic history in the nineteenth and twentieth centuries neglect the role of entrepreneurs and managers to a remarkable degree. Cf. K. Borchardt, *Die Industrielle Revolution in Deutschland* (Munich, 1972: translated as 'Germany, 1700–1914', in C. M. Cipolla (ed.), *Fontana Economic History of Europe*, IV, 1: *The Emergence of Industrial Societies, Part One* (London and Glasgow, 1973), 76–160); F. W. Henning, *Die Industrialisierung in Deutschland, 1800–1914* (Paderborn, 1973); Henning, *Das industrialisierte Deutschland, 1914–1972* (Paderborn, 1974).

7 Cf. H. Mottek, 'Zum Verlauf und zu einigen Hauptproblemen der industriellen Revolution in Deutschland', in Mottek *et al.*, *Studien zur Geschichte der industriellen Revolution in Deutschland* (Berlin, 1960), 11–63; W. G. Hoffmann, 'The Take-Off in Germany', W. W. Rostow (ed.), *The Economics of Take-Off into Sustained Growth* (London, 1964), 95–118; Henning, *Die Industrialisierung in Deutschland*, 111ff. Stressing economic development before the industrial revolution: F. Mendels, 'Proto-Industrialization: The First Phase of the Industrialization Process', *Journal of Economic History*, XXXII (1972), 241–61.

8 Cf. H. A. Winkler (ed.), *Organisierter Kapitalismus: Voraussetzungen und Anfänge* (Göttingen, 1974).

9 For the concept of the 'manufactory', cf. H. Freudenberger and F. Redlich, 'The Industrial Development of Europe', *Kyklos*, XVII (1964), 372–403, esp. 386–92.

10 The concepts used here are a little different from definitions which emphasize the division of labour rather than geographical centralization as the main criterion to distinguish between the putting-out system and the manufactory; such definitions draw the line between the putting-out system and the manufactory at the point where the traditional pattern of the division of labour (as inherited from the craft system and surviving within the developing putting-out system) is transformed and refined by the putter-out, thus transforming the dependent artisan into a decentralized process worker. See, for example, H. Krüger, *Zur Geschichte der·Manufakturen und der Manufakturarbeiter in Preussen* (Berlin, 1958), 178–96, and other authors in the Marxist tradition. According to this definition many decentralized enterprises which in our

terminology were putting-out enterprises are regarded as (decentralized) manufactories; on the basis of this conceptual position (which is not used in this chapter) it becomes possible to speak of a 'manufactory period' (*Manufakturperiode*) (sixteenth to eighteenth centuries), preceding industrial capitalism. Against this definition is the difficulty of determining empirically exactly when the traditional pattern of work division typical of the craft system (which was changing too, after all) turned into the patterns characteristic of the manufactory; normally this was a gradual process. In addition, if one considers the great importance which the concentration of workers in the factory – and with it the division between home and place of work – had both for the tasks of entrepreneurs and managers and for the social circumstances of the workers, there is much to be said for the definition used here, which is shared by many works on the subject. Cf. E. Schremmer, *Die Wirtschaft Bayerns* (Munich, 1970), 472ff; J. Kermann, *Die Manufaktur im Rheinland, 1750–1833* (Bonn, 1972), 79ff. Using this narrower definition we reject the notion of a 'manufactory period', since manufactories in this sense were much less numerous than putting-out enterprises, and since they were normally not the organizations out of which the factories of the industrial revolution developed (see pp. 507–10, below).

11 Cf. K. H. Kaufhold, 'Umfang und Gliederung des deutschen Handwerks', in W. Abel *et al.*, *Handwerksgeschichte in neuer Sicht* (Göttingen, 1970), 33ff.

12 Cf. R. Forberger, *Die Manufaktur in Sachsen* (Berlin, 1958), 289.

13 In the burgeoning cloth industry area around Monschau in 1760, only 5 per cent of the capital was in machinery, the rest being in stock, outstanding debts, and obligations: cf. M. Barkhausen, 'Staatliche Wirtschaftslenkung und freies Unternehmertum im westdeutschen und im nord- und südniederländischen Raum bei der Entstehung der neuzeitlichen Industrie im 18. Jahrhundert', *Vierteljahrschrift für Sozial- und Wirtschaftsgeschichte*, XLV (1958), 168–241, esp. 197.

14 Manufactory entrepreneurs are discussed extensively here because typologically they are most similar to the industrial entrepreneurs and managers of the industrial revolution.

15 There were certainly many manufactory entrepreneurs who did not run the distribution themselves but sold to local wholesale dealers. Cf. O. Reuter, *Die Manufaktur im fränkischen Raum* (Stuttgart, 1961), 116f. One may assume that this was not so much ex-shopkeepers and putting-out entrepreneurs, but rather ex-craftsmen and people from other backgrounds.

16 Cf. Barkhausen, 'Staatliche Wirtschaftslenkung'; M. Barkhausen, 'Der Aufstieg der rheinischen Industrie im 18. Jahrhundert und die Entstehung eines industriellen Grossbürgertums', *Rheinische Vierteljahrsblätter*, XIX (1954), 135–78; K. Wolf, 'Stages in Industrial Organization', *Explorations in Entrepreneurial History*, 2nd ser., I (1963), 125–41; W. Zorn, *Handels- und Industriegeschichte Bayerisch-Schwabens, 1648–1870* (Augsburg, 1961), 205ff.

17 Kermann, *Die Manufaktur im Rheinland*, 606; Reuter, *Die Manufaktur im fränkischen Raum*, 142.

18 One thinks of silver and iron-ore mines; foundries; iron- and copper-hammering, bell-moulding, sheet-iron, and steel-wire works; powder mills; sulphur works; etc. Cf. Reuter, *Die Manufaktur im fränkischen Raum*, 178ff; W. Sombart, *Der moderne Kapitalismus*, 3 vols. (Munich and Leipzig, 1919–27), II, 740ff. One can dispute whether these enterprises should be called 'manufactories': cf. *ibid.* and G. Jahn, 'Die Entstehung der Fabrik', *Schmollers Jahrbuch*, LXIX (1949), 94 ff.

19 A case in point is the founding of an integrated cloth manufactory in about 1700 by the Lutheran cloth dealer Arnold Schmitz, who had had to leave Catholic Aachen: cf. Barkhausen, 'Staatliche Wirtschaftslenkung', 190.

20 Cf. F. Redlich, 'A German Eighteenth Century Iron Works during Its First

Hundred Years', *Bulletin of the Business Historical Society*, XXVII (1953), 69–96, esp. 71, 76f, and 79.

21 Cf. K. Abraham, *Der Strukturwandel im Handwerk in der ersten Hälfte des 19. Jahrhunderts* (Cologne, 1955), 115; K. Groba, *Der Unternehmer im Beginn der Industrialisierung Schlesiens* (Breslau, 1936), 6, 12 f.; Schremmer, *Die Wirtschaft Bayerns*, 523ff; O. Dascher, *Das Textilgewerbe in Hessen–Kassel vom 16. bis 19. Jahrhundert* (Marburg, 1968), esp. 62ff; H. Rachel and P. Wallich, *Berliner Grosskaufleute und Kapitalisten*, 2nd edn, 3 vols. (Berlin, 1967), II, 209ff, 253ff, and 351f; Krüger, *Zur Geschichte der Manufakturen*, 63ff and 233ff. In general on the connection between relative backwardness and mercantilist state intervention, see A. Gerschenkron, *Europe in the Russian Mirror* (Cambridge, 1970), esp. 86ff; on the positive correlation between relative backwardness and the trend towards largeness in industrial organization, A. Gerschenkron, *Economic Backwardness in Historical Perspective* (Cambridge, Mass., 1962), 5–51, esp. 10, 15f, and 26.

22 Cf. Rachel and Wallich, *Berliner Grosskaufleute*, 134–80, on the warehouse entrepreneur Johann Andreas Kraut; examples from Hessen–Kassel in Dascher, *Das Textilgewerbe*, 57ff and 81ff; from Franconia in Reuter, *Die Manufaktur im fränkischen Raum*, 22, 74, and 93; Forberger, *Die Manufaktur in Sachsen*, 211f, on seventy private associations in Saxony.

23 Cf. Rachel and Wallich, *Berliner Grosskaufleute*, 209–24; another less marked example of such a manufacturing entrepreneur with diversified property in Dascher, *Das Textilgewerbe*, 66.

24 Cf. W. Treue, 'Das Verhältnis von Fürst, Staat und Unternehmer in der Zeit des Merkantilismus', *Vierteljahrschrift für Sozial- und Wirtschaftsgeschichte*, XLIV (1957), 27 and 37ff; H. Müller, *Geschichte des VEB Stahl- und Walzwerks Riesa* (Berlin, 1961), 39ff, 49ff, 60, 62, and 65f.

25 Cf. Zorn, *Handels- und Industriegeschichte*, 206ff and 275: in Bavarian Swabia the rise of outsiders without marrying into a local family was a phenomenon not of the seventeenth and eighteenth centuries, but only of the nineteenth; cf. Barkhausen, 'Staatliche Wirtschaftslenkung'; Barkhausen, 'Der Aufstieg der rheinischen Industrie'; H. Kellenbenz, 'Unternehmertum in Südwestdeutschland', *Tradition*, X (1965), 175.

26 Cf. the example in Kellenbenz, 'Unternehmertum', 174; Schremmer, *Die Wirtschaft Bayerns*, 569ff; Forberger, *Die Manufaktur in Sachsen*, 272ff.

27 Cf. Dascher, *Das Textilgewerbe*, 81ff; Schremmer, *Die Wirtschaft Bayerns*, 508, 515, and 517 (Bavaria remained firmly attached to the Roman Catholic religion and so did not profit as other German states did from the religious persecutions and the emigrations of Huguenots and other minority religious groups which followed them).

28 These generalizations are based on the studies by Dascher, Forberger, Kellenbenz, Krüger, Rachel and Wallich, Schremmer, and Treue, cited above, and also G. Slawinger, *Die Manufaktur in Kurbayern, 1740–1833* (Stuttgart, 1966).

29 Cf. Freudenberger and Redlich, 'Industrial Development of Europe', 392–7; Reuter, *Die Manufaktur im fränkischen Raum*; Kilby, *Entrepreneurship and Economic Development*, 35.

30 Schremmer, *Die Wirtschaft Bayerns*, 522; Reuter, *Die Manufaktur im fränkischen Raum*, 15f.

31 Cf. F. Decker, *Die betriebliche Sozialordnung der Dürener Industrie im 19. Jahrhundert* (Cologne, 1964), 13–45; cf. also A. Thun, *Die Industrie am Niederrhein und ihre Arbeiter*, 2 vols. (Leipzig, 1879).

32 Cf. F. Zunkel, *Der rheinisch–westfälische Unternehmer, 1834–1879* (Cologne and Opladen, 1963), 15f; A. Eyberg, 'Umwelt und Verhalten der Unternehmer des Oberbergischen Kreises im 19. Jahrhundert' (unpublished dissertation, Cologne,

1955), 10ff, 27ff, and 54ff; F. Hellwig, 'Unternehmer und Unternehmensform im saarländischen Industriegebiet', *Jahrbücher für Nationalökonomie und Statistik*, CLVIII (1943), 404 and 413ff; Sombart, *Der moderne Kapitalismus*, 712. On the Hoesch Iron and Steel Works, Ltd, cf. *Eisen- und Stahlwerke Hoesch Aktiengesellschaft in Dortmund, 1871–1921* (Dortmund, n.d.), 1–3.

33 Forberger, *Die Manufaktur in Sachsen*, 272–7 and 286–93; H. Blumberg, *Die deutsche Textilindustrie in der industriellen Revolution* (Berlin, 1965), 132–44.

34 Cf. A. Schwemann, 'Friedrich Wilhelm Graf von Reden', *Beiträge zur Geschichte der Technik und Industrie*, XIV (1924), 22–39; K. Fuchs, *Vom Dirigismus zum Liberalismus: Die Entwicklung Oberschlesiens als preussisches Berg- und Hüttenrevier* (Wiesbaden, 1970), 33–69, 94, and 135f; Redlich, *Der Unternehmer*, 251ff and 292. However, it seems doubtful that Prussian state ownership of the mines on the Rhine and Ruhr was more advantageous for the economic growth of the region than the private alternative would have been.

35 Slawinger, *Die Manufaktur in Kurbayern*, 68; Schremmer, *Die Wirtschaft Bayerns*, 572; Reuter, *Die Manufaktur im fränkischen Raum*; 152; Rachel and Wallich, *Berliner Grosskaufleute*, 223, 256, and *passim*; L. Baar, *Die Berliner Industrie in der industriellen Revolution* (Berlin, 1966), 40–73.

36 On the long tradition of famous entrepreneurial families and dynasties: Zunkel, *Der rheinisch–westfälische Unternehmer*, 13ff; Hellwig, 'Unternehmer und Unternehmensform', 407ff and 413; H. Kaelble, *Berliner Unternehmer während der frühen Industrialisierung* (Berlin and New York, 1972), 59, 33, and 55. H. Beau says that of 300 entrepreneurs of the Rhineland and Westphalia in the period 1790–1870, 251 (or five-sixths) were the sons of economically independent families (*Das Leistungswissen des frühindustriellen Unternehmertums in Rheinland und Westfalen* (Cologne, 1959), 71). Nearly 50 per cent of outstanding businessmen born in the nineteenth century and listed in a general biographical encyclopedia (cf. note 40 below) came from businessmen's families: W. Stahl, *Der Elitekreislauf in der Unternehmerschaft* (Frankfurt and Zürich, 1973), 104–23. Cf. Dascher, *Das Textilgewerbe*, 84f, on the family relationships between early manufactory entrepreneurs and the entrepreneurs of the industrial revolution in Hessen.

37 Cf. F. W. Henning, 'Die Einführung der Gewerbefreiheit und ihre Auswirkungen auf das Handwerk in Deutschland', in Abel *et al.*, *Handwerksgeschichte in neuer Sicht*, 148, on the restrictive effect of the concession system in Bavaria, even in the 1850s.

38 Cf. L. Beutin, 'Die märkische Unternehmerschaft in der frühindustriellen Zeit', *Westfälische Forschungen*, X (1957), 65; Beau, *Das Leistungswissen*, 48ff; Kaelble, *Berliner Unternehmer*, 19f; for more details cf. Stahl, *Der Elitekreislauf*, 179–191.

39 Cf. Redlich, *Der Unternehmer*, 334ff; R. Engelsing, 'Bremisches Unternehmertum', *Schriften der Wittheit zu Bremen*, II (1958), 9–23.

40 Stahl, *Der Elitekreislauf*, 206–21; O. Kindermann, 'Das Sozialprofil deutscher Unternehmer im 19. Jahrhundert anhand der NDB' (unpublished manuscript, Münster, 1975), 80. The figures of Stahl and Kindermann are based on samples of entrepreneurs included in the first volumes of the *Neue Deutsche Biographie*.

41 On the over-representation of Protestants among West German entrepreneurs: W. Däbritz, Führende Persönlichkeiten des rheinisch–westfälischen Wirtschafts- und Soziallebens', in O. Most *et al.* (eds.), *Wirtschaftskunde für Rheinland und Westfalen* (Berlin, 1931), 113f; Hellwig, 'Unternehmer und Unternehmensform', 412 (this emphasizes the strong representation of Lutherans, not Calvinists, among the Saarland entrepreneurs); Zunkel, *Der rheinisch–westfälische Unternehmer*, 29ff (emphasizes the importance of the Calvinist ethic for the spirit of capitalism and the bourgeois concept of work, and also the minority situation of the Rhineland Protestants and

their descent from persecuted immigrants); Kaelble, *Berliner Unternehmer*, 79f., on the over-representation of Jews among Berlin entrepreneurs of the industrial revolution (50 per cent, compared with a proportion of 2–4 per cent in the whole population); cf. also Sombart, *Der moderne Kapitalismus*, III, 21f. For their regional origin: F. Eulenburg, 'Die Herkunft der deutschen Wirtschaftsführer', *Schmollers Jahrbuch*, LXXIV (1954), 86ff; Stahl, *Der Elitekreislauf*, 179ff.

42 We cannot discuss here whether these restrictions on access to entrepreneurial positions had a generally restricting effect on economic growth.

43 Cf. Redlich, *Der Unternehmer*, 296f.

44 See the data and descriptions of the social and occupational origins of entrepreneurs in Kaelble, *Berliner Unternehmer*, 30–124, which demonstrates the extensive exclusion of members of the lower classes. See pp. 510–11 above, and note 57 below.

45 Cf. Redlich, *Der Unternehmer*, 281–98 ('Europäische Aristokratie und wirtschaftliche Entwicklung'); W. Zorn, 'Unternehmertum und Aristokratie in Deutschland', *Tradition*, VIII (1963), 241–54; Braun, 'Zur Einwirkung soziokultureller Umweltbedingungen', 253ff.

46 Cf. H. Sachtler, *Wandlungen des industriellen Unternehmertums in Deutschland seit Beginn des 19. Jahrhunderts*, published dissertation (Halle–Wittenberg, 1937), 8; Groba, *Der Unternehmer*, 28ff; Redlich, *Der Unternehmer*, 336ff; C. Matschoss, *Die Maschinenfabrik R. Wolf Magdeburg–Buckau, 1862–1912* (Magdeburg, 112), 2f, on the disappointment of a grammar-school teacher when his son became an engineer at the turn of the century; K. Helfferich, *Georg von Siemens*, 3 vols. (Berlin, 1923), III, 153 and 159, for the contempt of a civil servant even in 1870 for his son, a director of the Deutsche Bank ('Mein Sohn, der *Kommis*').

47 Cf. K.-H. Manegold, 'Das Verhältnis von Naturwissenschaften und Technik im 19. Jahrhundert im Spiegel der Wissenschaftsorganisation', in *Geschichte der Naturwissenschaften und der Technik im 19. Jahrhundert* (Düsseldorf, 1969), 141–87, esp. 160ff.

48 For an example, see the quotation from a Saxon newspaper in 1830, in E. Dittrich, 'Ferdinand Hartmann', in Dittrich (ed.), *Lebensbilder sächsischer Wirtschaftsführer* (Leipzig, 1941), 134f; on the Prussian encouragement to industry: I. Mieck, *Preussische Gewerbepolitik in Berlin, 1806–44* (Berlin, 1965); for the later period: J. Kocka, *Unternehmensverwaltung und Angestelltenschaft am Beispiel Siemens* (Stuttgart, 1969), 525ff; R. Tilly, 'Los von England: Probleme des Nationalismus in der deutschen Wirtschaftsgeschichte', in H. Giesch and H. Sauermann (eds.), *Quantitative Aspekte der Wirtschaftsgeschichte* (Tübingen, 1968); K. W. Hardach, 'Anglomanie und Anglophobie während der Industriellen Revolution in Deutschland', *Schmollers Jahrbuch*, XCI (1971), 153–81; and in general, A. Gerschenkron, *Economic Backwardness*, 25.

49 C. Matschoss, *Preussens Gewerbeförderung und ihre grossen Männer* (Berlin, 1921); Kocka, *Unternehmensverwaltung*, 56.

50 This change is illustrated by the appearance of the putting-out enterprise, the manufactory, and the factory as institutions with purely economic functions, in contrast to the craft works and the artisans' guilds, which combined economic functions with social, cultural, and to some extent also political ones. Cf. Schremmer, *Die Wirtschaft Bayerns*, 571f.

51 Krüger, *Zur Geschichte der Manufakturen*, 242, demonstrates how far the newly won wealth and luxury of the manufacturing entrepreneurs in the last third of the eighteenth century were used for show, and how the new wealth did not respect traditional status differences between the bourgeoisie and the aristocracy. But the limits upon the emancipation of successful entrepreneurs from the traditional social structure are demonstrated by the vigour of their continued striving after the traditional symbols of success, such as titles and aristocratic life-styles.

52 Cf. Braun, 'Zur Einwirkung soziokultureller Umweltbedingungen', 277–81.

53 Cf. O. Simon, *Die Fachbildung des Preussischen Gewerbe- und Handelsstandes im 18. und 19. Jahrhundert* (Berlin, 1902).

54 W. Zorn, 'Typen und Entwicklungskräfte deutschen Unternehmertums', *Vierteljahrschrift für Sozial- und Wirtschaftsgeschichte*, XLIV (1957), 56–77, cited in K. E. Born (ed.), *Moderne deutsche Wirtschaftsgeschichte* (Cologne and Berlin, 1966), 25–41, esp. 30ff; Kaelble, *Berliner Unternehmer*, 54f; R. Bendix, *Work and Authority in Industry* (New York, 1956), 251f; on the differentiation between founders, heirs, and commissioned entrepreneurs, which forms the basis of the following discussion, cf. Kaelble, *Berliner Unternehmer*, 38ff and 76ff.

55 Exceptions in Sachtler, *Wandlungen des industriellen Unternehmertums*, 9ff; Engelsing, 'Bremisches Unternehmertum', 54; Redlich, *Der Unternehmer*, 308f.

56 Cf. A. Eyberg, 'Umwelt und Verhalten', 132; also Beau, *Das Leistungswissen*, 18.

57 According to preliminary comparisons in Kaelble, *Berliner Unternehmer*, 110ff. We refer here to mobility within one generation, and the early entrepreneurs' own occupational origins. Investigation of mobility between successive generations, using as a yardstick the occupational status of the entrepreneurs' fathers, leads to similar results (*ibid.*, 30ff and 97ff, and pp. 512–14 above). This is in contrast to earlier assumptions, e.g. Sachtler's often-cited calculations (*Wandlungen des industriellen Unternehmertums*, 7ff) which suggest a much higher degree of mobility in the industrial revolution, but which are not very useful because of their inexact and unclear categorization.

58 For the Rhineland cf. Zunkel, *Der rheinisch–westfälische Unternehmer*, 25. Of 126 industrial entrepreneurs in Berlin (before 1870), the largest occupation of origin was that of trader ('*Kaufmann*') with 59, followed by craftsman (50), college graduate (12), chemist (3), officer or landowner (1 each): cf. Kaelble, *Berliner Unternehmer*, 42.

59 Cf. Blumberg, *Die deutsche Textilindustrie*, esp. 62ff and 132–44; Baar, *Die Berliner Industrie*, 151ff; Dittrich, *Lebensbilder sächsischer Wirtschaftsführer*, 48ff and 128–42; H. Wutzmer, 'Die Herkunft der industriellen Bourgeoisie in Preussen in den vierziger Jahren des 19. Jahrhunderts', in Mottek *et al.*, *Studien zur Geschichte der industriellen Revolution*, 147 and 158ff; Beau, *Das Leistungswissen*, 61 and 67–9; A. Thun, *Die Industrie am Niederrhein*, I, p. 38.

60 Cf. G. Schmoller, *Zur Geschichte des Kleingewerbes im 19. Jahrhundert* (Halle, 1870), 648ff; Baar, *Die Berliner Industrie*, 75–83.

61 Cf. Kaelble, *Berliner Unternehmer*, 42 and 45; Beau, *Das Leistungswissen*, 14ff.

62 Beau, *loc. cit.*; W. Köllmann, *Friedrich Harkort*, I: *1793–1838* (Düsseldorf, 1964).

63 Cf. W. Köllmann, 'Frühe Unternehmer', in W. Först (ed.), *Ruhrgebiet und neues Land* (Cologne and Berlin, 1968), 16ff and 22ff; W. Däbritz, 'Führende Persönlichkeiten', 110f, 114ff, 117ff, and 120–3; W. Herrmann, *Entwicklungslinien montanindustrieller Unternehmungen im rheinisch–westfälischen Industriegebiet* (Dortmund, 1954), 14 and 22; Hellwig, 'Unternehmer und Unternehmensform', 404 and 410f; H. Schacht, 'Zur Finanzgeschichte des Ruhrkohlen-Bergbaus', *Schmollers Jahrbuch*, XXXVII, 3 (1913), 162–9.

64 Cf. M. L. Hartsough, 'Business Leaders in Cologne in the Nineteenth Century', *Journal of Economic and Business History*, III (1929–30), 232–52; B. Kuske, *Mevissens Stellung in der Wirtschaftsentwicklung* (Cologne, 1921); A. Bergengrün, *David Hansemann* (Berlin, 1901), 158ff.

65 Cf. Kaelble, *Berliner Unternehmer*, 49f.

66 Cf. (e.g.) *ibid.*, 48f and 50f; H. Witt, *Die Triebkräfte des industriellen Unternehmertums vor hundert Jahren und heute* (Hamburg, 1929), 91f; Hellwig, 'Unternehmer und Unternehmensform', 410f; A. Krüger, *Das Kölner Bankiergewerbe vom Ende des 18. Jahrhunderts bis 1875* (Essen, 1925), 33ff.

67 Cf. Engelsing, 'Bremisches Unternehmertum', 98ff.

68 Cf. K. Wiedenfeld, *Das Persönliche im modernen Unternehmertum*, 59f, with regard to Alfred Krupp and Werner Siemens; Sachtler, *Wandlungen des industriellen Unternehmertums*, 7; Beau, *Das Leistungswissen*, 56; Engelsing, 'Bremisches Unternehmertum', 95f.

69 Zorn, 'Typen und Entwicklungskräfte', 31.

70 Beau (*Das Leistungswissen*, 69) has estimated that of 400 enterprises in the Rhineland–Westphalian industrial area, 266 were run by businessmen and technicians together, 78 by technicians alone, and 56 by businessmen alone. He found that in the mining industry 91 out of 108 enterprises were such partnerships, and in the textiles industry 83 out of 120. His results are probably biased and may underestimate the *proportion* of businessmen and partnerships, not their absolute numbers, because he adopts a very broad concept of the entrepreneur which seems to include many very small entrepreneurs of a craftsman nature, as well as larger master craftsmen.

71 Quantitative evidence in this connection is given in G. Hahn, *Untersuchungen über die Ursachen von Unternehmensmisserfolgen*, published dissertation (Cologne, 1956), 40–1. Also, on the overwhelming proportion of ex-artisans among entrepreneurs, see W. Huschke, *Forschungen über die Herkunft der thüringischen Unternehmerschicht des 19. Jahrhunderts* (Baden-Baden, 1962), 9ff; Dascher, *Das Textilgewerbe*, 85.

72 Cf. Engelsing, 'Bremisches Unternehmertum', 95f, and Dittrich, *Lebensbilder sächsischer Wirtschaftsführer*, 50, on the origins of Bremen and Saxon entrepreneurs in declining crafts and marginal craft shops; Dittrich, *op. cit.*, 58–73 on G. T. Bienert (1813–94) as an impressive example – a miller's son (orphaned at an early age) who rose to be a milling entrepreneur with 250 employees; cf. also C. Matschoss, 'Franz Dinnendahl (1775–1826)', in *Rheinisch-westfälische Wirtschaftsbiographien*, 1 (Münster, 1932), 357–72; Sachtler, *Wandlungen des industriellen Unternehmertums*, 9ff; F. D. Marquardt, 'Sozialer Aufstieg, sozialer Abstieg und die Entstehung der Berliner Arbeiterklasse, 1806–1848', *Geschichte und Gesellschaft*, 1 (1975), 43–77, esp. 57ff.

73 Cf. Kaelble, *Berliner Unternehmer*, 42; A. Schröter and W. Becker, *Die deutsche Maschinenbauindustrie in der industriellen Revolution* (Berlin, 1962), 64ff; Wutzmer, 'Die Herkunft der industriellen Bourgeoisie', 152, 156f, and 161.

74 Cf. Engelsing, 'Bremisches Unternehmertum', 98ff; Jahn, 'Die Entstehung der Fabrik', 210–21; Baar, *Die Berliner Industrie*, 142ff.

75 Stahl, *Der Elitekreislauf*, 237–45.

76 Cf. Köllmann, 'Frühe Unternehmer', 143ff. Cf. Dittrich, *Lebensbilder sächsischer Wirtschaftsführer*, 143ff.

77 There were of course many exceptions. Cf. Blumberg, *Die deutsche Textilindustrie*, 132ff, on the larger craft yarn-producing shops, which became worsted-yarn factories; see also examples of the sometimes continuous, sometimes abrupt transition from craft shop to factory in E. Klein, 'Zur Frage der Industriefinanzierung im frühen 19. Jahrhundert', in H. Kellenbenz (ed.), *Öffentliche Finanzen und privates Kapital im späten Mittelalter und in der ersten Hälfte des 19. Jahrhunderts* (Stuttgart, 1971), 123ff.

78 The majority of Berlin engineering entrepreneurs – most of whom were ex-artisans – did not originate in Berlin. Cf. Kaelble, *Berliner Unternehmer*, 23.

79 Cf. K. H. Schmidt, 'Bestimmungsgründe und Formen des Unternehmenswachstums im Handwerk', in Abel *et al.*, *Handwerksgeschichte in neuer Sicht*, 245–51; K. Assmann, 'Verlag – Manufaktur – Fabrik', in *ibid.*, 202–29; O. Borst, 'Staat und Unternehmer in der Frühzeit der Württembergischen Industrie', *Tradition*, XI (1966), 126, 155, and 161f; Rachel and Wallich, *Berliner Grosskaufleute*, 351; G. Luntowski, 'Lüneburger Unternehmer im 19. Jahrhundert', *Tradition*, XI (1966), 201–17; H. Kellenbenz, 'Unternehmertum in Südwestdeutschland', 173 and 187.

80 Cf. Beutin, 'Die märkische Unternehmerschaft', 66; Beau, *Das Leistungswissen*,

14f; Eyberg, *Umwelt und Verhalten*, 51ff; Jahn, 'Die Entstehung der Fabrik', 201-21.

81 Cf. Schröter and Becker, *Die deutsche Meschinenbanindustrie*, 195-8. Examples: Dittrich, *Lebensbilder sächsischer Wirtschaftsführer*, 170 and 250f; Köllmann, 'Frühe Unternehmer', 39; for an example of an artisan foundation surviving as a family concern, S. Haubold, *Entwicklung und Organisation einer Chemnitzer Maschinenfabrik*, published dissertation (Bonn, 1939).

82 Cf. C. Matschoss, *Männer der Technik* (Berlin, 1925), 128f, 243f, and 299 (with many other examples); Kaelble, *Berliner Unternehmer*, 66ff.

83 Cf. P. Lundgreen, *Techniker in Preussen während der frühen Industrialisierung: Ausbildung und Berufsfeld einer entstehenden sozialen Gruppe* (Berlin, 1975), 190f.

84 Cf. Eyberg, *Umwelt und Verhalten*, 51ff; Groba, *Der Unternehmer*, 22f; Zunkel, *Der rheinisch-westfälische Unternehmer*, 28f.

85 Cf. B. Knochenhauer, *Die oberschlesische Montanindustrie* (Gotha, 1927), 107-46; A. Perlick, *Oberschlesische Berg- und Hüttenleute* (Kitzingen, 1953); U. Lohse, 'Guido Graf Henckel von Donnersmarck und seine industriellen Schöpfungen', *Stahl und Eisen*, XXXVII (1917), 156-61.

86 Kaelble, *Berliner Unternehmer*, 55f. These figures are of course not identical with the self-recruitment rates of entrepreneurs as a social group. A large number of entrepreneurs were the sons of businessmen yet did not take over their fathers' enterprises, either because they had already established themselves independently or had to give precedence to a brother, or for other reasons. See *ibid.*, 59, and H. Kaelble, 'Sozialer Aufstieg in Deutschland, 1850-1914', *Vierteljahrschrift für Sozial- und Wirtschaftsgeschichte*, LX (1973), 52. From a top group of 235 German entrepreneurs (1800-70), 54 per cent were the sons of entrepreneurs. Only army officers had a higher self-recruitment rate!

87 Engelsing, *Bremisches Unternehmertum*, 67 (particularly about the Bremen shipowners); examples and a similar conclusion in Witt, *Die Triebkräfte des industriellen Unternehmertums*, 103ff; W. Berdrow, *Alfred Krupp*, 2 vols. (Berlin, 1928); E. Schröder, 'Alfred Krupp', in *Rheinisch-westfälische Wirtschaftsbiographien*, V (Münster, 1953), 46-78.

88 On F. W. Grundmann (1804-87) as director of the Tiele–Winckler administration, cf. Perlick, *Oberschlesische Berg- und Hüttenleute*, 158-61; on the Rhineland examples: Köllmann, 'Frühe Unternehmer', 17f, 20, 32, and 39; W. O. Henderson, 'W. Th. Mulvany, an Irish Pioneer in the Ruhr', *Explorations in Entrepreneurial History*, VI (1953), 230-45; A. Bein, *Friedrich Hammacher: Lebensbild eines Parlamentariers und Wirtschaftsführers, 1824-1904* (Berlin, 1932), 36ff; Kaelble, *Berliner Unternehmer*, 63 and 73ff; on Kaselowsky: Lundgreen, *Techniker in Preussen*, 329.

89 Cf. Groba, *Der Unternehmer*, 8f.

90 One should read the story of the life of Gottlieb Traugott Bienert (1813-94) in Dittrich, *Lebensbilder sächsischer Wirtschaftsführer*, 58-73, for an idea of this extremely hard-working miller's deep-seated urge to succeed, and of his eventual rise; see also the examples in Witt, *Die Triebkräfte des industriellen Unternehmertums*, 36 (A. Krupp, A. Busch) and in Eyberg, *Umwelt und Verhalten*, 56 (P. W. E. Steinmüller), for the driving force of unaccepted poverty.

91 C. Matschoss (ed.), *Werner Siemens*, 2 vols. (Berlin, 1916), I, pp. 28f and 30f.

92 Cf. Dittrich, *Lebensbilder sächsischer Wirtschaftsführer*, 250; Witt, *Die Triebkräfte des industriellen Unternehmertums*, 40ff.

93 As a representative example of a liberal who saw private success and the general good in a harmonious two-sided relationship, see Werner Siemens (Kocka, *Unternehmensverwaltung*, 81); on Camphousen's nationalism: Hartsough, 'Business Leaders in Cologne', 342. For Siemens, 'the great technical business houses were summoned to

use their full power so that the industry of their land could take the leading place in the great competition of the civilized world, or at least the place appropriate for the nature and position of their land' (*Lebenserinnerungen*, 17th edn (Munich, 1966), 298). On nationalistic, anti-British feeling as a motivation or justification of economic success on the part of German entrepreneurs of the industrial revolution, see L. Hatzfeld, 'Der Anfang der deutschen Drahtindustrie', *Tradition*, VI (1961), 250 n.63; elements of a civilizing and also rational vision of development in David Hansemann's plea for the railway, *Die Eisenbahnen und deren Aktionäre in ihrem Verhältnis zum Staate* (Leipzig and Halle, 1837); on the publication of the discussions of the board of the Rheinische Eisenbahn-Gesellschaft, see K. Kumpmann, *Die Entstehung der Rheinischen Eisenbahn-Gesellschaft, 1830–1844* (Essen–Ruhr, 1910), 182f.

94 For an analysis of these attitudes on the part of industrialists of the Rhineland and Westphalia, cf. Zunkel, *Der rheinisch-westfälische Unternehmer*, 66ff; *ibid.*, 30ff, on the connection between Calvinism and the work ethic; see above all Weber, 'Die protestantische Ethik', 17ff; but note too Hellwig, 'Unternehmer und Unternehmens-form', 412, who also describes a greater economic activity on the part of the Protestant bourgeoisie in the Saar region but emphasizes that these families were Lutheran.

95 Thun, *Die Industrie am Niederrhein*, I, pp. 75f, on the Aachen textile-factory-owners around 1870; on the entrepreneur Hansemann's criticism of the public's obsession with profits as early as 1837, see A. Bergengrün, *David Hansemann*, 193ff; on the public's desire for speculation: Zunkel, *Der rheinisch-westfälische Unternehmer*, 52ff; Rachel and Wallich, *Berliner Grosskaufleute*, III, 229; Kaelble, *Berliner Unter-nehmer*, 92 and 94.

96 F. Harkort in Witt, *Die Triebkräfte des industriellen Unternehmertums*, 75.

97 Krupp in *ibid.*, 45.

98 Matschoss, *Werner Siemens*, I, p. 218; and cf. *ibid.*, II, 911.

99 Cf. Redlich, *Der Unternehmer*, 322ff; Zorn, 'Typen und Entwicklungskräfte', 35f; W. O. Henderson, 'England und die Industrialisierung Deutschlands', *Zeitschrift für die gesamte Staatswissenschaft*, CVIII (1952), 264–94; Beau, *Das Leistungswissen*, 37–45 and 68; F. Redlich, *Die volkswirtschaftliche Bedeutung der deutschen Teerfarbenindustrie* (Munich and Leipzig, 1914), 1ff; W. Kroker, *Wege zur Verbreitung technologischer Kenntnisse zwischen England und Deutschland in der zweiten Hälfte des 18. Jahrhunderts* (Berlin, 1971), esp. 49ff and 109ff; M. Schumacher, *Auslandsreisen deutscher Unternehmer 1750–1851, unter besonderer Berücksichtigung von Rheinland und Westphalen* (Cologne, 1968).

100 See, for example, Groba, *Der Unternehmer*, 9, on the attempt of the Silesian Count von Maltzan (1733–1817), who was so fascinated by his English experiences that he tried to create a Silesian Manchester on his estates, starting with nothing, and failed. Similarly, the products of Harkort in the 1820s probably owed their failure in the marketplace partly to the fact that they were technically very advanced and followed the English example too faithfully. Carl Gottlieb Haubold's pioneering engineering plant in Saxony failed repeatedly, in spite of using the best English methods, because of this discrepancy between imported technology and local demand. Cf. Dittrich, *Lebensbilder sächsischer Wirtschaftsführer*, 143ff, esp. 150ff. And the Bochumer Verein, though technically consistently successful, had to survive years without a profit before it gradually produced financial success as well.

101 Harkort failed as a businessman; but, fascinated as he was by the example of England, he served as a many-sided stimulator and propagandist of technical–industrial progress. The engineering factory-owner Haubold eventually pressured the Saxon textile putting-out entrepreneurs into mechanizing and buying his machines. Dinnen-dahl ran after the ploughs of the Westphalian miners – who were still part-time farmers – and implored them to let him build a steam engine for their mine. The

steel-producer Alfred Krupp worked in the early years as his own commercial traveller, and with great energy.

102 The basis idea (which certainly needs to be tested through detailed studies) with some variations is found in D. S. Landes, 'The Structure of Enterprise in the Nineteenth Century', in XIe Congrès International des Sciences Historiques (Stockholm, 21-8 August 1960), *Rapports* (Uppsala, 1960), v, 121.

103 Cf. Beutin, *Die märkische Unternehmerschaft*, 67ff; Beau, *Das Leistungswissen*, 19ff; Zunkel, *Der rheinisch-westfälische Unternehmer*, 69ff and 75ff; Kaelble, *Berliner Unternehmer*, 60ff.

104 Cf. K. Borchardt, 'Zur Frage des Kapitalmangels in der ersten Hälfte des 19. Jahrhunderts in Deutschland', *Jahrbücher für Nationalökonomie und Statistik*, CLXXIII (1961), 401-21; R. Tilly, 'Germany 1815-1870', in R. Cameron *et al.*, *Banking in the Early Stages of Industrialization* (New York, 1967), 151-82; H. Winkel, 'Kapitalquellen und Kapitalverwendung am Vorabend des industriellen Aufschwungs in Deutschland', *Schmollers Jahrbuch*, XC, 1 (1970), 275-301; Klein, 'Zur Frage der Industriefinanzierung', 118-28.

105 Lundgreen, *Techniker in Preussen*, 198, 202f, 209-11, 228, and 267.

106 Hahn, *Untersuchungen*, 81.

107 Haubold's engineering factory showed a profit which fluctuated between 6 per cent and 83 per cent of the capital indicated in the accounts, in the years 1841-6. The factory was founded in 1837: in 1842 it had a fixed capital of only 8,000 talers and a liquid capital of only 1,000; by 1847, these figures had been raised through self-financing to 36,000 and 3,500 talers. The telegraph works of Siemens & Halske in Berlin was founded in 1847 with 6,843 talers, and only in 1863 acquired its first steam machine; from 1 October 1847 to 1 January 1850 its profit was 32,000 talers. The engineering factory of similar size which Borsig founded in Berlin in 1837 cost 67,500 talers. Wilhelm Zais's large cotton-spinning and weaving works was founded in Cannstadt in 1835 with 100,000 guilders (about 57,000 talers). Cf. Haubold, *Entwicklung und Organisation einer Chemnitzer Maschinenfabrik*, 30; Kocka, *Unternehmensverwaltung*, 59; Rachel and Wallich, *Berliner Grosskaufleute*, III, 182; Klein, 'Zur Frage der Industriefinanzierung', 120.

108 Cf. Bergengrün, *David Hansemann*, 190; Arthur von Mayer, *Geschichte und Geographie der deutschen Eisenbahnen von ihrer Entstehung bis auf die Gegenwart, 1890* (Berlin, 1891), I, 192, for the erroneous assessments and calculations of Nuremberg businessmen when they founded the first German railway (Nuremberg-Fürth) in 1835.

109 Family members were also asked to guarantee bonds. Cf. P. Neubaur, *Matthias Stinnes und sein Haus* (Mülheim, n.d.), 304ff, as an impressive example.

110 The cautious response of Beuth and the Prussian government towards technicians and entrepreneurs seeking financial credits is shown very clearly in Lundgreen, *Techniker in Preussen*, 210; Klein, 'Zur Frage der Industriefinanzierung', 126; W. Fischer, *Der Staat und die Industrialisierung in Baden* (Berlin, 1962), 156ff. On the large estate-owners: H. Winkel, *Die Ablösungskapitalien aus der Bauernbefreiung in West- und Süddeutschland* (Stuttgart, 1968); on the private bankers: Krüger, *Das Kölner Bankiergewerbe*; Rachel and Wallich, *Berliner Grosskaufleute*, III, 184 (about the Schickeler brothers); Klein, 'Zur Frage der Industriefinanzierung', 121ff (with examples from South and Southwest Germany); P. Schwartz, *Die Entwicklungstendenzen im deutschen Privatbankiergewerbe*, published dissertation (Strassburg, 1915), 42-7 (on Saxony and Berlin); on the participation of private banks in the joint-stock companies of the pre-1848 period: P. C. Martin, 'Frühindustrielles Gewerbe in der Rechtsform der AG', in W. Fischer (ed.), *Beiträge zu Wirtschaftswachstum und Wirtschaftsstruktur im 16. und 19. Jahrhundert* (Berlin, 1971), 208f; in general: Tilly, 'Germany 1815-1870', 159ff.

111 Cf. Landes, 'The Structure of Enterprise', 117f.

112 Cf. Martin, 'Frühindustrielles Gewerbe', 196ff; K. Bösselmann, *Die Entwicklung des deutschen Aktienwesens im 19. Jahrhundert* (Berlin, 1939), covering only the period up to 1850; cf. Siemens, *Lebenserinnerungen*, 297, and Hellwig, 'Unternehmer und Unternehmensform', 414, on the reserved attitude of leading entrepreneurs towards the share system.

113 Figures (certainly not accurate in detail) from E. Engel, *Die erwerbsthätigen juristischen Personen insbesondere die Actiengesellschaften im preussischen Staate* (Berlin, 1876), 10f: 143 million talers (61 per cent of the total share capital of *c.* 225 million) was invested in twenty-seven railway companies. Bösselmann, (*Die Entwicklung des deutschen Aktienwesens*, 201) estimates the capital invested in the Prussian railway system at 156 million talers; cf. also P. C. Martin, 'Die Entstehung des preussischen Aktiengesetzes von 1843', *Vierteljahrschrift für Sozial- und Wirtschaftsgeschichte*, LVI (1969), 500–2, with corrected figures up to 1843; cf. also H. Thieme, 'Statistische Materialien zur Konzessionierung von Aktiengesellschaften in Preussen bis 1867', *Jahrbuch für Wirtschaftsgeschichte*, 1960, part 2, 286–300.

114 Cf. H. D. Krampe, *Der Staatseinfluss auf den Ruhrkohlenbergbau in der Zeit von 1800 bis 1865* (Cologne, 1961).

115 Cf. Martin, 'Frühindustrielles Gewerbe'; Herrmann, *Entwicklungslinien montanindustrieller Unternehmungen*, 14f.

116 All figures from Engel, *Die erwerbsthätigen juristischen Personen*, 10–17.

117 Cf. Schacht, 'Zur Finanzgeschichte des Ruhrkohlen-Bergbaus', 162–85; Blumberg, 'Die Finanzierung', in Mottek *et al.*, *Studien zur Geschichte der industriellen Revolution*, esp. 185 and 196; F. Schunder, *Tradition und Fortschritt* (Stuttgart, 1959).

118 Sombart, *Der moderne Kapitalismus*, II, 110ff (quotation p. 120).

119 I am indebted for this information to Herman Freudenberger of Tulane University in New Orleans.

120 Cf. *Allgemeines Landrecht*, II, 8, sections 483, 562, 566, 567–613, and 642ff. The relevant provisions were again in the *Allgemeine Deutsche Handelsgesetzbuch* of 1861 and the *Handelsgesetzbuch* of 1900.

121 Cf. Hahn, *Untersuchungen*, 80f and 89–93; Decker, *Die betriebliche Sozialordnung*, 51ff and 69; Kocka, *Unternehmensverhaltung*, 95; Dittrich, *Lebensbilder sächsischer Wirtschaftsführer*, 152f and 161; Thun, *Die Industrie am Niederrhein*, I, pp. 40ff.

122 A short account of the bookkeeping methods at Siemens & Halske in Berlin around 1860 is given in Kocka, *Unternehmensverhaltung*, 97; Haubold, *Entwicklung und Organisation*, 44f, on the Chemnitz engineering factory of Haubold, where (although the factory was founded in 1837) they introduced depreciation only in 1874, by which time the capital was already over 110,000 talers.

123 E. Roeksy, *Die Verwaltung und Leitung von Fabriken* (Leipzig, 1878), 7.

124 C. G. Otto, *Buchführung für Fabrikgeschäfte* (Berlin, 1850); C. G. Gottschalk, *Die Grundlage des Rechnungswesens und ihre Anwendung auf industrielle Anstalten* (Leipzig, 1865); E. Stern, *Vollständige Anleitung zur Buchführung für die Gewerbtreibenden und kleinere Fabrikanten* (Darmstadt, 1867).

125 Cf. Thun, *Die Industrie am Niederrhein*, I, 38, on the criticism of Aachen textile industrialists for technical incompetence about 1870; Engelsing, 'Bremisches Unternehmertum'; Beau, 47ff, 52ff, and 58ff.

126 The following paragraphs are based on J. Kocka, 'Management und Angestellte im Unternehmen der Industriellen Revolution', in R. Braun *et al.* (eds.), *Gesellschaft in der industriellen Revolution* (Cologne and Berlin, 1973), 162–201.

127 On early examples of works rules, cf. Fischer, *Der Staat und die Industrialisierung*, 356f (for 1837, 1838, and 1845); O. Neuloh, *Die deutsche Betriebsverfassung und ihre Sozialformen bis zur Mitbestimmung* (Tübingen, 1956), 154ff (on Krupp); on the further

extension of works rules, *ibid.*, 79. Cf. the office rules of Harkort's '*Mechanische Werkstätte*' (1830) in Köllmann, *Friedrich Harkort*, 66f and 187f. On the 'first basic law of administration for the direction of large industrial works' (1872), see E. Schröder, 'Alfred Krupp's Generalregulativ', *Tradition*, I (1956), 35–57. Business regulations and instructions appeared at Siemens' from the 1850s and 60s.

128 Thus the former military officer W. Siemens, quoted in Kocka, 'Management und Angestellte', 178.

129 Thus Werner Siemens in 1868, *ibid.*, 175.

130 Cf. L. H. A. Geck, *Die sozialen Arbeitsverhältnisse im Wandel der Zeit* (Berlin, 1931); E. Michel, *Sozialgeschichte der industriellen Arbeitswelt* (Frankfurt, 1953); Decker, *Die betriebliche Sozialordnung*; L. Puppke, *Sozialpolitik und soziale Anschauungen frühindustrieller Unternehmer in Rheinland und Westfalen* (Cologne, 1966); G. Adelmann, *Die soziale Betriebsverfassung des Ruhrbergbaus vom Anfang des 19. Jahrhunderts bis zum Ersten Weltkrieg* (Bonn, 1962).

131 See J. Kocka, 'Industrielles Management: Konzeptionen und Modelle in Deutschland vor 1914', *Vierteljahrschrift für Sozial- und Wirtschaftsgeschichte*, LVI (1969), 332–72. However, there was earlier a literature on the technical problems of individual branches of industry, discussions of questions of company law and workers' problems, and, from the 1850s onwards, books on factory accountancy.

132 A. Emminghaus, *Allgemeine Gewerkslehre* (Berlin, 1868), 9 and 164. In fact, the small and medium-sized textile, metalworking, and paper plants in Düren introduced written work and factory regulations only when they were made compulsory by law in 1891 (Decker, 'Die betriebliche Sozialordnung', 61).

133 H. J. Habakkuk, *Industrial Organisation since the Industrial Revolution* (Southampton, 1968), 4–15; Wiedenfeld, *Das Persönliche im modernen Unternehmertum*, 59ff; T. Vogelstein, 'Die finanzielle Organisation der kapitalistischen Industrie', in *Grundriss der Sozialökonomik*, VI, 2nd edn (Tübingen, 1923), 390f and 393ff.

134 Cf. Schröter and Becker, *Die deutsche Maschinenbauindustrie*, 199ff, who emphasize that the German engineering factories around 1860 were in advance even of the English in the development of specialized drawing offices. Kocka, *Unternehmensverwaltung*, 135ff, on the development of the departmental structure at Siemens', and the problems of direction which followed.

135 Cf. Dittrich, *Lebensbilder sächsischer Wirtschaftsführer*, 150ff (on Haubold, who clearly recognized this difference between Germany and England around 1830).

136 On the Gutehoffnungshütte, cf. E. Maschke, *Es entsteht ein Konzern* (Oberhausen, 1969), 19–31; on the great diversification of Harkort's '*Mechanische Werkstätte*' around 1820: Köllmann, 'Frühe Unternehmer', 11ff; on Borsig's far-reaching diversification around 1840: Witt, *Die Triebkräfte des industriellen Unternehmertums*, 93; on the Silesian foundations: Fuchs, *Vom Dirigismus zum Liberalismus*, 32ff; on the mining industrialists of the Saar: Hellwig, 'Unternehmer und Unternehmensform', 409 and 415; cf. also Herrmann, *Entwicklungslinien montanindustrieller Unternehmungen*, 10 and 22ff; on early foundations 'auf der grünen Wiese': Martin, 'Frühindustrelles Gewerbe', 204–6.

137 Cf. O. Schwarz, 'Die Betriebsformen der modernen Grossindustrie', *Zeitschrift für die gesamte Staatswissenschaft*, XXV (1869), 595.

138 Hansen, *Gustav von Mevissen*, I, p. 408.

139 Cf. B. H. Strousberg, *Strousberg und sein Wirken von ihm selbst geschildert* (Berlin, 1876), 405–21; G. Reitböck, 'Der Eisenbahnkönig Strousberg', *Beiträge zur Geschichte der Technik und Industrie*, XIV (1924), 65–84; and particularly the comparison between B. H. Strousberg and J. I. Merès in F. Redlich, 'Two Nineteenth-Century Financiers and Autobiographers', *Economy and History*, X (1967), 37–128, esp. 113–28.

140 Strousberg could not employ either of the two. On the one hand, he had no tightly knit extended family but was rather a much-travelled man, new to Germany; on the other hand, he was the anti-bureaucratic type *par excellence*.

141 Cf., for example, J. Kocka, 'Family and Bureaucracy in German Industrial Management', *Business History Review*, XLV (1971), 137–40; Kaelble, *Berliner Unternehmer*, 28; Decker, *Die betriebliche Sozialordnung*, 30; Dittrich, *Lebensbilder sächsischer Wirtschaftsführer*, 60ff and 252ff; Eyberg, *Umwelt und Verhalten*, 127f.

142 Cf. Strousberg, *Strousberg und sein Wirken*, 158ff; Kumpmann, *Die Entstehung der rheinischen Eisenbahn-Gesellschaft*, 165ff, 178ff, 180f, 183ff, and 245ff. With regard to this influence of the state bureaucracy, the development of railway management in Germany differed from that in America: cf. A. D. Chandler, 'The Railroads', *Business History Review*, XXXIX (1965), 16–40. In general, see Kocka, 'Family and Bureaucracy', 140ff (with examples from the Siemens company). See also C. Helfer, 'Über militärische Einflüsse auf die industrielle Entwicklung Deutschlands', *Schmollers Jahrbuch*, LXXXIII (1963), 597–609.

143 In a private letter to his brother Carl, 28 February 1870, in Kocka, *Unternehmensverwaltung*, 90.

144 Cf. W. G. Hoffmann *et al.*, *Das Wachstum der deutschen Wirtschaft seit der Mitte des 19. Jahrhunderts* (Berlin, 1965), 63, 204ff, and 454ff; R. Wagenführ, *Die Industriewirtschaft* (Berlin, 1933), 56ff; A. Spiethoff, *Die wirtschaftlichen Wechsellagen*, 2 vols. (Tübingen and Zürich, 1955); J. A. Schumpeter, *Business Cycles*, 2 vols. (New York, 1939), vol. I.

145 These structural alterations are part of a general and complex process of socio-economic change, which has been described as the transition to 'organized capitalism'. Cf. J. Kocka, 'Organisierter Kapitalismus oder Staatsmonopolistischer Kapitalismus?', in H. A. Winkler (ed.), *Organisierter Kapitalismus: Voraussetzungen und Anfänge* (Göttingen, 1973), 19–35; and the articles by Wehler, Winkler, *et al.* in the same volume.

146 Cf. Sombart, *Der moderne Kapitalismus*, III, 835–8.

147 The syndicate's domination of the market was almost perfect during the whole period: its proportion of the market was between 80 and 90 per cent. Cf. K. Wiedenfeld, *Ein Jahrhundert rheinischer Montanindustrie, 1815–1915* (Bonn, 1916), 111; W. N. Parker, 'Entrepreneurship, Industrial Organization, and Economic Growth', *Journal of Economic History*, XIV (1954), 384ff.

148 W. Rathenau, *Von kommenden Dingen* (Berlin, 1918), 144. This is what W. Sombart criticized as an example of alienation (cf. Sombart's *Der Bourgeois* (Munich and Leipzig, 1913), 212ff).

149 See, for example, Werner Siemens in a private letter to his brother Carl in 1884: 'The mere making of money . . . is certainly very pleasant but does not form the basis of our business and gives no guarantee of survival. But I wish to make at least the Berlin business continue as a lasting family institution!' (Matschoss, *Werner Siemens*, II, p. 837).

150 On the following, more precisely in: J. Kocka, 'Siemens und der aufhaltsame Aufstieg der AEG', *Tradition*, XVII (1972), 125–42; Kocka, *Unternehmensverwaltung*, 319–35.

151 It should be emphasized that salaried entrepreneurs also developed an identification with 'their' concerns which made them reluctant to enter larger combines; they too were eventually compelled to do so by more aggressive rivals. Cf. Wiedenfeld, *Das Persönliches im modernen Unternehmertum*, 92f; H. Böhme, 'Emil Kirdorf', *Tradition*, XIII (1968), 286 and 290ff.

152 One example out of many is the development of the family engineering concern of Haubold in Chemnitz, which was founded in 1837 and which in 1939

employed *c.* 1,200 workers: Haubold, *Entwicklung und Organisation*, esp. 64 (on family policy as a limit to expansion and diversification).

153 For example, the pure smelting and rolling works in the Ruhr territory which refused, for whatever reasons, to expand through acquisition or internal development into mixed concerns were swallowed up by less reluctant competitors in the process of concentration in that region before 1914; cf. Wiedenfeld, *Ein Jahrhundert rheinischer Montanindustrie*, 129f. It may be that there is here an important difference between certain German and French developments. In France, joint-stock companies outside family control may have been too few in number, and those few not strong enough, to have any effect in weakening the family orientation of the others: and, as we have outlined, that close family orientation could have a retarding effect on the economy as a whole. In Germany, however – in part because industrialization was first 'delayed' and then very sudden – joint-stock companies that were not outgrowths of older family enterprises did emerge in sufficient numbers and with adequate strength, in the sectors mentioned, from the middle third of the century onwards. On France, see D. S. Landes, 'French Entrepreneurship and Industrial Growth in the Nineteenth Century', *Journal of Economic History*, XI (1949).

154 For the theoretical basis of this connection, cf. Penrose, *Theory of the Growth of the Firm*, esp. 65–151.

155 Wiedenfeld, *Ein Jahrhundert rheinischer Montanindustrie*, 77–152; H. G. Heymann, *Die gemischten Werke im deutschen Grosseisengewerbe* (Stuttgart and Berlin, 1904); A. Tross, *Der Aufbau der Eisen- und eisenverarbeitenden Industrie-Konzerne Deutschlands* (Berlin, 1923).

156 Cf. Kocka, *Unternehmensverwaltung*, 319ff and 368ff; Redlich, *Die volkswirtschaftliche Bedeutung*, 8f and 18–23; J. J. Beer, *The Emergence of the German Dye Industry* (Urbana, Ill., 1959), 94ff and 115ff.

157 On the following paragraph: Wiedenfeld, *Das Persönliche im modernen Unternehmertum*, 73ff; Haubold, *Entwicklung und Organisation*, 53–64; H. von Beckerath, *Der moderne Industrialismus* (Jena, 1930), 61f; Sombart, *Der moderne Kapitalismus*, III, 793f.

158 Cf. *ibid.*, III, 784–829; Vogelstein, *Die finanzielle Organisation*, 390–412. M. Stemme-Sogemeier, *Bielefeld und seine Industrie* (Trautheim, 1953), 52ff; E. Landauer, *Handel und Produktion in der Baumwollindustrie* (Tübingen, 1912); E. Landauer, 'Über die Stellung des Handels in der modernen industriellen Entwicklung', *Archiv für Sozialwissenschaften und Sozialpolitik*, XXXIV (1912), 879–92; J. Kocka, 'Expansion–Integration–Diversifikation: Wachstumsstrategien industrieller Grossunternehmen in Deutschland vor 1914', in H. Winkel (ed.), *Industrie und Gewerbe im 19. und 20. Jahrhundert* (Berlin, 1975), 203–26.

159 Cf. K. Wiedenfeld, *Kartelle und Konzerne* (Berlin and Leipzig, 1927); H. Levy, *Industrial Germany: A Study of Its Monopoly Organizations and Their Control by the State* (New York, 1966). Figures from: W. Wagenführ, *Kartelle in Deutschland* (Nuremberg, 1931), p. xiii; H. König, 'Kartelle und Konzentration', in H. Arndt (ed.), *Die Konzentration in der Wirtschaft*, 2nd edn, 2 vols. (Berlin, 1960), I, pp. 303–32, esp. 310f; V. Holzschuher, 'Soziale und ökonomische Hintergründe der Kartellbewegung' (unpublished dissertation, Erlangen/Nuremberg, 1937); E. Maschke, *Grundzüge der deutschen Kartellgeschichte bis 1914* (Dortmund, 1964); R. Liefmann, *Kartelle und Trusts und die Weiterbildung der volkswirtschaftlichen Organisation* (Stuttgart, 1910); Liefmann, *Kartelle, Konzerne und Trusts*, 9th edn (Stuttgart, 1930). A good case study: H. Lüthgen, *Das Rheinisch–westfälische Kohlensyndikat in der Vorkriegs-, Kriegs- und Nachkriegszeit und seine Probleme*, (Leipzig and Erlangen, 1926). *Ibid.*, 229, on the relatively steady price movements in coal under the syndicate 1893–1914, compared to the previous years; and A. Klotzbach, *Der Roheisenverband* (Düsseldorf, 1926),

262ff, on the greater price stability of syndicated pig iron in Germany compared with English and American prices.

160 Cf. H. Rosenberg, *Grosse Depression und Bismarckzeit* (Berlin, 1967); H. Kaelble, *Industrielle Interessenpolitik in der Wilhelminischen Gesellschaft: Centralverband Deutscher Industrieller, 1895–1914* (Berlin, 1967); K. Saul, *Staat, Industrie, Arbeiterbewegung im Kaissereich, 1903–1914* (Düsseldorf, 1974).

161 Cf. A. Weber, *Die rheinisch–westfälischen Provinzialbanken und die Krisis* (Leipzig, 1903), 337: of eighteen industrial corporations of the Rhineland and Westphalia founded in the years 1896–1900 and quoted on the Berlin stock exchange in 1901, sixteen emerged from the conversion of previously existing private companies, and only two were new foundations.

162 Cf. O. Jeidels, *Das Verhältnis der deutschen Grossbanken zur Industrie mit besonderer Berücksichtigung der Eisenindustrie* (Leipzig, 1905); E. Riesser, *Die deutschen Grossbanken und ihre Konzentration* (Jena, 1910); M. Gehr, *Das Verhältnis zwischen Banken und Industrie in Deutschland seit der Mitte des 19. Jahrhunderts bis zur Bankenkrise von 1931*, published dissertation (Stuttgart, 1959).

163 Cf. Sombart, *Der moderne Kapitalismus*, III, 213f; Hoffmann *et al.*, *Das Wachstum der deutschen Wirtschaft*, 454ff and 773ff; R. Passow, *Die wirtschartliche Bedeutung und Organisation der Aktiengesellschaften* (Jena, 1907), 7–12.

164 Cf. *ibid.*, 127–211, for an analysis of the law and reality of the constitutions of joint-stock companies before 1914; F. Eulenburg, 'Die Aufsichtsräte der deutschen Aktiengesellschaften', *Jahrbuch für Nationalökonomie und Statistik*, XXXII (1906), 92–109; Sombart, *Der moderne Kapitalismus*, III, 740f; Jeidels, *Das Verhältnis der deutschen Grossbanken zur Industrie*, 143ff.

165 Cf. Jeidels, *op. cit.*, 162–268.

166 Kirdorf quotation in *Schriften des Vereins für Sozialpolitik*, CXVI (Leipzig, 1916), 285; further: Kocka, *Unternehmensverwaltung*, 429ff; Gehr, *Das Verhältnis zwischen Banken und Industrie*, 62ff; Jeidels, *Das Verhältnis der deutschen Grossbanken zur Industrie*, 233ff and 258–72; Wiedenfeld, *Das Persönliche in modernen Unternehmertum*, 104–7; Carl Fürstenberg, *Die Lebensgeschichte eines deutschen Bankiers* (Wiesbaden, 1961), 165f, 175, and 394f; W. Hagemann, 'Das Verhältnis der deutschen Grossbanken zur Industrie' (unpublished dissertation, Berlin, 1931), 18ff. On the rates of self-financing: W. G. Hoffmann, 'Die unverteilten Gewinne der Aktiengesellschaften in Deutschland, 1871–1957', *Zeitschrift für die gesamte Staatswissenschaft*, CXV (1959), 271–91, esp. 277 and 281f; Kocka, *Unternehmensverwaltung*, 327; R. Tilly, 'The Growth of Large-Scale Enterprise in Germany since the Middle of the Nineteenth Century', in H. Daems and H. van der Wee (eds.), *The Rise of Managerial Capitalism* (The Hague, 1974), 145–69. Cf. also R. Hilferding, *Das Finanzkapital* (Vienna, 1910).

167 Cf. A. Riedler, *Emil Rathenau und das Werden der Grosswirtschaft* (Berlin, 1916), 30ff and 144ff; Manegold, 'Das Verhältnis von Naturwissenschaften und Technik', 164–87; K. H. Manegold, *Universität, Technische Hochschule und Industrie* (Berlin, 1970).

168 In 1825–75 there appeared eleven chemical institutes in German universities: they educated chemists before the modern chemical industry appeared. Cf. Sombart, *Der moderne Kapitalismus*, III, 890.

169 Cf. Beer, *Emergence of the German Dye Industry*, 57–93; Kocka, *Unternehmensverwaltung*, 139f; Manegold, 'Das Verhältnis von Naturwissenschaften und Technik', 179ff.

170 Cf. W. Treue, 'Erfinder und Unternehmer', *Tradition*, VIII (1963), 255–71; W. Treue, *Eugen Langen und Nic. August Otto: Zum Verhältnis von Unternehmer und Erfinder, Ingenieur und Kaufmann* (Munich, 1963).

171 Cf. H. Hartmann, *Education for Business Leadership: The Role of the German*

'*Hochschulen*' (Paris, 1955), 18ff; H. Hartmann, 'Die Akademiker in der heutigen Unternehmerschaft', *Tradition*, IV (1959), 133–48.

172 Cf. Beer, *Emergence of the German Dye Industry*, 91f; Kocka, *Unternehmensverwaltung*, 363ff; on similar trends in the mining industry: Wiedenfeld, *Das Persönliche im modernen Unternehmertum*, 66ff.

173 Cf. F. Pinner, *Emil Rathenau und das elektrische Zeitalter* (Leipzig, 1918), 126ff; F. Redlich, *Die volkswirtschaftliche Bedeutung der deutschen Teerfarbenindustrie* (Munich and Leipzig, 1914), 8f; Beer, *Emergence of the German Dye Industry*, 94ff.

174 Cf. Kocka, 'Industrielles Management', 337ff.

175 Cf. F. E. Farrington, *Commercial Education in Germany* (New York, 1914), 23; *ibid.*, 144, on the higher commercial schools.

176 In detail: Kocka, 'Industrielles Management', 347ff; F. Redlich, 'Academic Education for Business', *Business History Review*, XXXI (1957), 35–91, esp. 48ff; A. Isaac, *Die Entstehung der wissenschaftlichen Betriebswirtschaftslehre in Deutschland seit 1898* (Berlin, 1923); W. Böhme, 'Ein Vierteljahrhundert Verband Deutscher Diplom-Kaufleute e. V.', *Der Diplom-Kaufmann*, X (1930), 247–59; Hartmann, *Education for Business Leadership*, 18ff.

177 Cf. Kocka, 'Industrielles Management', 356–60 and 365ff.

178 The example of Siemens in Kocka, *Unternehmensverwaltung*, 363–82 and 547ff; on the inter-war period: O. H. von der Gablentz, 'Industriebürokratie', *Schmollers Jahrbuch*, L (1926), 539–72.

179 For details and sources, cf. Kocka, 'Industrielles Management', 347–56; on similar arguments from German entrepreneurs of the 1950s: Hartmann, *Authority and Organization*.

180 Cf. Neuloh, *Die deutsche Betriebsverfassung*, 151ff.

181 Cf., for example, Fürstenberg, *Die Lebensgeschichte eines deutschen Bankiers*, 135, on the importance of 'leitende Persönlichkeit'.

182 Cf. A. D. Chandler, *Strategy and Structure* (Cambridge, Mass., 1962), for this type of structure and also for the more decentralized type discussed below.

183 Cf. Kocka, 'Family and Bureaucracy', 152–5.

184 Cf. J. Huret, 'Die A.E.G.', *Organisation*, X (1908), 608f; examples from the 1920s given in R. T. Brady, *The Rationalization Movement in German Industry: A Study in the Evolution of Economic Planning* (Berkeley, Calif., 1933), 121, 172f, and 178f; Maschke, *Es entsteht ein Konzern*, 62f (on the decentralizing policy of Paul Reusch at the Gutehoffnungshütte); Kocka, 'Family and Bureaucracy', 152–5 (on Siemens & Halske).

185 Cf. the concept of 'entrepreneurial enterprise', referring to an intermediate stage of company development from the 'personal enterprise' to the 'managerial enterprise' proper, in A. D. Chandler and H. Daems, 'Introduction', in Daems and van der Wee (eds.), *Rise of Managerial Capitalism*, 5f.

186 Cf. H. Böhme, 'Emil Kirdorf', 284f and 290; and in general, Kocka, 'Industrielles Management', 341f.

187 Cf. Schmoller, 'Wesen und Verfassung der grossen Unternehmungen', in *Zur Social- und Gewerbepolitik*, 388–94; J. Burnham, *The Managerial Revolution* (Westport, Conn., 1972; repr. of New York, 1941 edn); a critical survey of some attitudes to salaried entrepreneurs is found in H. Pross, *Manager und Aktionäre in Deutschland* (Frankfurt, 1965), 12–42; J. Meynaud, *Technocracy* (London, 1964).

188 Cf. Rathenau, *Von kommenden Dingen*, 140ff; W. Rathenau, *Reflexionen* (Leipzig, 1912), 81ff; W. von Moellendorff, *Deutsche Gemeinwirtschaft* (Berlin, 1916).

189 Cf. Granick, *Der europäische Manager*, 62ff. This achronistic contempt for salaried entrepreneurs seems certainly to have disappeared by the 1960s.

190 For the most recent period, and for some social changes which cannot be

discussed here, see M. M. Postan, *An Economic History of Western Europe, 1945–1964* (London, 1967), 290ff.

191 On Kirdorf, see H. Böhme, 'Emil Kirdorf'; on Jencke, W. A. Boelcke (ed.), *Krupp und die Hohenzollern in Dokumenten* (Frankfurt, 1970), 118–34 and 277; on Hugenberg, D. Guratzsch, *Macht durch Organisation* (Düsseldorf, 1973); on Hilger, Perlick, *Oberschlesische Berg- und Hüttenleute*, 161f.

192 As an estimate for the time after 1945, see Postan, *Economic History*, 275ff; on the other hand, J. Schumpeter, 'Der Unternehmer in der Volkswirtschaft von heute', in B. Harms (ed.), *Strukturwandlungen der deutschen Volkswirtschaft*, 2 vols. (Berlin, 1928), I, pp. 295–312.

193 Cf. K. Hax, 'Wandlungen der Gewinnvorstellungen', in *Gestaltwandel der Unternehmung* (Berlin, 1954), 209.

194 In the literature of social science the new salaried entrepreneurs are often compared with the 'tycoons' of the industrial revolution, and in this way sharp contrasts are drawn between the leading salaried staff of the twentieth century and the owner–entrepreneurs of the nineteenth. Thus: P. A. Baran and P. M. Sweezy, *Monopoly Capital* (New York and London, 1968), 29ff (on the American side). This is a problematic summary, at least for the German situation, since such speculative 'tycoons' were by no means the dominant type of entrepreneur in the industrial revolution. Particularly in this field there was a strong continuity between the industrial revolution and organized capitalism.

195 Cf. Hoffmann, 'Die unverteilten Gewinne der Aktiengesellschaften'; on the policy of the AEG management towards the AGM; Pinner, *Emil Rathenau*, 384ff; W. Rathenau, *Zur Kritik der Zeit* (Berlin, 1919), 207. But it should be emphasized that the large family concerns of the nineteenth and twentieth centuries did not behave very differently in this respect.

196 See, with regard to England, C. Ericson, *British Industrialists: Steel and Hosiery 1850–1950* (London, 1959); a study is forthcoming, by T. Pierenkemper, on Westphalian industrialists (coal-mining and heavy industry) in the late nineteenth and early twentieth centuries.

197 Sombart, *Der moderne Kapitalismus*, III, 19ff (with examples). Sachtler (*Wandlungen des industriellen Unternehmertums*, 41) investigated the origins of 1,300 directors and owner–entrepreneurs listed in the *Reichshandbuch der Deutschen Gesellschaft* (Berlin, 1930–1) and came to the following classifications of origins (unfortunately without exact definitions):

Origin	Salaried entrepreneurs	Owner–entrepreneurs
Workers, petty-bourgeois	12 per cent	8 per cent
Middle class (*Mittelstand*)	34 per cent	25 per cent
Upper class	34 per cent	12 per cent
Large-scale entrepreneurs	20 per cent	55 per cent

But cf. Stahl, *Der Elitekreislauf*, 104, 126, 155, 160. In this sample of better-known entrepreneurs the salaried businessmen, on the whole, had fathers with slightly higher-ranking occupations than the owner–entrepreneurs.

198 Cf. Sachtler, *Wandlungen des industriellen Unternehmertums*, 41; similar results in Stahl, *Der Elitekreislauf*, 228ff.

199 The investigation of leading entrepreneurs by H. Kaelble ('Sozialer Aufstieg', 52) does not indicate any marked increase in recruitment from the lower and lower-middle classes to the leading groups of entrepreneurs of the late nineteenth and early twentieth centuries. Other evidence suggests that more sons of civil servants and salaried men of higher ranking, in general, were among salaried entrepreneurs than

among owner–entrepreneurs, while the sons of craftsmen and traders were more frequent among owner–entrepreneurs. Cf. Stahl, *Der Elitekreislauf*, 104 and 155.

200 The next section is based on Kocka, *Unternehmensverwaltung*, 383–459; Rathenau, 'Geschäftlicher Nachwuchs', in *Zur Kritik der Zeit*, 206–28; Sombart, *Der moderne Kapitalismus*, III, 3–22 and 736–47; Beckerath, *Der moderne Industrialismus*, 37ff, 58ff, and 231ff; Wiedenfeld, *Das Perösonliche im modernen Unternehmertum*, 101ff; Stahl, *Der Elitekreislauf*, 245 (on age patterns) and *passim*.

201 For a survey of the legal competence of these organs and their historical development, and of the various company forms (including the GmbH, which we have not dealt with here), see A. Hueck, *Gesellschaftsrecht*, 17th edn (Munich, 1975).

202 Cf. Beckerath, *Der moderne Industrialismus*, 60f and 233f; Kocka, *Unternehmensverwaltung*, 383–462; on the composition of supervisory boards around 1905, Eulenburg, 'Die Aufsichtsräte'.

203 Cf. Sombart, *Der moderne Kapitalismus*, III, 738.

204 Cf. J. Herle, *Die Stellung des Verbandsgeschäftsführers in der Wirtschaft* (Berlin, 1926); Beckerath, *Der moderne Industrialismus*, 242f.

205 From Sombart, *Der moderne Kapitalismus*, III, 746f.

Bibliographies

EDITORS' NOTE

In accordance with the established practice of the Cambridge series of histories, the bibliographies printed below are selective and incomplete. Their purpose is not to list all the publications bearing directly or indirectly on the subject, but to enable the readers to study some of the topics in greater detail. As a rule, books and articles superseded by later publications have not been included, and references to general treatises indirectly relevant to the subject-matter of individual chapters have been reduced to the minimum. As most of the chapters are not new pieces of research, but summaries and interpretations of knowledge already available in secondary literature, references to original sources have either been left out altogether or have been confined to the principal and most essential classes of evidence.

Within the limits set by these general principles, the individual contributors were given the freedom of composing and arranging bibliographies as they thought best. The 'layout' of the bibliographical lists, therefore, varies from chapter to chapter.

CHAPTER II

Capital Formation in Great Britain

Sections I and II list the most important books and articles dealing specifically with the estimation of capital formation and the capital stock in Britain in the period 1760–1860. These lists do not cover the supply of finance for this process of capital formation (cf. p. 631 note 3 above) or the extensive theoretical literature on the general contribution of capital to economic growth, and they do not include the numerous works which refer to capital formation as part of a more general discussion of the industrial revolution.

Section III indicates other works cited in the notes which have been particularly helpful as sources of data or of general information, though many of these works are not primarily concerned with the estimation of capital accumulation.

I. General Works

BEEKE, H. *Observations on the Produce of the Income Tax*. 1800.

COLQUHOUN, P. *A Treatise on the Wealth, Power and Resources of the British Empire*, 1815.

CROUZET, F. 'Capital Formation in Britain during the Industrial Revolution', in Crouzet (ed.), *Capital Formation* (below).

CROUZET, F. (ed.). *Capital Formation in the Industrial Revolution*. 1972.

DEANE, P. M. 'Capital Formation in Britain before the Railway Age', *Economic Development and Cultural Change*, IX (1961); reprinted in Crouzet (ed.), *Capital Formation* (above).

—— 'New Estimates of Gross National Product for the United Kingdom, 1830–1914', *Review of Income and Wealth*, XIV (1968).

—— 'The Role of Capital in the Industrial Revolution', *Explorations in Entrepreneurial History*, X (1972–3).

DEANE, P. M., and W. A. COLE. *British Economic Growth, 1688–1959*. 1962; 2nd edn 1967.

DEANE, P. M., and H. J. HABAKKUK. 'The Take-Off in Britain', in W. W. Rostow (ed.), *The Economics of Take-Off into Sustained Growth*. 1963.

Economist. 'The Annual Accumulations of Capital in the United Kingdom', *Economist*, December 1863.

GAYER, A. D., W. W. ROSTOW, and A. J. SCHWARTZ. *The Growth and Fluctuations of the British Economy, 1790–1850*. 1953.

GIFFEN, R. *The Growth of Capital*. 1889.

HIGGINS, J. P. P., and S. POLLARD (eds.). *Aspects of Capital Investment in Great Britain, 1750–1850*. 1971.

LOWE, J. *The Present State of England*. 1823.

PEBRER, P. DE. *Taxation, Revenue, Expenditure, Power, Statistics and Debt of the Whole British Empire*. 1833.

POLLARD, S. 'Fixed Capital in the Industrial Revolution in Britain', *Journal of Economic History*, XXIV (1964); reprinted in Crouzet (ed.), *Capital Formation* (above).

—— 'The Growth and Distribution of Capital in Great Britain, c. 1770–1870', in *Third International Conference of Economic History* (Munich 1965). 1968.

SPACKMAN, W. S. *An Analysis of the Occupations of the People, showing the Relative Importance of the Agricultural, Manufacturing, Shipping, Interests*. 1847.

II. Works Dealing with Specific Sectors

BLAUG, M. 'The Productivity of Capital in the Lancashire Cotton Industry in the Nineteenth Century', *Economic History Review*, 2nd ser., XIII (1961).

CAIRNCROSS, A. K., and B. WEBER. 'Fluctuations in Building in Great Britain, 1785–1849', *Economic History Review*, 2nd ser., IX (1956).

CHALKLIN, C. W. *The Provincial Towns of Georgian England: A Study of the Building Process, 1740–1820*. 1974.

CHAPMAN, S. D. 'Fixed Capital Formation in the British Cotton Industry, 1770–1815', *Economic History Review*, 2nd ser., XXIII (1970).
—— 'Industrial Capital before the Industrial Revolution', in Harte and Ponting (eds.), *Textile History and Economic History* (below).
CRAIG, R. S. 'Capital Formation in Shipping', in Higgins and Pollard (eds.), *Aspects of Capital Investment* (above).
GINARLIS, J. E. 'Road and Waterways Investment in Britain, 1750–1850'. Unpublished Ph.D. thesis, University of Sheffield, 1970.
HADFIELD, C. *The Canal Age*. 1968.
HOLDERNESS, B. A. 'Capital Formation in Agriculture', in Higgins and Pollard (eds.), *Aspects of Capital Investment* (above).
—— 'Landlord's Capital Formation in East Anglia, 1750–1870', *Economic History Review*, 2nd ser., XXV (1972).
JENKINS, D. T. *The West Riding Wool Textile Industry, 1770–1835: A Study of Fixed Capital Formation*. 1975.
KENWOOD, A. G. 'Railway Investments in Britain, 1825–75', *Economica*, XXXII (1965).
—— 'Port Investments in England and Wales, 1851–1913', *Yorkshire Bulletin of Economic and Social Research*, XVII (1965).
MITCHELL, B. R. 'The Coming of the Railway and United Kingdom Economic Growth', *Journal of Economic History*, XXIV (1964).
SHANNON, H. A. 'Bricks – A Trade Index, 1785–1849', *Economica*, I (1934).
SWANN, D. 'The Pace and Progress of Port Investment in England, 1660–1830', *Yorkshire Bulletin of Economic and Social Research*, XII (1960).

III. OTHER WORKS CITED

BOOTH, C. 'Occupations of the People of the United Kingdom', *Journal of the Royal Statistical Society*, XLIX (1886).
BOREHAM, A. J., and J. R. BELLERBY. 'Farm Occupiers' Capital in the United Kingdom before 1939', *Farm Economist*, VII, 6 (1953).
CAIRNCROSS, A. K. *Home and Foreign Investment, 1870–1913*. 1953.
CARTER, A. 'Dutch Foreign Investment, 1738–1800', *Economica*, XX (1953).
CENTRAL STATISTICAL OFFICE. *National Accounts Statistics: Sources and Methods*. 1968 (cited in the notes as 'Sources and Methods').
—— *National Income and Expenditure*. Annual.
CLAPHAM, J. H. *An Economic History of Modern Britain*. 3 vols. 1926–38.
DEANE, P. M. *The First Industrial Revolution*. 1965.
DYOS, H. J. *Victorian Suburb*. 1961.
FEINSTEIN, C. H. *Domestic Capital Formation in the United Kingdom, 1920–1938*. 1965.
—— *National Income, Expenditure and Output of the United Kingdom, 1856–1965*. 1972.
GIFFEN, R. 'On Recent Accumulations of Capital in the United Kingdom', *Journal of the Royal Statistical Society*, XII (1878).
HARRIS, W. J. 'A Comparison of the Growth of Wealth in France and England, specially with reference to their Agricultural Systems', *Journal of the Royal Statistical Society*, LVII (1894).
HARTE, N. B., and K. G. PONTING (eds.). *Textile History and Economic History: Essays in Honour of Miss Julia de Lacy Mann*. 1973.
HAWKE, G. R. *Railways and Economic Growth in England and Wales, 1840–1870*. 1970.
HITCHCOCK, H.-R. *Early Victorian Architecture in Britain*. 1954.
HOBHOUSE, H. *Thomas Cubitt, Master Builder*. 1971.
HOFFMANN, W. *British Industry, 1700–1950*. 1955.
HUTCHINS, J. G. B. *The American Maritime Industries and Public Policy, 1878–1914*. 1941.
IMLAH, A. H. *Economic Elements in the Pax Britannica*. 1958.
JACKMAN, W. J. *The Development of Transportation in Modern England*. 1916.
LAW, H., and D. K. CLARK. *Construction of Roads and Streets*. 8th edn. 1914.
MCCULLOCH, J. R. *A Statistical Account of the British Empire*. 1837; 4th edn, 1854.
MACPHERSON, D. *Annals of Commerce, Manufactures, Fisheries and Navigation*. 1805.

MAYWALD, K. 'An Index of Building Costs in the United Kingdom, 1845–1938', *Economic History Review*, 2nd ser., VII (1954–5).
—— 'The Construction Costs and the Value of the British Merchant Fleet, 1850–1938', *Scottish Journal of Political Economy*, III (1956).
MINGAY, G. E. *English Landed Society in the Eighteenth Century*. 1963.
MITCHELL, B. R. *Abstract of British Historical Statistics*. 1962.
OLSEN, D. J. *Town Planning in London*. 1964.
PAGET, F. A. 'Report on . . . Steam Road-Rolling', in Law and Clark (eds.), *Construction of Roads* (above).
POOLE, G. BRAITHWAITE. *Statistics of British Commerce*. 1852.
SIGSWORTH, E. M. *Black Dyke Mills*. 1958.
SINCLAIR, SIR JOHN. *The History of the Public Revenue of the British Empire*. 3rd edn. 1804.
Sources and Methods: see Central Statistical Office (above).
STAMP, J. C. *British Incomes and Property*. 1916.
SUMMERSON, SIR JOHN. *Georgian London*. 1945; 2nd edn, 1962.
THOMPSON, F. M. L. *English Landed Society in the Nineteenth Century*. 1963.
—— *Hampstead: Building a Borough, 1650–1964*. 1974.
THOMPSON, R. J. 'An Inquiry into the Rent of Agricultural Land in England and Wales during the Nineteenth Century', *Journal of the Royal Statistical Society*, LXX (1907).
TOOKE, T., and W. NEWMARCH. *A History of Prices*. 6 vols. 1838–57.
WALSH, J. H. *A Manual of Domestic Economy*. 1857.

CHAPTER III

Labour in Great Britain

ADAMS, L. P. *Agricultural Depression and Farm Relief in England, 1813–1852*. 1932; repr. 1965.
ADAMS, W. E. *Memoirs of a Social Atom*. 1903; repr. 1968.
AIKIN, JOHN. *A Description of the Country from Thirty to Forty Miles round Manchester*. 1795.
ALISON, WILLIAM PULTENEY. *Observations on the Management of the Poor in Scotland*. 2nd edn. 1840.
—— *Reply to the Pamphlet Entitled Proposed Alteration of the Scottish Poor Law*. 1840.
—— *Reply to Dr Chalmers' Objections*. 1841.
ANDERSON, J. *Observations on the Means of Exciting a Spirit of National Industry*, 1777.
ANDREWS, C. BRUYN (ed.). *The Torrington Diaries*. 4 vols. 1935–8.
[ARBUTHNOT, JOHN]. *An Inquiry into the Connection between the Present Price of Provisions and the Size of Farms. By a Farmer*. 1773.
ASHTON, T. S. 'Some Statistics of the Industrial Revolution in Britain', *Manchester School*, XVI (1948).
—— *An Economic History of England: The Eighteenth Century*. 1955.
—— *Economic Fluctuations in England, 1700–1800*. 1955.
ASHTON, T. S., and J. SYKES. *The British Coal Industry in the Eighteenth Century*. 1929.
ASPINALL, A. *Early English Trade Unions*. 1949.
BAIRD, C. R. 'On the Poorest Class of Operative in Glasgow in 1837', *Journal of the Royal Statistical Society*, I (1838–9).
BAMFORD, SAMUEL. *Autobiography*. 2 vols. 1967 edn (first published 1839–41).
BARTON, JOHN. *Observations on . . . the Condition of the Labouring Classes of Society*. 1817; repr. 1934.
—— *An Inquiry into the Causes of the Progressive Depreciation of Agricultural Labour in Modern Times*. 1820.
—— *In Defence of the Corn Laws*. 1833.

BEALES, H. L. 'The Historic Context of the Essay on Population', in D. V. Glass (ed.), *Introduction to Malthus*. 1953.
BIENEFELD, M. A. 'A Study of the Course of Change in the . . . Hours of Work of Manual Workers in Certain British Industries . . . from the Eighteenth Century to the Present Day'. Unpublished Ph.D. thesis, London, 1969.
—— *Working Hours in British Industry: An Economic History*. 1972.
BLAUG, M. *Ricardian Economics: A Historical Study*. 1958.
—— 'The Myth of the Old Poor Law and the Making of the New', *Journal of Economic History*, XXIII, 2 (1963).
BOOTH, CHARLES. *Life and Labour of the People in London*. 2 vols. 1889; and 17 vols. 1903.
BOWLEY, A. L. 'The Statistics of Wages in the United Kingdom during the Last Hundred Years', articles in various issues of *Journal of the Royal Statistical Society*, LXI–LXIII (1898–1900).
—— *Wages in the United Kingdom in the Nineteenth Century*. 1900.
—— *The Division of the Product of Industry*. 1919.
—— *The Change in the Distribution of the National Income, 1880–1913*. 1920.
—— *Wages and Incomes since 1860*. 1937.
BOWLEY, A. L., and A. R. BURNETT-HURST. *Livelihood and Poverty*. 1915.
BOWLEY, MARIAN. *Innovations in Building Materials*. 1960.
—— *The British Building Industry: Some Studies in Response and Resistance to Change*. 1966.
BRASSEY, THOMAS (LORD BRASSEY). *Work and Wages*. 1894 edn (first published 1872).
BRIGGS, ASA, and J. SAVILLE (eds.). *Essays in Labour History*. 1960.
BROOKE, D. 'Railway Navvies on the Pennines, 1841–1871', *Journal of Transport History*, n.s., III (1975).
BROTHWELL, J. F. 'The Theoretical Basis for the Phillips Curve', *Bulletin of Economic Research*, XXIV (1972).
BROWN, E. H. PHELPS, and MARGARET H. BROWNE. *A Century of Pay*. 1968.
BROWN, E. H. PHELPS, and P. E. HART. 'The Share of Wages in National Income', *Economic Journal*, LXII (1952).
BUCKATZSCH, E. J. 'Places of Origin of a Group of Immigrants into Sheffield, 1624–1799', *Economic History Review*, 2nd ser., II, 3 (1950).
—— 'The Constancy of Local Populations and Migration in England before 1800', *Population Studies*, V, 1 (1951).
BURET, EUGÈNE. *De la misère des classes laborieuses en Angleterre et en France*. 2 vols. 1840.
BURNESS, W. *Essay on the Elements of British Industry*. 1848.
BURNETT, J. *Useful Toil: Autobiographies of Working People from the 1820's to the 1920's*. 1974.
BURT, ROGER. *Cornish Mining*. 1969.
BURT, ROGER (ed.). *Industry and Society in the South-West*. 1970.
BUTTERWORTH, E. *Historical Sketches of Oldham*. 1856.
BYTHELL, DUNCAN. *The Handloom Weavers*. 1969.
CAIRD, J. *English Agriculture in 1850–51*. 2nd edn. 1968.
CAIRNCROSS, A. K. 'Internal Migration in Victorian England', *Manchester School*, XVII (1949).
CHALKLIN, C. W. *The Provincial Towns of Georgian England*. 1974.
CHALLINOR, RAYMOND, and BRIAN RIPLEY. *The Miners' Association: A Trade Union in the Age of the Chartists*. 1968.
CHALMERS, THOMAS. *The Christian and Civic Economy of Large Towns*. 3 vols. 1821–6.
CHALONER, W. H. *The Skilled Artisans during the Industrial Revolution, 1750–1850*. Historical Association pamphlet. 1969.
CHAMBERS, J. D. 'Enclosure and Labour Supply in the Industrial Revolution', *Economic History Review*, 2nd ser., V (1953).
—— *Nottinghamshire in the Eighteenth Century*. 2nd edn. 1965.
—— *Population, Economy and Society in Pre-Industrial England*, 1972.
CHAMBERS, J. D., and G. E. MINGAY. *The Agricultural Revolution, 1750–1880*. 1966.
CHAMBERS, WILLIAM. *Memoir of Robert Chambers with Autobiographical Reminiscences*. 1872.

CHAPMAN, S. D. 'The Transition to the Factory System in the Midland Cotton Industry', *Economic History Review*, 2nd ser., XVIII (1965).
—— *The Early Factory Masters*. 1967.
CHURCH, R. A. 'Labour Supply and Innovation, 1800–1860: The Boot and Shoe Industry', *Business History*, XII, 1 (1970).
CLAPHAM, J. H. *Economic History of Modern Britain*. 3 vols. 1926–39; repr. 1964.
—— 'Work and Wages', in G. M. Young (ed.), *Early Victorian England*. 2 vols. 1934; repr. 1963.
CLEGG, H. A., ALAN FOX, and A. F. THOMSON. *A History of British Trade Unions since 1889*, I: *1889–1910*. 1964.
COATS, A. W. 'Changing Attitudes to Labour in the Mid-Eighteenth Century', *Economic History Review*, 2nd ser., XI (1958).
—— 'The Classical Economists and the Labourer', in Jones and Mingay (eds.), *Land, Labour and Population in the Industrial Revolution*.
COBDEN, JOHN C. *The White Slaves of England*. 1853.
COLE, G. D. H. *Attempts at General Union*. 1953.
—— *Studies in Class Structure*. 1955.
COLE, G. D. H., and A. W. FILSON (eds.). *British Working-Class Movements: Select Documents, 1789–1875*. 1965 edn (first published 1951).
COLLIER, F. *The Family Economy of the Working Class in the Cotton Industry, 1784–1833*. 1964.
COLLINS, E. J. T. 'Labour Supply and Demand in European Agriculture, 1800–1880', in E. L. Jones and S. J. Woolf (eds.), *Agrarian Change and Economic Development*. 1969.
—— 'Harvest Technology and Labour Supply in Britain, 1790–1870', *Economic History Review*, 2nd ser., XXII (1969).
—— 'Harvest Technology and Labour Supply in Britain, 1790–1870'. Unpublished Ph.D. thesis, Nottingham, 1970.
COLQUHOUN, PATRICK. *A Treatise on Indigence*. 1806.
COOKE-TAYLOR, R. W. *The Modern Factory System*. 1841.
COONEY, E. W. 'The Origins of the Victorian Master Builders', *Economic History Review*, 2nd ser.; VIII (1955).
COONTZ, SYDNEY H. *Population Theories and the Economic Interpretation*. 1961.
CORRY, B., and D. LAIDLER. 'The Phillips Relation: A Theoretical Explanation', *Economica*, XXXIV, 134 (1967).
DAVID, PAUL A. 'Labour Productivity in English Agriculture, 1850–1914: Some Quantitative Evidence on Regional Differences', *Economic History Review*, 2nd ser., XXIII, 3 (1970).
DEANE, P., and W. A. COLE. *British Economic Growth, 1688–1959*. 1962.
DERRY, T. K. 'The Repeal of the Apprenticeship Clause of the Statute of Apprentices', *Economic History Review*, III (1931–2).
DESAI, ASHOK V. *Real Wages in Germany, 1871–1913*. 1968.
DEVEY, JOSEPH. *The Life of Joseph Locke*. 1962.
[DODD, WILLIAM]. *The Labouring Classes of England*. 1847.
DRAKE, MICHAEL (ed.). *Population in Industrialization*. 1969.
DUCKHAM, BARON F. 'Serfdom in Eighteenth Century Scotland', *History*, LIV (1969).
DYER, G. *Complaints of the People of England*, 1793.
EDWARDS, J. K. 'Norwich Bills of Mortality, 1707–1830', *Yorkshire Bulletin*, XXI (1969).
EDWARDS, M. M. *The Growth of the British Cotton Trade, 1780–1815*. 1967.
ENGELS, F. *Condition of the Working Class in England*. 1845; repr. 1958.
FAIRLIE, S. 'The Corn Laws and British Wheat Production, 1829–76', *Economic History Review*, 2nd ser., XXII (1969).
FAUCHER, LÉON. *Manchester in 1844: Its Present Condition and Future Prospect*. 1844.
—— *Etudes sur l'Angleterre*. 2nd edn. 1856.
FEI, J. C. H., and G. RANIS. *Development of the Labor Surplus Economy*. 1964.
FEINSTEIN, C. H. 'Changes in the Distribution of the National Income in the United Kingdom since 1860', in Marchal and Ducros (eds.), *Distribution of the National Income*.

FELKIN, W. 'The Labouring Classes in the Township of Hyde, Cheshire', *Journal of the Royal Statistical Society*, I (1838–9).

FEYNES, R. *History of the Northumberland and Durham Miners*. 1873; repr. 1923.

FISCHER, J. C. *Tagebücher*. 1951.

FISCHER, W. 'Innerbetrieblicher und sozialer Status der frühen Fabrikarbeiterschaft', *Forschungen zur Sozial- und Wirtschaftsgeschichte*, VI (1964).

FONG, H. D. *The Triumph of the Factory System*. 1932.

FRASER, W. H. *Trade Unions and Society: The Struggle for Acceptance, 1850–1880*. 1974.

FURNISS, E. S. *The Position of the Labourers in a System of Nationalism*. 1920; repr. 1957.

FUSSELL, G. E., and M. COMPTON. 'Agricultural Adjustment after the Napoleonic Wars', *Economic History*, IV (1939).

GASH, N. 'Rural Unemployment, 1815–1834', *Economic History Review*, VI (1935).

GASKELL, P. *The Manufacturing Population of England*. 1833.

—— *Artisans and Machinery*. 1836; repr. 1968.

GHOSH, R. N. 'The Colonization Controversy: R. J. Wilmot-Horton and the Classical Economists', in Shaw (ed.), *Great Britain and the Colonies*.

GILBOY, E. W. *Wages in Eighteenth-Century England*. 1934.

GONNER, E. C. K. *Common Land and Enclosure*. 2nd edn. 1965.

GREG, W. R. 'English Socialism' (1850), in *Mistaken Aims and Attainable Ideals of the Artisan Class*. 1876.

GUEST, JOHN. *Compendious History of the Cotton Manufacture*. 1823; repr. 1968.

HABAKKUK, H. J. *American and British Technology in the Nineteenth Century*. 1962.

—— *Population Growth and Economic Development since 1750*. 1971.

HAMILTON, E. J. 'Profit Inflation and the Industrial Revolution, 1751–1800', *Quarterly Journal of Economics*, LVI (1942).

HAMMOND, J. L., and B. HAMMOND. *The Village Labourer, 1760–1832*. 1912.

—— *The Skilled Labourer, 1760–1832*. 1920 edn.

HANDLEY, J. E. *The Irish in Scotland, 1798–1845*. 2nd edn. 1945.

HARRISON, R. J. *Before the Socialists*. 1965.

HARTWELL, R. M. (ed.). *The Industrial Revolution*. 1970.

HASBACH, W. *A History of the English Agricultural Labourer*. 1908.

D'HAUSSEZ, BARON. *Great Britain in 1833*. 1833.

HAWKE, G. R. *Railways and Economic Growth in England and Wales, 1840–1870*. 1970.

HEAD, SIR GEORGE. *A Home Tour through the Manufacturing Districts of England in the Summer of 1835*. 1968 edn.

HENDERSON, W. O. (ed.). *Industrial Britain under the Regency: The Diaries of Escher, Bodmer, May and de Gallois*. 1968.

HICKS, J. R. *Value and Capital*. 1946.

HILL, SIR FRANCIS. *Georgian Lincoln*. 1966.

HILL, R. L. *Toryism and the People, 1832–46*. 1929.

HILTON, W. S. *Foes to Tyranny: A History of the Amalgamated Union of Building Trade Workers*. 1963.

HINDMARSH, L. 'Condition of the Agricultural Labourers in the Northern Division of Northumberland', *Journal of the Royal Statistical Society*, I (1838–9).

HINES, A. G. 'Trade Unions and Wage Inflation in the United Kingdom, 1893–1961', *Review of Economic Studies*, XXXI (1964).

—— 'Unemployment and the Rate of Change of Money Wage Rates in the United Kingdom, 1862–1963: A Reappraisal', *Review of Economics and Statistics*, L, I (1968).

HOBSBAWM, E. J. 'The British Standard of Living, 1790–1850', *Economic History Review*, 2nd ser., X (1957).

—— 'Customs, Wages and Work-Load in Nineteenth Century Industry', in Briggs and Saville (eds.), *Essays in Labour History*.

—— *Labouring Men*. 1964.

HOBSBAWM, E. J., and GEORGE RUDÉ. *Captain Swing*. 1969.

HOLMES, J. M., and D. J. SMYTH. 'The Relation between Unemployment and Excess Demand for Labour: An Examination of the Theory of the Phillips Curve', *Economica*, XXXVII, 148 (1970).

HOPKINSON, G. G. 'The Development of Lead Mining and of the Coal and Iron Industries in North Derbyshire and South Yorkshire, 1700–1850'. Unpublished Ph.D. thesis, Sheffield, 1958.

HOUSE, J. W. 'North-Eastern England: Population Movements and the Landscape since the Early 19th Century' (cyclostyled). 1954.

HOWELL, GEORGE. *The Conflicts of Capital and Labour.* 1878.

HUGHES, EDWARD. *North Country Life in the Eighteenth Century.* 2 vols. 1952.

HUGHES, J. R. T. *Fluctuations in Trade, Industry and Finance.* 1960.

HUNT, E. H. 'Labour Productivity in English Agriculture, 1850–1914', *Economic History Review*, 2nd ser., XX (1967).

—— 'Quantitative and Other Evidence in Agriculture, 1850–1914', *Economic History Review*, 2nd ser., XXIII (1970).

—— *Regional Wage Variations in Britain, 1850–1914.* 1973.

JOHN, A. H. *The Industrial Development of South Wales, 1750–1850.* 1950.

—— 'Farming in Wartime, 1793–1815', in Jones and Mingay (eds.), *Land, Labour and Population in the Industrial Revolution.*

JONES, E. L. 'The Agricultural Labour Market in England', *Economic History Review*, 2nd ser., XVII (1964).

—— 'The Agricultural Origins of Industry', *Past and Present*, no. 40 (1968).

JONES, E. L., and G. E. MINGAY (eds.). *Land, Labour and Population in the Industrial Revolution.* 1967.

KALDOR, N. 'Economic Growth and the Problem of Inflation, II', *Economica*, XXVI, 104 (1959).

KAY, J. P. 'Earnings of Agricultural Labourers in Norfolk and Suffolk', *Journal of the Royal Statistical Society*, I (1838–9).

KEELING, FREDERIC. *Child Labour in the United Kingdom.* 1914.

KEYNES, J. M. 'Relative Movements of Real Wages and Output', *Economical Journal*, XLIX (1939).

KINDLEBERGER, C. P. *Foreign Trade and the National Economy.* 1962.

—— *Europe's Postwar Growth: The Role of Labor Supply.* 1967.

KINGSFORD, P. W. *Victorian Railwaymen.* 1970.

KITTRELL, E. R. 'The Development of the Theory of Colonization in English Classical Political Economy', in Shaw (ed.), *Great Britain and the Colonies.*

KNOWLES, K. G. J. C., and D. J. ROBERTSON. 'Differences between the Wages of Skilled and Unskilled Workers, 1880–1950', *Bulletin of the Oxford Institute of Statistics*, XIII (1951).

KUCZYNSKI, J. *Die Geschichte der Lage der Arbeiter unter dem Kapitalismus.* 40 vols. 1962–8.

LASLETT, PETER. *The World We Have Lost.* 1971 edn (first published 1965).

LAW, JOHN. *Money and Trade.* 1705.

LEEDS TOWN COUNCIL. Statistical Committee. 'Report upon the Condition of the Town of Leeds and of Its Inhabitants', *Journal of the Royal Statistical Society*, II (1839–40).

LEIFCHILD, J. R. *Our Coal and Our Pits.* 1856.

LEWIS, J. PARRY. *Building Cycles and Britain's Growth.* 1965.

LEWIS, RICHARD A. *Edwin Chadwick and the Public Health Movement, 1832–1854.* 1952.

LEWIS, W. A. 'Economic Development with Unlimited Supplies of Labour', *Manchester School*, XXII (1954).

—— *Socialism and Economic Growth.* 1971.

LIPSEY, R. G. 'The Relation between Unemployment and the Rate of Change of Money Wages in the United Kingdom, 1862–1957', *Economica*, XXVII, 105 (1960).

LIPSEY, R. G., and M. D. STEUER. 'The Relations between Profits and Wage Rates', *Economica*, XXVIII, 108 (1961).

LOFTUS, P. J. 'Labour's Share in Manufacturing', *Lloyds Bank Review*, XCII (1969).

LONDON AND CAMBRIDGE ECONOMIC SERVICE and *The Times*. 'The British Economy: Key Statistics, 1902–1966'.

LOUIS, HENRY. 'The Pitmen's Yearly Bond', *Transactions of the North of England Institute of Mining*, LXXX (1930).

LUDLOW, J. M., and LLOYD JONES. *The Progress of the Working Class, 1832–1867.* 1867.

MACASKILL, JOY. 'The Chartist Land Plan', in Asa Briggs (ed.), *Chartist Studies.* 1959.

McCORMICK, B. 'Hours of Work in British Industry', *Industrial and Labour Relations Review*, XII (1959).

McCORMICK, B., and J. E. WILLIAMS. 'The Miners and the Eight-Hour Day, 1863–1910', *Economic History Review*, 2nd ser., XII (1959).

McCULLOCH, J. R. *A Descriptive and Statistical Account of the British Empire.* 2 vols. 3rd edn. 1847.

—— *A Treatise on the Circumstances which Determine the Rate of Wages and the Condition of the Labouring Classes.* 2nd edn. 1854; repr. 1963.

M'DOUALL, P. M. 'Statistics of the Parish of Ramsbottom, nr Bury, Lancashire', *Journal of the Royal Statistical Society*, I (1838–9).

McKEOWN, T., and R. G. BROWN. 'Medical Evidence relating to English Population Changes in the Eighteenth Century', in D. V. Glass and D. E. Eversley (eds.), *Population in History.* 1965.

MALTHUS, T. R. *Essay on the Principle of Population.* 2 vols. 3rd edn. 1806.

—— *Principles of Political Economy.* 2nd edn. 1836; repr. 1936.

MAYHEW, H. *London Labour and the London Poor.* 4 vols. 1861.

MARCHAL, JEAN, and BERNARD DUCROS (eds.). *The Distribution of National Income.* 1968.

MARSHALL, J. D. 'The Lancashire Rural Labourer in the Early Nineteenth Century', *Transactions of the Lancashire and Cheshire Antiquarian Society*, LXXI (1961).

MARSHALL, W. *A Review of the Reports to the Board of Agriculture for the Northern Department of England.* 1808.

MARX, KARL. *Capital*, vol. I. Everyman edn. 2 parts. 1930; repr. 1957.

—— *Capital*, vol. III. Chicago edn. 1909.

MATHER, F. C. *After the Canal Duke*, 1970.

MATHIAS, PETER. *The First Industrial Nation: The Economic History of Britain, 1700–1914.* 1969.

MATTHEWS, R. C. O. *Economic Fluctuations in Great Britain, 1833–1842*, 1954.

MEEK, R. L. *Marx and Engels on Malthus.* 1953.

MENDELS, F. F. 'Proto-Industrialization: The First Phase of the Industrialization Process', *Journal of Economic History*, XXXII (1972).

MERTTENS, F. 'The Hours and Cost of Labour in the Cotton Industry at Home and Abroad', *Transactions of the Manchester Statistical Society*, 1893–4.

MINGAY, G. E. 'The Size of Farms in the Eighteenth Century', *Economic History Review*, 2nd ser., XIV (1962).

MITCHELL, B. R., and P. DEANE. *Abstract of British Historical Statistics*, 1962.

MORGAN, VALERIE. 'Agricultural Wage Rates in Late Eighteenth-Century Scotland', *Economic History Review*, 2nd ser., XXIV (1971).

MORRIS, MAX (ed.). *From Cobbett to the Chartists, 1815–1848.* 1948.

MOSLEY, JOHN V. 'Poor Law Administration in England and Wales, 1830 to 1850, with Special Reference to the Problem of the Able-Bodied Labourer'. Unpublished Ph.D. thesis, London, 1976.

NATIONAL ASSOCIATION FOR THE PROMOTION OF SOCIAL SCIENCE. *Trades' Societies and Strikes.* 1860.

National Income and Expenditure. Central Statistical Office blue books: annual.

NEALE, R. S. 'Class and Class Consciousness in Early Nineteenth-Century England: Three Classes or Five', *Victorian Studies*, XII (1968–9).

Notes to the People (journal), ed. Ernest Jones, vols. I–II (1851–2); repr. 1967.

NURKSE, R. *Capital Formation.* 1953.

OHKAWA, K., and R. MINAMI. 'The Phase of Unlimited Supplies of Labour', *Hitotsubashi Journal of Economics*, V, I (1964).

OWEN, R. *On the Employment of Children in Manufactories* (1818), repr. in *New View of Society*, ed. G. D. H. Cole. 1927.

—— *Life of Robert Owen, by Himself.* 1920 edn.

PAPPÉ, H. O. 'Wakefield and Marx', in Shaw (ed.), *Great Britain and the Colonies.*

PEACOCK, A. J. *Bread or Blood.* 1965.

PELLING, HENRY. *Popular Politics and Society in Late Victorian Britain.* 1968.

PERKIN, HAROLD. *The Origins of Modern English Society, 1780–1880.* 1969.

PHILLIPS, A. W. 'The Relation between Unemployment and the Rate of Change of Money Wage Rates in the United Kingdom, 1861–1957', *Economica*, XXV, 100 (1958).

PIMLOTT, J. A. R. *The Englishman's Holiday: A Social History.* 1947.

PINCHBECK, IVY. *Women Workers and the Industrial Revolution, 1750–1850.* 1930.

POLE, WILLIAM. *The Life of Sir William Fairbairn, Bart.* 1877.

POLLARD, S. 'Trade Unions and the Labour Market, 1870–1914', *Yorkshire Bulletin of Economic and Social Research*, XVII (1965).

POLLARD, S., and D. W. CROSSLEY. *The Wealth of Britain, 1085–1966.* 1968.

PORTER, G. R. *Progress of the Nation.* 3rd edn. 1851.

POSTGATE, R. W. *The Builders' History.* 1923.

PRESSNELL, L. S. (ed.). *Studies in the Industrial Revolution.* 1960.

PREST, A. R. 'National Income of the United Kingdom, 1870–1946', *Economic Journal*, LVIII (1948).

PREST, J. *The Industrial Revolution in Coventry.* 1960.

PROTHERO, I. J. 'Chartism in London', *Past and Present*, no. 44 (1969).

—— 'London Chartists and the Trades', *Economic History Review*, 2nd ser., XXIV, 2 (1971).

RADCLIFFE, WILLIAM. *Origin of the New System of Manufacture.* 1828.

RAZZELL, P. E. 'Statistics and English Historical Sociology', in Hartwell (ed.), *The Industrial Revolution.*

REDER, M. W. 'The Size Distribution of Earnings', in Marchal and Ducros (eds.), *The Distribution of National Income.*

REDFORD, A. *Labour Migration in England, 1800–1850.* 2nd edn. 1964.

RICARDO, D. *The Works and Correspondence of David Ricardo*, ed. P. Sraffa and M. H. Dobb. 11 vols. 1951–73.

RICHARDSON, C. 'Irish Settlement in Mid-Nineteenth-Century Bradford', *Yorkshire Bulletin of Economic and Social Research*, XX (1968).

RIMMER, W. G. 'Working-Men's Cottages in Leeds, 1770–1840', *Thoresby Society*, XLVI (1960).

ROBINSON, J. *An Essay on Marxian Economics.* 1942; repr. 1947.

ROGERS, J. E. THOROLD. *Six Centuries of Work and Wages.* 1894.

RONDEAU, C. 'The Autonomous Influence of Institutional Determinants of the Movement of Money Wages in the United Kingdom, 1862–1938'. Unpublished Ph.D. thesis, London, 1969.

ROUTH, GUY. *Occupation and Pay in Great Britain, 1906–1960.* 1965.

ROWNTREE, B. SEEBOHM. *Poverty: A Study of Town Life.* 1901.

RULE, JOHN G. 'Some Social Aspects of the Cornish Industrial Revolution', in Burt (ed.), *Industry and Society in the South-West.*

SCOTT, HYLTON. 'The Miners' Bond in Northumberland and Durham', *Proceedings of the Society of Antiquaries of Newcastle-upon-Tyne*, 4th ser., XI (1947).

SEMMEL, B. 'The Philosophic Radicals and Colonialism', in Shaw (ed.), *Great Britain and the Colonies.*

SHAW, A. G. L. (ed.). *Great Britain and the Colonies, 1815–1865.* 1970.

SIGSWORTH, E. M. 'A Provincial Hospital in the Eighteenth and Early Nineteenth Centuries', *College of General Practitioners, Yorkshire Faculty Journal*, June 1966.

SIMOND, L. *Journal of a Tour and Residence in Great Britain during the Years 1810 and 1811.* 2 vols. 1815.

SIMPSON, J. B. *Capital and Labour in Coal Mining.* 1900.

SMELSER, NEIL J. *Social Change in the Industrial Revolution.* 1959.

SMITH, ADAM. *Wealth of Nations*, ed. J. R. McCulloch. 1863 edn.

SOMERVILLE, ALEXANDER. *The Autobiography of a Working Man.* 1848; repr. 1967.

SOTIROFF, G. (ed.). *Economic Writings.* 2 vols. 1962–3.

STATISTICAL SOCIETY OF LONDON, COMMITTEE OF. 'State of the Working Classes in the Parishes of St Margaret and St John, Westminster', *Journal of the Royal Statistical Society*, III (1840–1).

STATISTICAL SOCIETY OF MANCHESTER, 'Report on the Condition of the Population in Three Parishes in Rutlandshire', *Journal of the Royal Statistical Society*, II (1839–40).

STEFFEN, G. *Studien zur Geschichte der englischen Lohnarbeiter*. 3 vols. 1901.

STEUART, SIR JAMES. *An Inquiry into the Principles of Political Œconomy*. 2 vols. 1767; repr. 1966.

STYLES, PHILIP. 'The Evolution of the Law of Settlement', *University of Birmingham Historical Journal*, IX (1963).

SYMONS, JELINGER C. *Arts and Artisans at Home and Abroad*. 1839.

TAYLOR, A. J. 'The Sub-Contract System in the British Coal Industry', in Pressnell (ed.), *Studies in the Industrial Revolution*.

TAYLOR, JAMES STEPHEN. 'The Mythology of the Old Poor Law', *Journal of Economic History*, XXIX (1969).

THACKRAH, C. TURNER. *The Effects of Arts, Trades and Professions . . . on Health and Longevity*. 1832.

THOMAS, R. L., and P. M. STONEY. 'Unemployment Dispersion as a Determinant of Wage Inflation in the U.K., 1926–1966', *Manchester School*, XXXIX (1971).

THOMAS, W. E. S. 'Francis Place and Working-Class History', *Historical Journal*, V (1962).

THOMIS, M. I. *Politics and Society in Nottingham, 1785–1835*. 1969.

THOMPSON, E. P. *The Making of the English Working Class*. 1963.

—— 'Time, Work Discipline and Industrial Capitalism', *Past and Present*, no. 38 (1967).

THOMPSON, E. P., and EILEEN YEO. *The Unknown Mayhew*. 1971.

Torrington Diaries: see Andrews, C. B. (above).

TREBLE, J. H. 'The Place of the Irish Catholics in the Social Life of the North of England, 1829–51'. Unpublished Ph.D. thesis, Leeds, 1968.

—— 'Irish Navvies in the North of England, 1830–1880', *Transport History*, VI (1973).

TURNBULL, G. *A History of Calico Printing in Great Britain*. 1939.

TUCKER, JOSIAH. *Reflections on the Present Low Price of Coarse Wools*. 1782.

UMEMURA, MATAJI. 'Agriculture and Labour Supply in Japan in the Meiji Era', *The Developing Economies*, III, 3 (1965).

UNWIN, MRS COBDEN (ed.). *The Hungry Forties: Life under the Bread Tax*. 1904.

VANDERKAMP, J. 'The Phillips Relation: A Theoretical Explanation – A Comment', *Economica*, XXXV, 138 (1968).

VESTER, M. *Die Entstehung des Proletariats als Lernprozess*. 1970.

[WADE, JOHN]. *History of the Middle and Working Classes*. 1833.

WAKEFIELD, EDWARD GIBBON. *England and America*. 2 vols. 1833.

—— *The Collected Works of Edward Gibbon Wakefield*, ed. M. F. Lloyd Pritchard. 1968.

WALKER, F. A. *The Wages Question*. 1887.

WALLAS, G. *Francis Place, 1771–1854*. 1908.

WARD, JAMES. *Workmen and Wages at Home and Abroad*. 1868.

WARD, J. T. *The Factory Movement, 1830–1855*. 1962.

—— *The Factory System*. 2 vols. 1970.

WEBB, S., and B. WEBB. *History of Trade Unionism*. 1902 edn.

WEBER, A. F. *The Growth of Cities in the 19th Century*. 1899.

WILES, R. C. 'The Theory of Wages in Later English Mercantilism', *Economic History Review*, 2nd ser., XXI (1968).

WILLIAMS, J. E. *The Derbyshire Miners*. 1962.

WING, CHARLES. *Evils of the Factory System, Demonstrated by Parliamentary Evidence*. 1837; repr. 1967.

WOODWARD, J. H. 'Before Bacteriology – Deaths in Hospitals', *College of General Practitioners, Yorkshire Faculty Journal*, Autumn 1969.

WOOTTON, BARBARA. *The Social Foundations of Wage Policy*. 1955.

[WRIGHT, THOMAS]. *Some Habits and Customs of the Working Classes, by a Journeyman Engineer*. 1867; repr. 1967.

YOUNG, ARTHUR. *A Farmer's Tour through the East of England*. 4 vols. 1771.

—— *Political Arithmetic*. 1774.

YOUNG, G. M. (ed.). *Early Victorian England*. 2 vols. 1934; repr. 1963.

YOUNGSON, A. J. *The Making of Classical Edinburgh, 1750–1850*. 1966.

CHAPTER IV

Industrial Entrepreneurship and Management in Great Britain

Because the chronological period of much of this chapter is the same as that of Professor David S. Landes's contribution to volume VI of this *History*, 'Technological Change and Development in Western Europe' (subsequently expanded into *The Unbound Prometheus*) – which must serve as the best general introduction to the industrial environment within which the British entrepreneur operated – it has been deemed unnecessary to provide here a bibliography which would, in essence, simply reproduce Professor Landes's remarkably comprehensive list. All that is attempted is to indicate the main secondary sources upon which this brief, exploratory essay has depended. These are roughly divided into seven main groups, which are not mutually exclusive and none of which is by any means exhaustive.

1. INDUSTRIAL STRUCTURE AND ORGANIZATION

AARONOVITCH, S. *Monopoly. A Study of British Monopoly Capitalism*. London, 1955.

AARONOVITCH, S., and MALCOLM C. SAWYER. 'The Concentration of British Manufacturing', *Lloyds Bank Review*, no. 114 (October 1974), 14–23.

ARMSTRONG, A., and A. SILBERSTON. 'Size of Plant, Size of Enterprise and Concentration in British Manufacturing Industry, 1935–58', *Journal of Royal Statistical Society*, ser. A, CXXVIII, 3 (1965), 395–420.

ASHWORTH, W. 'Changes in the Industrial Structure, 1870–1914', *Yorkshire Bulletin of Economic and Social Research*, XVII, 1 (May 1965), 61–74.

BANNOCK, G. *The Juggernauts: The Age of the Big Corporation*. London, 1971.

BULL, GEORGE, and ANTHONY VICE. *Bid for Power*. London, 1958.

BURN, DUNCAN (ed.). *The Structure of British Industry*. 2 vols. Cambridge, 1958.

COMMITTEE ON INDUSTRY AND TRADE (Balfour Committee). *Factors in Industrial and Commercial Efficiency*. London, 1927.

DUNNING, J. H., and C. J. THOMAS. *British Industry: Change and Development in the Twentieth Century*. London, 1961.

EVELY, R., and I. M. D. LITTLE. *Concentration in British Industry*. Cambridge, 1960.

GEORGE, K. D. 'Changes in British Industrial Concentration, 1951–58', *Journal of Industrial Economics*, XV, 3 (July 1967), 200–11.

—— 'A Note on Changes in Industrial Concentration in the United Kingdom', *Economic Journal*, LXXXV (1975), 124–8.

GEORGE, K. D., and A. SILBERSTON. 'The Causes and Effects of Mergers', *Scottish Journal of Political Economy*, XXII (1975), 179–93.

VAN DER HAAS, H. *The Enterprise in Transition: An Analysis of European and American Practice*. London, 1967.

HABAKKUK, H. J. *Industrial Organisation since the Industrial Revolution: The Fifteenth Fawley Foundation Lecture*. Southampton, 1968.

HANNAH, LESLIE. 'Takeover Bids in Britain before 1950: An Exercise in Business "Pre-History"', *Business History*, XVI (1974), 65–77.

—— 'Mergers in British Manufacturing Industry, 1880–1918', *Oxford Economic Papers*, n.s., XXVI (1974), 65–77.

—— *The Rise of the Corporate Economy*. London, 1976.

HANNAH, LESLIE (ed.). *Management Strategy and Business Development: An Historical and Comparative Study*. Papers presented at a conference on management history, June 1975. London, 1976.

HART, P. E., and S. J. PRAIS. 'The Analysis of Business Concentration: A Statistical Approach', *Journal of the Royal Statistical Society*, ser. A, CXIX (1956), 150–81.

HART, P. E., M. A. UTTON, and G. WALSHE. *Mergers and Concentration in British Industry*. Cambridge 1973.

INDUSTRIAL REORGANISATION CORPORATION. *First Report and Accounts* (December 1966 – March 1968). London, 1968.

KINDLEBERGER, C. P. *Economic Growth in France and Britain, 1851–1950*. Cambridge, Mass., 1964.

KITCHING, JOHN. 'Why Acquisitions are Abortive', *Management Today*, November 1974, 82–7 and 148.

LEAK, H., and A. MAIZELS. 'The Structure of British Industry', *Journal of the Royal Statistical Society*, CVIII, 1–2 (1945), 142–207.

LUCAS, A. F. *Industrial Reconstruction and the Control of Competition: The British Experiments*. London, 1937.

LYDALL, H. F. 'Aspects of Competition in Manufacturing Industry', *Bulletin of the Oxford University Institute of Statistics*, XX (1958), 320–37.

—— 'The Growth of Manufacturing Firms', *Bulletin of the Oxford University Institute of Statistics*, XXI (1959), 85–111.

McCLELLAND, W. G. 'The Industrial Reorganisation Corporation, 1966–71: An Experimental Prod', *The Three Banks Review*, no. 94 (June 1972), 23–42.

MARSHALL, A. *Industry and Trade*. London, 1920.

MENNELL, WILLIAM. *Takeover: The Growth of Monopoly in Britain, 1951–61*. London, 1962.

NEWBOULD, G. D. *Management and Merger Activity*. Liverpool, 1970.

NEWBOULD, G. D., and ANDREW S. JACKSON. *The Receding Ideal*. Liverpool, 1972.

POLLARD, S. *The Development of the British Economy, 1914–1950*. London, 1962.

POSTAN, M. M. *An Economic History of Western Europe, 1945–1964*. London, 1967.

PLUMMER, ALFRED. *New British Industries in the Twentieth Century: A Survey of Development and Structure*. London, 1937.

PRAIS, S. J. 'A New Look at the Growth of Industrial Concentration', *Oxford Economic Papers*, n.s., XXVI (1974), 273–88.

REDDAWAY, W. B. 'An Analysis of Take-overs', *Lloyds Bank Review*, no. 104 (April 1972), 8–19.

SAMUELS, J. M. (ed.). *Readings on Mergers and Takeovers*. London, 1972.

SAWYER, MALCOLM C. 'Concentration in British Manufacturing Industry', *Oxford Economic Papers*, n.s. XXIII, 3 (November 1971), 352–75.

SILVERMAN, H. A. (ed.). *Studies in Industrial Organisation*. London, 1946.

SINGH, AJIT. *Take-overs: Their Relevance to the Stock Market and the Theory of the Firm*. Cambridge, 1971.

SMITH, RANDALL, and DENNIS BROOKS. *Mergers Past and Present*. London, 1963.

STACEY, NICHOLAS A. H. *Mergers in Modern Business*, 2nd, rev. edn. London, 1970.

SUTHERLAND, A. *The Monopolies Commission in Action*. Cambridge, 1969.

TURNER, G. *Business in Britain*. London, 1969.

UTTON, M. A. 'The Effect of Mergers on Concentration: U.K. Manufacturing Industry, 1954–65', *Journal of Industrial Economics*, XX (1971–2), 42–58.

—— 'On Measuring the Effects of Industrial Mergers', *Scottish Journal of Political Economy*, XXI (1974), 13–26.

—— 'Mergers and the Growth of Large Firms', *Bulletin of the Oxford University Institute of Economics and Statistics*, XXXIV (1972), 189–97.

—— 'Some Features of the Early Merger Movements in British Manufacturing Industry', *Business History*, XIV, 1 (January 1972), 51–60.

WALSHE, G. *Recent Trends in Monopoly in Great Britain*. Cambridge, 1974.

WHITTINGTON, G. 'Changes in the Top 100 Quoted Manufacturing Companies in the United Kingdom, 1948 to 1968', *Journal of Industrial Economics*, XXI (1972–3), 17–34.

WRIGHT, J. F. 'The Capital Market and the Finance of Industry', in G. D. N. Worswick and P. H. Ady (eds.), *The British Economy in the Nineteen-Fifties*. Oxford, 1962. 461–501.

2. Studies of Particular Industries and Regions

Allen, G. C. *The Industrial Development of Birmingham and the Black Country*. London, 1929.

Andrews, P. S., and E. Brunner. *Capital Development in Steel*. Oxford, 1952.

Ashton, T. S. *Iron and Steel in the Industrial Revolution*, 2nd edn. Manchester, 1951.

Bartlett, J. N. 'The Mechanisation of the Kidderminster Carpet Industry', *Business History*, ix, 1 (January 1967), 49–67.

Bellamy, Joyce M. 'Cotton Manufacture in Kingston Upon Hull', *Business History*, iv, 2 (June 1962), 91–108.

Birch, Alan. *The Economic History of the British Iron and Steel Industry, 1784–1879*. London, 1967.

Bremner, D. *The Industries of Scotland: Their Rise, Progress and Present Condition*. London, 1869.

Burn, D. L. 'The Genesis of American Engineering Competition', *Economic History*, ii (1931), 292–311.

—— *The Economic History of Steelmaking, 1867–1939*. Cambridge, 1940.

Burnham, T. H., and G. O. Hoskins. *Iron and Steel in Britain, 1870–1930*. London, 1943.

Buxton, Neil K. 'Entrepreneurial Efficiency in the British Coal Industry between the Wars', *Economic History Review*, 2nd ser., xxiii, 3 (December 1970), 476–97.

Chapman, S. D. *The Early Factory Masters*. Newton Abbot, 1967.

—— 'Fixed Capital Formation in the British Cotton Industry, 1770–1815', *Economic History Review*, 2nd ser., xxiii, 2 (August 1970), 235–66.

—— 'Enterprise and Innovation in the British Hosiery Industry, 1750–1850', *Textile History*, v (1974), 14–37.

—— 'Working Capital in the British Cotton Industry, 1770–1850'. Unpublished paper presented at Ealing Business History Conference, 1975.

Chapman, Sydney J. *The Lancashire Cotton Industry: A Study in Economic Development*. Manchester, 1904.

Church, R. A. 'The Effect of the American Export Invasion on the British Boot and Shoe Industry, 1885–1914', *Journal of Economic History*, xxviii (1968), 223–54.

—— 'Labour Supply and Innovation, 1800–1860: The Boot and Shoe Industry', *Business History*, xii, 1 (January 1970), 25–45.

—— 'The British Leather Industry and Foreign Competition, 1870–1914', *Economic History Review*, 2nd ser., xxiv, 4 (November 1971), 543–70.

Clapham, J. H. *The Woollen and Worsted Industries*. London, 1907.

Clow, Archibald, and Nan L. Clow. *The Chemical Revolution: A Contribution to Social Technology*, London, 1952.

Coleman, D. C. *The British Paper Industry, 1495–1860*. Oxford, 1958.

Duckham, Baron F. *History of the Scottish Coal Industry, i: 1700–1815*. Newton Abbot, 1970.

Edwards, M. M. *The Growth of the British Cotton Trade, 1780–1815*. Manchester, 1967.

Ellis, C. Hamilton. *Nineteenth Century Railway Carriages*. London, 1949.

Farnie, D. A. 'The English Cotton Industry, 1850–1896'. Unpublished M.A. thesis, University of Manchester, 1953.

Forward, E. A. *Handbook of the Collections Illustrating Land Transport*, iii: *Railway Locomotives and Rolling Stock, part 2: Descriptive Catalogue*. London, 1948.

Glover, F. J. 'The Rise of the Heavy Woollen Trade of the West Riding of Yorkshire in the Nineteenth Century', *Business History*, iv, 1 (December 1961), 1–21.

Gulvin, Clifford. *The Tweedmakers: A History of the Scottish Fancy Woollen Industry, 1600–1914*. Newton Abbot, 1973.

Hamilton, Henry. *An Economic History of Scotland in the Eighteenth Century*. Oxford, 1963.

Harrison, A. E. 'The Competitiveness of the British Cycle Industry, 1890–1914', *Economic History Review*, 2nd ser., xxii (1969), 287–303.

Harte, N. B., and K. G. Ponting (eds.). *Textile History and Economic History: Essays in Honour of Miss Julia de Lucy Mann*. Manchester, 1973.

HELM, ELIJAH. 'The Alleged Decline of the British Cotton Industry', *Economic Journal*, II (1892), 735–44.

KIRBY, M. W. 'The Lancashire Cotton Industry in the Inter-War Years: A Study in Organisational Change', *Business History*, XVI (1974), 145–9.

LENMAN, BRUCE, and KATHLEEN DONALDSON. 'Partners' Incomes, Investment and Diversification in the Scottish Linen Area, 1850–1921', *Business History*, XIII, 1 (January 1971), 1–18.

McCLOSKEY, DONALD M. 'Productivity Change in British Pig Iron, 1870–1939', *Quarterly Journal of Economics*, LXXXII, 2 (May 1968), 281–96.

—— *Economic Maturity and Entrepreneurial Decline: British Iron and Steel, 1870–1913*. Cambridge, Mass., 1973. (See note 171 to this chapter, above.)

McKENDRICK, NEIL. 'The Victorian View of the Midland Potteries', *Midland History*, 1 (1971), 34–47.

MANN, J. DE L. *The Cloth Industry in the West of England from 1640 to 1880*. Oxford, 1971.

MINCHINTON, W. E. *The British Tinplate Industry: A History*. Oxford, 1957.

MUSSON, A. E., and E. ROBINSON. 'The Origins of Engineering in Lancashire', *Journal of Economic History*, XX (1960), 209–32.

OLIVER, J. L. *The Development and Structure of the Furniture Industry*. London, 1966.

ORSAGH, T. G. 'Progress in Iron and Steel: 1870–1913', *Comparative Studies in Society and History*, III (1960–1), 216–30.

POLLARD, SIDNEY. 'British and World Shipbuilding. 1890–1914: A Study in Comparative Costs', *Journal of Economic History*, XVII (1957), 426–44.

RAINNIE, G. F. (ed.). *The Woollen and Worsted Industry: An Economic Analysis*. Oxford, 1965.

ROBERTSON, A. J. 'The Decline of the Scottish Cotton Industry', *Business History*, XII, 2 (July 1970), 116–28.

ROBERTSON, P. L. 'Technical Education in the British Shipbuilding and Marine Engineering Industries, 1863–1914', *Economic History Review*, 2nd ser., XXVII (1974), 225–35.

SANDBERG, LARS G. 'Movements in the Quality of British Cotton Textile Exports, 1815–1913', *Journal of Economic History*, XXVIII (1968), 1–27.

—— 'American Rings and English Mules: The Role of Economic Rationality', *Quarterly Journal of Economics*, LXXXIII, 1 (February 1969), 25–43.

—— *Lancashire in Decline*. Columbus, Ohio, 1974.

SAUL, S. B. 'The American Impact on British Industry, 1895–1914', *Business History*, III, 1 (January 1960), 19–38.

—— 'The Motor Industry in Britain', *Business History*, V, 1 (December 1962), 22–44.

—— 'The Market and Development of the Mechanical Engineering Industries in Britain, 1860–1914', *Economic History Review*, 2nd ser., XX (1967), 111–30.

SHAPIRO, SEYMOUR. *Capital and the Cotton Industry*. Ithaca, N.Y., 1967.

SHIMMIN, ARNOLD N. 'Distribution of Employment in the Wool Textile Industry in the West Riding of Yorkshire', *Journal of the Royal Statistical Society*, LXXXIX (1926), 96–118.

SIGSWORTH, E. M. 'The West Riding Wool Textile Industry and the Great Exhibition', *Yorkshire Bulletin of Economic and Social Research*, IV, 1 (1952), 21–31.

SMITH, ROLAND. 'The Lancashire Cotton Industry and the Great Depression, 1873–1896'. Unpublished Ph.D. thesis, University of Birmingham, 1954.

TAYLOR, A. J. 'Concentration and Specialisation in the Lancashire Cotton Industry, 1825–50', *Economic History Review*, 2nd ser., 1 (1949), 114–22.

THOMAS, JOHN. *The Rise of the Staffordshire Potteries*. Bath, 1971.

THOMSON, A. G. *The Paper Industry in Scotland*, Edinburgh, 1974.

TIMMINS, S. (ed.). *The Resources, Products and Industrial History of Birmingham and the Midland Hardware District*. London, 1866.

TRINDER, BARRIE. *The Industrial Revolution in Shropshire*. London, 1973.

TURNBULL, G. *A History of the Calico Printing Industry of Great Britain*. Altrincham, 1951.

TURNER, GRAHAM. *The Car Makers*. London, 1963.

URE, A. *The Cotton Manufacture of Great Britain*. 2 vols. London, 1836.

VAIZEY, JOHN. *The History of British Steel*. London, 1974.

VAMPLEW, WRAY. 'Scottish Railways and the Development of Scottish Locomotive Building in the Nineteenth Century', *Business History Review*, XLVI (1972), 320–38.

WARNER, SIR FRANK. *The Silk Industry of the United Kingdom: Its Origin and Development.* London, 1921.

WILSON, R. G. *Gentlemen Merchants: The Merchant Community in Leeds, 1700–1830.* Manchester, 1971.

WOLFF, KLAUS H. 'Textile Bleaching and the Birth of the Chemical Industry', *Business History Review*, XLVIII (1974), 143–63.

3. THE FIRM: STRUCTURE, GROWTH, OWNERSHIP, AND CONTROL

ASHTON, T. S. 'The Growth of Textile Businesses in the Oldham District, 1884–1924', *Journal of the Royal Statistical Society*, LXXXIX (1926), 567–83.

BLEASE, J. G. 'Institutional Investors and the Stock Exchange', *District Bank Review*, no. 151 (September 1964), 38–64.

BOLTON REPORT. *Report of the Committee of Inquiry on Small Firms.* Cmnd 4811. London, 1971.

BOSWELL, JONATHAN. *The Rise and Decline of Small Firms.* London, 1972.

CHANNON, DEREK F. *The Strategy and Structure of British Enterprise.* London, 1973.

CHILD, JOHN. *The Business Enterprise in Modern Industrial Society.* London, 1969.

CLAPHAM, J. H. *An Economic History of Modern Britain.* 3 vols. Cambridge, 1926–38.

DAEMS, HERMAN, and HERMAN VAN DER WEE (eds.). *The Rise of Managerial Capitalism.* Louvain, 1974.

FLORENCE, P. S. 'The Statistical Analysis of Joint Stock Company Control', *Journal of the Royal Statistical Society*, CX, 1 (1947), 19–26.

—— *Ownership, Control and Success of Large Companies.* London, 1961.

—— *The Logic of British and American Industry. A Realistic Analysis of Economic Structure and Government.* 2nd edn. London, 1961.

GALAMBOS, LOUIS. 'Business History and the Theory of the Growth of the Firm', *Explorations in Entrepreneurial History*, 2nd ser., IV (1966), 3–16.

HUNT, B. C. *The Development of the Business Corporation in Britain, 1800–1877.* Cambridge, Mass., 1936.

JEFFERYS, J. B. 'Trends in Business Organisation in Great Britain Since 1856'. Unpublished Ph.D. thesis, University of London, 1938.

—— 'The Denomination and Character of Shares, 1855–1885', *Economic History Review*, XVI (1946), 45–55.

KAYSEN, C. B. 'The Social Significance of the Modern Corporation', *American Economic Review*, XLVII (1957), 311–19.

LANDES, D. S. 'The Structure of Enterprise in the Nineteenth Century. The cases of Britain and Germany' in Comité International des Sciences Historiques, XLe Congrès International des Sciences Historiques, Stockholm, *Rapports*, V: *Histoire contemporaine*. Uppsala, 1960. 107–28.

LEVI, LEONE. 'On Joint Stock Companies', *Journal of the [Royal] Statistical Society*, XXXIII (1870), 1–37.

LEVY, A. B. *Private Corporations and their Control*, 2 vols. London, 1950.

MACROSTY, H. W. 'Business Aspects of British Trusts', *Economic Journal*, XII (1902), 347–66.

—— *The Trust Movement in British Industry.* London, 1907.

MACGREGOR, D. H. 'Joint Stock Companies and the Risk Factor', *The Economic Journal*, XXXIX (1929), 491–505.

MACHLUP, FRITZ. 'Theories of the Firm: Marginalist, Behavioral, Managerial', *American Economic Review*, LVII, 1 (March 1967), 1–33.

MARWICK, W. H. 'The Limited Company in Scottish Economic Development', *Economic History*, III (1937), 415–29.

MELMAN, S. *Dynamic Factors in Industrial Productivity.* Oxford, 1956.

MERRITT, A. J. and M. E. LEHR. *The Private Company Today.* London, 1971.

MIDGLEY, K. 'How Much Control do Shareholders Exercise?', *Lloyds Bank Review*, no. 114 (October 1974), 24–37.

MILLER, HARRY. *The Way of Enterprise: A Study of the Origins, Problems and Achievements in the Growth of Post-War British Firms*. London, 1963.

MONSON, R. J., J. S. CHIU, and D. E. COOLEY. 'The Effect of Separation of Ownership and Control on the Performance of the Large Firm', *Quarterly Journal of Economics*, LXXXII (1968), 435–51.

NAPIER, T. B. 'The History of Joint Stock and Limited Liability Companies', in *A Century of Law Reform* (London, 1901), 380–415.

NICHOLS, THEO. *Ownership, Control and Ideology*. London, 1969.

PARKINSON, HARGREAVES. *Ownership of Industry*. London, 1951.

PAYNE, P. L. 'The Emergence of the Large-Scale Company in Great Britain, 1870–1914', *Economic History Review*, 2nd ser., XX, 3 (December 1967), 519–42.

SAVILLE, J. 'Sleeping Partnership and Limited Liability, 1850–1856', *Economic History Review*, 2nd ser., VIII, 3 (April 1956), 418–33.

SCOTT, BRUCE R. 'The Industrial State: Old Myths and New Realities', *Harvard Business Review*, LI (1973), 133–48.

SHANNON, H. A. 'The Coming of General Limited Liability', *Economic History*, II (1931), 267–91.

—— 'The First Five Thousand Limited Companies and Their Duration', *Economic History*, II (1932), 396–424.

—— 'The Limited Companies of 1866 and 1883', *Economic History*, IV (1932–3), 290–307.

SHENFIELD, BARBARA. *Company Boards: Their Responsibilities to Shareholders, Employees and the Community*. London, 1971.

SPIEGELBERG, RICHARD. *The City: Power without Accountability*. London, 1973.

STOPFORD, JOHN M. 'The Origins of British-Based Multinational Manufacturing Enterprises', *Business History Review*, XVLIII (1974), 303–35.

TEW, BRIAN, and R. F. HENDERSON (eds.). *Studies in Company Finance: A Symposium on the Economic Analysis and Interpretation of British Company Accounts*. Cambridge, 1959.

THOMAS, W. A. *The Provincial Stock Exchanges*. London, 1973.

TODD, GEOFFREY. 'Some Aspects of Joint Stock Companies, 1844–1900', *Economic History Review*, IV (1932–3), 46–71.

WELBOURNE, E. 'Bankruptcy Before the Era of Victorian Reform', *Cambridge Historical Journal*, IV (1932), 51–62.

WILLIAMSON, OLIVER E. 'Managerial Discretion, Organisational Form and the Multi-division Hypothesis' in R. Marris and A. Wood (eds.), *The Corporate Economy*. London, 1971. 343–86.

4. THE ENTREPRENEUR: DEFINITION, MOTIVATION, RECRUITMENT, AND ROLE

AITKEN, H. G. J. 'The Future of Entrepreneurial Research', *Explorations in Entrepreneurial History*, 2nd ser., I, 1 (Fall 1963), 3–9.

ALDCROFT, D. H. 'Investment in and Utilisation of Manpower: Great Britain and Her Rivals, 1870–1914', in Barrie M. Ratcliffe (ed.), *Great Britain and Her World, 1750–1914: Essays in Honour of W. O. Henderson*. Manchester, 1975.

AMES, E., and N. ROSENBERG. 'Changing Technological Leadership and Industrial Growth', *Economic Journal*, LXXIII (1963), 13–31.

ATKINSON, J. W., and B. F. HOSELITZ. 'Entrepreneurship and Personality', *Explorations in Entrepreneurial History*, X, 3–4 (April 1958), 107–12.

ASHTON, T. S. *The Industrial Revolution*. Oxford, 1948.

BALDWIN, W. L. 'The Motives of Managers, Environmental Restraints, and the Theory of Managerial Enterprise', *Quarterly Journal of Economics*, LXXVIII (1964), 238–56.

BARRITT, D. P. 'The Stated Qualifications of Directors of Larger Public Companies', *Journal of Industrial Economics*, V (1956–7), 220–4.

BENDIX, REINHARD. *Work and Authority in Industry: Ideologies of Management in the Course of Industrialization*. New York, 1956.

—— 'A Study of Managerial Ideologies', *Economic Development and Cultural Change*, V, 2 (1957), 118–28.

BRADBURN, N. M., and D. E. BERLEW. 'Need for Achievement and English Industrial Growth', *Economic Development and Cultural Change*, X (1961), 8–20.

CHAPMAN, S. J., and F. J. MARQUIS. 'The Recruiting of the Employing Classes from the Ranks of the Wage-Earners in the Cotton Industry', *Journal of the Royal Statistical Society*, LXXV (1912), 293–306.

CHILD, JOHN. 'Quaker Employers and Industrial Relations', *Sociological Review*, XII, 3 (November 1964), 293–315.

COCHRAN, T. C. 'The Entrepreneur in Economic Change', *Behavioral Science*, IX (1964).

COLE, G. D. H. 'Self-Reliance and Social Legislation', *The Listener*, 20 May 1948.

COPEMAN G. *Leaders of British Industry: A Study of the Careers of more than a Thousand Public Company Directors*. London, 1955.

—— *The Chief Executive and Business Growth*. London, 1971.

CROUZET, FRANÇOIS. 'Capital Formation in Great Britain during the Industrial Revolution', in F. Crouzet (ed.), *Capital Formation in the Industrial Revolution*. London, 1972. 162–222.

DENISON, E. F. *Why Growth Rates Differ*. Washington, 1967.

ELLIS, HAVELOCK. *A Study of British Genius*. London, 1904.

ERICKSON, CHARLOTTE. *British Industrialists: Steel and Hosiery, 1850–1950*. Cambridge, 1959.

EVANS, G. H., jun. 'A Theory of Entrepreneurship', *Journal of Economic History*, II, Suppl. (1942), 141–6.

—— 'The Entrepreneur and Economic Theory: A Historical and Analytical Approach', *American Economic Review*, XXXIX (1949), 336–48.

EVERSLEY, D. E. C. 'The Home Market and Economic Growth in England, 1750–1780', in E. L. Jones and G. Mingay (eds.), *Land, Labour and Population in the Industrial Revolution: Essays Presented to J. D. Chambers*. London, 1967. 206–59.

FLINN, M. *Origins of the Industrial Revolution*. London, 1966.

—— 'Social Theory and the Industrial Revolution', in Tom Burns and S. B. Saul (eds.), *Social Theory and Economic Change*. London, 1967. 9–34.

GERSCHENKRON, ALEXANDER. Review of E. E. Hagen's *On the Theory of Social Change*. *Economica*, new ser., XXXII (1965), 90–4.

GRANICK, DAVID. *The European Executive*. New York, 1962.

HAGEN, E. E. *On the Theory of Social Change*. London, 1964.

HANS, N. *New Trends in Education in the Eighteenth Century*. London, 1951.

HARBISON, FREDERICK. 'Entrepreneurial Organisation as a Factor in Economic Development', *Quarterly Journal of Economics*, LXX (1956), 364–79.

HARTWELL, R. M. 'Business Management in England during the Period of Early Industrialisation: Inducements and Obstacles', in R. M. Hartwell (ed.), *The Industrial Revolution*. Oxford, 1970. 28–41.

HOBSBAWM, E. J. 'Custom, Wages and Work-Load in Nineteenth-Century Industry', in *Labouring Men* (London, 1964), 344–70.

—— *Industry and Empire*. Harmondsworth, 1969 (first published London, 1968).

HOSELITZ, B. F. 'Entrepreneurship and Capital Formation in France and Britain since 1700', in *Capital Formation and Economic Growth*, NBER Special Conference Series, 6. Princeton, 1955. 291–337.

—— *Sociological Aspects of Economic Growth*. New York, 1960.

JENKINS, HESTER, and D. CARADOG JONES. 'Social Class of Cambridge University Alumni of the 18th and 19th Centuries', *British Journal of Sociology*, I, 2 (June 1950), 93–116.

KILBY, PETER (ed.). *Entrepreneurship and Economic Development*. New York, 1971.

LEES, J. P. 'The Social Mobility of a Group of Eldest-Born and Intermediate Adult Males', *British Journal of Psychology*, XLII (1952), 210–21.

LEES, J. P. and STEWART, A. H. 'Family or Sibship Position and Scholastic Ability', *Sociological Review*, V (1957), 85–106.

LEIBENSTEIN, HARVEY. 'Allocative Efficiency vs. "X-Efficiency"', *American Economic Review*, LXI (1966), 392–415.

LEWIS, ROY, and ROSEMARY STEWART. *The Boss: The Life and Times of the British Business Man.* London, 1961.

MCCLELLAND, D. C. *The Achieving Society.* Princeton, 1961.

MANTOUX, P. *The Industrial Revolution in the Eighteenth Century.* London, 1923.

MARRIS, ROBIN. *The Economic Theory of 'Managerial' Capitalism.* London, 1964.

MATHEW, W. M. 'The Origins and Occupations of Glasgow Students, 1740–1839', *Past and Present*, no. 33 (April 1966), 74–94.

PENROSE, EDITH. *The Theory of the Growth of the Firm.* Oxford, 1959.

PERKIN, HAROLD. *The Origins of Modern English Society.* London, 1969.

POLLARD, S. 'Fixed Capital in the Industrial Revolution in Britain', *Journal of Economic History*, XXIV (1964), 299–314.

PUMPHREY, R. E. 'The Introduction of Industrialists into the British Peerage: A Study in Adaptation of a Social Institution', *American Historical Review*, LXV (1959), 1–16.

REDLICH, F. 'Economic Development, Entrepreneurship and Psychologism: A Social Scientist's Critique of McClelland's *Achieving Society*', *Explorations in Entrepreneurial History*, 2nd ser., I, 1 (Fall 1963), 10–35.

ROSENBERG, NATHAN. 'The Direction of Technical Change: Inducement Mechanisms and Focusing Devices', *Economic Development and Cultural Change*, XVIII, 1, part 1 (October 1969), 1–24.

RUBINSTEIN, W. D. 'British Millionaires, 1809–1949', *Bulletin of the Institute of Historical Research*, XLVIII (1974), 202–23.

RUTTAN, V. 'Usher and Schumpeter on Invention, Innovation and Technological Change', *Quarterly Journal of Economics*, LXXIII (1959), 596–606.

SAMPSON, ANTHONY. *The New Anatomy of Britain.* London, 1971.

SAWYER, J. E. 'The Social Basis of the American System of Manufacturing', *Journal of Economic History*, XIV, 4 (Fall 1954), 361–79.

SMALLEY, ORANGE. 'Variations in Entrepreneurship', *Explorations in Entrepreneurial History*, 2nd ser., I (1964), 250–62.

SMILES, AILEEN. *Samuel Smiles and his Surroundings.* London, 1956.

SMITH, M. BREWSTER. Review of D. C. McClelland's *The Achieving Society*, *History and Theory*, III (1964), 371–81.

STANWORTH, PHILIP, and ANTHONY GIDDENS (eds.). *Elites and Power in British Society.* Cambridge, 1974.

SUTTON SMITH, BRIAN, and B. G. ROSENBERG. *The Sibling.* New York, 1970.

THOMPSON, E. P. *The Making of the English Working Class.* London, 1963.

——— 'Time, Work-Discipline and Industrial Capitalism', *Past and Present*, no. 38 (December 1967), 56–97.

WILES, P. J. D. *Price, Cost and Output.* Oxford, 1961.

5. THE ENTREPRENEUR: GENERAL ASSESSMENT OF PERFORMANCE

ALDCROFT, D. H. 'The Entrepreneur and the British Economy, 1870–1914', *Economic History Review*, 2nd ser., XVII, 1 (August 1964), 113–34.

——— 'Technical Progress and British Enterprise, 1875–1914', *Business History*, VIII, 2 (July 1966), 122–39.

——— (ed.). *The Development of British Industry and Foreign Competition, 1875–1914.* London, 1968.

BROWN, E. H. PHELPS, and MARGARET H. BROWNE. *A Century of Pay.* London, 1968.

BYRES, T. J. 'The Scottish Economy During the Great Depression, 1873–1896'. 2 vols. Unpublished B.Litt. thesis, University of Glasgow, 1962.

——— 'Entrepreneurship in the Scottish Heavy Industries, 1870–1900', in P. L. Payne (ed.), *Studies in Scottish Business History.* London, 1967.

COLEMAN, D. C. 'Gentlemen and Players', *Economic History Review*, 2nd ser., XXVI (1973), 92–116.

GRAY, H. G., and SAMUEL TURNER. *Eclipse or Empire?* London, 1916.

HABAKKUK, H. L. *American and British Technology in the Nineteenth Century.* Cambridge, 1962.

HARLEY, C.K. 'Skilled Labour and the Choice of Technique in Edwardian Industry', *Explorations in Economic History*, XI (1974), 391–414.

HOFFMAN, ROSS. *Great Britain and the German Trade Rivalry, 1875–1914*. Philadelphia, 1933.

JEWKES, JOHN. 'Is British Industry Inefficient?', *The Manchester School*, XIV, 1 (1946), 1–16.

JOHNSTON, J. 'The Productivity of Management Consultants', *Journal of the Royal Statistical Society*, ser. A, CXXVI, 2 (1963), 237–49.

KINDLEBERGER, C. P. 'Obsolescence and Technical Change', *Bulletin of the Oxford University Institute of Statistics*, XXIII, 3 (December 1961), 281–97.

LANDES, DAVID S. 'Entrepreneurship in Advanced Industrial Countries: The Anglo-German Rivalry', in *Entrepreneurship and Economic Growth*, Papers presented at a conference sponsored jointly by the Committee on Economic Growth of the Social Science Research Foundation and the Harvard University Research Center in Entrepreneurial History, Cambridge, Mass. 12–13 November 1954.

—— 'Technological Change and Development in Western Europe, 1750–1914', in *Cambridge Economic History of Europe*, VI: *The Industrial Revolutions and After*. Cambridge, 1965.

—— *The Unbound Prometheus: Technological Change and Industrial Development in Western Europe from 1750 to the Present*. Cambridge, 1969.

LEVINE, A. L. *Industrial Retardation in Britain, 1880–1914*. London, 1967.

McCLOSKEY, DONALD M. 'Did Victorian Britain Fail?' *Economic History Review*, 2nd ser., XXIII (1970), 446–59.

—— (ed.). *Essays on a Mature Economy: Britain after 1840*. Papers and Proceedings of the MSSB Conference on the New Economic History of Britain, 1840–1930. London, 1971.

McCLOSKEY, DONALD M., and LARS G. SANDBERG. 'From Damnation to Redemption: Judgments on the Late Victorian Entrepreneur', *Explorations in Economic History*, IX, 1 (Fall 1971), 89–108.

PAYNE, P. L. *British Entrepreneurship in the Nineteenth Century*. London, 1974.

SIGSWORTH, ERIC M. 'Some Problems in Business History, 1870–1914', in C. J. Kennedy (ed.), *Papers of the Sixteenth Business History Conference*. Lincoln, Nebraska, 1969. 21–37.

TUCKER, K. A. 'Business History: Some Proposals for Aims and Methodology', *Business History*, XIV (1972), 1–16.

WILSON, CHARLES. 'The Entrepreneur in the Industrial Revolution in Britain', *Explorations in Entrepreneurial History*, VII, 3 (February 1955), 129–45.

—— 'Economy and Society in Late Victorian Britain', *Economic History Review*, 2nd ser., XVIII (1965), 183–98.

6. MANAGERS AND MANAGEMENT

ACTON SOCIETY TRUST. *Management Succession: The Recruitment, Selection, Training and Promotion of Managers*. London, 1956.

CHILD, JOHN. *British Management Thought*. London, 1969.

CLARK, D. G. *The Industrial Manager: His Background and Career Pattern*. London, 1966.

CLEMENTS, R. V. *Managers: A Study of their Careers in Industry*. London, 1958.

HANNAH, LESLIE. 'Managerial Innovation and the Rise of the Large-Scale Company in Interwar Britain', *Economic History Review*, 2nd ser., XXVII (1974), 252–70.

HANNAH, LESLIE (ed.). *Management Strategy and Business Development: An Historical and Comparative Study*. London, 1976.

HUME, L. J. 'Jeremy Bentham on Industrial Management', *Yorkshire Bulletin of Economic and Social Research*, XXII, 1 (May 1970), 3–15.

JENKS, L. H. 'Early Phases of the Management Movement', *Administrative Science Quarterly*, V (1960–1), 421–47.

LEE, G. A. 'The Concept of Profit in British Accounting, 1760–1900', *Business History Review*, XLIX (1975), 6–36.

McGIVERING, I. C., D. G. J. MATTHEWS, and W. H. SCOTT. *Management in Britain.* Liverpool, 1960.

NATIONAL ECONOMIC DEVELOPMENT COUNCIL. *Management Recruitment and Development.* London, 1965.

POLLARD, S. *The Genesis of Modern Management.* London, 1965.

STEWART, ROSEMARY, PAULINE WINGATE, and RANDALL SMITH. *The Human Effects of Mergers: The Impact on Managers.* London, 1964.

TAYLOR, B., and K. MACMILLAN (eds.). *Top Management.* London, 1973.

TILLETT, A., T. KEMPNER, and GORDON WILLS (eds.). *Management Thinkers.* London, 1970.

URWICK, L. and E. F. L. BRECH. *The Making of Scientific Management.* 2 vols. London, 1949.

WILLIAMSON, HAROLD F. (ed.). *Evolution of International Management Structure.* Newark, N.J., 1975.

7. STUDIES OF PARTICULAR FIRMS AND ENTREPRENEURS

ADDIS, J. B. *The Crawshay Dynasty: A Study in Industrial Organisation and Development, 1756–1867.* Cardiff, 1967.

ALFORD, B. W. E. *W.D. & H.O. Wills and the Development of the U.K. Tobacco Industry, 1786–1965.* London, 1973.

ANON. [various authors]. *Fortunes Made in Business.* 3 vols. London, 1884–7.

ANON. *James Finlay and Company Limited, Manufacturers and East India Merchants, 1750–1950.* Glasgow, 1951.

ASHTON, T. S. 'The Records of a Pin Manufactory, 1814–21', *Economica*, V (1925), 281–92.

—— *An Eighteenth Century Industrialist: Peter Stubs of Warrington, 1756–1806.* Manchester, 1939.

BARKER, T. C. *Pilkington Brothers and the Glass Industry.* London, 1960.

BOYSON, RHODES. *The Ashworth Cotton Enterprise: The Rise and Fall of a Family Firm, 1818–1880.* Oxford, 1970.

CAMPBELL, R. H. *Carron Company.* Edinburgh and London, 1961.

CHALONER, W. H. 'Robert Owen, Peter Drinkwater and the Early Factory System in Manchester, 1788–1800', *Bulletin of the John Rylands Library*, XXXVII (1954), 78–102.

CHAPMAN, DENNIS. 'William Brown of Dundee, 1791–1864: Management in a Scottish Flax Mill', *Explorations in Entrepreneurial History*, IV, 3 (1952), 119–34.

CHAPMAN, S. D. 'The Peels in the Early English Cotton Industry', *Business History*, XI, 2 (July 1969), 61–89.

—— 'James Longsdon (1745–1821), Farmer and Fustian Manufacturer: The Small Firm in the Early English Cotton Industry', *Textile History*, I, 3 (December 1970), 265–92.

—— *Jesse Boot of Boots the Chemists.* London, 1974.

CHECKLAND, S. G. *The Mines of Tharsis.* London, 1967.

—— *The Gladstones: A Family Biography, 1764–1851.* Cambridge, 1971.

CHURCH, R. A. 'An Aspect of Family Enterprise in the Industrial Revolution', *Business History*, VIII, 2 (July 1966), 120–5.

—— 'Messrs Gotch & Sons and the Rise of the Kettering Footwear Industry', *Business History*, VII (1966), 140–9.

—— *Kenricks in Hardware: A Family Business, 1791–1966.* Newton Abbot, 1969.

COLEMAN, D. C. *Courtaulds: An Economic and Social History.* 2 vols. Oxford, 1969.

CORLEY, T. A. B. *Quaker Enterprise in Biscuits: Huntley & Palmers of Reading, 1822–1972.* London, 1972.

DANIELS, G. W. 'The Balance Sheets of Three Limited Companies in the Cotton Industry', *The Manchester School*, III, 2 (1932), 77–84.

DONNACHIE, I. L., and JOHN BUTT. 'The Wilsons of Wilsontown Ironworks (1779–1813): A Study in Entrepreneurial Failure', *Explorations in Entrepreneurial History*, 2nd ser., IV (1966–7), 150–68.

FARNIE, D. A. 'John Rylands of Manchester', *Bulletin of the John Rylands University Library of Manchester*, LVI, 1 (Autumn 1973), 93–129.

FITTON, R. S., and A. P. WADSWORTH. *The Strutts and the Arkwrights, 1758–1830*. Manchester, 1958.

GLOVER, F. J. 'History of Messrs Wormalds and Walker Ltd, Dewsbury'. Unpublished Ph.D. thesis, University of Leeds, 1959.

HEATON, H. 'Benjamin Gott and the Industrial Revolution in Yorkshire', *Economic History Review*, III, 1 (1931–2), 45–66.

JOHN, A. H. (ed.). *The Walker Family: Ironfounders and Lead Manufacturers, 1741–1893*. London, 1951.

JONES, ROBERT, and OLIVER MARRIOTT. *Anatomy of a Merger: A History of G.E.C., A.E.I. and English Electric*. London, 1970.

LEE, C. H. 'M'Connel and Kennedy, Fine Cotton Spinners'. Unpublished M.Litt. thesis, University of Cambridge, 1966.

—— *A Cotton Enterprise, 1795–1840: A History of M'Connel and Kennedy, Fine Cotton Spinners*. Manchester, 1972.

LOGAN, JOHN C. 'The Dumbarton Glass Works Company: A Study in Entrepreneurship', *Business History*, XIV, 1 (January 1972), 61–81.

LLOYD, HUMPHREY. *The Quaker Lloyds in the Industrial Revolution*. London, 1975.

MCKENDRICK, NEIL. 'Josiah Wedgwood: An Eighteenth-Century Entrepreneur in Salesmanship and Marketing Techniques', *Economic History Review*, 2nd ser., XII, 3 (April 1960), 408–33.

—— 'Josiah Wedgwood and Factory Discipline', *Historical Journal*, IV, 1 (1961), 30–55.

—— 'Josiah Wedgwood and the Factory System', *Proceedings of the Wedgwood Society*, no. 5 (1963), 1–29.

—— 'Josiah Wedgwood and Thomas Bentley: An Inventor-Entrepreneur Partnership in the Industrial Revolution', *Transactions of the Royal Historical Society*, XIV (1964), 1–33.

—— 'Josiah Wedgwood and Cost Accounting in the Industrial Revolution', *Economic History Review*, 2nd ser., XXIII, 1 (April 1970), 45–67.

MACKENZIE, N. H. 'Cressbrook and Litton Mills, 1779–1835', *Derbyshire Archaeological Journal*, LXXXVIII (1968), 1–25.

MORRIS, W. R. (Lord Nuffield). 'Policies that have Built the Morris Business', *Journal of Industrial Economics*, II, 3 (August 1954), 193–206.

MORTON, JOCELYN. *Three Generations in a Family Textile Firm*. London, 1971.

MUSSON, A. E. 'An Early Engineering Firm: Peel, Williams & Co. of Manchester', *Business History*, III, 1 (December 1960), 8–18.

—— *Enterprise in Soap and Chemicals, Joseph Crosfield and Sons Ltd, 1815–1965*. Manchester, 1965.

NAMIER, L. B. 'Anthony Bacon, M.P., An Eighteenth Century Merchant', in W. E. Minchinton (ed.), *Industrial South Wales*. London, 1970. 59–106.

O'HAGEN, H. OSBORNE. *Leaves from My Life*. 2 vols. London, 1929.

OWEN, ROBERT. *The Life of Robert Owen, written by Himself*. London, 1857.

PAFFORD, ELIZABETH R., and JOHN H. P. PAFFORD. *Employer and Employed: Ford Ayrton & Co. Ltd, Silk Spinners*. Edington, Wilts., 1974.

PAYNE, P. L. *Rubber and Railways in the Nineteenth Century*. Liverpool 1961.

PIGOTT, S. *Hollins: A Study of Industry, 1784–1949*. Nottingham, 1949.

RAISTRICK, A. *Dynasty of Iron Founders*. Newton Abbot, 1970.

RAPP, DEAN. 'Social Mobility in the Eighteenth Century: the Whitbreads of Bedfordshire, 1720–1815', *Economic History Review*, 2nd ser., XXVII (1974), 380–94.

READER, W. J. *Imperial Chemical Industries: A History*. I: *The Forerunners, 1870–1926*. Oxford, 1970. II; *The First Quarter-Century, 1926–1952*. Oxford, 1975.

REID, SIR WEMYSS. *Memoirs and Correspondence of Lyon Playfair*. London, 1900.

RICHARDSON, H. W. and J. M. BASS. 'The Profitability of Consett Iron Company before 1914', *Business History*, VII, 2 (July 1965), 71–93.

RIDEN, PHILIP. *The Butterfly Company, 1790–1830*. Wingerworth, Chesterfield, 1973.

RIMMER, W. G. *Marshalls of Leeds, Flax Spinners, 1788–1886*. Cambridge, 1960.

ROBERTSON, A. J. 'Robert Owen, Cotton Spinner: New Lanark, 1800–1825', in S. Pollard and J. Salt (eds.), *Robert Owen, Prophet of the Poor*. London, 1971. 135–165.

ROBINSON, ERIC. 'Boulton and Fothergill, 1762–1782 and the Birmingham Export of Hardware', *University of Birmingham Historical Journal*, VII (1959), 60–79.

—— 'Eighteenth Century Commerce and Fashion: Matthew Boulton's Marketing Techniques', *Economic History Review*, 2nd ser., XVI, 1 (August 1963), 39–60.

ROLL, E. *An Early Experiment in Industrial Organisation, Being a History of Boulton & Watt, 1775–1805*. London, 1930.

SCOTT, J. D. *Vickers: A History*. London, 1962.

SIGSWORTH, Eric M. *Black Dyke Mills*. Liverpool, 1958.

SMITH, ROLAND. 'An Oldham Limited Liability Company, 1875–1896', *Business History*, IV, 1 (December 1961), 34–53.

STONE, WILLARD E. 'An Early English Cotton Mill Cost Accounting System: Charlton Mills, 1810–1889', *Accounting and Business Research*, no. 13 (Winter 1973), 71–8.

SUTTON, G. B. 'The Marketing of Ready Made Footwear in the Nineteenth Century. A Study of the Firm of C. and J. Clark', *Business History*, VI, 2 (June 1964), 93–112.

TRIPP, BASIL H. *Renold Limited, 1956–67*. London, 1969.

TURNER, G. *The Leyland Papers*. London, 1971.

TYSON, R. E. 'The Sun Mill Company Limited: A Study in Democratic Investment, 1858–1959'. Unpublished M.A. thesis, University of Manchester, 1962.

WEDGWOOD, HENSLEIGH C. 'Josiah Wedgwood, Eighteenth-Century Manager', *Explorations in Entrepreneurial History*, 2nd ser., II, 3 (Spring–Summer 1965), 205–26.

WELLS, F. A. *Hollins and Viyella: A Study in Business History*. Newton Abbot, 1968.

WILSON, A. S. 'The Origin of the Consett Iron Company, 1840–1864', *Durham University Journal*, N.S. XXXIV (1972), 90–102.

WILSON, CHARLES. *The History of Unilever: A Study of Economic Growth and Social Change*. 2 vols. London, 1954.

—— *Unilever, 1945–65: Challenge and Response in the Post-War Industrial Revolution*. London, 1968.

WILSON, CHARLES, and WILLIAM READER. *Men and Machines: A History of D. Napier & Son, Engineers, Ltd, 1808–1958*. London, 1958.

CHAPTER V

Capital Investment and Economic Growth in France, 1820–1930

AFTALION, A. *Les Crises périodiques de surproduction*. Paris, 1913.

BARDET, J. P., et al. *Le Bâtiment: Enquête d'histoire économique, XIVe–XIXe siècles*. Paris and The Hague, 1971.

BERTHET, J., J. J. CARRÉ, P. DUBOIS, and E. MALINVAUD. 'Sources et origines de la croissance française au milieu du XXe siècle'. First draft, mimeographed; Paris, June 1965. (See below, Carré et al., *La Croissance française*.)

BOURGEOIS-PICHAT, J. 'Evolution de la population française depuis le XVIIIe siècle', *Population*, VI, 4 (1951).

BOUTIN, M. E. 'La Propriété bâtie', *Journal de la Société de Statistique de Paris*, July 1891.

BOUVIER, J., F. FURET, and M. GILLET. *Le Mouvement du profit en France au XIXe siècle*. Paris and The Hague, 1965.

BROSSELIN, M. 'Evaluation de la production intérieure de bois d'oeuvre, 1840–1912'. Unpublished thesis, University of Dijon, 1972.

CAHEN, MME. 'Evolution de la population active en France depuis cent ans', *Etudes et Conjoncture*, 'Economie française', no. 3 (May–June 1953).

CAIRNCROSS, A. K. *Home and Foreign Investment, 1870–1913*. Cambridge, 1953.

CARON, F. *Histoire de l'exploitation d'un grand réseau: La Compagnie du Chemin de Fer du Nord, 1846–1937*. Paris and the Hague, 1973.

—— 'Investment Strategy in France', in H. Daems and H. van der Wee (eds.), *The Rise of Managerial Capitalism*. Louvain, 1974.

CARRÉ, J. J., P. DUBOIS, and E. MALINVAUD. *La Croissance française: Un Essai d'analyse économique causale de l'après-guerre*. Paris, 1972. (The definitive version of Berthet *et al.*, 'Sources et origines', above.)

CHEVALIER, L. *La Formation de la population parisienne au XIXe siècle*. Paris, 1950.

COLSON, C. *Cours d'économie politique*. 1st edn. Paris, 1903.

CROUZET, F. 'Un Indice de la production industrielle française au XIXe siècle', *Annales*, XXV, 1 (January–February 1970).

DAUZET, P. *Le Siècle des chemins de fer en France*. Paris, 1948.

DENUC, J. 'Dividendes, valeur mobilière et taux de capitalisation des valeurs mobilières françaises', *Bulletin Statistique Générale de la France*, XIII, 4 (1934).

DÉSERT, G. 'Aperçus sur l'industrie française du bâtiment au XIXe siècle', in Bardet *et al.*, *Le Bâtiment*.

DESSIRIER, J. 'Chemin de fer et progrès technique', *Année Ferroviaire*, 1952.

DOLLFUS, J. *De l'industrie cotonnière*. Paris, 1855.

DUON, M. *Documents sur le problème des logements à Paris*. Institut National de Statistique et des Etudes Economiques (INSEE). Paris, 1946.

DUPEUX, G. 'La Croissance urbaine en France au XIXe siècle', *Revue d'Histoire Economique et Sociale*, LIII, 4 (1975).

DUPIN, C. *Les Forces productives de la France*. Paris, 1827.

'Evolution des conditions de logement depuis cent ans', *Etudes et Conjoncture*, October–November 1957.

FEINSTEIN, C. H. 'Home and Foreign Investment: Some Aspects of Capital, Finance and Income in the United Kingdom, 1870–1914'. Unpublished Ph.D. thesis, University of Cambridge, 1959.

FEIS, H. *Europe: The World's Banker, 1870–1914*. Rev. edn. New York, 1965.

FLAGEOLLET, M. 'Les Débuts de l'industrie automobile française: Panhard et Levassor'. Unpublished thesis, University of Paris (Nanterre), 1970.

FLAUS, L. 'Fluctuations de la construction urbaine, 1830–1940', *Journal de la Société de Statistique de Paris*, 1949.

FOVILLE, A. DE. *La France économique*. Paris, 1887.

FRIDENSON, P. *Histoire des usines Renault*. Paris, 1972.

GAILLARD, J. *Paris: La Ville, 1852–1870*. Lille and Paris, 1976.

GILLE, B. *La Sidérurgie française au XIXe siècle*. Paris and Geneva, 1968.

GIRARD, L. *La Politique des travaux publics du Second Empire*. Paris, 1952.

GRIPON-LAMOTHE, G. *Historique du réseau des chemins de fer français*. Paris, 1904.

HALBWACHS, M. *Les Expropriations et le prix des terrains à Paris, 1860–1900*. Paris, 1909.

HUBER, M., H. BUNLÉ, and F. BOVERAT. *La Population française*. Rev. edn. Paris, 1965.

JAMES, A. M. 'Sidérurgie et chemins de fer en France', *Cahiers de l'ISEA* (Institut de Science Economique Appliquée), ser. T 5, no. 158 (February 1965).

JEANNENEY, J. M., and C. A. COLLIARD. *Economie et droit de l'électricité*. Grenoble, 1950.

KUZNETS, S. 'International Differences in Capital Formation and Financing', in M. Abramovitz (ed.). *Capital Formation and Economic Growth*. New York, 1956.

LAURENT, R. *L'Octroi de Dijon au XIXe siècle*. Paris, 1960.

LÉVY-LEBOYER, M. *Les Banques européennes et l'industrialisation internationale dans la première moitié du XIXe siècle*. Paris, 1964.

—— 'La Croissance économique en France au XIXe siècle: Résultats préliminaires', *Annales*, XXIII, 4 (1968).

—— 'L'Héritage de Simiand: Prix, profit, et termes de l'échange au XIXe siècle', *Revue Historique*, no. 493 (1970).

—— 'La Décélération de l'économie française dans la seconde moitié du XIXe siècle', *Revue d'Histoire Economique et Sociale*, XLIX, 4 (1971).

—— 'La Balance des paiements et l'exportation des capitaux français, 1820–1940', in *La Position internationale de la France: Aspects économiques et financiers, XIXe et XXe siècles*. Paris and The Hague, 1977.

LUBELL, H. *The French Investment Program: A Defense of the Monnet Plan*. Paris, 1952.

LUCAS, F. *Etude sur les voies de communication*. Paris, 1873.

MAIRESSE, J. *L'Evaluation du capital fixe productif: Méthodes et résultats*. Collections de l'INSEE, ser. C, nos. 18–19. Paris, 1972.

MARCZEWSKI, J. 'Some Aspects of the Economic Growth of France, 1660–1958', *Economic Development and Cultural Change*, IX, 3 (1961).

—— 'Le Produit physique de l'économie française de 1789 à 1913', *Cahiers de l'ISEA*, ser. AF 4, no. 163 (July 1965).

MARKOVITCH, T. J. 'L'Industrie française de 1789 à 1964', *Cahiers de l'ISEA*, ser. AF 6, no. 174 (June 1966), and ser. AF 7, no. 179 (November 1966).

MARNATA, F. *Les Loyers des bourgeois de Paris, 1860–1958*. Paris, 1961.

MASSÉNAT-DEROCHE, L. *L'Automobile aux Etats-Unis et en Angleterre*. Paris, 1910.

MAYER, J. 'La Croissance du revenu national français', *Cahiers de l'ISEA*, ser. D 7 (1949).

MAYWALD, K. 'The Construction Costs and the Value of the British Merchant Fleet, 1850–1938', *Scottish Journal of Political Economy*, III, 1 (1956).

MERGER, M. 'La Consommation chaumontaise'. Unpublished thesis, University of Dijon, 1970.

MERLIN, P. *L'Exode rural*. Paris, 1971.

MICHALET, C. A. *Les Placements des épargnants français de 1815 à nos jours*. Paris, 1968.

MORSEL, H. 'Les Industries hydro-électriques de la région alpine', in Centre National de la Recherche Scientifique, *L'Industrialisation en Europe au XIXe siècle*. Lyons, 1970.

PERROUX, F. 'Matériaux pour une analyse de la richesse privée en France, 1826–1914', in Proceedings of Congress of Castelgandolfo, *Cahiers de l'ISEA*, ser. D 7 (1953).

—— 'Prise de vue sur la croissance de l'économie française, 1780–1950', in S. Kuznets (ed.), *Income and Wealth*, ser. V. London, 1955.

PICARD, A. *Traité des chemins de fer*. Paris, 1887.

PIQUET-MARCHAL, O. *Etude économique des chemins de fer d'intérêt local*. Paris, 1964.

PUPIN, R. *La Richesse française devant la guerre*. Paris, 1916.

RIBOUD, P. 'Les Grands Réseaux de chemin de fer français de 1884 à 1937', *Revue Générale des Chemins de Fer*, 1938.

ROUSSEAU, E. 'Rapport d'examen des demandes des constructeurs et des armateurs', in *Commission Extra-parlementaire de la Marine Marchande*. Paris, 1903.

SAUVY, A. 'Rapport général au Conseil Economique sur le revenu national', *Journal Officiel*, 7 April 1954.

—— 'Le Revenu des Français au XIXe siècle', *Population*, XX, 5 (1965), and XXVII, 1 (1971).

SAUVY, A. *Histoire économique de la France dans l'entre-deux-guerres*. 3 vols. Paris, 1965–72.

SCHWARZ, H. 'L'Industrie de l'automobile', *Journal Officiel: Documents Administratifs*, 26–7 August 1936.

SOCIÉTÉ NATIONALE DES CHEMINS DE FER FRANÇAIS (SNCF). 'Principales Statistiques des chemins de fer depuis 1821'. Internal document, 1964.

TERNY, G., et al. *L'Evolution de longue période des dépenses publiques françaises*. Paris, 1974.

THUILLIER, G. *Georges Dufaud et les débuts du grand capitalisme dans la métallurgie, en Nivernais, au XIXe siècle*. Paris, 1959.

TOUTAIN, J. C. 'Les Transports en France de 1830 à 1965', *Cahiers de l'ISEA*, ser. AF 9, no. 8 (September–October 1967).

VIAL, J. *L'Industrialisation de la sidérurgie française, 1814–1864*. 2 vols. Paris and The Hague, 1967.

VINCENT, L. A. 'Evolution de la production intérieure brute en France de 1896 à 1938', *Etudes et Conjoncture*, XVII, 11 (1962).

—— 'Population active, production et productivité dans 21 branches de l'économie française, 1896–1962', *Etudes et Conjoncture*, XX, 2 (February 1965).

—— 'Les Comptes nationaux', in Sauvy (ed.), *Histoire économique de la France*, vol. III.

ZYLBERMAN, E. 'La Croissance et les comptes économiques de la France sous le Second Empire'. Unpublished thesis, University of Paris, 1969.

CHAPTER VI

Labour in the French Economy since the Revolution

This bibliography should not be regarded as exhaustive. It is designed to cover only the most important works, most of which themselves contain important bibliographies.

I. GENERAL WORKS

The works of Emile Levasseur, which date from the end of the nineteenth century and the beginning of the twentieth, have not since been rivalled in the scale of their design; if some developments appear inadequate in the light of more recent economic concepts, certain trends of research are much concerned with contemporary historiography. It is therefore necessary to begin with:

LEVASSEUR, EMILE. *La Population française.* 3 vols. Paris, 1889–92.
—— *Histoire des classes ouvrières et de l'industrie en France de 1789 à 1870.* 2nd edn. 3 vols. Paris, 1904.
—— *Questions ouvrières et industrielles en France sous la IIIe République.* Paris, 1907.
Several general demographic studies contain much empirical material about France; among the most useful are:
CHEVALIER, LOUIS. *Démographie générale.* Paris, 1951.
LANDRY, A. *Traité de démographie.* Paris, 1945.
PRESSAT, ROLAND. *L'Analyse démographique.* 2nd edn. Paris, 1969.
REINHARD, M., A. ARMENGAUD, and J. DUPAQUIER. *Histoire générale de la population mondiale.* Paris, 1968.
Traditional economic histories of France (such as that by Henri See) give little space to the problems of the labour force apart from the following, which deal only with the twentieth century:
PARODI, MAURICE. *L'Economie et la société française de 1945 à 1970.* Paris, 1971.
SAUVY, ALFRED (ed.). *Histoire économique de la France dans l'entre-deux-guerres.* 3 vols. Paris, 1965–72.
On the general history of French population there are two excellent recent small books which provide a synthesis of research and cover the most important issues:
ARMENGAUD, A. *La Population française au XXe siècle.* 3rd edn. Paris, 1970.
—— *La Population française au XIXe siècle.* Paris, 1971.
These do not replace the following earlier studies:
BOURGEOIS-PICHAT, JEAN. 'Evolution générale de la population française depuis le XVIIIe siècle', *Population,* VI, 4 (1951), 635–62.
—— 'Note sur l'évolution générale de la population française depuis le XVIIIe siècle', *Population,* VII, 2 (1952), 319–29.
HUBER, M., H. BUNLÉ, and F. BOVERAT. *La Population de la France: Son évolution et ses perspectives.* 4th edn. Paris, 1965.
TOUTAIN, J. C. 'La Population de la France de 1700 à 1959', *Cahiers de l'ISEA,* ser. AF, no. 3 (January 1963).
More limited in chronological coverage but also important is:
POUTHAS, CHARLES H. *La Population française pendant la première moitié du XIXe siècle.* INED Travaux et Documents, 25. Paris, 1956.

The frequent citation of articles in the journal *Population,* published since 1946 by the Institut National des Etudes Démographiques (INED), shows its importance as a source for French demographic history.

Demographic Trends and General Structure of the French Population

'De la France d'avant-guerre à la France d'aujourd'hui: 25 ans d'évolution de la structure économique et sociale française', special number of *Revue d'Economie Politique*, LIII (1939), notably pp. 9–87.

ARMENGAUD, A. 'Mouvement ouvrier et néo-malthusianisme au début du XXe siècle', *Annales de démographie historique*, 1966, 7–21.

DUPAQUIER, JACQUES. 'Problèmes démographiques de la France napoléonienne', *Revue d'Histoire Moderne et Contemporaine* (special number, 'La France à l'époque napoléonienne'), XVII (1970), 339–58.

FAGE, ANITA. 'La Révolution française et la population', *Population*, VIII, 2 (1953), 311–38.

IBARROLA, JÉSUS. *Les Incidences des deux conflits mondiaux sur l'évolution démographique française.* Grenoble, 1964.

LE ROY LADURIE, EMMANUEL. 'Révolution française et "funestes secrets"', *Annales Historiques de la Révolution Française*, XXXVII (1965), 386–400.

REINHARD, M. 'La Révolution française et le problème de la population', *Population*, I, 3 (1946), 419–27.

—— 'Bilan démographique de l'Europe 1789–1815', in *Comité International des Sciences Historiques, XIIe Congrès… Vienne 1965, Rapports*, I: *Grands thèmes*, Vienna, n.d., 451–71.

SAUVY, ALFRED. *Richesse et population.* Paris, 1943.

VINCENT, PAUL. 'Conséquences de six années de guerre sur la population française', *Population*, I, 3 (1946), 429–40.

Trends in the Active Population

In addition to Toutain's article 'La Population de la France de 1700 à 1959', cited above, the basic article remains:

CAHEN, MME. 'Evolution de la population active en France depuis cent ans d'après les dénombrements quinquennaux', *Etudes et Conjoncture*, 'Economie française', no. 3 (May–June 1953), 230–88.

together with the following:

CREBOUW, YVONNE. 'Recherches sur l'évolution numérique de la main d'oeuvre industrielle depuis un siècle, 1866–1972', 3 vols. Unpublished thesis, Paris, 1967 (typescript).

FOURASTIÉ, JEAN (ed.). *Migrations professionelles: Données statistiques sur leur évolution en divers pays de 1900 à 1955.* INED Travaux et Documents, 31. Paris, 1957.

NIZARD, ALFRED. 'La Population active selon les recensements depuis 1946', *Population*, XXVI, I (1971), 9–61.

VIMONT, CLAUDE. *La Population active, évolution passée et prévisions.* Paris, 1960.

On more limited aspects:

DARIC, JEAN. 'Vieillissement de la population et prolongation de la vie active', *Population*, I, I (1946), 69–78.

—— 'La Population féminine active en France et à l'étranger', *Population*, II, I (1947), 61–6.

—— 'Le Travail des femmes: Professions, métiers, situations sociales et salaires', *Population*, X, 4 (1955), 675–90.

HOUDAILLE, J. 'La Structure professionnelle en France au début du XIXe siècle', *Population*, XXV (1970), 1289–93.

PERITZ, ERIC. 'La Jeunesse dans la population active de la France', *Population*, VIII, 3 (1953), 527–54.

PRESSAT, ROLAND. 'La Population active de la France: Premiers résultats du recensement de 1962', *Population*, XVIII, 3 (1963), 473–88.

SAUVY, ALFRED. 'Les Tendances de la population active en France', *Population*, X, 3 (1955), 413–26.

—— 'Développement économique et répartition professionnelle de la population', *Revue d'Economie Politique*, LXXVI (1966), 372–96.

On the economic context of changes in the active population during the nineteenth century, some recent works have clarified the processes and phases of industrial growth: above all

LÉVY-LEBOYER, MAURICE. *Les Banques européennes et l'industrialisation internationale dans la première moitié du XIXe siècle*. Paris, 1964.

—— 'Les Processus d'industrialisation: Le Cas de l'Angleterre et de la France', *Revue Historique*, CCXXXIX, 2 (April–June 1968), 281–98.

See also

CROUZET, FRANÇOIS. 'Un Indice de la production industrielle française au XIXe siècle', *Annales ESC*, XXV, 1 (January–February 1970), 56–99.

MARKOVITCH, T. J. 'L'Industrie française de 1789 à 1964', *Cahiers de l'ISEA*, ser. AF 5 and AF 6 (1966).

There is much to be gleaned from the main studies in economic and social history which have been published since the Second World War by (among others) P. Léon, C. Fohlen, A. Armengaud, and P. Vigier.

The formation of the industrial proletariat is less well documented, but the following general works should be noted:

ARIÈS, PHILIPPE. *Histoire des populations françaises et de leurs attitudes devant la vie depuis le XVIIIe siècle*. Paris, 1948.

CROUZET, FRANÇOIS. 'Agriculture et Révolution industrielle: Quelques réflexions', *Cahiers d'Histoire*, XII, 1 and 2 (1967), 67–86.

DUVEAU, GEORGES. *La Vie ouvrière en France sous le Second Empire*. Paris, 1946.

FOURASTIÉ, JEAN. 'Le Personnel des entreprises: Remarques de démographie et de sociologie', *Population*, XV, 2 (1960), 289–300.

FRIEDMANN, GEORGES (ed.). *Villes et campagnes*. Ecole Pratique des Hautes Etudes, VIe Section. Paris, 1953.

LEFRANC, GEORGES. *Histoire du travail et des travailleurs*. Paris, 1957.

MAUCO, GEORGES. *Les Migrations ouvrières en France au début du XIXe siècle*. Paris, 1932.

Among recent works limited to one region or to a particular occupational sector, see the following:

AGULHON, MAURICE. *Une Ville ouvrière au temps du socialisme utopique: Toulon de 1815 à 1851*. Paris and The Hague, 1970.

CHEVALIER, LOUIS. *La Formation de la population parisienne au XIXe siècle*. Paris, 1950.

GILLE, B. 'La Formation du prolétariat ouvrier dans l'industrie sidérurgique française', *Revue d'Histoire de la Sidérurgie*, IV, 4 (1963), 244–51.

HARDACH, GERT H. 'Les Problèmes de main d'oeuvre à Decazeville', *Revue d'Histoire de la Sidérurgie*, VIII, 1 (1967), 51–68.

—— *Der soziale Status des Arbeiters in der Frühindustrialisierung*. Berlin, 1969.

TREMPÉ, ROLAND. *Les Mineurs de Carmaux, 1848–1914*. 2 vols. Paris, 1971.

VIAL, JEAN. *L'Industrialisation de la sidérurgie française, 1814–1864*. 2 vols. Paris and The Hague, 1967.

WRIGLEY, E. A. *Industrial Growth and Population Change: A Regional Study of the Coalfield Areas of North-West Europe in the Later Nineteenth Century*. Cambridge, 1961.

IMMIGRATION

For the nineteenth century and the beginning of the twentieth, the fundamental work remains:

MAUCO, GEORGES. *Les Etrangers en France: Leur rôle dans l'activité économique*. Paris, 1932.

On the post-war period, see:

CHEVALIER, LOUIS. 'L'Immigration en France, 1950–1960', *Population*, XVI, 1 (1961), 113–16.

GRANOTIER, BERNARD. *Les Travailleurs immigrés en France*. Paris, 1970.

LANNES, XAVIER. *L'Immigration en France depuis 1945*. Publications du Groupe de Recherches pour les Migrations Européennes. The Hague, 1953.

'Les Etrangers en France', special number of *Esprit*, XXXIV, 1, no. 348 (April 1966), particularly the following articles:

CLAVIÈRE, PHILIPPE. 'Les Immigrants dans l'économie française', 862–8.

PROST, ANTOINE. 'L'Immigration en France depuis cent ans', 532–45.

On more limited aspects, see the following:

FAIDUTTI-RUDOLPH, ANNE-MARIE. *L'Immigration italienne dans le Sud-Est de la France.* Etudes et Travaux de Méditerranée. 2 vols. Gap, 1964.

SAUVY, ALFRED. 'Evaluation des besoins de l'immigration française', *Population*, 1 (1946), 91 ff.

It should be said that a large-scale inquiry has recently been launched into the role of immigration in the formation of the French labour force in the nineteenth and twentieth centuries. This is organized through the Centre National de la Recherche Scientifique, under the direction of Georges Dupeux; some results have been presented in two recent sessions of the Institut Francais d'Histoire Sociale.

EDUCATION AND PROFESSIONAL TRAINING

The essential recent works are:

GUINOT, JEAN-PIERRE. *Formation professionnelle et travailleurs qualifiés depuis 1789.* Paris, 1946.

and, above all,

PROST, ANTOINE. *L'Enseignement en France, 1800–1967.* Paris, 1968.

which contains an extensive bibliography and constitutes the best and most recent synthesis as well as being in its own right a most stimulating essay on the past and present problems of education in France.

ANGEVILLE, COMTE A. D'. *Essai sur la statistique de la population française.* Bourg, 1836; reprint, Paris, The Hague, and New York, 1969 (with an important introduction by Emmanuel Le Roy Ladurie).

DUVEAU, GEORGES. *La Pensée ouvrière sur l'éducation pendant la Seconde République et le Second Empire.* Paris, 1948.

FLEURY, MICHEL, and PIERRE VALMARY. 'Les Progrès de l'instruction élémentaire de Louis XIV à Napoléon III', *Population*, XII, 1 (1957), 71–92 (which resurrects the research of Maggiolo, ignored since E. Levasseur).

GONTARD, MAURICE. *L'Enseignement primaire en France de la Révolution à la Loi Guizot (1789–1833).* Lyon, 1955.

VILAR, PIERRE. 'Enseignement primaire et culture populaire en France sous la IIIe République', in Louis Bergeron (ed.), *Niveaux de culture et groupes sociaux*, Proceedings of a conference at the Ecole Normale Supérieure, Paris, 7–9 May 1966. Paris, 1967.

VIMONT, CLAUDE, and JACQUES BAUDOT. 'Les Titulaires d'un diplôme d'enseignement technique ou professionel dans la population active de 1962', *Population*, XX, 5 (1965), 783–4.

On the 'production' of French technical 'cadres', there is much to be found in:

CAMERON, RONDO. *La France et le développement économique de l'Europe, 1800–1914.* Paris, 1966 (abridged French translation of the original edition, Princeton, N.J., 1961).

Finally, maps which are very important for all aspects of the subject are to be found in:

BOUJU, P. M., G. DUPEUX, *et al. Atlas historique de la France contemporaine, 1800–1965.* Paris, 1966.

CHAPTER VII

Entrepreneurship and Management in France in the Nineteenth Century

Business history has not attracted much attention among French economic historians in recent years and can be considered as still in its infancy in France. Much more attention has been given to topics in macro-economics, such as trends and fluctuations in prices or economic activity or, more recently, economic growth. This explains the shortage of information in this field.

Most surviving business archives, at least for large firms and for those in Paris, are now kept in the Archives Nationales in Paris (in series AQ), where an index of the files is available. Some depositories of the *départements* also include business archives (to be found, for the most part, in series E).

Statistical data on business firms are available in some periodical publications:

Compte rendu général de l'administration de la justice civile et commerciale en France pendant l'année . . . (annual), which starts in 1825 and continues through the nineteenth century. It provides, for each *département*, the yearly number of new companies and bankruptcies, but unfortunately without giving the amount of capital involved.

Compte rendu des travaux des ingénieurs des mines pendant l'année . . . (annual); and

Resumé des travaux statistiques de l'administration des mines en . . . (annual), published by the Ministry of Public Works from 1834. It includes reports and statistics on mines, quarries, iron and steel plants, foundries, and blast furnaces, for each département, providing the most complete set of information on any given branch of this industry.

Other data are to be found in the short-lived review *Histoire des Entreprises*, published semi-annually from 1957 to 1964 by the Centre de Recherches Historiques of the Ecole Pratique des Hautes Etudes.

Many firms have published monographs for their centenaries or bicentenaries, but these are rarely useful, being mainly apologias with little data of scientific value. Among the few important monographs are the following (full bibliographical data in the 'List of Works Cited' below):

LÉON, 'Deux siècles d'activité minière et métallurgique'.
LÉON, 'Crises et adaptations de la métallurgie alpine'.
THUILLIER, *Georges Dufaud*.
FOHLEN, *Une Affaire de famille au XIXe siècle*.
CARON, *Histoire de l'exploitation d'un grand réseau*.

General problems of the industrial firm are considered in the following works:

GILLE, *Recherches sur la formation de la grande entreprise capitaliste*.
GILLE, *La Sidérurgie française au XIXe siècle*.
BOUVIER, *Le Crédit Lyonnais de 1863 à 1882*.
BOUVIER, FURET and GILLET, *Le Mouvement du profit en France*.
FOHLEN, *L'Industrie textile au temps du Second Empire*.
LÉVY-LEBOYER, *Les Banques européennes*.
VIAL, *L'Industrialisation de la sidérurgie française*.
Charbon et Sciences Humaines.

For a discussion of the various factors affecting the growth of French industry and the role of entrepreneurship, see Kindleberger, *Economic Growth in France and Britain*, with extensive bibliography on the 'behavioural hypothesis' of Landes and others.

A summary of the question has been given in Fohlen, 'The Industrial Revolution in France, 1700–1914'.

List of Works Cited

BOUVIER, J. *Le Crédit Lyonnais de 1863 à 1882*. 2 vols. Paris, 1961.
—— '*Rapports entre systèmes bancaires et entreprises industrielles*', in the colloquium *L'Industrialisation en Europe au XIXe siècle*, held at Lyons, 7–10 October 1970. Paris, 1972.
BOUVIER, J., F. FURET and M. GILLET. *Le Mouvement du profit en France au XIXe siècle: Matériaux et études*. Paris and The Hague, 1965.
CAMERON, R. E. 'Economic Growth and Stagnation in France, 1815–1914', *Journal of Modern History*, xxx (1958–9).
—— *France and the Economic Development of Europe, 1800–1914*. Princeton, N.J., 1961.
CAMERON, R. E. (ed.). *Banking in the Early Stages of Industrialization*. New York and Oxford, 1967.

CARON, F. *Histoire de l'exploitation d'un grand réseau: La Compagnie du Chemin de Fer du Nord, 1846–1937.* Paris and The Hague, 1973.

CHANDLER, A. D. *Strategy and Structure: Chapters in the History of Industrial Enterprise.* Cambridge, Mass., 1962.

CHAPTAL, J. A. *De l'industrie française.* 2 vols. Paris, 1819.

Charbon et Sciences Humaines. Proceedings of a colloquium held by the Faculty of Letters of the University of Lille in May 1963. Paris, 1966.

CLOUGH, S. B. 'Retardative Factors in French Economic Development in the 19th and 20th Centuries', *Journal of Economic History*, Suppl. III (1946), 91–102.

COBDEN, R. *Political Writings.* 2 vols. London, 1867.

COQUELIN, C. 'Des sociétés commerciales en France et en Angleterre', *Revue des Deux-Mondes*, III (1843), 397–437.

EARLE, E. M. (ed.). *Modern France: Problems of the Third and Fourth Republics.* Princeton, N.J., 1951.

FOHLEN, C. *Une Affaire de famille au XIXe siècle: Mequillet-Noblot.* Paris, 1955.

—— *L'Industrie textile au temps du Second Empire.* Paris, 1956.

—— 'Sociétés anonymes et développement capitaliste', *Histoire des Entreprises*, VI and VIII (1960–1).

—— 'The Industrial Revolution in France, 1700–1914', in *The Fontana Economic History of Europe*, IV. London 1970.

GILLE, B. 'Les Problèmes du crédit en Alsace et les milieux financiers parisiens (1825–1848)', *Revue d'Alsace*, XCV (1956).

—— *La Banque et le crédit en France de 1815 à 1848.* Paris, 1959.

—— *Recherches sur la formation de la grande entreprise capitaliste, 1815–1848.* Paris, 1959.

—— *La Sidérurgie française an XIXe siècle.* Paris and Geneva, 1968.

GILLET, M. *Les Charbonnages du nord de la France.* Paris, 1973.

KEMP, T. *Industrialization in Nineteenth Century Europe.* London, 1969.

KINDLEBERGER, CHARLES P. *Economic Growth in France and Britain, 1851–1950.* Cambridge, Mass., 1964.

LANDES, D. S. 'French Entrepreneurship and Industrial Growth in the Nineteenth Century', *Journal of Economic History*, IX (1949), 45–61.

—— 'French Business and the Businessmen: A Social and Cultural Analysis', in Earle (ed.), *Modern France.*

—— 'Vieille banque et banque nouvelle: La Révolution financière du XIXe siècle', *Revue d'Histoire Moderne et Contemporaine*, III (1956), 204–22.

—— 'New Model Entrepreneurship in France and Problems of Historical Explanation', *Explorations in Entrepreneurial History*, I (1963).

—— *The Unbound Prometheus: Technical Change and Industrial Development in Western Europe from 1750 to the Present.* Cambridge, 1969.

LÉON, P. 'Deux siècles d'activité minière et métallurgique en Dauphiné: L'Usine d'Allevard, 1675–1870', *Revue de Géographie Alpine*, XXXVI (1948), 215–58.

—— 'Crises et adaptations de la métallurgie alpine: L'Usine d'Allevard, 1869–1914', *Cahiers, d'Histoire*, 1963, 6–35 and 141–64.

LEVASSEUR, P. *Histoire des classes ouvrières en France depuis la conquête de Jules César jusqu'à la Révolution.* 2 vols. Paris, 1859.

—— *Histoire des classes ouvrières en France depuis 1789 jusqu'à nos jours.* 2 vols. Paris, 1867.

LÉVY-LEBOYER, M. *Les Banques européennes et l'industrialisation internationale dans la première moitié du XIXe siècle.* Paris, 1964.

LHOMME, J. *La Grande Bourgeoisie au pouvoir (1830–1880).* Paris, 1960.

MORSEL, H. 'L'Innovation technique dans les Alpes françaises du Nord de 1870 à 1921', *Bulletin du Centre d'Histoire Economique et Sociale de la Région Lyonnaise*, II (1970).

PARSONS, T. *The Structure of Social Action.* New York and London, 1936.

—— *Essays in Sociological Theory*, 2nd edn. New York, 1958.

RIPERT, G. *Aspects juridiques du capitalisme moderne*, 2nd edn. Paris, 1951.

SAWYER, J. E. 'Strains in the Social Structure of Modern France', in Earle (ed.), *Modern France.*

THUILLIER, G. 'Pour une histoire bancaire régionale: En Nivernais, de 1800 à 1880', *Annales ESC*, 1955.
—— *Georges Dufaud et les débuts du grand capitalisme dans la métallurgie, en Nivernais, au XIXe siècle*. Paris, 1959.
—— *Aspects de l'économie nivernaise*. Paris, 1966.
TILLY, R. *Financial Institutions and Industrialization in the Rhineland, 1815–1870*. Madison, Wisconsin, 1966.
VIAL, J. *L'Industrialisation de la sidérurgie francaise, 1814–1864*. 2 vols. Paris and The Hague, 1967.

CHAPTER VIII

Capital Formation in Germany in the Nineteenth Century

AUBIN, H. and W. ZORN (eds.). *Handbuch der deutschen Wirtschafts- und Sozialgeschichte.* 2 vols. Stuttgart, 1976.
BLUMBERG, H. *Die deutsche Textilindustrie in der industriellen Revolution.* East Berlin, 1965.
BORCHARD, KARL. 'Staatsverbrauch und öffentliche Investitionen in Deutschland, 1780–1850'. Doctoral dissertation, University of Göttingen, 1968.
BORCHARDT, KNUT. 'Zur Frage des Kapitalmangels in der ersten Hälfte des 19. Jahrhunderts in Deutschland', *Jahrbücher für Nationalökonomie und Statistik*, CLXXIII (1961); reprinted in Braun *et al.* (eds.), *Industrielle Revolution*.
—— *Hundert Jahre Rheinische Hypothekenbank*. Frankfurt, 1971.
BRAUN, R., *et al.* (eds.). *Industrielle Revolution: Wirtschaftliche Aspekte*. Cologne, 1972.
BRINKMANN, CARL. 'The Place of Germany in the Economic History of the Nineteenth Century', *Economic History Review*, 1933.
BROCKHAGE, B. *Zur Entwicklung des preussisch–deutschen Kapitalexports*, part I: *Der Berliner Markt für ausländische Staatspapiere 1816 bis um 1840*. Staats- und sozialwissenschaftliche Forschungen, 148. Leipzig, 1910.
BRY, GERHARD. *Wages in Germany, 1871–1945*. Princeton, 1960.
VON CIRIACY-WANTRUP, S. *Agrarkrisen und Stockungsspannen: Zur Frage der langen 'Wellen' in der wirtschaftlichen Entwicklung*. Berlin, 1936.
DIETERICI, C. F. W. *Der Volkswohlstand im preussischen Staat*. Berlin, 1846.
—— *Handbuch der Statistik des preussischen Staates*. Berlin, 1861.
DIETERICI, C. F. W. (ed.). *Mitteilungen des statistischen Bureaus in Berlin*, II, 12–14 (1849).
ENGEL, ERNST. 'Die Viehhaltung im preussischen Staate in der Zeit von 1816 bis mit 1858', *Zeitschrift des Königlichen Preussischen Statistischen Bureaus*, I, 8 (1861).
—— *Das Zeitalter des Dampfes in technisch–statistischer Betrachtung*, Berlin, 1879–80; 2nd edn, 1881.
FAIRLIE, SUSAN. 'The Nineteenth-Century Corn Laws Reconsidered', *Economic History Review*, 2nd ser., XVIII (1965).
VON FINCKENSTEIN, GRAF, M. W. *Die Entwicklung der Landwirtschaft in Preussen und Deutschland, 1800–1930*. Würzburg, 1960.
FISCHER, W. (ed.). *Beiträge zu Wirtshaftswachstum und Wirtschaftsstruktur im 16. und 19. Jahrhundert*. Berlin, 1971.
FRANZ, G. 'Landwirtschaft, 1800–1850', in Aubin and Zorn (eds.), *Handbuch der deutschen Wirtschafts- und Sozialgeschichte*, II.
FREMDLING, RAINER. 'Eisenbahnen und deutsches Wirtschaftswachstum, 1840–79'. Unpublished dissertation, University of Münster, 1974. (Published under the same title, Dortmund, 1975: references above are to the unpublished version.)
GADOR, R. 'Die Entwicklung des Strassenbaues in Preussen 1815–1875 unter besonderer Berücksichtigung des Aktienstrassenbaues'. Unpublished dissertation, Free University of Berlin, 1966.
VON DER GOLTZ, T. *Geschichte der deutschen Landwirtschaft*. 2 vols. Stuttgart, 1903; reprinted Aalen, 1963.

HANSEMANN, D. *Preussen und Frankreich.* Leipzig, 1833.

HELFFERICH, KARL. *Deutschlands Volkswohlstand, 1888–1913.* Berlin, 1913.

HELLING, G. 'Berechnung eines Index der Agrarproduktion in Deutschland im 19. Jahrhundert', *Jahrbuch für Wirtschaftsgeschichte*, no. 4 (1965).

HENNING, F.-W. 'Kapitalbildungsmöglichkeiten der bäuerlichen Bevölkerung im 19. Jahrhundert', in Fischer (ed.), *Beiträge zu Wirtschaftswachstum und Wirtschaftstruktur.*

HIGGINS, J., and S. POLLARD. *Aspects of Capital Investment in Great Britain, 1750–1850.* London, 1971.

HIRSCHMAN, A. *The Strategy of Economic Development.* New Haven, Conn., 1958.

HOFFMANN, W. *Growth of Industrial Economies,* transl. W. O. Henderson and W. H. Chaloner. Manchester, 1958.

—— 'The Take-Off in Germany', in Rostow (ed.), *The Economics of Take-Off into Self-Sustained Growth.*

HOFFMANN, W., and J. Müller. *Das deutsche Volkseinkommen 1851–1957.* Tübingen, 1959.

HOFFMANN, W., et al. *Das Wachstum der deutschen Wirtschaft seit der Mitte des 19. Jahrhunderts.* Berlin, Heidelberg, and New York, 1965.

HOHORST, GERD. 'Bevölkerungsentwicklung und Wirtschaftswachstum in Preussen, 1816 bis 1914'. Dissertation, University of Münster, 1974.

HOLTFRERICH, C. *Quantitative Wirtschaftsgeschichte des Ruhrkohlenbergbaus im 19. Jahrhundert: Eine Führungssektoranalyse.* Dortmund, 1973.

IPSEN, G. 'Die preussische Bauernbefreiung als Landesausbau', *Zeitschrift für Agrargeschichte und Agrarsoziologie*, II (1954).

JACOBS, A., and H. RICHTER. *Die Grosshandelspreise in Deutschland von 1792 bis 1934.* Sonderhefte des Instituts für Konjunkturforschung. Berlin, 1935.

JANTKE, C., and D. HILGER. *Die Eigentumslosen, der deutsche Pauperismus und die Emanzipationskrise in Darstellungen und Deutungen der zeitgenössischen Literatur.* Freiburg and Munich, 1965.

JOCHIMSEN, R. *Theorie der Infrastruktur: Grundlagen der marktwirtschaftlichen Entwicklung.* Tübingen, 1966.

JOSTOCK, P. 'The Long-Term Growth of National Income in Germany', *Studies in Income and Wealth*, ser. v. London, 1955.

KAUFHOLD, K. 'Handwerk und Industrie, 1800–1850', in Aubin and Zorn (eds.), *Handbuch der deutschen Wirtschafts- und Sozialgeschichte*, II.

KINKEL, HANS-JÜRGEN. 'Kapitalbildung und Finanzierungsprobleme im Ruhrgebiet, 1830–1880'. Unpublished diploma thesis, University of Münster, 1968.

KIRCHHAIN, G. 'Das Wachstum der deutschen Baumwollindustrie im 19. Jahrhundert'. Doctoral dissertation, University of Münster, 1971 (privately published in photocopy).

KLEIN, E. *Geschichte der deutschen Landwirtschaft im Industriezeitalter.* Wissenschaftliche Paperbacks, I. Wiesbaden, 1973.

KLEMENT, D. *Strukturwandlungen des Kapitalstocks nach Anlagearten in Deutschland seit der Mitte des 19. Jahrhunderts.* Tübingen, 1967.

KOSELLECK, R. *Preussen zwischen Reform und Revolution: Allgemeines Landrecht, Verwaltung und soziale Bewegung.* Stuttgart, 1967.

KRUG, L. *Betrachtungen über den Nationalreichtum der preussischen Staaten.* 2 vols. Berlin, 1805; reprinted Aalen, 1967.

KRUG, L., and L. VON MÜTZELL. *Neues topographisch–statistisch–geographisches Wörterbuch des preussischen Staates.* 6 vols. Halle, 1825.

KUCZYNSKI, JÜRGEN. *Die Geschichte der Lage der Arbeiter unter dem Kapitalismus*, I–II. East Berlin, 1961–2.

KUTZ, MARTIN. 'Die deutsch–britischen Handelsbeziehungen von 1790 bis zur Gründung des Zollvereins', *Vierteljahrschrift für Sozial- und Wirtschaftsgeschichte*, September 1969.

KUZNETS, SIMON. *Modern Economic Growth: Rate, Structure, Spread.* New Haven, Conn., 1966.

LANDES, DAVID. 'Die Industrialisierung in Japan und Europa: Ein Vergleich', in Wolfram Fischer (ed.), *Wirtschafts- und sozialgeschichtliche Probleme der frühen Industrialisierung.* Berlin, 1968.

LÜTGE, FRIEDRICH. *Deutsche Sozial- und Wirtschaftsgeschichte*, 3rd edn. Berlin, Heidelberg, and New York, 1966.

LUTZ, F. A., and D. C. HAGUE (eds.). *The Theory of Capital*. London, 1961.

MARTIN, P. C. 'Frühindustrielles Gewerbe in der Rechtsform der AG', in Fischer (ed.), *Beiträge zu Wirtshaftswachstum und Wirtschaftsstruktur*.

MEITZEN, A. *Der Boden und die landwirtschaftlichen Verhältnisse des preussischen Staates nach dem Gebietsumfange vor 1866*, 8 vols. Berlin, 1868–1908 (esp. vol. III, 1871).

MOTTEK, HANS. *Wirtschaftsgeschichte Deutschlands: Ein Grundriss*. 2 vols. East Berlin, 1957 and 1964.

PARKER, W. N. 'Productivity Growth in American Grain Farming: An Analysis of Its 19th-Century Sources', in R. W. Fogel and Stanley I. Engerman (eds.), *The Reinterpretation of American Economic History*. New York, Evanston, San Francisco, and London, 1971.

PARKER, W. N. and E. L. JONES (eds.), *European Peasants and Their Markets*. Princeton, 1975.

PRIMACK, M. 'Land Clearing under Nineteenth-Century Techniques: Some Preliminary Calculations', *Journal of Economic History*, XXII (1962).

PRUSSIA. Preussisches Ministerium für Handel, Gewerbe und öffentliche Arbeiten. Technisches Eisenbahnbureau. *Statistische Nachrichten von den preussischen Eisenbahnen*, I–XXVII. Berlin, 1855–80.

—— Königliches Preussisches Statistisches Bureau. *Tabellen und amtliche Nachrichten für das Jahr 1849*, I–VI. Berlin, 1853.

——. —— *Tabellen und amtliche Nachrichten über den preussischen Staat*. Berlin, 1858.

——. —— *Jahrbuch für die amtliche Statistik des preussischen Staates*, V. Berlin, 1883.

VON REDEN, F. W. *Erwerbs- und Verkehrsstatistik des Königstaats Preussen*. Darmstadt, 1853.

—— *Deutschland und das übrige Europa*. Wiesbaden, 1854.

—— *Finanz-Statistik*. 3 vols. Darmstadt, 1856.

RITTER, U. *Die Rolle des Staates in den Frühstadien der Industrialisierung: Die preussische Industrieförderung in der ersten Hälfte des 19. Jahrhunderts*. Berlin, 1961.

ROSTOW, W. W. *The Stages of Economic Growth*. Cambridge, 1960.

ROSTOW, W. W. (ed.). *The Economics of Take-Off into Self-Sustained Growth*. New York and London, 1963.

SAX, E. *Die Eisenbahnen:* vol. III of *Die Verkehrsmittel in Volks- und Staatswirtschaft*, 2nd edn. Berlin, 1922.

SCHUMPETER, J. *Business Cycles: A Theoretical, Historical and Statistical Analysis of the Capitalist Process*. 2 vols. New York, 1939.

SERING, M. *Geschichte der preussisch–deutschen Eisenzölle von 1818 bis zur Gegenwart*. Staats- und sozialwissenschaftliche Forschungen, 3. Leipzig, 1882.

SPIETHOFF, A. *Die wirtschaftlichen Wechsellagen: Aufschwung, Krise, Stockung*. 2 vols. Tübingen, 1955.

TILLY, RICHARD. 'The Political Economy of Public Finance and Prussian Industrialization, 1815–1866', *Journal of Economic History*, XXVI (1966).

—— 'Los von England: Probleme des Nationalismus in der deutschen Wirtschaftsgeschichte', *Zeitschrift für die gesamte Staatswissenschaft*, CXXIV (1968).

—— 'Soll und Haben: Recent German Economic History and the Problem of Economic Development', *Journal of Economic History*, XXIX (1969).

TOWNE, M. and E. RASMUSSEN. 'Farm Gross Product and Gross Investment in the Nineteenth Century', in National Bureau of Economic Research, *Trends in the American Economy in the Nineteenth Century*. Studies in Income and Wealth, 24. Princeton, 1960.

UCKE, A. 'Die Agrarkrise in Preussen während der zwanziger Jahre dieses Jahrhunderts'. Doctoral dissertation, University of Halle, 1887.

UNGEWITTER, F. H. *Die preussische Monarchie*. Berlin, 1859.

VON VIEBAHN, G. *Statistik und Geographie des Regierungs-Bezirks Düsseldorf*. Düsseldorf, 1836.

—— *Statistik des zollvereinten und nördlichen Deutschlands*. 3 vols. Berlin, 1862.

WAGENBLASS, H. *Der Eisenbahnbau und das Wachstum der deutschen Eisen- und Maschinenbauindustrie, 1835 bis 1860*. Stuttgart, 1973.

WAGENFÜHR, R. *Die industriewirtschaftlichen Entwicklungstendenzen der deutschen und internationalen Industrieproduktion 1860 bis 1932.* Sonderhefte des Instituts für Konjunkturforschung, 31. Berlin, 1933.

ZORN, W. 'Die wirtschaftliche Struktur der Rheinprovinz um 1820', *Vierteljahrschrift ür Sozial- und Wirtschaftsgeschichte*, IV, 3 (1967).

CHAPTER IX

Labour in German Industrialization

ABEL, W. 'Der Pauperismus in Deutschland', in Abel *et al.* (eds.), *Wirtschaft, Geschichte und Wirtschaftsgeschichte.*

ABEL, W., *et al.* (eds.). *Wirtschaft, Geschichte und Wirtschaftsgeschichte.* Stuttgart, 1966.

ABRAHAM, K. *Der Strukturwandel im Handwerk in der ersten Hälfte des 19. Jahrhunderts.* Cologne, 1955.

ADELMANN, G. *Die soziale Betriebsverfassung des Ruhrbergbaus vom Anfang des 19. Jahrhunderts bis zum ersten Weltkrieg.* Bonn, 1962.

—— 'Strukturwandlungen der rheinischen Leinen- und Baumwollgewerbe zu Beginn der Industrialisierung', *Vierteljahrschrift für Sozial- und Wirtschaftsgeschichte*, LIII (1966).

ANGEL-VOLKOV, S. 'The "Decline of the German Handicrafts" – Another Reappraisal', *Vierteljahrschrift für Sozial- und Wirtschaftsgeschichte*, LXI, 2 (1974).

ANTON, G. K. *Geschichte der preussischen Fabrikgesetzgebung bis zu ihrer Aufnahme durch die Reichsgewerbeordnung.* Berlin, 1953.

ASHLEY, W. J. *The Progress of the German Working Classes in the Last Quarter of a Century.* London, 1904.

BAAR, L. *Die Berliner Industrie in der Industriellen Revolution.* East Berlin, 1966.

BECKER, W. 'Die Bedeutung der nichtagrarischen Wanderungen für die Herausbildung des industriellen Proletariats in Deutschland, unter besonderer Berücksichtigung Preussens von 1850 bis 1870', in H. Mottek (ed.), *Studien zur Geschichte der industriellen Revolution in Deutschland.* East Berlin, 1960.

BENDIX, R. *Work and Authority in Industry.* New York, 1956.

BERNAYS, M. 'Berufswahl und Berufsschicksal des modernen Industriearbeiters', *Archiv für Sozialwissenschaft und Sozialpolitik*, XXXV (1912).

BERNHARD, E. 'Auslese und Anpassung der Arbeiterschaft', *Schmollers Jahrbuch*, XXXV (1911).

BERNHARD, L. *Die Akkordarbeit in Deutschland.* Leipzig, 1903.

BIENKOWSKI, L. VON. 'Untersuchungen über Arbeitseignung und Leistungsfähigkeit der Arbeiterschaft einer Kabelfabrik', *Schriften des Vereins für Sozialpolitik*, CXXXIV (1910).

BLUMBERG, H. *Die deutsche Textilindustrie in der industriellen Revolution.* East Berlin, 1965.

BOLTE, K. M. *Deutsche Gesellschaft im Wandel.* Opladen, 1967.

BOLTE, K. M., *et al. Struktur und Wandel der Gesellschaft.* Opladen, 1970.

BORCHARDT, K. 'Zum Problem der Erziehungs- und Ausbildungsinvestitionen im 19. Jahrhundert', in H. Aubin *et al.* (eds.), *Beiträge zur Wirtschafts- und Stadtgeschichte.* Wiesbaden, 1965.

—— 'Regionale Wachstumsdifferenzierung in Deutschland im 19. Jahrhundert unter besonderer Berücksichtigung des West–Ost Gefälles', in Abel *et al.* (eds.), *Wirtschaft, Geschichte und Wirtschaftsgeschichte.*

—— *The Industrial Revolution in Germany.* London, 1970.

BORN, K. E. *Staat und Sozialpolitik seit Bismarcks Sturz, 1890–1914.* Wiesbaden, 1957.

—— 'Sozialpolitische Probleme und Bestrebungen in Deutschland von 1848 bus zur Bismarckschen Sozialgesetzgebung', *Vierteljahrschrift für Sozial- und Wirtschaftsgeschichte*, XLVI (1959).

BRADY, R. A. *The Rationalization Movement in German Industry.* Berkeley, Calif., 1933.

BREPOHL, W. *Industrievolk im Wandel von der agraren zur industriellen Daseinform dargestellt am Ruhrgebiet.* Tübingen, 1957.

BROWN, E. H. PHELPS and MARGARET H. BROWNE. *A Century of Pay.* London, 1968.

BRY, GERHARD. *Wages in Germany, 1871–1945.* Princeton, 1960.

BUCHHOLZE, E. W. *Ländliche Bevölkerung an der Schwelle des Industriezeitalters: Der Raum Braunschweig als Beispiel.* Stuttgart, 1966.

BURGDORFER, F. 'Migrations across the Frontiers of Germany', in W. F. Willcox (ed.), *International Migrations.* 2 vols., II. New York, 1931.

CONZE, W. 'Vom "Pöbel" zum "Proletariat": Sozialgeschichtliche Voraussetzungen für den Sozialismus in Deutschland', *Vierteljahrschrift für Sozial- und Wirtschaftsgeschichte,* XLI (1954).

CREW, D. 'Definitions of Modernity: Social Mobility in a German Town, 1880–1901', *Journal of Social History,* VII, 1 (Fall 1973).

CROON, H. 'Die Einwirkung der Industrialisierung auf die gesellschaftliche Schichtung der Bevölkerung im Rheinisch–Westfälischen Industriegebiet', *Rheinische Vierteljahrsblätter,* XXIX (1955).

DAWSON, W. H. *The German Workman.* London, 1906.

—— *Industrial Germany.* London, 1912.

DECKER, F. *Die betriebliche Sozialordnung der Dürener Industrie im 19. Jahrhundert.* Cologne, 1965.

DESAI, A. V. *Real Wages in Germany, 1871–1913.* Oxford, 1968. An exceptionally penetrating work.

DETHLOFF, J. 'Das Handwerk in der kapitalistischen Wirtschaft', in Harms (ed.), *Strukturwandlungen der deutschen Volkswirtschaft,* II.

EHRENBERG, R. 'Der Gesichtskreis eines deutschen Fabrikarbeiters', *Thünen Archiv,* I (1906).

—— 'Schwäche und Stärkung neuzeitlicher Arbeitsgemeinschaften', *Archiv für exacte Wirtschaftsforschung,* III (1911).

ENGELSING, R. 'Lebenshaltungen und Lebenshaltungskosten im 18. und 19. Jahrhundert in den Hansestadten Bremen und Hamburg', *International Review of Social History,* 1966.

Enquete-Ausschuss: Verhandlungen und Berichte des Unterausschusses für Arbeitsleistung (Ausschuss zur Untersuchung der Erzeugungs- und Absatzbedingungen der deutschen Wirtschaft). Berlin, 1930.

FISCHER, W. 'Die Rolle des Kleingewerbes im wirtschaftlichen Wachstumsprozess in Deutschland, 1850–1914', in Fischer, *Wirtschaftliche und soziale Probleme der gewerblichen Entwicklung im 15.–16. und 19. Jahrhundert.* Stuttgart, 1968.

—— *Wirtschaft und Gesellschaft im Zeitalter der Industrialisierung.* Göttingen. 1972. A collection which includes many of Fischer's pioneering studies on the structure of the labour force in early industrialization.

FISCHER, W. (ed.). *Wirtschafts- und sozialgeschichtliche Probleme der frühen Industrialisierung.* Berlin, 1968.

—— *Beiträge zu Wirtschaftswachstum und Wirtschaftsstruktur im 16. und 19. Jahrhundert.* Berlin, 1971.

FISCHER, W., and P. CZADA. 'Wandlungen in der deutschen Industriestruktur im 20. Jahrhundert', in G. A. Ritter (ed.), *Entstehung und Wandel der modernen Gesellschaft.*

FORBERGER, R. *Die Manufaktur in Sachsen vom Ende des 16. bis zum Anfang des 19. Jahrhunderts,* East Berlin, 1958.

—— 'Zur Auseinandersetzung über das Problem des Überganges von der Manufaktur zur Fabrik', in Deutsche Akademie der Wissenschaften zu Berlin (eds.), *Beiträge zur Deutschen Wirtschafts- und Sozialgeschichte des 18. und 19. Jahrhunderts.* East Berlin, 1962.

GAINSBOROUGH COMMISSION. *Life and Labour in Germany.* London, 1906.

GERMANY. Kaiserliche Statistische Amt. *Statistik des deutschen Reichs.* 2nd ser., various dates.

GÖHRE, P. *Three Months in a Workshop.* London, 1895 (translation of *Drei Monate Fabrikarbeiter* (Leipzig, 1891)).

GRANDKE, H. 'Die vom Verein für Sozialpolitik veranstalteten Untersuchungen über

die Lage des Handwerks in Deutschland, mit besonderer Rücksicht auf seine Konkur-
renzfähigkeit gegenüber der Grossindustrie', *Schmollers Jahrbuch*, XXI (1897).

GRUMBACH, F., and H. KÖNIG. 'Beschäftigung und Löhne der deutschen Industriewirtschaft, 1888–1954', *Weltwirtschaftliches Archiv*, LXXIX (1957).

GÜNTHER, A. 'Die Arbeitszeit in der Grosseisenindustrie', *Soziale Praxis*, XXI, 46 (15
August 1912).

GÜNTHER, A., and R. PREVOT. 'Die Wohlfahrtseinrichtungen der Arbeitgeber in
Deutschland und Frankreich', *Schriften des Vereins für Sozialpolitik*, CXIV (1905).

HARDACH, K. 'Anglomanie und Anglophobie während der industriellen Revolution in
Deutschland', *Schmollers Jahrbuch*, XCI (1971).

—— 'Some Remarks on German Economic Historiography and Its Understanding
of the Industrial Revolution in Germany', *Journal of European Economic History*, I
(1972).

HARMS, B. (ed.). *Strukturwandlungen der deutschen Volkswirtschaft*. 2 vols. Berlin, 1928.

HARTWICK, H. H. *Arbeitsmarkt, Verbände und Staat, 1918–1933*. Berlin, 1967.

HEBERLE, R., and F. MEYER. *Die Grossstädte im Strome der Binnenwanderung*. Leipzig, 1937.

HEISS, C. 'Auslese und Anpassung der Arbeiter in der Berliner Feinmechanik', *Schriften
des Vereins für Sozialpolitik*, CXXXIV (1910).

HENDERSON, W. O. *Britain and Industrial Europe, 1750–1870*. Liverpool, 1954; 2nd edn,
Leicester, 1965.

HESSE, H. 'Die Entwicklung der regionalen Einkommensdifferenzen im Wachstumsprozess der deutschen Wirtschaft vor 1913', in W. Fischer (ed.), *Beiträge zu Wirtschaftswachstum*.

HINKE, H. 'Auslese und Anpassung der Arbeiter im Buchdruckergewerbe mit besonderer
Rücksichtnahme auf die Setzmaschine', *Schriften des Vereins für Sozialpolitik*, CXXXIV
(1910).

HINZE, K. *Die Arbeiterfrage zu Beginn des Modernen Kapitalismus in Brandenburg–Preussen*.
Berlin, 1927; reprinted Berlin, 1963.

HIRSCHBERG, E. *Die soziale Lage der arbeitenden Klassen in Berlin*. Berlin, 1897.

HOFFMANN, W. G. 'Der tertiäre Sektor im Wachstumsprozess', *Jahrbücher für Nationalökonomie und Statistik*, CLXXXIII (1969).

—— 'Die Phillips-Kurve in Deutschland', *Kyklos*, XXII (1969).

HOFFMANN, W. G., *et al. Das Wachstum der deutschen Wirtschaft seit der Mitte des 19.
Jahrhunderts*. Berlin, 1965. The indispensable statistical compilation, but full of heroic
assumptions about the quality of the data.

IPSEN, G. 'Die preussische Bauernbefreiung als Landesausbau', *Zeitschrift für Agrargeschichte und Agrarsoziologie*, II (1954).

J., R. 'Erlebnisse eines Metalldrehers', *Thünen–Archiv*, II (1909).

JANTKE, C., and D. HILGER. *Die Eigentumslosen, der deutsche Pauperismus und die Emanzipationskrise in Darstellungen und Deutungen der zeitgenössischen Literatur*. Freiburg and
Munich, 1965.

KAELBLE, H. 'Sozialer Aufstieg in Deutschland, 1850–1914', *Vierteljahrschrift für Sozial-
und Wirtschaftsgeschichte*, LX (1973).

KAELBLE, H., and H. VOLKMANN. 'Konjunktur und Streik während des Übergangs zum
Organisierten Kapitalismus', *Zeitschrift für Wirtschafts- und Sozialwissenschaften*, XCII
(1972).

KAUFHOLD, K. H. 'Das preussische Handwerk in der Zeit der Frühindustrialisierung', in
W. Fischer (ed.), *Beiträge zu Wirtschaftswachstum*.

KESSLER, G. 'Die Lage der deutschen Arbeiterschaft seit 1914', in Harms (ed.), *Strukturwandlungen der deutschen Wirtschaft*, I.

KISCH, H. 'The Textile Industries in Silesia and the Rhineland: A Comparative Study in
Industrialisation', *Journal of Economic History*, XIX (1959).

—— 'From Monopoly to Laissez Faire: The Early Growth of the Wupper Valley Textile Trades', *Journal of European Economic History*, I (1972).

KISTLER, F. *Die wirtschaftliche und soziale Verhältnisse in Baden, 1849–1870*. Freiburg, 1954.

KNAUERHASE, R. 'The Compound Steam Engine and Productivity Changes in the
German Merchant Fleet, 1871–87', *Journal of Economic History*, XXVIII (1968).

KNODEL, JOHN E. *The Decline of Fertility in Germany, 1871–1939*. Princeton, 1974.
KOCKA, J. *Unternehmensverwaltung und Angestelltenschaft am Beispiel Siemens, 1847–1914*. Stuttgart, 1969.
KÖLLMANN, W. *Sozialgeschichte der Stadt Barmen im 19. Jahrhundert*. Tübingen, 1960.
—— *Bevölkerung in der industriellen Revolution*. Göttingen, 1974. A collection of Köllmann's indispensable essays on population, migration, and social structure.
KRAUS, A. *Die Unterschichten Hamburgs in der ersten Hälfte des 19. Jahrhunderts: Entstehung, Struktur und Lebenverhältnisse*. Stuttgart, 1965.
KREUGER, H. *Zur Geschichte der Manufakturen und der Manufakturarbeiter in Preussen*. Berlin, 1958.
KUCZYNSKI, J. *Die Geschichte der Lage der Arbeiter unter dem Kapitalismus*. 38 vols. East Berlin, 1961– . Almost all directly or indirectly relevant.
KUCZYNSKI, R. R. *Der Zug nach der Stadt: Statistische Studien über Vorgänge der Bevölkerungsbewegung im deutschen Reich*. Stuttgart, 1897.
—— *Die Entwicklung der gewerblichen Löhne seit der Begründung des deutschen Reichs*. Berlin, 1909.
—— *Arbeitslohn und Arbeitszeit in Europa und Amerika, 1870–1909*. Berlin, 1913.
KÜHNE, H. 'Der Arbeitseinsatz im Vier Jahres Plan', *Jahrbücher für Nationalökonomie und Statistik*, CXLVII (1937).
LAMPRECHT, H. 'Über die soziale Herkunft der Handwerker', *Soziale Welt*, III (1951).
LANDE, D. 'Arbeits- und Lohnverhältnisse in der Berliner Maschinenindustrie zu Beginn des 20. Jahrhunderts', *Schriften des Vereins für Sozialpolitik*, CXXXIV (1910).
LANDES, D. S. 'Technological Change and Development in Western Europe, 1750–1914', in *Cambridge Economic History of Europe*, VI. Cambridge, 1965.
LANGE, E. 'Die ortsüblichen Tagelöhne gewöhnlicher Tagearbeiter im deutschen Reiche', *Archiv für soziale Gesetzgebung und Statistik*, VI (1893).
LAZARSFELD, P. F. *Jugend und Beruf*. Jena, 1931.
LEUCKE, O. 'Über einige Bestimmungsgründe der Lohnverdienste', *Archiv für exacte Wirtschaftsforschung*, III (1911).
Life and Labour in Germany: see Gainsborough Commission.
LLOYD, G. I. H. 'Labour Organisation in the Cutlery Trade of Solingen', *Economic Journal*, XVIII (1908).
LÖSCH, A. *Bevölkerungswellen und Wechsellagen*. Jena, 1936.
LUDWIG, K. H. 'Die Fabrikarbeit von Kindern im 19. Jahrhundert', *Vierteljahrschrift für Sozial- und Wirtschaftsgeschichte*, LII (1965).
McCREARY, E. C. 'Social Welfare and Business: The Krupp Welfare Program, 1860–1914', *Business History Review*, XLII, I (1968).
MOMBERT, P. 'Die Arbeits- und Lohnverhältnisse der Angestellten der Düsseldorfer Strassenbahnen', *Schriften des Vereins für Sozialpolitik*, XCIX (1902).
—— 'Der innerstaatliche Bevölkerungsausgleich', *Allgemeines statistisches Archiv*, XXIII (1933–4).
MÖNCKMEIER, W. *Die deutsche überseeische Auswanderung*. Jena, 1912.
MORGENSTERN, MAX. 'Auslese und Anpassung der industrieller Arbeiterschaft, betrachtet bei den Offenbacher Lederwarenarbeitern', *Schriften des Vereins für Sozialpolitik*, CXXXV (1912).
MOTTEK, H. *Wirtschaftsgeschichte Deutschlands: Ein Grundriss*. 2 vols. East Berlin, 1957 and 1964.
MUSGRAVE, P. W. *Technical Change: The Labour Force and Education*. Oxford, 1967.
NEUSS, E. *Entstehung und Entwicklung der Klasse der besitzlosen Lohnarbeiter in Halle*. East Berlin, 1958.
NOYES, P. H. *Organization and Revolution: Working Class Associations in the German Revolutions of 1848–49*. Princeton, 1966.
OBERMANN, K. 'Zur Rolle der Eisenbahnarbeiter im Prozess der Formierung der Arbeiterlöhne in Deutschland', *Jahrbuch für Wirtschaftsgeschichte*, 1970, part 2.
ORSAGH, T. J. 'Löhne in Deutschland, 1871–1913', *Zeitschrift für die gesamte Staatswissenschaft*, CXXV, 3 (1969).
PIEPER, L. *Die Lage der Bergarbeiter im Ruhrrevier*. Stuttgart, 1903.

PLATZER, H. J. 'Die Steigerung der Erwerbsziffer in Deutschland', *Jahrbücher für National-ökonomie und Statistik*, CXXXV (1931).

PUPPKE, L. *Sozialpolitik und soziale Anschauungen frühindustrieller Unternehmer in Rheinland und Westfalen*. Cologne, 1966.

QUANTE, P. *Die Abwanderung aus der Landwirtschaft*. Kiel, 1958.

—— 'Die Bevölkerungsentwicklung der preussischen Ostprovinzen im 19. und 20. Jahrhundert', *Zeitschrift für Ostforschung*, VIII (1959).

REUTER, O. *Die Manufaktur im fränkischen Raum*. Stuttgart, 1961.

RIMLINGER, G. 'The Legitimation of Protest: A Comparative Study in Labour History', *Comparative Studies in Society and History*, II (1960).

RITTER, G. A. (ed.). *Entstehung und Wandel der modernen Gesellschaft*. Berlin, 1970.

RITTER, U. P. *Die Rolle des Staates in den Frühstadien der Industrialisierung*. Berlin, 1961.

SAMUELSON, JAMES. *The German Working Man*. London, 1869.

SCHMITZ, W. 'Regelung der Arbeitszeit und Intensität der Arbeit', *Archiv für exacte Wirtschaftsforschung*, IV (1912).

SCHMOLLER, G. *Zur Geschichte der deutschen Kleingewerbe im 19. Jahrhundert*. Halle, 1870.

SCHOFER, L. 'Patterns of Worker Protest: Upper Silesia, 1865–1914', *Journal of Social History*, V, 4 (1972).

SCHOTT, S. *Die grossstädtischen Agglomerationen des deutschen Reichs, 1871–1910*. Breslau, 1912.

SCHRÖTER, A., and W. BECKER. *Die deutsche Maschinenbauindustrie in der industriellen Revolution*. East Berlin, 1962.

SCHUMACHER, M. *Auslandsreisen deutscher Unternehmer, 1750–1851, unter besonderer Berücksichtigung von Rheinland und Westfalen*. Cologne, 1968.

SCHUMANN, F. 'Die Arbeiter der Daimler-Motoren-Gesellschaft, Stuttgart–Unter-türkheim', *Schriften des Vereins für Sozialpolitik*, CXXXV, I (1911).

SLAWINGER, G. *Die Manufaktur in Kurbayern*. Stuttgart, 1965.

SOMBART, W. *Der moderne Kapitalismus*. 2nd edn. 5 vols. Munich and Leipzig, 1916; reprinted Berlin, 1955.

SPIETHOFF, A. *Die wirtschaftlichen Wechsellagen: Aufschwung, Krise, Stockung*. 2 vols. Tübingen, 1955.

Statistik des deutschen Reichs: see Germany, Kaiserliche Statistische Amt.

STEARNS, P. N. 'Adaptation to Industrialization: German Workers as a Test Case', *Central European History*, III (1970).

—— 'Die Herausbildung einer sozialen Gesinnung im Frühindustrialismus', in P. C. Ludz (ed.), *Soziologie und Sozialgeschichte*. Opladen, 1972.

—— 'Measuring the Evolution of Strike Movements', *International Review of Social History*, XIX, I (1974).

STEGLICH, W. 'Eine Streiktabelle für Deutschland 1864–1880', *Jahrbuch für Wirtschafts-geschichte*, 1960 (no. 2).

STRAUSS, H. *Die Lage und die Bewegung der Chemnitzer Arbeiter in der ersten Hälfte des 19. Jahrhunderts*. East Berlin, 1960.

STUDDERS, H. *Die Facharbeiterfrage in der Kriegswirtschaft*. Hamburg, 1938.

SYRUP, F. 'Studien über den industriellen Arbeiterwechsel', *Archiv für exacte Wirts-chaftsforschung*, IV (1912).

—— *Arbeitseinsatz und Arbeitslosenhilfe in Deutschland*. Berlin, 1936.

TEUTEBERG, H. J. *Geschichte der industriellen Mitbestimmung in Deutschland*. Tübingen, 1961.

THUN, A. *Die Industrie am Niederrhein und ihre Arbeiter*. 2 vols. Leipzig, 1879.

TILLY, R. 'Popular Disturbances in Nineteenth Century Germany: A Preliminary Survey', *Journal of Social History*, IV (1970).

TODT, E. *Die gewerkschaftliche Betätigung in Deutschland, 1850–1859*. East Berlin, 1950.

UHDE, K. *Die Produktions-Bedingungen der deutschen und englischen Steinkohlen Bergbaues*. Jena, 1907.

UHEN, L. *Gruppenbewusstsein und informelle Gruppenbildungen bei deutschen Arbeitern*. Berlin, 1964.

VOIGT, P. 'Die Hauptergebnisse der neuester deutschen Handwerksstatistik von 1895', *Schmollers Jahrbuch*, XXI (1897).

WALKER, M. *Germany and the Emigration*. Cambridge, Mass., 1964.
WEHLER, H.-U. 'Theorieprobleme der modernen deutschen Wirtschaftsgeschichte (1800–1945)', in G. A. Ritter (ed.), *Entstehung und Wandel der modernen Gesellschaft*.
WIEDFELDT, O. *Statististische Studien zur Entwicklungsgeschichte der Berliner Industrie von 1720 bis 1890*. Leipzig, 1898.
WÖRISHOFFER, F. *Die soziale Lage der Fabrikarbeiter in Mannheim*. Karlsruhe, 1891.
WOYTINSKY, W. 'Arbeitslosigkeit und Kurzarbeit', *Jahrbücher für Nationalökonomie und Statistik*, CXXXIV (1931).
WRIGLEY, E. A. *Industrial Growth and Population Change*. Cambridge, 1960.
WUNDERLICH, F. *Farm Labour in Germany, 1810–1945*. Princeton, 1961.
ZIMMERMANN, W. 'Zur sozialen Lage der Eisenbahner in Preussen', *Schriften des Vereins für Sozialpolitik*, XCIX (1902).
ZORN, W. 'Typen und Entwicklungskräfte deutschen Unternehmertums', in K. E. Born (ed.), *Moderne deutsche Wirtschaftsgeschichte*. Cologne, 1966.
ZWAHR, H. 'Zur Konstituierung des Proletariats als Klasse: Strukturuntersuchung über das Leipziger Proletariat während der industriellen Revolution', in H. Bartel and E. Engelberg (eds.), *Die grosspreussisch–militäristische Reichsgründung, 1871*, I. East Berlin, 1971.

CHAPTER X

Entrepreneurs and Managers in German Industrialization

ABEL, W., et al. *Handwerksgeschichte in neuer Sicht*. Göttingen, 1970.
ABRAHAM, K. *Der Strukturwandel im Handwerk in der ersten Hälfte des 19. Jahrhunderts*. Cologne, 1955.
ADELMANN, G. *Die soziale Betriebsverfassung des Ruhrbergbaus vom Anfang des 19. Jahrhunderts bis zum Ersten Weltkrieg*. Bonn, 1962.
—— 'Führende Unternehmer im Rheinland und in Westfalen, 1850–1914', *Rheinische Vierteljahrsblätter*, XXXV (1971).
ARNDT, H. (ed.). *Die Konzentration in der Wirtschaft*. 2nd edn. 2 vols. Berlin, 1971.
ARPS, L. *Deutsche Versicherungsunternehmer*. Karlsruhe, 1968.
BAAR, L. *Die Berliner Industrie in der industriellen Revolution*. Berlin, 1966.
BARAN, P. A., and P. M. SWEEZY. *Monopoly Capital*. New York and London, 1968.
BARKHAUSEN, M. 'Der Aufstieg der rheinischen Industrie im 18. Jahrhundert und die Entstehung eines industriellen Grossbürgertums', *Rheinische Vierteljahrsblätter*, XIX (1954).
—— 'Staatliche Wirtschaftslenkung und freies Unternehmertum im westdeutschen und im nord- und südniederländischen Raum bei der Entstehung der neuzeitlichen Industrie im 18. Jahrhundert', *Vierteljahrschrift für Sozial- und Wirtschaftsgeschichte*, XLV (1958).
BEAU, H. *Das Leistungswissen des frühindustriellen Unternehmertums in Rheinland und Westfalen*. Cologne, 1959.
BECKERATH, H. VON. *Der moderne Industrialismus*. Jena, 1930.
BEER, J. J. *The Emergence of the German Dye Industry*. Urbana, Illinois, 1959.
BEIN, A. *Friedrich Hammacher: Lebensbild eines Parlamentariers und Wirtschaftsführers, 1824–1904*. Berlin, 1932.
BENDIX, R. *Work and Authority in Industry*. New York. 1956.
BERDROW, W. *Alfred Krupp*. 2nd edn. 2 vols. Berlin, 1928.
BERGENGRÜN, A. *David Hansemann*. Berlin, 1901.
BEUTIN, L. *Geschichte der südwestfälischen Industrie- und Handelskammer zu Hagen und ihre Wirtschaftslandschaft*. Hagen, 1956.
—— 'Die märkische Unternehmerschaft in der frühindustriellen Zeit', *Westfälische Forschungen*, X (1957).
BIERMANN, B. *Die soziale Struktur der Unternehmerschaft*. Stuttgart, 1971.

BLAICH, F. *Kartell- und Monopolpolitik im Kaiserlichen Deutschland.* Düsseldorf, 1973.

BLUMBERG, H. *Die deutsche Textilindustrie in der industriellen Revolution.* Berlin, 1965.

BOELCKE, W. A. (ed.). *Krupp und die Hohenzollern in Dokumenten.* Frankfurt, 1970.

BÖHME, H. 'Emil Kirdorf', *Tradition*, XIII (1968) and XIV (1969).

—— *Deutschlands Weg zur Grossmacht.* 2nd edn. Cologne, 1972.

BÖHME, W. 'Ein Vierteljahrhundert Verband Deutscher Diplom-Kaufleute e. V.', *Der Diplom-Kaufmann*, X (1930).

BORCHARDT, K. 'Zur Frage des Kapitalmangels in der ersten Hälfte des 19. Jahrhunderts in Deutschland', *Jahrbücher für Nationalökonomie und Statistik*, CLXXIII (1961).

—— *Die industrielle Revolution in Deutschland.* Munich, 1972. English translation 'Germany, 1700–1914', in C. M. Cipolla (ed.), *Fontana Economic History of Europe*, IV (London and Glasgow, 1973).

BORN, K. E. (ed.). *Moderne deutsche Wirtschaftsgeschichte.* Cologne and Berlin, 1966.

BORST, O. 'Staat und Unternehmer in der Frühzeit der Württembergischen Industrie', *Tradition*, XI (1966).

BÖSSELMANN, K. *Die Entwicklung des deutschen Aktienwesens im 19. Jahrhundert.* Berlin, 1939.

BOURCART, J. J. *Die Grundsätze der Industrieverwaltung.* Zürich, 1874.

BRADY, R. A. *The Rationalization Movement in German Industry: A Study in the Evolution of Economic Planning.* Berkeley, Calif., 1933.

BRAUN, R. *Industrialisierung und Volksleben.* Erlenbach and Zürich, 1960.

—— *Sozialer und kultureller Wandel in einem ländlichen Industriegebiet.* Erlenbach and Zürich, 1965.

—— 'Zur Einwirkung soziokultureller Umweltbedingungen auf das Unternehmerpotential und das Unternehmerverhalten', in Fischer (ed.), *Wirtschafts- und sozialgeschichtliche Probleme.*

BRINKMANN, C. *Zur Wirtschaftsgeschichte der deutschen Unternehmungen.* Berlin, 1942.

BURNHAM, J. *The Managerial Revolution.* New York, 1941 (repr. Westport, Conn., 1972).

—— *Das Regime der Manager.* Stuttgart, 1948.

CAMERON, R. E. 'Founding the Bank of Darmstadt', *Explorations in Entrepreneurial History*, VIII (1955–6).

CHANDLER, A. D. *Strategy and Structure.* Cambridge, Mass., 1962.

—— 'The Railroads', *Business History Review*, XXXIX (1965).

CHANDLER, A. D., and F. REDLICH. 'Recent Developments in American Business Administration and Their Conceptualization', *Business History Review*, XXXV (1961).

COCHRAN, T. C. 'The Entrepreneur in Economic Change', *Explorations in Entrepreneurial History*, 2nd ser., III (1965–6).

DÄBRITZ, W. 'Führende Persönlichkeiten des rheinisch–westfälischen Wirtschafts- und Soziallebens', in O. Most *et al.* (eds.), *Wirtschaftskunde für Rheinland und Westfalen.* Berlin, 1931.

DAEMS, H., and H. VAN DER WEE (eds.). *The Rise of Managerial Capitalism.* The Hague, 1974.

DASCHER, O. *Das Textilgewerbe in Hessen–Kassel vom 16. bis 19. Jahrhundert.* Marburg, 1968.

DECKER, F. *Die betriebliche Sozialordnung der Dürener Industrie im 19. Jahrhundert.* Cologne, 1964.

DITTRICH, E. (ed.). *Lebensbilder sächsischer Wirtschaftsführer.* Leipzig, 1941.

EICHHOLTZ, D. *Junker und Bourgeoisie vor 1848 in der preussischen Eisenbahngeschichte.* Berlin, 1962.

EMMINGHAUS, A. *Allgemeine Gewerkslehre.* Berlin, 1868.

ENGEL, E. *Die erwerbsthätigen juristischen Personen insbesondere die Actiengesellschaften im preussischen Staate.* Berlin, 1876.

ENGELSING, R. 'Bremisches Unternehmertum', *Schriften der Wittheit zu Bremen*, II (1958).

EULENBURG, F. 'Die Aufsichtsräte der deutschen Aktiengesellschaften', *Jahrbücher für Nationalökonomie und Statistik*, XXXII (1906).

—— 'Die Herkunft der deutschen Wirtschaftsführer', *Schmollers Jahrbuch*, LXXIV, 1 (1954).

EYBERG, A. 'Umwelt und Verhalten der Unternehmer des Oberbergischen Kreises im 19. Jahrhundert'. Unpublished dissertation, Cologne, 1955.

FARRINGTON, F. E. *Commercial Education in Germany*. New York, 1914.

FISCHER, W. *Der Staat und die Industrialisierung in Baden*. Berlin, 1962.

—— *Herz des Reviers*. Essen, 1965.

—— *Wirtschaft und Gesellschaft im Zeitalter der Industrialisierung*. Göttingen, 1972.

FISCHER, W. (ed.). *Wirtschafts- und Sozialgeschichtliche Probleme der frühen Industrialisierung*. Berlin, 1968.

FORBERGER, R. *Die Manufaktur in Sachsen*. Berlin, 1958.

FREUDENBERGER, H. 'Die Struktur der frühindustriellen Fabrik', in Fischer (ed.), *Wirtschafts- und Sozialgeschichtliche Probleme*.

FREUDENBERGER, H., and F. REDLICH. 'The Industrial Development of Europe', *Kyklos*, XVII (1964).

FUCHS, K. *Vom Dirigismus zum Liberalismus: Die Entwicklung Oberschlesiens als preussisches Berg- und Hüttenrevier*. Wiesbaden, 1970.

FÜRSTENBERG, C. *Die Lebensgeschichte eines deutschen Bankiers*. Wiesbaden, 1961.

GABLENTZ, O. H. VON DER. 'Industriebürokratie', *Schmollers Jahrbuch*, L (1926).

GEBHARD, G. *Ruhrbergbau*. Essen, 1957.

GECK, L. H. A. *Die sozialen Arbeitsverhältnisse im Wandel der Zeit*. Berlin, 1931.

GEHR, M. *Das Verhältnis zwischen Banken und Industrie in Deutschland seit der Mitte des 19. Jahrhunderts bis zur Bankenkrise von 1931*. Published dissertation. Stuttgart, 1959.

GERSCHENKRON, A. 'Social Attitudes, Entrepreneurship, and Economic Development', *Explorations in Entrepreneurial History*, VI (1953–4).

—— *Economic Backwardness in Historical Perspective*. Cambridge, Mass., 1962.

—— *Europe in the Russian Mirror*. Cambridge, 1970.

Gestaltwandel der Unternehmung. Nürnberger Hochschulfestwoche 1953. Berlin, 1954.

GOTTSCHALK, C. G. *Die Grundlage des Rechnungswesens und ihre Anwendung auf industrielle Anstalten*. Leipzig, 1865.

GRANICK, D. *The European Executive*. New York, 1962.

GROBA, K. *Der Unternehmer im Beginn der Industrialisierung Schlesiens*. Breslau, 1936.

GURATZSCH, D. *Macht durch Organisation: Die Grundlegung des Hugenbergschen Presseimperiums*. Düsseldorf, 1973.

HABAKKUK, H. J. *Industrial Organisation since the Industrial Revolution*. Southampton, 1968.

HAGEMANN, W. 'Das Verhältnis der deutschen Grossbanken zur Industrie'. Unpublished dissertation, Berlin, 1931.

HAHN, G. *Untersuchungen über die Ursachen von Unternehmensmisserfolgen*. Published dissertation. Cologne, 1956.

HANSEMANN, D. *Die Eisenbahnen und deren Aktionäre in ihrem Verhältnis zum Staate*. Leipzig and Halle, 1837.

HANSEN, J. *Gustav von Mevissen, 1815–1899*. 2 vols. Berlin, 1906.

HARBISON, F., and C. A. MYERS. *Management in the Industrial World*. New York, 1964.

HARDACH, K. 'Anglomanie und Anglophobie während der Industriellen Revolution in Deutschland', *Schmollers Jahrbuch*, XCI (1971).

HARTMANN, H. *Education for Business Leadership: The Role of the German 'Hochschulen'*. Paris, 1955.

—— 'Managers and Entrepreneurs: A Useful Distinction?' *Administrative Science Quarterly*, III (1958–9).

—— *Authority and Organization in German Management*. Princeton, 1959.

—— 'Die Akademiker in der heutigen Unternehmerschaft', *Tradition*, IV (1959).

HARTMANN, H., and W. WIENOLD. *Universität und Unternehmer*. Gütersloh, 1963.

HARTSOUGH, M. L. 'Business Leaders in Cologne in the Nineteenth Century', *Journal of Economic and Business History*, III (1929–30).

HATZFELD, L. 'Der Anfang der deutschen Drahtindustrie', *Tradition*, VI (1961).

HAUBOLD, S. *Entwicklung und Organisation einer Chemnitzer Maschinenfabrik.* Published dissertation. Bonn, 1939.

HELFER, C. 'Über militärische Einflüsse auf die industrielle Entwicklung Deutschlands', *Schmollers Jahrbuch,* LXXXIII (1963).

HELFFEREICH, K. *Georg von Siemens.* 3 vols. Berlin, 1923.

HELLWIG, F. *Karl Ferdinand Freiherr von Stumm-Halberg.* Heidelberg, 1936.

—— 'Unternehmer und Unternehmensform im saarländischen Industriegebiet', *Jahrbücher für Nationalökonomie und Statistik,* CLVIII (1943).

HENDERSON, W. O. 'England und die Industrialisierung Deutschlands', *Zeitschrift für die gesamte Staatswissenschaft,* CVIII (1952).

—— 'W. Th. Mulvany, an Irish Pioneer in the Ruhr', *Explorations in Entrepreneurial History,* V (1953).

HENNING, F. W. 'Die Einführung der Gewerbefreiheit und ihre Auswirkungen auf das Handwerk in Deutschland', in Abel *et al., Handwerksgeschichte in neuer Sicht.*

—— *Die Industrialisierung in Deutschland, 1800–1914.* Paderborn, 1973.

—— *Das industrialisierte Deutschland, 1914–1972.* Paderborn, 1974.

HERLE, J. *Die Stellung des Verbandsgeschäftsführers in der Wirtschaft.* Berlin, 1926.

HERRMANN, W. *Entwicklungslinien montanindustrieller Unternehmungen im rheinisch–westfälischen Industriegebiet.* Dortmund, 1954.

HEYMANN, H. G. *Die gemischten Werke im deutschen Grosseisengewerbe.* Stuttgart and Berlin, 1904.

HILFERDING, R. *Das Finanzkapital.* Vienna, 1910.

HIRSCHMAN, A. O, *The Strategy of Economic Development.* New Haven, Conn., 1958.

HOESCH IRON AND STEEL WORKS, LTD. *Eisen- und Stahlwerke Hoesch Aktiengesellschaft in Dortmund, 1871–1921.* Dortmund, n.d.

HOFFMANN, W. G. 'Die unverteilten Gewinne der Aktiengesellschaften in Deutschland, 1871–1957', *Zeitschrift für die gesamte Staatswissenschaft,* CXV (1959).

—— 'The Take-Off in Germany', in W. W. Rostow (ed.), *The Economics of Take-Off into Self-Sustained Growth.* London and New York, 1963.

HOFFMANN, W. G., et al. *Das Wachstum der deutschen Wirtschaft seit der Mitte des 19. Jahrhunderts.* Berlin, 1965.

HOLZSCHUHER, V. 'Soziale und ökonomische Hintergründe der Kartellbewegung'. Unpublished dissertation, Erlangen/Nuremberg, 1937.

HUECK, A. *Gesellschaftsrecht.* 17th edn. Munich and Berlin, 1975.

HURET, J. 'Die A.E.G.', *Organisation,* X (1908).

HUSCHKE, W. *Forschungen über die Herkunft der thüringischen Unternehmerschicht des 19. Jahrhunderts.* Baden-Baden, 1962.

ISAAC, A. *Die Entstehung der wissenschaftlichen Betriebswirtschaftslehre in Deutschland seit 1898.* Berlin, 1923.

ISAY, R. *Die Geschichte der Kartellgesetzgebung.* Berlin, 1955.

JAEGER, H. *Unternehmer in der deutschen Politik, 1890–1918.* Bonn, 1967.

—— 'Gegenwart und Zukunft der historischen Unternehmerforschung', *Tradition,* XVII (1972).

—— 'Business History in Germany: A Survey of Recent Developments', *Business History Review,* XLVIII (1974).

JAHN, G. 'Die Entstehung der Fabrik', *Schmollers Jahrbuch,* LXIX (1949).

JEIDELS, O. *Das Verhältnis der deutschen Grossbanken zur Industrie mit besonderer Berücksichtigung der Eisenindustrie.* Leipzig, 1905.

KAELBLE, H. *Industrielle Interessenpolitik in der Wilhelminischen Gesellschaft: Centralverband Deutscher Industrieller, 1895–1914.* Berlin, 1967.

—— *Berliner Unternehmer während der frühen Industrialisierung.* Berlin and New York, 1972.

—— 'Sozialer Aufstieg in Deutschland, 1850–1914', *Vierteljahrschrift für Sozial- und Wirtschaftsgeschichte,* LX (1973).

KELLENBENZ, H. 'Unternehmertum in Südwestdeutschland', *Tradition,* X (1965).

KELLENBENZ, H., and K. VAN EYLL. *Die Geschichte der unternehmerischen Selbstverwaltung in Köln, 1797–1914.* Cologne, 1972.

KERMANN, J. *Die Manufaktur im Rheinland, 1750–1833*. Bonn, 1972.

KINDERMANN, O. 'Das Sozialprofil deutscher Unternehmer im 19. Jahrhundert anhand der NDB'. Unpublished manuscript, Münster, 1975.

KISCH, H. *Prussian Mercantilism and the Rise of the Krefeld Silk Industry*. Philadelphia, 1968.

—— 'The Textile Industries in Silesia and the Rhineland', *Journal of Economic History*, XIX (1968).

KLAVEREN, J. VAN. 'Die Manufakturen des Ancien Régime', *Vierteljahrschrift für Sozial- und Wirtschaftsgeschichte*, II (1964).

—— *Die Industrielle Revolution und das Eindringen des Fabrikanten in den Handel*. Dortmund, 1971.

KLEIN, E. 'Zur Frage der Industriefinanzierung im frühen 19. Jahrhundert', in H. Kellenbenz (ed.), *Öffentliche Finanzen und privates Kapital im späten Mittelalter und in der ersten Hälfte des 19. Jahrhunderts*. Stuttgart, 1971.

KLOTZBACH, A. *Der Roheisenverband*. Düsseldorf, 1926.

KLUITMANN, L. *Der gewerbliche Geld- und Kapitalverkehr im Ruhrgebiet im 19. Jahrhundert*. Bonn, 1931.

KNOCHENHAUER, B. *Die oberschlesische Montanindustrie*. Gotha, 1927.

KOCKA, J. *Unternehmensverwaltung und Angestelltenschaft am Beispiel Siemens, 1844–1914*. Stuttgart, 1969.

—— 'Industrielles Management: Konzeptionen und Modelle in Deutschland vor 1914', *Vierteljahrschrift für Sozial- und Wirtschaftsgeschiche*, LVI (1969).

—— 'Family and Bureaucracy in German Industrial Management', *Business History Review*, XLV (1971).

—— 'Siemens und der aufhaltsame Aufstieg der AEG', *Tradition*, XVII (1972).

—— 'Management und Angestellte im Unternehmen der Industriellen Revolution', in R. Braun *et al.* (eds.), *Gesellschaft in der industriellen Revolution*. Cologne and Berlin, 1973.

—— 'Organisierter Kapitalismus oder Staatsmonopolistischer Kapitalismus?' in Winkler (ed.), *Organisierter Kapitalismus*.

—— 'Expansion–Integration–Diversifikation: Wachstumsstrategien industrieller Grossunternehmen in Deutschland vor 1914', in Winkel (ed.), *Industrie und Gewerbe im 19. und 20. Jahrhundert*.

KÖLLMANN, W. *Sozialgeschichte der Stadt Barmen im 19. Jahrhundert*. Tübingen, 1960.

—— *Friedrich Harkort*, I: *1793–1838*. Düsseldorf, 1964.

—— 'Frühe Unternehmer', in W. Först (ed.), *Ruhrgebiet und neues Land*. Cologne and Berlin, 1968.

KRAMPE, H. D. *Der Staatseinfluss auf den Ruhrkohlengergbau in der Zeit von 1800 bis 1865*. Cologne, 1961.

KROKER, W. *Wege zur Verbreitung technologischer Kenntnisse zwischen England und Deutschland in der zweiten Hälfte des 18. Jahrhunderts*. Berlin, 1971.

KRÜGER, A. *Das Kölner Bankiergewerbe vom Ende des 18. Jahrhunderts bis 1875*. Essen, 1925.

KRÜGER, H. *Zur Geschichte der Manufakturen und der Manufakturarbeiter in Preussen*. Berlin, 1958.

KUH, F. *Der selbständige Unternehmer*. Berlin, 1918.

KUMPMANN, K. *Die Entstehung der Rheinischen Eisenbahn-Gesellschaft, 1830–1844*. Essen–Ruhr, 1910.

KUSKE, B. *Mevissens Stellung in der Wirtschaftsentwicklung*. Cologne, 1921.

LANDAUER, E. *Handel und Produktion in der Baumwollindustrie*. Tübingen, 1912.

—— 'Über die Stellung des Handels in der modernen industriellen Entwicklung', *Archiv für Sozialwissenschaft und Sozialpolitik*, XXXIV (1912).

LANDES, D. S. 'French Entrepreneurship and Industrial Growth in the Nineteenth Century', *Journal of Economic History*, IX (1949).

—— 'Entrepreneurship in Advanced Industrial Countries: The Anglo-German Rivalry', in *Entrepreneurship and Economic Growth*. Cambridge, Mass., 1954.

—— 'The Structure of Enterprise in the Nineteenth Century', in XIe Congrès International des Sciences Historiques (Stockholm, 21–8 August 1960), *Rapports*, V. Uppsala, 1960.

LANDES, D. S. *The Unbound Prometheus*. Cambridge, 1969.

—— (ed.). *The Rise of Capitalism*. New York and London, 1966.

LEVY, H. *Industrial Germany: A Study of Its Monopoly Organizations and Their Control by the State*. New York, 1966.

LIEFMANN, R. *Kartelle und Trusts und die Weiterbildung der volkswirtschaftlichen Organisation*. Stuttgart, 1910.

—— *Kartelle, Konzerne und Trusts*. 9th edn. Stuttgart, 1930.

LOHSE, U. 'Guido Graf Henckel von Donnersmarck und seine industriellen Schöpfungen', *Stahl und Eisen*, XXXVII (1917).

LUNDGREEN, P. *Techniker in Preussen während der frühen Industrialisierung: Ausbildung und Berufsfeld einer entstehenden sozialen Gruppe*. Berlin, 1975.

LUNTOWSKI, G. 'Lüneburger Unternehmer im 19. Jahrhundert', *Tradition*, XI (1966).

LÜTHGEN, H. *Das Rheinisch-westfälische Kohlensyndikat in der Vorkriegs-, Kriegs- und Nachkriegszeit und seine Probleme*. Leipzig and Erlangen, 1926.

MANEGOLD, K.-H. 'Das Verhältnis von Naturwissenschaften und Technik im 19. Jahrhundert im Spiegel der Wissenschaftsorganisation', in *Geschichte der Naturwissenschaften und der Technik im 19. Jahrhundert*. Düsseldorf, 1969.

—— *Universität, Technische Hochschule und Industrie*. Berlin, 1970.

MARBURG, T. F. 'Government and Business in Germany: Public Policy toward Cartels', *Business History Review*, XXXVIII (1964).

MARQUARDT, F. D. 'Sozialer Aufstieg, sozialer Abstieg und die Entstehung der Berliner Arbeiterklasse, 1806–1848', *Geschichte und Gesellschaft*, I (1975).

MARTIN, P. C. 'Die Entstehung des preussischen Aktiengesetzes von 1843', *Vierteljahrschrift für Sozial- und Wirtschaftsgeschichte*, LVI (1969).

—— 'Frühindustrielles Gewerbe in der Rechtsform der AG', in W. Fischer (ed.), *Beiträge zu Wirtschaftswachstum und Wirtschaftsstruktur im 16. und 19. Jahrhundert*. Berlin, 1971.

MARX, K. *Das Kapital*. 3 vols. Berlin, 1962–4.

MASCHKE, E. *Grundzüge der deutschen Kartellgeschichte bis 1914*. Dortmund, 1964.

—— *Es entsteht ein Konzern*. Oberhausen, 1969.

MATSCHOSS, C. *Die Maschinenfabrik R. Wolf Magdeburg–Buckau, 1862–1912*. Magdeburg, 1912.

—— *Preussens Gewerbeförderung und ihre grossen Männer*. Berlin, 1921.

—— *Männer der Technik*. Berlin, 1925.

MATSCHOSS, C. (ed.). *Werner Siemens*. 2 vols. Berlin, 1916.

MAUERSBERG, H. *Deutsche Industrien im Zeitgeschehen eines Jahrhunderts*. 2 vols. Stuttgart, 1966.

MAYER, A. VON. *Geschichte und Geographie der deutschen Eisenbahnen von ihrer Entstehung bis auf die Gegenwart, 1890*. 2 vols. Berlin, 1890–1.

MENDELS, F. 'Proto-Industrialization: The First Phase of the Industrialization Process', *Journal of Economic History*, XXXII (1972).

MEYNAUD, J. *Technocracy*. London, 1964.

MICHEL, E. *Sozialgeschichte der industriellen Arbeitswelt*. 4th edn. Frankfurt, 1960.

MIECK, I. *Preussische Gewerbepolitik in Berlin, 1806–44*. Berlin, 1965.

MOELLENDORF, W. VON. *Deutsche Gemeinwirtschaft*. Berlin, 1916.

MOTTEK, H. *Wirtschaftsgeschichte Deutschlands: Ein Grundriss*. 2 vols. Berlin, 1972.

MOTTEK, H., *et al. Studien zur Geschichte der industriellen Revolution in Deutschland*. Berlin, 1960.

MÜLLER, H. *Geschichte des VEB Stahl- und Walzwerks Riesa*. Berlin, 1961.

NEUBAUR, P. *Matthias Stinnes und sein Haus*. Mülheim, n.d.

NEULOH, O. *Die deutsche Betriebsverfassung und ihre Sozialformen bis zur Mitbestimmung*. Tübingen, 1956.

NUSSBAUM, H. *Unternehmer gegen Monopole*. Berlin, 1966.

OSTHOLD, P. *Die Geschichte des Zechenverbandes, 1908–1933*. Berlin, 1934.

OTTO, C. G. *Buchführung für Fabrikgeschäfte*. Berlin, 1830.

PARKER, W. N. 'Entrepreneurship, Industrial Organization and Economic Growth', *Journal of Economic History*, XIV (1954).

Passow, R. *Die wirtschaftliche Bedeutung und Organisation der Aktiengesellschaften*. Jena, 1907.

Penrose, E. T. *The Theory of the Growth of the Firm*. Oxford, 1959.

Perlick, A. *Oberschlesische Berg- und Hüttenleute*. Kitzingen, 1953.

Pinner, F. *Emil Rathenau und das elektrische Zeitalter*. Leipzig, 1918.

Postan, M. M. *An Economic History of Western Europe, 1945–1964*. London, 1967.

Pross, H. *Manager und Aktionäre in Deutschland*. Frankfurt, 1965.

Pross, H., and K. W. Boetticher. *Manager des Kapitalismus*. Frankfurt, 1971.

Puppke, L. *Sozialpolitik und soziale Anschauungen frühindustrieller Unternehmer in Rheinland und Westfalen*. Cologne, 1966.

Rachel, H., and P. Wallich. *Berliner Grosskaufleute und Kapitalisten*. 3 vols. 2nd edn. Berlin, 1967.

Rathenau, W. *Reflexionen*. Leipzig, 1912.

—— *Zur Kritik der Zeit*. Berlin, 1912.

—— *Von kommenden Dingen*. Berlin, 1918.

Redlich, F. *Die volkswirtschaftliche Bedeutung der deutschen Teerfarbenindustrie*. Munich and Leipzig, 1914.

—— 'A German Eighteenth Century Iron Works during Its First Hundred Years', *Bulletin of the Business Historical Society*, xxvii (1953).

—— 'Academic Education for Business', *Business History Review*, xxxi (1957).

—— *Anfänge und Entwicklung der Firmengeschichte und Unternehmerbiographie*. Baden-Baden, 1959.

—— *Der Unternehmer*. Göttingen, 1964.

—— 'Two Nineteenth-Century Financiers and Autobiographers', *Economy and History*, x (1967).

—— *Steeped in Two Cultures: A Selection of Essays*. New York, 1971.

Reichshandbuch der Deutschen Gesellschaft. Berlin, 1930–1.

Reichwein, R. *Funktionswandlungen der betrieblichen Sozialpolitik*. Cologne, 1965.

Reitböck, G. 'Der Eisenbahnkönig Strousberg', *Beiträge zur Geschichte der Technik und Industrie*, xiv (1924).

Reuter, O. *Die Manufaktur im fränkischen Raum*. Stuttgart, 1961.

Rexhausen, F. *Der Unternehmer und die volkswirtschaftliche Entwicklung*. Berlin, 1960.

Rheinisch–westfälische Wirtschaftsbiographien. Münster, 1932 ff.

Riedler, A. *Emil Rathenau und das Werden der Grosswirtschaft*. Berlin, 1916.

Rieker, K. 'Die Konzentrationsentwicklung in der gewerblichen Wirtschaft', *Tradition*, v (1966).

Riesser, E. *Die deutschen Grossbanken und ihre Konzentration*. 3rd edn. Jena, 1910.

Roesky, E. *Die Verwaltung und Leitung von Fabriken*. Leipzig, 1878.

Röseler, K. 'Unternehmer in der Weimarer Republik', *Tradition*, xiii (1968).

Rosenberg, H. *Grosse Depression und Bismarckzeit*. Berlin, 1967.

Sachtler, H. *Wandlungen des industriellen Unternehmertums in Deutschland seit Beginn des 19. Jahrhunderts*. Published dissertation. Halle–Wittenberg, 1937.

Salin, E. 'The Schumpeterian Theory and Continental Thoughts', in D. L. Spencer and A. Woroniak (eds.), *The Transfer of Technology to Developing Countries*, New York, 1967.

Saul, K. *Staat, Industrie und Arbeiterbewegung im Kaiserreich, 1903–1914*. Düsseldorf, 1974.

Schacht, H. 'Zur Finanzgeschichte des Ruhrkohlen-Bergbaus', *Schmollers Jahrbuch*, xxxvii, 3 (1913).

Schmoller, G. *Zur Geschichte des Kleingewerbes im 19. Jahrhundert*. Halle, 1870.

—— *Zur Social- und Gewerbepolitik*. Leipzig, 1890.

Schremmer, E. *Die Wirtschaft Bayerns*. Munich, 1970.

Schriften des Vereins für Sozialpolitik, cxvi. Leipzig, 1916.

Schröder, E. 'Alfred Krupp's Generalregulativ', *Tradition*, i (1956).

Schröter, A., and W. Becker. *Die deutsche Maschinenbauindustrie in der industriellen Revolution*. Berlin, 1962.

Schumacher, M. *Auslandsreisen deutscher Unternehmer, 1750–1851, unter besonderer Berücksichtigung von Rheinland und Westfalen*. Cologne, 1968.

SCHUMPETER, J. *Theorie der wirtschaftlichen Entwicklung*. Munich, 1911.
—— 'Der Unternehmer in der Volkswirtschaft von heute', in B. Harms (ed.), *Struktur-wandlungen der deutschen Volkswirtschaft*. 2 vols. Berlin, 1928.
—— *Business Cycles*. 2 vols. New York, 1939.
—— *Capitalism, Socialism, and Democracy*. New York, 1950.
—— *History of Economic Analysis*. New York, 1954.
SCHUNDER, F. *Tradition und Fortschritt*. Stuttgart, 1959.
SCHWARTZ, P. *Die Entwicklungstendenzen im deutschen Privatbankiergewerbe*. Published dissertation. Strassburg, 1915.
SCHWARZ, O. 'Die Betriebsformen der modernen Grossindustrie', *Zeitschrift für die gesamte Staatswissenschaft*, XXV (1869).
SCHWEMANN, A. 'Friedrich Wilhelm Graf v. Reden', *Beiträge zur Geschichte der Technik und Industrie*, XIV (1924).
SERLO, W. *Westduetsche Berg- und Hüttenleute und ihre Familien*. Essen, 1938.
SIEBERT, P. *Gottlieb Daimler*. 4th edn. Stuttgart, 1950.
SIEMENS, G. *Der Weg der Elektrotechnik. Geschichte des Hauses Siemens*. 2nd edn. 2 vols. Freiburg, 1961.
SIEMENS, W. *Lebenserinnerungen*. 17th edn. Munich, 1966.
SIMON, O. *Die Fachbildung des preussischen Gewerbe- und Handelsstandes im 18. und 19. Jahrhundert*. Berlin, 1902.
SLAWINGER, G. *Die Manufaktur in Kurbayern, 1740–1833*. Stuttgart, 1966.
SOMBART, W. *Der Bourgeois*. Munich and Leipzig, 1913.
—— *Der moderne Kapitalismus*. 3 vols. (first published 1916–27). Munich and Leipzig. I: 3rd edn, 1919; II: 6th edn, 1924; III: 1st edn, 1927.
SPIETHOFF, A. *Die wirtschaftlichen Wechsellagen*. 2 vols. Tübingen and Zürich, 1955.
STAHL, W. *Der Elitekreislauf in der Unternehmerschaft*. Frankfurt, 1973.
STEMME-SOGEMEIER, M. *Bielefeld und seine Industrie*. Trautheim, 1953.
STERN, E. *Vollständige Anleitung zur Buchführung für die Gewerbtreibenden und kleinere Fabrikanten*. Darmstadt, 1867.
STROUSBERG, B. H. *Strousberg und sein Wirken von ihm selbst geschildert*. Berlin, 1876.
TEUTEBERG, H. J. *Geschichte der Industriellen Mitbestimmung in Deutschland*. Tübingen, 1961.
THIEME, H. 'Statistische Materialien zur Konzessionierung von Aktiengesellschaften in Preussen bis 1867', *Jahrbuch für Wirtschaftsgeschichte*, 1960, part 2.
THUN, A. *Die Industrie am Niederrhein und ihre Arbeiter*. 2 vols. Leipzig, 1879.
TILLY, R. 'Germany, 1815–1870', in R. Cameron et al., *Banking in the Early Stages of Industrialization*. New York, 1967.
—— 'Los von England: Probleme des Nationalismus in der deutschen Wirtschafts-geschichte', in H. Giesch and H. Sauermann (eds.), *Quantitative Aspekte der Wirt-schaftsgeschichte*. Tübingen, 1968.
—— 'The Growth of Large-Scale Enterprise in Germany since the Middle of the Nineteenth Century', in Daems and van der Wee (eds.), *Rise of Managerial Capitalism*.
TREUE, W. 'Das Verhältnis von Fürst, Staat und Unternehmer in der Zeit des Merkan-tilismus', *Vierteljahrschrift für Sozial- und Wirtschaftsgeschichte*, XLIV (1957).
—— *Die Geschichte der Ilseder Hütte*. Peine, 1960.
—— *Eugen Langen und Nic. August Otto: Zum Verhältnis von Unternehmer und Erfinder, Ingenieur und Kaufmann*. Munich, 1963.
TROSS, A. *Der Aufbau der Eisen- und eisenverarbeitenden Industrie-Konzerne Deutschlands*. Berlin, 1923.
TURIN, G. *Der Begriff des Unternehmers*. Zürich, 1947.
UFERMANN, P., and C. HÜGELIN. *Stinnes und seine Konzerne*. Berlin, 1924.
VISSER, D. 'The German Captain of Enterprise', *Explorations in Entrepreneurial History*, 2nd ser., VI (1968–9).
VOGELSTEIN, T. 'Die finanzielle Organisation der kapitalistischen Industrie', in *Grundriss der Sozialökonomik*, VI. 2nd edn. Tübingen, 1923.
WAGENBLASS, H. *Der Eisenbahnbau und das Wachstum der deutschen Eisen- und Maschinen-bauindustrie, 1835–1860*. Stuttgart, 1973.

WAGENFÜHR, H. *Kartelle in Deutschland.* Nuremberg, 1931.

WAGENFÜHR, R. *Die Industriewirtschaft.* Berlin, 1933.

WAGON, E. *Die finanzielle Entwicklung deutscher Aktiengesellschaften von 1870–1900.* Jena, 1903.

WATANABE, H. 'Die Wuppertaler Unternehmer in den Dreissiger Jahren des Neunzehnten Jahrhunderts', *Hokudai Economic Papers*, III (Hokkaido, 1972–3).

WEBER, A. *Die rheinisch–westfälischen Provinzialbanken und die Krisis.* Leipzig, 1903.

WEBER, M. 'Die protestantische Ethik und der Geist des Kapitalismus' (1905), in *Gesammelte Aufsätze zur Religionssoziologie*, I. 5th edn. Tübingen, 1963.

WEHLER, H.-U. 'Probleme der deutschen Wirtschaftsgeschichte', in *Krisenherde des Kaiserreichs, 1871–1918.* Göttingen, 1970.

WIEDENFELD, K. *Das Persönliche im modernen Unternehmertum.* Leipzig, 1911.

—— *Ein Jahrhundert rheinischer Montanindustrie, 1815–1915.* Bonn, 1916.

—— *Kartelle und Konzerne.* Berlin and Leipzig, 1927.

WINKEL, H. *Die Ablösungskapitalien aus der Bauernbefreiung in West- und Süddeutschland.* Stuttgart, 1968.

—— 'Kapitalquellen und Kapitalverwendung am Vorabend des industriellen Aufschwungs in Deutschland', *Schmollers Jahrbuch*, XC (1970).

WINKEL, H. (ed.). *Industrie und Gewerbe im 19. und 20. Jahrhundert.* Berlin, 1975.

WINKLER, H. A. (ed.). *Organisierter Kapitalismus: Voraussetzungen und Anfänge.* Göttingen, 1974.

WITT, H. *Die Triebkräfte des industriellen Unternehmertums vor hundert Jahren und heute.* Hamburg, 1929.

WOLF, K. 'Stages in Industrial Organization', *Explorations in Entrepreneurial History*, 2nd ser., I (1963).

WUTZMER, H. 'Die Herkunft der industriellen Bourgeoisie in Preussen in den vierziger Jahren des 19. Jahrhunderts', in Mottek *et al., Studien zur Geschichte der industriellen Revolution.*

ZORN, W. 'Typen und Entwicklungskräfte deutschen Unternehmertums', *Vierteljahrschrift für Sozial- und Wirtschaftsgeschichte*, XLIV (1957).

—— *Handels- und Industriegeschichte Bayerisch–Schwabens, 1648–1870.* Augsburg, 1961.

—— 'Unternehmertum und Aristokratie in Deutschland', *Tradition*, VIII (1963).

ZUNKEL, F. *Der rheinisch–westfälische Unternehmer, 1834–1879.* Cologne and Opladen, 1963.

CHAPTER XI

Labour and Capital in the Scandinavian Countries in the Nineteenth and Twentieth Centuries

ÅBERG, YNGVE. *Produktion och produktivitet i Sverige 1861–1965.* Uppsala, 1969.

ADAMSON, ROLF. *Järnavsättning och bruksfinansiering 1800–1860.* Göteborg, 1966.

AHVENAINEN, JORMA. 'The Competitive Position of the Finnish Paper Industry in the Inter-War Years', *Scandinavian Economic History Review*, XXII (1974).

ATTMAN, ARTUR. *Fagerstabrukens historia: Adertonhundratalet.* Uppsala, 1958.

BAGGE, GÖSTA, ERIK LUNDBERG, and INGVAR SVENNILSON. *Wages in Sweden, 1860–1930.* Stockholm, 1933.

BERGSTRÖM, VILLY. *Den ekonomiska politiken i Sverige och dess verkningar.* Stockholm, 1969.

BJERKE, JUUL. *Langtidslinjer i norsk økonomi 1865–1960.* Samfunnsøkonomiske studier, 16. Oslo, 1966.

BJERKE, KJELD. 'The National Product of Denmark 1870–1952', *Income and Wealth*, v. London, 1955.

BJERKE, KJELD, and NIELS USSING. *Studier over Danmarks nationalprodukt 1870–1950.* Copenhagen, 1958.
BOURNEUF, ALICE. *Norway: The Planned Revival.* Cambridge, Mass., 1958.
BRISMAN, SVEN. 'Affärsbankerna i Danmark och Norge', *Ekonomisk tidskrift,* XI (1911).
BULL, EDVARD. *Arbeidermiljø under det industrielle gjennembrudd.* Oslo, 1958.
COHN, EINAR. *Privatbanken i Kjøbenhavn gennem hundrede aar, 1857–1957.* Copenhagen, 1957.
DAHMÉN, ERIK. *Ekonomisk utveckling och ekonomisk politik i Finland.* Helsinki, 1963.
—— *Entrepreneurial Activity in Swedish Industry, 1919–1939.* Cambridge, Mass., 1970.
DRAKE, MICHAEL. *Population and Society in Norway, 1735–1865.* Cambridge, 1969.
Emigrationen fra Norden indtil I. Verdenskrig. Reports to the Meeting of Scandinavian Historians, Copenhagen 1971. Copenhagen, 1971.
FLEETWOOD, ERIN E. *Sweden's Capital Imports and Exports.* Geneva, 1947.
FRIDLIZIUS, GUNNAR. *Swedish Corn Export in the Free Trade Era.* Lund, Sweden, 1957.
—— 'Sweden's Exports, 1850–1960', *Economy and History,* IV (1963).
FURRE, BERGE. *Norsk historie 1905–1940.* Oslo, 1972.
GÅRDLUND, TORSTEN. *Svensk industrifinansiering under genombrottsskedet 1830–1913.* Stockholm, 1947.
GASSLANDER, OLLE. *History of Stockholm's Enskilda Bank to 1914.* Stockholm, 1955.
GUSTAFSSON, BO. *Den norrländska sågverksindustrins arbetare 1890–1913.* Uppsala, 1965.
HAMMARSTRÖM, INGRID. *Stockholm i svensk ekonomi 1850–1914.* Stockholm, 1970.
HANSEN, SVEND AAGE. *Early Industrialization in Denmark.* Copenhagen, 1970.
—— *Økonomisk vækst i Danmark.* 2 vols. Copenhagen, 1972–4.
HEDIN, LARS-ERIK. 'Some Notes on the Financing of the Swedish Railroads', *Economy and History,* X (1967).
HENRIKSEN, OLE BUS, and ANDERS ØLGAARD. *Dansk udenrigshandel 1874–1958.* Copenhagen, 1960.
HILDEBRAND, KARL-GUSTAF. *Erik Johan Ljungberg och Stora Kopparberg.* Uppsala, 1970.
—— *I omvandlingens tjänst: Svenska Handelsbanken 1871–1955.* Stockholm, 1971.
—— *Banking in a Growing Economy.* Stockholm, 1971.
HODNE, FRITZ. 'Growth in a Dual Economy – the Norwegian Expansion, 1814–1914', *Economy and History,* XVI (1973).
—— *An Economic History of Norway, 1815–1970.* Bergen, 1975.
HÖÖK, ERIK. *Den offentliga sektorns expansion 1913–1958.* Uppsala, 1962.
JOHANSSON, ÖSTEN. *The Gross Domestic Product of Sweden and Its Composition, 1861–1955.* Stockholm, 1967.
JÖRBERG, LENNART. *Growth and Fluctuations of Swedish Industry, 1869–1912.* Lund, Sweden, 1961.
—— 'Structural Change and Economic Growth: Sweden in the 19th Century', *Economy and History,* VIII (1965).
—— 'The Industrial Revolution in the Nordic Countries', in *Fontana Economic History of Europe,* IV. London, 1970.
JÖRBERG, LENNART, and OLLE KRANTZ. 'Scandinavia, 1914–1970', in *Fontana Economic History of Europe,* VI. London, 1975.
JUNGENFELT, KARL G. *Löneandelen och den ekonomiska utvecklingen.* Uppsala, 1966.
JUTIKKALA, EINO. *Bonden i Finland genom tiderna.* Helsinki, 1963.
JUTILA, K. T. *The Agricultural Depression in Finland during the Years 1928–35.* Helsinki, 1937.
KALELA, JORMA. 'Torpare och småbrukare i finländsk politik från storstrejken till 1930-talskrisen', *Historisk tidskrift för Finland,* 1974.
KEILHAU, WILHELM. *Det norske folks liv og historie,* VIII: *Tidsrummet 1814 til omkring 1840.* Oslo, 1929.
—— *Ibid.* IX: *Tidsrummet 1840 til omkring 1875.* Oslo, 1931.
—— *Ibid.* X: *Tidsrummet fra omkring 1875 til omkring 1920.*
—— *Det norske folks liv og historie i vår egen tid.* Oslo, 1938.
KING, MERVYN A. 'Economic Growth and Social Development – the Finnish Achievement', *Ekonomiska samfundets tidskrift,* XXVII (1974).

KNOELLINGER, CARL ERIK. *Fackföreningar och arbetsmarknad i Finland*. Helsinki, 1959.
KOCK, KARIN. *Kreditmarknad och räntepolitik 1924–1958*, 2 vols. Stockholm, 1961–2.
KRANTZ, OLLE, and CARL-AXEL NILSSON. 'Relative Income Levels in the Scandinavian Countries', *Economy and History*, XVII (1974).
—— *Swedish National Product, 1861–1970*. Lund, Sweden, 1975.
Kriser och krispolitik i Norden under mellankrigstiden. Reports to the Meeting of Scandinavian Historians, Uppsala 1974. Uppsala, 1974.
KUUSE, JAN. *Interaction between Agriculture and Industry: Case Studies of Farm Mechanisation and Industrialisation in Sweden and the United States, 1830–1930*. Göteborg, 1974.
LIEBERMAN, SIMA. *The Industrialization of Norway, 1800–1920*. Oslo, 1970.
LINDAHL, ERIK, EINAR DAHLGREN, and KARIN KOCK. *National Income of Sweden, 1861–1930*. Stockholm, 1937.
LINDBECK, ASSAR. *Svensk ekonomisk politik: Problem och teorier*. Stockholm, 1975.
LUNDBERG, ERIK. *Konjunkturer och ekonomisk politik*. 2nd edn., Stockholm, 1958.
—— *Instability and Economic Growth*. New Haven, Conn., 1968.
LUNDBERG, ERIK (ed.). *Svensk finanspolitik i teori och praktik*. Lund, Sweden, 1971.
LUNDBERG, ERIK, and TORKEL BACKELIN (eds.). *Ekonomisk politik i förvandling*. Stockholm, 1970.
LUNDBERG, LARS. *Kapitalbildningen i Sverige 1861–1965*. Uppsala, 1969.
MADDISON, ANGUS. *Economic Growth in the West*. New York, 1964.
MARTINIUS, STURE. *Agrar kapitalbildning och finansiering 1833–1892*. Göteborg, 1970.
—— *Jordbruk och ekonomisk tillväxt i Sverige 1830–1870*. Göteborg, 1970.
MEINANDER, NILS. *Penningpolitik under etthundrafemtio år, Finlands Bank, 1811–1961*. Helsinki, 1963.
MILWARD, ALAN S. *The Fascist Economy in Norway*. Oxford, 1972.
MILWARD, ALAN S., and S. B. SAUL. *The Economic Development of Continental Europe, 1780–1870*. London, 1973.
MODIG, HANS. *Järnvägarnas efterfrågan och den svenska industrin 1860–1914*. Uppsala, 1971.
MONTGOMERY, ARTHUR. *The Rise of Modern Industry in Sweden*. Stockholm, 1939.
—— *Svensk och internationell ekonomi 1913–1939*. Malmö, 1954.
NILSSON, CARL-AXEL. *Järn och stål i svensk ekonomi 1885–1912*. Lund, 1972.
NORWAY, CENTRAL BUREAU OF STATISTICS. *Historisk statistikk 1968*. Norges Offisielle Statistikk, XII: 245. Oslo, 1969.
OHLSSON, LENNART. *Utrikeshandeln och den ekonomiska tillväxten i Sverige 1871–1966*. Stockholm, 1969.
ÖHMAN, BERNDT. *Svensk arbetsmarknadspolitik 1900–1947*. Stockholm, 1970.
ÖSTLIND, ANDERS. *Svensk samhällsekonomi 1914–1922*. Stockholm, 1945.
PHILIP, KJELD. *En fremstilling og analyse af den danske kriselovgivning 1931–1938*. Copenhagen, 1939.
PIHKALA, ERKKI. *Suomen ulkomaankauppa 1860–1917*. Helsinki, 1970.
PIPPING, HUGO E. *Finlands näringsliv efter andra världskriget*. Helsinki, 1954.
RASMUSSEN, POUL NØRREGAARD. 'Den offentlige sektor gennem 100 år', *Nationaløkonomisk Tidsskrift*, 1972.
RYGG, NICOLAI. *Norges Banks historie*. 2 vols. Oslo, 1929–35.
SCHILLER, BERNDT. *Storstrejken 1909: Förhistoria och orsaker*. Göteborg, 1967.
SCHYBERGSON, PER. 'Joint Stock Companies in Finland in the Nineteenth Century', *Scandinavian Economic History Review*, XII (1964).
—— *Hantverk och fabriker: Finländsk konsumtionsvaruindustri 1815–1870*. 3 vols. Åbo and Helsinki, 1972–4.
SEJERSTED, FRANCIS. *Historisk introduksjon til økonomien*. Oslo, 1973.
—— *Ideal, teori og virkelighet: Nicolai Rygg og pengepolitikken i 1920-årene*. Oslo, 1973.
SEMMINGSEN, INGRID. 'Emigration from Scandinavia', *Scandinavian Economic History Review*, XX (1972).
SILENSTAM, PER. *Arbetskraftsutbudets utveckling i Sverige 1870–1965*. Uppsala, 1970.
SÖDERLUND, ERNST (ed.). *Swedish Timber Exports, 1850–1950*. Stockholm, 1952.
—— *Skandinaviska Banken i det svenska bankväsendets historia 1864–1914*. Stockholm, 1964.

STEEN, SVERRE. *Det gamle samfunn.* Det frie Norge, 4. Oslo, 1957.
STOLTZ, GERHARD. *Økonomisk utsyn 1900–1950.* Samfunnsökonomiske studier, 3. Oslo, 1955.
STONEHILL, ARTHUR. *Foreign Ownership in Norwegian Enterprises.* Samfunnsökonomiske studier, 14. Oslo, 1965.
SVENDSEN, KNUD ERIK, SVEND AAGE HANSEN, ERLING OLSEN, and ERIK HOFFMEYER. *Dansk pengehistorie.* 2 vols. Copenhagen, 1968.
SWEDEN, CENTRAL BUREAU OF STATISTICS. *Statistisk översikt av det svenska näringslivets utveckling åren 1870–1915.* Stockholm, 1919.
—— —— *Historisk statistik för Sverige.* 3 vols. Stockholm, 1955–72.
—— —— *Historisk statistik för Sverige: Översiktstabeller.* Stockholm, 1960.
—— Federation of Swedish Industries. *Sveriges industri.* Stockholm, 1967.
TVEITE, STEIN. *Jord og gerning.* Kristiansand, 1959.
—— 'Hamburg og norsk naeringsliv 1814–1860', *Historisk Tidsskrift* (Oslo), XLII (1963).
UTTERSTRÖM, GUSTAF. *Jordbrukets arbetare*, 2 vols. Stockholm, 1957.
VALEN-SENSTAD, FARTEJN. *Norske landbruksredskaper 1800–1850-aarene.* Lillehammer, 1964.
YOUNGSON, A. J. *Possibilities of Economic Progress.* Cambridge, 1955.

INDEX

Aachen, 518; coal-field accidents, 486; machine-breaking, 464; revolt against truck system, 482; textile factories, 718n95, 720n125

Aachen–Munich insurance company, 400

Abbé, Ernst, professor of physics, 571, 572

Åberg, Yngve, 614

absenteeism, 477

absentee landlords, 653n86

absolutism, 515; absolutist princes, and entrepreneurs, 502–3, 504–5, 506, 509, 512

Abstract of Turnpike Trust Expenditure, 60

Abstracts of Highway Expenditure, 60

accountancy, 235, 543–5; banking influence on, 373, 568; books on, 721; central accounting, 578; in family enterprises, 196; in French railway companies, 375; laws regulating, 358; pre-specialist, 374, 507, 544; progress after 1870, 572; in a Welsh factory, 366

accountants, 196; as directors, 206, 213, 223, 680nn201, 209

see also bookkeeping

acquisition of firms, *see* mergers

advertising, 573, 677

AEG (Allgemeine Elektrizitäts-Gesellschaft), 557, 558–9, 569, 573, 587

Aftalion, A., 268, 282

agriculture

France: agricultural tradition and industrialization, 348; bank finance for, 368; dependence of industry on, 269; employers' union, 301; equipment, 236; joint-stock companies, 356; migration from/to, 245, 305–8, 325, 334, 340, immigrant labour in, 321, 335–6; output, 281, 289–91, and investment, 292–5; proportion of population employed in, 304, 305–6, 325, 326, 344–5, collapse of pre-eminence, 340; stagnation, 231, 232; surplus of labour, 304–5, 'reserve army', 307

    Agricultural Labour Service, 321

Germany: aristocratic enterprise in, 514; buildings, 396, 397–8, 399, 404–5, 428, 429, and livestock, 397; capital formation, 387–8, 429; capital-intensity, 398, 428; depressions, 386, 442; 'golden age' of, 695n8; investment, 396–8, feed–seed investment, 397; productivity, 473, annual gross product, 397; reforms, 384; role in industrialization, 396, 428

agricultural labour: children, 467; hours of labour, 484; immigrants employed in, 442; migration from, 468, 469–70, proportion of population employed in, 445

agricultural processing industries, 486

    see also agriculture: Prussia

Great Britain, 48–50, 139–48; capital formation in, 31, 32, 36, 40–1, 48–9, 74–6; capital stock, 49–50; improvements, 92, 93; malthusian theory and, 98; migration from, 102, 107, 140–1, to coal mines, 137; 'new' agriculture, 82, 116, 127, 144–5; share of national wealth, 88–9; technical changes, 142, 144; works and buildings, 37–8, 48–9

    agricultural labour, 115, 119, 143–6; an 'internal reservoir' for whole economy, 139, 144, 147, 149; living standards, 161; output per head, 650n23; piecework, 157; political repression, 145, 146; proportion of population employed in, 139–41; wages, 37, 60, 99, 101–2, 103–4, 145–6, 650n25; women and children, 123

    ancillary occupations, 142

    Royal Commission on (1896), 643n159; Select Committee (1833), 652nn63, 75, 659nn223, 225, 660n258, (1836), 659n223

Ireland, 115; Irish agricultural labour in England, 104, 112, 140

Prussia, 388–96, 429–34; agrarian reforms, 384; buildings, 393; capital accumulation, 425, 428; capital formation, 388, 393–4; capital-intensity, 388; capital shortage, 697n31; capital stock, 393; depressions, 389, 428; improvements, 388, 392; investment, 388, 395, 427–8, seed reinvestment, 389, 391; livestock, 392, 395, 432–3; population, 441; production, 384–5, 389, 393–6, 429, 434, productivity, 392; role in industrialization, 385, 396; seed inputs, 390, 430; subsidies for, 702n109; a surplus sector, 384, 385, 395, 698n37; *see also* agriculture: Germany

Scandinavia: ancillary occupations, 591, 599; credit unions for, 598; depressions, 592; dominance of, in economy, 592, 613; individual enterprise in, 598; investment, 598, 604,

transport (*cont.*)
  Germany: capital formation, 422; and
    enterprise, 552, 580; growth, 422;
    investment, 410, 411, 417–18, 567;
    labour force, 446, migrant, 468, tips
    for, 483; productivity, 473
      Prussia, 427
  Great Britain: capital formation, 31, 32,
    39–42, 58–65, 74–6, 93–4; growth,
    210–11; for labour, 108; share of
    national wealth, 88–9; wages, 161,
    170
  Scandinavia, 591, 604–5, 614
  see also canals and waterways; infra-
    structure; railways; roads and high-
    ways
Trist, *see* Norton, Trist, and Gilbert
truck system, 162, 464, 482, 486
Truman, brewing entrepreneur, 187
Tunisia, 335
Turnbull, R. E., 71, 643n159
turnips, 70, 389, 392, 430, 431, 697n28
turnpike roads, 30, 59–61, 145, 639n110,
  640n111
  Select Committee on Turnpike Trusts
    and Tolls (1836), 61
'twelve industries' (commodities), production of, 420–1, 425–6, 438–9,
  702n107
Tyson, R. E., 671n103

Ulmer, Henri, 327
unemployment and underemployment, 11
  France: in 1930s, 324, 330; under-
    employment, 309, 344
  Germany: cyclical or seasonal, 488–9;
    before 1850, 528, in 1920s, 488, in
    1930s, 476, 489; through labour
    disputes, 478; underemployed as
    labour reserve, 388
  Great Britain: in agriculture, 145–6;
    cyclical, 126, 127, 175; disguised,
    101–2, 115, 123, 124, 142, 144, 162; in
    exporting industries, 125–7; involun-
    tary, 629n11; poverty caused by, 172;
    seasonal, 125; structural, 126, 127;
    underemployment, 124, 127–8; un-
    employed as labour reserve, 189; and
    wages, 175–6, 177
  Scandinavia: agricultural, 615; in 1920s
    and 30s, 615–16, 618; in 1950s,
    621
Ungewitter, F. H., 412
Unilever, 223, 225, 229, 680n209, 683n236
Union of German Employers' Associa-
  tions, 475
Union of German Engineers, 458

United Kingdom, *see* Great Britain
United States of America, 201, 209, 347,
  388, 485, 514
  big business, 375; family business,
    380
  canals, 356
  entrepreneurs, 217, 687n287
  hours of labour and output, 12
  immigration, 321–2, 442
  industrial planning, 226
  influence on European industrial
    growth, 531
  International General Electric Com-
    pany, 217
  joint-stock companies, 203, 585
  labour markets, 452
  Louisiana Purchase, 20
  management techniques, 214, 228, 574,
    575
  mechanization, 456; machine tools and
    mechanics, 451; technical achieve-
    ment, 672n117
  multi-divisional structure, 225, 226
  natural resources, 21
  real-wage index, 472; share of wages in
    national product, 168
  shipbuilding, 64, 65, 641nn134, 136
  technical education, 571
  yarn production, 208
United Steel Company, 682n222, 683n232
United Turkey Red Company, 210
universities, 224, 571, 572, 583, 724n168;
  see also education
Upper Silesia, 462, 469, 479
urban development
  France, 243, 252, 260; Paris, 248
  Germany, 408–9; Prussia, 401, 405,
    408–9
  Great Britain, 43–7 and notes; adverse
    effects, 106, 124, 162; migration from
    country to town, 105–6; streets and
    squares, 135; villages turned to towns,
    118; urban land rent, 73
  Scandinavia, 595, 600

value added, 4, 5, 17, 171, 602; in agriculture, 395
vehicles, 77, 215
  see also automobiles; carriages
Verdoorn, P. J., 12
vertical integration, 552, 560, 577
vertical shaft, *see* coal industry
Vial, Jean, 365, 380
Vickers, Thomas, 204, 217
Vickers, a limited liability company, 204,
  217
  Metropolitan Vickers, 683n238

DATE DUE

30 505 JOSTEN'S